POLITICS UK

Eighth Edition

Bill Jones and Philip Norton

With contributed material by Colin Copus, Byron Criddle, Oliver Daddow, Russell Deacon, David Denver, Anneliese Dodds, Wyn Grant, Kevin Hickson, Michael Holmes and Richard Kelly

And concluding articles by Mark Garnett, Robert Hazell, Michael Moran, Jonathan Powell, Peter Riddell and Peter Waller

Routledge
Taylor & Francis Group

LONDON AND NEW YORK

First edition published 1991 by Philip Alan Ltd
Second and Third editions published 1994 and 1998 by Prentice Hall
Fourth edition published 2001 by Pearson Education Limited
Seventh edition published 2010 by Pearson Education Limited

Eighth edition published 2014
by Routledge
2 Park Square, Milton Park, Abingdon, Oxon OX14 4RN

and by Routledge
711 Third Avenue, New York, NY 10017

Routledge is an imprint of the Taylor & Francis Group, an informa business

British Library Cataloguing in Publication Data
A catalogue record for this book is available from the British Library

Library of Congress Cataloging in Publication Data
Politics UK / [edited by] Bill Jones and Philip Norton; with additional material by:
Oliver Daddow, Kevin Hickson, David Denver, Byron Criddle, Richard Kelly, Russell Deacon,
Colin Copus, Anneliese Dodds, Wyn Grant, Michael Holmes and concluding essays by,
Mark Garnett, Peter Riddell, Robert Hazell, Peter Waller, Jonathan Powell. – Eighth edition.
    pages cm
  ISBN 978-1-4479-2140-0
  1. Great Britain–Politics and government–1997–   I. Jones, Bill, 1946–
JN231.P69 2013
320.941–dc23

                                                            2013019172

ISBN: 978-1-4479-2140-0 (pbk)

Typeset in Minion Pro
by Graphicraft Limited

For Carolyn

Bill Jones

For my students

Philip Norton

BRIEF CONTENTS

PART 1 CONTEXT

PART 2 DEFINING THE POLITICAL WORLD

PART 3 THE REPRESENTATIVE PROCESS

PART 4   THE LEGISLATIVE PROCESS

PART 5   THE EXECUTIVE PROCESS

PART 6   THE POLICY PROCESS

CONTENTS

PART 1   CONTEXT

PART 2   DEFINING THE POLITICAL WORLD

PART 3   THE REPRESENTATIVE PROCESS

PART 4   THE LEGISLATIVE PROCESS

PART 5   THE EXECUTIVE PROCESS

PART 6   THE POLICY PROCESS

CONTRIBUTORS

Colin Copus is Professor of Local Politics and Director of the Local Governance Research Unit in the Department of Public Policy, De Montfort University. His main research interests are: local party politics, local political leadership, the changing role of the councillor, and small party and independent politics. He also researches and writes on English national identity and English governance. He has recently concluded two major research projects: the first a Leverhulme-funded project exploring the role and impact of small political parties, independent politics and political associations in local government; the second, a Nuffield-funded comparative project examining the roles, responsibilities and activities of councillors across Europe. He has worked closely with practitioners in local government and with policymakers, having recently worked with the Political and Constitutional Reform Committee of the House of Commons, on a codification of central and local government relationships. Colin is the author of two major books: *Leading the Localities: Executive Mayors in English Local Governance* (Manchester University Press 2006); and *Party Politics and Local Government* (Manchester University Press 2004). He has also served as a councillor on a London Borough council, a county and a district council and three parish councils.

Byron Criddle is Emeritus Reader in Politics at Aberdeen University. His co-authored publications on British politics include various editions from 1995 to 2005 of *Parliamentary Profiles*, four editions of the *Almanac of British Politics* (between 1995 and 2007), and contributions to the Nuffield series of British General Election studies from 1983 to 2010.

Oliver Daddow is Reader in International Politics at the University of Leicester. He was educated at Oxford University and the University of Nottingham and has previously worked in the Defence Studies Department, King's College London, and the Department of Politics, History and International Relations, Loughborough University. He has also been a Visiting Scholar in the Center for British Studies, University of California, Berkeley.

His research interests are in British foreign policy, Euroscepticism and the uses of history in foreign policy-making. He is the author of *New Labour and the European Union: Blair and Brown's Logic of History* (Manchester University Press 2011), *Britain and Europe since 1945: Historiographical Perspectives on Integration* (Manchester University Press 2004) and *International Relations Theory: The Essentials* (Sage 2013). He edited *Harold Wilson and European Integration: Britain's Second Application to Join the European Economic Community* (Frank Cass 2003) and, with Jamie Gaskarth, co-edited *British Foreign Policy: The New Labour Years* (Palgrave Macmillan 2011). With Mark Bevir and Ian Hall he co-convenes the British International Studies Association's Working Group on Interpretivism in International Relations. Together, they have co-edited the 2013 Special Issue of *British Journal of Politics and International Relations* on Interpreting British Foreign Policy and are co-editing a new book, *Interpreting Global Security* (Routledge 2013).

Russell Deacon is currently a Professor in Welsh Governance and Modern Political History in the Department of History and Classics at Swansea University. He has been a civil servant and worked in the Welsh Assembly on policy creation. Professor Deacon has written widely on devolution and written a number of books on this area including: *Devolution in Great Britain* (2006) and *Devolution in the United Kingdom* (2012). He is also a political historian who specialises on the Welsh Liberal Party and the wider Liberal Democrats. His most recent publication in this respect is *A History of the Welsh Liberal Party* (2013). Professor Deacon is also a director for the Welsh political and business think tank *Gorwel*.

David Denver is Emeritus Professor of Politics at Lancaster University. He is the author of a well-known text – *Elections and Voters in Britain* – which has gone through various editions, as well as numerous other books and articles on elections.

Anneliese Dodds is Senior Lecturer in Public Policy within the School of Languages and Social Sciences at Aston University. She is the author of *Comparative Public Policy* (Palgrave 2012) and numerous articles on comparative and UK social and public policy.

Mark Garnett is Senior Lecturer in Politics at the University of Lancaster. His many books on British politics and society include *From Anger to Apathy: The British Experience since 1975* (Jonathan Cape 2007).

Wyn Grant is Professor of Politics at the University of Warwick and is the author of *Economic Policy in Britain* (2002). He is a regular commentator for radio and print media on economic policy issues.

Robert Hazell is Professor of Government and the Constitution, and founder of the Constitution Unit in the School of Public Policy at University College London. In 2011 he led a research project into the UK's new coalition government, with Peter Waller and others, published as Hazell and Yong, *The Politics of Coalition: How the Conservative-Liberal Democrat Government Works* (Hart 2012).

Kevin Hickson is senior lecturer in politics at the University of Liverpool where he teaches and researches British politics, with particular emphasis

on political ideologies and political economy. He is the author/editor of eight books and numerous chapters and journal articles.

Michael Holmes is Senior Lecturer in European politics at Liverpool Hope University. His research work has focused on the political systems and structures of the European Union, with particular emphasis on how EU integration has impacted on political parties across Europe.

Bill Jones joined the Extra-Mural Department at Manchester University in 1972 as the person in charge of politics and government, serving as Director 1987–92. His books include *The Russia Complex* (on Labour and the USSR); *British Politics Today* (which ran through seven editions before being republished with the suffix *The Essentials* in 2010); *Political Issues in Britain Today* (five editions); *Debates in British Politics* (with Lynton Robins, 2001); and *The Dictionary of British Politics* (2nd edition 2010). He was Vice Chair and Chair of The Politics Association 1979–85, being made a Life Fellow in 2001. He suffered a stroke while jogging in 1992 and took medical retirement from Manchester. In 2006 he took up a part-time teaching position at Liverpool Hope University being made a professor in 2009. He also occasionally broadcasts on radio and television and runs a political blog: *Skipper*.

Richard Kelly is Head of Politics at Manchester Grammar School. He has authored or co-authored eight books relating to British party politics, including *Conservative Party Conferences* (MUP 1989) and *Changing Party Policy in Britain* (Blackwell 1999). He has also contributed to *Conservative Century* (OUP 1994); *Conservatives in Crisis* (MUP 2003) and *Retrieving the Big Society* (Wiley-Blackwell 2012).

Michael Moran is emeritus professor of government at the University of Manchester. His publications include *Politics and Governance in the UK* (Palgrave, 2nd edn 2011), *After the Great Complacence: financial crisis and the politics of reform*

(Oxford University Press 2011, co-author) and *Business, Politics and Society* (Oxford University Press 2009).

Philip Norton (Lord Norton of Louth) is Professor of Government and Director of the Centre for Legislative Studies at the University of Hull, as well as being a member of the House of Lords. He is the author or editor of 30 books. He was the first chair of the House of Lords Constitution Committee. He has been described in *The House Magazine* – the journal of both Houses of Parliament – as 'our greatest living expert on Parliament'.

Jonathan Powell is founder and CEO of Inter Mediate, an NGO devoted to conflict resolution working in Africa, Latin America, Asia and the Middle East. He was Tony Blair's Chief of Staff from 1995 to 2007 and chief British negotiator in Northern Ireland. He has published *The New Machiavelli: How to wield power in the modern world* and *Great Hatred Little Room: Making peace in Northern Ireland* and will publish in 2014 *Talking to Terrorists: How to end armed conflict.*

Peter Riddell is Director of the Institute for Government and until mid-2010 had been a journalist for 40 years, working on the *Financial Times* and *The Times*, for most of the time about politics. He has written seven books on British politics and has close ties to the academic world, with two honorary doctorates, as a Fellow of the Royal Historical Society and member of the Academy of Social Sciences. He was appointed to the Privy Council in 2010 to serve on the detainees' inquiry and was made a CBE in 2012.

Peter Waller is a former senior civil servant who is now an honorary research fellow at the Constitution Unit UCL where he carries out political research, largely focused on Whitehall and Westminster. He has recently worked on projects on public appointments, the coalition and the role of special advisers in Government.

PROFILES

GUIDED TOUR

The eighth edition of **Politics UK** is packed with features expressly designed to enhance your understanding and enjoyment of British politics. Here are just a few:

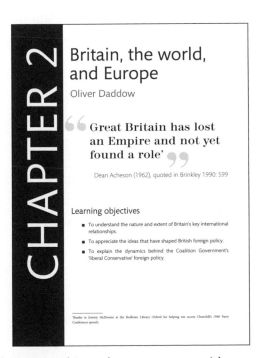

Each eye-catching chapter opens with a set of **Learning objectives**, which list the topics covered and outline what you should understand by the end of the chapter.

Profile boxes, found throughout the book, focus on particular individuals who have helped develop our understanding of what politics is, or who have played a significant role in British politics. A list of these profiles is shown on page xx.

Throughout the text you will find emboldened **Key terms and phrases** highlighted for which you will find full definitions in the **Glossary**.

Towards the end of chapters you will find the **Britain in context** feature, which looks at the issues covered within a chapter in the context of global politics and provides a useful comparative angle on the key issues in British politics.

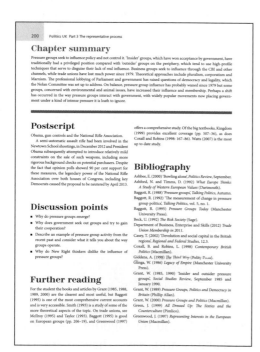

Chapter summaries consolidate the ideas and topics covered in the chapter and are followed by **Discussion points** that prompt you to consider and develop your own responses to various political issues.

You will also find annotated suggestions for **Further reading** and **Useful websites** at the end of each chapter.

AND ANOTHER THING . . .

The riots of August 2011: anger, or apathy?

On 6 August 2011 more than a hundred local residents marched from the Broadwater Farm Estate in North London to the Tottenham police station. The demonstration was held in protest at the police shooting on 4 August of Mark Duggan, a well-known local figure. The police's explanation of Duggan's death was disputed by other eye-witnesses, and his friends and relatives rejected allegations that he had been a prominent gangster. The protest march was intended to be peaceful, but ended in violence amid further allegations of police misconduct. The police were attacked with a variety of missiles, buildings were set on fire and shops were looted.

Whatever the circumstances of Duggan's death, the incident evoked memories of disorder in the same area in October 1985. Broadwater Farm had been the scene of serious rioting after a local woman had died during a police search of her house. A police officer caught up in the ensuing violence had been killed. In 1985, as in 2011, unrest had undoubtedly been accentuated by racial factors. The situation on 6 August was extremely volatile, and the police response was cautious. As a result, it seemed to many observers that looters had taken control of the streets. Over the next few days trouble affected many London boroughs, then radiated out to places like Birmingham, Leeds, Manchester and Nottingham. In Croydon on 8 August a large furniture store was torched, along with other buildings. Attacks on police personnel occurred in many places, though unlike in 1985 no officer was killed.

The British weather was partly responsible for a lull in the unrest on 10 August, by which time Parliament had been recalled and David Cameron had returned from holiday to chair emergency meetings. It was announced that plastic bullets would be made available to the police for purposes of crowd-control; that, and a massive increase in police numbers, helped to deter potential rioters. Having looked as if it was ungovernable on 8 August, four days later England had returned to something like normality. But apart from numerous injuries and grievous damage to various properties, the deaths of five people were attributed to incidents during that short, surreal period.

Britain (and especially England) has a long history of civil disorder. For those who examine recent rioting with any care, the incidents of 2011 provide ample grounds for speculation. Leaving aside the special circumstances of Broadwater Farm in 1985, these things seem to happen at ten-year intervals, like the census. In 1981 riots in Bristol and Brixton, south London had triggered unrest in many English towns and cities. A decade after the 1981 riots there was serious trouble in Oxford and on Tyneside. Yet that disorder had been localised. Just before the 2001 general election there was racist-inspired violence in parts of Lancashire and Yorkshire; but again these outbreaks had been short-lived and geographically limited.

What made 2011 different from 1991 and 2001? In the riots of 1981 the perceived abuse of police powers, especially against representatives of ethnic minorities, was a precipitating factor. By 2011 a series of reports into racist attitudes within the police service had been effective to some extent. Yet rioting took place in areas where the police had taken steps to adopt a more sensitive style of policing. One novel factor in 2011 was the availability of the internet and social networking sites, which aroused considerable excitement within the media. However, electronic communication probably just made it easier for rioters to coordinate their activities; they could not have created the initial urge to riot.

A plausible conclusion is that the riots of 1991 and 2001 were localised because they were triggered by local grievances, while in 1981 and 2011 something more general was in play. In 1981 Britain was enduring a period of mass unemployment, under an apparently inflexible government. In 2011, it could be argued, the governing coalition of Conservatives and Liberal Democrats had revived this approach, proposing spending cuts which would greatly increase unemployment and make life much more difficult for those who were already dependent on benefits. Although some sections of the media quickly identified 2011 rioters who were anything but poor, detailed research showed that the majority came from deprived areas.

The 2010 British General Election took place against the background of widespread public disorder in Greece. This was provoked largely by the *prospect* of 'austerity' measures similar to those advocated by Britain's Coalition

---

Each part concludes with a thought-provoking feature entitled **And another thing . . .** These articles are authored by leading political thinkers and take a sideways glance at some of the key issues under debate in contemporary British politics.

EPILOGUE

Coalition government in the UK: how has it been?

Bill Jones, May 2013

> **The Coalition Parties will work together effectively to deliver our programme, on the basis of goodwill, mutual trust and agreed procedures which foster collective decision-making and decision-making while reflecting each party's identity.**
> (Coalition Agreement for Stability and Reform, May 2010)

> **It's because the Conservatives really know capitalism doesn't work and the Liberal Democrats think it actually does, that the coalition government has survived so far.**
> (Jeremy Hardy, comedian, 24 November 2012, York Theatre Royal)

> **The initial bright-eyed vow that served as the defining mission of the coalition – to eradicate the deficit by 2015, thereby winning re-election as a reward for clearing up the economic mess – has turned to dust.**
> (Jonathan Freedland, the *Guardian*, 6 December 2012)

When the 6 May election results produced no overall winner, a rather unseemly wrestling match took place between the three biggest parties in the Commons as to who would ally with whom. David Cameron, as leader of the biggest party, could have claimed the right to lead a minority government and to try and hang on until another election would have given him a chance to achieve a workable majority. However, this would not have been a strong government, and it was widely appreciated that the nature of Britain's economic crisis required a government able to take unpopular measures. Cameron came to favour a coalition, as linking with the Lib Dems would have given him protection against his dissatisfied right wing which felt strongly – still does – that his *Big Society*-themed election campaign 'lost' them an election

against a failing Labour government led by the disastrously unpopular Brown that they should have won easily. So, he made his 'big, open and comprehensive offer' to the Liberal Democrats and talks began.

Brown, no doubt devastated at losing the election, must have been surprised to still be 'in play' the day after polling. But his position was much less favourable. First, to assemble a majority he would need to do deals with a rainbow-coloured group of smaller parties, some of whom – the SNP for instance – would be likely to pull the plug if their demands were ignored. Second, by any commonsense measure Labour had 'lost' the election and, as several of the party's leading figures made clear during Brown's negotiations, voters were unlikely to accept the continuation in government of a party which had served 13 years, had been seriously unpopular for some time and had been soundly beaten in the national contest for control of Westminster.

The 'consummation' of the Tory–Lib Dem love affair in the Rose Garden of Number 10 was much lampooned as a 'gay' political marriage, so affectionate did Nick and Dave appear to be. The ridicule concealed not a little astonishment also as the Lib Dems had operated politically to the left of Labour post 2005 with reasonably well-entrenched positions on: favouring welfare payments and redistributing wealth; being opposed to increased tuition fees for university study; stoutly defending civil liberties and opposing New Labour's tightening of the screw on terrorist suspects; encouraging closer integration of the UK with the EU; and forging ahead with constitutional change, especially voting reform.

Given that the Conservatives had been moving to the right on most of these issues for some years, the emergence of a Coalition Agreement, somewhat grandly entitled a 'Programme for Government', did cause eyebrows to be

---

New to this edition is an **Epilogue** offering a final word and alternative perspective on how the Coalition is working in practice. This feature offers a fully updated account of events summarising the relationships and developments of the Coalition government.

PREFACE

Politics is an exciting subject. We, the authors, are naturally biased in thinking it offers students very special attractions. It is a subject you digest with your breakfast each morning; its complex canvas unfolds with the daily papers, the *Today* programme, the broadcast news, not excluding possible viewings of blogs; by the evening new details have been painted in and the picture subtly, sometimes dramatically, has changed.

Politics is unpredictable, dynamic; it affects us, it is about us. In one sense the canvas *is* us: a projection of ourselves and our aspirations, a measure of our ability to live together. Given what can happen when it goes wrong – a ruler like Pol Pot or Saddam Hussein, for example – politics is arguably the most important focus there is in the study of the human condition. We hope that this volume on the politics of the United Kingdom does the subject some kind of justice.

This book is designed to provide a comprehensive introduction to British politics for both the general reader and the examination candidate. With the latter group in mind, we fashioned a text for the first edition that was unusual by British standards. When we studied A-level politics, all those years ago, the transition from GCSE-level to A-level was quite difficult. This was hardly surprising, because many of the A-level texts were the same as those we went on to study at university, partly because of shared assumptions about A-level and university students. It was believed that we should be treated as mature intellects (good), but also that it was up to us to extract meaning from the texts which, in the name of standards, made few concessions to our possible unfamiliarity with the subject (not so good). In these circumstances it is hardly surprising that so many aspiring university students gave up before the intrinsic interest of the subject could capture them.

Things have improved since then, in the world of textbooks remarkably so. Syllabuses have become much wider and now embrace stimulating new areas such as political sociology and current political issues. This has helped authors produce more interesting work but a revolution has also taken place on the production side. *Politics UK*, when it came out in 1990, was arguably the first book to embrace the American approach of providing a comprehensive course textbook with a plethora of new features such as photographs, diagrams, tables and illustrative figures.

Since then most of our rival textbooks on British politics have adopted similar styles, and if imitation is the highest form of flattery, we are greatly flattered. The book has moved through seven successful editions and this is the eighth. The key features of this new edition are as follows.

■ The fourth edition was comprehensively 'Europeanised': each chapter was looked at and amended to take account of the EU impact and influence – all this material has been accordingly updated for the seventh edition.

■ 'Updating' means covering developments over the four years since the last edition, of course – including the 2010 election – but older examples are still cited in some cases; there are continuities in British politics and the whole of the post-war period is used as a kind of laboratory in which political behaviour is observed.

- Many of the chapters in this eighth edition have been completely rewritten, and all chapters not rewritten have been comprehensively updated up to, where possible, spring 2013.

- The book contains an alphabetical Glossary defining all the key terms highlighted in the text.

- The comparative approach to politics has become increasingly popular over the last decade and, while this is not expressly a comparative text, we have included a 'Britain in context' box for each chapter which provides a limited version of this kind of input.

- The book's presentation has been augmented by the inclusion of many tables and diagrams from the quality press. The comment and debate at the end of each major part have been written, as before, by distinguished guest writers. This time they are:

  - **Jonathan Powell**, former diplomat then Chief of Staff to Tony Blair in Downing Street.

  - **Professor Robert Hazell**, UCL and founder of its Constitution Unit.

  - **Mark Garnett**, well known author on British Politics and academic, who is Senior Lecturer at University of Lancaster.

  - **Peter Waller**, former senior civil servant and now research fellow at UCL.

  - **Peter Riddell**, former columnist and assistant editor at *The Times* and now Director of Institute for Government.

  - **Professor Michael Moran**, distinguished academic author of major research on British politics and the economy based at University of Manchester.

The chapters on Parliament in this book have always been authoritative and up to date; they are even more so since Philip Norton became a member of the House of Lords himself in 1998. We have to thank those reviewers who commented so usefully on draft chapters of this book and thereby helped to improve them. We hope teachers and students find the book as useful and stimulating as previous editions.

Thanks are due to all the contributors and to the staff at Pearson Education who have proved remarkably helpful and professional, especially Dawn Phillips who has been central to the book's preparation and has dealt with all the problems of coordinating busy academics including late submissions, with great patience and good humour. She has been a highly professional breath of fresh air and we are very grateful to her.

Bill Jones

Philip Norton

ACKNOWLEDGEMENTS

The authors and publishers wish to thank the reviewers who offered valuable feedback on draft chapters of the text, namely:

Dr Victoria Honeyman, University of Leeds

Dr Peter Lynch, University of Stirling

Dr Joanna McKay, Nottingham Trent University

David S. Moon, University of Liverpool

Dr Nick Randall, Newcastle University

Mark Stuart, University of Nottingham

Professor Paul Webb, University of Sussex

We are also grateful to the following for permission to reproduce copyright material:

Figures

Figure 2.1 from Foreign and Commonwealth Office (2006) Active Diplomacy in a Changing World, http://collections.europarchive.org/tna/20080205132101/fco.gov.uk/Files/kfile/ozintpriorities2006Chap2.pdf, contains public sector information licensed under the Open Government Licence (OGL) v1.0.http://www.nationalarchives.gov.uk/doc/open-government-licence/open-government; Figure 2.2 from UN Security Council: functions and powers, http://www.un.org/docs/sc/unsc_functions.html; Figure 2.3 from Aims of the Council of Europe http://www.coe.int/aboutcoe/index.asp?page=nosObjectifs, 2012; Figures on pp. 8, 95 from *Women in Public Life, the Professions and the Boardroom* (Cracknell, R., 2012), House of Commons Library, contains Parliamentary information licensed under the Open Parliament Licence v1.0, Charts 1, 2, 3 within Box 6.2; Figure 7.3 from *Political Change in Britain*, 2nd edn, Palgrave Macmillan (Butler, D.E. & Stokes, D., 1974); Figure 7.4 adapted from data from *BES*; Figure 10.1 from Pressure groups and the policy process, *Social Studies Review*, vol. 3 (5) (Grant, W., 1988), reproduced with permission from the California Council for Social Studies; Figure 10.2 from Insider and outsider pressure groups, *Social Studies Review*, vol. 1 (1) (Grant, W., 1985), reproduced with permission from the California Council for Social Studies; Figure 10.5 from *Labour Force Survey* (Office for National Statistics) Chart 3.1, Source: Office for National Statistics licensed under the Open Government Licence v.1.0; Figure 13.1 from The constitution in flux, *Social Studies Review*, 2 (1) (Norton, P., 1986), reproduced with permission from the California Council for Social Studies; Figure 20.1 adapted from 'Local government in England and Wales' by Gray, A. (1970) in, *British Politics Today* (Jones, B. and Kavanagh, D. (eds) 1979); Figure 22.1 from 'The policy making process' by Burch, M. (1979) in, *British Politics Today* (Jones, B. and Kavanagh, D., 1979), Manchester University Press; Figure 22.3 from *Pressure Groups Today*, Manchester University Press (Baggott, R. 1995); Figures 23.2, 23.3 from *Digest 4: Information on the Criminal Justice System in England and Wales* (Barclay, G. and Tavares, C., 1999), Home Office Research, Development and Statistical Directorate, contains public sector information licensed under the Open Government Licence v1.0; Figure 26.1 from The policy-making process (Clarke, M.), *British Foreign Policy: Tradition, Change and Transformation*, p. 86 (Figure 4.1) (Smith, M., Smith, S. and White, B. (eds) 1988), reproduced by kind permission of Unwin Hyman Ltd; © M. Smith, S. Smith and B. White 1988.

Tables

Table 3.1 adapted from Gross value added per head of population (capita) for the four countries of the UK in 2010, http://www.ons.gov.uk/ons/rel/regional-accounts/regional-gross-value-added--income-approach-/december-2011/index.html, © Crown copyright 2011, source: Office for National Statistics licensed under the Open Government Licence v.1.0; Table 3.2 adapted from Gross value added per capita for the English regions (2010), http://www.ons.gov.uk/ons/rel/regional-accounts/regional-gross-value-added--income-approach-/december-2011/index.html, © Crown copyright 2011, source: Office for National Statistics licensed under the Open Government Licence v.1.0; Table 7.5 adapted from Data from, *British Election Study (BES) face-to-face post-election survey* (2010), The original data have been weighted to reflect the actual turnout in the election; Tables 7.7, 7.8, 7.9, 7.10 adapted from data from, *British Election Study (BES) post-election internet survey* (2010);

Table 8.3 adapted from Based on a lecture by Professor David Denver; Tables 9.1, 9.3 from Criddle, B. in *The British General Election of 2010* (Kavanagh, D. & Cowley, P., 2010), Macmillan; Tables 11.4, 11.5 adapted from data from, http://privatewww.essex.ac.uk/tquinn/index.html (Quinn, T.); Table 11.6 adapted from From Blue Labour to Red Tories: party factions in Britain today, *Politics Review*, 22 (4) (Kelly, R., 2013), reproduced in adapted from by permission of Philip Allan (for Hodder Education); Table 12.2 from *Devolution in the United Kingdom*, Edinburgh University Press (Deacon, R., 2012); Table 12.7 adapted from Office for National Statistics, 2008, source: Office for National Statistics licensed under the Open Government Licence v.1.0; Table 12.8 adapted from data from Eurostat, March 2012; Table 14.1 adapted from data from Ipsos/MORI, copyright © Ipsos MORI, reproduced with permission; Table 15.1 from B. Criddle 'More Diverse, Yet More Uniform', in *The British General Election of 2010* (D. Kavanagh and P. Cowley (eds) 2010), reproduced with permission of Palgrave Macmillan; Table 15.2 from B. Criddle 'MPs and candidates', in *The British General Election of 2005*, p.159 (D. Kavanagh and D. Butler (eds) 2005), Reproduced with permission of Palgrave Macmillan; Table 15.3 from the House of Commons Sessional Information Digests, 2001–10 © Parliamentary Copyright. Parliamentary copyright material is reproduced with the permission of the Controller of Her Majesty's Stationery Office (HMSO) on behalf of Parliament, contains public sector information licensed under the Open Government Licence (OGL) v1.0. http://www.nationalarchives.gov.uk/doc/open-government-licence/open-government; Table 15.4 from the House of Commons Sessional Information Digest, 2010–12, © Parliamentary Copyright. Parliamentary copyright material is reproduced with the permission of the Controller of Her Majesty's Stationery Office (HMSO) on behalf of Parliament., Contains public sector information licensed under the Open Government Licence (OGL) v1.0.http://www.nationalarchives.gov.uk/doc/open-government-licence/open-government; Table 17.1 from www.parliament.co.uk, Contains Parliamentary information licensed under the Open Parliament Licence v1.0; Table 17.2 from House of Lords Library Note, Work of the House of Lords: Statistics, LLN 2012/009, 2012, www.parliament.co.uk, contains Parliamentary information licensed under the Open Parliament Licence v1.0; Table 20.2 adapted from *Lost! 90 per cent of councillors in 35 years: Are county-wide unitaries effectively the end of UK local government?* (Game, A.), Paper presented to the PSA Local Politics Specialist Group University of Birmingham; Table 20.5 from New Local Government Network 2003 (updated 2012); Table 20.6 from nlgn.org.uk, New Local Government Network;

Table 21.1 adapted from Ministry of Justice, Judicial Salaries from 1 April 2010, Crown Copyright material is reproduced with permission under the terms of the Click-use Licence; Table 21.2 adapted from *Appointments and Diversity: A Judiciary for the 21st Century, Ministry of Justice, Consultation Paper CP19/2011*, p. 7 (2011), Contains public sector information licensed under the Open Government Licence v1.0; Table 24.1 adapted from *Government expenditure by function* (OECD 2012); Table 24.1 adapted from data from Office for National Statistics, 2011a, Source: Office for National Statistics licensed under the Open Government Licence v.1.0; Table 27.5 adapted from European Parliament Information Office in the UK (www.europarl.org.uk); Table 27.7 adapted from UK election statistics: 1918–2012, *House of Commons Library Research Paper 12/43*, pp. 33–4 (McGuinness, F., Cracknell, R., Davies, M., Taylor, M., 2012), contains Parliamentary information licensed under the Open Parliament Licence v1.0.

Text

Extract on page 10 from If I ruled the world, *Prospect*, Issue 188 (Pinker, S.); Box 1.2 from A Doctor Writes: Politicians' Pride is a Medical Disorder, *Guardian*, 28/3/2009 (Boseley, S.); Box 6.3 from *Sex and Power: Who Runs Britain?* (2006), Equal Opportunities Commission, the copyright and all other intellectual property rights in the material to be reproduced are owned by, or licensed to, the Commission for Equality and Human Rights, known as the Equality and Human Rights Commission ('the EHRC'); Box 6.4 from Feminist debates, ideology: feminism, *Politics Review*, 12 (4) (Bryson, V.), reproduced with permission of Philip Allan Updates, reproduced by permission of Philip Allan (Hodder Education); Box 6.5 from Landmarks in History of British Feminism, http://www.wrc.org.uk, Women's Resource Centre; Extract on page 144 from Commons Sketch: Blair lays on the therapy for the teracotta army, *Guardian*, 3/11/1999 (Hoggart, S.) © Guardian Newspapers Limited, reprinted with permission; Extract 8.2 from Less than four years old with fewer than 60 staff . . . 7.3 million unique users to 18.4 million, *Guardian*, 6/4/2009 (Pilkington, E.); Extract on page 185 from Protester who 'slimed' Mandelson given caution, *Guardian*, 10/4/2009 (Summers, D.); Box 10.3 from Extract from We must stand up to the creeping tyranny of the group veto, *Guardian*, 2/3/2006 (Garton Ash, T.); Box 10.9 from Extract from Labour's fatuous war against the countryside has been an abject failure, *The Observer*, 26/2/2006 (Cohen, N.); Extract on page 384 from Constitution Committee, House of Lords, Cabinet Office Inquiry: Minutes of Evidence, Wednesday 4 November 2009, http://www.publications.parliament.uk/pa/ld/lduncorr/const041109ev10.pdf,   contains

Parliamentary information licensed under the Open Parliament Licence v1.0; Box 22.1 from British industrial policy remains plagued by the antidote fallacy, *The Guardian*, 24/12/2012 (Professor Karel Williams, Manchester Business School); Box 23.1 from What Really Causes Crime?, *The Guardian*, 12/7/2002 (Polly Toynbee), © Guardian Newspapers Limited 2002, reprinted with permission.

Picture credits

The publisher would like to thank the following for their kind permission to reproduce their photographs:

(Key: b – bottom; c – centre; l – left; r-right; t – top)

Alamy Images: Clive Sawyer 39, David Levenson 438, Ingram Publishing 91, Justine Kase 375, Mark Baigent 521, One Image 341, Pictorial Press 504, Reportage/Archival 104, 106, Reportage/Archival 104, 106, Richard Franklin (front cover), Rolf Richardson 344; **BBC Motion Gallery:** 32; **Corbis:** 283, Adam Woolfitt 305, Tim Graham Picture Library 275; **DK Images:** Ian Aitken © Rough Guides 557, Jamie Marshall 251, Joe Cornish 221, Lucy Claxton 295, 391, Stephen Oliver 273, 327, 373, Suzanne Porter © Rough Guides 437; **Getty Images:** 23l, 29l, 46, 61, 487t, AFP 108, Carlde Jouza/ AFP 510, Mondadori 60, Popperfoto 44, Wire Image 86; **Guardian News and Media Ltd:** 72, 79, 85; **iStockphoto:** 203, 249, Kuzma 137, stocknshares 116, Tillsonburg 179; **James Davies:** 470b; **John Foxx Images:** Imagestate 485; **Oliver Daddow:** 24; **Pearson Education Ltd:** Debbie Rowe 19, Jules Selmes 3, 413, MindStudio 537, Richard Smith 501, Sozaijiten 71, 159, 465; **Press Association Images:** 186, 471, Charles Dharapak 29r, Chris Radburn 207, Claude Haller/ Empics 75, Dave Thompson 74, David Jones 213, 487b, Dominic Lipinski 147, 533, Doug Peters 146, Fiona Hanson 150, Jeremy Slewyn 379, Johnny Green 542, Ken McKay 144, Lewis Whyld 145, Matt Crossick 545, Nick Ansell 383, PA Wire 313, Sean Dempsey/PA Wire 418, Stefan Rousseau 234, The Labour Party 492; **Rex Features:** Richard Gardner 212, Richard Wintle 210, Startraks 93, 140; **Richard Kelly:** 211; **Shutterstock. com:** 360b 417, David Fowler 23r, Nicku 42; **TopFoto:** 65, 92, 103, 470t, Universal Pictorial Press Photo 189, Uppa 192, 442; **UNOG Library, League of Nations Archives:** 22

All other images © Pearson Education

In some instances we have been unable to trace the owners of copyright material, and we would appreciate any information that would enable us to do so.

PART 1

CONTEXT

CHAPTER 1

Political concepts and perspectives

Bill Jones

> " There has never been a perfect government, because men have passions; and if they did not have passions, there would be no need for government "
>
> Voltaire, *Politique et legislation*

Learning objectives

- To establish some understanding of the discipline of political science to provide context for understanding the rest of the book.

- To discuss the nature of politicians and the reasons why they choose their profession.

- To explain and illustrate the concept of politics and how political ideas often rest on assumptions about human nature.

- To explain the importance of certain further core concepts.

- To provide a brief overview of topics covered in the book.

The concept of politics defined and discussed

Politics is far from being a popular area of activity; politicians rank below those modern pariahs estate agents, in some opinion polls. They are often held to be, among other failings: self-serving, venal, dishonest, power-obsessed people who are more likely to be a danger to society rather than its salvation. Politics, and its politicians, have changed over the years, both in its practices and the way it is regarded. Long before the **democratic** era, it is fair to say, politicians were mostly people who had seized control by force and exercised it in their own interests. **Power** was often used merely to reflect the will and the glory of the chief conqueror and the changing nature of his whims.

Since those days a number of changes have occurred:

1 Rulers who are interested only in power for themselves have become a recognised phenomenon against whom society must protect itself. Aristotle, the Greek philosopher, argued that 'man is by nature a political animal' who required a robust system of law to be kept in check.

2 He also argued that government was best undertaken by a relatively disinterested group of well-educated men: in effect, a stratum of cultured gentlemen.

3 Two groups, long assumed to be excluded from the governing class – the very poor (originally slaves) and women – are no longer regarded as incapable of being responsible, though neither is as well represented as numbers would merit. Because these groups often derive so little from the systems under which they live, they can end up not participating and adopting anti-social attitudes and behaviour.

4 Democracy – or a system whereby every citizen is entitled to some kind of say in their own government – has become widely accepted as desirable, especially in developed countries in Europe and North America and, increasingly, in large parts of the rest of the world. However, it does not follow that every country will prove successfully receptive to democratic politics, as the modern instances of attempts to introduce democracy to Iraq and Afghanistan demonstrate. Nor does it follow that voters, even in well-established democracies, will especially value their own system of government, as declining **turnout** figures in the UK in recent decades make clear.

Defining politics

What precisely did Aristotle mean when he said man is by nature a *political* animal? The word is much used and most people think they know what it means, but usually they cannot give a clear explanation. A typical reply might be that it is concerned with: 'Political parties, you know, Labour and Conservatives.' Clearly this is factually correct but it does not take us very far towards a definition as many things have connections to political parties. No, to extract a clear definition we have to examine what things occur when 'politics' is definitely present.

For example, the following 'news items' can all be said to involve 'politics' at some level:

1 Father seeks to influence soccer manager to give his son a place in the team.
2 Chancellor ignores union claims for increased salaries.
3 Oil prices continue to rise as war spreads in Middle East.
4 Thousands demonstrate in favour of climate change measures.

The first example illustrates that politics operates at a 'micro' level; we speak of the 'politics' of the family or 'small groups'. The second is drawn from the mainstream of what we regard as 'political': a government minister taking a decision on something.

From these and the other two examples it can be seen that 'politics' entails:

- a strong element of conflict and its resolution;
- a struggle for scarce and finite resources;
- the use of various methods of persuasion or pressure, to achieve a desired outcome.

So, if we can move towards a definition, it might be constructed as:

Politics is a process that seeks to manage or resolve conflicts of interest between people, usually in a peaceful fashion. In its general sense it can describe the interactions of any group of individuals, but in its specific sense it refers to the many and complex relationships that exist between state institutions and the rest of society.

Politicians and their ambition

'Politics is a spectator sport,' writes former Tory MP, the late Julian Critchley (1995: 80). An enduring question that exercises us spectators is 'Why are they doing it?' The great eighteenth-century man of letters, Dr Johnson, in his typically blunt fashion, said politics was 'nothing more nor less than a means of rising in the world', a comment which the 2009 scandal of MPs exploiting their expenses allowances might seem to validate. But we know somehow that mere self-interest is not the whole truth. Peter Riddell, formerly a columnist at *The Times*, in his wonderfully perceptive book *Honest Opportunism* (1993), looks at this topic in some detail. He quotes nineteenth-century Prime Minister, Benjamin Disraeli, who perhaps offers a more rounded and believable account of his interest in politics to his Shrewsbury constituents: 'There is no doubt, gentlemen, that all men who offer themselves as candidates for public favour have motives of some sort. I candidly acknowledge that I have and I will tell you what they are: I love fame; I love public reputation; I love to live in the eye of the country.'

Riddell also quotes former Chancellor of the Exchequer, F.E. Smith, who candidly gloried in the 'endless adventure of governing men'. For those who think that these statements were merely expressions of nineteenth-century romanticism,

What does government do?

Leading British sociologist and adviser to Prime Minister Tony Blair, Anthony Giddens, explained what government does in terms of representing diverse interests in the country and providing a publicly protected forum for the reconciling of such interests. It also provides a variety of public functions in the form of welfare payments to the needy and, through the police, security from theft and attack. It regulates markets in the interests of the public and guards against the growth of harmful monopolies. It provides a system of law, educates the young, builds roads, railways and other infrastructure. It also engages with other countries and regulates trade.

Source: Giddens (1998: 47–8)

The hubris syndrome

Symptoms of the 'hubris' or overweening pride syndrome are as follows:

- A narcissistic propensity to see one's world primarily as an arena in which to exercise power and seek glory.
- A disproportionate concern with image and presentation.
- A messianic manner.
- Excessive confidence in one's own judgement and contempt for advice.

- Exaggerated self-belief, bordering on omnipotence.
- A belief that one is accountable solely to history or God.
- Loss of contact with reality; often associated with progressive isolation.
- Restlessness, recklessness and impulsiveness.

Extracted from Sarah Boseley's 'A Doctor Writes: Politicians' Pride is a Medical Disorder', The *Guardian*, 28 March 2009

Riddell offers the example of Labour intellectual, Richard Crossman's, comment that politics is a 'never ending adventure – with its routs and discomfitures, rushes and sallies', its 'fights for the fearless and goals for the eager'. He also includes former Conservative Deputy Prime Minister, Michael Heseltine, whom he once heard, irritated, asking at one of Jeffrey Archer's parties in 1986: 'Why *shouldn't* I be Prime Minister then?'

The tendency of politicians to explain their taste for politics in terms of concern for 'the people' is seldom sincere. In the view of journalist Henry Fairlie this is nothing more than 'humbug'. Cabinet Minister, William Waldegrave, agrees: 'Any politician who tells you he isn't ambitious is only telling you he isn't for some tactical reason; or more bluntly, telling a lie – I certainly wouldn't deny that I wanted ministerial office; yes, I'm ambitious.' As if more proof were needed, former Labour Foreign Secretary, David Owen, once said on television that 'Ambition drives politics like money drives the international economy.' Ambition, of course, is good for society only if it works for the general good; if it is purely self-inclined we end up with the likes of Saddam Hussein. As Edmund Burke noted: 'Ambition can creep as well as soar.' Politics is also an all-consuming obsession for some people. Writing in The *Guardian*, 11 March 2006, Michael Heseltine, again that famously ambitious Conservative politician who narrowly missed gaining the top prize, probably spoke for all those bitten by the political bug when he said: 'Politics is a life sentence. It's an obsessive, all demanding, utterly fascinating, totally committing profession – stimulating, satisfying, stretching.' Given the unusual confidence and self-absorption the pursuit of politics requires, it is not surprising that politicians can fall prey to 'hubris' (see Box 1.2 above).

Riddell goes on in his book – now dated but important as it discerned an important trend – to analyse how the ambitious political animal has slowly transformed British politics. He follows up and develops Anthony King's concept of the 'career politician', observing that a decreasing number of MPs had backgrounds in professions, or 'proper jobs' in Westminster parlance, compared with those who centred their whole lives on politics. The jobs of these people were of secondary importance, merely anticipating or supporting the Westminster career. In 1951 the figure was 11 per cent; by 1992 it was 31 per cent. By contrast, the proportion of new MPs with 'proper jobs' fell from 80 per cent to 41 per cent.

Many of this new breed begin life as researchers for an MP or in a party's research department, then proceed to seek selection as a candidate and from there enter into parliament and, from then on, ever onwards and upwards. The kind of MP who enters politics in later life is in steep decline; the new breed of driven young professionals has tended to dominate the field, proving firmer of purpose and more skilled in execution than those for whom politics is a later or learned vocation. The kind of businessman who achieves distinction in his field and then goes into politics is now a rarity rather than the familiar figure of the nineteenth century or the earlier decades of the twentieth century.

Ambition to hubris: a short journey?

Lord David Owen trained as a doctor and became an MP in 1966. He was made Labour Foreign Secretary at the precocious age of 38. His subsequent resignation from the party and involvement in the short-lived Social Democratic Party denied him the senior role in government which many had predicted. There is little doubt his career was adversely affected by the perception that he was an arrogant man, impatient with views with which he did not agree. So, his 2007 book, *The Hubris Syndrome: Bush, Blair and the Intoxication of Power* (he also wrote a paper on the same subject for the journal of the Royal Society of Psychiatrists in March 2009), made interesting reading for students of politics. He identifies the tendency to be intoxicated with power as an occupational hazard in politics and names as 'sufferers', Prime Ministers Lloyd George, Neville Chamberlain, Thatcher, Blair and US president George Bush.

Owen, who admits to have exhibited elements of the syndrome himself, believes he has discerned a medical condition:

> I have seen the isolation – this extraordinary pressure under which leaders in business or in politics live, with shortages of sleep – a generally very high-pressured existence. I'd liken it to . . . a long-distance runner. You go through a pain threshold and something changes. The public are way ahead. The man in the street starts to say the prime minister has 'lost it'. They put it all down to adrenaline. They see these people as supercharged.

Are politicians viewed generally with too much cynicism?

Certainly politics and its practitioners, according to many opinion polls, are seen in the present day, variously, as untrustworthy, self-seeking, power mad or cynical manipulators. My own view is that the cynicism has been excessive. Most politicians are quite decent people, trying hard to make a difference for the better. One of the problems is that in a 24–7 news age the media know that negative stories about political transgressions, whether sexual, financial or merely concerning incompetence, will attract great interest. The public loves to have someone to blame for things they do not like – high prices, poor public services, inflation, or whatever – and too often, perhaps, politicians are on the receiving end.

For example, Labour Home Secretary Jacqui Smith received a terrible press in late March 2009 when it transpired her husband had bought two 'blue' movies and charged them to his wife's parliamentary expenses. The media really went to town; the minister was not directly involved but was at the same time embroiled in another well-publicised dispute as to which was her 'main home' for expenses purposes. The accumulation of such stories tends

to construct a default negative image of MPs, garnished perhaps by a national tradition or habit of sometimes savagely non-deferential, satirical criticism of our rulers. There is much evidence to suggest we are excessively cynical about our politicians, but the history of their own behaviour makes it clear that they should be treated with, at minimum, a cautious discrimination. I think the closest to the truth I have found was encapsulated by Estelle Morris, a Labour Education Secretary who resigned in 2002. Upon being elevated to the Cabinet she asked a colleague what its members were 'really like' and received the reply:

> The good news is they are just like all the rest of us; but the bad news is . . . they are just like all the rest of us.

Democracy is not easy

Britain is one of the oldest democracies, evolved, almost by accident it sometimes seems, from a system of absolute monarchy around the eleventh century. However, democracy insists on some quite stringent requirements which are not always achievable. Below some of the major problems associated with democracy are identified.

Participation   Democracy is founded upon the assumption that citizens will join in the process, at least to the extent of voting. In the early years of the twentieth century, voting turnout was high – sometimes over 80 per cent (85 per cent in 1950) and it stayed over the 70 per cent mark for most elections in the second half of that century. However, in 1997 it dropped to 71 per cent and in 2001 to a worrying 59.2 per cent. It did recover to 62 per cent in 2005 and 65 per cent in 2010, but these figures were much lower than the post-1945 figures. Moreover, in elections for the new Police and Crime Commissioners, 15 November 2012, average turnout was less than 15 per cent. Most worrying of all is that, while older voters tend to vote still in high percentages, younger cohorts do not and surveys reveal they do not feel any particular civic duty to do so. David Denver's chapter on voting behaviour gives more detail and discussion on this topic (Chapter 7).

Party membership   Parties need members to disseminate information and run campaigns, but membership levels of our two main parties have shrunk from close to a million each in the 1950s to barely a third of a million each in the present day.

Knowledge   Democracy assumes voters are aware of political parties as well as their candidates and have some insight into the issues involved in the democratic debate and election issues. If they do not, it is easier for politicians to ignore the need to communicate the truth and harder for voters to ensure they are casting their votes wisely. Unfortunately many voters have only tenuous understanding of political issues. It has to be said some issues are extraordinarily complex – for example, whether the UK should ever join the euro, or how the pound sterling can co-exist with a currency so embattled during 2011–12. Consequently, the efficacy of our democracy is often questioned.

Funding   Political parties cost money to support and elections are not cheap either. While the **state** pays for the latter, the parties are supposed to be responsible for their own funding. With falling membership both main parties became dependent on rich donors, raising the concern that this gives them undue **influence**. The alternative – state aid – as practised in many other countries, is not popular in Britain since politicians themselves are not especially esteemed. Attempts to solve the problem have been tried over the past decade but so far without any conclusive agreement being reached.

Lying in politics   In 2005 journalist Peter Oborne wrote *The Rise of Political Lying*, a wickedly comprehensive analysis of this topic. Unfortunately, in a democracy, despite the protestations of our politicians that they speak only the truth, there is a tendency for lying to be almost endemic. This is because in a democracy some politicians are quite frankly dishonest and mendacious and this is greatly to be regretted. But these are other explanations. The disparate positions of different political groupings sometimes make it necessary for politicians to bend the truth to make agreement acceptable to all: peace in Northern Ireland, for example, might have proved wholly elusive if this process has not been allowed to occur. On other occasions the truth has to be concealed for the public good, as in times of war, for national security and even in delicate financial matters when volatile markets can make or break economies.

Sovereignty   Rousseau pointed out that the British electorate only has true power over national decision-making **sovereignty** on election days; once they have voted, power is virtually immune from popular influence.

Elites   As Robert Michels observed with his 'iron law of **oligarchy**', outwardly democratic forms are usually subverted by small elites who come to control all the major institutions.

Media   The media now dominates the conduct of democratic politics, and politicians, with their media manipulators or 'spin doctors', have been able to disguise and obfuscate the real issues when it has suited them.

Key concepts in the study of politics

What is a concept?

A concept is usually expressed by a single word or occasionally by a phrase. Just to delve briefly into the philosophy of conceptual analysis, concepts are frequently general in nature, representing a specific function or category of objects. As Andrew Heywood (1994: 4) explains:

> a concept is more than a proper noun or the name of a thing. There is a difference between talking about a chair, a particular and unique chair, and holding the concept of a 'chair', the idea of a chair. The concept of a chair is an abstract notion, composed of the various features which give a chair its distinctive character – in this case, for instance, the capacity to be sat upon.

It follows, therefore, that the concept of a 'parliament' refers not to a specific parliament in a given country but to the generality of them – the abstract idea underlying them. By the same token, as we grow up, we come to attribute meaning and function to everyday objects through learning the appropriate concepts – plates, cups, windows, doors and so forth. Without these concepts we would be totally confused, surrounded by a mass of meaningless phenomena. In one sense concepts are the meaning we place on our surrounding world, impose on it, to enable us to deal with it. Similarly, we come to understand the political world through concepts that we learn from our reading, the media and our teachers. Over the years we come to extend them and refine them in order to achieve a sophisticated understanding, to become 'politically literate'. To use a slightly different analogy, concepts are like the different lenses opticians place in front of us when attempting to find the one that enables us to see most effectively. Without them we cannot bring a blurred world into focus; with them we achieve, or hope to achieve, some clarity and sharpness.

Power and authority and other ideas

These are two central ideas in the study of politics and need to be understood from the outset.

Power   In essence this means the ability to get someone else to do what they otherwise would not have done. This could be achieved through direct coercion: threatening or delivering violence; pointing a gun at someone. While this relationship might be widely reflected in relations between states, it is rare, except in brutal tyrannies, for it to occur within organised states. Here there is a system for the management of disputes and usually this precludes the use of force or coercion, except as a background resort if all else fails.

US political scientists, Bachrach and Baratz (1981), argued that power is more subtle than this: decisions made by politicians not to do things were just as important as those actually made. If a matter is deliberately marginalised or ignored completely then considerable power is being exercised in keeping the matter off the political agenda. Political philosopher Karl Marx argued that those with control over wealth and its production effectively ruled society as they were able, through their control of the main institutions of society, to permeate it with the values upon which their own power rested. Thus, in his view, rich capitalists were able to win acceptance for their economic system as unarguable 'commonsense'.

Authority   This is the acceptance by someone of another's right to tell them what to do – for example, a police officer or a judge. In other words this is *power* with the crucial added ingredient of legitimacy. For it to work the means whereby authority is granted – a process of discussion in an elected parliament – and the related institutions must be regarded as legitimate and authoritative. Few governments can survive without this characteristic.

Interests   This term relates to what politicians are concerned to achieve. It could be more resources for a specific group in society, or more generally a class of people. It could be the reversal of a political decision – for example, withdrawal from the EU – or it might be the obtaining of a place of status and power in government or merely an honour like a knighthood or a peerage. George Orwell in his dystopic novel, *Nineteen Eighty-Four*, suggests politicians are basically concerned to accumulate power, often for its own sake (see above, Politicians and their ambition). Certainly history can offer up any number of despots and tyrants – Hitler, Stalin, Saddam Hussein, Gaddafi – who would fit this bill, but in a democracy, to some extent an antidote to political **tyranny**, safeguards are usually built in to prevent such a leader from gaining power.

Actors   This term is often used to describe people who participate in politics: the *dramatis personae* of the process, which has often been likened to a performance or a game. Indeed US Senator Eugene McCarthy once wittily suggested that:

> Being in politics is like being a football coach. You have to be smart enough to understand the game and dumb enough to think it's important.

Legislature   This is the element of government in a democracy which is usually elected by a society to discuss and pass the laws by which it wishes to be governed. It is the election which provides the democratic authority the government needs to govern effectively. So, in the case of the UK, it is Parliament, comprising the Commons, Lords and the Queen. It hardly needs saying that, at the time of writing, only the first element is democratically elected.

Executive   This element is responsible for implementing the policies and laws produced by the legislature. In the Westminster model of government the government is formed by the party winning a majority at a general election. In the US model the President is elected separately and has a **legitimacy** similar to that of the legislature, producing a relationship between them which is essentially one of conflict and cooperation through debate and negotiation.

Judiciary   This is the part of government which interprets the laws, running the legal system of courts and the machinery of justice. It also handles appeals against alleged miscarriages of justice and rules whether laws are compatible with EU law which, since 1972, has taken precedence over domestic law by virtue of the terms of the 1957 Treaty of Rome which originally founded the European Union.

Some political concepts are merely descriptive, for example 'election', but others embody a 'normative' quality – they contain an implication of what 'ought' to be done. Such a concept is:

Democracy   This notion of citizen ability to elect and remove government goes back to the Greeks who pioneered it in their city states. Churchill famously said of democracy that:

> No one pretends that democracy is perfect or all wise. Indeed, it has been said that democracy is the worst form of government, except for all the others that have been tried from time to time.

In Britain it evolved out of conflicts between an absolute monarchy and an advisory council-cum-parliament reflecting the wealth all monarchs at that time needed to rule. After centuries of gradually emerging authority the latter refused to endorse the royal will and a short but bitter Civil War (1642–49) – in which parliamentary forces took the field under Oliver Cromwell against royalist armies – saw the king deposed and executed in 1649. In 1660 the monarchy was restored but had lost its supremacy to Parliament which was now set on a trajectory of increasing and decisive control over government business. The 1832 'Great Reform Act' laid the foundations for the democratic representation that has continued to evolve to the present day.

Representation   This is another normative idea, central to democracy in that it enables large societies to be ruled to a degree, admittedly tenuous when few are interested in politics, by every citizen. The authors of the American Revolution adopted Reverend John Mayhew's resonant 1750 phrase – 'No Taxation without Representation' – as the banner of their cause because they believed the right to levy taxes could legitimately be obtained only through the consent of the American peoples' elected representatives.

Precisely what form **representation** takes is another matter as there is more than one possibility. The explanations below unpack the different nuances of the term.

1 'Altruistic': here someone will allegedly seek to protect and advance the interests of a group in society – for example, the poor. Whether such stated objectives – for example, by MPs – are genuine, however, will always be a matter of judgement for voters.

2 'Delegate representative': this is when someone is obligated to represent voters' views in a defined way.

3 'Judgement representative': this version, wholly antithetical to item 2 above, is forever connected to the orator and theorist Edmund Burke who, in 1774, told his electors in Bristol:

> Your representative owes you, not his industry only, but his judgement; and he betrays, instead of serving you, if he sacrifices it to your opinion.

This approach risks being elitist in that it assumes the representative better knows what is good for his/her electors than they do.

4 'Revolutionary or "class" representative': this is usually associated with Marxist notions that free enterprise **capitalism** benefits the middle classes but effectively brainwashes working-class voters to the fact of their own exploitation. Marxists argue that only those revolutionaries who are aware of the proletariat's *genuine* interests can truly represent them.

5 'Educated representative': this is the view that voters require substantial knowledge of current affairs before they can properly vote. But if education is to be the criterion for representation, then why not select those who excel in competitive exams to represent us in government, like the mandarins of imperial China? (see Heywood 1994: 178–9).

6 Representation as microcosm: American President John Adams (1735–1826) argued that the legislature should reflect every facet of society, becoming: 'a portrait in miniature of the people at large, as it should think, feel, reason and act like them'. This is a rather narrow view, however, which suggests a man cannot represent a woman or someone of one social class represent a voter from another.

In the British system representation is accepted as a fundamental requirement but no single interpretation is entrenched. Rather – perhaps in tune with Britain's pragmatic traditions – aspects of several of the above can be discerned. Apart from the occasional exceptions, British politicians are relatively non-corrupt compared with most other countries and take their representative duties seriously. Labour veteran Tony Benn has argued for the delegate approach to representation, but for his fellow parliamentarians the Burkean view is the more accepted; the revolutionary approach has never been widely supported in Britain; and, while most MPs are well educated, it is not thought that a high level of education is an essential prerequisite either for an MP or for a voter.

Human nature   This idea is central to the study of politics, that how human beings behave depends on their essential nature, so philosophers have speculated upon its essence. Thomas Hobbes, for example, was pessimistic: he felt that without the protective constraints of civilised society, the selfish nature of human beings would make life 'solitary, poor, nasty, brutish and short'. There would be no security of property, 'no thine and mine distinct; but only that to be everyman's, that he can get; and for so long as he can keep it'. Others did not agree. French philosopher Jean Jacques Rousseau argued that it was the evils of modern society itself which were responsible for its own dysfunctions. Karl Marx too was an optimist on this topic, arguing that mankind was much better than it appeared because of the corrupting effects of the harsh economic system of privately owned capital. Marx believed that human nature was the rogue product of a sick society, asserting: 'Environment determines consciousness'. It followed that changing the social environment for the better would improve human nature too.

Charles Darwin's (1809–82) theory of evolution encouraged some, like Herbert Spencer (1820–1903), to argue that this notion of the 'survival of the fittest' validated capitalism as the way in which the human species was developing itself and to argue against government interference with the 'natural order' of things. Too much of it and a revolution would be needed to correct the imbalance.

Holocaust and human violence   Many would adduce last century's two world wars, the Holocaust, 9/11, the Iraq war and the spread of international crime and terrorism as evidence that mankind has never lived through a more violent or bloodier era. However, the controversial evolutionary biologist, Steven Pinker, begs to differ in his massively well-researched book, *The Better Angels in our Nature: The Decline of Violence in History and its Causes*. A thumbnail sketch by Pinker of his own argument is as follows:

The medieval rate of homicide was 35 times the rate of today, and the rate of death in tribal warfare 15 times higher than that. Collapsed empires, horse-tribe invasions, the Crusades, the slave trade, the wars of religion, and the colonisation of the Americas had death tolls which, adjusted for population, rival or exceed those of the world wars. In earlier centuries the wife of an adulterer could have her nose cut off, a seven-year-old could be hanged for stealing a petticoat, a witch could be sawn in half, and a sailor could be flogged to a pulp. Deadly riots were common enough in 18th-century England to have given us the expression 'to read the riot act', and in 19th-century Russia to have given us the word 'pogrom'. Deaths in warfare have come lurchingly but dramatically downward since their post-war peak in 1950. Deaths from terrorism are less common in today's 'age of terror' than they were in the 1960s and 1970s, with their regular bombings, hijackings, and shootings by various armies, leagues, coalitions, brigades, factions and fronts.

(Steven Pinker, *Prospect*, November 2011)

Pinker therefore, dares to suggest that the growth of moral repugnance at torture and violence together with less barbarous civil punishment practices, has actually caused beneficial changes in human nature. Some call him a Panglossian optimist (after Voltaire's absurdly naïve character in his *Candide*), but others welcome his well-supported contention that improving human nature is by no means a lost cause.

Nationalism　It would be wrong to assume that nationalism, or passionate support for one's country has *always* been around. The extension of loyalty to a common ethnicity within a common territory, all sharing a common history and culture, including struggle against common foes, arrived around 250 years ago and was facilitated greatly by industrialisation and modern economies. In the case of England it probably arrived earlier, around Elizabethan times; in Shakespeare's *Henry V* we have the king exhorting, 'Cry God for Harry, England and St George!'

The French Revolution of 1789 asserted the notion that everyone is endowed with certain **natural rights** – for example, the right of people to govern themselves, and that a national community should be allowed to rule itself. This helped breath fire into a number of national movements in the nineteenth century including those of Belgium, Greece and Poland, not to mention the unifying nationalism of Italy and Germany. England, and its wider expression, Britain, has tended to pride itself on not being especially nationalistic, and on this side of the Atlantic, American patriotism is often seen as rather too overt and crude. Yet, fierce sentiments do exist just below the surface, as in the raucous support for the national football team and the 'Euro-scepticism' expressed towards the EU demonstrate.

Class　Every society becomes stratified sooner or later into those with power and those without. The Greeks and Romans had slaves; Saxon and Norman nobility in England had serfs and peasants working their estates; and by the nineteenth century there were great masses of people

Human nature – Milgram's experiment

The experimental psychologist Stanley Milgram conducted a historic experiment in 1963 which suggested that – even though we might think it's the last thing we might do – virtually everyone is capable of being disturbingly cruel in response to presumed authority. He set up a situation in which people, more or less at random, were invited to join an alleged test involving someone tied to a chair. The participant was told by a man in a white coat who appeared to have scientific authority to ask the pinioned person some questions and to administer electric shocks if the answers were wrong. The subject of the test was, in fact, an actor who shouted and writhed in response to the shocks. The participant, however, was told to continue with the shocks notwithstanding the subject's screams right up to an allegedly fatal level of 450 volts. Most of them did so without serious complaint. This experiment, essentially into human nature, showed, somewhat bleakly, that most of us are capable of behaving like guards in concentration camps if we accept the authority of the person directing us to apply sadistic or even fatal force.

working in factories owned by a small group of super-rich businessmen. For Karl Marx the formation of different classes and the consequent conflict between them was the motive force of history, constantly changing the present society into the future one. Studying British society in the industrial era of the eighteenth and nineteenth centuries he discerned a small property-owning middle class (or *bourgeoisie*) controlling the lives of a vast new working class (or *proletariat*). His analysis was so profound, detailed and acute he immediately influenced thinking on society all over Europe, yet he did much more.

Marx believed the duty of a philosopher was not just to study society but to *change* it. He went on to argue that in the age of capitalism the rich would so exploit the poor that in the end the latter would rise up, cast off their shackles and commence a process whereby members of the working class would seize control of their own destinies. It followed, according to Marx, that the duty of progressive people everywhere was to assist this historical process and help provide the vanguard of the working-class revolution.

Today the British working class has halved in size since the *early* twentieth century and the middle class has burgeoned. John Major, when he became Prime Minister in 1990, tried to argue that Britain was now 'classless', but few accept this complacent analysis which so favours the group in power. Andrew Adonis and Stephen Pollard, in their book *A Class Act* (1997), show how a new 'super class' emerged on US-style salaries – half a million a year or more for top executives – and how another group – sometimes called an 'underclass' – has emerged at the bottom, living in poverty, substantially on welfare benefits. Attempts by New Labour after 1997 to remove class inequalities entailed massive expenditures on welfare services, but the evidence is that the inequalities remain huge: only the rate of change has been arrested. With an Eton-educated Prime Minister in Downing Street, class is still very much a live political issue in the UK.

Freedom   This elusive concept divides into 'freedom from' and 'freedom to': negative and positive freedom. It is imperative that people are free from the fear, persecution and imprisonment of a tyrannical regime, but also important that people are not prevented by circumstances – birth, education, poverty – from having the chance to realise their potential as human beings. While both left and right can agree on the avoidance of the former, they differ sharply over the latter.

The nineteenth-century liberal philosopher, T.H. Green (see Wemde 2004), first argued, in modern times, for 'positive freedom'. He believed that anyone prevented from realising his or her full potential was in a real sense 'unfree'. He defined freedom as the ability of people to 'make the best and most of themselves'. If they were not able to do this then

they were not free. This definition, so attractive to socialists as it implied direct assistance to the needy, in theory opened up the whole field of government intervention, especially via welfare services. Such a formulation of the concept also carries with it the clear implication that wealth should be redistributed to give more chances to more people: for example, an unemployed man would be able to feed his family, via benefits, until he could find a new job.

Opponents of this approach, echoing classical liberals, claim that it is self-defeating: the government takes away the individual's incentive to improve his or her lot; it takes away the freedom of employers to employ workers at rates the market requires; it is part, in fact, of a subtle, incremental tyranny. In the twentieth century Friedrich Hayek (2001) and the economist Milton Friedman (1962) argued this case passionately, insisting that such a position was the 'road to servitude'. Sir Keith Joseph, a disciple of both thinkers, stated flatly that 'poverty is not unfreedom'.

Defenders insist that unless individuals are empowered to realise their personal potential, then they are not truly free. They also argue that the kind of freedom right-wingers and classical liberals want is the freedom of the strong to dominate the weak, or, as R.H. Tawney (1931) vividly put it, 'the freedom of the pike is death to the minnows'.

Equality   This is another two-pronged concept, comprising 'equality of opportunity' and 'equality of outcome'. The left prefer the latter, the right the former. Both agree on the need for equality of opportunity and both sign up to it in respect of the law, gender, race and career choices; the problem lies with the 'outcome' bit. The right maintain that we already have full equality in respect of all the items mentioned. They cite the fact that anyone can proceed educationally, whatever their circumstances, provided they are dedicated and put in the effort. The left counter that the claim is disingenuous in that, while the odd one or two might manage to climb to the top from very humble beginnings, the majority fail miserably.

Meanwhile, those born in comfortable and supportive middle-class families not only do much better in terms of education and career, but also in terms of gaining positions of power in society: director's boardrooms, senior ranks of the armed forces, journalism, civil service and academe not to mention Parliament and the Cabinet. If the analogy of a race is used, children from poor backgrounds, with less caring parents, start it from some distance behind those from privileged backgrounds who are given a flying start.

Left-wingers have argued that the 'playing field' should be level for everyone and have urged more equal salaries or redistribution via taxation and state benefits. This provokes the right-wing riposte that such actions remove incentives: if people can survive easily on benefits, they will not feel the need to work and improve themselves. In consequence, society will be the poorer and those who have worked hard will see their reward highly taxed so that the lazy can benefit. Wilkinson and Pickett' 2009 book, *The Spirit Level*, identified **inequality** as a major source of social dysfunction worldwide. Its opening paragraph reads as follows:

> It is a remarkable paradox that, at the pinnacle of human material and technical achievement, we find ourselves anxiety-ridden, prone to depression, worried about how others see us, unsure of our friendships, driven to consume and with little community life. Lacking the relaxed social contact and satisfaction we all need, we seek comfort in over-eating, obsessive shopping and spending, or become prey to obsessive alcohol, psychoactive medicines and illegal drugs.

The appearance of *The Spirit Level* in early 2009, caused many hearts on the left of centre to beat faster as it seemed at best to prove and at minimum to reinforce some of the fundamental truths such people have always maintained. What the book asserts is that relative socio-economic inequality is extremely harmful and at the heart of most of our acute social problems.

The book illustrates this thesis with a plenitude of diagrams and tables so that, by the end of the book, the truth of their argument seems to be beyond doubt. In a nutshell, the authors argue that the wider the socio-economic gap in a country, the greater the social dysfunction regarding: child wellbeing and educational achievement, anxiety levels, mental health and drug abuse, levels of self-esteem, social deviance and incarceration, life expectancy and, even, obesity. Critics accuse the authors of selectively choosing countries to study which support their main thesis but this they robustly deny and refute.

Social justice   Who should get what in society? This concept causes as much disagreement and very similar debate as that over equality. Marx's ideal communist society was supposed to deliver: 'From each according to his ability, to each according to his needs.'

At the heart of this notion of social justice is that large accumulations of wealth, side by side with poverty and ill-health, are not justifiable. It follows, according to this approach, that wealth should be redistributed in society and, indeed, between nations. On the other hand, even left-wing theorists agree that some economic inequality is necessary to make the economic system work, so the real debate concerns how much redistribution is needed to achieve justice.

One influential thinker on the Left has been John Rawls, whose book *A Theory of Justice* (1999) has occasioned much debate. He asked us to consider what distribution of goods – what rewards would go to whom – we would endorse if we were rational people planning a society but, crucially, were *unaware* of our own capacities. In this way it would be possible to prevent people from favouring their own talents and strengths – for example, preventing a clever person from advocating a meritocracy or a physically strong person a free-for-all society. This ensures that any decisions reached would be neutral. Rawls argues that all would agree on the desirability of the greatest possible degree of liberty in which people would be able to develop their talents and fulfil their life plans. In addition, however, Rawls posits the '*difference principle*', whereby he maintains that social and economic inequalities – differences in wealth, income and status – are only just if they work to the advantage of the most *disadvantaged* members of society and only if they can be competed for fairly by all. Rawls argues that in such a situation rational people would choose, through a sense of insecurity, a society in which the position of the worst-off is best protected; this would be a market economy in which wealth is redistributed through tax and welfare systems up to the point when it becomes a disincentive to the economic activity. (It has to be said, however, that some poor people oppose high taxation and the benefits public expenditure can give to the poor because they hope one day to be rich and do not wish their bounty to be reduced by the depredations of the taxman.)

On the Right Robert Nozick (1974) has been an influential theorist, arguing that wealth is justifiable if it is justly acquired in the first place (for example, has not been stolen) and has been justly transferred from one person to another. He goes on to argue that if these conditions have not been met, the injustice should be rectified. Nozick rejects the notion of 'social justice', the idea that inequality is somehow morally wrong. If transfers of wealth take place between one group in society and another, it should be on the basis of private charity, made on the basis of personal choice. Nozick's views do not necessarily bolster right-wing views on property, however, as the rectification principle could imply the redistribution of much wealth, especially when it is considered that so much of the wealth of the West has been won at the expense of plunder and slavery in Third World countries.

BOX 1.4

BRITAIN IN CONTEXT

Conceptual dissonance

The former publisher and infamous fraud, Robert Maxwell, once wrote a series of hagiographic studies of East European leaders which sold extremely well in their own countries but showed a strange disinclination to fly from the shelves anywhere else. In the book he wrote about the notorious Romanian leader, Nicolae Ceausescu (1918–89), Maxwell, in an interview incorporated into the text, asks 'Mister President, tell me, why do your people love you so?' This question and its unperturbed reply illustrate the fact that different people have different takes on commonly understood ideas. Maxwell, driven by the self-interest of selling copies in Romania, probably knew the man was a vicious autocrat; Ceausescu in turn probably genuinely believed he was loved, as his famous look of incomprehension indicated when crowds in front of his palace began angrily to interrupt one of his interminable speeches in 1989, a short time before he was deposed and shot. Both men, totally absorbed in their own false worlds, no doubt perceived the world differently from the people they exploited. But such 'conceptual dissonance' tends to occur between nations as well as between different kinds of people.

In many cases this flows from the vastly different histories experienced by countries. France, for example, has never quite recovered from its 1789 revolution founded upon the great ideas of 'Liberty, Equality and Fraternity'. Consequently, new arrivals to France have become citizens of the republic on an equal standing with everyone else. Such legal even-handedness is wholly admirable, one might think, but in the autumn of 2005 its limits were exposed when French leaders, especially Jacques Chirac (President of France 1995–2007) seemed to refuse to believe that the young men of the Muslim faith, many of North African provenance, who were rioting in the suburbs of Paris and other big cities, suffered from severe racial discrimination and disproportionate economic hardship. So deeply ingrained was this belief in equality that no separate social statistics were available regarding France's constituent minorities. They were just the same so there were no separate figures.

Another example of conceptual dissonance is provided by the difference between Western and Muslim societies. In the West free speech is a hallowed principle, defended even if it offends some people holding deep religious beliefs. For fundamentalist Muslims such tolerance is not possible. Anything which reflects what they see as disrespect for the prophet Mohammed they interpret not as merely a difference of viewpoint or maybe satirical humour, but as unforgivable blasphemy. The case of the Danish cartoons published in a right-wing newspaper in November 2005 well illustrated this difference in perception, only one of many between the two cultures. Muslim groups protested and there were violent protests worldwide.

In Japan, still influenced by its ancient culture, the world is also perceived in a different way from in the West. For example, social hierarchy is deemed in some situations to be as important as equality, so that people seated at a dinner table will place the person believed by a group to be the most senior and important in the place of honour while other guests will be placed according to their perceived rank and place in society.

The USA, created in the heat of a revolution against the perceived tyranny of George III, places huge stress on the need for democracy. This helps explain why the USA elects far more public officials than the UK; for example, judges, as well as mayors and sheriffs, are widely elected in America but not in the UK. It might also explain why President George W. Bush and his advisers believed so passionately in disseminating democracy in the Middle East. They believed it would lead to greater moderation, acceptance of the West and happiness for the Arab citizens concerned. For a long while it seemed this assumption had tragically misfired in the case of Iraq, invaded in 2003, whereupon it descended into chaos for several years. At the time of writing (2013) Iraq seems relatively peaceful but the cost has arguably been prohibitive.

Analysing the political process

To illustrate some of the concepts used in the understanding of the political process a hypothetical situation is posited below and its implications considered. A major national newspaper breaks a story that Kevin Broadstairs, a Conservative Cabinet minister, has been having an affair with an actress. The PM issues a statement in support of his colleague and old friend from university days. However, more embarrassing details hit the front pages of the tabloids, including the fact that the same actress has also been carrying on with a senior member of the Opposition. The 1922 Committee (the controlling body of Conservative MPs) meets, and influential voices call for a resignation.

This not unfamiliar situation can be analysed as follows:

- *Interests*: The PM needs to appear above suspicion of 'favouritism' but also needs to show that he is loyal and not a hostage to either groups of backbenchers or the press. Broadstairs obviously has an interest in keeping his job, retaining respect within his party and saving his rocky marriage. The governing party needs to sustain its reputation as the defender of family values. The press wishes to sell more newspapers.

- *Actors*: In this situation they are potentially numerous: the PM, Broadstairs, the actress, her former lovers, backbench MPs, editors, television producers, the Opposition, Mrs Broadstairs and (unfortunately) her children, the Church, feminists and anyone else willing to enter the fray.

- *Power*: The power relationship in these circumstances is naturally influenced by the ability of each side to enforce threats. The PM has the power of political life or death over the minister but would like to show his strength by resisting resignation calls; Broadstairs effectively has no power in this situation and is largely dependent on the PM's goodwill and possible press revelations.

- *Authority*: No one questions the PM's right to sack Broadstairs. However, the press's right to force resignations is very much resisted by politicians. The ultimate authority of the governing party to call for the minister's head is also not questioned.

- *Political process*: Will Broadstairs survive? Our minister in this situation is a hostage to the discretion of his mistress and other people either involved or perceiving an interest in the affair.

The outcome will depend on the following:

- *Political will*: How prepared are the PM and Broadstairs to stand firm against resignation calls? How long could he hold out once the 1922 Committee has given the thumbs down? How long would this committee stay silent as it saw the issue eroding voter support? How effective would Broadstairs' enemies in his own party be in hastening his downfall?

- *Influence*: How much influence does the PM have in Fleet Street? The evidence suggests that political sympathies of a paper count for nothing when a really juicy scandal is involved. Even right-wing papers carried full coverage of sleaze stories relating to John Major's Government. Does Broadstairs have a body of support on the back benches, or is he a 'loner'?

- **Manipulation**: How good is the minister at coping with the situation? Can he make a clean breast of it, like Paddy Ashdown regarding his extramarital affair in January 1992, and survive with reputation arguably enhanced? Can he handle hostile press conferences and media interviews (as David Mellor did with aplomb – though they did not save his political career ultimately)? Can the minister call up old favours on the back benches?

Let's suppose that things quieten down for a few days, the PM defends his friend at Question Time and the wife says she'll stand by her man. If this was all there was to it, Broadstairs would survive and live to fight again, albeit with his reputation and prospects damaged. We saw that in the somewhat similar David Mellor case in 1992 the revelations kept on coming (much to public amusement and his embarrassment), but the crucial revelations concerned acceptance of an undeclared free holiday by the minister. After this, backbench calls for a resignation and an excited press ensured that Mellor had to go.

The political process in this case is a little haphazard and depends to some extent on each day's tabloid headlines. It will also depend on the PM's judgement as to when the problem has ceased to be an individual one and has escalated to the point when his own judgement and the political standing of his party are in question. Alastair Campbell, Blair's famously powerful press secretary, reckoned that if public criticism of a minister continued after 14 days then, even if blameless, the minister would have to resign as such publicity prevents the minister from functioning as the government requires. Once that point has been reached it is only a matter of time before the minister's career is over. There was much in ex-Prime Minister Harold Wilson's tongue-in-cheek comment that 'much of politics is presentation, and what isn't, is timing'.

Plan of the book

This opening chapter has discussed the meaning of politics, the nature of politicians and key concepts in the study of politics. The rest of the book, organised in six parts, follows directly from the definition we adopted on page 4.

Politics is about conflicting interests: Part 1 provides the historical, social and economic contexts from which such conflicts emerge in Britain; Part 2, on ideology, examines the intellectual basis of such conflicts. Politics is centrally concerned with how state institutions manage or resolve conflicts within society: Parts 3, 4 and 5 deal respectively with the representative, legislative (law-making) and executive (law-implementing) processes whereby such management takes place or is attempted. Finally, Part 6 examines how these institutions handle the major policy areas.

Chapter summary

This introductory chapter explains that politics is about the management and resolution of conflicts about what people want to do and achieve. It looks at the career of politicians and seeks to explain career motivations as well as attendant dangers. The study of the subject focuses on how this process is performed, especially the way individuals relate to the state. Key concepts in the study of politics are explained including power, authority, equality, representation, democracy, freedom, democracy and social justice.

Discussion points

- Why do you think people go into politics and make it their life's work?
- Think of a typical political scenario and analyse it in the way demonstrated in the chapter.
- Which interpretation of equality and social justice seem most appealing to you?

Further reading

Crick's classic work (2000) is invaluable reading, as an accompaniment to this book, as is Duverger (1966). Leftwich (1984) is worth reading as an easy-to-understand initiation, and Laver (1983) repays study too. Renwick and Swinburn (1989) is useful on concepts, though Heywood (1994) is by any standards a brilliant textbook. Axford et al. (1997) is also well worth looking into. Riddell (1993) is both highly perceptive and very entertaining – a must for anyone wondering if the subject is for them. O'Rourke (1992) is a humorous but insightful book. Oliver (1992) is an amusing collection of silly quotations from politicians. Michael Moran's book (Moran 2011) offers a subtle and authoritative introduction.

Bibliography

Adonis, A. and Pollard, S. (1997) *A Class Act: The Myth of Britain's Classless Society* (Hamish Hamilton Ltd).

All, A.R. and Peters, B.G. (2000) *Modern Politics and Government* (Macmillan), Chapter 1.

Axford, B., Browning, G.K., Huggins, R., Rosamond, B. and Turner, J. (1997) *Politics: An Introduction* (Routledge).

Bachrach, P. and Baratz, M. (1981) 'The two faces of power', in F.G. Castles, D.J. Murray and D.C. Potter (eds) *Decisions, Organisations and Society* (Penguin).

Crick, B. (2000) *In Defence of Politics* (Continuum).

Critchley, J. (1995) *A Bag of Boiled Sweets* (Faber and Faber).

Dearlove, J. and Saunders, P. (2000) *Introduction to British Politics* (Polity Press), Chapter 1.

Duverger, M. (1966) *The Idea of Politics* (Methuen).

Friedman, M. (1962) *Free to Choose: A Personal Statement* (Secker and Warburg).

Gamble, A. (2000) *Politics and Fate* (Polity Press).

Giddens, A. (1998) *The Third Way* (Polity Press).

Hague, R., Harrop, M. and Breslin, S. (2000) *Comparative Government and Politics* (Palgrave).

Hayek, F.A. (2001) *The Road to Serfdom* (Routledge Classics).

Healey, D. (1990) *The Time of My Life* (Penguin).

Heywood, A. (1994) *Political Ideas and Concepts* (Macmillan).

Jones, B. (2005) *The Dictionary of British Politics* (Manchester University Press).

Kingdom, J. (1999) *Government and Politics in Britain* (Polity Press).

Lasswell, H. (1936) *Politics, Who Gets What, When, How?* (McGraw-Hill).

Laver, M. (1983) *Invitation to Politics* (Martin Robertson).

Leftwich, A. (1984) *What is Politics? The Activity and its Study* (Blackwell).

Minogue, K. (2000) *Politics: A Very Short Introduction* (Oxford University Press).

Moran, M. (2011) *Politics and Governance in the UK* (Palgrave).

Nozick, Robert (1974) *Anarchy, State and Utopia* (Blackwell).

Oborne, P. (2005) *The Rise of Political Lying* (Free Press).

Oliver, D. (1992) *Political Babble* (Wiley).

O'Rourke, R.J. (1992) *Parliament of Whores* (Picador).

Orwell, G. (1955) *Nineteen Eighty-Four* (Penguin).

Owen, David (2007) *The Hubris Syndrome: Bush, Blair and the Intoxication of Power* (Politicos).

Pinker, S. (2007) *The Better Angels in our Nature* (Viking).

Rawls, John (1999) *A Theory of Justice*, revised edn (Belknap).

Renwick, A. and Swinburn, I. (1989) *Basic Political Categories*, 2nd edn (Hutchinson).

Riddell, P. (1993) *Honest Opportunism* (Hamish Hamilton).

Robins, S. (2001) *The Ruling Asses* (Prion).

Tawney, R.H. (1931) *Equality* (Unwin).

Wemde, Ben (2004) *T.H. Green's Theory of Positive Freedom: From Metaphysics to Political Theory* (Imprint Academic).

Wilkinson, R. and Pickett, K. (2009) *The Spirit Level* (Penguin).

Zakaria, F. (2004) *The Future of Freedom* (Norton).

Useful websites

British Politics page: www.ukpol.co.uk

Euro Consortium for Political Research: www.essex.ac.uk/ecpr

International Political Science Association: www.ipsa-aisp.org/

Political Science resources: www.socsciresearch.com/r12html

UK Political Studies Association: www.psa.ac.uk

Blogs

Bill Jones's blog: http://skipper59.blogspot.com/

Norman Geras: http://normblog.typepad.com

Guido Fawkes: http://5thNovember.blogspot.com/

CHAPTER 2

Britain, the world, and Europe

Oliver Daddow

> " **Great Britain has lost an Empire and not yet found a role'** "

Dean Acheson (1962), quoted in Brinkley 1990: 599

Learning objectives

- To understand the nature and extent of Britain's key international relationships.

- To appreciate the ideas that have shaped British foreign policy.

- To explain the dynamics behind the Coalition Government's 'liberal Conservative' foreign policy.

Thanks to Jeremy McIlwaine at the Bodleian Library Oxford for helping me access Churchill's 1948 Party Conference speech.

Britain is a major global political, diplomatic and economic actor by virtue of its imperial history, its membership of key **international organisations**, forward-leaning defence posture and the City of London's position as a leading financial centre. With such a vast web of connections have come real and lasting debates about the most appropriate role for Britain in the world, especially since decolonisation after the Second World War and the turn to Europe as a forum in which Britain tries to exert global influence through its **foreign policy**. Some suggest Britain should safeguard its national interest by working more closely with its partners in the European Union. Others argue that Britain should continue to think and act globally, particularly by cultivating the '**special relationship**' with the United States. In reality very few British leaders have wanted to make a decision in favour of one over the other, performing a difficult foreign policy balancing act as a result. Although their language may change, it is clear that the leaders of all the main political parties continue to see Britain as a 'force for good' in the world by virtue of working the country's Commonwealth, US and EU connections. However, with the age of austerity prompting severe budget cuts across all departments of government a question remains. Can Britain any longer afford a globally engaged foreign policy when it does not have the means to back its good intentions with financial muscle?

Introduction

Britain's global outlook

Former US Secretary of State Dean Acheson's scathing assessment of the state of British foreign policy in 1962 continues to rankle with British politicians of all the major parties. Membership of many of the world's leading regional and international organisations gives Britain a profile and influence that very few other states can match. However, the image of a former great power only slowly and reluctantly coming to terms with its fall from grace has come to characterise assessments of Britain's place in the world by observers from within and outside the country. In no small measure the criticisms act as a useful reality check to politicians from across the board who have continually claimed 'great' global status for Britain in the face of many facts to the contrary, not least the country's decreasing ability to finance an influential global role since the end of the Second World War in 1945. This chapter will study the tension between the rhetoric and reality in British foreign policy as they pertain to discussions about its role in the world, and some of the paradoxes this has thrown up over the decades since 1945.

The Foreign and Commonwealth Office currently manages nearly 270 diplomatic posts in 170 countries, employing 14,000 staff in missions ranging from large embassies to smaller consulates (FCO 2011). Britain aside, France is the only other state that enjoys membership of all the institutions shown in Figure 2.1. However, membership of a given international organisation does not necessarily guarantee influence over its outlook, policies, working methods or activities on the ground. Nor do the British seem as comfortable working with their partners in some international organisations as they do in others. For example, in the aftermath of the Second World War Britain was a founder member, and enthusiastic advocate, of the United Nations (UN) and the North Atlantic Treaty Organization (NATO) but was rather more hesitant about joining what since 1993 has been the European Union (EU). The EU was formerly known as the European Economic Community (EEC), created by France, Germany, Italy, Belgium, the Netherlands and Luxembourg (the last three known as the Benelux states) when they signed the Treaty of Rome in 1957; Britain joined the EEC in 1973. Accounting for the organisational framework within which Britain's global relationships play out helps us to understand both the scope and limits of Britain's role in the world. It also provides crucial insights into the debates surrounding the nature and conduct of British foreign policy today when the financial resources being dedicated to government work across the board are being dramatically squeezed following the stringent government spending cuts announced in the 2010 Comprehensive Spending Review.

The United Nations

Britain was one of the founder members of the UN in October 1945 and has an Ambassador permanently stationed at the UN headquarters in New York, heading the UK's Mission to the United Nations. Together with France, the US, Russia and China, Britain is one of five Permanent Members of the UN Security Council (the P5 of the UNSC), giving it an influential voice in helping the UN's effort to uphold peace and security around the globe through diplomacy, information gathering and the deployment of military force. Ten other states are voted onto the Security Council for a period of two years each, making for a total of 15 states on the UNSC at any one time: the core or permanent members circled by ten non-permanent members (UN undated) (Figure 2.2).

The P5 members have an effective veto over substantive issues that come before the Security Council, giving them significant leverage in core UN discussions and debates (Table 2.1). Since the establishment of the P5 the heaviest users of the veto (Global Policy Forum undated a) have been Russia (124 times) and the US (82 times). This reflects the geopolitical standoff between the Russian and American blocs that developed over nearly 50 years after the establishment of the UN during what was known as the **Cold War**. Britain has used the veto 32 times, the last time in December 1989 along with France and the US over a resolution on the situation in Panama. Other resolutions vetoed by the UK in the 1980s included such issues as sanctions against South Africa, where Britain exercised its veto on several occasions, and over the Falkland Islands (Global Policy Forum undated b). We can see that P5 members tend to use the veto where they deem resolutions to be potentially damaging to their vital national interest, usually but not always defined in security terms.

The European Union

Like many of the international organisations considered in this chapter, the origins of the EU lay in the determination of leading European nation-states after 1945 to avoid sliding into another destructive war, as had occurred twice in the first half of the twentieth century. The wider security context was also an important stimulus and was noticeable in American policy-making circles (see Lundestad 2000; McGuire and Smith 2008). As the Cold War between Russia and the US gathered momentum, Washington strategists wanted to see Europeans building up their national defences as a means of deterring a potential attack from the East, in the event that the 'cold' war turned 'hot'. Attention on the western side of the Iron Curtain became fixed on how to solve the 'German question' and in particular how to tie Germany

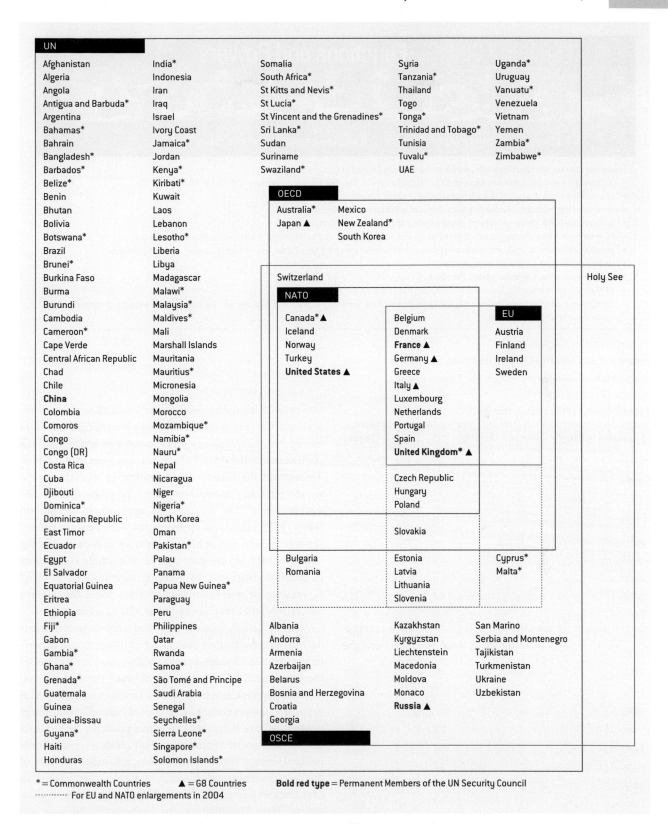

UN

Afghanistan	India*	Somalia	Syria	Uganda*
Algeria	Indonesia	South Africa*	Tanzania*	Uruguay
Angola	Iran	St Kitts and Nevis*	Thailand	Vanuatu*
Antigua and Barbuda*	Iraq	St Lucia*	Togo	Venezuela
Argentina	Israel	St Vincent and the Grenadines*	Tonga*	Vietnam
Bahamas*	Ivory Coast	Sri Lanka*	Trinidad and Tobago*	Yemen
Bahrain	Jamaica*	Sudan	Tunisia	Zambia*
Bangladesh*	Jordan	Suriname	Tuvalu*	Zimbabwe*
Barbados*	Kenya*	Swaziland*	UAE	
Belize*	Kiribati*			
Benin	Kuwait			
Bhutan	Laos			
Bolivia	Lebanon			
Botswana*	Lesotho*			
Brazil	Liberia			
Brunei*	Libya			
Burkina Faso	Madagascar			
Burma	Malawi*			
Burundi	Malaysia*			
Cambodia	Maldives*			
Cameroon*	Mali			
Cape Verde	Marshall Islands			
Central African Republic	Mauritania			
Chad	Mauritius*			
Chile	Micronesia			
China	Mongolia			
Colombia	Morocco			
Comoros	Mozambique*			
Congo	Namibia*			
Congo (DR)	Nauru*			
Costa Rica	Nepal			
Cuba	Nicaragua			
Djibouti	Niger			
Dominica*	Nigeria*			
Dominican Republic	North Korea			
East Timor	Oman			
Ecuador	Pakistan*			
Egypt	Palau			
El Salvador	Panama			
Equatorial Guinea	Papua New Guinea*			
Eritrea	Paraguay			
Ethiopia	Peru			
Fiji*	Philippines			
Gabon	Qatar			
Gambia*	Rwanda			
Ghana*	Samoa*			
Grenada*	São Tomé and Principe			
Guatemala	Saudi Arabia			
Guinea	Senegal			
Guinea-Bissau	Seychelles*			
Guyana*	Sierra Leone*			
Haiti	Singapore*			
Honduras	Solomon Islands*			

OECD

Australia*   Mexico
Japan ▲   New Zealand*
    South Korea

Switzerland   Holy See

NATO

		EU
Canada* ▲	Belgium	
Iceland	Denmark	Austria
Norway	**France** ▲	Finland
Turkey	Germany ▲	Ireland
United States ▲	Greece	Sweden
	Italy ▲	
	Luxembourg	
	Netherlands	
	Portugal	
	Spain	
	United Kingdom* ▲	
	Czech Republic	
	Hungary	
	Poland	
	Slovakia	
Bulgaria	Estonia	Cyprus*
Romania	Latvia	Malta*
	Lithuania	
	Slovenia	

Albania	Kazakhstan	San Marino
Andorra	Kyrgyzstan	Serbia and Montenegro
Armenia	Liechtenstein	Tajikistan
Azerbaijan	Macedonia	Turkmenistan
Belarus	Moldova	Ukraine
Bosnia and Herzegovina	Monaco	Uzbekistan
Croatia	**Russia** ▲	
Georgia		

OSCE

* = Commonwealth Countries   ▲ = G8 Countries   **Bold red type** = Permanent Members of the UN Security Council
---------- For EU and NATO enlargements in 2004

Figure 2.1 Membership of international organisations as at March 2006

Source: Foreign and Commonwealth Office (2006) *Active Diplomacy in a Changing World*,
http://collections.europarchive.org/tna/20080205132101/fco.gov.uk/Files/kfile/ozintpriorities2006Chapt2.pdf

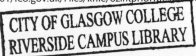

UN SECURITY COUNCIL Functions and Powers

UN Home | Security Council Home | Daily Programme | Webcast

Under the Charter, the functions and powers of the Security Council are:
- to maintain international peace and security in accordance with the principles and purposes of the United Nations;
- to investigate any dispute or situation which might lead to international friction;
- to recommend methods of adjusting such disputes or the terms of settlement;
- to formulate plans for the establishment of a system to regulate armaments;
- to determine the existence of a threat to the peace or act of aggression and to recommend what action should be taken;
- to call on Members to apply economic sanctions and other measures not involving the use of force to prevent or stop aggression;
- to take military action against an aggressor;
- to recommend the admission of new Members;
- to exercise the trusteeship functions of the United Nations in 'strategic areas';
- to recommend to the General Assembly the appointment of the Secretary-General and, together with the Assembly, to elect the Judges of the International Court of Justice.

Figure 2.2 UN Security Council: functions and powers
Source: http://www.un.org/Docs/sc/unsc_functions.html

Table 2.1 Use of the veto in the P5

Period	China*	France	Britain	US	USSR Russia	Total
Total	6	18	32	82	124	261
2008	1	–	–	–	1	2
2007	1	–	–	–	1	2
2006	–	–	–	2	–	2
2005	–	–	–	–	–	–
2004	–	–	–	2	1	3
2003	–	–	–	2	–	2
2002	–	–	–	2	–	2
2001	–	–	–	2	–	2
2000	–	–	–	–	–	0
1999	1	–	–	–	–	1
1998	–	–	–	–	–	0
1997	1	–	–	2	–	3
1996	–	–	–	–	–	0
1986–95	–	3	8	24	2	37
1976–85	–	9	11	34	6	60
1966–75	2	2	10	12	7	33
1956–65	–	2	3	–	26	31
1946–55	(1*)	2	–	–	80	83

* Between 1946 and 1971 the Chinese seat on the Security Council was occupied by the Republic of China (Taiwan), which used the veto only once, to block Mongolia's application for membership in 1955. The first veto exercised by the present occupant, the People's Republic of China, was therefore not until 25 August 1972.

into an institutional framework that would allow it to recover economically and politically without becoming once more an aggressive, expansionist power capable of destabilising the continental landmass of Europe as it had been under Hitler. Throughout the history of **integration** in western Europe we see economic means being used for political ends. The assumption of this 'functionalist' approach to integration (Haas 1958) is that creating interdependence between nation-states is a sound way of helping them see how damaging the selfish actions of one state can be to a whole community of states; furthermore, by working together and 'pooling' sovereignty in international institutions states can achieve collectively what they would not be able to achieve alone.

Various British Conservative and Labour governments decided to remain aloof from Europe's integrationist experiments for over 25 years. Britain finally joined in 1973 under the Conservative Government of Edward Heath, following two failed applications in the 1960s. Despite giving rhetorical support to the general idea of a 'United Europe', Westminster politicians have been cautious about involving Britain in a project they worried could potentially create a supranational political union. Britain was, however, a founder member of the intergovernmental Council of Europe, established in May 1949 with nine other states: Belgium, Denmark, France, Ireland, Italy, Luxembourg, the Netherlands, Norway and Sweden (Figure 2.3). In September 1959 the European Court of Human Rights was established in Strasbourg to ensure that states meet the obligations they sign up to when they join the Council.

- to protect human rights, pluralist democracy and the rule of law;

- to promote awareness and encourage the development of Europe's cultural identity and diversity;

- to find common solutions to the challenges facing European society;

- to consolidate democratic stability in Europe by backing political, legislative and constitutional reform.

Figure 2.3 Aims of the Council of Europe

Source: Council of Europe updated. Reaffirmed in the Warsaw Declaration of May 2005 (Council of Europe 2005)

In Britain, support for the Council of Europe was cross-party and came from such influential figures as wartime leader Winston Churchill (The Churchill Society undated) and Labour's Foreign Secretary at the time of its establishment, Ernest Bevin, who said it would inspire 'something new and hopeful in European life' (Bevin 1949).

The Clement Attlee Labour Government of 1945–51 decided not to take Britain into the European Coal and Steel Community (ECSC).

Formally created by the Paris Treaty of April 1951, the ECSC put control of the two industries vital to a nation's war-making capacity in the hands of a European decision-making body, the High Authority. Its founder members were 'the Six' that would later found the EEC: France, Germany, Italy and the Benelux states. When the Conservatives were returned to power under Winston Churchill in 1955 there were high hopes that he would alter Labour's negativity towards European integration. However, they continued the extra-European focus in the nation's postwar foreign policy by keeping Britain out of the EEC. Instead, in 1960, Britain helped found the European Free Trade Association (EFTA) along with Austria, Denmark, Norway, Portugal, Sweden and Switzerland. The Conservative administration in London saw EFTA as a means of protecting the British economy from the potentially harmful impact of being outside the trading bloc created by the Six; to the EEC Europeans, however, this move looked like a hostile effort to torpedo their ambitious designs at birth. Britain consequently lost a lot of the goodwill it had built up among the countries of western Europe and for many years remained outside the EEC club (Ellison 2000). By 1960 it was fair to say that Europe was at 'sixes and sevens': the six of the EEC against the seven of EFTA.

The creation of EFTA could not disguise the increasingly evident weaknesses in the British economy, and civil servants

PROFILE

Clement Attlee (1883–1967)

Clement Attlee was leader of the Labour Party for two decades, 1935–55, and served as Prime Minister 1945–51, having been Deputy Prime Minister in Winston Churchill's National Coalition Government during the Second World War. The Attlee governments are best remembered for putting in place a large-scale **nationalisation** programme in Britain and for founding the welfare state, including such key and enduring institutions as the National Health Service (NHS). Attlee largely left foreign policy in the hands of his ebullient Foreign Secretary, Ernest Bevin (1881–1951), although he took a close interest in British moves to develop an independent nuclear weapon and to found the postwar international security architecture such as NATO. Attlee and Bevin have been called 'Cold Warriors' every bit as frequently as their Conservative peers from the time (see for instance Taylor 1990), showing the strength of the **consensus** about Britain's role in the world that emerged and consolidated in the early years after the Second World War.

PROFILE

Edward Heath (1916–2005)

Edward Heath was leader of the Conservative Party 1965–75 and Prime Minister during a turbulent period at home and abroad in 1970–74, particularly with regard to the economy and fraught industrial relations. Heath served in the Royal Artillery during the Second World War and this strongly moulded his belief that international cooperation was necessary to overcome some of the worst excesses of nationalism and insecurity in international affairs. He was particularly exercised about how to resolve the 'German problem' in European and global politics. Heath was a critic of Eurosceptics who he believed yearned for Empire and wrongly kept Britain out of the early steps of European integration, and his maiden speech in Parliament in 1950 was on the virtues of Britain joining the European Coal and Steel Community. Heath was proud to have been the Prime Minister who finally helped Britain into the EEC in 1973 and tried to manage foreign policy expectations by talking of Britain as 'a medium power of the first rank' (quoted in Harvey 2011: 5).

This art installation in the Council of Ministers building in Brussels caused something of a stir when it was unveiled in January 2009 to mark the beginning of the Czech Presidency of the EU. It looks like a huge plastic modelling kit, with each of the 27 pieces representing a stereotype of the EU member states. France was on strike ('grève') and Sweden an item of flatpack furniture, while the Bulgarian sculpture had to be covered up (middle right of the image above left) because of complaints about the country being depicted as a 'Turkish toilet' (Gavrilova 2009). Britain, meanwhile, was an empty space (above right). Twelve years after Tony Blair came to power aiming to help Britain be more comfortable working with Europe, key planks of his strategy, such as joining the single currency, had never been put in place. As one former government insider put it: 'By the general election of 2005 Britain was no closer to joining the euro than it had been in 2001 and arguably further away than in 1997' (Price 2005: 366). Psychologically as well as politically it is doubtful if many in Britain feel truly at home in Europe.

Entropa, David Cerny, Justus Lipsius Building Brussels, 1 January to 31 June 2009

Source: Author's photos.

and politicians in London soon began to notice a marked divergence between the performance of the British economy and those inside the EEC. Not just this: Britain's trade patterns were shifting markedly from Commonwealth states to states in western Europe. During the 1960s Britain twice applied to join the EEC but was rebuffed by France's use of the veto to block Britain's accession (Ludlow 1997; Daddow 2003). After the second '*non*' the British left their application on the table and the Conservatives under Edward Heath were finally able to take Britain into the EEC in 1973.

These troubled decades in Britain's European policy set the tone for much of what has followed, with the British routinely struggling to accept the idea of a European future and tending to opt out of new plans for integration, notably the single European currency, the euro. The huge backbench rebellion by Conservative Members of Parliament in October 2011 over a proposal to hold a **referendum** on Britain's EU membership demonstrates the continued ability of the Europe question to be a thorn in the side of Britain's leading political parties (Taylor 2011; Watt 2011). Further-

more, the economic crisis in the Eurozone has reinvigorated Euroscepticism in Britain and this will continue to make 'Europe' a divisive and controversial issue in British foreign policy discussions, especially in the build-up to the much talked about referendum on the EU scheduled to be held during the parliament of 2013–20.

The North Atlantic Treaty Organization

In contrast to the EU, Britain is an enthusiastic participant in the North Atlantic Treaty Organization (NATO), not least because of American membership. Being active in NATO allows London to express its whole-hearted support for Britain's bilateral relationship with the US, forming the axis which 'arguably runs at the heart of the alliance' (Beech 2011: 350). Britain was a founder member of NATO, set up in April 1949 to promote the goals of the Atlantic Charter: freedom, security and prosperity for signatory countries, built on the principles of democracy, individual liberty and the rule of law (NATO 1949). The UK delegation to NATO is based in Brussels, headed by an Ambassador and staffed by civil servants from the Foreign Office, the Ministry of Defence and the three armed services: Army, Navy and Air Force. NATO membership was attractive to Attlee's postwar Labour Government for two principal reasons.

The first and most immediate concern facing British foreign policy-makers when NATO was created was to safeguard the country's security against the potential of attack by Germany and (perhaps more urgently) Russia, as the Cold War heightened East–West tensions in Europe in the later 1940s. Article 5 of the North Atlantic Treaty set down the principle that 'an armed attack against one or more of [the signatories] in Europe or North America shall be considered an attack against them all'. In this event all other NATO members would come to the aid of the party under attack, using armed force if necessary (NATO 1949). Following the terrorist attacks on US soil in September 2011 Article 5 was invoked for the first time in NATO history on 4 October 2011.

The second reason why NATO was attractive to Britain was that it had US membership. With the US on board the organisation possessed military as well as diplomatic credibility and played to the instinctive Atlanticism of British Foreign Secretary Bevin and Prime Minister Attlee. Essentially a product of the Cold War, since the collapse of the Soviet bloc in 1989 NATO has spent a good deal of time defining and redefining its role for the twenty-first century (Medcalf 2008). Since 2003 NATO has expanded both its membership (currently 28 countries) and its military infrastructure so that it can play a constructive part in what are known as 'out-of-area' operations in places such as the Balkans, Afghanistan, the Darfur region of Sudan and, more recently, the successful **intervention** in Libya under Operation Unified Protector from March to October 2011 (NATO 2011).

The Organization for Security and Cooperation in Europe

The Organization for Security and Cooperation in Europe (OSCE) is an intergovernmental body dealing with early warning, conflict prevention, crisis management and post-conflict rehabilitation – the kinds of issues that military organisations such as NATO are ill-equipped to deal with. Originally founded by the Helsinki Act of 1975 at the Conference on Security and Co-operation in Europe (CSCE), it originally sought to promote dialogue between states of the East and states of the West. At the end of the Cold War the CSCE helped the newly independent states in central and eastern Europe make the transition to democracy and free market economies, as well as dealing with internal and external threats to their security and stability (OSCE, undated: 1). The OSCE has a comprehensive three-fold definition of security, working across these dimensions to fulfil its missions: traditional political–military security, economic security and environmental and human security. The methods it uses are equally wide-ranging, from dialogue and security-building, election monitoring and promoting press freedom, through to arms control and environmental activities. You can see in Figure 2.1 that the OSCE is the largest of the specifically security-focused international organisations with 56 members (as of March 2009). Crucially, it is the only organisation outside the UN that brings the US and Russia to the same table.

As with the other international organisations covered here, the UK has a formal delegation based at the OSCE headquarters in Vienna, and this represents the UK at the weekly meetings of the Permanent Council, works on arms control, and with the OSCE's human rights institutions, notably the Office for Democratic Institutions and Human Rights (ODIHR), 'to promote human rights and democracy through project work, election observation missions and legislative advice in participating States'. The Coalition Government has maintained New Labour's focus on promoting human rights in a rules-based international system, clearly set out in the Foreign Office's annual human rights report (for instance FCO 2010).

The Organisation for Economic Cooperation and Development

Britain has been a member of the Organisation for Economic Co-operation and Development (OECD) since 1961. The forerunner to the OECD was the Organisation for European Economic Co-operation, set up in 1948 to administer Marshall Aid funds from the US to help western European states recover from the ravages of the Second World War. The aim of the OECD is to help its members achieve **sustainable economic growth** and employment and more broadly to contribute to global economic stability and expansion by encouraging free trade practices in the developed and developing worlds (OECD undated a). The OECD also gathers together a huge quantity of economic statistics, reports and publications that help London's decision-makers shape the country's foreign economic policy (OECD undated b).

Circles, pivots and bridges: ideas about British foreign policy

Understanding how Britain's external outlook is expressed through its membership of international organisations is one way of understanding Britain's place in the world today. For a more complete picture, however, it is important to appreciate how this practice has been influenced by shifting ideas about Britain's role in the world. In something of an ongoing cycle, ideas help inform the practice which in turn impacts back upon ideas about British foreign policy, so that disentangling the one from the other can be problematic. This section will trace the evolution of British foreign policy thinking by studying two periods. In the first and by far the longer of the two periods we see the big ideas about Britain's role in the world taking shape and entrenching themselves within the political class and public mind at large. This is the imperial period which lasted roughly from the end of the American War of Independence in 1783 to the middle of the twentieth century when Britain developed and managed a sprawling global empire only to see it collapse after the Second World War. The second period began with the election of the Tony Blair-led Labour Government of 1997 which tried, perhaps more than any of its predecessors, to help Britain come to terms with its decline as a 'great' global power. New Labour privileged the ethical dimensions of British foreign policy, making the case for a combination of hard-headed pragmatism and active interventionism to protect British citizens and innocent civilians from harm in trouble spots around the world. Paradoxically, however, ideas about Empire and Britain's status as a major global player have died hard in Establishment Britain and it is doubtful whether New Labour successfully managed to implement a truly post-imperial foreign policy for Britain. David Cameron's Coalition Government has, broadly, accepted the fundamentals of New Labour's foreign policy thinking but badged it differently – 'liberal Conservatism'.

From Empire to decolonisation

At the height of British Empire in the nineteenth and early twentieth centuries, the one idea that dominated British foreign policy thinking was the importance to Britain of possessing and expanding the British Empire. This Empire was constructed after the United States Congress declared in July 1776 that the 13 American colonies which were then at war with Britain would henceforth be independent from Britain – that is, not formally part of the British Empire. Instead of concentrating on its transatlantic Empire, the British threw themselves into fresh imperialist expansion in key strategic locations such as India and the countries of sub-Saharan Africa, so that by the years between the First and Second World Wars the British Empire stretched over one-quarter of the land surface of the earth and contained one-fifth of its population. As one scholar of Britain's role in the world has observed:

> Empire for more than a century was the most important transnational space inhabited by the British and it had a profound impact on British politics, particularly on the way British people thought about race, and about the role of the British state in the world.
>
> (Gamble 2003: 62)

It was both a formal and informal Empire. It was formal in that the British controlled the various colonies which made up the Empire and locked them into an informal economic sphere 'dominated by British companies, and a currency sphere in which the pound sterling was the accepted master currency' (Gamble 2003). The British maintained their domination of global trade by encouraging worldwide acceptance of the principle of the liberal economic order – the free movement of goods, capital and people (Gamble 2003: 79–80) backed by 'a sufficient exertion of power (notably the Navy's "gunboat diplomacy") to secure an open market in which contracts would be enforceable' (Clarke 1996: 13–14). It may seem anachronistic today, but politicians such as Lord Curzon, Viceroy of India 1899–1905, could contentedly claim in the Victorian era that the British Empire was 'the greatest force for good the world has ever seen' while academic historians such as J.R. Seeley at Cambridge could publicly talk of Britain's civilising 'destiny' without fear of contradiction or dissent from the governing elites in Establishment Britain (Schama 2002: 262).

In the years 1950–4 the Empire–Commonwealth accounted for some 49 per cent of Britain's imports and accepted 54 per cent of British exports (Kennedy 1985: 335); in 1956 45 separate governments were controlled by what was then the Colonial Office (Cross 1968: 325). By 1960, however, Harold Macmillan (Conservative Prime Minister 1957–63) identified the growing strength of what he called 'this African national consciousness' which became in the minds of London's foreign policy-makers a symbol that attitudes towards the necessity and desirability of empires were changing at home and abroad. Macmillan observed that: 'The wind of change is blowing through this continent, and whether we like it or not, this growth of national consciousness is a political fact . . . and our national policies must take account of it' (Macmillan 1960). One year later Macmillan applied to take Britain into the EEC, citing structural shifts in Britain's trading patterns from Commonwealth to Empire as a significant factor in the Government's thinking about Britain's policy towards European integration (Camps 1964: 231). Continuing economic crises culminating in the devaluation of sterling in November 1967 helped prompt a second, and again unsuccessful, application, this time by Harold Wilson (Labour Prime Minister 1964–70 and 1974–76). Britain was finally accepted into the EEC club in 1973, and this lengthy process appeared to show that the country's leaders and public had come round to accepting the reduced role and status of a regional power, commensurate with its economic capabilities.

Another demonstration can be seen in the 1964–70 Wilson Government's deep defence cuts which included withdrawing British forces from bases east of the Suez Canal in 1967 (Alexander 2003). This move appeared to indicate Britain's inability to cling to Empire as an outlet for its global power and prestige. Indeed in one interpretation it 'symbolized Labour's determination to leave the Empire behind' altogether (Gamble 2003: 209). However, while the rapid dissolution of Empire over a period of little more than 20 years from the retreat from India and Burma in 1947–8 may have signalled the end of the 'formal' Empire, the values and national purposes Britain had tried to inculcate through the possession of its overseas territories as far afield as Canada, Africa, Asia and Australia left a deep psychological legacy. Echoes of Empire continue to be heard in British foreign policy thinking to this day (Calvocoressi 2009: 177). The 'winds of change' might have blown through the Empire, but had they blown through the corridors of the Foreign Office and Downing Street in London? When considering British foreign policy it is important to ask whether the Wilson years were quite the turning point they sometimes seem, given the persistence of great power pretensions from 1945 to the present.

Churchill's 'three circles' and Britain's 'great' world role

The Second World War proved how futile it was for Britain to hold on to far-flung territories which drained vital resources from its economy at a time when national self-determination movements in Asia and Africa were bringing the ethics of imperial foreign policies into the realm of public and political debate the world over. Britain had already suffered serious economic upheaval with the end of the gold standard in September 1931, when the link between the one-to-one exchange value of the pound and gold was finally broken for good. For an economic system that had been in operation since the early eighteenth century and which had survived (just) the upheaval of the First World War, it was a sign of the economic turbulence of the times that the British had to admit defeat and that the pound was no longer deemed to be as valuable as gold. A more immediate and, in national security terms, potentially more devastating challenge to British power and prestige came from the rise of the Axis powers, Germany, Italy and Japan in the 1930s. The Second World War (1939–45) drained Britain economically. Historian Simon Schama estimates that fighting the war cost Britain £7,000 million ($7 billion), or a quarter of its economy, with defence spending accounting for some 10 per cent of gross domestic product by 1945 (Schama 2002: 540). By the end of hostilities the serious problems afflicting the economy in Britain typified the situation across Europe where all the major players were deemed to be on the verge of economic, not to mention political and social, collapse (Ellwood 1996).

How would the British react to being forced into relying on a now superior economic power, the US, to bail it out of its economic travails and help provide for its continuing national security against a potentially resurgent Germany and a hostile Russia? One idea that took hold came from then Opposition leader, Winston Churchill, in his speech to the Conservative Party Conference in 1948, the theme of which was how to provide for national security when 'the state of the world and the position of our country in it, have sunk to levels which no one could have predicted' (Churchill 1948: 149). In a short passage midway through the speech, Churchill suggested that the British had a unique role to play in the world by virtue of being 'the only country which has a great part to play in every one' of 'three great circles among the free nations and democracies' (all quotations in this section are from Churchill 1948: 153) (Figure 2.4).

Churchill's first circle, 'naturally', was the British Commonwealth and Empire which he had earlier in the speech described as 'the foundation of our Party's political belief'. The second circle was 'the English-speaking world in which we, Canada, and the other British Dominions play so important a part'. Last on Churchill's list was 'United Europe' and this might have been symbolic, especially given the time Churchill spent in the speech discussing the need for close British ties with the US and his comments on the importance of Empire. But what gets forgotten about this speech is that prior to setting out his model Churchill had eulogised the principle of European integration and stressed that 'there is absolutely no need to choose between a United Empire and a United Europe. Both are vitally and urgently necessary.' More evident in the speech than any denigration of the European ideal was Churchill's view that, of all the countries in the world, Britain was uniquely placed to play an active global role by virtue of its worldwide diplomatic entanglements. Its European connections would provide a

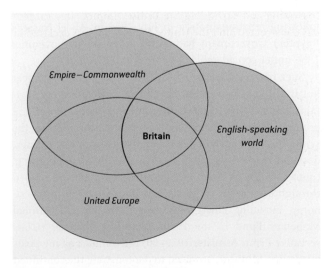

Figure 2.4 Churchill's three circles

prop to, rather than the end of, the nation's outward-looking foreign policy agenda.

Churchill's approach to understanding Britain's role in the world has proved remarkably popular whichever main **political party** has been in power, Labour or Conservative. Even as the British economy fell into a state of disrepair British leaders have never quite been able to give up on the idea that Britain can play out a globally important role for the good not only of Britain but the world itself. A few illustrations from across the post-1945 period nicely illustrate this gap between rhetoric and reality. Churchill's contemporaries such as Attlee and Bevin, overseeing the development of the atomic bomb and dealing with a host of imperial problems and military flashpoints around the world, did not disappoint those with exalted expectations of the role Britain could play globally after 1945, even as the facts of the matter were becoming clearer. For example, while negotiating a huge postwar US bailout to Britain, Foreign Secretary Bevin was adamant that the money would be used to prevent Britain becoming a second-class power and that, in fact, Britain could retain its power and influence with regard to the US and USSR (Taylor 1990: 74–5).

Returning to power after the Attlee-Bevin years, the Churchill governments of 1951–55 saw an opportunity to enact their global great power pretensions, even though by 1952 the Cabinet was openly debating the link between national poverty and foreign policy in times of economic downturn (Hurd 2011: 343). Churchill's Foreign Secretary, Anthony Eden, actively espoused the three circles model in his speech to the Party conference in 1953, evidence that 'the rhetoric lingered on' because it drew on an imperialist mentality 'which he shared with millions' (Hurd 2011: 346). Taking over from Churchill in April 1955, Eden (Prime Minister 1955–57) set about resorting to traditional and rather blunt instruments of British diplomacy in places such as Egypt. It resulted in the Suez Crisis, when a planned invasion in cahoots with France to reoccupy the Suez Canal following renationalisation in July 1956 by Abdel Nasser's Egyptian Government had to be called off in November 1956 under considerable pressure from the US.

Suez marked the end of Anthony Eden's political career but it did less than might have been expected to end Britain's extensive rhetorical commitment to global power and prestige. Harold Wilson, who as we have seen oversaw the symbolically important defence cutbacks from east of Suez, declared in 1964: 'we are a world power or we are nothing' (quoted in Taylor 1990: 133) and this sentiment was echoed through even some of the darkest days for the British economy, including emergency loans from the International Monetary Fund in the 1970s. Margaret Thatcher (Conservative Prime Minister 1979–90) did as much as any postwar Prime Minister, however, to demonstrate the continued vitality of great power pretensions beneath the surface of defence cutbacks and acceptance of a more coherent role for Britain, centring on membership of the EEC. Britain's 1982 invasion of the Falkland Islands, 8,000 miles across the Atlantic, to reclaim disputed British territory that had been captured by the Argentinians in April of that year, led to her pronouncement in a speech at Cheltenham on 3 July that: 'We have ceased to be a nation in retreat' (Thatcher 1993: 235).

Even though the outcome of the conflict was a close-run thing, it helped Thatcher launch an attack on the 'decline' thesis, and its political and public reception showed how the nation still yearned for 'the reproduction of past glories' (Taylor 1990: 123). Enthusiastically donning the Churchillian guise of war leader, Thatcher used this foreign policy adventure to claim that 'Great Britain is great again' (quoted in Reynolds 1991: 261) and harked back to history to ram this point home at Cheltenham: 'we rejoice that Britain has rekindled that spirit which has fired her for generations past and which today has begun to burn as brightly as before' (Thatcher 1993: 235). John Major, Margaret Thatcher's successor as Prime Minister (1990–7), continued like his predecessors to tread a fine line between recognising economic and political reality while at the same time advancing the case for a major **world role** for Britain. Reflecting in his autobiography on Britain's membership of the UNSC the (then) Group of Seven (G7) industrial nations, the nation's hugely effective armed forces, the 'special bonds' of Commonwealth and our 'close links' with the US, Major writes that 'our voice counted at the top table. I was determined to ensure that it should continue to do so' (Major 1999: 495–6). As with so many Prime Ministers and Foreign Secretaries from 1945 onward, this snapshot of Major's foreign policy outlook shows how the British political class has been hooked on the idea of maintaining global pretensions seemingly against all odds. The tensions that have emerged from aspiring to play out a 'great' global role in the face of severe economic problems have broadly come to be captured in the Establishment consensus that, in the words of Douglas Hurd (Conservative Foreign Secretary 1989–95), Britain had 'punched above its weight' in world affairs since 1945 (quoted in Harvey 2011). Had the time come by the end of 18 years of Conservative government in 1997 to accept this assessment and reduce Britain's global great power pretensions? The following sections will study how and why New Labour and then the Coalition Government have struggled to come up with a convincing answer.

Updating the three circles model: Blair's 'bridge', 1997–2010

As we move further away from the war years 1939–45 we might have expected to see a drop in the popularity of the

Churchill analogy as Britain's reduced resources shaped expectations about what was achievable externally. As Britain did less around the world, the pressure would ease on the nation to be everywhere trying to do everything. However, we have already seen that leaderships on both the Labour and Conservative side were fixated by the idea of a great global role. What about a 'new' Labour leader in Tony Blair actively looking to refashion a 'new' image for Britain centred on 'constructive engagement' with the EU, reminiscent of Edward Heath's approach – would he fare any better? Tony Blair reshaped Churchill's three circles model to take account of the geostrategic context of British foreign policy at the turn of the twenty-first century. Blair replaced Empire with the US but made much the same kinds of claim as Churchill about Britain occupying 'pivotal' or special place in the world as an arbiter between Europe, the US and the wider world. Blair's thinking on foreign policy came to centre on the idea that Britain could act as a 'bridge' between Europe (meaning the EU) and the US. In this vision for British foreign policy Britain would maintain its centrality in world affairs by being a Churchill-esque point of contact between Brussels and the national capitals in Berlin, Paris, Rome and so forth on the one hand, and Washington on the other. Blair's thinking was plain to see in 1997, with the 'bridge' in place as a blunt fact of international life: 'We are the bridge between the US and Europe. Let us use it. When

Britain and America work together on the international scene, there is little we can't achieve' (Blair 1997).

Even in speeches where Blair pushed the British to accept a European future he could not resist the bridge analogy: 'we are stronger in Europe if strong with the US. Stronger together. Influential with both. And a bridge between the two' (Blair 1999b). Blair's unwavering public support for George W. Bush's decision to undertake military operations to overthrow Saddam Hussein in March 2003 caused huge controversy within European–American relations, and Britain's decision to support the US aroused great hostility in other leading EU countries such as France and Germany. Undeterred, Blair was still expounding the 'bridge' idea in November 2004, albeit with slightly less confidence than he had done in previous years:

> We have a unique role to play. Call it a bridge, a two-lane motorway, a pivot or call it a damn high wire, which is often how it feels; our job is to keep our sights firmly on both sides of the Atlantic.
>
> (Blair 2004)

Tony Blair's successor Gordon Brown (Labour Prime Minister June 2007 to May 2010) had ably supported this approach to British **identity** and role in the world and, as expected, made little alteration to the policies and rhetoric devised by Tony Blair and his foreign secretaries. In appointing the

Tony Blair spent a lot of time trying to convince the British people and a global audience that Britain was uniquely well placed to act as a bridge between the US and the EU. Not everyone was convinced that his approach was either feasible or desirable. Here are some of the main criticisms levelled at the 'bridge' idea:

1 **A product of New Labour's 'Third Way' style of thinking which sets up artificial binaries and seeks to synthesise them by heading down the middle – part of a 'big tent' political strategy.** One exponent of this view was Robin Cook Foreign Secretary 1997–2001 who noted: 'The concept of a bridge is perfectly tailored for New Labour, as a bridge cannot make choices, but by definition is in the middle' (Cook 2003: 133). Ian Bache and Andrew Jordan are of the same view that Blair's positioning of Britain 'did not eliminate the Atlanticism of the past. Rather, the third way involved transcending such dilemmas' (Bache and Jordan 2006: 8). But did the third way in foreign policy open more questions than it answered?

2 **Avoids making a difficult decision between a more transatlantic or more European direction for British foreign policy: the view from Europe.** Gerhard Schröder, German Chancellor 1998–2005, made the point at an EU–US summit in June 2001 that the problem with Blair's bridge was that the traffic only seemed to flow in one direction (in Seldon 2005: 615). In this view the US had disproportionate influence over the policies and suggestions Blair tried to convince the Europeans to take on board, but Blair did not put European thinking to Washington with anything like the same gusto. Nor did Blair spend enough time selling his strategy to France or Germany or conversely persuading the Americans that the Europeans should be brought on board with regard to decision making in the 'war on terror' (Garton Ash 2003).

3 **Blair said it but didn't mean it, and when push came to shove over Iraq Blair showed his true, Atlanticist, colours.** Like Robin Cook, Clare Short is another ex-government minister turned critic. Short was Head of the Department for International Development, DfID, from May 1997 to May 2003 when she resigned over British policy on Iraq. In her memoirs she writes that 'Blair insists that the UK is a bridge between the US and the EU but over Iraq he demonstrated a total incapacity to act as a bridge' and in the end Britain became nothing more than 'a mouthpiece of the US' (Short 2005: 273 and 296). Christopher Meyer was British Ambassador to the US at the time of the Iraq invasion. His judgement is that already by January 2003 'Blair's famous bridge between Europe and America was sinking beneath the waves' (Meyer 2006: 261).

4 **Blair said and meant it but was unable to put the words into practice: British over-confidence.** By the beginning of 2003, his biographer Anthony Seldon writes, 'While the bridge support was crumbling on the far side of the Atlantic, the always insecure base on the European side was simultaneously disintegrating' (Seldon 2005: 589). In this interpretation Blair failed to convince either the Europeans *or* the Americans that Britain could be a viable go-between. Nor, crucially, could he match the 'hawks' in Washington for influence over Bush's foreign and defence policy thinking. As one former State Department official put it regretfully: 'we typically ignore them and take no notice – it's a sad business' (quoted in Baldwin and Webster 2006).

Figure 2.5 Blair's 'bridge' collapses?

Source: Getty Images

'I come in friendship to renew, for new times our special relationship that is founded on our shared history, our shared values and, I believe, our shared futures.' (Brown 2009)

'. . . in millions of interactions every day – including our massive business relationship – our people forge friendships together. That's what makes this relationship special. But what makes it essential is that it's not just about history or sentiment. It is a living, working partnership. It is essential to our security. It is essential for our prosperity.' (Cameron 2010)

'The disparity in strength meant that the relationship was always more important for the British than the American partner. (Cradock 1997: 52)

How do we judge whether or not the 'special relationship' exists in anything other than the language used to express this elusive quality to bilateral relations between policy-makers in London and Washington? As one critic of the term has put it, 'Politicians are so well practised in massaging each other's egos that the rhetoric about the relationship is poured out automatically regardless of the reality' (Dickie 1994: Preface, 10). Is the Anglo-American relationship solidly built on permanent and enduring features of international politics such as shared history, values, language, economic outlook, and strategic proximity in times of war and conflict? Or are the short-term effects of personal relations between Prime Ministers and Presidents and their respective teams just as important? Do the obvious periods of synchronicity between the countries, for example under Winston Churchill and Franklin D. Roosevelt, Margaret Thatcher and Ronald Reagan, outweigh the periods of turbulence in the relationship, for example between Harold Wilson and Lyndon B. Johnson?

Thinking more widely, is there a certain 'X-Factor' that marks the Anglo-American relationship apart from America's relations with other states in and outside the EU, such as Germany and Japan? Is the relationship more a feature of British foreign policy rhetoric than American, and therefore too one-sided to be deployable as a valid concept that captures the true nature of relations between the two countries? After all, as Dimbleby and Reynolds pointed out in the title of their 1988 book on the subject, the countries are literally 'oceans apart' in more than the odd way culturally and on more than the occasional political issue. At the heart of this question lies the problem of how we measure the quality of diplomatic relations between the two states and then how we compare that outcome against measures for other of the UK and US's bilateral relationships. Henry Kissinger suggested in 1982 that Anglo-American relations are better off being described as a 'durable partnership' (Kissinger 1982) – do you agree?

How 'special' is 'special'?

Source: http://mtblog.newyorker.com/online/blogs/newsdesk/ObamaBrown.jpg

strongly Blairite David Miliband as Foreign Secretary Brown signalled that little would change under his stewardship. Indeed, Brown was so taken with trying to solve the serious economic crisis that hit economies around the world in 2008 that foreign policy took rather a back seat. Brown developed new priorities around such favoured ideals as aid and development to the poorest regions of the world, but on the 'big' issues such as Afghanistan, Iraq and Britain's relations with the EU and US Brown continued where Blair left off.

Siginificantly for our purposes in this chapter, Brown and Miliband alighted on the idea of Britain being at the 'hub' of global political and economic relations, indicating their Churchillian-style conviction that Britain could yet play an exceptional role in international politics (on Brown and Miliband see Daddow 2011b: 243–53).

A 'force for good': British foreign policy from Blair to Cameron

In the previous section we saw how Tony Blair tried to update Churchill's idea of the three circles of British foreign policy for the twenty-first century. This went hand-in-hand with a whole host of other ways in which the New Labour Government from May 1997 set about refashioning Britain for life in the fast-paced twenty-first century. 'New' Labour as the governing party liked to be known, wanted to fashion a 'New' Britain which could build on the best aspects of the country's past but also move beyond that in terms of a fresh appreciation of the nation's role in an era of globalisation and complex interdependence. Churchill's 'three circles' were not quite forgotten but they were thought about in a new light. The question is: did Blair and his team succeed in forging a post-imperial foreign policy? We will take each plank of the New Labour foreign policy agenda in turn, and assess how the Government set about modernising British foreign policy by devising new ways of conceptualising and speaking about Britain's role in the world. We will suggest that the Conservative–Liberal Coalition Government formed in June 2010 signed up to much, but perhaps not all, of what New Labour had in mind for British foreign policy.

Ethics and foreign policy

On 12 May 1997, just 10 days into New Labour's governance of Britain, Foreign Secretary Robin Cook launched a 'New Mission Statement' for the Foreign Office. This was to be part of New Labour's wider approach to government, wishing it to be 'businesslike'. The New Mission Statement went hand-in-hand with a Strategic Defence Review (SDR). Published in July 1998, the SDR sought to align British military capabilities and defence posture more closely with its foreign policy objectives (McInnes 1998), and was built on the characteristic New Labour promise of 'radical change and solid planning' (Robertson 1998: 4). The SDR was updated in 2002 to account for the impact of the events of '9/11' on the global security environment (Cm 5566 Vol. I, 2002). The New Mission Statement set down four goals for British foreign policy, what Cook called his 'contract with the British people on foreign policy' (Cook 1997). The first goal of British foreign policy should be to safeguard national security, particularly but not exclusively through NATO membership. Cook's second goal was economic – to boost British prosperity by promoting UK business abroad and encouraging exports (the Coalition Government has gone even further in this regard). The third goal was to protect the environment and improve the quality of life in Britain. The fourth goal was the most commented upon: 'to secure the respect of other nations for Britain's contribution to keeping the peace of the world and promoting democracy around the world . . . Our foreign policy must have an ethical dimension . . .' with human rights at its centre (Cook 1997). This latter goal went to the very heart of what New Labour felt 'modern' Britain should be about. It believed the country should command respect from other states in the international arena not because of its superior coercive power (the tenets of an imperial foreign policy backed by 'gunboat diplomacy') but because Britain stands out as a beacon, a 'force for good in the world' (Cook 1997).

Doctrine of the international community

In truth, Cook's idea of the 'ethical dimension' never really took off in a serious or sustained way, not least because Prime Minister Blair hesitated to give it enthusiastic backing over a prolonged period of time. Meanwhile, issues such as arms sales to countries with dubious human rights records soon took the gloss off Cook's high-blown rhetoric and rather overshadowed developments that elsewhere had much positive impact (see, for example, *Guardian* 2001). Over New Labour's first term in office (1997–2001) the 'ethical dimension' was quietly dropped, yet New Labour remained rhetorically committed to the liberal idea that Britain should act as a 'force for good' in the world. Blair's regular commitment of UK armed forces to military interventions for humanitarian purposes – for example, in Kosovo in 1999 and Sierra Leone in 2000 – stand out as hard examples of the expeditionary impulse in British foreign policy under New Labour (Daddow 2009). These operations were seen by Blair as instances of the 'international community' in operation. As he saw it, in an era of increased interdependence between states British national interests could be affected negatively by the actions of evil leaders, rogue states or destabilising intra-state conflicts in apparently remote parts of the globe. For example, drugs cultivated from poppies in Afghanistan could appear on Britain's streets because of the speed of modern-day travel and the problems of policing porous national borders; terrorists were gaining ever easier access to the raw materials to make devastating weapons such as 'dirty bombs'. Blair believed collective action could and should be undertaken to sort out humanitarian crises and the problems of crime and international terrorism at source, if such action was judged likely to succeed. He went on to set out the 'circumstances in which we should get actively involved in other people's conflicts': Are we sure of our case? Have all diplomatic options been exhausted? Can military operations be 'sensibly and prudently undertaken'? Are we in it for the long term? And are there national interests involved? (Blair 1999a).

While deemed controversial in some quarters, the 'Blair doctrine' garnered much support 'as the best way of defending our interests and the moral way of promoting our values' (Powell 2007). For instance, the Foreign Office's 2008 Mission Statement, 'Better World, Better Britain' updated and refined Labour's internationalist approach which continued to shape New Labour's foreign policy thinking under Prime Minister Gordon Brown and Foreign Secretary David Miliband from June 2007 to June 2010. Indeed, at the launch of Labour's 2008 National Security Strategy (NSS), Gordon Brown followed in Blair's footsteps by making the case for an 'all risks' approach to understanding and protecting national

During the Kosovo conflict Blair met refugees at a camp in Macedonia to hear their experiences. Both he and Cherie Blair 'were clearly moved by the whole experience' (Campbell 2007: 387) and according to many observers this visit marked a turning point in his commitment to intervention for humanitarian purposes (Seldon 2005: 401). Over Kosovo, Blair became widely regarded as the leader of the Western alliance, much to the chagrin of the Americans

Source: http://news.bbc.co.uk/1/hi/uk_politics/407709.stm; BBC Photo Library

security because 'no country is in the old sense far away when the consequences of regional instability and international terrorism . . . reverberate quickly around the globe' (cited in McCormack 2011: 118).

A liberal Conservative foreign policy

Before coming to power in 2010 Prime Minister David Cameron and Foreign Secretary William Hague were adamant that in government they would pursue what they called a liberal Conservative foreign policy; 'Liberal, because Britain must be open and engaged with the world, supporting human rights and championing the cause of democracy and the rule of law at every opportunity. But Conservative, because our policy must be hard-headed and practical, dealing with the world as it is and not as we wish it were' (Conservative Party 2010: 109). Sceptical of what the Conservative Party election manifesto wrote off as 'grand utopian schemes for remaking the world', Cameron and Hague sought to differentiate their approach from New Labour's and in the process also challenged significant elements of previous Conservative Party thinking (Beech 2011: 358). However, they could not escape the new interventionist 'paradigm' that had taken a hold of British foreign policy. The reason, said Hague, was the pragmatic realisation that the world had moved on and the Conservative Party had to move with the times: 'In Britain, [Tony Blair's] "Liberal interventionism" has generated much debate but to varying degrees all of us have subscribed to it' (Hague 2009).

The major foreign policy crisis that the 2010 Government initially had to deal with – Libya – proved him correct and entrenched the interventionist ideal still closer to the heart of British foreign policy thinking.

Thus, it seems fair to suggest that continuity rather than change has most been in evidence in the conduct of the Coalition Government's foreign policy since 2010, which we can see in three main ways. First, the Coalition Government has accepted New Labour's interpretation that globalisation hugely affects the UK national security by bringing problems from apparently remote parts of the world to Britain's door. **Multilateralism** continues to play a central part in British foreign policy thinking. William Hague in particular has trumpeted the challenges facing foreign policy in a 'networked world' (Hague 2010) and sought to engage with new social media such as Twitter in a bid to reach parts of the national and international communities other Foreign Secretaries could not reach. For example, on 9 June 2011 Hague conducted a 'Twitter chat' on Libya. Insecurity as a product of porous national borders and the growing scale of transnational threats is what the Government's Strategic Defence and Security Review (SDSR) has sought to address (see below).

Second, the Coalition Government has embraced the engaged New Labour interventionist posture and justified a 'war of choice' in Libya accordingly as being of benefit to the British national interest. Cameron and French President Nicolas Sarkozy's handling of the Libyan crisis was a good example of prominent European nations taking a lead in coordinating international efforts to combat human rights abuses, especially on Europe's doorstep where the Americans are less keen to tread. At the same time, there is something in Justin Morris's predication that Cameron will remain more cautious than Blair about intervening in the affairs of another state for acts that fall short of genocide, and the Coalition's 'propensity to resort to force will be markedly less than that exhibited by the governments of Tony Blair' (Morris 2011: 341). After Iraq, the British public's appetite for interventions without clear and obvious purpose appears to be limited at best and this has served to limit any Blair-style adventures (into Syria or Iran for example) on the part of David Cameron.

Third, as outlined in the Government's 2010 Strategic Defence and Security Review (SDSR), the Coalition Government remains committed to pursuing a nostalgically inclined 'great' role for Britain, echoing leaders back to Churchill and since, as we have seen in this chapter. Its opening line reads: 'Our country has always had global responsibilities and global ambitions' (HM Government 2010a: foreword). Even in times of stringent financial austerity the idea that Britain might retrench from its global outlook is anathema to Whitehall decision-makers. As a *Times* commentator noted of Hague's hugely ambitious July 2009 speech on doing everything from revivifying the Commonwealth to engaging more deeply with the emerging 'BRIC' economies (Brazil, Russia, India and China), 'Britain faces the question of whether, after Iraq, financial crisis and recession, it chooses to be a shrunken power. Hague's answer is 'no' (cited in Daddow 2011a: 234). Following the Eurozone crisis, even the idea that Britain

might take on the role of a regional power (wholeheartedly inside the EU) with global interests is a discussion the Government seems unwilling to have – referendum or no referendum on Britain's membership of the EU.

To knock the square peg of an enhanced global outlook into the round hole of financial crisis the Government has sought to do what it feels it needs to protect its national interest on the world stage more strategically, reforming its working methods and increasing cross-department collaboration, particularly with regard to the role of the Department for International Development. The Coalition Government has also preached the merits of a commercial foreign policy in an age of ansterity. Here we find echoes of the 1998 SDR's call for defence and foreign policy to be conducted jointly, more 'smartly' and in a more 'business-like' fashion. Early warning about the likely eruption of security threats, the Government believes, will necessitate less frequent and costly action to rectify the consequences of such instability spreading disorder around the globe. Meanwhile, William Hague has committed himself to strengthening 'the long-term capability and international effectiveness of the Foreign and Commonwealth Office as an institution as the heart of government' (Hague 2011). After what he sees as the organisation's untimely decline during the Blair years, Hague's effort to put a gloss on the role of the FCO will face the same budgetary challenges as his Government's wider attempt to carve out a leading role for Britain in the world.

Chapter summary

This chapter began by exploring the history and legacy of Britain's key international relationships, focusing on its involvement in key international organisations: the UN, EU, NATO, the OSCE and OECD. It moved on to explore the key ideas that have shaped contemporary British foreign policy thinking, centring on Winston Churchill's alluring 'three circles' model of Britain's place in the world and New Labour's updating of that line of thought through its concept of Britain acting out the role of a 'bridge' on the world stage. The final part surveyed the transition from Labour to the Coalition Government, particularly the continued emphasis on interventionism within British foreign policy discourse under the new guise of a liberal Conservative foreign policy.

Discussion points

- Do you think Britain still warrants its place as a Permanent Member of the UN Security Council?
- How much global influence does Britain gain from its membership of (a) NATO and (b) the OSCE?
- Will an in/out referendum on OK membership of the EU settle the Europe question in British politics?
- What are the principal ideas that have helped shape British foreign policy since 1945? Are these ideas relevant today?

- Did the 2003 invasion of Iraq show that Britain still places too much emphasis on its 'special relationship' with the United States?
- Explain how Britain has tried to act as a 'force for good' in the world since 1997. Has it succeeded?
- How does a liberal Conservative foreign policy posture differ from an 'ethical' foreign policy?
- What impact has 'globalisation' had on the definition of the British 'national interest' over the past two decades?

Further reading

Coverage of the general themes, issues and controversies in British foreign policy considered in this chapter can be found in Jamie Gaskarth (2013), John Dickie (2007), David Sanders (1990), Robert Holland (1991) and Paul Kennedy (1985), with a useful focus on the impact of decolonisation on Britain's image of itself as a Great Power in Heinlein (2002). On the strategic, political and economic dimensions of the British Empire see P.J. Cain and A.G. Hopkins (1993) and Eric Hobsbawm (1990); on the notion of the 'two' British Empires – at home and abroad – see Marshall (2001) and Bayly (2001). Ferguson (2004) gives a good overview of Britain's wider imperial experiences. On the 'special relationship' and the myths that surround it see John Charmley (1995), David Dimbleby and David Reynolds (1988), and especially John Baylis (1997) on the slipperiness of the concept. Britain's troubled attempts to come to terms with the idea of European unity are documented in John Young (2000) and Hugo Young (1998), while Daddow (2011b) traces New Labour's troubled attempts to reach a new consensus on the matter. Stephen George's famous thesis (1998) is that Britain has been Europe's 'awkward partner' – even after joining the organisation.

Good surveys of New Labour's foreign policy include Richard Little and Mark Wickham-Jones (2000), Mark Curtis (2003), Paul Williams (2005) and Daddow and Gaskarth (2011). Rhiannon Vickers shows the party political roots of this foreign policy trajectory within the Labour Party (2011), while Anne Deighton (2005) shows the strong links between Blairite and Churchillian thinking on British foreign policy. On the 'ethical' foreign policy see Nicholas Wheeler and Tim Dunne (1998) and for critiques of this agenda see Christopher Hill (2001) and especially David Chandler (2003). William Wallace (2005) critiques Blair's endeavour to situate Britain as a 'bridge' between Europe and America. Reflections on the SDR can be found in Cornish and Dorman (2009).

The foreign policy of the 2010 Coalition Government is well covered in Dodds and Elden (2008), Beech (2011) and Morris (2011). The SDSR receives critical treatment in Dover and Phythian (2011), while the negative implications of Britain's gradual disengagement from the Europe's common effort at defence cooperation is charted in O'Donnell (2011). David Cameron has explained the principles of liberal Conservatism in foreign policy (see for instance, Cameron 2006 and William Hague 2009).

On the causes and conduct of the American Revolution see Wood (2003). The history, structure and functions of the UN are detailed in Baehr and Gordenker (2005) and Thomas Weiss (2012) considers how to improve the UN machine. NATO's post-Cold War identity crisis is well covered in Moore (2007), Smith (2006), Sloan (2010) and Webber and Hyde-Price (2011). For an alternative approach to the OSCE's role in promoting security see Sandole (2007).

Bibliography

Alexander, P. (2003) 'Commonwealth Crises and the Second Application', in Daddow, O.J. (ed.) (2003) *Harold Wilson and European Integration: Britain's Second Application to Join the EEC* (Frank Cass) pp. 188–210.

Bache, I. and Jordan, A. (2006) 'Britain in Europe and Europe in Britain', in I. Bache and A. Jordan (eds) *The Europeanization of British Politics* (Palgrave Macmillan) pp. 3–16.

Baehr, P.B. and Gordenker, L. (2005) *The United Nations: Reality and Ideal*, 4th edn (Palgrave Macmillan).

Baldwin, T. and Webster, P. (2006) 'US State Department official – relationship is one-sided', *The Times*, 30 November, http://www.timesonline.co.uk/tol/news/politics/article1088295.ece, first accessed 23 March 2009.

Baylis, J. (1997) *Anglo-American Relations since 1939: The Enduring Alliance* (Manchester University Press).

Bayly, C.A. (2001) 'The Second British Empire', in R.N. Winks, (ed.) (2001) *The Oxford History of the British Empire: Historiography* (Oxford University Press) pp. 54–72.

Beech, M. (2011) 'British Conservatism and Foreign Policy: Traditions and Ideas Shaping Cameron's Foreign Policy', *British Journal of Politics and International Relations*, vol. 13, no. 3, pp. 348–63.

Bevin, E. (1949) Opening address at Council of Europe, 5 May, http://www.coe.int/t/dc/av/audio_archive_bevin_en.asp, accessed 24 October 2011.

Blair, T. (1997) Speech at the Lord Mayor's Banquet, London, 10 November.

Blair, T. (1999a) 'Doctrine of the International Community', Economic Club, Chicago, 22 April, http://www.number-10.gov.uk/output/Page1297.asp, first accessed 6 September 2005.

Blair, T. (1999b) Speech about Britain in Europe, 14 October, http://webarchive.nationalarchives.gov.uk/20091006031459/number10.gov.uk/page1461, accessed 28 October 2011.

Blair, T. (2004) Speech at the Lord Mayor's Banquet, London, 15 November, http://217.154.230.218/NR/rdonlyres/23B6E38C-DC30-48D8-BAC3-E256351AF119/0/MC_SP_lmbanquetblair_04.pdf, accessed 28 October 2011.

Brinkley, D. (1990) 'Dean Acheson and the "Special Relationship": The West Point Speech of December 1962', *The Historical Journal*, vol. 33, no. 3, pp. 599–608.

Brown, G. (2009) Speech to US Congress, 4 March, http://www.number10.gov.uk/Page18506, first accessed 23 March 2009.

Cain, P.J. and Hopkins, A.G. (1993) *British Imperialism: Crisis and Deconstruction 1914–1990* (Longman).

Calvocoressi, P. (2009) *World Politics since 1945*, 9th edn (Pearson Education Limited).

Cameron, D. (2006) Speech at the British American Project, 11 September, 'A new approach to foreign affairs: liberal conservatism', http://www.conservatives.com/News/Speeches/2006/09/Cameron_A_new_approach_to_foreign

_affairs__liberal_conservatism.aspx, accessed 28 October 2011.

Cameron, D. (2010) Joint press conference with Barack Obama, 26 May, http://www.number10.gov.uk/news/uk-us-relationship-essential/, accessed 28 October 2011.

Campbell, A. (2007) *The Blair Years: Extracts from the Alastair Campbell Diaries* (Hutchinson).

Camps, M. (1964) *Britain and the European Community 1955–1963* (Oxford University Press).

Chandler, D. (2003) 'Rhetoric Without Responsibility: The Attraction of Ethical Foreign Policy', *British Journal of Politics and International Relations*, vol. 5, no. 3, pp. 295–316.

Charmley, J. (1995) *Churchill's Grand Alliance: The Anglo-American Special Relationship 1940–1957* (Hodder and Stoughton).

Churchill, W. (1948) Official proceedings of Conservative Party Conference, Bodleian Library Special Collections, shelf mark NUA 2/1/56, pp. 149–56.

Clarke, P. (1996) *Hope and Glory: Britain 1900–1990* (Allen Lane/The Penguin Press).

Cm 5566 Vol. I (2002) 'The Strategic Defence Review: A New Chapter', July, http://www.mod.uk/NR/rdonlyres/79542E9C-1104-4AFA-9A4D-8520F35C5C93/0/sdr_a_new_chapter_cm5566_vol1.pdf, first accessed 17 March 2009.

Conservative Party (2010) General Election manifesto, 'Invitation to Join the Government of Britain', http://media.conservatives.s3.amazonaws.com/manifesto/cpmanifesto2010_lowres.pdf, accessed 28 October 2011.

Cook, R. (1997) 'Robin Cook's speech on the government's ethical foreign policy', Guardian Unlimited, http://www.guardian.co.uk/world/1997/may/12/indonesia.ethicalforeignpolicy, first accessed 20 October 2006.

Cook, R. (2003) *The Point of Departure* (Simon and Schuster).

Cornish, P. and Dorman, A. (2009) 'Blair's wars and Brown's Budgets: From Strategic Defence Review to Strategic Decay in Less than a Decade', *International Affairs* vol. 85, no. 2, pp. 247–61.

Council of Europe (undated) http://www.coe.int/aboutCoe/index.asp?page=nosObjectifs, accessed 24 October 2011.

Council of Europe (2005) Warsaw Declaration, 17 May, http://www.coe.int/t/dcr/summit/20050517_decl_varsovie_en.asp, accessed 24 October 2011.

Cradock, P. (1997) *In Pursuit of British Interests: Reflections on Foreign Policy under Margaret Thatcher and John Major* (John Murray).

Cross, C. (1968) *The Fall of the British Empire 1918–1968* (Book Club Associates).

Curtis, M. (2003) *Web of Deceit: Britain's Real Role in the World* (Vintage).

Daddow, O.J. (ed.) (2003) *Harold Wilson and European Integration: Britain's Second Application to Join the EEC* (Frank Cass).

Daddow, O. (2009) '"Tony's War"?: Blair, Kosovo and the Interventionist Impulse in British Foreign Policy', *International Affairs*, vol. 85, no. 3, pp. 547–60.

Daddow, O. (2011a) 'Conclusion', in O. Daddow and J. Gaskarth (eds) (2011) *British Foreign Policy: The New Labour Years* (Palgrave Macmillan), pp. 221–35.

Daddow, O. (2011a) 'Conclusion', in O. Daddow and J. Gaskarth (eds) (2011) *British Foreign Policy: The New Labour Years* (Palgrave Macmillan).

Daddow, O. (2011b) *New Labour and the European Union: Blair and Brown's Logic of History* (Manchester University Press).

Daddow, O. and Gaskarth, J. (eds) (2011) *British Foreign Policy: The New Labour Years* (Palgrave Macmillan).

Deighton, A. (2005) 'The foreign policy of British Prime Minister Tony Blair: radical or retrograde?', Centre for British Studies, Humboldt University, Berlin, 11 July, http://www.gbz.hu-berlin.de/publications/working-papers/downloads/pdf/WPS_Deighton_Blair.pdf, first accessed 3 March 2009.

Dickie, J. (1994) *'Special' No More: Anglo-American Relations, Rhetoric and Reality* (Weidenfeld and Nicolson).

Dickie, J. (2007) *The New Mandarins: How British Foreign Policy Works* (I.B. Tauris).

Dimbleby, D. and Reynolds, D. (1988) *An Ocean Apart: The Relationship between Britain and America in the Twentieth Century* (BBC Books).

Dodds, K. and Elden, S. (2008) 'Thinking Ahead: David Cameron, the Henry Jackson Society and British Neo-conservatism', *British Journal of Politics and International Relations*, vol. 10, no. 3, pp. 347–63.

Dover, R. and Phythian, M. (2011) 'Lost Over Libya: The Strategic Defence and Security Review – An Obituary', *Defence Studies*, vol. 11, no. 3, pp. 420–44.

Ellison, J. (2000) *Threatening Europe: Britain and the Creation of the European Community 1955–58* (Macmillan).

Ellwood, D.W. (1996) *Rebuilding Europe: Western Europe, America and Postwar Reconstruction* (Addison Wesley Longman Limited).

FCO (2006) *Active Diplomacy for a Changing World: The UK's International Priorities*, FCO Command Paper, CM 6762, March, Chapter 2, p. 26, http://www.libertysecurity.org/IMG/pdf/fullintpriorities2006.pdf accessed 12 October 2011.

FCO (2008) Mission Statement, 'Better World, Better Britain', http://www.fco.gov.uk/resources/en/pdf/mission-statement, accessed 17 March 2009.

FCO (2009b) 'Organisation for Security and Co-operation in Europe', http://www.fco.gov.uk/en/about-the-fco/what-we-do/building-strong-relationships-ol/international-partners/osce, first accessed 16 March 2009.

FCO (2010) 'Human Rights and Democracy: the 2010 FCO Report', http://s3-eu-west-1.amazonaws.com/htcdn/Human-Rights-and-Democracy-The-2010-Foreign-Commonwealth-Report.pdf, accessed 26 October 2011.

FCO (2011) 'Who We Are', http://www.fco.gov.uk/en/about-us/who-we-are/, accessed 12 October 2011.

Ferguson, N. (2004) *Empire: How Britain Made the Modern World* (Penguin).

Gamble, A. (2003) *Between Europe and America: The Future of British Politics* (Palgrave Macmillan).

Garton Ash, T. (2003) 'Blair's bridge', *Guardian*, 4 September, http://www.guardian.co.uk/politics/2003/sep/04/iraq.iraq, accessed 23 March 2009.

Gaskarth, J. (2013) *British Foreign Policy* (Polity).

Gavrilova, D. (2009) 'Entropa: Art of Politics, Heart of a Nation', Open Democracy, 19 January, http://www.opendemocracy.net/article/entropa-art-of-politics-heart-of-a-nation, accessed 28 April 2013.

George, S. (1998) *The Awkward Partner: Britain in the European Community*, 3rd edn (Oxford University Press).

Global Policy Forum (undated a), 'Changing patterns in the use of the veto in the Security Council', http://www.globalpolicy.org/component/content/article/102/32810.html, accessed 24 October 2011.

Global Policy Forum (undated b), 'Subjects of UN Security Council votes', http://www.globalpolicy.org/images/pdfs/Z/Tables_and_Charts/vetosubj.pdf, accessed 24 October 2011.

Guardian (2001), Leader, 'Putting ethics on the map', 9 April, http://www.guardian.co.uk/politics/2001/apr/09/ethical-foreignpolicy.politicalnews, accessed 18 September 2012.

Haas, E.B. (1958) *The Uniting of Europe: Political, Social and Economic Forces, 1950–1957* (Stanford University Press).

Hague, W. (2009) Speech at the International Institute for Strategic Studies, London, 'The Future of British Foreign Policy', 21 July, http://www.conservatives.com/News/Speeches/2009/07/William_Hague_The_Future_of_British_Foreign_Policy.aspx, accessed 28 October 2011.

Hague, W. (2010) Speech at the Foreign and Commonwealth Office, London, 1 July, 'British Foreign Policy in a Networked World', http://www.conservatives.com/News/Speeches/2010/07/William_Hague_Britains_Foreign_Policy_in_a_Networked_World.aspx, accessed 28 October 2011.

Hague, W. (2011) Speech on the Foreign and Commonwealth Office, London, 8 September, 'The best diplomatic service in the world: strengthening the Foreign and Commonwealth Office as an institution', http://www.fco.gov.uk/en/news/latest-news/?id=652930982&view=Speech, accessed 28 October 2011.

Harris, M. (2011) 'Time for a Lib Dem foreign policy Orange Book?', Huff Post: Politics United Kingdom, 4 July, http://www.huffingtonpost.co.uk/matthew-harris/time-for-a-lib-dem-foreign-policy_b_889856.html, accessed 31 October 2011.

Harvey, M. (2011) 'Perspectives on the UK's Place in the World', Chatham House Europe Programme Paper 2011/01, December, http://www.chathamhouse.org/sites/default/files/public/Research/Europe/1211pp_harvey.pdf, accessed 18 September 2012.

Heinlein, F. (2002) *British Government Policy and Decolonisation 1945–1963: Scrutinising the Official Mind* (Frank Cass).

Hill, C. (2001) 'Foreign Policy', in Anthony Seldon (ed.) *The Blair Effect: The Blair Government 1997–2001* (Little, Brown and Company) pp. 331–53.

HM Government (2010a) 'Securing Britain in an Age of Uncertainty: The Strategic Defence and Security Review', http://www.direct.gov.uk/prod_consum_dg/groups/dg_digitalassets/@dg/@en/documents/digitalasset/dg_191634.pdf, accessed 28 October 2011.

HM Government (2010b) 'The Coalition: Our Programme for Government', http://www.conservatives.com/News/News_stories/2010/05/The_Coalitions_Programme_for_Government.aspx, accessed 28 October 2011.

Hobsbawm, E.J. (1990) *Industry and Empire* (Penguin).

Holland, R. (1991) *The Pursuit of Greatness: Britain and the World Role, 1900–1970* (Fontana).

Hurd, D. (2011) *Choose Your Weapons: The British Foreign Secretary – 200 Years of Argument, Success and Failure* (Phoenix).

Kennedy, P. (1985) *The Realities Behind Diplomacy: Background Influences on British External Policy 1865–1980* (Fontana).

Kissinger, H. (1982) Speech at Royal Institute of International Affairs, *Executive Intelligence Review*, 11 January, http://www.larouchepub.com/other/2002/2901_kissinger.html, first accessed 9 July 2002.

Little, R. and Wickham-Jones, M. (eds) (2000) *New Labour's Foreign Policy: A New Moral Crusade?* (Manchester University Press).

Ludlow, N.P. (1997) *Dealing with Britain: The Six and the First UK Application to the EEC* (Cambridge University Press).

Lundestad, G. (1997) *'Empire' by Integration: The United States and European Integration, 1945–1997* (Oxford University Press).

Macmillan, H. (1960) Speech to South African Parliament, 3 February, http://africanhistory.about.com/od/erindependence/p/wind_of_change2.htm, accessed 28 October 2011.

Major, J. (1999) *John Major: The Autobiography* (HarperCollins).

Marshall, P.J. (2001) 'The First British Empire', in R.N. Winks (ed.) (2001) *The Oxford History of the British Empire: Historiography* (Oxford University Press) pp. 43–53.

McCormack, T. (2011) 'From "Ethical Foreign Policy" to National Security Strategy: Exporting Domestic Incoherence', in O. Daddow and J. Gaskarth (eds) *British Foreign Policy: The New Labour Years* (Palgrave Macmillan), pp. 103–22.

McGuire, S. and Smith, M. (2008) *The European Union and the United States: Competition and Convergence in the Global Arena* (Palgrave Macmillan).

McInnes, C. (1998) 'Labour's Strategic Defence Review', *International Affairs*, vol. 74, no. 4, pp. 823–45.

Medcalf, J. (2008) *Going Global or Going Nowhere?: NATO's Role in Contemporary International Security* (Peter Lang).

Meyer, C. (2006) *DC Confidential* (Phoenix).

Moore, R.R. (2007) *NATO's New Mission: Projecting Stability in a post-Cold War World* (Praeger).

Morris, J. (2011) 'How Great is Britain? Power, Responsibility and Britain's Future Global Role', *British Journal of Politics and International Relations*, vol. 13, no. 2, pp. 326–47.

NATO (1949) 'The North Atlantic Treaty', 4 April, http://www.nato.int/cps/en/natolive/official_texts_17120.htm, accessed 26 October 2011.

NATO (2011) 'NATO and Libya – Operation Unified Protector', http://www.nato.int/cps/en/natolive/topics_71652.htm, accessed 26 October 2011.

O'Donnell, C.M. (2011) 'Britain's Coalition Government and EU Defence Cooperation: Undermining British Interests', *International Affairs*, vol. 87, no. 2, pp. 417–33.

OECD (undated a) 'History', http://www.oecd.org/document/63/0,3746,en_2649_201185_1876671_1_1_1_1,00.html, accessed 26 October 2011.

OECD (undated b) 'Statistics Portal', http://www.oecd.org/statsportal/0,3352,en_2825_293564_1_1_1_1_1,00.html, accessed 26 October 2011.

OSCE (undated) 'The OSCE at a Glance', http://www.osce.org/secretariat/24704, accessed 26 October 2011.

Powell, J. (2007) 'Why the West should not fear to intervene', *Observer*, 18 November, http://www.guardian.co.uk/commentisfree/2007/nov/18/comment.foreignpolicy, first accessed 11 September 2008.

Price, L. (2005) *The Spin Doctor's Diary: Inside Number Ten with New Labour* (Hodder and Stoughton).

Reynolds, D. (1991) *Britannia Overruled: British Policy and World Power in the Twentieth Century* (Longman).

Robertson (1998) Introduction to Strategic Defence Review (1998), http://www.mod.uk/NR/rdonlyres/65F3D7AC-4340-4119-93A2-20825848E50E/0/sdr1998_complete.pdf, first accessed 17 March 2009.

Sanders, D. (1990) *Losing an Empire, Finding a Role: British Foreign Policy since 1945* (Macmillan).

Sandole, D.J.D. (2007) *Peace and Security in the Postmodern World: The OSCE and Conflict Resolution* (Routledge).

Schama, S. (2002) *A History of Britain, Vol. 3: The Fate of Empire 1776–2000* (BBC Worldwide Ltd).

Seldon, A. (2005) *Blair* (The Free Press).

Short, C. (2005) *An Honourable Deception?: New Labour, Iraq, and the Misuse of Power* (The Free Press).

Sloan, S.R. (2010) *Permanent Alliance?: NATO and the Transatlantic Bargain from Truman to Obama* (Continuum Publishing).

Smith, M.A. (ed.) (2006) *Where is NATO Going?* (Routledge).

Taylor, P.J. (1990) *Britain and the Cold War: 1945 as Geopolitical Transition* (Pinter).

Taylor, S. (2011) 'Cameron hit by backbench rebellion over EU', *European Voice.com*, http://www.europeanvoice.com/article/2011/october/cameron-hit-by-backbench-rebellion-over-eu/72406.aspx, accessed 26 October 2011.

Thatcher, M. (1993) *The Downing Street Years* (HarperPerennial).

The Churchill Society (undated), Churchill speech in Zurich, 19 September 1946, http://www.churchill-society-london.org.uk/astonish.html, accessed 24 October 2011.

UN (undated) 'Charter of the United Nations Chapter V: The Security Council', http://www.un.org/en/documents/charter/chapter5.shtml, accessed 24 October 2011.

Vickers, R. (2011) *The Labour Party and the World, Vol. 2: Labour's Foreign Policy since 1951* (Manchester University Press).

Wallace, W. (2005) 'The Collapse of British Foreign Policy', *International Affairs*, vol. 82, no. 1, pp. 56–68.

Watt, N. (2011) 'David Cameron rocked by record rebellion as Europe splits Tories again', http://www.guardian.co.uk/politics/2011/oct/24/david-cameron-tory-rebellion-europe?newsfeed=true, accessed 26 October 2011.

Webber, M. and Hyde-Price, A. (eds) (2011) *Theorising NATO* (Routledge).

Weiss, T.G. (2012) *What's Wrong with the United Nations (and how to fix it)*, 2nd edn (Polity Press).

Wheeler, N.J. and Dunne, T. (1998) 'Good International Citizenship: A Third Way for British Foreign Policy', *International Affairs*, vol. 74, no. 4, pp. 847–70.

Williams, P.D. (2005) *British Foreign Policy under New Labour, 1997–2005* (Palgrave Macmillan).

Wood, G.S. (2003) *The American Revolution: A History* (Weidenfeld and Nicolson History).

Young, H. (1998) *This Blessed Plot: Britain and Europe from Churchill to Blair* (Macmillan).

Young, J.W. (2000) *Britain and European Unity 1945–1999*, 2nd edn (Macmillan).

Useful websites

Britain in NATO: http://www.fco.gov.uk/resources/en/pdf/4103709/5476465/britain-in-nato.pdf

Council of Europe: http://www.coe.int/lportal/web/coe-portal

EFTA: http://www.efta.int/

EU: http://europa.eu/index_en.htmGlobal Policy

Forum: http://www.globalpolicy.org/

NATO: http://www.nato.int/

ODIHR: http://www.osce.org/odihr

OECD: http://www.oecd.org/home/0,3305,en_2649_201185_1_1_1_1_1,00.html, including OECD statistics portal: http://www.oecd.org/statsportal/0,3352,en_2825_293564_1_1_1_1_1,00.html

OSCE: http://www.osce.org/

OSCE YouTube channel: http://www.youtube.com/user/osceSDSR: http://www.direct.gov.uk/prod_consum_dg/groups/dg_digitalassets/@dg/@en/documents/digitalasset/dg_191634.pdf

UK Delegation to NATO: http://uknato.fco.gov.uk/en/

UN: http://www.un.org/en/

CHAPTER 3

The social and economic context

Kevin Hickson

> " **There is no such thing as society** "
>
> Margaret Thatcher

Learning objectives

- To examine the changing social and economic structures in Britain, setting them in their historical context.

- To discuss the major characteristics of British society and the impact they have on British politics including class, national identity, ethnicity and multiculturalism, age and gender.

- To examine the nature of British economic decline in a long-term perspective since 1945 and the immediate context of the banking crisis of 2007–8 and the ongoing recession.

The aim of this chapter is to analyse the changing social and economic context of British politics. At one time it may have been possible to study British politics without reference to the domestic social and economic context. The study of politics would have included a legal and historical discussion of the constitution and the major political institutions such as the Monarchy, Houses of Parliament, political parties and pressure groups. Such 'institutional' analysis has its place but is limited without situating institutions within the wider social and economic framework which shape political action and are shaped by it in a dialectical relationship (the two interacting and shaping each other). This is very clear when we examine the major factors which affect the support for political parties and the determination of General Election outcomes. It is also relevant to current political debate over the condition of the economy. Towards the end of this chapter we will discuss in some detail the politics of the banking crisis and subsequent recession which is arguably the major issue facing politicians at the moment.

It was also once the case that the study of British politics was done in a fairly isolated way with little focus on international developments. The traditional A-level syllabus tended to focus on British political institutions and processes in way which barely touched on developments outside of the UK. However, the process of European integration and debates over the extent to which we now live in a globalised world have had a massive impact on British politics. The banking crisis of 2007–8 and the subsequent recession is partly domestic, but also international. Equally, the crisis in the Eurozone affects Britain even though we are not a member of the single currency. If it was ever the case that the Westminster Parliament was sovereign and British government had complete executive control over the actions of those who lived within its territorial borders then it is certainly no longer the case. The decline of British power, both military and economic as discussed below, has taken Britain from once being the world's dominant power to being a mid-ranking power.

However, it should also be noted that Britain remains a major international power and has not been a passive observer of wider developments. Therefore, although it is important to stress the increasingly interdependent world that Britain inhabits what should also be kept in mind is the way that domestic factors impact on British politics. Hence, this chapter will examine the social and economic context of British politics but will also draw on international issues where relevant.

The chapter will begin with a discussion of the major social characteristics and cleavages that impact on British politics, starting with the traditional one of social class and the extent to which it has been a factor with declining salience. We will then go on to discuss other social issues such as the changing role of gender, the rise of an ageing society, and the rise of multiculturalism and ethnicity.

After that, the chapter will discuss the economic context, placing recent developments into a broader historical context of decline and crisis in the British economy which are recurring themes in British politics and culminating in the banking crisis of 2007 and 2008 and the ongoing difficulties.

Social context: stability and identity

Compared to a number of other countries Britain, or more specifically England, has remained relatively stable in its political arrangements. It is true that events such as the signing of the Magna Carta (1215), the Wars of the Roses (1455–85), the English Civil War (1642–51) and the so-called 'Glorious Revolution' of 1688 were periods of political upheaval. As a result of these events Britain emerged with a constitutional monarchy, subordinate to the House of Commons and the dominance of the Protestant faith. However, Britain was able to manage the great nineteenth-century social and economic transformations of industrialisation and urbanisation relatively easily compared to other countries where there were corresponding political crises. The franchise (vote) was extended gradually until 1918 when all men over 21 and women over 30 were given the legal right vote in General Elections (parity being established in 1928). Despite the often remarked class divisions which existed in Britain, these were managed relatively easily and there was very little risk of political

revolution along the lines of France in 1789 or Russia in 1917. The class system was also relatively stable and this was often the feature of satire in Britain, such as the famous *Frost Report* sketch (1966), featuring a representative of the upper, middle and working classes each claiming to know and accept their place within the social hierarchy.

Wales

This long-term historical stability was also a feature of other social and cultural cleavages in the United Kingdom. Wales merged completely into political Union with England in 1542. Despite recurrent demands for national self-determination the Welsh have tended to express their nationalism in more cultural rather than political forms: the demand for Welsh language tuition and so forth, rather than outright independence. There was a majority against a devolved legislative body being established in the referendum of 1979. Devolution was granted following a further referendum in 1997 with the establishment of the Welsh Assembly. This was followed more recently by the granting of more powers to the Assembly.

Scotland

Scotland was formally brought into the Union in the eighteenth century with the Act of Union of 1707 although it retained distinct legal, educational and ecclesiastical structures. Although there were always those who demanded greater independence, it was not until the 1960s that the cause of Scottish nationalism grew. Even then there was an insufficient majority for a Scottish Parliament in the 1979 referendum and the Scottish Parliament was not established until 1999. Unlike the situation in Wales, however, this has not led to the end of demands for greater independence, and the greatest challenge to the UK is now the referendum on the political future of Scotland to be held in 2014. The continuing force of Scottish nationalism is testament not just to the political skills of Alex Salmond as leader of the Scottish National Party but also to the significant differences which exist in the social and economic contexts of Scotland when compared to England.

Ireland

Ireland was different. The Union between Ireland and the rest of the UK occurred much later, in 1801. The South of Ireland was then granted independence in 1922 and there has been recurring violence in Northern Ireland between those who wanted a united Ireland and those who wished to remain part of the Union with England, Scotland and Wales. The crucial difference between Northern Ireland and other parts of the UK is that the main social divide was not one of social class but rather religion. Hence, once again we should be careful when discussing the social and economic context of UK politics since the constituent parts of the UK have different characteristics, with Northern Ireland being the most notable of all.

In a broader historical context, therefore, what is striking about the UK is the strong degree of economic and social stability. Conflicts within the UK, with the exception of Ireland, have been generally very easy to reconcile although important social and economic variations remain.

In many ways it is much easier to identify what is unique about the social, economic, cultural and political contexts of Northern Ireland, Scotland and Wales. It is harder to identify the key aspects of English identity, not least because of its varying social and economic contexts in different parts of the country.

What does it mean to be English?

This is a question which politicians across the political spectrum have, for different reasons, often tried to avoid. Labour depends on Scottish and Welsh MPs to form a majority at Westminster. The Conservatives have traditionally supported the Union and wish to avoid an association with an emerging English nationalism as they do not wish to appear extreme.

However, some commentators have sought to develop a clearer sense of Englishness, although this has proved complicated for several reasons.

The first is that a single English identity has found it difficult to bridge significant regional economic and social disparities. England has several distinctive regional social and economic contexts. The South-east of England (London and the area immediately around it) is far more prosperous than the rest of England, and is far more densely populated. The economy of the South-west is based largely on agriculture and tourism, with much lower population density. Broadly speaking, England becomes gradually poorer the further away from the South-east you go. The South-east region dominates the English economy, with the majority of financial services being located there, while declining manufacturing has mainly been an issue which has affected the North and the Midlands as these were historically the areas which were more industrialised (about which I return below).

Table 3.1 Gross value added per head of the population (capita) for the four countries of the UK in 2010

Rank	Place	GVA per capita (£)
1	England	20,974
2	Scotland	20,220
3	Northern Ireland	15,651
4	Wales	15,145

Source: http://www.ons.gov.uk/ons/rel/regional-accounts/regional-gross-value-added-income-approach-/december-2011/index.html

Table 3.2 Gross value added per capita for the English regions (2010)

Rank	Place	GVA per capita (£)
1	Greater London	35,026
2	South-east	21,924
3	East	18,996
4	South-west	18,669
5	East Midlands	18,090
6	North-west	17,381
7	West Midlands	17,060
8	Yorkshire and the Humber	16,917
9	North-east	15,744

Source: http://www.ons.gov.uk/ons/rel/regional-accounts/regional-gross-value-added-income-approach-/december-2011/index.html

In 2009, 51.8 million people lived in England, compared to 5.2 million in Scotland, 3 million in Wales and 1.8 million in Northern Ireland. Population density is also much higher in England with 392 people per square kilometre compared to just 66 people per square kilometre in Scotland. Of the UK's population 26 per cent live in London and the South-east.

Culturally, however, England does not fit neatly into regions. Although there have been efforts to foster a clearer sense of regional identity, most people do not think in terms of regionalism. This was clear in the failed referendum on an assembly for the North-east region in 2004. People have affinity to their immediate home area and often to their county, but not to their region. Therefore, it has proven very difficult to fit these economic and cultural variations into a single English identity.

Social class

As stated above, the major historical division in British society is that of social class. The British class system was never fully related to economic status and the relationship to the means of production as the nineteenth-century revolutionary socialist philosopher Karl Marx believed. It was also about schooling, accent, manners, dress and so on. In other words, it wasn't just 'economic' class but also 'social'.

The British class system usually distinguished between three social classes. The first was the *upper class* or aristocracy. This was numerically the smallest social class and identified by the possession of large landed estates and by genealogy – the ability to trace one's family tree back

PROFILE

Karl Marx (1818–83)

Karl Marx was a German-born philosopher who argued that class within the capitalist system was divided between the bourgeoisie who owned the means of production and a proletariat who, in the absence of owning productive wealth, had to sell their labour. Arguably, this was an oversimplification of the British class system which stressed more the social aspects of class than the narrowly economic. The most likely cause of this was the persistence of a socially significant aristocracy.

through the generations. The aristocracy was the dominant political class up until the late nineteenth century when they were challenged by the new, industrial and commercial middle class.

However, while the nobility in other countries were often toppled by political revolution, in Britain the upper classes proved much more adaptable to change, often succeeding in absorbing the rising middle class rather than excluding it, thus avoiding social conflict.

Consequently, the aristocracy has survived in Britain even though its political power as a class had been removed. Until the election of Edward Heath in 1964 Conservative leaders mainly came from aristocratic families. All Conservative Prime Ministers after the Second World War came from the aristocracy: Winston Churchill (1951–55), Anthony Eden (1955–57) and Alec Douglas-Home (1963–64), and to a lesser extent Harold Macmillan (1957–63). In this regard David Cameron, who was elected leader in 2005, marks a return to an earlier type of Conservative leader after the more 'meritocratic' leaderships of Edward Heath, Margaret Thatcher, John Major, William Hague, Iain Duncan Smith and Michael Howard. The last formal vestige of the aristocracy in the political system is the remaining hereditary peers in the House of Lords – those who were there through birthright, and survived the attempt by Tony Blair's Labour Government to remove all hereditary peers after a compromise was reached. In the counties there are still some ceremonial roles played by leading families.

The middle class emerged in the industrial revolution with the rise of new factory and mill owners and with the need to have more professional people in the new towns and cities. The middle class remained a minority through much of the twentieth century, but with **de-industrialisation** and the rise of a 'service' economy the middle classes have become much bigger. Closely related to the idea of being middle class is the notion of meritocracy. While the aristocracy used to rule through privilege and inheritance, the middle class is open to talent, with the top senior managerial and professional occupations supposedly filled through equality of opportunity. However, critics of meritocracy have always argued that it neglects the social and economic barriers which some face when entering the labour market.

In contrast, the working class was the largest social class created by the industrial revolution with vast armies of factory workers in the nineteenth and early-to-mid-twentieth centuries. But with the decline in manufacturing and the need for a more skilled labour force in new hi-tech industries the traditional working class has declined markedly.

It is important to make a distinction between real and subjective notions of social class and between the economic and psychological understandings of class. While it may be the case that social and economic inequality remains significant in Britain with large-scale variations in income and wealth, perceptions about social class have changed. According to a YouGov opinion poll conducted in 2010 over 66 per cent of respondents said that they were middle class, whereas 30 per cent believed that they were working class. This was down by 10 per cent from ten years previously. Moreover, 80 per cent thought that social class used to matter, whereas only 50 per cent still thought it did. Successive politicians and Prime Ministers have sought to argue that social class no longer matters, and these figures would seem to suggest that perceptions of social class no longer have the force which they once had.

We have therefore moved from a 'pyramid' form of social structure with a small upper class at the top and a large working class at the bottom to a social structure more like a diamond with a few at the top and the bottom but with the majority somewhere in the middle.

One alleged consequence of this change to the social class structure has been the fragmentation of traditional class-based voting for political parties. The Conservative Party was traditionally supported by the middle class, and Labour by the working class. There were always some working-class Conservative voters, for reasons of **deference** or because they supported right-wing policies. There were also some middle-class voters who supported Labour, especially those who worked in the **public sector**.

However, the Labour Party twice faced long periods of Opposition, between 1951 and 1964 and again between 1979 and 1997 when it was argued that their traditional working-class base was shrinking. One possible explanation for the creation of 'New' Labour was that it was an attempt to come to terms with the fragmentation of the Labour Party's traditional working-class vote. One of the most notable features of the 2010 General Election results was the fact that for the first time Labour got more middle-class votes than working-class votes.

Is there an underclass?

A persistent feature of political debate since at least the 1970s is the existence, or not, of an 'underclass'. The underclass consists of those who are particularly poor and live in severely depressed urban areas. However, the term is usually used not just to describe those living in poverty, but also to ascribe certain psychological characteristics, attributing to those who belong to it certain socially deviant behaviours. Those who wish to argue that there is such an underclass assert that there is a section of society which is not only separate in terms of its social and economic position, being poor and unemployed, but is also morally separate: that is to say, those who constitute the underclass are poor and unemployed because of their own moral failings. For some commentators, mostly but not exclusively from the right, such moral failure is encouraged by the welfare state which (they say) discourages people from working.

This debate has become a particular feature of US and British politics, in both of which countries the 'New Right' has become particularly strong. Advocates of the New Right wish to see an extension of **free market** economics, with minimal state intervention. It was associated with the Reagan Administration in America (1981–89) and the Thatcher Government in Britain (1979–90). Margaret Thatcher stated that she wished to see a return to 'Victorian values' such as hard work, thrift and self-help. The development of the welfare state after 1945, she said, undermined these human virtues and replaced them with a dependency **culture**. From the 1980s onwards governments have increasingly used a harsh rhetoric when discussing those who are poor, or at least sections of the poor: those who were 'undeserving' of help from government.

Although the argument about an undeserving underclass originated on the right of the political spectrum, it has also been a feature of Labour Party discourse since the 1990s in the era of 'New' Labour.

In terms of policy solutions the New Right and New Labour sought to strengthen the responsibilities of those who were on benefits, and impose tougher sanctions on those who could not demonstrate that they were actively seeking employment.

At the same time, public opinion towards welfare has hardened. According to the 2010 Social Attitudes Survey, although there was concern with the gap between the rich and the poor, this did not feed through to policy, with more people saying that poverty was less the fault of the government and more of individuals.

However, there are critics of the underclass thesis who argue that there are wider social and economic issues which need to be considered such as the decline of manufacturing which has left certain areas facing high unemployment and a tendency towards low-waged, low-skilled employment opportunities in many large towns and cities. Moreover, some commentators point to the demonisation of the poor. The word 'chav' is frequently used as a pejorative term against sections of the working class by the right-wing press and social commentators. Although it derives from the Romani word for child 'chavi' it has increasingly been seen as standing for the phrase 'council house and violent'. The idea has been challenged by the left-wing writer Owen Jones in his book *Chavs*.

Multicultural Britain

The other major factor which has inhibited a sense of English identity is that England, and Britain more generally, has become more multicultural.

The official religion in Britain has been Protestant since the Tudor Reformation. The official Church is the Church of England, with numerous other Nonconformist Protestant faiths and Catholicism ever present, their influence waxing and waning.

This has been more prevalent in some areas than others. A key factor in the Northern Ireland troubles from the 1960s onwards was the conflict between Catholics and Protestants. Some cities in the rest of the UK have also been prone to religious sectarianism, notably Glasgow and Liverpool. In the rest of the UK most people have described themselves with greater or lesser commitment as 'Church of England'.

However, two developments have challenged the once dominant position of Anglicanism. The first is the declining church attendance figures since the end of the Second World War. A 2007 study showed that attendance at church was declining, with just 15 per cent attending once a month compared to over half the population 50 years ago. Of those who do attend church regularly an increasing proportion are elderly and middle class. Overall, church attendance in Britain was recorded as the fourth lowest in the European Union. However, the same report also found that a significant number of people still regarded themselves as Christians even if they did not attend regular church services. Fifty-eight per cent of respondents called themselves Christian, compared to 33 per cent who termed themselves atheists and agnostics.

At the same time Britain has become multi-faith and multicultural, after the first significant arrival of non-whites from the Empire in the late 1940s with the *Empire Windrush* arriving in 1948 carrying nearly 500 passengers from Jamaica wishing to establish homes in the UK. Further immigration followed in the 1950s and 1960s as the British Empire was wound up, former colonies were granted independence and the Commonwealth was established. In more recent years immigration has tended to come mainly from eastern Europe with the expansion of the European Union. This is demonstrated by the fact that for those living in the UK but born elsewhere, Poland is now the second highest country of birth after India. Britain has proven an attractive place for immigrant communities, offering a higher standard of living and political stability.

The 2001 census showed that over 92 per cent of the population was white, with a total of 4.6 million non-whites. This was in fact an increase from the 1991 census and further rises are likely, with studies suggesting that 20 per cent of the population will be minority ethnic by 2051.

Of course, this is a national average and the figures vary considerably as ethnic minority communities tend to be concentrated in particular parts of the UK, including several parts of London, Birmingham, Leicester, Slough and Luton. It is possible that Leicester will become the first city in the UK to have a non-white majority by 2015. Other parts of the UK remain overwhelmingly white.

There are several positive effects from immigration. Britain has become more pluralistic with more people of other faiths and of no faith. Immigration has been shown to have several economic benefits, particularly at times of economic growth when there are shortages of labour in certain sectors of the economy. Moreover, immigration creates greater cultural diversity. For liberals this has been a blessing as they welcome diversity and pluralism in society.

Despite this there have been those who have warned of the negative consequences of immigration. The most notable example was the right-wing Conservative politician, Enoch Powell, who in 1968 delivered the so-called 'Rivers of Blood' speech in Birmingham, in which he said that there would be civil unrest along the lines of the United States of America (where the civil rights leader Martin Luther King had just been assassinated) if immigration was not curbed. Powell was sacked from the Shadow Cabinet never to hold ministerial office again, although he continued to attract some support by speaking out on these issues.

Margaret Thatcher also referred to people feeling as if they were 'swamped' by immigrants in an interview in 1978 while she was still Leader of the Opposition. However, after being warned off the issue by her senior colleagues she never returned to this theme as Prime Minister.

PROFILE

Enoch Powell (1912–98)

Enoch Powell had distinguished academic and military careers before becoming a Conservative MP and served in a number of ministerial positions, but is most famous for his views expressed on the subject of immigration, especially his so-called 'Rivers of Blood' speech of 1968. He became increasingly critical of Britain's membership of the EEC. In the first General Elections of 1974 he encouraged people to vote Labour as that party promised a referendum on Britain's membership of the EEC. He subsequently became an Ulster Unionist MP.

A statement on the issue came from the Labour peer, Maurice Glasman, who argued that white, working-class people are concerned about the level of immigration and called for a temporary immigration freeze. This followed the incident during the 2010 General Election campaign when Gordon Brown had been stopped by a lady, Mrs Duffy, saying that there was a concern that immigrants had taken jobs that would otherwise have gone to locals. He was recorded on a microphone saying that she was a 'bigot'.

Enoch Powell, Birmingham, 1968 'We must be mad, literally mad, as a nation to be permitting the annual inflow of some 50,000 dependants, who are for the most part the material of the future growth of the immigrant descended population. It is like watching a nation busily engaged in heaping up its own funeral pyre.'

Margaret Thatcher, interview, 1978, people of Britain 'might be rather swamped by people of a different culture'.

Maurice Glasman, interview, 2011 'Britain is not an outpost of the UN. We have to put the people in this country first.'

What is striking about all three cases is that each time the issue of immigration is raised it causes controversy. Some have argued that there is frequently a silence on the issue among mainstream politicians.

It has therefore been regarded as a more extremist political issue with the National Front (founded 1967), the British National Party (founded in 1982 following a split with the NF) and the English Defence League (founded in 2009) being three of the most prominent organisations on the far right of British politics with an anti-immigration stance.

Occasional civil unrest has been a feature of areas with high immigration including the urban riots of the early 1980s and again in 2011, but poverty was often seen as the main cause of such unrest rather than immigration. Immigration remains an issue in elections, but open racial tension at least is not a regular feature of modern British society.

The ageing society

Another important development in modern British society is that the elderly population is growing significantly. Fifteen per cent of the UK population is now over 65, compared to 11 per cent in 1951 and 5 per cent in 1911. This proportion is likely to carry on rising. Moreover, life expectancy is increasing, which means that more of the elderly population are living into their eighties and nineties. Improved standards of healthcare and reductions in poverty mean that people are able to live longer. Average life expectancy for men is now 78.2 years and 82.3 years for women, although there are considerable variations between richer and poorer parts of the UK.

Discussion of the ageing society is usually expressed in negative terms. The pension age has been raised as the cost of financing state pension schemes increases rapidly. Private pension schemes have frequently come under strain. For those living in their own homes until old age there is a need for carers, provision of meals and local transport, while for those unable to fend for themselves there are the costs associated with residential care and increased hospitalisation. The working population will have to work longer as the cost of an elderly society increases.

However, it can also be pointed out that the elderly population will in the future be fitter and more able to contribute to economic and social wellbeing rather than merely being passive citizens.

A major political issue, and one not always directly addressed because of its complexity and unpopularity, is how best to pay for the costs of an elderly society. While all would accept that it is a major issue and imposes a particular burden on public expenditure, serious decisions are often delayed as governments tend to think in the short-term.

Gender

A further long-term change in British society has been the increased independence of women.

The feminisation of British politics has been a consistent feature since the end of the nineteenth century. The first cause, associated with the Suffragettes and Suffragists, was the extension of the vote to women. Women were able to vote in local elections from the 1880s. The vote was nearly granted to women in General Elections prior to the First World War, but they had to wait until 1918 after their involvement in the war effort made it impossible for opponents to resist any longer. The first woman who took her seat in the House of Commons was Nancy Astor in 1919 and the first woman Cabinet Minister, Margaret Bondfield, was appointed in 1929. The first, and so far only woman Prime Minister was Margaret Thatcher who was elected in 1979.

However, female representation has always been much lower than that of their male counterparts. Various positive measures have been enacted to address this with mixed success. In the General Election of 2010, 143 female MPs were elected, 22 per cent of the total number of MPs. The majority

Nancy Astor (1879–1964)

Nancy Astor was the first woman to sit in the House of Commons and was a Conservative. She was born in America. She married the wealthy Waldorf Astor and lived at Cliveden in Buckinghamshire which served as a hospital in both world wars and was also associated with the pursuit of the Appeasement policy of the 1930s when British governments sought a diplomatic agreement with Nazi Germany. She was known as a strongly independent-minded MP and perhaps for that reason never rose to high office, making numerous controversial remarks.

of these (81) were Labour, reflecting the fact that the party is the only one to have women-only shortlists. Hence, parliamentary representation is still considerably lower than the proportion of women in society.

After the granting of political rights a further feminist cause, associated with 'second wave feminism' in the 1960s and 1970s, was one of equal economic and social rights, notably equal pay. Legislation was introduced to enforce this but women's pay remains lower than men's and fewer women occupy top jobs including government ministers, business executives and top public sector jobs. Roughly 70 per cent of women are now in employment, significantly higher than was the case in earlier decades. However, while only one in every six men is in part-time work, roughly half of all women in work are employed part-time. The average pay of women is considerably lower than for men (see the *Social Trends* website).

The decline of the British economy

Just as British society has been subject to change and international pressure, so too has the British economy.

When studying the British economy over the course of the twentieth century a persistent theme is that of 'decline'.

What does 'decline' mean?

The decline of Britain from the world's leading imperial power in the Victorian age can be measured in two ways.

The first is *absolute* decline in terms of the fall of Britain from its once dominant position. Britain has been overtaken by other leading powers, most notably the United States of America and the Soviet Union after the end of the Second World War in 1945 and, more recently, it has been eclipsed as the leading power in Europe and now further challenged by the emergence of new powers, most notably China. If Britain was once the world's pre-eminent superpower, it is now very much in the second division of world powers, unable to act independently in military conflicts.

Alternatively, British decline can be understood in *relative* terms. This is the meaning of the term 'decline' when applied to the British economy. Here decline is not absolute but relative to others. The British economy continued to expand but at a slower rate than other major economies. Hence it declined relatively but not absolutely.

The economy has continued to expand and people are now much wealthier than they once were. In 1957 Harold Macmillan, the Conservative Prime Minister, boasted that 'most of our people have never had it so good', a claim he repeated as he went on to win a landslide General Election victory in 1959. For the first time they could afford to purchase their own homes, motor cars and 'white goods' such as fridges, freezers and washing machines, which previous generations had not been able to afford.

Further prosperity in the 1980s included the acceptance that most people would take at least one foreign holiday a year, and a shareholding democracy was encouraged by Margaret Thatcher, in the name of 'popular capitalism'. New Labour boasted that it had cured the trade cycle of its fluctuating periods of boom and bust. There would be no more boom and bust under New Labour.

However, this masked a more complex situation. First, not everyone benefited from these changes, and certainly not to an equal amount. Inequality grew significantly, especially during the 1980s and 1990s as the gap between the rich and poor widened. It did not narrow noticeably during the Labour Government of 1997 to 2010. While the rich benefited most from economic changes since 1979, those on an average level saw a slight increase, but the poor started to fall behind.

Second, it has been clear from at least the 1950s that, although the British economy was expanding, it was not doing so as quickly as its major competitors. This was already established by the time Macmillan boasted of Britain's economic performance. This is the meaning of *relative decline* – that the British economy was growing in absolute terms over time, but was starting to lag behind other leading capitalist economies. From being the world's leading economy in the nineteenth century it is now the eighth leading economy and the third in Europe.

Government responses to decline

The need to reverse Britain's economic decline was to be a major theme of economic policy debate from the early 1960s. Two broad phases can be identified.

The first was the move to greater government intervention and planning. This began under the Conservative Government of Macmillan who was influenced by the idea of **corporatism**, where business leaders, the trade unions and the government would determine economic policy through a policy of bargaining and compromise. The National Economic Development Council was established for this purpose. The subsequent Labour Government, led by Harold Wilson, added to this agenda by establishing new government departments, such as the Ministry of Technology and the Department of Economic Affairs, and unveiling the National Plan which proposed higher economic growth through more government intervention.

In the 1970s Edward Heath, who had been Conservative Leader since 1965, initially appeared to move in a more free-market direction but reverted to a more interventionist approach in the face of a deteriorating economy. When Labour was returned to office in 1974 they adopted the Social Contract, essentially a deal between the trade unions and the Government along the lines that, in return for the trade unions forgoing wage increases, the Government would implement new welfare measures which would benefit their members. The 1970s was a period of high inflation and it was believed that the Social Contract would reduce it by controlling wages. The extent to which inflation was caused by high wages was open to dispute. Some believed that higher wages were the consequence of rising inflation as people tried to maintain living standards. After several years of pay restraint the Social Contract broke down decisively in 1978–9 with the so-called 'Winter of Discontent', when workers went on strike for higher pay.

Prior to 1979, therefore, government intervention was viewed positively. The government could and should intervene in the economy in order to stimulate growth, thereby raising living standards. In the 1970s this approach came under pressure with mounting economic problems and finally the election of a more resolutely right-wing Conservative Government in 1979.

Thatcherism

Thatcherism marked the start of the second broad response to relative economic decline. The new policy was much more critical of the role of government intervention in the economy and blamed it for Britain's poor economic performance. Planning didn't work because it could not respond to changing consumer demand and the needs of the **private**

sector. Whereas markets were dynamic, government was slow to respond. Instead things should be left to the market, as free as possible from government control and meddling. Taxes were cut, especially income tax, for higher earners in the expectation that this would unleash their entrepreneurial talents. Trade unions were subject to a raft of measures designed to curtail their powers, and membership of trade unions fell significantly over the course of the 1980s and 1990s. Government expenditure and borrowing were cut and 'red tape' on business was lifted. Government intervention was seen as the problem and the free market as the solution.

The transition to a free-market form of capitalism was very difficult. There was a recession in the early 1980s and unemployment peaked at over 3 million. Urban riots were a notable feature of Britain in the early 1980s. By the middle of the decade the economy was in a period of growth and the new rich of the City of London (or 'Yuppies') were a symbol of Britain's new-found wealth. However, as noted above, inequality soared and the idea that the British economy had now turned the corner was challenged by a further recession in the late 1980s and early 1990s.

New Labour

The arrival of 'New' Labour marked the broad acceptance of these Thatcherite reforms to economic policy, granting independence to the Bank of England and its Monetary Policy Committee to set interest rates, supposedly free from political interference, so that an anti-inflationary stance was seen as the primary objective of economic policy ahead of a reduction in unemployment. There was no reversal of trade union legislation or the **privatisation** agenda of the Thatcher and Major years. Indeed, the Labour Government extended the Private Finance Initiative whereby the building of new hospitals and schools would be funded by loans from the private sector.

On the other hand, there were attempts to reduce unemployment, especially youth and long-term unemployment through the New Deal, whereby the government would invest in education and training schemes to help people back in to work. There was record spending on the National Health Service and on education, the introduction of the first-ever national minimum wage and significant redistribution from rich to poor through various taxation measures. These last were sometimes referred to as 'stealth taxes' because they were often more hidden and indirect forms of taxation compared to the more traditional method of redistribution through income tax.

The gap between rich and poor, however, did not narrow. If New Labour was not a straightforward continuation of Thatcherism, it was far from being a traditional Labour government. This is partly explained by the passage of time. Labour had been out of power for 18 years and in that time Britain had changed significantly in the face of a radical reforming Conservative Government, as had the world. New Labour believed that it was constrained to a greater degree than previous Labour governments because it now operated under conditions of '**globalisation**'. The global finance markets had to be placated, while corporations were no longer tied to one single country, but instead had become multinational in their operations. The role of national governments under global conditions was to maintain the confidence of finance markets and the inward investment of multinational corporations. In order to do this it had to maintain relatively low tax rates and competitive, deregulated markets.

The climate of ideas

From this overview of British economic policy since 1945 what is clear is the importance of the role of ideas. Three dominant ideas, or paradigms, can be identified in British economic policy since 1945.

The first is **Keynesianism**, associated with the work of the economist John Maynard Keynes (1883–1946). Keynes argued that the market is inefficient and can become trapped in a cycle of troughs or recessions. At these times the market is, by itself, inadequate and cannot recover. In order to recover, it needs the assistance of government intervention in the form of pumping money into the economy to stimulate activity. This money is borrowed and then repaid once the economy expands. It assumes a positive role for government, and inspired politicians in Britain from both the Labour and the Conservative parties during the Second World War, when Keynes became an advisor to the Treasury, and after 1945.

The apparent failures of government intervention and Keynesian economics in the 1970s led on to the second paradigm of economic liberalism in the 1980s and 1990s. Economic liberals had a much more positive view of the market and its ability to regulate itself. They considered that government intervention distorted the market and made it more inefficient and unable to respond. The solution was a reduced role for government. Particularly influential here were the political economists Friedrich von Hayek and Milton Friedman. Hayek argued that government intervention distorted markets and imposed arbitrary rules restricting individual freedom, which could only be secured in the market when we could choose what to buy and sell. Friedman developed the idea of monetarist economics, the idea that Keynesian-style interventions at times of economic downturn created higher inflation but did nothing in the

long term to reduce unemployment. The role of government should be limited to the control of the money supply while everything else should be left to the market. These ideas proved very influential on Margaret Thatcher as Prime Minister after 1979.

It has been much debated whether New Labour marked the continuation of the economic liberal paradigm or its replacement with something else. Although there was no obvious return to a Keynesian strategy, or at least not until the banking crisis discussed below, policies such as the minimum wage were anathema to economic liberals. Some have argued that New Labour embarked on a 'Third Way' in economic policy, using economic liberal policies to achieve more traditional Labour values.

Between 1945 and the early 2000s the economic context changed dramatically as Britain went through several distinctive policy phases, and from a substantial manufacturing economy to a largely service-based one. In 1979 the largest sector in the British economy was manufacturing, employing 7.1 million people compared to just 2.9 million people employed in finance and business. By 2009 this had been transformed. Now 6.4 million people were employed in finance and business compared to 2.9 million people working in manufacturing. Although the decline in manufacturing was stark, Britain remains one of the leading manufacturing countries in the world with particular strengths in pharmaceuticals and aerospace.

The banking crisis and beyond

As manufacturing declined in Britain, especially from the 1980s onwards, politicians of both major parties argued that the financial services sector was the dynamic force of British capitalism.

Margaret Thatcher relaxed the regulations on banks and the rules relating to their credit policies. The growth in the City was astronomical and the new wealth of the financial services sector came to epitomise the 1980s. The Labour Party remained cautious in its dealings with the City of London, but after the 1992 General Election defeat went on a charm offensive believing that unless they won the support, or at least managed to eradicate the suspicion which City financiers and businesspeople more generally had of the Labour Party, they would not win another General Election.

When Gordon Brown granted operational independence to the Monetary Policy Committee of the Bank of England to set interest rates in 1997 he also established the Financial Services Authority (FSA) to regulate the work of the banks and other financial institutions. There was a significant reliance on the financial services sector in Britain during the years of Labour Government after 1997. According to some of its critics, the Labour Government lacked a similar concern with the manufacturing sector. For instance, when Brown unveiled the 'five tests' which would have to be met to determine whether Britain would enter the European single currency, one was specifically about whether it would be in the interests of the City (the others were the compatibility of business cycles, flexibility, investment and jobs). There was not another 'test' specifically related to manufacturing.

Although there were some criticism of the economic policy of New Labour, this was often marginal as the economy continued to grow at a relatively high rate and the increased tax revenue available for public spending kept coming in.

The City now became noted for its high-risk culture, particularly among the investment arms of the major banks in the search for vast profits and the payment of large bonuses to anyone who generated profits in this way. Additionally, private consumption was funded through increased personal debt. The early years of the new millennium were ones in which debt – personal and corporate – soared.

The system was high risk and economic expansion depended on the extensive use of credit. The tipping point occurred in 2007 and 2008 when loans in America for 'sub-prime' mortgages (loans to those who may have difficultly repaying) could not be financed. Banking collapses followed in America and Britain leading to a subsequent **recession** and a corresponding crisis in the Eurozone. A policy of deflation has resulted and the boom years now look a long way away. The current economic context is therefore much less rosy than if this chapter had been written say ten or even five years ago, although we can see that the seeds of the current economic downturn were present even then, albeit hidden from view.

In order to understand the current crisis it is necessary to consider two questions.

What is the meaning of 'crisis'?

The meaning most commonly attached to 'crisis' is a dramatic moment, one of urgency and suspense in which it is not clear what is going to happen. The crisis may be one of, or within, capitalism: an economic crisis; but the way in which the crisis is resolved is open to the manipulation of political actors. Although journalists tend to think of crises as frequent and temporary phenomena, academic historians and political scientists prefer to think of them as more long term: an impasse which cannot easily be resolved. It may well be that the current economic crisis is a more long-term one and the solution to it still looks difficult to find.

Recessions can be V-shaped, in which the decline and recovery happen quickly. They can also be U-shaped, where the recovery can be longer coming and can be uneven while at the bottom. One feature of the current economic context and debate is that we have now been through a 'double-dip' recession which takes more a W-shape. The final, and worst, form of recession is an L-shape. There is current uncertainty as to whether the recovery will take a long time and, indeed, whether there will ever be a recovery to where the economy stood before the crash.

Who is to blame?

One final consideration of the current economic context is: who is the blame for the mess?

Politicians in Britain naturally seek to blame one another. The Conservative-Liberal Democrat Coalition which came into office in 2010 blames the previous Labour Government for failing to control public spending. The large debts which were inherited are seen as the consequence of Labour's profligacy in government. Increasing public spending and debt in the good times meant that there was nothing from which to draw when things got worse.

Similarly, the Labour Party blames the current government for cutting spending too fast and too deep at a time when the economy is already weak, thus killing off any growth potential that the economy may have had when the General Election took place and taking Britain back into another recession.

What is striking about this debate is how quickly what was originally a crisis in the markets became a crisis of the state. Government spending and/or economic management is seen as the cause of the problems in the economy. If banks were going to be bailed out anyway, there was no incentive to avoid risk. The riskier the operation, the more likely it was that the government would have to intervene if the gamble didn't pay off.

A second striking feature of this debate is the lack of a clear economic strategy for getting Britain (and the wider world) back out of recession. For some, the size of the debt is the problem. If this isn't cut, it will lead to a situation where the British economic context is more like that of Spain or Italy, or possibly even Greece, where the credit-rating agencies decide that the economy is not performing well. Consequently, the price Britain pays for its debt repayments will increase as creditors demand higher interest for an apparently greater risk. Moreover, as the public sector contracts, there will be greater scope for the private sector to expand and produce wealth.

Meanwhile, others argue that the crisis is more one of growth. A focus on immediate deficit reduction stifles growth, whereas a growing economy is better able to repay its debts as more people are in employment, paying taxes rather than claiming welfare payments. Hence, the size of Britain's debt at the moment is not falling despite cuts to expenditure.

The most obvious target for blame has been the bankers who indulged in such high-risk activities. Public anger against bankers has risen in response to particularly newsworthy cases. Fred Goodwin had been Chief Executive of the Royal Bank of Scotland, but resigned in 2008 just before it was announced that RBS had made a loss of £24.1 billion, the greatest losses in British corporate history. He had been knighted in 2004 for services to banking but was stripped of his knighthood in 2012. A second particularly notable example is Bob Diamond, the former Chief Executive of Barclays, who was forced to resign after his bank was found to have concealed the real rate of interest it was paying. One particularly controversial aspect to these cases and those of many senior and middle-ranking investment bankers was the huge salaries, bonuses and pensions they have received. The increased concern over high pay has reopened a debate over inequality in Britain, and one recent work has sought to highlight the link between inequality and social wellbeing (Wilkinson and Pickett, *The Spirit Level*).

Conclusion

British society and the economy continue to change at a dramatic rate. The economy, for a long time in a period of expansion, has entered a notably bleak period in which it has been seen as being particularly susceptible to wider international economic developments and an overreliance on its financial service sector. The days when Britain was a powerhouse of manufacturing have gone and the future is uncertain. The immediate question of what the solution is to the economic crisis, and the longer-term question of what sort of economy Britain should become have yet to be answered.

The British social structure has also changed. The once overriding importance of social class has dwindled, with fewer people thinking of themselves in explicitly class terms. The traditional class pyramid with a few people at the top widening out into a broad base of the working class has become more diamond-shaped. Most people are now part of a large middle strata with a few remaining at the top and a few at the bottom. Debate over the future of British society has tended to focus on the reasons why some have got stuck at the bottom, and the economic crisis has now sparked some discussion over the extent to which those at the top are deserving of their vast salaries as they have moved further away from those in the middle. In place of class other social cleavages have emerged. These include ethnicity and multi-culturalism, changing gender roles and the increased proportion of elderly people. All of these things provide opportunities but also challenges. So far, despite the occasional warnings from those concerned by the pace of change, British society has adapted quietly and effectively to such challenges.

Chapter summary

This chapter has examined the major social and economic features of contemporary British politics. It has done so in the belief that, although politicians still have major choices to make, they make these choices within certain social and economic contexts and constraints. In order to make sense of the social and economic context of British politics, it was necessary to look at wider international developments, as Britain is no longer an isolated country, if indeed it ever was. Britain is a mid-ranking power with an economic structure and historical legacy which makes it particularly susceptible to changes from outside of its political borders.

In the course of the chapter it has been apparent that both the British economy and society have changed dramatically. In terms of its social structure, the class system has become more fragmented and self-perceptions of the importance of class have declined. In turn this has impacted on the political parties who have to appeal for votes from a more complex electorate. Other social distinctions have become more important. These include changing gender roles, an ageing society, ethnicity and multiculturalism, and changing perceptions of nationhood in the constituent parts of the United Kingdom.

The economic context in Britain has been shaped by the idea of decline since at least the late 1950s and the longer-term transition from a manufacturing economy to a service-based economy, with a particular stress on the financial services sector. Periods of boom have been interspersed with periods of recession but the current recession (at the time of writing), following the global financial crisis, is a particularly deep one and the future is uncertain.

Discussion points

- 'Social class is still the predominant characteristic of British society.' Discuss.
- Is it still meaningful to talk about Britishness given the increased diversity of British society?
- What is meant by the 'decline' of the British economy and can it be cured?
- Who is to blame for Britain's current economic malaise?

Further reading

There are a number of historical studies of postwar Britain. On society see A.H. Halsey and J. Webb (eds) *Twentieth Century British Social Trends* (2000). On politics see D. Childs, *Britain since 1939: Progress and Decline* (2002). On the issues concerning economic decline see A. Gamble, *Britain in Decline* (1994); G. Bernstein, *The Myth of Decline: The Rise of Britain since 1945* (2004) and R. English and M. Kenny (eds) *Rethinking British Decline* (1999).

On the politics of class see A. Adonis and S. Pollard, *A Class Act: The Myth of Britain's Classless Society* (1997). On race see J. Solomon, *Race and Racism in Britain* (2003). A provocative study of the 'underclass' is *Chavs: The Demonisation of the Working Class* (2012) by Owen Jones.

For discussions of contemporary economic and social problems see A. Gamble, *The Spectre at the Feast* (2009); W. Hutton, *Them and Us* (2011); R. Wilkinson and K. Pickett, *The Spirit Level: Why Equality is Better for Everyone* (2009) and S. Lansley, *The Cost of Inequality* (2012). For a recent statement from a Conservative perspective see J. Norman, *The Big Society* (2010).

Bibliography

Adonis, A. and Pollard, S. (1997) *A Class Act: The Myth of Britain's Classless Society* (Hamish Hamilton).

Bernstein, G. (2004) *The Myth of Decline: The Rise of Britain since 1945* (Pimlico).

Childs, D. (2002) *Britain since 1939: Progress and Decline* (Palgrave).

English, R. and Kenny, M. (eds) (1999) *Rethinking British Decline* (Macmillan).

Gamble, A. (1994) *Britain in Decline*, 4th edn (Macmillan).

Gamble, A. (2009) *The Spectre at the Feast* (Macmillan).

Halsey, A.H. and Webb, J. (eds) (2000) *Twentieth Century British Social Trends* (Macmillan).

Hutton, W. (2011) *Them and Us* (Abacus).

Jones, A. (2012) *Chavs: The Demonisation of the Working Class* (Verso).

Lansley, S. (2012) *The Cost of Inequality* (Gibson Square).

Norman, J. (2010) *The Big Society* (University of Buckingham Press).

Solomon, J. (2003) *Race and Racism in Britain* (Palgrave).

Wilkinson, R. and K. Pickett (2009) *The Spirit Level: Why Equality is Better for Everyone* (Allen Lane).

Useful websites

The government's National Statistics Online (http://www.ons.gov.uk/ons/index.html) is an invaluable source of statistical information. Annual editions of *Social Trends* are published online at http://data.gov.uk/dataset/social_trends and the British Social Attitudes Survey is available at http://www.britsocat.com/Home.

For economic data and reports see the Institute of Fiscal Studies (IFS) website www.ifs.org.uk and comparative data is available from the Organisation for Economic Co-operation and Development (OECD) at www.oecd.org

The riots of August 2011: anger, or apathy?

On 6 August 2011 more than a hundred local residents marched from the Broadwater Farm Estate in North London to the Tottenham police station. The demonstration was held in protest at the police shooting on 4 August of Mark Duggan, a well-known local figure. The police's explanation of Duggan's death was disputed by other eyewitnesses, and his friends and relatives rejected allegations that he had been a prominent gangster. The protest march was intended to be peaceful, but ended in violence amid further allegations of police misconduct. The police were attacked with a variety of missiles, buildings were set on fire and shops were looted.

Whatever the circumstances of Duggan's death, the incident evoked memories of disorder in the same area in October 1985. Broadwater Farm had been the scene of serious rioting after a local woman had died during a police search of her house. A police officer caught up in the ensuing violence had been killed. In 1985, as in 2011, unrest had undoubtedly been accentuated by racial factors. The situation on 6 August was extremely volatile, and the police response was cautious. As a result, it seemed to many observers that looters had taken control of the streets. Over the next few days trouble affected many London boroughs, then radiated out to places like Birmingham, Leeds, Manchester and Nottingham. In Croydon on 8 August a large furniture store was torched, along with other buildings. Attacks on police personnel occurred in many places, though unlike in 1985 no officer was killed.

The British weather was partly responsible for a lull in the unrest on 10 August, by which time Parliament had been recalled and David Cameron had returned from holiday to chair emergency meetings. It was announced that plastic bullets would be made available to the police for purposes of crowd-control; that, and a massive increase in police numbers, helped to deter potential rioters. Having looked as if it was ungovernable on 8 August, four days later England had returned to something like normality. But apart from numerous injuries and grievous damage to various properties, the deaths of five people were attributed to incidents during that short, surreal period.

Britain (and especially England) has a long history of civil disorder. For those who examine recent rioting with any care, the incidents of 2011 provide ample grounds for speculation. Leaving aside the special circumstances of Broadwater Farm in 1985, these things seem to happen at ten-year intervals, like the census. In 1981 riots in Bristol and Brixton, south London had triggered unrest in many English towns and cities. A decade after the 1981 riots there was serious trouble in Oxford and on Tyneside. Yet that disorder had been localised. Just before the 2001 general election there was racist-inspired violence in parts of Lancashire and Yorkshire; but again these outbreaks had been short-lived and geographically limited.

What made 2011 different from 1991 and 2001? In the riots of 1981 the perceived abuse of police powers, especially against representatives of ethnic minorities, was a precipitating factor. By 2011 a series of reports into racist attitudes within the police service had been effective to some extent. Yet rioting took place in areas where the police had taken steps to adopt a more sensitive style of policing. One novel factor in 2011 was the availability of the internet and social networking sites, which aroused considerable excitement within the media. However, electronic communication probably just made it easier for rioters to coordinate their activities; they could not have created the initial urge to riot.

A plausible conclusion is that the riots of 1991 and 2001 were localised because they were triggered by local grievances, while in 1981 and 2011 something more general was in play. In 1981 Britain was enduring a period of mass unemployment, under an apparently inflexible government. In 2011, it could be argued, the governing coalition of Conservatives and Liberal Democrats had revived this approach, proposing spending cuts which would greatly increase unemployment and make life much more difficult for those who were already dependent on benefits. Although some sections of the media quickly identified 2011 rioters who were anything but poor, detailed research showed that the majority came from deprived areas.

The 2010 British General Election took place against the background of widespread public disorder in Greece. This was provoked largely by the *prospect* of 'austerity' measures similar to those advocated by Britain's Coalition

Government. On this view, it could be argued that, although not all the 2011 English rioters were poor, their response to the killing of Mark Duggan was a pre-emptive strike against a government which proposed to make ordinary people, rather than the bankers who had caused the economic crisis, the primary victims of 'austerity'.

Were the outbreaks of August 2011, then, primarily effusions of political anger? Subsequent research conducted jointly by the London School of Economics and the *Guardian* newspaper suggests that political issues were a major contributing factor (*Reading the Riots*, 2011). The study reported that participants in the riots had mentioned several specific issues, particularly those affecting young people (such as the decision to increase university tuition fees). Eighty per cent of rioters claimed that 'government policy' was an 'important' cause of the riots, ranking third as a motivating factor behind 'poverty' and 'policing', and just ahead of 'unemployment' (all of which, of course, could be linked to government policy).

Useful though it is, the LSE/*Guardian* research should be treated cautiously: it was based on interviews with rioters who were rationalising their actions in hindsight. Helpfully, the study included the results of a *Guardian*/ ICM poll which asked members of the general public to nominate the factors which *they* judged to be important. While the rioters ranked government policy third out of the fifteen reasons for the riots, the public placed it eleventh. For the public, the joint top-ranking factors were 'criminality' and 'bad parenting' (both mentioned by 86 per cent of respondents), with 'moral decline' a close third.

It is hardly surprising that rioters and non-rioters disagreed sharply on their responses. More interesting are the cases where the perceptions of the rioters corresponded closely with the views of non-participants. Thus, almost the same high proportion (about three-quarters) thought that 'media coverage' was important – suggesting that many rioters took to the streets because they had seen footage of others doing so. More than two-thirds of the public identified 'boredom' as an important factor, and this proportion was matched among the rioters.

In 2007 the present author argued (in *From Anger to Apathy*, Jonathan Cape) that since the mid-1970s there has been a significant change in the British mentality. Before that time, material considerations had been important for most citizens, but by the end of the 1980s the country had been engulfed by a 'consumerist' ethos. Sensing this development, politicians like Tony Blair tended to assume that, whatever members of the public chose to tell opinion pollsters, their real reason for preferring one party over

another was founded on material self-interest. This mood was clearly linked to a sensational decline in electoral turnout, especially at the 2001 General Election when less than 60 per cent of registered voters chose to participate. It was not just that the 2001 outcome was inevitable long before the campaign started; despite superficial disagreements on issues like Europe, there could be no rational expectation that a change of government would have made much difference to the average voter.

On the surface, the events of August 2011 seemed to challenge the argument that the 'Anger' of the late 1970s and early 1980s had been replaced by 'Apathy'. However, on closer inspection the riots – or rather, the lootings – of 2011 add weight to the notion of a 'consumerised' British public. It was noted at the time that looters concentrated on outlets for fashionable accessories rather than necessities. From this perspective, the most eye-catching finding of the LSE/*Guardian* study was that clear majorities (more than 70 per cent) of the general public and the rioters themselves accepted that 'greed' was a significant motivation for the August 2011 disorders.

The 2010 British General Election saw an increase in turnout, from 61.3 per cent in 2005 to 65.1 per cent. However, for the first time since 1992, the election of 2010 was always going to be very close; various methods had been introduced to make voting easier; and in 2010 televised debates were held between the three main party leaders. In combination, these factors should have ensured a much higher turnout in 2010 – something close to the 77.7 per cent registered in 1992. While in 1981 a significant proportion of rioters felt thoroughly alienated from the orthodox political process, the evidence of the 2011 riots suggests that many of the participants had no quarrel with the mainstream majority beyond the fact that they lacked the material resources to join it. Others, in the excitement of the moment, decided to steal items that they could have acquired legally because they thought they would get away with it.

Thus, the 2011 riots are best understood as fundamentally different from all other outbreaks of disorder in the years since 1979. Beginning with violent expressions of anger, very quickly they lapsed into a series of copy-cat incidents, drawing in bored and frustrated people on the margins of a consumer society. As such, though they clearly had a political dimension, they also illustrate the sense of disengagement which is the leading theme of the last two decades in British politics.

by Mark Garnett

PART 2

DEFINING THE POLITICAL WORLD

Ideology and the liberal tradition

Bill Jones

> " The ideas of economists and political philosophers, both when they are right and when they are wrong, are more powerful than is commonly understood. Indeed, the world is ruled by little else. Practical men, who believe themselves to be quite exempt from any intellectual influences, are usually slaves of some defunct economist "
>
> John Maynard Keynes

Learning objectives

- To clarify the concept of ideology.
- To trace the transition of new ideas from their 'revolutionary' inception to accepted orthodoxy.
- To show how classical liberalism developed into new liberalism, the creed that set the social agenda for the next century.

This chapter begins by discussing what we mean by the term '**ideology**'. It goes on to explain how 'liberal' ideas entered the political culture as *heresies* in the seventeenth and eighteenth centuries but went on to become the *orthodoxies* of the present age. Classical liberalism in the mid-nineteenth century is examined together with the birth of modern liberalism in the early twentieth century. So-called 'liberal' ideas therefore provide the architecture of our beliefs in a democratic society; we hold our political views, discuss and debate them within a framework of ideas acquired hundreds of years ago.

Introduction

What is ideology?

Ideology as a concept is not easy to define. Perhaps it is helpful to regard ideology as 'applied philosophy'. It links philosophical ideas to the contemporary world, it provides a comprehensive and systematic perspective whereby human society can be understood, and it provides a framework of principles from which policies can be developed.

For up to two decades after 1945 it seemed as if political ideas as a factor in British politics was on the wane; 'ideologies' are systems of belief which embody political ideas like 'socialism', 'conservatism', 'fascism' or 'communism'. The coalition comradeship of the war had drawn some of the sting from the sharp conflicts about ideas between the two major political parties, and in its wake the Conservatives had conceded – without too much ill grace – that Labour would expand welfare services and nationalise a significant sector of the economy. Once in power after 1951, the Conservatives presided over their socialist inheritance of a **mixed economy** and a welfare state. Both parties seemed to have converged towards a general consensus on political values and institutions: there was arguably more to unite than to divide them. By the end of the 1950s some commentators – notably the American political scientist Daniel Bell – were pronouncing 'the end of ideology' (see Bell 1960) in Western societies.

However, the faltering of the British economy in the 1960s, exacerbated in the early 1970s by the rise in oil prices, industrial unrest and raging inflation, reopened the ideological debate with a vengeance. A revived Labour Left hurled contumely at their right-wing Cabinet colleagues for allegedly betraying socialist principles. Margaret Thatcher, meanwhile, Leader of the Opposition after 1975, began to elaborate a position far to the right of her predecessor Edward Heath (Prime Minister, 1970–4 – see Profile, page 23). The industrial paralysis of the 1978–9 'winter of discontent' provided a shabby end for Jim Callaghan's Labour Government and a perfect backcloth against which Thatcher's confident assertions could be projected. From 1979 to 1990 ideology in the form of Thatcherism or the New Right triumphed over what has subsequently been labelled the 'postwar consensus' on the mixed economy and the welfare state.

Individuals support ideologies for a variety of reasons: moral commitment – often genuine, whatever cynics might say – as well as self-interest. It is entirely possible for a businessman, for example, to believe quite genuinely, that a pro-business set of policies by a party is good not only for him but for the nation as a whole. Clearly, ideology will mean more to political activists; it has to be recognised that most people are ill-informed on political matters, or not especially interested in them. However, the broad mass of the population is not completely inert. During election campaigns they receive a crash course in political education, and leaving aside the more crass appeals to emotion and unreason, most voters are influenced to some extent by the ideological debate. The party with the clearest message that seems most relevant to the times can win elections, as Labour discovered in 1945, the Conservatives in 1979 and Labour again in 1997.

Classifying ideologies

This is a difficult and imperfect science, but the following two approaches should help to clarify it.

The horizontal left–right continuum

This is the most familiar classification, used and abused in the press and in everyday conversations. It arose from the seating arrangements adopted in the French Estates General in 1789, where the aristocracy sat to the right of the King and the popular movements to his left. Subsequently the terms have come to represent adherence to particular groups of principles. Right-wingers stress freedom, or the right of individuals to do as they please and develop their own lives and personalities without interference, especially from governments – which history teaches are potentially tyrannical. Left-wingers believe that this kind of freedom is only won by the strong at the expense of the weak. They see equality as the more important value and stress the collective interest of the community above that of the individual.

The implications of these principles for economic policy are obviously of key importance. Right-wingers champion free enterprise, or capitalism: the rights of individuals to set up their own businesses, to provide goods and services and to reap what reward they can. Left-wingers disagree. Capitalism, they argue, creates poverty amid plenty – much better to move towards collective ownership so that workers can receive the full benefit of their labour. Politicians in the centre dismiss both these positions as extreme and damaging to the harmony of national life. They tend to argue for various combinations of left and right principles or compromises between them: in practice, a mixed economy plus efficient welfare services. The left–right continuum therefore relates in practice principally to economic and social policy.

Left	Centre	Right
Equality	Less inequality	Freedom
Collectivism	Some collectivism	Individualism
Collective ownership	Mixed economy	Free enterprise

BOX 4.1

Left and right discussed

In his book *The Third Way* (1998), Anthony Giddens suggests left and right are less than adequate terms. He points out that what was once left can now be right – such as nineteenth-century free-market views. He quotes the Italian writer Bobbio, who argues that politics is adversarial and that 'left and right' encapsulates the familiar idea of bodily opposites, i.e. the left and right arms. He goes on to say that when ideas are evenly balanced most people accept the dichotomy, but when one ideology seems 'the only game in town' neither side finds the terms suitable. The strong ideology seeks to claim it is the 'only' alternative, while the weaker tries to strengthen its position by absorbing some elements of the stronger side and offering them as its own, producing a 'synthesis of opposing positions with the intentions in practice of saving whatever can be saved of one's own position by drawing in the opposing position and thus neutralising it'. Both sides then present their views as beyond the old left/right distinction and as something totally new and exciting. Giddens comments that 'the claim that Tony Blair has taken over most of the views of Thatcherism and recycled them as something new is readily comprehensible from

such a standpoint'. Giddens insists that the 'left' is not just the opposite of 'right': the core of the former is concerned with social justice or 'emancipatory' politics, while the right has shifted to anti-global and even racist positions.

He goes on to accept that socialism is no longer valid as a 'theory of economic management' and that in consequence the right/left distinction has lost relevance. Now people face 'life politics' decisions such as those connected with nuclear energy, work, global warming, devolution and the future of the EU, none of which fits easily into the old dichotomy. By talking of the 'radical centre', Giddens suggests that 'major gains' can be derived as it 'permits exchange across political fences which were much higher'. So to look at welfare reform, it is not merely an argument about high or low spending but comprises 'common issues facing all welfare reformers. The question of how to deal with an ageing population isn't just a matter of setting pension levels. It requires more radical rethinking in relation to the changing nature of ageing.'

Source: Giddens (1998: 37–46)

The vertical axis or continuum

The inadequacies of the left–right continuum are obvious. It is both crude and inaccurate in that many people can subscribe to ideas drawn from its whole width and consequently defy classification. H.J. Eysenck suggested in the early 1950s that if a 'tough' and 'tender' axis could bisect the left–right continuum, ideas could be more accurately plotted on two dimensions. In this way ideological objectives could be separated from political methodology – so tough left-wingers, e.g. communists, would occupy the top left-hand quarter, tough right-wingers, e.g. fascists, the top right-hand quarter, and so on.

Political parties and the left–right continuum

Despite its inadequacies, the left–right continuum is useful because it is commonly understood (though see Box 4.1). It will be used as a guide to the following sections, but first a word on the way in which political parties relate to the political spectrum.

For most of the postwar period, the major ideological divisions have not occurred between the two big parties but within them. The Labour Party has covered a very wide spectrum from the revolutionary Left to the cautious social democrat Right. Similarly, two major Conservative schools of thought developed in the late 1970s: traditional ('wet') conservatism and the New Right or Thatcherite conservatism. The centre ground was dominated for many years by the Liberal Party, but during the 1980s it was augmented by the Social Democratic Party (which split off from the Labour Party in 1981) and then was fragmented when the merger initiative following the 1987 General Election resulted in the awkward progeny of the Social and Liberal Democrats plus the rump Social Democratic Party led defiantly by David Owen until May 1990, when the party formally folded.

The liberal tradition

Since then, like so many other political labels coined as forms of abuse ('tory' was once a name given to Irish outlaws), the word 'liberalism' has lost any derogatory connotations it might have caused in the nineteenth century and fully traversed the ground between vice and virtue. Now liberalism denotes opinions and qualities that in this country are generally applauded. Most people would like to think they are 'liberal' in the sense of being open-minded, tolerant, generous or rational. This is partly because the ideas of the English liberal philosophers from the mid-seventeenth to the mid-nineteenth centuries became accepted as dominant elements in our political culture. These were the ideas that helped to create our 'liberal democratic' political system in the late nineteenth century and since then have provided its philosophical underpinnings.

Interestingly by contrast, in the USA the term came to assume a pejorative meaning in the early 1980s, when the Republicans successfully linked it to being 'soft on communism' and therefore anti-American (see Box 4.2); in March 2006 the film actor George Clooney's statement that he was indeed a 'liberal' consequently contained a note of defiance.

An important distinction clearly has to be made between liberal with a small 'l' and the Liberalism associated with the party of the same name until the 1987 merger. The Liberal Party always claimed a particular continuity with 'liberal' philosophical ideas; but so deeply ingrained have these views become that most political parties also owe them substantial unacknowledged philosophical debts. For their part, liberals have made contributions to political, social and economic thinking that have been hugely influential and have been plundered shamelessly by other parties. It makes sense, therefore, to begin with some consideration of the liberal tradition of both the philosophical 'l' and party political 'L' variety.

Philosophical liberalism

Bertrand Russell attributes the birth of English liberal thought in part to the French philosopher René Descartes (1596–1650). His famous proposition 'I think, therefore I am' made 'the basis of knowledge different for each person since for each the starting point was his own existence not that of other individuals or the community' (Russell 1965: 579). To us such propositions seem unexceptional, but in the mid-seventeenth century they were potentially revolutionary because they questioned the very basis of feudal society and religious belief. This relied on unquestioning acceptance of the monarch's divine right to rule, the aristocracy's hereditary privileges and the Church's explanation of the world together with its moral leadership. Feudal society was in any case reeling from the impact of the Civil War (1642–9), the repercussions of which produced a limited **constitutional monarchy** and the embryo of modern parliamentary government. Descartes had inaugurated a new style of thinking.

Rationality

The English philosopher, John Locke (1632–1704) did much to set the style of liberal thinking as rational and undogmatic. He accepted some certainties, such as his own existence, God and mathematical logic, but he respected an area of doubt in relation to most propositions. He was inclined to accept differences of opinion as the natural consequences of free individual development. Liberal philosophers tended to give greater credence to facts established by scientific enquiry – the systematic testing of theories against reality – rather than to assertions accepted as fact purely on the basis of tradition. In the present day, evolutionary biologist Richard Dawkins, uses similar rational argument, though in a far-more passionate and far-reaching fashion, to deny the validity of religion (see *The God Delusion*, 2006).

Toleration

This lack of dogmatism was closely connected with a liberal prejudice in favour of **toleration** and compromise. Conflicts between Crown and Parliament, Catholicism and Protestantism had divided the country for too long, they felt: it was time to recognise that religious belief was a matter of personal conscience, not a concern of government.

Natural rights and the consent of the governed

This idea emerged out of the 'contract' theorists of the seventeenth and eighteenth centuries. These thinkers believed that each individual had made a kind of agreement to obey the government in exchange for the services of the state, principally (according to Thomas Hobbes) 'security' or protection from wrong-doing. It was not suggested that anything had actually been signed; the idea was more of an application of the legal concept of rights to the philosophical realm. It was all a far cry from an earlier English philosopher Sir Robert Filmer's (1588–1653) doctrine that the 'divine authority' of monarchs to receive absolute obedience could be traced back to Adam and Eve, from whom all monarchs were originally descended.

Individual liberty

The idea of natural rights was closely allied to the concept of individual **liberty**, which had already been established by the eighteenth century: freedom from arbitrary arrest, search and taxation; equality before the law; jury trials, freedom of thought and expression, freedom to buy and sell.

Such liberties in practice were protected by **constitutional** checks and balances, limited government and representation. The great liberal philosopher, John Stuart Mill (1806–73), established the classic liberal view on liberty when he argued that anyone should be free to do as they wish unless their actions impinge on the freedom of someone else (see Box 4.2).

Constitutional checks and balances

The French Enlightenment philosopher Baron Montesquieu argued something destined to influence not only John Locke but all future democratic government: that to ensure that *executive* power was not exercised arbitrarily by the monarch, the law-making or *legislative* arm of government should be separate, independent and removable by the community. The courts, or *judiciary*, should also be separate. This

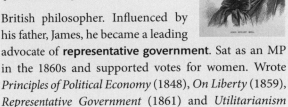

John Stuart Mill (1806–73)

British philosopher. Influenced by his father, James, he became a leading advocate of **representative government**. Sat as an MP in the 1860s and supported votes for women. Wrote *Principles of Political Economy* (1848), *On Liberty* (1859), *Representative Government* (1861) and *Utilitarianism* (1863).

doctrine of the 'separation of powers' informed liberal enthusiasm for written constitutions (although, ironically, Britain has never had a written constitution or, indeed, an effective separation of powers, ironically a mistaken analysis by Montesquieu).

Limited government

Instead of the absolute power that Filmer argued the monarch was free to exercise, liberal philsophers, mindful of past abuses, sought to restrict the legitimacy of government to a protection of civil liberties. It was held to be especially important, though, that government did not interfere with the right to property or the exercise of economic activity.

BOX 4.2

Libertarianism

For some people the central aim of political activity should be the defence of freedom, that everyone owns their own body, life and property and has the right to do as they please with them. This is essentially the J.S. Mill position, but the assertion of the individual right to freedom above all else leads to some unusual political positions. For example, some argue that the state needs to defend the freedom of others to certain rights – welfare support, for example – but for libertarians this involves an unacceptable imposition of taxes by the government, demands backed by force and hence 'tyrannical'.

They also argue against any kind of censorship, the military draft, the minimum wage, laws on sexual behaviour, drug use and immigration controls while supporting free trade and prostitution. Robert Nozick's much admired 1974 work, *Anarchy, State and Utopia*, elaborated some of these positions including the view of taxation as 'forced labour'. Translated into the more conventional political world, libertarianism appeals partly to the anarchic left who resent any controls but perhaps more powerfully to the right and, because it implicitly entails disobedience to the law and a complete 'rolling back' of the state, the far right. In the USA some groups have established themselves as libertarian enclaves in conventional society, seeking to be true to their visions and in the process rejecting the whole concept and machinery of government with its controls, regulation and impositions. At this point left-wing anarchism and right-wing libertarianism meet in a variety of intriguing ways.

Representation

It followed that if the legislature was to be removable then it needed to be representative. Many liberal Whigs – inclined to support Parliament rather than the monarch – in the eighteenth century believed that Parliament was generally representative of the nation, even though the franchise was small and usually based on a highly restrictive property qualification. However, such positions were destined to be eroded by the inherent logic of natural rights: if everyone had equal rights then surely they should have an equal say in removing a government not of their liking?

The influence of the liberal philosophers perhaps seems greater in retrospect than it was, because they were often seeking to justify and accelerate political trends that were already well under way. Nevertheless, such liberal notions were of key importance and provide ideas still used as touchstones in the present day.

Some commentators, such as Eccleshall (1984, 1986) and Gamble (1981), see liberalism as providing the philosophical rationale for modern capitalist society. Certainly the idea of individual freedom, property rights and limited government suited the emergent entrepreneurial middle classes who were destined to come of political age in the next century. However, liberal views on government have enjoyed a general acceptance not just in Britain but also in the USA, western Europe and elsewhere. They have provided the commonly accepted ground rules of democratic behaviour, the 'procedural values' of toleration, fair play and free speech that Bernard Crick, the great modern advocate of citizenship, argued should be positively reinforced in our society via our classrooms. They have provided in one sense an 'enabling' ideology that all major parties have accepted. Indeed, it is in some ways surprising that a creed originating in an agrarian, largely non-industrialised country should have provided a political framework that has survived so tenaciously and indeed triumphantly into the present day.

Classical liberalism

The American and French Revolutions applied liberal principles in a way that shocked many of their more moderate adherents. The Napoleonic interlude caused a period of reaction, but during the mid- to late-nineteenth century classical liberalism took shape. Claiming continuity with the early liberals, this new school was based on the economic ideas of the Scot, Adam Smith (1723–90) and the radical English philosophers Jeremy Bentham (1748–1832), James Mill (1773–1836) and his prodigy of a son, John Stuart Mill. Liberalism with a capital 'L' then took the stage in the form of the Liberal Party, a grouping based on the Whigs, disaffected Tories – the group which, in the eighteenth-century

parliament, supported the king – and the Manchester Radicals led by Richard Cobden and John Bright.

Classical liberalism was characterised by the idea of the independent, rational and self-governing citizen as the basic unit of society. For liberals, this concept now represented a goal or vision to be worked for. Liberals hoped that through the erosion of aristocratic privilege and the moral transformation of the working class, social differences would give way to a new society of equals.

Human nature

The liberal view of human nature was fairly optimistic. John Stuart Mill, for example, doubted whether working for the common good would induce citizens to produce goods as efficiently as when self-interest was involved. His awareness of human selfishness perhaps underlay his advice against too rapid a rate of social progress. However, at the heart of liberal philosophy was a belief in the potential of human nature to change into Locke's *civilised reasonable human being*, capable of being educated into responsible citizenship. Many liberals felt that such an education would take a great many years but that it was possible, especially through direct involvement of citizens in the economy and the political system.

Freedom

Classical liberalism retained the emphasis on freedom. In his essay *On Liberty*, for example, Mill felt: 'It was imperative that human beings should be free to form opinions and to express their opinions without reserve.' The only constraint should be that in the exercise of his freedom, an individual should not impinge upon the freedom of others.

Utilitarianism

Jeremy Bentham (1748–1832) took the **rationality** of liberal philosophy to new levels with his science of utilitarianism. His approach was based on what now seems an extraordinarily simplistic view of human psychology. He argued that human beings were disposed to seek pleasure and avoid pain. While they sought what was best for themselves they frequently made mistakes. The role of government therefore was to assist individuals in making the correct choices, in enabling the achievement of the 'greatest happiness for the greatest number'. While Bentham embraced the *laissez-faire/capitalist* economic system as highly utilitarian, he believed that most laws and administrative arrangements reflected aristocratic privilege and therefore were in need of reform. His ideas were criticised as simplistic and his Panopticon – a model prison based on his philosophy – was generally seen

Box 4.3

Manchester Radicals

This school of thought was based on the form of capitalism pioneered in the great textile city of Manchester. It's leaders were Richard Cobden and John Bright, both MPs for many years. They advocated free trade (i.e. trade without tariffs) as an end to **imperialism** and war, which they condemned as the playground of aristocratic elites.

as risible by other philosophers, but he had a pervasive influence on Liberal legislators in the nineteenth century.

Minimal government – middle-class values

Bentham's influence paradoxically led to far-reaching legal and administrative reforms: for example, the regulatory framework for mines and factories. However, other liberals were strongly opposed to such regulation both as a violation of laissez-faire principles and as an interference in the moral education of the poor. Liberals such as the social Darwinist Herbert Spencer (1820–1903) argued that welfare provision was wrong in that it sheltered the poor from the consequences of their behaviour. 'Is it not manifest', he argued, 'that there must exist in our midst an immense amount of misery which is a normal result of misconduct and ought not to be dissociated from it?' State support for the poor was therefore a dangerous narcotic likely to prevent the right lessons being learned. The stern lesson that classical liberals wished to teach was that the poorer classes would face the penalties of poverty unless they adopted the values and lifestyles of their economic superiors: thrift, hard work, moderate indulgence and self-improving pastimes. His famous quotation sums up his approach: 'To protect people from the consequences of their folly, is to people the world with fools.'

Bentham and James Mill (1773–1836) introduced arguments in favour of representative government. Bentham dismissed the natural rights argument as 'nonsense on stilts'. His own utilitarian reasoning was that such a form of government was the most effective safeguard for citizens against possibly rapacious rulers or powerful 'sinister interests'. As both men believed individuals to be the best judge of where their own interests lay, they favoured universal franchise (although Mill sought to restrict it to men over 40). His son, J.S. Mill (1806–73), is probably the best-known advocate of representative government. He urged adult male and female suffrage, but to guard against a 'capricious and impulsive' House of Commons he advised a literacy qualification for voting and a system of plural voting whereby educated professional people would be able to cast more votes than ill-educated workers. Mill also believed that a participatory **democracy** and the sense of responsibility it would imbue

would contribute towards the moral education of society: 'Democracy creates a morally better person because it forces people to develop their potentialities.'

Laissez-faire economics

Laissez-faire economics was predicated on the tenet of individual freedom: it asserted that the ability to act freely in the marketplace – to buy and sell property, employ workers and take profit – was central to any free society. Adam Smith's (1723–90) broadsides against the trade protection of the eighteenth-century **mercantilist** system provided the clearest possible statement of the case for economic activity free from political restrictions. According to Smith, producers should be allowed to supply products at the price consumers are willing to pay. Provided that competition was fair, the 'invisible hand' of the market would ensure that goods were produced at the lowest possible price commensurate with the quality consumers required. Producers would be motivated by selfish pursuit of profit but would also provide social 'goods', through providing employment, creating wealth and distributing it in accordance with the energy and ability of people active in the economic system. Smith believed that government intervention and regulation would impede this potentially perfect self-adjusting system. Liberals were not especially worried by the inequalities thrown up by laissez-faire economics or claims that employers 'exploited' employees. Classical liberals were opposed to inherited financial advantages but not so concerned with the differences created by different performances in relation to the market. They favoured the meritocracy of the market: they were the high priests of capitalism.

Peace through trade

Liberals, especially the so-called Manchester Radicals, also applied their free-trade principles to foreign affairs. Richard Cobden, for example, regarded diplomacy and war as the dangerous pastimes of the aristocracy. His answer to these perennial problems was 'to make diplomacy open and subject to parliamentary control', eliminate trade barriers, and encourage free trade worldwide. Commerce, he argued, was peaceful and beneficial, and it encouraged cooperation and contact between nations. If the world were a completely open market, national economies would become more integrated and interdependent and governments would be less likely to engage in conflicts or war.

'New liberalism'

The emphasis of classical liberalism was on laissez-faire, wealth production, toleration of inequality, minimal welfare, individual responsibility and moral education. Towards the end of the nineteenth century, however, liberals themselves began to move away from their own ascetic economic doctrines. John Stuart Mill had argued that government intervention was only justified to prevent injury to the life, property or freedom of others. To some liberals it appeared that capitalist society had become so complex and repressive that the freedom of poor people to develop their potential was being restricted: even if they were inclined to emulate their middle-class betters their capacity to do so was held back by poverty, poor health and education, and squalid living and working conditions. Liberal thinkers began to shift their emphasis away from 'negative' freedom – freedom from oppression – towards providing 'positive' freedom – the capacity of people to make real choices regarding education, employment, leisure and so on. In the modern day the political philosopher Isaiah Berlin sharpened this distinction in his famous 'Two Concepts of Liberty' essay, which distinguished between a British-derived 'freedom from' and a Rousseau-derived 'freedom to'.

State responsibility for welfare

The English philosopher, T.H. Green (1836–82) helped to initiate this movement for positive action to assist the poor by calling for a tax on inherited wealth. Alfred Marshall (1842–1924), another English thinker, believed that capitalism now provided such material plenty that it had the capacity to redistribute some of its largesse to the disadvantaged so that they would be able genuinely to help themselves to become self-reliant. But it was the distinguished Liberal philosopher and sociologist, L.T. Hobhouse (1864–1929) who perhaps marked the key shift of Liberals towards paternalism:

> The state as over-parent is quite as truly liberal as socialistic. It is the basis of the rights of the child, of his protection against parental neglect, of the equality of opportunity which he may claim as a 'future citizen'.

Hobhouse insisted that his version of paternalism should not be oppressively imposed; he favoured a basic minimum standard of living that would provide 'equal opportunities of self-development'. He followed Green in proposing taxation to finance such welfare innovations as health insurance and pensions. The great Liberal victory of 1906 enabled the Government to implement many of these new measures. Thereafter Liberals became firm advocates of **welfarism**; in 1942, the Liberal William Beveridge produced his famous blueprint for the postwar welfare state.

The mixed economy: Hobsonian and Keynesian economics

Government intervention of a different kind was proposed by the economist, J.A. Hobson (1858–1940). He was the first major liberal economist (he later became a socialist) to argue that capitalism was fatally flawed. Its tendency to produce a rich minority who accumulated unspent profits and luxury goods meant that the full value of goods produced was not consumed by society. This created slumps and, indirectly, the phenomenon of economic imperialism. Capitalists were forced by such under-consumption to export their savings abroad, thus creating overseas interests with political and colonial consequences. Hobson argued that the state could solve this crisis with one Olympian move: redirect wealth from the minority to the poor via progressive taxation. The section of society most in need would then be able to unblock the mechanism which caused overproduction and unemployment, thus making moral as well as economic sense.

J.M. Keynes (1883–1946) (see Profile) completed this revolution in liberal economic thought by arguing that demand could be stimulated not by redistribution of wealth to the poor but by government-directed investment in new economic activity. Confronted by a world recession and massive unemployment, he concentrated on a different part of the economic cycle. He agreed that the retention of wealth by capitalists under a laissez-faire economic system lay at the heart of the problem, but he believed the key to be increased investment, not increased consumption. Instead of saving in a crisis, governments should encourage businessmen to invest in new economic activity. Through the creation of new economic enterprises wealth would be generated, consumption increased, other economic activities stimulated and unemployment reduced. He envisaged a mixed economy in which the state would intervene with a whole range of economic controls to achieve full employment and planned economic growth. Keynes was not just concerned with the cold science of economics: his view of the mixed economy would serve social ends in the form of alleviated hardship and the extension of opportunity. But while Keynes was unhappy with capitalism in the 1930s he did not propose to replace it – merely to modify it. He was

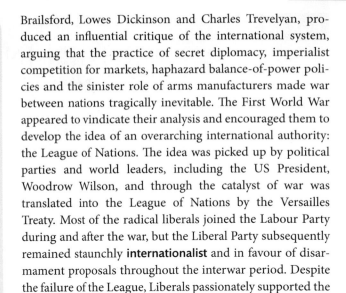

John Maynard Keynes (1883–1946)

Born in Cambridge, Keynes was the son of an academic. He was educated at Eton and King's College, Cambridge, where he mixed in avant-garde intellectual circles, such as the 'Bloomsbury group', and taught sporadically. He served in the India Office (1906–8) and later wrote his first book on this subject. In the First World War he advised the Treasury and represented it at the Versailles Treaty negotiations but resigned over the terms proposed. His essay *The Economic Consequences of the Peace* (1919) brought his powerful radical intellect to the notice of the country's ruling élite. He attacked Churchill's restoration of the gold standard in 1925, and the unemployment caused by the Depression inspired his most famous work, *A General Theory of Employment, Interest and Money* (1936). His views won support on the left and in the centre as well as helping to inspire the New Deal policies of Roosevelt in the USA.

Keynes married a Soviet ballerina and with her father founded the Vic-Wells ballet. In 1943 he established the Arts Theatre in Cambridge. In the same year he played a leading role in the Bretton Woods agreement, which set up a new international economic order, the establishment of the International Monetary Fund and negotiations following the ending of lend-lease (a financial agreement whereby aid was channelled to the UK during the war) after the war to secure a major loan to help Britain to survive the rigours of the immediate postwar world. Most people achieve only a fraction in their lifetimes of what Keynes managed to do. He was one of the truly great figures of the century, and his influence lives on today.

no egalitarian, unlike socialist economists, and disagreed with Hobsonian calls for wealth redistribution, which he felt would adversely affect the incentives to achieve which human nature required: 'for my own part I believe there is social and psychological justification for significant inequalities of income and wealth' (Keynes 1985: 374).

Internationalism

During the early twentieth century radical liberals, such as J.A. Hobson, Norman Angel, E.D. Morel, C.R. Buxton, H.N. Brailsford, Lowes Dickinson and Charles Trevelyan, produced an influential critique of the international system, arguing that the practice of secret diplomacy, imperialist competition for markets, haphazard balance-of-power policies and the sinister role of arms manufacturers made war between nations tragically inevitable. The First World War appeared to vindicate their analysis and encouraged them to develop the idea of an overarching international authority: the League of Nations. The idea was picked up by political parties and world leaders, including the US President, Woodrow Wilson, and through the catalyst of war was translated into the League of Nations by the Versailles Treaty. Most of the radical liberals joined the Labour Party during and after the war, but the Liberal Party subsequently remained staunchly **internationalist** and in favour of disarmament proposals throughout the interwar period. Despite the failure of the League, Liberals passionately supported the United Nations which emerged in the wake of the Second World War.

Further development of democratic government

The New Liberals were no less interested than their predecessors in the development of representative democracy through extension of the franchise and the strengthening of the House of Commons. Lloyd George's device of including welfare proposals in his 1909 Budget – a measure that the House of Lords had traditionally passed 'on the nod' – precipitated a conflict between the two chambers that resulted in the House of Lords' power being reduced from one of absolute veto over legislation to one of delay only. In the early 1920s the Liberal Party gave way to Labour as the chief opposition party, returning 159 MPs in 1923, 59 in 1929 and only 21 in 1935. The dramatic decline in the party's fortunes coincided with its support for a change in the electoral system from the 'first-past-the-post' system, which favoured big parties, to alternatives that would provide fairer representation to smaller parties, such as the Liberals, with thinly spread national support.

This chapter has so far sought to emphasise the centrality of the liberal (note small 'l') tradition in the evolution of modern British political thought. In the eighteenth century it helped to establish reason, toleration, liberty, natural rights and the consent of the governed in place of religious dogma, feudal allegiance and the divine right of monarchs to rule. In the nineteenth century it added representative, democratic government with power shared between various elements. Having provided key guidelines for our modern system of government, classical liberalism argued for minimal government intervention in social policy and an economy run essentially in harmony with market forces.

BOX 4.4

BRITAIN IN CONTEXT

Liberal values

It is seductively easy to believe that the beliefs under-pinning one's own system of government are somehow 'natural', 'universal' and superior to those of other cultures. Probably the most famous statement of liberal values is enshrined in the Declaration of Independence made by the 'thirteen united states of America' in 1776, beginning:

> We hold these truths to be self-evident, that all men are created equal, that they are endowed by their Creator with certain unalienable Rights, that among these are Life, Liberty, and the pursuit of Happiness. That to secure these rights, Governments are instituted among Men, deriving their just powers from the consent of the governed.

These few words embody much of the liberal thinking of Hobbes (his views were a mixture of the liberal and illiberal), Locke, Paine, Rousseau and other thinkers associated with the impending French Revolution. 'Life, liberty and the pursuit of happiness' were considered to be 'self-evident' truths, reflecting universal rights owned by all humans. At the time, when it was believed monarchs ruled with the authority of God who had decreed a natural order and social hierarchy, such views were wholly unorthodox and revolutionary; as much as the armies of Napoleon they unseated the established order in Europe and set the movement towards democracy in train.

As the new order took shape, what once was heretical became at first acceptable and then, by degrees, the new unchallenged orthodoxy. Citizens in Britain and the USA do not question these 'inalienable rights' which are enshrined in law and constitution; though in the USA the term 'liberal' has acquired pejorative overtones through the efforts of Republicans to identify Democrats with 'un-American' (and hence unpatriotic) socialist ideas.

However, elsewhere in the world, such liberal values did not pass unchallenged. Communist countries claimed such beliefs were merely one of the means whereby property-owning capitalists fooled the exploited working classes into accepting gross inequalities. In more recent times fundamentalist Muslim movements have condemned Western liberalism as a sign of the West's decadence and corruption. They do not subscribe to notions of free speech, but believe government should be a direct exten-sion of their religion. This has given birth to a 'theocracy' in Iran, powerful internal movements in Muslim states and worldwide movements like al-Qaeda which seek to destroy the West; all this reinforcing the analysis of Samuel P. Huntington's exceptional book *The Clash of Civilizations and the Remaking of World Order* (Touchstone Books, 1997).

We should not, therefore, assume that liberal values are automatically right, and we should remember that:

1 Even cherished values – such as freedom of speech – are not absolute; Western countries all legislate to place limits on some kinds of expression.

2 Some Muslim countries do not accept liberal values but regard religious values as absolute, thus producing powerful conflicts with secular views of government (read Orhan Pamuk's novel *Snow* for excellent insights into these conflicts).

3 Before we reject such opposing views we should remember that even in 1776 (our Christian) God's name was invoked as the source of liberal values.

The New Liberals, however, engineered a new intellectual revolution. They argued for government intervention to control an increasingly complex economy that distributed great rewards and terrible penalties with near-random unfairness. They also saw commerce not as the healing balm for international conflicts but as the source of the conflicts themselves. The irony is that the Liberals Keynes and Beveridge proved to be the chief architects of the postwar consensus between Labour and Conservatives, while, as we shall see, Margaret Thatcher wrought her revolution not through application of traditional conservatism but through a rediscovery of classical liberalism.

John Rawls and *A Theory of Justice*

The contribution of US scholar John Rawls (1921–2002) to liberal thinking has been hugely important (see also section on 'social justice', Chapter 1). Some regard the reserved US academic as the greatest philosopher of the twentieth century while others consider his ideas fatally flawed and that, like Herbert Spenser, once also seen as a dominant thinker at the opposite send of the political spectrum, his reputation is not destined to last. Rawls was concerned to establish a methodology for discerning social justice: what constituted a *fair* way of living with others. To do this he employed an innovative method, not dissimilar from early social contract theorists.

The *Original Position* and *The Veil of Ignorance*

Rawls asked us to think what kind of a society people might choose, if they were, as yet, outside society – which he calls the *Original Position* – and unaware of what position they might occupy within it – *The Veil of Ignorance*. This ignorance would extend to whether a person in this new society is to be very rich or poverty stricken, male or female, disabled or fully abled, healthy or sickly, heterosexual or homosexual, highly intelligent or unintelligent, good looking or ugly, overflowing with talents or relatively unskilled. This device is similar to that used by my mother when settling disputes between myself and my brother over fair shares of treats – for example a cake. She would tell one of us to divide the cake and the other to choose his slice. Not wanting to disadvantage himself, each brother has every incentive to make a scrupulously fair division. If one does not know the outcome of such a procedure, one is led by this arrangement to accept principles of *fairness* and *equality*. Rawls was not content with this method alone but specified what he regarded as appropriate principles.

Principles

He specified a *Liberty Principle* whereby everyone had a fundamental right to basic liberties which should be sacrosanct.

Difference principle

This principle is the key part of Rawls' system and specifies that inequalities are only justifiable if they assist the worst off. So this recognises that human beings often require incentives to work harder but aims to restrict any subsequent advantage to that person unless it contributes to the welfare of the very poorest in society. So, huge bankers' bonuses could only be justified for Rawls if the poorest benefited from them. Moreover, he did not consider that gifted people – sportsmen, musicians, writers – should benefit from their gifts unless the same condition applied. He saw such talents of birth as the products purely of good fortune, a condition which if absent, should not penalise those not similarly endowed.

Clearly such a scheme of ethical thinking justifies taxation and the welfare state, so liberals fastened onto Rawls' innovative thinking to reinforce support for the emergent shape of developed societies and to refute the criticisms they received from the right.

Fukuyama and the end of history

No account of the development of the liberal tradition in politics can end without some reference to Francis Fukuyama (1952–), the formerly obscure official in the US State Department who argued in articles and a book (1992) that the liberal tradition had developed to the extent that, allied to free-enterprise economics, it had eclipsed all its rivals on the left and right – communism, fascism, socialism – thus producing the 'universalisation of Western Liberal democracy as the final form of human government'.

He founded his reasoning on the Hegelian notion that civilisations successively develop, resolve internal conflicts and change for the better. The 'end of history' is when a point is reached whereby conflict is eradicated and the form of society best suited to human nature has evolved.

The importance of the article lay partly in its timing. The British Empire took a couple of decades to expire, but Stalin's collapsed in a few years at the end of the 1980s. The intellectual world was deafened by the crashing of rotten regimes and astonished by the apparent vibrancy of their democratic successors. Moreover, after decades of defending liberal values against a grey and predatory communist bloc, the Western intelligentsia responded warmly to a thesis that appeared to say 'we've won'. Fukuyama's bold thesis fitted the facts and suited the mood of the times. Even in Britain the triumph of Thatcher in three successive elections between 1979 and 1987 seemed to reflect the thrust of the argument and her stated resolve to destroy socialism in her country. However, Fukuyama's thesis seems to ignore the exponential forces for change that are transforming society at breakneck speed: computer technology and the information revolution; the huge pressure on finite world resources; the spread of nuclear weapons; and the increasing concentration of wealth in a few hands, leading to the huge and growing gap between rich and poor. Who is to say that these forces will not undermine the liberal consensus and positions and possibly usher in a new authoritarianism? Moreover, as Samuel P. Huntington's book, *The Clash of Civilizations and the Remaking of World Order*, suggested, the world could now be engaged in a struggle between the values of the West and the more traditional and narrow values of Islam.

To assume that the liberal underpinnings of many of the world's political systems will survive can be seen as at best naïve and at worst complacent.

Chapter summary

Ideology is a kind of applied philosophy. It can be classified on the right–left continuum, a flawed but still much-used form. The liberal tradition, based on rights, freedom and representation, developed from the seventeenth century and set the ground rules for political activity during the nineteenth and twentieth. Classical liberalism elevated the market economy, but the New Liberalism, which was concerned to protect society from its excesses, still provides the rationales for the welfare state and the mixed economy. John Rawls produced a philosophical defence of liberal political structures and Fukuyama adduced the theory that liberalism had finally triumphed. However, the faltering of Western economies over the past half century has posed new questions to both of these philosophical positions.

Discussion points

- Are there better ways of classifying ideology than the left–right continuum?
- What are the grounds for thinking that all human beings have rights?
- Should government resist interfering in the economy?
- Have the Liberals been exploited/robbed in ideological terms by the other two big parties?
- Offer a critique of Rawls' Difference Principle.
- Defend the Fukuyama thesis that the evolution of political systems has reached its end-point in liberal democratic free enterprise.

Further reading

Two excellent books are available that introduce politics students to ideology: Adams (1999) is well written and subtly argued, while Heywood (1998) is also essential reading. Useful in general terms are Eccleshall (1984) and Gamble (1981). Plant (1991) is more difficult but no less rewarding. On utilitarianism and liberalism, the texts by J.S. Mill (1971, 1975, 1985a, 1985b) are as good a starting point for understanding liberalism as any. Eccleshall (1986) lays some claim to be the definitive text, but Arblaster (1984) and Manning (1976) address wider readerships. Fukuyama (1992) elaborates the 'end of history' theory. Fareed Zakaria's *The Future of Freedom* (2004) is a quite brilliant book on threats to liberal democracy. An excellent and clear introduction to a wide variety of philosophical ideas, including political ones, is to be found in Nigel Warburton's (2011) *A Little History of Philosophy*.

Bibliography

Adams, I. (1999) *Political Ideology Today*, 2nd edn (Manchester University Press).

Arblaster, A. (1984) *The Rise and Fall of Western Liberalism* (Blackwell).

Bell, D. (1960) *The End of Ideology* (Free Press).

Dawkins, R. (2006) *The God Delusion*, Bantam.

Eccleshall, R. (1984) *Political Ideologies* (Hutchinson).

Eccleshall, R. (1986) *British Liberalism* (Longman).

Fukuyama, F. (1992) *The End of History and the Last Man* (Hamish Hamilton).

Gamble, A. (1981) *An Introduction to Modern Social and Political Thought* (Macmillan).

Giddens, A. (1998) *The Third Way* (Polity Press).

Hattersley, R. (1989) 'Endpiece: nous and nostalgia', The *Guardian*, 30 September 1989.

Heywood, A. (1998) *Political Ideologies: An Introduction*, 2nd edn (Macmillan).

Huntington, S.P. (1996) *The Clash of Civilizations and the Remaking of World Order* (University of Oklahoma Press, also in paperback published by Touchstone Books, 1997).

Keynes, J.M. (1971) *The Economic Consequences of the Peace*, Vol. II of his *Collected Works* (Palgrave Macmillan; first published 1919).

Keynes, J.M. (1985) *A General Theory of Employment, Interest and Money*, Vol. VII of his *Collected Works* (Macmillan; first published 1936).

Manning, D.J. (1976) *Liberalism* (St Martin's Press).

Mill, J.S. (1971) *Utilitarianism* (Everyman; first published 1863).

Mill, J.S. (1975) *Representative Government* (Oxford University Press; first published 1861).

Mill, J.S. (1985a) *On Liberty* (Penguin; first published 1859).

Mill, J.S. (1985b) *Principles of Political Economy* (Penguin; first published 1848).

Nozick, R. (1974) *Anarchy, State and Utopia* (Blackwell).

Pamuk, O. (2004) *Snow* (Faber and Faber).

Plant, R. (1991) *Modern Political Thought* (Blackwell).

Russell, B. (1965) (first published in 1946) *The History of Western Philosophy* (Unwin).

Sutherland, J. (1999) 'How Blair discovered defeat by definition', The *Guardian*, 25 October 1999.

Warburton, Nigel (2011) *A Little History of Philosophy* (Yale University Press).

Zakaria, F. (2004) *The Future of Freedom* (Norton).

Useful websites

http://libertarianism.com

http://www.iep.utm.edu/ (Internet Encyclopedia of Philosophy)

CHAPTER 5

Political ideas: the major parties

Bill Jones

> " **Party spokesmen say not what they mean but what they have agreed to say** "
>
> Michael Portillo, The *Observer*, 2 March 2003

Learning objectives

- To explain the provenance of Conservatism and the ideology of capitalist free enterprise, to explain the difference between 'one nation' and **neo-liberal** Conservatism, and to assess the impact of Margaret Thatcher on her party's ideas.

- To trace the origins of Labour thinking to the rejection of nineteenth-century **capitalism**, to describe its maturing into corporate **socialism** and revisionism plus the left-wing dissent of the 1970s and 1980s, and to analyse the impact of Labour's rapid move into the centre and the apparent embrace of neo-Thatcherite and communitarian ideas by Tony Blair. Also to sketch in some of the changes in Labour thinking since its defeat at the May 2010 election.

- To sum up the message of the Liberal Party over the years, including its alliance with the SDP and evolution into the Liberal Democrats.

In the aftermath of the Second World War some commentators felt that the two major political parties in Britain were 'converging' ideologically. Daniel Bell, the American sociologist, wrote of 'the end of ideology', and in the 1970s a postwar 'consensus' was discerned between the two parties on the desirability of a welfare state and a mixed economy. Britain's relative economic decline inclined both parties to adopt more radical remedies that drew on their ideological roots. Margaret Thatcher swung the Conservatives violently to the right, while Labour went radically to the left in the early 1980s. Once Thatcher had gone in 1990, Major adopted a less overtly ideological stance, while Labour, following the failed experiment of Michael Foot as leader (1981–83), successively under Neil Kinnock, John Smith and Tony Blair moved rapidly into the centre. This chapter analyses the evolution of the ideas of the major parties and brings up to date their most recent changes.

Introduction

The Conservative Party

CONSERVATIVES

Source: Courtesy of the Conservative Party
(www.conservatives.com)

Key elements of Conservatism

Lord Hailsham (1959) has described 'Conservatism' as not so much a philosophy as an 'attitude'. However, it is possible to discern a number of key tenets on which Conservative policies have been based:

1 *The purpose of politics is social and political harmony*: Conservatives have traditionally believed that politics is about enabling people to become what they are or what they wish to be. They also believe in a balance, a harmony in society, a measured **pragmatism** that has always kept options open. Like Edmund Burke, they have tended to believe that 'all government . . . is founded on compromise'.

2 *Human nature is imperfect and corruptible*: This quasi-religious notion of 'original sin' lies at the heart of Conservatism, leading its supporters to doubt the altruism of humankind beyond close family, to perceive most people as more interested in taking than giving, and to see them as fairly easy to corrupt without the external discipline of strong government and other social forces.

3 *The* **rule of law** *is the basis of all freedom*: Law restricts freedom, yet without it there would be no freedom at all. This is because without limitations to actions motivated by humankind's selfish and aggressive nature, the consequence would be anarchic chaos. Limiting freedom via the law is therefore the basis of freedom. It follows that accepting the authority of the law is the precondition of all liberty.

4 *Social institutions create a sense of society and nation*: Social and political institutions help to bind together imperfect human beings in a thing called *society*. Living together constructively and happily is an art, and this has to be learned. At the heart of the learning process lies the family and the institution of marriage. The royal family, Conservatives used to believe (less so now perhaps), provides an idealised and unifying 'micro-model'. At the macro level is the idea of the 'nation', ultimately a cause worth dying for.

5 *Foreign policy is the pursuit of state interests in an anarchic world*: States exhibit all the dangerous characteristics of individuals plus a few even more unpleasant ones of their own. A judicious defence of national interests, advise Conservatives, is the best guide for any country in the jungle of international relations.

6 *Liberty is the highest political end*: Individuals need freedom to develop their own personalities and create their own destinies. Conservatives agree with J.S. Mill that this should entail freedom from oppression by others. Such freedom should be limited only when it begins to encroach upon the liberty of others. It should not embrace the 'levelling' of wealth, as advocated by socialists, as this redistribution would be imposed upon a reluctant population by the state (see also Chapter 1).

7 *Government through checks and balances*: 'Political liberty', said Tory Lord Chancellor Lord Hailsham, 'is nothing else than the diffusion of power.' This means in practice institutions that divide power between them, with all having a measure of independence, thus preventing any single arm of government from being over-mighty.

8 *Property*: Conservatives, like David Hume, believe that the right to property is the 'first principle of justice' on which the 'peace and security of human society entirely depend'. Norton and Aughey (1981) take this further, arguing that owning property is in itself an 'education. It enlightens the citizens in the value of stability and shows that the security of small property depends upon the security of all property' (1981: 34). The Conservative policy of selling council houses reflected this belief in that it is assumed that people will cherish their houses more once they enjoy personal ownership.

9 **Equality of opportunity** *but not of result*: Conservatives believe everyone should have the same opportunity to better themselves. Some will be more able or more motivated and will achieve more and accumulate more property. Thus, an unequal distribution of wealth reflects a naturally unequal distribution of ability. Norton and Aughey (1981) maintain that the party is fundamentally concerned with justifying inequality in a way that 'conserves a hierarchy of wealth and power and make[s] it intelligible to democracy' (1981: 47). To do this, Conservatives argue that inequality is necessary to maintain incentives and make the economy work; equality of reward would reward the lazy as much as the industrious.

10 *One nation*: Benjamin Disraeli, the famous nineteenth-century Conservative Prime Minister, added a new element to his party's philosophy by criticising the 'two nations' in Britain, the rich and the poor. He advocated an alliance between the aristocracy and the lower orders to create one nation. His advice was controversial and has come to be seen as synonymous with the liberal approach to Conservatism.

11 *Rule by elite*: Conservatives have tended to believe the art of government is not given to all; it is distributed unevenly, like all abilities, and is carefully developed in families and outside these most commonly in good schools, universities and the armed forces.

12 *Political change*: Conservatives are suspicious of political change as society develops organically as an infinitely complex and subtle entity; precipitate change could damage irreparably things of great value. Therefore, they distrust the system builders such as Marx, and the root-and-branch reformers such as veteran Labour ideologue Tony Benn. But they do not deny the need for all change; rather they tend to agree with the Duke of Cambridge that the best time for it is 'when it can be no longer resisted', or with Enoch Powell that the 'supreme function of a politician is to judge the correct moment for reform'.

The impact of Thatcherism

This collection of pragmatic guides to belief and action was able to accommodate the postwar Labour landslide, which brought nationalisation, the managed Keynesian economy, close cooperation with the trade unions and the welfare state. The role of Harold Macmillan, Prime Minister (1957–63) was crucial here. In the 1930s he wrote *The Middle Way*, a plea for a regulated laissez-faire economy that would minimise unemployment and introduce forward economic planning. He was able to accept many of the reforms introduced by Labour and reinterpret and implement them for his own party during his time as its leader.

The *postwar consensus* continued with little difference over domestic policy for the next decade and a half, embracing the effective consensus between Harold Macmillan and Labour leader, Hugh Gaitskell; and Labour premier Harold Wilson and his Tory successor in 1970, Edward Heath. However, when the economy began to fail in relation to competitors in the late 1960s and early 1970s a hurricane of dissent began to blow up on the right of the Conservative Party – in the person of Margaret Thatcher. She had no quarrel with traditional positions on law, property and liberty, but she was passionately convinced of a limited role for government (although not necessarily a weak one); she wanted to 'roll back' the socialist frontiers of the state. She was totally uninterested in checks and balances but wanted to maximise her power to achieve the things she wanted. She opposed contrived 'equality' and favoured the functional inequalities – she called them '*incentives*' – required by a dynamic economy. She had scant respect for the aristocracy as she admired only ability and energy – qualities, it cannot be denied, she owned in abundance. She was not in favour of gradual change but wanted radical alterations, *in her lifetime*. She was a revolutionary within her own party, which still, even in 2013, has not stopped reverberating from her impact.

Thatcherite economics

1 Margaret Thatcher was strongly influenced by Tory intellectual Sir Keith Joseph (1918–94), who was in turn influenced by the American 'Chicago' economist Milton Friedman (1912–2006). He urged that to control inflation it was merely necessary to control the supply of money and credit circulating in the economy.

2 Joseph was also a disciple of Friedrich von Hayek, who believed that freedom to buy, sell and employ, i.e. economic freedom, was the foundation of all freedom. Like Hayek, he saw the drift to collectivism as a bad thing: socialists promised the 'road to freedom' but delivered instead the 'high road to servitude'.

3 Hayek and Friedman agreed with the classical Scottish economist and philosopher, Adam Smith and the classical liberals that, if left to themselves, market forces – businessmen using their energy and ingenuity to meet the needs of customers – would create prosperity. To call this 'exploitation' of the working man, as socialists did, was nonsense, as businessmen were the philanthropists of society, creating employment, paying wages and endowing charities. When markets were allowed to work properly they benefited all classes: everyone benefited, even the poor: 'the greatest social service of them all', said Thatcher, 'is the creation of wealth.'

4 Thatcher believed strongly that:

   (i) state intervention destroyed freedom and efficiency through taking power from the consumer – the communist 'command' economies were inefficient and corrupt, protecting employment through temporary and harmful palliatives, and controlling so much of the economy that the wealth-producing sector became unacceptably squeezed;

   (ii) state welfare was expensive, and morally weakening in that it eroded the self-reliance she so prized, and was, in addition, monopolistic, denying choice as well as being less efficient than private provision.

5 Trade unions were one of Thatcher's bêtes noires: major enemies. She saw them as undemocratic, reactionary vested interests that regularly held the country to ransom in the 1970s. She was determined to confront and defeat them.

6 Her defence of national interests was founded in a passionate patriotism, which sustained her support for the armed forces and the alliance with the USA. During the Falklands War she showed great composure and courage in taking risks and ultimately triumphing. The reverse side of this was her preference for the US link over the European Union, which she suspected of being a Trojan horse for German plans to dominate the whole continent.

Thus, Margaret Thatcher drove a battering ram through traditional Conservatism, but economically it was a return to the classical liberalism of the early to mid-nineteenth century (see Chapter 4). Many claimed to have been converted to her ideas, but the 1980s witnessed a tough internal battle, which the Prime Minister eventually won, between her and the so-called 'wet' wing of the party, which still hearkened back to the inclusive 'one nation' strand of the party's thinking, characterised by Harold Macmillan and Ted Heath.

The Major years

When John Major succeeded Margaret Thatcher following the virtual 'coup' in November 1990, many thought he would be the best hope of stern and unbending Thatcherism, but he seemed much more conciliatory, more concerned with the un-Thatcherite aim of achieving unity – for example, a 'classless society' – even at the cost of compromise. As the years passed, however, it became apparent that this initial analysis was far from what was actually to happen. Major's Government was almost wholly circumscribed by the ideas of his predecessor. As Heywood has pointed out, the Major Government accepted her ideas; there was no conflict with 'wets', and even Heseltine, Clarke and Patten had accepted the unchallenged supremacy of markets by the mid-1990s. Moreover, he took her ideas further even than she dared in her day, privatising British Rail and introducing the market principle into many hitherto forbidden areas of the welfare state. The changes were in style rather than substance. In the 1980s Thatcherism adopted a 'heroic' mode, smashing socialism and the power of the trade unions; it was like a continuous war or revolution as the Prime Minister tried to change 'the hearts and minds of the nation'. Major replaced that style with a 'managerial' version. However, he also added another element: a renewed emphasis on morality (the 'back to basics' campaign, which in the event backfired), obligation and citizenship. Conservatives have long been worried by the downside of market forces: growing inequality, the emergence of an underclass, insecurity at work and the loss of the 'feel-good factor', or the sense of the nation 'being at ease with itself' to use Major's phrase. There was a feeling in the mid-1990s that the nation's social fabric was in dire need of repair. Added to this market individualism plus an emphasis on morality had been a shift towards a 'Little Englanderism' and a near loathing of all things European – though Major himself was relatively pro-EU. Most commentators did not believe Major was this kind of right-wing politician by instinct, but that he was forced to adjust his position on Europe quite drastically by the viscerally determined Eurosceptic minority, which, through his tiny majority, held the balance of power.

Major was criticised from many parts of the party: 'poor judgment and weak leadership' (The Sun); 'drifting with the intellectual tide' (Thatcher); 'He is not a natural leader, he cannot speak, he has no sense of strategy or direction' (Lord Rees Mogg, editor of The Times); 'a nice bloke but not up to the job' (Kenneth Clarke, his Chancellor 1993–97); and, the cruellest cut, 'the government gave the impression of being in office but not in power' (Norman Lamont, his Chancellor 1990–93).

Hague's new start

As soon as the Conservatives lost the 1997 election so calamitously, Major resigned and a contest was held for a new leader. In the end, genial ex-Chancellor Kenneth Clarke was judged too pro-EU, and MPs chose the relatively unknown and untested William Hague. He was, at least for those who regretted the demise of Thatcher, firm on the subject of Europe: he would have very little of it and would not join the emergent European single currency for at least a parliamentary term, if ever. Those who mocked this narrow, 'Little England' perspective were frustrated when his party won the European elections handsomely in June 1999. Subsequently Michael Portillo, the right-winger many felt would have

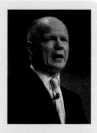

PROFILE

William Hague (1961–)

English Conservative politician. Made his debut with a precocious speech at the 1977 conference. After Oxford, he worked as a management consultant and then became MP for Richmond in his native Yorkshire. He was seen as suitably opposed to Europe in 1997 and was preferred to Kenneth Clarke as leader. His early years were difficult with successes inside the Commons but rarely in the country. In the election of 2001 he stuck to his Eurosceptic guns throughout the campaign but could only persuade the nation to return one more Conservative MP. He resigned, with remarkably good grace, shortly after the election defeat. After that he busied himself with brilliant after-dinner speaking, an acclaimed biography of the Younger Pitt and occasional broadcasting. In December 2005, however, David Cameron summoned him back to his party's **front bench** as Shadow Foreign Secretary and unofficial Deputy Leader. After the May 2010 election he took up the post of Foreign Secretary.

won the leadership had he not astonishingly lost his huge majority to novice Labour candidate Stephen Twigg, had effectively reinvented himself as the quintessence of the 'Compassionate Conservatism' its leaders now claimed to embrace. However, this flirtation with a softer image did not last for the party as a whole; the Conservative High Command – alarmed by polls flat-lining at one-third of the vote – were worried that the party's core vote was about to crumble. In October 1999 Hague unveiled his 'Commonsense Revolution', a bundle of right-wing measures focusing on five 'guarantees': to cut taxes as a share of the national income; to keep out of the single currency until at least the end of the next parliamentary session and to demand opt-outs on measures not in the national interest; a 'parent's guarantee' whereby inefficient heads could be dismissed; a 'patient's guarantee' setting maximum times for treatment; and a get-tough guarantee on work dodgers, who would lose all benefit if they refused work after eight weeks. In fact, the conference represented a surprising swing back towards Thatcherism. The lady herself appeared and was cheered to the echo by the ageing delegates as well as praised in speeches that pointedly and hurtfully ignored the contributions made by the premier of seven years, John Major. Most of the right-wing press applauded the party's rediscovery of its identity – being right-wing, Eurosceptic and proud of it. But others were not so sure. That shrewd commentator Peter Riddell wrote that:

> The more William Hague roused his party faithful in Blackpool, the more he led them away from power . . . [his] main achievement . . . may have been to deepen the divisions within his own party and to reduce still further its chances of winning the next election.
>
> (*The Times*, 12 October 1999)

Riddell, not for the first time, proved remarkably prescient: in June 2001 Labour's second landslide occurred. Hague resigned and a contest for the leadership of the Tories took place amid some acrimony. According to the new rules for electing a leader, the parliamentary party held a series of ballots to find the two candidates between whom the party faithful would choose. Portillo soon fell by the wayside, foundering, it seemed, on his admission of a homosexual experience when a student at Cambridge. It was left to Kenneth Clarke, again, to battle it out with the inexperienced right-winger, Iain Duncan Smith. The latter's Euroscepticism, tough line on crime and general Thatcherite orthodoxy proved much more attractive, in the judgement of the ageing party membership, compared with the liberal one-nation approach of Clarke – despite his obvious political gifts – who lost by a two-to-one majority.

PROFILE

Michael Portillo (1953–)

Conservative politician. Educated at Cambridge. Worked for the Conservative Research Department, 1976–9, and as junior minister in various departments until he became a Cabinet minister in the early 1990s. Was defeated in the 1997 election and missed his chance to lead the party then. Worked hard at being an advocate of 'caring Conservatism' before becoming adopted as a candidate in the safe seat of Kensington. Made Shadow Chancellor in late 1999. 'Re-invented' himself as a caring, inclusive one-nation Conservative with speeches, television programmes and an admission of a student-day homosexual experience. This last caused trouble with older Conservatives; when Portillo stood for the leadership after Hague's resignation, Norman Tebbit made a thinly veiled attack on his sexuality, and the modernisers' hope was defeated at the Commons stage (according to the new procedure) before party members were able to vote on the two nominees.

The Iain Duncan Smith effect

'IDS', as he is known, began his tenure as leader by striving to make an impression in the Commons, but Blair proved too dominant and his opponent too unsure of his ground to 'win' even a few of the weekly Prime Minister's Question Time encounters. What made it worse was that so many of the well-known Conservatives either had retired (e.g. Tebbit, Baker, Fowler), had not been keen on serving under Duncan Smith (e.g. Clarke, Hague), or were still stigmatised by association with the 'bad old days' of the Conservative's 18 years in power (e.g. Howard, Gummer). Despite his defeat in the leadership contest, Portillo's influence remained as a voice calling for 'modernisation' of the Conservative message: a more inclusive attitude to women, gays and ethnic minorities; a distancing from anything resembling racism on immigration policy; an acceptance of the need to modernise and improve public services; and a less dogmatic hostility to all things European. Once again the dead weight of lumpen party opinion on key policy issues served to retard any progress. Duncan Smith's ineffectual orthodoxy was soon found to be out of touch in the polls, and in the spring of 2002, at the party's Harrogate conference, IDS effected a neat volte-face on policy, calling for a compassionate attitude towards the 'vulnerable' in society, a decentralisation of power to the regions and a supportive attitude towards the public services. However, shifting towards a new policy position is one thing; communicating it, via an unknown Shadow Cabinet, is another: the polls still flat-lined at just over 30 percentage points. The new leader faced immense difficulty in convincing voters that his party was not, as he complained, 'nasty, extreme and strange' (*Observer* 2 July 2002). At the party conference later in the year, the new party chairman, Theresa May, urged the party to lose its '*nasty*' image: evidence of her support for the modernisation camp. However, the *éminence grise* of this tendency featured again in February 2003 when Michael Portillo complained bitterly at the peremptory sacking of the chief executive of the party, Mark MacGregor. The outbreak of war against Iraq the following month enabled Duncan Smith to occupy familiar Conservative territory – pro-armed forces and pro-USA – although such a position precluded political exploitation of Prime Minister Blair's discomfort in prosecuting a war unpopular in the country and even more so in his own party; Kenneth Clarke's backing of an 'anti-war' horse over Iraq scarcely helped to strengthen the embattled leader's position. Discontent with IDS grew in the run-up to the 2003 party conference and soon afterwards he lost a crucial party vote of confidence. Michael Howard, the right-wing former Home Secretary, was selected in his place.

The Michael Howard interlude

On Thursday 6 November 2003 the man who came sixth in the 1997 leadership challenge was, remarkably, elected unopposed to the leadership of his party. Despite his reputation for being a right-winger, Howard stressed his desire to

continue IDS's emphasis on social justice with policies aimed at helping the disadvantaged. This was accompanied by calls for zero tolerance policing, more spending on drug treatment for addicts and an increase in the basic state pension. His concerns regarding Europe were underlined by renewed calls for a referendum on the proposed new constitution for the EU.

From the outset, Howard proved reasonably effective at Prime Minister's Questions, but found it hard to resist the need to bolster up the core vote and did little to move the party into the electorally crucial centre ground. The party continued to languish in the polls as the General Election approached in 2005. The party continued to lack a distinctive message right up to polling day on 5 May and duly paid the price when the votes were counted. The Conservatives won 33 more seats but had to sit back and watch an unpopular government led by a gifted but mistrusted Tony Blair maintain its hold on the Commons to the extent of an overall majority of 66. Howard, the old professional, seasoned politician, had hoped to lead a renaissance of Toryism but had proved to be merely a stop-gap leader of a party which some perceived to be in terminal decline. Howard resigned quite soon but stayed on to preside over the election of his successor. This period – May to October – saw much soul searching during which most party members came to realise that drastic change was necessary. The Conservative Policy Exchange **think tank** produced a devastating report on the party, highlighting its unpopularity, lack of contact with modern society and hopeless image as a party favouring middle-class people in the shires and the South-east. Figure 5.1, drawn from the report, reveals how people viewed their own political position on the left–right continuum and then

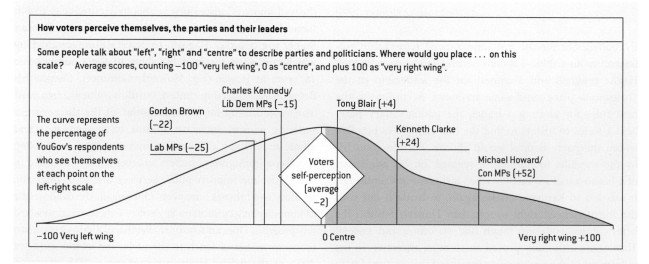

Figure 5.1 How voters perceive themselves, the parties and their leaders
Source: From Policy Exchange (2005) *The Case for Change*, May 2005. Reproduced with permission

superimposed their estimates of where leading politicians stood. Inevitably the majority of people occupy the centre ground, indicating where any party wishing to win an election needs to project its messages. Howard was perceived as being quite far to the right – his MPs also. Kenneth Clarke, on the other hand, was seen as substantially closer to the centre. Gordon Brown was located slightly to the right of Labour MPs and to the left of Charles Kennedy. And Tony Blair? His brilliant sense of where the centre of political gravity lies enabled him to sit astride the middle of the graph, four points to the right of dead centre.

The election of David Cameron, December 2005

The Conservative Party conference in October 2005 at Blackpool indicated that the party had finally realised that major change to the party and its thinking was necessary before an election win could be contemplated. The declared leadership candidates were able to address the delegates and make an initial pitch. Howard had influenced his own succession by placing members of the new young liberal or 'moderniser' group in his party to major positions in the Shadow Cabinet – George Osborne (34) to Shadow Chancellor and David Cameron (39) to Education – and allowing them to make an impression before the leadership contest in the autumn. Osborne, it seemed, had already decided not to run but to manage the campaign of his old Etonian friend, Cameron. Parallels with Tony Blair's rise to power were already being made before Cameron delighted the conference with a speech he had learnt by heart and delivered, apparently spontaneously, without notes. David Davis, the former minister in his mid-50s, who had assembled what many thought to be an impregnable lead among declared MPs, tried to follow suit but, compared with the sparkling, inspiring rhetoric of his rival, appeared lacklustre and dull. Cameron went on to win easily the MPs' ballot and then to win over the party for the membership ballot on 5 December, which he won by a margin of two to one. On 6 December he took on Blair at PMQs and, in an excellent, witty debut performance, told him 'you were the future once'.

Cameron seeks to 'rebrand' and move into the centre ground

Cameron, while copying the informal, media-friendly style of the younger Tony Blair, was careful to steer clear of specific policy commitments, though it was clear his period in power would see a jettisoning of the party's much beloved positions on a number of issues. Cameron and his coterie of 'Notting Hill Set' colleagues were very keen to change the brand image of the party. During the 2005 election, focus groups had revealed that members who liked a policy position when it was explained to them changed their mind when they discovered it was a Conservative party policy. Concerted efforts were made to banish the notion of the 'nasty party', the idea of a bigoted, intolerant group of richer, older people who wanted power merely to advance their own interests and outdated way of life. Consequently Cameron let it be known his name was not David but 'Dave'; that he cared deeply about special-needs childcare (his NHS-cared-for disabled son, Ivan, died in February 2009); that he cared about the environment (cycling to the Commons, snow-sledding in the Arctic, appointing environmentalist Zac Goldsmith to an advisory position); that he cared about world poverty (Bob Geldof's turn to be included); and that the party no longer hated gays and opposed civil partnerships.

In late December Oliver Letwin declared that his party favoured redistribution of wealth, and shortly afterwards Cameron shifted its position on immigration from opposition to qualified support for those incomers essential to the economy. Cameron also addressed the key area of tax cuts. It seemed Conservatives now would basically accept the 4 per cent increase in basic taxation since 1997 as necessary to sustain public services at requisite levels. He also declared that cuts would have to come in the wake of economic stability, a reversal of the Thatcherite view that the latter is a condition for the achievement of the former. And the party would no longer be the natural adjunct of the free enterprise economy: henceforward, the party would stand up to as well as be a supporter of business'.

The new boy was careful, however, to keep the core vote onside with a judicious dash of Euroscepticism. True, he wished to bury the party's civil war over the EU, which he deemed irrelevant now that the proposed new constitution had been rejected by France and Holland. He nevertheless wanted the Conservative Party to end its membership of the European People's Party, a right-wing grouping which nevertheless favoured rather too much integration. Instead, his party helped create the anti-federalist Reformist's grouping which contained parties subscribing to some homophobic and anti-semitic sentiments. Perhaps his biggest break with the past, however, was to declare, in an echo of John Rawls (see Chapter 4) that the litmus test for social policies should be what they could do for the disadvantaged: many older Tories must have felt an onset of apoplexy at that.

Like Blair in the mid-90s Cameron set up a number of study groups to review policy areas. Opinion polls almost immediately registered a lead for Labour, albeit a slender one at that early stage. Blair must have realised at once that the political situation had changed drastically and that he no longer could expect a free ride in his domination of the centre ground. But Cameron too did not face an easy ride; right-wing commentator, Melanie Phillips, writing in the *Daily Mail*, believed his prospectus 'leaves millions of natural

Conservatives effectively disenfranchised – and even worse demonized as dinosaurs by the party that is supposed to represent them'.

Wise old commentators judged such opposition to be precisely what Cameron needed. Blair had risen to public prominence through his brilliant victory over party traditionalists concerning Clause Four. Lacking any similar dragons to slay, Cameron needed to overcome opposition from the older cohorts as represented, for example, by Lord Tebbit, one of Thatcher's most loyal and true-blue Conservative followers; it would be by overcoming such opposition that his party would be seen to have changed. As the 2010 election approached Cameron and his advisers sought to position themselves on the major questions of the day: reduce government 2009 debt of £175 billion to reduce interest rates on further borrowing; blame Labour for the recession triggered by the 2007 US banking crisis; protect the NHS and education budgets but offer deep cuts elsewhere to reduce the deficit; and on the EU to sustain Eurosceptical rhetoric but reject any talk of a referendum on the Lisbon Treaty or membership of the EU by abandoning the referendum idea. In their election campaign these ideas received great emphasis within the framework of its alleged theme – the 'Big Society' – the involvement of ordinary people in their own government. This theme, the brainchild of Cameron's strategist Steve Hilton, was derided by more traditional Tories but staunchly expounded by the boss himself.

Conservatives in power

Once installed as Prime Minister in the Coalition Government in May 2010, Cameron set about presenting his Government as a radical one, determined to not only clear the nation's indebtedness, but to transform it both constitutionally and socially so that its 'Broken Society' could be repaired. However, his ability to deliver on campaign promises was hampered by two major factors: the absence of funding, given its spending cuts programme; and the vetoing power of the centrist Liberal Democrats with whom Conservatives – at the time of writing – share the Coalition.

1 *Stewardship of the economy*: Throughout most of Labour's final period in power, the Conservative Party more or less endorsed Labour's **fiscal** policy regarding taxation and spending but, as the recession bit after 2007, George Osborne pursued twin policies of blaming Labour for the recession and the level of government indebtedness. From supporting a basically Keynesian approach to the recession-hit economy he outlined a more Hayekian one of severe cuts in spending to reduce the huge deficit. This he justified in terms of the need to balance the books and to satisfy the bond markets (which lend huge amounts to

governments) that money lent to the UK should not carry a prohibitive interest rate. Many critics, not just Labour, argued the economy was too weak for such rapid withdrawals of demand and would slide back into the recession in which it had languished in 2008–9. Osborne was deaf to such entreaties and continued with his strategy, despite near negative economic growth in 2010–13. However, his Autumn Statement 2011 did announce a detailed (£32 billion) package to reflate the economy, closer to the Keynesian line advocated by many of his earlier critics.

2 *Social policy*: Most of public spending comprises the issue of pensions and benefits plus funding of schools, hospitals and other public services. Because the recipients of these services are largely the lower paid, spending cuts have a direct impact on their lives. Critics of the Coalition Government cited this fact to challenge the Government's assertion that cuts would be 'fair' and would not disadvantage those most in need. Inevitably this aspiration proved hard to fulfil. Meanwhile, the Secretary for Social Security, Iain Duncan Smith, translated from unsuccessful party leader into the banner holder of a transformation of the benefits system, was yet, in early 2013 to introduce his Universal Credit, designed to ensure those on benefits will always be better off by being in employment.

3 *Big Society*: By any standards this was an unlikely task for any government to take on and by 2013 there were few signs of the policy evident anywhere. This was partly because cuts to charity budgets curtailed what voluntary community contributions were already being made, partly because changes to planning laws limited rather increased public participation, and partly because nobody, even at the midpoint of the parliament, was sure what the policy entailed.

4 *Europe*: This is the area where, after the economy, the most contentious policies were pursued. Given that the subject had divided the party under John Major and was partly the cause of the electoral defeat in 2001, Cameron was keen to play Europe down as an issue: to accept the UK was part of the EU but not to appear in any way proactive in supporting the international body. Events, however, were not destined to assist him after his accession to the premiership. In 2009 Cameron and his Foreign Secretary, Willian Hague, were relieved that the EU-strengthening Lisbon Treaty was ratified by all members, thus allowing them to rule out a UK referendum in November 2008.

However, in October 2011 a vote was taken on the holding of a referendum on EU membership itself. Cameron argued that, when the EU was trying to cope with a catastrophic crisis in its common currency, the euro, such a vote would be unhelpful for European partners. While Cameron was able to defeat the motion, 81 of his MPs voted for it, suggesting the Eurosceptics' reach still extended through much of his party. This became clear in December when Cameron went to yet another Brussels summit seeking to ensure the euro's survival, despite the desperate risk that countries like Greece, Italy, Spain and Portugal might be forced to default on their government debts. Germany and France sought to set up financial arrangements to bail out countries in difficulties and to apply tougher disciplines on the 17-nation eurozone.

Cameron was keen to ensure additional regulation did not impinge upon the profitable working of the City of London and, when his plea for special treatment was peremptorily refused, he used his veto to prevent any treaty being signed. It seems likely the other 26 EU countries will eventually reach their own agreement, and Cameron's attempt to ring-fence London's financial pre-eminence will probably not prevent its interests being harmed. But Cameron's 'Churchill-like' stand proved hugely popular with his party which cheered him to the echo at this next appearance in the Commons; a bounce in the polls suggested many voters agreed with his EU-defying stance.

In November 2012 Cameron opposed any increase in the EU budget but was faced by a Commons vote – in which Labour voted with the Tory Eurosceptics – demanding he should insist on a reduction of the budget. With *Prospect* magazine in June 2012, showing 40 per cent of Conservative voters considering voting for UKIP, the political spectrum was being dragged to the right. Moreover, a *Guardian* poll on 17 November 2012 revealed 56 per cent of voters favouring withdrawal from the EU, and with sizeable minorities in both Labour and the Lib Dems agreeing, all parties faced the need to reflect this new lurch towards the sceptics' position.

The Labour Party and socialism

Source: Courtesy of the Labour Party (www.labour.org.uk)

Socialism

Socialism developed as a critique and alternative to capitalism and its political expression, Conservatism. It focused on economics as the key activity, but the full sweep of its message provided guidance on virtually all aspects of living.

Critique of capitalism

Socialism asserted that capitalism 'exploited' the working masses by selling the fruits of their labour, taking the lion's share of the revenue and paying only subsistence wages. This produced huge disparities in income between the suburban-living rich and the urban-based poor. Because the ruling capitalists dominate all the institutions of the state, argued Karl Marx, whose analysis was more influential in Britain than his prescriptions, they subtly intrude their values into all walks of life, and a complex web of mystifications produces a 'false consciousness' in which the working class believes, wrongly, that its best interests are served by supporting capitalist values. Capitalist championing of 'individualism' and 'freedom' are mere cloaks, he claimed, for the exploitation of the weak by the strong. The ruthlessness of the system induces similar qualities within society. Wage labour merely relieved employers of any residual obligations they might have felt towards their workers. By living in large urban settlements, working men were alienated from each other, while the automating of industry denied workers any creative input or satisfactions. A final criticism was that capitalism with its booms and slumps was inevitably inefficient and inferior to a planned economy. Socialists argued that two large antagonistic classes emerge in capitalist societies: a small, wealthy ruling class and a large impoverished proletariat, living in the cities, which actually created the wealth which for the most part benefited the already wealthy.

Underlying principles of socialism

Socialism developed out of this critique of nineteenth-century capitalism. The principles underlying the new creed included the following:

1 *Human nature is basically good*: People wish to live together peacefully and cooperatively, according to this view; it is only the selfish competitive economic system of capitalism that distorts man's innate qualities.

2 *'Environment creates consciousness'*: It followed from this Marxist axiom that a superior environment will create a superior kind of person: change the environment and you change the person.

3 *Workers create the wealth*: They are entitled to receive the full fruits of their efforts and not the small fraction that the rich, bourgeois factory owners pay them.

4 *Equality*: Everyone has the right to start off in life with the same chances as everyone else; the strong should not exploit their advantage and impose themselves on the weak.

5 *Freedom*: The poor need more resources for the playing field of life to be level and thus be truly free.

6 *Collectivism*: Social solidarity should take the place of selfish individualism.

The Labour Party

Labour in power

Labour held power briefly in the 1920s and began to formulate a more pragmatic, less emotional and more coherent version of socialism. During the 1930s and the war years socialist thinkers who were also active politicians such as Hugh Dalton (1887–1962) and Herbert Morrison (1888–1965) developed what has since been called 'corporate socialism', comprising:

1 *Keynesian economics*: Management of the economy, using investment to cure slumps and squeeze out unemployment.

2 *Centralised planning of the economy*: This was the corollary of the Keynesian approach; it had worked brilliantly during the 1939–45 war and would do the same for the peace, promised Labour.

3 *Nationalisation*: Morrison devised this approach based on bringing an industry out of private and into public control via a board accountable to Parliament. Once in power, Labour nationalised 20 per cent of the economy, including the major utilities.

4 *Welfare state*: Labour established the National Health Service and expanded universal social services into a virtual 'welfare state' in which the state had obligations to citizens 'from the cradle to the grave'.

5 *Mixed economy*: The extent of nationalisation was not defined but, unlike the Soviet command economies, it was intended to maintain a private sector, albeit one subordinate to the public.

6 *Socialist foreign policy*: The trauma of two world wars convinced Labour that a new approach was needed based on disarmament and international collective security. The USSR, however, proved resistant to fraternal overtures from a fellow left-wing government, and ultimately Labour's combative Foreign Secretary, Ernest Bevin (1881–1952), was forced to encourage the USA into the NATO alliance.

Revisionism

Anthony Crosland (1918–77), along with others like Gaitskell, Healey and Jenkins, was not content, like Morrison, to declare cynically that 'socialism is what the Labour government does'. In his *The Future of Socialism* (1956), he asserted that Marx's predictions of capitalist societies polarising before revolutions established left-wing government had been proved hopelessly wrong; the working class had ignored revolutions and had been strengthened by full employment. The business class had not fought the advance of socialism but had been *tamed* by it. Crosland argued that the ownership of the economy was no longer relevant, as salaried managers were now the key players.

He attacked another sacred cow by maintaining that nationalisation was not necessarily the most effective road to socialism and that other forms of collective ownership were more effective. He concluded that Labour should now concentrate its efforts on reducing inequality through progressive taxation and redistributive benefits and – the key proposal – reducing class differences through an end to selection in education. In practice, revisionism was Labour's policy for the next 30 years, but when in government in the 1970s its possibly fatal flaw was exposed: it was dependent on an expanding economy, and when this fell into decline, public expenditure cuts became inevitable.

The left wing of the party, however, never accepted revisionism, and first Aneurin (Nye) Bevan, then Michael Foot, opposed the new drift towards a diluted ideology. In the 1960s Wilson defied the Left in the parliamentary party, but when it teamed up with the trade unions, trouble was in store for the 1970s administrations under both Wilson and Callaghan. Led by Tony Benn, the Left now offered an alternative economic strategy based on workers' control, extended state control of the economy, in effect, **participatory democracy** at all levels of national life; all this plus fresh injections of funds into the welfare state, encouragement of extra-parliamentary activity, and unilateral abandonment of nuclear weapons. The revisionist leadership tried to ignore the Left, but when the 1979 General Election was lost to a new and militantly ideological leader, Margaret Thatcher, the Left insisted that a similar return to the roots of socialist ideology was necessary. With the revisionist leadership defeated and discredited, the Left made its move, managing to translate its candidate, Michael Foot, into leader in 1980, plus imposing a radically left-wing set of policies on the party. This resulted in the 1983 manifesto being dubbed by Gerald Kaufman 'the longest suicide note in history'. More significantly, the Left's ascendancy led to the defection of an important centre-right section of the party to form the Social Democratic Party (see Box 5.1). The conventional view is that the new party split the anti-Tory vote and helped to keep Thatcher in power for a decade. However, the party's history as written by Ivor Crewe and Anthony King (1995) concluded that this transient new force, if anything, reduced the Tory majority.

Neil Kinnock, elected as Foot's successor, was a child of the Left but soon recanted, dismissing its prescriptions as 'Disneyland thinking'. He assiduously began to nudge his

BOX 5.1

Social Democratic Party

On 1 August 1980 Shirley Williams, David Owen and Bill Rodgers published their famous 'Gang of Three' statement: an open letter in the *Guardian* 'rejecting class war, accepting the mixed economy and the need to manage it efficiently'. After the Wembley conference of 1981 which passed rule changes strengthening the power of left-wing activists over candidate selection and the party leadership, the Gang of Three was joined by Roy Jenkins to form the Social Democratic Party (SDP). Over the next few months over two dozen Labour MPs made the same journey, joined by a solitary Conservative. The SDP fought the 1983 election in 'Alliance' with the small Liberal Party, garnering 26 per cent of the vote but less than 4 per cent of the seats. The much wished for breakthrough in 1987 failed when they mustered only 22 per cent. A formal merger of the two parties was delayed by personality problems posed largely by David Owen, but by 1988 the future Liberal Democrats had emerged, albeit for a while with a defiant Owenite rump. The SDP was formed in a blaze of publicity and 'breaking the mould' rhetoric, but a genuine alternative was probably not on offer. In one sense its message represented an amalgam of policies picked up across the political spectrum. Decentralisation was close to the Liberal, Bennite and Green position; SDP views on the market economy and trade unions were close to Margaret Thatcher's position – she actually praised Owen for being 'sound' on both – and on social policy and defence the SDP was close to the position of the Callaghan Government, to which the SDP leaders had once belonged. This is not to say that the SDP lacked a carefully worked out and detailed programme, merely that it lacked a distinctive alternative or even radical quality. History will judge the SDP as a party of protest with a limited appeal outside the middle classes.

party towards the centre ground via a series of policy reviews, which essentially accepted the 'efficiency and realism' of the market as the best model of economic organisation. It was implicit in this new analysis – although hotly denied – that socialism was no longer relevant; even the word disappeared from party policy documents. When he lost the crucial 1992 election, Kinnock resigned and John Smith continued this 'desocialising' work. When Smith died tragically of a heart attack in May 1994, Tony Blair was elected leader and soon placed his stamp on a party denied power for nearly 15 years.

Views of Labour leaders

As for Tony Blair, I still think, as I thought when I first met him, we're lucky to have him – both the Labour Party and the nation. He might have gone off and joined the Social Democrats and no-one would have heard of him again.

Michael Foot, The *Observer*, 6 September 1996

My view of Christian values has led me to oppose what I perceived to be a narrow view of self-interest that Conservatism – particularly in its modern, more right-wing form – represents.

Tony Blair, September 1995

Having already abandoned its former policies of opposition to the European Community/Union, unilateral nuclear disarmament and nationalisation, Blair shifted the party even further to the right by attacking the power of trade unions in the party. He waged a spectacularly successful war against the 'collective ownership' Clause Four in the party's constitution, drafted by Sidney Webb in 1917:

To secure for the workers by hand or by brain the full fruits of their industry and the most equitable distribution thereof that may be possible upon the basis of the common ownership of the means of production, distribution, and exchange, and the best obtainable system of popular administration and control of each industry or service.

Clause Four rewritten

The iconic clause, so fundamental that it was inscribed on membership cards, was replaced in April 1995 at a special conference by a massive majority. The new clause endorsed a 'dynamic economy, serving the public interest'; a 'just society which judges its strength by the condition of the weak as much as the strong'; 'an open democracy, in which government is held to account by the people'; and where 'decisions are taken as far as practicable by the communities they affect'.

Not content with this, Blair later drew the party away from the social democratic heartland of full employment and welfare spending: it was deemed that the requisite high taxation would never be endorsed by middle-class voters – remember that Labour was caught out badly by the Conservatives over tax in 1992 – and it was believed that the world's economy had changed. With modern technology the economy has become globalised so that flows of capital can break companies and even currencies in minutes. To maintain policies of high taxation, it was believed, risks massive withdrawals of capital by speculators and investors from any economy contemplating such socialistic measures.

There was now no alternative to Thatcher's economics; '**New Labour**' had effectively embraced tax cuts, low inflation, a market economy plus encouragement of entrepreneurial activity and some privatisation. Thatcherism, in a sense, had 'won'. Tony Blair flirted for a while with Will Hutton's idea of a 'stakeholder society', that everyone, individuals and groups, should have some investment in society, and everyone should feel part of their community at all levels, economic, cultural and social; the idea withered through business opposition to any wider role. The other biggish idea supported by Blair was constitutional reform; Labour embraced devolved assemblies for both Scotland and Wales plus reform of the House of Lords and a referendum on the electoral system. However, the changes were not without major flaws, none more so than the unresolved, so-called 'West Lothian question', whereby Scottish MPs would have the ability to vote on English issues but English MPs do not have the ability to reciprocate as the internally elected assembly would assume this role (see Chapter 14). The Lords reform agenda stalled after the virtual abolition of hereditary peers and the chamber continued in its half-reformed way. As for reforming the voting system, the results of the Jenkins Report continued to gather dust as the party swung against the idea.

Blairism

The massive endorsement of New Labour in the General Election of 1 May 1997 was fulfilment of the strategy conceived and implemented by Tony Blair and his close collaborators Peter Mandelson and Philip Gould to move the Labour Party into a position where it embraced the market economy and removed the fear of old-style socialism felt by the middle-class occupants of 'Middle England'. 'Blairism' was vaguely expressed and lent itself to wide interpretation, but some commentators disagreed and claimed that Blairism boasted a coherent philosophical framework and was a well worked-out 'project'. Socially it is based on the idea of communitarianism. At university, Blair was very interested in the ideas of John McMurray, a Scottish philosopher who

took issue with the modish idea of 'individualism', that the individual has choices and freedoms and is an autonomous unit. McMurray argued the contrary, that, as Adams puts it:

> People do not exist in a vacuum; in fact, they only exist in relation to others. The completely autonomous self of liberal theory is a myth. People's personalities are created in their relationships with others, in the family and the wider community. By pursuing the interests of society as a whole we benefit individuals including ourselves.
>
> (Adams 1998: 148–9)

Blair argued that people should build communities based on the idea of responsibility, a sense of duty towards others maybe less fortunate and a recognition that one's actions have repercussions and may require reparation. Old Labour tended to see poor people as 'victims of the system'; to speak of them having responsibilities is to borrow from another right-wing lexicon. Blair also subscribed to the idea of a *Third Way*. Apart from being an alternative to socialism and pro-capitalist ideology, it was never clearly defined. Another participant has been the eminent sociologist Anthony Giddens, highly regarded by Blair, who wrote, *The Third Way: The Renewal of Social Democracy*. This argues that the old definitions of left and right are obsolete (see Chapter 4) and that in the world of globalisation a new approach is required. He defines the overall aim of Third Way politics as helping citizens to:

> pilot their way through the major revolutions of our time: globalisation, transformations in personal life and our relationship to nature . . . One might suggest as a prime motto for the new politics, 'No rights without responsibilities'.
>
> (Giddens 1998: 64–5) (see also Box 5.2)

Blair in power

For the first two years in power, Gordon Brown kept the brake firmly on expenditure, but after the 2001 election Labour embarked in 2002 on the spending of over £100 billion over the following years, marking for many a welcome return to Old Labour orthodoxy. However, the event that transformed Labour during the early months of 2003 was the war on Iraq. Tony Blair had decided to stand 'shoulder to shoulder' with George W. Bush after the horrific attacks on the World Trade Center on 11 September 2001, but the extent of his loyalty to a right-wing president advised by Republican hawks was anathema to many Labour MPs. When it proved impossible to muster a United Nations Security Council majority for the war in March, 139 MPs supported a hostile motion and Robin Cook resigned from the Cabinet. Left-wing critics spoke of a leadership contest. Such speculation proved

BOX 5.2

How 'new' is New Labour?

A number of scholars have considered this question but the approach of Steven Fielding of Nottingham University (2003) is perhaps the most useful for this chapter's purposes. Fielding argues that New Labour is in reality part of the continuous development of social democratic thinking over the last century and a half. He denies the claim, associated with Roy Hattersley for one, that New Labour was a kind of 'coup' involving Blair, Mandelson and Gould and also denies the idea that New Labour was, in fact, all that new. His case is that New Labour was less to do with high-profile personalities and more to do with social democratic adaptations to the constantly fluid nature of international economics. As he sees it, New Labour was an attempt to reconcile a system which produced winners and losers with the ideas of equality, justice and efficiency. This last was the crucial lacuna in socialism as Attlee's nationalisation produced overmanned, loss-making state behemoths. Labour began to view the economy not so differently from Conservatives as something where growth and productivity had to be encouraged.

When this apparent attempt failed in a welter of strikes in 1979, the left swung back to bedrock and a right-wing Conservative government was elected. When voters rejected the left in 1983 and 1987, new thinking was set in train which nudged ever closer to an acceptance of market forces and a capitalist economy.

Writing some years into Labour's period in power, Fielding concluded:

> The party at the start of the twenty-first century may be a highly cautious social democratic organization; but recognizably social democratic it remains. If the state has advanced modestly and in novel ways since 1997, Labour's purpose in office is the same as it ever was: to reform capitalism so that it may better serve the interests of the majority.
>
> *Source*: Fielding (2003: 217)

premature but Blair's blind support for US foreign policy was squeezing support in his own New Labour power base (see also Chapter 26).

Blair's legacy

As it became obvious there was not much time left, Blair seemed to obsess with leaving a lasting 'legacy'. While he would have loved it to include a shiny new health and education service, polls showed voters relatively unimpressed and Labour critics furious at his encouragement of private sector invasion of such public sector citadels. For so many people, whatever their party loyalties, the debacle of the Iraq war will be emblazoned on Blair's grave. But this would be unfair. His tireless efforts in Northern Ireland arguably proved crucial in winning an admittedly fragile settlement which saw a new Executive formed before he left office. Secondly, Blair caused the Conservatives to desert the aridities of Thatcherism. He had stolen Tory clothes to an extent but had subtly re-attired his party as liberal, tolerant and dedicated to improving the condition of the less well-off majority. As leader followed leader the Conservatives finally got the message: they would have to change, just as Labour did from the mid-80s. David Cameron was the result. Now the litmus test for a new policy is, ostensibly at least, what it can do for the disadvantaged. Homophobia is out; environmentalism is very much in; pro-business yes, but at a distance; tax cuts maybe but not until the economy can sustain them. Already the signs of Blair's greatest legacy perhaps are evident in our present politics: Thatcher finished off left-wing socialism but Blair badly weakened right-wing Conservatism: a legacy of which any left-leaning politician can be proud. Cameron and Osborne, moreover, both admired Blair; in rebranding and repositioning their party, they absorbed much of Blairism, just as Blair had done the same with Thatcherism.

Gordon Brown's period in power

Brown's period as Prime Minister lasted only from June 2007, so he did not have much time to implant any characteristic elements. Indeed his many critics claimed he lacked any real vision of what his party should offer the country.

Economy

His critics' voices were partially stilled by his reaction to the banking crisis of 2007 and the subsequent recession. He took confident strides in a Keynesian direction, channelling huge amounts of money into the banking system as a 'fiscal stimulus' to ensure that the threatened collapse did not occur. There is some justification for believing his claim that other nations followed his lead. The problem with such a policy was that it helped build up huge levels of debt which imposed heavy interest repayment obligations. In the run-up to the election Labour argued that continued investment in the economy was necessary to avoid an even deeper recession. Brown's arguments were undermined to an extent, in autumn 2009, when it became clear the UK economy was not emerging from recession as robustly as other developed nations like the USA, Germany, France and Japan. Labour argued strongly that they were not to blame for the recession, and that the expenditure cuts proposed by the Tories would cause a fragile recovery to collapse into even deeper recession. Opinion polls suggest the Conservatives won this particular 'blame game' and Labour, at the time of writing (2013), has still to re-establish a reputation for economic competence.

Public expenditure

Labour insisted in late 2009 that it would maintain public spending to sustain recovery and protect recipients of services. This was undermined however by Treasury plans indicating severe cuts in planned Labour expenditure from 2011 onwards.

Foreign policy

Labour took a positive view on the EU, supporting the Lisbon Treaty and seeking to ridicule Conservative hostility. On Afghanistan they offered continued support to the war but were damaged by accusations that British troops had not been properly equipped to fight the Taliban.

Long period in power: 1997–2010

As for the Tories in 1997, Labour suffered from the fact that they had been in power for three terms (over 12 years) and voters were tired of them. Frequent examples of poor or incompetent government received considerable publicity and fuelled fears of a major rejection at the 2010 election. In the event, Labour was fortunate to survive May 2010 with 258 seats when a total meltdown threatened. After an extended leadership contest Ed Miliband stood against his elder brother for the top job and, surprisingly, won, with the votes of the unions proving decisive in Labour's **electoral college** system.

Ed Miliband as leader

Since the autumn of 2010 Miliband has tried hard to make an impact but most commentators would agree, he has yet to make a genuine breakthrough. On 25 September Miliband junior set out his stall in his conference speech.

He began by stating the party would have to reject some of the assumptions it had embraced over the last 30 years.

> These crises point to something deep in our country. The failure of a system. A way of doing things So the task of leadership in this generation is no ordinary task. It is to chart a new course. And strike a new bargain in our country.

He admitted some of Labour's acceptance of Thatcherism had been right – for example, the sale of council houses and rules on the closed shop. 'But while some of it was right, too much of what happened was based on the wrong values.'

Some New Labour policies were still appropriate, he argued:

> We changed the fabric of our country but we did not do enough to change the values of our economy. You believe rewards should be for hard work. But you've been told we have to tolerate the wealthiest taking what they can. And what's happened? Your living standards have been squeezed by runaway rewards at the top.
>
> This approach had led to a bad result. In our economy, you've been told the fast buck is ok. And what's happened? We've ended up with a financial crisis and you've ended up footing the bill. You believe in a society where everybody is responsible for their actions. But you've been told that if companies are big enough or powerful enough they can get away with anything. And what's happened? Big vested interests like the energy companies have gone unchallenged, while you're being ripped off.

In essence, Ed Miliband was laying out a plan to engineer a renaissance in human nature, to change the moral basis of the economy and society. While the *Guardian* readers listening might have celebrated the moral sweep of his vision, even the most optimistic must have feared for its achievability. The speech certainly had the feel of a bright new dawn; he did not mention 'socialism' but it seemed he was calling for it in all but name. Given 'socialism' is now widely seen as a failed ideology, some thought Miliband's vision was unrealistic. Tony Blair, in a big spread in The *Sun* in June 2011, thundered that Ed would never win except from the centre and under the banner of New Labour.

Box 5.3

Recent Labour schools of thought

Blue Labour: This school of thought attracted a brief period of attention but it is unclear if it contributed anything of benefit to Miliband's cause. It was launched by Maurice (later Lord) Glasman in April 2009 and his approach, worked out in seminars held in Oxford and London, gathered the support of a variety of respected figures: James Purnell, former Cabinet minister for Work and Pensions and chairman of the left-leaning Institute for Public Policy Research (IPPR); Jon Cruddas, independent-minded Labour MP; Marc Stears, Oxford philosopher; Jonathan Rutherford, professor of Cultural Studies, Middlesex University; and Chuka Umuna, MP and Shadow for Business, Innovation and Skills. Miliband's debt to this approach could be seen in Glasman's call for 'reciprocity, mutuality and solidarity', a call, almost, to retrieve values from the 'utopian' period of socialist thought. Glasman was calling for a rejection of New Labour's embrace of the markets and the centralisation which had characterised the party post-1945. Labour was enjoined to reconnect with local communities all over the country. Glasman was calling for the devolution of power to local communities to create 'participatory local democratic socialism' whereby local communities ally themselves against impersonal market forces. 'The purpose of democracy is to allow people organised in local communities, to choose whatever course of action they deem most speaks to their needs' (Beech and Hickson 2012: 21). 'Mutualism', based on cooperation and sharing benefits, is the core economic message rather than the current banking and big corporations. However, Glasman also called for measures to protect Labour's traditional working-class constituency by limiting immigration, and at a fringe 2011 conference meeting he criticised public-sector trade unions. But by the autumn of that year, Glasman had already burnt his boats in an interview with Mary Riddell in the *Daily Telegraph*. Asked whether he would support a total ban on immigration he replied: 'Yes. I would add that we should be more generous and friendly in receiving those [few] who are needed. To be more generous, we have to draw the line.'

This proved too much for Cruddas and Rutherford; Marc Stears confessed himself to be 'deeply distressed' by the comments and Dan Hodges in *The New Statesman*, 20 July, pronounced the effective end of Blue Labour.

The Purple Book: contributors to this book like Peter Mandelson, argue, more in the spirit of New Labour, against embracing 'out of date notions of class politics'. It urges acceptance of the complex globalised world and the consumerist culture and the creation of attractive policy proposals. Once the economy has recovered, this approach hopes, Labour's prospects will also recover.

Black Labour: this product of the Policy Network think tank, urges on Labour realistic approaches to fiscal prudence and tight expenditure controls. With its economic competence re-established, Labour will have a good chance of winning in 2015 once the Coalition's cuts have rendered voters hostile to its constituent parties.

The Liberal Democrats

LIBERAL DEMOCRATS

Source: Courtesy of the Liberal Democrats Party (www.libdems.org.uk)

After the war the Liberal Party continued to decline politically but still offered an alternative to voters in the centre of political ideas. At heart the party still adhered to the ideas of 'new liberalism' covered in Chapter 4, with emphases on individual liberty, equality, a mixed economy, a developed welfare state and a reformed, democratised system of government. Under the skilful successive leaderships of Jo Grimond, Jeremy Thorpe and David Steel, the party survived the postwar decades but hardly prospered. Then in 1981, as we have seen, it joined forces with the breakaway SDP to form the 'Alliance'. It was not difficult to unite on policies, which were very close; rather it was personalities who caused the foundering of this short-lived collaboration (see Box 5.1). In 1987 the two elements of the Alliance formally merged and fought the 1992 election as the Liberal Democrats. Its manifesto, *Changing Britain for Good*, called for a shift of power to the consumer and ordinary citizen, the development of worker shareholding and a market economy in which the market is the 'servant and not the master'. In addition, the party repeated the traditional

PROFILE

Paddy Ashdown
(1941–)

Former leader of Liberal Democrats. Formerly captain in the Marines, he saw active service in Borneo. He also learned to speak Mandarin Chinese as part of the diplomatic corps 1971–6. Won Yeovil in 1983 as a Liberal and became leader of merged party in 1988. He worked hard to build a close relationship with Labour. Lib-Dems won 46 seats in the 1997 General Election, after which Ashdown retired as leader. Charles Kennedy took over in 1999. Ashdown was appointed by the UN as International High Representative in Bosnia from May 2002 to 2006. His remains a highly influential voice in the Liberal Democrats.

call for reform of the voting system and **devolution** of power to the regions. Following the 1992 general election its new leader, Paddy Ashdown (elected in 1988), made steady progress with a replacing of 'equidistance' between the two big parties with a policy of open cooperation with Labour; in 1996, a joint Labour/Lib-Dem committee was set up to liaise on constitutional reform.

The strong showing by the Liberal Democrats in the 1997 general election buttressed the claim of that party to be the de facto, left-of-centre conscience of the new Blair order regarding constitutional reform and the nurturing of the welfare state, especially the educational system. The Lib Dems joined a Cabinet committee tasked with studying the future of constitutional reform – a tempting whiff of power perhaps for a party starved of it since the paltry sniff provided by the Lib–Lab pact of 1977–9. In 1999 Paddy Ashdown stood down after a distinguished period as leader of Britain's third party. His successor was the amiable Charles Kennedy, popular on quiz shows and a witty, clubbable man. He rejected suggestions to take up a left-of-Labour stance as the kind of *cul de sac* that had ruined Labour in the early 1980s. Instead he chose a 'business as usual' policy of 'constructive opposition' to Tony Blair with a view to replacing the Conservatives as the official opposition to the Labour Government. In an interview with the US magazine *Talk*, Blair said that his biggest mistake in May 1997 had been not to ask Ashdown to join his Cabinet, although with such a huge majority it was politically impossible to deny even a single post to his own party.

In the 2005 election Kennedy fought his usual relaxed campaign, offering an anti-war stance over Iraq, increased taxation for the very rich, and no tuition fees for university students. This worked well in constituencies where Labour was the Lib-Dem target, and 12 seats were won in this way. However, what attracted former Labour voters did not work the same magic in the close Lib-Dem–Conservative seats: only three were won while five were lost.

This election of 62 MPs, though welcome, still carried a sense of feeling of a missed opportunity; in addition there developed a sense that the party was losing what momentum it had gained at the election and all this contributed towards a whispering campaign against Kennedy. Complicating the situation, by the time of the autumn party conference a new wing was identified in the expanded 62-strong ranks of the Lib Dems: a group leaning more to the right, epitomised by *The Orange Book* of essays written by MPs and activists favouring a greater acceptance of market forces. Kennedy found his attempts to keep both factions happy were failing and by November senior party colleagues were said to be briefing against him.

Kennedy finally admitted the chief accusation against him – that he had a drinking problem – and a few days later, when the pressure did not abate, stood down in early January 2006. In the resultant, chaotic contest Simon Hughes and Chris Huhne waged a lively campaign, but the veteran Sir Menzies (Ming) Campbell won quite easily in the end, in March 2006. When he in turn proved unable to offer a new direction and higher poll ratings, he too resigned in October 2007. Another contest took place and this time the young, good-looking Nick Clegg was the choice. He too had difficulty making an impact, but he led the way in his 2008 conference in suggesting tax cuts; a nudge perhaps in the direction likely to win seats in the South-east from the Conservatives. However, the Lib Dems had much for which to hope and fight; **psephological** predictions of a hung parliament in the 2009–10 election raised much talk of which side he would swing to in any resultant coalition negotiations. The political positions of the Lib Dems have never seemed to matter very much, as power has always seemed so far away. However, the possible prospect of a hung parliament made their evolving policy positions for once into matters of intense interest.

Coalition partners after May 2010

Clegg's decision to enter a Conservative-led Coalition Government worried many of his close colleagues, not to mention the substantial number of voters who had voted for his party, primarily to keep the Conservatives *out* of power. The Coalition Agreement of May 2010 found, surprisingly, much on which to agree but certain key areas were destined to cause problems:

1 *Health*: The agreement promised to sustain funding but to end '**top-down**' reorganisation. Unfortunately this was precisely what Tory Health Minister Andrew Lansley had in mind, not to mention an expansion of private sector involvement in the NHS. After Lib Dems condemned some of these proposed changes and agonised debate took place within the Government, a 'pause for thought' was announced in May 2011.

2 *Constitutional reform*: Nick Clegg was given responsibility for this, in his role as Deputy Prime Minister, and his party were more than a little hopeful that the agreed referendum on the introduction of the Alternative Vote system would be won and would open the way to the introduction of **proportional representation**, a system which would greatly advantage smaller parties and possibly deliver the Lib Dems a decisive role in creating Coalition Governments. David Cameron, it had been widely rumoured, had promised, in deference to his Coalition partners, to take a back seat in the Conservative's 'No' campaign. However, his party persuaded him the AV system might prove a disaster to future Tory hopes of ruling alone, so he threw himself into the campaign, and an issue on which only a few months earlier the country had been evenly balanced was voted down by a majority of two to one.

3 *Europe*: After voting reform the Liberal Democrats' most fervent passion is reserved for the EU. So, the party was devastated in December 2011 when Cameron returned from the 8th–9th Brussels summit convened to save the euro, having vetoed the proposed treaty changes and effectively alienated the UK from the rest of the 26 members.

In conclusion

The Lib Dems still nominally subscribe to a left-of-centre agenda, closer to Labour than the Conservatives but the more market-oriented 'Orange Book' faction has found coalition Government to its liking; in practice, the party has had to stand by and watch its dearest tenets attenuated by the exigencies of Coalition Government. Its dilemma is that this stance has massively eroded its popular support so that, at the time of writing, it is constrained even from ending the coalition arrangement as electoral oblivion would be the likely consequence.

The ideology of the Coalition project

The influential Conservative MP, Douglas Carswell, was quoted in the *Sunday Times* 18/11/12 as writing:

> Bad government rules. A Conservative–Liberal Democrat coalition ought to have worked – it could

have been transformative. By fusing together Conservative ideas about the free market with the Liberal tradition of political radicalism, the government could have become a watershed administration . . . But instead of change, too often the coalition has perpetuated the status quo.

Viewed from the ideological viewpoint this seems naïve indeed. To assert that such different ideological traditions could be so easily 'fused' stretches credibility. The Liberal Democrats have never been too keen on the free market and their 'radicalism' has often required substantial public expenditure to be translated into reality. Given the Tory argument that public expenditure requires deep and rapid cuts, the project was always going to be hugely problematic, even before constitutional reform and diametrically opposed views on the EU are considered.

United Kingdom Independence Party (UKIP)

'Ukip is a sort of a bunch of . . . fruitcakes and loonies and closet racists,' said David Cameron on LBC Radio in October 2006. But with 13 MEPs at the 2009 Euro elections – outpolling Labour – and beating the Liberal Democrats in polls, not to mention a number of electoral contests (not least coming second in the Eastleigh by-election, February 2013) plus a clutchful of council seats, UKIP now deserves to be considered a 'mainstream' party rather than the 'party of protest' as once described by party leader, Nigel Farage in 2006. Farage is a former Conservative Party member and the party's policies sit close to the right end of that party's spectrum of ideas. Farage describes the other three mainstream parties as basically 'social democratic', while his party offers genuine opposition to such approaches. Foremost among its policies is withdrawal from the EU, but it has also elaborated a number of policies to compile a full election manifesto. It proposes: a 'flat rate' tax of 31 per cent with no bands for different levels of earning; restrictions on the selling of British companies overseas; cuts in pay for politicians and officials; a *voucher* system for education with more emphasis on the 3Rs; an extra 40 per cent on defence; and a war on multiculturalism and political correctness.

With 56 per cent in an autumn 2012 poll favouring EU withdrawal and up to 40 per cent of Tory voters in another admitting they were considering voting UKIP, Conservatives are fearful of the votes UKIP might take from them in 2015 and whether these 'fruitcakes and loonies' will deny them the overall majority they crave.

BOX 5.4

BRITAIN IN CONTEXT

Mainstream ideas and the political spectrum

As explained in Chapter 4, the political spectrum is usually represented from left to right, with unregulated free enterprise on the right and an anarchic or a communally owned economy on the left. Many of the ideas on the fringes – anarchism on the left or fascism on the right – would be regarded as extreme in the present day and unlikely to hold centre stage. Ideas likely to feature in the 'mainstream' of politics will usually be in the centre ground, that group of ideas which at any one time represents the general consensus of what people believe to be reasonable or legitimate political objectives.

Objectives which fall outside the mainstream are not automatic lost causes: repeated advocacy or changed circumstances can draw them into the centre – like anti-union legislation and privatisation during the early 1980s in the UK. During that same period the political spectrum was at its broadest in Britain with a near command economy being urged on Labour's left and a minimalist free enterprise state on the Thatcherite right. Since then ideological differences have narrowed significantly but they are still wider in Britain than in the USA.

Naturally right-wing pro-capitalist ideas are powerful in the USA, often seen as the 'headquarters' of world free enterprise thinking. By the same token 'left-wing' ideas, together with the US mainstream, are further to the right than in the UK. Americans have traditionally regarded any left-wing idea as the thin end of a communist wedge and therefore to be resisted as 'unpatriotic', or not sufficiently 'American'. So even state-funded health services, commonplace in Europe, are seen from across the Atlantic as 'socialist' and therefore slightly sinister. Some theorists explain the weakness of US left-wing thinking as the consequence of 'hegemonic' right-wing ideas –

ideas so deeply ingrained and powerful they squeeze the life out of any alternatives. It is certainly true that both major parties in the USA stoutly support free enterprise economics: even the Democrats urge economic growth and support business, though not with the passion of the true-believing Republicans.

Within Europe political spectrums, as in Britain, have tended to shift rightwards. Capitalism is no longer seen as a system which necessarily disadvantages large groups of people, but rather as the motor of dynamic economic growth from which all can benefit. Consequently, communism faded away in the wake of the Cold War and most brands of left-wing socialism tended to follow suit. Former communist countries display a fascinating mix of ideas in their spectrums. During communism, as in most authoritarian regimes, the political spectrum was very narrow, containing virtually no options for genuine change.

Once the old pro-Moscow regimes imploded, however, they were replaced by volatile new democracies in which, as in Russia, wild nationalism was present together with some surviving residual old-style communism. Many Russians, relieved at the passing of communism, were alarmed by their new combustible democracy and associated social dislocation. They gratefully accepted the promise of security which the former KGB chief Putin offered as president, even if political choices were once again heavily circumscribed. It would seem to be the case that a wide political spectrum, offering the chance of usually limited change at any particular time, is a characteristic of democracies. Authoritarian regimes do not tend to offer much choice and seek to shrink their spectrums into an unchanging narrowness.

Chapter summary

Conservatism is more than mere pragmatism in the ruling interest. It also includes a concern for unity, harmony and balance in a society based on property, equal opportunity, elite rule and gradual change. Margaret Thatcher gave major prominence to the neo-liberal strand in Conservatism, which stressed the primacy of markets in economics. Major returned to the rhetoric of 'one nation' Conservatism but contained the practice of Thatcherism. Labour began as a socialist party dedicated to the replacement of capitalism by a collectively owned economy, but in government translated this into nationalisation, a policy of doubtful success. In opposition during the 1980s it gradually shed its socialist clothes and donned those of the free market and restricted public spending: in effect a compromise with Thatcherism. Liberal Democrats inherited the 'new liberal ideas' of the early twentieth century to which they added an initial disposition to work with the Labour Party in office, something which faded after the invasion of Iraq in 2003.

Discussion points

- To what extent was Margaret Thatcher a Conservative?
- Did John Major contribute anything distinctive to Conservative thinking?
- Did Labour sell out its principles during the 1980s?
- Is there room for a distinctive third set of political ideas in Britain, and do the Lib Dems offer them?
- To what extent did the political ideologies of the Conservative and Liberal Democrat parties genuinely overlap when the Coalition Government was being negotiated in May 2010?

Further reading

Andrew Heywood's *Political Ideologies* (1998) is a valuable though dated source, as is the similar book by Ian Adams (1998). The Giddens book, *The Third Way*, has been criticised as being too vague, but it is chock full of interesting ideas and more than repays a careful reading.

Moran's *Politics and Governance in the UK* (2011) has an excellent chapter 15 on this topic which is recommended.

Tim Bale's *The Conservative Party: From Thatcher to Cameron* (2013) is a brilliant book published by Polity Press.

Bibliography

Adams, I. (1998) *Ideology and Politics in Britain Today* (Manchester University Press).

Ashbee, E. and Ashford, N. (1999) *US Politics Today* (Manchester University Press).

Bale, T. (2013) *The Conservative Party: From Thatcher to Cameron*, Polity Press.

Beck, U. (2013) *German Europe*. Polity Press.

Beech, M. and Hickson, K. (October 2012) Which Path for Labour? *Political Insight*, Political Studies Association, pp. 20–24.

Beer, S.H. (1982) *Britain Against Itself* (Faber).

Cooke, G., Lent, A., Painter, A. and Sen, H. (2011) *In the Black Labour* (Policy Network).

Crewe, I. and King, A. (1995) *SDP: The Birth, Life and Death of the Social Democratic Party* (Oxford University Press).

Crosland, C.A.R. (1956) *The Future of Socialism* (Jonathan Cape).

Driver, S. and Mantell, L. (1998) *New Labour: Politics after Thatcherism* (Pluto Press).

Field, F. (1995) *Making Welfare Work* (Institute of Community Studies).

Fielding, S. (2003) *The Labour Party* (Palgrave).

Foley, M. (1994) *Ideas that Shape Politics* (Manchester University Press).

Foote, G. (1997) *The Labour Party's Political Thought* (Manchester University Press).

Giddens, A. (1998) *The Third Way: The Renewal of Social Democracy* (Policy Press).

Glasman, M., Rutherford, J., Stears, M. and White, S. (2011) *The Labour Tradition and the Politics of Paradox* (LW Online Books).

Gould, B. (1989) *A Future for Socialism* (Jonathan Cape).

Gould, P. (1998) *The Unfinished Revolution* (Little, Brown).

Hazell, R. and Young, B. (2012) *The Politics of Coalition* (Hart).

Hailsham, Lord (1959) *The Conservative Case* (Penguin).

Heywood, A. (1998) *Political Ideologies*, 2nd edn (Macmillan).

Howell, D. (1980) *British Social Democracy* (Croom Helm).

Hutton, W. (1998) *The Stakeholding Society* (Polity Press).

Kelly, R. (1999) 'The Third Way', *Politics Review*, September.

Kelly, R. (1999) *British Political Parties Today* (Manchester University Press).

Marshall, P. and Laws, D. (2004) *The Orange Book: Reclaiming Liberalism* (Profile Books).

Moran, M. (2011) *Politics and Governance in the UK* (Palgrave).

Norton, P. and Aughey, A. (1981) *Conservatives and Conservatism* (Temple Smith).

Policy Exchange (2005) *The Case for Change* (Policy Exchange).

Russell, A. (2004) *Neither Left nor Right – the Liberal Democrats and the Electorate* (Manchester University Press).

Smith, C. (1998) *Creative Britain* (Faber and Faber).

Tressell, R. (1965) *The Ragged Trousered Philanthropists* (Panther; first published 1914).

Tucker, K. (1998) *Anthony Giddens and Modern Social Theory* (Sage).

Whiteley, P. and Seyd, P. (1992) *Labour's Grass Roots: the Politics of Party Membership* (Clarendon).

Useful websites

Centre for Policy Studies: www.cps.org.uk/
Conservative Party: www.conservatives.com/
Institute of Economic Affairs: www.iea.org.uk/
Institute of Public Policy Research: www.ippr.org.uk
Labour Party: www.labour.org.uk/
Liberal Democrats: www.libdems.org.uk/

CHAPTER 6

Political ideas: themes and fringes

Bill Jones

> **Under capitalism, man exploits man. Under communism it's just the opposite**
>
> John Kenneth Galbraith

Learning objectives

- To explain and put into context the themes of:
  - feminism;
  - national identity;
  - environmentalism.

- To identify, analyse and elucidate the political fringe on the far left and far right.

- To explain the intellectual source of ideas characterising the political fringe.

The first chapter looked at political concepts, the fourth ideology, and then party political ideas were examined in Chapter 5. This sixth chapter on political ideas addresses three major themes – **feminism**, **national identity** and **environmentalism**. This is followed by the rarefied world of the political fringe, represented by a colourful assemblage of small parties that are not always easy to identify; they may be seen selling their newspapers on the street or taking part in street demonstrations or even contesting national elections. However, their intellectual roots are often connected to major philosophical themes and, while they might operate outside the party conference forums now, in the future they might well be the leaders on stage.

Gender issues

Any woman whose IQ hovers above her body temperature must be a feminist.

Rita Mae Brown, author

In 1980 a United Nations report stated:

While women represent 50 per cent of the world's population, they perform nearly two-thirds of all working hours, receive one-tenth of world income and own less than 1 per cent of world property.

Despite the existence of a worldwide feminist movement, the position of women worldwide has improved very slightly, since the dawn of feminism in the late eighteenth century. The rights of women were implicit in the recognition of the rights of 'men', but thinkers such as Locke did not include women in their scheme of things. Rousseau did, however (while treating his own wife very badly), and in 1792 Mary Wollstonecraft's *A Vindication of the Rights of Women* (see Wollstonecraft, 1967) articulated their rights explicitly (see Profile) just as the French Revolution was asserting the rights of oppressed people everywhere. Whether women were 'oppressed' or not was a moot point. Most men assumed that women existed to perform domestic roles: producing and rearing children and caring for their husbands as well as doing all the household chores. Probably most women at the time would have agreed, had they ever thought themselves important enough to be consulted. They had no possibility of pursuing careers, voting or participating in public life. Their consolation was the power they exercised through this domestic role, influencing their men-folk, maybe even dominating them, behind the scenes. But the legal position of women at this time was dire: they had no right to divorce (unlike their husbands); they had no right to marital property; and their husbands could beat them quite legally – even rape them should they wish. Moreover, men regularly used prostitutes while preaching fidelity for their wives and divorcing them when this failed, on their side, to be upheld. In 'exchange' women were praised for their femininity and sensitivity and were idealised by the notion of romantic love. An unequal relationship indeed.

Emergent socialist ideas supported the position of women. Friedrich Engels argued in his book *The Origin of the Family, Private Property and the State* (1884) that the pre-historical position of women had been usurped by men so that property now was passed on through the male line instead of the female because men wished to pass on property to their sons. The exploitative relationship between the propertied class and the proletariat was mirrored within the family by the relationship between men and women. A socialist revolution would sweep away private property and remove the economic basis of the exploitative monogamous marriage.

PROFILE

Mary Wollstonecraft (1757–97)

Mary Wollstonecraft was an Anglo-Irish writer and is often cited as the first modern feminist. At the age of 28 she wrote a semi-autobiographical novel, *Maria*. She moved to London to become the 'first of a new genus' of women, a full-time professional writer and editor specialising in women and children. She was closely associated with the group of radical reforming writers called the English Jacobins, where she met her future husband, the philosopher William Godwin, often regarded as a forerunner of the *anarchist* movement. In her book *A Vindication of the Rights of Women* (1792) she argued for equal rights for women in society, especially regarding educational opportunities. Her daughter with Godwin was Mary Shelley, the author of *Frankenstein*. Because she lived with two other men before she married Godwin, her unconventional lifestyle at the time caused some outrage, which tainted her reputation throughout the nineteenth century. Eventually, however, her pioneering feminism was recognised and appreciated for its eloquent and brave articulation of ideas which are now part of the mainstream.

During the nineteenth century the women's movement, such as it was, concentrated on gaining the vote, the belief being that, once this citadel had fallen, the other injustices regarding the imbalance of political and legal rights compared with men would soon be remedied.

To an extent these early feminists were operating with the grain of history, as the franchise for men was being progressively extended at this time. Nevertheless, it took a bitter and militant struggle for the 'Suffragettes', led by Emmeline and Christabel Pankhurst, to win through: in 1918 women received the vote, but only if they fulfilled certain educational and property qualifications and were, bizarrely it now seems, over the age of 30. They finally achieved equal political rights in 1928, but this did not automatically transform their position, or make any difference at all in the short and medium term. The women's movement subsided for a number of decades, but the impact of another world war, where women once again played leading roles on the home front, advanced their claims for better treatment. Simone de Beauvoir's *The Second Sex* (1952) attacked the asymmetry whereby men were defined as free independent beings and women merely in terms of their relationships with men.

The so-called 'second wave' of feminism began with Betty Friedan's *The Feminine Mystique* (1963). This major work rejected the myth that women were different and were happy being the domestic adjuncts of their husbands. Having nominally equal rights did not deliver real equality in a world controlled by men and discriminating against women. In the late 1960s and 1970s the work of Germaine Greer (*The Female Eunuch*, 1971) and Kate Millett (*Sexual Politics*, 1969) moved the focus of debate from the wider world of career and public life to the micro-worlds that we all inhabit. Greer developed some of the ideas of Herbert Marcuse (1964, 1969a, 1969b), who argued that Western society was sexually repressed. She suggested that women had absorbed the male idea of their sexuality as soft and yielding – a kind of sex image stereotype – while their true and possibly quite different nature was not allowed to be expressed and fulfilled. Connected with this went an assertion of lesbianism as a socially demonised activity.

Instead of their living out expected roles, Greer was insisting that people could be true to themselves, being 'male' or 'female' according to their own natures. Millett's emphasis was on how women are brainwashed into accepting a given image of *themselves* regarding their role and even their appearance. This image, according to her, was a reflection of 'patriarchy': constructed by men with their interests to the fore. What was attributed to gender roles was in fact no more than a socially constructed role that women were induced to accept from birth via a battery of socialising agencies, including family, tradition, law, the media and popular culture. Women were forced to accept a narrow, constricting role of being gentle, caring mother figures whose job was to tend their men. Alternatively, they were seen as whores and temptresses, equally subservient but this time more dangerous. Millett also directed attention at the family and home, pointing out that here was the most important arena in which the male controlled the key sexual relationship, dominating the female; following from this is the key feminist phrase, that 'the personal is the political'.

In the 1970s it was observed that liberal feminists, who believed that reform and a high degree of equality were possible in society as it is, coexisted with socialist feminists, who believed that the main inequality was still between classes and not the sexes. They believed that major changes to the economy and society were necessary before women could be truly free. A third group soon emerged: the **radical feminists**. For them the problem lies not in society or the economy but in human nature or, more precisely, male human nature. The problem with women, in other words, is men. In *The Dialectic of Sex* (1980, originally published 1971), Shulamith Firestone perceived a fundamental oppression of women by men as a result of their biological role. Sexual domination therefore both precedes and exceeds economic exploitation. What she advocates is a 'sexual revolution much larger than – inclusive of – a socialist one' to 'eradicate the tapeworm of exploitation'. She argues for a restructuring of society through science, whereby children would be produced artificially and looked after communally so that women's physical and psychological burdens would be removed and they would be free for the first time in history.

BOX 6.1

Sexual inequality at work

According to LSE research reports back in February 2000 and January 2001, a woman earns on average £250,000 less than a man during a lifetime. This is partly because women workers tend to be concentrated in low-paid jobs, but also because they are paid less than men for doing the same work and routinely denied access to bonus payments and pension schemes.

In November 2012 the BBC reported evidence from the Fawcett Society saying that 'women still earn 14.9% less on average than men for the same job. But it says this gap could widen as public sector cuts push women into the private sector, where the gap is wider. The warning coincides with a survey which suggests that a woman can earn £423,000 less than a man in her career.'

Susan Brownmiller – *Against our Will* (1975) – shifts the focus to the violence that men use to threaten women; the fear of rape is used to maintain male dominance, and rapists act for all men in demonstrating the consequences of non-compliance. Other feminist writers, such as Andrea Dworkin and Dale Spender – often called 'supremacists' – assert female moral superiority and argue that the world would be better if women were in control. Often this type of feminist will be **separatist** in relation to men; their lesbianism consequently has a political quality to it. For them men are not necessary for women, and women who live with men are 'man identified' instead of being 'woman identified'.

It is often said that since the 1970s the women's movement has lost some momentum. Certainly the tone has become milder; Greer (1985) and Friedan (1982) have both disappointed radicals by writing approvingly of domesticity and childrearing. The New Right in the USA and UK, moreover, have reinforced 'traditional values' of women's roles and the desirability of marriage (and by implication the subversive effects of one-parent families) to hold society together. In their book *Contemporary Feminist Politics* (1993), Lovenduski and Randall applauded the progress made by the women's movement in permeating institutions and professions and in disseminating feminist values so effectively that they have become widely accepted as orthodoxies. However, they lament the failure to replace activists when they bow out of activity, and the internecine squabbling and fragmentation that have weakened the movement. The strong showing of women candidates in the 1997 General Election – women MPs virtually doubled from 62 to 120, most of them Labour – cheered campaigners for more female representation and those who defended the special Labour measures to favour women candidates in winnable seats. However, some feminists criticised 'Blair's babes', as they were dubbed, as performing a decorative but non-feminist role in the governing party. Comparisons are made on the Labour side with the fiercely effective Barbara Castle and on the Conservative side with the legendary Thatcher. Box 6.2 provides chapter and verse on employment and political life in the UK showing that, while much has been achieved in the recent past, women are still at a definite disadvantage compared to men. However, as long as men in prominent public positions in UK life continue to issue provocative statements, British feminists will feel they still have much to achieve. This by Dominic Raab MP (Conservative) is a good example of the genre as these recent quotations illustrate:

> Maybe it's time men started burning their briefs, to put to an end once and for all what Emmeline Pankhurst used to call 'the double standard of sex morals'.

> Feminists are now amongst the most obnoxious bigots.

> From cradle to grave, men are getting a raw deal. They work longer hours, die earlier and retire later than women.

BOX 6.2

Women in public life

Position (year)	% women
MPs (2012)	22
Lords (2012)	22
Cabinet (2012)	22
Government (2012)	17
MSPs (2011)	35
AMs (2011)	40
MLAs (2011)	19
Board of public bodies (2010–11)	36
Senior civil service (2011)	35
Justice of the Supreme Court (2011)	9
GPs (2010)	45
NHS consultants (2010)	31
Secondary head teachers (2010)	37
University professors (2009–10)	19

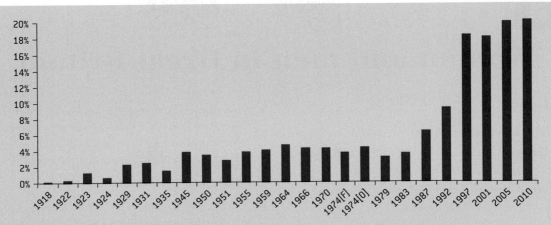

Proportion of female MPs, 1918–2010

Gwyneth Dunwoody broke Barbara Castle's record for longest continuing service as a female MP, having been elected in 1974 (she was also a Member between 1966 and 1970) and serving until her death in April 2008. Harriet Harman is currently the longest serving female MP, having been elected in the Peckham by-election in 1982.

Female councillors (England), 1997–2010 (%)

	1997	2001	2004	2006	2008	2010
Councillors	28	29	29	30	31	31
Leader/Deputy Leader	0	0	0	18	21	21

Source: Local Government Association, *National Census of Local Authority Councillors in England*, various years.

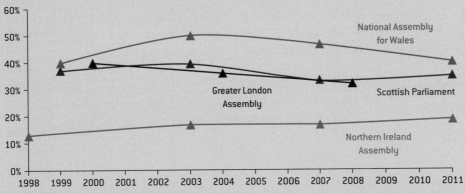

Women elected to devolved bodies, 1998–2011

Source: House of Commons Library, *Women in Public Life, the Professions and the Boardroom*, March 2012

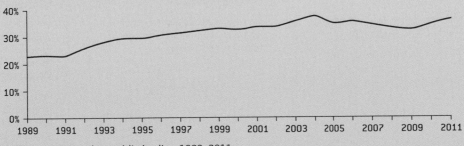

Women appointed to public bodies, 1989–2011

Source: House of Commons Library, *Women in Public Life, the Professions and the Boardroom*, March 2012

BOX 6.3

Women and men in Great Britain

Employment

- 46 per cent of people in the labour market are women.
- In the 16–64 age group, two-thirds of women and over three-quarters of men are in employment.
- Nearly half of women (44 per cent) and about one in ten men who work are part time.

Parents and carers

- Of mothers of under-fives, 52 per cent were in employment, and two-thirds of those working as employees were part time.

- Since there are almost 4.7 million under-eights in England and just over a million places with childminders in full day care or in out-of-school clubs, there are four children for each place in these types of provision.

Pay and income

- Average hourly earnings for women working full time are 18 per cent lower than for men working full time, and for women working part time hourly earnings are 40 per cent lower.

Source: Equal Opportunities Commission (2006) *Sex and Power: Who Runs Britain?*

BOX 6.4

Feminist debates

This is a schematic summary of the main strands of feminist thought. It is important to understand that these strands are not rigidly separate, that some writers could be entered in more than one category, and that in recent years there has been a significant convergence of apparently competing approaches.

Type of feminism	Key concepts	Goals	Key writers
Liberal	Rights, equality	The same rights and opportunities as for men, with a focus on the public sphere	*Classic:* Mary Wollstonecraft John Stuart Mill *Recent:* Betty Friedan Naomi Wolf Natasha Walter
Radical	Patriarchy, 'the personal is political', sisterhood	Radical transformation of all spheres of life to liberate women from male power. Replace or displace men as the measure of human worth	Kate Millett Andrea Dworkin Catherine MacKinnon Germaine Greer
Socialist and Marxist	Class, capitalism, exploitation	An economically just society in which all women and men can fulfil their potential	*Classic:* William Thompson Friedrich Engels Alexandra Kollontai Sylvia Pankhurst *Recent:* Michelle Barrett Juliet Mitchell Sheila Rowbotham Lynne Segal Anne Phillips

Type of feminism	Key concepts	Goals	Key writers
Black	Interactive and multiple oppressions, solidarity, black	An end to the interconnecting oppressions of gender, 'race' and class	*Classic:* Maria Stewart Julia Cooper *Recent:* Patricia Hill Collins bell hooks Angela Davis Heidi Mirza
Postmodern	Fragmentation, discourse, deconstruction, differences	Overcoming binary oppositions. Free-floating, fluid gender identities. However, the idea of a final goal is rejected in principle	Judith Butler Julia Kristeva Joan Scott Denise Riley Michelle Barrett

Source: Valerie Bryson (2003) 'Feminist debates, ideology: feminism', *Politics Review*, Vol. 12, No. 4, April 2003. Reproduced with permission from Philip Allan Updates

As if this was not enough to worry about, an article (criticised by several feminist writers) by Professor Alison Wolf, of Kings College London, in a March 2006 edition of *Prospect* magazine, maintained that new attitudes in the workplace are in effect 'killing feminism':

In the past, women of all classes shared lives centred on explicitly female concerns. Now it makes little sense to discuss women in general. The statistics are clear: among young, educated, full-time professionals, being female is no longer a drag on earnings or progress.

Wolf goes on to argue that total commitment to career diverts the crucial resource of female talent away from the caring professions like teaching, prevents them from volunteering and thus minimises 'female altruism', and dissuades many women from having children.

BOX 6.5

Landmarks in history of British feminism

1 1870 The Married Women's Property Act first allowed women to own their own property. Until that year a woman's property transferred to her husband and remained so after a divorce.

2 1903 The Women's Social and Political Union is set up in Manchester by Emmeline Pankhurst, her daughters Christabel and Sylvia plus Annie Kearney.

3 1906 The National Federation of Women Workers is set up by Mary MacArthur.

4 1909 Trades Boards Act fixes minimum wages in most exploitative trades, especially those involving women workers.

5 1913 Massive rally held in Hyde Park in support of votes for women.

6 1918
   a) Women over 30 given right to vote.
   b) Parliamentary Qualification of Women Act enables women to stand as MPs.
   c) (Countess) Constance Markiewicz elected first woman MP for Sinn Fein.

7 1921 Unemployment benefit extended to include allowances for wives.

8 1922 Law of Property Act allows husbands and wives to inherit property equally.

9 1923 Matrimonial Causes Act makes grounds for divorce same for men and women.

10 1928 All women given right to vote on same basis as men.

11 1929 'Flapper Election' as thousands of women turn out to vote.

12 1941 National Service Act introduces conscription for women (war work) as well as men.

13 1958 Life Peerages Act entitles women to sit in Lords for first time.

14 1967
    a) Abortion Act passed, making it legal under certain conditions.
    b) Contraceptive pill becomes available through Family Planning Clinics.

15 1968 Women striking at Dagenham win fight for equal pay with men.

16 1970
    a) First Women Liberation Conference held at Ruskin College.
    b) Equal Pay Act makes it illegal to pay women less than men for same work.

17 1975
    a) Sex Discrimination Act makes it illegal to discriminate against women in work, education and training.
    b) Employment Protection Act delivers statutory maternity provision.

18 Equal Opportunities Act passed to oversee Equal Pay and Sex Discrimination Acts.

19 1979 Margaret Thatcher becomes first woman Prime Minister.

20 1982 30,000 women gather at Greenham Common Peace Camp.

21 1997 Election sees 101 women elected to Commons.

Source: Women's Resource Centre (http://www.wrc.org.uk/)

National identity: the English/British sense of who they are

All countries have some sense of identity – where they have come from, who they are, what they stand for – and, just like individuals, most encounter problems in finding satisfactory answers. The USA, for example, comprising a multitude of different elements, often recent arrivals, experiences a fragile sense of unity and coherence – undermined by overt and covert racism – which constantly has to be reinforced by what to Europeans may seem like manic statements of patriotism. France too has been undergoing an identity crisis in recent years, with its famed sense of equality, dating back to the 1789 revolution, being questioned especially by Muslim immigrant groups who declare they are not in any real sense equal when they suffer from racism and widespread unemployment. The British also are undergoing problems in deciding who they are, what they are for and to whom they belong.

Andrew Gamble, in *Between Europe and America* (2003), addresses this topic and analyses the way in which this sense of identity has changed over the years. He argues that England was at the heart of this identity, expanding to absorb Wales, Scotland and, until 1922, Ireland. After losing the 13 colonies, the Empire enjoyed its biggest expansion in the nineteenth century, embracing one-quarter of the world's population and one-quarter of its territory.

The Empire created an extensive ruling elite and a world-view which also embodied a degree of smug superiority that often irritated the rest of the world. However, the massive losses of the First World War sapped the nation's power and, even though the postwar settlement expanded the Empire, it had lost its stability. The Second World War involved the sacrifice of much of the wealth which the Empire represented and by 1945 it was living on borrowed time. The refusal of the US to support Britain's involvement in the attempt to regain the Suez Canal in 1956 was the signal for the further winding-up of the imperial dream which independence to India in 1947 had initiated. Those schoolchildren who had felt a thrill of pride in seeing the 1950s map of the world coloured with so much red had soon to adjust to a much more humble role.

Along with imperial decline came its economic concomitant: a slow sinking of Britain from 'workshop of the world' to 'sick man of Europe'. During the seventies the sour mood of the times infected a workforce which became increasingly uncooperative and demanding of higher wages just when the country could no longer afford them. The result was a major upsetting of the postwar settlement whereby agreed increased taxes funded a welfare state and included trade unions as a valued partner of government. Margaret Thatcher set about enthroning the role of markets, removing the inefficient nationalised industries, curbing the over-powerful unions and rolling back the state. However, the effects of this harsh medicine on Scotland and Wales gave added power to the arguments for independence in these countries. When Tony Blair was elected in 1997, the stage was set for the partial dismantling of the constitution – devolution – posing a number of questions about the concept of Britain. 'England' is no longer synonymous with 'Britain' now new identities have been assumed by the nations of the Celtic fringe, each with their separate assemblies. Since Alex Salmond's nationalists won a majority in the 2011 elections, a referendum on Scottish independence may pave the way for exactly that, with complex repercussions for any 'British' sense of identity.

At the same time there is an internal questioning of identity caused by the inflow of immigrants, initially from the Empire and Commonwealth after 1945, and latterly by economic and political refugees from poorer and strife-torn countries during the latter part of the century. This growing band of ethnic minorities has changed the nature of British cities and arguably made the country a 'multicultural' society. But there are evident strains, sometimes violent, between immigrants and their British neighbours; many resist this loss of their old identity and argue that such people are at heart 'foreigners'. Lord Norman Tebbit controversially demanded that, when cricket teams arrived from their home countries, Commonwealth immigrants should support the English side. In practice, immigrants and their descendants now tend to assume a dual identity of 'black British' or 'British Asian'.

Yet another thread in this complex reworking of identities is the European Union. At the 'Congress of Europe' in May 1948 Winston Churchill made the chairman's address, including the words: 'I hope to see a Europe where men and women of every country will think of being European and wherever they go in this wide domain will truly feel, "I am at home".' The truth is that neither he nor Ernest Bevin, Labour Foreign Secretary from 1945 to 1951, actually believed all the warm words they said about a united Europe. Like US diplomats, they recognised a degree of unity as necessary to resist the Soviet threat and were not opposed to a closer coming together should the nations concerned wish it; the problem was that Britain, when it came down to it, did not.

Bevin had explained in 1946 that Britain saw herself as a 'great power', adding that 'the very fact we have fought so hard for liberty, and paid such a high price, warrants our retaining that position' (Gamble 2003: 189). So, Europe was seen as something separate from Britain, which still sat at the 'big boys' table. When the European Iron and Steel Community was established in 1950 – the organisational template, as it turned out, for the later European Community – Britain loftily stood aside, refusing to allow any mere Europeans to decide how these nationalised concerns should be run. The same thing happened with the developments up to 1957 when the Treaty of Rome established the new

experiment in supranationalism. Clement Attlee mischievously summed up a dominant British political class view of Europe when he said:

> The so-called Common Market of six nations. Know them all well. Very recently, this country spent a great deal of blood and treasury rescuing four of 'em from attacks by the other two.

It is no surprise that Britain initially was not interested, but then the devastating American rebuff of Suez, plus the signs that British capitalism was unable to keep pace with the new dynamic customs-union based in Brussels, brought about a dramatic change of emphasis and potential allegiance. Britain applied in May 1960 and received another rebuff, this time courtesy of General De Gaulle, who repeated the trick in 1967. Running behind the bus trying to catch it and then being thrown off when we did was not the best early experience to have of this economically integrated Europe. We finally made it in 1972 when the General had left the stage and a staunchly Europhile Ted Heath was able to manufacture a majority Commons vote for entry.

Nonetheless, dissent was by no means stilled. At first it was the Labour left which cavilled at this 'capitalist club', but under Thatcher it was the right-wing Conservatives who developed their disaffection and eventually gave full expression to an anti-European position. They could not begin to accept that the British identity, forged by a thousand years of history, a worldwide empire and heroic struggles against tyranny, could be meekly subsumed into what Margaret Thatcher liked to call 'the Belgian Empire'. Against what proved to be her better judgement she acceded to measures of greater integration (for example, the Single European Act in 1987) but then, after leaving office, became an avid and bitter cheerleader for the Eurosceptic cause. Polls showed that upwards of a third of Britons came to agree with her, and by 20 November 2012 56 per cent of respondents in a poll stated their willingness to withdraw completely. British public opinion, no doubt soured by the long-running 'Eurozone Crisis', seemed to have shifted into radical Eurosceptic mode at the time of writing.

The dilemma for Britain's changing sense of identity emerged starkly during the 1980s and 1990s. The Tory right preferred America to Europe: the American attitude to economics, welfare and, indeed, the management of world order. When Labour entered government, many felt their identification would swing back towards our partners in Europe. Certainly Blair subscribed to the Social Chapter upon which Conservative sceptics had poured so much vitriol and joined in the EU (as it was called after Maastricht in 1992) summits, but his desire for Britain to join the common currency, the euro, was prevented (in retrospect presciently) by his Chancellor Gordon Brown to whom Blair

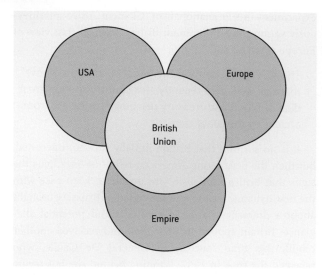

Figure 6.1 The Four Circles of England: in his *Between Europe and America* (2003) Andrew Gamble (pp. 30–4) quotes Churchill's view that Britain lay at the touching point of three circles – Empire, Europe and America. Gamble argues that since devolution, a fourth, that of the 'British Union' should be added

had conceded virtual control of the economy. So, entry into the EU's inner counsels was prevented; EU opponents were pleased and hoped Labour would maintain the pro-American bias favoured by many Conservatives. Brown, in any case, was a warm admirer of the American economic model and had tried hard to keep employment 'flexible', unlike many EU countries where pro-worker employment laws hold down productivity. But the biggest shifting of Gamble's 'four spheres' occurred after the 9/11 attack on the World Trade Center in New York (see Figure 6.1).

'Britishness'

Linda Colley (2005) in her book, *Britons: Forging the Nation 1707–1837*, argues that British people, known as such since the Act of Union 1707 with Scotland, tend to have a 'layered' sense of being British plus an often even closer identity like Scottish, Welsh, Northern Irish, Asian or Caribbean; oddly perhaps, 'English' is more often regarded as interchangeable with 'British'. Polling evidence suggests that the 'British' layer has given way to the connecting identity, so that many now feel more English, Scottish and so forth than the composite 'British', the 'glue' which holds together the traditional idea of the 'United Kingdom'. The IPPR opinion study, *The Dog that Finally Barked* (January 2012), confirmed these trends, indeed, discerning an emergent *revival* 2000–11 of 'English' conscious-ness, based on dissatisfaction with the devolution settlement.

More particularly it springs from a sense of resentment, no doubt sharpened in recessionary times, that the 'Celtic fringe receive proportionately more per capita funding than

the English': 45 per cent of respondents said Scotland gets 'more than its fair share of public spending'; 52 per cent of the English sample indicated they felt Scotland's economy benefits more than England's from being in the union; 80 per cent support full fiscal autonomy ('devo-max') for Scotland whereby it would spend only the taxes raised within its own borders. Moreover a majority was shown for the proposal that 'Scottish MPs should not be allowed to vote in the House of Commons on laws that affect England'.

For a few years after devolution occurred English voters seemed content with it, but now only one in four supports the status quo and 59 per cent do not trust the government to advance the long-term interests of England. According to the report:

> English voters appear to want what we call an 'English dimension' to the country's politics – that is, distinct governance arrangements for England as a whole.
>
> (IPPR 2012: 2)

While many people still see themselves as 'British-English', an increasing number of English people see themselves as more the latter than the former. Moreover, the survey suggests that the stronger the feeling of 'Englishnes', the stronger the desire for an 'English dimension' in their **governance**.

Green thinking

The ecological perspective rejects philosophies of the right, left and centre as more similar than dissimilar. Sir Jonathon Porritt (a former senior government environment adviser) characterises them collectively as '**industrialism**': this 'super-ideology . . . conditioned to thrive on the ruthless exploitation of both people and planet, is itself the greatest threat we face' (Porritt 1984). Conservatives, socialists and centre politicians argue about rival economic approaches – individualism versus collectivism and how the cake of national income should be sliced up and distributed – but they all agree that the size of the cake should be increased through vigorous economic growth. This is the central proposition that the Greens most emphatically reject. 'Industrialism', they say, is predicated on the continuous expansion of goods and services and on the promotion of even more consumption through advertising and the discovery of an increasing range of 'needs'. It creates great inequalities in which a rich and envied minority set the pace in lavish and unnecessary consumption while a sub-stantial number – in many countries a majority – are either unemployed or live in relative, perhaps dire, poverty. The Conservatives have presided over an increase in income differentials but have offered economic growth as a panacea: more for the rich and more for the poor. Porritt observes:

If the system works, i.e. we achieve full employment, we basically destroy the planet; if it doesn't, i.e. we end up with mass unemployment, we destroy the lives of millions of people . . . From an industrial point of view it is rational to . . . promote wasteful consumption, to discount social costs, to destroy the environment. From the Green point of view it is totally irrational, simply because we hold true to the most important political reality of all: that all wealth ultimately derives from the finite resources of our planet.

(Porritt 1984: 46–7)

The Green view goes on to adduce a number of basic principles:

1 *A world approach*: All human activity should reflect appreciation of the world's finite resources and easily damaged ecology.

2 *Respect the rights of our descendants*: Our children have the right to inherit a beautiful and bountiful planet rather than an exhausted and **polluted** one.

3 *Sufficiency*: We should be satisfied with 'enough' rather than constantly seeking 'more'.

4 *A conserver economy*: We must conserve what we have rather than squander it through pursuit of high-growth strategies.

5 *Care and share*: Given that resources are limited, we must shift our energies to sharing what we have and looking after all sections of society properly.

6 *Self-reliance*: We should learn to provide for ourselves rather than surrendering responsibility to specialised agencies.

7 *Decentralise and democratise*: We must form smaller units of production, encourage cooperative enterprises and give people local power over their own affairs. At the same time, international integration must move forward rapidly.

Porritt maintains that this amounts to a wholly alternative view of rationality and mankind's existence. He contrasts the two world-views of industrialism and **ecology** in Table 6.1.

Inevitably, the other major parties have done all they can to climb aboard the Green band-wagon, cloaking their

Table 6.1 Two worlds: industrialism versus ecology

Industrialism	Ecology
The environment	
Domination over nature	Harmony with nature
Environment managed as a resource	Resources regarded as strictly finite
High energy, high consumption	Low energy, low consumption
Nuclear power	Renewable sources of energy
Values	
An ethos of aggressive individualism	Cooperatively based communitarian society with emphasis on personal autonomy
Pursuit of material goods	Move towards spiritual, non-material values
Rationality and packaged knowledge	Intuition and understanding
Patriarchal values, hierarchical structure	Post-patriarchal feminist values, non-hierarchical structure
Unquestioning acceptance of technology	Discriminating use and development of science and technology
The economy	
Economic growth and demand stimulation	Sustainability, quality of life and simplicity
Production for exchange and profit	Production for use
High income differentials	Low income differentials
A free-market economy	Local production for local need
Ever-expanding world trade	Self-reliance
Employment as a means to an end	Work as an end in itself
Capital-intensive production	Labour-intensive production
Political organisation	
Centralisation, economies of scale	Decentralisation, human scale
Representative democracy	Direct democracy, participative involvement
Sovereignty of nation-state	Internationalism and global solidarity
Institutionalised violence	Non-violence

Source: Adapted from Porritt (1984) *Seeing Green*, pp. 216–17

Global warming

Of all the many dangers facing the world's environment, it has been the problem of global warming that has most exercised environmentalists and governments in recent years.

The scientific argument on 'greenhouse' gases

It is an obvious fact that the earth receives its warmth from the sun. However, certain gases within the earth's atmosphere have been crucial in helping retain the sun's heat over the billions of years life has been evolving. Some of the sun's heat is reflected back into space but the retention of a portion of this heat, absorbed by the gases, has enabled the earth to achieve a temperature ideal for supporting life. Indeed, without such gases the average temperature of the world would have been $-15°C$ instead of $+18°C$.

In 1898 the Swede Svante Arrhenius calculated that a doubling of CO_2 would increase world temperatures by 5–6°C. In 1988 the UN established the Intergovernmental Panel on Climate Change. The IPCC's latest estimate is of a warming of between 1.4 and 5.8°C by 2100 depending on what is done to curb gas emissions (IPCC 2001). Other studies suggest even higher rates of warming.

Consequences of global warming

The earth's temperature has provided the conditions in which humans have evolved and flourished, but rapidly rising temperatures would cause deforestation, the loss of fishing stocks, the collapse of many crops, outbreaks of many more destructive tropical storms, the melting of vast permafrosted areas (which would also release massive new stored reserves of CO_2) and the gradual melting of the ice-caps, causing catastrophic rises in sea level amounting to over 200 feet.

The developing world

The surging economies of China and India – often using CO_2-rich emitting energy production methods – hugely increase the threats, but it is hard for the developed world to insist that poorer countries forego the benefits and comforts which the West has enjoyed for many years. In 1997 an agreement was reached at Kyoto whereby signatories agreed to reduce emissions to 5 per cent below the 1990 levels by 2010; in practice this means a reduction of 29 per cent in all greenhouse gases. Developing countries were excluded from this requirement, but the biggest problem lay with the reluctance of the USA to ratify the agreement.

With only 5 per cent of the world's population, the world's biggest economy emits a quarter of the world's CO_2. George W. Bush, originally an oil man and advised by many more, refused to accept the Kyoto Protocol. One of his advisers, Myron Ebell, claimed the whole global warming story was a scare tactic created by Europe to enable their ailing economies to compete more effectively against the USA. Barack Obama, elected in 2008, basically accepted the arguments and pledged to reverse Bush's policy on this issue. Few Greens, by 2012, were satisfied that he had.

Scepticism about global warming remains despite the fact that 99 per cent of scientists in this area of study insist it is a fact. Scientists point out that of the warmest 20 years ever experienced, 16 have happened during the last quarter-century and match almost precisely increases in CO_2 as a proportion of the atmosphere. Temperature increases of that kind are unprecedented and are conclusive evidence that we do have an acute problem which could conceivably lead to the ending of all human life.

The United Kingdom

The UK was an enthusiastic signatory of Kyoto and at first made good progress towards the agreed goal, assisted by a switch of power stations from coal to gas. The 2005 Labour manifesto set a target of 20 per cent, well above the required Kyoto level, but as the deadline has approached performance has declined. On 28 March 2006, Margaret Beckett, the then Environment Secretary, announced that reductions were likely to be in the range 15–18 per cent instead, blaming increased economic growth and the rise in oil prices which had caused many power stations to return to coal use. Since then recession-affected economic shrinkage will probably reduce emissions in the UK and worldwide.

policies in light green clothes and shamelessly stealing the rhetoric of the environmentalists.

As it currently stands, the Greens' political programme is unlikely to fall within the 'art of the possible' (see below). It has established some support among students, and in 1994 it gained four council seats, but, before 2010, its best parliamentary performance was in 1989, when it managed 6.1 per cent of the vote in Lambeth, Vauxhall. In May 2003 Greens won seven seats in the Scottish Parliament. In the 2005 General Election the Greens fielded 202 candidates but not one got elected – hardly a launching pad for power – but, as the writer Malcolm Muggeridge (1903–90) once pointed out, 'utopias flourish in chaos', and if global warming continues unchecked accompanied by more environmental chaos, it may well be the Greens who inherit politically what is left of the earth, if it is not already too late by then. In May 2010 the Greens were hugely encouraged when Caroline Lucas became the party's first MP for Brighton Pavilion. This foothold, not to mention their MP's persuasive powers, has increased the attention paid to the party and they will hope to build on this success at the next election.

The political fringe

The political fringe is the name given to those small factions and groups that often do their political work outside the conference halls of the main parties rather than within them. Those who belong are often determined ideologues, given to regular argument in groups prone to splits and factions. They do have some intrinsic interest, however, as microcosms of political ideas and conflicts. It must also be remembered that in the early part of this century the Labour Party was just such a small faction, snapping around the heels of the Liberal Party. Yet, within a couple of decades it was actually in power and destined to be there – with a huge majority – as the new millennium started.

Far left

Marx, Lenin and Stalin

Most far-left groups owe their intellectual debts to Karl Marx; he argued that under a capitalist economy rich property owners so drive down wages in pursuit of profits and a competitive edge that a vast army of impoverished workers will eventually rise up and sweep away the whole corrupt system. Once private property had been abolished, working people would begin to live new and better lives in an economy in which people would work willingly for each other and not reluctantly for an employer. It did not quite work out that way.

After the Marxist takeover of power in Russia in 1917, a period of great hardship and economic instability followed. Lenin established a political system based on centralised control supported by a network of secret police. He believed in the need for a 'vanguard party' of professional revolutionaries to lead the masses – who were deluded by agencies of capitalism into a 'false consciousness' – when the time came. There had to be rigid discipline and acceptance of the vanguard party's 'dictatorship of the proletariat' while it implemented socialism. Communists claimed that this was the transitional stage the USSR had achieved by the early 1920s, when Lenin died.

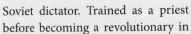

Joseph Stalin (1879–1953)

Soviet dictator. Trained as a priest before becoming a revolutionary in Georgia, Russia. Was secretary to Lenin's Communist Party and after his death deviously manipulated his enemies out of power while placing his own supporters in key positions. Became unchallenged dictator in 1930s and tried to neutralise Hitler by doing a deal with him. Hitler broke the agreement and attacked the USSR in 1941. After initial reverses the Soviets fought back under Stalin's leadership and defeated Hitler. Despite his brutal behaviour Stalin won friends on the left in Western countries, who persisted in believing his propaganda and seeing him as a force for progress.

Leon Trotsky (1879–1940) – advocate of 'worldwide revolution' – was Lenin's heir apparent, but the dogged, apparently unintellectual Joseph Stalin, Secretary of the Party, was cleverer than his brilliant colleague. He urged 'socialism in one country' rather than working for an unlikely international conflagration; he outmanoeuvred his rivals and plotted ruthlessly, succeeding in presenting Trotsky as a traitor to the revolution. Stalin eventually drove Trotsky into exile in Mexico, where his agents succeeded in assassinating him in 1940 (see Profile).

Stalin, by then, had become a brutal dictator, both paranoid and obsessed with power, claiming to be implementing **communism** but in reality imposing industrialisation, collective farming and his own tyrannical rule on a reluctant and starving peasantry. Anyone less than obsequiously worshipful of their leader was imprisoned, exiled or shot.

Overseas communist parties were employed essentially to assist the development of the 'home of socialism', and any deviation from the party line was punished by expulsion or worse. Critics argue that Marx might have analysed the workings of capitalism correctly, but failed to take account of the element in human nature, as exemplified so horrifyingly by Stalin, which yearns for power and is willing to use any means to achieve and retain it.

This is the legacy, despite its drawbacks, inherited by extreme left-wing parties in Britain. The Communist Party of Great Britain (CPGB) was founded in 1920 and became the willing tool of Moscow's message in this country, interpreting all the shifts in the official line and condemning anyone perceived as an enemy of the USSR. Members managed to survive the astonishing volte-face when Stalin ceased to oppose Hitler as first priority and signed a deal with him in 1939 to partition Poland. Once Hitler had invaded Soviet Russia in 1941, British communists breathed a sigh of relief; they were at last able to luxuriate in a vast amphitheatre of approving views as the whole country applauded the heroic Soviet effort. After the war, the party won two seats – Mile End and West Fife – but Stalin's expansion into eastern Europe, his blockade of Berlin in 1948 and the crushing (after his death) of the Hungarian rising in 1956 by the Soviet military machine, not to mention

Khrushchev's denunciation of Stalin in his secret speech to the 20th Party Congress, substantially disillusioned communists and Moscow 'fellow travellers' alike. The Cold War effectively ruined the chances of communist parties achieving power anywhere in Europe, and they began to wither and atrophy.

In the 1970s and 1980s opposition to communism in eastern Europe intensified, and the accession of the liberal Mikhail Gorbachev to power in Moscow was the signal for bloodless revolutions throughout the former communist bloc, with only China, Cuba, Vietnam and Laos being spared. The CPGB split into a hard-line, pro-Moscow rump and a liberal 'Euro-communist' wing, with the latter seizing control. It tried to transform itself into 'an open, democratic party of the new pluralistic and radical left'. In 1991 it ceased to be the CPGB and renamed itself the Democratic Left, though with little public support. Some of its former supporters, however, stuck with the party paper, *The Morning Star*, and founded the Communist Party of Britain – to little political effect: it has never fought a parliamentary election.

All this is not to say Marxism does not still influence the left; Marx's understanding of the capitalist system was too acute for that – but his prescription for the future was too vague and based upon faulty assumptions of human nature. As one wit once said: 'Marx was right about what was wrong, but wrong about what was right.'

PROFILE

Leon Trotsky (1879–1940)

Leon Trotsky was a Russian Jewish revolutionary politician born in the Ukraine. He was arrested for being a Marxist at the age of 19 but escaped from Siberia in 1902. After teaming up with Lenin, he became president of the first soviet in St Petersburg after the abortive 1905 revolution. He escaped to the West but returned to Russia in March 1917 to assist Lenin in organising the Bolshevik Revolution in November of the same year, leading the 5 million-strong Red Army in the ensuing civil war. A **charismatic** leader, Trotsky should have succeeded Lenin in 1924, but his theories of permanent world revolution were less well suited to the times than Stalin's pragmatic 'socialism in one country'. He was eventually exiled in 1929, being assassinated in Mexico with an ice pick in 1940 by an agent of Moscow. His ideas live on, but mostly on the radical intellectual fringe in developed countries.

Trotskyism

A number of Trotskyite bodies sprang up during and after Trotsky's lifetime, calling for worldwide revolution. Ted Grant, a South African, was involved with some of them, such as the Militant Labour League, in the 1930s. With Peter Taafe, Grant set up the *Militant* newspaper and adopted the tactic of 'entryism', the idea being to infiltrate members of a 'Militant Tendency' (notice only a 'tendency' and not a separate party, which would have breached Labour rules) into the decaying structure of the 1960s Labour Party. The idea then was to seize leadership at the grass-roots level and, in theory, the country once the time for revolution arrived. The Tendency virtually controlled Liverpool City Council in the 1980s, and two members, Dave Nellist and Terry Fields, were elected MPs, plus Pat Wall for Bradford in 1987 (died 1990). They advocated a number of radical measures, including nationalisation of the top 200 companies, extension of state control over the whole economy, workers' control in state-owned industries, nationalisation of the media, a slashing of defence spending, withdrawal from the EC and abolition of the House of Lords. In 1992 the Tendency expelled its guru Ted Grant, ending its policy of entryism; the movement gave way to Militant Labour, still attempting to influence the Labour Party, but most of the prominent members had faded away and the MPs not only lost their seats but were first expelled from the party. However, Militant MPs, while exercising little influence during their time in the Commons, did impress with their dedication, hard work and refusal to accept more salary for themselves than a skilled worker.

The Workers' Revolutionary Party

Another Trotskyist thread into the colourful tapestry of the far left was provided by 'The Club', a grouping, led by Gerry Healy, which left the Revolutionary Socialist Party in 1947 to infiltrate the Labour Party. Healy was soon expelled from Labour for his Trotskyite views, and put his energies into a new party to express and promote the views of his hero. The idea, as with all such parties, is to build up battle-hardened cadres to seize power when capitalism collapses, as it must. Its newspaper, *Newsline*, was rumoured in the seventies to be funded by Libya's Colonel Gaddafi. Membership was never high and suffered from Healy's imperious and eccentric leadership style, which led to the WRP actually splitting into two versions in the eighties and to his finally being deposed shortly afterwards. Celebrity members such as Vanessa Redgrave and her brother (the late) Corin, who stood as candidates in 1974 and 1979, gave the party a high media profile. The WRP still exists, led by Sheila Torrence, and still publishes *Newsline*.

The Socialist Workers' Party

Tony Cliff, who founded the Socialist Workers' Party, left the Labour Party at the beginning of the 1960s. His party has concentrated on international revolution, and international links are stressed. Paul Foot (1938–2004), nephew of Michael and a national columnist, was a high-profile and persuasive member. The SWP prints a newspaper, *Socialist Worker*, touted by young converts in many British cities and towns.

It was also behind the Anti-Nazi League, set up to fight the growth of European Nazism in the 1970s and then revived in 1992 after the rise of the BNP in Britain. These initiatives won an influx of new members; since that heyday it has shrunk, though it remains active in fighting its causes and supporting Respect (see page 106) in local elections.

The Socialist Labour Party

This was formed in 1996 by miners' leader Arthur Scargill following his failure to prevent the rewriting of Clause Four at Labour's conference in 1995. 'We recognise only two classes in society, both of which are recognised by their relationship to the means of production', he explained. 'Our problems are the result of a rotten capitalist system.' Accordingly, his party favours common ownership of the economy, full employment, a four-day week, a ban on non-essential overtime, retirement at 56, restoration of union rights, abolition of the monarchy, House of Lords and public schools, and withdrawal from the EU. Only 500 attended the launch in May 1996. Scargill fought for the seat of Newport East against Alan Howarth in 1997 and for Hartlepool against Peter Mandelson in 2001 but polled negligibly.

The Socialist Alliance

This was a novel 'umbrella' organisation of left-wing parties that fought the 2001 General Election. It was chaired by Dave Nellist, the former Militant MP, and its manifesto was both a scathing critique of New Labour as no better than Thatcherism and a hard-won (far-left groups find it hard to agree) common agenda for an 'alternative to the global, unregulated free market'. However, the results did not augur well for future growth and success. The candidates who stood received very low percentages of the vote and the Alliance seemed to have closed down in 2005, although its website promises it is 'coming back'.

BOX 6.7

The strange case of *Living Marxism*

This journal of the left appeared in the late 1960s but became the mouthpiece of the Revolutionary Communist Party (RCP) which sought to produce the familiar 'vanguard' of the masses. Once the Cold War ended in the early 1990s, LM became a voice of controversial ideas under the influence of sociology professor, Frank Furedi and former social worker, Clare Fox. Her Institute of Ideas complemented LM and sought to involve mainstream intellectuals in seminars and conferences. So, we see here an extreme left-wing faction, morphing into new forms and becoming a broader cultural movement which eventually, ironically, joined hands with US right-wing libertarian think tanks known as The Freedom Network. Trotsky would have been surprised.

Respect: The Unity Coalition

This body was set up in 2004 as a result of collaboration between George Galloway, the SWP and members of the Muslim Association of Britain to campaign principally against the ongoing war in Iraq. Galloway was formerly the talented but maverick MP for a Glasgow constituency, expelled from Labour in 2004 for calling on British troops to disobey orders. He fought a clever, though much criticised, campaign in Hackney and Bethnal Green against the sitting MP, Oona King, and won a sensational victory. Apart from its anti-war stance, Respect offered a left-wing socialist prospectus including the end of privatisation and 'the bringing back into democratic public ownership of the other public services'. In March 2012 Galloway won a sensational by-election in Bradford West; on 21 April on the BBC's *Week at Westminster*, Galloway confidently spoke of the possibility of a 'national nervous breakdown that might destroy the old parties', citing the fact that, since 1950, 30 per cent fewer voters opt for the two big parties and that PR voting in Scotland and Wales had made the smaller parties more visible.

Perhaps he spoke too soon: he was badly damaged by comments he made about rape in the context of the Julian Assange case in August 2012, following which Respect's leader, Salma Yaqoob, resigned.

John Callaghan, the authority on the far left, judges that 'far left politics is dying in its Leninist form and has moved into Green and anti-globalisation movements involving former militants from Muslim communities' (e-mail to author, 8 April 2006). But he makes a shrewd point when he points out that far-left politics often act as an apprenticeship for future mainstream politicians, citing Alan Milburn and Stephen Byers (former Trotskyists) and John Reid (former member of the CPGB).

Far right

Fascism

This set of ideas, developed by Benito Mussolini in the 1920s and supplemented by Adolf Hitler in the 1930s, was founded on xenophobic nationalism and total submission to the state. Democracy was scorned as the language of weakness and mediocrity; a one-party totalitarian state led by a charismatic leader was the preferred alternative. The leader and his team were seen as the result of an evolving process whereby the best people and ideas won through. It followed that the same thing happened when nations fought; war was the means whereby nations grew and developed. Hitler added a racial twist: the Aryans were the founding race of Europe, a race of conquerors, and the Germans their finest exemplars; all other races were inferior; the Jews in particu-

lar were lower than vermin and should therefore be cast out and possibly destroyed. In the stressful inter-war years, racked by economic depression and unemployment, these unwholesome ideas seemed attractive and full of hope to many who faced despair as their only alternative. It is emotionally satisfying perhaps to blame one's troubles on a single group in society, especially one that is quite easily recognisable physically and very successful economically and culturally. It has also to be said that such ideas flourished in the fertile soil of a German culture sympathetic to anti-semitism.

PROFILE

Adolf Hitler (1889–1945)

German dictator. Was originally an Austrian who tried to make a living as an artist. Fought in the First World War and set up the racist, expansionist Nazi movement in the 1920s. Came to power in the early 1930s and set about dominating Europe via threats, invasions and finally all-out war. In 1942 he dominated the continent, but his decision to invade Russia and to declare war on the USA eventually proved his downfall. Still retains his admirers on the political fringe.

In Britain, Sir Oswald Mosley founded a party that evolved into the British Union of Fascists (1932–43), offering himself as the strong charismatic national leader who would end the party bickering and lead the country into new successes. Mosley proposed that employers and workers should combine in the national interest and work in harmony; strikes and lock-outs should be banned; all major elements in the productive process should work together to plan the economy (corporatism). Moreover, he argued that the British Empire would provide all the things the country needed, and imports that could be made in Britain would be banned. Parliament and the old parties would be reformed and MPs would be elected according to occupational groups. Once elected, Parliament would pass on power to the leader to introduce the 'corporate state'. Parties and Parliament would be ended; everyone and everything would be 'subordinated to the national purpose'. Mosley's anti-semitism was disguised in Britain, but his coded references to 'alien influences' were clear enough to most Britons;

he favoured sending all the Jews in the world to a barren reservation. When it was revealed that Hitler's remedy to his self-invented 'Jewish problem' had been genocide of the most horrifying kind, a revulsion set in against fascist ideas. But they have proved unnervingly resilient and still appear in the present time in a different form.

The National Front

In 1967 the National Front (NF) was formed. Its central message was a racist one, warning against dilution of the British race via intermarriage with other races of different colour which it believed would produce an inferior breed of Briton. Repatriation of black Britons was the answer offered. At the level of theory, however, the Jews were offered as the main threats, being characterised as an international conspiracy to subvert Western economies and introduce communism before setting up a world government based in Israel. This side of the NF and its utter contempt for democracy was disguised in public expressions, but it exercised considerable appeal to young men with a taste for violence and racial hatred. It later changed its name to the National Democrats. In 1983 the 'New' NF – later the British National Party – was born; this is dedicated to infiltration and is more secretive, having many contacts with neo-Nazi groups abroad and many terrorist groups too. Football supporters are often infiltrated by NF members, and in 1994 a friendly football match between Ireland and England was abandoned following thuggish violence instigated by the NF. A related body called Combat 18 (the number in the name relates to the order in the alphabet of Hitler's initials: AH) openly supports Nazi ideas and embraces violence as a political method.

The British National Party

As previously, the General Election of May 1997 saw the usual multicoloured rainbow of fringe joke candidates. But for the far left and far right as well as the pranksters the result was widespread loss of deposits; voters may flirt with the fringe from time to time, but when the election arrives they revert, perhaps fortunately, to 'sensible' voting. In May 2002 the BNP won three council seats in Burnley – the biggest electoral victory for the far right in two decades. The party's new leader, Nick Griffin, with his articulate style and Cambridge education (see quotation from the *Observer* below), gave the party a credibility with arguments that exploited the feelings of poor indigenous voters that somehow immigrants were not only changing the nature of their localities but also receiving favoured treatment. This was argued with particular success in respect of asylum seekers, an issue much loved by the tabloids. These developments

worried the mainstream parties, which were keen to nip this electoral upturn in the bud.

A senior BNP figure explained the new tactics of the fringe party:

> The BNP has deliberately become increasingly sophisticated in the last few years to ensure ballot box success. . . . The irony is that it's New Labour who have shown us how to do it; we learnt from them that a party could change without losing its support base. New Labour dropped Old Labour in much the same way as we've moved on from the so-called 'skinhead' era. We realized that the type of recruit we needed in the modern world was completely different to the sort we needed when we were engaging in street level activity.
>
> (Kevin Scott, North-East Director BNP, quoted in the *Observer*, 20 April 2003)

The same issue of the *Observer* also published the facts that 13 of the BNP's 28 regional directors or branch organisers in 2002 had criminal records for offences that included assault, theft, fraud, racist abuse and possession of drugs and weapons. In 2004 a BBC undercover reporter recorded a speech in Keighley by Nick Griffin in which he said:

> These 18-, 19- and 25-year-old Asian Muslims are seducing and raping white girls in this town right now . . . It's part of their plan for conquering countries. They will expand into the rest of the UK as the last Whites try and find their way to the sea. Vote BNP so the British people really realize the evil of what these people have done to our country.

This speech, and a similar one by a former Leeds City Council candidate, faced charges of behaviour likely to incite racial hatred in January 2006, but both defendants were sensationally acquitted when the cases came to court in 2006.

The BNP sought to make 2009 a 'breakthrough year' for the far right. Immigration issues still rankled among those made unemployed by the recession of that year, and the BNP benefited from the widespread backlash of distrust of politics. In the Euro-elections of June Labour came third behind UKIP, but more worrying for many in the party was the fact that the lower turnout in the North-west had enabled the BNP to win two MEPs and therefore take a place of sorts on the national stage, rather than occupying its usual fringe position.

Following this, the BBC felt obliged to invite the BNP leader Nick Griffin to participate in *Question Time*, the popular BBC show which provides something of a national showcase for different political viewpoints. The decision was fiercely contested by the likes of Peter Hain who claimed a

BNP leader Nick Griffin celebrates his 2009 election as one of eight MEPs (Members of the European Parliament) for the North-west of England

Source: Getty Images/AFP.

The reason why the EDL's adoption of Islamophobia is particularly significant is that unlike the 1970s, when the National Front was embracing antisemitism, there are now sections of the media and the British establishment that are relatively sympathetic towards Islamophobia. It is not difficult to look through the media and find quite hostile views towards Islam and Muslims. That is fundamentally different to the 1970s, when very few newspapers or politicians were endorsing the NF's antisemitic message.

(*Guardian*, 28 May 2010)

British Freedom Party

Founded in October 2010 and attracting members from the EDL and the BNP, its chairman is Paul Weston, who toured the USA in 2011. So far its activities seem to have been below the radar of the mainstream media.

English Democrats

This party was formed by Robin Tilbrook in 2002, from a number of smaller parties and factions. Despite its right-wing sounding name it seems to be more a 'nationalist' party focused on reforming the constitution so that England as an entity is better represented with its own distinctive parliament. So far it has not made much impression electorally but did flag up 7.2 per cent of the vote in the Haltemprice and Howden by-election in 2008.

Radical Islam

This branch of 'fringe' thinking has come into sharp focus since 9/11 and the 7/7 bombings in London. Radical Islam sees it as the will of Allah to establish a world caliphate, to convert unbelievers either by persuasion or force. While such ideas seem to find little purchase in the USA, the 7/7 bombers were all second-generation immigrants to Britain from the Leeds area and ostensibly seemed well-integrated into British society. It seems economically deprived areas of immigrant settlement nourish radicalism with converts – like the Shoe Bomber, Richard Reid – particularly likely to take the extremist road.

Al Muhajiroun was a 1986 group led by Omar Bakri Muhammad which praised the 9/11 attacks and was banned under the 2006 Terrorism Act with Bakri expelled from the UK; however, it is believed the also banned *Saviour Sect* is essentially a reformed version of *al Muhajiroun*. Abu Hamza al-Masri, a convicted terrorist, founded the Islamic Council of Britain, 11 September 2002, with the goal of 'implementing sharia law in Britain'. Other radical groups often are UK branches of transnational Islamic bodies like *Hizb ut-Tahrir*,

'clueless BBC is giving the BNP the legitimacy it craves' and quoted Griffin's own claim that his party aimed to 'defend rights for Whites with well-directed boots and fists'.

Nevertheless, it is hard to deny the BBC were acting within the democratic traditions of the country. In the event, the programme, on 22 October 2009, provoked much interest. Griffin was attacked by panel members (including Jack Straw and Chris Huhne) and the audience, and was generally felt to have been exposed as a incoherent, second-rate politician. But his party had received a major publicity boost though to no discernible electoral advantage.

English Defence League (EDL)

The EDL originated from a group in Luton responding in March 2009, to an Islamic Al Muhalajiroun demonstration against Royal Anglian Regiment troops returning from the Afghan War. Membership or branch numbers are not known, though EDL organisers claim 100,000 members; figures closer to a quarter of that number might be more realistic. The group is allegedly dedicated to peaceful demonstrations, but its clashes with far-left groups have been anything but, as is proved by the violence between EDL supporters and Asian and Black groups in Leicester in October 2010. As the EDL has become a familiar element of the far right, violence has broken out at events in various parts of the country, including Stoke on Trent in January 2010 and Dudley in July of the same year.

It is significant that Islamophobia is the main thrust of EDL thinking. Mathew Goodwin, academic expert on the far right comments:

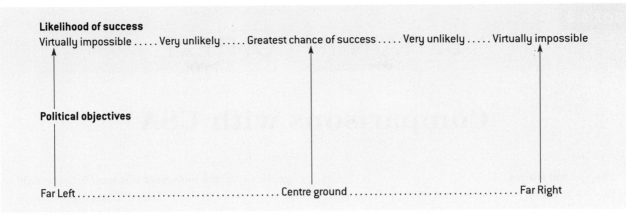

Figure 6.2 The art of the possible

an ostensibly peaceful grouping which some have claimed is a breeding ground for those who go on to adopt more extremist convictions.

The art of the possible

Politicians on the fringe have made a conscious or unconscious decision regarding the 'art of the possible', Bismarck's acute definition of politics. As Figure 6.2 illustrates, political objectives on the extremes have little chance of success; the best chances exist in the political centre. It is the big mainstream parties that tend to set the agenda and to go on to successfully achieve the items on it. Changing Labour's Clause Four on common ownership was held to be beyond the art of the possible for a long time after Gaitskell's attempt failed in the late 1950s. Later, Callaghan referred to the issue as 'theological', but Blair decided that such a change was necessary to convince the public that Labour was no longer dangerously radical. His brilliant campaign in 1994 to change the clause to some extent redefined the art of the possible (Figure 6.2) in the Labour Party. Items on the far left or right are either unattainable or achievable only if circumstances change radically and, usually, rapidly. Voting studies show that the majority of people regard themselves as occupying the 'centre ground' in politics, and those parties which successfully compete for its control usually go on to win elections.

Parties on the fringe have two possible strategies to pursue. First, they can eschew any real chance of winning power and seek merely to change the hearts and minds of citizens to provide the context in which radical change can occur. Early socialists performed this role effectively until the creed became a credible alternative in the mid-twentieth century. Even so, it took over 100 years for socialism to win an electoral victory in Britain, so activists of this type have

to be genuinely dedicated to change in the future; few are so patient. Alternatively, the less patient can seek to short-circuit the normal process of propagandising and winning over opinions by manipulating the democratic process. The really extreme activists on the right and left seek to set a revolutionary set of events in train and to seize power rather as the Bolsheviks did in Russia in 1917. As people usually need a substantial period to change their minds completely, this strategy usually requires the use of force, with all its attendant unpredictability and dangers. The early British communists and the Militants sought to reach the same objective through 'entryism': to drive their Trojan horse into a big party, Labour, and to win power through subterfuge. Seemingly underhand, this is not too disreputable a strategy given that the right-wing Conservatives led by Thatcher in the 1970s managed to achieve something similar by using the democratic machinery and then steering the party in a radical direction. Left-wing Labour tried a similar exercise in the early 1980s but was rebuffed so sharply by the electorate in 1983 that it left the way open for New Labour, maestros of the centre ground. So, the late radical socialist journalist Paul Foot sought to pursue the 'long haul' route of gradually changing social attitudes through education and exhortation. His uncle, Michael, also a fiery left-winger in his youth, decided to compromise and became a mainstream politician in the 1970s with a seat in the Cabinet and later a period as party leader. Time alone will tell how successful the agitators of the present will prove in the future, though those who articulate a 'green' perspective have seen their ideas move rapidly from the extreme left to somewhere much closer to the centre ground in a matter of only two to three decades. Moreover, in the local and devolved assembly elections votes are often cast for parties on the political fringe, provoking the thought that maybe some of those groups on the fringe are destined in the near future to join the mainstream.

BOX 6.8

BRITAIN IN CONTEXT

Comparisons with USA

Themes and fringes

Box 5.4 in the last chapter focused on the political spectrum, my case being that in the USA it is not especially wide with very little support for left-of-centre positions. However, this should not be taken to imply that there are no groups occupying positions substantially to the left and right. Far from it.

The Socialist Party of America was born at the turn of the nineteenth century. Its leader, Eugene Debs, not only went to jail for his beliefs but stood for President on more than one occasion, yet never quite managed to poll a million votes. He was succeeded by Norman Thomas, a graduate of Princeton and a lay minister who also stood for the highest office, but did no better than Debs in the end.

During the 1930s Roosevelt's New Deal, with its extensive government intervention in the economy, was implicitly socialist, but after the Second World War the backlash began with any left-wing idea being associated with communism and 'un-American' activities. The resultant McCarthyite witch hunts of the 1950s further weakened the left, but the socialist tradition survives in the form of The Socialist Party of the USA – not a major force, with affiliates in only 18 states. The Communist Party of the USA is even smaller and more ineffective. But there is, at the present time, the Progressive Coalition of House of Representatives members, numbering about 60, who subscribe to a socialistic set of ideas. However, the only real force on the left is the Democratic Party, and this tends to deter those tending to the left from switching support to a small party with no chance of achieving power. Almost certainly, however, the groups on the far right are more powerful than those on the left. The extraordinary rise of the Tea Party within the context of the Republican Party galvanised the American right shortly after Obama's election in 2008. Led by the likes of Sarah Palin and Glen Beck, the *Fox News* presenter, the grouping led a ferocious attack upon Obama and his party, focusing not just on taxes but on opposition to immigrants, legalised abortion and the idea of gay marriage. However, the movement was too far to the right and its influence probably helped Obama to overcome the appeal of the Republican candidate in November 2012, Mitt Romney.

One variety of socialism, the National Socialist Movement (NSM), is in fact on the far right, being admirers of Nazi Germany and the policies of Hitler. But the main blanket term for the far right is the 'Patriot Movement'. This takes in the militias which operate in well over half of the states together with the rifle clubs and survivalist clubs. These groups, many of them steeped in ultra-nationalism and anti-semitism, were influential in motivating John McVeigh, the Oklahoma Bomber. The worrying aspect of such right-wing groupings is that they reject the *legitimacy* of government, its right to issue laws and levy taxes. Similarly, groups representing the Afro-American minority in the 1960s and 1970s, like the Black Panthers and the Weathermen, refused to accept government authority and were prepared to use violence as a method.

Another characteristic of US society not reflected to the same degree in the UK is the 'culture wars' within it. Here we see groups who believe that a changing society which includes a large number of single-parent families, a variety of races and people of contrasting sexual preferences requires a more liberal and flexible set of values, especially towards sexuality and abortion. Other groups, however, often motivated by religious convictions, hotly resist such a move and are determined, for example, to reverse the Supreme Court ruling which makes abortion legal.

Often supported by their churches, a large section of American society feel that family values are under severe attack and need to be defended against the compromised attitudes of current urban life, reinforced by the media and popular music. Almost 40 per cent of Americans regularly attend church and, under George W. Bush, such leanings have acquired political significance. In Britain only about 5 per cent of people attend church and religion generally has scant infiuence.

Chapter summary

Feminism is concerned with the unequal position of women in society and falls into liberal, socialist and radical categories. Nationalism emerged in the nineteenth century and, while it is now contested by internationalism, still retains much of its destructive force. Green thinking applies environmentalism to politics, calling for a revolutionary change in the way developed societies live. Far-left fringe groups tend to draw on the ideas of Marx and Trotsky; their relevance has declined since the anti-communist revolutions, but many followers still keep up the struggle. Far-right groups tend to be neo-fascist and racialist; their support is small but their influence subversive.

Discussion points

- Has feminism achieved any major victories, and if so what are they?
- What problems are there in defining the British identity?
- Is nationalism more dangerous than terrorism?
- What chance is there of the Greens ever winning power in the UK?
- Why do you think people join fringe political groups?

Further reading

Lovenduski and Randall (1993) is a thorough review of feminism in Britain; the political ideas books by Adams (1993) and Heywood (1992) have good sections on nationalism; and Dobson (1990) and Porritt (1984) are good on ecology. An excellent study of totalitarianism is Arendt (1951). On fascism, also recommended is Cheles et al. (1991); Thurlow (1986) is a history of British fascism to the present day. For the anatomy of the far right see Matthew Goodwin's (2011) *New British Fascism: Rise of the British National Party: The Rise of the British National Party (BNP)* (Extremism and Democracy).

Bibliography

Adams, I. (1993) *Political Ideology Today* (Manchester University Press).

Adams, I. (1998) *Ideology and Politics in Britain Today* (Manchester University Press).

Arendt, H. (1951) *The Origins of Totalitarianism* (Allen and Unwin).

Bentley, R., Dorey, P. and Roberts, D. (2003) *British Politics Update 1999–2002* (Causeway Press).

Brownmiller, S. (1975) *Against our Will: Men, Women and Rape* (Simon and Schuster).

Bryson, V. (2003) 'Feminist debates, ideology: feminism', *Politics Review*, Vol. 12, No. 4, April 2003.

Callaghan, J. (1987) *The Far Left in British Politics* (Blackwell).

Cheles, L., Ferguson, M. and Wright, P. (1991) *Neo-Fascism in Europe* (Longman).

Colley, L. (2005) *Britons: Forging the Nation 1707–1837* (Yale University Press).

de Beauvoir, S. (1968) *The Second Sex* (Bantam; first published 1952).

Dobson, A. (1990) *Green Political Thought* (Unwin Hyman).

Dowds, M. and Young, J. (1996) *13th British Social Attitudes Survey* (SPCR).

Engels, F. (2010) *The Origin of the Family, Private Property and the State* (Penguin Classics; first published 1884).

Equal Opportunities Commission (2006) *Sex and Power: Who Runs Britain? 2006* (Equal Opportunities Commission).

Ferguson, N. (2003) *Empire* (Allen Lane).

Firestone, S. (1980) *The Dialectic of Sex* (Women's Press).

Friedan, B. (1963) *The Feminine Mystique* (Norton).

Friedan, B. (1982) *The Second Stage* (Norton).

Gamble, A. (2003) *Between Europe and America* (Palgrave).

Giddens, A. (1998) *The Third Way* (Polity).

Goodwin, M. (2011) *New British Fascism: Rise of the British National Party* (Routledge).

Greer, G. (1971) *The Female Eunuch* (Granada).

Greer, G. (1985) *Sex and Destiny* (Harper and Row).

Heywood, A. (1992) *Political Ideologies* (Macmillan).

House of Commons Library (2012) *Women in Public Life, the Professions and the Boardroom*, 9 March.

Hussein, E. (2007) *The Islamist* (Penguin).

Intergovernmental Panel on Climate Change (IPCC) (2001) *Climate Change 2001* (United Nations).

Institute of Public Policy Research (IPPR) (2012) *The Dog that Finally Barked*, January.

Lovenduski, J. and Norris, P. (2003) 'Westminster women: the politics of presence', *Political Studies*, Vol. 51, No. 1, March.

Lovenduski, J. and Randall, V. (1993) *Contemporary Feminist Politics* (Oxford University Press).

Marcuse, H. (1964) *One Dimensional Man* (Beacon).

Marcuse, H. (1969a) *An Essay on Liberation* (Penguin).

Marcuse, H. (1969b) *Eros and Civilisation* (Sphere).

Millett, K. (1969) *Sexual Politics* (Granada).

Nozick, R. (1974) *Anarchy, State and Utopia* (Blackwell).

Paglia, C. (2006) *Break, Blow, Burn* (Vintage).

Porritt, J. (1984) *Seeing Green* (Blackwell).

Reid, J.R. (2004) *The United States of Europe* (Penguin).

Thurlow, R. (1986) *Fascism in Britain* (Blackwell).

Wolf, A. (2006) 'Working girls', *Prospect*, April.

Wollstonecraft, M.A. (1967) *A Vindication of the Rights of Women* (Norton; originally published 1792).

Useful websites

Anti-Nazi League: www.anl.org.uk/campaigns.html

Green Party: www.greenparty.org.uk

National Democrats:
www.netlink.co.uk/users/natdems/

Searchlight Magazine:
www.searchlightmagazine.com/default.asp

Socialist Alliance: www.socialistalliance.net

Socialist Workers' Party: www.swp.org.uk

Workers' Revolutionary Party: www.wrp.org.uk

Women's Resource Centre: http://www.wrc.org.uk/

The declining reach of the mainstream media

Every few years a scandal erupts in British public life – and an inquiry is set up under a judge, a professor or retired civil servant at which the failings of those in responsible positions are revealed. Shock and horror and much hand-wringing follows. The authorities are usually found to have been negligent, complacent and say they have already taken steps to ensure that it will never happen again. The list of inquiries – Lynskey, Franks, Cullen, May, Saville, Laming Anderson, Hutton, and Chilcot – provides footnotes to British political history. The names are remembered even when the details have been forgotten.

However, few have been as spectacular, revealing, and occasionally lurid as the inquiry into 'the culture, practices and ethics of the press' under Lord Justice Leveson which held public hearings from November 2011 until mid-2012. The inquiry was set up in July 2011 by David Cameron following the outcry over the allegations of phone hacking by the *News of the World* and of illicit payments by the press to the police. Because of a large number of arrests and later criminal charges relating both to phone hacking and payments to the police and public authorities, Lord Leveson had concentrated on: 'the culture, practices, and ethics of the press, including contacts between the press and politicians and the press and the public; to consider the extent to which the current regulatory regime has failed and whether there has been a failure to action upon any previous warnings about media misconduct'.

There are varying models of inquiry – from groups of privy counsellors (generally to look at matters involving intelligence), via one-offs under a retired public servant, to formal judicial inquiries. Leveson was established under the Inquiries Act 2005 which adopts court-like procedures including the use of barristers to question, and the designation of core participants entitled to formal legal representation. These included media organisations, the police, and victims of media intrusion.

The hearings were divided into four modules: the press and the public; the press and the police; the press and politicians; and the future, including possible regulatory changes. Overall, 184 witnesses appeared. It was a roll-call of the celebrity, media, police and political worlds (I gave evidence on politicians relations with the press, based on my long experience as a political correspondent and commentator).

The inquiry was criticised by many in the media for being a show trial, while Michael Gove, the Education Secretary, and a former journalist himself, warned that the proceedings were having a 'chilling effect' on free speech. Some newspapers were said to be holding back on some stories, and the way they were treated, while the inquiry was under way. Moreover, Lord Leveson was accused of being naïve about the way the press worked. Many newspaper groups argued that they themselves were innocent of phone hacking and other dubious or illegal practices and sought to isolate News International, the owner of the *News of the World* before its closure in July 2011, which was getting most of the criticism.

The public hearings were revealing at several levels. First, within the constraints of multiple police arrests, and then charges, there were the allegations about the bad, even illegal, practice of parts of the media. Several victims described their anger and bitterness at being violated by phone hacking and other intrusions into family tragedies. It was a pretty black picture. These disclosures contrasted with the claims of newspaper witnesses who insisted, in classic fashion for such inquiries, that any errors were the work of a minority, that improvements had already been made and that standards were, anyway, getting better. However, the impression of respectability and high standards was undermined by candid witnesses, from former *News of the World* reporters to a media proprietor such as Richard Desmond who said he did not know what the word 'ethical' meant.

Second, the inquiry highlighted the very close relationships between certain, mainly tabloid, papers, and the police – some now subject to criminal investigations but others involving a blurring of ethical boundaries between journalists and contacts, especially those employed by the state.

Third, and most damaging for politicians, the evidence revealed how close many prominent Conservative and Labour figures were to Rupert Murdoch and his senior team at News International. There were frequent social contacts. Most famously David Cameron had 'country suppers' in Oxfordshire with Rebekah Brooks, the former chief executive of News International, and exchanged text messages with her, ending 'DC LOL'. Tony Blair and Gordon Brown had also had close contacts with News International executives and logs were released of meetings between senior ministers and media executives.

So, apart from the various allegations of criminal wrongdoing, the Leveson inquiry triggered a bout both of soul-searching and of self-righteousness by the media. As in many other parts of public life, when a stone is lifted on previously hidden behavior, the revelations can be unsavoury. Yet, as I argued in my book, *In Defence of Politicians – in spite of themselves* (Biteback, 2011): 'Politicians and the media are locked in an embrace of mutual dependency, occasional friendship, frequent suspicion and barely hidden bitterness and scorn.' They cannot live without each other but the relationship will always be tense, and often abusive.

There is a barely disguised contempt on both sides. The media, and particularly, but not exclusively the tabloid papers, often treat politicians as being inherently on the make, and the take. There is frequently no attempt to differentiate between what is in the public interest and what is essentially private, even though it may interest the public. Coverage of government is often either narrowly partisan and fails to appreciate the hard choices facing ministers, whichever party is in office. There is a blame culture which fails to take account of the inherent risks faced by any decision-maker.

The resentment was summed up by Tony Blair in one of his valedictory speeches as Prime Minister shortly before he left office in June 2007, when he described parts of the media as like a 'feral beast'. His argument – reflected in much of the argument surrounding Leveson – was that the press has put scandal, sensation and division ahead of straight reporting – though what is straight often lies in the eye of the reader.

There is something in these charges – too much for the comfort of many journalists. But a robust, inquisitive press is vital to holding to account politicians and others in power. There is plenty to be exposed and challenged. And regulation always includes the threat that investigation will be suppressed. Yet many tabloid exposures – including those involving questionable or even illegal techniques – are not about major public issues or scandals but about the private lives of celebrities. Most of the press witnesses

defined free speech as an absolute. But other witnesses argued that there were other interests to be taken into consideration. Moreover, free speech is for individuals not institutions. Lord Leveson himself was concerned that any new regulator should not only be independent of the government and of Parliament but also of the press.

The underlying assumption in this debate is that the press matters. It is not just proprietors, editors and columnists who behave as if they are vitally important defenders of freedom and arbiters of the direction of Britain. So too often do politicians themselves. They increasingly see themselves as the weaker half of the relationship and assiduously court media potentates as well as working journalists. Ministers pretend to be interested in the papers' leaders and editors' opinions, in many cases in my experience often ill-informed.

Both sides exaggerate the influence of newspapers enormously, and, to some extent, of television. For all the claims by the *Sun* to have 'won' the 1992 election for the Tories, there is little evidence to back this up. More persuasively, newspapers, particularly tabloids, follow their readers rather than lead them. Their influence is greater, cumulatively, on issues and in shaping political attitudes; for instance, on Europe, immigration and towards recipients of welfare payments. The most revealing trend is, however, the decline in sales of newspapers, by more than a fifth between 2004 and 2010 with sales of some of the tabloids down by much more. The number of viewers of the main BBC and ITV evening news bulletins has dropped by more than a half. The huge growth in the number of television outlets; the ability to watch any programme when you want to do so; the arrival of DVDs; and, above all, the development of the internet, blogging, tweets and social networking in all its forms have transformed the way people receive information. Of course, some of the most successful websites are run by conventional media groups. But the relationship between politicians and the media has changed fundamentally. There is no longer a national conversation with people watching the same programmes and reading the same papers. In that respect, the Leveson inquiry had been looking at the abuses and behaviour of established media which are growing less influential by the day.

by Peter Ridell

← WAY IN

POLLING

STATION

PART 3

THE REPRESENTATIVE PROCESS

CHAPTER 7

Elections and voting

David Denver

> " Elections rule the political process but not the government's policy. They decide who rules; they do not rule themselves "
>
> Ian Gilmour, 1971: 136

Learning objectives

- To understand the purposes and importance of elections in Britain.

- To be aware of the variety of electoral systems in use in the UK.

- To have a grasp of how and why turnout has varied over time, from place to place and from individual to individual.

- To be aware of how and why support for different parties has varied over time, from place to place and from individual to individual.

It almost goes without saying that general elections are major events in the political life of the United Kingdom, giving rise to greatly increased political activity, discussion, interest and media coverage. For about a month before polling day the campaign dominates news coverage in the mass media – almost to the point of saturation. Day by day the activities of the party leaders are reported, opinion polls charted, individual constituencies analysed, policies dissected and so on. In 2010, for the first time, the campaign featured live televised debates involving the leaders of the three major parties and these attracted large audiences – 9.6 million viewed the first, 4.2 million the second (broadcast on Sky) and 8.6 million the third. On election night itself the main television channels and radio stations provide special all-night programmes to report, analyse and discuss the results and, next day, the front pages of all newspapers worthy of the name are entirely devoted to election news. By the time a general election is over there must be very few people in the country unaware that something important has been going on.

Elections in Britain are not confined to choosing Members of Parliament (and hence a government), however. In addition, there are elections in Scotland, Wales and Northern Ireland for devolved legislatures, local elections across the whole country for councils and mayors, and also elections to the European Parliament. Although none of these generates the intensity of coverage or the level of excitement and interest among the electorate that general elections do – with European elections coming bottom of the list in this respect – they all attract considerable media coverage and involve many thousands of people in campaigning and standing for office. Millions of citizens make the effort to vote in them.

What, the naïve might ask, is all the fuss about? The answer is, of course, that elections are important. In the first place, they are central to democratic political systems. It is through elections that citizens participate directly in the political process and, by electing representatives, the people ultimately determine the personnel and policies of governments. Only a government which is elected by the people is a legitimate government and elections are the mechanisms by which governments are held accountable. At least once every five years general elections enable the people to pass judgement on the performance of the incumbent government and vote either to keep it in office or 'throw the rascals out'. In short, it is the existence of free, competitive elections which distinguishes political systems that we normally call 'democratic' from others.

Second, despite the cautionary note sounded by Ian Gilmour (a former Conservative MP, Cabinet minister, thinker and author who died in 2007) in his comment quoted on the title page of this chapter, elections are important because they make a difference to the policies pursued by governments and hence to the lives of most people. Exactly how and how much elections affect what governments do is a matter of some debate. Voters themselves disagree about how much difference it makes when one party rather than another wins an election, and it is certainly true that governments of any party are constrained by external events over which they have little control. It is obvious, also, that local and European Parliament elections make much less difference than general elections. It is clear, however, that the results of general elections (and also elections to the devolved legislatures) significantly affect what happens subsequently. Indeed, elections are so central to politics that, as David Butler (1998: 454) observed, 'History used to be marked off by the dates of kings . . . Now it is marked by the dates of [general] elections.'

Electoral systems

Elections, then, enable individual citizens to participate directly in politics by choosing representatives at various levels. Voters will have different preferences, of course, and so there has to be an agreed mechanism whereby individual choices are aggregated in order to arrive at a result. In other words, elections involve a particular **electoral system**.

Until fairly recently, almost all public elections in the UK were conducted under what is formally known as the single member, simple plurality system (SMSP). Each electoral district (constituency) has a single representative, and he or she wins by virtue of getting most votes (a simple **plurality**) in the area concerned. This is more commonly known – in an analogy with horse-racing – as the **first-past-the-post system** (FPTP). For a candidate to get past the winning post he or she needs to get more votes than any other candidate – even if it is only one vote more – whether or not this represents a majority of those who voted. Indeed, in the 2010 General Election only just over a third of MPs elected obtained a majority of votes in their constituencies and in Norwich South the successful Liberal Democrat won less that 30 per cent of the votes cast.

For various reasons, however, assorted other electoral systems have been introduced in recent years. The reasons include trying to bolster popular support for devolution in Scotland and Wales; ensuring representation for the different communities in Northern Ireland; complying with European Union regulations; and keeping the Liberal Democrats in a governing coalition with Labour in Scotland. The effect is that the former **hegemony** of FPTP has long gone and the UK has become a veritable laboratory for anyone interested in the operation and impact of different electoral systems. Those currently in use are listed in Table 7.1 and briefly explained in Box 7.1.

Table 7.1 Electoral systems in the UK

System	Body elected
Single member, simple plurality (First-past-the-post)	House of Commons Some English/Welsh local authorities
Multi-member, simple plurality	Some English/Welsh local authorities
Additional member system (aka Mixed member proportional)	Scottish Parliament Welsh Assembly London Assembly
Single transferable vote	Northern Ireland Assembly All Scottish councils
Regional party (closed) lists	European Parliament
Supplementary vote	Mayors in England

There is an extensive literature on the properties and effects of different electoral systems and considerable debate among enthusiasts about the various alleged good and bad points of each (see, for example, Farrell 2001). Unusually, this debate reached the public realm in 2011 when there was a referendum on whether the method of electing the House of Commons should change from FPTP to the alternative vote (AV) method. In the event, the electorate gave AV a massive thumbs down, by 68 per cent to 32 per cent and, in the process, probably ensured that no further attempt will be made to move away from FPTP for many years to come.

This is not the place to examine the pros and cons of different electoral systems. It is important to note, however,

BOX 7.1

Electoral systems

Under the **additional member** (or **mixed member proportional**) **system**, voters have two votes. One is used to choose a constituency representative (on the basis of first-past-the-post in the UK case) while the other is cast for a party list (within regions in the cases of Scotland and Wales). The list votes are used to 'top up' those elected in constituencies so that the distribution of representatives across parties within the relevant area is broadly proportional to the share of list votes received. Generally, this means that no single party is able to win a majority of seats but in the Scottish Parliament election of 2011 the SNP defied the odds by winning 69 of the 129 seats (53 constituencies and 16 list seats).

The single transferable vote (STV) requires multi-member electoral districts. In Scotland, for example, all local council wards elect three or four councillors. Voters list their choices in order of preference (using as few or as many choices as they please). To be elected, a candidate needs to reach a specified quota of votes (the total number of valid votes divided by the number of seats at stake plus one, all plus one). If no candidate reaches the quota then the votes of the bottom candidate are re-allocated on the basis of second preferences. Similarly 'surplus' votes are re-allocated when a candidate exceeds the quota. The system produces proportional outcomes, which makes it difficult for a single party to win a majority of seats. Of the 32 Scottish councils only two had a single party in control following the first STV elections in 2007.

A **regional party list system** is used for European Parliament elections in the UK (except in Northern Ireland where STV is employed). The regions elect a number of members (ranging in 2009 from 3 in the North-east to 10 in the South-east). The parties put forward a list of candidates and voters vote for one list or another. The list is 'closed' in the sense that voters cannot opt for individuals within the lists, just the list as a whole. The party winning the most votes gets the first seat and its vote total is then divided by two. The party which then has the most votes gets the next seat and its vote is divided by two. This process continues with the divisor being increased by one every time a party wins a seat until all the seats are allocated. The system produces broadly proportional results within regions.

The **supplementary vote system** allows voters to indicate a first and second choice among candidates. If no candidate has a majority (more than 50 per cent) of first preferences then all but the top two candidates drop out and their votes are transferred on the basis of second preferences (if these are for one of the top two). In the election for London mayor in 2008, for example, Boris Johnson had 42.5 per cent of first preference votes but when the second preferences of those who dropped out were transferred he had 53.2 per cent and was elected.

The **alternative vote system**, which was the subject of a nationwide referendum in May 2011, is based on single member constituencies. Rather than plumping for one candidate, as in first-past-the-post, however, voters indicate an order of preference. A candidate obtaining more than 50 per cent of first preferences is elected. Otherwise, the last-placed candidate drops out and his or her votes re-allocated among the rest on the basis of second preferences. This continues until a candidate has more than 50 per cent of votes.

that there is no 'ideal' system. A preference for one sort or another ultimately comes down to making value judgements about what we want a system to achieve. Is it important to ensure fair representation of parties or is it better to have a system that increases the likelihood of a single-party majority government, which can be clearly held accountable by the people? Is the link between individual MPs and constituencies something worth preserving? Should voters be able to discriminate among candidates of the same party or should parties determine the order in which their candidates should be elected? These and other questions raise issues about which people will disagree and hence they will have different views about which electoral system is 'best'.

Electoral trends

In looking at election results in the UK, psephologists (specialists in electoral analysis) are usually interested in three features: the level of turnout (the percentage of the eligible electorate which turns out to vote), the level of support for the various parties and the resultant make-up of the body concerned in party terms. The first two of these have both temporal and spatial dimensions – that is, they vary over time and across different areas of the country. In this section patterns of change over the past 50 years or so are considered.

Percentage turnout figures for general elections between 1964 and 2010 are given in Table 7.2 and illustrated in Figure 7.1. From the 1964 election to 1997 turnout was always more than 70 per cent and fluctuated within a relatively narrow range. Although there was a tendency for more people to vote when a close contest was expected and

Table 7.2 Turnout (%) in general elections, 1964–2010

1964	77.1	1987	75.3
1966	75.8	1992	77.7
1970	72.0	1997	71.4
1974 (Feb)	78.8	2001	59.4
1974 (Oct)	72.8	2005	61.4
1979	76.0	2010	65.8
1983	72.7		

fewer when the result seemed a foregone conclusion, to a considerable extent these fluctuations appear to be almost random. In 2001, however, turnout dropped sharply to 59.4 per cent and recovered only slightly in 2005. Although easy Labour victories were expected in these elections, this is not enough to explain the very low level of participation. In 2010 a much closer contest was in prospect and turnout increased significantly. Nonetheless, it remained markedly lower than was normal before the turn of the century. Possible explanations for this change will be discussed below.

Summary statistics for party vote shares in the same elections are given in Table 7.3 and illustrated in Figure 7.2. Perhaps the most striking development over the period is the increased fragmentation of party support. In the 1960s the Conservatives and Labour utterly dominated elections, together winning almost 90 per cent of votes. Thereafter, the political centre (initially the Liberal Party, which later formed the 'Alliance' with the Social Democratic Party and later still became the Liberal Democrats) figured more prominently while support for 'Others' (including the SNP in Scotland, Plaid Cymru in Wales, UKIP, the BNP and the Green Party) also became more significant. By 2010 the two major parties could muster only 65 per cent of votes

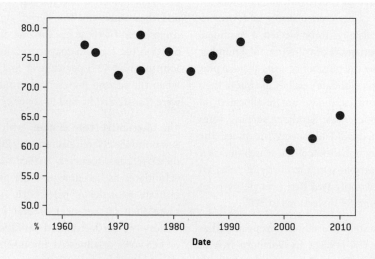

Figure 7.1 UK turnout in general elections, 1964–2010

Table 7.3 Party shares of votes in general elections, 1964–2010

	1964 %	1966 %	1970 %	Feb. 1974 %	Oct. 1974 %	1979 %	
Conservative	43.4	41.9	46.4	37.9	35.8	43.9	
Labour	44.1	48.0	43.1	37.2	39.3	36.9	
Liberal	11.2	8.5	7.5	19.3	18.3	13.8	
Others	1.3	1.6	3.0	5.6	6.6	5.4	
	1983 %	1987 %	1992 %	1997 %	2001 %	2005 %	2010 %
Conservative	42.4	42.3	41.9	30.7	31.7	32.4	36.1
Labour	27.6	30.8	34.4	43.2	40.7	35.2	29.0
Liberal Democrats	25.4	22.6	17.8	16.8	18.3	22.0	23.0
Others	4.6	4.3	5.9	9.3	9.3	10.4	11.9

Notes: The figures for the Liberal Democrats in 1983 and 1987 are for the 'Alliance' between the Liberals and the Social Democratic Party (SDP).

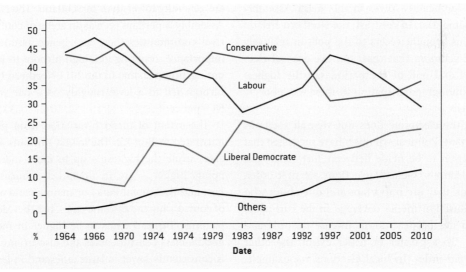

Figure 7.2 Party shares of vote in UK general elections, 1964–2010

between them. Britain used to be the archetypal two-party system; in the twenty-first century such a description is clearly inadequate. This conclusion is reinforced if elections other than general elections are considered. In the European Parliament elections of 2009, for example, of the 69 seats at stake in Britain 13 were taken by UKIP, two by the BNP and two by the Greens. In the Scottish Parliament election of 2011 the SNP won an outright majority of seats. The BNP have won a number of council seats in different parts of the country.

In general elections, however, the electoral system has ensured that the party fragmentation among voters has been reflected in the composition of the House of Commons to only a very limited extent. Excluding Northern Ireland MPs,

the Conservatives and Labour together won over 98 per cent of seats in the 1960s and in 1970. From 1974 through to 1992 the figure hovered around 95 per cent but then fell to 91 per cent in 1997 and 90 per cent in 2001. In 2005 and 2010 the proportions were, respectively, 88 and 89 per cent. In the latter election the Conservatives did not have an overall majority (more seats than all the other parties combined) and were forced to enter a coalition with the Liberal Democrats. There has been enough fragmentation in the House of Commons, therefore, to have important consequences for the conduct of government and politics. It remains to be seen, however, whether – both among voters and in the legislature – the trend towards greater fragmentation will continue in future.

Turnout

Aggregate variations

As well as varying over time, election turnout varies according to the type of election involved and also from place to place. Table 7.4 shows the percentage turnout at different types of election in the UK between 2005 and 2010 and it is apparent that they do not attract the same level of interest on the part of the electorate. The lowest turnout in this period was for the 2009 European Parliament elections (34.7 per cent) and these have consistently held the wooden spoon (even though the low level of interest in European elections has been partially disguised by holding them on the same day as local elections in both 2004 and 2009). Turnout in local elections themselves in England and Wales never reached 40 per cent, although this was easily exceeded in the 2008 London mayoral contest. Turnout in the 2007 Scottish Parliament election, on the other hand, was well over 50 per cent but it was significantly lower in the Welsh Assembly elections of the same year. In contrast, the Northern Ireland Assembly elections brought voters to the polls in relatively large numbers. Excluding that case, the two general elections at the start and end of the period saw the highest turnouts, even although participation in these was poor by historical standards.

Clearly, then, the electorate does not view all elections as equally important. Political scientists have suggested that there is a distinction to be made between 'first-order' and 'second-order' elections. General elections are first-order. Most people think they are important and care about who wins; there is saturation media coverage in the run-up to polling day; and the parties mount intense national and local campaigns. To a greater or lesser extent, the other contests are second-order. In local elections, for example, not a great deal appears to be at stake – voters could be forgiven for thinking that it doesn't really make an enormous difference which party controls their council – and there is little media coverage. Characteristically, turnout is lower in second-order elections. To conceive of UK elections in terms of a first-order/second-order dichotomy is to oversimplify matters, however. Some elections are more second-order than others. The European Parliament, for example, is seen as remote by people in the UK, its routine activities are virtually unreported in the British media and it seems to make little difference whoever is elected. Unsurprisingly, turnout in the relevant elections is poor. On the last occasion that European elections were held on their own (1999) UK turnout was a paltry 24 per cent. The Scottish Parliament, on the other hand, has extensive powers – so it matters who wins – and elections to it generate considerable interest within Scotland. This is reflected in the relatively high turnout. The

Table 7.4 Turnout in UK elections, 2005–10

	%
General Eection 2005	61.4
English locals 2006	36.6
Scottish Parliament 2007	53.9
Welsh Assembly 2007	46.4
Northern Ireland Assembly	63.5
English locals 2007	38.3
English/Welsh locals 2008	35.6
London mayor 2008	45.3
English locals 2009	39.3
European Parliament 2009	34.7
General Election 2010	65.8

Welsh Assembly has more restricted powers and turnouts are generally lower than in Scotland. The Northern Ireland Assembly is perhaps seen as an arena of conflict between the rival communities there and hence assumes considerable importance, resulting in a high turnout in 2007. It is worth noting, however, that in the 2011 Northern Ireland elections turnout fell to a level roughly on a par with Scotland at 54.5 per cent.

The extent of turnout variation from place to place is illustrated in Box 7.2. The lowest turnouts are in **inner city** areas while the highest – up to more than 30 percentage points higher – are in upmarket suburbs (Renfrewshire East and Richmond Park) or mainly rural areas. These are, of course, only the extreme cases, but they do reflect general patterns. Turnout tends to be higher in more prosperous, middle-class constituencies and also in more rural areas; it is consistently lower in large cities and in less affluent areas with higher levels of social housing. This pattern is very well established and has changed little over the last 50 years at least. In addition, it is also evident in local and devolved elections. Overlaying these differences based on the social composition of constituencies, however, the marginality or safeness of a seat also matters. Electors are more inclined to go to the polls in places where the contest is likely to be close than in places that are rock-solid for one party or another. This is largely due to the fact that parties campaign harder in areas where the result may be in doubt than in those where they have no chance or expect to cruise to victory. In the 2010 election, for example, in constituencies (N = 169) where the winning party had a majority of 10 per cent or less in 2005 (estimated in the case of constituencies with changed boundaries) the mean turnout was 67.7 per cent, while in those where the relevant majority was over 30 per cent (N = 110) 2010 turnout was 61.1 per cent.

BOX 7.2

Highest and lowest constituency turnouts in the 2010 General Election

Lowest	%	Highest	%
Manchester Central	45.6	Renfrewshire East	78.8
Leeds Central	46.4	Westmorland and Lonsdale	77.6
Birmingham Ladywood	49.8	Richmond Park	77.0
Glasgow North East	50.0	Winchester	76.2
Blackley and Broughton	50.5	Devon Central	76.2

Variations in turning out

Looking at and analysing variations in aggregate turnout across time, space and types of election is certainly fascinating. In the end, however, the decision to vote or not is made by individuals. In order to discover who votes and who doesn't and to begin to explain why, we need to turn to survey data.

There are three main approaches to explaining why some people vote while others don't. The first concentrates on the social locations and circumstances of individual voters. It suggests that the resources that underpin political participation (knowledge, skills and time) are unevenly distributed across different social groups, as are levels of involvement in community networks. As a result, different sorts of people differ in their propensity to vote. The second derives from rational choice theory and directs attention to the costs and benefits of voting, suggesting that turnout will be greater when there are more incentives to vote (for example, living in a marginal rather than a safe seat) and costs are kept at a minimum. A third approach focuses on the connections between parties and voters. It is concerned with how parties mobilise voters and the impact of voters' identification with parties.

Differences in turnout across a variety of social groups are illustrated in Table 7.5, which has figures for the 2010 election. As has been the case for some time, there is no significant difference in the turnouts of men and women. On the other hand, married people and those who have been widowed were much more inclined to vote than the unmarried. This has been the case for a long time and it is only partly to do with age. Middle-class groups voted more heavily than the working class, the better off more than the worse off, owner-occupiers more than renters and those with a university degree or professional qualification more

Table 7.5 Turnout of social groups in 2010

	%		%
Sex		**Housing**	
Men	64	Owner-occupiers	74
Women	63	Renters	44
Marital status		**Highest education qualification**	
Married	74	None	54
Widowed	75	Occupational qualification	61
Live with partner	47	GCSE (or equivalent)	59
Separated/divorced	59	A level (or equivalent)	64
Single/never married	51	Professional qualification	70
		Degree	73
Occupation		**Age**	
Professional and managerial	78	18–24	45
Other non-manual	64	25–34	52
Manual	52	35–44	62
		45–54	67
Income		55–64	71
Lowest third	56	65+	79
Middle third	66		
Top third	79		

Source: Data from British Election Study (BES) 2010 face-to-face post-election survey. The original data have been weighted to reflect the actual turnout in the election

than those without. The clear division in turnout between the relatively well-off, well-educated professional middle classes on the one hand and the less well-educated manual working class on the other is a relatively new phenomenon and certainly was not in evidence in the 1960s when national survey studies of voting began. Perhaps the most striking figures in the table, however, are those for age. The turnout of the youngest voters in 2010 was only 45 per cent, but this increased steadily with age and reached 79 per cent among those aged 65 and above. A simple, practical explanation for the heavy turnout of the oldest group is that it might just be a consequence of the fact that, since most are retired, they have more time to go to the polling station. At a more general level, however, it is widely suggested that as people get older they become more involved in the political process and acquire a greater sense of responsibility.

The approach which focuses on the costs and benefits of voting suggests an arresting conclusion: it is irrational to vote. Voting involves some costs (it takes time, for example) but there is no obvious benefit. The chances of one person's vote making a difference to the constituency result – never mind the overall national outcome – and hence obtaining some benefit from electing the party that he or she prefers, are infinitesimal. The question, therefore, is not why some people don't vote but why anyone does!

The answer is that rather than voting for what we might term *instrumental* reasons, many of those who participate in elections have a *normative* motivation – that is, they vote because they see voting as part of a citizen's duty. In 2010 a large majority of British Election Study (BES) pre-election respondents agreed that it is every citizen's duty to vote (75 per cent) and most also said that they would feel guilty if they didn't vote (56 per cent). Unsurprisingly those who believe that voting is a duty are much more likely to turn out than those who do not. Perhaps more important, younger people have a much weaker sense of civic duty in respect of voting than those who are older. Among 18–24-year olds, 58 per cent believed that voting is a duty and 31 per cent would feel guilty if they didn't vote. These figures rise steadily with age to reach 88 per cent and 73 per cent among the over 65s. We have here an important source of age differences in turnout. Conceptions of duty also help to explain turnout differences between the married/widowed and others.

Turning to the connections between parties and voters, surveys in the UK have always found that the more strongly someone identifies with or supports a party, the more likely they are to vote. This is not difficult to understand; people who are strong party supporters are more likely to want to demonstrate their support by voting than those with a less strong commitment or none at all. Voting, for them, is *expressive*. In the 2010 election BES figures show a turnout of 85 per cent among strong party **identifiers**, 78 per cent for the fairly strong, 60 per cent for the not very strong identifiers and 39 per cent for those with no identification.

The turnout of strong identifiers has not changed a great deal since the 1960s – decline is concentrated in the other groups. The problem is that there are now many fewer strong identifiers than there used to be. In the 1960s over 40 per cent of voters had a very strong party identification and only about 10 per cent had no attachment. In 2010, according to the BES internet poll, the respective figures were 18 per cent and 16 per cent. So, the group with the highest turnout has been decreasing in size while the one with the lowest turnout has grown. This is a major cause of the markedly lower turnouts in the UK since the turn of the century.

After the 2001 election there was much hand-wringing among the 'chattering classes' over what was to be done about low turnout. Government responses have largely focused on the process of voting, such as allowing easier access to postal voting. This approach implicitly assumes that lowering the costs of voting will improve turnout. In practice, however, this makes little difference. It is much more difficult to do anything about the really important sources of poor turnout – a decline in the sense of civic duty among younger voters and weakening commitment to parties among the electorate as a whole.

Party support

Aggregate variations

Like turnout, levels of party support vary in different types of election and from place to place, as well as over time. We have already seen that support for 'others' in general elections has increased since 1964. Nonetheless, the major parties usually do even worse in 'second-order' elections. The best example is European Parliament elections. In these elections, in 2009, the Conservatives, Labour and Liberal Democrats between them won 56 per cent of the votes (and 49 of the 72 seats) as compared with 88 per cent in the General Election held a year later. Within Scotland and Wales, support for the SNP and Plaid Cymru is noticeably stronger in the devolved elections than in UK general elections. In the 2010 General Election these parties garnered 20 per cent and 11 per cent of the votes within their respective countries. Just a year later in the elections for the Scottish Parliament and Welsh Assembly the figures were 45 per cent and 19 per cent. The second-order theory suggests that smaller parties do better in these elections than in general elections because control of the UK government is not at stake. Voters are more willing to indulge themselves by deserting the major parties because it simply doesn't matter very much who wins. While this rings true for European and, perhaps, local elections, it is certainly far from the whole story as far as devolved elections are concerned.

The merest glance at constituency election results is enough to confirm the rather obvious point that party performances vary from place to place (and the same is true of wards in local elections). Elections would be rather boring if they didn't! The extent of variation across constituencies is truly enormous. In the 2010 General Election, for example, the Conservative vote share ranged from 4.4 per cent in Na h-Eileanan an Iar (Western Isles) to 62.8 per cent in Richmond (Yorks), Labour's from 2.3 per cent in Westmorland and Lonsdale to 66.6 per cent in Coatbridge, Chryston and Bellshill and that for the Liberal Democrats from 5 per cent in Glasgow East to 62 per cent in Orkney and Shetland. Anyone with more than a passing interest in British politics will be aware that, on the whole, the Conservatives do better in more affluent, middle-class areas and in rural and suburban constituencies. Labour, on the other hand, does better in poorer and more working-class areas and in more urban areas. Support for the Liberal Democrats is less predictable than that for the two larger parties, although they tend to do badly where Labour is strong and get more support in the same sorts of constituencies that usually favour the Conservatives.

Overlaying these broad patterns, however, there is a clear regional dimension to party support in the UK. Table 7.6 shows figures from the 2010 election for Scotland, Wales, Northern Ireland and the nine 'standard' regions of England. Northern Ireland is clearly *sui generis*, as the major parties do not contest elections there, and the nationalist parties make Scotland and Wales distinctive. Nonetheless, with the exception of London, the so-called 'North–South divide' remains in evidence. Labour's strongest areas outside London are Scotland, Wales and the three northernmost English regions. In each of these it was the largest party in terms of popular support. On the other hand, Labour trailed the

Conservatives in the Midlands and came a poor third in the south and east of England. Conservative support across regions is a mirror image of that for Labour but the Liberal Democrats have a relatively even spread of support across the country although, as usual, in 2010 they did rather better than average in the South-west and South-east of England and, on this occasion, rather poorly in Scotland. A North–South division is even more apparent in terms of seats won. In Scotland, Wales and northern England, despite making gains, the Conservatives won only 52 seats compared with 171 for Labour and 25 for the Liberal Democrats. In the Eastern, South-east and South-west regions, by contrast, the tally was 162 for the Conservatives, 10 for Labour and 23 for the Liberal Democrats.

There is a considerable literature on the 'North–South divide' and a number of explanations for it have been suggested. For example, the proportion of broadly middle-class people has tended to increase in the South and in rural areas and, relatively speaking, to decrease in the North, Scotland and urban areas. It remains the case, however, that even within classes there are significant regional differences in party choice. A more fruitful approach is the argument that regional behaviour, even within classes, is a product of regional variations in economic wellbeing which are themselves a result of uneven regional economic development. Put crudely, Scotland and the North have simply not been as prosperous as the South especially since the decline of heavy industry. It is worth remembering, however, that even in the nineteenth century the Tories were weaker in Scotland, Wales and the North than they were in the South, so that an explanation focusing on recent economic trends is not entirely satisfactory. Core-periphery theory offers a broader perspective. This suggests that the 'core' – London and the South-east – dominates other areas (the 'periphery')

Table 7.6 Party shares of votes in 2010 in regions (row %)

	Con	Lab	Lib Dem	SNP/PC	Other
Scotland	16.7	42.0	18.9	19.9	2.5
Wales	26.1	36.2	20.1	11.3	6.3
Northern Ireland	–	–	–	–	100.0
North-east	23.7	43.6	23.6	–	9.1
North-west	31.7	39.4	21.6	–	7.3
Yorkshire/Humber	32.8	34.3	22.9	–	10.0
East Midlands	41.2	29.8	20.8	–	8.2
West Midlands	39.5	30.6	20.5	–	9.4
Eastern	47.1	19.6	24.0	–	9.3
London	34.5	36.6	22.1	–	6.8
South-east	49.3	16.2	26.2	–	8.3
South-west	42.8	15.4	34.7	–	7.1

culturally, economically and politically. Peripheral regions are poorer, suffer more in times of economic depression, have worse housing conditions and so on. As a result they tend to favour radical, non-establishment parties. This theory certainly does not fit the British case perfectly; for example, London itself is 'the core of the core' but is not particularly fertile ground for the Conservatives. However, it does offer some clues to understanding the geographical pattern of voting.

Explaining party choice: class and party identification

'A person thinks, politically, as he (sic) is socially. Social characteristics determine political preference.' That was the blunt conclusion of the first-ever survey study of voting behaviour in the USA (Lazarsfeld et al., 1968 edition: 27). Much influenced by this, early British studies also focused on the connection between social location and party choice. Although a variety of interesting relationships were found to be significant (involving, for example, age, sex, religious denomination and housing tenure), the strongest social influence on party choice was found to be **occupational class**. Middle-class voters were heavily Conservative while about two-thirds of the working class voted Labour. Writing in 1967, Peter Pulzer could conclude, in a much-quoted sentence, that 'Class is the basis of British party politics; all else is embellishment and detail' (1967: 98). Social determinism was never the whole story, however. For example, this approach has difficulty in accounting for the (often large) minorities who do not conform to group voting norms and it offers no clue to as to which of the many social groups to which people belong will be decisive in determining party support.

In the late 1960s and early 1970s, a more refined explanatory theory of party choice was put forward by David Butler and Donald Stokes (1969, 1974). This 'Butler-Stokes model', summarised in Figure 7.3, involves party identification as well as class voting. Party identification refers to a sense of attachment to a party, a feeling of commitment to it, being a supporter of the party and not just someone who happens to vote for it from time to time. The starting point of the model is the class and party of voters' parents, and this is underpinned by the theory of political socialisation, which suggests that families are particularly important in transmitting political attitudes and beliefs to succeeding generations. Most people, in the 1950s and 1960s were brought up to think of themselves as supporters of one party or another (with upwards of 40 per cent of the electorate describing themselves as *very strong* party supporters) and thus developed an enduring loyalty to a party which they would support, for the most part, through thick and thin. Although Butler and Stokes allowed for short-term factors to affect party choice – particular issues, party leaders, government performance, for example – they emphasised that class and party identification were the strongest influences on party choice and, since these didn't change much, electoral stability rather than volatility was to be expected.

Although it was widely accepted as a powerful explanation of party choice in the 1950s and 1960s, the relevance of the Butler-Stokes model began to decline almost as soon as the second edition of their book was published. The first development was a sharp decline in the level of class voting. Various measures of the overall level of class voting have been developed, the simplest of which is known as the 'Alford index'. Scores on this index range from zero (the same proportions vote Conservative and Labour in each class) to 100 (all manual workers vote Labour and all non-manual workers Conservative). In 1964 and 1966 the scores were 42 and 43 respectively. In the 1970s the average score was 31.5, in the 1980s 25.0 and in the 1990s 23.5. In the 2001, 2005 and 2010 elections the scores were 23, 18 and 17. Whichever measure of class voting is used, a similar story of long-term decline is evident. From a situation in which there was a

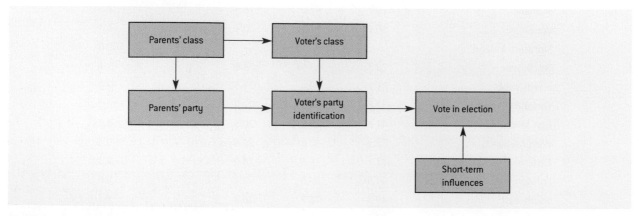

Figure 7.3 Butler-Stokes model of party choice

Table 7.7 Social characteristics and party choice in 2010 (row percentages)

	Conservative	Labour	Liberal Democrat	Other
Occupational class				
Professional and managerial	40	26	26	8
Other non-manual	38	30	23	9
Manual	30	37	19	14
Housing tenure				
Owner-occupier	40	29	23	9
Private renter	29	28	33	9
Social renter	26	40	19	14
Age				
18–24	29	29	36	7
25–34	35	28	32	6
35–44	33	35	24	9
45–54	32	35	22	11
55–64	41	26	20	13
65+	47	25	17	11
Sex				
Male	35	30	24	11
Female	38	30	24	8
Religion				
None	32	29	28	11
Anglican	49	26	17	8
Church of Scotland	25	39	17	19
Roman Catholic	32	42	19	8
Nonconformist	42	27	24	7
Non-Christian	38	32	25	5
Ethnicity				
White British	38	29	23	10
Asian	23	39	35	3
Black	12	60	23	5

Note: Data are from the BES post-election internet survey. In almost all cases the numbers on which the percentages are based are very large. The exception relates to ethnicity where there are only 197 Asian and 108 black respondents.

clear, if imperfect, **alignment** between class and party there has been a progressive **dealignment**.

Table 7.7 shows party choice by occupational class in the 2010 General Election together with patterns among other social categories of interest (the 'embellishment and detail', in Pulzer's phrase). Class still makes some difference. Professionals, managers and other non-manual workers were more likely to vote Conservative (and Liberal Democrat) and less likely to vote Labour than manual workers. The differences are relatively small, however, and no class came near to giving one of the parties 50 per cent of its votes. Housing tenure is related to class and here again there are differences. Perhaps the most interesting is that there seems

to have been relatively strong support for the Liberal Democrats among those privately renting their accommodation. This is probably related to age. Younger people were much more inclined to support the Liberal Democrats who were, indeed, the most popular party among 18–24-year-olds. While that is relatively unusual (Labour is normally the most popular among the youngest voters), the heavy support for the Conservatives among older voters is not. The days when women were clearly more Conservative and less willing to vote Labour than men (the 'gender gap') have long gone and the differences between them in 2010 were very minor. In terms of religious affiliation, Anglicans (overwhelmingly Church of England) were the most strongly

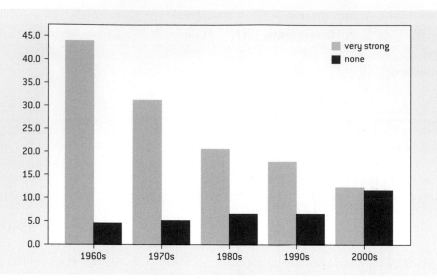

Figure 7.4 Strength of party identification, 1964–2010
Source: BES

Conservative group, followed by nonconformists. Catholics, on the other hand, were more inclined to vote Labour. The strongest support for the Liberal Democrats was among those claiming no religious affiliation, while the high figure for 'other' among Church of Scotland adherents is explained by support for the SNP. Finally, the figures for ethnicity show that the Conservatives were very weak among black voters and clearly worse than average among those of Asian origins. Labour was strongly preferred by the former but the Liberal Democrats ran Labour close among the latter, which may have been a consequence of the incumbent Labour Government's policies on Iraq and Afghanistan.

Looking at the voting choices of different groups of the electorate is certainly interesting and a good deal of effort has gone into explaining why certain groups display distinctive patterns of party support. In fact, however, even taking together all the categories shown in Table 7.7 does not take us very far in explaining party choice. The statistical procedures that enable us to come to such a conclusion are complicated but if, for example, we wanted to predict whether survey respondents voted Conservative or for another party in 2010 then, without knowing anything at all about them, we would be right in 63 per cent of cases if we simply assumed that none of them voted Conservative. If we knew their occupation, tenure, age, sex, religion and ethnicity then our prediction would improve to only 65 per cent of cases. If we tried to predict which of the three major parties a person supported, we would be correct in fewer than half of the cases.

The second development undermining the Butler-Stokes model of party choice has been a steady decline in the strength of party identification amongst the electorate. Figure 7.4 shows the mean percentages identifying 'very strongly' with a party and having no party identification in BES election surveys grouped by decade. It is immediately apparent that there has been a sharp and steady decline in the proportion of electors claiming to be strong party supporters. At the same time, the proportion with no party identification has increased – more than doubling over the period – although the great majority of people retain some sort of attachment to a party. The important point is that the attachment is much weaker than it used to be. Analysts have suggested that this trend is a consequence of interactions between social changes – including developments in the occupational and industrial structure – and more obviously political changes – including the unimpressive performance of governments, television coverage of politics and changes in party rhetoric to try to appeal to a very broad spectrum of voters. Whatever the reasons for weakening party identification, it has important effects. Weaker party identifiers – of whom there are now more than ever – are less likely to vote than those with a strong attachment and also much less likely to stick with their party through thick and thin.

Explaining party choice: valence voting

Class and **partisan dealignment** together seriously undermined the explanation of party choice that had seemed to work very well until the 1970s. As a result, electoral analysts began to put more weight on voters' opinions, assessments and judgements when explaining party choice. There was no consensus, however, about which opinions were most important or, indeed, about what the new approach to voting should be called – the terms used included 'issue voting', 'policy voting', 'instrumental voting', 'pocket-book voting' and 'consumer voting'.

In their report on the 2001 General Election, however, the BES team developed and elaborated a more general explanation of party choice, which they christened a 'valence politics' model. This quickly won general acceptance in the electoral studies community (Clarke et al. 2004). The starting point for the theory is a distinction originally made by Butler and Stokes between what they called 'position' issues and 'valence' issues. Position issues are those on which people take different positions (for or against electoral reform, for example, or for or against Britain's membership of the European Union). Valence issues are ones on which nearly everyone takes the same side. Not many favour increased crime, for example, or want the National Health Service to be abolished. Since the 1960s, the argument goes, politics has come increasingly to be about valence issues – the differences between the parties on position issues, or on ideology more generally, have become relatively small as they all crowd into the 'middle ground'. For voters deciding which party to support, then, the question is not which party has the ideological or policy positions that they favour but which is likely to be most competent at achieving the goals that are widely shared among all voters (such as reduced crime, a healthy economy, a well-run health service).

The next stage in the argument emphasises the importance of party leaders. Given that most voters neither think nor know all that much about politics, they tend to seek ways of simplifying political choices. Evaluating the competence of the various parties on various issues is a fairly complex activity. On the other hand, we are used to judging people and so many voters simplify their electoral choice by focusing on party leaders. Evaluating leaders is a short-cut to evaluating party competence and is made all the easier by the fact that the media bombard us with information about the leaders. Whereas most voters used to evaluate leaders largely on the basis of their pre-existing party preference, evaluations of leaders now strongly influence their choice of party.

The final element in the valence politics model of voting relates to party identification. Despite the clear decline in the strength of partisanship in Britain over the years, party identification stubbornly remains a statistically important influence on party choice in elections. Initially at least, this would appear to be something of a problem for the valence politics argument since, as traditionally conceived, party identification has little to do with judgements or evaluations. Rather, it reflects a sort of 'tribal' loyalty. Valence theorists suggest, however, that it should be understood as an underlying preference that is continually updated. As

Table 7.8 Vote in 2010 by party best to handle most important problem

	Best party				
	Conservative	Labour	Lib Dem	Other	None/DK
Vote	%	%	%	%	%
Con	84	2	7	33	26
Lab	3	79	10	21	29
Lib Dem	9	17	80	13	34
Other	2	2	4	33	11

Source: BES internet surveys

people's store of information, evaluations and reactions to events changes then so does their underlying party preference. In this interpretation party identification is dynamic rather than an unchanging loyalty.

Evidence of the importance of valence or performance considerations in recent elections is plentiful (see Clarke et al. 2004, 2009). Table 7.8 shows the impact of valence issues in 2010. In the run-up to the election, BES respondents were asked to name what they thought was the most important issue facing the country and which party would be best at handling the issue that they had identified. Understandably, almost 50 per cent nominated the economy and associated problems such as the credit crunch and national debt. Three other valence issues – crime, immigration and the NHS – were mentioned by 20 per cent, so that together these four issues accounted for 7 in 10 of all responses. Table 7.8 shows the votes of these respondents cross-tabulated with the party they thought best able to deal with the problem.

There is a very clear relationship. Overwhelmingly people voted for the major party that they thought would best handle the issue that they had nominated as the most important. The association is strongest in the case of those who thought the Conservatives were the most competent but the others are not far behind. The real advantage gained by the Conservatives in the election, however, was that rather more people thought that they would be best on these issues (31 per cent) than thought the same of Labour (25 per cent) or the Liberal Democrats (8 per cent).

Table 7.9 focuses on evaluations of the party leaders. Respondents were asked which of the three they thought would make the best Prime Minister and the table shows how their responses were related to their choice of party. Again, the relationship is strong, especially in the case of Gordon Brown and David Cameron. As before, however, Labour's problem was that, although people who thought Brown would be the best Prime Minister were very likely to vote Labour, there were rather more people who thought that Cameron would be best. In opinion polls throughout the campaign the latter was consistently ahead on the 'best

Table 7.9 Vote in 2010 by choice for best Prime Minister

	Best Prime Minister			
	Brown	**Cameron**	**Clegg**	**Don't know**
Vote	%	%	%	%
Con	1	82	5	14
Lab	82	2	14	30
Lib Dem	13	9	75	34
Other	5	7	6	22

Source: BES internet surveys

Prime Minister' question, and in the BES survey used here he was preferred by 39 per cent of respondents compared with 30 per cent for Brown and 16 per cent for Clegg (the remainder saying that they didn't know).

The evidence in Tables 7.8 and 7.9 is certainly consistent with the valence or performance politics interpretation of party choice. The difficulty is that it is also consistent with the older theory based on party identification. People who identify with a party would be expected to think that it is the best to handle virtually any problem (because it is 'their' party) and that the party leader would be the best person to be Prime Minister (because he or she is 'their' leader). To take the discussion further, therefore, we need to incorporate party identification into the analysis and also, possibly, control for social factors. Doing so by means of cross-tabulations is cumbersome, however, and produces results which are difficult to explain and to present clearly. Table 7.10, the final table in this chapter, therefore, is based on a statistical technique known as binary logistic regression which enables us to assess the impact of each of a number of variables on (in this instance) party choice while holding all the other variables in the analysis constant. This sounds frightening (and the statistics involved certainly are) but interpreting the results of such analyses is not too difficult.

Table 7.10 Logistic regression analysis of party choice in 2010

	Conservative versus others	Labour versus others	Lib Dem versus others
Occupation (ref. = prof. and managerial)			
Other non-manual	–	1.23	0.76
Manual	–	1.44	0.69
Age (ref. = 18–24)			
Aged 25–44	1.80	–	–
Aged 45–64	2.12	0.69	–
Aged 65+	2.70	0.60	–
Party identification (ref. = none)			
Conservative	3.47	0.21	0.40
Labour	0.35	3.99	0.61
Lib Dem	0.22	0.46	4.69
Other	0.38	0.51	0.05
Best party on issues (ref. = none/DK)			
Conservative	2.26	0.61	0.60
Labour	0.37	1.74	0.75
Lib Dem	0.38	0.51	2.54
Other	–	–	0.43
Best Prime Minister (ref. = don't know)			
David Cameron	9.94	0.19	0.31
Gordon Brown	0.09	4.68	0.31
Nick Clegg	0.54	0.42	4.00
% correctly classified	90.8	88.9	85.4

Note: See accompanying text for guidance in interpreting this table. Only significant odds ratios ($p < 0.05$) are shown.

Source: BES 2010 internet surveys

Table 7.10 presents three analyses – one for voting for each party versus voting for any other. This is necessary as in this statistical technique the variable to be analysed (party choice) can only have two values (Conservative/not Conservative, for instance). For each of the five explanatory factors analysed (occupation, age, party identification, best party on issues and best Prime Minister) a reference category is specified ('Don't Know' in the case of best Prime Minister, for example). The figures shown for each remaining category are odds ratios, which measure how more or less likely someone in the category was to vote for the party concerned than someone in the reference category. A ratio of less than 1 indicates that people in that category were less likely to vote for the party, while a ratio greater than 1 means that they were more likely to do so. Thus, those aged 65 and over were almost three times (2.70) more likely to vote Conservative than those aged 18–24 (the reference category). As noted above, the results take account of a number of explanatory factors at the same time. Thus, we can assess the impact of opinion as to the best Prime Minister on party choice while taking account of age, occupation, party identification and best party on issues.

When the other factors are taken into account, occupation has no effect on the likelihood of voting Conservative. On the other hand, other non-manuals and manual workers were somewhat more likely to vote Labour and less likely to vote Liberal Democrat than the reference category (professional and managerial groups). The impact of age is patchy – there are no significant effects for voting Liberal Democrat, but older age groups were less likely to vote Labour and more likely to vote Conservative, even taking everything else into account. The party identification figures are much as expected – those who identify with a party were much more likely to vote for it and much less likely to vote for another party. The same is true of assessments of the best party to handle important issues. These opinions remain a significant influence on party choice, although the coefficients are not particularly large. When it comes to best Prime Minister it can be seen that, net of all other influences, those who opted for Cameron were almost ten times more likely than those with no opinion to vote Conservative, those who opted for Brown almost five times more likely to vote Labour and those choosing Clegg four times more likely to vote Liberal Democrat. These coefficients indicate very substantial effects. There is strong evidence, therefore, that the performance or valence politics explanation of party choice goes a long way in explaining voting in the 2010 election.

Conclusion

It is not the case, of course, that everyone nowadays votes on the basis of evaluations of the relative competence of the parties or of the party leaders. There remain, no doubt, plenty of people who are long-term supporters of a party and always vote for it no matter what. There are assuredly also some voters who have clearly worked out positions on central (or even not so central) policy issues or take a particular ideological position and make their decisions in elections on that basis. There may even be a few voters who still think of politics in class terms. There are also numerous other influences on voting that need to be taken into account – the mass media and campaigning, for example. Nonetheless, valence concerns have clearly increased in importance among the electorate and this has a number of consequences. For one thing, the fact that the fortunes of their parties are to a considerable extent riding on the shoulders of the party leaders makes for a tough life for them. These days, the penalty for electoral failure is swift demotion. Moreover, in choosing leaders, parties increasingly have to pay attention to the electoral appeal of likely candidates (rather than ideology, standing in the party or even the ability to govern, for example). Even so, electoral appeal can dissipate rapidly. Evaluations of leaders can be more volatile than more settled attitudes towards parties. For example, in September 2007, according to IpsosMori, 44 per cent of the public were satisfied with the performance of the Prime Minister, Gordon Brown, and 26 per cent dissatisfied. Less than a year later, in July 2008, 21 per cent were satisfied and 72 per cent dissatisfied. Under valence voting, then, the popularity of parties can fluctuate to a much greater extent and more quickly than was the case when party loyalties were more fixed. That certainly makes life more exciting (as well as more complicated) for election-watchers.

I noted at the outset that elections allow the people to participate in politics and, in that context, the relatively low turnouts in recent general elections remain disappointing. On the other hand, the main purpose of general elections is to enable the people to hold governments to account – to pass judgement on the performance of the incumbents and vote either to keep them in office or replace them. When party choice was largely based on class and inherited partisanship, it is not clear that elections actually fulfilled this function very well. With the development of more widespread valence or performance voting, the claim that elections are key mechanisms of popular control can be more easily substantiated.

Chapter summary

Elections are central to the political system of the UK, ultimately enabling citizens to hold to account their representatives at national, sub-national and local levels. Turnout in elections has tended to decline, and this is probably a result of a declining sense of citizen duty among the electorate and a weakening of party identification. In explaining patterns of party support, the social characteristics of voters are no longer as important as they once were. Instead, more emphasis is placed on how voters evaluate the performance of the governing party and their reactions to party leaders.

Discussion points

- Should voting in general elections be made compulsory?
- Why are the outcomes of UK general elections unpredictable?
- Why have party leaders become more important influences on voters' decisions?

Further reading

The themes covered in this chapter are explored in greater detail in Denver, Carman and Johns (2012) *Elections and Voters in Britain*, 3rd edn (Palgrave). Detailed studies of the 2010 elections include Kavanagh and Cowley (2010) *The British General Election of 2010* (Palgrave); Geddes and Tonge (eds) (2010) *Britain Votes 2010* (Oxford University Press) and Allen and Bartle (2011) *Britain at the Polls 2010* (Sage). The most recent BES report is Clarke, Sanders, Stewart and Whiteley (2009) *Performance Politics and the British Voter* (Cambridge University Press), although this may prove difficult reading to those inexperienced in the field.

Bibliography

Butler, D. (1998) 'Reflections on British Elections and Their Study', *Annual Review of Political Science*, Vol. 1, pp. 451–64.

Butler, D.E. and Stokes, D. (1969) *Political Change in Britain*, 1st edn (Macmillan).

Butler, D.E. and Stokes, D. (1974) *Political Change in Britain*, 2nd edn (Macmillan).

Clarke, H., Sanders, D., Stewart, M. and Whiteley, P. (2004) *Political Choice in Britain* (Oxford University Press).

Clarke, H., Sanders, D., Stewart, M. and Whiteley, P. (2009) *Performance Politics and the British Voter* (Cambridge University Press).

Farrell, D. (2001) *Electoral Systems: A Comparative Introduction* (Palgrave Macmillan).

Gilmour, I. (1971) *The Body Politic*, revised edn (Hutchinson).

Lazarsfeld, P., Berelson, B. and Gaudet, H. (1968) *The People's Choice*, 3rd edn, first published 1944 (Columbia University Press).

Pulzer, P.G. (1967) *Political Representation and Elections in Britain* (George Allen & Unwin).

Useful websites

Useful websites include www.electoralcommission.gov.uk/ and www.pollingreport.co.uk/

CHAPTER 8

The mass media and political communication

Bill Jones

> " I am absolved of responsibility. We journalists don't have to step on roaches. All we have to do is turn on the light and watch the critters scuttle "

P.J. O'Rourke on the duties of journalists in relation to politics, 1992: xix

Learning objectives

- To explain the workings of the media: press and broadcasting.

- To encourage an understanding of how the media interact and influence voting, elections and the rest of the political system.

- To discuss how the pluralist and Marxist dominance theories help to explain how the media operate and influence society.

Without newspapers, radio and pre-eminently television – not to mention more recently the internet and social media like Twitter – the present political system could not work. The **media** are so all-pervasive that we are often unaware of the addictive hold they exert over our attentions and the messages they implant in our consciousness on a whole range of matters of which politics is but one. This chapter assesses the impact of the mass media upon the workings of our political system, together with some different theories about how they operate in practice.

The mass media

The term 'mass media' embraces books, pamphlets and film but is usually understood to refer to newspapers, radio and television. This is not to say that films, theatre, art and books are not important, but perhaps the influence of the latter three media are usually less instant and more long term. For example the novels of Dickens did not cause instant change, but did help create the climate in which change eventually took place. Since the 1950s television has eclipsed newspapers and radio as the key medium. That statement has to be qualified, however, as the internet- and Web-carried social media are increasingly important in political communication. These are not as important as television currently, but the gap is definitely closing.

Surveys indicate that three-quarters of people identify television as the most important single source of information about politics. On average British people now watch over 20 hours of television per week, and given that 20 per cent of television output covers news and current affairs, a fair political content is being imbibed. Indeed, the audience for the evening news bulletins regularly exceeds 20 million. Surveys used regularly to show that over 70 per cent of viewers trust television news as fair and accurate, while only one-third trusted newspapers. This degree of trust in television, however, was gravely shaken by a number of scandals in 2010–12.

Public trust in mass media

A YouGov survey in November 2012 on trust in the media showed television still the most trusted medium but not to the same extent as before:

- 64% of UK adults saw TV as the most trusted media outlet
- 58% said the same about radio
- 38% trusted newspapers, while 25% thought the same about magazines
- Interestingly, websites saw a high level of trust (55%)
- But blogs are trusted by under one in ten people (9%)
- Facebook and Twitter are trusted by only 15% of UK people as a place to get trusted media content, despite their huge numbers of users

Source: YouGov, 14 November 2012

From the spoken to the written (and then broadcast) word

Television is now such a dominant medium that it is easy to forget that its provenance has been relatively recent. During the seventeenth and early eighteenth centuries, political communication was mainly verbal: between members of the relatively small political elite; within a broader public at election times; within political groups such as the seventeenth-century Diggers and Levellers; and occasionally from the pulpit. Given their expense and scarcity at the time, books, pamphlets and **broadsheets** had a limited, although important, role to play; they played a part during the Civil War (1640–49), and at the end of the eighteenth century pamphlets were very important in disseminating radical, not to say revolutionary, ideas.

The **Industrial Revolution** drew workers in from the land into crowded urban spaces where they, arguably, enjoyed a higher standard of living but were scarcely so contented they were not receptive to reformers and travelling speakers, like the Wiltshire farmer Harry 'Orator' Hunt. He delivered inspiring speeches on parliamentary reform in London and elsewhere including St Peter's Fields in Manchester in August 1819, where the crowd was charged by mounted troops in the 'Peterloo Massacre' resulting in 15 people dead and 650 injured. The Chartists pursuing similar objectives attracted big audiences and also, like the Anti-Corn Law League, disseminated pamphlets via the new postal system.

Next in the chronology of development came the inception of mass circulation newspapers – *The Times*, the *Telegraph*, *Daily Mail*, *Express* and the *Daily Mirror* – which provided information on current affairs for the newly enfranchised masses. The **press barons** – Northcliffe, Beaverbrook and Rothermere – were courted by politicians for the influence they were believed to wield; in consequence, they were showered with honours and often given government jobs to further enhance their invariably enormous egos. Table 8.1 provides recent circulation figures for the national dailies.

By tradition the British press has been pro-Conservative. In 1945 the 6.7 million readers of Conservative-supporting papers outnumbered the 4.4 million who read Labour papers. During the 1970s, the **tabloid** the *Sun* increased the imbalance to the right, and by the 1992 election the Labour-supporting press numbered only the *Guardian* and the *Daily Mirror*, with the vast majority of dailies and Sundays supporting the government party: 9.7 million to 3.3 million. Major's Government however, at the fag-end of the Conservatives' 18 years in power, saw its 'brand' deteriorate markedly. Ejection from the ERM in 1992, endless squabbles with the rebellious Eurosceptics and a deluge of sleaze saw to it that the press began to realign behind Labour's charismatic new leader, Tony Blair. In 1995 the *Sun* caused a sensation by deciding to desert Major and back Blair. It should be noted that by this time a large proportion of the reading public had decided to change sides, and it could be argued that editors were merely making a commercial judgement in changing sides too (see Table 8.2 showing changes of allegiances in the 2001 and 2005 general elections).

Table 8.1 Circulation of daily newspapers, February 2012

Title	Average sale	Percentage change year on year	Percentage change month on month
The *Daily Mirror*	1,122,563	−5.99	2.78
Daily Record	276,003	−10.06	0.55
Daily Star	624,029	−15.02	1.22
The *Sun*	2,751,219	−8.35	8.71
Daily Express	586,707	−8.31	−1.63
Daily Mail	2,011,283	−5.86	0.82
The *Daily Telegraph*	596,180	−8.45	1.56
Financial Times	319,757	−16.53	−4.20
The *Herald*	46,479	−10.80	0.24
The *Guardian*	229,753	−17.74	−0.15
i	243,321	82.30	9.74
The *Independent*	117,084	−36.72	−2.06
The *Scotsman*	39,331	−9.30	1.77
The *Times*	405,113	−11.40	−0.96
Racing Post	47,741	−5.02	−4.60

Source: Press Gazette

Table 8.2 Circulation of Sunday newspapers, February 2012

Title	Average sale	Percentage change year on year	Percentage change month on month
Daily Star on Sunday	644,804	103.59	0.69
Sunday Mail	370,355	1.10	1.40
Sunday Mirror	1,753,202	60.43	3.01
The People	770,772	53.89	−1.22
Sunday Express	607,894	10.47	−3.02
Sunday Post	302,388	−4.88	0.18
The *Mail on Sunday*	1,921,010	−1.89	0.63
Independent on Sunday	124,428	−18.44	−3.09
The *Observer*	264,321	−15.87	−0.88
Scotland on Sunday	50,726	−9.83	11.11
Sunday Herald	31,106	−27.80	7.95
The *Sunday Telegraph*	461,772	−6.92	1.97
The *Sunday Times*	967,975	−6.87	3.48

Source: Press Gazette

Quality press and the tabloids

All the instincts of the working class are Tory: on race, patriotism, you name it. It's just that they happen to vote Labour. Murdoch understands that which is why the Sun has been so successful.

(Lord Bernard Donoghue quoted in Chris Mullin, *A View from the Foothills*, 2009: 397–8)

Anyone can see the UK press has 'quality' newspapers like *The Times*, *Telegraph*, *Guardian*, *Financial Times* and *Independent*, with their Sunday extensions, the 'mid-tabloids' like the *Mail* and *Express* and the tabloids like the *Sun*, *Mirror* and *Star*. Each type of product is aimed at and caters for a particular demographic: educated middle class, lower middle class and working class respectively.

PROFILE

Rupert Murdoch (1931–)

Australian media magnate. Educated at Oxford, where briefly he was a Marxist. Learned newspaper business in Australia but soon acquired papers in Britain, most famously the *Sun*, the *News of the World*, *The Times* and the *Sunday Times*. His company News International also owns Sky TV, and he owns broadcasting outlets all over the world, including China. Blair and Murdoch seem to get on well and he regularly calls to see the man he helped to elect in 1997. Even during the war in Iraq the *Sun* remained solidly behind Blair. His career and reputation took a big blow when his *News of the World* title was shown to have used phone hacking to acquire stories. Despite a close to 3 million a week circulation, the title was discontinued.

Decline of newspaper readership

Sunday paper sales declined from 17 million to 15 million in the period 1990–98, while dailies declined from 15 million to 13 million. Britain is still a nation addicted to newspapers but the habit is declining. The reasons for this are connected with the preference of the young to read newspapers, if at all, free online and their tendency not to acquire the habit of reading a daily newspaper; the competition for the nation's attention in the form of sport, computer games, celebrity gossip and social networks; and the increasing cost of newspapers, with the 'qualities' now costing over a pound per copy. Daily newspapers, with few exceptions, have lost readership at a rate of 2–3 per cent per year according to the OECD report of June 2010. In November 2011 the 11 daily newspapers sold an average of 8.89 million per day, including the surprisingly successful *Independent's* spin-off, the minimalist 'I'; this figure represented a 6.7 per cent decline on the previous year. The rate of decline is therefore accelerating. However, the free morning paper, *Metro*, increased its circulation across the country by 2.42 per cent and 4.42 per cent in London.

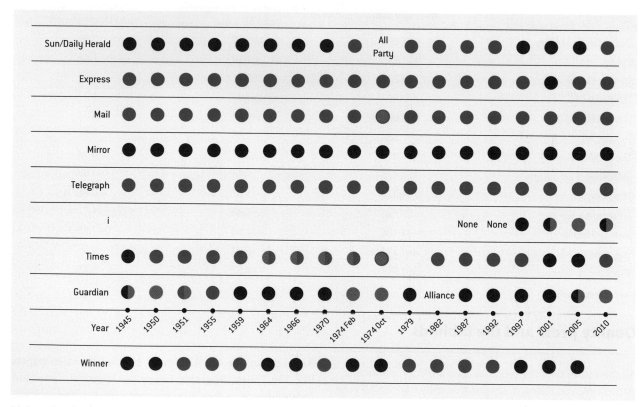

Main national newspaper support elections from 1945–2010
[key: red = Labour; blue = Conservative; yellow = Liberal]
Source: Guardian, 4 May 2010

Tabloids

The declining market helps explain the razor-sharp competition among tabloids. Experience suggests that 'sleaze' stories sell papers, leading to invasions of privacy and associated controversy. The explosion of a national obsession with celebrity has also heavily influenced tabloid content, with the *Star* becoming more like a celeb gossip magazine than a traditional newspaper. The 'qualities' affect to disapprove of such stories but gleefully join in once these stories have, in their opinion, entered the mainstream.

However, there is more to tabloids than lightweight stories; they sell by the millions, and even if a vote is bought through blackening a politician's name, it counts as much as any other on election day. Media experts working for parties read the tabloids very carefully and react accordingly. In elections going back to the 1980s a close correlation was noted between issues run by the Conservatives and lead stories in the tabloids; it was known that certain tabloid editors had close links with Conservative Central Office. Tony Blair had long been convinced of the political importance of the tabloids; his press secretary, Alastair Campbell, was known chiefly as a tabloid journalist, though with much political savvy. Cameron too initially chose a tabloid man for the same role – the ill-fated Andy Coulson, forced to resign in February 2011, in connection with the phone hacking scandal (see below).

Leveson inquiry and report, November 2012

The revelations, via a persistent *Guardian* investigation, were finally widely accepted as true in 2011, that major newspapers – especially those run by Rupert Murdoch's News International group – had been breaking the law through hacking into the phones of public figures. Most of the press withheld support for the story until the revelation that the parents of murdered teenager Milly Dowler had also been victims. This caused public revulsion and led to a wide-ranging public inquiry headed by Lord Justice Leveson in July 2011 into the culture, practices and ethics of the British press. Scores of witnesses gave verbal evidence over the following year; the judge's massive three-volume report came out on 29 November 2012. It found that: phone hacking was not confined to 'one or two practitioners of the "dark arts"'; news stories had been pursued 'recklessly', causing 'devastating' damage to families like the Dowlers; famous people had been viewed as 'fair game' for intrusive reporting which violated their 'entitlement to any sort of private life'; and that complainants had been ignored. In addition he dismissed the press's lobbying for self-regulation and that News International's excessive closeness to the police had caused some 'wrong' decisions to be made.

The report recommended:

- a press regulator independent of both politicians and the press, supported by 'statutory underpinning';
- a statutory obligation of the government to 'protect freedom of the press' and to allow for an independent regulator organised by the industry;
- fines for misconduct would not exceed £1 million and the watchdog would have 'sufficient powers to carry out investigations into suspected serious or systemic breaches of the code';
- an arbitration process regarding civil claims against the press which 'should be fair, quick and inexpensive';
- membership would not be mandatory but those who do not join would be policed by Ofcom, the watchdog for broadcasters.

Reaction to Leveson

Reaction was mixed, with David Cameron, supported by most of the press, balking at the statutory element as a 'Rubicon' he felt should not be crossed in the interests of free speech. His Deputy, Nick Clegg, openly disagreed and insisted statutory foundations were essential for any watchdog to be effective. Ed Miliband agreed with Clegg, thus producing a potentially dangerous rift in the Coalition Government. (See p. 156 for New Press Regulatory Framework.)

Broadcasting

Hitler, Baldwin and Roosevelt exploited the radio successfully during the interwar years, and during the war Churchill's use of the radio must have been worth quite a few divisions to the war effort so inspiring did it prove. Some politicians, surprisingly including Neville Chamberlain, were adept at speaking to the cameras of Pathé News; others, equally surprisingly, like Oswald Mosley, were not. During the war, films like *In Which We Serve*, starring Noel Coward, were effective vehicles for wartime propaganda. Broadcasts of the fledgling television service were stopped during the war and were slow to restart; not so in the USA where television was quickly recruited for political service.

The clearest example was in 1952 when Richard Nixon bought 30 minutes of airtime to clear his name of financial impropriety with his famous 'Checkers' broadcast. Offering himself as a hard-working, honest person of humble origins,

Nixon finished his talk by telling viewers how his daughter had received a puppy as a present: he did not care what 'they say about it, we're gonna keep it!' (see quotation below). This blatant appeal to sentiment and his playing the 'victim' role proved spectacularly successful and confirmed Nixon's vice-presidential place on the Eisenhower ticket. Later on, television ironically contributed to Nixon's undoing through the famous televised debates with Kennedy during the 1960 presidential election contest. Despite an assured verbal performance – those listening on the radio thought he had bested Kennedy – Nixon, the favourite, looked shifty with his 'five o'clock shadow' and crumpled appearance. Kennedy's good looks and strong profile gave him a clear edge. Politicians the world over looked, listened and learned that how you appear on television counts for as much as what you say (see below, Television and the image).

Richard Nixon – the 'Checkers' speech

I should say this: Pat doesn't have a mink coat, but she does have a respectable Republican cloth coat. One other thing I should probably tell you, because if I don't they'll be saying this about me too. We did get something, a gift, after the election . . . a little cocker spaniel in a crate all the way from Texas . . . And our little girl, Trisha, the six-year-old, named it Checkers. And you know, the kids love that dog, and I just want to say this right now, that regardless of what they say about it, we're gonna keep it!

Richard Nixon, US Vice-President, in the 'Checkers speech' (cited in Green 1982)

The British Broadcasting Corporation (BBC) was founded in 1926 as a public corporation. John Reith, its first Director General, set a high moral tone – 'to inform, educate and entertain' – the vestiges of which can still perhaps be discerned within the corporation's output. In 1955, however, the BBC's monopoly was broken when ITV came into being, followed by commercial radio in 1973.

The BBC was granted a second television channel (BBC2) in 1964; a second ITV channel (Channel 4) began broadcasting in 1982, and Channel 5 in 1997. In February 1989 Rupert Murdoch's Sky Television began broadcasting using satellite technology. After a quiet start the new technology took hold and was operating at a profit by 1993. Many of the channels offer old films and popular programme repeats from the USA, but *Sky News* established itself in the eyes of the public and politicians as a respectable and competent 24-hour news channel which stands comparison with the BBC's equivalent rolling service.

The media, entertainment and political significance

. . . popular entertainment engagement with politics matters because of how it shapes political values and images, which in turn influence perception and experience of the world.

(John Street 2011: 101)

In his excellent book on the mass media, John Street (2011) argues powerfully that 'entertainment' is more than mere enjoyment. Soaps, dramas, even game shows exert a subtle, unrecognised influence on the way we interpret the world and form our political views. Evidence of its importance is gained by recalling how prohibitive autocratic governments are regarding certain kinds of art or entertainment. Communist governments tended to see certain films and pop music, even jazz, as subversive Western decadence; Islamic governments tend to be the same, though for different, religious reasons. In such political systems the media are used to present a benign, munificent role of the state, thereby seeking to pre-empt opposition and encourage conformity.

Street points out that the West was not immune from this; the CIA maintained a busy file on John Lennon after he arrived to live in New York (Street 2011: 93). He also argues that satire is often used in the USA to:

. . . pit the assumptions of the commonplace against the pretensions of the politicians and their aides. Everyday common sense is offered as a counterweight to the elite being out of touch.

(Street 2011: 88–9)

Depictions of greed, hypocrisy and incompetence in satirical drama – reflecting a generally cynical analysis – are used to criticise Western political systems on behalf of the public. Soap operas might seem like routine, relaxing airtime for viewers but Street cites studies suggesting how they play important social roles. For example, they can be the vehicles for key values – the primacy of the family, the desirability of helping neighbours and others in need, the importance of recognising the essential humanity of relative 'outsiders' like immigrants or gays (Street 2011: 95–9). He also observes how sport is used to create and reinforce national identities as well as being used by media moguls like Murdoch to establish their presence in the media marketplace. Just as the works of Charles Dickens, through highlighting the condition of the poor, prepared the emotional and ideological context in which socialism could develop, so the media perform the crucial functions of informing and fashioning our political culture.

Television has transformed the electoral process

Since the 1950s television has become the most important media element in general elections. Unlike in the USA, political advertising is not allowed on British television, but party political broadcasts are allocated on the basis of party voting strength. These have gained in importance during elections and become increasingly sophisticated, and some – like the famous Hugh Hudson-produced party political broadcast on Neil Kinnock in 1987 – can have a substantial impact on voter perceptions. More important, however, is the extensive news and current affairs coverage, and here US practice is increasingly being followed:

1 *Professional media managers ('spin doctors')* – such as Labour's Peter Mandelson – have become increasingly important. Brendan Bruce, Conservative Director of Communications 1989–91, comments: 'The survival of entire governments and companies now depends on the effectiveness of these advisers yet few outside the inner circles of power even know these mercenaries exist or what their true functions are' (Bruce 1992: 128). Street observes how British politics has become 'packaged' and more like the American model with its 'large army of professionals (speech writers, pollsters, advertising executives, film makers and so on)' (Street 2011: 237).

2 *Political meetings* have declined. Political leaders now follow their US counterparts in planning their activities in the light of likely media coverage. The hustings – open meetings in which debates and heckling occur – have given way to stage-managed rallies to which only party members have access. Entries, exits and ecstatic applause are all meticulously planned with the all-ticket audience as willing and vocal accomplices.

3 **Soundbites**: Given television's requirements for short, easily packaged messages, political leaders insert pithy, memorable passages into their daily election utterances – the so-called 'soundbite' – in the knowledge that this is what television wants and will show in their news broadcasts and summaries throughout the day.

4 *Party political broadcasts (PPBs)* comprise slots allocated to the parties either on the basis of their voting performance at the previous election or on the number of candidates they are fielding. The first was made by Lord Samuel for the Liberals in 1951 but they were seldom skilfully made until 1987 when film director Hugh Hudson made a film of Neil Kinnock which impressively

raised his personal ratings. In 1997 Major vetoed a PPB which represented Blair as a Faust-like figure, prepared to sell his principles for electoral victory. In recent years PPBs have declined further in importance. During the 1980s they averaged nine minutes in length but by 2005 this figure had come down to a mere two-and-a-half minutes.

Television has influenced the form of political communication

Broadcasting – especially television – has had a transforming impact on political processes. Two minutes of exposure on peak-time television enables politicians to reach more people than they could meet in a lifetime of canvassing, handshaking or addressing public meetings. Alternatively, speaking on BBC Radio 4's early morning *Today* programme gains access to a largely up-market audience of over one million opinion formers and decision makers (Margaret Thatcher always listened to it and once rang in, unsolicited, to comment). In consequence, broadcasting organisations have become potent players in the political game: As for politicians, to command attention in our living rooms, they have to be relaxed, friendly, confidential – they have to talk to us as individuals rather than as members of a crowd (Queen Victoria used to complain Gladstone addressed her as if she were a public meeting). Long speeches are out. On television, orators are obsolete. Political messages have to be compressed into spaces of two to three minutes – often less. Slogans and key phrases have become so important that speech writers are employed to think them up; the playwright Ronald Millar, for example, was thus employed and helped to produce Margaret Thatcher's memorable 'The lady's not for turning' speech at the 1981 Conservative Party Conference (available on YouTube).

Television and the image

Since the arrival of television, appearances have been crucial. Bruce (1992) quotes a study that suggested 'the impact we make on others depends on . . . how we look and behave – 55 per cent; how we speak – 38 per cent and what we say only 7 per cent. Content and form must therefore synchronise for, if they don't, form will usually dominate or undermine content' (1992: 41). So we saw Harold Wilson smoking a pipe to pre-empt what his adviser Marcia Williams felt was an overly aggressive habit of using his fist to emphasise a point.

Margaret Thatcher was the first leading politician to take image building totally professionally under the tutelage of her personal media guru, (later Sir) Gordon Reece. Peter

Mandelson, Labour's premier **spin doctor** of the 1980s and 1990s, commented (author interview, 1992) that by the mid-1980s 'every part of her had been transformed: her hair, her teeth, her nose I suspect, her eyebrows. Not a part of Mrs Thatcher was left unaltered.' Every politician now has a career reason to be vain.

In addition politicians seek to establish an image or *brand* for their parties. A negative image can contaminate policy as the Conservatives found out after nearly a decade in opposition. Theresa May claimed Tories were seen as the 'nasty party', ungenerous, illiberal and uncaring for the poor. Consequently David Cameron, when he became leader in 2005, worked extremely hard to associate his party with liberal attitudes towards gays, the environment and the disadvantaged. Once 'rebranded' he faced an ongoing problem as prime minister trying to prevent negative images returning as he led cuts in public services and, in his 2012 budget, tax cuts for the richest 1%. I went to the CBI conference in Birmingham to hear the Prime Minister speak, and there on a giant TV screen . . . was our very own Big Brother. This Big Brother smiles a lot in a self-deprecating kind of way. He uses 'um' and 'well' as a rhetorical device, to convince us he's not reading out a prepared text, but needs to pause to work out exactly what he means. There is a prepared text of course but he adds to it phrases such as 'I really think' and 'you know I really have to tell you' and 'in my view'. This is the new oratory. The old politicians told us they were right, and that there was no room for doubt, the new politician is not telling us truths, but selling us himself . . . His message is that you should take him on trust; you should believe him because you love him.

(Simon Hoggart, 'Commons Sketch: Blair lays on the therapy for the terracotta army', the *Guardian*, 3 November 1999. © Guardian Newspapers Limited, reprinted with permission)

Television party leader debates, 2010

The most famous televised political debates were between Nixon and Kennedy in 1960, but it took another half century for Britain to copy this particular American innovation. The reason? Probably because Gordon Brown, running way behind in the polls, thought his mastery of policy detail would win the viewers over; Cameron agreed because his mastery at PMQs convinced him he could best Brown in this context too. On 15 April the first debate took place and, with 10 million people tuning in, it transformed the campaign. Missing the supportive noise of his own MPs, Cameron was below par; Brown was maybe a touch better than expected; but the revelation of the debate was Nick Clegg. As the leader of the third party, Clegg was a relative unknown to most voters so his bravura performance had a major impact. Setting himself apart from the two big

A televised debate with party leaders
Source: Press Association/Ken McKay

traditional parties, he was able, helped by his youthful good looks and media confidence, to manufacture a sense of freshness and optimism regarding change for the better. Liberal Democrat poll ratings surged to over 30 per cent, transforming a two-horse race into a three-horse one.

> More fluent and comfortable in the format than an unusually constipated Cameron and a stolid Gordon Brown, Clegg grabbed 'change' from the Tory and 'fairness' from Labour.
>
> (Andrew Rawnsley, *Observer*, 9 May 2010).

'Cleggmania' had broken out but, sadly for his followers, it was short-lived. Clegg was ferociously attacked by the Tory press and from Labour sources too; during the remaining two debates Cameron seemed to 'learn' the rules of this new game and ended up, by many judges, the overall 'winner'. On election day those heady Lib Dem poll predictions were replaced by an actual substantially lower score of 24 per cent: respectable by previous standards but evidence that support won through the media can prove 'soft' and easily eroded by time and the political rough and tumble. However, many Conservative strategists felt Cameron's decision to debate on television was another fatal misjudgement contributing to his party's failure to win an expected overall majority.

Television images: Blair v Brown

These two Labour Prime Ministers had hugely contrasting images. Blair's was chameleon to a degree; keen to appeal to everyone, he tried to be all things to all men: blokish with demotic speech, sipping a cup of tea in photo shoots; serious when reading the lesson at important funerals; aggressive and witty at PMQs; statesmanlike if addressing the UN. On television he was a natural, able to convey relaxed good humour. He was also more than a little vain, seeking to dress 'young' in tight jeans and allegedly using fake tan from time to time.

Brown was totally different: shy in public and often dishevelled; unable to project in public the warmth or wit his friends saw in private. At PMQs he was regularly bested by the more Blair-like Cameron, and his speaking style, aggressive and incisive in Opposition, proved lacklustre and pedestrian in government. Supporters claimed he was honest – not trying to be someone he was not like Blair – and serious in order to address the serious issues of the day. All the polling evidence, however, shows Brown failed to impress, charm or win over the majority of British voters, who clearly respond to a little well-crafted wooing, even if it is at times a little obvious. Brown also lacked basic political nous, leaving a microphone on live when confiding to an aide that a loyal Labour voter, Gillian Duffy, he had just interviewed was a 'bigot' (see photograph).

Gillian Duffy and Gordon Brown

Source: Press Association/Lewis Whyld

Broadcasters have usurped the role of certain political institutions

Local party organisation is less important now that television can gain access to people's homes so easily and effectively. However, the message is a more centralised national one, concentrating on the party leadership rather than local issues and local people. The House of Commons has lost some of its informing and educative function to the media. Ministers often prefer to give statements to the media rather than to Parliament – often on the 'Green' just outside the House – and television interviewers gain much more exclusive access to ministers than the House of Commons can ever hope for. Even public discussion and debate are now purveyed via radio and television programmes such as the BBC's *Today*, *Newsnight* and *Question Time*.

The appointment of party leaders

Clement Attlee was famously taciturn in front of the cameras and Winston Churchill never took to it, but Harold Macmillan flirted with television, conducting a stilted 'interview' in Number 10 in the run-up to the 1959 election. From here on, elections became televisual and the ability to shine on television a qualification for the top political jobs. So, Harold Wilson was good, Ted Heath not so much so; Jim Callaghan was competent, Margaret Thatcher became so; John Major was average; Blair was brilliant. Gordon Brown tried hard but could not overcome some kind of innate shyness and lack of confidence. Significantly, David Cameron's 'without notes' speech at the 2006 Tory conference was the launch pad for his campaign and as leader he has proved a very good media performer as well as crushingly effective at PMQs – the aspect of the Commons most featured on news bulletins. Street argues (Street 2011: 244) that we have seen the emergence of a *'celebrity politics'* in which the politicians 'mimic the style of pop stars and film stars, in an attempt to make themselves look more attractive to increasingly disillusioned voters and media' (ibid.: 236).

Personnel

Unsurprisingly, the media and politics have become more closely interrelated, with media professionals such as David Steel, Tony Benn, Bryan Gould, Austin Mitchell and Peter Mandelson going into politics, and Robert Kilroy-Silk, Brian Walden, Michael Portillo and Matthew Parris moving out of politics and into the media. The apotheosis of this tendency was represented by former US President Ronald Reagan, who used his actor's ability to speak lines to the camera to compensate, arguably, for other political inadequacies.

Spin doctors

New Labour is extremely relaxed about people becoming filthy rich.

(Peter Mandelson, 1998)

These potent new actors on the political stage focus their energies on ensuring that the media give the desired interpretation of events or statements (see Street 2011: Chapter 9). Their provenance is usually thought to have been during the 1980s when the *New York Times* used the term in an October 1984 article to describe smartly dressed men and women who moved among crowds at political events and sought to explain what their political boss had *really* meant to say. Since then the popular idea is of somewhat shadowy figures moving around and choreographing press conferences or on the phone to television executives cajoling and bullying to get their way. The results are usually believed to be a distortion of the truth and to have fuelled the lack of trust in the political process. Malcolm Tucker, the profane, ruthless but entirely fictional spin doctor in the satirical sitcom *The Thick of It* reflected something of this popular view.

New Labour and spin

While other prime ministers faced world wars or major economic crisies, I have faced the modern media.

Tony Blair in Richards 2010: 195

One student of the media quoted a senior Labour spin doctor as saying: 'Communications is not an afterthought to our policy. It's central to the whole mission of New Labour' (Barnett and Gaber 2001: 116). So, it is hardly surprising that Labour was demonised as the party that invested too much in presentation, in 'spin'. Roy Greenslade, writing in the *Guardian* on 6 June 2002, argued that it all began in response to the way Neil Kinnock was treated by the right-wing press during the 1980s, attacked as a 'windbag', weak and incompetent. The *Sun*, *Mail* and *Express* pulled no punches and built up their coverage – much of it based on no evidence – thoughout the decade. Leading up to the 1992 election, the *Sun*'s editor, Kelvin McKenzie, went to town two days before polling day, devoting nine pages to its 'Nightmare on Kinnock Street' feature. 'It's *The Sun* wot won it' was the gloatingly triumphant headline following the result.

Maybe the reaction of Mandelson and his colleagues to this onslaught is understandable. Together with Alastair Campbell, Blair's press secretary, he insisted slurs were rebutted and retractions given. The right-wing media soon discovered they were being matched, and criticisms of 'New Labour spin' became commonplace. Unfortunately this aggressive media policy continued into government, and what had been an asset rapidly became a liability as voters began to doubt the veracity of government statements and statistics.

'Spin is still everywhere', wrote Sir Bernard Ingham, Thatcher's fearsome spin doctor, in the *Sunday Times* (16 March 2003), 'and because of spin, Blair has forfeited the trust of the nation and . . . parliament.' Opinion polls gauging public trust in Blair certainly reinforced such a judgement, and some even attributed the shockingly low turnout in the 2001 election to a collapse of voter belief in what the government was saying.

It would be foolish to accuse New Labour of inventing spin; even before the advent of mass media, governments sought to offer the best possible interpretations of their actions. Yet, for all its expertise, Blair's operation lacked subtlety. Campbell acquired too high a profile as the demonic 'spinner' and even featured as the subject of a televised profile. Blair too once asked in a leaked memo for 'more eye-catching initiatives' to combat Conservative policy statements. After the non-discovery of weapons of

PROFILE

Alastair Campbell (1957–)

Tony Blair's press secretary. Educated at Cambridge; had a career in tabloid journalism before joining Blair's personal staff. Often referred to as the 'real Deputy Prime Minister', he had constant access to his boss, and his words were held to carry the authority of the PM. He was well known to journalists and he used charm and threats to get his own way. In 2003 he was incensed when accused via a BBC interview of 'sexing up' the intelligence dossier used to justify the decision to go to war in Iraq. He was exonerated eventually but the ensuing media furore – during which he was accused of vindictiveness against the BBC – proved to be his swansong as he stepped down in the autumn of that year, still defiant and largely contemptuous of the nation's media.

PROFILE

Peter Mandelson (1954–)

He was educated at Hendon County Grammar School and at Oxford. He was made Labour's director of communications in 1985 and was a close ally of Neil Kinnock in moving the party into the centre. He played an important role in the 1987 and 1992 general elections when he himself was elected MP for Hartlepool. He advised Tony Blair on his leadership campaign in 1994 following John Smith's death, though secretly. With Blair and Brown he became, along with these young politicians, an architect of New Labour. He served in the Cabinet twice but in July 2004 Blair announced that his old friend was to be sent to Brussels as the UK's European Trade Commissioner. With Blair gone, most thought the *Prince of Darkness's* time in the spotlight was over. However, Gordon Brown, known as Mandelson's sworn enemy, amazed everyone by calling him back into the Cabinet in October 2008 as Business Secretary and virtual Deputy Prime Minister.

mass destruction in Iraq, after Blair had cited them as the justification for invasion in 2003, the association of New Labour with 'spin' was compounded.

Peter Oborne's critique of 'manipulative populism'

The well-known columnist, author and broadcaster, Peter Oborne, wrote a swingeing attack on the 'supplanting of parliamentary democracy' . . . 'a regime of media hype, spin doctors and skullduggery' (*The Triumph of the Political Class*). He recalls that Stanley Baldwin and Clement Attlee were Prime Ministers who worked through their ministers – who are the people who actually wield the legal power of government – and Parliament. It followed that the Chief Whip was the person on whom the PM relied most heavily for support in his political battles.

Oborne (2007: 53) recalls Brown's promise to:

bring back cabinet government, respect civil service impartiality, restore the primacy of parliament and to abandon the dark political arts at which the team of political assassins around Blair had so excelled.

However, Brown did none of these things and Cameron's ill-fated appointment of Andy Coulson – former editor of the

News of the World – did not at the time suggest any real change if a new regime was to enter Downing Street. Oborne also explains that the elevation of Campbell and Coulson was due not necessarily to mere media strategies, but to the new nature of the media. It is now so all-encompassing, such a constant and demanding presence, that it has become the instrument of a new kind of politics. Parliament is supposed to be the body which ultimately determines policy and decisions but the media is now so powerful it can apply a range of influences: certainly delays, sometimes vetoes as well as urge courses of action. Oborne cites the vivid phrase coined by Anthony Barnett to describe this new way in which we are governed: 'manipulative populism'.

Tabloidisation of television

Studies have shown the reduction of peak time current affairs television since the 1980s and some have argued there has been a progressive 'dumbing down' of the medium. Possible explanations for this, offered by Leach et al. (2003: 164–5), are that:

1 Television competition has taken its cue from print journalism where falling sales have induced a 'race to the bottom'.

2 Newspapers are chasing younger readers and hope the snappy, abbreviated style, peppered with items about celebrities and the like, will prove attractive to this demographic.

3 Rupert Murdoch's influence of the mass media. For example, when Elvis Presley died *The Times* did not cover the funeral in 1977 as it was deemed inappropriate, but after Murdoch took over in 1981 two journalists were sent to cover Bob Marley's last rites.

4 Increased competition from satellite and cable plus internet-carried material has forced more populist policies.

The phone-hacking scandal, 2011–12

The Leveson inquiry into the ethics and practices of the press occasioned by the phone-hacking scandal was set up by David Cameron in July 2011. However, the story began in 2005 when *News of the World* journalists 'hacked' into the mobile phones of member of the royal family in pursuit of stories; royal editor Clive Goodman and his colleague Glen Mulcaire pleaded guilty to these crimes; they were imprisoned for four and six months respectively. The editor of the Sunday tabloid denied any knowledge of their 'rogue' behaviour, repeating his denials in front of a Commons' Select committee. However, the mutterings that such ignorance was not believable in any conscientious editor did not cease and Nick Davies of the *Guardian* eventually unearthed evidence proving that royal phone hackings were not isolated offences and that senior staff must have known about it.

In the summer of 2011 the senior staff of News International (NI) appeared before the Media and Culture Committee where their main defence was, again, that they knew nothing about such murky matters, despite the fact that, in the light of emerging evidence, it was an explanation almost impossible to sustain. NI could no longer deny that phone hacking had been a widespread practice within the Sunday tabloid; it closed the *News of the World* on 7 July and in February 2011 launched a replacement, the *Sun on Sunday*. By then a major inquiry into press ethics and practices under Justice Leveson had been set up and its hearings attracted considerable publicity. In March 2012, Deputy Assistant Commissioner of the Metropolitan Police, Sue Ackers, astonished the inquiry by describing a 'culture of illegal payments at the *Sun*' to officials in 'all areas of public life'. The outcome of this scandal is a much tougher regulatory agency than the Press Complaints Commission, though one not warmly supported by the press itself.

The media and pressure groups

Just as individual politicians influence the media and seek their platforms to convey their messages, so do pressure groups as they seek to influence government policy. Pressure group campaigners such as gay rights campaigner, Peter Tatchell, and Tony Juniper, formerly leader of Friends of the Earth, are expert and knowledgeable about massaging the form in which the press and television like to receive stories. Because it has been so successful, much pressure group activity now revolves around the use of the media. For example, anti-blood-sports campaigners use yellow smoke when trying to disrupt hunting events as they know television responds well to it.

The mass media and voting behaviour

Jay Blumler et al.'s (1978) judgement that 'modern election campaigns have to a considerable extent become fully and truly television campaigns', was probably a decade late. But what impact do the mass media have on the way in which

citizens cast their votes? Does the form that different media give to political messages make any major difference? Substantial research on this topic has been undertaken, although with little definite outcome. One school of thought favours the view that the media do very little to influence voting directly but merely reinforce existing preferences.

Blumler and McQuail (1967) argued that people do not blandly receive and react to political media messages, but instead apply a filter effect. Denver (1992: 99) summarises this effect under the headings of selective exposure, perception and retention.

1 *Selective exposure*: Many people avoid watching altogether when politics appear on television or in the press, while those who are interested favour those newspapers or television programmes that support rather than challenge their views.

2 *Selective perception*: The views and values that people have serve to 'edit' incoming information so that they tend to accept what they want to believe and ignore what they do not.

3 *Selective retention*: The same editing process is applied to what people choose to remember of what they have read or viewed.

The variety of media, moreover, act in a variety of ways as Table 8.3 suggests.

However, the filter-reinforcement thesis seems to assign too minor a role to such an all-pervasive element. It does not seem to make 'common' sense. In an age when party preferences have weakened and people are voting much more instrumentally, according to issues, then surely the more objective television coverage has a role to play in switching votes? Is it reasonable to suppose the filter effect negates all information that challenges or conflicts with established positions? If so, then why do parties persist in spending large sums on party political broadcasts? Some empirical data support a direct-influence thesis, especially in respect of television:

1 Professor Ivor Crewe maintains that during election campaigns up to 30 per cent of voters switch their votes,

Table 8.3 The press, television and political influence

Television	Press
Balanced	Partisan
Trusted	Not trusted
Mass audience	Segmented audience
'Passive' audience politically	'Active' audience
Most important source of information	Secondary source

Source: Professor David Denver

so despite the surface calm in 1983 and 1987 there was considerable 'churning' beneath the surface. These two elections may have been unusual in any case: the before and after campaign variations were much larger in 1979, 1974 and 1970 although not in the landslide 1997 election.

2 Many studies reveal that the four weeks of an election campaign provide too short a time over which to judge the impact of the media. Major shifts in voting preference take place between elections, and it is quite possible, or even probable, that media coverage plays a significant role.

Focus groups

Much has been written about New Labour and focus groups, and a great deal of it has been uncomplimentary. They have been cited as evidence of Labour's concern with the superficial, with adapting policy on the basis of marketing expediency and not principle – in other words, as the thin end of the wedge that Old Labour critics argue has robbed the party of its moral purpose and integrity. This point of view was hotly refuted by the chief enthusiast for the technique in the Blairite party: the late Philip Gould, former advertising expert, who wrote a fascinating book on the evolution of the 'new' party and its march to power (Gould 1999). In the following extract he explains the technique and his own reasons for having faith in it:

> The eight or so members of the group will have been recruited by a research company according to a formal specification: who they voted for in the last election, their age, their occupation . . . I do not just sit there and listen. I challenge, I argue back, I force them to confront issues. I confront issues myself. I like to use the group to develop and test ideas.
>
> (Gould 1999: 327–8)

The permanent campaign

In 2000 Ornstein and Mann edited a book entitled *The Permanent Campaign, and its Future*. The provenance of the phrase lay in 1982 with Sidney Blumenthal, who used it to describe the emergent style of media coverage in the USA. Assiduous USA watchers in New Labour's elite seem to have absorbed the new approach and made it their own: 'a nonstop process of seeking to manipulate sources of public approval to engage in the act of governing itself' (Hugh Heclo in Ornstein and Mann 2000: 219). In other words, government and campaigning have become indistinguishable. The tendency now is for parties in government to view each day as something to be 'won' or 'lost'.

Assessing the effect of the media

Judging the effect of the media on voting behaviour is very difficult, because it is so hard to disentangle it from a myriad of factors such as family, work, region and class that play a determining role. However, it seems fair to say that:

1 *The media reinforce political attitudes*: This is important when the degree of commitment to a party can prove crucial when events between elections, as they always do, put loyalties to the test.

2 *The media help to set the agenda of debate*: This 'framing' of the political agenda can be seen on Radio 4's *Today* programme which regularly bases its items on news stories picked from the day's papers. During election campaigns party press conferences attempt to achieve this, but the media do not always conform, and between elections the media, especially the print media, play a much more important agenda-setting role.

3 *Media reportage has some direct impact* on persuading voters to change sides, but research has not yet made clear whether this effect is major or marginal.

Theories and the mass media

The mass media and the theory of pluralist democracy

If the mass media have such a transforming impact on politics, then how have they affected the fabric of British democracy? It all depends on what we mean by democracy. The popular and indeed 'official' view is that our elected legislature exerts watchdog control over the executive and allows a large degree of citizen participation in the process of government. This **pluralist** system provides a free market of ideas and a shifting, open competition for power between political parties, pressure groups and various other groups in society. Supporters of the present system claim that not only is it how the system ought to work (a normative theory of government) but it is, to a large extent, also descriptive: this is how it works in practice.

According to this view, the media play a vital political role:

1 They report and represent popular views to those invested with decision-making powers.

2 They inform society about the actions of government, educating voters in the issues of the day. The range of newspapers available provides a variety of interpretations and advice.

3 They act as a watchdog of the public interest, defending the ordinary person against a possibly over-mighty government through their powers of exposure, investigation and interrogation. To fulfil this neutral, disinterested role, it follows that the media need to be given extensive freedom to question and publish.

This pluralist view of the media's role, once again both normative and descriptive, has been criticised under the following points.

Do ownership and control influence media messages?

Excluding the BBC, the media organisations are substantially part of the business world and embrace profit making as a central objective. This fact alone severely prejudices media claims to objectivity in reporting the news and reflecting popular feeling. In recent years ownership has concentrated markedly. About 80 per cent of newspaper circulation is in the hands of four conglomerates: Associated Newspapers, owned by the Rothermere family and controlling the *Daily Mail* and the *Mail on Sunday*; the Mirror Newspaper Group, owning the *Mirror*, *Sunday Mirror* and *Sunday People*; United Newspapers, owning the *Express*, the *Sunday Express*, the *Star* and the *Standard*; and News International, severely wounded by the phone-hacking scandal (see above) owning *The Times*, *Sunday Times* and the *Sun*. These latter-day press barons and media groups also own rafts of the regional press and have strong television interests: Murdoch, for example, owns Sky Television (for a fuller analysis see Street 2011: Chapter 6).

Nor is the press especially accountable: the Press Council used to be a powerful and respected watchdog on newspaper editors, but it tended to acquiesce meekly in the concentration of ownership on the grounds that the danger of monopoly control is less unacceptable than the bankruptcy of familiar national titles. Moreover, since the *Sun* regularly flouted its rulings, the council lost even more respect and was unable, for example, to prevent the private lives of public figures being invaded by tabloid journalists to an alarming degree. Following the report of the Leveson inquiry into the press regulation of the press will be significantly strengthened.

Television evinces a much clearer distinction between ownership and control and fits more easily into the pluralist model. The BBC, of course, is government-owned, and in theory at least its board of governors exercises independent

PROFILE

Christopher Meyer, (1944–)

Chairman of the Press Complaints Commission, Oxbridge-educated Meyer is a career diplomat who stepped in to take over the PCC chair when Lord Wakeham became enmired in the 2002 Enron scandal. He served in Moscow, Brussels, Bonn and Washington and is fluent in all the relevant languages. In the 1980s, he was the chief Foreign Office spokesman under Geoffrey Howe and then took over as chief press officer. It is said that Meyer was pivotal in building a good relationship between Blair and Bush in the wake of the latter's controversial election – though much of this could be explained by good personal chemistry. In 2005 he published memoirs entitled *DC Confidential* which distributed insights into the way in which Blair operated (not good on detail), Prescott (poor on expressing himself), Jack Straw ('more to be liked than admired') and sundry other ministers whom he described as 'pygmies'. Apart from these personal swipes, however, there was little of substance in the book and Meyer survived calls for him to resign his PCC post.

control. Independent television is privately owned, and this ownership is becoming more concentrated, but the Independent Broadcasting Authority (IBA) uses its considerable legal powers under the 1981 Broadcasting Act to ensure 'balance' and 'due accuracy and impartiality' on sensitive political issues. This is not to say that television can be acquitted of the charge of bias – as we shall see below – but merely that television controllers are forbidden by law to display open partisanship and that those people who own their companies cannot insist on particular editorial lines.

News values are at odds with the requirements of a pluralist system

In order to create profits, media organisations compete for their audiences, with the consequent pursuit of the lowest common denominator in public taste. In the case of the tabloids this means the relegation of hard news to inside pages and the promotion to the front page of trivial stories such as sex scandals, royal family gossip and the comings and goings of soap opera stars. The same tendency has been apparent on television, with the reduction of current affairs programmes, their demotion from peak viewing times and the dilution of news programmes with more 'human interest' stories. As a result of this tendency it can be argued that the media's educative role in a pluralist democracy is being diminished. Some would go further, however, and maintain that the dominant news values adopted by the media are in any case inappropriate for this role. The experience of successful newspapers has helped to create a set of criteria for judging newsworthiness that news editors in all branches of the media automatically accept and apply more or less intuitively. The themes to which the public are believed to respond include:

1 *Personalities*: People quickly become bored with statistics and carefully marshalled arguments and relate to stories that involve disagreement, personality conflicts or interesting personal details.

2 *Revelations*: Journalist Nicholas Tomalin once defined news as the making public of something that someone wished to keep secret. Leaked documents, financial malpractice and sexual peccadilloes, e.g. the revelation that John Major had a four-year affair with Edwina Currie, are assiduously reported and eagerly read.

3 *Disasters*: The public has both a natural and a somewhat morbid interest in such matters.

4 *Visual back-up*: Stories that can be supported by good photographs (or film footage on TV) will often take precedence over those that cannot be so supported.

5 *Celebrities*: Increasingly over the past two decades news items relating to celebrities have become of great interest to readers. Consequently media outlets seek to link their content to celebrity of some kind.

It is commonly believed that newspapers which ignore these ground rules will fail commercially and that current affairs television which tries too hard to be serious will be largely ignored and described, fatally, as 'boring'. There is much evidence to suggest that these news values are based on fact: that, perhaps to our shame, these are the themes to which we most readily respond. However, it does mean that the vast media industry is engaged in providing a distorted view of the world via its concentration on limited and relatively unimportant aspects of social reality.

BOX 8.1

Bias, broadcasting and the political parties

Harold Wilson was notoriously paranoid about the media and believed that not only the press but also the BBC was 'ineradicably' biased against him, full of 'card-carrying Tories', in the words of Michael Cockerell. Perhaps it is being in government that explains it, as in the 1980s it was Margaret Thatcher and her 'enforcer' Norman Tebbit who seemed paranoid. He launched ferocious attacks on the corporation, calling it 'the insufferable, smug, sanctimonious, naive, guilt-ridden, wet, pink, orthodoxy of that sunset home of that third-rate decade, the sixties'.

Answering questions in the House can be stressful amid all the noise, but ultimately the barbs can be ignored and the questions avoided easily. But on radio or television well-briefed interviewers can put politicians on the spot. This is why ministers of both parties have complained so vehemently about *Today* presenter John Humphrys and *Newsnight's* Jeremy Paxman. Cockerell explains that Humphrys is not a 'politically motivated questioner; his aim is to strip away the public relations gloss and to use his own sharp teeth to counter pre-rehearsed soundbites' (*Guardian*, 28 May 1996).

This probably gets to the heart of the perennial conflict between politicians and the media. Politicians in power ideally would like to control the media – Mrs Thatcher once said she did not like short interviews but would like instead to have four hours of airtime on her own – and resent the criticism that they receive from journalists and interviewers. In a pluralist democracy it is indeed the job of the media to make government more accountable to the public, and perhaps it is when politicians do not like it that the media are doing their jobs most effectively (see also Street 2011: Chapter 1).

The lobby system favours the government of the day

The pluralist model requires that the media report news in a truthful and neutral way. We have already seen that ownership heavily influences the partisanship of the press, but other critics argue that the lobby system of political reporting introduces a distortion of a different kind. Some 150 political journalists at Westminster are known collectively as 'the lobby'. In effect, they belong to a club with strict rules whereby they receive special briefings from government spokesmen in exchange for keeping quiet about their sources. Supporters claim that this is an important means of obtaining information that the public would not otherwise receive, but critics disagree. Anthony Howard, the veteran political commentator, has written that lobby correspondents, rather like prostitutes, become 'clients' or otherwise 'instruments for a politician's gratification' (Hennessy 1985: 9). The charge is that journalists become lazy, uncritical and incurious, preferring to derive their copy from bland government briefings – often delivered at dictation speed.

Television companies are vulnerable to political pressure

Ever since the broadcasting media became an integral part of the political process during the 1950s, governments of all complexions have had uneasy relationships with the BBC, an organisation with a worldwide reputation for excellence and for accurate, objective current affairs coverage. Margaret Thatcher, however, took government hostility to new lengths; indeed, 'abhorrence of the BBC appeared for a while to be a litmus test for the Conservativeness of MPs' (Negrine 1995: 125). Governments seek to influence the BBC in three major ways. First, they have the power of appointment to the corporation's board of governors. The post of chairman is especially important; Marmaduke Hussey's appointment in 1986 was believed to be a response to perceived left-wing tendencies (according to one report, he was ordered by Norman Tebbit's office to 'get in there and sort it out – in days and not months'). Second, governments can threaten to alter the licence system (although former Home Secretary Willie Whitelaw knew of no occasion when this threat had been used): Margaret Thatcher was known to favour the introduction of advertising to finance the BBC, but the Peacock Commission on the financing of television refused to endorse this approach. Third, governments attempt to exert pressure in relation to particular programmes – often citing security reasons. The range of disputes between the Thatcher governments and the BBC is unparalleled in recent history. In part this was a consequence of a dominant, long-established and relatively unchallenged Prime Minister as well as Thatcher's determination to challenge the old consensus – she long suspected that it resided tenaciously within the top echelons of the BBC.

Theories of class dominance

The Glasgow University Media Group

On the basis of their extensive programme analyses, the Glasgow University Media Group suggest that television coverage of economic news tends to place the 'blame for society's industrial and economic problems at the door of the workforce. This is done in the face of contradictory evidence, which when it appears is either ignored [or] smothered' (1976: 267–8). Reports on industrial relations were 'clearly skewed against the interests of the working class and organised labour . . . in favour of the managers of industry'. The Glasgow research provoked a storm of criticism. In 1985, an academic counterblast was provided by Martin Harrison (1985), who criticised the slender basis of the Glasgow research and adduced new evidence that contradicted its conclusions. The Glasgow research is often cited in support of more general theories on how the media reinforce, protect and advance dominant class interests in society. Variations on the theme were produced by Gramsci, in the 1930s by the Frankfurt School of social theorists and in the 1970s by the sociocultural approach of Professor Stuart Hall (for detailed analysis see McQuail 1983: 57–70; Watts 1997), but the essence of their case is summed up in Marx's proposition that 'the ideas of the ruling class are in every epoch the ruling ideas'. He argued that those people who own and control the economic means of production – the ruling class – will seek to persuade everyone else that preserving status quo values and institutions is in the interests of society as a whole.

The means employed are infinitely subtle and indirect, via religious ideas, support for the institution of the family, the monarchy and much else. Inevitably the role of the mass media, according to this analysis, is crucial. Marxists totally reject the pluralist model of the media as independent and neutral, as the servant rather than the master of society. They see the media merely as the instrument of class domination, owned by the ruling class and carrying their messages into every home in the land. It is in moments of crisis, Marxists would claim, that the fundamental bias of state institutions is made clear. In 1926, during the General Strike, Lord Reith, the first Director General of the BBC, provided some evidence for this view when he confided to his diary, 'they want us to be able to say they did not commandeer us, but they know they can trust us not to be really impartial' (see also Street 2010: 289–301).

Which of the two models – pluralist or class dominance – better describes the role of the media in British society?

From the discussion so far, the pluralist model would appear inadequate in a number of respects. Its ability to act as a fair and accurate channel of communication between government and society is distorted by the political bias of the press, the lobby system, news values and the tendency of television to reflect consensual values. Moreover, the media are far from being truly independent: the press is largely owned by capitalist enterprises, and television is vulnerable to government pressure of various kinds. Does this mean that the dominance model is closer to the truth? Not really.

1 As former editor of *ITN News*, David Nicholas observes, 'trying to manipulate the news is as natural an instinct to a politician as breathing oxygen', but because politicians try does not mean that they always succeed. People who work in the media jealously guard their freedom and vigorously resist government interference (Tyne Tees TV, April 1986).

2 The media may tend to reflect consensual views, but this does not prevent radical messages regularly breaking into the news – sometimes because they accord with news values themselves. Television also challenges and criticises the status quo at the humorous level: for example, in the form of the satirical *The Thick of It* and at the serious level in the form of the BBC's regular *Panorama* programme.

3 Programmes such as *Rough Justice* and *First Tuesday* in the past have shown that persistent and highly professional research can shame a reluctant establishment into action to reverse injustices – as in the case of the Guildford Four, released in 1989 after 15 years of wrongful imprisonment.

4 News values do not invariably serve ruling-class interests, otherwise governments would not try so hard to manipulate them. And even the most serious of the quality newspapers will join the feeding frenzy of a scandal once it has taken hold.

Each model, then, contains elements of the truth, but neither comes near the whole truth. Which is the nearer? The reader must decide; but despite all its inadequacies and distortions the pluralist model probably offers the better framework for understanding how the mass media interact with the British political system. It is clear that certain parts of the media – the quality press, the political weeklies, BBC, ITN and Sky News, BBC Radios 4 and 5 plus the little-watched Parliament Channel – all contribute greatly towards an informed democracy. It is also clear that other parts – the daily and Sunday tabloids, commercial radio – in relative terms do not, though, as we have seen, the more subtle influence of entertainment programmes like soaps and game shows do have to be taken into account.

Language and politics

All this modern emphasis on technology can obscure the fact that in politics language is still of crucial importance. Taking the example of Northern Ireland, we have seen how the precise meaning of words has provided a passionate bone of contention. When the IRA announced its ceasefire in 1994, its opponents insisted it should be a 'permanent' one. However, the paramilitary organisation did not wish to abandon its ability to use the threat of violence as a negotiating counter and refused to comply, insisting that its term 'complete' ceasefire was as good as the British government needed or would in any case get. Gerry Adams, president of the political wing of the IRA, Sinn Fein, had a similar problem over his attitude towards bombings. His close contact with the bombers made it impossible for him to condemn the bombing of Manchester in June 1996, so he used other less committing words like 'regret' or 'unfortunate'. Another aspect is tone of voice, which can bestow whole varieties of meaning to a statement or a speech. Sir Patrick Mayhew, for example, John Major's Northern Ireland Secretary, specialised in being 'calm'.

The new media

1 *Information*: It is now possible to download immense amounts of up-to-date information about political issues via the internet.

2 *E-mail*: It is possible to communicate with politicians and the politically active all over the world, extending enormously the scope of political action.

3 *Interactive democracy*: By being hooked up to the internet, it might be possible for politicians or government in democracies to seek endorsement for policies directly from the people. This would have all kinds of drawbacks: for example, it could slow down the political process even more than at present in developed countries; it could give a platform to unsavoury messages from racists and power-seeking ideologues; it might enthrone the majority with a power it chooses to abuse. But these opportunities exist, and it is virtually certain that they will be experimented with if not adopted in the near future.

4 *Blogs*: It is now possible for anyone to set up their own website and issue opinions and information to the world on a regular basis. In the year 2005 it was calculated that 80,000 weblogs (blogs) were created and their rate of increase has now become exponential. Many younger people now use such sources as a matter of course, and some – like the US Drudge Report – break new stories or

influence election campaigns. Fareed Zakaria offers this insight into the implications of the revolution currently taking place (see also Box 8.2):

> Today's information revolution has produced thousands of outlets for news that make central control impossible and dissent easy. The Internet has taken this process another huge step forward, being a system where, in the columnist Thomas Friedman's words, 'Everyone is connected but no one is in control.'
>
> (Zakaria 2004: 17)

However, the internet still has some way to go before the existing media are usurped. Most blogs are manned by one or two people only; they do not have the same income as mainstream media; their scoops are still rare and often confined to fringe issues and political gossip. But, as Box 8.3 suggests, in the USA maybe the locus of power is shifting much faster than in the UK.

5 *Mobile phones*: Virtually everyone now owns a mobile phone and this fact, together with the onrush of technology, has produced the transmission of more and more different types of information via their tiny screens. Some political parties have issued text messages to phone owners, but in 2006 more possibilities were opened up by the mobile provider which announced the results of an experiment whereby television had been broadcast direct to mobile phone subscribers. Despite the smallness of the screens, the trial was declared successful with thousands of mobile owners watching several hours of television a week – though most of it at home rather than on the move. Inevitably news and political content will in future be imbibed via this unlikely route and will become yet another facet of the political media.

6 *Online pressure groups*: in recent years a number of online organisations have sprung up – Avaas in the USA, 38 Degrees in the UK – which solicit support for (mostly) left-of-centre causes and compile impressively large online petitions which are used to pressurise decision-makers.

7 *Twitter*: This relatively new social medium launched in 2006 whereby users can post brief messages of no more than 140 characters. In the UK it is used for comment and occasionally revelations as in the North Wales child abuse case when various suggestions as to who the alleged senior Tory official involved might be. Abroad these short, text-like messages were used by the initiators of the 2011 'Arab Spring' to coordinate movements in countries like Egypt, Tunisia and Iran. Many politicians use their Twitter accounts for political purposes. George Galloway has 150,000 'followers' on Twitter, over twice the population of the average constituency.

Writing in *The Times* on 17 October 2012, Tony Blair's former spin doctor, Alastair Campbell, delivered his incisive judgements on how the new media have transformed the political landscape.

1 'The speed of change is breathtaking. Facebook, founded in 2004 recently recorded its one billionth devotee. YouTube, created in 2005, now has more videos downloaded in one month than three US TV networks created

---

BOX 8.2

Blogs come of age: The Huffington Post

Starting in 2005 as a blog initiated by, amongst others, Arianna Huffington, Greek-born, Oxbridge-educated and oil millionaire divorcee, the 'HuffPo' has been making waves in the USA for some time. This is partly because its owner, once the scourge of the right, has swung to the left and now champions Obama. Moreover, while print journalism licks its wounds at redundancies and closures, the liberal blog had just announced, in April 2009, a $1.7 million fund to help fill the gap left by the disappearing investigative news teams. The rise of this blog has been astonishing and it now calls itself an 'internet newspaper', does its own investigations and provides mainstream news and comment:

> Less than four years old and with fewer than 60 staff (including seven news reporters), it is now a competitor to the New York Times, 158 years old and with more than 1,000 journalists. According to the ratings website Comscore, in February the HuffPo drew more than a third of the Times's traffic: 7.3 million unique users to 18.4 million.
>
> (Ed Pilkington, *Guardian, Media Guardian*, 6 April 2009)

in 60 years. Twitter launched in 2006 has more than 900 million users with 800,000 joining every day. The number of British people on Twitter, 10 million – has overtaken the number buying a daily newspaper.'

2 'Where (the Democrats' Obama campaign) did use Facebook brilliantly was in identifying supporters and turning them into activist ambassadors. In an era when people believe politicians and journalists less than they used to, they still respect each other. And therein lies the power of social media as a political force – a tech version of old-fashioned, word-of-mouth campaigning.'

3 'What they (politicians) really fear is losing control. . . . Nobody controls how the message lands. What this offers politicians is the opportunity to communicate directly without having to rely on elites of the old media. That is both emancipating and democratic . . . Today the agenda changes by the hour, often with a big gap between what the media deem newsworthy and what the public decide is "most viewed" or "most read".'

4 'Today governments are having to adapt to changes driven by technology and the personalisation of communications. If they don't, the results can be seismic.'

5 'There is an inescapable momentum behind the flow of political power to individuals and movements which recognise no national boundaries . . . [Politicians] must understand that the only voice they can control is their own, and they must be prepared for the voters' response to echo across the digital world.'

BOX 8.3

BRITAIN IN CONTEXT

The media

The nature of the media in any country is usually a reflection of its political character. Democracies believe in freedom of speech and hence in open media, though politicians in democracies seek constantly to manipulate the media to their own advantage. In authoritarian systems the media are usually heavily controlled in terms of what newspapers can print or broadcasters can say on air.

The media in the UK play a similar role to those in the USA. The major difference is that in the latter, candidates can buy airtime to show their own political ads and to issue 'attack ads' to weaken opposing candidates. As such ads are very expensive; this gives an advantage to campaigns which are well funded. Indeed, many candidates in the USA and incumbent legislators, governors and so forth, spend much of their energies raising campaign cash. The phenomenon of 'spin doctors' was more or less invented in the USA where sculpting messages or media images for mass consumption has been something of a growth industry; they have since been disseminated worldwide to wherever democratic elections are regularly held. Much campaign output is either 'semi-mediated' like the presidential debates or 'mediated' in news broadcasts, but in the latter case candidates and their aides have become clever in gaining favourable media attention.

Many media critics claim that in the US the media favour the right in that they reflect and reinforce attitudes wholly accepting of the status quo. They point to Fox News, owned by Rupert Murdoch which, leans towards a Bush interpretation of issues and news stories. However, Fox News and its right-wing partisan output did nothing for Mitt Romney's unsuccessful campaign for the White House in November 2012. As in the UK debate, others deny any bias and argue the media are essentially free to state views and opinions. But this argument attains a worldwide dimension when ownership of the media is examined. Huge media conglomerates like Murdoch's News Corporation or Berlusconi's Mediaset control media in other countries and there is concern that some political control is thereby connected. Murdoch, for example, broadcasts satellite television into China and has agreed to some censorship controls demanded by the government of that country.

Such control worries those concerned to spread freedom and democracy. Alastair Campbell, above, analyses the growing impact of blogs and Twitter and celebrates their democratic nature. But autocratic governments fear such freedom, are aware of its actual and potential power and will use coercive methods to neutralise it: imprisoning bloggers and tracking down dissident Twitter users. However, the advantage of the new media is their ubiquity and range; despite his best efforts President Bashar al Assad of Syria was unable to prevent mobile phone videos of his army's atrocities from reaching the outside world.

Chapter summary

The spoken voice was the main form of political communication until the spread of newspapers in the nineteenth century. Broadcasting introduced a revolution into the way politics is conducted as its spread is instant and its influence so great. New political actors have emerged specialising in the media, and politicians have learned to master their techniques. Press news values tend to influence television also, but the latter is more vulnerable to political pressure than the already politicised press. Class dominance theories suggest that the media are no more than an instrument of the ruling class, but there is reason to believe that they exercise considerable independence and are not incompatible with democracy.

Postscript

New post-Leveson press regulatory framework agreed: After 100 hours of late night negotiation – and concessions made by David Cameron – the three parties hammered out an agreement which was eventually agreed (18 March 2013). A new regulator, underpinned by a Royal Charter, rather than statutory law, would have the power to levy fines of up to £1m and ensure that apologies by errant newspapers are prominently displayed. However, after all that effort at hammering out a deal, the publishers of *The Times*, *The Sun*, *The Daily Telegraph*, *The Daily Mail*, *The Mirror* and *The Express* rejected the three parties' plan and complicated matters by producing their own rival plan for a voluntary regulator (26 April 2013).

Discussion points

- Should British political parties be allowed to buy political advertising on television?
- Has televising Parliament enhanced or detracted from the efficacy of Parliament?
- Does television substantially affect voting behaviour?
- Do the media reinforce the political status quo or challenge it?
- Should interviewers risk appearing rude when confronting politicians?
- How important have blogs and online pressure groups become in disseminating news and comment?

Further reading

By far the best current study of the mass media is by John Street, whose second edition appeared in 2011. It is clearly written, comprehensive and takes an international perspective rather than a narrowly national one. Another very useful study is Negrine (2008), and Budge et al. (2007) provide two excellent chapters (13 and 14). The two most readable studies of leadership, the media and politics are both by Michael Cockerell (Cockerell 1988; Cockerell et al. 1984). Bruce (1992) is good on the behaviour of politicians in relation to the media. Blumler and Gurevitch (1995) is an essay on the crisis of communication for citizenship and as such is an interesting source of ideas. See Jones (1993) on the television interview. The most brilliant and funny book about the press is still Chippendale and Orrie's history of the *Sun* (1992).

Bibliography

Barnett, S. and Gaber, I. (2001) *Westminster Tales: The 21st Century Crisis in Political Journalism* (Continuum).

Bilton, A., Bennett, K., Jones, P., Skinner, D., Stanworth, M. and Webster, A. (1996) *Introductory Sociology*, 3rd edn (Macmillan).

Blumler, J.G. and Gurevitch, M. (1995) *The Crisis of Public Communication* (Routledge).

Blumler, J.G. and McQuail, D. (1967) *Television in Politics* (Faber and Faber).

Blumler, J.G., Gurevitch, M. and Ives, J. (1978) *The Challenge of Election Broadcasting* (Leeds University Press).

Bruce, B. (1992) *Images of Power* (Kogan Page).

Budge, I., Crewe, I., McKay, D. and Newton, K. (2007) *The New British Politics* (Longman).

Campbell, A. '140 Reasons why Politicians are Out of Touch', *The Times*, 17 October 2012.

Chippendale, P. and Orrie, C. (1992) *Stick it Up Your Punter* (Mandarin).

Cockerell, M. (1988) *Live from Number Ten* (Faber and Faber).

Cockerell, M., Walker, D. and Hennessy, P. (1984) *Sources Close to the Prime Minister* (Macmillan).

Cohen, N. (1999) The *Observer*, 24 October 1999.

Cronkite, W. (1997) *A Reporter's Life* (Knopf).

Denver, D. (1992) *Elections and Voting Behaviour*, 2nd edn (Harvester Wheatsheaf).

Donovan, P. (1998) *All Our Todays: Forty Years of the Today Programme* (Arrow).

Fowler, N. (1991) *Ministers Decide: A Memoire of the Thatcher Years* (Chapmans).

Franklin, B. (1999) *Tough on Sound-bites, Tough on the Causes of Sound-bites: New Labour News Management* (Catalyst Pamphlet).

Franklin, B. (2004) *Packaging Politics: Political Communication in Britain's Media Democracy* (Edward Arnold).

Geddes, A. and Tonge, J. (1997) *Labour's Landslide* (Manchester University Press).

Glasgow University Media Group (1976) *Bad News* (Routledge and Kegan Paul).

Gould, P. (1999) *The Unfinished Revolution* (Abacus).

Green, J. (1982) *Book of Political Quotes* (Angus and Robertson).

Harrison, M. (1985) *TV News: Whose Bias* (Hermitage, Policy Journals).

Hennessy, P. (1985) *What the Papers Never Said* (Political Education Press).

Hoggart, S. (1999a) 'Commons Sketch: Blair lays on the therapy for the terracotta army', The *Guardian*, 3 November 1999.

Hoggart, S. (1999b) 'Commons Sketch: no joke for No. 10 when Hague gag hits the target', The *Guardian*, 11 November 1999.

Ingham, B. (2003) 'The wages of spin', *Sunday Times*, 16 March (adapted from The *Wages of Spin*, John Murray, 2003).

Jones, B. (1993) '"The pitiless probing eye": politicians and the broadcast political interview', *Parliamentary Affairs*, January.

Jones, B. (2000) 'Media and government', in Pyper, R. and Robins, L. (eds) *United Kingdom Governance* (Palgrave Macmillan).

King, A. (ed.) (1997) *New Labour Triumphs: Britain at the Polls* (Chatham House).

Leach, R., Coxall, B. and Robins, L. (1998) *British Politics* (Palgrave).

Lloyd, J. (2004) *What the Media are Doing to Our Politics* (Constable).

Marr, A. (1999) 'And the news is . . . electric', The *Observer*, 17 October.

McQuail, D. (1983) *Mass Communication Theory: An Introduction* (Sage).

Mullin, C. (2009) *A View from the Foothills* (Profile Books).

Negrine, R. (1995) *Politics and the Mass Media*, 2nd edn (Routledge).

Negrine, R. (2008) *The Transformation of Political Communication, Continuities and Change in Media and Politics* (Palgrave).

Newton, K. (1992) 'Do voters believe everything they read in the papers?', in Crewe, I., Norris, P., Denver, D. and Broughton, D. (eds) *British Elections and Parties Yearbook* (Harvester Wheatsheaf).

Oborne, P. (2007) *The Triumph of the Political Class* (Simon & Schuster).

Ornstein, N. and Mann, T. (2000) *The Permanent Campaign, and its Future* (AET).

O'Rourke, P.J. (1992) *Parliament of Whores* (Picador).

Richards, S. (2010) *Whatever it Takes: the Real Story of Gordon Brown and New Labour* (Fourth Estate).

Seyd, P. and Whiteley, P. (1992) *Labour's Grass Roots* (Clarendon Press).

Seymore-Ure, C. (1974) *The Political Impact of the Mass Media* (Constable).

Street, J. (2011) *Mass Media, Politics and Democracy*, 2nd edn (Palgrave).

Watts, D. (1997) *Political Communication Today* (Manchester University Press).

Whale, J. (1977) *The Politics of the Media* (Fontana).

Wring, D. and Deacon, D. (2005) 'The election unspun' in Geddes, A. and Tonge, J., *Britain Decides* (Palgrave).

Zakaria, F. (2004) *The Future of Freedom* (Norton).

Useful websites

UK Media Internet Directory: Newspapers: www.mcc.ac.uk/jcridlan.htm
Daily Telegraph: www.telegraph.co.uk
The *Independent*: www.independent.co.uk
The Times: www.the-times.co.uk
Guardian: www.guardian.co.uk
The Economist: www.economist.co.uk
BBC Television: www.bbc.co.uk
BBC charter review: www.bbc.charterreview.org.uk
ITN: www.itn.co.uk
CNN: www.cnn.com

Blogs

http://skipper59.blogspot.com/ (run by the author of this chapter)
http://5thnovember.blogspot.com/
http://normblog.typepad.com/
http://samizdata.net/blog/ http://
http://chickyog.blogspot.com/
http://oliverkamm.typepad.com
http://www.huffingtonpost.co.uk/
http://www.thedailybeast.com/

Parliamentary representation

Byron Criddle

> " The most perfect political community is one in which the middle class is in control, and outnumbers both of the other classes "
>
> Aristotle

Learning objectives

- To distinguish between political representation and demographic representation.

- To analyse changes in the demographic composition of the House of Commons over time.

- To assess how far the social characteristics of the major parties' MPs remain distinct, and to what extent they have sought to change them.

- To consider whether a lack of demographic representativeness matters.

The central representative function of the House of Commons is to represent the political parties for whom voters have voted at general elections, and so to determine the political complexion of the government. An additional if essentially unrelated consideration is that the Members of Parliament elected to represent the parties should in their social characteristics reflect those of the wider electorate; that they should be representative demographically as well as politically. This they have never been. The chapter analyses the traditionally unrepresentative pattern of the social characteristics of MPs, notes changes to them over time, and examines attempts to make MPs more representative, particularly of a balance between the sexes and of ethnic diversity. Finally, there is consideration of whether a socially unrepresentative House of Commons matters.

Introduction

Political representation

The key consideration in a parliament being 'representative' is its political representativeness; the requirement that the composition of the elected legislature conforms to the political wishes of the voters. In Britain, in an age of universal suffrage this has come to involve voters choosing to vote for candidates of different political parties in precise geographical areas, or constituencies. Once elected, the Members of Parliament are expected to support the party for which they were elected, whether that party has formed a government or is a party in opposition, while at the same time being available to deal with matters of concern to any of the voters in their constituencies regardless of the voters' party preference. But in this mix of political and geographical representation, it is the partisan identity of the MP that determines their legislative behaviour, because the prime purpose of electing an MP is to determine the political complexion of the government. Constitutionally, all other considerations are secondary (see Box 9.1).

However, beyond an assumed essential requirement of political representation, is the further, if lesser, concern institutionally that the elected legislature should be representative of the electorate in a demographic sense: that those elected to it should comprise in their personal characteristics a microcosm of the wider society in terms of salient social categories such as class, ethnicity, language or religion (see Box 9.2). The legitimacy of democratic institutions may come to depend on concern being shown for such demographic representation, particularly if there is a perception amongst the electorate that a significant link can be assumed between a politician's social characteristics, whether class, race or sex, and their political attitudes, beliefs and behaviour.

Whatever the claims for the merits of demographic representation, and noting the potential incompatibility between the paramount role of an MP loyally representing a party, and also representing a social identity that might involve breaching that party loyalty, the hard reality is that in all liberal democracies those who occupy positions in the political elite whether as ministers or Members of Parliament are overwhelmingly drawn from the ranks of the relatively privileged and never comprise a cross-section of the population, whether in class, sex or race. Notwithstanding the high-minded view, dating from Aristotle, that there is an obligation on all citizens to participate politically for the good of the whole as well as for the good of the individual, high levels of participation should not be expected (Aristotle, *The Politics*, 1962 edition).

Likewise, an American study distinguished between three ranks of **political participation**, with the 'apathetics' at the bottom, who do not even vote but who comprise about

---

BOX 9.1

Political representation

Under the British system of parliamentary government, the government needs, by convention, the support of a majority of MPs in the House of Commons. This has come to mean the support of the MPs of the party that has secured a majority of the seats in a general election. Parliamentary government therefore involves the disciplined support of the government by those MPs elected under the label of the majority party. MPs, both of the winning party and of the opposing losing parties, will by their election be seen as mandated to represent their parties' political **manifesto** on which they campaigned in the election. This, the mandate model of representation, prioritises party unity and party discipline over other representational duties, such as the role of an MP as a geographical representative, and as a channel for constituents' views if those views are significantly at odds with the Member's political identity. Traditionally, to stray from party political loyalty on substantive issues in significant votes is to breach party discipline and to compromise an MP's career by denying preferment as government ministers, or, *in extremis*, putting at risk the continued endorsement by their party without which they could not expect to gain re-election. Thus a mix of **mandate** and ambition makes the party political identity of an MP their overwhelmingly salient characteristic as a representative.

A critique of this view of the MP as politically mandated and tied by party discipline is that voters do not necessarily vote rationally for party policies as presented at an election, or at least not for all of them, and thus have not mandated MPs politically. They may well have voted habitually, without any regard for party policy. It compromises too the historical view of the MP as a territorial representative, representing all constituents regardless of their identity, background or political allegiance.

Box 9.2

Demographic representation

Demographic representation involves a parliament being representative in the sense that its members comprise a microcosm of the population. It is claimed that parliaments should comprise proportions of important sub-groups equivalent to the presence of those sub-groups (social class, sex, race, language or religion), among the wider electorate. Underlying the call for representatives to mirror the social characteristics of the electorate is the assumption that, where a social group has distinct political interests, parliamentary representatives drawn from their ranks will be more effective. Thus, working-class MPs will better represent working-class voters, and women better represent the concerns of women. That the social characteristics of an electorate should at least find some reflection in the constitution of an elected assembly is not unreasonable, even though, for example, 'the concerns of women' might be defined differently by rival political parties, so that the presence of more women MPs might not affect the traditional and predominant salience of party identity when women MPs vote on gender-related issues.

It is possible that calls for a more socially representative parliament in Britain have grown for two reasons. First, that with the decline in the class alignment of voting which traditionally structured the competition of the major parties and mobilised the voters, there is now room for other social identities, such as ethnicity or gender, to structure voting. Second, that the decline of deference towards politicians in general, has created a populist demand for MPs who, to quote a Conservative Party official, 'look more like the country they are governing'.

An increase in rebellious voting in recent parliaments has also invited speculation about possible links between MPs' dissident behaviour and their personal and social characteristics.

---

30 per cent of the population; the 'spectators', who vote and follow politics to some extent and amount to about 60 per cent, and at the top the 'gladiators', comprising some 5 per cent as the small minority of activists who staff the political parties and from whose ranks the political elite is recruited (Milbrath and Goel 1977). Crucially, far from being a cross-section of society, they are essentially people with 'resources', the haves, rather than the have nots.

A comprehensive study of political participation in Britain (Parry et al. 1992) attributed political participation to the possession of individual resources, such as material wealth, education, skills, and group networks, all of which can be used by an individual to promote their own interests by political action. Put simply, those in higher social groups have assets such as higher education, professional status, money, time, communication skills and networks of contacts, which cumulatively create confidence and are a spur to ambition. The uneven distribution in society of such resources explains the lack of political participation among less resourced groups such as manual workers, women and those in ethnic minorities. However, one corrective for a lack of individual resources can be access to group resources, such as those provided by trade unions for those of their members who lack personal resources such as money and education, but who can, with union financial support and education, obtain the time and confidence to rise from manual occupations into political careers. Thus can be explained the career of the under-resourced, educationally deprived merchant seaman, John Prescott, who rose through his union to acquire a safe Labour parliamentary seat in 1970, enabling a career spanning 40 years, 10 as Deputy Prime Minister (1997–2007).

However, such examples are rare, and more visible is the impact of substantial personal resources of the sort that enabled the multi-millionaire businessman Sir James Goldsmith to create his own eurosceptic Referendum Party, running candidates across the country in 1997; and the businessman Lord Ashcroft whose millions financed Conservative campaigning in key target seats in the 2010 election.

Resources apart, political activism at the top can also be prompted by inherited political interest, although such an inheritance is also more likely to be found among already highly resourced individuals. David Cameron, who became Prime Minister in 2010, had three MPs among his forebears, as well as being a direct descendant of King William IV, and the Labour Party leader Ed Miliband was both the son of a politics professor and the brother of another MP. Many politicians have politics and the affairs of state in their blood. With these facts in mind, the quest for demographic representation, for a socially cross-sectional House of Commons may well seem highly unrealistic, yet continuing concern over social unrepresentativeness was displayed in a BBC television documentary in January 2011.

'Posh and posher: why public school boys run britain'

This assertion about a 'posh and posher' British political elite, was made by the journalist Andrew Neil (who repeated it in an article headed 'The Fall of the Meritocracy' in *The Spectator*, 29 January 2011). It involved the claim that the composition of the Cameron Government of 2010 was evidence of increasing social elitism in British politics, because David Cameron was the first Eton- and Oxford-educated Prime Minister since 1964, that the number of public-school educated MPs and, specifically, of Etonians had increased, and that the post-1945 meritocracy which saw the rise of state grammar-school-educated politicians had ground to a halt. The first five post-war Prime Ministers between 1945 and 1964 had all been privately educated: Clement Attlee, Winston Churchill, and then three Etonians – Anthony Eden, Harold Macmillan and Alec Douglas-Home. But then, for 33 years after that (from 1964 to 1997), came five Prime Ministers, Harold Wilson, Edward Heath, James Callaghan, Margaret Thatcher, and John Major – the last Conservative Prime Minister before Cameron – all of whom were state-educated and upwardly socially mobile.

Historically, the Conservative Party in the House of Commons had been overwhelmingly dominated by the rich and high born. In the earlier twentieth century its MPs were drawn exclusively from the high-status professions of the military and law, and from landowning and business. In the 1918 parliament 27 per cent were Etonians, a figure down from 43 per cent pre-1914. In the last pre-Second World War House of Commons elected in 1935, two-fifths of Conservative MPs were aristocrats, whether peers in their own right, heirs to peerages, younger sons of peers, blood relations of peers, or related by marriage to peers, landed gentry or baronets (Haxey 1939). Great political families with centuries of representation were still present, such as the Stanleys (Earls of Derby), the Cecils (Marquesses of Salisbury) and the Cavendishes (Dukes of Devonshire). The latter family supplied in successive generations the Duke's eldest son as MP for the local West Derbyshire constituency, so making their stately home, Chatsworth, a family seat in two senses. In the 1935 House of Commons the Cavendish family provided by blood or marriage a total of nine MPs, including the businessman and Etonian Harold Macmillan who had married the Duke's daughter. He, an MP (with some interruption) between 1924 and 1964, and Prime Minister between 1957 and 1963, was in turn related to three more MPs – a son, son-in-law and grandson – who sat between 1950 and 2001.

If not aristocracy, plutocracy prevailed in the prewar House of Commons. The names of captains of industry abounded: Austin (cars), Palmer (biscuits), Lyle (sugar), Vickers (shipbuilding), Hornby (toy trains), Guinness (brewing), Nicholson (distilling), Borwick (baking powder). In many cases, like the landed aristocrats, the industrial magnates represented the site of their commercial activity, such as the brewer Sir Richard Wells occupying the Bedford constituency from 1922 to 1945.

MPs effectively bought their seats, as recalled by the aristocratic diplomat Duff Cooper's thwarted attempt to get selected at Stroud in 1924 when his offer of a customary donation to local party funds – in this case of £300 (the equivalent in 2012 of £14,000) was trumped by a higher bidder.

Deference to wealth and status abounded, with an occasion later recalled by the journalist and postwar Labour MP, Tom Driberg, involving two old ladies arriving at a polling station in Bournemouth in the 1930s and one of them asking, 'Can you tell us where servants vote for Sir Henry Page-Croft?', who was the sitting Conservative MP, an Eton- and Cambridge-educated company director.

After the Second World War this plutocratic pattern was undermined by the party banning seat-purchasing, putting an upper limit on an MP's donation to party funds of £50 per annum (though that was still the equivalent of twice the average monthly wage at the time), and ending the practice of constituency officers raising the matter of financial contributions from aspiring candidates until after their selection. Nevertheless, elitism lingered, so that in the county of Devon in 1955, of six Conservative-held rural seats, four were held by Etonians and one by a Harrovian. But the sixth seat, Totnes, was held by an electrician, Ray Mawby, who was the first Conservative MP ever to come direct from a manual job, and while very few former manual workers have subsequently been elected as Conservative MPs, there was after the 1950s a clear trend away from elitism as measured by educational characteristics.

Thus, the percentage of Conservative MPs from private schools fell from 78 per cent in 1951 to 54 per cent in 2010; of Oxford or Cambridge graduates from 52 to 34 per cent, and of Etonians from 24 to 6.5 per cent, as revealed in the graphs, which analyse the party after five elections in which it obtained approximately similar totals of MPs, and following which it formed a government. The trend away from private school and Oxbridge education was even more marked in successive new intakes of MPs: in 2010 only 50 per cent of new MPs had attended private schools, compared to 55 per cent in 1992, and only 27 per cent were Oxbridge graduates compared to 43 per cent in 1992.

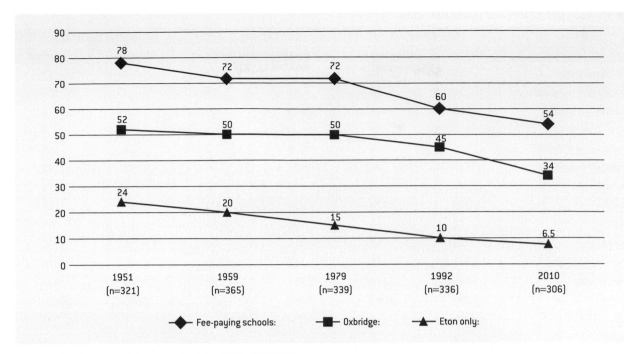

Figure 9.1 Education of Conservative MPs, 1951–2010 (%)

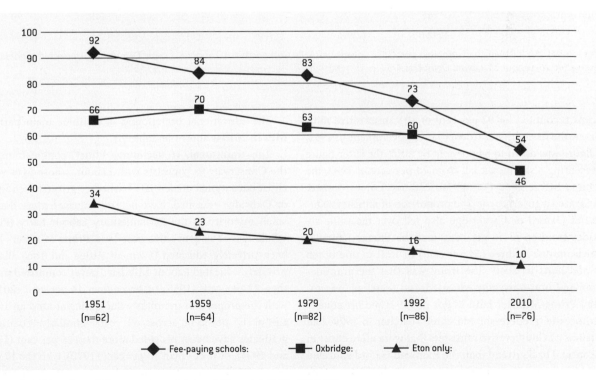

Figure 9.2 Education of Conservative ministers (MPs only), 1951–2010 (%)

Within the private school contingent of Conservative MPs there was also a trend away from the more prestigious schools: in Table 9.1 Eton, Harrow and Winchester are listed separately because in earlier years products of these high-status schools dominated the Conservative benches. Thus, in 1959, 105 MPs had attended these three schools, and made up 40 per cent of the private school contingent; equivalent figures for 2010 were 25 (15 per cent).

The same downward trajectory from elitism was evident in the composition of Conservative governments. While private

Table 9.1 Education of MPs and candidates, 2010

	Conservative		Labour		Liberal Democrat	
	Elected	**Unelected**	**Elected**	**Unelected**	**Elected**	**Unelected**
Secondary school	15	34	27	41	2	47
Secondary + poly/coll	25	26	42	59	4	106
Secondary + univ	100	172	153	209	29	316
Private school	5	1	–	1	1	4
Private sch + poly/coll	16	6	2	2	4	5
Private sch + univ	145	86	34	49	17	81
Unknown	–	–	–	12	–	15
Total	306	325	258	373	57	574
Oxford	72	28	30	21	10	35
Cambridge	32	18	15	17	6	36
Other universities	141	212	142	220	30	326
All universities[1]	245	258	187	258	46	397
	(80%)	(80%)	(73%)	(70%)	(80%)	(70%)
Eton	20	5	–	–	1	3
Harrow	3	1	–	–	–	–
Winchester	2	2	–	–	–	–
Other private schools	141	85	36	52	21	87
All private schools	166	93	36	52	22	90
	(54%)	(29%)	(14%)	(14%)	(40%)	(16%)

[1] Of graduates, the following had attended post-1992 universities: MPs: Conservative 4, Labour 6, Liberal Democrat 0; Unelected candidates: Conservative 26, Labour 24, Liberal Democrat 44.

schools accounted for 92 per cent of all Conservative ministers in the first postwar Conservative government in 1951, the figure was down to 54 per cent by 2010, the latter figure representing a significant fall from 73 per cent in 1992, the last time before 2010 that a Conservative Prime Minister had formed a government. The proportion of ministers educated at Oxford or Cambridge also fell over the same six decades from 66 to 46 per cent, and the Etonian complement from one in three (34 per cent) in 1951 to one in ten (10 per cent) in 2010. The irony was that the grammar school and non-university educated, and therefore 'meritocratic', Prime Minister John Major in 1992, and his equally 'meritocratic' predecessor Margaret Thatcher in 1979, had led teams of Conservative ministers that were more elitist in educational background than the Eton and Oxford educated David Cameron's Conservative ministers in 2010. Cameron's parliamentary party was also the least public school and Oxbridge-educated Conservative Party in modern times, and the Conservative ministers in his government comprised the least elitist group of any post-1945 Conservative government. Thus the 'posh and posher' claim was exposed as journalistic hyperbole. There was a persistent pattern of eroding elitism: still 'posh' relatively, but certainly not 'posher'.

The educational background of all three main parties' MPs in 2010 is shown in Table 9.1.

The traditional, if declining, 'elitist' composition of the Conservatives contrasts with Labour, whose MPs with elitist educational credentials – whether privately schooled or Oxbridge-educated, have never comprised more than a small minority of the **Parliamentary Labour Party (PLP)**. While two of Labour's five post-1945 Prime Ministers had been privately educated (Clement Attlee and Tony Blair), privately-educated Labour MPs have never comprised more than 22 per cent (1955) or fewer than 14 per cent (2010), with the proportion trendlessly fluctuating around an average of 17 per cent across 60 years. Similarly, Oxbridge graduates have never provided more than 25 per cent (1970 and 1974), or fewer than 13 per cent (1970), with the 17 per cent in 2010 close to the post-1951 average of 18 per cent.

Liberal Democrat MPs' educational profile is situated midway between the two larger parties. In 2010 40 per cent of their 57 MPs had been privately educated, and 28 per cent had attended Oxford or Cambridge, and these figures had not fluctuated significantly over the elections since 1992, when the party rose to a total of 20 MPs, a figure more than doubled in four subsequent elections.

Table 9.2 Graduate MPs, 1951–2010 (%)

	Conservative	Labour	Liberal Democrat
1951	65	41	
1955	63	40	
1959	60	40	
1964	63	42	
1966	67	50	
1970	63	54	
1974f	67	53	
1974o	69	57	
1979	68	57	
1983	71	53	
1987	70	56	
1992	73	61	75
1997	81	66	70
2001	83	67	70
2005	81	64	79
2010	80	73	80

What did change from the 1950s, apart from the decline in elitist credentials on the Conservative side, was the proportion of all MPs who were graduates, as shown in Table 9.2. This generally reflected the changing social composition of the PLP as middle-class redbrick graduates came to replace the declining numbers of manual workers, though many such Labour MPs had risen from working-class backgrounds through the state grammar school system introduced nationally after 1944. By 2010 virtually all MPs were graduates of one sort or another, reflecting a society characterised in its younger age groups by a system of mass higher education, though the relative, if diminishing, elitism of Conservative MPs remained.

Occupations of MPs

If the educational profile of the House of Commons reflects some evidence of convergence across the parties on a high proportion of graduates and a reduction – if not removal – of the more elitist Oxbridge element in Conservative ranks, Table 9.3, showing the occupation of MPs in 2010, confirms how the two major parties still have distinct occupational characteristics, the main features of which have been historically apparent across the postwar decades, as shown in Table 9.4.

Table 9.4 depicts similar proportions of Conservative and Labour MPs drawn from the professions, and very dissimilar proportions from business, and from manual occupations. But even in the professional category there has been an important distinction, as is visible in the detailed breakdown in Table 9.3, between the Conservatives' private sector professionals such as lawyers, and Labour's public sector professionals from teaching or public administration, mirroring the traditional ideological difference between the parties on private and public enterprise. To talk of a 'middle-class-dominated House of Commons' is very misleading given this sectoral divide between the State and the Market – between 'The *Guardian*' middle class, and 'The *Daily Telegraph*' middle class. This distinction is more starkly revealed in the high proportion of Conservatives drawn from business, and the virtual absence of any Labour MPs with commercial experience – fewer than 10 per cent in all elections since 1970.

Equally distinctive historically has been the significant proportion of between a third and a quarter, until the 1990s, of Labour MPs from manual occupations, even though these numbers had declined steeply to under 10 per cent by 2010. This latter figure, as with others in Table 9.3, is less than definitive. Classification of occupations requires judgement in the many cases where MPs have had more than one type of occupation, and may in the case of manual workers have become trade union officials and so classified in the 'miscellaneous' section of Table 9.3. But the decline of Labour's once most defining attribute, the manual worker, is clear.

In the pre-war era, when the Conservatives reflected plutocracy with their MPs drawn exclusively from the law, the army, business and the land, Labour was a party of wholly working-class stamp. In 1918 at the first election held under full manhood suffrage and female voting over 30, of the 59 Labour MPs elected, all but one was sponsored (i.e. financed) by the trade union covering the manual trade in which they had worked, and even the one MP who wasn't so sponsored was of working-class origin. Twenty-six of the fifty-nine were coal miners. At the last pre-war election in 1935, 70 per cent of the 154 Labour MPs were former manual workers, a third of them miners.

Thereafter, the Parliamentary Labour Party (PLP)'s social profile changed with Labour's replacement of the Liberal Party as the leading opposition to the Conservatives. Prominent middle-class Liberal political families, such as the Benns and the Foots, transferred their allegiance to Labour, and the 1945 electoral landslide drew other ambitious middle-class radicals into the party. Table 9.4 plots the subsequent continuous decline of the PLP's phalanx of working-class MPs, a decline accompanying that of the country's industrial base and of the blue-collar unions affiliated to the party, whose sponsoring of MPs was discontinued following the 1995 Nolan Commission's report on MPs involvement with outside interests. Previously, union sponsorship had provided the all-important 'group resources'

Table 9.3 Occupation of MPs and candidates, 2010

	Conservative		Labour		Liberal Democrat	
	Elected	**Unelected**	**Elected**	**Unelected**	**Elected**	**Unelected**
Professions						
Barrister	27	20	9	10	2	14
Solicitor	29	19	17	44	2	20
Doctor/Dentist/Optician	6	6	2	6	1	12
Architect/Surveyor	6	1	–	1	1	4
Civil/chartered engineer	2	3	4	6	–	16
Accountant	13	17	2	7	2	18
Civil service/local govt	2	9	13	35	3	38
Armed services	15	3	1	1	–	7
Teachers: university	–	4	9	7	4	23
Poly/college	–	1	12	9	–	13
School	4	18	14	29	6	65
Other consultant	3	5	3	6	1	15
Science/research	–	1	3	7	–	4
Total	*107*	*107*	*89*	*168*	*22*	*249*
	(35%)	*(33%)*	*(35%)*	*(45%)*	*(39%)*	*(43%)*
Business						
Company director	50	30	4	5	3	20
Company executive	50	38	4	18	4	37
Commerce/insurance	10	15	1	6	3	35
Managerial/clerical	2	9	5	13	–	18
General business	8	21	6	6	–	33
Management consultant	5	11	–	2	1	4
Total	*125*	*124*	*20*	*50*	*11*	*147*
	(40%)	*(38%)*	*(8%)*	*(13%)*	*(20%)*	*(26%)*
Miscellaneous						
Miscellaneous white collar	2	19	15	22	4	50
Politician/political organiser	31	22	52	44	7	31
Union official	–	–	29	20	–	–
Journalist/publisher	18	21	15	19	5	26
Public relations	11	11	3	9	2	14
Charity/voluntary sector	2	7	13	22	3	21
Farmer	8	4	–	–	2	3
Housewife	–	–	–	–	–	5
Student	–	4	–	–	–	10
Total	*72*	*88*	*127*	*136*	*23*	*160*
	(24%)	*(27%)*	*(49%)*	*(37%)*	*(40%)*	*(28%)*
Manual worker	*2*	*6*	*22*	*16*	*1*	*11*
	(1%)	*(2%)*	*(9%)*	*(4%)*	*(2%)*	*(2%)*
Unknown	–	–	–	3	–	7
Grand total	*306*	*325*	*258*	*373*	*57*	*574*

Table 9.4 Occupational categories of MPs, 1951–2010 (%) (professions, business, miscellaneous, and manual)

	Conservative				Labour				Liberal Democrat			
	Prof	Bus	Misc	Man	Prof	Bus	Misc	Man	Prof	Bus	Misc	Man
1951	41	37	22	–	35	9	19	37				
1955	46	30	24	1	36	12	17	35				
1959	46	30	23	1	38	10	17	35				
1964	48	26	25	1	41	11	16	32				
1966	46	29	23	1	43	9	18	30				
1970	45	30	24	1	48	10	16	26				
1974f	44	32	23	1	46	9	15	30				
1974o	46	33	20	1	49	8	15	28				
1979	45	34	20	1	43	7	14	36				
1983	45	36	19	1	42	9	16	33				
1987	42	37	20	1	40	8	22	29				
1992	39	38	22	1	42	8	28	22				
1997	37	39	23	1	45	9	33	13	50	24	24	2
2001	39	36	25	1	43	8	36	12	52	27	19	2
2005	38	38	23	1	40	7	43	10	40	29	29	2
2010	35	40	24	1	35	8	49	9	39	20	40	2

Note: f and o refer to the two elections in 1974 (February and October).

needed to promote the parliamentary ambitions of manual workers, and in the 1950s and 1960s over a third of all Labour MPs enjoyed union sponsorship. Even before its discontinuance, however, the practice had grown of unions sponsoring middle-class professional MPs, such as the Scottish aristocrat and former schoolteacher, Tam Dalyell, already an MP of 17 years standing when acquiring the sponsorship of the railwayman's union (NUR) in 1979. By that time, 20 per cent of Labour's sponsored MPs were graduates with no previous occupational involvement with the sponsoring union, so reducing the practice of union sponsorship to a financial resource for ambitious middle-class professionals. By 1987 two-thirds of sponsored Labour MPs had no experience of manual work, a symbol no doubt of de-industrialisation, and yet by 2010, the Commons' proportion of former manual workers, at under 10 per cent, was significantly lower than the third of the working population still employed in manual occupations.

The professional politician

A significant development in recent decades has been the expansion of an occupational category of absolutely no demographic significance, but rather an outgrowth of the trade of politics itself – the career politician. Table 9.3 shows 52 (20 per cent) of Labour and 31 (10 per cent) of Conservative MPs categorised as 'politicians', but many more such people are hidden throughout the table, classified by their 'first or foremost' occupation as, say, a lawyer or a teacher. In 2010 a quarter of all MPs had at some time had a political job. In the words of the former parliamentary press gallery journalist, Peter Riddell:

> The British parliament, and hence government, is increasingly dominated by career politicians, by men and a few women who have dedicated most of their adult lives to entering the Commons, staying there and advancing to become ministers or spokesmen . . . The signs are many and varied. They include the growth of ancillary political jobs – public affairs consultants, special advisers, full-time union officials, full-time council leaders . . . (and) the willingness to commit yourself to fighting several seats before entering the Commons; the desire of most to stay at Westminster, and the high rate of recidivism by defeated MPs seeking to return . . . The range and experience of MPs is narrower than in the past, and their dedication to politics is greater . . . Moreover, in part because of the skills developed from an early age and in part because of the degree of commitment, these career politicians are the ones who tend to rise fastest and furthest at Westminster . . . Their careers

at Westminster are the centre of their lives, both financially and socially. There is no longer a self-perpetuating aristocracy which regards service in parliament and government as part of their inherited duties. . . . The rise in the pay of MPs and the growth of ancillary political occupations has meant that more people can be full-time politicians, whereas in the past only those in government or financially supported by trade unions could survive financially without other income, either from business interests or inherited wealth.

(Riddell 1996)

The professionalisation of politics, has been assisted by increasing specialisation in all occupations. No longer, therefore, does an ambitious barrister take some years out of his chambers to be an MP, if to do so will damage his professional reputation at a lawyer. Equally, to leave a managerial position in a company to embark on a risky political career is to undermine the steady rise of a corporate man. Likewise, a university lecturer seeking to rise within his profession will not be helped by the distraction of a dalliance with politics. The amateur, in all trades, is a thing of the past.

In the view of the journalist and author, Peter Oborne (2007), who has a more negative view of career politicians whom he sees as comprising a 'political class':

They tend not to have significant experience of industry, commerce or civil society. . . . The Conservative MP, Boris Johnson, worked as a management consultant after leaving university. 'Try as I might', he later stated, 'I could not look at an overhead projection of a growth/profit matrix and stay conscious'. The only Cabinet minister in Tony Blair's 1997 administration known to have had any experience of work in the commercial sector was the Deputy Prime Minister, John Prescott, who had been a ship's steward in the 1950s. He was joined in the Cabinet in due course by Alan Milburn, whose commercial experience was limited to a brief period running Days of Hope, a Marxist bookshop known by its patrons as Haze of Dope . . . Milburn was nevertheless handed the task of running the National Health Service, the largest employer in the world outside the Indian Railways and the Red Army . . . So far as could be discovered, not one of the Gordon Brown Cabinet in June 2007 had any commercial experience.

(Oborne 2007: 6–7)

Allowing for journalistic hyperbole, Oborne makes a point about the lack of managerial experience on the part of **professional politicians**, and lists a range of policy failures (military interventions, rail nationalisation, IT failures in government administration) allegedly attributable to it. Yet, in the wake of the classic career politicians David Cameron and Ed Miliband, they arrive in increasing numbers in successive new intakes of MPs, a process stimulated by the opportunity given to lay the foundations of a political career by the Conservative and Labour parties each remaining in government for long periods since 1979. Time had thus been given for the would-be careerist, after graduating often in Politics or its Oxford equivalent PPE (Politics, Philosophy and Economics), to work for an MP or as a party staffer, and then as a SPAD (special adviser) to a Cabinet minister; then, after careful screening within the party machine for reliability and ideological soundness, to move seamlessly into a parliamentary seat, even, as in some Labour cases in 2010, into the seat vacated by the very minister for whom they previously worked, a pattern reminiscent of the pre-war Dukes of Devonshire inserting their son and heir into the family seat of West Derbyshire.

Sex and ethnicity

Campaigners for demographic representation have prioritised the objective of increasing the proportion of women MPs in order to reflect the fact that women comprise 52 per cent of the population. Women have always been under-represented in the House of Commons, because of their lack of resources. As argued by one of the leading academic feminist advocates of increased numbers of women MPs, 'women are, on average, and as a result of gendered socialisation and the gendered division of labour, likely to have fewer resources than men, whether that is the necessary free time to engage in politics, money to fund selection and election campaigns, and, or lower levels of political ambition, confidence and experience' (Childs and Webb 2012: 71). Table 9.5 shows the paucity of numbers of women MPs before the early 1990s and their perceptible rise thereafter. The key explanation for low totals of women politicians lies in a shortage of both supply of and demand for women candidates, a matter to be examined below.

As with women MPs, so with those from ethnic minorities, whose historically low totals are shown in Table 9.6.

Table 9.5 Women MPs, 1945–2010

	Conservative		Labour		Liberal/LibDem		Others	Total	
		%		%		%			%
1945	1	0.5	21	5.3	1	8.3	1	24	3.8
1950	6	2.0	14	4.4	1	11.1	–	21	3.4
1951	6	1.7	11	3.7	–		–	17	2.7
1955	10	2.9	14	5.0	–		–	24	3.8
1959	12	3.3	13	5.0	–		–	25	4.0
1964	11	3.6	18	5.6	–		–	29	4.6
1966	7	2.8	19	5.2	–		–	26	4.1
1970	15	4.6	10	3.4	–		1	26	4.1
1974f	9	3.0	13	4.3	–		1	23	3.6
1974o	7	2.5	18	5.6	–		2	27	4.3
1979	8	2.4	11	4.1	–		–	19	3.0
1983	13	3.2	10	4.8	–		–	23	3.5
1987	17	4.5	21	9.0	2	11.7	1	41	6.3
1992	20	6.0	37	13.7	2	10.0	1	60	9.2
1997	13	7.9	101	24.2	3	6.5	3	120	18.2
2001	14	8.0	95	23.0	3	5.8	4	118	17.9
2005	17	8.6	98	27.7	10	16.1	3	128	19.8
2010	49	15.7	81	31.6	7	12.3	6	143	22.0

Table 9.6 Ethnic minority MPs

	Con	Lab	Lib	Total
[1]Pre-1945	1	1	1	3
1945–83	–	–	–	–
1987	–	4	–	4
1992	1	5	–	6
1997	–	9	–	9
2001[2]	–	12	–	12
2005	2	13	–	15
2010	11 (3.6%)	16 (6%)	–	27 (4.2%)

1 1892 Liberal; 1895 Conservative; 1922 Labour-supported Communist
2 A Lib Dem MP sat from 2004 to 2005.

Changing political recruitment: supply and demand explanations

The supply and demand model distinguishes between factors influencing the supply of candidates seeking selection to contest parliamentary elections, and factors affecting the demand for them from the party selectors who make the choice at constituency level. On the demand side the model assumes judgements about an aspiring candidate's personal attributes: their appearance, fluency, qualifications, experience and character. Because candidates are rarely known to local selectors, assumptions are made about them on the basis of their general characteristics, whether they are barristers, public-school educated, manual workers, women, or from an ethnic minority. These considerations are termed 'direct discrimination'. Additionally, there will be 'imputed discrimination', whereby selectors might themselves approve the candidate but claim that they would not meet the approval of the wider electorate: a woman would lose votes, particularly in a mining constituency; a farmer would be inappropriate in a suburban constituency; and a BME (black and minority ethnic) candidate would be rejected in an overwhelmingly white area. Aside from such imputed discrimination accounting for low demand for candidates with specific personal characteristics, the generally high demand for candidates with verbal fluency explains the popularity among selectors of the 'talking professionals' or 'chattering classes' such as lawyers, teachers and journalists. Given such candidates' possession of all the necessary resources, of education, time, social status, skills and contacts, they proliferate as MPs.

On the supply side, the under-representation of certain categories is explained by the low numbers of such people seeking a political career. The resource-poor, such as women, those in ethnic minorities and manual workers do not come forward in sufficient numbers within the 'pool of eligibles', the list of approved would-be candidates maintained by the parties' headquarters, from whom selections are made. Consequently the pool of aspiring politicians is far from constituting a cross-section of society.

With obvious implications for the number of women and ethnic minority MPs, the major parties have sought to manipulate their supply and to stimulate demand for them. As the party traditionally committed to equality, Labour led the way before the 1992 election in introducing the mandatory shortlisting of at least one woman in selection conferences, and then before 1997 introducing all-women shortlists (AWS), which completely skewed demand for women candidates by precluding male ones altogether, in half of all the target seats the party expected to gain, and in those seats from which the sitting Labour MP was retiring. Though successfully challenged in the courts by two excluded men under the Sex Discrimination Act (1975) and temporarily suspended before the 1997 election, all-women shortlists were legalised in 2002 by way of the Sex Discrimination (Election Candidates) Act (which excluded party political candidate selections from sex discrimination legislation), and were applied rigorously thereafter to secure the selection of women in the party's industrial heartlands where traditionally powerful male-dominated blue collar unions had blocked women's selection. It was in part to overcome prejudice from the male-dominated industrial unions that Labour had also introduced in 1994 a system of 'one member one vote' in candidate selection conferences, to open up the choice to all party members rather than confining voting to delegates representing party branches and affiliated unions, which was the system hitherto for candidate selection, and which had traditionally been used by union delegates to secure selection of union-sponsored candidates. By targeting selection in safe and winnable seats with AWS, Labour achieved a significant rise in numbers of women MPs. With the stated aim of increasing women's share of the PLP from 28 per cent in 2005 to 40 per cent in 2010 – an ambitious task given the expected defeat of many of its sitting women MPs – the party effectively imposed AWS across its industrial heartlands, including the Northeast, and South Wales, where historically few women MPs had ever been elected. The skewing of supply to negate low demand in this way had been helped by a notable conflict before the 2005 election in the selection at Blaenau Gwent, where a well-known local male candidate, Peter Law, who was expecting to inherit the seat from the retiring MP, had

been excluded by an all-women shortlist, had stood as an independent against the selected woman, and won, so costing Labour one of its safest seats.

'A parliamentary party that would look like the country it is governing'

To achieve the demographically laudable objective reflected in this Conservative Party official's statement about candidate selection processes before the 2010 election, the Conservatives had to rival Labour's visually impressive relative feminisation of its Commons benches (see Table 9.5) in successive elections after 1992. A party by tradition culturally resistant to sex-equality objectives, it nevertheless needed to attend to problems with the supply of, and demand for, women candidates. Low demand for Conservative women candidates had been associated with a dislike of aspiring professional women candidates by the ageing, non-career women who were numerous among the local constituency membership and who held to a traditional view of the domestic division of labour. Equally, low supply meant that only 27 per cent of the party's approved candidates list – the pool of eligibles from which constituencies drew when picking a candidate – were women.

In 2006 to stimulate demand the party created a 'Priority List' (or 'A list') of 100 aspiring candidates evenly composed of women and men, and required selections in target seats and in vacant Conservative-held seats to be made from that gender-balanced list and not from the larger male-dominated main approved list. While it did not guarantee the selection of women as Labour's AWS did, a reduced, gender-balanced pool of eligibles together with a requirement for gender-balanced shortlists, with the shortlisting guided by central party officials, clearly made female selection more likely. Nevertheless, it met with resistance from the grass roots and from ambitious local male aspirants, and was eventually replaced by reversion to selection from the traditional full list of approved candidates, though with the requirement for gender-balanced shortlists remaining.

A further innovation in Conservative selection procedures before the 2010 election was the open primary, where registered voters who were not party members were able to vote in the final selection meeting, but with the decision taken being subject to the subsequent endorsement of a party-only meeting. These were held in 116 constituencies, only 15 of which were Conservative-held, but where 48 of the seats were subsequently gained by the party at the election, 22 of them by women. More audacious still were selections in the two Conservative-held constituencies of Totnes and Gosport, by means of an all-postal ballot, in which all registered voters in the constituency were invited to select from the shortlisted candidates. In Totnes a woman, Sarah Wollaston, a GP who had not long been a party member, was chosen from a shortlist of one man and two women (with both her rivals being established local councillors), and in Gosport from a gender-balanced list of four (with one of the men from the BME community) another woman, Caroline Dinenage, was also chosen. Although turnout in these postal primaries was low (25 per cent at Totnes and 18 per cent at Gosport), the intention was to demonstrate the party's openness to the wider public and to counterbalance any reluctance among the party membership to select women.

Through centralised intervention with advice and guidance and managed shortlisting, Conservative women MPs were trebled in number (to 49) and doubled in percentage (to 16 per cent – see Table 9.5) in 2010, so ending Labour's ownership of the feminising agenda established by the so-called 'Blair's babes' elected in 1997. In 1997 over 80 per cent of all women MPs were Labour; after 2010, it was 57 per cent.

That the Liberal Democrats made little contribution to the total of women MPs, apart from the 10 they elected in 2005, owed much to the party's lack of seats, and hence the opportunity to prioritise women, and a related reluctance to go further than merely requiring a presence of women on shortlists. However, the combined efforts of Labour and the Conservatives ensured that the proportion of women in the House of Commons by 2010 was, at 22 per cent, close to the European mean of 25 per cent, this notwithstanding the use in most European states of proportional electoral systems more conducive to prioritising the election of women (Gallagher et al. 2011).

Even more remarkable than the increase in the number of Conservative women MPs in 2010 was the election of 11 black and minority ethnic (BME) Conservative MPs, where previously there had been no more than three in the entire post-1945 period, one elected in 1992 (and defeated in 1997), and two more elected in 2005 (see Table 9.6). Labour's near-monopoly of BME representation owed much to fundamental facts of electoral behaviour and political geography. Most non-white voters were in lower-income groups and voted Labour, and were concentrated in inner-city constituencies traditionally held by Labour, so that it was easy to match BME candidates to seats with large BME electorates. Of Labour's 16 BME MPs in 2010 only five represented seats in which fewer than 20 per cent of

the electorate were non-white, and most of the others had majorities or near-majorities of BME electors.

The Conservatives in contrast had no seats where a particular demand for minority ethnic candidates could be so assumed, and in the safe all-white seat of Cheltenham in 1992 a black candidate, John Taylor, had been defeated after an acrimonious dispute in the local party. But in the run-up to the 2010 election, as with gender, so with race. Party headquarters encouraged a pool of aspiring BME candidates, seven of whom were put on the priority 'A list', brought them to the attention of constituencies where MPs were retiring, and saw their selection and election in six traditionally safe Conservative seats, all with miniscule proportions of non-white voters. Given a traditional absence of any grass-roots demand for such candidates in areas such as the Surrey stockbroker belt, it was probable that much exhortation was applied by the party's headquarters staff, one of whom, the retiring MP for Stratford-on-Avon, John Maples, who was in overall charge of the Conservative candidates selection process, had revealingly declared that he:

> would like to be able to run this like a dictator. I would achieve what I want. I could get the right candidates in the right seats, the right percentages of women and ethnic minority candidates, but the party is not going to wear that, and each (constituency) association has autonomy.

The relative influence of the centre and the periphery in Conservative selection procedures has long been hard to measure, and seen as a 'secret garden', but perhaps not insignificantly John Maples' replacement as MP for Stratford-on-Avon, was one of the party's nine new ethnic-minority MPs, Nadhim Zahawi, a businessman of Iraqi-Kurdish origin.

The Conservatives' rivalling of Labour in 2010 in the number of ethnic minority MPs, though remarkable, did have its limitations. Of the 11 Conservative non-white MPs, only two were women, and neither of them from a Muslim background, whereas of Labour's 16, seven were women, three of them of Pakistani parentage, and by all three being professional women (two barristers and one political aide), they were representative of modernising tendencies within the Muslim community. In this way Labour's attention to improving the representation of ethnic diversity was still ahead of the Conservatives.

The occupational background of the BME MPs elected in 2010 did nothing to change the two parties' standard patterns. Of the 11 Conservatives, three were lawyers, three bankers, three businessmen, one an accountant and one a politician; and of Labour's 16, seven were lawyers, four politicians, one a civil servant, one a dentist, two professional engineers and one a manual engineer.

BOX 9.3

Ethnic minority MPs, 1892–2011

Conservative[1]

1. Mancherjee Bhownaggree
   1895–1906
   Bethnal Green NE

2. Nirj Deva
   1992–97
   Brentford & Isleworth

3. Adam Afriyie
   2005–
   Windsor

4. Shailesh Vara
   2005–
   Cambridgeshire NW

5. Rehman Chishti
   2010–
   Gillingham & Rainham

6. Helen Grant
   2010–
   Maidstone & The Weald

7. Sam Gyimah
   2010–
   Surrey E

8. Sajid Javid
   2010–
   Bromsgrove

9. Kwasi Kwarteng
   2010–
   Spelthorne

10. Priti Patel
    2010–
    Witham

11. Alok Sharma
    2010–
    Reading W

12. Paul Uppal
    2010–
    Wolverhampton SW

13. Nadhim Zahawi
    2010–
    Stratford-on-Avon

Labour

1. Shapurji Saklatvala[2]
   1922–23, 1924–29
   Battersea N

2. Diane Abbott
   1987–
   Hackney N & Stoke Newington

3. Paul Boateng
   1987–2005
   Brent S

4. Bernie Grant
   1987–2000
   Tottenham

5. Keith Vaz
   1987–
   Leicester E

6. Ashok Kumar
   1991–92, 1997–2010
   Middlesbrough S & Cleveland E

7. Piara Khabra
   1992–2007
   Ealing Southall

8. Oona King
   1997–2005
   Bethnal Green & Bow

9. Mohammed Sarwar
   1997–2010
   Glasgow C

10. Marsha Singh
    1997–2012
    Bradford W

11. Mark Hendrick
    2000–
    Preston

12. David Lammy
    2000–
    Tottenham

13. Parmjit Dhanda
    2001–10
    Gloucester

14. Khalid Mahmood
    2001–
    Birmingham Perry Barr

15. Dawn Butler
    2005–2010
    Brent S

16. Sadiq Khan
    2005–
    Tooting

17. Shahid Malik
    2005–10
    Dewsbury

18. Virendra Sharma
    2007–
    Ealing Southall

19. Rushana Ali
    2010–
    Bethnal Green & Bow

20. Shabana Mahmood
    2010–
    Birmingham Ladywood

21. Lisa Nandy
    2010–
    Wigan

22. Chi Onwurah
    2010–
    Newcastle-on-Tyne C

23. Yasmin Quereshi
    2010–
    Bolton SE

24. Anas Sarwar
    2010–
    Glasgow C

25. Chuka Umunna
    2010–
    Streatham

26. Valerie Vaz
    2010–
    Walsall S

27. Seema Malhotra
    2011–
    Feltham & Heston

Liberal / Liberal Democrat

1. Dadabhai Naoraji 1892–5 Finsbury C
2. Parmjit Singh Gill 2004–5 Leicester S

1 Jonathan Sayeed was Conservative MP for Bristol E (1983–92) and Mid-Bedfordshire (1997–2005), but wished not to be classified as an ethnic minority MP.
2 Shapurji Saklatvala was first a Labour, and then a Labour-supported Communist MP.

Does representativeness matter?

However demographically 'unrepresentative' a party's MPs may appear to be, it is not clear that electoral sanctions follow. The Conservatives won over half – 11 out of 20 – of all the general elections following the first held on a complete adult franchise in 1929, and were only badly defeated in four others (in 1945, 1966, 1997 and 2001). But it is true that two of the bad defeats were in the recent past, and despite all the efforts under the Cameron leadership to broaden the candidate base, the party failed to win outright in 2010. It is likely that, in an age of disillusion with politics and politicians and with a complete collapse of the deference political elites enjoyed until the 1960s, the populist targeting of a 'posh' leadership finds a receptive audience.

Yet, it is doubtful either that representativeness is possible, or that in any case the social characteristics of MPs affect their legislative behaviour. On the first point, David Butler, the leading academic analyst of British electoral politics, has written:

> To what degree should a legislature be representative? Most people would like their legislature to contain spokesmen from all significant classes within the community, (but) in practice politicians are still drawn from a narrow segment of the population, notwithstanding the desire of all parties to offer a diverse and representative selection of candidates. They come overwhelmingly from the ranks of the male, the middle aged and the middle class. The bias in recruitment tells something about the values of selection committees in the constituencies, but it also touches a larger problem. Less than one voter in six admits to great interest in politics and even of these the overwhelming majority would have no taste for a political career. The 'eligibles' are so small a segment of the population that they could not possibly be representative.
>
> (Butler and Kavanagh 1974: 211)

On the second point, the co-author of the established series of British general election studies, Dennis Kavanagh has observed:

> From all the available data on social background it is not immediately obvious what its implications are for the behaviour and values of politicians. Will a better educated House (of Commons) be more ideological, more interested in abstract ideas? In the case of Labour, does the decline in the number of former manual workers and the embourgeoisment, when elected, of former workers, lead to a deradicalisation of views, as Michels claimed at the beginning of the (twentieth) century? Has the reduction of MPs from upper class backgrounds led to a decline of the 'One Nation' outlook on the Conservative benches? We do not know, but it seems most implausible that there should be a strong correlation between broad social background characteristics and values.
>
> (Kavanagh 1992: 12–32)

Despite the populist assumption – reflected in the 'posh and posher' charge – that an Etonian Prime Minister would represent the interests of his privileged background, it is not impossible that there is a relationship between inherited 'old' money and a moderately paternalistic 'One Nation' Conservatism, as distinct from a connection between self-made 'new' money and a Thatcherite anti-statist individualism. The Etonian, Harold Macmillan, had argued for state interventionist Keynesianism in his book *The Middle Way* in the 1930s depression, and the cover of the memoirs of another moderate Etonian, Sir Ian Gilmour, who was dropped as a minister by Margaret Thatcher for being 'wet', depicted him accompanying her on a ballroom floor with the caption, 'Dancing With Dogma'. Of the Conservative Etonian MPs elected in 2010 one, Kwasi Kwarteng, was, as were a number of others, a banker, but he was also black, of Ghanaian parentage. Another, Zac Goldsmith, despite being a multimillionaire, was an ardent campaigner against environmental degradation, who had pledged to resign his seat if the Cameron Government went back on its opposition to a third runway at Heathrow, and was also the sixteenth most rebellious Conservative MP in the first three years of the 2010 parliament. In short, it was unclear what were the non-purely-partisan political implications in being an Old Etonian Conservative MP.

To muddy the Etonian waters still further, of Labour's two Etonian MPs in the 2001–5 parliament, Mark Fisher and Tam Dalyell, Fisher was the eleventh most dissident Labour MP, with 74 rebellious votes, and Dalyell the nineteenth with 53 – out of a total of 218 Labour MPs rebelling at least once (Cowley 2005).

Nonetheless, the drive for demographic representation had been dominated for 20 years essentially by the call for more women MPs, for which four reasons are given. First, with women comprising half the population, for reasons of justice. Second, with a male-dominated parliament 'looking wrong' and undermining the legitimacy of the institution, for symbolic reasons. Third, because women, disliking the adversarial nature of political debate, bring a different, more

BOX 9.4

Reasons why women's presence in politics is said to matter

The justice argument claims that women's absence from elected political forums is evidence of a prima facie case of injustice that should be redressed. This argument does not rely upon the representatives having any differential impact upon politics; it matters simply that women are present.

The second argument is that the presence of women in political forums is important for symbolic reasons. An overwhelmingly male political body 'looks wrong' and suggests that women are not capable of being representatives. In addition, women's presence enhances, and their absence diminishes, the legitimacy of the political institution. Again, this argument does not require that the newly present women representatives make a difference in a substantive sense, although they may be said to have some effect as role models.

The third argument is that women will bring a different, more consensual, style to politics.

Finally, and most contested, is the argument that women representatives are more likely than male representatives to act for women. It is this latter argument that engages many feminists and underpins the presumption that the presence (in 1997) of 120 women MPs (including Labour's 101 women MPs) meant that women would be better represented (Childs 2005: 8).

---

consensual style to politics; and fourth, that they make a substantive difference by acting *for* women in a way male representatives do not. The fourth point is the nub of the feminist case; that women MPs make a difference in policy and legislative terms (see Box 9.4 for fuller presentation of these reasons).

Some of these claims were tested after the large influx of 65 new Labour women MPs, taking the party's total to 101, in 1997; first, that women 'do politics differently', preferring cooperation to conflict, collaboration to hierarchy, and setting greater store by loyalty. These assumptions appeared to be confirmed by the very low rate of dissident voting among the 65 new women, only 11 of whom rebelled in the 1997–2001 parliament. The low incidence of dissent at 17 per cent of new women MPs, contrasted with 34 per cent of new men MPs, and 44 per cent of all Labour MPs (Cowley 2002). However, challenging the claimed link between sex and loyalty was the fact that longer-serving women Labour MPs had high rates of rebelliousness indistinguishable from those of longer-serving male MPs. An MP's propensity to rebel is affected by many considerations, including ambition and (a related factor) relative youth, but personal factors such as sex appear unrelated. In the words of the leading analyst of dissident Commons voting: 'being a woman per se did not make one less likely to rebel' (Cowley 2002: 118).

Symbolically challenging too the claim that 'women represent women', all 65 bar one of Labour's new women MPs in 1997 famously accepted legislation cutting benefits paid to lone parents (invariably women). It was, however, a standard feminist argument that the 'presence of women' made a difference, that they were more liberal within each of the major parties, were more concerned with social policy, prioritised constituency work, and were more likely to take a pro-woman line than men. Also, when a 'critical mass' of women MPs was achieved, women MPs would cease aping the macho style of a male-dominated House. It was noted that three-quarters of the new Labour women in 1997 identified themselves as 'feminist', and it was claimed that they 'feminised the agenda' of the 1997–2001 Labour Government. It was further noted that Conservative women MPs in the 2001–05 parliament took a prominent part in debates on gender-related legislation such as equal pay and human reproduction, and yet without compromising the expectation that parliamentary voting on such matters was structured by party affiliation (Childs and Webb 2012). Given a Labour Party committed to a feminist perspective and a Conservative Party with a more traditional ethos, it was likely that the specificity of party prevailed over sex to prevent any uniform definition of the 'substantive representation of women'.

Clearly, however, concern for demographic representation has risen. First, the old ideological basis of party competition having faded, and tribal identities having weakened, the major parties now seek votes across the electorate. The waning of class identity has increased the salience of other identities, such as sex and ethnicity, making voters more open to mobilisation around them. Second, there has been a decline in party discipline in recent parliaments, with MPs more likely to vote against their party. While such disloyalty falls well short of MPs compromising the balance between government and opposition in key votes, and with the average size of back-bench revolts being in single figures, it does inevitably invite attention to the individual MPs who are rebelling and to seek any possible connection between their errant behaviour and the personal characteristics that may explain it.

Chapter summary

The social characteristics of Conservative and Labour MPs were transformed across the eight decades following the achievement of full adult franchise in 1929. An initial contrast between aristocratic and plutocratic Conservative MPs and proletarian Labour MPs was replaced from the 1940s onwards by a seemingly 'middle-class'-dominated House, but where great diversity was masked by apparent uniformity. The Conservative middle-class MP was privately educated, had been (if a graduate) to an elite university, and was in a high-status private profession or in business. The Labour middle-class MP was likely to have enjoyed upward social mobility into a state sector profession such as teaching, and attended a state school and a redbrick university. Notwithstanding the clear trend in the Conservative Party to a much less elitist educational background, a trend increasingly clear with each new intake of Conservative MPs, this is not a picture of middle-class uniformity.

Uniformity was more apparent in other respects. Growing numbers of MPs of all parties were professional politicians, and following the lead given by Labour, there were increasing numbers of MPs who were women or were from ethnic minorities. As the House of Commons came to give a visual impression of greater social diversity, it was less clear however, what political implications greater social representativeness implied. Concern for the enhanced 'legitimacy' of Parliament, and notions of greater 'justice' may have been met without any significant difference having been made to the way MPs performed their role as partisan representatives of political parties.

Nevertheless, in politics, perception is all, and there remain symbolic grounds for a socially representative parliament in order to sustain its legitimacy and authority in an era of declining confidence in, or even disillusionment with, democratic institutions.

Discussion points

- What problems have the parties encountered in making their parliamentary representatives more diverse, and how successful have they been?
- Has the social composition of the House of Commons become more uniform or more diverse, or both?
- Is there a feminised style of politics and do women MPs make a substantive difference?
- How does a 'supply and demand' model explain the unrepresentative social composition of the House of Commons?
- Does the unrepresentativeness of MPs matter?

Further reading

Analysis of the social composition of the House of Commons and description of any changes in candidate selection processes is contained in the chapter headed 'MPs and candidates' in the successive studies of general elections since 1951 under the authorship of Butler et al. (1980) and Kavanagh and Cowley (2010). Explanations for the socially unrepresentative composition of the House of Commons with particular reference to a 'supply and demand' model is contained in Norris and Lovenduski (1995).

The phenomenon of the professional or career politician is analysed in the article by King (1981) and in Riddell (1993, 2011), Oborne (2007) and Paxman (2002). Concern for increasing the number of women MPs and claims for the impact of an increased women's presence is to be found in Childs (2005), Childs and Webb (2012) and Norris (1996).

Assessment of links, if any, between MPs' social characteristics and their legislative behaviour may be explored by combining the analysis of parliamentary rebellions in Cowley (2002, 2005, 2011) with biographical profiles of MPs in Roth and Criddle (1997–2005), Vachers (2006) and Waller and Criddle (2007, and earlier editions 1996, 1999, 2002).

Bibliography

Aristotle (1962 edition) *The Politics* (Penguin).

Birch, A. (1964) *Representative and Responsible Government* (Allen and Unwin).

Butler, D. (1952) *The British General Election of 1951* (Macmillan).

Butler, D. (1955) *The British General Election of 1955* (Macmillan).

Butler, D. and Rose, R. (1960) *The British General Election of 1959* (Macmillan).

Butler, D. and King, A. (1965) *The British General Election of 1964* (Macmillan).

Butler, D. and King, A. (1966) *The British General Election of 1966* (Macmillan).

Butler, D. and Pinto-Duschinsky, M. (1970) *The British General Election of 1970* (Macmillan).

Butler, D. and Kavanagh, D. (1974) *The British General Election of February 1974* (Macmillan).

Butler, D. and Kavanagh, D. (1975) *The British General Election of October 1974* (Macmillan).

Butler, D. and Kavanagh, D. (1979) *The British General Election of 1979* (Macmillan).

Butler, D. and Kavanagh, D. (1983) *The British General Election of 1983* (Macmillan).

Butler, D. and Kavanagh, D. (1987) *The British General Election of 1987* (Macmillan).

Butler, D. and Kavanagh, D. (1992) *The British General Election of 1992* (Macmillan).

Butler, D. and Kavanagh, D. (1997) *The British General Election of 1997* (Macmillan).

Butler, D. and Kavanagh, D. (2001) *The British General Election of 2001* (Macmillan).

Butler, D. and Kavanagh, D. (2005) *The British General Election of 2005* (Macmillan).

Butler, D. and Pinto Duschinsky, M., 'Does unrepresentativeness matter?', in Layton-Henry, Z. (1980) *Conservative Party Politics* (Macmillan).

Childs, S. (2005) *New Labour's Women MPs* (Routledge).

Childs, S. and Webb, P. (2012) *Sex, Gender and the Conservative Party* (Macmillan).

Childs, S. and Lovenduski, J., 'Political Representation', in Colis, K. et al. (2012) *Oxford Handbook on Gender and Politics* (Blackwells).

Cowley, P. (2002) *Revolts and Rebellions: Party Voting Under Blair* (Politico's).

Cowley, P. (2005) *The Rebels* (Politico's).

Cowley, P. 'Political Parties and the Party System', in Heffernan R. et al. (2011), *Developments in British Politics* (Palgrave Macmillan).

Cowley, P. and Stuart, M. (2012) *The Bumper Book of Coalition Rebellions* (Nottingham University).

Cowley, P. and Stuart, M. (2013) Cambo Chained: Dissension amongst the Coalition's Parliamentary Parties, 2012–13 (Nottingham University).

Criddle, B. 'Members of Parliament', in Seldon, A. and Ball, S. (1994) *The Conservative Century* (Oxford University Press).

Evans, E. (2008) 'Supply or Demand: Women Candidates and the Liberal Democrats', *British Journal of Politics and International Relations*, 10(2008), pp. 590–606.

Gallagher, M., Laver, M. and Mair, P. (2011) *Representative Government in Modern Europe* (McGraw-Hill).

Guttsman, W.L. (1968) *The British Political Elite* (MacGibbon and Kee).

Gidings, P. (ed.) (2005) *The Future of Parliament* (Palgrave Macmillan).

Haxey, S. (1939) *Tory MP* (Gollancz).

Kavanagh, D. (1992) 'The Political Class and its Culture', *Parliamentary Affairs*, vol. 45, pp. 12–32.

Kavanagh, D. and Cowley, P. (2010) *The British General Election of 2010* (Macmillan).

King, A. 'The Rise of the Career Politician and its Consequences', *The British Journal of Political Science*, vol. 2, no. 3, July 1981.

Krook, M.L. (2009) *Quotas for Women in Politics* (Oxford University Press).

Lovenduski, J. and Norris, P. (eds) (1996) *Women in Politics* (Oxford University Press).

Mactaggart, F. (2000) *Women in Parliament: Their Contribution to Labour's First 1000 Days* (Fabian Society).

McIlveen, R. (2009) 'Ladies of the Right: An Interim Analysis of the A List', *Journal of Elections, Public Opinion and the Parties*, 19.2 (May 2009), pp. 147–59.

Mellors, C. (1978) *The British MP: A Socio-Economic Study of the House of Commons* (Saxon House).

Michels, R. (1962) *Political Parties* (New York Free Press).

Milbrath, L. and Goel, M. (1977) *Political Participation* (Rand McNally).

Norris, P. (1996) *Women in Politics* (Oxford University Press).

Norris, P. and Lovenduski, J. (1995) *Political Recruitment: Gender, Race and Class in the British Parliament* (Cambridge University Press).

Oborne, P. (2007) *The Triumph of the Political Class* (Simon and Schuster).

Parry, G., Moyser, G. and Day, N. (1992) *Political Participation and Democracy in Britain* (Cambridge University Press).

Paxman, J. (2002) *The Political Animal: An Anatomy* (Michael Joseph).

Phillips, A. (1995) *The Politics of Presence* (Oxford University Press).

Ranney, A. (1965) *Pathways to Parliament* (University of Wisconsin Press).

Riddell, P. (1993) *Honest Opportunism: The Rise of the Career Politician* (Hamish Hamilton).

Riddell, P. (2011) *In Defence of Politicians* (Biteback).

Ross, J.F.S. (1944) *Parliamentary Representation* (Yale University Press).

Roth, A. and Criddle, B. Parliamentary Profiles A–Z, various volumes 1997–2005 (Parliamentary Profiles).

Rush, M. (1969) *The Selection of Parliamentary Candidates* (Thomas Nelson).

Searing, D. (1994) *Westminster's World* (Harvard).

Saggar, S. (2002) *Race and Representation: Ethnic Pluralism and Electoral Politics* (Manchester University Press).

Squires, J. and Wickham Jones, M. (2001) *Women in Parliament* (Equal Opportunities Commission).

Vachers Parliamentary Profiles (2006) (Dods Parliamentary Communications).

Waller, R. and Criddle, B. (2007) *The Almanac of British Politics*, 8th edn (Routledge).

Useful websites

The Speaker's Conference on Parliamentary Representation (2010): http://www.publications.parliament.uk

http://www.revolts.co.uk

http://www.theyworkforyou.com.mps

http://www.dodonline.co.uk

http://www.publicwhip.org.uk

http://operationblackvote

http://en.wikipedia.org

CHAPTER 10

Pressure groups

Bill Jones

> " **Ten people who speak make more noise than ten thousand who are silent** "
>
> Napoleon Bonaparte

Learning objectives

- To explain that formal democratic government structures conceal the myriad hidden contacts between government and organised interests.

- To analyse and explain the way in which groups are organised and operate.

- To introduce some familiarity with theories regarding this area of government–public interaction.

- To provide some specific examples of pressure group activity.

The Norwegian political scientist Stein Rokkan, writing about his country's system, said 'the crucial decisions on economic policy are rarely taken in the parties or in Parliament'. He judged 'the central area' to be 'the bargaining table' where the government authorities meet directly with trade union and other group leaders. 'These yearly rounds of negotiations mean more in the lives of rank and file citizens than formal elections.'

British politics is not as consensually well organised or cooperative as the Norwegian model, but there is a central core of similarity regarding pressure group influence. Accordingly, this chapter examines the way in which organised groups play their part in the government of the country. Democratic government predicates government by the people, and politicians often claim to be speaking on behalf of public opinion. But how do rulers learn what people want? Elections provide a significant but infrequent opportunity for people to participate in politics. These are (now) held every five years, but pressure groups provide continuous opportunities for such involvement and communication.

Definitions

Interest or **pressure groups** are formed by people to protect or advance a shared interest. Like political parties, groups may be mass campaigning bodies, but whereas parties have policies for many issues and, usually, wish to form a government, groups are essentially sectional and wish to influence government only on specific policies.

Historical background

The term 'pressure group' is relatively recent, but organised groups tried to influence government long before the modern age of representative democracy. The Society for Effecting the Abolition of the Slave Trade was founded in 1787 and under the leadership of William Wilberforce and Thomas Clarkson succeeded in abolishing the slave trade in 1807. In 1839, the Anti-Corn Law League was established, providing a model for how a pressure group can influence government. It successfully mobilised popular and elite opinion against legislation that benefited landowners at the expense of the rest of society and in 1846 achieved its objective after converting the Prime Minister of the day, Sir Robert Peel, to its cause. It proved wrong the cynical dictum that the interests of the rich and powerful will invariably triumph over those of the poor and weak and strengthened the supporters of Britain's (at that time nascent) representative democracy. In the twentieth century the scope of government has grown immensely and impinges on the lives of many different social and economic sectors. After 1945 the development of the mixed economy and the welfare state drew even more people into the orbit of government. Groups developed to defend and promote interests likely to be affected by particular government policies. For its own part, government came to see pressure groups as valuable sources of information and potential support. The advent of modern media have provided a vast amphitheatre in which pressure groups can compete on equal terms with the political parties, to deliver their messages to the public. The variety of modern pressure groups therefore reflects the infinite diversity of interests in society. A distinction is usually drawn between the following:

1 **Sectional** or **interest groups**, most of which are motivated by the particular economic interests of their members. Classic examples of these are trade unions, professional bodies (e.g. the British Medical Association) and employers' organisations (e.g. The Engineering Employers' Federation).

2 **Cause** or **promotion groups**, which exist to promote an idea not directly related to the personal interests of its members. Wilberforce's was such a group, and in modern times the Campaign for Nuclear Disarmament (CND),

the Child Poverty Action Group (CPAG) and the Society for the Protection of the Unborn Child (SPUC) can be identified. Of the environmental groups, the Ramblers' Association, Greenpeace and Friends of the Earth are well-known examples.

Other species of pressure group include:

■ *Peak associations*: These are umbrella organisations that represent broad bands of similar groups such as employers (the Confederation of British Industry, CBI) and workers (the Trades Union Congress, TUC).

■ *'Fire brigade' groups*: So called because they form in reaction to a specific problem and disband if and when it has been solved; the Anti-Corn Law League might be seen as an early example.

■ *Episodic groups*: These are usually non-political but occasionally throw themselves into campaigning when their interests are affected: for example, sports clubs campaigning for more school playing fields.

■ *Online pressure groups*: These new lobbying phenomena have sprung up in the latter half of last decade. Best known internationally is Avaaz, usually focusing on abuses of power, torture and war crimes and mustering hundreds of thousands of signatures to bring pressure to bear, often with remarkable success. In the UK 38 Degrees led by David Babbs performs a rather similar role.

Membership of sectional groups is limited to those who are part of the specific interest group – for example, coal miners or doctors. In contrast, support for a cause such as nuclear disarmament or anti-smoking can potentially embrace all adults. However, the two types of group are not mutually exclusive. Some trade unions take a stand on political causes: for example (in the past), on apartheid in South Africa, on poverty or sexual equality. Some members of cause groups may have a material interest in promoting the cause – for example teachers in the Campaign for the Advancement for State Education. It should be noted that pressure groups regularly seek to influence each other to maximise impact and often find themselves in direct conflict over certain issues, for example, and most obviously, Forest which defends the rights of smokers and ASH, the anti-smoking body.

Civil society and groups

Civil society has a long provenance in political thought, being related to the seventeenth-century notion of a 'state of nature', which humans (in theory only) inhabited before entering the protective confines of the state (see Chapter 4). The idea of such an independent social entity enabled the likes of Hobbes and Locke to argue that citizens had the right to overthrow a corrupt or failing government. Civil society was held to comprise relationships in society which were not overtly political: those of family, business, church and, especially according to the modern sense of the term, *voluntary organisations*. These relationships help people to live together, cooperating, compromising; accepting both leadership and responsibility; providing the very basis of democratic activity; and training members in the art of democratic politics. Some commentators have argued that, while citizen protest led to the overthrow of communist governments, the absence of a strong or 'thick' civil society in eastern European countries has hindered their transition from totalitarian to democratic society. The ability to form organisations independent of the state is one of the hallmarks and, indeed, preconditions of a democratic society. A study by sociologists Ashford and Timms (1992) revealed substantial membership of groups in the UK, including 16 per cent in church or religious organisations, 14 per cent in trade unions, 17 per cent in sporting organisations and 5 per cent in environmental or ecological groups.

'Bowling alone'

One American student of civil society, Robert Putnam (1995), offers a rather depressing analysis in his essay 'Bowling alone'. He points out that despite rising levels of education – usually associated with increased participation – involvement with voluntary bodies in the USA was in decline: parent–teacher association membership had fallen from 12 million in 1982 to 5 million in 1995; unions, churches and many other bodies reported similar declines; and even the percentage who dined with neighbours dropped from 72 per cent in 1974 to 61 per cent in 1993. The title of his essay derived from the statistic that while the numbers involved in bowling between 1980 and 1993 increased by 10 per cent, the number playing in league teams plummeted by 40 per cent: Americans were 'bowling alone'.

Putnam saw this as merely one symptom of 'disengagement': fading away of groups; the decline of solidarity and trust; and a detachment from the political process evidenced in falling turnouts at elections. Some bodies have huge memberships but, as Putnam shows in the USA, these are often 'passive memberships' where someone pays an annual subscription but attends no meetings. If Britain is anything like America – and it often mimics trends a few years removed – a slow decline in pressure group activity and a 'thinning' of civic society would seem to be a worrying possibility.

A report by the Institute of Education in February 2003 on voluntary group membership suggested worrying similarities

with our transatlantic cousins. The study was based on three birth cohorts – 1946, 1958 and 1970. The first group produced a figure of 60 per cent membership, the second only 15 per cent and those born in 1970 a mere 8 per cent.

However, political scientist Peter Hall's research suggested British levels of participation were higher than the USA. Even more reassuringly, the 'Citizen Audit 2000–2001' programme at Sheffield University suggested that, despite the low turnout in the 2001 General Election, the 'British public is politically engaged'. Its findings, based on interviews with 13,000 people, found that three-quarters had engaged in one or more political activities, more particularly – including contributing and raising money for civic societies; boycotting products on moral grounds; while 2.5 million had taken part in a public demonstration. A more recent Cabinet Office paper (Hilton et al. 2010) offers a bullish assessment of the current state of British civil society. It noted that while some bodies had declined in membership – Mothers' Union, political parties and church congregations, for example – the number of charities registered since 1960 is 180,000, while civil societies in 2007 numbered an impressive 870,000. It also suggested 'passive' membership often reflected the trust of members that the body concerned had the competence to act effectively. The paper concluded 'civic participation is currently vibrant' (ibid.:).

Pressure groups and government

Okay, you've convinced me. Now go out there and bring pressure on me.

(President Franklin D. Roosevelt
in response to a business delegation)

The relationship between interest groups and government is not always or even usually **adversarial**. Groups may be useful to government. Ministers and civil servants often lack the information or expertise necessary to make wise policies, or indeed the *legitimacy* to ensure that they are implemented effectively. They frequently turn to the relevant representative organisations to identify defects in existing policies and seek suggestions as to how things might be improved. They sound out group leaders about probable resistance to a new line of policy. Moreover, an interest group's support, or at least acceptance, for a policy can help to 'legitimise' it and thus maximise its chances of successful implementation. If bodies involved in a new law refuse to cooperate and organise against it – as in the case of the poll tax in 1990 – a law can become unenforceable. The accession to power of Labour in May 1997 raised the spectre of union influence once again dominating policy, as in the 1970s. Blair was emphatic that unions, like any other group seeking influence, would receive 'fairness but no favours'. Indeed, Blair seemed more concerned to woo business groups than the electorally unpopular unions, so much so that Wyn Grant, an authority on pressure groups, has judged New Labour governments more pro-business than any in his lifetime.

In the several stages of the policy process, groups have opportunities to play an important role (see also Chapter 21):

1 At the initial stage they may put an issue on the policy agenda (e.g. environmental groups promoted awareness of the dangers to the ozone layer caused by many products and have forced government to act).

2 When governments issue Green Papers (setting out policy options for discussion) and White Papers (proposals for legislation), groups may **lobby** backbenchers or civil servants.

3 In Parliament, groups may influence the final form of legislation. As we can see from Figure 10.1, groups are involved at virtually every stage of the policy process.

Insider–outsider groups

Groups are usually most concerned to gain access to ministers and civil servants – the key policy-makers. Pressure group techniques are usually a means to that end. When government departments are formulating policies there are certain groups they consult. The Ministry of Agriculture, Fisheries and Food, when it existed under that name, was in continuous and close contact with the National Farmers' Union. Indeed, in 1989, in the wake of the salmonella in eggs scandal, when Health Minister Edwina Currie said on television that 'most egg production' in the country was so infected, it was alleged by some that the ministry neglected the interests of consumers compared with those of the producers. Wyn Grant (1985) has described groups that are regularly consulted as 'insider groups'; in the study of pressure groups this has become possibly the most important distinction. A good example of a new insider group is the TaxPayers' Alliance (see Box 10.1), although some claim it is so close to the Conservative Party it is effectively a wing of it.

On the other hand, the Campaign for Nuclear Disarmament, for example, mounts public campaigns largely because it has no access to Whitehall; in Grant's language it is an 'outsider group'. Not only does it lack specialist knowledge on foreign policy or defence systems, but the policies it advocates are flatly opposed to those followed by every postwar British government. Grant's classification of groups is summarised in Figure 10.2.

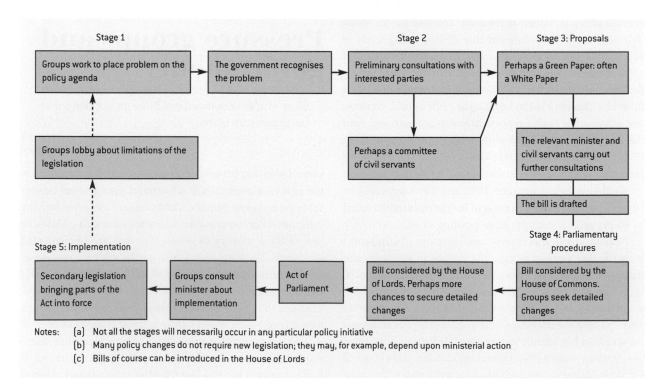

Figure 10.1 Pressure groups and the policy process

Source: From W. Grant (1988) 'Pressure groups and the policy process', *Social Studies Review*, vol. 3, no. 5. Reproduced with permission from the California Council for Social Studies

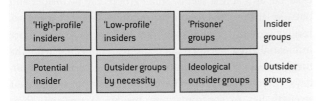

| 'High-profile' insiders | 'Low-profile' insiders | 'Prisoner' groups | Insider groups |
| Potential insider | Outsider groups by necessity | Ideological outsider groups | Outsider groups |

Figure 10.2 Grant's typology of pressure groups

Source: From W. Grant (1985) 'Insider and outsider pressure groups', *Social Studies Review*, vol. 1, no. 1. Reproduced with permission from the California Council for Social Studies

To gain access to the inner sanctums of decision making, groups usually have to demonstrate that they possess at least some of the following features:

1 *Authority*, which may be demonstrated in the group's ability to organise a majority of its potential members. The National Union of Mineworkers spoke for nearly 100 per cent of miners for many years, but its authority was weakened not just by the fall-off in membership after its disastrous 1983–4 miners' strike-against the Thatcher Government's pit closure programme – but also by the formation in 1985 of the breakaway Union of Democratic Miners. Similarly, the authority of the teachers' unions has been weakened because of the divisions between so many different groups. Overwhelming support by members for their group leadership's policies is another guarantor of authority.

2 *Information*: Groups such as the British Medical Association and the Howard League for Penal Reform command an audience among decision makers because of their expertise.

3 *The compatibility of a group's objectives with those of the government*: For example, trade unions traditionally received a more friendly hearing when pressing for favourable trade union legislation or state intervention in industry from a Labour than from a Conservative government. The TUC always received short shrift from Margaret Thatcher, who made no effort to disguise her

BOX 10.1

TaxPayers' Alliance: pressure group or Tory front?

'Since it was launched in 2004 the Alliance has become arguably the most influential pressure group in the country . . .' So wrote the *Guardian*, 10 October 2009, in a major article on the new phenomenon, written in the wake of the Conservative Party conference in Manchester.

'The idea of tearing down the walls of big government as Cameron did in his speech on Thursday is something we have been talking about for years,' said its chief executive, Matthew Elliott, yesterday. 'The Tory party has moved on to our agenda.'

The TPA also claimed authorship of George Osborne's public sector pay freeze and that no public sector worker should earn more than the Prime Minister without the Chancellor approving it. The TPA also urge the wholesale abandonment of cherished Labour achievements: the secondary school building programme, child benefit and Sure Start centres for young children.

The media too – especially the right-wing press – have proved deliriously receptive to its messages:

'In the last year the *Daily Mail* quoted the TPA in 517 articles. The *Sun* obliged 307 times, once bizarrely on page 3 when a topless Keeley parroted the TPA's line against energy taxes. The *Guardian* mentioned the group 29 times.'

The term 'Alliance' suggests that the TPA has some kind of democratic legitimacy, that it represents the voting public in some kind of genuine fashion. Indeed, it claims to be: 'the guardian of taxpayers' money, the voice of the taxpayer in the media and their representative at Westminster'. The *Guardian* had investigated the TPA's sources for its £1 million annual funding and discovered 60 per cent of it comprised donors giving £5,000 or more to the Conservative Party. Moreover, one of the group's directors lives abroad and does not pay any UK tax.

Perhaps inevitably after this Labour sources called foul. Former Deputy Prime Minister, John Prescott, denounced it as 'nothing more than a front for the Conservative Party', calling on the BBC – which regularly interviews TPA staff – to clarify its umbilical links to the Tories when its representatives are quoted or interviewed.

The Chief Executive of the TPA, Matthew Elliot, dismissed the attack, claiming it was as hard on the Conservative councils who wasted money as it was on Labour and pointing out its donors had once given to Labour in its earlier days.

hostility or even contempt. But even when likely to receive a friendly hearing, groups seeking access to the policy process are not advised to put forward demands that the government regards as unreasonable.

4 *Compatibility of group objectives with public sympathies*: A group out of sympathy with public views – for example, advocating the housing of convicted paedophiles in residential areas – is unlikely to gain inner access to decision making.

5 *Reliable track record for sensible advice in the past* (and the ability, through knowledge of Whitehall, to fit in with its procedures and confidential ethos): most insider groups, like the BMA, CBI and NFU, fit this profile.

It goes without saying that most groups aspire to be *insiders* rather than *outsiders*.

6 *Possession of powerful sanctions*: Some groups of workers are able to disrupt society through the withdrawal of their services. The ability of electricians to inflict injury on society was.

It goes without saying that most groups aspire to be *insiders* rather than *outsiders*

But becoming and remaining an insider group requires the acceptance of constraints. Group leaders, for example, should respect confidences, be willing to compromise, back up demands with evidence and avoid threats (Grant 1989, 1990). Grant accepts that this typology is not quite as

clear-cut as it at first seems. Some groups can be insider and outsider at the same time – for example, Greenpeace. Also, insider groups, in the present day, are not invariably more influential than outsider ones: groups connected with the fuel crisis of 2000 brought the country to a standstill within days. Direct action groups have shown their power but their strength lies in confrontations; insider groups win their battles out of the limelight and often on better terms.

Being on the inside is still thought by many to be better than on the outside, though this does amount to a kind of 'pact with the devil' that groups sign with government. If government fails to deliver the influence that group leaders expect, they can find themselves in trouble with their membership. Alternatively, they can become so closely associated with a particular government policy that they can lose credibility if that policy fails (but see below for Grant's recent thinking on the evolution of group relations with government).

Pressure group methods can be seen on a continuum running from peaceful methods to violent ones (see Figure 10.3). Anyone working for a pressure group, especially if it is a local one focusing on, say, a planning issue, will find themselves working hard at routine chores such as stuffing envelopes, ringing up supporters, delivering publicity and collecting signatures on petitions. However, other groups use different techniques. Trade unions use or threaten to use the 'denial of function' approach; in practice, this means going on strike, a kind of holding to ransom of those who benefit

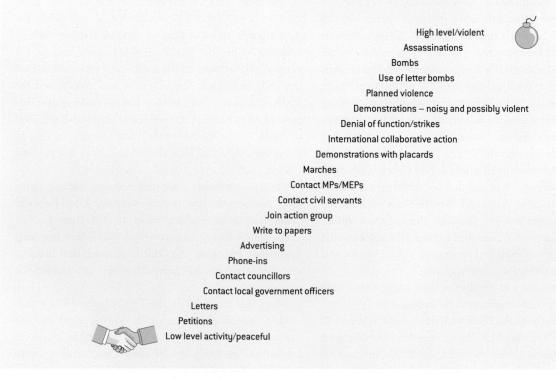

Figure 10.3 Pressure groups methods continuum

from their labour. In some cases, however, such methods encounter moral restraints; for example, should nurses refuse to look after patients in support of a pay dispute? Few would find this easy. Other groups are concerned to test the law. The Ramblers' Association, for example, is quite happy to ignore notices from landowners denying them access if the notices are not legal; in such circumstances, its members are happy to assert their legal rights and to clear any obstructions that may have been put in place. However, they stop short of actually breaking the law. Other groups are prepared to go even further. Some anarchist groups deliberately break the law as part of a strategy of undermining law and order and existing civil society; others do so to attract the publicity of a court case and possibly a 'martyred' period in jail for an activist: for example, Fathers 4 Justice.

Such groups and sentiments are still rare. Most groups concentrate their efforts at the peaceful end of the spectrum, but a change in the political culture is discernible over the last couple of decades.

The growth (and increasing respectability) of direct action

Some groups either are so passionate or have become so impatient with the slow-moving wheels of government that they have deliberately used high-profile and illegal tactics. Brian Cass, the chief executive of Huntingdon Life Sciences, which conducts experiments on animals, was once beaten by animal rights activists wielding baseball bats and in April 2003 won a court injunction to prevent protesters from approaching within 50 yards of employees' homes. However, the best known of such extremists have probably been the protesters against the Newbury bypass and, later, the new runway at Manchester Airport. Unlike the stereotypical scruffy lefties, these are often respectable, middle-aged, middle-class people or their nice children. In consequence, the protesters were often not criticised but lauded and turned into minor folk heroes like Daniel Hooper, who under his activist name of 'Swampy' back in the late 1990s, featured in many protests.

Perhaps the endorsement of 'respectable' middle-class opinion is crucial in terms of how the media cover such stories. The Greenham Common women – often muddy, strident, scruffily dressed and with crew-cut hair – who camped outside US cruise missile bases in the UK during the 1980s were generally given negative coverage, especially by the right-wing press. Perhaps this new militancy is part of a growing awareness of political power among ordinary citizens. It also suggests that a sea-change has occurred regarding citizens' view of themselves (see Box 10.8).

Terror tactics

Some groups have opted to use a version of terror to advance their ideas. The Animal Liberation Front has regularly used violence to protest against experiments on animals, the staff and property of Huntingdon Life Sciences providing frequent targets (see also Box 10.2). In June 1999 the direct action collective, Reclaim the Streets (RTS) group demonstrated in central London. In the *Observer* (31 October) one of the participants explained: 'There are a lot of us who now recognize we can't pick individual battles; we have to take on the whole system.' RTS proved influential and in 2012 demonstrations under its name took place in Finland, Ireland and Belgium.

A curious example of a pressure group which was undermined by members prepared to use extremist methods is Fathers 4 Justice. This was formed in December 2002 by marketing executive Matt O'Connor who had suffered from legal decisions denying him access to his children after divorce. His idea was to use high profile but basically amusing stunts to win public attention: 'ordinary dads doing extraordinary things'. After a number of harmless stunts, the organisation overstretched itself when on 18 January 2006 it transpired that a group connected with Fathers 4 Justice had planned to kidnap Tony Blair's five-year-old son Leo. The idea, it seemed, was to hold him for a while and then set him free unharmed, but Matt O'Connor was dismayed: 'We do peaceful direct action with a dash of humour. We're in the business of uniting dads with their kids, not separating them.' He indicated that his group would cease to function. In April 2009 a member of climate change group, Plane Stupid, was cautioned by police after she threw green custard over Peter Mandelson She commented:

> Despite the harmless and comic nature of my antics, the police informed me that throwing custard over an un-elected government minister could be seen as a public order offence and have cautioned me accordingly . . . Climate change is the greatest threat we have ever faced through which millions will lose their lives and livelihoods.
>
> (*Guardian*, 10 April 2009)

Aiming for the power points

Pressure groups seek to influence the political system at the most accessible and cost-effective 'power points'. The obvious target areas include:

BOX 10.2

The case of Darley Oaks Farm and Gladys Hammond

In October 2004, thieves stole the body of Gladys Hammond, mother-in-law to Christopher Hall, owner of a farm in Staffordshire which bred guinea pigs for scientific experimentation. In 2005 four activists were charged with conspiracy to backmail. The leader of the group was revealed as Jon Ablewhite, a clergyman's son, who had led a six-year campaign against the farm. He was a charismatic character, six feet plus, according to a fellow activist: motivated and organised – 'amicable and educated, just the type you need'. When the farm eventually stopped breeding guinea pigs he was ecstatic, saying: 'Factory farming is on the same moral level as the Holocaust because of the systematic abuse and killing of these animals. Don't forget that Goebbels learned from factory farmers and used their methods to execute the Jews.' Mrs Hammond's remains were recovered in 2006 and reburied on 31 May.

Jon Ablewhite, accused of desecration of Gladys Hammond's grave
Source: Chris Radburn / PA / Empics

1 *The public at large*: Groups seek to raise money, train staff, attract and mobilise membership, to assist in group activities and to apply pressure on their behalf.

2 *Other pressure group members*: Groups with similar objectives will often duplicate membership, e.g. the various environmental groups. Moreover, such groups can combine forces over particular campaigns such as the Countryside Alliance, which coordinated a heterogeneous collection of groups against Labour's threatened ban on fox hunting 2004–7 (see Box 10.9).

3 *Political parties*: Groups will seek to influence the party that seems most sympathetic to its views. Inevitably trade unions – the historical crucible of the labour movement – look to Labour, and business groups tend to concentrate on the Conservatives (see below). Constitutional reform groups such as Charter 88 initially looked to the Liberal Democrats but, as such support was already solid, it embarked on a successful campaign to convert the Labour Party. Interestingly, the Campaign for Nuclear Disarmament achieved a similar conversion back in the 1960s and in the early 1980s but never achieved its objective, as Labour decided to abandon such a policy during the later part of the decade. For its part, the Countryside

Alliance tended to work within the ambit of the Conservative Party as does the TaxPayers' Alliance.

4 *Parliament*: Especially the House of Commons, but in recent years increasingly the House of Lords. The Commons is more attractive to groups as this is where the important debates on legislation occur. Groups often draft amendments for friendly MPs – often asked to hold voluntary office – to submit in Parliament. MPs are also sought – and this may be their most important function for some groups – for their ability to provide access to even more important people, such as the increasingly important Select Committees and (especially) regular meetings with ministers and civil servants. This ability to provide access – sometimes at a price – has been at the centre of the rows over sleaze that dogged Major's government and has also affected Blair's administration. The Academic Study of Parliament Group surveyed a number of groups, discovering that over three-quarters were in regular contact with MPs; some 60 per cent said the same of members of the Lords.

In July 2012 an opportunity was introduced for the public to intervene in legislation. The public can now move amendments during a new 'public reading stage'

Violence as a political weapon

Writing in the *Guardian* on 14 November 2005, columnist Gary Younge discussed the riots devastating French suburbs and considered the efficacy of violent means to achieve political ends. He quoted African-American abolitionist Frederick Douglass's aphorism that: 'Power concedes nothing without a demand. It never did and it never will.' He pointed out that the mostly unemployed ethnic minorities, living in rundown estates and suffering racial discrimination, had nothing to lose, but their actions immediately won concessions and government actions designed to alleviate their problems. Younge comments that 'none of this would have happened without the riots'. Any amount of peaceful measures would have attracted feeling attention but it was the damage to property and the threat to life which galvanised the French government. He went on to assert that: 'When all non-violent, democratic means of achieving a just end are unavailable, redundant or exhausted, rioting is justifiable', but he goes on to add: 'Rioting should be neither celebrated nor fetishised, because it is a sign not of strength but of weakness. Like a strike, it is often the last and most desperate weapon available to those with the least power.' He warns that rioting easily becomes an end in itself and something which can polarise, divide and set loose murder and mayhem in society. He issues something like a partial endorsement of violence as a political weapon, urging that it be used with restraint and economy. Yet, critics might suggest to him, the problem is that using the threat of chaos to win concessions is perilously close to unleashing the real thing.

Also addressing this topic, Professor Timothy Garton Ash, writing in the *Guardian* on 2 March 2006, perceived the emergence of a 'group veto' by groups who say:

> We feel so strongly about this that we are going to do everything we can to stop it. We recognize no moral limits. The end justifies the means. Continue on this path and you must fear for your life . . .
>
> If the intimidators succeed, then the lesson for any group that strongly believes in anything is: shout more loudly, be more extreme, threaten violence, and you will get your way.
>
> Inch by inch, paragraph by paragraph, we are becoming less free.

He concludes that any point of view which does not threaten harm should be tolerated – even right-wing historian David Irving's Holocaust denials – but that any person or group which urges 'kill the Jews!' or 'kill the Muslims!' should be 'met with the full rigour of the law'.

---

allowing the public to draft laws line by line via a website. Suggestions are collated by civil servants and considered by peers and MPs during the passage of the bill (*Sunday Times*, 8 July 2012).

5 *Ministers and civil servants*: Clearly, ministers and their civil servants are natural targets for groups. Regular access provides 'insider' status and potentially composition of the policy-making 'triangle' also comprising ministers and civil servants (see Box 10.4 and Chapter 21).

6 *European Union (EU)*: Pressure group activity is like a river in that it seeks out naturally where to flow. Since power has shifted to Brussels so groups have automatically shifted their focus too. In the early days, when there was no elected European Parliament, their activities helped to reduce the '**democratic deficit**' (Greenwood 1997: 1), but since the Single European Act (SEA) in 1986 groups have played an increasingly important role as the competence of EU institutions has expanded to include the environment and technology. The Maastricht Treaty of 1992 also extended EU powers into health and consumer protection. The Commission has calculated that there are 3,000 interest groups in Brussels, including more than 500 Europe-wide federations and employing 10,000 personnel (Greenwood 1997: 3). In addition there are over 3,000 lobbyists, a huge increase in just a few years. These lobbyists and groups – especially the business ones – invest the substantial resources needed to set up shop in the heart of Belgium because they feel the stakes are so high. The EU can make decisions that deeply affect, among others, the work and profits of fishermen, farmers and the tobacco industry, as well as the conditions of employment of trade unionists. Greenwood discerns five areas of EU activity that attract group pressure:

■ *Regulation*: Much of the EU's output of directives comprises rules governing the way the consumer is served. Indeed, in some sectors the bulk of new regulatory activities now takes place not in Whitehall but in Brussels.

Box 10.4

Lobbying government

The USA is not the only country where massive corporate power can exert a near controlling influence over legislation. In Britain too corporations are especially adept, through their superior resources, at making contact with key decision-makers. Maybe this is where the most important influencing of government occurs.

A good example is provided by the insurance industry in the wake of Labour's 2008 Pensions Act which aimed to provide pensions for lower-paid workers in permanent or temporary employment. Writing in the *Guardian*, 10 July 2012, Nick Mathieson wrote:

> Intense lobbying by the insurance industry succeeded in persuading the government to water down a new pension scheme designed to help the lower paid save for retirement, leaving the scheme 'fighting with one arm behind its back'. Three senior insurance executives, two Whitehall sources familiar with the situation and two pension campaigners confirmed that the ground-breaking, not-for-profit scheme, due to come into force in October, was neutered by an industry that feared 'unfair competition'.

Bowing further to industry pressure, the government imposed a £4,400 annual cap on the combined contributions employers and employees can make to the scheme, meaning employers with staff earning above £55,000 will be forced to use additional schemes.

On 9 July 2012, the same journalist reported on a study which revealed the City of London spent £92 million in 2011 on lobbying politicians and regulators in 'an economic war of attrition' which has won it many battles including:

- the killing of government plans to establish a watchdog to police quoted corporations;
- reducing corporation taxes on banks' overseas subsidiaries, saving the finance industry billions.

The study showed 129 organisations engaging in lobbying for the finance sector with 800 employees. The fact that half of the Conservative Party's funding comes from the City must help lobbying activities more than a little. It is small wonder proposals in the annual Budget often disappear before the resultant Finance Acts in the summer. Nor is it surprising that in the wake of the financial meltdown in 2007–9 the promises to reform the banking industry have been so slow and half-hearted.

- *Promotion*: For example, the development of key technologies to support export drives.
- *Integration*: Such as the measures to advance free and fair competition in the Single Market.
- *Funding*: Such as the Structural Funds to reduce regional imbalances or funds for research activities.
- *Enablement*: Such as measures to support environmental improvement.

The SEA and Maastricht Treaty expanded the power of the European Parliament and made it possible for it to amend legislation; pressure groups directed their attentions accordingly. However, the major source of group interest remains the Commission, a relatively small number of officials who can be influenced via the usual processes of presentations, briefing documents, networks, lunches and so forth. Some directorates are more receptive than others, but on the whole the institutions of the EU expect to be lobbied and welcome such attentions on the grounds that people wishing to influence measures usually represent those who will be affected by them and

hence are likely to make useful inputs. The cross-sectoral federations are often consulted as they are thought to be broadly representative: for example, UNICE (Union of Industrial Confederations of Europe), the highly influential EUROCHAMBRES (the association of European Chambers of Commerce), and ETUC (European Trade Union Confederation).

7 *The media*: The director of the charity Child Poverty Action once said that 'coverage by the media is our main strategy' (Kingdom 1999: 512). Such a statement could equally be made by virtually all pressure groups outside those few insider groups at the epicentre of government policy and decision making. Unless influence is virtually automatic, any group must maximise its ability to mobilise the public to indicate its authority, its power and potential sanction; influencing the public can be achieved only via the media. Therefore ensuring that group activities catch the eye of the media is the number one priority.

8 *Informal contacts and the Establishment*: So far the contacts mentioned have been ones that are in the public domain; it is quite possible that most would have a written minutes

of proceedings. However, the world does not function just on the basis of formal, minuted meetings. Britain is a relatively small island with a ruling elite drawn substantially from the 7 per cent of the population who are educated in public schools. It might be claimed that such a critique is a little old-fashioned, but many argue that the deep connections of class, blood, marriage, shared education and leisure pursuits link decision makers in the country in a way that makes them truly, in the words of sociologist John Scott (1991), a 'ruling class'. In addition, when not in their clubs they can meet in other elite leisure places such as the opera at Covent Garden, Glyndebourne and Henley. This form of the 'Establishment' still exists and still exerts much influence; arguably the tendency for even New Labour to be agnostic over the social provenance of its elite members helps extend its influence. It is impossible to reckon the influence of such informal contacts, but some, especially the Marxists, claim that this is how the really big decisions are always made: in private and in secret between fellow members of the closely interlinked networks of the ruling elite. What follows in public is merely the democratic window dressing for self-interested fixing. The evidence cited in Box 10.4 suggests there might be more than a grain of truth in this analysis.

PROFILE

Robin Butler (1938–)

Former Secretary to the Cabinet. Educated at Oxford, from where he joined the Treasury. Worked in private offices of Wilson and Heath before rising to Permanent Secretary in the Treasury and then Secretary to the Cabinet 1988–97. Perhaps appropriately for Britain's top civil servant, Butler seemed to epitomise many of the ideals of the British ruling elite: he was the well-rounded man (he was also a rugby blue); he was apparently modest, articulate and effortlessly able while at the same time being 'infinitely extendable': able to cope with any crisis or any demands on his time or intellect. In 2005 he issued his report into the intelligence on which the decision to go to war in Iraq was based, a report which contained a degree of criticism rare for such a senior member of the Establishment, though his solution was scarcely revolutionary: a return to traditional Cabinet government where papers are tabled and discussed with minutes taken and circulated. He was a non-executive director of HSBC bank 1998–2008.

Factors determining effectiveness

The effectiveness of pressure groups is also a function of organisational factors. They need:

- a coherent organisational structure;
- high-quality and efficient staff (these days they recruit direct from the best universities);
- adequate financial resources;
- good leadership;
- clear strategy;
- first-class media skills.

Economic interest groups are usually well financed, but cause groups can often command significant annual income also; charities in 2008 managed to raise nearly £50 billion. In addition, cause groups can compensate for shoestring resources by attracting high-quality committed leadership; for example, in the recent past, Jonathon Porritt (Friends of the Earth), Frank Field (CPAG), Mike Daube (ASH) and perhaps the most effective popular campaigner of them all, Des Wilson of Shelter and many other causes.

Good organisation is also of key importance, and the best pressure groups are as efficiently organised as any business, with high-class staff recruited from the best universities.

Issue attention cycle

The American political scientist Anthony Downs has suggested that the media and the public's receptivity to pressure group messages is another potent factor influencing effectiveness. He pointed out that the new cause groups must run the gauntlet of the 'issue attention' cycle (see Figure 10.4). The pre-problem stage is followed by alarmed discovery, coupled with the feeling that something could and should be done. When it becomes clear, as it usually does, that progress will not be easy, interest declines and this is when the pressure group faces its toughest tests. This has certainly been true of environmental, nuclear disarmament and AIDS campaigns, but all three of these reveal that with new discoveries and fresh events the issue attention cycle can be rerun – possibly frequently over time.

Economic interest groups

The policies of the government in such areas as interest and exchange rates, taxation, spending, trading policy and

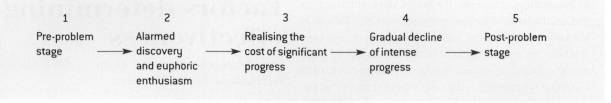

Figure 10.4 The issue attention cycle

Source: A. McCulloch (1998) 'Politics and the environment', *Talking Politics*, Autumn 1998. Reproduced with permission from The Politics Association

industrial relations are important in providing the context for the economy. Two of the most powerful interest groups that try to influence these policies are business and trade unions.

Business

Business is naturally deeply affected by government economic policies, and it is understandable that its representatives will seek to exert influence. Many firms depend on government handouts, subsidies and orders and will seek to influence the awarding of contracts.

In one sense any sizeable business organisation acts like a pressure group. **Multinational companies** – many with turnovers larger than those of small countries – make their own regular and usually confidential representations to government. When conditions for trading appear more favourable in another country, they pack up and move their whole operation, often within months. The threat to do this and deny employment is a potent weapon which such large companies use to barter advantages from governments.

Strength in unity

Particular industries often form federations, such as the Society of Motor Manufacturers or the Engineering Employers' Federation, and seek strength in unity. The Confederation of British Industry (CBI) was formed in 1965 and since that date has acted as an overall 'peak' organisation to provide a forum for discussion – it holds an annual conference – and to represent the views of members to government. It has a membership of 15,000, employs several hundred staff and has an annual budget of some £5 million. The CBI is dominated by big companies, and this helps to explain the 1971 breakaway Small Business Association (later the Federation of Small Businesses). For much of Margaret Thatcher's first term of office her policies of high interest and exchange rates damaged manufacturing industry, and the CBI criticised her for it. On one famous occasion, the then Director General of the CBI, Sir Terence Beckett, called for a 'bare-knuckle' fight

to make Margaret Thatcher change her deflationary policies, but his violent rhetoric abated after a stormy confrontation with that formidable lady Prime Minister. Under Tony Blair's business-friendly Labour administration the CBI under Adair Turner was generally supportive of government policy, while his highly extrovert, near demagogic successor, Digby Jones, was more critical of government.

The Institute of Directors is a more right-wing and political campaigning body. It opposed price and income restraints, which the CBI was prepared to support in the 1970s, and it vigorously supported the Conservative government's policies of privatisation, cutting public spending and encouraging free-market economics. Other organisations, such as Aims of Industry, are used as means of raising support and indirectly revenue for the Conservative Party. Although no business group has a formal association with the Conservative Party, a number of major firms do make financial contributions. Many businesses utilise the informal contacts mentioned above, especially when the Conservatives are in power, as this tends to open up the channels of communication between government and business. These may take the form of whispers in the ears of government ministers at dinner parties, in gentlemen's clubs and elsewhere.

Trade unions

Trade unions perform two distinct roles. The first is political. Since they helped to form the Labour Party in 1900 they have played, and still play, a decisive role in the internal politics of that party (see Box 10.5). Trade unions are overtly involved in party politics more deeply than any other interest group.

The second role of individual trade unions is industrial bargaining, to represent the interests of their members on pay and working conditions in negotiations with employers. Three-quarters of all unions are affiliated to the Trades Union Congress (TUC), which speaks for the trade union movement as a whole. In the past this function has involved unions directly in the political life of the country.

BOX 10.5

Labour and the unions

Ever since February 1900, when the Labour Representation Committee, the embryo of the party, was formed, trade unions have played a key role and are the category of pressure group most closely involved in mainstream politics.

- *Affiliation*: Half of all trade unions are affiliated to the party including the majority of the big unions: e.g., CWU, Unite and USDAW. Other unions can have more complex relationships with the party: UNISON has a general political fund as well as an affiliated one.

- *Money link*: A union's political fund receives money from members along with their subscriptions unless they specifically 'contract out'. Unions, if affiliated, decide how much to give to Labour from their funds. One calculation in 2005 was that contributions collected in this fashion and donated to Labour amounted to £24 million between 2002 and 2005, comprising half of the funding the party needs annually. Unions tend to be unpopular with voters (despite the fact so many voters are members) so Conservative jibes that Labour is 'in the pocket of union paymasters' have an important resonance.

- *Membership*: Each union decides how many members it wishes to say pay the political levy. Those union members who pay the levy can join the party at a reduced rate.

- *Representation*: Union '**block votes**' – leaders casting votes on behalf of affiliated members – used to dominate conference voting decisions, but the proportion allowed to count by the block votes was reduced to only 50 per cent in 1996, and the party's stated aim is to achieve '**one member, one vote**' eventually.

- *Electoral College*: Labour leaders are elected by an electoral college in which unions, MPs and constituency members have one-third of the vote each. Ed Miliband won his close contest against his brother in autumn 2010 through his assiduous wooing of the union sector, causing leading members of the party to urge a change in the voting system.

- *Volunteers*: These provide the foot soldiers of the Labour Party; nearly three-quarters of trade unionists are party members and over half voted Labour at the last two elections.

- *Problems in Blair's second and third terms*: Blair's predilection for 'modernising' public services by involving private companies in their operations won him few friends in the unions, especially the new breed of leaders he now faced, who had not experienced the dog years of Labour's opposition to Thatcher. The 2004 *Warwick Agreement* established agreement on key principles with the Labour Government on pay and holiday pay, pensions and other workplace issues.

Various attempts were made by Labour and Conservative governments to win the agreement of unions to pay policies that would keep inflation in check and the cost of British exports competitive in overseas markets. By the late 1960s Harold Wilson had become so exasperated with striking trade unions that he proposed measures to curb their tendency to strike and cripple the economy. However, his White Paper 'In Place of Strife' was attacked by the unions, and James Callaghan led a successful revolt against it in the Cabinet, destroying the authority of Wilson's Government. Ted Heath's administration after 1970 worked hard to solve the problem of union disruption and eventually tried a statutory (i.e. passing new laws) approach, but this foundered hopelessly and resulted in an election in 1974, which he lost. Labour back in power tried to stem the rocketing inflation by engineering a 'Social Contract' with the unions whereby they agreed to restrain wage demands in exchange

for favourable policies on pensions, low pay and industrial legislation. This succeeded to an extent and for a while the UK had a pay regime that was almost Scandinavian in its harmony between business and workers, but in 1978 Callaghan's call for a 5 per cent limit was rejected by the unions, and his Government descended into the ignominy of the 'winter of discontent' (January–February 1979) with, infamously, bodies left unburied and operating theatres without electricity.

Subsequently, Margaret Thatcher introduced a series of laws that emasculated union power: five Employment Acts and the 1984 Trade Union Act. These made unions liable for the actions of their members and rendered their funds liable to seizure by the courts, as the miners found to their disadvantage in 1984 when their lack of a strike ballot made them liable to sequestration of assets. Their bitter strike slowly ran out of steam and they suffered a humiliating defeat, which set the tone for union dealings with government for the rest of the decade. Days lost through strikes fell to an all-time low, and a kind of industrial peace held sway, although at the cost of much bitterness. Margaret Thatcher refused to consult with the unions, and their occasional meetings proved to be cold and wholly unproductive. Unemployment helped to reduce the size of union membership by 3 million (a quarter) from 1979 to 1989. Thatcher's crusade against the unions had a major impact on British politics, especially her refusal to settle with Arthur Scargill's over the Miners Strike 1984–85.

This drawn-out divisive, bitter and violent confrontation split the nation and struck a blow against union power from which it has never recovered. Tony Blair did nothing to reassert union power and did his best to keep it at arm's length. The then TUC General Secretary John Monks accepted in 1997 that: 'We know there will be no special tickets to influence based on history and sentiment.' Blair and Brown went on to suffer little industrial disruption during their periods in power. After 2001 a new more militant cohort of union leaders emerged including Dave Prentis at Unison, Bob Crow at Rail Maritime and Transport Workers, Mark Sewotka at Public and Commercial Services union; and perhaps the most vocal since the Coalition Government came to power in 2010.

The growth of part-time work, mostly by women, did not help to swell membership much either, as such workers are notoriously difficult to organise. To minimise the impact of recession and shrinkage, some unions decided to merge, such as UNISON in 1993, the 1.3-million member public service organisation. Unite was formed on 1 May 2007, by the merger of Amicus and the once all powerful Transport and General Workers' Union. Unite is led by probably the most militant current union leader, Len McCluskey, who called for strikes and 'civil disobedience' during the 2012 Olympics. Such calls attracted widespread condemnation across the political spectrum (including Labour leader Ed Miliband) and the idea received little support. Indeed, unions in the UK seemed to be far less militant in their response to the economic recession and government public spending cuts than those in countries like Greece, France and Spain.

PROFILE

Len McClusky (1960–)

Born in Anfield, Liverpool, McClusky went to Cardinal Godfrey School and worked as a docker in Liverpool for over a decade. He became a shop steward and campaign organizer at 19 for the TGWU. He supported the far-left Militant during the 1980s but did not become a member; he joined the Labour Party when he was 10 years old. He was elected General Secretary of Unite after the merger with Amicus in 2007. He acquired the soubriquet 'Red Len' after the extended Unite dispute with British Airways and became a bogey figure for the right-wing press after calling for militant action during the London Olympics.

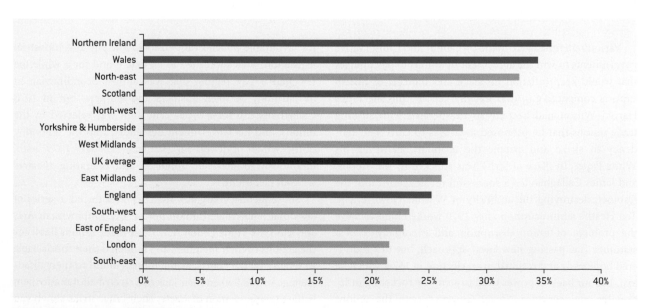

Figure 10.5 Trade union density by nation and region, 2010
Source: Labour Force Survey, Office for National Statistics

BOX 10.6

Union membership

- Union membership hit 13 million in 1979 (see Figure 10.5) but the recessions of the eighties and nineties saw falls associated with the jobs which had disappeared. Membership at 6.4 million is now closer to interwar levels.

- The percentage of the workforce in unions declined from 32.4 per cent in 1995 to 29.8 per cent in 2000, 28.5 per cent in 2005 and 26.0 per cent in 2011.

- Private sector union membership fell to 2.5 million in in 2011 and in the public sector to 3.9 million.

- The TUC is the umbrella body representing the majority of trade unions. There are 58 affiliated unions with a total of about 6.5 million members, around half of whom are represented by two unions: Unite or UNISON.

- Unite is the biggest union following the merger between Amicus, GMB and TGWU in 2007.

The growth of professional lobbying

One of the striking features of recent years has been the rapid growth of professional lobbying companies. These offer to influence policy and effect high-level contacts in exchange for large amounts of money. Often, the lobbyists are selling the excellent contacts they have made during a previous career in Parliament or the civil service. In this respect, Britain has once again moved towards the American model; on Capitol Hill, this kind of activity has been an accepted part of political life for decades.

In Britain over 60 lobbying organisations have been set up, ranging from the small Political Planning Services to the large (now defunct) Ian Greer Associates. Most major public relations companies have lobbying operations, either in-house or via an established lobbying company. Over 30 Conservative MPs worked for lobbyists before the Nolan Report; consultancies could pay anything up to and beyond £10,000 per year. There has been pressure for the regulation of such agencies (in Washington, they have to be registered). Westminster lobbyists can charge clients around £30,000 a year for a 'full service', including lobbying ministers, civil servants and MPs to push their case.

Lord Nolan and the removal of sleaze

Sleaze is not an invention of New Labour by any means and its roots go back at least a decade and a half. On 15 January 1990 the Granada TV programme *World in Action* broadcast its report on MPs and outside interests. It quoted Richard Alexander MP, who had placed an advertisement in the House of Commons magazine as follows: 'Hard working backbench Tory MP of ten years standing seeks consultancy in order to widen his range of activities.' The programme was only one of several investigations at that time and

later of how MPs used 'consultancy', often for commercial interests; in effect they were paid to apply pressure through their network of contacts in Parliament and Whitehall. In 1994 the *Sunday Times* approached two MPs, under the guise of being a commercial interest, and asked them to place questions on its behalf in exchange for money. In the ensuing media row the newspaper was criticised by many Conservative MPs for its underhand tactics, but the two MPs concerned, Graham Riddick and David Tredinnick, were the object of much more widespread and impassioned obloquy. A commission on 'standards in public life' – 'sleaze' according to the popular media – was set up by John Major under the judge Lord Nolan. This reported in the autumn of 1995 and was debated in November. Nolan suggested curbs on the economic activity of MPs and urged that they be obliged to reveal the extent of their earnings. On 6 November, Nolan's proposals were agreed and a new system was introduced whereby MPs are:

- obliged to disclose earnings, according to income bands;

- forbidden from tabling questions and amendments on behalf of outside interests;

- restricted in what they can say in the chamber on behalf of such interests;

- obliged to register all details of contracts with a new and powerful Parliamentary Commissioner (since March 1996).

However, the subject of sleaze was not excluded from the news even after Nolan, much as Major would have appreciated this. The *Guardian* newspaper ran a story accusing a junior trade minister, Neil Hamilton, of accepting money when a back-bench MP in exchange for asking questions and being in the employ of the well-known lobbying company Ian Greer Associates, the then agent of the owner of Harrods, Mr Mohamed Al Fayed. Al Fayed was running a campaign to prevent the tycoon Tiny Rowlands from regaining control of the store, and he also desperately wanted to

Box 10.7

Coalition and lobbyists

Simon Jenkins in the *Guardian* marvelled in August 2011 at how soft a touch the Coalition Government was proving for lobbyists of varying kinds.

> The Coalition Government, which started in a spirit of reformist radicalism, is proving one whose inexperience and shaky majority leaves it vulnerable to lobbyists . . .

The construction industry scored the most remarkable successes. With plummeting local council budgets, it struggled to protect its prestige projects by stressing the embarrassment of their cancellation. Hence such costly survivals as the high-speed rail line, London's Crossrail and, the grand daddy of them all, the Olympics.

---

win British citizenship. Hamilton declared that he would sue (as he had successfully and sensationally against the BBC when *Panorama* had accused him of fascist tendencies).

However, in October 1996, in a major climb-down, he announced the withdrawal of his action on grounds of finance. The *Guardian* responded by calling him a 'liar and a cheat' on its front page. The story continued when the subject was referred to the Standards and Privileges Committee. Hamilton was trounced in the General Election by the anti-corruption independent candidate Martin Bell. The memory of Conservative sleaze did not go away but Labour too came in for criticism. In January 2009 Labour initiated an inquiry into allegations by the *Sunday Times* that four of its Members in the House of Lords had taken money for moving amendments to legislation passing through the chamber. Again the CPS decided to take no action.

Scandals regarding government favours or influence

Both Labour and Conservative parties have a history of highly embarrassing political scandals involving individuals or organisations seeking favours or influence.

Cash for honours, 2006

This scandal arose in early 2006 when the House of Lords Appointments Commission rejected a number of nominees on the grounds that they had loaned large sums to the cash-strapped governing Labour Party. A loophole in the law

enabled loans to be made without the need for transparency attached to cash donations; it was suspected the lenders had issued the loans as a quid pro quo for a promise of an honour. Both major parties had taken advantage of this lacuna in the law. Following the shameless selling of honours by Lloyd George, a 1925 Act had made such trades illegal and, following initiatives by SNP and Plaid Cymru MPs, a police investigation ensued which led to the arrest of, among others, Tony Blair's fundraiser, Lord Levy and the questioning of Blair himself. In the end the investigation, led by Assistant Commissioner John Yates, failed to result in prosecutions, through lack of direct evidence and on 17 July 2007 the case was dropped. But much embarrassment had been caused, the rumour mill worked overtime and the reputation of the government, not to mention Blair himself, had taken severe hits.

Cash for influence, March 2012

> Secret corporate lobbying is the next big scandal waiting to happen.
>
> (David Cameron, March 2010)

This juicy scandal was the result of an undercover operation by the *Sunday Times*. Posing as multi-million pound hedge-fund managers from a Liechtenstein-based company, the reporters met with the Tory Party's then Treasurer, Peter Cruddas head of a spread-betting firm, CMC Markets. Unwittingly caught on camera, he explained to the 'businessmen' that regular donations could win access to private dinners with ministers. While a hundred grand would usher them into the company of medium-level ministers, 'premier league' donations of £250,000 would buy them Number 10 and Chequers dinners with Cameron and Osborne; they would be allowed to ask 'practically any question you want'

– it would be 'awesome for your business'. This sale of access was said to earn the Conservatives, £5 million a year.

The result was exceptional embarrassment for the Tories. Cameron was forced to reveal who had attended such dinners and the rank odour of sleaze was difficult to disguise. A new attempt to reform the funding of political parties was made, though little practical resulted on this vexed issue.

Pressure groups and democracy

Do pressure groups contribute towards a healthier democracy? As in the debate over the media in Chapter 8, it depends on what is meant by 'democracy'. The commonly accepted version of British representative or pluralist democracy accords the media a respected if not vital role. According to this view:

1 Pressure groups provide an essential freedom for citizens, especially minorities, to organise with like-minded individuals so that their views can be heard by others and taken into account by government.

2 They help to disperse power downwards from the central institutions and provide important checks against possibly over-powerful legislatures and executives.

3 They provide functional representation according to occupation and belief.

4 They allow for continuity of representation between elections, thus enhancing the degree of participation in the democratic system.

5 They provide a 'safety valve', an outlet for the pent-up energies of those who carry grievances or feel hard done by.

6 They apply scrutiny to government activity, publicising poor practice and maladministration.

However, some claim that groups operate in a way that harms democracy. They claim the following:

1 The freedom to organise and influence is exploited by the rich and powerful groups in society; the poor and weak often have to rely on poorly financed cause groups and charitable bodies.

2 Much influence is applied informally and secretly behind the closed doors of ministerial meetings, joint civil service advisory committees or informal meetings in London clubs. This mode of operating suits the powerful insider groups, while the weaker groups are left outside and have to resort to ineffective means such as 'knocking on the door' through merely influencing public opinion.

3 By enmeshing pressure groups into government policy-making processes, a kind of 'corporatism' (see below) has been established that 'fixes' decisions with ministers and civil servants before Parliament has had a chance to make an input on behalf of the electorate as a whole.

4 Pressure groups are often not representative of their members and in many cases do not have democratic appointment procedures for senior staff.

5 Pressure groups are essentially sectional – they apply influence from a partial point of view rather than in the interests of the country as a whole. This tendency has led some political scientists to claim that in the 1970s Britain became harder to govern (King 1975b), exacerbating conflict and slowing down important decision-making processes.

Theoretical perspectives

Pluralism

This approach is both descriptive in that it claims to tell us how things are and normative in that it believes this is generally a good way for things to be. The importance of pressure group activity was first recognised by commentators in this country in the 1950s, taking their lead (as so often before and since) from an American scholar, on this occasion Robert Dahl, who believed that major decisions were taken in an American democracy – where power was widely dispersed and shared – through negotiation between competing groups. In 1957 British journalist Paul Johnson said pretty much the same thing about his own country, adding 'Cabinet ministers are little more than the chairmen of arbitration committees'. American scholar, Samuel Beer (1911–2009), with his concept of 'new group politics', supported this view, believing the wartime controls, in which groups voluntarily aided the government in getting things done, to have survived the peace with the 'main substance' of political activity taking place between the 'public bureaucrats' of the government and the 'private bureaucrats . . . of the great pressure groups'. However, this pluralist approach was soon much criticised for claiming that power was equally dispersed and that access to government was open. Critics maintained that rich business interests would always exercise disproportionate influence and win better access.

BOX 10.8

The importance of citizen campaigning

Des Wilson was probably the best-known popular campaigner in the country – during the 1960s and 1970s – before he became a 'poacher turned gamekeeper' and joined the public relations staff of British Airports Authority. On a Tyne Tees TV programme in 1986 he explained his own philosophy on citizen campaigning and suggested ten guidelines for people wishing to become involved in such campaigns.

It is very important to remember that the very existence of campaigners, the fact that people are standing up and saying 'No, we don't want this, this is what we want instead', is terribly important because it makes it impossible for the political system to claim that there is no alternative to what they are suggesting.

Citizen organisations are about imposing citizen priorities on a system which we have set up which doesn't always act as well for us as it should. The more we can impose human values by maintaining surveillance, getting involved in organisations, being prepared to stand up and be counted, the better. Even if we are beaten the important thing is that the case has been made, the voice has been heard, a different set of priorities has been set on the table.

Our movement is, if you like, the real opposition to the political system because I believe all the political parties are actually one political system which runs this country. If we are not satisfied, it's no use just switching our vote around and it's no use complaining 'They're all the same, those politicians'. We can create our own effective opposition through our own lives by standing up and making demands on our own behalf.

Guidelines for campaigners

1 *Identify objectives*: Always be absolutely clear on what you are seeking to do. It is fatal to become sidetracked and waste energy on peripheral issues.

2 *Learn the decision-making process*: Find out how decisions are made and who makes them.

3 *Formulate a strategy*: Try to identify those tactics that will best advance your cause and draw up a plan of campaign.

4 *Research*: Always be well briefed and work out alternative proposals to the last detail.

5 *Mobilise support*: Widespread support means more political clout and more activists to whom tasks can be delegated.

6 *Use the media*: The media are run by ordinary people who have papers or news bulletins to fill. They need good copy. It helps to develop an awareness of what makes a good story and how it can be presented attractively.

7 *Attitude*: Try to be positive, but also maintain a sense of perspective. Decision makers will be less likely to respond to an excessively strident or narrow approach.

8 *Be professional*: Even amateurs can acquire professional research, media and presentational skills.

9 *Confidence*: There is no need to be apologetic about exercising a democratic right.

10 *Perseverance*: Campaigning on local issues is hard work: this should not be underestimated. Few campaigns achieve their objectives immediately. Rebuffs and reverses must be expected and the necessary resilience developed for what might prove to be a long campaign.

Source: Jones (1986)

Policy networks

This theory was constructed by political scientists Richardson and Jordan, with considerable help from Rod Rhodes. It suggested that groups and other sources of advice were crucial to the formation of policy. They saw departments constructing 'policy communities' with stable membership of just a few insider groups; policy would flow from this community in consultation with ministers and officials. A looser collection of groups was discerned in 'issue networks'. These comprised a shifting membership of groups and experts who were only occasionally consulted and were – to use American parlance – 'outside the loop' (see also Chapter 21).

Corporatism

Corporatism – sometimes prefixed by 'neo-' or 'meso-' (Smith 1993: Chapter 2) – was in some ways a development of **pluralism** in that it perceived a contract of sorts taking place between the most powerful groups in the country, rather as Beer saw happening in the war, whereby the government exchanged influence with the groups for their agreement to deliver member compliance. In the Scandinavian countries and Germany, something very like this contract had already become a regular part of the political process.

Corporatism, in one sense, was a means of bridging the gap between a capitalist economy and the socialist notions of planning and democratic consultation. To some extent this altered analysis matched the transition in Britain from a governing Conservative Party, whose ethos was against intervention, to a Labour one, whose ethos was in favour. The drift towards something called 'corporatism' was perceived at the time and criticised by left-wingers such as Tony Benn and centrists such as David Owen.

The Marxist analysis of pressure groups

Marxists would argue that the greater role accorded to the state in corporatism is only an approximation of the real control exercised by business through the state; as Marx said, 'the state is nothing but an executive committee for the bourgeoisie'. The whole idea of pluralist democracy, therefore, is merely part of the democratic window-dressing that the ruling economic group uses to disguise what is in reality its hegemonic control. Naturally, according to this view, the most potent pressure groups will be the ones representing business, while trade unions, for the most part, will be given a marginal role and will in any case act as 'duped' agents of the capitalist system, labouring under the 'false consciousness' that they are not being exploited. Certainly the scandal over 'cash for influence' in 2012 detailed above provides some evidence that Marx's analysis was at least partly right.

New Right

According to the New Right analysis, shared by Margaret Thatcher, pressure groups do not enhance democracy as they are primarily interested in their own concerns and not those of wider society. They represent only a section of society, usually the producers, and leave large groups, such as the consumers, unrepresented. Also according to this view, pressure groups 'short-circuit' the proper working of the system by promiscuously influencing the legislature and the executive so that the former cannot properly represent the interests of all and the latter cannot implement what has been decided.

From the politics of production to the politics of consumption

At a conference at Salford University in March 2002, Professor Wyn Grant explained the evolution of pressure groups since the end of the Second World War. He perceived four phases:

1 *1945–60, establishment politics*: This occurred in response to the vast Keynesian extension of government intervention in the economy and the life of the country via the welfare state. Groups representing staff in these new public sector activities negotiated closely with governments of both colours and established rules as well as conventions of behaviour.

2 *1960–1979, tripartism*: Emergence of a new generation of cause groups. Government consultation with business and unions became formalised into tripartism, but cause groups were beginning to change with an explosion of membership for environmental groups.

3 *1979–1997, tripartite and professional groups downgraded*: Mrs Thatcher felt that she did not need advice from groups and resisted the close contact they demanded. She also saw herself on a mission to dismantle the privilege and unfair practices that characterised many professions and their representative bodies. Insider groups still operated, but they were even less visible and were often disappointed.

4 *1997–, Third Way?* Tony Blair started by appearing willing to consult widely, although with definite care in respect of the unions. However, the rise of well-organised popular movements like the fuel protesters in September 2000, the Countryside Alliance and the Anti-War Movement in March 2003 revealed that 'outsider' groups were usurping the previously dominant role of insider groups: the former can now fill the streets and affect policy through delay or even effect reformulation. Grant assesses the Blair Government as the most pro-business government (accepting of the disciplines of globalisation) since the war – more so even than Thatcher. He also suggests that a major shift had taken place from the 'politics of production' to the 'politics of collective consumption'. The former involved struggles over the 'fruits of the production process' via elite bargaining, tending to use 'corporatism' to affect sectional issues. The latter, by contrast, uses the internet to organise dispersed support, tends to concentrate on 'public goods' and core social values (e.g. GM crops), and tends to be very media-driven (e.g. the fuel crisis of September 2000).

BOX 10.9

Banning fox hunting

In his 1997 manifesto, Tony Blair promised to ban fox hunting, and the Commons voted to do so in November 1997 by 411 votes to 151. However, the House of Lords rejected the bill and shortly afterwards the Countryside Alliance and its allies mobilised an impressive campaign involving a mass march to London. The political problem for Blair was that his backbenchers saw the issue more as a 'class' issue and the advantages of a ban began to look less attractive once the pressure groups involved mounted a mass opposition, which also persuaded sceptical middle-class voters that maybe hunting was something which should be allowed after all.

In June 2001 a commitment to a ban was repeated in Labour's manifesto; in March 2002, the Lords voted for the middle-way 'licensed option'. Then, in September 2002 an unusual approach was taken by the Rural Affairs Minister Alun Michael. He invited a number of the protagonists in the debate to air their views over three days under his chairmanship. After the three days Michael announced that a bill would be drawn up shortly. It would bring fox hunting within the ambit of animal welfare legislation, which bans unnecessary cruelty. It was intended that local tribunals would decide where hunting performed a useful purpose to farmers or the landscape, outweighing suffering caused to animals.

On Sunday 22 September 2002 a huge demonstration was mounted by the Countryside Alliance in London. Called the Liberty and Livelihood March, it involved over 400,000 marchers: the biggest demonstration ever in the British capital at the time. It would seem that no government can ignore such a mobilisation of opinion in the 24/7 media age. Blair did ignore protesters over Iraq but paid a heavy political price. The Government retreated from the outright ban for which many of its supporters craved, and the resultant Hunting Bill sought to allow hunting to proceed on a licensed basis. The legislative part of the saga was ended in November 2004 when Speaker Martin invoked the Parliament Act – used for only the fourth time since 1949 when it was passed – meaning that the ban on fox hunting came into force in February 2005. Since then the issue has subsided somewhat, though it seems some local hunts insist on riding out and stretching the law to its absolute limits, if not beyond on some occasions.

Writing in the *Observer* on 26 February 2006, Nick Cohen argued that:

> The anti-hunting law that aroused so much passion is now producing contempt and indifference. Only one hunt has closed and hunters behave as if the 700 hours of parliamentary debate that preceded the ban was so much wasted breath . . . The difficulty was always that the anti-hunters weren't trying to protect foxes, but punish a particular kind of hunter: the Tory toff with red coat and redder face. . . . Today a farmer can still shoot or snare a fox, but if he goes after it with more than two dogs, the police will arrest him. That's the theory. In practice, the police have arrested hardly anyone.

In September 2010 Tony Blair admitted in his memoirs that the fox hunting ban was a 'mistake'.

Yet, despite the fervent propaganda of the Countryside Alliance, a poll published on 26 December 2012 showed public opinion, if anything, has hardened against hunting with 76 per cent against the legalisation of fox-hunting. Futhermore, the Heythrop Hunt, patronised by David Cameron himself, was successfully prosecuted in December 2012 by the RSPCA for cruelty and fined £4,000. Owen Paterson, the Environment Secretary, admitted on the same day as the poll appeared that a vote repealing the ban was unlikely in 2013: 'There's only a point having a vote if you're going to win.'

BOX 10.10

BRITAIN IN CONTEXT

Pressure/interest groups

Most political systems contain concentrations of power which can exert some control over the system as a whole or over specific policies. This is true for democracies and autocracies alike, though the respective roles played by groups in both types of government differ greatly.

'Lobbies', as interest groups are called in the US – the most important of which are based in K Street, Washington DC – have a particularly high profile for a number of reasons. First, the three separate institutions of government – legislature, executive, judiciary – invite access in Washington and in their state-level equivalents, not to mention the primaries and related campaigns which groups can influence through financial contributions. Second, lobbyists are accepted as legitimate players in the political system, advancing views in a free society. Thirdly, interests surrounding presidents have tended to occupy favoured places in the White House. Thus, civil rights bodies flourished and advanced their causes when Kennedy and Johnson were in office; while oil interests, especially the Halliburton company, won contracts and powerful executive offices for former employees under Bush.

The downside of all this activity is the constant suspicion that wealthy interests are winning favours in exchange for cash payments – either direct to politicians or indirectly via election campaign funds. Jack Abramoff, a colourful and hugely influential Washington lobbyist, was put on trial in 2006 for effectively bribing powerful politicians to make decisions in the interests of his clients. Court cases are rare but serve to confirm the 'tip of the iceberg' suspicion that this has become almost an accepted part of the way in which American politics works.

Because US politics, not unlike those of the UK, are so open, the accusation of 'corporatism' – when state and interest groups combine to dominate decision-making – is seldom made. Countries regarded as much more corporatist are usually found in Europe, examples being Austria, Denmark, Germany, Finland and Ireland.

At the other end of the political scale autocratic governments do not usually allow formal access to groups. Less well-developed countries, especially those in Africa, face the constant danger that the military – often the most powerful group in the country – will step in to take over, or at least do the bidding of a dictator who does not have national interests closest to his heart. On the other hand, even a regime like that of the Chinese will consult widely with its doctors before changing its medical arrangements or with its businessmen and women before joining international trade organisations. Dictators should beware: if the needs of their people are constantly and flagrantly ignored, history suggests they will invariably rise up and cast off the shackles. Countless examples can be cited from Latin America, Africa and in the 1980s eastern Europe where, for example, the Romanian leader Ceausescu was overthrown and summarily executed.

In recent years the advance of globalisation has seen the emergence of hundreds of NGOs or 'non-government organisations' that may be associated with global bodies like the United Nations or the World Bank, with charities like Oxfam and Médecins sans Frontières, or with environmental issues like Greenpeace.

Chapter summary

Pressure groups seek to influence policy and not control it. 'Insider' groups, which have won acceptance by government, have traditionally had a privileged position compared with 'outsider' groups on the periphery, which tend to use high-profile techniques that serve to disguise their lack of real influence. Business groups seek to influence through the CBI and other channels, while trade unions have lost much power since 1979. Theoretical approaches include pluralism, corporatism and Marxism. The professional lobbying of Parliament and government has raised questions of democracy and legality, which the Nolan Committee was set up to address. On balance, pressure group influence has probably waned since 1979 but some groups, concerned with environmental and animal issues, have increased their influence and membership. Perhaps a shift has occurred in the way pressure groups interact with government, with widely popular movements now placing government under a kind of intense pressure it is loath to ignore.

Postscript

Obama, gun controls and the National Rifle Association.

A semi-automatic assault rifle had been involved in the Newtown School shootings in December 2012 and President Obama subsequently attempted to introduce relatively mild constraints on the sale of such weapons, including more rigorous background checks on potential purchasers. Despite the fact that opinion polls showed 90 per cent support for these measures, the legendary power of the National Rifle Association over both houses of Congress, including key Democrats caused the proposal to be neutered by April 2013.

Discussion points

- Why do pressure groups emerge?
- Why does government seek out groups and try to gain their cooperation?
- Describe an example of pressure group activity from the recent past and consider what it tells you about the way groups operate.
- Why do New Right thinkers dislike the influence of pressure groups?

Further reading

For the student the books and articles by Grant (1985, 1988, 1989, 2000) are the clearest and most useful, but Baggott (1995) is one of the most comprehensive current accounts and is very accessible. Smith (1993) is a study of some of the more theoretical aspects of the topic. On trade unions, see McIlroy (1995) and Taylor (1993). Baggott (1995) is good on European groups (pp. 206–19), and Greenwood (1997)

offers a comprehensive study. Of the big textbooks, Kingdom (1999) provides excellent coverage (pp. 507–36), as does Coxall and Robins (1998: 167–86). Watts (2007) is the most up to date study.

Bibliography

Ashbee, E. (2000) 'Bowling alone', *Politics Review*, September.

Ashford, N. and Timms, D. (1992) *What Europe Thinks: A Study of Western European Values* (Dartmouth).

Baggott, R. (1988) 'Pressure groups', *Talking Politics*, Autumn.

Baggott, R. (1992) 'The measurement of change in pressure group politics', *Talking Politics*, vol. 5, no. 1.

Baggott, R. (1995) *Pressure Groups Today* (Manchester University Press).

Beck, U. (1992) *The Risk Society* (Sage).

Department of Business, Enterprise and Skills (2012) *Trade Union Membership in 2011*.

Casey, T. (2002) 'Devolution and social capital in the British regions', *Regional and Federal Studies*, 12.3.

Coxall, B. and Robins, L. (1998) *Contemporary British Politics* (Macmillan).

Giddens, A. (1998) *The Third Way* (Polity Press).

Glinga, W. (1986) *Legacy of Empire* (Manchester University Press).

Grant, W. (1985, 1990) 'Insider and outsider pressure groups', *Social Studies Review*, September 1985 and January 1990.

Grant, W. (1989) *Pressure Groups, Politics and Democracy in Britain* (Phillip Allan).

Grant, W. (2000) *Pressure Groups and Politics* (Macmillan).

Green, J. (1999) *All Dressed Up: The Sixties and the Counterculture* (Pimlico).

Greenwood, J. (1997) *Representing Interests in the European Union* (Macmillan).

Hall, P. (1999) 'Social capital in Britain', *British Journal of Political Science*, vol. 29, no. 3, pp. 417–61.

HMSO, *Modernising Government*, March 1999, Cmnd 4310.

Hilton, M., McKay, J. Crowson, N. and Monhot, J.-F. (2010) *'The Big Society': Civic participation and the state of modern Britain* (Cabinet Office Strategy Unit Paper).

Inglehart, R. (1977) *The Silent Revolution: Changing Values and Political Styles among Western Publics* (Princeton University Press).

Jones, B. (1986) *Is Democracy Working?* (Tyne Tees Television).

Jenkins, S. (2011) 'The Maths of Coalition Has Opened the Door to Lobbyists', the *Guardian*, 11 August 2011.

King, A. (1975a) 'Overload: problems of governing in the 1970s', *Political Studies*, June.

King, A. (1975b) *Why Is Britain Becoming Harder to Govern?* (BBC Books).

Kingdom, J. (1999) *Government and Politics in Britain* (Polity Press).

McIlroy, J. (1995) *Trade Unions in Britain Today* (Manchester University Press).

McLeod, R. (1998) 'Calf exports at Brightlingsea', *Parliamentary Affairs*, vol. 51, no. 3.

Moran, M. (1985) 'The changing world of British pressure groups', *Teaching Politics*, September.

Nye, J. (1997) 'In government we don't trust', *Foreign Policy*, Autumn.

Pahl, R. and Winkler, J. (1974) 'The coming corporatism', *New Society*, 10 October.

Paxman, J. (1991) *Friends in High Places* (Penguin).

Political Studies Association News, vol. 13, no. 5, March 2003.

Putnam, R.D. (1995) 'Bowling alone', *Journal of Democracy*, January.

Reeves, R. (1999) 'Inside the violent world of the global protestors', the *Observer*, 31 October.

Scott, J. (1991) *Who Rules Britain?* (Polity Press).

Simpson, D. (1999) *Pressure Groups* (Hodder & Stoughton).

Smith, M. (1993) *Pressure, Power and Policy* (Harvester Wheatsheaf).

Taylor, R. (1993) *The Trade Union Question in British Politics* (Blackwell).

Duncan Watts (2007) *Pressure Groups* (Politics Study Guides) April.

Useful websites

Directory of 120 NGO websites:
www.oneworld.org/cgi-bin/babel/frame.pl
Amnesty International: www.amnesty.org
Countryside Alliance:
www.countryside-alliance.org/index.html
Friends of the Earth: www.foe.co.uk
Greenpeace: www.greenpeace.org.uk
Outrage!: www.outrage.org.uk
Trades Union Congress: www.tuc.org.uk
Blog: http://skipper59.blogspot.com/

CHAPTER 11

Political parties

Richard Kelly

"If the parties fail . . . then democracy fails"

Houghton Report on political parties, 1976

Learning objectives

- To illuminate the crisis of British political parties.

- To explain the continuation of this crisis since the 2010 General Election.

- To assess the impact of the crisis upon Britain's party system.

- To examine how the main parties have responded to this crisis since 2010.

- To analyse the impact of party politics within the Coalition.

- To consider the extent to which there is an inter-party consensus.

- To evaluate recent changes in party organisation.

- To contemplate the revival of party politics.

The previous edition of *Politics UK* identified a 'crisis' afflicting Britain's major political parties – one arising from a schism between the parties and the voters they aim to represent. This chapter will argue that, far from abating, this crisis continued well beyond the General Election of 2010. It will therefore show that the main parties remain unpopular, inspect their (largely indifferent) electoral performances, and consider how this has affected the nature of our party system. It will then chart the main parties' response to their lack of public support and expose the emergence of fresh, intra-party rivalries. Vital new trends affecting the locus of power inside the major parties will also be explored, along with the possibility that these trends – when allied to Britain's economic woes – could offer an 'accidental solution' to the crisis of party politics in the UK.

Introduction

Party politics in crisis

The 'crisis' of British political parties is, essentially, one of reputation – or, more specifically, the parties' reputation among voters. Put simply, our political parties have fallen into disrepute among those they seek to serve. The implications of this cannot be underrated, for two basic reasons. First, Britain's political system has long accorded a central role to political parties: British government is generally about *party* government while British elections are generally about *party* voting. Second, most political systems rely ultimately on the consent of the governed – and, given the current reputation of British political parties, there are reasons to suspect that, here in the UK, such consent is fading.

The unpopularity (*qua* crisis) of British political parties can be demonstrated by a number of examples, which have been extant for some time in our political culture. Yet they have all been dramatically underlined during the second decade of the twenty-first century.

Dwindling electoral interest

As indicated in the previous paragraph, elections – particularly general elections – are party-based affairs, defined by party campaigns, party leaders and party candidates. Consequently, public disenchantment with political parties may well produce public disengagement from elections. And, in recent general elections, there has been ample evidence that this has happened.

In the eight general elections between 1945 and 1970 the average voter turnout was 77 per cent. Yet, at the three general elections between 2001 and 2010 it was just 61 per cent. Indeed, it was telling that even in 2010, when many commentators hailed a 'surge' of interest, the turnout was still only 65 per cent – lower than at any postwar general election before 2001. Of particular concern were voters aged 18–24, where turnout was a mere 44 per cent. In other words, despite what seemed to be one of the more interesting general elections of recent years, most first-time voters could not be bothered to vote for *any* political party.

The problem of low turnout was compounded by the problem of low registration. Research unveiled by the Electoral Commission in December 2011 showed that up to 6 million adults were yet to put themselves on the **electoral register**. Again, it seemed unlikely that such indifference towards elections could be separated from an indifference towards their principal protagonists (i.e. political parties).

Dwindling allegiance/membership

Underlying such figures was a sharp decline in the number of voters claiming some allegiance to a party. In 1964 42 per cent of voters 'strongly identified' with a political party; yet during the 2010 General Election campaign only 31 per cent claimed even a 'fairly strong' affiliation (*ICM*, 21 April 2010). This lack of empathy has been reflected in the parties' membership figures. British political parties are mass membership bodies with almost any adult having the right to join. Yet, since the 1960s fewer and fewer voters have taken the opportunity.

In Labour's leadership contest of 2010 fewer than 127,000 **constituency Labour Party (CLP)** members registered a vote in the party's **electoral college** (see Table 11.1) – a marked fall from the 270,000 recorded when CLP members were first allowed to choose a Labour leader in 1983 (Quinn 2012). Neither can the two other main parties gloat. In their submission to the Electoral Commission in late 2011 the Liberal Democrats admitted to just under 49,000 members – a 25 per cent fall since 2010 alone – while the Conservatives look unlikely to recover the million-plus membership they had as recently as 1982. According to their own submission to the Commission, the Tories by October 2011 had fewer than 177,000 members.

Dubious funding and propriety

Dwindling membership has affected party funding, in a way that further affects the parties' popularity. Fewer members mean fewer subscriptions; and fewer subscriptions mean greater reliance upon institutional funding and plutocratic donations (Koss 2010).

A report on party finance in November 2011 by the Committee on Standards in Public Life found that since the 2010 General Election 85 per cent of Labour's revenue had come from trade union donations – a 50 per cent rise since 2001. Likewise, 51 per cent of donations to the Conservative Party were now derived from institutions or individuals based in the City of London (see Table 11.2). The Committee's findings were endorsed by the Bureau of Investigative Journalism, which found that the Conservative Party received donations of over £50,000 from 50 individual donors based in the City. According to the Bureau, these donors thereby qualified for the party's 'Leader's Group', which facilitated 'regular and intimate meetings with the Prime Minister' (*Guardian*, 7 October 2011).

At a time when both parties were required to make tough decisions about economic policy, these figures did little to reassure voters that decisions would be reached objectively, free of influence from vested interests. Indeed, an ICM poll found that most voters thought the main parties were 'in the pockets' of pressure groups, corporations and wealthy individuals (*Sunday Telegraph*, 18 December 2011).

Often encapsulated by the word 'sleaze', this issue was given extra resonance towards the end of the last parliament

Table 11.1 The 2010 Labour leadership contest

	PLP (a)	CLPs (b)	Affiliated (c)	Total
The count: round 1 (d)				
David Miliband	13.9%	14.7%	9.2%	37.8%
Ed Miliband	10.5%	9.9%	13.8%	34.3%
Ed Balls	5%	3.4%	3.4%	11.8%
Andy Burnham	3%	2.8%	2.8%	8.7%
Diane Abbott	0.9%	2.4%	4.1%	7.4%
The count: round 2 (e)				
David Miliband	14%	15.1%	9.8%	38.9%
Ed Miliband	11.1%	11.1%	15.2%	37.5%
Ed Balls	5.2%	3.8%	4.2%	13.2%
Andy Burnham	3%	3.3%	4.1%	10.4%
The count: round 3 (f)				
David Miliband	15.8%	16.1%	10.9%	42.8%
Ed Miliband	12.1%	12.4%	16.7%	41.2%
Ed Balls	5.4%	4.8%	5.7%	16%
The count: round 4 (g)				
Ed Miliband	15.5%	15.2%	19.9%	50.65%
David Miliband	17.8%	18.1%	13.4%	49.35%
Turnout:	98.5%	71.7%	9%	

Notes:

(a) The Parliamentary Labour Party (PLP) comprises Labour MPs and MEPs and casts a third of votes in this electoral college system.

(b) Members of constituency Labour parties (CLPs) cast a third of votes in the electoral college.

(c) Affiliated members (also casting a third of voices) come mainly from trade unions sponsoring the Labour Party, plus a small number of socialist societies.

(d) The votes are cast and counted according to the Alternative Vote system, where voters express numerical preferences. If no candidate has a majority of first preferences after the first count, the bottom-placed candidate – in this case, Abbott – is eliminated and his/her supporters' 2nd preference votes added to the remaining candidates' totals.

(e) As still no candidate had a majority, the bottom-placed candidate – now Burnham – was eliminated and his supporters' 2nd or (if their 2nd preferences were for Abbott) 3rd preferences added to the remaining candidates' totals.

(f) As still no candidate had a majority, the bottom-placed candidate – now Balls – was eliminated and his supporters' 2nd or (if their secondary preferences were for Abbott or Burnham) 3rd or 4th preferences added to the remaining candidates' totals.

(g) Ed Miliband's victory was anomalous for a number of reasons. First, only after the 4th round of counting was he the most popular candidate. Second, he was never the preferred candidate of the PLP or CLPs – only, in effect, of the trade unions, whose members seem the least committed members of the Labour movement (see turnout). Third, he may have only overtaken his brother on account of voters' 3rd or 4th preferences; the seriousness of such votes is open to question.

(h) Labour's electoral college system is a long way from the one-member-one-vote model. First, it is possible for those who are members of more than one section (like most MPs) to cast more than one vote. Second, votes do not carry equal weight. Although each section represents a third of the electoral college, a vote cast in the PLP section (comprising a few hundred votes) is more influential than one cast in either the CLP section (comprising less than 200,000 eligible voters) or the affiliated trade union section (comprising about 360,000 eligible voters).

when, thanks to an exposé by the *Daily Telegraph*, hundreds of party MPs were shown to have exploited Parliament's Additional Costs Allowance (Mullin 2010). Following the 2010 General Election, six party politicians – Eliot Morley, David Chaytor, Eric Ilsley, Jim Devine, Lord Taylor and Lord Hanningfield – were duly prosecuted under criminal law and given custodial sentences. As *Private Eye* noted (12 March 2012), in proportional terms this meant that Members of the 2005 parliament were four times more likely to be jailed than ordinary members of the public. The imprisonment in 2013 of Chris Huhne – a former cabinet minister who perverted the course of justice – did little to improve the standing of party politicians in Britain.

Table 11.2 Party finance: ending the big donor culture

Report by Committee on Standards in Public Life (chair: Sir Christopher Kelly), November 2011

Principal recommendations:
■ Donations to parties from individuals or institutions should be capped at £10m
■ Campaign spending by parties should be capped at £25.4m
■ Trade unionists should 'opt into' political affiliation (rather than 'opt out' as at present)
■ State aid to parties should be increased by up to £23m over a five-year period
■ State aid should be distributed on a cash-for-votes basis after general elections (£3 per voter, for each party winning seats)
Reactions:
■ Conservative leadership opposed cap on donations (the party secured over £2 million donations during 2010–11 alone)
■ Conservative leadership opposed cap on campaign spending (the party spend £16.6 million in 2010, twice as much as Labour and more than all other parties combined)
■ Labour leadership opposed reforms to trade union political affiliation (although Ed Miliband later proposed a £50,000 cap on all donations)
■ Lib Dem leadership opposed increased state aid (Nick Clegg stated 'at a time of cuts elsewhere, it is not the time to ask voters to stump up extra for political parties')

The crisis underlined: parties and electoral performance

The parties' unpopularity was demonstrated vividly by the their performance at the 2010 General Election (Mitchell et al. 2012). The Conservatives may have regained office but for many it was a hollow victory. For the fourth successive general election they failed to gain even 40 per cent of the votes cast and an overall majority of seats. This means, of course, that many of today's voters were not even born when the Conservatives last won a parliamentary majority. Though clearly not as bad as Labour's performance, historically the Conservative performance in 2010 was dismal: the party won fewer votes than Labour in 1992 (when Labour was thought to have lost ignominiously) and fewer votes than Edward Heath's Conservative Party in the two general elections of 1974 (once thought the nadir of Conservative fortunes).

Outside southern England, the Conservative performance was again abject: Birmingham, Bradford, Leeds, Leicester, Liverpool, Manchester, Newcastle and Sheffield remained bereft of Conservative MPs, while in Scotland the party won just 17 per cent of votes and one seat. Indeed, by 2011, it was quipped, there were more pandas in Scotland than Conservative MPs. The Tories also had grave concerns about their performance among first-time voters, where they won just 30 per cent support, and among women voters under the age of 35, where the party came third with just 28 per cent of votes (Childs and Webb 2011).

Labour's performance in 2010 was arguably the second worst in its history, though this was partially eclipsed by the help it received from the Westminster electoral system (Labour's vote share in 2010 was 3 per cent lower than the Tories' in 2005; yet Labour in 2010 won 258 seats, compared to the Tories' 198 in 2005). Nevertheless, Labour left government with 5 million fewer votes than when it arrived in 1997, and attracted more votes in 1987 when it lost by a landslide. There were also signs that Labour was again struggling outside its traditional heartlands. Excluding Greater London, Labour polled just 16 per cent of votes in southern England (thus coming third) and won just 10 of the 197 constituencies. 'Southern discomfort', first diagnosed in the 1980s and alleviated by Tony Blair in the 1990s, was clearly afflicting Labour again by 2010 (Radice and Diamond 2010).

The Liberal Democrats seemed to have been regressing ever since the early stages of the 2010 General Election campaign. The impact of Nick Clegg's barnstorming performance in the first of the televised leader debates could not be sustained and on polling day 2010 the party made little progress. Britain's third party won fewer seats than in 2005, and fewer votes than in the general elections of the 1980s. Indeed, had it not been for the hung parliament which resulted, the 2010 General Election might have been regarded as one of its most disappointing performances. The surge of Lib Dem support, predicted by some opinion polls in the early part of the campaign, simply never happened.

For a party normally happy to appear centre-left, being in alliance with the Tories would always cause problems among some former supporters. And, by 2011 it was clear that Liberal Democrats were bearing the brunt of public hostility

seats in 2010 (rising to 11 in 2012 following a by-election victory for Respect's George Galloway).

Beyond Westminster, the impact of 'other' parties was even more profound. Britain's MEPs now included politicians from eight different parties, including the British National Party, Green Party and United Kingdom Independence Party. Indeed, UKIP was the second most popular party in the 2009 European elections and, by 2012, plausibly aspired to eclipse the Liberal Democrats at a future general election. Plaid Cymru, meanwhile, was part of the Welsh Assembly Government until 2011 and boasted a 23 per cent increase in membership between 2011 and 2012 (Plaid Cymru 2012). The 2011 Welsh Assembly elections, however, prompted a fraught leadership election and a concurrent identity crisis throughout the party – one that centred on the credibility of a Welsh nation-state and the extent to which Plaid attracted only Welsh-speaking voters (Sandry 2011). The election of Leanne Wood, a republican with strong socialist leanings, suggested that Plaid was prepared to embark upon a new and radical direction (see Table 11.3).

When arguing that the term 'three-party system' is inadequate, the most obvious illustration came in respect of the Scottish National Party and its performance at the 2011 Scottish Parliament elections. After four years as a minority administration in Edinburgh, the SNP was re-elected with a majority of seats and 44 per cent of votes. This result had implications not just for the other main Scottish parties, all of whom were plunged into leadership contests (see Table 11.4), but the very survival of the UK, prompting David Cameron to demand a referendum on Scottish independence a few months later.

As it was unclear how much public support there was for an independent Scotland, the SNP's momentum always relied heavily on the charismatic leadership of Alex Salmond. There was also a lingering suspicion that the SNP's growing support came not from those preoccupied with a Scottish

Split down the middle: former Lib Dem leader Charles Kennedy objected to Nick Clegg's coalition with the Conservatives.

to Coalition policies. During the postwar era, Britain's third party had often benefited from an aura of moral superiority; from an impression that its politicians were uncorrupted by power and thus able to restore integrity to politics. By 2012 this advantage had almost completely disappeared.

Impact upon the party system

Having once been a straightforward two-party affair, the nature of Britain's party system had been unclear for almost half a century; and recent elections have done little to clarify matters. Certainly, there was little to link the party competition of the 1950s with the outcome of the 2010 General Election: 86 MPs came from parties other than Labour and the Conservatives; only 65 per cent of voters backed Labour or Conservative candidates; and (as in 2005) neither of the two main parties achieved even 40 per cent of the votes.

Indeed, in many parts of Britain the term 'main two parties' was a misnomer given that Labour or Tory candidates were pushed into third (sometimes fourth) place in over a third of constituencies. A further break with the past came in terms of class voting. Assuming the terms are still significant, only one-third of working-class/blue-collar voters voted Labour (compared to over two-thirds in the 1960s) and fewer than 40 per cent of middle-class/white-collar voters backed the Conservatives (compared to over 70 per cent in the 1960s). Any notion of a 'revived' two-party system was also made to look naïve by the 'devolution' elections of 2011, when the Tories failed to record even a quarter of the votes cast in Scotland and Wales.

With three parties having governed the UK during the course of 2010, Lib Dem supporters were keen to hail the advent of a three-party system. Yet, while the collapse of the two-party system was undeniable, the idea of a three-party system seemed simplistic. Even in the House of Commons, there were no fewer than 10 parties winning

Table 11.3 Party leadership contests in Wales, 2011–12

Welsh Conservative Party, July 2011 (all-member ballot)

Andrew Davies 53.1%

Nick Ramsay 46.7%

NB: 'Welsh Conservative leader' refers to the leader of the Conservative group in the Welsh National Assembly

Plaid Cymru, March 2012 (all-member ballot)

	1st count	2nd count
Leanne Wood	2879	3326
Elin Jones	1884	2494
Dafydd Elis-Thomas	1278	–

The count was conducted under the Alternative Vote electoral system (see notes for Table 11.1)

Table 11.4 Party leadership contests in Scotland, 2011

(NB: In the case of all parties, the term 'leader' refers to the parties' leaders in the Scottish Parliament)

Labour				
	Elected members	**Individual members**	**Affiliated members**	**Total**
Johann Lamont	53.3%	36.6%	65.4%	51.8%
Ken Macintosh	41.3%	53.1%	26.4%	40.3%
Tom Harris	3.2%	10.3%	8.2%	7.9%

Labour's contest was conducted on an electoral college basis, with each of the three sections casting a third of the votes. 'Elected members' comprised Members of the Scottish Parliament, plus MPs and MEPs from Scottish constituencies. 'Individual members' refers to members of Scottish constituency Labour parties. 'Affiliated members' refers mainly to trade unionists, resident in Scotland, who have paid a political subscription to their trade unions. See note (h) on Table 11.1 for general arguments about the electoral college system.

Conservatives		
	1st count	**2nd count**
Ruth Davidson	2278	2983
Murdo Fraser	2096	2417
Jackson Carlow	830	
Margaret Mitchell	472	

NB: The contest was conducted on a one-member-one-vote basis and the results determined by the Alternative Vote system (see notes on Table 11.1)

Source: T. Quinn: http://privatewww.essex.ac.uk/tquinn/index.html

nation-state, but from ex-Labour voters looking for an alternative centre-left berth. Disconnected from a Tory-led government at Westminster, and disgruntled by the record of New Labour, such voters might have been drawn by the leftish tendencies of Salmond's administration (as shown by its curtailment of prescription charges and its extension of free residential care for the elderly). But the rejection of independence in a referendum could occasion a crisis of identity for the SNP, especially as centre-left parties are not in short supply for Scottish voters (Mitchell et al. 2012).

The success of the SNP has naturally encouraged talk of a multi-party system. Yet, when trying to ascertain the 'true' nature of the UK's party system, the most accurate response might be that no such 'system' actually exists. Systems, after all, denote predictability and uniformity; yet modern party competition seems defined by fluctuations and asymmetrical outcomes (Driver 2011). At the 2010 General Election, for example, there was a swing of 9 per cent against Labour in the north-east of England but a 2 per cent swing towards Labour in Scotland. At the same election, there was even inconsistency within particular cities: in Birmingham, for example, the 10 per cent swing against Labour in Erdington was accompanied by virtually no anti-Labour swing in Edgbaston. In short, the relationship between parties and voters seemed anything but systematic – a trend exacerbated by the growing importance of individual party candidates, particularly after the parliamentary expenses scandal.

The crisis addressed: parties and policies since 2010

In the wake of the 2010 General Election, the parties acknowledged room for improvement in terms of electoral support, and tried to bring this about through a careful review of their policies and underlying doctrines. However, there were two extraordinary things about this reaction. The first was its universality; the second was its methodology.

First, in the aftermath of a general election it is quite normal for *opposition* parties to undertake a process of self-examination: this will normally involve recognition of past mistakes, a public show of humility, a degree of reorganisation and, eventually, a much-trumpeted relaunch. What made the aftermath of 2010 unusual was that *all* the main Westminster parties, including the two parties in government, seemed to embark upon such navel-gazing – a clear reflection of the fact that no party had indisputably 'won' the General Election. The crisis in the relationship between parties and voters had seemingly produced an endemic crisis within the parties themselves.

Second, in marked contrast to Blair's creation of New Labour after 1994, or Cameron's 'decontamination' of the Tories after 2005, this self-examination was not especially centralised or coordinated. This particular development will be explored later in the chapter, in the section dealing with party organisation.

Next Labour: in the red or back to black?

After 2010, Labour – or *Next Labour*, to use its new leader's phrase – seemed far from clear about its future course, with a myriad of internal factions appearing to surface and resurface (Heppell and Hill 2012). Even the self-styled 'left' had two separate tendencies. On the one hand, there was the *Old Left*, embodied by MPs like Michael Meacher, John McDonnell and Dennis Skinner, and advertised by the **Tribune** and *Socialist Campaign* groups. For them, the 'crisis of capitalism' after 2007, and the widespread vilification of the financial sector that followed, were a vindication of their long-standing belief in extensive public ownership, a class-based approach to politics, and a new symbiotic relationship between Labour and the trade unions.

On the other hand, there was the *New Left*, exemplified by seasoned politicians like Ken Livingstone, new MPs like Lisa Nandy, and party factions like the **Compass Group**. In one respect, the New Left agreed with New Labour: the traditional working class was no longer enough to propel a left-wing party into power and, in a **cosmopolitan** society and globalised economy, Labour could not just preach the virtues of nationalisation and class struggle. Yet, in terms of prescription, there was a sharp divergence from the Blairites – the neo-socialists arguing that Labour should update its support for the underdog by creating a new coalition of 'marginalised' groups such as ethnic and religious minorities, the disabled, and those striving for gay, lesbian and bisexual equality. This idea was far from novel and recalled the politics of Livingstone's Greater London Council in the 1980s. Livingstone's defeat by Boris Johnson in the 2012 London mayoral contest, on a night when Labour triumphed in local elections elsewhere, also implied that the idea had little electoral mileage.

Table 11.5 Selection of Labour candidate for London mayoral election, 2012

	Individual members	**Affiliated members**	**Total**
Ken Livingstone	66%	71%	68.6%
Oona King	34%	29%	31.4%

NB: 'Individual members' refers to Labour's constituency members, plus its MPs and MEPs, in Greater London constituencies. 'Affiliated members' refers to members of affiliated trade unions and socialist societies resident in Greater London.

Source: T. Quinn: http://privatewww.essex.ac.uk/tquinn/index.html

Somewhat fresher thinking emerged from a section of the party that became known as *Blue Labour*. Grouped around academics like Maurice Glasman and MPs like Jon Cruddas, Blue Labour agreed with the left that the party should be more trenchant in its critique of capitalism. Yet the angle they chose was meant to engage those of a conservative, as well as egalitarian, disposition. Blue Labour highlighted not just capitalism's effect on equality, but also its alleged contempt for history, heritage and identity. As Cruddas argued in 2012, 'We need to talk more about conserving our traditions, valuing the places we live in, and sustaining our ways of life'.

Linking 'viral capitalism' to conservative fears about immigration, the relaxation of greenbelt laws, airport extensions and high-speed rail links, Blue Labour argued that the left should stand for continuity and **conservation** as well as a more regulated form of capitalism (Davies 2011). These assertions were linked to a renewed argument for the 'mutual society', where power was localised and accountable, and where individualism was checked by personal responsibility (Glasman 2011). Following the 2011 riots in English cities, some close to Blue Labour were prepared to enter further into territory normally associated with Conservatives. Ex-minister David Lammy, for instance, linked the riots to the decline of marriage-based families, the absence of father-figures for many Afro-Caribbean young men, and the 'confused' moral messages emanating from Christian churches in the inner-cities (Lammy 2011).

Blue Labour was to be challenged in September 2011 by the emergence of *Purple Labour*. Purporting to represent 'neo-Blairism', enfolding ex-ministers like David Miliband and rising stars like Rachel Reeves (see Profile), and centred largely upon the **Progress** Group, it was inclined to state that New Labour needed updating rather than cremating. Rejecting the arguments of Labour's left, Purple Labour argued it was time for 'rethinking not reassurance', especially on the reform of public services (Miliband 2012). Yet, *contra* Blue Labour, Purple Labour also dismissed anything that smacked of cultural conservatism, arguing that 'Next Labour' must be progressive, tolerant and fully committed to a more cosmopolitan society (Philpott 2011).

Like Blue Labour, Purple Labour's spokespeople had concerns about the EU's austerity programme, favouring instead a 'pro-growth' strategy. Yet, unlike Blue Labour, Purple Labour claimed that any alternative to the EU's austerity programme must come from within the EU itself, with no slackening of Britain's relationship with Brussels. For that reason, most Blairites rejoiced at the advent of a new French President in 2012 – François Hollande's victory being seen as a lodestar for both 'Next Labour' and a renewed yet progressive EU.

PROFILE

Rachel Reeves (1979–)

Elected MP for Leeds West in 2010, Rachel Reeves has been widely tipped as Labour's first woman leader (allowing for the caretaker role performed by Margaret Beckett in 1994 and Harriet Harman in 2010). Following her arrival at Westminster, she quickly achieved front-bench status as shadow pensions minister and impressed MPs with her grasp of financial policy – a reflection, it was said, of her Oxford degree in PPE and her LSE Masters degree in Economics. Ed Miliband promoted her to shadow chief secretary to the Treasury in October 2011: a signal achievement for one who had been in Parliament less than two years.

The economics of 'Next Labour' were also addressed by a party section known as **Black Labour**, based on the title of a paper (*In The Black Labour*) produced by Policy Network, and lauded by party luminaries like Alastair Darling. Arguing that greater equality and social justice required prosperity, and that prosperity required fiscal conservatism, Black Labour argued that Labour would not be taken seriously until it matched the Coalition's pledge to erase the deficit in public finances. For Black Labour, the party's main task was to create an alternative, 'progressive' programme of spending reduction, more attuned to society's neediest elements and more consistent with egalitarian objectives (Cooke et al. 2011).

Amid these internal debates, Miliband's own allegiance was unclear. While the left was heartened by his attacks on 'predator capitalism', he still appeased Purple Labour by championing 'the squeezed middle', and by supporting a cap on union donations to the party. And while he appeased Blue Labour by inviting Jon Cruddas to oversee Labour's Policy Review, he also impressed Black Labour by supporting the Government's freeze on public sector pay. All this aroused predictable opposition from certain trade unions, who bemoaned the advent of 'White Flag Labour'. Indeed, the GMB later withdrew more than £500,000 of its donations to Labour and even considered a break from the party altogether (*Guardian*, 11 June 2012).

The Conservatives: no end to division

When he became Conservative leader in 2005, David Cameron hoped that, by the time he reached Downing Street, his party would be rebranded, re-energised and sure of its future direction (Snowdon 2010; Bale 2011). Although Cameron reached Downing Street, it was unclear if his ambitions for the party were achieved. Indeed, in the wake of regaining office, the battle for the party's soul seemed to resume with a new *brio*.

Irrespective of the General Election result, this was always likely to happen. The demise of economic optimism by 2009 had obviated the first few years of the Cameron project, one that involved 'sharing the proceeds of growth', promoting 'general wellbeing' and letting 'sunshine win the day' (Beech and Lee 2009). Instead, austerity left Conservatives muddled and divided about what they stood for, with the party divisions of 2010 only concealed by a hearty appetite for power.

This lack of ideological clarity helped account for the party's election campaign in 2010 – one that seemed infinitely less cogent than its previous 'Opposition-to-government' campaign in 1979. The party's uncertainty was duly compounded by its failure to win a majority of seats – notwithstanding a presentable leader, a long spell of fraught Labour government, and a lavishly funded campaign.

As a result, David Cameron did not have the luxury normally afforded a party leader who has just become Prime Minister: a grateful and pliable party. Instead, he found himself presiding over fresh Conservative divisions arising from three broad tendencies within the party: *Thatcherites, pre-Thatcherites* and *post-Thatcherites*.

From the first two tendencies, there were clear hints that the party should look backwards for inspiration. *Thatcherites* like David Davies, Liam Fox and Michael Fallon claimed that the recipe used in the 1980s (economic liberalism plus social and constitutional conservatism) remained pertinent 30 years on. This message was articulated by two new party groupings launched in the autumn of 2012: **Conservative Voice**, aiming to harness Thatcherism's supporters in both the parliamentary and extra-parliamentary Conservative Party, and **Blue Collar Conservatism**, a group of about 60 Tory MPs seeking to 're-build links with the striving working class voters that Margaret Thatcher instinctively understood' (*Daily Telegraph*, 1 November 2012).

Meanwhile, the much smaller *pre-Thatcherite* tendency (embodied by elder statesmen like Kenneth Clarke and Lord Heseltine) harked back even further to the 'one nation' Toryism of Macmillan, Baldwin and Disraeli. These Conservatives, supported outside Parliament by the *Tory Reform Group*, were generally supportive of Cameron's centrist agenda, even though their attitude to the EU – normally sympathetic – was at odds with both the leadership and bulk of party members. Nonetheless, this Tory tendency was heartened by Clarke's presence in Cabinet and by Heseltine's appointment to head a government inquiry into economic growth. Heseltine duly reported in late 2012 and proposed a range of new, state-led initiatives (including a 'National

Red message, blue background: Jesse Norman MP (standing) and Tracey Crouch MP defend the Big Society.
Source: Manchester Grammar School.

Growth Council') – all of which bore strong echoes of Conservatism in the post-war/pre-Thatcher era.

Post-Thatcherites, meanwhile, argued for a genuinely new form of Conservatism, one that reflected the peculiar circumstances of the post-Blair era. Yet there remained disagreement over what this 'modern' Conservatism should involve. As a result, there emerged two rival 'modernist' tendencies: **Red Tories** and **liberal Conservatives**.

Reflecting the title of a book by philosopher Philip Blond, fuelled by the think tank Respublica, and represented by senior Tories like Iain Duncan Smith, the Red Tories were eager to refute Thatcherism's supposed view of society – viz: that there was 'no such thing'. Like the left, they claimed that individuals were largely shaped by society, with 'broken' societies often being responsible for delinquency and disorder. Like the left too, they were ready to accept a link between capitalism and some of the forces that poisoned society – such as 'ruthless' materialism and 'amoral' consumerism (Blond 2010).

Unsurprisingly, this tendency was the most strongly linked to the party's flagship theme of a Big Society – one involving a network of local and largely voluntary communities, and recalling Edmund Burke's vision of 'little platoons' (Edwards 2012). Red Tories also placed great faith in conservative morality – especially in relation to marriage and families – and seemed to argue that, in terms of welfare provision, local

voluntary effort was better than mandatory state services (Norman 2010). In terms of their support for localism and mutualism, Red Tories certainly had strong echoes of Blue Labour. Yet, in terms of delivery, they clearly preferred old-fashioned paternalism to democratic accountability.

Even though it had sympathy for the concept of 'one nation', it would be a mistake to see Red Toryism as just another form of pre-Thatcherite Conservatism – for two reasons. First, Red Tories had little or no sympathy for the EU; indeed, some of their MPs espoused views that seemed very close to those of UKIP. Second, as their support for 'voluntarism' implied, Red Tories were highly sceptical about statist solutions to both the 'broken society' and the 'broken economy' (Kelly and Crowcroft 2012). Accordingly, they were quick to denounce the record of Conservative governments in the 1960s and early 1970s – and even quicker to denounce the 'pro-growth' ideas unveiled by Lord Heseltine in 2012.

The party's other post-Thatcherite group could be termed *liberal Conservatives* in that they sought to combine economic liberalism (which Thatcherism supports) with social liberalism (which Thatcherism rejects). These Conservatives were quite close ideologically to the Nick Clegg/David Laws wing of the Liberal Democrats (see Table 11.6), were happy to extend the Coalition beyond one term, and were dubbed by some authors as 'Orange Book Conservatives' (King 2011; Kelly 2012).

Linked to the **Bright Blue** faction outside Parliament, and the Free Enterprise Group inside Parliament (chaired by Kwasi Kwarteng – see Profile), this tendency sought to marry laissez-faire capitalism to a more laissez-faire stance on personal lifestyle and morality, supporting tax cuts and deregulation alongside a defence of reforms like gay marriage (Webb and Childs 2011). Consequently, these liberal Conservatives were rather cautious about the Big Society, fearing that a stress on communalism could actually boost tribalism and reactionary social attitudes. As one new MP remarked, 'the little platoons are not always liberal platoons' (Kelly 2013). There was also concern that 'localism' could lead to 'anti-business' planning laws which, though pleasing to rural and suburban Tories, might obstruct the market-led recovery that liberal Conservatives extolled. Finally, in a further nod to liberal thinking, such Conservatives were keen to modernise the political system and generally supported Lords reform, elected police commissioners and the spread of elective mayors (McAnulla 2012).

These broad intra-party differences were still transcended by the single issue of Europe. However, the division was no longer the Eurosceptic/Europhile division that enfeebled previous Conservative Prime Ministers. Instead, the new Euro-division was mainly one of **Eurosceptics** versus *Europhobes*. Eurosceptics, rallied by the **Fresh Start Group** of MPs, and encompassing both Red Tories like Jesse Norman and liberal Conservatives like Kwarteng, wanted a 'looser and larger' Europe that led to 'more trade and fewer rules' (Davis et al. 2011). Europhobes, including both Red Tories like Tracey Crouch and liberal Conservatives like Douglas Carswell, were said to anticipate Britain's withdrawal from the EU altogether – a wish evident among many of the 81 Tory MPs who defied Cameron in 2011 by voting for a referendum on Britain's EU membership. As the *Conservative Home* website revealed, their action was backed by a majority of Conservative members – 68 per cent of whom believed that Britain should leave the EU (*Sunday Telegraph*, 13 November 2011).

Liberal Democrats: orange books to red boxes

As Nick Clegg waved from the steps of 10 Downing Street, before entering for the first time as Deputy PM, he was effectively waving farewell to his party's past – one unsullied by the murky compromises of government (Jones 2010). Yet, though his party's coalition with the Tories shocked and dismayed many, it was only the culmination of a strategy that began with Clegg's leadership of his party in 2007. The chapters written for the party's **Orange Book** in 2004, by Clegg and allies like Ed Davey, were not simply contributions to the debate about liberalism; they were written in anticipation of New Labour's collapse and a new, centre-right coalition (Marshall and Laws 2004; Gerard 2011).

Visions of a 'progressive project' – beloved by Paddy Ashdown and other previous Lib Dem leaders – were thus shelved in favour of a new stress on markets, privatisation and individual choice. Increased tax thresholds, rather than increased benefits, were duly commended as a weapon against poverty. However, far from uniting the party round a new market-friendly settlement, the 'Orange Book revolution' served to make a diverse party a more divided one – especially as many Lib Dem politicians owed their position to ex-Labour voters.

These divisions were inevitably worsened by the formation of the Coalition and some of the policies it pursued. In early 2012 such divisions were highlighted by the launch of a new Lib Dem grouping, Liberal Left. Comprising party peers like Lord Oakeshott and ex-MPs like Evan Harris, it aimed to bolster existing 'progressive' factions, such as the **Beveridge Group**, and 'non-Orange' Lib Dem MPs like Tim Farron (see Profile). Generally, however, Lib Dems were increasingly reconciled to the problems of government, mindful of the power it bestowed. And, despite the party's schisms, there were still many areas where the party was unanimous.

It remained unanimous on the issue of electoral reform, insisting the 2011 referendum result was a 'no' to Alternative Vote rather than proportional representation.

PROFILE

Kwasi Kwarteng (1975–)

Born in 1975 and rated as one of the Conservative Party's sharpest thinkers, Kwasi Kwarteng combines an education that is classically Tory (Eton, Oxbridge) with a parentage that is anything but (Ghanaian). His career since graduating has been similarly eclectic, working as a financial analyst in the City and writing a less than complimentary book about the British Empire. Kwarteng entered Parliament as MP for Spelthorne in 2010 and, along with four other new Tory MPs, co-authored a book (*After the Coalition*) which charted new and radical directions for the party. By 2012 he was chair of the Free Enterprise Group – a collection of Tory MPs keen on drastically reducing state involvement in the economy. Many commentators predict he will be the first Conservative Cabinet minister of African Caribbean descent.

Table 11.6 Main intra-party divisions since 2010

Faction/tendency	Associated groups/politicians
Labour	
Old Left:	Tribune Group, Socialist Campaign Group, Tony Benn, Dennis Skinner
New Left:	Compass, Ken Livingstone, Diane Abbott, Lisa Nandy
Blue Labour:	Jon Cruddas, Maurice Glasman, Frank Field
Purple Labour:	Progress Group, David Miliband, Stephen Twigg, Rachel Reeves
Black Labour:	Policy Network, Alistair Darling, Liam Byrne, Stella Creasey
Conservative	
Pre-Thatcherites:	Tory Reform Group, Kenneth Clarke, Nicholas Soames, Michael Heseltine
Thatcherites:	Conservative Voice, Blue Collar Conservatism, Liam Fox, David Davies, Michael Fallon
Post-Thatcherites: (a) Red Tories: (b) Liberal Conservatives:	Respublica, Iain Duncan Smith, Jesse Norman, Tracey Crouch Bright Blue, Free Enterprise Group, Boris Johnson, Nick Boles
Liberal democrats	
Orange Book Liberals:	Nick Clegg, David Laws, Danny Alexander, Ed Davey
Social Liberals:	Beveridge Group, Liberal Left, Simon Hughes, Tim Farron

Source: R. Kelly, *Politics Review*, 22,4

It unanimously supported Lords reform, and applauded Clegg's attempt (albeit a doomed one) in 2012. It unanimously defended European integration and vigorously condemned Cameron's veto of a new EU treaty in December 2011. In addition, as such condemnation showed, it unanimously backed Clegg's strategy of 'differentiation' – one that was meant to advertise differences between the two Coalition parties, while putting the doctrine of **collective responsibility** into cold storage.

PROFILE

Tim Farron (1970–)

Born in 1970 and MP for Westmorland and Lonsdale since 2005, Tim Farron was elected President of the Liberal Democrats in late 2010. As a member of the party's left-leaning Beveridge Group, Farron carries appeal to those Lib Dems aiming to 'decontaminate' the party after the Con–Lib coalition. Known for being bright and genial, Farron is seen as someone who could reconnect Lib Dems with their centre-left heritage. Yet, as MP for an historically Tory constituency, he can also appeal to more conservative voters. He is open about his Christian faith and, while a defender of gay marriage, was quick to defend the integrity of those who opposed it.

Parties in government: from 'winner takes all' to 'win some, lose some'

By the summer of 2013 both governing parties would have had sensed achievements and setbacks in government: hardly surprising in a coalition. Yet in a political culture attuned to single party government and the ethos of 'winner takes all', the new ethos – 'win some, lose some' – was still hard to take for many MPs and party activists.

Most Conservatives were pleased with the fiscal conservatism of economic policy and the cuts in corporation tax. They were also reassured by the advent of free schools (semi-detached from state control), the cap on non-EU immigration, the 2012 Welfare Reform Act (with its cap on welfare payments) and the 5 per cent reduction in the top rate of income tax. On the other hand, Tories were frustrated by the Coalition's failure to effect a raft of key Conservative policies, like the restoration of marriage tax allowance (MTA), the reform of inheritance tax and the repeal of the Human Rights Act (Norton 2012). There was also Tory frustration at the Government's failure to implement fully the recommendations of the 2011 Beecroft Report, which would have abetted the hiring and firing of employees and thus (according to many Tories) a supply-side recovery. Eurosceptics, meanwhile, were delighted by

Cameron's veto of a new EU Treaty in 2011, but resentful that he did not question Britain's membership of the EU *per se* – even with the travails of the Eurozone.

These Tory frustrations naturally seemed to vindicate the influence of Liberal Democrats, which seemed to include: diluting Andrew Lansley's NHS reforms; ensuring MTA did not return; averting academic selection in free schools; and containing Euroscepticism in the wake of the Eurozone crisis. Neither was Lib Dem influence purely negative: the Coalition's raising of the income tax threshold to almost £10,000, its 'tycoon tax' (ensuring no more than 25 per cent of income was subject to tax relief), and its pupil premium for disadvantaged schoolchildren all echoed long-standing Lib Dem ambitions.

However, the party's reputation was grievously injured by the Coalition's decision not to scrap student tuition fees, thus aborting a key Lib Dem policy at the 2010 election. Party activists were also frustrated by the shelving of Vince Cable's 'mansion tax' (on properties worth over £2 million), and the scuppering of Lords reform by Tory MPs. However, as Clegg asserted at the party's 2011 conference, it could still claim to be 'punching above its weight' in terms of public policy, and thereby fulfilling a new and paradoxical role: 'constructive opposition to Conservatism while in government' (*Guardian*, 22 September 2011).

The Lib Dems in government thus embodied a hybrid political strategy: being more 'compassionate' than the Tories as a party of government while – simultaneously – being more 'constructive' than Labour as a party of opposition. The outcome was that, within the Coalition, party differences became increasingly overt – and the direction of government increasingly unclear. Defence Secretary Philip Hammond, for example, announced that the UK was moving towards a replacement for Trident – only to be publicly corrected by Nick Clegg. Tory Environment Minister John Hayes declared a moratorium on wind-farms – only to be publicly contradicted by Environment Secretary Ed Davey. All this suggested that Britain had not so much a coalition, in which two parties sunk their differences, as two parallel party governments, each pursuing their own (often conflicting) agendas.

The good, the big and the open: towards a new consensus?

As explained in the 7th edition of *Politics UK*, there was a significant convergence of the main parties' policies between 2005 and 2010. At the heart of this convergence lay a recognition of serious tensions within British society, a desire

that such tensions should be ended, and (*pace* Margaret Thatcher) an insistence that 'society' did indeed exist.

Cameron had been quick to sense that concern for 'society' had political mileage – hence his stress on the 'Big Society' after 2006 (Elliott and Hanning 2012). However, in the wake of England's 2011 riots other parties were not prepared to let Conservatives monopolise the issue. Ed Miliband posited 'the Good Society' (one that rejected both the 'undeserving rich' and 'undeserving poor') and, at the 2012 Labour conference, co-opted the nineteenth-century Tory ideal of 'one nation'. Nick Clegg, meanwhile, exalted an 'Open Society' that was more 'accountable' (justifying his latest essay at Lords reform) and 'inclusive' (allowing him to oppose a couples' tax allowance that excluded the unmarried).

The acknowledgement of 'society' connected to a broad consensus over law and order, with all parties accepting the mantra of 'tough on crime, tough on the causes of crime'. This was a significant shift by the Conservative Party, exemplified in government by Ken Clarke's preference (while Justice Secretary) for rehabilitation rather than imprisonment of offenders. Cameron's declaration of support for gay marriage offered further evidence of a centre-left, rather than Conservative, consensus in social policy. For Conservatives, it was a reminder that, while Thatcherism may have won the economic arguments of the 1980s, the liberal-left had won many of the arguments pertaining to culture and social policy.

However, even Thatcher's economic victory – *laissez faire* over *dirigisme* – seemed questionable by 2012. Following Miliband's attack on 'predator capitalism', Cameron seemed to follow suit, castigating 'crony capitalism' and instigating the removal of Fred Goodwin's knighthood (for decisions Goodwin made while leading the nationalised Royal Bank of Scotland). By early 2012 all the main parties had rejected 'uncontrolled' capitalism and were professing the case for extra regulation. The only difference seemed to be over the form this regulation should take: state interference, as Labour seemed to favour, or the 'John Lewis' model (self-regulation and shareholder control) admired by the two Coalition parties. There was also growing consensus, among the two main parties at least, that there should be no extra regulation from Europe. Encouraged by the Eurozone crisis, Labour MPs voted in 2012 to cut the EU budget – thus effectively becoming more Eurosceptic than a Conservative Prime Minister (who merely wanted it frozen).

Although the emergence of a fresh consensus was hard to dispute, it was not easy to categorise. On the one hand, growing cross-party agreement on the need for cuts in public spending, and Ed Miliband's diminishing enthusiasm for a neo-Keynesian alternative, showed that any return to a social democratic consensus was fanciful. On the other hand, widespread clamour for more regulation of markets, controversy surrounding tax cuts for the 'rich', and a universal recognition of 'society' were hardly consistent with a Thatcherite hegemony.

In the quest to define the new consensus, the concept of a 'social market' could yet prove helpful. It is hardly a new concept: it was advanced by a number of continental centre parties in the early postwar era. Yet its central assumption – that capitalism should be managed so as to ensure greater social cohesion – seemed highly pertinent to UK politics by 2012. Amid economic turbulence and social unrest, Westminster's politicians may have been arguing as ferociously as ever. Yet, beneath the adversarial rhetoric, there were signs that they were moving towards a social market *rapprochement*.

Party organisation: a Bagehot-based analysis

The organisation of political parties has two imperatives. The first is to service a party's leaders and members as they perform party business. The second is to determine the distribution of power within the party concerned. In respect of this second imperative, the key question normally concerns the extent to which an organisation promotes intra-party democracy and, *inter alia*, political participation.

When assessing party organisation from this angle, it is useful to adopt an approach taken to the British constitution by Walter Bagehot in 1867 – one that distinguished between the 'dignified' and 'efficient' versions of how things worked. For Bagehot, the former version pointed to formality and official structures; the latter to political dynamism and the 'real' locus of power. Since 2010, this distinction has seemed increasingly apt for Britain's major political parties.

Power in the parties: the dignified version

Within both the Labour and Conservative parties there have been developments arising from formal, structural change. The greatest impact of this was felt in the Conservative Party as a result of an *ad hoc* initiative from David Cameron in the summer of 2009. Keen to restore his own party's credibility during the MPs' expenses scandal, Cameron announced that the Conservative system for selecting parliamentary candidates would be 'opened up'. More specifically, this would allow involvement from those previously uninvolved in the party, while according more influence to ordinary members

over local party officials. In most of the constituencies yet to choose candidates, this meant the final decision being made in a one-member-one-vote ballot. In some (like Totnes, Macclesfield and Gosport) it involved the local party arranging an 'open primary' where the choice was made by voters rather than party members.

The effect of these reforms was significant, but perhaps not in the way Cameron envisaged. It meant that, among the 148 Tory MPs elected for the first time in 2010, a sizeable batch owed their position to ordinary party members (and, in some cases, ordinary voters) rather than party elites. This, in turn, meant that the party's newly elected MPs had few qualms about defying their front bench, especially now it was part of a Coalition none of their voters had endorsed.

One early indication of this was when they helped prevent Cameron from changing the rules of the 1922 Committee (thus ensuring that ministers were still excluded). New MPs were also prominent among the 81, 91 and 136 Tories rebelling on the EU (2011), Lords reform (2012) and gay marriage (2013) respectively. By 2012, in fact, most new Conservative MPs had voted against their leadership in Parliament at least once. The launch of a new 'loyalist' grouping of Tory MPs – the **301 Group** – was a recognition that Tory MPs were anything but united.

Although there has been no comparable impact, the debate over organisational reform has been more extensive inside the Labour Party. This was predictable: parties no longer governing the country tend to get interested in how they govern themselves. For such parties the nature of reform invariably links to their perception of why they lost the previous general election. For Labour after 2010 it was perceived that voters saw it as divided, sleazy and unrepresentative of society. The notion of it being divided and sleazy led to a weakening of the Parliamentary Party (PLP), while the notion of it being unrepresentative led to plans for a new, 'fourth estate' within the party.

In the case of the PLP Miliband had stated it was 'important we no longer have the distraction of internal elections . . . and that we talk to the public rather than ourselves' (*Guardian*, 10 March 2011). He evidently saw the PLP's traditional shadow cabinet elections as a threat to this goal, and formally proposed their abolition: 196 Labour MPs duly voted for this curtailment of party democracy, with just 41 voting against. It pointed to a crisis of confidence among those who had spearheaded a doomed election campaign, and meant Miliband would be spared the problem afflicting many of Labour's previous Opposition leaders: having to include on their front bench MPs they did not rate, but who had their own mandate from the party.

Meanwhile, a wider-ranging survey of party organisation – culminating in the document *Refounding Labour to Win* – was conducted by the party's National Executive

Committee. This too sought to have a humbling effect on the PLP – first, by prescribing the 'duties' of Labour MPs within a PLP 'code of conduct'; second, by making trade union membership compulsory for PLP members; and third, by denying requests that, in a future Labour leadership contest, Labour MPs would 'shortlist' candidates before it was opened up to the party outside Parliament (as is the case with Conservative leadership contests).

In terms of power in the party, Labour MPs were evidently facing their greatest challenge for 30 years. After losing office it is not uncommon for a party's MPs to face challenges from extra-parliamentary activists. Yet, with Labour after 2010, it was hard not to conclude that this was also a backlash against the parliamentary expenses scandal, especially as most of those tarnished (and later prosecuted) were from Labour's benches. It was also unclear whether the new party leader would have been the sturdiest defender of PLP interests. Miliband, after all, was the first Labour leader to get the job despite, rather than because of, fellow Labour MPs (see Table 11.1).

One of Refounding Labour's boldest proposals concerned the creation of a new party section. Intended to supplement the existing three 'estates' (PLP, CLPs and **affiliated** groups like trade unions), the new section would be known as Registered Supporters, and would include those who were prepared to pledge Labour their electoral support, but without actually joining the party. The initial suggestion was that, once these Registered Supporters numbered at least 50,000, they should receive 3–10 per cent of votes in both the college and the party's annual conference.

However, if a new element were to be introduced in such a way, the party's existing three elements would have to lose influence. Although NEC modernisers thought the loss could be borne by trade unions, the unions themselves were not eager to dilute their own power. So, Labour's 2011 conference voted for the 'principle' of Refounding Labour's reforms but left most of the details to be resolved (or not) in the three years ahead. This also applied to the proposal that, in future, either the leader or deputy leader must be a woman.

Power in the parties: the efficient version

In the past, party reorganisation has usually been harnessed to a review of party policy – with party elites being in charge of both. This was true of Labour after 1994, when Blair's Partnership in Power reorganisation was linked to the advent of 'Third Way' policies, and the Conservatives after 1997, when William Hague created a 'fresh structure' that would service his 'fresh Conservatism' (Bale 2012). Even when policy and organisation were challenged by 'outsider' groups

– like the Campaign for Labour Party Democracy after 1979 – it was done through established party channels, such as the parties' annual conferences (Faucher-King 2005).

After 2010, however, official party organisation was strangely de-aligned from party debates about policy and philosophy. Instead, some of the most fertile policy discussions seemed to occur away from official party structures, centring upon a myriad of party groups that were informal, unofficial and on-line (e.g. Labour Democratic Network, Lib Dem Voice and Conservative Home). Driven by the so-called '**clicktivists**', these party groups gestated and communicated via blogs, Facebook, Twitter and other examples of the new media, largely short-circuiting the formal party machines (Carswell 2012). The implication was that, beyond what Bagehot might have termed their 'dignified' organisations, the major parties were showing a surprising level of energy and initiative, spawned by a new generation of irreverent, computer-savvy activists. As Tim Montogomerie, editor of Conservative Home, stated, 'We give Tory members more of a voice than they had in the pre-internet age . . . this site is like a conference fringe that never stops' (Observer, 12 February).

All this pointed to a new, 'organic' model of party organisation that challenged the 'oligarchic model' posited by R.T. McKenzie's British Political Parties in 1955, which asserted that power in the parties lay mainly with their parliamentary leaders. This alternative, 'organic model' suggested that party activity in Britain could be undergoing both a quiet revolution and a modest revival.

The crisis of party politics: an accidental solution?

When the Power inquiry of 2006 examined political parties, its diagnosis was critical but unoriginal: the parties, it claimed, were uninspiring, unresponsive and unpopular. The solutions Power advanced were equally passé, betraying (in the liberal traditions of John Stuart Mill) a breezy, bourgeois faith in enlightened elites. The parties' leaders, Power claimed, should promptly 'instigate' reform, 'reassess' party structures, 'empower' ordinary members and 'reconnect' with the wider public. The intended outcome may have been democratic; yet the route prescribed was decidedly top-down (Fairclough et al. 2007).

Six years after the Power report, there were reasons to believe that party politics was regaining traction. Yet this seemed to have happened in an unplanned – even accidental – way, circumventing both party elites and official party organisations. As indicated earlier, a look at the internal workings of Britain's main parties, specifically their informal grass-root activity, revealed no shortage of vitality and initiative. Likewise, their members' approach to policy discussion since 2010 – informal, anarchic, cybernetic – seemed quintessentially modern in character, as well as impressively vibrant. With this in mind, the shrunken number of party members can be misleading, causing quantity to be confused with quality. While it is undeniable that party members today are less numerous, they seem increasingly sophisticated and, in relation to party leaders, decreasingly deferential (Whiteley 2011).

Furthermore, if parties represent 'big picture' politics – focusing on society as a whole rather than aspects of it – they are helped by the fact that 'big picture' politics is again compelling. For much of the previous two decades, it used to be argued that party politics suffered from a 'culture of contentment' and a sense we had reached the 'end of history' (Schmitt and Holmberg 1995). Encouraged by widespread affluence, and a sense that the broad status quo was inevitable, ideological disputes about the *nature* of society were supplanted by forensic quarrels about its *details*. In terms of political participation, this inevitably led to a growth of pressure groups and protest movements rather than engagement with political parties.

However, following the high-profile, socio-economic 'accidents' of recent years – notably the 'credit crunch' of 2008, the summer riots of 2011 and the recurrent euro crisis of 2012 – commentators discerned a new public interest in the general nature of capitalism and society (Edwards 2012). This should not have been surprising. When social and economic conditions worsen, the public usually renews its interest in the 'big picture' – and the ability of governments to shape it. Furthermore, despite the growth of pressure groups, the only organisations which can democratise those governments are political parties. This could and should lead to greater public interest in party politics, and what parties would do with the state apparatus they aspire to control.

Such renewed interest would be even more conceivable were the parties to offer significantly different solutions, thus dispelling notions that they were 'all the same'. This possibility cannot be discounted. Earlier in the chapter, it was observed that, despite considerable similarities in party policy, there were also burgeoning differences – notably about the role of the state in securing economic and social stability. Should Britain's economy worsen, making existing positions redundant, those party differences could widen, especially given the *chutzpah* of modern party activists. In a climate defined by polarised parties and desperate voters, party politics in Britain could easily undergo a renaissance. By 2012 there were signs that party members, at least, understood that possibility.

Box 11.1

BRITAIN IN CONTEXT

Parties in retreat

If British party politics is defined by a lack of public interest, then it suffers a problem common to Western democracies. In the USA, for example, various studies show a long-term trend from party politics to single-issue protest movements (Meisel and Bering 2012). It might be assumed that, in younger democracies, there would be greater engagement with parties competing for office. Yet, even here, electoral turnout has generally been no healthier than in the UK (for example, 49 per cent in the Polish parliamentary elections in 2011, 59 per cent in the Slovakian parliamentary elections of 2012). Another aspect of British party politics seen elsewhere is the rejection of the centre-left. Despite the election of a Socialist Party president in France, and the re-election of a Democrat president in America, at the end of 2012 social democratic parties were still out of power in 22 out of 27 EU countries. This may relate to the historic faith of centre-left parties in bold, governmental solutions – a faith that may seem less tenable given the traumas of a supra-national currency in Europe.

Chapter summary

The 2010 General Election did little to relieve the crisis of British party politics: by postwar standards, none of the major parties secured much trust from voters. In the two years that followed, only the Scottish National Party could claim much in the way of momentum. The three main UK parties, meanwhile, struggled to secure a clear identity that would separate them from their rivals and impress voters. However, the onset of economic recession produced, among sections of all parties, more intellectual vitality than seen for several decades. Exploiting new information technology, this surge of energy flowed largely from informal channels set up by party members rather than official structures overseen by party leaders. This development had obvious implications for the 'power in the parties' debate and suggested that the oligarchic model of party organisation – axiomatic between 1997 and 2010 – was being challenged by a more organic arrangement. But it also offered the promise of a revival in party politics generally, underwritten by a new public interest in capitalism and the 'bigger picture' of political life.

Discussion points

- Why have political parties alienated voters?
- Is it still possible to speak of a 'British party system'?
- What are the differences within and between the main parties?
- Have the two Coalition parties betrayed or upheld their values?
- Has there been a redistribution of power inside the main parties?
- Is party politics poised to revive?

Further reading

Both Driver (2011) and Clark (2012) provide solid, up-to-date overviews of political parties in Britain, while the relationship between parties and voters is analysed and updated by Dalton, Farrell and McAllister (2011) and Kavanagh and Cowley (2010).

The definitive study of the Conservative Party recently is provided by Bale (2011), although the studies edited by Heppell and Seawright (2012), and the biography written by Elliott and Hanning (2012), merit attention. Ideological and philosophical developments in or around the Conservative Party are closely examined by Blond (2010), Bright Blue (2012), King (2011), Webb and Childs (2011) and the essays edited by Edwards (2012).

Recent developments in the Labour Party are assessed by Griffiths and Hickson (2010), contributions to the debate about 'Next Labour' are offered by Cooke et al. (2011), Davies (2011), and the essays edited by Philpott (2011), while Radice and Diamond (2010) provide a partisan analysis of Labour's relationship with voters. An authoritative account of the party's new leadership is delivered by Hasan and Macintyre (2011).

The recent impact of the Liberal Democrats is evaluated by Gerard (2011) and the essays edited by Beech and Lee (2011), while the record of the Scottish and Welsh nationalist parties is surveyed by Mitchell et al. (2012) and Sandry (2011) respectively. Organisational and financial developments within the parties are examined by Koss (2010), Quinn (2012) and Whiteley (2011).

Bibliography

Bale, T. (2011) *The Conservatives Party from Thatcher to Cameron* (Polity).

Bale, T. (2011) *The Conservatives Since 1945: The Drivers of Party Change* (Oxford University Press).

Beech, M. and Lee, S. (eds) (2011) *The Cameron-Clegg Government* (Palgrave Macmillan).

Beech, M. and Lee, S. (eds) (2009) *The Conservatives Under David Cameron: Built to Last?* (Palgrave Macmillan).

Blond, P. (2010) *Red Tory* (Faber and Faber).

Bright Blue (2012) *Tory Modernisation 2.0* (Bright Blue Publications).

Carswell, D. (2012) *The End of Politics and the Birth of iDemocracy* (Biteback).

Childs, S. and Webb, P. (2011) *Sex, Gender and the Conservative Party* (Palgrave Macmillan).

Clarke, A. (2012) *Political Parties in the UK* (Palgrave Macmillan).

Cooke, G., Lent, A., Painter, A. and Sen, H. (2011) *In The Black Labour* (Policy Network).

Cruddas, J. (2012) 'Building the new Jerusalem', *New Statesman*, 28 September.

Dalton, R., Farrell, D. and McAllister, I. (2011) *Political Parties and Democratic Linkage* (Oxford University Press).

Davies, R. (2011) *Tangled Up in Blue* (Ruskin Publishing).

Davis, D., Binley, B. and Baron, J. (2011) *The Future of Conservatism* (Biteback).

Driver, S. (2011) *Understanding British Party Politics* (Polity).

Edwards, J. (ed.) (2012) *Retrieving the Big Society* (Wiley-Blackwell).

Elliott, F. and Hanning, J. (2012) *Cameron: Practically a Conservative* (Fourth Estate).

Fairclough, P., Kelly, R. and Magee, E. (2007) 'The Power Inquiry', in *UK Government and Politics Annual Survey 2007* (Philip Allan).

Faucher-King, F. (2005) *Changing Parties: an Anthropology of British Political Party Conferences* (Palgrave Macmillan).

Gerard, J. (2011) *The Clegg Coup* (Gibson Square).

Glasman, M. (2011) 'I'm blue and true to Labour', *Guardian*, 8 April 2011.

Griffiths, S. and Hickson, K. (eds) (2010) *British Party Politics and Ideology after New Labour* (Palgrave Macmillan).

Hasan, M. and Macintyre, J. (2011) *Ed: The Milibands and the Making of a Labour Leader* (Biteback).

Heppell, T. and Hill, M. (2012) 'Labour in Opposition' in Heppell, T. and Seawright, D. (eds) *Cameron and the Conservatives, The Transition to Coalition* (Palgrave Macmillan).

Houghton Committee Report on Financial Aid to Political Parties (1976), Cmnd 6601 (HMSO).

Jones, T. (2010) *The Revival of British Liberalism: from Grimond to Clegg* (Palgrave Macmillan).

Kavanagh, D. and Cowley, P. (2010) *The British General Election of 2010* (Palgrave Macmillan).

Kelly, P. (2012) 'Red or Orange? The Big Society in the New Conservatism' in Edwards, J., *Retrieving the Big Society* (Wiley-Blackwell).

Kelly, R. (2013) 'From Blue Labour to Red Tories', *Politics Review*, vol. 22, no. 4.

Kelly, R. and Crowcroft, R. (2012) 'From Burke to Burkha: Conservatism, Multiculturalism and the Big Society' in Edwards, J., *Retrieving the Big Society* (Wiley-Blackwell).

King, P. (2011) *The New Politics: Liberal Conservatism or Same Old Tories?* (Polity).

Koss, M. (2010) *The Politics of Party Funding* (Oxford University Press).

Kwarteng, K., Patel, P., Raab, D., Skidmore, C. and Truss, E. (2011) *After The Coalition* (Biteback).

Labour Party (2011) *Refounding Labour to Win: a party for the new generation*, www.labour.org.uk

Lammy, D. (2011) *Out of the Ashes* (Guardian Books).

March, L. (2011) *Radical Left Parties in Europe* (Routledge).

Marshall, P. and Laws, D. (ed.) (2004) *The Orange Book: Reclaiming Liberalism* (Profile Books).

McAnulla, S. (2012) 'Liberal Conservatism: Ideological Coherence', in Heppell, T. and Seawright, D. (eds) *Cameron and the Conservatives* (Palgrave Macmillan).

McKenzie, R.T. (1955) *British Political Parties* (Heinemann).

Meisel, L. and Bering, J. (2012) *The Oxford Handbook of American Political Parties and Interest Groups* (Oxford University Press).

Miliband, D. (2012) 'The dead end of the Big State', *New Statesman*, 6 February.

Mitchell, J., Bennie, L.G. and Johns, R. (2012) *The Scottish National Party* (Oxford University Press).

Mullin, C. (2010) 'The great Parliamentary expenses crisis' in Jones, B. and Norton, P., *Politics UK*, 7th edn (Pearson).

Norman, J. (2010) *The Big Society* (Buckingham University Press).

Norton, P. (2012) 'Coalition Cohesion' in Heppell, T. and Seawright, D. (eds) *Cameron and the Conservatives* (Palgrave Macmillan).

Philpott, R. (ed.) (2011) *Purple Labour* (Biteback).

Plaid Cymru (2012) *Moving Forward: Renewing Plaid for Wales*, www.plaidcymru.org.

Quinn, T. (2012) *Electing and Ejecting Party Leaders in Britain* (Palgrave Macmillan).

Radice, G. and Diamond, P. (2010) *Southern Discomfort Again* (Fabian pamphlets).

Sandry, A. (2011) *Plaid Cymru: An Ideological Analysis* (Welsh Academic Press).

Schmitt, H. and Holmberg, S. (1995) 'Political Parties in Decline?' in Klingemann, H. and Fuchs, D., *Citizens and the State* (Oxford University Press).

Snowdon, P. (2010) *Back From The Brink: The Inside Story of the Tory Resurrection* (Harper Press).

Webb, P. and Childs, S. (2011) 'Wets and dries resurgent? Intra-party alignments among contemporary Conservative members', *Parliamentary Affairs*, vol. 64, no. 3.

Whiteley, P. (2011) *Political Participation in Britain* (Palgrave Macmillan).

Useful websites

www.conservativehome.co.uk
www.labourdemocraticnetwork.org
www.leftfootforward.org
www.libdemvoice.org

CHAPTER 12

Devolution

Russell Deacon

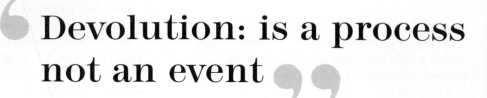

> **Devolution: is a process not an event**

Former Welsh Secretary Ron Davies (1999: 2)

Learning objectives

- To define devolution and note the various devolutionary models.

- To explain the background and role of nationalism and the subsequent drive towards political devolution and independence within the UK.

- To cover the story of how devolution evolved across the United Kingdom and Northern Ireland.

- To assess some of the key events and developments in devolutionary politics in the first four electoral cycles of devolution.

- To explore some of the major impacts on the politics of the UK from the advent of devolution.

What then is **devolution**? At a basic level devolution is simply the devolving of powers from the centre to the periphery. It is important to note that this does not involve transferring sovereignty from Westminster, which therefore makes it distinctly different from federalism. In the case of the United Kingdom devolution therefore means transferring powers from Westminster and Whitehall to the devolved bodies and administrative offices across the United Kingdom. The process of devolution can be categorised as three discrete processes:

1 *Administrative*: the process by which power is transferred to allow specific functions to be carried out;

2 *Executive*: the process by which power is transferred to enable policy decisions to be made;

3 *Legislative*: the process by which the power to make laws is conferred on another body.

Devolution, originally a side interest for mainstream UK politicians, has brought forward the central constitutional question of the last 90 years. If Scotland votes for independence in 2014, there will no longer be a UK, and British politics will have to undertake a fundamental change. Yet, the topic of devolution is not as modern as its may sound. It has dominated politics at various periods over the last 120 years, and has caused wars, the splitting of political parties and the downfall of governments. Since wide-scale political

Introduction

devolution arrived in the United Kingdom and Northern Ireland at the end of the last century, the whole nature of British politics itself has undergone an evolutionary change. As the media in the United Kingdom tends to be dominated by those based around London, many people may not be aware of the extent of the changes to our political system or the variation in policy output over the last decade.

The United Kingdom and Northern Ireland has had administrative devolution for over a century. This expanded over time so that by the 1990s it covered all of the UK. Executive and legislative devolution, outside of Northern Ireland, however, are of a more recent occurrence. This type of devolution has had a far greater impact on the politics of the UK. Since 2011 all of the nations in the United Kingdom, apart from England, have legislatures that can make their own primary laws. It is this sort of executive and legislative devolution (often referred to as political devolution) that is examined in this chapter.

Theory

In 2005 Jennifer Todd, drawing upon the work of around 20 of the most prominent academics who had commented on devolution since the mid-1970s, highlighted three models of territorial politics which provide us with a way to assess devolutionary change.

The first model is that of 'state realism'. Within this model the state has adapted its power and sovereignty to take account of changing political realities. This new form of devolution is, therefore, simply the older dual polity whereby the centre allowed a certain practical autonomy on local issues to its peripheries, while retaining control over 'high politics'. Under this model, however, the divide between the centre and the periphery is not clear-cut and therefore the older 'mainframe' of the unitary state may be under intolerable strain and crack.

The second model considers devolution to be driven by 'European regionalism'. This model indicates that nations within the UK move from 'state centred' to 'European determined linkage politics'. This means that, within a European context, nations such as Scotland, Wales and Northern Ireland need the UK Parliament less and less as they are able to interact directly with the European Union, without needing to go through Westminster. In turn, the European Union and European Commission require regions or nations in order to determine their policy output such as the establishment of European regional development funding or support for cultural and linguistic policies. In the case of the United Kingdom part of this packaging involves the identification and recognition of the constituent nations.

The final model sees devolution as a 'renewal of imperial legacies'. Here the Westminster government, just as it did with its colonies in the last century, transfers more and more sovereignty and powers to the devolved nations. The strategy behind this is that in time they will become dominions independent in their own right. This may well soon be the case with Scotland. Those advocating this model also point to Northern Ireland as an example of this. Here the Westminster government would be glad to be rid of its responsibilities for this troubled province. The main drawback to this theory, however, is that all mainstream British political parties constantly advocate their commitment to maintaining the union.

Nationalism and the drive towards political devolution

Nationalism in the United Kingdom is normally related to those groups that believe that either the nation or putative nation is at the centre of a political system of government. Due to the fact that political boundaries in the British Isles have been fairly constant for the last five centuries, national identities have had time to develop and take a firm historical root. Even in Ireland, where the political boundaries were only firmly established in 1922, the national identity focuses on whether its citizens feel themselves to be Irish or British Irish nationals. And each side forms its own brand of nationalism, accordingly.

One of the common misconceptions of both academics and historians is to label only those groups that desire independence for their own nation, such as Plaid Cymru in Wales and the Scottish National Party (SNP) in Scotland, as nationalists. This extends to *Mebion Kernow* in Cornwall or, in the case of Ireland, desiring union with another nation, either the Irish Republic or the UK. As many of us know, nationalism in the British Isles is both wider and more complex than this. In the nineteenth century the Liberal Prime Minister, William Gladstone, was the originator of 'Home Rule – all round', meaning in essence devolution for all of the nations of the British Isles. After this was defeated by the Liberal Unionists, who split from their own party and the Conservatives, Liberal nationalism emerged once more in Scotland and Wales in the late Victorian and Edwardian era. The Young Scot's Society and *Cymru Fydd* (Wales to be) were both Liberal Party nationalist movements that pursued devolutionary policies which sought to place their own nations at the centre of their own political systems. Nationalism has continued in the Liberal Party and subsequently in the Liberal Democrat Party with a desire for a federal system of government for the United Kingdom. Within the Labour Party, initially supportive of devolution, this desire was much reduced, particularly after the Russian Revolution and the First World War produced left-wing proponents who advocated the need for international socialism and an end to nationalist divisions. It, nevertheless, maintained a distinct presence within the Labour Party from then on, despite the strong unionist tendency that existed in the Labour Party after the First World War. British and English nationalism have been ever-present in the Conservative Party. There have even on occasions been elements of support for Scottish nationalism within the party. This, however, was never the case in Wales, and it was only after the Conservative Party had evolved in the Welsh Assembly for more than a decade that Welsh Conservative Assembly Members there became stronger advocates of further Welsh devolution. A number of prominent Welsh Conservatives, particularly at Westminster, still remain staunchly unionist in outlook (British nationalist).

In Ireland nationalism has always been viewed from a different perspective when compared to perceptions in England, Wales and Scotland. This is the nationalism, which on both sides had blood on its hands, through centuries of religious warfare and rebellions against the British crown. This did not occur anywhere else in Great Britain after the last Jacobean revolt in Scotland in 1745. First, Irish nationalism simply and unwaveringly demanded home rule. As this desire was rejected by the Westminster Parliament, so Irish nationalism became more violent. Irish nationalism then developed into Catholic nationalism pursuing the ideal of a united and independent Ireland. This was in turn countered by Protestant nationalism (Unionism) which sought to keep Ireland within the United Kingdom. The two then opposed each other in a bloody quasi civil war that lasted on and off for much of the twentieth century. Among certain sectors of the community this hostility still remains under the surface and can burst into bloody rioting, particular during the 'marching season'.

In Wales and Scotland a new type of nationalism developed in the years before the Second World War. This was the nationalism of independence rather than home rule. By the end of the century it would eclipse the nationalism which exists within the three mainstream UK parties. In 1925, Plaid Cymru was formed and then in 1934 the Scottish Nationalist Party (SNP) was created. Both had had their origins in other nationalist organisations but it was these new parties that came to represent the mainstream independence nationalism of their respective nation states. Political scientists, however, do not always refer directly to them as 'nationalist' parties. This label they reserve for those anti-immigrant parties or groups, normally on the far political right such as the BNP and the English Defence League. Instead, Plaid Cymru and the SNP are referred to by them as 'ethnoregionalist' parties. This means that they represent a specific regional/national group within a larger nation state, in this context the Welsh and the Scottish peoples in the United Kingdom. In the political world and in the media, however, they remain defined as nationalist parties, but students of politics should be aware there is a clear distinction between nationalist and ethnoregionalist parties. Having stated this, however, they are still referred to by their commonly known label – 'nationalist party' – in this chapter.

While in Northern Ireland the nationalist parties fully displaced the mainstream British political parties, this has never been the case in Scotland or Wales. Here, for decades after their foundation, both Plaid Cymru and the SNP struggled to make any political progress. It was only with Plaid Cymru's by-election win in Carmarthen in 1966 and the SNPs similar by-election win in Hamilton in 1967 that the modern period of Scottish and Welsh nationalism associated with a drive towards independence started. This nationalist impact was seen to be so sudden and potentially damaging electorally to the Labour Party, which traditionally relied on their Scottish and Welsh seats to counteract the Conservatives majority of the English seats, that they set up a Royal Commission under Lord Kilbrandon to examine the issue of devolution. When Kilbrandon reported back in 1973 it was to a Conservative government under Edward Heath that was lukewarm to political devolution. It was some five years later, under the Labour Government of James Callaghan and after much political turmoil, that the referendums on Scottish and Welsh devolution were held. The devolution referendum was defeated in Wales in 1979, and in Scotland an insufficient majority was gained to carry it forward. The Labour Government then fell to a vote of no confidence. It became the first government to fall on an issue of devolution since William Gladstone's Liberal Government had split on Irish Home Rule almost a century before.

Two months later, in the 1979 General Election, the Conservatives won and the pro-devolution Liberals, Plaid

Cymru and the SNP lost between them 13 of their 29 MPs. The SNP was reduced from 11 to just two seats in the process. The victorious Conservatives had honed their campaigning skills in the Scottish and Welsh referendums and increased their seats in these nations at the pro-devolutionists' expense. The new government under Margaret Thatcher was unashamedly pro-unionist. A month after their victory the Conservatives reversed the devolutionary mechanisms. The political fortunes of the pro-devolutionists were now put on hold for two decades.

Ireland

The historical events that resulted in the formation of the province of Northern Ireland (Ulster) already fill many volumes. Bearing this in mind, therefore, the historical elements so instrumental in understanding the politics of Northern Ireland can only be touched upon here briefly. Ulster has been a constant reminder of the British Isles' violent, sectarian and turbulent past transported into modern times. The religious wars between Catholics and Protestants that faded from the British mainland more than four centuries ago have yet to die in Northern Ireland. Politics there today therefore remains almost totally divided between political parties which were formed on a religious basis. The Catholic nationalists are republicans who seek a union with the Catholic Irish Republic, while the Protestants seek to maintain the union with the protestant United Kingdom (unionists). The only parties that are non-sectarian are the 'Alliance Party', which is linked to the British Liberal Democrats and attracts limited support in Northern Ireland and the Green Party. In short, therefore after the Anglo-Irish Treaty of 1922, Northern Ireland broke away from Southern Ireland (Eire) and from then onwards has developed a separate political identity. It was given its own parliament, known by the place in which it was prominently located – Stormont. Until 1972 Stormont ran the province, with near autonomy from Westminster, as part of the United Kingdom with its own Prime Minister, the last of whom was Brian Faulkner.

Stormont, however, was a Protestant-controlled parliament that supported the mechanisms of a protestant state while maintaining as strict a segregation as that occurring between black and white citizens in the southern United States until the late 1960s. The Catholics, inspired by the American black civil rights movement, sought their own civil rights during the 1960s, mainly through their own political party, the Social Democratic and Labour Party (SDLP). This movement was heavily resisted by the Stormont government and enforced by the almost exclusively Protestant-manned Royal Ulster Constabulary (RUC) and their auxiliary policemen (B Specials). This produced a situation that became ever more violent and began a period known as 'the

Troubles'. At its height in 1972, 467 people were killed, 323 of them civilians. The atrocities of that year became infamous in Irish history and included events such as: Bloody Sunday, Bloody Friday, McGurk's Bar, Kelly's Bar, Callender Street and Abercorn. For the next three and a half decades, while the British Army and Royal Ulster Constabulary fought the Irish Republican Army (IRA), and the various other **paramilitary organisations**, the politicians (sometimes closely connected to **paramilitaries**, particularly Sinn Féin with the IRA), British and Irish Prime Ministers and the occasional American President, tried every 'carrot and stick' method they could conceive of to end the Troubles. Justice for those caught up in the Troubles would, however, never come for many and for others it would take decades. It would not be until 2010, for instance, that the truth behind Bloody Sunday was fully revealed in the Saville Inquiry – almost 40 years after the event.

The current Northern Ireland peace process began with the signing of the Good Friday Agreement (named after the day it was signed) and its subsequent approval by a Northern Ireland referendum in May 1998. This created the devolved Northern Ireland Assembly, which officially came into being in December 1999. Because of the previous problems with Northern Ireland politics, such as the **gerrymandering** of constituency boundaries, the Assembly's elections were under STV, the most proportional system possible. The Good Friday Agreement meant that all of the main political parties would in future have to share power in any Northern Ireland government. The largest political party would take the most senior First Minister's post and the second largest that of Deputy First Minister. But within a short space of time after opening the peace process ground to a halt once more. A row in February 2000 between the political parties over weapons **decommissioning** led to a four-month suspension of the Assembly.

A further crisis came in July 2001 when David Trimble, the Assembly's First Minister and leader of the moderate Ulster Unionist Party (UUP), resigned out of frustration at the IRA's failure to decommission their weapons. He returned later that year when the IRA began to put its 'weapons beyond use'. The Northern Ireland Assembly then resumed business for a short period. Then, in July 2002 the IRA made an unprecedented apology for 'non-combatant' deaths. However, Trimble resigned again three months later after the discovery of incriminating documents in Sinn Féin's party offices. Britain then resumed **direct rule** of Northern Ireland with the Prime Minister postponing the next Assembly elections until November 2003. In these elections, the more radical unionist Ian Paisley's Democratic Unionist Party (DUP), which opposed the Good Friday Agreement, displaced the UUP as the biggest party in the Assembly. At the same time, Sein Féin replaced the moderate SDLP as the main Catholic (republican) party. As the rest of British politics was moving towards the political centre, Northern Ireland's was moving to the political extremes.

For a long while after the elections there was stalemate once more. In December 2004, remarkably, it seemed as though Mr Paisley might become the new First Minister, with Sinn Féin's Martin McGuinness (the former head of the IRA) as Deputy First Minister. But a bank raid and a brutal murder, both blamed on the IRA, wrecked the deal.

In Britain's General Election of May 2005 the Democratic Unionists gained parliamentary seats at Mr Trimble's expense, and Sinn Féin escaped punishment for the IRA's misdemeanours by also increasing their share of the vote. But the British government's hasty welcome to the IRA's promise in July 2005 to 'end the armed campaign' enraged Unionists and pushed them further away from cooperation. Consequently, there was no devolved Assembly between the 2003 and 2007 elections. When the 2007 Northern Ireland Assembly elections occurred, the DUP and Sein Féin were now the main political parties in Northern Ireland. It could therefore only be with their cooperation that Northern Ireland's Assembly would restart. Political progress was now stuck on the thorny issue of law and order in Northern Ireland. By now, via the 2006 St Andrews Agreement, the RUC had been disbanded and replaced with the Police Service of Northern Ireland (PSNI), which had a much larger number of Catholic officers in it. Yet, this still lacked the required republican support, something that was essential for Ulster's future.

In January 2007 Sein Féin voted to support policing in Northern Ireland for the first time in the party's history. This broke the political log jam and enabled the DUP to remove a vital political barrier and join the government with them. At the same time Tony Blair was using the 'stick' of introducing water charges for Northern Ireland, which all Northern Irish parties opposed, and Gordon Brown, then Chancellor, offered the 'carrot' of £1 billion extra funding if an Executive was formed. The strategy worked, and the DUP leader Ian Paisley, at the age of 81, now saw his moment in history and finally joined with his lifelong republican foes in a joint administration. He became the First Minister and Martin McGuinness the Deputy First Minister. Considering neither had even spoken to each other prior to their agreeing to share office, they got on remarkably well. It seemed as though the threat of sectarian division had finally been removed from Northern Irish politics.

Then in May 2008 Northern Ireland got a new First Minister – Peter Robinson, the long-time deputy leader of the DUP, acceded, as Ian Paisley stood down. Sinn Féin then refused to nominate Martin McGuinness as Deputy First Minister unless the DUP agreed to the devolution of justice. Gordon Brown intervened and Gerry Adams was called to Number 10 to try and find a compromise. Between May and November the Executive did not meet, and during this period the image of devolution took a nosedive with the Northern Irish general public. An accommodation was eventually reached in which the DUP agreed with Sinn Féin to make the police answerable to an Northern Irish justice minister in time, but both Sinn Féin and the DUP ruled themselves out of this post. In the event it was the former Alliance Party leader David Ford, who in April 2010 became Northern Ireland's first justice minister since 1972.

The main issue to the threaten the DUP–Sinn Féin-led administration after 2008 was not one of political violence or sectarianism but was instead related to the personal life of the First Minister, Peter Robinson. The First Minister's wife, Iris, who was also a DUP MP and Member of Legislative (Northern Ireland) Assembly (MLA), was involved in an affair with a teenage man. The subsequent revelations led to Iris stepping out of politics and Peter having to step down for a while 'clearing' his name in certain 'irregular' aspects of the affair. In the 2010 General Election the voters of Robinson's Belfast East constituency punished him electorally by removing him as an MP in favour of the Alliance candidate Naomi Long. In the 2011 Northern Ireland Assembly elections, however, he topped the STV list and was elected on the first count, restoring his support in his constituency, thus ensuring that he would become the longest-serving Northern Irish First Minister with his Sinn Féin Deputy Martin McGuinness an even longer-serving Deputy Minister.

Currently, devolution in Northern Ireland remains more stable than at any time since the early 1960s. The government of Northern Ireland has remained united on issues such as condemning political violence, resisting financial cuts from Westminster and encouraging economic development in Ulster. Together they have been able to do things not possible in the decades of conflict. They have, for instance, been able to promote tourism in Northern Ireland. This has been done by harnessing their historic and cultural legacy not to 'the Troubles' but to events such as the centenary of sinking of the ocean liner *Titanic* (build in Belfast) and the setting of popular TV shows such as *Small Island* and *Game of Thrones*. Northern Ireland has consequently become a popular cruise destination. Yet, despite this progress there still remains the possibility of instability:

■ The economic problems suffered by Ireland and the overall UK recession have depressed the Northern Ireland economy. In the past unemployment, particularly among the young, has increased sectarian violence, which still occurs across Northern Ireland from time to time.

■ Some paramilitaries such as the Real and Continuity IRA continue to mount operations. The killing of soldiers, policemen and prison officers reminds Northern Ireland that some people seem to never wish to abandon the gun.

Table 12.1 Northern Ireland Assembly results, 1998–2011 (108 seats)

Party	1998	2003	2007	2011
Social Democratic and Labour Party (SDLP)	24	18	16	14
Ulster Unionist Party (UUP)	28	30 (33)*	18	16
Democratic Unionist Party (DUP)	20	27 (24)*	36	38
Sinn Féin	18	24	28	29
Alliance	6	6	7	8
Others	12	3	3	3

* Three UUP defections to the DUP.

Source: Deacon 2012

- The Westminster government's Parliamentary Voting System and Constituencies Act 2011 was set to reduce the number of MLAs (Members of Legislative Assembly) to 96, in line with the reduction in Westminster constituencies. Following a dispute in the Westminster Coalition Government, however, the Liberal Democrats said they would no longer support the reduction. The original electoral system combined with the number of MLA positions available ensured that virtually all political opinions were included in the Assembly. A reduction of MLAs, therefore, could lead to the exclusion of some parties, which may drive them back to political violence as a form of representation.

- Some Unionist voices such as former DUP MEP and now Traditional Unionist Voice (TUV) MLA Jim Allister remain opposed to power sharing and are still popular amongst sections of the unionist community. Their views could once more stop power sharing in other parties such as the DUP, whose own membership and support base still retain a degree of scepticism towards power sharing.

- The three mainland British political parties remain outside Northern Irish politics. The Conservative Party unsuccessfully attempted to have joint candidates with the UUP in elections. The Alliance Party's one MP, Naomi Long, sits as an opposition member in Westminster and not with her sister party, the Liberal Democrats, in government. Although the Labour Party does enjoy close relations with the SDLP, it still does not have direct representation in Ulster. The Northern Irish parties frequently vote with the opposition in Westminster. This means that, unlike elsewhere in the UK, there continues to be no Northern Irish MPs serving in the Westminster government, keeping its representatives outside the British government.

Scotland

On 15 October 2012 the British Prime Minister, David Cameron and the First Minister of Scotland, Alex Salmond,

signed a joint agreement allowing for a referendum on Scottish independence in the autumn of 2014. The event signalled the start of a process of events that could lead to the most important events in the history of the United Kingdom since the Anglo-Irish Treaty in 1921. If the Scottish people vote for independence, it would reverse the events of the past 500 years in bringing the nations of the United Kingdom closer together politically. At the start of the seventeenth century Scotland and England became joined. In March 1603 the English Queen Elizabeth I died and King James of Scotland became King of England and Ireland. This happened in a smooth transition of power quite different from most previous changes of monarch in both Scotland and England. James now concentrated his reign in England and for the rest of his life he only visited Scotland once more, in 1617. This demonstrated the start of a transition of power to England that went on for the next century and beyond.

When the Scottish Parliament was abolished with the Act of Union in 1707, the event was described by the Scottish Lord Chancellor, James Ogilvy, as like the 'end of an old song'. Yet, the distinctive tune of Scotland and Scottishness did not end with the demise of its parliament. The Scottish church, education and legal systems remained separate from those in England and Wales. From 1885 onwards there was also a separate government department and minister for Scotland. Unlike the positions of Northern Ireland and Wales, there was never any doubt over Scotland's existence as a country separate from England. Over time much of the government's business in Scotland was transferred from London to the Scottish Office in Edinburgh. From 1926 the Scottish Secretary also sat in the Cabinet. Therefore, by the time the Second World War arrived, the Scottish Office already represented a substantially devolved administrative department.

For the first seven decades of the twentieth century there were sporadic attempts to push forward political devolution for Scotland amongst all of the parties in Scotland. This was strongest in the Scottish Liberals and the Scottish National Party (SNP), but there were also politicians in the Labour

Box 12.1

Scotland Act 2012

Aside from formally changing the name of the 'Scottish Executive' to the 'Scottish Government' this Act introduced the following new powers to the Scottish Parliament:

- New Scottish rate of income tax – up to 10p in the pound;
- Devolution of stamp duty land tax;
- Devolution of landfill tax;
- Power to create new taxes;
- New borrowing powers of about £5 billion of the budget;
- Legislative power over air weapons;
- Responsibility for drink-driving and speed limits;
- A role in appointments in broadcasting and the Crown Estate;

- New procedure for Scottish criminal cases that go to the UK Supreme Court.

A number of these powers were not immediate and will have to await introduction in 2015 onwards. In order to gain the SNP government's consent for the Act to be enforced in Scotland, the Westminster Coalition Government had dropped plans to return certain powers to Westminster. They also agreed to review the role of the UK Supreme Court in Scottish criminal cases, and accepted that new borrowing limits would be reviewed regularly. Also, on fiscal issues they stated that they would now consult on whether the Scottish government should be able to issue its own money bonds.

and Conservative (Unionist) parties who supported political devolution. They were, however, kept in check by a far more powerful unionist tendency in their respective parties that endured in Labour's case into the late 1970s and in the Conservatives into the late 1990s. The rise of the SNP and Plaid Cymru as a political threat to Labour, in particular, had lead to the establishment of a Royal Commission under Lord Kilbrandon by Harold Wilson's Government in the late 1960s. The Kilbrandon Commission was set up to consider all aspects of devolution across Great Britain. It was to the Conservative Government of Edward Heath the recommendations of the Kilbrandon Commission were given in 1973. This led in turn to the failed devolution referendum of 1 March 1979. Confusingly, the referendum was actually won but failed to reach a vital 40 per cent threshold of the total Scottish population needed to vote in favour of a Scottish Parliament. In the event only 36 per cent of the total Scottish electorate had voted 'yes'. During this period some interesting questions were raised in respect of Scottish devolution that were never effectively answered until over three decades later (see Box 12.1).

The 1980s and 1990s saw a succession of unionist Thatcherite Scottish Secretaries who proved both unpopular and a boom for Scottish nationalism. The introduction of the hugely controversial and unpopular community charge (poll tax) in Scotland, a year before it occurred in England and Wales, also fuelled the feeling that the nation had become something of a testing ground for Thatcherism. Attempts by the last Conservative Scottish Secretary in the

1990s, Michael Forsyth, to increase and improve administrative devolution, while also giving a greater role to Westminster's Scottish Committees, did little to reduce the public and political mood for increased political devolution. From the mid-1980s onwards opinion poll after poll indicated that the Scottish population wanted a Scottish parliament, and as time went on, this idea became more rather than less popular.

In March 1989 the Scottish Labour and Liberal Democrat parties, together with a number of minor parties, trade unions, the churches and civil organisations formed the Scottish Constitutional Convention. As the body was only concerned with political devolution rather than independence, the SNP refused to join it. John Smith, George Robertson and Donald Dewar for the Labour Party and David Steel and Jim Wallace for the Scottish Liberal Democrats were the key political figures behind the move towards a Scottish parliament. The Convention published its report setting out the ground for a proportionally elected primary law making and tax raising Scottish parliament in November 1995 entitled *Scotland's Parliament, Scotland's Right*. With the Conservatives and Unionists totally removed from Scottish Westminster politics after the 1997 General Election, a referendum was held in September, which saw a massive majority in favour of a Scottish parliament (of those who voted 74.3 per cent were for the parliament and 60.2 per cent supported tax-raising powers). The combined anti-devolutionist forces of both Scottish Labour and Conservative MPs present in 1979 had now gone, which was reflected in the size of the 'yes' vote.

The first Scottish elections were on 6 May 1999 and saw a turnout of 58 per cent. Some 73 Members of the Scottish Parliament (MSPs) were elected by the traditional Westminster-style, first-past-the-post system and an additional 56 MSPs elected through AMS (the proportional electoral Additional Member System) in eight Scottish regions. The results were significant because:

- these were the first elections to a Scottish parliament in three centuries;

- no one party gained a majority, which was not unexpected from the new proportional election; therefore, it was though that a coalition government would always operate in future;

- it saw the UK's first Green Party parliamentarian, on the regional list for the Lothians;

- the first Scottish Socialist Party member was also elected – Tommy Sheridan – in the Glasgow region;

- the rebel Labour MP Denis Canavan was elected in Falkirk West. He had been deselected by his own party, then stood against them and won. His success would encourage other Labour members not selected to do the same, not only in Scotland but also in Wales and London.

After the election was held, the process of forming the first Scottish government began. The government in Scotland was initially referred to as 'The Scottish Executive' but later became the 'Scottish government' under section 12(1) of the Scotland Act 2012. It is legally separate from the legislature and similar to the position in the Westminster Parliament. For the first three terms no one political party gained an overall majority at a Scottish parliamentary election (see Table 12.2). In fact, the electoral system had been designed with this in mind, with those in the Scottish Constitutional Convention wary of using the same electoral system that had allowed the Labour Party to dominate Scottish elections since the 1950s. It was envisaged, therefore, that coalition governments would be the future of Scottish politics, thus forcing a moderation of any one political party's ambitions and ensuring more consensus politics. It was not a surprise to political commentators, therefore, that after the 1999 and 2003 Scottish elections it was a Labour–Liberal Democrat coalition which formed and signed two four-year cooperation agreements. The first was called *Partnership for Scotland*, followed by the unimaginatively titled *A Partnership for a Better Scotland* in August 2003.

Labour's Donald Dewar became the first politician to take the title of First Minister in Scotland and the Scottish Liberal Democrats' Jim Wallace, was his Deputy. Dewar, who was seen as one of the 'fathers of Scottish devolution' died suddenly of a brain haemorrhage on 11 October 2000.

He was replaced by Henry McLeish in April 2001. McLeish, however, resigned on 8 November 2001 due to the so-called 'Officegate' expenses row, which centred on the sub-letting of his constituency office in Glenrothes. He, in turn was replaced by the Motherwell and Wishaw Member of the Scottish Parliament (MSP), Jack McConnell. For the next five and half years the Scottish coalition executive worked effectively together through a series of policy and legislative changes which saw Scotland pursing significantly different policies to those in England. The problems over the introduction of university tuition fees, with both sides taking differing views (Labour for them, Scottish Liberal Democrats against) led to an independent commission being established that determined in favour of university tuition fees not being introduced. The new Parliament building at Holyrood also became something of a scandal, costing ten times its original estimate. Both the architect Enric Miralles and the First Minister Donald Dewar who had been responsible for the original proposals, however, were dead by the time Lord Fraser's inquiry into the building had been undertaken. This meant the key decision makers escaped any direct accountability.

From the outset the Scottish Parliament had been established with the power to create its own (primary) laws. This meant that laws could be made in three different ways via Executive Bills, Committee Bills and MSP's Bills. The vast majority of legislation, as with the Westminster Parliament, is through Executive Bills. These Acts have helped provide Scotland with laws as diverse as those giving free long-term care for the elderly to those abolishing fox hunting and establishing STV as a method of election for Scottish local government.

The 2003 Scottish General Election had been significant for continuing the Lab–Lib coalition government and widening the number of political parties present in the Parliament to six, but the 2007 election saw an end to this, and the 2011 election would later consolidate this change. In the 2007 election the SNP gained 20 more seats. Its leader,

Table 12.2 Scottish General Election parliamentary elections results, 1999–2011: constituency and regional list lists

Party	1999	2003	2007	2011
Labour	56	50	48	37
Scottish National Party	35	27	47	69
Conservative & Unionist	18	18	17	15
Scottish Liberal Democrat	17	17	16	5
Scottish Green Party	1	7	2	2
Scottish Socialists	1	6	0	0
Independents	1	3	1	1
Others	0	1	0	0

Source: Deacon 2012

Alex Salmond, returned to the Parliament after a four-year gap during which he had been leading his party at Westminster. The SNPs' gains had been at the expense of the other political parties, in particular the minority parties who had lost 12 of their 14 MSPs. Just as after the previous two Scottish elections, the largest minority party needed a coalition partner. The Conservatives and the Labour Party, however, would not consider going into coalition with the SNP. The Scottish Liberal Democrats also refused to join them in coalition, because of their policy of not supporting a pro-independence party. The SNP, therefore, formed a minority government with Scottish Green Party support, but still 16 seats short of a majority. For the next four years the SNP minority government struggled on in trying to fulfil its own agenda, often only after lengthy negotiations with the opposition parties. In August 2009 the SNP Justice Secretary, Kenny MacAskill, freed the terminally ill Lockerbie bomber, Abdelbasset Ali al-Megrahi, on compassionate grounds. This caused a storm of protest across the political spectrum but in particular in the United States, from President Obama downwards. On 22 September 2009 the SNP was overwhelming defeated in a vote on its handling of Ali al-Megrahi's release. Although the SNP continued as a minority government, it was felt that Scotland's international standing had been damaged and that the lessons of the Ali al-Megrahi affair would have to be looked at carefully if Scotland was ever itself to become an independent sovereign nation. It would be nearly three more years before Megrahi died, during which the SNP was constantly criticised nationally and internationally over this action.

In the Westminster General Election of 2010, although the SNP now came second in turns of the popular vote, it was the Scottish Liberal Democrats who gained 11 seats to the SNP's 6. Labour once again remained the dominant political power in the Westminster election with some 41 seats (70 per cent). Despite the fact that in Scotland they won just one seat, in England, however, it was the Conservatives that won the majority of seats. The electoral arithmetic meant that they together with the Liberal Democrats formed the new Westminster Coalition. As the Conservatives were the minority Westminster party in Scotland, it would fall to the Scottish Liberal Democrats to fill the Cabinet posts from Scottish MPs. Amongst these Danny Alexander briefly became the first Liberal Secretary of State for Scotland since 1932. Because of a Westminster Cabinet resignation, Alexander then became Chief Secretary to the Treasury with Michael Moore becoming the new Scottish Secretary. Moore then set about trying to establish a Westminster Coalition political agenda for Scotland while also being squeezed between the increasingly acrimonious relationship between the SNP and Westminster Coalition governments' differing political agendas for Scotland's future.

While the 2010 Westminster elections had been good for the Scottish Liberal Democrats the 2011 Scottish parliamentary elections were the exact opposite (see Table 12.2). The 2007 election had squeezed the minor parties in Scottish politics in favour of the SNP; now it would the three main British parties who were squeezed electorally. The Westminster Coalition government and its agenda of spending cuts was going down badly in Scotland. The SNPs own spending plans had been much reduced by cuts to the Scottish block grant, and in these elections the SNP made sure that the electorate was aware of that fact. In the event the SNP stormed ahead at the expense of the Conservatives, Labour and especially the Scottish Liberal Democrats. The latter were reduced to a rump of just five MSPs from their previous 17 seats. The SNP government under Salmond's leadership gained 23 seats to stand on 69 seats and gained over half the Scottish parliamentary seats in the process (54 per cent). Scotland now had the first majority government in any of the devolved nations. This was with a proportional electoral system that was designed to ensure that a party with less than 50 per cent of the vote would not gain the majority of the seats. The SNP had won around 45 per cent of the vote. Although within a year and a half the SNP would lose three MSPs over a suspension and resignations, they were still able retain to majority government by two MSPs. While Scottish Labour, Conservative and Liberal Democrat leaders tendered their resignations in 2011, Salmond set forward on his second term of government with the satisfaction that the electorate had given his party a majority to pursue their dream of an independent Scotland.

From the outset the centrepiece of the SNP government's programme has been its commitment to having a referendum on independence, its so-called 'National Conversation' (see Box 12.2). There was, however, a Commission being undertaken by Sir Kenneth Calman, Chancellor of the University of Glasgow (The Commission on Scottish Devolution). While the Commission and its eventual recommendations were endorsed by both Labour and Coalition governments at Westminster, the SNP government in Holyrood was much more lukewarm on them, demanding instead full fiscal autonomy.

When the Calman Commission had reported back in June 2009, it indicated that after ten years, Scottish devolution could be declared to be a 'success'. Calman, however, also recommended that the Parliament should further evolve and that Holyrood should take charge over much more of its own revenue raising. In future half the income tax raised in Scotland as well as stamp duty, landfill tax and air passenger duty should be collected by the Scottish government and form a third of its budget. The Calman Commission also said the Scottish Parliament should control other areas such as national speed limits, drink-driving laws and airguns legislation.

The SNP Government criticised Calman for not giving the Scottish Parliament full fiscal powers, while the other parties criticised the SNP in turn for being selective in the parts of Calman they pushed to be implemented immediately. When the Coalition Government at Westminster came into power in 2010, they were quick to act on Calman and a new Scotland Bill was then scrutinised by both the Scottish and Westminster Parliaments. The bill, however, could not come into law until the SNP Government endorsed it. Despite the fact that the Westminster Government had refused a number of SNP demands, including the devolution of corporation tax, the Scottish Secretary Michael Moore was able to get the bill accepted by the SNP with some minor modifications

(see Box 12.1), to become the Scotland Act 2012. If all proceeds according to plan and Scotland does not vote for independence in 2014, the changes brought about by the Act will result in the Scottish government raising around 35 per cent of its own expenditure with the rest coming from a Westminster block grant. While this was occurring, the Scottish and Westminster governments were negotiating over the terms of an independence referendum (Box 12.2).

The large-scale Scottish Government budget cuts required as part of the Westminster Coalition Government's attempts to reduce the UK budget deficit had already strained relations with the SNP and Coalition Government. This was despite David Cameron's commitment to a 'respect agenda' in Westminster's devolved government relations when coming into power in 2010. Regardless of these cuts, it is Scottish

Box 12.2

Scottish influence on UK politics – the West Lothian Question

From the introduction of the *Authorised King James's Version of the Bible* (1611), the standard text for the Church of England for more than 250 years, to the succession of Scottish Prime Ministers such as Sir Henry Campbell Bannerman, Ramsay MacDonald, Andrew Bonar Law, Sir Alex Douglas Home, and Gordon Brown, Scottish influence on British politics has been substantial. There have been an even greater number of Scottish Cabinet ministers at Westminster and leaders of other British political parties such as the Liberals/Liberal Democrats (four of their seven postwar leaders and two of their four Westminster Coalition Cabinet members came from Scottish seats).

Yet the Scottish influence over British politics hasn't always been welcomed. In 1978 the anti-devolutionist Scottish Labour MP Tam Dalyell introduced what became known as *The West Lothian Question*. This concerned what right he had to vote on laws related to England and Wales, when English and Welsh MPs could not vote on issues related to 'West Lothian'. This was because they are devolved from the Westminster Parliament to the Scottish Parliament. This issue has remained contentious to this day. It even concerned Gordon Brown the former Prime Minister, and the Chancellor Alastair Darling whose constituencies are in Scotland. Later on it also impacted on the Liberal Democrats who had two Cabinet members

with Scottish seats (Danny Alexander and Michael Moore). Their votes have been used on the divisive issue of tuition fees for English students on a number of occasions by all of the main Westminster parties. This has been done even though those Scottish MPs voting for these fees are unable to vote on the same issue in Scotland, which itself, does not levy fees. In January 2004 the Labour Government only won a vote on top-up fees for England by the use of its Scottish MPs:

In 2005 the number of Scottish MPs at Westminster was reduced from 72 to 57, as part of the attempts to address the situation. This, however, did not end the problem, but only alleviated it. None of the three main political parties would end the right of Scottish MPs to vote on English-only bills. The Coalition Government, however, set up a West Lothian Commission in January 2012 under Sir William McKay in order to consider how the House of Commons might deal with legislation which affects only part of the United Kingdom, following the devolution of certain legislative powers to the Scottish Parliament, the Northern Ireland Assembly and the National Assembly for Wales.

Whether McKay and his five other commissioners could end a problem that has now stretched over five decades, or whether the break-up of the UK itself may end the problem, remains to be seen.

independence, however, which set to dominate the devolved political agenda in Scotland until 2015 as the politicians divide into the 'yes' and 'no' camps.

Wales

Prior to the Acts of Union between 1536–42 under Henry VIII Wales was not one nation but a patchwork quilt of crown lands and Marcher lordships. Therefore, until Welsh nationalism re-emerged in the latter half of the nineteenth century, Wales had always been integrated closely into England. To all intents and purposes Wales ceased to be a nation and instead became a series of counties almost fully assimilated into England. During the late nineteenth century the Liberal Prime Minister William Gladstone was the first British leader to accept that Wales was a nation distinct from England. Liberal MPs such as Henry Richard, Tom Ellis and David Lloyd George pushed forward Welsh nationalism and, consequently, the Liberal governments between 1905 and 1916 saw the establishment of many of the trappings of nationhood including a National Library, National Museum and the establishment of Welsh regiments and symbolism in the army.

Despite the founding of Plaid Cymru (Party of Wales) in 1925, Welsh nationalism at a parliamentary level remained mainly in the Welsh elements of the Liberal or Liberal National Party. The Labour Party, which under the Merthyr Tydfil MP, Keir Hardie (1900–16), had been pro-devolution after the First World War, turned almost wholly against it. Those few Labour MPs who were pro-devolution did so against a rising tide of unionism. Nevertheless, despite this strong unionist stance, the Llanelli MP Jim Griffith, the deputy leader of the Labour Party, who was pro-devolution, was able to persuade Harold Wilson and the wider Labour Party to establish both a Welsh Office and a Welsh Secretary in the Cabinet in 1964. This began the period of significant executive devolution in Wales.

The Conservatives in Wales always remained hostile to Welsh devolution, with no significant figure emerging as a pro-Welsh devolutionist during the twentieth century. Thus, with the vast majority of Welsh MPs being hostile or indifferent to Welsh devolution and the Welsh Liberals reduced to just one MP (Emlyn Hooson) by 1966, Welsh nationalism was only fully reignited when the Plaid Cymru President and their political hero, Gwynfor Evans, was elected to Carmarthen in 1966. From now on Plaid Cymru was seen as a direct threat to the Labour Party in Wales, who soon realised that it had to do something to combat the appeal of the rising nationalist tide. As we noted earlier, this resulted in the establishment of the Kilbrandon Commission in 1968 and the subsequent failure of the St David's Day devolution referendum in 1979. The referendum had only occurred in the first place because of the minority Labour government's reliance on Welsh Liberal and Plaid Cymru MPs to stay in power.

A few months after the 1979 referendum result, a General Election saw Margaret Thatcher's Conservative government elected. It then controlled politics in Wales from London for the next 18 years. Although they always remained opposed to political devolution, the various Conservative Welsh secretaries enhanced administrative devolution. This included establishing the use of the Barnett formula (Box 12.3) which determined government funding for Wales, the extension of administrative devolved powers in

Box 12.3

Barnett formula

The Barnett formula was brought in as a funding mechanism for the devolved administrations prior to their expected arrival in 1979. The funding formula from the Westminster government to the proposed devolved bodies was established by Joel Barnett, then the Labour Chief Secretary to the Treasury. It was based loosely on the population sizes of Scotland, Wales and England (10:5:85). The Barnett formula remains controversial, with politicians in England claiming it is over-generous, whereas those in Scotland and Wales claim that it actually reduces the amount provided for them as time goes on, the 'Barnett Squeeze'. Despite these claims, the Barnett formula has only undergone slight alterations since it was introduced in 1979, but there is a consensus that this central funding needs to be reformed for the devolved nations. The Calman Commission in Scotland and the Silk Commission in Wales have both produced extensive recommendations on increasing their respective nations' fiscal autonomy. This will in turn diminish or even eventually end the need for the existence of the Barnett formula. Both Scotland and Wales's legislatures have also been given the power to borrow money when tax-raising powers have been devolved to them. This is in addition to the Barnett formula.

Wales and the reforming of Welsh local government into a system of 22 unitary authorities. Only Nicholas Edwards (1979–87), the first of the Thatcher–Major period Welsh Secretaries, however, was actually a Welsh MP. During the last ten years of Conservative rule in Wales, therefore, the succession of Welsh Secretaries with English constituencies, including Peter Walker, John Redwood and William Hague, fuelled resentment of a new era of English **colonialism** by those 'unaccountable quasi-colonial governors' who ruled via a series of unelected **quangos**. During this period the Welsh Labour Party continued to win the majority of Welsh seats, but remain powerless against their Conservative foes. This was enough to persuade many within the Labour Party to support devolution and, accordingly, by the time of the General Election of 1997, the party had become committed to introducing an elected Welsh Assembly in its first term.

When the Labour Party included an element of proportional representation in its plans for the Welsh Assembly (the Additional Member System), it was enough to persuade Plaid Cymru and the Welsh Liberal Democrats to endorse their plans in the referendum. With the Conservatives routed in the 1997 General Election, losing all of their Welsh seats, and the Labour anti-devolution MPs silenced, there was no effective opposition to the Yes campaign. This helped them win a narrow victory, by just 6,721 votes (0.3 per cent of the total vote). Wales was then given a National Assembly of some 60 elected members (40 constituency members and 20 proportional members – list members). This Assembly, unlike that in Scotland and Northern Ireland, would only have the power to amend secondary legislation, rather than to originate its own primary legislation.

The former Labour leader, Ron Davies, who led the Yes campaign did not become the First Secretary (changed in 2001 to First Minister) as envisaged. Davies had been forced to resign after a personal scandal and a new leader was needed. Thus, when the dust settled after the 1999 Welsh Assembly elections, it was Alun Michael, Ron Davies' replacement as Welsh Secretary and Tony Blair's loyal right-hand man in Wales who became the First Secretary. He had won a controversial Labour Party election competition against Rhodri Morgan to become Davies' replacement. Michael led a minority government in the Welsh Assembly

and had initially refused to go into coalition with the Welsh Liberal Democrats, preferring to govern alone. As his party lacked a majority by three seats, it was only a matter of time before they were defeated. This came over a vote of no confidence concerning his ability to gain matched-funding from the Westminster government's Treasury to secure European Objective One funding to Wales. Gordon Brown, then Chancellor, did not give his support in time and Michael resigned. He was replaced by Rhodri Morgan in an unelected leadership contest. Morgan then gained the required finance from the Treasury and formed a coalition government with the Welsh Liberal Democrats led by Michael German (later Lord German). This was the Welsh Liberals' first taste of governing political power since 1945.

The Lab–Lib Welsh Assembly coalition government (2000–2003) was significant mainly for introducing a limitation on top-up fees for students and free entry to museums in Wales that began to distinguish Welsh government policy from that of England's. The Welsh coalition government also established a number of commissions to examine controversial aspects of Welsh Assembly coalition policy. The Rees Commission, for instance, provided a compromise solution to student tuition fees, and the Sunderland Commission looked at the future of Welsh local government. It was the Richard Commission (chaired by the Labour peer Lord Richards) which was established to examine the Assembly's powers and the adequacy of its electoral systems.

The 2003 Welsh Assembly elections had seen Labour gain exactly half of the Assembly seats with the opposition gaining the other half. Lord Dafydd Elis Thomas immediately accepted the Presiding Officer's post once more. He had been the Presiding Officer (the Assembly's equivalent of the House of Commons Speaker) in the 1999–2003 Assembly. As the Presiding Officer can only vote in the Assembly's plenary sessions as a casting vote in the event of a tie, Thomas's decision meant that Labour now had an effective majority of one. They did not need to form a coalition. Rhodri Morgan was once more elected as First Minister and the Assembly set out to follow a Labour policy agenda, which among other things, included the abolition of prescription fees in Wales and the introduction of a 5p charge on plastic shopping bags.

When the Richard Commission reported back in 2004, it was after the Welsh Lab–Lib coalition government had come to an end. They recommended that the Assembly be given full law-making powers and that it increase the number of Assembly Members to 80, to be elected by STV. Richard also recommended that the Welsh Assembly be formally divided on a parliamentary legislature and executive basis: the so-called 'separation of powers' familiar in most legislatures. While the Labour Party was happy to accept the last recommendation, it did not want to accept

Table 12.3 Welsh Assembly election results, 1999–2011: constituency and regional list lists

Year	1999	2003	2007	2011
Labour	28	30	26	30
Plaid Cymru	17	12	15	11
Conservatives	9	11	12	14
Welsh Liberal Democrats	6	6	6	5
Independents/others	0	1	1	0

the first two. Accordingly, the electoral arrangements were ignored and the law-making powers were reduced to a complicated, staged implementation of primary powers which still had to go through Westminster before the legislative competence orders (LCOs) came into place. The LCO process gave the Westminster government the right to determine which Welsh primary legislation was selected and how long it would take to go through Westminster. In the event the LCO process proved to be ineffective, with even non-controversial laws taking years to pass through the process and anything even slightly controversial not even getting past the starting block. The failure of the LCO process, however, did have one very important side effect. It convinced all of the political parties' Welsh Assembly representatives that, for primary law making to be effective, it needed to be undertaken within Wales. Thus, when the March 2011 primary power referendum took place in Wales, all of the Welsh Assembly members supported the Yes campaign, which won by a majority of almost two to one.

At the start of 2005, amid much controversy about ever-rising costs – from £12 million to £24 million – the Assembly moved into a purpose-built legislative chamber on Cardiff Bay's waterfront. Then, in May, the Labour Assembly Member, Peter Law, contested his own Blaenau Gwent seat against the official Labour 'all-women shortlist' candidate. Law won the seat but in the process was expelled from the Labour Party. The Labour Party was now in a minority in the Assembly but they limped on in government for the next two years suffering a number of defeats and having to come to 'arrangements' with the other political parties in order to get their policies and budget through. This provided an important reminder to the Labour Party of the instability of one-party minority government.

The 2007 Assembly elections, now entitled the 'Welsh General Election', once again saw no one party gain a majority, with Labour remaining the largest party, but with five seats short of a majority. It was then a whole month before the parties examined fully the various possible combinations possible and the result was somewhat of a surprise for everyone including the political parties themselves. Labour joined together with its bitter political foe, Plaid Cymru, in what was termed the Red–Green Alliance (Red the colour of Labour and Green that of Plaid Cymru) under the agreed policy for government the *One Wales Agreement*. Rhodri Morgan once more became the First Minister and Plaid Cymru's leader, Ieuen Wyn Jones, the Deputy Minister. On 1 December 2009 Morgan was replaced by Carwyn Jones (see Profile), the Counsel General for Wales, in a three-cornered Labour leadership election. Morgan left office at the age of 70 with a popularity rating of 65 per cent (who thought he was doing a good job). Not only was Morgan's popularity much higher than that of his political opponents in Wales, it was almost unprecedented in British politics for a politician to leave office while still being so popular.

At the centre of the Red–Green Alliance agreement between the parties was the establishment of another commission – the All Wales Convention. This was to examine how the proposed referendum in Wales on obtaining full primary law making would be best won. The Commission was chaired by the former British Ambassador to the United Nations, Sir Emyr Jones Parry. Although the All Wales Convention reported back in November 2009, it would be another 16 months before the actual referendum was held. The Welsh Assembly unanimously passed the required trigger vote in February 2010, but the May 2010 British General Election and the arrival of a new coalition Conservative Welsh Secretary, Cheryl Gillan, delayed actual setting of the referendum date. Partly to save money and partly to enhance turnout for the British AV (alternative vote) referendum it was decided to hold both referendums on the same day, in March 2011. The desire for full law-making powers in Wales has risen over the last quarter of the 2000s (see Table 12.4). The fact that all of the main Welsh political parties now also supported primary law-making powers for Wales helped produce a decisive victory for the Yes campaign and put Wales on a near par with Scotland and Northern Ireland for its primary law-making powers.

Initially, the Labour government in Westminster under Tony Blair had tried to control the policy outputs of the Welsh Assembly. Over time, however, this wish to control had diminished and Wales was allowed to very much go its own way. Here Labour worked with both the Welsh Liberal Democrats and later Plaid Cymru to pursue agreed policy agendas in a way that was still alien to the Labour governments of Westminster. The ten years of Welsh devolution had also shown that there was a demand from within the Welsh Assembly and across the Welsh public for greater

Table 12.4 The desire to see primary law-making powers for Wales

Institution (figures are percentages)	2007	2008	2009	2011*
In favour of turning assembly into full law-making parliament	47	49	52	63.5
Against turning assembly into full law-making parliament	44	42	39	36.5
Don't know	9	9	9	–

* March 2011 Referendum result on law-making powers.

Source: Based on data from BBC Wales/ICM polls, June 2007, February 2008, February 2009

devolution. This, however, had been resisted and limited by the more unionist elements within the Welsh Labour Party rather than the British Labour Party, in the ways it had previously done. The Welsh Labour MPs, conscious of their loss of power and status, continued to resist further advances in devolution. Yet, the demand for increased powers remained solid in Wales and it is therefore likely that the Welsh Assembly will develop into a parliament similar to the Scottish model. By 2009 opinion polls were already indicating that the Welsh electorate now thought that the Welsh Assembly government had the greatest influence on their lives, itself an indication of just how much it had embedded itself into Welsh life. This didn't mean, however, that it should be the case. On the question of which elected body should have the most power, an ICM poll carried out in March 2012 by *The Commission on Devolution in Wales* indicated that the majority of the Welsh population still believed it should be the Westminster government (54 per cent) with only 31 per cent stating it should be the Welsh government.

PROFILE

Carywn Jones (1967–)

Held a number of Welsh government ministerial posts until becoming Welsh Labour leader and First Minister in 2009. Jones is a fluent Welsh speaker who was born in Swansea and was educated as a barrister, It was at Aberystwyth University that he joined the Labour Party, during the 1984 Miners Strike. Jones was elected to Bridgend County Borough Council in 1995 and became the Assembly Member there in 1999. Jones subsequently proved himself as one of the loyal Labour stalwarts during the minority Welsh Labour government 2005–7 and the coalition government between Labour and Plaid Cymru 2007–11.

In 2009, following the resignation of Rhodri Morgan, Jones won the subsequent Labour leadership election in the first round with 52 per cent of the vote over his two opponents. Jones subsequently led his party in the 2011 Welsh Assembly elections where they gained exactly half of the seats and then formed a minority government. After the Coalition Government's win in Westminster and the problems associated with the post-2008 economic crisis, relations between Cardiff and London became a lot more tempestuous than under his predecessor Rhodri Morgan.

The relationship between the Welsh and Coalition governments took a rapid downturn after the 2010 General Election. Wales became the only part of the United Kingdom still governed by the Labour Party. In the 2011 elections the party once more gained exactly half of the vote they had in 2003 and formed a minority government under Carwyn Jones. These elections also saw a significant fall in support for the Welsh Liberal Democrats and Plaid Cymru and a rise in support for the Conservatives, who now became the official opposition in Wales. Both Westminster and Cardiff became openly critical of each other's policies. Relations reached their most hostile point in the summer of 2012 when the Welsh Education Secretary ordered the re-grading of the English GCSE papers in Wales, while his counterpart in Whitehall – Education Secretary, Michael Gove – did not. This caused a national outcry, as did Gove's unilateral declaration to scrap the GCSE without first consulting the Welsh or Northern Ireland Education Ministers. Both nations also use the same GCSE qualification. The political tensions that had remained hidden or suppressed during the period when Labour were in control in both London and Cardiff have now come very much into the open.

As Labour had been re-elected to be the Welsh government in 2011, it was their legislative agenda that led the new primary powers agenda. The first law to go through the Welsh Assembly was on 3 July 2012, entitled the Local Government Byelaws (Wales) Act. Interference from Westminster did not stop, however, as almost straightaway the UK Attorney General asked the Supreme Court to decide whether parts of the bill were within the Assembly's powers to grant. Although the Attorney General also has this power for Scotland and Northern Ireland, it had never been enacted with respect to their legislative processes. This direct interference in a devolved government's primary legislative process was therefore unprecedented, something that became even more controversial when there were moves to do the same to the second piece of primary legislation on the Welsh language. In the event, because of the legal challenge, the second piece of legislation on the Welsh language confusingly ended up becoming the first piece of Welsh legislation to receive royal assent in November 2012.

Devolution and the European Union (EU)

Jennifer Todd's models of devolution, cited earlier in this chapter, sees devolution in the UK in part as a need to adapt to the EU's desire of 'European regionalism'. In turn, opinion polls across the United Kingdom have sometimes stated

Box 12.4

Independence

There are no political parties advocating independence for Northern Ireland, whereas there are those who advocate it for Wales, Scotland and even England. In a YouGov/ITV Wales Poll in February 2012 only 10 per cent of those polled supported independence in Wales. In similar polls this figure had stood at between 20 and 13 per cent in 1997, 2001, 2003 and 2009. Even in Plaid Cymru opinion is split as to whether the party should pursue independence or not. This is not the case in Scotland, however. Here the SNP, as the government, have succeeded in bringing forward a referendum on the question of independence for Scotland for the autumn of 2014. All of the main UK parties reject full independence for Scotland. While Labour and the Conservatives would like to see enhanced powers and fiscal responsibilities for the Scottish Parliament, the Liberal Democrats would like to see it with a central role in a federal parliament. In October 2012 the Sir Menzies Campbell (the former Liberal Democrat leader) Commission published *Federalism: the best future for Scotland*. It proposed 'a strong Scotland within the United Kingdom' with control over most domestic policy issues. Only the Liberal Democrats, however, see federalism as a viable alternative to independence. The other political parties see it as a choice between enhanced devolution or independence. As part of the increased devolution there have been two main further choices on offer:

1 'Devo max' which would put the Scottish Parliament in full control of income tax, corporation tax, most welfare spending and take a geographical share of oil revenues;

2 'Devo plus' which would leave pensions, VAT and national insurance in the hands of the Westminster government but the Scottish Parliament in charge of all other taxes.

In October 2012 an agreement was made between the Westminster and Scottish governments, which paved the way for a referendum on Scottish independence in the autumn of 2014. Although the October and December 2012 opinion polls in Scotland indicated that only around 30 per cent of voters supported independence, there was still a further two years of campaigning to go on both sides. There were also a number of other considerations to take into account for any UK nation to become independent. These are some of the main ones:

1 *What would the breakaway countries put in their new constitutions?* These would state the rights and obligations of the citizens of the newly independent country. The UK currently doesn't have a codified constitution, but any newly independent country would certainly need one.

2 *Who would be the head of state?* Would it remain the Queen or would they become a republic? Plaid Cymru remains a republican party, while the SNP is monarchist.

3 *Which currency would they use?* An independent country joining the European Union would almost certainly have to join the euro, although the SNP wishes to retain the use of sterling.

4 *Setting up new administration and legal systems.* Taxes would now all be collected within the independent country and the majority of laws would also be made there. This would mean creating a full administrative and legal infrastructure.

5 *Rebalancing the remaining countries in the union.* Those countries that remain in the union may feel dominated by England, and may need to set up a federal system of government in order to enable the union to survive.

6 *TV and radio.* The independent nation would have to set up its own broadcasters. Would they still rely on a TV licence or would they be paid for by other means?

7 *Borders controls would have to be introduced.* The newly independent country would be obliged to join the European free travel area, which Britain has opted out of.

8 *The national flag.* The Union Jack would go and the new national flag would have to fly over all public buildings.

9 *What would the remaining countries be called?* They could no longer be called 'Great Britain'.

10 *Defence.* Would the independent countries create their own armies, air forces and navies and allow the British army to remain there? Plaid Cymru remains pacifist, while the SNP now favours joining NATO.

11 *Nuclear deterrent.* Would the newly independent country still rely on the British nuclear deterrent? Both the SNP and Plaid Cymru are opposed to the use of nuclear weapons.

Table 12.5 Who has the most influence on Wales?

Institution	1999	2003	2009
Assembly government	26	22.4	40
UK government	24.5	57.9	29.2
Local councils	7	15	15.8
European Union	36.5	4.7	8
Don't know	6	0	7

Sources: Based on data from 1999 poll The Economist Newspaper Limited, London (6 November 1999); 2003 poll Richard Commission; 2009 poll, BBC Wales/ICM poll (24 February 2009)

that the EU is the most important influential political body on their lives (see Table 12.5). The level of trust in the EU across the UK has also increased over time. The Eurobarometer, which judges public opinion across the EU, has indicated that the awareness of and interest in the EU amongst the devolved nations is considerably higher than the UK average (see Table 12.6).

Prior to political devolution to the non-English nations in the United Kingdom, there were three territorial departments (Northern Ireland, Scottish and Welsh Offices) with connections to the European Commission. This was mainly through four different processes:

1 The direct links and setting-up of administrative processes required by the process of administering the Common Agricultural Policy and the European structural funds (European Social Fund and European Regional Development Funds);

2 The establishment of, or support for, territorial offices in Brussels, such as the Wales Information Centre. These acted as information-gathering and lobbying organisations;

3 The secondment of territorial departments' civil servants to the European Commission and UKREP (the United Kingdom's Embassy to the European Commission);

4 The territorial departments' ministers attending Council of Ministers meetings and their inclusion in the Westminster government's Cabinet European Committee.

The EU referred to the territorial departments, when they existed and later on to the English Regional Assemblies as 'subnational' authorities (SNAs). As those SNAs that covered the territorial departments gained political devolution, the Westminster government committed itself to include them in the EU policy process. Although the UK government was keen to retain a single UK position on all EU issues, it did allow the non-English devolved bodies considerable access to the UK's EU policy-making mechanisms. It also allowed Scotland and Northern Ireland primary legislative competence over many of those areas of responsibility that had been devolved and which were affected by EU policy. Wales, lacking the primary legislative powers, did not gain this same responsibility until 2011.

The relationship between the three devolved bodies and the Westminster government was developed through an inter-administration memorandum of understanding (MoU) in 2001 between the Office of the Deputy Prime Minister, then John Prescott, and the three devolved bodies. The MoU laid down a concordat for coordinating EU policy across the United Kingdom. In essence, the relationship meant that the Westminster government allowed the devolved bodies full integration into the process, provided that the devolved bodies respected the confidentiality of the process and kept any discussions concerning this EU policy process within the designated processes. It took some while for the Whitehall departments to fully remember that they had a duty to consult with the devolved bodies about relevant EU issues. Ultimately, as the UK lacks a constitutional court to resolve differences, the devolved SNAs can only have their own EU policy ambitions satisfied by successfully lobbying the Westminster government. As we saw earlier, this happened in Wales in 2000 when the Assembly successfully lobbied the Westminster government for additional resources to match fund EU structural funds. This was too late, however, to save the career of the Labour First Secretary, Alan Michael, who lost a vote of no confidence over this issue.

The main area of access to, and influence upon, EU policy making, therefore, remains the Westminster government. The SNAs also have a presence in the EU's Committee of the Regions, which represents all 74 of the EU's designated regions. This body acts as a mechanism for the regions

Table 12.6 Interest in EU affairs in the devolved nations/regions

	Wales %	Scotland %	Northern Ireland %	Greater London %	UK average %
Interested/fairly interested in European affairs	54.7	53.7	54.9	59.2	52.8
Voted in the last European elections	33.5	39.2	48.3	34.4	33.8
Believe that the EU should take a role in tackling:					
Climate change	86.1	81.2	83	79.3	80.4
Terrorism	92.2	86.3	86.3	83.4	85.6
Protecting human rights	88.4	88.6	85	86.7	84.8

Source: Based on data from Eurobarometer (2009) 'Attitudes towards the EU in the United Kingdom', FlashEurobarometer 207, July 2009

to influence overall policy. All of the politically devolved SNAs have offices in Brussels to serve as their eyes and ears with the Commission and Parliament. These offices, however, are not used on the whole to bypass the Westminster government but instead act as an additional resource and information gatherer for each body. Officially, therefore, the UK government regards them as part of the extended UKREP family rather than independent agencies, and they have consequently been given the requisite diplomatic status.

There are a number of different characteristics in the devolved bodies' and EU policy making. As the UK has what is known as 'asymmetrical' (unequal) devolution and varying national interests or attitudes to the EU, policy creation differs. Thus, while fishing is an important issue in Scottish–EU relations, it is of little importance in Wales. On the other hand, while the issue of ensuring that the European Parliament accepts Welsh as a fully recognised language is important to Wales–EU relations, even the Welsh acknowledge it is of no importance to the other devolved nations. At the same time the Westminster government will often pay more attention to the opinions of a nation it regards as having more expertise in a given area. Asymmetrical devolution also means that the regions of England do not have the same impact on the EU process as do the other three nations. Within the SNAs themselves the specific attention paid to EU issues also varies. For example, despite the fact that the Mayor of London is responsible for administering the European Structural Funds, there is no specific committee on the GLA to scrutinise European issues directly. Instead it goes through the other committees. The case is the same in the Northern Ireland Assembly. Scotland and Wales, however, have both committees and ministers responsible for EU policy making.

The devolved bodies have also been able to interpret EU policies according to their own criteria on occasions, setting the rules even if they have not been sanctioned by the European Commission. In February 2009, for instance, the Northern Ireland Assembly allocated farm modernisation payments on a 'first come, first served' basis, which saw thousands of farmers waiting outside the Department of Agriculture's offices for days. Although the European Commission stated the projects should only receive funding on 'objective criteria, rather than a first come, first served basis', the Northern Ireland Assembly still interpreted matters in its own way. This has caused considerable confusion, which might not have occurred had there existed a centralised UK policy. The issue of potential Scottish independence also poses a whole set of questions on the relationship between the UK and the EU, specifically if Scotland is not part of the EU and is an independent country in its own right (see Box 12.2).

England and its regions

England under the flag of St George is seen from the outside as being one homogenous nation. There are, however, strong regional identities, which politicians can only ignore at their peril. People in numerous English towns, cities and councils have their own distinct identities as strong as any national ones. Politicians have long been aware of this English regional distinctiveness that is particularly acute in counties such as Cornwall and Yorkshire and cities such as Liverpool, Manchester and London. Politicians, however, have been split as to how to deal with the distinctiveness. Over the past decade they have sought to tackle it by supporting it with regional political and administrative devolution. They have embraced local identity through the local government authority reorganisation with the re-establishment of old counties such as Rutland and old county borough councils such as Reading and Oxford. Unionists within both the Labour and Conservative parties, however, have sought to have minimum English regional identity and instead retain a strong unitary parliament in Westminster.

The recent origins of English devolution go back to a Speaker's conference in 1920 which decided the best solution to the problems of the devolutionary pressures in Ireland was 'Home Rule all round' for all of the British Isles nation states. The Labour and Conservative governments of that period did not agree with this notion, however. Therefore, devolution of administrative power in England took on a slow process. In the 1930s came the embryos of devolved government from the Special Areas Act 1934 that classified specific areas of the England according to their economic deprivation. Then during the Second World War England was divided into regional government areas for defence and other administrative purposes under regional governors. In the 1960s the Regional Economic Planning Councils and Regional Economic Planning Boards were set up under Harold Wilson's Labour Government. In the 1970s the Kilbrandon Commission had suggested regional elected authorities for England, but the measure did not go forward after the failure of Scottish and Welsh devolution in 1979. Then, under Margaret Thatcher's Conservative Government, Urban Development Corporations were set up in the 1980s. All devolved some elements of administrative power from Whitehall to the regions but the boundaries of the different organisations often did not coincide. At the same time the Thatcher government had become increasingly frustrated with the Labour-controlled metropolitan authorities and the Greater London Council (led by Ken Livingstone) acting as alternative centres of power and undermining their own government. They therefore abolished them all in 1986 leaving the large English metropolitan areas without an elected layer of government to control cross-borough activities.

In implementing the so-called 'European regionalism' model of devolution, it was the arrival of the EU's reforms to its Structural Funds (which provide economic assistance to specified regions) that required settled and administratively integrated regional offices. Therefore in 1994, under Prime Minister John Major, the 10 Government Offices of the Regions were established with the purpose of bringing together those elements of central government that needed to be integrated in order to make use of the EU's structural funds. When Labour came into power they turned these Government Offices into Regional Development Agencies that had Regional Chambers (RCs) above them. The RCs in the English regions were made up of appointed local government councillors, people from business and industry and other local notables. When they were established at the start of the century, it was thought that this would be a temporary measure and that in time they would replaced by democratically elected members. The thrust beyond English devolution in Tony Blair's Government came almost wholly from John Prescott, the Deputy Prime Minister. English devolution fell under his direct remit.

When Jack Straw had been the Labour Home Secretary in charge of the devolutionary process at the start of New Labour's 1997 term in office, he had defined what was called 'the triple lock' on the progress of English political devolution. This stated that if an English region wanted political devolution:

- it would have to petition to become a directly elected assembly;

- Parliament would have to legislate for this;

- the electorate in the region would have to approve these measures in a referendum.

With Wales, Scotland and then Northern Ireland gaining devolution, England became one of the few countries in Europe without a form of regional government. This changed marginally in 2000, when a referendum was passed which established an elected mayor for London and an elected London Regional Authority (see Box 12.5). This did not apply to the rest of England, however. Prescott was therefore keen to see this spread to other English regions even if it didn't comply with Jack Straw's triple lock. Opinion polls had indicated that there was a demand for English regional government. This was highest in the North-east and North-west. In 2002 Prescott brought out the Government White Paper, *Your Region, Your Choice: Revitalising the English Regions* which was followed by the White Paper, *Your Region, Your Say*. This set out the case for elected regional chambers in the English regions but not all at once. Instead,

it would be a step-by-step approach with the regions with the strongest identity going first. The Regional Assemblies (Preparations) Act 1993 went through Westminster and it was then planned to have all postal referendums in the North-west, North-east and Yorkshire and Humberside. Problems with postal voting during the European elections in June 2004 meant that the referendum on English devolution was scaled down to just one region – the North-west.

On the 4 November 2004 a referendum was held in the English North-east. The support for the concept of a regional assembly there failed by almost five to one. The two No campaigns which ran there had successfully defeated the Yes campaign on similar issues to those that had resulted in the Welsh people rejecting their Assembly referendum in 1979. These revolved around the perception that they didn't want any more politicians, the assembly wasn't powerful enough, their regional identity wasn't strong enough, most Labour and Conservative politicians remained against it, as did local government, which feared being scrapped or marginalised.

The negative vote in the North-east in effect killed off English devolution. The Regional Chambers were subsequently scrapped by the Labour Government soon after the negative North-east referendum result. Although the RDAs were initially kept by Labour, they were in turn scrapped in March 2012 by the Coalition Government, who regarded them as expensive bureaucratic bodies lacking any real sense of purpose. In their own defence, however, the RDAs pointed out that for each £1 invested in them they had generated a further £4.50 of economic development. Committed to a policy of 'localism' rather than regionalism, however, the Westminster Coalition Government replaced the RDAs with local enterprise partnerships (LEPs). These are voluntary partnerships of local government and business based on unitary authority or county level areas. There are currently some 39 of these LEPs replacing 8 of the RDAs. The ninth RDA, for London, was merged with the GLA. It is still too early to say whether or not the demise of the RDAs and the rise of the LEPs is beneficial for English economic development. A report by Lord Heseltine in October 2012 advocated that the government use the LEPs

Table 12.7 Public spending as share of GDP, UK countries and London, 2006

Nation/region	2005–6
United Kingdom	43.0%
England	40.9%
London	33.4%
Wales	62.4%
Scotland	54.9%
Northern Ireland	71.3%

Source: Office for National Statistics 2008

Box 12.5

Personality politics: the Mayor of London

There is one area of England that does have its own devolved government. That is London, with the Greater London Authority (GLA). The GLA is made up of a directly elected Mayor and a separately elected Authority. The Mayor of London controls a number of the capital's major public bodies. He sets the budget for the Metropolitan Police Service (MPS), Transport for London (TfL), the London Fire and Emergency Planning Authority (LEFPA), the London Development Agency (LDA) and the Greater London Authority (GLA). Over his four-year term the Mayor is responsible for around £60 billion of expenditure.

Even before its inception, the position of elected Mayor of the authority became one of personality politics. Ken Livingstone, the former Labour leader of the GLC saw himself as the rightful heir to the Mayor of the GLA. He was not selected by Labour in its controversial selection context, but stood and won as an Independent against the official Labour candidate. For the next eight years Livingstone ran London with both success and personal controversy, often in the process ignoring the role of the GLA as a scrutinising body. It was Livingstone who introduced the successful traffic congestion charge and also helped gain the Olympics for London in 2012.

Livingstone was defeated in 2008 by a Conservative politician as colourful in character as himself, Boris Johnson. The former MP for Henley on Thames and editor of *The Spectator* magazine, Johnson had established a reputation for political mishaps and general buffoonery. Nevertheless, this only added spice to his appeal as a candidate and he was duly elected by a majority of 139,772 votes. In 2012 Johnson or 'Boris' as he was now commonly known was re-elected with a decreased majority of 62,538.

The London-based media has engaged with the London Mayoral election to a degree unparalleled in British politics, outside the British General Elections. They have also helped promote 'Borismania', so that the Conservative Mayor has become the most popular Conservative both inside and outside of his party. Yet, critics point out that the media often ignores the 'true' facts about Boris's successes. The London Olympics, for instance, had been secured for London three years before Boris's arrival. The London Bike Hire Scheme (known as Boris bikes) was actually first proposed by the Liberal Democrat Authority Member, Lynne Featherstone, in 2001. Despite this opposition criticism, however, Boris remains a political figure who is able to project his voice far beyond London.

to stimulate the English economy at a local level and in the process transfer £49 billion of central government funding to a local level. The report was enthusiastically accepted by the government and indicated that there is still a desire to support a form of devolution in England, albeit at a sub-regional level.

Table 12.8 GDP per inhabitant UK countries and London, 2009

Nation/region	GDP per inhabitant, euros	GDP as a percentage of the EU average
United Kingdom	27,700	113.1
London	46,300	189.2
Wales	20,100	82.0
Scotland	26,500	108.4
Northern Ireland	21,100	86.4

Source: Eurostat, March 2012 (there is no separate figure for England)

Conclusions

There has now been a decade and a half of devolution in the United Kingdom from which we can measure its impact on the UK political system. The foremost of these are:

■ Relations between central and devolved governments have become increasingly acrimonious, particularly when either the Westminster Coalition Government or devolved government acts unilaterally or as a fall-out from the recent economic cuts to devolved block grants. The system of arrangements for dealing with Scottish, Welsh and Northern Irish matters, relying on departmental concordats, bilateral and informal links largely amongst officials rather than ministers has not always worked as it should.

■ Devolution has not helped the nations and regions converge (Tables 12.7 and 12.8). These disparities have remained as wide as under the strictly unionist state.

- To date, the constituent parts of the United Kingdom have not broken away from each other as was predicted by the anti-devolutionists. In Scotland, where the SNP has successfully secured a referendum on independence for 2014, the break-up of the United Kingdom, however, is now a distinct possibility.

- Most of the political parties who are represented in the devolved bodies were not happy with the initial product of devolution. There have therefore been constant revisions and proposals for revisions of the constitutional devolution settlements.

- In 2011 the SNP became the first political party to gain the majority of the seats in a devolved government election. Elsewhere coalition government and/or **electoral pacts** have become the norm. The Northern Ireland Assembly is designed to be in a permanent coalition government. The Welsh Assembly has consisted of coalition governments for two of its four terms. This has moved the devolved governments and British politics closer to the current Westminster and European style of politics.

- The success of coalition devolved governments across all of the devolved executives has proved that proportional representation does not lead to unstable government, as had previously been claimed be the case, if it was ever introduced in Westminster.

- A whole new generation of young and female politicians who would have been unable to progress through the existing political system to Westminster has emerged. This has greatly reduced the gender imbalance in British

politics. At the same time there has been the opportunity for the advancement of minor parties such as the Greens, who had not been represented at Westminster prior to 2011 thereby increasing the diversity of the political system.

- With the proposals to devolve more fiscal powers and with the all-devolved bodies (excluding the GLA) having primary legislative powers devolution has become more symmetrical. Although those in the Conservative and Labour parties would deny it, the UK appears to be evolving into a more federal-style system of government and away from the mainly unitary form that has existed for the past 200 years. Thus, although only the Scottish Parliament has the name 'parliament' within it, the Welsh and Northern Ireland Assemblies have also become parliaments.

- Policy and service differences between the devolved nations and England have intensified, particularly in certain aspects of healthcare and education. This has caused regional jealousy and animosity.

- While devolutionary powers outside England have increased, in England devolution has moved towards a sub-regional level of localism. This means that the problems caused by not having effective devolution in England, such as economic inequality and the failure to solve the West Lothian question, still cannot be resolved effectively.

- Personality politics, particularly in London, has caught the attention of the media, thus creating unprecedented interest in devolved politics. This media obsession, however, often obscures the real nature of the politics involved.

Chapter summary

At the start of this chapter we looked at Todd's three models of devolution. Of those models the current type of devolution in Britain appears to be moving towards Todd's 'renewal of imperial legacies' model. As we have noted in this chapter, there has been a constant transfer of powers and policy areas to the devolved nations. This is set to continue with the devolution of tax raising and borrowing powers, enabling these nations to develop in a similar way to the dominion models of Britain's imperial past. Whether this in time develops into a federal system or the splitting-up of the United Kingdom entirely, will probably be evident by 2014. Currently, Westminster maintains a strong presence over taxation, international affairs, commerce and the economy and many social welfare issues. It may well continue to undertake these roles in the 'imperial legacy model'. There will, however, need to be further adjustments to the structure of government in the United Kingdom. Currently the civil service, for instance, remains loyal to no single devolved government but instead to the crown. This would clearly alter substantially under a federal model or independence.

Although the break-up of the United Kingdom, which was predicted to be caused by devolution, has not yet occurred it is more likely now than at any time since the 1920s. If Scotland does become independent after the 2014 referendum, it will alter both the shape and very nature of British politics in a more radical way than virtually any event for the past 400 years. The political textbooks will have to be rewritten and a new era of politics will start in the United Kingdom. Even if this does not occur, British politics post-2014 is likely to be very different from when devolution occurred just 15 years earlier.

Discussion points

- How have policy differences affected the lives of citizens in the respective nation states in terms of issues such as education and health?
- Has devolution resulted in the end of the concept of Britishness and the rise of the individual nation state?
- Why do you think that English nationalism still remains a relatively minor political force?
- Will Scottish independence result in the 'Balkanisation' of the UK?
- Has devolution caused British politics to become more European and less Anglo-Saxon in nature?
- What will be the likely evolution of devolution by 2025?

Further reading

Those who wish to have a brief overall picture of devolution and its developments should read *Devolution in the United Kingdom*, 2nd edition by Russell Deacon. A more comprehensive coverage of devolutionary history can be found in *Devolution in Britain Today*, also by Russell Deacon. Those students who wish to examine the devolved politics of a particular region or nation now have a wealth of texts to choose from, including official publications and reports of the devolved bodies themselves. Edinburgh University Press, Manchester University Press and the University of Wales Press specialise in these, as do publishers such as Welsh Academic Press. In particular, the reports produced by the Institute of Welsh Affairs, Gorwel and the Constitution Unit of the University of London are particularly useful.

Bibliography

Aughey, A. (2007) *The Politics of Englishness* (Manchester University Press).

Cash, J.D. (2010) *Identity, Ideology and Conflict: The Structuration of Politics in Northern Ireland* (Cambridge University Press).

Cairney, P. (2011) *The Scottish Political System Since Devolution* (Imprint Academic).

Curtis, J. and Syed, B. (2009) *Has Devolution Worked? The verdict from policy makers and the public* (Manchester University Press).

Davies, R. (1999) *Devolution: A Process Not an Event*, Vol. 2 of *Gregynog Paper* (Institute of Welsh Affairs).

Deacon, R. (2002) *The Governance of Wales: The Welsh Office and the Policy Process 1964–99* (Welsh Academic Press).

Deacon, R. (2006) *Devolution in Britain Today* (Manchester University Press).

Deacon, R. (2012) *Devolution in the United Kingdom* (Edinburgh University Press).

Dixon, P. and O'Kane, E. (2011) *Northern Ireland Since 1969* (Longman).

Devine, T. (ed.) (2008) *Scotland and the Union 1707–2007* (Edinburgh University Press).

Eurobarometer (2009) 'Attitudes towards the EU in the United Kingdom', FlashEurobarometer 209, July.

McEvoy, J. (2008) *The Politics of Northern Ireland* (Edinburgh University Press).

Osmond, J. (2007) *Crossing the Rubicon: Coalition Politics Welsh Style* (Institute of Welsh Affairs).

Todd, J. (2005) 'A new territorial politics in the British Isles?', in Coakely, J., Laffan, B. and Todd, J. (2005) *Renovation Or Revolution? New Territorial Politics in Ireland and the United Kingdom* (University College Dublin Press).

Travers, T. (2004) *The Politics of London: Governing An Ungovernable City* (Palgrave Macmillan).

Useful websites

Devolution websites

General

Democracy Live BBC Politics coverage, detailed and up-to-date devolution coverage: http://news.bbc.co.uk/democracylive.

Devolution Matters – A blog posting by Dr Alan Trench that gives regular summaries and comment of the latest events in devolution across the UK: http://devolutionmatters.wordpress.com.

University College London's Constitution Unit's devolution programme: http://constitution-unit.com.

The Economic and Social Research Council ran a large-scale research project from 2000 to March 2006 on 'Devolution and Constitutional Change Programme' which covers early devolutionary issues: http://www.devolution.ac.uk.

England

The Department for Communities and Local Government is the government department responsible for English devolution/decentralization: http://www.communities.gov.uk/corporate/.

The Greater London Authority and London Mayor's official website: http://www.london.gov.uk/who-runs-london/authority.

Northern Ireland

Northern Ireland Assembly: http://www.niassembly.gov.uk.

Northern Ireland Executive (government): http://www.northernireland.gov.uk.

For more information about politics in Northern Ireland: http://www.belfasttelegraph.co.uk.

Scotland

The Scottish Parliament website: www.scottish.parliament.uk.

The Scottish Government's website: http://home.scotland.gov.uk/home.

The Audit Scotland website which also provides details of problems or areas of concern in Scottish governance: www.audit-scotland.gov.uk.

Site of the Scottish National Party (SNP): www.snp.org.

Wales

Gorwel: Welsh economic think tank that covers devolved issues relating to the Welsh economy and public affairs: http://www.gorwel.co.

Institute for Welsh Affairs (Welsh think tank): http://www.iwa.org.uk.

The National Library of Wales has a substantial website on Welsh political history: http://www.llgc.org.uk/ymgyrchu/map-e.htm.

National Assembly for Wales: http://www.assemblywales.org.

Welsh Government: http://www.wales.gov.uk.

How well has Coalition Government worked?

The 2010 election result can best be described as an 'accident waiting to happen'.

It was an accident in that – as the great ranks of disgruntled commentators have endlessly parroted – 'no one voted for the Coalition'.

It was also waiting to happen in that since 1970 the percentage of the electorate voting for the two main parties has been in long-term decline, with Labour and the Conservatives currently receiving less than 70 per cent of all votes, whereas 90 per cent plus was previously the norm. Despite this, we staggered on until 2010 with either the Tories or Labour getting a majority of seats. But that was never going to happen indefinitely. With the smaller parties collectively getting over 80 seats out of 650 at the last four elections, there is a strong chance that we will not see a return to one-party government any time soon.

So, on the face of it, coalitions are here to stay, and both the major parties are going to have to get used to it. In the early days of May 2015 the odds are we will be faced with the sight of parties negotiating with each other to identify what combination of parties can best cobble together a working majority, which means it is worth looking at our first full coalition since the war and seeing how well it has worked. The Constitution Unit at UCL had an opportunity to consider that as we were granted unique access to both Whitehall and Westminster to talk to those involved and see what they thought about it.[1]

Has it worked well for the political parties?

Normally politics is a zero sum game – in which losses for one party must mean gains for someone else. But as we get ready for the next election, we are actually faced with a somewhat bizarre situation in which none of the parties feel they have done well out of the coalition.

Most obviously perhaps, the Liberal Democrats could well face electoral meltdown. This is the curse of all third parties, as widely demonstrated throughout Europe. A significant proportion of the votes of any third party come from those who are fed up of the two main parties – but once the third party enters government, the advantage of being different evaporates. If the Government is successful, the major party gets the credit. But if it fails, the electorate blames the party which has had to sacrifice most of its principles and ideas simply to be in government. Yet, even if the Lib Dems lose seats, they could still find themselves in a king-maker position if the next election is again indecisive. Moreover, the argument that they have restrained a Tory government from being excessively right wing will potentially attract new voters – as will the argument that they are the best chance of avoiding a single-party Labour government.

The Conservatives have had their coalition troubles too. There have been numerous revolts by Tory backbenchers who can say they are acting to defend traditional Tory values. The early argument that a coalition would provide protection for David Cameron against his right wing has been undermined by the greater freedom the right wing thinks it has to express its views. At the same time, the fact of the coalition allowed the Tories to re-enter 10 Downing Street – and after 13 years of Labour governments from 1997 to 2010 they have re-established the Tory party as a credible brand for a government. The argument that they deserve a chance to govern on their own will attract some voters at least. One real risk, however, which also seems a risk for Labour though perhaps less acutely, is that at least some constituency parties will only be interested in selecting anti-Coalition candidates where vacancies occur.

In addition, the Labour Party cannot be sure that *not* being in the Coalition has strengthened their position with the electorate. They have the advantage of being in Opposition during the prolonged recession. But they have a new leader who can readily be portrayed by the other two main parties as being inexperienced in the harsh realties of government, and they will have to find a stance for the next election which is critical of both the Tories and the Lib Dems – but not so critical that they rule out any chance of a coalition with the Lib Dems.

---

1 Now available as *The Politics of Coalition* by Robert Hazell, Ben Yong and others: http://www.ucl.ac.uk/constitution-unit/constitution-unit-news/080612

So, the zero sum game has not gone away. Unless the electorate suddenly votes in great numbers for fourth parties and nationalists – possible but not probable – it seems inevitable that the three main parties will be perceived after the 2015 election as having benefited or suffered from the Coalition – but we just don't know yet who the winners and loser will be.

Has it worked well for Whitehall?

The efficient running of Whitehall might not seem to many politicians to be more important than the health of their political party, but it actually matters considerably. If a political party is divided by feuding and disharmony, it has little impact on the delivery of government. But if government itself is bogged down in factionalism, then everyone is potentially affected.

The evidence at this stage – from our interviews with members of the Coalition and their civil servants – is that the internal processes of government have been working well. Tory ministers have worked harmoniously with Lib Dem ministers and vice versa. Mutual respect was widely reported. Indeed there might be a positive paradox here in that there were constant echoes of the old political adage that the real enemies of any politician are those within his or her own party, not in another party. We were certainly told time and time again that the Coalition was far more harmonious than the predecessor Labour Government with its famous splits between Blairites and Brownites.

This does not mean that there have not been numerous disputes and controversies – as with all governments, coalition or single party – but at no point have events really come anywhere close to undermining the basic message that the Coalition will find the necessary compromises to fulfil its clear intention for the current Parliament and Government to last until 2015.

And has it worked well for the country?

Frankly, our view is that the Coalition has served the country surprisingly well. That is not a verdict you will see much reference to in the press because there is limited readership for positive stories about politics. And such is the public dissatisfaction with politicians of all types that the appetite for praise of them is limited.

But facts are facts. First it is easy to forget that the Coalition was formed in the midst of an economic crisis over the future of the euro. So there was a need to form a stable government and to form it quickly. It is to the credit of those involved that they produced a workable government with a clear programme for action within five days – a time which has even been criticised since for being too short.

Second, almost three years on from that the UK still has a strong government with a solid working majority. And the Coalition Government – most clearly in its first 12 months – also proved a decisive government, delivering a reform agenda which was more significant than most governments achieve. When you consider the most obvious alternative – a period of minority Tory government followed by a second election which might well also have been indecisive – the country has been well served.

Obviously none of this means that coalition has suddenly proved a superior form of government to one delivered by a single party. Certainly the key economic problems have not gone away. In the long run the fact that we have had a relatively strong government capable of making tough decisions will be of no consolation if those decisions prove to be the wrong ones.

It still seems hard to deny the Coalition a positive report. It has worked and worked well. And those who argued prior that coalitions would be disastrous, leading to weak and indecisive government, have simply been proved wrong.

But back to the underlying arithmetic. While it is a safe bet that at the next General Election the vast majority of MPs will come from the recognised parties, there is no reason to think that the long-term growth of minor parties will not continue. So, even if the Lib Dems lose many of their 22 per cent of votes at the last election, the idea that the disaffected Lib Dem voters will switch decisively to Labour or the Tories seems implausible. No one should be surprised if a third of the electorate decline to vote Labour or Tory. And, if they do, the odds are strongly in favour of another coalition.

That doesn't mean, of course, that we will have the same relatively straightforward outcome that we had at the 2010 election. One huge advantage in forming the coalition in 2010 was that the arithmetic meant that a coalition was only really possible between the Tories and the Lib Dems – but that such a coalition would have a solid majority. It is entirely possible – perhaps probable – that the 2015 election will make such a solid two-party coalition impossible and we will be faced with no party able to secure a solid working majority – leading to a coalition with a tiny majority and tiny parties potentially being in government. The fact that our first coalition government has been a benign one is no guide whatsoever to the future.

By Robert Hazell and Peter Waller

Part 4 represents a turning point in this book. The earlier sections have addressed more theoretical aspects of British politics; later ones deal with the core institutions of the country. To help manage this transition more easily two short sections follow on the way in which the key functions of government – legislative, executive and judicial – relate to each other, utilising a comparison with the very different system used by the USA. The second section explains how the different institutions of government are responsible and answerable, ultimately to the voters at election time.

Two overviews of the British political system

The functions of government

It is helpful to contrast the British political system with that of the USA. It is well known that the eighteenth-century framers of the US constitution wrote into their 1787 document a strict separation of powers. The legislature (Congress) and the executive (the Presidency) were to be elected separately for terms of differing length, with the **judiciary** (the Supreme Court) appointed by the President for life. In diagrammatic form, the functions can be represented by three separate and independent circles (see Figure 1).

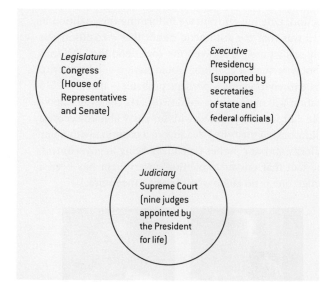

Figure 1 Functions of government: USA

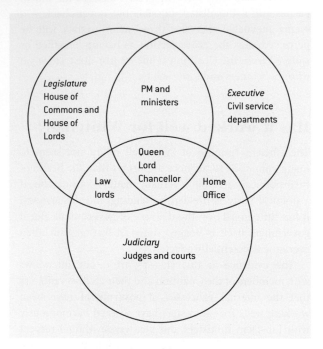

Figure 2 Functions of government: UK

The purpose of this arrangement was to disperse power to institutions that would check each other and ensure that no branch of government became over-mighty. In Britain, however, there never was such a separation. The three functions overlap significantly. To change or re-elect a government there is only one election and that is to the legislative chamber, the House of Commons. After the election, the majority party in that chamber invariably forms the executive. The crucial overlap between the legislative and executive spheres therefore comprises Prime Minister, Cabinet and the other 70 or so junior ministers. Until 2006, the judiciary was similarly appointed by the executive: not by the Prime Minister but by the Lord Chancellor, the government's chief law officer, who sat in the Cabinet and presided over the House of Lords (see Figure 2).

The US constitution ensures that the President cannot be overthrown by Congress – except through impeachment – but looser party discipline means that the President cannot regularly command congressional support for his policies; indeed, like Presidents Bush, for a while, and Clinton, his party may be in the minority in Congress. The British Prime Minister, in contrast, has more power: provided that the support of the majority party is sustained, he or she leads both the executive and legislative arms of government. However, loss of significant party support can bring down the British Prime Minister, as it did Chamberlain in May 1940 and Thatcher in 1990. This possibility clearly acts as a constraint upon potential prime ministerial action, but the fact is that parties in government very rarely even threaten to unseat their leaders, because they fear the electoral consequences of apparent disunity.

The executive's power is further reinforced by the doctrine of parliamentary sovereignty, which enables it to overrule any law – constitutional or otherwise – with a simple majority vote; and considerable residual powers of the monarch via the royal prerogative. The power of the House of Lords of legislative delay only (other than for bills originating in the Lords), and local government's essentially subservient relationship to Westminster, complete the picture of an unusually powerful executive arm of government for a representative democracy.

Representative and responsible government

Represented in a different way, the British political system can be seen as a circuit of representation and **responsibility**. Parliament represents the electorate but is also responsible to it via elections. In their turn, ministers represent majority opinion in the legislature (although they are appointed by the Prime Minister, not elected) and are responsible to it for their actions in leading the executive. Civil servants are not representatives but as part of the executive are controlled by ministers and are responsible to them. Figure 3 illustrates the relationship.

This, of course, is a very simplistic view, but it does express the underlying theory of how British government should work. The reality of how the system operates is infinitely more complex, as Figure 4 – itself highly simplified – seeks to illustrate. Earlier chapters have explained how the different elements of British government operate in practice:

1 Parliament provides the forum, the 'playing field' on which the ordered competition of democratic government is publicly conducted.

2 Political parties dominate the system, organising the electorate, taking over Parliament and providing the ministers who run the civil service.

3 The Prime Minister as leader of the majority party can exercise considerable personal power and in recent years has become more akin to a presidential figure.

4 The judiciary performs the important task of interpreting legislation and calling ministers and officials to account if they act without statutory authority.

5 Civil servants serve ministers, but their permanence and their professionalism, their vested interests in searching for consensus and defending departmental interests raise suspicions that they occasionally or even regularly outflank their ministerial masters.

6 Pressure groups infiltrate the whole gamut of government institutions, the most powerful bypassing Parliament and choosing to deal direct with ministers and civil servants. (See Chapter 10.)

7 The media have increasingly usurped the role of Parliament in informing the public and providing a forum for public debate. Television is a potent new influence, the impact of which is still to be fully felt. (See Chapter 8.)

Does the reality invalidate the theory? It all depends upon how drastically we believe Figure 4 distorts Figure 3. Indeed, Marxists would declare both to be irrelevant in that business pressure groups call the shots that matter, operating behind the scenes and within the supportive context of a system in which all the major actors subscribe

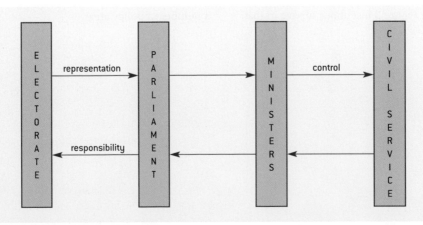

Figure 3 Representative and responsible government

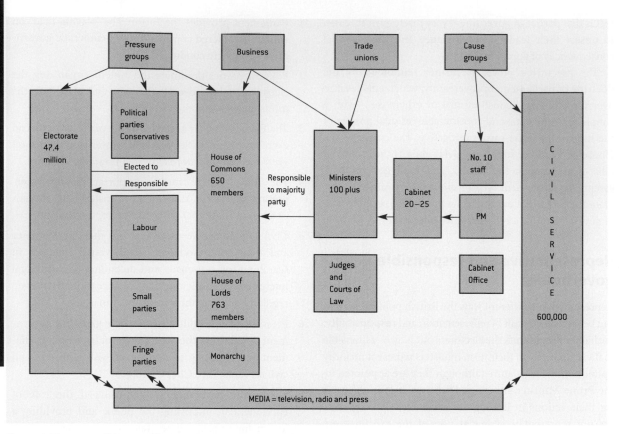

Figure 4 Elements of UK central government

to their values. Former Cabinet minister Tony Benn would argue that the executive has become so dominant at the expense of the legislature that the PM's power can be compared with that of a medieval monarch. As we have seen, Britain's constitutional arrangements have always allowed great potential power – potential that strong Prime Ministers like Margaret Thatcher have been keen and able to realise when given the time. But I would maintain, and cite in support of the analyses offered by the authors of this book, that the essential features of the democratic system portrayed in Figure 3 just about survive in that:

- party-dominated governments are removable;
- Parliament still applies watchdog controls (and just occasionally reminds the executive by biting);
- the electorate has a choice between parties;
- civil servants ordinarily seek to obey their political masters;
- pressure groups influence but do not dictate.

Part 4 explains how the legislative system works; Part 5 explains the executive process; and Part 6 looks at a number of policy areas.

PART 4

THE LEGISLATIVE PROCESS

CHAPTER 13

The changing constitution

Philip Norton

> " The British Constitution has always been puzzling and always will be "
>
> Queen Elizabeth II

Learning objectives

- To identify the sources and key components of the British constitution.

- To analyse the nature of the debate about the British constitution.

- To consider the major changes and modifications made to the constitution in recent years.

- To detail the arguments for and against some of the major changes that have taken place or are proposed to the constitution, including electoral reform.

- To address the problems faced by political parties as a consequence of constitutional change.

Introduction

In the quarter-century following the Second World War, the constitution rarely figured in political debate. It was seen as the preserve more of lawyers than of politicians. In the last three decades of the century, it became a subject of political controversy. Demands for reform of the constitution grew. Many of those demands were met by the Labour Government elected in May 1997, with major changes being made to the constitutional framework of the country. Less expectedly, more constitutional change took place under the Coalition Government formed following the General Election of 2010. Changes under both governments were extensive, but adhered to no particular approach to constitutional change. Despite the changes to the nation's constitutional arrangements, some critics demand further change. The changes that have taken place have created problems for the three main political parties.

The constitution

What, then, is a **constitution**? What is it for? What is distinctive about the British constitution? Where does it come from? What are the essential constituents of the 'traditional' constitution? What challenges has it faced in recent years? What changes have been made to it? What are the problems posed to the political parties by such changes? And what is the nature of the debate taking place about further constitutional change?

Definition and sources

What is a constitution? A constitution can be defined as the aggregation of laws, customs and **conventions** that determines the composition and powers of organs of the state (such as government, Parliament and the courts) and regulates the relationship of the various state organs to one another and to the private citizen.

What are constitutions for? Constitutions vary in terms of their purpose. A constitution may be constructed in such a way as to embody and protect fundamental principles (such as individual liberty), principles that should be beyond the reach of the transient wish of the people. This is referred to as **negative constitutionalism** (see Ivison 1999). This tends to be reflected in presidential systems of government (see Bradley, Ziegler and Baranger 2007); the United States is a notable example. A constitution may be constructed in order to ensure that the wishes of the people are paramount. This is referred to as **positive constitutionalism**. Here, there are few, if any, restraints on the people's elected representatives. This tends to be reflected in parliamentary systems of government (Bradley, Ziegler and Baranger 2007). The UK falls primarily in this category.

What form do constitutions take? Most, but not all, are drawn up in a single, codified document. Some are short, others remarkably long. Some embody provisions that exhort citizens to act in a certain way ('It shall be the duty of every citizen . . .'); others confine themselves to stipulating the formal structures and powers of state bodies. Processes of interpretation and amendment vary. Most, but not all, have entrenched provisions: i.e. they can only be amended by an extraordinary process beyond that normally employed for amending the law.

The British constitution differs from most in that it is not drawn up in a single codified document. As such, it is often described as an 'unwritten' constitution. However, much of the constitution does exist in 'written' form. Many Acts of Parliament – such as the European Communities Act 1972, providing the legal basis for British membership of the European Community, and the Constitutional Reform Act 2005, creating a Supreme Court – are clearly measures of constitutional law. Those Acts constitute formal, written –

and binding – documents. To describe the constitution as unwritten is thus misleading. Rather, what Britain has is an uncodified constitution.

Even in countries with a formal, written document, 'the constitution' constitutes more than the simple words of the document. Those words have to be interpreted. Practices develop, and laws are passed, that help to give meaning to those words. To understand the contemporary constitution of the United States, for example, one has to look beyond the document to interpretations of that document by the courts in the USA, principally the US Supreme Court, and to various acts of Congress and to practices developed over more than 200 years. The constitutions of most countries thus have what may be termed a 'primary source' (the written document) and 'secondary sources' (judicial interpretation, legislative acts, established practice). The UK lacks the equivalent primary source. Instead, the constitution derives from sources that elsewhere would constitute secondary sources of the constitution. Those sources are four in number (see Figure 13.1). They are:

1 *statute law*, comprising Acts of Parliament and subordinate legislation made under the authority of the parent Act;

2 *common law*, comprising legal principles developed and applied by the courts, and encompassing the prerogative powers of the crown and the law and practice of Parliament;

3 *conventions*, constituting rules of behaviour that are considered binding by and upon those who operate the constitution but that are not enforced by the courts or by the presiding officers in the Houses of Parliament;

4 *works of authority*, comprising various written works – often but not always accorded authority by reason of their age – that provide guidance and interpretation on uncertain aspects of the constitution. Such works have persuasive authority only.

Statute law is the pre-eminent of the four sources and occupies such a position because of the doctrine of **parliamentary sovereignty**. Under this judicially self-imposed concept, the courts recognise only the authority of Parliament (formally the Queen-in-Parliament) to make law, with no body other than Parliament itself having the authority to set aside that law. The courts cannot strike down a law as being contrary to the provisions of the constitution. Statute law, then, is supreme and can be used to override common law.

Amendment

No extraordinary features are laid down in Parliament for the passage or amendment of measures of constitutional law. Although bills of constitutional significance usually have their committee stage on the floor of the House of Commons, rather than in a public bill committee (see Chapter 15), there is no formal requirement for this to happen. All bills have

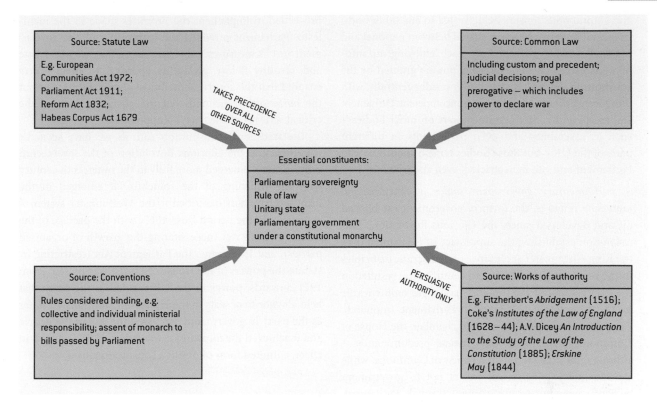

Figure 13.1 The traditional constitution: sources and constituents

Source: P. Norton (1986) 'The constitution in flux', *Social Studies Review*, vol. 2, no. 1. Reproduced with permission from the California Council for Social Studies

to go through the same stages in both Houses of Parliament and are subject to simple majority voting. As such, the traditional constitution is, formally, a **flexible constitution**.

However, as we shall see, there are two recent developments that challenge this flexibility: membership of the European Community/Union and the incorporation of the European Convention on Human Rights into British law. The devolution of powers to elected assemblies in different parts of the United Kingdom may also be argued to limit, in effect, the capacity of Parliament to pass any legislation it wishes.

The traditional constitution: essential constituents

The traditional constitution existed for most of the twentieth century. It had four principal features. Although, as we shall see, these features have been challenged by changes in recent years, each nonetheless remains formally in place:

1 *Parliamentary sovereignty* has been described as the cornerstone of the British constitution. As we have seen, it stipulates that the outputs of Parliament are binding and cannot be set aside by any body other than Parliament itself. The doctrine was confirmed by the Glorious Revolution of 1688 and 1689, when the common lawyers combined with Parliament against the King. Since the Settlement of 1689 established that the King was bound by the law of Parliament, it followed that his courts were also so bound.

2 *The rule of law* was identified by nineteenth-century constitutional lawyer A.V. Dicey as one of the twin pillars of the constitution and is generally accepted as one of the essential features of a free society. However, it is logically subordinate to the first pillar – parliamentary sovereignty – since Parliament could pass a measure undermining or destroying the rule of law. It is also a matter of dispute as to what the term encompasses. In terms of the law passed by Parliament, it is essentially a procedural doctrine. Laws must be interpreted and applied by an impartial and independent **judiciary**; those charged under the law are entitled to a fair trial; and no one can be imprisoned other than through the due process of law. However, there is some dispute as to how far the doctrine extends beyond this, not least in defining the extent of the power of the state to regulate the affairs of citizens.

3 *A unitary state* is one in which formal power resides exclusively in the national authority, with no entrenched

and autonomous powers being vested in any other body. In federal systems, power is shared between national and regional or state governments, each enjoying an autonomous existence and exercising powers granted by the constitution. In the UK state power resides centrally, with the Queen-in-Parliament being omnicompetent. Parliament can create and confer certain powers on other bodies – such as assemblies and even parliaments in different parts of the UK – but those bodies remain subordinate to Parliament and can be restricted, even abolished, by it.

4 *A parliamentary government under a constitutional monarchy* refers to the form of government established by, and developed since, the Glorious Revolution. That revolution established the supremacy of Parliament over the King. The greater acceptance of democratic principles in the nineteenth and twentieth centuries has resulted in the enlargement of the franchise and a pre-eminent role in the triumvirate of Queen-in-Parliament (monarch, Commons, Lords) for the elected chamber, the House of Commons. 'Parliament' thus means predominantly – although not exclusively – the House of Commons, while 'parliamentary government' refers not to government by Parliament but to government through Parliament. Ministers are legally answerable to the crown but politically answerable to Parliament, that political relationship being governed by the conventions of collective and individual **ministerial responsibility**. A government is returned in a general election and between elections depends on the confidence of a majority of Members of Parliament both for the passage of its measures and for its continuance in office.

Three of these four features (parliamentary sovereignty, unitary state, parliamentary government) facilitated the emergence of strong, or potentially strong, government. A government secure in its majority in the House of Commons was usually able to enact measures that were then binding on society and which could not be set aside by any body other than Parliament itself. There were no other forms of government below the national enjoying autonomous powers (the consequence of a unitary state). No other actors at national level were able to countermand the elected House of Commons, be it the crown or the House of Lords (the consequence of the growth of parliamentary government under a constitutional monarchy) or the courts (the consequence of the doctrine of parliamentary sovereignty). The United Kingdom thus enjoyed a centralised system of government.

That system of government, made possible by the essential features of the constitution, was variously described as the Westminster system of government. At the heart of the system was the Cabinet, sustained by a party majority in the House of Commons. Each party fought a general election on the basis of a party manifesto and, if elected to office, it

proceeded to implement the promises made in the manifesto. Parliament provided the legitimacy for the government and its measures, subjecting those measures to debate and scrutiny before giving its approval to them. *Party* ensured that the government almost always got its way, but the *party system* ensured that the government faced the critical scrutiny of the party in opposition.

The traditional constitution can, as we have seen, be traced back to the Glorious Revolution of the seventeenth century, but it emerged more fully in the nineteenth century with the widening of the franchise. It emerged in the form we have just described – the Westminster system – essentially in the period from 1867, with the passage of the second Reform Act (necessitating the growth of organised parties), and 1911, when the Parliament Act (restricting by statute the powers of the House of Lords) was passed. From 1911 onwards, power in the UK resided in the party that held a majority of seats in the House of Commons. In so far as the party in government expressed the will of the people and it achieved the measures it wanted, the UK acquired, in effect, a limited form of positive constitutionalism.

Challenges to the traditional constitution

The traditional constitution was in place from 1911 to 1972. Although it was variously criticised in the years between the two world wars, especially in the depression of the 1930s, it went largely unchallenged in the years immediately after the Second World War. The nation's political institutions continued to function during the war, and the country emerged victorious from the bitter struggle. In the 1950s the nation enjoyed relative economic prosperity. There appeared little reason to question the nation's constitutional arrangements. That changed once the country began to experience economic recession and more marked political conflict. The constitution came in for questioning. If the political system was not delivering what was expected of it, was there not then a case for changing the system itself? The issue of constitutional reform began to creep onto the political agenda.

Since 1970, the traditional constitution has faced three major challenges. Each has had significant consequences for the nation's constitutional arrangements. The first was membership of the European Community (now the European Union). The second was the constitutional changes introduced by the Labour Government elected in May 1997. The third was the constitutional reforms implemented by the Coalition Government after May 2010.

Membership of the European Community/Union

A juridical dimension

The United Kingdom became a member of the European Community (EC) on 1 January 1973. The Treaty of Accession was signed in 1972 and the legal basis for membership provided by the European Communities Act 1972. The motivation for joining the Community was essentially economic and political. However, membership had major constitutional consequences, primarily because it:

- Gave the force of law not only to existing but also to all future European law. As soon as regulations are agreed, they have binding applicability in the UK. The assent of Parliament is not required. That assent has, in effect, been given in advance under the provisions of the 1972 Act. Parliament has some discretion as to the form in which European directives are to be implemented, but the discretion refers only to the form and not to the principle.

- Gave European law precedence over UK law. In the event of a conflict between European law and UK law, the former takes precedence. The full effect of this was only realised with some important court cases in the 1990s (Fitzpatrick 1999). In the *Factortame* case of 1990–1, the European Court of Justice held that the courts in the UK could suspend the provisions of an Act of Parliament, where it appeared to breach EC law, until a final determination was made. In the case of *Ex Parte EOC*, in 1994, the highest domestic court, then the appellate committee of the House of Lords, struck down provisions of the 1978 Employment Protection (Consolidation) Act as incompatible with EC law (Maxwell 1999).

- Gave the power to determine disputes to the courts. Where there is a dispute over European law, the matter is resolved by the courts. Questions of law have to be decided by the European Court of Justice (ECJ), now the Court of the European Union, which sits in Luxembourg. Where a question of European law reaches the highest domestic court of appeal (until 2009 the House of Lords, since then the Supreme Court), it has to be referred to the Luxembourg Court for a definitive ruling. Lower courts may ask the Court of the European Union for a ruling on the meaning of treaty provisions. All courts in the UK are required to take judicial notice of decisions of the European Court.

The effect of these changes has been to challenge the doctrine of parliamentary sovereignty. The decisions of Parliament can, in certain circumstances (where they conflict with European law), be set aside by a body or bodies other than Parliament itself – namely, the courts. In sectors that now fall within the competence of the European Union, it can be argued that the UK now has something akin to a written constitution – that is, the treaties of the European Union.

The doctrine of parliamentary sovereignty remains formally in place because Parliament retains the power to repeal the European Communities Act. The European Court is able to exercise the power it does because an Act of Parliament says that it can. However, the effect of repealing the 1972 Act would be to take the UK out of the European Union. The claim that Parliament retains the power to repeal the 1972 Act appears to be accepted by most constitutional lawyers (and there is provision in the Lisbon Treaty for member states to withdraw from membership), but the longer the Act remains in force the more the doctrine of parliamentary sovereignty will be challenged and may eventually fade away.

A political dimension

As a consequence of membership, the constitution thus acquired a new juridical dimension, one that challenged the doctrine of parliamentary sovereignty. At the same time, it also acquired a new political dimension, one that challenged the decision-making capacity of British government. Under the terms of entry, policy-making power in various sectors of public policy passed to the institutions of the European Community. Subsequent treaties have served both to extend the range of sectors falling within the competence of the EC and to strengthen the decision-making capacity of the European institutions.

The Single European Act, which came into force in 1987, produced a major shift in the power relationship between the institutions of the Community and the institutions of the member states, strengthening EC institutions, especially through the extension of qualified majority voting (QMV) in the Council of Ministers. The Act also brought about a shift in the power relationships within the institutions of the Community, strengthening the European Parliament through the extension of the cooperation procedure, a procedure that provides a greater role for the Parliament in Community law making. Further shifts in both levels of power relationship were embodied in the Treaty on European Union (the Maastricht Treaty), which took effect in November 1993. This established a European Union with three pillars, extended the sectors of public policy falling within the competence of the European Community, and established a new co-decision procedure for making law in certain areas, a procedure that strengthened again the position of the European Parliament. It now became a partner, with the Council of Ministers, in law making. A further strengthening of the position of the EC, now the European

Union, took place with the implementation in 1999 of the Amsterdam Treaty, in 2003 of the Nice Treaty, and in December 2009 with the consolidation of the EU's powers in the Lisbon Treaty. These treaties variously extended the competences of the EU, reformed the Union's institutional structures, and – in the case of the Lisbon Treaty – drew together the pillars into one entity. The European Union has thus been characterised by the absence of any steady state in constitutional terms: there has been almost continual pressure for further change, with attendant consequences for the member states.

As a result of membership of the European Union, the British government is thus constrained in what it can do. The government and Parliament could block new treaty provisions (primary legislation) – which require unanimous approval of the member states – but are constrained in seeking to block or change legislation introduced under the existing treaties (secondary legislation). Where proposals for secondary legislation are laid before the Council of the European Union (formerly the Council of Ministers), the UK minister may be outvoted by the ministers of the other member states. A decision may thus be taken that is then enforced within the UK, even if it does not have the support of the British government and Parliament. If the government takes an action that appears to be incompatible with EU law, it can be challenged in the courts and then required to bring itself into line with EU law. An Act of Parliament, as we have seen, does not take precedence over European law. Membership of the European Community – now the European Union – has thus added a new element to the constitution, one that does not fit easily with the existing features of that constitution.

Constitutional reform under the Blair Government

Background to reform

The 1970s and 1980s witnessed growing demands for reform of the existing constitution. The system of government no longer appeared to perform as well as it had in the past. The country experienced severe economic problems (inflation, rising unemployment), industrial disputes, civil unrest in Northern Ireland and some social unrest at home (riots in cities such as Bristol and Liverpool). The political process also came under pressure. Turnout declined in general elections. The proportion of electors voting for either of the two major parties fell. Two general elections took place in one year (1974), with no decisive outcome. A Labour government elected with less than 40 per cent of the vote in October 1974 was able to implement a series of radical measures.

Critics of the constitution argued the case for change. Some politicians and lawyers made the case for an entrenched Bill of Rights – putting rights beyond the reach of simple

majorities in the two Houses of Parliament. The case for a Bill of Rights was put by Lord Hailsham in a 1976 lecture, subsequently published in pamphlet form under the title *Elective Dictatorship*. Some politicians wanted a new electoral system, one that produced a closer relationship between the proportion of votes won nationally and the proportion of seats won in the House of Commons. The case for a new electoral system was made in an influential set of essays, edited by Professor S.E. Finer in 1975. Finer argued that a system of proportional representation would put an end to partisanship and help get rid of the policy discontinuity that results when one party replaces another in government.

There were also calls for power to be devolved to elected assemblies in different parts of the United Kingdom and for the use of referendums. Both changes, it was argued, would push decision making down from a centralised government to the people. The Labour Government elected in 1974 sought, unsuccessfully, to pass measures providing for elected assemblies in Scotland and Wales. The Government did make provision for the first UK-wide referendum, held in 1975 on the issue of Britain's continued membership of the European Community.

The demands for change were fairly disparate and in most cases tied to no obvious intellectually coherent approach to constitutional change. However, as the 1980s progressed, various coherent approaches developed (Norton 1982, 1993). These are listed in Box 13.1. Each approach had its advocates, although two of them, the high Tory and Marxist approaches, were overshadowed by the other approaches. The corporatist, or group, approach was more to the fore in the 1970s, when a Labour government brought representatives of trade unions and business into discussions on economic policy. It retained some advocates in the 1980s. The socialist approach, pursued by politicians such as former Labour Cabinet minister Tony Benn, had a notable influence in the Labour Party in the early 1980s, the Labour manifesto in the 1983 General Election adopting an essentially socialist stance. The New Right approach found some notable supporters in the Conservative Party, notably Cabinet minister Sir Keith Joseph; it also had some influence on the Prime Minister, Margaret Thatcher.

However, the two most prominent approaches were the liberal and the traditionalist. The liberal approach was pursued by the Liberal Party and by its successor party, the Liberal Democrats. It also attracted support from a much wider political spectrum, including some Labour supporters and even some ex-Marxists. In 1988 a constitutional reform movement, Charter 88, was formed (the year of formation was deliberate, being the tercentenary year of the Glorious Revolution) to bring together all those who supported a new constitutional settlement.

The liberal approach made much of the running in political debate. However, the traditional approach was the more influential of the two by virtue of the fact that it was the approach adopted by the Conservative Government. Although Prime Minister Margaret Thatcher supported reducing the public sector, she nonetheless maintained a basic traditionalist approach to the constitution. Her successor, John Major, was a particularly vocal advocate of the traditional approach. Although the period of Conservative government from 1979 to 1997 saw some important constitutional changes – such as a constriction of the role of local government and the negotiation of new European treaties (the Single European Act and the Maastricht Treaty) – there was no principled embrace of radical constitutional change. The stance of government was to support the existing constitutional framework.

As the 1990s progressed, the debate about constitutional change largely polarised around these two approaches. The collapse of communism, the move from Labour to New Labour in Britain and the demise of Margaret Thatcher as leader of the Conservative Party served to diminish the impact of several of the other approaches. As the liberal approach gained ground, so supporters of the traditional approach began to put their heads above the parapet in support of their position.

Supporters of the liberal approach argued that a new constitution was needed in order to push power down to the individual. Power was too heavily concentrated in public bodies and in special interests. Decentralising power would limit the over-mighty state and also be more efficient, ensuring that power was exercised at a more appropriate level, one more closely related to those affected by the decisions being taken. Supporters of the traditional approach countered this by arguing that the traditional constitution had attributes that, in combination, made the existing arrangements preferable to anything else on offer. The attributes were those of coherence, accountability, responsiveness, flexibility and effectiveness. The system of government, it was argued, was coherent: the different parts of the system were integrated, one party being elected to office to implement a programme of public policy placed before electors. The system was accountable: electors knew who to hold to account – the party in government – if they disapproved of public policy; if they disapproved, they could sweep the party from office. The system was responsive: knowing that it could be swept out at the next election, a government paid attention to the wishes of electors. Ministers could not ignore the wishes of voters and assume they could stay in office next time around as a result of post-election bargaining (a feature of some systems of government). The system was flexible: it could respond quickly in times of crisis, with measures being passed quickly with all-party agreement. The system was also effective: government could govern and could usually be assured of parliamentary approval of measures promised in the party's election manifesto. Government could deliver on what in effect was a contract with the electors: in return for their support, it implemented its promised package of measures.

The clash between the two approaches thus reflected different views of what the constitution was for. The liberal approach, in essence, embraced negative constitutionalism. The constitution was for constraining government. The traditional approach embraced a qualified form of positive constitutionalism. The Westminster system enabled the will of the people to be paramount, albeit tempered by parliamentary deliberation. The qualification is a crucial one, at the heart of the Westminster system.

Reform under a Labour government

In the 1970s, Labour politicians tended to adopt an essentially traditionalist stance. There was an attempt to devolve powers to elected assemblies in Scotland and Wales and the use of a national referendum, but these were not seen as part of some coherent scheme of constitutional reform. The referendum in particular was seen as an exercise in political expediency. In the early 1980s the influence of left-wing activists pushed the party towards a more socialist approach to the constitution. Under the leadership of Neil Kinnock, the party was weaned off this approach. It began to look more in the direction of the liberal approach. The longer the party was in opposition, the more major constitutional reform began to look attractive to the party. It was already committed to devolution. In its socialist phase, it had adopted a policy of abolishing the House of Lords. It moved away from that to committing itself to removing hereditary peers from the House and introducing a more democratic second chamber. Having previously opposed electoral reform, some leading Labour MPs began to see merit in introducing proportional representation for parliamentary elections. John Smith, leader from 1992 to 1994, committed a future Labour government to a referendum on the issue of electoral reform. The party also began to move cautiously towards embodying rights in statutory form: in 1992 it favoured a charter of rights. It also committed itself to strengthening local government.

The move towards a liberal approach was apparent in the Labour manifesto in the 1992 and 1997 general elections. In both elections, the Conservatives embraced the traditional approach and the Liberal Democrats the liberal approach. The constitution was one subject on which it was generally acknowledged that there was a clear difference in policy between the parties.

Looking in greater detail at the Labour Party's proposals in the 1997 manifesto, the party advocated:

- devolving power to Scotland and Wales;
- removing hereditary peers from the House of Lords;
- incorporating the European Convention on Human Rights into British law;
- appointing an independent commission to recommend a proportional alternative to the existing electoral system;

BOX 13.1

Approaches to constitutional change

High Tory

This approach contends that the constitution has evolved organically and that change, artificial change, is neither necessary nor desirable. In its pure form, it is opposed not only to major reforms – such as electoral reform, a Bill of Rights and an elected second chamber – but also to modifications to existing arrangements, such as the introduction of departmental select committees in the House of Commons. Its stance on any proposed reform is thus predictable: it is against it. The approach has been embraced over the years by a number of Conservative MPs.

Socialist

This approach favours reform, but a particular type of reform. It seeks strong government, but a party-dominated strong government, with adherence to the principle of intra-party democracy and the concept of the mandate. It wants to shift power from the existing 'top-down' form of control (government to people) to a **'bottom-up'** form (people to government), with the party acting as the channel for the exercise of that control. It favours sweeping away the monarchy and the House of Lords and the use of more elective processes, both for public offices and within the Labour Party. It is wary of, or opposed to, reforms that might prevent the return of a socialist government and the implementation of a socialist programme. It is thus sceptical of or opposed to electoral reform (potential for Coalition Government), an entrenched Bill of Rights (constraining government autonomy, giving power to judges) and membership of the European Union (constraining influence, sometimes viewed as a capitalists' club). For government to carry through socialist policies, it has to be free of constitutional constraints that favour or are dominated by its opponents. The most powerful advocate of this approach has been former Labour Cabinet minister Tony Benn.

Marxist

This approach sees the restructuring of the political system as largely irrelevant, certainly in the long run, serving merely to delay the collapse of capitalist society. Government, any government, is forced to act in the interests of finance capital. Changes to the constitutional arrangements may serve to protect those interests in the short term but will not stave off collapse in the long term.

Whatever the structures, government will be constrained by external elites, and those elites will themselves be forced to follow rather than determine events. The clash between the imperatives of capitalism and decreasing profit rates in the meso-economy determines what capitalists do. Constitutional reform, in consequence, is not advocated but rather taken as demonstrating tensions within the international capitalist economy. This approach has essentially been a 'pure' one, with some Marxists pursuing variations of it and some taking a more direct interest in constitutional change.

Corporatist

The corporatist, or group, approach seeks the greater incorporation of groups into the process of policy making in order to achieve a more consensual approach to public policy. The interdependence of government and interest groups – especially sectional interest groups – is such that it should be recognised and accommodated. A more integrated process can facilitate a more stable economic system. Supporters of this approach have looked to other countries, such as Germany, as examples of what can be achieved. This approach thus favours the representation of labour and business on executive and advisory bodies and, in its pure form, the creation of a functionalist second chamber. It was an approach that attracted support, especially in the 1970s, being pursued in a mild form by the Labour Government from 1974 to 1979 and also being embraced, after 1972, by Conservative Prime Minister Edward Heath.

New Right

This approach is motivated by the economic philosophy of the free market. State intervention in economic affairs is viewed as illegitimate and dangerous, distorting the natural forces of the market and denying the consumer the freedom to choose. The state should therefore withdraw from economic activity. This viewpoint entails a contraction of the public sector, with state-owned industries being returned to the private sector. If institutions need reforming in order to facilitate the free market, then so be it: under this approach, no institution is deemed sacrosanct. Frank Vipert, the former deputy director of the free-market think tank, the Institute of Economic Affairs, has advocated a 'free market written constitution'.

It is an approach associated with several politicians on the right wing of the Conservative Party, such as John Redwood.

Liberal

Like the New Right approach, this is a radical approach to constitutional change. It derives from traditional liberal theory and emphasises the centrality of the individual, limited government, the neutrality of the state in resolving conflict and consensual decision making. It views the individual as increasingly isolated in decision making, being elbowed aside by powerful interests and divorced from a governmental process that is centralised and distorted by partisan preferences. Against an increasingly over-mighty state, the individual has no means of protection. Hence, it is argued, the need for radical constitutional change. The liberal approach favours a new, written constitution, embodying the various reforms advocated by Charter 88 (now part of a wider reform movement, Unlock Democracy), including a Bill of Rights, a system of proportional representation for elections, an elected second chamber, and a reformed House of Commons. In its pure form, it supports federalism rather than devolution. Such a new constitutional settlement, it is argued, will serve to shift power from government to the individual. The only reform about which it is ambivalent is the use of referendums, some adherents to this approach seeing the referendum as a device for oppression by the majority. It is an approach pursued by Liberal Democrats, such as Shirley Williams, and by some Labour politicians.

Traditional

This is a very British approach and derives from a perception of the 'traditional' system as fundamentally sound, offering a balanced system of government. It draws on Tory theory in its emphasis on the need for strong government and on Whig theory in stressing the importance of Parliament as the agent for setting the limits within which government may act. These emphases coalesce in the Westminster model of government, a model that is part descriptive (what is) and part prescriptive (what should be). Government, in this model, must be able to formulate a coherent programme of public policy – the initiative rests with government – with Parliament, as the deliberative body of the nation, subjecting the actions and the programme of government to rigorous scrutiny and providing the limits within which government may govern. This approach recognises the importance of the House of Commons as the elected chamber and the fact that the citizen has neither the time nor the inclination to engage in continuous political debate. There is thus a certain deference, but a contingent deference, to the deliberative wisdom of Parliament. The fact that the Westminster model is prescriptive means that traditionalists – unlike high Tories – will entertain change if it is designed to move present arrangements towards the realisation of that model. They also recognise with Edmund Burke that 'a state without the means of some change is without the means of its conservation' and are therefore prepared to consider change in order to maintain and strengthen the existing constitutional framework. Over the years, therefore, traditionalists have supported a range of incremental reforms, such as the introduction of departmental select committees in the House of Commons, but have opposed radical reforms – such as electoral reform – which threaten the existing framework. There is wariness about membership of the European Union, with involvement accepted as long as it does not pose a major threat to the existing domestic arrangements for decision making. It is an approach pursued by many mainstream Conservative politicians and by some Labour MPs.

- holding a referendum on the voting system;
- introducing a system of proportional representation for the election of UK members of the European Parliament;
- legislating for an elected mayor and strategic authority for London;
- legislating to give people in the English regions power to decide by referendum, on a region by region basis, whether they wanted elected regional government;
- introducing a Freedom of Information Bill;
- holding a referendum if the government recommended joining a single European currency;
- setting up a parliamentary committee to recommend proposals to modernise the House of Commons.

Following its election to office in 1997, the New Labour Government moved to implement its manifesto promises. In the first session (that is, the first year) of the new parliament, it achieved passage of legislation providing for referendums in Scotland and Wales. In these referendums, electors in Scotland voted by a large majority for an elected parliament with legislative and some tax-varying powers. Voters in Wales voted narrowly for an elected assembly to determine spending in the Principality of Wales (see Table 13.1). The Government then introduced measures to provide for an

Table 13.1 Referendum results in Scotland and Wales, 1997

Scotland		
	A Scottish Parliament	*Tax-varying powers*
Agree	1,775,045 (74.3%)	1,512,889 (63.5%)
Disagree	614,400 (25.7%)	870,263 (36.5%)
Turnout: 60.4%		
Wales		
	A Welsh Assembly	
Yes	559,419 (50.3%)	
No	552,698 (49.7%)	
Turnout: 50%		

elected parliament in Scotland and an elected assembly in Wales. Elections to the new bodies were held on 6 May 1999, and Scotland and Wales acquired new forms of government. The government also introduced legislation providing for a new 108-member assembly in Northern Ireland with a power-sharing executive. This, along with other unique constitutional arrangements, including a North/South Ministerial Council and a Council of the Isles, had been approved by electors in Northern Ireland in a referendum in May 1998.

In the first session the Government also achieved passage of the Human Rights Act, providing for the incorporation of most provisions of the European Convention on Human Rights into British law, thus further reinforcing the new judicial dimension of the British constitution. It also achieved passage of a bill providing for a referendum in London on whether or not the city should have an elected mayor and authority. The referendum in London, in May 1998, produced a large majority in favour of the proposal: 1,230,715 (72 per cent) voted 'yes' and 478,413 (28 per cent) voted 'no'. The turnout, though, was low: only 34.1 per cent of eligible electors bothered to vote. The House of Commons appointed a Select Committee on Modernisation. Within a year of its creation, it had issued seven reports, including one proposing various changes to the way legislation was considered in Parliament. The Government also introduced a bill providing for a closed member regional list system for the election of British Members of the European Parliament (MEPs). This was complemented by the use of the additional member system (AMS) for elections to the Scottish Parliament and the Welsh Assembly, and by the use of the single transferable vote (STV) for the Northern Ireland Assembly (see Ministry of Justice 2008).

At the end of 1997 the Government appointed a Commission on the Voting System to make a recommendation on a proportional alternative to the existing first-past-the-post system for electing the House of Commons. The commission, chaired by Liberal Democrat peer Lord Jenkins, was asked to report within a year and did so. It considered a range of options but recommended the introduction of

an electoral system known as the alternative vote plus ('AV Plus'). Under this system, constituency MPs would be elected by the alternative vote but with top-up MPs, constituting between 15 and 20 per cent of the total number of members, being elected on an area-wide basis (such as a county) to ensure some element of proportionality.

In the second session of Parliament, the Government achieved passage of the House of Lords Act. Taking effect in November 1999, the Act removed most hereditary peers – more than 500 – from membership of the House of Lords. At the same time as introducing the House of Lords Bill, the Government established a Royal Commission on the Reform of the House of Lords, under a former Conservative minister, Lord Wakeham, to make recommendations for a reformed second chamber once the hereditary peers had gone. The commission was asked to report within a year and did so. It recommended that a proportion of the membership of the second chamber be elected by popular vote.

The Government also achieved passage of three other measures of constitutional note during the parliament. The Greater London Authority Act brought into being an elected mayor and a strategic authority for the metropolis. The additional member electoral system was employed for election of Assembly members and the supplementary vote (SV) for election of the mayor. (The successful candidate in the first election for mayor was Ken Livingstone.) The Freedom of Information Act opened up documents held by public authorities, with certain exceptions, to public scrutiny. The Political Parties, Elections and Referendums Act created a new Electoral Commission, stipulated new rules governing donations to political parties and introduced provisions to cover the holding of referendums. Given that referendums had been promised on various issues, the measure was designed to ensure some consistency in the rules governing their conduct.

After a reforming first Parliament, constitutional change appeared to take a back seat to other measures introduced by the Blair Government. However, a further major change was enacted at the end of the second Parliament, one not envisaged in the party's manifesto. The Constitutional Reform Act 2005 provided that the Lord Chancellor (a Cabinet minister at the head of the judiciary) need not be a lawyer or a peer. It also transferred the judicial powers of the Lord Chancellor (a political appointee) to the Lord Chief Justice (a senior judge) and created a new Supreme Court. Instead of the highest court of appeal being law lords sitting in a judicial committee of the House of Lords, it was now to be an independent body sitting separately from a legislative chamber. The court came into being in October 2009, housed in the old Middlesex Guildhall in Parliament Square. The change was described by the new President of the Court, Lord Phillips of Worth Matravers, as 'essentially one of form, not of substance' (*Financial Times*, 10 September 2009). It involved principally a transfer of personnel, the law lords moving from the House of Lords to the new court.

Further change came about as a result of political settlement in Northern Ireland in 2007 – Democratic Unionist leader Ian Paisley agreeing to go into a power-sharing government in the province with Sinn Fein member Martin McGuinness – and with Gordon Brown becoming Prime Minister in succession to Tony Blair. Whereas Blair had emphasised wider constitutional change, largely external to Parliament – though having notable consequences for Parliament – Brown focused on changes designed to strengthen Parliament in calling government to account and in enhancing its links with the public (Norton 2008). He introduced a *Governance of Britain* agenda, with Parliament at the heart of it. There were various initiatives, but the principal legislative manifestation was the enactment in 2010 of the Constitutional Reform and Governance Act, designed to transfer the prerogative power of treaty making from the crown (in effect, the government) to Parliament. It also put the civil service on a statutory basis. The government also pressed for further reform of the House of Lords.

In a little over a decade, the Labour Government thus saw through major changes to the country's constitution. These changes variously modified, reinforced or challenged the established tenets of the traditional constitution. Each tenet was affected in some way by the changes shown in Table 13.2.

Parliamentary sovereignty, already challenged by British membership of the European Community, was further challenged by the incorporation of most provisions of the European Convention on Human Rights (ECHR). This gave the courts an added role, in effect as protectors of the provisions of the convention. If a provision of UK law was found by the courts to conflict with the provisions of the ECHR, a court could issue a declaration of incompatibility. It was then up to Parliament to act on the basis of the court's judgement. Further treaties transferred more policy competences to the EU.

The rule of law was strengthened by the incorporation of the ECHR. The effect of incorporation could be seen as providing a little more balance between the twin pillars of the constitution identified by Dicey (parliamentary sovereignty and the rule of law). The courts could now protect the rule of law against Parliament in a way that was not previously possible. The transfer of powers from the Lord Chancellor to the Lord Chief Justice, and the creation of a supreme court, was also designed to demonstrate judicial independence.

The unitary state was challenged by the creation of elected assemblies in Scotland, Wales and Northern Ireland. In Scotland the new Parliament was given power to legislate on any matter not reserved to the UK Parliament. It was also given power to vary the standard rate of taxation by 3p in the pound. The UK Parliament was expected not to legislate on matters that fell within the competence of the Scottish Parliament. The powers previously exercised by the Welsh Office were devolved to a National Assembly for Wales. Provision for the transfer of more powers was made by the Government of Wales Act 2006. Legislative and administrative powers were also provided for a new Northern Ireland Assembly: elections to the assembly were held in 2007. The devolution of such powers raised questions as to the extent to which Parliament should intervene in matters that were exclusive to a part of the UK other than England. As such, devolution may be seen to limit, in effect, the flexibility of the traditional constitution. As we have seen (Chapter 12), devolution also serves to reinforce the juridical dimension to the constitution, giving the courts a role akin to constitutional courts in determining the legal competence of the new assemblies.

The creation of these devolved bodies also challenged some of the basic tenets of a parliamentary government under a constitutional monarchy. Decision-making power was being hived off to bodies other than the British Cabinet. Some decision-making competences had passed to the institutions of the European Union, others to elected bodies in different parts of the United Kingdom. There was also an enhancement of the powers of the courts at the expense of the government and Parliament. The coherence inherent in central parliamentary government was being challenged.

Table 13.2 Changes to the established tenets of the traditional constitution

Tenets	Affected by
Parliamentary sovereignty	Incorporation of ECHR Ratification of Amsterdam, Nice and Lisbon Treaties
Rule of law	Incorporation of ECHR Creation of a supreme court
Unitary state	Creation of Scottish Parliament, National Assembly for Wales and Northern Ireland Assembly
Parliamentary government under a constitutional monarchy	Use of referendums New voting systems in different parts of the UK Removal of hereditary peers from the House of Lords Freedom of Information Act Modernisation of the House of Commons Transfer of prerogative powers

Parliamentary government was also challenged by the use of referendums. Referendums provide for electors, rather than Parliament, to determine the outcome of particular issues. Opponents of a new electoral system also argued that, if the proposals for electoral reform were implemented, the capacity of the political system to produce accountable government would be undermined. The removal of most hereditary peers proved controversial – not least, and not surprisingly, in the House of Lords – although the full consequences for parliamentary government were not apparent: in the event, it proved to be a more independent House, willing to challenge the House of Commons. Reforms proposed to strengthen the House of Commons had some, albeit limited, effect.

Reform under the Coalition Government

Had a Conservative government been elected in the 2010 General Election, there would not likely have been major constitutional change. The Conservative election manifesto had some proposals for constitutional change, but the party was wedded primarily to the traditional approach. However, the failure of the party to win an overall majority and the decision of the party leader, David Cameron, to seek negotiations with the Liberal Democrats to form a coalition changed fundamentally the scope for change. The two parties held, as we have seen, notably opposing views on constitutional reform. The negotiations almost foundered on the issue of electoral reform (Laws 2010: 104–5; Norton 2011a: 156–7). However, agreement was eventually reached (see Wilson 2010; Norton 2011b) with a Coalition Agreement published that embodied a disparate programme of constitutional and political reform (HM Government 2010: 26–8). The key features of the agreement were:

- five-year fixed-term Parliaments;
- a referendum bill on electoral reform (the AV system) and the creation of fewer and equal-sized constituencies;
- power to recall MPs;
- a committee to bring forward proposals for a wholly or mainly elected second chamber on the basis of proportional representation;
- reform of the House of Commons based on the report of the Select Committee on the Reform of the House of Commons (the Wright Committee);
- a commission to consider the 'West Lothian question';
- petitions that achieved 100,000 signatures to be eligible for debate in the House of Commons.

The first session of the new Parliament saw the passage of the Fixed-term Parliaments Act, stipulating that the next general election was to take place on 7 May 2015 and on the first Thursday in May every five years thereafter. This removed the Prime Minister's discretion to request an elec-

Table 13.3 Result of the referendum on the voting system, 2011

Question: At present, the UK uses the 'first past the post' system to elect MPs to the House of Commons. Should the 'alternative vote' system be used instead?

Yes	6,152,607	32.1%
No	13,013,123	67.9%
Turnout:	42.4%	

tion within the five-year maximum life span of a Parliament. Under the Act, an early election could only be triggered if the House of Commons passed a motion of no confidence in the government (and no new government could be formed within 14 days) or if the House voted, by a two-thirds majority of all MPs, for an early election. It constituted a significant change in the nation's constitutional arrangements and was unusual in that, in respect of a vote of no confidence in the government, it was translating a convention into statute.

The session also saw the enactment of the Parliamentary Voting System and Constituencies Act. This provided for a referendum on the introduction of the Alternative Vote in elections to the House of Commons and for the reduction in the size of the House of Commons from 650 to 600 with effect from the 2015 General Election, with the constituencies to be equal in size, with no deviation from the average by more or less than 5 per cent. As a consequence of the Act, a referendum on AV was held on 5 May 2011. After a bitter campaign, the No vote triumphed decisively, achieving more than two-thirds of the vote (Table 13.3). The referendum was distinctive for being a binding referendum: Parliament had prescribed that the result, whatever it was, would take effect. It was not seeking the advice of the electorate but instead handing it over to electors. Had there been a majority voting Yes, even if only by a majority of one, the Alternative Vote would have been introduced for elections to the House of Commons.

The Government also published a draft House of Lords Bill, providing for a 300-member second chamber, with 80 or 100 per cent of its members elected by the single transferable vote (STV) and each serving single, non-renewable 15-year terms. The draft bill was sent to a Joint Committee of the two Houses for examination and, following its report in April 2012, the Government introduced a House of Lords Reform Bill to replace the existing House of Lords with a largely elected chamber, elected under a regional list system.

The Government also achieved passage of a European Union Act providing for referendums to be held on any treaty changes that entailed a transfer of power or competence from the UK to the European Union. This was a measure very much favoured by the Conservatives. A UK Bill of Rights Commission was also established to investigate the creation of a UK Bill of Rights that incorporated or built on the UK's obligations under the ECHR and protected and extended liberties. This again was a Conservative initiative, many Conservative MPs being wary of the Human Rights Act and wanting to replace it with a distinctly British Bill of Rights. The extent to which this would or could supplant, as opposed to supplement, the European Convention was not clear. The commission was to report by the end of 2012. Another product of Conservative preferences was the appointment at the start of 2012 of a commission to examine the 'West Lothian question' – the situation where MPs from Scotland could vote on English laws, as on education, but MPs from England could not vote on the equivalent Scottish law.

Reform also took place in the House of Commons. From the start of the new Parliament, the chairs of select committees were elected by all MPs and the members of committees by the members of the parliamentary parties, thus moving power from the party whips to backbenchers. A backbench business committee was elected, enabling a committee of the House to decide business on 35 days of the year, moving power from the government's business managers to backbench MPs. The government also introduced an e-petition site: any petition attracting 100,000 votes or more was sent to the backbench business committee to consider if the topic should be allocated for debate in the House.

In the negotiations leading to the creation of the Coalition, the perception was that the Liberal Democrats had got the better of the deal on constitutional issues and the Conservatives the better of the deal on economic issues. However, the loss of the AV referendum made the balance in favour of the Liberal Democrats less obvious. The abandonment of the House of Lords Reform Bill in August 2012 – the result of sustained opposition to the bill from Conservative backbenchers – further strained relations between the coalition partners. In retaliation for the loss of the bill, the leader of the Liberal Democrats, Deputy Prime Minister Nick Clegg, announced that his party would vote against the orders to implement the recommendations of the Boundary Commission.

Complicating the ever-changing constitutional framework was the future of Scotland within the United Kingdom. In 2011 the Scottish Nationalist Party achieved an absolute majority of seats in the Scottish Parliament and could claim a political mandate to hold a referendum in Scotland on whether it should become an independent nation *or* acquire far greater powers than at present while remaining in the UK, this latter option being dubbed 'devo max'. However, the British government, supported by the Labour opposition, made clear that the power to call a referendum resided with the UK government, constitutional issues being reserved to Westminster under the Scotland Act. The British government favoured a referendum solely on the issue of independence, not 'devo max', and wanted it earlier than preferred by the SNP Scottish government. Agreement was reached that

there should be a referendum in 2014 on a single question on Scotland remaining within the UK. However, potential for conflict remained over the actual wording of the question and both pro and anti campaigns got under way in preparation for the referendum campaign.

By 2013 the constitutional framework of the UK had thus undergone notable change under the Coalition Government, with more changes in prospect. The 2010 General Election had not resulted in the return of a Conservative government and essentially a steady-state approach to the constitution. Instead, it produced a government that adopted a similar, active approach to constitutional change to that of its predecessor.

The collective effect of these changes has been to modify the Westminster constitution, though arguably not destroy it. Formally, each of the elements of the constitution remains in place:

1 The doctrine of parliamentary sovereignty may be challenged by incorporation of the ECHR, but formally Parliament is not bound by the rulings of the courts. The courts may issue declarations of incompatibility, but it is then up to Parliament to act on them. Parliament retains the formal power not to take any action (even if the reality is that it will act on them).

2 The minister responsible for introducing the Human Rights Act – the Lord Chancellor, Lord Irvine – conceded that the Human Rights Act 'may be described as a form of higher law' but stressed that the Act decrees that the validity of any measure passed by Parliament is unaffected by any incompatibility with the ECHR. 'In this way, the Act unequivocally preserves Parliament's ability to pass Bills that are or may be in conflict with the convention' (House of Lords *Hansard*, written answer, 30 July 2002).

3 Devolution may challenge the concept of a unitary state, but ultimate power still resides with the centre. Devolved powers – indeed, devolved institutions – may be abolished by Parliament. The Westminster Parliament can still legislate for the whole of the UK, even in areas formally devolved. (Indeed, it variously does legislate in devolved areas, albeit at the invitation of the devolved institution – the Scottish Parliament, for example, may invite the UK Parliament to extend the provisions of a bill affecting England and Wales to Scotland.)

4 Parliament decides whether referendums are to be held and, if so, on what basis. Referendums are normally advisory – Parliament is not bound by them – but Parliament can prescribe that they are binding, as was the case with the 2011 referendum on the electoral system. If they are advisory, it is then for Parliament to decide whether to act on the outcome, though it would be somewhat perverse to ignore how the people have voted.

5 The creation of a Supreme Court has entailed moving law lords out of the House of Lords and into a new building, across the road in Parliament Square. The physical separation may over time affect the culture of the relationship between the court and the executive, but the change confers no new powers to strike down Acts of Parliament.

6 The Fixed-term Parliament Act limits the powers of the Prime Minister in calling a general election, but does not affect the principle that the government rests on the confidence of the House of Commons for its continuance in office. A government may be turned out of office by MPs passing a vote of no confidence.

7 A new electoral system, especially if one of proportional representation, has the potential to undermine the accountability inherent in the present system, but in the event no new system has been introduced, the referendum in 2011 resulting in a large majority opposing a modification to the existing system. Though new electoral systems have been employed for other bodies (including the election of newly created police commissioners in 2012, chosen by the Supplementary Vote), the first-past-the-post system remains in place for the election of members of the House of Commons.

Although the practical effect of some of the changes may be to challenge and, in the long run, undermine the provisions of the Westminster constitution, the basic provisions remain formally in place. The fact that they have been modified or are under challenge means that we may be moving away from the traditional constitution: however, as yet, no new constitution has been put in its place. The traditional approach to the constitution has lost out since 1997, but none of the other approaches can claim to have triumphed.

Parties and the constitution

In the wake of the General Election of 1997, the stance of the parties on constitutional issues was clear. The Labour Party had been returned to power with a mandate to enact various measures of constitutional reform. The party's election manifesto was frequently quoted during debate on those measures, not least during debate on its House of Lords Bill. The Conservative Party remained committed to the traditional approach to the constitution. It had proposed no major constitutional reform in its election manifesto and was able to take a principled stand in opposition to various measures introduced by the Labour Government. The Liberal Democrats were wedded to the liberal approach and could claim some intellectual purity in advocating that approach.

Though some critics claimed that there was not much to choose between the parties, in the sphere of constitutional reform there was a marked division, one that was especially marked between the Conservatives and Liberal Democrats.

However, the actions taken by the parties in government have created difficulties for them in delineating a clear approach to constitutional change. Though they have been responsible, as we have seen, for substantial changes to the British constitution, their actions bear little correlation to any of the approaches to constitutional change outlined in Box 13.1.

The Labour Party

For the Labour Party in office, there were two problems. One was practical: that was, trying to implement all that it had promised in its election manifesto. A three-figure parliamentary majority in the period from 1997 to 2005 was not sufficient to stave off problems. The narrowness of the vote in the referendum in Wales in 1997 appeared to deter ministers from moving quickly to legislate for referendums in the English regions. When, in 2002, Deputy Prime Minister John Prescott published a White Paper on regional government, the proposals were cautious, providing for regional referendums on a rolling basis. It was recognised that not all regions would necessarily vote for a regional assembly. Initially, referendums in three regions were planned, but this was then reduced to one. When, in the first regional referendum, in the North-east in 2004, there was a decisive 78 per cent 'no' vote, the policy was effectively put on hold. The proposal for a referendum on a new electoral system encountered opposition. The report of the Commission on the Voting System in 1998 attracted a vigorous response from both Labour and Conservative opponents of change – one report suggested that at least 100 Labour MPs, including some members of the Cabinet, were opposed to electoral reform – and this appeared to influence the the government. No referendum was held during the parliament and none was promised in the party's 2001 and 2005 election manifestos. The House of Lords Bill encountered stiff opposition in the House of Lords and the government was unable (and in this case largely unwilling) to mobilise a Commons majority to carry through further change. The Freedom of Information Bill ran into opposition from within the ranks of the government itself, various senior ministers – including Home Secretary Jack Straw – not favouring a radical measure. When the bill was published in 1999, it was attacked by proponents of open government for not going far enough.

There was also a practical problem in that not all those reforms that were implemented had the desired effect. Far from undermining support for nationalist parties, devolution in Scotland provided the basis for the SNP to emerge as the largest single party in the 2007 elections to the Scottish

Parliament and form a minority administration and then, in 2011, to win an absolute majority of seats – 69 out of 129 in the Parliament – and form the first majority administration in Scotland. Following the indecisive outcome of the 2007 elections to the National Assembly for Wales, a Labour–Plaid Cymru coalition was formed. Some of the judgments of the courts, interpreting the Human Rights Act, were heavily criticised by ministers (Norton 2007a). And, as we have noted, the House of Lords proved more assertive following implementation of the House of Lords Act (Russell and Sciara 2007), with the Government suffering a string of defeats.

The constitution thus did not change in quite the way that the party had intended. This practical problem also exacerbated the second problem. The party was unable to articulate an intellectually coherent approach to constitutional change. It had moved away from both the socialist approach and the traditional approach and some way towards the liberal approach. However, it only partially embraced the liberal agenda. It was wary of a new system for elections to the House of Commons and appeared to have dropped the idea by the time of the 2001 election. The Government hesitated to pursue regional assemblies in England. It set up a Royal Commission to consider reform of the House of Lords but – until a vote by MPs in 2007 favouring a largely or wholly elected House – it was reluctant to embrace demands for an elected second chamber. Some ministers opposed any change that might challenge the primacy of the House of Commons, in which the Government had a parliamentary majority. In respect of both devolution and the incorporation of the European Convention on Human Rights, the Government ensured that the doctrine of parliamentary sovereignty remained in place.

Although the Labour Government was able to say what it was against, it was not able to articulate what it was for, at least not in terms of the future shape of the British constitution. What was its approach to the constitution? What did it think the constitution was for? What sort of constitution did it wish to see in place in five or ten years? When these questions were put to ministers, they normally avoided answering them. As Prime Minister, Tony Blair avoided making speeches on the subject (Theakston 2005: 33). However, in a debate on the constitution in the House of Lords in December 2002, the Lord Chancellor, Lord Irvine, did concede that the Government did not have an overarching approach, arguing instead that the Government proceeded 'by way of pragmatism based on principle'. The three principles he identified were:

- To remain a parliamentary democracy, with the Westminster parliament supreme and within that the Commons the dominant chamber.

- To increase public engagement with democracy, 'developing a maturer democracy with different centres of power, where individuals enjoy greater rights and where the government is carried out close to the people'.
- 'To devise a solution to each problem on its own terms.'

(House of Lords Hansard, 18 December 2002, Vol. 642, col. 692; www.publications.parliament.uk/pa/ld200203/ldhansrd/vo021218/text/21218-05.htm)

The problem with these 'principles' is that they are not obviously compatible with one another: the first two are in conflict as to where power should reside – should it be in Westminster or in other centres of power? – and the third is a let-out clause, enabling policy to be made up as one goes along.

The government thus lay open to the accusation that it had no clear philosophical approach, nothing that would render its approach predictable or provide it with a reference point in the event of things going wrong. Opponents were thus able to claim that it has been marching down the path – or rather down several paths – of constitutional reform without having a comprehensive map and without any very clear idea of where it was heading. Tony Blair took one path and Gordon Brown another, but with neither articulating a clear destination.

The Conservative Party

The Conservative Party encountered a problem, first in opposition and then, more substantively, in government. In opposition it was able to adopt a consistent and coherent position. It supported the traditional approach to the constitution. It was therefore opposed to any changes that threatened the essential elements of the Westminster system of government. It was especially vehement in its opposition to proposals for electoral reform, mounting a notable campaign against the recommendations of the Commission on the Voting System in 1998. It opposed devolution, fearing that it would threaten the unity of the United Kingdom. It opposed the House of Lords Bill, not least on the grounds that the Government had not said what the second stage of reform would be.

However, it was clear that as and when it was returned to government, the constitution would be very different to that which it had been defending when last in government. How was a future Conservative government to respond to the constitutional changes made under the Labour Government? Should a future Conservative government go for the reactionary, conservative or radical option (Norton 2005)? That is, should it seek to overturn the various reforms made by the Labour Government, in effect reverting to the status quo ante (the **reactionary** option)? Should it seek to conserve the constitution as it stood at the time the Conservatives regained power (the conservative option)? Or should it attempt to come up with a new approach to constitutional change (the radical option)? Party leader William Hague made a speech on the constitution in 1998, effectively ruling out the reactionary option, but neither he nor any of his successors as party leader addressed what stance the party would take if returned to office.

The failure to articulate a clear approach was in any event overtaken by events in 2010. The failure to achieve an absolute majority of seats in the general election produced negotiations with the Liberal Democrats in order to form a coalition. The obvious problem was that, as we have noted, the parties took diametrically opposed views on the constitution. The result was a compromise. That compromise bore no relationship to any approach to constitutional change. The nature of the agreement drawn up by the negotiators (HM Government 2010) reflected the fact that those engaged in the negotiations had no strong grasp of the constitution. The agreement stated 'We will put a binding motion before the House of Commons stating that the next general election will be held on the first Thursday of May 2015'. This reflected the rushed nature of the negotiations. No binding motion was ever brought forward because there was no one to be bound by such a binding motion. (The royal prerogative cannot be constrained simply by a motion of the House of Commons.) The changes proposed were sufficient to achieve political agreement, but they bore no relationship to the preferred position of either party.

The result was that a Conservative-dominated Coalition Government embarked on significant constitutional change that lacked coherence and bore little relationship to the stance of the party on constitutional change. There was major disquiet in Conservative ranks in Parliament over approving the referendum on the electoral system, over the passage of the Fixed-term Parliaments Bill, and over House of Lords reform. Managing the parliamentary party was the immediate concern of the Conservative leadership. However, in the long term the party faced the problem it encountered when it was in opposition. As and when it was returned to government with an absolute majority, what stance was it to take? Should it seek to conserve that which existed, and which it had changed, when it was in coalition, or should it seek to revert to what had previously existed, repealing in particular the Fixed-term Parliaments Act? Like the Labour Government, it had embarked on constitutional changes that lacked intellectual coherence and without a clear view of where it was going.

The Liberal Democrats

The Liberal Democrats, as we have seen, could claim to be in the strongest position on issues of constitutional change. They embraced the liberal approach to constitutional change. When Labour was in office, they were able to evaluate the Government's reform proposals against the liberal agenda. Given that the Government fell short of pursuing a wholly liberal agenda, they were able to push for those measures that the Government had not embraced. Their stance was thus principled and consistent.

However, they faced a major problem in 2010. They were invited to participate in negotiations leading to a coalition. The party was keen to be in government – the last time Liberals had been part of a peacetime government was in 1922 – and would look irresponsible at a time of economic crisis if they refused. They therefore engaged in discussions that necessarily entailed compromising on their intellectual purity. The main goal of the party was a new electoral system based on proportional representation. The compromise, as we have seen, was a referendum on AV, which essentially pleased neither party: the Conservatives wanted no change, and so disliked holding a referendum, and the Liberal Democrats wanted more than AV. The referendum on AV was seen as half-a-loaf from the Liberal Democrat perspective, essentially as a stepping stone to later, more radical change. In the event, the No vote in the 2011 referendum killed off hopes of achieving electoral reform in the foreseeable future. The other prize was seen as an elected House of Lords, but that failed to materialise, the Government abandoning its House of Lords Reform Bill rather than face protracted debate and sustained opposition from Conservative MPs.

The party thus found itself in government, but the price for being part of the policy-making process was to abandon its highly principled position on constitutional change. It was not clear what the future route could be to reclaiming and achieving the liberal approach to constitutional change.

The continuing debate

The constitution remains an issue of debate. It does so at two levels. One is at the wider level of the very nature of the constitution itself. What shape should the British constitution take? How plausible are the various approaches to constitutional change? The Conservatives, as we have seen, favour the traditional approach but have had to compromise in order to form a government. The Liberal Democrats favour the liberal approach, but they too have had to compromise in order to be in government. The Labour Party wants to move away from the Westminster model but have not articulated the type of constitution they wish to achieve for the United Kingdom.

The other level is specific to various measures of constitutional change. Some changes have been made to the constitution. Other changes are advocated, not least – although not exclusively – by advocates of the liberal approach. Supporters of change want, among other things, to see the introduction of a system of proportional representation for parliamentary elections. Opponents, as they did during the 2011 referendum, continue to advance the case for the first-past-the-post method of election (see Box 13.2). Following the 2010 General Election, a Coalition Government was formed, the result of post-election bargaining and a government for which no voter had an opportunity to vote. Opponents of a new electoral system argue that this is exceptional under the existing electoral system, but would likely become the norm under a PR system of election. The use of referendums, and the promise of their use on particular issues, has spurred calls for their more regular use. Opponents are wary of any further use; some are opposed to referendums on principle (see Box 13.3). The role of the second chamber also generates considerable debate. Should there be a second chamber of Parliament? Most of those engaged in constitutional debate support the case for a second chamber but do not agree on the form it should take. Should it be wholly or partly elected? Or should it be an appointed House? (See Chapter 18.) The reforms pursued by successive governments since 1997 have not put an end to debate about the future of the British constitution. If anything, they have given it new impetus, leaving the issue of the constitution very much on the political agenda.

The relationship between the debate about the constitution and about particular measures of constitutional reform throws up a vital question. Should specific reforms derive from a clear view of what the constitution, as a constitution, should look like in five or ten years? Or should the shape of the constitution be determined by specific changes made on the basis of their individual merits?

Electoral reform (proportional representation)

The case for

- Every vote would count, producing seats in proportion to votes.

- It would get rid of the phenomenon of the 'wasted vote'.

- It would be fairer to third parties, ensuring that they got seats in proportion to their percentage of the poll.

- On existing voting patterns, it would usually result in no one party having an overall majority – thus encouraging a coalition and moderate policies.

- A coalition enjoying majority support is more likely to ensure continuity of policy than changes in government under the existing first-past-the-post system.

- A coalition enjoying majority support enjoys a greater popular legitimacy than a single-party government elected by a minority of voters.

- Coalitions resulting from election by proportional representation can prove stable and effective.

The case against

- Very few systems are exactly proportional. Little case to change to a relatively more proportional system than the existing system unless other advantages are clear.

- A system of proportional representation would give an unfair advantage to small parties, which would be likely to hold the balance of power.

- The government is most likely to be chosen as a result of bargaining by parties after a general election and not as a deliberate choice of the electors.

- It would be difficult to ensure accountability to electors in the event of a multi-party coalition being formed.

- Coalitions cobbled together after an election – and for which not one elector has definitively voted – lack the legitimacy of clear electoral approval.

- There is no link between electoral systems and economic performance.

- Coalitions resulting from election under a system of proportional representation can lead to uncertainty and a change of coalition partners.

- Bargaining between parties can produce instability, but coalitions can also prove difficult for the electorate to get rid of.

- There is popular support for the consequences of the existing electoral system – notably a single party being returned to govern the country.

- 'Proportional representation' is a generic term for a large number of electoral systems: there is no agreement on what precise system should replace the existing one.

BOX 13.3

Referenda

The case for

- A referendum is an educational tool – it informs citizens about the issue.

- Holding a referendum encourages people to be more involved in political activity.

- A referendum helps to resolve major issues – it gives a chance for the voters to decide.

- The final outcome of a referendum is more likely to enjoy public support than if the decision is taken solely by Parliament – it is difficult to challenge a decision if all voters have a chance to take part.

- The use of referendums increases support for the political system – voters know they are being consulted on the big issues. Even if they don't take part, they know they have an opportunity to do so.

The case against

- Referendums are blunt weapons that usually allow only a simple answer to a very general question. They do not permit explanations of why voters want something done nor do they usually allow alternatives to be considered.

- Referendums undermine the position of Parliament as the deliberative body of the nation.

- There is no obvious limit on when referendums should be held – if one is conceded on the issue of Europe, why not also have referendums on immigration and capital punishment? With no obvious limit, there is the potential for 'government by referendum'.

- Referendums can be used as majoritarian weapons – being used by the majority to restrict minorities.

- There is the difficulty of ensuring a balanced debate – one side may (indeed, is likely to) have more money and resources.

- There is the difficulty of formulating, and agreeing, a clear and objective question.

- Research shows that turnout in referendums tends to be lower than that in elections for parliamentary and other public elections. In the UK, for example, there have been turnouts of less than 50 per cent in the referendums on having a London mayor (1998) and on the Alternative Vote (2011).

- Referendums are expensive to hold and are often expensive ways of not deciding issues – if government does not like the result it calls another referendum (as has happened in both Denmark and Ireland over ratification of European treaties).

BOX 13.4

BRITAIN IN CONTEXT

A distinctive constitution

The United Kingdom is distinctive for having an uncodified constitution. The laws, rules and customs determining how it is to be governed are not drawn up in a single document. This is a distinction it shares with only two other countries: Israel and New Zealand. Other states have drawn up codified documents as a consequence of being newly formed or having to start afresh, having broken away from a colonising power or having been defeated in battle. Britain has not suffered a distinctive

constitutional break since the seventeenth century. An attempt to impose a codified, or 'written', constitution during the period of the Protectorate was abandoned with the restoration of the monarchy in 1660. When James II fled the country in 1688, he was deemed to have abdicated and those responsible for inviting his daughter and son-in-law, Mary and William of Orange, to assume the throne were keen to stress continuity in the nation's constitutional arrangements. The nation's constitutional foundations thus pre-date the creation, starting with the USA in the eighteenth century, of formal codified constitutions.

There are other distinctive features of the nation's constitutional arrangements. Many countries have entrenched constitutions: that is, they are amendable only through some extraordinary process, such as a two-thirds majority in the legislature and/or approval by the people in a referendum. In the UK laws that change the nature of the constitution – such as the Human Rights Act 1998 – go through the same process as those that determine that it is an offence to leave the scene of an accident.

In terms of the basic structure of government, the UK is also distinctive, but not unique, in having a particular form of parliamentary government. Some systems are presidential, where the head of government and the legislature are elected separately and where neither depends on the other for continuation in office. In a parliamentary system the head of government and other ministers derive their positions through election to the legislature

– they are not elected separately – and they depend for their continuation in office on the confidence of the legislature. There are two basic types of parliamentary government: the Westminster parliamentary system and the continental. The Westminster model stresses single-party government, elected normally through a first-past-the-post electoral system, with two major parties competing for the all-or-nothing spoils of electoral victory. The continental parliamentary system places stress on consensus politics, with Coalition Government derived from elections under electoral systems of proportional representation. The Westminster model has been exported to many Commonwealth countries, though a number have departed from it; New Zealand, for example, has adopted a system of proportional representation. There are also various hybrid presidential–parliamentary systems, where the president is directly elected but a government, under a prime minister, is formed through elections to the legislature. France has a hybrid system; hybrid systems have been adopted by a number of democracies in central and eastern Europe.

Chapter summary

The British constitution remains distinctive for not being codified in a single document. It is drawn from several sources and retains the main components that it has developed over three centuries. Although little debated in the years between 1945 and 1970, it has been the subject of dispute – and of change – in the years since. Proponents of reform have argued that existing constitutional arrangements have not proved adequate to meet the political and economic challenges faced by the United Kingdom. They have pressed for reform, and various approaches to change have developed. Debate has polarised around two approaches: the liberal, favouring a new constitutional settlement for the United Kingdom; and the traditional, favouring retention of the principal components of the existing constitution.

The constitution has undergone significant change as a result of British membership of the EC/EU, the election of a Labour government in May 1997 and the creation of a Coalition Government in 2010. The juridical dimension of the constitution has been strengthened as a result of the incorporation of the European Convention on Human Rights into British law; by the devolving of powers to elected bodies in different parts of the UK, the courts acting in effect as constitutional courts for the devolved bodies; and by the creation of a supreme court. New European treaties have resulted in more policy-making power passing upwards to the institutions of the European Union. Devolution has seen some powers pass downwards to elected bodies in Scotland, Wales and Northern Ireland. The consequence of these changes has been to change the contours of the 'traditional', or Westminster, model of government, although not destroying the model altogether.

The constitution remains a subject of political controversy, posing problems for each of the main political parties. Governments since 1997 have pursued change but have done so on a pragmatic basis, embracing no particular approach to change. The British constitution has changed significantly in recent years and continues to be the subject of demands for further change, but its future shape remains unclear.

Discussion points

- How does the constitution of the United Kingdom differ from that of other countries? What does it have in common with them?
- Which approach to constitutional change do you find most persuasive, and why?
- How convincing are the principal arguments against holding referendums?
- Is electoral reform desirable?
- What are the main obstacles to achieving major constitutional change in the United Kingdom?

Further reading

For the principal features of the contemporary constitution, see, for example, Alder (2011).

For an overview of constitutional change in the twentieth century, see the contributions to Bogdanor (2003) and Norton (2011c). Works addressing constitutional change under the Labour Government are King (2007) and Bogdanor (2009). King tends to take a more critical view; the constitution, in his view, is 'a mess'. Bogdanor sees the old system being replaced by a new one. On the constitution under the Coalition Government, see Bogdanor (2011).

Also useful are Oliver (2003) and Jowell and Oliver (2011). Johnson (2004) and Marquand (2004) offer critical reflective analyses. On Conservative and Labour approaches to the constitution, see Norton (2005, 2007b, 2008).

Articles covering aspects of constitutional change can also be found in scholarly journals, not least *Public Law* and *Parliamentary Affairs*, as well as in student magazines such as *Politics Review*.

There are various useful publications that address specific issues. Most of these are identified in subsequent chapters (The crown, Chapter 14; House of Commons, Chapters 15 and 16; House of Lords, Chapter 17; The judiciary, Chapter 21). Chapter 21 also addresses issues arising from membership of the European Union, the incorporation of the European Convention on Human Rights, devolution and the Constitutional Reform Act. On electoral reform, see Ministry of Justice (2008). On referendums, see Butler and Ranney (1994) and Qvortrup (2005).

Bibliography

Alder, J. (2011) *Constitutional and Administrative Law*, 8th edn (Palgrave Macmillan).

Benn, T. (1993) *Common Sense* (Hutchinson).

Bogdanor, V. (ed.) (2003) *The British Constitution in the Twentieth Century* (Oxford University Press/British Academy).

Bogdanor, V. (2009) *The New British Constitution* (Hart Publishing).

Bogdanor, V. (2011) *The Coalition and the Constitution* (Hart Publishing).

Bradley, A.W., Ziegler, K.S. and Baranger, D. (2007) 'Constitutionalism and the Role of Parliaments', in Ziegler, K.S., Baranger, D. and Bradley, A.W. (eds) *Constitutionalism and the Role of Parliaments* (Hart Publishing).

Brazier, R. (1994) *Constitutional Practice*, 2nd edn (Oxford University Press).

Butler, D. and Ranney, A. (1994) *Referendums around the World* (AEI Press).

Finer, S.E. (ed.) (1975) *Adversary Politics and Electoral Reform* (Wigram).

Fitzpatrick, B. (1999) 'A Dualist House of Lords in a Sea of Monist Community Law', in Dickson, B. and Carmichael, P. (eds) *The House of Lords: Its Parliamentary and Judicial Roles* (Hart Publishing).

Foley, M. (1999) *The Politics of the British Constitution* (Manchester University Press).

Hailsham, Lord (1976) *Elective Dictatorship* (BBC).

HM Government (2010) *The Coalition: our programme for government* (The Cabinet Office).

Institute for Public Policy Research (1992) *A New Constitution for the United Kingdom* (Mansell).

Ivison, D. (1999) 'Pluralism and the Hobbesian Logic of Negative Constitutionalism', *Political Studies*, vol. 47, no. 1.

Johnson, N. (2004) *Reshaping the British Constitution* (Palgrave Macmillan).

Jowell, J. and Oliver, D. (2011) (eds) *The Changing Constitution,* 7th edn (Oxford University Press).

King, A. (2007) *The British Constitution* (Oxford University Press).

Labour Party (1997) *New Labour: Because Britain Deserves Better* (Labour Party).

Laws, D. (2010) *22 Days in May* (Biteback).

Marquand, D. (2004) *The Decline of the Public: The Hollowing Out of Citizenship* (Polity Press).

Maxwell, P. (1999) 'The House of Lords as a Constitutional Court – the Implications of Ex Parte EOC', in B. Dickson and P. Carmichael (eds) *The House of Lords: Its Parliamentary and Judicial Roles* (Hart Publishing).

Ministry of Justice (2008) *Review of Voting Systems: The Experience of New Voting Systems in the United Kingdom since 1997*, Cm 7304 (The Stationery Office).

Norton, P. (1982) *The Constitution in Flux* (Blackwell).

Norton, P. (1993) 'The Constitution: Approaches to Reform', *Politics Review*, vol. 3, no. 1.

Norton, P. (2005) 'The Constitution', in K. Hickson (ed.) *The Political Thought of the Conservative Party Since 1945* (Palgrave Macmillan).

Norton, P. (2007a) 'The Constitution: Fragmentation or Adaptation?' in Rush, M. and Giddings, P. (ed.) *The Palgrave Review of British Politics 2006* (Palgrave Macmillan).

Norton, P. (2007b) 'Tony Blair and the Constitution', *British Politics*, vol. 2.

Norton, P. (2008) 'The Constitution under Gordon Brown', *Politics Review*, vol. 17, no. 3.

Norton, P. (2011a) 'The Con-Lib Agenda for the "New Politics" and Constitutional Reform', in Lee, S. and Beech, M. (eds), *The Cameron-Clegg Coalition* (Palgrave Macmillan).

Norton, P. (2011b) 'The Politics of Coalition', in N. Allen and J. Bartle (eds), *Britain at the Polls 2010* (Sage).

Norton, P. (2011c) (ed.) *A Century of Constitutional Reform* (Wiley-Blackwell).

Oliver, D. (2003) *Constitutional Reform in the UK* (Oxford University Press).

Qvortrup, M. (2005) *A Comparative Study of Referendums: Government By the People*, 2nd edn (Manchester University Press).

Ranney, A. and Butler, D. (1994) *Referendums Around the World. The Growing Use of Democracy* (AEI Press).

Royal Commission on the Reform of the House of Lords (2000) *A House for the Future*, Cm 4534.

Russell, M. and Sciara, M. (2007) 'Why Does the Government get Defeated in the House of Lords? The Lords, the Party System and British Politics', *British Politics*, vol. 2.

Theakston, K. (2005) 'Prime Ministers and the Constitution: Attlee to Blair', *Parliamentary Affairs*, vol. 58, no. 1.

Wilson, R. (2010) *5 Days to Power* (Biteback).

Useful websites

Organisations with an interest in constitutional change

Constitution Unit: www.ucl.ac.uk/constitution-unit
Electoral Reform Society: www.electoral-reform.org.uk
Campaign for Freedom of Information: www.cfoi.org.uk
Unlock Democracy: www.unlockdemocracy.org.uk/

Reports

Independent Commission on the Voting System (the Jenkins Commission): www.archive.official-documents.co.uk/document/cm40/4090/4090.htm.

Ministry of Justice, *The Governance of Britain*, Cm 7170: www.official-documents.gov.uk/document/cm71/7170/7170.asp.

Ministry of Justice, *Review of Voting Systems: The Experience of New Voting Systems in the United Kingdom since 1997*, Cm 7304: www.official-documents.gov.uk/documents/cm73/7304/7304.asp.

Royal Commission on the Reform of the House of Lords (the Wakeham Commission), *A House for the Future*: www.archive.official-documents.co.uk/document/cm45/4534/4534.htm.

Government departments with responsibility for constitutional issues

Ministry of Justice: www.justice.gov.uk.
Home Office: www.homeoffice.gov.uk.

Other official bodies

The Electoral Commission: www.electoralcommission.org.uk.

European bodies

European Convention on Human Rights: www.echr.coe.int.

CHAPTER 14

The crown

Philip Norton

> " The sovereign has, under a constitutional monarchy such as ours, three rights – the right to be consulted, the right to encourage, the right to warn "
>
> Walter Bagehot, *The English Constitution*

Learning objectives

- To identify the place of the monarchy in British constitutional history.

- To detail the political significance of 'the crown'.

- To outline the roles that citizens expect the monarch to fulfil and the extent to which they are carried out.

- To outline criticisms made of the monarchy – and the royal family – in recent years.

- To look at proposals for change.

I t is an extraordinary fact, often overlooked, that Britain's representative democracy evolved over a thousand years out of an all-encompassing monarchy underpinned by the religious notion of the divine right of kings. The monarchical shell remains intact, but the inner workings have been taken over by party political leaders and civil servants. The shell itself has been the subject of critical comment, especially in recent years. This chapter analyses the emergence of the modern monarchy and considers its still important functions together with the arguments of the critics.

The monarchy

The crown is the symbol of all executive authority. It is conferred on the monarch. The monarchy is the oldest secular institution in England and dates back at least to the ninth century. In Anglo-Saxon and Norman times, the formal power that the crown conferred – executive, legislative and judicial – was exercised personally by the monarch. The King had a court to advise him and, as the task of government became more demanding, so the various functions were exercised on the King's behalf by other bodies. Those bodies now exercise powers independent of the control of the monarch, but they remain formally the instruments of the crown. The courts are Her Majesty's courts and the government is Her Majesty's government. Parliament is summoned and prorogued by royal decree. Civil servants are crown appointees. Many powers – prerogative powers – are still exercised in the name of the crown. The monarch exercises few powers personally, but those powers remain important. However, the importance of the monarchy in the twenty-first century derives more from what it stands for than from what it does.

The monarchy has been eclipsed as a major political institution not only by the sheer demands of governing a growing kingdom but also by changes in the popular perception of what form of government is legitimate. The policy-making power exercised by a hereditary monarch has given way to the exercise of power by institutions deemed more representative. However, the monarchy has retained a claim to be a representative institution in one particular definition of the term. It is this claim that largely defines the activities of the monarch today.

The concept of representation

The monarchy predates by several centuries the emergence of the concept of representation. The term 'representation' entered the English language through French derivatives of the Latin *repraesentare* and did not assume a political meaning until the sixteenth century. It permits at least four separate usages (see Birch 1964; Pitkin 1967):

1 It may denote acting on behalf of some individual or group, seeking to defend and promote the interests of the person or persons 'represented'.

2 It may denote persons or assemblies that have been freely elected. Although it is not always the case that persons so elected will act to defend and pursue the interests of electors, they will normally be expected to do so.

3 It may be used to signify a person or persons typical of a particular class or group of persons. It is in this sense that it is used when opinion pollsters identify a representative sample.

4 It may be used in a symbolic sense. Thus, individuals or objects may 'stand for' something: for example, a flag symbolising the unity of the nation.

The belief that free election was a prerequisite for someone to claim to act on behalf of others grew in the nineteenth century. Before then, the concept of 'virtual representation' held great sway. This concept was well expressed by Edmund Burke. It was a form of representation, he wrote,

> in which there is a communion of interests, and a sympathy in feelings and desires, between those who act in the name of any description of people, and the people in whose name they act, though the trustees are not actually chosen by them.
>
> (Pitkin 1967: 173)

It was a concept challenged by the perception that the claim to speak on behalf of a particular body of individuals could not be sustained unless those individuals had signified their agreement, and the way to signify that agreement was through the ballot box. This challenge proved increasingly successful, with the extension of the franchise and, to ensure elections free of coercion, changes in the method of election (the introduction of secret ballots, for example). By the end of the 1880s the majority of working men had the vote. By Acts of 1918 and 1928, the vote was given to women.

The extension of the franchise in the nineteenth and early twentieth centuries meant that the House of Commons could claim to be a representative institution under the first and second definitions of the term. The unelected House of Lords could not make such a claim. The result, as we shall see (Chapter 16), was a significant shift in the relationship between the two Houses. However, it was not only the unelected upper house that could not make such a claim. Nor could the unelected monarch. Nor could the monarch make a claim to be representative of the nation under the third definition. The claim of the monarch to be 'representative' derives solely from the fourth definition. The monarch stands as a symbol. The strength of the monarch as symbol has been earned at the expense of exercising political powers. To symbolise the unity of the nation, the monarch has had to stand apart from the partisan fray. The monarch has also had to stand aloof from any public controversy. When controversy has struck – as during the abdication crisis in 1936 and during periods of marital rift between members of the royal family in the 1990s – it has undermined support for the institution of monarchy and called into question its very purpose.

Royal ceremonial is symbolic of continuity with the past and of national unity
Source: Copyright © Pool/Tim Graham Picture Library/Corbis

Development of the monarchy

The present monarch, despite some breaks in the direct line of succession, can trace her descent from King Egbert, who united England under his rule in AD 829. Only once has the continuity of the monarchy been broken: from 1642, when Charles I was deposed (and later executed) until the Restoration in 1660, when his son Charles II was put on the throne, restoring the line of succession. The principle of heredity has been preserved since at least the eleventh century. The succession is now governed by statute and common law, the throne descending to the eldest son or, in the absence of a son, the eldest daughter. In 2012 the Government announced that there was agreement with other Commonwealth nations where the monarch is head of state that, in future, the first-born child, regardless of sex, should become monarch. If the monarch is under 18 years of age, a regent is appointed.

Although all power was initially exercised by the monarch, it was never an absolute power. In the coronation oath, the King promised to 'forbid all rapine and injustice to men of all conditions', and he was expected to consult with the leading men of his realm, both clerical and lay, in order to discover and declare the law and before the levying of any extraordinary measures of taxation. Such an expectation was to find documented expression in Magna Carta, to which King John affixed his seal in 1215 and which is now recognised as a document of critical constitutional significance. At the time it was seen by the barons as an expression of existing rights, not a novel departure from them.

The expectation that the King would consult with the leading men of the realm gradually expanded to encompass knights and burgesses, summoned to assent on behalf of local communities to the raising of more money to meet the King's growing expenses. From the summoning of these local dignitaries to court there developed a Parliament – the term was first used in the thirteenth century – and the emergence of two separate houses, the Lords and the Commons.

The relationship of crown and Parliament was, for several centuries, one of struggle. Although formally the King's Parliament, the King depended on the institution for the grant of supply (money) and increasingly for assent to new laws. Parliament made the grant of supply dependent on the King granting a redress of grievances. Tudor monarchs turned to Parliament for support and usually got it; but the effect of their actions was to acknowledge the growing importance of the body. Stuart kings were less appreciative. James I and his successor, Charles I, upheld the doctrine of the **divine right** of kings: that is, that the position and powers of the King are given by God, and the position and

privileges of Parliament therefore derive from the King's grace. Charles' pursuit of the doctrine led to an attempt to rule without the assent of Parliament and ultimately to civil war and the beheading of the King in 1649. The period of republican government that followed was a failure and consequently short-lived. The monarchy was restored under Charles I's son, Charles II, in 1660, only to produce another clash a few years later.

Charles II's brother, James II, adhered to the divine right of kings and to the Roman Catholic faith. Both produced a clash with Parliament, and James attempted to rule by **royal prerogative** alone. A second civil war was averted when James fled the country following the arrival of William of Orange (James's Protestant son-in-law), who had been invited by leading politicians and churchmen. At the invitation of a new Parliament, William and his wife Mary (James's daughter) jointly assumed the throne. However, the offer of the crown had been conditional on their acceptance of the Declaration of Right – embodied in statute as the 1689 Bill of Rights – which declared the suspending of laws and the levying of taxation without the approval of Parliament to be illegal. As the historian G.M. Trevelyan observed, James II had forced the country to choose between royal absolutism and parliamentary government (Trevelyan 1938: 245). It chose parliamentary government.

The dependence of the monarch on Parliament was thus established, and the years since have witnessed the gradual withdrawal of the sovereign from the personal exercise of executive authority. Increasingly, the monarch became dependent on ministers, both for the exercise of executive duties and in order to manage parliamentary business. This dependence was all the greater when Queen Anne died in 1714 without an heir (all her children having died) and yet another monarch was imported from the continent – this time George, Elector of Hanover. George I was not especially interested in politics and in any case did not speak English, so the task of chairing the Cabinet, traditionally the King's job, fell to the First Lord of the Treasury. Under Robert Walpole this role was assiduously developed and Walpole became the most important of the King's ministers: he became 'prime minister'. Anne's dying without an heir and George's poor language skills facilitated the emergence of an office that is now at the heart of British politics.

George's grandson, George III, succeeded in winning back some of the monarchy's power later in the eighteenth century. It was still the King, after all, who appointed ministers, and by skilfully using his patronage he could influence who sat in the House of Commons. This power, though, was undermined early in the nineteenth century. In 1832 the Great Reform Act introduced a uniform electoral system, and subsequent Reform Acts further extended the franchise. The age of a representative democracy, displacing the concept of virtual representation, had arrived. The effect was to marginalise the monarch as a political actor. To win votes in Parliament, parties quickly organised themselves into coherent and highly structured movements, and the leader of the majority party following a general election became Prime Minister. The choice of Prime Minister and government remained formally in the hands of the monarch, but in practice the selection came to be made on a regular basis by the electorate.

Queen Victoria was the last monarch seriously to consider vetoing legislation (the last monarch actually to do so was Queen Anne, who withheld Royal Assent from the Scottish Militia Bill 1707). The year 1834 was the last occasion that a ministry fell for want of the sovereign's confidence; thereafter, it was the confidence of the House of Commons that counted. Victoria was also the last monarch to exercise a personal preference in the choice of Prime Minister (later monarchs, where a choice existed, acted under advice) and the last to be instrumental in pushing successfully for the enactment of particular legislative measures (Hardie 1970: 67). By the end of her reign it was clear that the monarch, whatever the formal powers vested by the constitution, was constrained politically by a representative assembly elected by the adult male population, the government being formed largely by members drawn from that assembly. Victoria could no longer exercise the choices she had been able to do when she first ascended the throne.

By the beginning of the twentieth century the monarch sat largely on the sidelines of the political system, unable to control Parliament, unable to exercise a real choice in the appointment of ministers, unable to exercise a choice in appointing judges. The extensive power once exercised by the King had now passed largely to the voters and to politicians. The elective power was exercised by voters on election day: between elections it was the Prime Minister who exercised many of the powers formally vested in the monarch. By controlling government appointments, the Prime Minister was able to dominate the executive side of government. And as long as he could command majority support in the House of Commons, he was able to dominate the legislative side of government. Power thus shifted from an unelected monarch to what one writer later dubbed an 'elected monarch' (Benemy 1965) – the occupant not of Buckingham Palace but of 10 Downing Street.

The shift to a position detached from regular partisan involvement, and above the actual exercise of executive power, was confirmed under Victoria's successors. 'Since 1901 the trend towards a real political neutrality, not merely a matter of appearances, has been steady, reign by reign' (Hardie 1970: 188). The transition has been facilitated by no great constitutional Act. Several statutes have impinged on the prerogative power, but many of the legal powers remain.

There is nothing in law that prevents the monarch from vetoing a bill or from exercising personal choice in the invitation to form a government. The monarch is instead bound by conventions of the constitution (see Chapter 13). Thus, it is a convention that the monarch gives her assent to bills passed by Parliament and that she summons the leader of the largest party following a general election to form a government. Such conventions mean that the actions of the monarch are predictable – no personal choice is involved – and they have helped to ease the passage of the monarch from one important constitutional position to another.

These changes have meant that we can distinguish now between 'the crown' and 'the monarch'. The former denotes the executive authority that formally rests with the monarch but is in practice exercised in the name of the monarch, and the latter is the individual who is head of state and performs particular functions. The separation of the two is significant constitutionally and has major political consequences.

Political significance of the crown

The transfer of power from monarch to a political executive meant that it became possible to distinguish between head of state and head of government. It also ensured that great political power rested with ministers. Prerogative powers, as we have seen, remain important. They are powers that have always resided in the crown and that have not been displaced by statute. Many such powers remain in existence, though just how many is not clear. There is no definitive list, though a parliamentary committee in 2004 did publish a list supplied by the government, setting out what it considered to be the main prerogatives. They included the summoning, prorogation and dissolution of Parliament; the appointment and deployment of armed forces; declarations of war; the giving of royal assent to bills; the negotiation and ratification of treaties; the appointment of ministers, civil servants, senior figures in the church (the monarch is supreme governor of the Church of England) and in the judiciary; and the recognition of foreign states.

Some of these have since been transferred from the crown to Parliament. The Constitutional Reform and Governance Act 2010 transferred the power to ratify treaties from the crown to Parliament. (It also put the civil service on a statutory basis.) The Fixed-term Parliaments Act 2011 removed the power of the crown to determine when, within a five-year maximum, a general election shall be held. As we have seen (Chapter 13), the conditions under which an early election may take place are determined by the provisions of the Act.

Although these changes reduced the number of powers vested in the crown (in effect, reducing the power of ministers), substantial prerogative powers still remain with ministers. The decision to go to war, to take one of the most, if not the most, important prerogative powers, remains with Government. Prime Minister Gordon Brown (2007–10) proposed that a parliamentary resolution be agreed, providing for the House of Commons to give its assent to committing armed forces to action abroad, but no resolution has yet been agreed.

The monarch is thus the person in whom the crown vests, but the powers inherent in the crown are exercised elsewhere, in most cases by her ministers. Those powers are usually exercised directly by ministers. In other words, the monarch does not even announce the decisions taken by ministers in her name. Announcements of new ministerial appointments are made directly from Downing Street. Decisions as to military action have also been announced by No. 10. In 1939 the announcement that Britain was at war with Germany was made not by the King, George VI, but by the Prime Minister, Neville Chamberlain. The decision to send a task force to repel the Argentine invasion of the Falkland Islands in 1982 was taken by Margaret Thatcher and the Cabinet. The Chief of Naval Staff told her that a force could retake the islands. 'All he needed was my authority to begin to assemble it. I gave it to him . . . We reserved for Cabinet the decision as to whether and when the task force should sail' (Thatcher 1993: 179). Announcements about the conflict were subsequently made from Downing Street or the Ministry of Defence. In 2003 decisions about joining with the USA in an attack on Iraq were taken by the Prime Minister, Tony Blair. Media attention focused on 10 Downing Street, not Buckingham Palace.

The prerogative is frequently exercised through rules, known as Orders in Council, that by virtue of their nature require no parliamentary authorisation. (Some Orders, though, are also made under statutory authorisation.) Orders in Council allow government to act quickly. Thus, for example, an Order in Council in 1982 allowed the requisitioning of ships for use in the campaign to retake the Falkland Islands. Not only are many prerogative powers exercised without the need for Parliament's approval, they are in many cases also protected from judicial scrutiny. The courts have held that many of the powers exercised under the royal prerogative are not open to judicial review.

Although the monarch will normally be kept informed of decisions made in her name, and she sees copies of state papers, she is not a part of the decision making that is involved. Nonetheless, the fiction is maintained that the decisions are hers. Peter Hennessy records that it was explained to him why the Table Office of the House of Commons would not accept parliamentary questions dealing with honours: 'It's the Palace', he was told (Hennessy 2000: 75). In other words, it was a matter for the Queen.

The maintenance of the royal prerogative thus puts power in the hands of the government. The government has, in effect, acquired tremendous powers, many of which it can exercise unilaterally. Parliament can question ministers about some aspects of the exercise of powers under the royal prerogative and could ultimately remove a government from office if dissatisfied with its conduct. However, so long as a government enjoys an overall majority in the House of Commons, it is unlikely to be much troubled about its capacity to exercise its powers.

Although the monarch now acts in a symbolic capacity, the country still has a form of medieval monarch – the Prime Minister. The monarch reigns, the Prime Minister rules. The Prime Minister enjoys the powers that he does because of the confluence of two things: a majority in the House of Commons and the royal prerogative.

The contemporary role of the monarchy

Given that the powers of the crown have almost wholly passed to the government, what then is the role of the monarch? Most people still believe that the monarchy has an important role to play in the future of Britain. In a MORI poll in January 2002, 80 per cent of those questioned said that the monarchy was important to Britain, as against 18 per cent who said that it was not. What, then, is the monarch's contemporary role? Two primary tasks can be identified. One is essentially a representative task: that is, symbolising the unity and traditional standards of the nation. The second is to fulfil certain political functions. The weakness of the monarch in being able to exercise independent decisions in the latter task underpins the strength of the monarchy in fulfilling the former. If the monarch were to engage in partisan activity, it would undermine her claim to symbolise the unity of the nation.

Symbolic role

The functions fulfilled by the monarch under the first heading are several. A majority of respondents in a poll in the late 1980s considered six functions to be 'very' or 'quite' important. As we shall see, the extent to which these functions are actually fulfilled by members of the royal family has become a matter of considerable debate. Two functions – preserving the class system and distracting people from problems affecting the country – were considered by most respondents as 'not very' or 'not at all' important.

Representing the UK at home and abroad

As a symbolic function, representing the country at home and abroad is a task normally ascribed to any head of state. Because no partisan connotations attach to her activities, the sovereign is able to engage the public commitment of citizens in a way that politicians cannot. When the President of the United States travels within the USA or goes abroad he does so both as head of state and as head of government; as head of government, he is a practising politician. When the Queen attends the Commonwealth Prime Ministers' conference, she does so as symbolic head of the Commonwealth. The British government is represented by the Prime Minister, who is then able to engage in friendly, or not so friendly, discussions with fellow heads of government. The Queen stays above the fray. Similarly, at home, when opening a hospital or attending a major public event, the Queen is able to stand as a symbol of the nation. Invitations to the Prime Minister or leader of an opposition party to perform such tasks run the risk of attracting partisan objection.

At least two practical benefits are believed to derive from this non-partisan role, one political, the other economic. Like many of her predecessors, the Queen has amassed considerable experience by virtue of her monarchical longevity. According to one of her Prime Ministers, Tony Blair: 'she has an absolutely unparalleled amount of experience of what it's like to be at the top of a government' (Hardman 2007: 168). In 2012 she celebrated her Diamond Jubilee as Queen. During her 60 years on the throne, she had been served by 12 Prime Ministers. As one MP noted, she had met nearly a quarter of all the Presidents of the United States throughout its history and had known a fifth of all British Prime Ministers (Simon Hughes, House of Commons: Official Report, 7 March 2012, col. 859). Two of her three most recent Prime Ministers (Tony Blair and David Cameron) had not been born when she ascended the throne. Her experience, coupled with her neutrality, has meant that she has been able to offer Prime Ministers detached and informed observations. (The Prime Minister has an audience with the Queen each week.) As an informed figure who offers no challenge to their position, she also offers an informed ear to an embattled premier: 'the Queen harbours a greater store of political knowledge and wisdom than any prime minister whose length of career is at the mercy of fickle voters' (Hamilton 2002: 17). The value of the Queen's role to premiers has been variously attested by successive occupants of Downing Street (see Shawcross 2002). These have included Labour Prime Ministers Harold Wilson, James Callaghan, and Tony Blair, who were especially warm in their praise. Blair said at the time of the Queen's golden wedding anniversary that he enjoyed his weekly audience with the Queen, not simply because of her experience but because she was an 'extraordinarily shrewd and perceptive observer of the world. Her advice is worth having' (*The Times*, 21 November 1997). Her questions, declared Gordon Brown 'are designed to get the best out of you' (Hardman 2011: 186). Her contact is not confined to the Prime Minister. The **Chancellor of the Exchequer** also sees her the night before a Budget speech. As Gordon Brown recalled when he was Chancellor: 'She knows over the years what works and what doesn't. Sometimes you go back and change a bit of your speech' (Hardman 2007: 170).

The political benefit has also been seen in the international arena. By virtue of her experience and neutral position, the Queen enjoys the respect of international leaders, not least those gathered in the Commonwealth, a body comprising more than 50 countries with over 2 billion inhabitants. During the 1980s, when relations between the British government led by Margaret Thatcher and a number of Commonwealth governments were sometimes acrimonious (on the issue of sanctions against South Africa, for example), she reputedly used her influence with Commonwealth leaders 'to ensure that they took account of Britain's difficulties' (Ziegler 1996). There were fears that, without her emollient influence, the Commonwealth would have broken up or that Britain would have been expelled from it. Her state visit to Dublin in 2011 – the first by a monarch since 1912 – was seen as a critical success in cementing the relationship of the United Kingdom and the Irish Republic. It was, declared one Labour MP, 'a very powerful symbol of reconciliation, which I believe will have a profound effect on healing the wounds that have disfigured life in the island of Ireland for generations' (Paul Flynn, House of Commons: Official Report, 7 March 2012, col. 870).

In terms of economic benefit, some observers claim – although a number of critics dispute it – that the Queen and leading members of the royal family (such as the Prince of Wales) are good for British trade. At home, royal palaces are major tourist attractions, though critics point out that Versailles – the royal palace in republican France – gets more visitors than Buckingham Palace. The symbolism, the history and the pageantry that surround the monarchy serve to make the Queen and her immediate family a potent source of media and public interest abroad. Royal (although not formal state) visits are often geared to export promotions, although critics claim that the visits do not have the impact claimed or are not followed up adequately by the exporters themselves. Such visits, though, normally draw crowds that would not be attracted by a visiting politician or industrialist.

Setting standards of citizenship and family life

For most of the present Queen's reign, this has been seen as an important task. The Queen has been expected to lead by example in maintaining standards of citizenship and family life. As head of state and secular head of the established Church, she is expected to be above criticism. She applies herself assiduously to her duties; even her most ardent critics concede that she is diligent (Wilson 1989: 190). In April 1947, at the age of 21, while still Princess Elizabeth, she said in a broadcast to the Commonwealth: 'I declare before you that my whole life, be it long or short, shall be devoted to your service.' She reiterated her vow when she addressed both Houses of Parliament in 2002 and again in 2012. She and members of the royal family undertake about 4,000 public engagements each year (Hardman 2007: 15); she has made more than 250 overseas visits. She is the patron of more than 620 charities and voluntary organisations. Other members of her family involve themselves in charitable activities. The Prince of Wales founded 18 out of 20 charities that form the 'Prince's Charities', a group of not-for-profit organisations. The Prince's Youth Business Trust has been responsible for funding the launch of 30,000 small businesses. The work of the Princess Royal (Princess Anne) as president of the Save the Children Fund helped to raise its international profile. Indeed, the name of a member of the royal family adorns the headed notepaper of about 3,000 organisations.

Up to and including the 1980s the Queen was held to epitomise not only standards of good citizenship, applying herself selflessly to her public duties, but also family life in a way that others could both empathise with and hope to emulate. (Queen Elizabeth the Queen Mother – widow of George VI – was popularly portrayed as 'the nation's grandmother'.) Significantly, during the national miners' strike in 1984, the wives of striking miners petitioned the Queen for help. However, the extent to which the Queen fulfils this role has been the subject of much publicised debate since the late 1980s. The problem lay not so much with the Queen personally but with members of her family. By 1992, the Queen was head of a family that had not sustained one successful lasting marriage. The Prince of Wales, as well as the Princess, admitted adultery. The Duchess of York was pictured cavorting topless with her 'financial adviser' while her daughters were present. By the end of the decade the divorced heir to the throne was attending public engagements with his companion, Camilla Parker-Bowles. In a MORI poll in January 2002, respondents were divided as to whether or not members of the royal family had 'high moral standards': 48 per cent thought that they did, and 44 per cent thought that they did not.

The claim to maintain high standards was also eroded by the collapse of a trial in 2002 involving the butler to Diana, Princess of Wales. The butler, Paul Burrell, was charged with stealing many items belonging to his late employer. The trial collapsed after it emerged that the Queen recalled a conversation with Burrell in which he said that he was storing items for safe-keeping. Following the collapse of the Burrell trial, a YouGov poll (17 November 2002) found that 17 per cent of respondents thought that 'recent revelations' had damaged the royal family 'a great deal' and 41 per cent 'a fair amount'.

Uniting people despite differences

The monarch symbolises the unity of the nation. The Queen is head of state. Various public functions are carried out in the name of the crown, notably public prosecutions, and as the person in whom the crown vests the monarch's name attaches to the various organs of the state: the government, courts and armed services. The crown, in effect, substitutes for the concept of the state (a concept not well understood or utilised in Britain), and the monarch serves as the personification of the crown. Nowhere is the extent of this personification better demonstrated than on British postage stamps. These are unique: British stamps alone carry the monarch's head with no mention of the name of the nation. The monarch provides a clear, living focal point for the expression of national unity, national pride and, if necessary, national grief.

This role is facilitated by the monarch largely transcending political activity. Citizens' loyalties can flow to the crown without being hindered by political considerations. The Queen's role as head of the Commonwealth may also have helped to create a 'colour-blind' monarchy, in which the welfare of everyone, regardless of race, is taken seriously. At different points this century, members of the royal family have also shown concern for the economically underprivileged and those who have lost their livelihoods – ranging from the 'something must be done' remark in the 1930s of the then Prince of Wales (later Edward VIII) about unemployment while visiting Wales to the work of the present Prince of Wales to help disadvantaged youths.

This unifying role has also acquired a new significance as a consequence of devolution. The crown remains the one unifying feature of the United Kingdom. The UK traditionally comprises one constitutional people under one crown and Parliament. The position of the UK Parliament is circumscribed by virtue of devolving powers to elected assemblies in different parts of the UK. The royal family anticipated the consequences of devolution by seeking funding for an enhancement of the royal offices and residence in Scotland. The Queen opened the Scottish Parliament as well as the National Assembly for Wales. In the event of conflict between a devolved government and the UK government, the Queen constitutes the one person to whom members of both governments owe an allegiance.

The extent to which this unifying feature remains significant was exemplified by the funeral of Queen Elizabeth the Queen Mother, who died in 2002 at the age of 101. The number of people queuing up to pay their respects as the Queen Mother's coffin lay in Westminster Hall, as well as those lining the route for the funeral, far exceeded expectations (see Box 14.1). When questioned as to why they were queuing for hours to pay their respects, some people responded by saying that it was because it enabled them to express their sense of identity as being British. The Queen's Golden and Diamond Jubilee celebrations, in 2002 and 2012, acted as a focal point for the expression of national identity, of bringing people together in a way that no other single national figure or institution could do.

However, the extent to which this role is fulfilled effectively does not go unquestioned. Critics, as we shall see, claim that the royal family occupies a socially privileged position that symbolises not so much unity as the social divisions of the nation. Although the royal household is known for having gays in its employ, and is an equal opportunities employer, critics have drawn attention to the dearth of employees in the royal household drawn from ethnic minorities. The 12,000 employees in the royal household are not especially well paid. In December 2012, for example, Buckingham Palace was advertising for a warden to help with engaging visitors to the royal collection at a salary of just over £14,860 a year pro rata and a security officer at Holyroodhouse (the Queen's official residence in Scotland) for £17,000 a year. There have been attempts to widen recruitment, but pay and conditions are not among the most competitive.

Allegiance of the armed forces

The armed services are in the service of the crown. Loyalty is owed to the monarch, not least by virtue of the oath taken by all members of the armed forces. It is also encouraged by the close links maintained by the royal family with the various services. Members of the royal family have variously served in (usually) the Royal Navy or the Army. Most hold ceremonial ranks, such as colonel-in-chief of a particular regiment. Prince Andrew was a serving naval officer and a helicopter pilot during the 1982 Falklands War. Prince Harry, as a serving army officer, saw action in Afghanistan in 2008 and 2012–13. Prince William, the heir to the Prince of Wales, is also a serving officer. The Queen takes a particular interest in military matters, including awards for service. In 2009 she instituted the Elizabeth Cross for widows of soldiers killed on active service or as a result of terrorist acts. Such a relationship helps to emphasise the apolitical role of the military and provides a barrier should the military, or more probably sections of it, seek to overthrow or threaten the elected government. (In the mid- to late 1970s, the press and some television programmes reported rumours that a number of retired officers favoured a coup in order to topple the Labour Government.) In the event of an attempted military coup, the prevailing view – although not universally shared – is that the monarch would serve as the most effective bulwark to its realisation, the Queen being in a position to exercise the same role as that of King Juan Carlos of Spain in 1981, when he forestalled a right-wing military takeover by making a public appeal to the loyalty of his army commanders.

Maintaining continuity of British traditions

The monarch symbolises continuity in affairs of state. Many of the duties traditionally performed by her have symbolic relevance: for example, the state opening of Parliament and – important in the context of the previous point – the annual ceremony of Trooping the Colour. Other traditions serve a psychological function, helping to maintain a sense of belonging to the nation, and a social function. The awarding of honours and royal garden parties are viewed by critics as socially elitist but by supporters as helping to break down social barriers, rewarding those – regardless of class – who have contributed significantly to the community. Hierarchy of awards, on this argument, is deemed less important than the effect on the recipients. The award of an MBE (Member of the Order of the British Empire) to a local charity worker may mean far more to the recipient, who may never have expected it, than the award of a knighthood to a senior civil servant, who may regard such an award as a natural reward for services rendered. Investiture is often as important as the actual award.

> To some it is a rather tiresome ordeal but to most a moving and memorable occasion. A fire brigade officer, who was presented with the British Empire Medal, spoke for many when he said: 'I thought it would be just another ceremony. But now that I've been, it's something I'll remember for the rest of my days'.
>
> (Hibbert 1979: 205)

During her reign, the Queen has conferred more than 400,000 honours and awards and more than 2 million people have attended royal garden parties or parties on behalf of charities, either at Buckingham Palace or Holyroodhouse in Edinburgh. Few decline the invitation.

Again, this function does not go unchallenged. The award of honours, for example, is seen as preserving the existing social order, the type of honour still being determined by rank and position. It is also seen as a patronage tool in the hands of the Prime Minister, given that only a few honours (Knight of the Garter, the Order of Merit and medals of the Royal Victorian Order) are decided personally by the Queen. However, both Buckingham Palace and Downing Street have sought to make some changes while preserving

BOX 14.1

Diamond Jubilee year, 2012

In 2002 the Queen's mother – Queen Elizabeth, the Queen Mother – died at the age of 101. It was estimated that 70,000 people would file past her coffin as she lay in state in Westminster Hall. In the event, 200,000 filed past. When the coffin was taken to Windsor for burial, it is estimated that more than 1 million people lined the route. An estimated 300 million people worldwide watched the funeral on television. The extent of popular interest took the media by surprise. The level of interest was demonstrated the same year as the Queen celebrated her Golden Jubilee. The celebrations culminated in a weekend of events, including a pop concert in the grounds of Buckingham Palace, a firework display, and a service of thanksgiving. An estimated 1 million people lined the Mall in London for the celebrations on the Saturday and a similar number were estimated to have lined the route for the Queen's visit to St Paul's Cathedral for the service of thanksgiving. Over a six-month period, there were 28 million hits on the Golden Jubilee website.

The celebrations appeared to tap popular support for the Queen as well as an opportunity to come together. Such sentiments appeared even more to the fore when the Queen celebrated her Diamond Jubilee in 2012. She became only the second British monarch to celebrate 60 years on the throne. Among the celebratory events were a pageant on the River Thames, with more than 1,000 boats taking part, and watched by an estimated 1.2 million people in central London. There was a Jubilee concert at Buckingham Palace – performers included Robbie Williams, JLS, Annie Lennox, Kylie Minogue, Sir Elton John and Sir Paul McCartney – and the official Diamond Jubilee song, 'Sing', reached number one in the single and album charts. The concert, broadcast on BBC1, attracted a peak audience in the UK of 17 million. The Jubilee website attracted over 2 million unique visitors and 7.6 million page views. The Monarchy Facebook page had over 1.8 million unique views.

The Diamond Jubilee appeared to tap popular support for the monarchy or may have been a factor in enhancing support for it. Held at a time of austerity, the celebrations – allied with the 2012 Olympic Games held in London – appeared to contribute to a feeling of goodwill at a time of political and economic uncertainty. The satisfaction with the Queen reached a record level, with 90 per cent saying that they were satisfied with the way she was doing her job; only 7 per cent said they were dissatisfied. As the Ipsos MORI report on the findings recorded, 'The Queen's rating is much higher than the ratings of David Cameron (40%) and Ed Miliband (40%) put together; no Prime Minister or party leader has ever scored more than 75% satisfaction in Ipsos MORI's polls'. The polls in that year found that support for the monarchy was higher than at any point in the previous 20 years. Public confidence in the monarch's long-term future was also at a 20-year high. The Director of Research at Ipsos MORI, Professor Roger Mortimore, noted that 'This has been a triumphant Jubilee year. After a rocky period in the 1990s, public support for the Monarchy and the Queen now looks as strong as it has been for many years. Most of the public now expect the Monarchy to survive well into the future, and that is probably the best guarantee that it will do so'.

The support was, as Professor Mortimore recorded, for 'the Monarchy and the Queen'. There is a difficulty in separating support for the institution from the person fulfilling the role of monarch. The performance of the Queen as monarch has generally won widespread admiration, demonstrated in the remarkably high levels of satisfaction. Underpinning support for the institution in the future is public support for the heir to the Prince of Wales – the Queen's elder grandson – Prince William. The marriage of Prince William and Kate Middleton in 2011 attracted widespread public interest. Polls in 2012 tapped the popularity of the couple, enhanced by the announcement in December 2012 that the Duchess of Cambridge (as Kate Middleton had become) was pregnant. In November 2012 just over 60 per cent of those questioned by Ipsos MORI said that, of the members of the royal family, they liked Prince William the most, followed by 48 per cent saying the Queen. (Prince Harry – Prince William's brother – came third and the Duchess of Cambridge came fourth.) Significantly for the future of the monarchy, older respondents tended to name the Queen, while younger ones tended to name younger members of the family.

After 60 years on the throne the Queen appeared to have established a basis of popular support for the continuation of the monarchy. Her health – and commitment to fulfilling her role as monarch – indicated that she may well continue to do so for some time.

The Duke and Duchess of Cambridge
Source: Corbis

continuity. Successive Prime Ministers have tried to make the honours system more inclusive – in recent years, for example, knighthoods have been conferred on head teachers – and the monarchy has sought to be more open. Since 1993 any member of the public has been able to nominate someone for an honour: nomination forms are available online.

Preserving a Christian morality

The Queen is supreme governor of the Church of England, and the links between the monarch and the church are close and visible. The monarch is required by the Act of Settlement of 1701 to 'joyn in communion with the Church of England as by law established'. After the monarch, the most significant participant in a coronation ceremony is the Archbishop of Canterbury, who both crowns and anoints the new sovereign. Bishops, as we have seen, are formally appointed by the crown. National celebrations led by the Queen will usually entail a religious service, more often than not held in Westminster Abbey or St Paul's Cathedral. The Queen is known to take seriously her religious duties and is looked to, largely by way of example, as a symbol of a basically Christian morality.

Preserving what are deemed to be high standards of Christian morality has been important since the nineteenth century, although not necessarily much before that: earlier monarchs were keener to protect the Church of England than they were to practise its morality. The attempts to preserve that morality in the twentieth century resulted in some notable sacrifices. Edward VIII was forced to abdicate in 1936 because of his insistence on marrying a twice-married and twice-divorced woman. In 1955 the Queen's sister,

Princess Margaret, decided not to marry Group Captain Peter Townsend because he was divorced. She announced that 'mindful of the Church's teaching that Christian marriage is indissoluble, and conscious of my duty to the Commonwealth, I have resolved to put these considerations before others'. However, two decades later, with attitudes having changed, the Princess herself was divorced. Her divorce was followed by that of Princess Anne and Captain Mark Phillips and later by that of the Duke and Duchess of York and the Prince and Princess of Wales. Following the death of Diana, Princess of Wales, the Prince of Wales began to be seen in public with his companion, Camilla Parker-Bowles. Although attitudes towards divorce have changed, divorces and separations in the royal family – and the heir to the throne admitting to adultery – have nonetheless raised questions about the royal family's capacity to maintain a Christian morality. The capacity to do so has also been challenged explicitly by the heir to the throne, Prince Charles, who has said that he would wish to be 'a Defender of Faiths, not the Faith'.

The stance of the Prince of Wales also reflects criticism by those who do not think that the royal family *should* preserve a morality that is explicitly or wholly Christian. Critics see such a link as unacceptable in a society that has several non-Christian religions and indeed a large secular element. The connection between the crown and the Christian religion may act against the crown being a unifying feature of the United Kingdom.

Those who think the royal family should preserve a strict Christian morality appear to be declining in number. This was reflected at the start of the twenty-first century in popular attitudes towards the relationship of Prince Charles and Camilla Parker-Bowles. Mrs Parker-Bowles was divorced and her former husband was still living. She and Prince Charles engaged in an affair while both were still married. In a YouGov poll in August 2002, when asked what they believed should happen at the end of the Queen's reign, a majority of respondents – 52 per cent – said that Prince Charles should become King and be allowed to marry Mrs Parker-Bowles. No less than 60 per cent would approve of the Archbishop of Canterbury allowing them to have a Church of England wedding (*Evening Standard*, 15 August 2002). In the event, they married in a civil ceremony in April 2005.

Exercise of formal powers

Underpinning the monarch's capacity to fulfil a unifying role, and indeed underpinning the other functions deemed important, is the fact that she stands above and beyond the arena of partisan debate. This also affects significantly the monarch's other primary task: that of fulfilling her formal duties as head of state. Major powers still remain formally with the monarch. Most prerogative powers, as we have seen, are now exercised by ministers on behalf of the crown. A number of other powers, which cannot be exercised by ministers, are as far as possible governed by convention. By convention, as we have seen, the monarch assents to all legislation passed by the two Houses of Parliament; by convention, she calls the leader of the party with an overall majority in the House of Commons to form a government. Where there is no clear convention governing what to do, the Queen acts in accordance with precedent (where one exists) and, where a choice is involved, acts on advice. By thus avoiding any personal choice – and being seen not to exercise any personal choice – the monarch is able to remain 'above politics'. Hence the characterisation of the monarch as enjoying strength through weakness. The denial of personal discretion in the exercise of inherently political powers strengthens the capacity of the monarch to fulfil a representative – that is, symbolic – role.

However, could it not be argued that the exercise of such powers is, by virtue of the absence of personal choice, a waste of time and something of which the monarch should be shorn? Why not, for example, as suggested by Blackburn (1999), codify existing practice in a way that requires no involvement by the monarch? There are two principal reasons why the powers remain vested in the sovereign.

First, the combination of the symbolic role and the powers vested in the crown enables the monarch to stand as a constitutional safeguard. As head of state and as commander-in-chief of the armed forces, the monarch could deny both legitimacy and support to anyone who sought to usurp the democratic institutions of the state. Thus, ironically, the unelected monarch – successor to earlier monarchs who tried to dispense with Parliament – serves as an ultimate protector of the political institutions that have displaced the monarchy as the governing authority (see Bogdanor 1995). The role of the Queen as a protector of democracy was emphasised in her Diamond Jubilee year by Labour MP Sir Gerald Kaufman. 'What she has done in making this United Kingdom a permanent democracy, a democracy that is impregnable, is perhaps the greatest of her many achievements' (House of Commons: Official Report, 7 March 2012, col. 862). In the same debate, another MP recalled the occasion when Margaret Thatcher's premiership was coming to an end and there were fears that she may try to call a general election to save herself, an act that her party, the Commons or the Cabinet would not have been able to prevent:

> The only person who could have stopped her was the Head of State and I believe all of us agree that the Queen's strength of character and the fact that she

had served many other Prime Ministers would give us full confidence that she was the best person in that situation or any situation when a Prime Minister decided to act in his or her interests rather than the interests of the country.

(House of Commons: Official Report, 7 March 2012, col. 870)

Second, retention of the prerogative powers serves as a reminder to ministers and other servants of the crown that they owe a responsibility to a higher authority than a transient politician. Ministers are Her Majesty's ministers; the Prime Minister is invited by the sovereign to form an administration. The responsibility may, on the face of it, appear purely formal. However, although the monarch is precluded from calling the Prime Minister (or any minister) to account publicly, she is able to require a private explanation. In *The English Constitution*, Walter Bagehot offered his classic definition of the monarch's power as being 'the right to be consulted, the right to encourage, the right to warn'. The Queen is known to be an assiduous reader of her official papers and is known often to question the Prime Minister closely and, on other occasions, the relevant departmental ministers. Harold Wilson recorded that in his early days as Prime Minister he was caught on the hop as a result of the Queen having read Cabinet papers that he had not yet got round to reading. 'Very interesting, this idea of a new town in the Bletchley area', commented the Queen. It was the first Wilson knew of the idea. More significantly, there are occasions when the Queen is believed to have made her displeasure known. In 1986, for example, it was reported – although not confirmed – that the Queen was distressed at the strain that the Prime Minister, Margaret Thatcher, was placing on the Commonwealth as a result of her refusal to endorse sanctions against South Africa (see Pimlott 1996; Ziegler 1996); she was also reported to have expressed her displeasure in 1983 following the US invasion of Grenada, a Commonwealth country (Cannon and Griffiths 1988: 620). Indeed, relations between the Queen and her first female Prime Minister were claimed to be strained (see Hamilton 2002), although Mrs Thatcher said that her relationship with the Queen was correct. The Queen is also believed to have signalled her displeasure when Prime Minister Tony Blair failed to include her in the itinerary of a visit to the UK by US President Bill Clinton (Pierce 1999). Nonetheless, former Prime Ministers have variously attested to the fact that the Queen is a considerable help rather than a hindrance, offering a private and experienced audience. She also serves as a reminder of their responsibility to some other authority than political party. She also stands as the ultimate deterrent. Although her actions are governed predominantly by convention, she still has the legal right to exercise them.

Criticisms of the monarchy

Various functions are thus fulfilled by the monarch and other members of the royal family. There has tended to be a high level of support for the monarchy and popular satisfaction with the way those functions are carried out. However, a high level of support for the institution of monarchy has not been a constant in British political history. It dropped during the reign of Queen Victoria when she withdrew from public activity following the death of Prince Albert. It dropped again in the 1930s as a result of the abdication crisis, which divided the nation. It increased significantly during the Second World War because of the conduct of the royal family and remained high in postwar decades. It dipped again in the 1990s: 1992 was described by the Queen as her *annus horribilis* (horrible year). The monarchy was no longer the revered institution of preceding decades, and its future became an issue of topical debate. Even at times of high popular support, it has never been free of criticism. In recent years the criticisms have been directed particularly at the activities of various members of the royal family.

Four principal criticisms can be identified: that an unelected monarch has the power to exercise certain political powers; that, by virtue of being neither elected nor socially typical, the monarchy is unrepresentative; that maintaining the royal family costs too much; and that the institution of monarchy is now unnecessary. The last three criticisms have become more pronounced in recent years.

Potential for political involvement

The actions of the sovereign as head of state are governed predominantly by convention. However, not all actions she may be called on to take are covered by convention. This is most notably the case in respect of the power to appoint a Prime Minister. Usually, there is no problem. As long as one party is returned with an overall majority, the leader of that party will be summoned to Buckingham Palace (or, if already Prime Minister, will remain in office). But what if there is a 'hung' parliament, with no one party enjoying an overall majority? In the General Election of 2010, no party emerged with an overall majority. The Prime Minister, Gordon Brown, remained in Downing Street and opened negotiations with the third largest party, the Liberal Democrats. Conservative leader, David Cameron, whose party had the largest single number of seats, did likewise. A Conservative–Liberal Democrat coalition was agreed and David Cameron was summoned to Buckingham Palace. But what would have happened if no agreement had been reached?

Such situations can pose a threat to the value that currently derives from the sovereign being, and being seen to be, above politics. She is dependent on circumstances and the goodwill of politicians in order to avoid such situations arising. The Queen was drawn into partisan controversy in 1957 and 1963 in the choice of a Conservative Prime Minister: the Conservatives at the time had no formal mechanism for selecting a new leader and no obvious leader had '**emerged**'. The embarrassment to the monarchy spurred the party to change its method of selecting its leader. In 2010 there was clear pressure on the parties to reach an agreement, not least to keep the Queen out of political controversy (Norton 2011: 244). There nonetheless remains the danger that circumstances may conspire again to make involvement in real – as opposed to formal – decision making unavoidable.

Given this potential, some critics contend that the powers vested in the monarch should be transferred elsewhere. Various left-of-centre bodies have advocated that some or all of the powers be transferred to the Speaker of the House of Commons. The proposal was advanced in 1996, in a Fabian Society pamphlet, by Labour parliamentary candidate Paul Richards, and again in 1998 by the authors of a pamphlet published by the left-wing think tank Demos (Hames and Leonard 1998). Defenders of the existing arrangements contend that the retention of prerogative powers by the crown has created no major problems to date – one constitutional historian, Peter Hennessy, in a 1994 lecture, recorded only five 'real or near real contingencies' since 1949 when the monarch's reserve powers were relevant (Marr 1995: 234; see also Bogdanor 1995) – and it serves as a valuable constitutional long-stop. Giving certain powers to the Speaker of the Commons would be to give them to a member of an institution that may need to be constrained and would probably make the election of the Speaker a much more politicised activity. Furthermore, the Speaker presently operates solely within the context of the House of Commons and has no remit that extends beyond it.

Unrepresentative

The monarchy cannot make a claim to be representative in the second meaning of the term (freely elected). Critics also point out that it cannot make a claim to be representative in the third meaning (socially typical). The monarchy is a hereditary institution and by its nature is of necessity socially atypical. Critics contend that social hierarchy is reinforced by virtue of the monarch's personal wealth. The Queen is believed to be among the world's richest women. Many of the functions patronised by the Queen and members of the royal family, from formal functions to sporting events, are also criticised for being socially elitist. Those who surround the royal family in official positions (the Lord Chamberlain, ladies-in-waiting and other senior members of the royal household), and those with whom members of the royal family choose to surround themselves in positions of friendship, are also notably if not exclusively drawn from a social elite. In the 1950s Lord Altrincham criticised the Queen's entourage for constituting 'a tight little enclave of British "ladies and gentlemen"' (Altrincham et al. 1958: 115). Various changes were made in the wake of such criticism – the royal family became more publicly visible, the presentation of débutantes to the monarch at society balls was abolished – but royalty remains largely detached from the rest of society. The closed nature of the royal entourage was attacked in the 1990s by Diana, Princess of Wales, who had difficulty adapting to what she saw as the insular and stuffy nature of the royal court. Even at Buckingham Palace garden parties, members of the royal family, having mixed with those attending, then take tea in a tent reserved for them and leading dignitaries. Focus groups, commissioned by Buckingham Palace in 1997, concluded that the royal family was out of touch because of their traditions and upbringing as well as remote because of 'the many physical and invisible barriers thought to have been constructed around them' (quoted in Jones 1998). In a MORI poll in 2002, 68 per cent of those questioned thought that the royal family was 'out of touch with ordinary people'; only 28 per cent thought that it was not.

Pressures continue for the institution to be more open in terms of the social background of the Queen's entourage and, indeed, in terms of the activities and background of members of the royal family itself. The public reaction to the death, in a car crash in 1997, of Diana, Princess of Wales – popular not least because of her public empathy with the frail and the suffering – and the findings from the focus groups (commissioned in the wake of the Princess's death) are believed to have been influential in persuading the Queen to spend more time visiting people in their homes and exploring how people live (for example, by travelling on the underground and by visiting a supermarket). Defenders of the royal family argue that it is, by definition, impossible for members of the family to be socially typical – since they would cease to be the royal family – and that to be too close to everyday activity would rob the institution of monarchy of its aura and charm. The conundrum was summarised by former Prime Minister, Sir John Major: 'To be part of the nation and yet apart from the nation is always a difficult balance' (Hardman 2011: 44).

Overly expensive

The cost of the monarchy has been the subject of criticism for several years. This criticism became pronounced in the 1990s. Until 2012 much but not all the costs of the monarchy were met from the civil list. This constituted a sum paid regularly by the state to the monarch to cover the cost of staff, upkeep of royal residences, holding official functions, and of public duties undertaken by other members of the royal family. (The Prince of Wales was not included: as Duke of Cornwall his income derives from revenue-generating estates owned by the Duchy of Cornwall.) Other costs of monarchy – such as travel and the upkeep of royal castles – were met by government departments through grants-in-aid from Parliament. In 1990, to avoid an annual public row over the figure, agreement was reached between the government and the Queen that the civil list should be set at £7.9 million a year for ten years. When the other costs of the monarchy – maintaining castles and the like – are added to this figure, the annual public expenditure on the monarchy was estimated in 1991 to exceed £57 million.

In the 1970s and 1980s accusations were variously heard that the expenditure was not justified, in part because some members of the royal family did very little to justify the sums given to them and in part because the Queen was independently wealthy, having a private fortune on which she paid no tax. (When income tax was introduced in the nineteenth century, Queen Victoria voluntarily paid tax. In the twentieth century, the voluntary commitment was whittled down and had disappeared by the time the Queen ascended the throne in 1952.) These criticisms found various manifestations. In 1988, 40 per cent of respondents to a Gallup poll expressed the view that the monarchy 'cost too much'. In a MORI poll in 1990 three out of every four people questioned believed that the Queen should pay income tax; half of those questioned thought the royal family was receiving too much money from the taxpayer. Certain members of the royal family became targets of particular criticism.

These criticisms became much louder in 1991 and 1992. They were fuelled by a number of unrelated developments. The most notable were the separation of the Duke and Duchess of York and – in December 1992 – of the Prince and Princess of Wales, following newspaper stories about their private lives. The result was that members of the royal family became central figures of controversy and gossip. In November 1992 fire destroyed St George's Hall at Windsor Castle, and the government announced that it would meet the cost of repairs, estimated at more than £50 million. Public reaction to the announcement was strongly negative. At a time of recession, public money was to be spent restoring a royal castle, while the Queen continued to pay no income tax and some members of the royal family pursued other than restrained lifestyles at public expense. A Harris poll found three out of every four respondents believing that ways should be found to cut the cost of the royal family.

Six days after the fire at Windsor Castle, the Prime Minister informed the House of Commons that the Queen had initiated discussions 'some months ago' on changing her tax-free status and on removing all members of the royal family from the civil list other than herself, the Duke of Edinburgh and the Queen Mother. The Queen herself would meet the expenditure of other members of the royal family. The following year, the Queen announced that Buckingham Palace was to be opened to the public, with money raised from entrance fees being used to pay the cost of repairs to Windsor Castle. These announcements served to meet much of the criticism, but the controversy undermined the prestige of the royal family. Critics continued to point out that most of the costs of the monarchy remained unchanged, funded by public money. They drew attention to the fact that the Queen was using novel devices of taking money from the public (entrance fees to the Palace) in order to fund Windsor Castle repairs rather than drawing on her own private wealth.

A further major change took place in 2012. Parliament enacted the Sovereign Grant Act 2011 to aggregate the different sources of support – the civil list and grants-in-aid. Under the Act the monarch and her successors are now funded by a Sovereign Grant which is linked to the net income surplus (or profit) of the Crown Estate. The Crown Estate comprises the income from crown lands that was surrendered to the Exchequer in the eighteenth century in return for government support. The Grant, which came into being in April 2012, is normally set equal to 15 per cent of the profit from the Crown Estate for two years previously.

By 2008–9 Head of State Expenditure was £41.5 million, a notable reduction in the costs compared with 10 years and, indeed, 20 years previously. In 2010–11 it was down further to £32.1 million. The Sovereign Grant for 2012–13 was set at £31 million. Buckingham Palace recorded that costs had been reduced as a result of increased income generation, deferral of property maintenance, and a pay freeze.

Defenders contend that the country obtains good value for money from the royal family and that much if not most of the money spent on maintaining castles and other parts of the national heritage would still have to be spent (rather like Versailles in France) even if there was no royal family. When such money is taken out of the equation, the public activities of the Queen and leading royals such as the Princess Royal are deemed to represent good value for public money. However, despite the various savings made, people in the UK have tended to be split as to whether the monarchy offers value for money. In November 2012, despite record levels of satisfaction with the Queen, 52 per cent of those questioned thought that the royal family should not receive as much money as it did, against 47 per cent who disagreed.

Unnecessary

Those who criticise the monarchy on grounds of its unrepresentative nature and its cost are not necessarily opposed to the institution itself. A more open and less costly monarchy – based on the Scandinavian model, with the monarch mixing more freely with citizens and without excessive trappings – would be acceptable to many. However, some take the opposite view. They see the monarchy as an unnecessary institution; the cost and social elitism of the monarchy are seen as merely illustrative of the nature of the institution. Advocates of this view have included the organisation Republic (www.republic.org.uk), and the *New Statesman* magazine. This approach is also taken by a number of writers. They include Tom Nairn in *The Enchanted Glass: Britain and its Monarchy*, Edgar Wilson in *The Myth of the British Monarchy*, Jonathan Freedland in *Bring Home the Revolution*, the contributors to Cyril Meadows, *Ending the Royal Farce*, Alastair Gray and Adam Tomkins in *How We Should Rule Ourselves*, and Stephen Haseler in *The Grand Delusion*.

Both Wilson and Haseler contend that the various arguments advanced in favour of the monarchy – its popularity, impartiality, productivity, capacity to unite, capacity to protect democratic institutions of state, and ability to generate trade – are all myths, generated in order to justify the existing order. To them and similar critics the monarchy forms part of a conservative establishment that has little rationale in a democratic society. For Haseler maintaining the monarchy is at the heart of the UK still seeing itself as a world power and an attempt by political leaders at 'imperial overreach' (Haseler 2012: xiv). Such critics would prefer to see the monarchy abolished. 'The constitutional case for abolishing the Monarchy is based mainly on the facts that it is arbitrary, unrepresentative, unaccountable, partial, socially divisive, and exercises a pernicious influence and privileged prerogative powers' (Wilson 1989: 178). The monarchy, declared the *New Stateman*, 'sits like the spider at the centre of a web of wealth and privilege . . . Its continued existence gives legitimacy to the deeply unequal way in which British society is structured' (*New Statesman*, 13 July 2009). Removing the monarchy, it said, would have huge symbolic value, 'confirming the people of Britain as citizens, not subjects'. Necessary functions of state carried out by the monarch could be equally well fulfilled, so critics contend, by an elected president. Most countries in the world have a head of state not chosen on the basis of heredity. So why not Britain?

Supporters of the institution of monarchy argue that, despite recent criticisms, the Queen continues to do a good job – a view that, according to opinion polls, enjoys majority support – and that the monarchy is distinctive by virtue of the functions it is able to fulfil. In a MORI poll in November

2012 satisfaction with the way the Queen was doing her job was at an all-time high (see Box 14.1). It is considered doubtful that an appointed or elected head of state would be able to carry out to the same extent the symbolic role, representing the unity of the nation. For a head of state not involved in the partisan operation of government, it is this role (representative in the fourth sense of the term) that is more important than that of being an elected leader. Indeed, election could jeopardise the head of state's claim to be representative in the first sense of the term (acting on behalf of a particular body or group). The monarch has a duty to represent all subjects; an elected head of state may have a bias, subconscious or otherwise, in favour of those who vote for him or her, or in favour of those – presumably politicians – who were responsible for arranging the nomination. The monarch enjoys a stature not likely to be matched by an elected figurehead in engaging the loyalty of the armed forces; and by virtue of her longevity and experience can assist successive Prime Ministers in a way not possible by a person appointed or elected for a fixed term. Hence, by virtue of these assets particular to the Queen, the monarch is deemed unique and not capable of emulation by an elected president. Although these assets may have been partially tarnished in recent years, it is argued that they remain of value to the nation.

Proposals for change

The monarchy has never been wholly free of critics. In the 1970s and 1980s those critics were relatively few in number. In the early 1990s they became far more numerous and more vocal. There were various calls for changes to be made in the institution of the monarchy and in the conduct of members of the royal family. Those most responsible for this situation arising were members of the royal family themselves. The marital splits, the antics of various royals, the public perception of some members of the royal family as 'hangers-on' (enjoying the trappings of privilege but fulfilling few public duties) and the failure of the Queen to fund the restoration of Windsor Castle herself contributed to a popular mood less supportive of the monarchy than before. This critical mood was tempered at the start of the new century.

Although the public standing of the monarchy improved, not least at the time of the Queen's Golden and Diamond Jubilees, calls for change continue to be made. Various options have been advanced. These can be grouped under four heads: abolition, reform, leave alone and strengthen.

Abolition

The troubles encountered by the royal family in the late 1980s and early 1990s appeared to influence attitudes toward the monarchy itself. As we have seen, the Queen described 1992 as her *annus horribilis* – her horrible year. That was reflected in popular attitudes towards the monarchy. Until the middle of 1992 fewer than 15 per cent of people questioned in various polls wanted to see the monarchy abolished. A Gallup poll in May 1992 found 13 per cent of respondents giving such a response. By the end of the year, the figure had increased to 24 per cent. In 1994, those favouring abolition gained the support of a leading magazine, *The Economist*.

Not only was there an increase in the percentage of the population expressing support for the abolition of the monarchy; there was also an increasing agnosticism among a wider public. In 1987, 73 per cent of respondents in a MORI poll thought that Britain would be worse off if the monarchy were abolished. In December 1992 the figure was 37 per cent; 42 per cent thought it would make no difference. The same poll found, for the first time, more people saying that they did not think that the monarchy would still exist in 50 years' time than saying it would: 42 per cent thought it would not, against 36 per cent saying it would.

However, those who argue the case for the retention of the monarchy appear still to have a considerable edge over those demanding abolition. The early 1990s represented the high point in terms of popular disaffection with royalty. Support for abolition of the monarchy has varied but usually no more than one in five express support for a republic. Those who do favour abolition are more likely to be found among the left-leaning members of the professional classes than the lower middle or working class: 'abolition of the monarchy is much more a demand of liberal intellectuals . . . than of the traditional working class left' (Mortimore 2002: 3). Although the proportion dipped in April 2005 (around the time of the marriage of Prince Charles), usually about seven out of ten people questioned favour retaining the monarchy (Table 14.1). Between 1992 and 2002, the proportion of the population believing the monarchy would not exist in 50 years' time outnumbered those believing that it would; since then, the proportion believing it will exist in 50 years' time has outnumbered those believing it will not. An Ipsos MORI poll in November 2012 found that 60 per cent believed it would exist in 50 years, against 27 per cent who believed that it would not.

Reform

Recent years have seen a growing body of support for some change in the nature of the monarchy and especially in the royal family. Some proposals for reform are radical. The authors of the Demos pamphlet, *Modernising the Monarchy*, argue the case not only for transferring the monarch's prerogative powers to the Speaker of the House of Commons but also for holding a referendum to confirm a monarch

Table 14.1 Attitudes towards the monarchy

Q. If there was a referendum on the issue, would you favour Britain becoming a republic or remaining a monarchy?

	Dec 1994	Aug 1998	Feb 2002	Apr 2005	Apr 2006	Apr 2011	Nov[1] 2012
Republic	20	16	19	22	18	18	16
Monarch	71	75	71	65	72	75	79
Don't know/other	9	9	10	13	10	7	5

1 Question in 2012: 'Would you favour Britain becoming a republic or remaining a monarchy?'

Source: Ipsos MORI

shortly after succeeding to the throne (Hames and Leonard 1998). There are some survey data to suggest that more people support the first of these proposals than oppose it. In a MORI poll in August 1998, 49 per cent thought that the powers should be removed, against 45 per cent who thought they should be retained.

There is also a desire for more general change in the way the monarch, and other members of the royal family, conduct themselves. This desire has been tapped by opinion polls as well as by the focus groups commissioned by Buckingham Palace. The public preference is for a more open and less ostentatious monarchy, with the Queen spending more time meeting members of the public, and with other members of the royal family, especially the 'minor royals', taking up paid employment (as some have) and blending into the community. A Granada TV deliberative poll in 1996, which involved interviewing people before and after discussing the subject with experts, found that the biggest percentage of affirmative responses was for the statement that 'members of the royal family should mix more with ordinary people'. The percentage agreeing was initially 66 per cent and, after discussion, it increased to 75 per cent. In a MORI poll in January 2002, 54 per cent of those questioned agreed with the statement that 'the monarchy should be modernised to reflect changes in public life'. Only 28 per cent felt that 'the monarch's role should remain broadly unchanged'.

There is also some support for a change in the order of succession. A small number of people favour the Queen abdicating in favour of Prince Charles, but the number is declining: it peaked in 1981 (48 per cent) and 1990 (47 per cent); since then, the proportion believing that she should remain Queen has exceeded 60 per cent. Some people also favour 'skipping a generation' and allowing Prince William, Prince Charles's elder son, to succeed to the throne in place of his father. In a MORI poll in September 1997, in the wake of the death of Diana, Princess of Wales, 54 per cent supported such a move: by November 1998, the percentage giving the same response was 34 per cent. The proportion increased markedly in March 2003 following the publication of the critical report on the way Prince Charles's household was run. By 2005 opinion was evenly divided. A MORI poll in

April 2005 found that 43 per cent favoured such a move against 40 per cent opposed. In June 2012, 36 per cent thought he should give up his right to succeed against 53 per cent who thought he should not.

However, it is not in the gift of the Prince of Wales to give up 'his right' to be the next monarch. The option of skipping a generation would require a change in the law. A decision by the Queen, or by Prince Charles upon or at the time of his succession to the throne, to abdicate is not one that can be taken unilaterally. Under the Act of Succession, Prince Charles will become King automatically on the death of his mother. There is no formal power to abdicate. That would require – as it did in 1936 – an Act of Parliament.

Another change that has variously been discussed, but which has less immediate relevance, is that of allowing the eldest child to succeed, regardless of gender. Though the Queen's eldest child is male and his eldest child is male, the marriage of Prince William in 2011 led to speculation as to what would happen if his first child was a girl. The Government announced its intention to legislate for the first born to succeed to the monarchy regardless of sex and in 2012, as we have noted, it announced it had achieved the agreement to such a change of the Commonwealth nations where the Queen was also head of state.

In 1996 it emerged that the senior members of the royal family, apparently prompted by Prince Charles, had formed a small group (the 'Way Ahead Group' composed of senior royals and Buckingham Palace officials) to meet to consider various changes to existing arrangements.

The measures taken by the Queen in recent years – notably the decision to pay income tax, to limit expenditure and to spend more time meeting ordinary members of the public – appear to enjoy popular support. The deliberations of the Way Ahead Group were designed also to bring the institution up to date and enhance such support. A Co-ordination and Research Unit, composed of officials, was also formed to act essentially as a royal think tank, since superseded by a body known as the Secretariat (Hardman 2011: 247). 'Charles Anson, the Queen's Press Secretary of the period, says that the reformers were pushing at an open door' (Hardman 2011: 25). The financial accounts (once highly secret) are now published, the Jubilee celebrations in both 2002 and 2012 were carefully planned, and junior royals have a somewhat lower public profile than before as well as receiving no support from public funds. In 2002 the Queen became the first member of the royal family to receive a gold disc from the recording industry: 100,000 copies of the CD of the *Party at the Palace*, produced by EMI, were sold within a week of release. More than half-a-million people 'like' her Facebook page. The Secretariat engage in thought as to how the royal family 'should be interacting with the rest of us' (Hardman 2011: 247).

Leave alone

The monarchy as it stands has some ardent admirers. Conservative MPs have generally moved quickly to defend the monarchy from criticism. When a Fabian Society pamphlet, *Long to Reign Over Us?*, was published in August 1996 (Richards 1996) advocating a referendum on the monarchy, a Conservative cabinet minister, Michael Portillo, immediately portrayed it as an attack on the institution of monarchy. 'New Labour should be warned that they meddle with the monarchy at the nation's peril', he declared. After 1997 some of the attempts by Prime Minister Tony Blair to encourage change also encountered criticism. In 1999 the leading historian, Lord Blake, declared: 'Reform has gone far enough . . . The monarchy is one of the fixed points of the British constitutional firmament. It cannot be subjected to constant change' (Pierce 1999).

Although this stance attracts support, it tends to be outweighed by those favouring some reform (a fact acknowledged in effect by the royal family in the creation of the Way Ahead Group). As we have seen, most people questioned in the MORI poll in January 2002 favoured some change; only 28 per cent wanted to leave the monarchy broadly unchanged. Those favouring modest reform appear to be in a majority among voters. It was also the stance favoured by the Labour Government under Tony Blair. 'Palace officials have been told clearly by Downing Street that there is strong political pressure for a much leaner monarchy' (Pierce 1999). Although some of the proposals emanating from Downing Street, such as reducing the ceremony of the state opening of Parliament, were resisted by Buckingham Palace (see Pierce 1999), the need for reform has generally been accepted by the royal family.

Strengthen

The final option is that of strengthening the role and powers of the monarchy. A Gallup poll in 1996 for the *Sunday Telegraph* tapped a body of support for giving the Queen a greater role. This was especially marked among working-class respondents and among the 16- to 34-year-old age groups: 57 per cent of working-class respondents thought that the Queen should be given 'a more substantial role in govern-

ment'; and 54 per cent of respondents aged 16 to 34 also thought that she should have a more substantial role (Elliott and McCartney 1996). The nature of the role was not specified. As we have seen, the potential for the Queen to be drawn into decision making exists. The exercise of some of these powers may not prove unpopular to a section of the population. It was notable in the 1996 poll that many respondents regarded the Queen as having superior skills to those of the then Prime Minister, John Major: 46 per cent thought that the Queen would make a 'better Prime Minister than John Major'; 39 per cent thought that she would make a better Prime Minister than Tony Blair; and 47 per cent of working-class respondents thought that she would run the country 'more wisely than politicians'.

There is thus some body of support for the Queen exercising more power in the political affairs of the nation. However, that view is not widely held among politicians, nor – as far as one can surmise – among members of the royal family. As we have seen, the strength of the monarchy rests largely on the fact that it is detached from the partisan fray and is not involved in having to exercise independent judgement. Having to make independent decisions would be popular with some but, and this is the crucial point in this context, not with all people. Those adversely affected by a decision would be unlikely to keep their feelings to themselves. The monarchy would be drawn into the maelstrom of political controversy, thus ridding it of its capacity to fulfil the principal functions ascribed to it.

Conclusion

The monarch fulfils a number of functions as head of state. Some of those functions are not peculiar to the monarch as head of state: they are functions that are typically carried out by a head of state. Supporters of the monarchy argue that a number of functions are particularly suited to the monarch and, in combination, could not be fulfilled by an elected or appointed head of state. The monarchy was under strain in the early 1990s as a result of various disconnected events, and its public standing declined markedly. The nature of the monarchy was further called into question following the death of the popular Diana, Princess of Wales, in August 1997. The Queen and other members of the royal family have responded to criticism by implementing changes in structures and activities designed to create a more open and responsive monarchy. The actions of the Queen and her family appeared to bear fruit, notably in the celebration of the Queen's Golden Jubilee in 2002 and especially her Diamond Jubilee in 2012.

There is no strong desire to get rid of the monarchy. There is, though, some scepticism about the future of the monarchy. However, the percentage of people thinking the monarchy will not exist in 100 years was, in April 2011, the lowest (42 per cent) since 1992. The proportion thinking it will still exist (37 per cent) was the highest since 1992. In November 2012 the percentage thinking it would exist in 100 years was even higher, exceeding the percentage believing it would not by 42 per cent to 38 per cent. The monarchy has proved remarkably adaptable, weathering some notable storms, and engaging popular support. It remains the most popular of the nation's political institutions. An Ipsos MORI poll in 2012, commissioned by Channel 4, found that, when asked what made them most proud to be British, more people opted for the royal family (28 per cent) than 'our system of democracy' (22 per cent).

BOX 14.2

BRITAIN IN CONTEXT

Presidents and monarchs

The United Kingdom is not unusual in having a monarchy. There are basically two types of head of state: presidents and hereditary rulers. Presidents are typically elected, though their role in government may vary. Some combine executive powers as head of government with formal ceremonial power as head of state; the President of the USA combines both. Some are predominantly ceremonial: that is, serving as head of state but not head of government; the President of Ireland is an example of this type. The same distinction can be drawn in terms of hereditary rulers. Some are both head of government and head of state. The number is now small, concentrated especially in the Middle and Far East, as powerful rulers over time have been overthrown, removed by popular vote or reduced to playing a largely ceremonial role. More than two-thirds of hereditary rulers have a predominantly or wholly ceremonial role, exercising few or no independent political powers. Most hereditary rulers take the title of king or queen, but some have the title of emir, grand duke, prince, sheik, or sultan; they are generally subsumed under the generic title of monarchs.

Monarchies account for less than one-quarter of the nations that now exist. There is a notable concentration of ceremonial monarchies in western Europe – Belgium, Denmark, the Netherlands, Norway, Spain, Sweden and the United Kingdom are monarchies; Luxembourg is a Grand Duchy and Monaco a principality. The number of countries with a monarch exceeds the number of monarchs, as some monarchs reign over more than one country: the Queen of Denmark, for example, is also Queen of Greenland. None, though, can match the British monarch, who is Queen of 16 countries and of a number of non-sovereign territories such as Bermuda, Gibraltar, the British Virgin Islands and the Falkland Islands.

Chapter summary

The monarchy remains an important institution in British political life. The monarch's transition from directing the affairs of state to a neutral non-executive role – with executive powers now exercised by ministers in the name of the monarch – has been a gradual and not always smooth one, but a move necessary to justify the monarch's continuing existence.

Transcending partisan activity is a necessary condition for fulfilling the monarch's symbolic ('standing for') role and hence a necessary condition for the strength and continuity of the monarchy. The dedication of the present monarch has served to sustain popular support for the institution. That support dropped in the 1990s, criticism of the activities of members of the royal family rubbing off on the institution of monarchy itself. Popular support for the institution remains and received a particular boost with the Queen's Golden Jubilee in 2002, the marriage of Prince William in 2011, and the Queen's Diamond Jubilee in 2012. However, most people when questioned want to see some change, favouring the monarchy and royal family being more open and approachable.

Discussion points

- What is the point in having a monarchy?
- Does the royal family represent value for money?
- What are the most important roles fulfilled by the Queen in contemporary society?
- What public role, if any, should be played by members of the royal family, other than the Queen?
- Should the monarchy be left alone, reformed or abolished?

Further reading

There are few substantial analyses of the role of the crown in political activity. The most recent scholarly analysis – that by Bogdanor (1995) – seeks to transcend recent controversy. The book provides a good historical perspective on the role of the monarchy as well as offering a defence of the institution. Hardie (1970) provides a useful guide to the transition from political involvement to neutrality; Hibbert (1979) also offers a useful overview. Lacey (1977, Golden Jubilee edition 2002) and Pimlott (1996, Golden Jubilee edition 2002) have produced useful and readable biographies of the Queen; several works appeared just prior to and during the Queen's Diamond Jubilee year, including Hardman (2011), Marr (2011), Bradford (2011) and Beddell Smith (2012). Bond (2012) offers a largely pictorial history. Shawcross (2009) has written a substantial official biography of Queen Elizabeth the Queen Mother. Recent books about the monarchy include Douglas-Home (2000) and Shawcross (2002). Strober and Strober (2002) offer quotations from people who have been close to the Queen during her reign. Hardman (2007) provides a guide to the royal family at work.

In terms of the debate about the future of the monarchy, the most recent reform tracts are those by Barnett (1994), Richards (1996) and Hames and Leonard (1998). The principal works arguing for abolition are Nairn (1988), Wilson (1989), Freedland (1999), Meadows (2003), Gray and Tomkins (2005), and Haseler (2012). The issue of the *New Statesman,* 13 July 2009, advocating abolition, also provides a substantial critique. On the case for monarchy, see Gattey (2002).

In terms of the controversies of the early 1990s, the book that sparked media interest in the state of the Prince of Wales's marriage was Morton (1992), followed later by a revised edition (Morton 1997). The biography of Prince Charles by Jonathan Dimbleby (1994) also contributed to the public debate. On the work undertaken by Prince Charles, see Morton (1998).

Bibliography

Altrincham, Lord, and others (1958) *Is the Monarchy Perfect?* (John Calder).

Bagehot, W. (2009) *The English Constitution (Oxford World's Classics)* (Oxford Paperbacks; originally published 1867).

Barnett, A. (ed.) (1994) *Power and the Throne: The Monarchy Debate* (Vintage).

Beddell Smith, S. (2012) *Elizabeth the Queen: The Life of a Modern Monarch* (Random House).

Benemy, F.W.G. (1965) *The Elected Monarch* (Harrap).

Birch, A.H. (1964) *Representative and Responsible Government* (Allen & Unwin).

Blackburn, R. (1992) 'The Future of the British Monarchy', in Blackburn, R. (ed.) *Constitutional Studies* (Mansell).

Blackburn, R. (1999) 'Monarchy and the Royal Prerogative', in Blackburn, R. and Plant, R. (eds) *Constitutional Reform* (Longman).

Bogdanor, V. (1995) *The Monarchy and the Constitution* (Oxford University Press).

Bond, J. (2012) *The Diamond Queen* (SevenOaks).

Bradford, S. (2011) *Queen Elizabeth: Her Life in Our Times* (Viking).

Cannon, J. and Griffiths, R. (1988) *The Oxford Illustrated History of the British Monarchy* (Oxford University Press).

Dimbleby, J. (1994) *The Prince of Wales. A Biography* (Little, Brown).

Douglas-Home, C. (2000) *Dignified and Efficient: The British Monarchy in the Twentieth Century* (Claridge Press).

Elliott, V. and McCartney, J. (1996) 'Queen Should have Real Power, say Britain's Youth', *Sunday Telegraph*, 21 April.

Freedland, J. (1999) *Bring Home the Revolution* (Fourth Estate).

Gattey, C.N. (2002) *Crowning Glory: The Merits of Monarchy* (Shepheard Walwyn).

Gray, A. and Tomkins, A. (2005) *How We Should Rule Ourselves* (Canongate Books).

Hames, T. and Leonard, M. (1998) *Modernising the Monarchy* (Demos).

Hamilton, A. (2002) 'Ten Out of Ten, Ma'am', *London Diplomat*, May/June.

Hardie, F. (1970) *The Political Influence of the British Monarchy 1868–1952* (Batsford).

Hardman, R. (2007) *Monarchy: The Royal Family at Work* (Ebury Press).

Hardman, R. (2011) *Our Queen* (Hutchinson).

Haseler, S. (2012) *The Grand Delusion* (I. B. Tauris).

Hennessy, P. (2000) *The Prime Minister: The Office and its Holders since 1945* (Allen Lane/Penguin Press).

Hibbert, C. (1979) *The Court of St James* (Weidenfeld & Nicolson).

Jones, M. (1998) 'Queen to Appoint Royal Spin Doctor to Boost Ratings', *Sunday Times*, 22 February.

Lacey, R. (1977) *Majesty* (Hutchinson).

Lacey, R. (2002) *Royal: Her Majesty Queen Elizabeth II*, The Jubilee Edition (TimeWarner).

Marr, A. (1995) *Ruling Britannica* (Michael Joseph).

Marr, A. (2011) *The Diamond Queen: Elizabeth II and Her People* (Macmillan).

Meadows, C. (ed.) (2003) *Ending the Royal Farce* (Republic).

Mortimore, R. (2002) 'The Monarchy and the Jubilee', *MORI: British Public Opinion Newsletter*, Spring, Vol. XXV, No. 1.

Morton, A. (1992) *Diana: Her True Story* (Michael O'Mara Books).

Morton, A. (1997) *Diana, Her True Story – In Her Own Words* (Michael O'Mara Books).

Morton, J. (1998) *Prince Charles: Breaking the Cycle* (Ebury Press).

Nairn, T. (1988) *The Enchanted Glass: Britain and its Monarchy* (Century Hutchinson Radius).

Norton, P. (2011), 'The Politics of Coalition', in Allen, N. and Bartle, J. (eds) *Britain at the Polls 2010* (Sage).

Pierce, A. (1999) 'Spin Meister of Royal Reform Trips up', *The Times*, 4 September.

Pimlott, B. (1996) *The Queen* (HarperCollins).

Pimlott, B. (2002) *The Queen: Elizabeth II and the Monarchy*, Golden Jubilee edition (HarperCollins).

Pitkin, H.G. (1967) *The Concept of Representation* (University of California Press).

Richards, P. (1996) *Long to Reign Over Us?* (Fabian Society).

Shawcross, W. (2002) *Queen and Country* (BBC).

Shawcross, W. (2009) *Queen Elizabeth the Queen Mother* (Macmillan).

Strober, D. and Strober, G. (2002) *The Monarchy: An Oral History of Elizabeth II* (Hutchinson).

Thatcher, M. (1993) *The Downing Street Years* (HarperCollins).

Trevelyan, G.M. (1938) *The English Revolution 1688–9* (Thornton Butterworth).

Wilson, E. (1989) *The Myth of the British Monarchy* (Journeyman/Republic).

Ziegler, P. (1996) 'A Monarch at the Centre of Politics', *Daily Telegraph*, 4 October.

Useful websites

Official royal websites

Royal family: www.royal.gov.uk
Online monthly magazine of the above: www.royalinsight.gov.uk
Prince of Wales: www.princeofwales.gov.uk
Duke of York: www.thedukeofyork.org/Home/Home.aspx
Crown Estate: www.crownestate.co.uk

Nominations for public honours

Nomination process: www.direct.gov.uk/en/ Governmentcitizensandrights/UKgovernment/ Honoursawardsandmedals/index.htm

Organisations favouring reform

Republic: www.republic.org.uk
Centre for Citizenship: www.centreforcitizenship.org

Organisation supporting the monarchy

Constitutional Monarchy Association: www.monarchy.net

Survey data on attitudes towards the Royal Family

MORI: www.mori.com/polls/indroyal.shtml

CHAPTER 15

The House of Commons at work

Philip Norton

> " [I]n matters other than legislation backbenchers have a much bigger part than the modern theory states "

Michael Foot

Learning objectives

- To explain the importance of the House of Commons in terms of its history and its functions.

- To detail the size and structure of the House.

- To consider the nature of the membership of the House.

- To identify and assess the means available to Members of Parliament to fulfil the functions ascribed to the House.

The House of Commons has its origins in the thirteenth century. At various times, it has played a powerful role in the affairs of the nation. Its most consistent activity has been to check the executive power. Its power has been limited by royal patronage and, more recently, by the growth of parties. It nonetheless remains an important part of the political process. It has to give its assent to measures of public policy. Ministers appear before it to justify their actions. It remains an arena for national debate and the clash of competing party views. It provides an important institutional constraint on the actions of government. Various means are available to the House to subject the government to scrutiny, though they vary in their effectiveness and, as we shall see in the next chapter, are the subject of critical debate.

Introduction

Origins of Parliament

Parliament has its origins in the thirteenth century. It was derived not from first principles or some grand design but from the King's need to raise more money. Its subsequent development may be ascribed to the actions and philosophies of different monarchs, the ambitions and attitudes of its members, external political pressures and prevailing assumptions as to the most appropriate form of government. Its functions and political significance have been moulded, though not in any consistent manner, over several hundred years.

Despite the rich and varied history of the institution, two broad generalisations are possible. The first concerns Parliament's position in relation to the executive. Parliament is not, and never has been on any continuous basis, a part of that executive. Although the Glorious Revolution of 1688 confirmed the form of government as that of 'parliamentary government', the phrase, as we have seen already (Chapter 13), means government through Parliament, not government by Parliament. There have been periods when Parliament has been an important actor in the making of public policy, not least for a period in the nineteenth century, but its essential and historically established position has been that of a reactive, or policy-influencing, assembly (Box 15.1; see Mezey 1979; Norton 2013): that is, public policy is formulated by the executive and then presented to Parliament for discussion and approval. Parliament has the power to amend or reject the policy placed before it, but it has not the capacity to substitute on any regular basis a policy of its own. Parliament has looked to the executive to take the initiative in the formulation of public policy, and it continues to do so.

The second generalisation concerns the various tasks, or functions, fulfilled by Parliament. Parliament is a multifunctional body. Not only does it serve as a reactive body in the making of public policy, it also carries out several other tasks. Its principal tasks were established within the first two centuries of its development. In the fourteenth century the King accepted that taxes should not be levied without the assent of Parliament. The giving of such assent was variously withheld until the King responded to petitions requesting a redress of grievances. At the same time Parliament began to take an interest in how money was spent and began to look at the actions of public servants. It became, in a rather haphazard way, a body for the critical scrutiny of government.

The development of Parliament

Knights and burgesses were summoned in the thirteenth century in order to give assent to the King's decision to raise extra taxes. They joined the King's court, comprising the leading churchmen and barons of the realm. In the fourteenth century the summoning of knights and burgesses became a regular feature of those occasions when the King summoned a 'parliament'. At various times during the century, the knights and burgesses sat separately from the churchmen and barons, so there developed two chambers – the Commons and the Lords.

The House of Commons became more significant in subsequent centuries. It was an important political actor during the Tudor reigns of the sixteenth century and a powerful opponent of the Stuart monarchs, who asserted the divine right of kings to rule, in the seventeenth. Clashes occurred between Parliament and Charles I – leading to the beheading of the King and a short-lived period of republican government under Oliver Cromwell – and, later, between Parliament and James II. The fleeing of James II in 1688

BOX 15.1

Types of legislature

- *Policy-making legislatures*: These are legislatures that not only can modify or reject measures brought forward by the executive but also can formulate and substitute policy of their own (e.g. the US Congress).

- *Policy-influencing legislatures*: These are legislatures that can modify and sometimes reject measures brought forward by the executive but lack the capacity to formulate and substitute policy of their own (e.g. UK Parliament, Portuguese *Assembleia da República*).

- *Legislatures with little or no policy effect*: These are legislatures that can neither modify nor reject measures brought forward by the executive, nor formulate and substitute policies of their own. They typically meet for only a short period each year to give formal approval to whatever is placed before them (e.g. former legislatures of eastern European communist states, such as East Germany).

allowed leading parliamentarians to offer the throne to James's daughter and son-in-law (Mary and William) on Parliament's terms, and the supremacy of Parliament was established. Henceforth, the King could not legislate – or suspend laws – without the assent of Parliament.

Parliament nonetheless continued to look to the executive power – initially the King, and later the King's ministers assembled in Cabinet – to take the initiative in formulating measures of public policy. When measures were laid before Parliament, assent was normally forthcoming. In the eighteenth century royal influence was employed, either directly or through the aristocratic patrons of 'rotten boroughs', to ensure the return of a House favourable to the ministry. This influence was broken in the nineteenth century. The 1832 Reform Act enlarged the electorate by 49 per cent and abolished many, although not all, rotten boroughs. The effect of the measure was to loosen the grip of the aristocracy on the House of Commons and to loosen the grip of the monarch on the choice of government. The last time a government fell for want of the monarch's confidence was in 1834. MPs entered a period when they were relatively independent in their behaviour, being prepared on occasion to oust ministers and sometimes governments (as in 1852, 1855, 1856 and 1866) and to amend and variously reject legislation. Except for the years from 1841 to 1846, party ties were extremely loose.

This so-called **Golden Age** was to prove short-lived. At that time, there was little public business to transact and what there was of it was reasonably easy to comprehend. Members were not tied overly to party and could make a judgement on the business before them. The consequence of the 1867 Reform Act, enlarging the electorate by 88 per cent, and of later Acts reducing corrupt practices, was to create an electorate too large, and too protected by the law, to be 'bought' by individual candidates. Extensive organisation was necessary to reach the new voters, and organised political parties soon came to dominate elections. For a winning party to govern effectively, its members in the House of Commons needed to be united, and by the end of the century cohesive party voting was a feature of parliamentary life. Party influence thus succeeded royal patronage in ensuring the assent of MPs for measures brought forward by ministers of the crown.

The effect on Parliament of the rise of a mass electorate was profound. Governments came to be chosen by the electorate, not – as had occasionally happened in preceding years – by the House of Commons. Popular demands of government engendered not only more measures of public policy, but more extensive and complex measures. By the turn of the century, Parliament lacked the political will and the institutional resources necessary to subject increasingly detailed government bills to sustained and effective scrutiny.

Albeit in a somewhat different form to earlier centuries, executive dominance had returned.

For the House of Commons, though, the developments of the nineteenth century served to confirm it as the pre-eminent component of the Crown-in-Parliament. The Glorious Revolution had established Parliament's supremacy over the King. The rise of the democratic principle in the nineteenth century established the supremacy of the elected House over the unelected. The House of Commons was clearly a representative chamber in that it was freely elected and in that its members were returned to defend and pursue the interests of electors (see Chapter 14). The House of Lords could claim to be representative in neither sense. The subordinate position of the House of Lords was confirmed by statute in the Parliament Act of 1911.

The position so established in the nineteenth century continued into the twentieth. The House of Commons remained – and remains – the dominant chamber in a Parliament dominated by party, with the initiative for measures of public policy resting with the Cabinet and with a party majority in the House ensuring the passage of those measures.

That sets the historical context. What, then, is the contemporary position of the House of Commons? What are the essential characteristics of the House – its members and its procedures? What functions does it fulfil? What tools does it have at its disposal to fulfil them? And to what extent have developments in recent years strengthened or weakened its capacity to carry out those functions?

The House of Commons

The size of the House of Commons has varied over time, ranging in the twentieth century from a high of 707 seats (1918–22) to a low of 615 (1922–45). The number was reduced in 1922 because of the loss of (most) Irish seats; it has varied in postwar years and from 1945 to 1974 stood at 630; because of the increase in the size of the population, it was increased in 1974 to 635, in 1983 to 650, in 1992 to 651 and in 1997 to 659. In 2001 there was the first reduction since 1922: the number of seats in Scotland went down from 72 to 59 to take account of the fact that Scotland had its own parliament. As a result, the number of seats in the 2005 Parliament was 646. The number increased to 650 in the Parliament of 2010.

Elections

Between 1715 and 1911, the maximum life of a Parliament was seven years and from 1911 to 2010 it was five years. An election could be called at any time within that period. The Fixed-term Parliaments Act 2011 provided instead for a fixed term of five years, other than in certain exceptional circumstances, such as the House of Commons passing a vote of no confidence and no new government being able to gain the confidence of the House. Under the Act the next general election after that of May 2010 is to take place on 7 May 2015.

Members (MPs) are returned for single-member constituencies. These have been the norm since the Reform Act of 1885, although 12 double-member constituencies survived until the General Election of 1950. The method of election employed is the 'first-past-the-post' system, with the candidate receiving the largest number of votes being declared the winner. This again has been the norm since 1885, although not until the General Election of 1950 (with the abolition of university seats, for some of which a system of proportional representation was used) did it become universal. All seats nowadays are contested by two or more candidates. Again, this is a relatively recent development. In elections before 1945 a significant fraction of members – an average of 13 per cent – were returned unopposed. As late as the 1951 election, four Ulster Unionist MPs were returned in uncontested elections.

Each constituency comprises a defined geographical area, and the MP is returned to represent all citizens living within that area. (University seats were exceptional: the constituencies comprised graduates of the universities, regardless of where they were living.) Constituency boundaries are at present drawn up and revised regularly by independent Boundary Commissions (one covering each country – England, Scotland, Wales and Northern Ireland); each commission is chaired formally by the Speaker of the House of Commons, although the essential work of leadership is undertaken by a deputy, who is a judge. An Electoral Commission, created by the Political Parties, Elections and Referendums Act 2000, reports on elections and referendums, oversees the registration of, and donations to, political parties, and seeks to raise public awareness of elections.

In 2011 the government achieved passage of the Parliamentary Voting System and Constituencies Act, which stipulated a reduction in the number of seats from 650 to 600 and provided that constituencies should have the same number of voters, plus or minus 5 per cent (with one or two specified exceptions). However, in 2012 the Liberal Democrat leader, Nick Clegg, announced that his party, despite being part of the Coalition, would vote against the recommendations of the Boundary Commissions for the new boundaries, and in 2013 both Houses voted not to implement the changes in the current Parliament.

Members

Although the House may constitute a representative assembly in that it is freely elected and MPs are returned to defend and pursue the interests of constituents, it is not a representative assembly in being typical in socio-economic terms of the population that elects it. The members returned to the House are generally male, middle-class and white. These characteristics have been marked throughout the twentieth century. The House has tended to become even more middle-class in the years since 1945. Before 1945, and especially in the early years of the century, the Conservative ranks contained a significant number of upper class and upper middle-class men of private means. The parliamentary Labour Party (the PLP) was notable for the number of MPs from manual working-class backgrounds: they constituted a little over half of the PLP from 1922 to 1935 and before that had been in an overwhelming majority (Rush 1979: 69–123). Since 1945 the number of business people on the Conservative benches has increased, as has the number of graduates, often journalists or teachers, on the Labour benches.

BOX 15.2

The atmosphere of the House

By the standards of the Palace of Westminster, the House of Commons (Figure 15.1) is not a particularly ornate chamber. Relatively new compared with the rest of the Palace – rebuilt after being destroyed on 10 May 1941 by enemy bombing – it has a fairly functional feel to it.

When it was rebuilt, there was a change in the style but not in the size. This meant that it was too small to accommodate every member. This has proved to be beneficial on two counts. First, on the rare occasions that the House is full, it conveys a sense of theatre: some members sit on the steps in the aisles, some crowd around the Speaker's chair, some stand in packed ranks at the bar of the House. Tension rises as the Prime Minister, or another senior minister, closes for the government and the Speaker rises to put the question. Members then troop into the voting lobbies either side of the chamber. If the outcome of the vote is uncertain, the tension is close to unbearable. After 10 to 15 minutes – sometimes longer – the tellers return and those representing the winning side line up on the right at the table, facing the Speaker. Once those on the winning side realise they have won, a massive cheer goes up. The most dramatic vote of recent history was on 28 March 1979, when the Labour Government lost a vote of confidence by one vote. There have been dramatic votes in the twenty-first century when the Labour Government came close to defeat, on the second reading of the

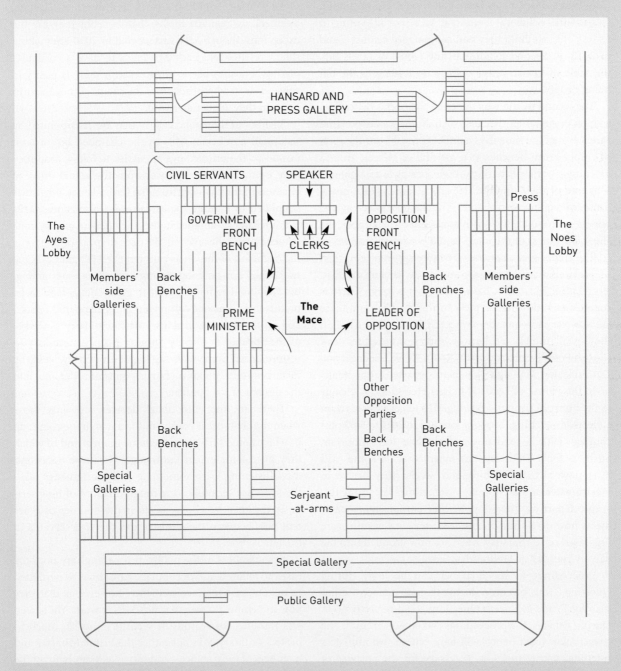

Figure 15.1 House of Commons seating plan

Education Bill in 2003 – even the government **whips** were not sure who had won – or the occasions when it was defeated: in 2005 on a provision to allow 90-day detention without trial and in 2009 on the resettlement rights in the UK of former Gurkha soldiers. Tensions were even higher in 2003 when the House voted on war with Iraq and it was not clear if Prime Minister Tony Blair – although assured of Conservative support – would be able to carry his own MPs with him. Under the Coalition Government, tense votes were held on tuition fees in 2010 – Liberal Democrat MPs (not all) voting in favour of something they had campaigned against – and in 2012 on Second Reading of the House of Lords Bill, the scale of Conservative opposition leading to the bill being dropped.

The second reason why the small chamber is better than a larger one is simply because such dramatic occasions are rare. Most of the time the chamber is notable for the rows of empty green benches as a handful of MPs sit around listening – or half-listening, or whispering to a neighbour – as one of their number delivers a speech from notes, sometimes quite copious notes. The chamber looks cavernous on such occasions. With a much larger chamber, the sheer emptiness of the place would be overwhelming.

The empty green benches are more apparent now than in previous decades. It is common to lament a fall in attendance. Most MPs have other things to do. There is sometimes little vital business in the chamber and there are now very few members who will attract a crowd when they speak: the big speakers of yesteryear are either dead (Enoch Powell, Edward Heath, Robin Cook, Michael Foot, Denis Healey, Margaret Thatcher), departed (Tony Benn) or in the House of Lords (Michael Heseltine). A change in the hours of sittings, allowing MPs to get away early on a Thursday evening (brought forward in 2012 to 5.00 pm) coupled with a tendency to schedule less important business for a Thursday, has meant that for some MPs it is now virtually a three-day week. They arrive in Westminster on the Monday – sometimes late in the day – and depart on Thursday. Neither parliamentary party meets now on a Thursday; indeed, very few meetings are organised on a Thursday. Most are now crowded into the day on Tuesday or Wednesday.

Proceedings in the chamber can be lively during Question Time, but even during that attendance – other than for Prime Minister's Questions – can be pretty poor. During debates, the proceedings can be notably dull. The government front bench will have one or two ministers listening, taking notes as necessary for the purpose of replying at the end. A government whip will be perched further along the bench, keeping an eye on proceedings, taking notes and liaising with the Chair about business. Their opposite numbers will be on the Opposition front bench. Notes or signals will variously pass between the whips, followed sometimes by a meeting behind the Speaker's Chair to fix some deal. Some MPs will wander in, look at what is going on and then depart. Some take their seats, stay a few minutes and go. A few will spend some time in the chamber and occasionally intervene to make a point. Some MPs (such as Labour MP Dennis Skinner) are regulars in the chamber, but they are the exceptions, though MPs first elected in 2010 are making their presence felt. Each MP tends to have a particular place where they like to sit, so even if there is plenty of space close to where they enter the chamber they move to the spot they are familiar with.

Visitors to the public gallery may be disappointed by the small number of MPs in the chamber, but at least nowadays the proceedings are easier to follow than they have ever been. One can work out the actual order of business in the chamber from the Order Paper, nowadays simplified to indicate the actual order of business. MPs still refer to one another in the third person and by constituency, but whenever an MP rises to speak or intervene the occupant of the Chair calls out the MP's name. Some exchanges can be enlightening as well as entertaining, but they tend to be exceptional. Proceedings tend to be predictable. Tensions can rise in an ill-tempered debate, and all the diplomatic skills – or disciplinary powers – of the Speaker or Deputy Speaker may be necessary to restore order. Some MPs try to get around the rules by raising partisan points on bogus points of order, much to the despair of the Speaker.

There are the exceptional debates, not just those when the chamber is packed but when an issue comes up in which some MPs have a genuine interest and of which they have some expert knowledge. On those occasions, those listening learn something and the minister takes the speeches seriously. One rough measure of how seriously the speech is being taken is the number of notes that pass between the minister and the civil servants in the official box.

For members of the public, proceedings are not only easier to follow than before but they are also now permitted to take notes. One inconvenience, however, is that they now sit behind a screen to watch MPs at work. The screen was installed for reasons of security – not so much to protect ordinary MPs but rather the Prime Minister and members of the Cabinet – and serves as a reminder of the difficult times in which public figures have to operate.

The shift in the background of Conservative MPs since 1945 is reflected in education as well as occupation. In 1945 just over 83 per cent of Conservative MPs had been educated at public schools – 27 per cent at Eton. Almost two-thirds – 65 per cent – had been to university, with half having gone to Oxford or Cambridge. Sixty-five years later – in the parliament elected in 2010 – 54 per cent were public-school educated, with just under 6 per cent having been at Eton; 80 per cent had been at university, the proportion having gone to Oxford or Cambridge comprising 34 per cent (see Table 15.1). The party has witnessed, particularly in the general elections in and since 1979, a growing number of newly elected candidates who have gone to state schools and then gone on to Oxbridge or some other university. The members of the parliamentary party are not socially typical, but they are somewhat more middle-class than the members elected in the years before 1979.

On the Labour side, the notable change in educational background has been the rise in the number of graduates. In 1945 just over one-third of Labour MPs (34 per cent) had been to university. By 1970 just over half of the PLP were university graduates. In the parliaments of Labour governments from 1997 onwards, approximately two out of every three Labour MPs had been to university, though the figure dipped slightly in 2005. In 1997 the figure was 66 per cent, in 2001 it was 67 per cent and in 2005 it was 64 per cent. In 2010 it reached 73 per cent (Table 15.1). Most of these were graduates of universities other than Oxford and Cambridge. The percentage of Oxbridge-educated Labour MPs has shown little change – the percentage educated at Oxbridge in 2010 (17 per cent) was almost identical to that of 1945.

These figures reflect the growing middle-class nature of the PLP. The percentage of manual workers in the party declined in each successive parliament until 1974, increased in 1979 and 1983, but then dropped back in subsequent elections. Only 17 per cent of new Labour MPs in 1992 were drawn from manual backgrounds. It declined further in subsequent elections, reaching its lowest percentage ever – 9 per cent – in 2010.

Indeed, there is something of a convergence between members on both sides in terms of education and background.

Table 15.1 University-educated MPs, 2010 (%)

Party	University (all)	Oxford and Cambridge
Labour	73	17
Conservative	80	34
Liberal Democrat	80	28

Source: B. Criddle (2010) 'More Diverse, Yet More Uniform', in D. Kavanagh and P. Cowley (eds) *The British General Election of 2010*. Reproduced with permission of Palgrave Macmillan

Of new MPs elected to the House of Commons, the vast majority – on both sides of the House – is university-educated, and a large proportion drawn not only from some middle-class occupation but from an occupation that is in the domain of politics or communication. Teachers, journalists and political staffers have been notable among the new intake of Labour MPs in and since 1997. In 2010, as Criddle recorded, 'at least a fifth of Labour MPs and some two-fifths of the new intake . . . came from previous employment as ministerial or Members aides' (Criddle 2010: 328). Business and the professions continue to dominate on the Conservative benches, though 16 per cent of the Tory MPs elected in 2010 had been political organisers, publishers or journalists.

This convergence also reflects the growth of the 'career politician' – the individual who lives for politics, who seeks entry to the House of Commons as early as possible and who seeks to stay in the House for as long as possible, ideally holding government office along the way (King 1981; Riddell 1993). Career politicians are contrasted with old-style MPs, who used to make a mark in other fields before becoming involved in politics and who could – and variously did – leave the House of Commons to pursue some other interest (for example, heading a major company or the family firm). The old-style members may have been ambitious in terms of government office, but they recognised that there was more to life than politics. For career politicians, politics is their life. The career politician has always existed in British politics, but their numbers have grown in recent years. They often (though not in all cases) hold a job in an area related to politics before seeking election. The consequence of the growth of the career politician is something we shall consider later.

Where there is a difference between the two sides is in terms of council experience and in terms of gender. Labour MPs are more likely to have served as local councillors. Of the new MPs elected in 1997, almost two-thirds of Labour MPs had served as councillors, compared with one-quarter of Conservative MPs. The new but relatively small Labour intake of 2001 also included a number of long-standing councillors, especially in safe Labour seats (Criddle 2002: 192). There are also many more women sitting on the Labour benches than on the Conservative (and Liberal Democrat) benches.

Women became eligible to sit in the House only in 1918. The number elected since then has been small. Between 1918 and 1974, the total number of women elected to the House was only 112 (including Countess Markievicz, the first woman elected but who, as a Sinn Féin candidate, did not take her seat). In the 1983 General Election 23 women were elected to the House; in 1987 the figure was 41 and in 1992 it was 60, still less than 10 per cent of the membership. The Labour Party in 1993 adopted a policy of all-women shortlists in a number of constituencies in order to boost the number of female Labour MPs. Although the policy was struck down by an employment tribunal in 1996 on the grounds that it breached sex discrimination legislation, this did not affect seats where female candidates had already been selected. As a result, a record number of female Labour MPs were elected in 1997: no less than 101, 64 of them elected for the first time. Labour replaced all-women shortlists with 50–50 short lists (half of the candidates female, the other half male) but this failed to push up the number of women candidates. In the 2001 election the number of women MPs dropped to 118. However, more were adopted for safe seats in the subsequent parliament and the number increased to 128 in 2005 and 143 in 2010, just over 22 per cent of the total.

The number of women MPs on the Labour benches is more marked than on the benches of other parties. Although Conservative leaders in recent decades have encouraged local parties to adopt female candidates, very few have done so. As leader, David Cameron introduced an A-list of candidates to promote women candidates and those drawn from ethnic minority backgrounds. This contributed to a notable increase in 2010 in the number of women sitting on the Conservative benches, women representing for the first time more than 15 per cent of the parliamentary party, though still notably lagging behind the number on the Labour benches. The Liberal Democrats have also had problems in getting more women elected; in 2005 they managed to double – from five to ten – the number of female MPs; again, an all-time high but one that represented only 16 per cent of Liberal Democrat MPs. However, three were defeated in 2010 – another had previously died – and only one new woman was elected.

The percentage of women MPs in the House of Commons in recent parliaments remains low compared to some other

Table 15.2 Women elected to Parliament, 2010

Party	Number of women MPs (2005 figure in parentheses)	
Labour	81	(98)
Conservative	49	(17)
Liberal Democrat	7	(10)
SNP	1	(0)
Democratic Unionists	0	(1)
Alliance	1	(0)
Sinn Fein	1	(1)
SDLP	1	(0)
Other	2	(1)
Total	**143**	**128**

Source: From B. Criddle (2010) 'More Diverse, Yet More Uniform', in D. Kavanagh and P. Cowley (eds) *The British General Election of 2010*, p. 319. Reproduced with permission of Palgrave Macmillan

countries – especially the Nordic countries – but it is now above the average (of 20.3 per cent) for national parliaments. Data compiled by the Inter-Parliamentary Union show that in 2012 the UK ranked sixty-third out of 190 national parliaments in terms of the proportion of women members.

The number of non-white MPs remains very small. For most of the twentieth century there were none at all. The first non-white MP was elected in 1892: Dadabhai Naoroji, an Indian, was elected as Liberal MP for Finsbury Central. Another Indian was elected as a Conservative three years later. A third sat from 1922 to 1929. There was then a 58-year gap. In 1987 four non-white MPs were elected. In 1992 the number increased to six (five Labour and one Conservative) and in 1997 to nine (all Labour), including the first Muslim MP and two Sikhs. The number has increased in subsequent parliaments and in 2010 there were 27 MPs elected from ethnic minority backgrounds: 16 were Labour and 11 were Conservative, including the first Conservative female Asian MP, Priti Patel. Labour provided the first three female Muslim MPs (Criddle 2010: 320–1).

One reason for the persistence of white, male MPs is the length of time that MPs typically serve in the House. Some MPs sit for 30 or 40 years. In the 2010 Parliament the Father of the House of Commons (the longest continuously serving MP), Conservative MP, Sir Peter Tapsell, had been first elected in 1959 and had continuous service since 1966. Another MP had been first elected in 1966. A total of 21 MPs had been first elected prior to 1980. A typical member sits for about 20 years. Given the growth in the number of career politicians, it is unlikely that this figure will decrease; if anything, the reverse. Even if parties are keen to replace existing MPs with candidates from a wider range of backgrounds, the opportunity to replace them does not necessarily come up very quickly. The length of service of legislators is a particular feature of the British House of Commons: MPs tend to serve as members longer than legislators in other comparable legislatures (see Somit and Roemmele 1995).

Members are paid an annual salary, but until 1912 they received no payment at all. Since then, they have been paid, but on a relatively modest basis. In 1954, for example, the salary was £1,250 and in 1964 it was increased to £3,250. In January 1996 an MP's salary was £34,086, fairly modest by international comparison – legislators in Italy, the USA, France and Germany were all paid considerably more (more than twice as much in Italy and the USA) – and by comparison with higher levels of management in the UK. (Ministers receive higher salaries.) In July 1996 MPs voted to increase their salaries by 26 per cent, to £43,000. The increase was controversial, and unpopular, but it still left MPs lagging behind the salaries of members of other comparable legislatures. The salary has been variously increased since and in 2012–13 it was £65,738. In 2011 responsibility for setting the level of pay was transferred from MPs to the Independent Parliamentary Standards Authority (IPSA), a body set up following a scandal over MPs' expenses in 2009.

Since the 1960s parliamentary facilities have also improved. In the mid-1960s an MP was guaranteed only a locker in which to keep papers and received no allowance, whether for hiring a secretary or even to cover the cost of telephone calls. If an MP was lucky enough to have an office, it was usually shared with several other MPs. A secretary had to be paid out of the MP's own pocket. A secretarial allowance (of £500) was introduced in 1969. This allowance evolved into an office cost allowance, allowing an MP to hire one and sometimes two secretaries and in most cases a research assistant (more often than not, part-time). In 2001 the office cost allowance was split into two: a staff cost allowance and an incidental expenses provision. Each MP could claim a staff cost allowance, enabling them to employ up to the equivalent of three full-time staff, but with the staff paid centrally by the House authorities and on agreed rates with standard contracts. Each MP could also claim a further £20,000 towards incidental expenses. MPs could claim travel expenses and, for those living outside London (and thus having to maintain two homes), an additional costs allowance. MPs with inner London constituencies receive a small London supplement. The additional cost allowance, as we shall see, became highly controversial in 2009 when details of claims made by MPs were published.

In the wake of the MPs' expenses scandal, a new regime was introduced. IPSA was created by the Parliamentary Standards Act 2009 and responsibility for paying expenses transferred to the new body. MPs can now claim for staffing (£144,000 for London area MPs and £137,200 for others), accommodation (for a second home either in London or within the constituency or 20 miles of its boundary, the figure depending on whether rented or mortgaged), office costs (up to £24,750 for London area MPs and £22,200 for others), as well as travel and subsistence. There are certain other allowable expenses, such as provision for those MPs with disabilities and a London area living allowance for Members sitting for London area seats or who do not claim the accommodation expenditure. All claims have to be authorised by IPSA and the sums claimed by each MP are published.

The physical space available to MPs has also increased. The parliamentary estate is much more than the Palace of Westminster. Buildings close to the Palace – including the former Scotland Yard buildings in Derby Gate, known as the Norman Shaw Buildings – were acquired for parliamentary use. More recently, buildings in Parliament Street – between Whitehall and Parliament Square – were taken over and redeveloped, retaining the exterior but with a modern and integrated complex of offices inside. They have the address of 1 Parliament Street. To these has been added a major purpose-built parliamentary building, Portcullis House, in Bridge Street, just across the road from the Elizabeth Tower (known until 2012 as the Clock Tower) housing Big Ben and linked to the Palace by an underground passage. Both the Norman Shaw buildings and 1 Parliament Street are linked to Portcullis House, so MPs can get from one part of the parliamentary estate to another without leaving the premises. The completion of Portcullis House, which includes rooms for committee meetings as well as suites of offices for MPs, meant that it was possible for every MP to have an individual office somewhere on the parliamentary estate.

Sittings of the House

The House to which Members are returned meets annually, each parliamentary session running normally for 12 months. Until the parliament returned in 2010, the session usually ran from November to November. When there was a spring election, this entitled either a short session (May to November) or a long one (May through to November of the following year). The Fixed-term Parliaments Act 2011 provided for May elections, so the Government decided that it was appropriate to have sessions running from May to May. To accommodate this, the first session of the new parliament was extended into an exceptional two-year one, running until May 2012. At the end of each session, the House is prorogued (formally adjourned). The effect of prorogation is to kill off unfinished public business; any bills that have not received the Royal Assent fall, though there is now provision for some bills to be carried over from one session to another.

There is a fairly regular cycle within each session. There is a summer recess, usually from late July through to the beginning of October, though in recent years there have been occasional two-week sittings in September. The House has a recess at Christmas, a half-term for a week in February, a recess in Easter and at Whitsuntide. The House usually sits for more than 150 days a year, a not unusual number compared with some other legislatures, such as those of the USA, Canada and France, although considerably more than most other legislatures. What makes it distinctive is the number of hours for which it sits: it sits usually for more than 1,200 hours a year. The figures for the period from 2001 to 2012 are given in Table 15.3. In previous parliaments, the sittings were sometimes longer, averaging nearly 1,500 hours in non-election sessions in the 1987–92 parliament. Other elected chambers are not able to compete with these figures.

Until 1999 the House sat at 2.30 pm on the first four days of the week and at 9.30 am on Fridays. On the first four days it usually rose by 10.30 pm. In an experiment started in

Table 15.3 The House of Commons: length of sittings, 2001–12

Session	Number of sitting days	Number of hours sat	Average length of sitting day
2001–2[a]	201	1,297	7 hours 40 minutes
2002–3	162	1,287	7 hours 57 minutes
2003–4	157	1,215	7 hours 44 minutes
2004–5[b]	65	535	8 hours 14 minutes
2005–6[a]	208	1,572	7 hours 33 minutes
2006–7	146	1,119	7 hours 40 minutes
2007–8	165	1,306	7 hours 55 minutes
2008–9	139	1,054	7 hours 35 minutes
2009–10[b]	60	540	7 hours 50 minutes
2010–12[c]	296	2,342	7 hours 57 minutes

(a) Long session following a spring general election.
(b) Short session following calling of a general election.
(c) Exceptional two-year session.

Source: From the House of Commons Sessional Information Digests, 2001–12. © Parliamentary Copyright. Parliamentary copyright material is reproduced with the permission of the Controller of Her Majesty's Stationery Office (HMSO) on behalf of Parliament

1999, it started meeting at 11.30 am on Thursdays (rising earlier in the evening, usually by 7.00 or 8.00 pm). Since then, sitting hours have moved to earlier in the day on all days bar Monday, the latest changes being implemented in October 2012. Since then, the House has sat at 2.30 p.m. on Mondays, and at 11.30 am on Tuesdays and Wednesdays, and 9.30 am on Thursdays (and Fridays, if sitting). The sitting time was brought forward on Tuesdays (from 2.30 pm) and Thursdays (from 10.30 am), the latter in order to enable the House to rise by 5.00 pm and for Members to get away to their constituencies, if they have not already departed.

Sittings may, in certain circumstances, be extended in order to transact particular business. Late or all-night sittings variously take place to get through the remaining stages of a bill. (If the House has an all-night sitting and is still sitting when the new day's sitting is scheduled to commence, then the business for that next day falls.) Late-night sittings became rare in the 1992–7 parliament but were employed again following the return of a Labour government in 1997 in order to get some of its major legislation through, but the change in sitting times was designed to reduce the need for such sittings. On Fridays, when **private members' bills** are normally discussed, the House rises at 3.00 pm. To give MPs more time to be in their constituencies, the House does not sit every Friday: ten Fridays each session are designated as non-sitting Fridays.

As a result of a change agreed by the House in 1999, there is also a 'parallel chamber', or 'main committee', allowing MPs to meet and discuss issues separate from the main chamber (see Box 15.3). This allows for non-contentious

issues to be debated. Meetings are held in the Grand Committee Room, just off Westminster Hall, and are known formally as meetings in Westminster Hall. The topics covered on Tuesdays and Wednesdays each week are proposed by private Members; the Thursday sitting is given over to a debate on a subject of general interest or a select committee report. All MPs can attend – as in the main chamber – although in practice few do so.

Functions

The principal function of the House is often seen as involvement in law making. It is, after all, classified as a legislature and the name means carrier, or giver, of law. In practice, as we have seen, the House essentially responds to the measures that the government brings forward. Furthermore, much of the time of the House is given over to business that has nothing directly to do with legislation. Question Time is now an established feature of the House. It is not part of the legislative process. When the House debates the economy or the government's industrial policy, those debates are not parts of the formal legislative process. The House has an important role to play in the legislative process, but it is clearly not its only role.

The principal functions of the House can be grouped under four headings: those of legitimisation, recruitment, scrutiny and influence, and expression. Several other functions can be identified (see Norton 2013) but these can largely be subsumed under these four broad headings.

Legitimisation

The primary purpose for which the representatives of the counties and boroughs (the communes) were first summoned was to assent to the King's demand for additional taxes. Subsequently, their assent also came to be necessary for legislation. The House has thus been, since its inception, a legitimising body.

The House fulfils the task of 'manifest legitimisation': that is, the overt, conscious giving of assent. In the UK the function has two elements: the giving of assent to bills and to requests for supply (money) and the giving of assent to the government itself. The government depends on the confidence of the House of Commons for its continuance in office. Until 2011, if the House withdrew its confidence, then by convention the government resigned or requested the dissolution of Parliament. Since the enactment of the Fixed-term Parliaments Act 2011, a **vote of no confidence** results in a general election, unless within 14 days a new government is formed and obtains a vote of confidence from the House.

The House proceeds on the basis of motions laid before it: for example, to give a bill a second reading or to agree to

Meetings in Westminster Hall

The Grand Committee Room is located just off Westminster Hall
Source: Copyright © Adam Woolfitt/Corbis

In December 1999 the House of Commons introduced a new form of meeting – meetings in Westminster Hall. These enable MPs to meet separately from the main chamber, and the gathering is sometimes described as a parallel chamber. (The parallel chamber is modelled on Australian experience.) Meetings in Westminster Hall are open to all MPs. They can come in as they can in the main chamber. The principal differences between the main chamber and the room used for the parallel chamber are of size and structure. The room used – the Grand Committee Room, located just off the cavernous Westminster Hall – is much smaller than the chamber of the House of Commons. It also differs in structure. MPs sit at desks arranged in a semicircle around a raised dais. The desks are fixed and have desktop microphones. Meetings are presided over by a Deputy Speaker or one of the MPs on the Panel of Chairs (senior MPs who are drawn on in order to chair public bill committees) and are usually used for discussing non-contentious business. Votes cannot be held. Meetings now take place on Tuesdays and Wednesdays from 9.30 to 11.30 a.m. and from 2.30 to 5.00 p.m. and on Thursdays from 1.30 to 4.30 p.m. On Tuesdays and Wednesdays there are short debates on topics raised by individual members. Thus, for example, on Wednesday, 12 September 2012 the topics covered were human rights violations, petrol prices (Wyre Forest), the aerospace industry, police officer reductions and protecting the Antarctic. Thursdays are given over to debates on select committee reports or subjects scheduled by the Backbench Business Committee. On Thursday 13 September 2012 the topic was the dairy industry, selected by the Backbench Business Committee. Attendance at meetings is low – usually a handful of MPs – not dissimilar to the chamber itself when unwhipped business is being taken.

The creation of the parallel chamber was controversial. Supporters see it as a way of allowing issues, for which there would otherwise be no time in the chamber, to be discussed. Most Conservative MPs voted against setting it up because they feared it would serve to distract attention from the chamber and absorb MPs' energies on minor issues. In the event, meetings of the new body have proved low-key, attracting virtually no media attention (the inaugural meeting was effectively ignored) and very little attention on the part of MPs. The chamber was initially employed on an experimental basis, but MPs subsequently voted to make it permanent. It was not seen as damaging to the main chamber and backbenchers have found it useful as a means of raising issues that they might not have the opportunity to raise in the main chamber. Each debate brings an issue to the attention of government, with a junior minister replying. The proceedings are published in *Hansard*.

an amendment to a bill. By approving such motions, the House gives its formal – manifest – assent. At the end of the debate (if there is one) on a motion, the Speaker of the House asks those supporting the motion to say 'aye', those opposing to say 'no'. If no dissenting voices are heard, the Speaker declares that 'the ayes have it'. If some MPs shout 'no' and persist then members divide (that is, vote). A simple majority is all that is necessary. (This is subject to two basic requirements: that at least 40 MPs – a quorum – are shown by the division to be present and that, in voting on a closure motion, at least 100 MPs have voted in favour.) Members vote by each trooping through one of two lobbies, known as the division lobbies (an 'aye' lobby and a 'no' lobby), where they are counted and their names recorded. The result of the vote is then announced in the chamber.

It is this accepted need for the House to confer legitimacy through giving its assent that constitutes the basic power of the House in relation to government. Initially, the knights and burgesses summoned to the King's court were expected to give assent. Gradually, members began to realise that, as a body, they could deny assent to supply and later to legislation. This formed the basis on which they could ensure the effective fulfilment of other functions. It remains the basis of the power of the House of Commons. Without the assent of the House, no measure can become an Act of Parliament. The contemporary point of contention is the extent to which the House is prepared to use its power to deny assent. Critics contend that the effect of the growth of party and hence party cohesion has largely nullified the willingness of the House to employ it.

The House also fulfils what Robert Packenham has termed the function of 'latent legitimisation'. According to Packenham, this derives from the fact that 'simply by meeting regularly and uninterruptedly, the legislature produces, among the relevant populace and élites, a wider and deeper sense of the government's moral right to rule than would otherwise have obtained' (Packenham, in Norton 1990: 87). However, it can be argued that such activity is necessary but not sufficient to generate such an underlying sense of legitimacy. Latent legitimacy can be said to derive from the House fulfilling the other functions expected of it (Norton 2013: Ch. 1). Given that Parliament not only sits regularly but has fulfilled a range of tasks expected of it for a considerable period of time, it is arguably a much stronger agent of latent legitimisation than many other legislatures. It would seem plausible to hypothesise that the function is weaker in a political system in which the legislature is a recent and conscious creation of resuscitation by the prevailing regime and fails to carry out tasks expected of it by the people.

Recruitment

Ministers are normally drawn from, and remain within, Parliament. The situation is governed solely by convention. There is no legal requirement that a minister has to be an MP or peer.

The practice of appointing ministers from those who sit in Parliament derives from expediency. Historically, it was to the King's benefit to have his ministers in Parliament, where they could influence, lead and marshal support for the crown. It was to the benefit of Parliament to have ministers who could answer for their conduct. An attempt was made early in the eighteenth century to prevent ministers from sitting in Parliament, but the legislation was superseded by another law allowing the practice to continue (Norton 2013: Ch. 3).

The convention that ministers be drawn from and remain within Parliament – predominantly now, by convention, the House of Commons – is a strong one inasmuch as all ministers are currently MPs or peers. It is extremely rare for a minister to be appointed who does not sit in either House and even rarer for that person to remain outside Parliament while in office: the person is either elevated to the peerage (nowadays the most used route) or found a safe seat to contest in a by-election. On occasion, one of the Scottish law officers – the Solicitor General for Scotland – was appointed from the ranks of Scottish lawyers and remained outside Parliament, but that was the exception that proved the rule. The post ceased to be part of the UK government following devolution.

The relationship between the House and ministers is governed by convention. Under the convention of individual ministerial responsibility, ministers are answerable to the House for their own conduct and that of their particular departments. Under the convention of collective ministerial responsibility, the Cabinet is responsible to the House for government policy as a whole. If it fails to maintains that confidence, and the House passes a vote of no confidence, then – as we have seen – a general election takes place unless a new government can be formed that enjoys the confidence of the House.

The fact that ministers remain in Parliament clearly has a number of advantages for government. Things have not changed that much from earlier centuries in that ministers can use their positions to lead and marshal their supporters. Ministers themselves add notably to the voting strength of the government, the so-called 'payroll vote' in the House.

Just over 90 ministers serve in the Commons and just over 20 in the Lords. With ministers' unpaid helpers – parliamentary private secretaries – added to the number, the payroll vote usually comprises between 30 to 40 per cent of MPs sat on the government side of the House. The government thus has a sizeable guaranteed vote to begin with. Party loyalty – and ambition for office – usually ensures that the votes of **backbenchers** follow those of ministers.

The convention that ministers be drawn from the ranks of parliamentarians has certain advantages for Parliament. It ensures that members are close to ministers, both formally and informally. Ministers can be questioned on the floor of the House; members can waylay them in the corridors and the division lobbies for private conversations. The fact that ministers remain as members of the House means that they retain some affinity with other members. MPs elevated to ministerial office retain their constituency duties.

Above all, though, the convention renders the House of Commons powerful as a recruiting agent. The route to ministerial office is through Parliament. In some other systems, the legislature is but one route to the top. In the USA, for example, there are multiple routes: cabinet ministers – and presidents – can be drawn from the ranks of business executives, academics, state governors, former army officers and lawyers. The US Congress enjoys no monopoly on recruitment to executive office. In the UK Parliament does have such a monopoly. Parliament is the exclusive route for those intending to reach the top of the political ladder. Those aspiring to ministerial office thus have to seek election to the House of Commons (or hope – often in vain – for a peerage) and have to make their mark in the House. The House also serves as an important testing ground for potential ministers and, indeed, for those on the ministerial ladder (see Norton 2013: Ch. 3). A poor performance at the despatch box can harm a minister's chances of further promotion. A consistently poor performance can result in the minister losing office. Conversely, a bravura performance may save a minister who is under pressure to go. For ambitious politicians, the chamber matters.

Scrutiny and influence

Scrutiny and influence are essentially conjoined functions. The House subjects both the measures and the actions of government to scrutiny. It does so through various means: debate, questioning and committee deliberations. If it does not like what is before it, it can influence the bill or the policy under consideration. It may influence solely by the force of argument. It may influence by threatening to deny assent (that is, by threatening to defeat the government). Ultimately, it may actually refuse its assent, denying the government a majority in the division lobbies.

These two functions are central to the activity of the House and absorb most of its time. Government business enjoys precedence on most days. The House spends most of its time discussing legislation and the policy and actions of ministers. Although the dominance of *party* has ensured that normally the government is assured a majority in divisions, the party *system* helps to ensure that government is subject to critical scrutiny from opposition parties in the House. The procedures of the House are premised on the existence of two principal parties, with each having the opportunity to be heard. Membership of all committees of the House replicates party strength on the floor of the House, thus ensuring that the Opposition has an opportunity to offer critical comments and to force government to respond at all stages of the parliamentary process.

Furthermore, scrutiny and influence may also take place outside, or despite, the context of party. MPs sit for particular constituencies. Although elected on a party label, they are nonetheless expected to ensure that government policy does not damage constituency interests. They may also be influenced by moral and religious views that ensure they pay careful attention to bills and government policies that run counter to their personal convictions. They may also listen to bodies outside Parliament – charities, consumer groups, professional organisations, companies – that have a particular interest in, or knowledge of, the subject under debate.

However, the extent to which the House actually fulfils these functions is a matter of dispute. Critics contend that the government stranglehold, via its party majority, ensures that the House is denied the means for sustained and effective scrutiny, and that, inasmuch as it may exert some limited scrutiny, that scrutiny is not matched by the capacity to influence government. MPs may consider and find fault with a particular measure but not then prove willing to use their power to amend or reject it.

Expression

The House serves not one but several expressive functions. Members serve to express the particular views and demands of constituents. An individual constituent or a group of constituents may be affected adversely by some particular policy or by the actions of some public officials. Constituents may feel that a particular policy is bad for the constituency or for the country. Contacting the local MP will usually result in the MP passing on the views to the relevant minister and may even result in the member raising the issue on the floor of the House. The pursuit of such cases by MPs ensures that they are heard and their points considered by ministers.

MPs also express the views of different groups in society as a whole. A range of issues that do not fall within the ambit of party politics are taken up and pursued by private members.

MPs may express the views of organised interests, such as particular industries or occupations. They may express the views of different sectors of society, such as students or the elderly. Many will give voice to the concerns of particular charitable, religious or moral groups. For example, some MPs have pressed for reform of the laws governing abortion, some have argued the case for liberalising the laws concerning homosexuality, and some want to strengthen the laws on road safety. These issues can be pursued by MPs through a number of parliamentary procedures (see Cowley 1998). In some cases, members table amendments to government bills. Another route is through the use of private members' bills. Although the more contentious the issue, the less likely the bill is to be passed, the debate on the bill serves an important function: it allows the different views to be expressed in an authoritative public forum, heard by the relevant minister and open to coverage by the mass media.

MPs, then, serve to express the views of constituents and different groups to the House and to government. MPs may also serve to express the views of the House and of government to constituents and organised groups. The House may reach a decision on a particular topic. Members may then fulfil an important role in explaining why that decision was taken. Members individually may explain decisions to constituents. **Select committees** of the House may, in effect, explain particular policies through their reports, which are read not just by government but also by groups with a particular interest in the committee's area of enquiry. The House thus has a tremendous potential to serve several expressive functions. The extent to which it does so is a matter of considerable debate. MPs have limited time and resources to pursue all the matters brought to their attention. The attention given to their activities by the media and by government may be slight. Many groups may bypass Parliament in order to express their views directly to ministers. Furthermore, it is argued, the views expressed by MPs on behalf of others are drowned out by the noise of party battle. By limiting the resources of the House and by keeping information to itself, the government has limited the capacity of the House to arm itself with the knowledge necessary to raise support for public policies.

These are the most important functions that may be ascribed to the House. The list is not an exhaustive one. Other tasks are carried out by the House. These include, for example, a disciplinary role (punishing breaches of privilege and contempt) and a small quasi-judicial role, primarily in dealing with private legislation (legislation affecting private interests, not to be confused with private members' legislation). Other functions often ascribed to the House can, as we have explained, be subsumed under the four main headings we have provided. However, two other functions, identified by Walter Bagehot in *The English Constitution* in 1867, have been lost by the House. One, the 'elective' function – that is, choosing the government – was held only briefly during the nineteenth century. Before then it was a function exercised by the monarch. Since then, it has passed largely, although not quite exclusively, to the electorate. The electorate chooses a government on a regular basis at general elections. The House retains the power to turn a government out through passing a motion of no confidence; but it is not a power it has exercised regularly – in the past century, it was used only in 1924 and 1979, opposition parties combining to turn out a minority government.

The other function is that of legislating. Initially, the need for the House to give its assent was transformed by members into the power to initiate measures, first through the presentation of petitions to the crown and later through the introduction of bills. This power was important in the nineteenth century, when the House could be described as sharing the legislative power with government. Even so, its exercise was limited. Most legislation introduced into the House was private legislation. Since then, public legislation has expanded as parties have become more powerful. Parties have ensured that the power to formulate – to 'make' – legislation rests with government, with the House then giving its assent. In so far as the House has retained a residual legislative power, it is exercised through the medium of private members' legislation. However, even that legislative power can be described now as one shared with government. Since 1959 no private member's bill that has been the subject of a vote at second reading (the debate on principle) has made it to the statute book without government providing time for it.

The means of scrutiny and influence

The functions that the House retains can be described as modest but appropriate to a reactive legislature. They have developed over time. But how well are they currently carried out? The principal functions of the House in relation to the executive are those of scrutiny and influence. The means available to the House to fulfil those functions are also at the disposal of members for expressing the views of their constituents and of wider interests. They can be grouped under two headings: legislation and executive actions.

Legislation

For Parliament the legislative process constitutes the consideration of a bill once it has been formally introduced. However, in recent years, some bills have been published in draft form and considered by a committee prior to formal introduction (Kennon 2004; Hansard Society 2004; Constitution Committee 2004; Norton 2013). Between 1997 and 2010, a total of 76 bills were published in draft, 16 per cent of the bills introduced in that period (Constitution Committee 2010: 7). The number peaked in the 2003–4 session, when 12 bills were published in draft, representing one in three of government bills for the session. Such scrutiny enables members to examine and comment before the government has decided on the final wording, and hence may be more willing to make changes before it commits itself to the measure. Despite considerable time pressures, bills subject to pre-legislative scrutiny have been variously amended as a result of recommendations by the committees considering them (Norton 2013). The committees engaging in such scrutiny have normally been departmental select committees.

When a bill is formally introduced into Parliament, it has to go through a well-established process involving debate and consideration in committee. About a third of the time of the House is taken up with debate on bills, though in recent sessions it has fallen to between 20 and 30 per cent. In the 2007–8 session it was 38 per cent, but it fell to under 30 per cent in the two remaining sessions of the parliament and remained under 30 per cent in the exceptionally long 2010–12 session (see Table 15.4). The bulk of this time is given over to government bills. (Private members' legislation usually occupies just under, or occasionally just over, 5 per cent of time on the floor of the House.) Every bill has to go through three 'readings' plus a committee and (usually) a report stage. The stages are shown in Table 15.5.

The first reading marks the formal introduction. No debate takes place. Indeed, at this stage there is not even a printed bill. All that is read out is the bill's title. Following first reading, the bill is printed. The second reading comprises a debate on the principle of the measure. Most government bills will be allocated a half or a full day's debate for second reading. Major bills, especially of constitutional significance, may be given two or more days for debate. In the 2012–13 session, for example, the House of Lords Reform Bill, to provide for a largely elected House of Lords, was accorded a two-day debate.

The debate itself follows a standard pattern: the minister responsible for the bill opens the debate, explaining the provisions of the bill and justifying its introduction. The relevant shadow minister then makes a speech from the Opposition front bench, outlining the stance of the opposition on the bill. After these two frontbench speeches, most members present tend to leave the chamber, usually leaving a small number of MPs to listen to the remaining speeches. Backbenchers from both sides of the House are then called alternately, plus usually a member from one or more of

Table 15.4 Time spent on the floor of the House, 2010–12

Business	Total time spent (hours:minutes)
Addresses other than Motions to annul or revoke Statutory Instruments	41.46
Government Bills	
Second readings: committed to public bill committee	151.32
Second readings: committal to **Committee of Whole House**	44.47
Committee of the Whole House	189.13
Consideration	174.10
Third reading	23.02
Lords amendments	60.48
Allocation of time motions	8.42
Committal and carry-over motions	–
Private Members' Bills	
Second readings (and all stages)	63.17
Later stages	12.23
Private Business three hours before the moment of interruption	16.27
Government Motions	
European Union Documents	27.49
Business Motions	7.44
General	83.08
Opposition Days	201.06
Opposition Motions in Government time (other than Motions to annul or revoke Statutory Instruments)	–
Private Members' Motions	
Substantive	2.11
Ten-Minute Rule	26.24
Adjournment, general and Standing Order No. 24 debates	
General debates	110.25
Daily	141.42
Standing Order No. 24 debates	7.57
Estimates (debates on Select Committee Reports)	25.43
Money Resolutions	1.44
Ways and Means	66.56
Motions for approval of Statutory Instruments	30.18
Motions to annul or revoke Statutory Instruments	–
No motion before the House	583.98
Questions to Ministers	200.43
Topical Questions	57.26
Urgent Questions	40.56
Statements	178.00
Speaker's Statements	0.52
Business Statements	51.19
Standing Order No. 24 Applications	0.25
Points of Order	28.13
Public Petitions	3.51
Miscellaneous (including suspensions of the proceedings)	24.13
Daily Prayers	24.25
TOTAL	2344.19

Source: House of Commons Sessional Information Digest, 2010–12

the minor parties, and the debate is then wound up with speeches from the Opposition and government front benches. (The House tends to fill up again for the winding-up speeches.) If the bill is contested, the House then divides. Debates, though not always predictable in content, are generally so in outcome: only three times in the past 100 years has the government lost a vote on second reading

(in 1924, 1977 and 1986). Speeches on occasion may influence some votes, even whole debates, but they are exceptional. A government sometimes loses the argument but not usually the vote.

Once approved in principle, the bill is then sent to committee for detailed scrutiny. Some bills, because of their constitutional significance or because of the need for

Table 15.5 Legislative stages

Stage	Where taken	Comments
First reading	On the floor of the House	Formal introduction: no debate
Second reading	On the floor of the House[a]	Debate on the principle
[Money resolution	On the floor of the House	Commons only]
Committee	In public bill committee in the Commons unless House votes otherwise (certain bills taken on the floor of the House); in Grand Committee or on the floor of the House in the Lords	Considered clause by clause; amendments may be made
Report[b]	On the floor of the House	Bill reported back to House; amendments may be made
Third reading	On the floor of the House	Final approval: no amendments possible in the Commons
Lords (or Commons) amendments	On the floor of the House	Consideration of amendments made by other House

(a) In the Commons, non-contentious bills may be referred to a committee.
(b) If a bill is taken in committee of the whole House in the Commons and no amendments are made, there is no report stage.

a speedy passage, will have their committee stage on the floor of the House. In most sessions the number is very small. The majority of bills are sent to a **public bill** committee. Up to 2006 bills were sent to standing committees. **Standing committees** were introduced in 1882 and became the norm in 1907. Despite the name, they were 'standing' only in name (Standing Committee A, Standing Committee B, etc.): their membership changed for each bill. The committees were limited not only by the fact that there was no permanent membership but by their inability to take evidence. Witnesses could not be summoned and written evidence received. The committees could only consider the bills before them. They proceeded by way of discussing amendments to clauses before agreeing the clauses. Each committee was structured like the chamber in miniature, one side facing the other, with ministers, shadow ministers and whips among the membership and with debate following party lines. Government backbenchers were encouraged to keep quiet to facilitate the passage of the bill, and opposition MPs encouraged to speak in order to challenge the government. Government defeats in committee were rare.

Because of the limitations of standing committees, their utilisation came in for considerable criticism. In 2006, following a report from the Select Committee on the Modernisation of the House of Commons, the House agreed a new procedure: the public bill committee (PBC). In dealing with private members' bills and certain other bills, they are similar to the old standing committees. However, they differ significantly in respect of government bills that have been introduced in the Commons and have been subject to a programme motion (stipulating the times at which stages have to be completed), but which have not had pre-legislative scrutiny (in other words, been before an

evidence-taking committee): in dealing with these bills, public bill committees are empowered to take both oral and written evidence. Within the time it has to consider a bill, the committee can determine what proportion of sittings will be devoted to taking evidence. In its evidence-taking, a committee is supported by the Scrutiny Unit, a body of specialists employed by the House, which also prepares briefing material for the committee.

The use of evidence-taking has been notable. In the 2007–8 session 229 witnesses appeared before 12 committees (Levy 2010: 538). As the use of public bill committees has developed, so MPs have tended to be better informed and more willing to engage in debating the provisions of the bill (Levy 2010: 539). As Jessica Levy has noted, 'Along with introducing the practice of direct questioning of witnesses (and the minister) in place of probing amendments, PBCs have proved more efficient than their standing committee predecessors' (Levy 2009: 49).

However, PBCs also have similarities with their predecessor standing committees. Each committee comprises between 16 and 50 members, though the norm is to appoint close to the minimum, other than for big bills like the Finance Bill. The membership is appointed anew for each bill. The membership thus lacks a corporate ethos. Each committee is chaired by a member of the Panel of Chairs, whose role is to preside in a manner similar to the Speaker; there is thus no leadership of the committee as a collective body. The membership reflects the party composition of the House, and ministers, shadow ministers and **whips** are appointed, with the government whips present to ensure, as in the chamber, that the government gets its business. One of the biggest constraints remains one of time. Committees are under pressure because of the number of bills introduced each session and the need to get them through usually by the end of the session. Several committees may therefore be appointed at roughly the same time. The need to get the business transacted by a stipulated date limits the time available to hear witnesses and, equally important, to digest what they have to say in time to influence debate on the amendments moved in committee (Levy 2010: 540–3).

After the committee stage, a bill returns to the House for the report stage. This provides an opportunity for the House to decide whether it wishes to make any further amendments and is often used by the government to introduce amendments promised during committee stage, as well as any last-minute (sometimes numerous) amendments of its own. There is, though, no report stage if a bill has been taken for its committee stage on the floor of the House and been passed without amendment.

There then follows the bill's third reading, when the House gives its final approval to the measure. Such debates are often short. If the bill is not contentious, there may be no debate at all. As can be seen from Table 15.4, debate on third reading occupies relatively little time. On completion of its third reading, the bill then goes to the House of Lords and, if the Upper House makes any amendments, the bill then returns to the Commons for it to consider the amendments. In most cases, the amendments are accepted. If not, the House of Lords usually gives way, though sometimes only after behind-the-scenes negotiations. Once both Houses have approved the bill, it then goes to the Queen for Royal Assent. Once that assent is given, then that, as far as Parliament is concerned, concludes the legislative process.

The process is fairly well established but much criticised (see, e.g., Brazier 2004), not only because of the inefficiencies of the committee procedure but also because of the time constraints imposed by government. In the past, after considerable time had been taken up by opposition MPs debating the early clauses of a bill in committee, the government would resort to a timetable, or guillotine, motion, imposing a timetable for the remaining provisions of a bill. Guillotine motions had been variously employed since 1887, but their increased use in the last quarter of the twentieth century attracted frequent condemnation. Because of the criticism, the two principal parties agreed in 1994 to a voluntary timetabling of bills. This meant that each bill was subject to an agreed timetable from the beginning, thus avoiding the need for a guillotine to be introduced at a later stage. However, this agreement was not sustained in the new parliament returned in May 1997 and the Labour Government variously resorted to the use of the guillotine, or what were termed 'programme motions', to get measures through. In 2000–1 new standing orders were introduced for programming motions, and programming is now a common and much

disputed feature of business. Programme motions differ from the previous use of the guillotine in that they are introduced and agreed by the House following the second readings of bills. Most government bills are now subject to such motions. The most stringent part of programming tends to be for consideration of Lords amendments, where it is not uncommon for a programme motion to stipulate that debate on the amendments, however many or important they are, is limited to one hour.

Bills thus follow a fairly predictable route. There are some variations: some non-contentious bills, for example, can be sent to a second reading committee, thus avoiding taking up valuable debating time on the floor of the House. Private members' bills are also treated differently, primarily in terms of timetabling. They have to go through all the stages listed, but time for their consideration on the floor of the House is extremely limited. Each session a ballot is held and the names of 20 private members are drawn. They are then entitled to introduce bills during the Fridays allocated to such bills, but only about the top half-dozen are likely to achieve full debates.

Bills constitute primary legislation. They often contain powers for regulations to be made under their authority once enacted. These regulations – known as 'delegated' or 'secondary' legislation and usually taking the form of what are termed 'statutory instruments' – may be made subject to parliamentary approval. (Under the affirmative resolution procedure, the regulation must be approved by Parliament in order to come into force; under the negative resolution procedure, it comes into force unless Parliament disapproves it.) Some regulations, though, only have to be laid before the House and others do not even have to be laid.

Given the growth of delegated legislation in postwar years – sometimes more than 1,500 statutory instruments are introduced in a session – the House has sought to undertake scrutiny of it (Norton 2013: Ch. 5). Detailed, and essentially technical, scrutiny is undertaken by a Select Committee on Statutory Instruments. However, there is no requirement for the government to wait for the committee to report on a regulation before bringing it before the House for approval, and on occasion – although not frequently – the government will seek approval before a regulation has been considered by the committee. Time for debate is also extremely limited, and much delegated legislation is hived off for discussion in a standing committee on delegated legislation. There is also a separate committee and procedure for dealing with regulatory reform orders, enabling primary legislation imposing a regulatory burden to be changed by order. There are also separate committees and procedures for dealing with draft European legislation: it is considered by a European Scrutiny Committee and, if recommended for debate, is discussed normally by one of three European committees.

Executive actions

Various means are employed to scrutinise and to influence the actions of government. These same means can be and usually are employed by MPs to express the views of constituents and different interests in society. The means essentially are those available on the floor of the House (debates and Question Time), those available on the committee corridor (select committees) and those available off the floor of the House (early day motions, correspondence, the parliamentary commissioner for administration, party committees and all-party groups). Some individually are of limited use. It is their use in combination that can be effective in influencing government.

Debates and Question Time

Most of the time of the House is taken up debating or questioning the actions of government. *Debates* take different forms. They can be on a substantive motion (for example, congratulating or condemning the policy of the government on a particular issue) or, in order to allow wide-ranging discussion (especially on a topic on which the government may have no fixed position), on an adjournment motion ('That this House do now adjourn'). For example, prior to the Gulf War at the beginning of 1991 the situation in the Persian Gulf was debated on an adjournment motion. After military action had begun, the House debated a substantive motion approving the action. Adjournment debates under this heading can be described as full-scale adjournment debates. They are distinct from the half-hour adjournment debates that take place at the end of every sitting of

the House. These half-hour debates take the form of a backbencher raising a particular issue and the relevant minister then responding. After exactly half an hour, the debate concludes and the House adjourns.

Debates are initiated by different bodies in the House. Most motions introduced by government are to approve legislation. However, the government occasionally initiates debates on particular policies. These can range from major issues of public policy, such as war in Iraq in 2003, to debate on essentially parliamentary matters, such as select committee nominations and the installation of the security screen in the public gallery. More frequently, debates are introduced by opposition parties. Twenty days each year are designated as Opposition Days. On 17 of these 20 days, the motion (or motions – a day's debate can be split into two) is chosen by the Leader of the Opposition. The remaining three days are given over to the other opposition parties. (Additional days are also occasionally found, and in the long 2010–12 session an additional 17 days were allocated.) There are also three estimates days each session, the choice of estimate for debate being made by a select committee of the House: the Liaison Committee, comprising the MPs who chair other select committees.

A notable innovation introduced at the start of the 2010 parliament was the creation of a Backbench Business Committee. This has taken over responsibility from government for allocating backbench business on 35 days, 27 of them on the floor of the House. The committee comprises backbench members – Labour MP Natascha Engel was elected by the House to chair it – and it invites backbench MPs to put forward proposals and has not been averse to selecting topics for debate that are controversial and not necessarily favourable to government. Among subjects selected for

The House of Commons in session.

Source: Press Asssociation

debate in the 2010–12 session were the war in Afghanistan, voting rights for prisoners, immigration, contaminated blood products, drugs policy, the Big Society, wild animals in circuses, whether there should be a referendum on continued membership of the European Union, and the disclosure of papers relating to the 1989 Hillsborough disaster. E-petitions that gain more than 100,000 signatures are also referred to the committee for consideration as subjects for debate, though the committee will also consider petitions with fewer signatures if there is support from a number of MPs.

Private members are also responsible for initiating the topics in the daily half-hour adjournment debates: on three days a week (four, if sitting on a Friday), members are selected by ballot, and on one the Speaker chooses the member. The member speaks for about 10–15 minutes, sometimes allowing time for one or two other Members to contribute briefly, before a junior minister responds. These backbenchers' occasions provide opportunities to raise essentially non-partisan issues, especially those of concern to constituents. Although they are poorly attended, they allow members to put an issue on the public record and elicit a response from government.

Whereas these half-hour adjournment debates are essentially opportunities for backbench MPs to get a detailed response from government, full-scale half-day or full-day debates initiated by government or opposition are very different and resemble instead the practice adopted in second reading debates. There are speeches from the two front benches, followed by backbench speeches alternating between the two sides of the House, followed by winding-up speeches from the front benches and then, if necessary, a vote. The term 'debate' is itself a misnomer. Members rarely debate but rather deliver prepared speeches, which often fail to take up the points made by preceding speakers. Members wishing to take part usually inform the Speaker in advance and can usually obtain some indication from the Speaker if and when they are likely to be called. There is a tendency for members not to stay for the whole debate after they have spoken. Members, especially backbenchers, frequently address a very small audience – sometimes no more than half a dozen MPs. There is a prevailing view in the House that attendance has dropped over recent years. MPs now have offices they can spend time in. There are competing demands on their time, and as the outcome of most votes is predictable – and members know perfectly well how they intend to vote – there appears little incentive to spend time in the chamber. Major set-piece debates – as on a motion of confidence – and a debate in which the outcome is uncertain can still attract a crowded chamber, some members having to sit on the floor or stand at the bar of the House in order to listen to the proceedings. Occasionally a particularly good speaker, such as Foreign Secretary William Hague, may attract members into the chamber. Such occasions are exceptional. On most days MPs addressing the House do so to rows of empty green benches.

Debates take place on motions. However, there is one form of business taken on the floor of the House that departs from the rule requiring a motion to be before the House. That is *Question Time*. This takes place on four days of the week – Monday to Thursday – when the House is sitting. It is the first substantive order of business once the House sits: it commences once prayers and some minor business – announcements from the Speaker, certain non-debatable motions concerning private legislation – are completed. It concludes exactly one hour after the House has commenced sitting.

Question Time itself is of relatively recent origin (see Franklin and Norton 1993). The first recorded instance of a question being asked was in the House of Lords in 1721, and the first printed notice of questions to ministers was issued in 1835. Question Time itself – a dedicated slot under the heading of 'Questions' on the order paper – dates from 1869. The institution of a dedicated slot for Prime Minister's Questions is of even more recent origin, dating from July 1961. From 1961 to 1997 the Prime Minister answered questions for 15 minutes on two days of the week (Tuesday and Thursday). In May 1997 the new Labour Prime Minister, Tony Blair, changed the procedure, answering questions for 30 minutes once a week on a Wednesday.

The practice of asking questions is popular with MPs, and the demand to ask questions exceeds the time available. Members are thus restricted in the number they can put on the order paper: no more than one to any one department on any day and no more than two in total on the day. (It is thus possible to have a question to the department answering before Prime Minister's Questions and one to the Prime Minister.) Questions can be tabled up to three working days in advance (four for those to the secretaries of state for Northern Ireland, Scotland and Wales) and are selected by a random physical and computer shuffle. Questions must be precisely that – statements and expressions of opinion are inadmissible – and each must be on a matter for which the minister has responsibility. There is also an extensive list of topics (including arms sales, budgetary forecasts and purchasing contracts) on which government will not answer questions. Ministers may also decline to answer on grounds of 'disproportionate cost'. At the beginning of 2012 the cost of answering an oral question was estimated to be £450. If the cost of answering a particular question was calculated to be £850 or more, then the minister may decline to answer on grounds of disproportionate cost.

The normal practice of tabling questions seeking answers to clear and specific questions tabled in advance was complemented in 2007 by the introduction of a new type of question. Towards the end of questions to a particular department, there are now 'topical questions'. These are not dissimilar to Prime Minister's Questions in that a member asks a minister an 'open' question – 'If he will make a statement on his departmental responsibilities' – and then supplementary questions can be on any aspect of the responsibilities of the department. The procedure enables questions to be raised that are current and provides an opportunity for opposition members to test ministers to ensure that they are fully briefed on issues affecting their departments.

Ministers answer questions on a rota basis, most ministries coming up on the rota every five weeks. The larger departments, such as the Treasury, are each allocated a full question time. Smaller departments are allocated only part of a question time (some may get 30 minutes, or even 10 minutes.) All questions tabled by members used to be printed on the order paper, a practice that was costly and largely pointless. The number tabled often ran into three figures, but the number of questions actually answered in the time available was usually fewer than 20. Following changes approved by the House in 1990, only the top 25 – fewer if the department is not taking up the whole of Question Time – are now printed.

The MP with the first question rises and says 'Question Number One, Mr Speaker' and then sits down. The minister rises and replies to the question. The MP is then called to put a follow-up – or 'supplementary' – question, to which the minister responds. Another member may then be permitted by the Speaker to put another supplementary. If an opposition **frontbencher** rises, he or she has priority. During Prime Minister's Question Time, the Leader of the Opposition is frequently at the despatch box and is permitted up to six interventions (prior to entering government in 2010, the leader of the Liberal Democrats was allowed three). The Speaker decides when to move on to the next question.

During an average session, about 3,000 to 5,000 questions will be tabled for an oral answer. In the 2008–9 session (the last normal-length session prior to 2012–13), the number was 4,113, though not all will be reached in Question Time. With supplementaries included, the questions actually answered will be in the region of 7,000.

Question Time is not the only opportunity afforded to MPs to put questions to ministers. Members can also table questions for written answer. These provide an opportunity to elicit more detailed answers than can be obtained through an oral question and are particularly useful for obtaining data from departments. The questions, along with ministers' answers, are published in *Hansard*, the official record of parliamentary proceedings. Members can table up to five priority written questions (for which a particular date for answer is specified, subject to three days' notice having been given) on any one day and as many non-priority questions as they wish. The average MP tables just over 100 a session. Exceptionally, some members table well in excess of 1,000. The number tabled each year has risen over the decades (see Franklin and Norton 1993: 27). By the 1990s some sessions

saw more than 40,000 questions being tabled. This figure has been far exceeded in the twenty-first century, with usually 50,000 to 70,000 being tabled in a year-long session. More than 73,000 were tabled in 2007–8.

Question Time itself remains an important opportunity for backbenchers to raise issues of concern to constituents and to question ministers on differing aspects of their policies and intentions. However, it has become increasingly adversarial in nature, with opposition frontbenchers participating regularly – a practice that has developed over the past 40 years – and with questions and supplementaries often being partisan in content. Some members view the proceedings, especially Prime Minister's Question Time, as a farce. However, it remains an occasion for keeping ministers on their toes (figuratively as well as literally), and it ensures that a whole range of issues is brought to the attention of ministers. It also ensures that much material is put on the public record that would not otherwise be available.

Select committees

The House has made greater use in recent years of select committees, appointed not to consider the particular details of bills (the task of public bill committees) but to consider particular subjects assigned by the House. Historically, they are well-established features of parliamentary scrutiny. They were frequently used in Tudor and Stuart parliaments. Their use declined in the latter half of the nineteenth century, the government – with its party majority – not looking too favourably on bodies that could subject it to critical scrutiny. For most of the twentieth century the use of such committees was very limited. The position changed in the 1960s and, more dramatically, in the 1970s.

The House has a number of long-standing select committees concerned with its privileges and internal arrangements. However, for the first half of the twentieth century, the House had only two major select committees for investigating the policy or actions of government: the Public Accounts Committee (PAC) and the Estimates Committee. Founded in 1861, the PAC remains in existence and is the doyen of investigative select committees. It undertakes post hoc (i.e. after the event) scrutiny of public expenditure, checking to ensure that it has been properly incurred for the purpose for which it was voted. The Estimates Committee was first appointed in 1912 for the purpose of examining ways in which policies could be carried out cost-effectively. In abeyance from 1914 to 1921 and again during the Second World War, it fulfilled a useful but limited role. It was abolished in 1971 and replaced by an Expenditure Committee with wider terms of reference.

The PAC and Estimates Committees were supplemented in the 1940s by a Select Committee on Statutory Instruments and in the 1950s by one on nationalised industries. There was a more deliberate and extensive use of select committees in the latter half of the 1960s, when the Labour Leader of the House, Richard Crossman, introduced several reforms to try to increase the efficiency and influence of the House. A number of select committees were established, some to cover particular policy sectors (such as science and technology) and others particular government departments (such as education). One was also appointed to cover the newly created Parliamentary Commissioner for Administration (PCA), better known as the *ombudsman*. However, the experience of the committees did not meet the expectations of their supporters. They suffered from limited resources, limited attention (from backbenchers, government and the media), limited powers (they could only send for 'persons, papers and records' and make recommendations), the absence of any effective linkage between their activities and the floor of the House, and the lack of a coherent approach to, and coverage of, government policy. Some did not survive for very long. The result was a patchwork quilt of committees, with limited coverage of public policy.

Recognition of these problems led to the appointment in 1976 of a Procedure Select Committee, which reported in 1978. It recommended the appointment of a series of select committees, covering all the main departments of state, with wide terms of reference and with power to appoint specialist advisers as the committees deemed appropriate. It also recommended that committee members be selected independently of the whips, the task to be undertaken by the Select Committee of Selection, the body formally responsible for nominating members. At the beginning of the new parliament in 1979, the Conservative Leader of the House, Norman St John-Stevas, brought forward motions to give effect to the Procedure Committee recommendations. By a vote of 248 to 12, the House approved the creation of the new committees. Initially, 12 were appointed, soon joined by committees covering Scottish and Welsh affairs. In the light of their appointment, various other committees were wound up. The PAC and the Committee on the Parliamentary Commissioner were retained. In 1980 a Liaison Select Committee, comprising predominantly select committee chairmen, was appointed to coordinate the work of the committees.

The 14 new committees began work effectively in 1980. Their number has fluctuated since, usually reflecting changes in departmental structure. Committees were also added to cover sectors or departments not previously covered, notably science and technology and, in 1994, Northern Ireland. With various restructuring of government departments, the number increased to 19 in 2005 and has remained at that number. There also exists the Committee on Arms Export Control (formerly known as the Quadripartite Committee), comprising four departmental select committees

(defence, foreign affairs, international development, and business, innovation and skills) which meets on occasion in order to examine strategic export controls. There are also several non-departmental select committees. These comprise principally 'domestic' committees – such as the Committee on Standards and Privileges and the Finance and Services Committee – but they also include investigative committees, such as the PAC, Environmental Audit, Public Administration, European Scrutiny and Statutory Instruments Committees. In 2009 nine regional committees were appointed to examine the regional strategies and the work of the regional bodies for the regions of England, but these were abolished in 2010.

The 19 departmental select committees appointed in the 2010 parliament are listed in Table 15.6. Each committee is established 'to examine the expenditure, administration and policy' of the department or departments it covers and of associated public bodies. Fourteen of the committees have 11 members, but defence, justice and Welsh Affairs have 12, the Treasury has 13, and Northern Ireland has 14. The chairs of the committees are shared between the parties, usually in rough proportion to party strength in the House.

Table 15.6 Departmental select committees, 2010–12 session

Committee	Chair
Business, Innovation and Skills	Adrian Bailey (Lab)
Communities and Local Government	Clive Betts (Lab)
Culture, Media and Sport	John Whittingdale (Con)
Defence	The Rt Hon. James Arbuthnot (Con)
Education	Graham Stuart (Con)
Energy and Climate Change	Tim Yeo (Con)
Environment, Food and Rural Affairs	Anne McIntosh (Con)
Foreign Affairs	Richard Ottaway (Con)
Health	The Rt Hon Stephen Dorrell (Con)
Home Affairs	Keith Vaz (Lab)
International Development	The Rt Hon. Malcolm Bruce (Lib Dem)
Justice	The Rt Hon. Sir Alan Beith (Lib Dem)
Northern Ireland Affairs	Laurence Robertson (Con)
Science and Technology	Andrew Miller (Lab)
Scottish Affairs	Ian Davidson (Lab)
Transport	Louise Ellman (Lab)
Treasury	Andrew Tyrie (Con)
Welsh Affairs	David C.T. Davies (Con)
Work and Pensions	Dame Anne Begg (Lab)

Before 2010 committee members were responsible for electing one of their own number from the relevant party to the chair, though the party leaders may (and normally did) engineer the appointment to the committee of a preferred candidate. However, a significant change was implemented at the start of the 2010 parliament. Following a recommendation from the Select Committee on Reform of the House of Commons (2009), the House agreed that the chairs of select committees should be elected by the House as a whole, and members of the committees elected by their respective party groups, thus removing the patronage of the party whips who had previously come to dominate the selection process. Election of the chairs in 2010 served to enhance the status of those elected and enshrine some degree of independence. Chairs were now beholden to colleagues in the House rather than to their party leadership.

Each committee has control of its own agenda and decides what to investigate. It has power to take evidence, and much of its time is spent questioning witnesses. Each committee normally meets once a week when the House is sitting in order to hold a public, evidence-taking session. Members sit in a horseshoe shape, MPs sitting around the horseshoe – not necessarily grouped according to party – with the witness or witnesses seated in the gap of the horseshoe. Each session will normally last up to two hours.

Committee practices vary. Some hold long-term inquiries, some go for short-term inquiries, and some adopt a mixture of the two approaches. Some will also summon senior ministers for a single session just to review present policy and not as part of a continuing inquiry. The Chancellor of the Exchequer, for example, appears each year before the Treasury Committee for a wide-ranging session on economic policy. Although committees cannot force ministers to attend, the attendance of the appropriate minister is normally easily arranged. So, too, is the attendance of civil servants, although they cannot divulge information on advice offered to ministers or express opinions on policy: that is left to ministers. Attendance by ministers and civil servants before committees is regular and frequent, although most witnesses called by committees represent outside bodies. In investigating a particular subject, a committee will call as witnesses representatives of bodies working in the area or with a particular expertise or interest in it. Figure 15.2 shows but part of the agenda of select committee meetings and witnesses in a typical week.

At the conclusion of an inquiry, a committee draws up a report. The report is normally drafted by the committee clerk – a full-time officer of the House – under the guidance of the chair. It is then discussed in private session by the committee. Amendments are variously made, although it is rare, though not unknown, for committees to divide along party lines. Once agreed, the report is published. The committees are prolific in their output. Between 1979 and 2005 over 400 reports would emanate from committees in each parliament. In the 2005–10 parliament, the figure reached 610.

Most reports embody recommendations for government action. Some of the recommendations are accepted. Others become subject to the 'delayed drop' effect: the government rejects or ignores a report but several years later, without necessarily acknowledging the work of the committee, implements some of the recommendations. Overall, only a minority of the recommendations emanating from committees will be accepted immediately and acted on by government. A more common response is to note a recommendation or to say that it is under review. A select committee has no formal powers to force the government to take any action on a report. All that the government is committed to do is to issue a written response to each report within 60 days of the report being published. The target is not always met.

The departmental select committees, like the House itself, are multifunctional. They serve several purposes. They have added considerably to the store of knowledge of the House. They provide an important means for specialisation by members. They serve an important expressive function. By calling witnesses from outside groups, they allow those groups to get their views on the public record. The evidence from witnesses is published. Reports are published in paper form and on the internet (www.parliament.uk; see under 'committees'). More time is now devoted to committee reports as a result of various Thursdays being devoted to debating them in Westminster Hall. The committees may take up the cases espoused by some of the groups, ensuring that the issue is brought onto the political agenda. The reports from the committees are read and digested by the groups, thus providing the committees with the potential to serve as important agents for mobilising support. Above all, though, the committees serve as important means for scrutinising and influencing government, especially the former. Ministers and civil servants know they may be called before committees to account for their actions. Committee sessions allow MPs to put questions to ministers in greater detail than is possible on the floor of the House. They give MPs the only opportunity they have to ask questions of officials. Not only will poor performances be noted – not least by the media – but also poor answers may attract critical comment in the committee's report. No minister or official wishes to be seen squirming in the face of difficult questions.

Select committees have thus developed as a major feature of parliamentary activity, with most MPs viewing that activity in a positive light. Their purview now even encompasses the Prime Minister. Prior to 2002 Prime Minister Tony Blair had refused requests to appear before the Public Administration Select Committee, citing the fact that his predecessors had not appeared before select

Science and Technology

9.15 am   *Subject*: Marine Science
           Witness(es): Professor Alan Rodger, Interim Director, British Antarctic Survey and Professor Ed Hill, Director, National Oceanography Centre

9.30 am   **Public Administration**
           Subject: Communicating and publishing statistics
           Witness(es): Andrew Dilnot CBE, Chair, UK Statistics Authority and Jil Matheson, National Statistician

9.30 am   **Work and Pensions**
           Subject: Governance and best practice in workplace pension provision
           Witness(es): Neil Carberry, Director for Employment and Skills, Confederation of British Industry and Tim Thomas, Head of Employment Policy,
           EEF; Andrew Vaughan, Chairman, Association of Consulting Actuaries, Kevin Wesbroom, Partner, Aon Hewitt, Jim Doran, Principal, Mercer and
           Will Aitken, Senior Consultant, Towers Watson

2.15 pm   **Environmental Audit**
           Subject: Insects and insecticides
           Witness(es): Professor Colin Brown, Advisory Committee on Pesticides, Professor Peter Matthiessen, Advisory Committee on Pesticides,
           Professor Richard Shore, Advisory Committee on Pesticides and Dr Bill Parker, Advisory Committee on Pesticides; Lord de Mauley,
           Parliamentary Under-Secretary of State, Department for Environment, Food and Rural Affairs, Professor Ian Boyd, Chief Scientific Adviser,
           Department of Environment, Food and Rural Affairs and Dave Bench, Director responsible for the Chemical Regulation Directorate and Chief
           Scientist, Health and Safety Executive

2.15 pm   **Treasury**
           Subject: Autumn Statement
           Witness(es): Simon Hayes, Chief UK Economist, Barclays, Simon Wells, Chief UK Economist, HSBC and Paul Mortimer-Lee, Global Head,
           Market Economics, BNP Paribas; Lee Hopley, Chief Economist, EEF and Professor Philip Booth, Editorial and Programme Director, Institute of
           Economic Affairs; Paul Johnson, Director, Institute for Fiscal Studies and Carl Emmerson, Deputy Director, Institute for Fiscal Studies;
           Professor Dieter Helm CBE, University of Oxford and New College Oxford and Mark Hellowell, Lecturer, School of Social and Political Science,
           University of Edinburgh

2.30 pm   **European Scrutiny**
           Subject: European Scrutiny system in the House of Commons
           Witness(es): Dr Katrin Auel, Institute for Advanced Studies, Vienna, Dr Julie Smith, University of Cambridge and Dr Ariella Huff, University
           of Cambridge

2.30 pm   **Defence**
           Subject: Annual Report and Accounts
           Witness(es): Jon Thompson, Permanent Under Secretary, MoD and David Williams, Acting Director General Finance

3.05 pm   **Procedure**
           Subject: Written question performance of the Department for Education
           Witness(es): Elizabeth Truss MP, Parliamentary Under Secretary of State, Department for Education and Hilary Spencer, Director of Strategy,
           Performance and Private Office Group, Department for Education

3.15 pm   **Public Accounts**
           Subject: London 2012 Olympic and Paralympic Games: Post-Games review
           Witness(es): Jonathan Stephens, Permanent Secretary, Department of Culture, Media and Sport, Dame Helen Ghosh DCB, Former Permanent
           Secretary, Home Office, Neil Wood, LOCOG, General Sir Nick Parker, Commander Land Forces, Ministry of Defence and Nick Buckles, Chief
           Executive Officer, G4S; Jonathan Stephens, Permanent Secretary, Department of Culture, Media and Sport, Denis Hone, Chief Executive Officer,
           LLDC and Richard Heaton, Permanent Secretary, Cabinet Office

4 pm   **Environment, Food and Rural Affairs**
           Subject: Rural Communities
           Witness(es): Holly Sims, Corporate Affairs Manager, Calor Gas, Graham Biggs MBE, Rural Services Network, John Slaughter, Director of External
           Affairs, Home Builders Federation and Sue Chalkley, Chief Executive, Hastoe Housing Association

4.10 pm   **Communities and Local Government**
           Subject: The performance of the Department
           Witness(es): Rt Hon Eric Pickles MP, Secretary of State, DCLG, Mark Prisk MP, Minister for Housing, DCLG, Nick Boles MP, Parliamentary Under
           Secretary of State, DCLG, Rt Hon Don Foster MP, Parliamentary Under Secretary of State and Brandon Lewis MP, Parliamentary Under Secretary
           of State, DCLG

Figure 15.2 Meetings of select committees, Wednesday, 12 December 2012

committees. In 2002 he reversed his stance and agreed to appear before the Liaison Committee to answer questions. His first appearance, for two-and-a-half hours, took place on 16 July. It is now standard practice that the Prime Minister appears before the committee, though in place of two lengthy sessions there are now three shorter ones. Each is devoted to covering particular topics. At the session on 3 July 2012, for example, the subjects covered were (i) the impact of the Eurozone crisis on the UK economy and public policy and (ii) civil service reform.

Despite these various strengths and advances, especially in 2010, limitations remain. The committees have limited powers and limited resources. They have the time and resources to investigate only a small number of issues. The number of reports they issue exceeds the time available on the floor of the House or in Westminster Hall to debate them. Most reports will not be mentioned on the floor of the House or even read by most MPs. Government is committed to providing a written response to committee reports but under no obligation to take action on the recommendations made in those reports. Also, although ministers and officials appear before committees, they do not necessarily reveal as much as the committees would like. Members are not trained in forensic questioning, and important lines of questioning may be neglected in order to give each member of the committee an opportunity to speak. Although the committees constitute a major step forward for the House of Commons, many MPs would like to see them strengthened.

Early day motions

Of the other devices available to members, early day motions (EDMs) are increasingly popular, although of limited impact. A member may table a motion for debate 'on an early day'. In practice there is invariably no time to debate such motions. However, they are printed and other MPs can add their names to them. Consequently, they are used as a form of parliamentary notice board. If a motion attracts a large number of signatures, it may induce the government to take some action or at least to pause, or it may seriously embarrass the government. This happens occasionally. An EDM in 2002–3 expressing concern over possible military action against Iraq attracted the signatures of more than 150 Labour MPs, which was seen as a signal that the Government might run into substantial opposition on its own side if it were precipitate in agreeing to use force to topple the Iraqi regime; the Government subsequently suffered the largest rebellious vote by backbenchers in the postwar era. Such occasions, though, are rare. EDMs are more often used for fulfilling a limited expressive function, allowing members to make clear their views on a range of issues, often reflecting representations made to them by people and groups outside the House. Examples of such EDMs are illustrated in Figure 15.3. The range of topics is extremely broad and the number of motions tabled an increasingly large one, exacerbated by motions unrelated to public policy – for example, congratulating particular sporting teams or individuals on their achievements.

In the 1970s and 1980s 300–400 EDMs were tabled each year. In the 1990s the number each year exceeded 1,000. In the 1992–7 parliament a total of 7,831 were tabled – an average of just over 1,500 a session. The number dipped in the 1997–2001 parliament, when 3,613, an average of just

over 900 a year, were submitted, but increased notably in the 2001–5 parliament when MPs put in a total of 6,767 – an average of 1,691 a session. The number has increased substantially since then, with over 2,000 a session being submitted. In the long 2005–6 session, 2,924 were tabled, in 2006–7 it was 2,385 and in 2007–8 the figure was 2,727. In the two-year 2010–12 session the number reached 3,024.

The consequence of excessive use of EDMs is that their value as a means of indicating strength of opinion on an issue of political significance is devalued. Their utility, which was always limited, is thus marginal, although not non-existent. Each is studied by the relevant government department and they still give MPs the opportunity to put issues of concern on the public record. An EDM which attracts more than 300 signatures – which rarely happens – will get noticed. Most of the rest will not.

Correspondence

The means so far considered have been public means by which MPs can scrutinise government and make representations to it. However, a number of private means exist, two official and two unofficial. One official means is through corresponding with ministers. Since the 1950s the flow of letters to MPs from constituents and a range of organisations (companies, charities and the like) has grown enormously. The flow increased significantly in the 1960s and increased dramatically in subsequent decades. In the late 1960s a typical MP would receive something in the region of 2,000 to 3,000 items of mail every year. In 2008, 4.1 million items of mail were delivered to the Palace of Westminster, 85 per cent of them going to the House of Commons: that averages out at nearly 5,500 items of mail per MP. However, the volume of letters has tended to go down as MPs' e-mail boxes start to fill, some MPs reporting receiving a three-figure number of e-mails in a typical day. Increasingly, e-mail is taking over from paper correspondence as the preferred means of contact. In 2011 the number of items of correspondence received in the Palace of Westminster was down to 2.6 million. E-mails remain an inexpensive means of communication, while the price of stamps continues to increase.

The usual method for an MP to pursue a matter raised by a constituent is by writing to the relevant minister, usually forwarding the letter from the constituent. Writing to a minister is one of the most cost-effective ways of pursuing constituency casework (see Norton and Wood 1993: Ch. 3). A letter invites a considered, often detailed response, usually free of the party pressures that prevail in the chamber; by being a private communication, it avoids putting a minister publicly on the defensive. Ministers are thus more likely to respond sympathetically in the use of their discretion than is the case if faced with demands on the floor of the House. Furthermore, there is no limit on the number of letters an

ISRAELI SETTLEMENTS IN OCCUPIED TERRITORIES

- Date tabled: 03.12.2012
- Primary sponsor: Russell, Bob
- Sponsors: Caton, Martin; Cunningham, Jim; Durkan, Mark; Edwards, Jonathan; Meale, Alan

That this House condemns the government of Israel for its announcement of plans to build a further 3,000 dwellings in the Occupied Territories of the West Bank and East Jerusalem in direct contravention of United Nations resolutions, the Geneva Convention and international law; and calls on the Government to work with other member states of the EU to cancel all trade agreements with Israel in response to that country's continued flouting of the will of the international community and all accepted international declarations.

Total number of signatures: 20

PYLONS ACROSS NORTH WEST WALES

- Date tabled: 29.11.2012
- Primary sponsor: Williams, Hywel
- Sponsors: Davies, Glyn; Llwyd, Elfyn; Lucas, Caroline; Owen, Albert; Williams, Roger

That this House notes that the National Grid is consulting on a new connection between Wylfa, Ynys Môn and Pentir in Gwynedd; believes that it is in the interests of the residents of north west Wales, visitors to the area and the Welsh tourism industry that this connection be under the sea; further notes the visual damage that an aerial connection would cause to the iconic landscapes of Gwynedd and Ynys Môn, including to areas in Eryri/Snowdonia, Afon Menai/the Menai Straits and including areas of outstanding natural beauty; and calls on the National Grid to identify an undersea connection as their preferred choice.

Total number of signatures: 9

SOCIAL SECTOR UNDER-OCCUPANCY

- Date tabled: 28.11.2012
- Primary sponsor: Morden, Jessica
- Sponsors: Esterson, Bill; Lammy, David; McCabe, Steve

That this House regrets that the measures to introduce size criteria restrictions to the calculation of housing benefit for working age claimants living in the social rented sector take no account of whether alternative accommodation is available; believes that this will result in cuts to the incomes of some of the poorest in society; notes that such measures fail to provide sufficient safeguards to protect the most vulnerable claimants and ensure that they are not pushed into poverty and homelessness; further believes that they will not achieve their aim of tackling under-occupancy; and further notes that they will risk costing more than they will save.

Total number of signatures: 28

EXPORTING FOR BRITAIN

- Date tabled: 26.11.2012
- Primary sponsor: Sheerman, Barry
- Sponsors: Bottomley, Peter; Hermon, Lady; Meale, Alan; Morrice, Graeme; Shannon, Jim

That this House recognises that exporting is good for Britain and welcomes the fact that businesses are engines of growth through exporting; further recognises the size and persistence of the UK's trade deficit and understands the need to rebalance the UK economy towards exports to secure recovery and long-term prosperity; welcomes the British Chambers of Commerce's role as lead supporter of international trade, delivering support and specialist advice to Britain's exporting community; and understands that businesses exporting play a crucial role in national recovery.

Total number of signatures: 41

Figure 15.3 Examples of early day motions to show how MPs use this device to draw attention to particular issues, 2012

MP can write, and those letters can usually be dictated at a time of the member's choosing. Letters from MPs to ministers are accorded priority in a department – each is circulated in a special yellow folder – and have to be replied to by a minister. If a letter fails to obtain the desired response, the member has the option of then taking the matter further, either by seeing the minister or by raising the matter publicly on the floor of the House.

Correspondence is a valuable and efficient means of ensuring that a matter is considered by a minister. A great many letters on a particular problem can alert a minister to the scale of that problem and produce action. Letter writing is also a valuable means of fulfilling an expressive function. Most constituents who write or e-mail do so to express a particular viewpoint or in order to obtain an authoritative explanation of why some action was or was not taken; only a minority write to try to have a particular decision changed. Contacting the MP in writing is a long-established, and now much used, means for citizens to have some input into the political process. Nonetheless, corresponding with Members has a number of limitations (see Norton 2013: Ch. 11). MPs are not always well versed in the subjects raised with them by constituents. Some lack sufficient interest, or knowledge of the political system, to pursue cases effectively.

Increasingly, they have difficulty finding the time to deal with all the matters raised by them.

Parliamentary Commissioner for Administration

Since the late 1960s MPs have had another option at their disposal in pursuing particular issues raised by constituents. The Parliamentary Commissioner for Administration – or ombudsman – was established under an Act of 1967 to investigate cases of maladministration within government. The office was subsequently extended so that the ombudsman is also the ombudsman for the health service.

The term 'maladministration' essentially covers any error in the way a matter is handled by a public servant: it does not extend to cover the merits of policies. The ombudsman considers only complaints referred by MPs: a citizen cannot complain directly. The Commissioner enjoys some protection in office in that he or she can only be removed by an address by both Houses of Parliament to the crown. (The first female ombudsman – Ann Abraham – was appointed in 2002 and was succeeded in 2011 by Dame Julie Mellor.) She can summon papers and take evidence under oath. When an inquiry is completed, she sends a copy to the MP who referred the case as well as to the relevant department. Her recommendations are normally acted on. However, she labours under a number of limitations: she has a limited remit, limited resources and limited access to certain files – she has no formal powers to see Cabinet papers. Perhaps most notably, she has no powers of enforcement. If she reports that officials have acted improperly or unjustly in the exercise of their administrative duties, it is then up to government to decide what action to take in response; if it fails to act, the only remaining means available to achieve action is through parliamentary pressure.

The number of cases referred to the ombudsman has increased over the years. Most complaints are deemed not to fall within her remit. In 2011–12 the ombudsman's office received almost 24,000 enquiries from the public. Of these, over 14,000 were to do with the NHS, and just over 6,000 to do with government departments and agencies. Nearly 5,000 of the cases received close scrutiny and 410 formal investigations were undertaken. (An investigation can encompass several complaints.) Most complaints were upheld and just over 1,700 remedies were sought and achieved.

The departments attracting the most parliamentary complaints were the Ministry of Justice, the Home Office and the Department of Work and Pensions. Many are not taken forward and in other cases inquiries are undertaken to see whether the body that is the subject of the complaint wishes to take action that meets with the approval of the complainant. This frequently happens. Although the relevant departments usually act on the ombudsman's recommendations – a failure to do so is rare – the government has since 2002 twice rejected recommendations that certain factual information should be released under the Code of Practice on Access to Government Information. In 2005 it rejected the findings in a case where some applicants to a scheme to compensate people interned by the Japanese in the Second World War were excluded because they or their parents were not born in the United Kingdom – a matter to which the ombudsman returned in 2011, telling the government to 'hang its head in shame' following repeated failings of the Ministry of Defence to deal fairly with the matter – and in 2006 rejecting the findings in a case on the handling of pension schemes.

The ombudsman reports to the Public Administration Committee in the Commons which can then, and variously does, pursue any matters that have not been resolved satisfactorily.

The Commissioner thus serves a useful service to MPs – and their constituents – but constitutes something of a limited last resort and one that has no direct powers of enforcement. MPs prefer to keep casework in their own hands and pursue it with government directly. For most members the preferred device for pursuing a matter with a minister remains that of direct correspondence.

Party committees

An important unofficial means of scrutinising and influencing government is that of party committees. These are unofficial in that they are committees of the parliamentary parties and not officially constituted committees of the House.

Each parliamentary party has some form of organisation, usually with weekly meetings of the parliamentary party. The two largest parties – Conservative and Labour – have traditionally had a sufficient number of members to sustain a series of committees. Conservative backbench committees were first established in the 1920s and established a reputation for being politically powerful (Norton 1979, 1994). The committees had elected officers and usually met weekly to discuss forthcoming business and topics of interest, often with invited speakers. Any Tory MP could attend and, if a controversial issue attracted a large audience, it signalled to the whips that there was a problem. However, the early 1990s witnessed a decline in attendance at meetings – members had many competing demands on their time – and the massive decline in the number of Conservative MPs in the 1997 General Election meant that the party had insufficient numbers to maintain the committees on the scale of previous decades. As a result, the number of committees was scaled down and a new practice instituted, with policy groups being created, covering such areas as the constitution and home affairs, sharing the same time slot and meeting on a rota basis.

Labour backbench committees traditionally lacked the clout of Conservative committees, but in the 1992–7 parliament the standing orders of the Parliamentary Labour Party (PLP) were changed in order to enhance the consultative status of the committees. Since 1997 Labour frontbenchers have consulted with backbench committees, some achieving a reputation for being assiduous in doing so. The committees also serve another purpose: they allow MPs to specialise in a particular subject. They enable an MP, through serving as officer of a committee, to achieve some status in the parliamentary party. This is often especially helpful to new members, giving them their first opportunity to make a mark in parliamentary life. It may also serve as a way of getting noticed for the purpose of being promoted to ministerial office. However, despite their attraction to MPs and their influence within party ranks, the committees have to compete for the attention of members – there are many other demands on members' time.

All-party groups

All-party groups, like party committees, are not formally constituted committees of the House. They are formed on a cross-party basis, with officerships being shared among members of different parties. They have proved particularly popular in recent decades. In 1988 there were 103 all-party subject groups. The number has grown massively since. By 2012 the number had grown to 432. (There are also 140 country groups, each bringing together MPs – and peers – with a special interest in the country or territory concerned.) Some of the groups, known as *all-party parliamentary groups*, are confined to a parliamentary voting membership; some – known as *associate parliamentary groups* – include non-parliamentarians. The subjects covered by these groups are diverse, including, for example, AIDS, alcohol abuse, breast cancer, compassion in dying, the constitution, electoral reform, gas safety, hill farming, Irish in Britain, mental health, rowing, universities, and tourism. Some exist in name only. Others are active in discussing and promoting a particular cause, some pressing the government for action. Among the more influential are the disability group, the long-established parliamentary and scientific committee, and the football group, which has been active in influencing policy on such issues as safety in sports grounds. The breast cancer group has been especially active in raising parliamentary awareness of the condition. Many of the all-party groups have links with relevant outside bodies – one study in 2012 found that over 300 received support from outside organisations (Ball and Beleaga 2012) – and can act as useful means of access to the political process for such groups.

Again, though, there are limitations. The sheer number of such groups – and other demands on MPs' time – means that relatively few attract a good attendance at meetings. The link with outside organisations has also been the subject of criticism, leading the Speakers of both Houses to set up an inquiry into their activity in 2011. The study that found that groups received outside support also discovered that 80 provided parliamentary passes to staff with outside interests. The links with outside groups have fuelled criticisms that some organisations are effectively using all-party groups as front organisations in order to get their case put before Parliament and pursued with ministers.

Having an impact?

In combination, then, a variety of means are available to MPs to scrutinise and influence government and through which they can serve to make known the views of citizens. The means vary in effectiveness and viewed in isolation may appear of little use. However, they are not mutually exclusive, and MPs will often use several of them in order to pursue a particular issue. An MP may write privately to a minister and, if not satisfied with the response, may table a question or seek a half-hour adjournment debate, or a full debate through the Backbench Business Committee. In order to give prominence to an issue, a member may table an EDM, speak in debate and bombard the minister with a series of written questions. They may seek to mobilise allies through the medium of an all-party group. The most effective MPs are those who know how to use these means in combination and – on occasion – which ones to avoid.

Through utilising the means available, an MP – or more especially MPs working in combination through a party group, all-party group, or ad hoc collaboration – may perform a service by highlighting features of government action that otherwise would not be exposed to public scrutiny. A select committee may extract information that would otherwise have remained hidden and may influence government through publication of a well-argued report. The Opposition may use its Opposition Days to highlight flaws in Government policy. All these activities in combination reflect an active House, one of the busiest in the world. MPs utilise the different mechanisms for the purpose of calling government to account. Ministers have to spend time in the House explaining their actions and policies and at times have to do under considerable pressure, especially if their policies are unpopular in the country and with their own supporters in the House. Nonetheless, some critics see the sum of the parts as greater than the whole. The House of Commons is a very active House, but some critics regard it as ineffective as a body for effectively fullfilling the functions ascribed to it. It has been subject to calls for reform. The pressures under which the House labours, and the demands for reform, are the subject of our next chapter.

BOX 15.4

BRITAIN IN CONTEXT

Ancient and large, but not unusual

The Westminster Parliament is distinctive because of its longevity. It is one of the oldest parliaments in the world. However, in terms of its place in the political system – especially in its relationship to the executive – it is not unusual. Of the types of legislature identified in Box 15.1, it is the first – that of *policy-making legislatures* – that is notable for not being a crowded category. Of national legislatures, only the US Congress has occupied the category for any continuous period of time. It is joined by the state legislatures of the USA and a few legislatures of more recent creation.

The category of *policy-influencing legislatures* is the crowded category and encompasses most legislatures in western Europe and the Commonwealth. It has also been swelled by the changes in the legislatures of the new democracies of southern, central and eastern Europe: previously they occupied the third category, that of *legislatures with little or no policy effect*, but – with democratisation– they have now moved up to occupy the second or even (sometimes briefly) the first category. The third category is now largely confined to dictatorships and one-party states, where legislatures exist for the purpose of giving assent to whatever is placed before them.

Within the category of policy-influencing legislatures, the UK Parliament is not ranked in the top reaches of the category: that is, there are other legislatures that utilise more extensively the capacity to amend or reject measures brought forward by the executive. The Italian parliament and the Scandinavian legislatures are among the strongest legislatures in the category. Westminster, like other Westminster-style legislatures, has less impact on public policy by virtue of the fact that it exists in a Cabinet-centred, two-party system, where the parties compete for the all-or-nothing spoils of electoral victory under a first-past-the-post electoral system. Continental parliamentary systems, utilising different electoral systems, place more stress on coalitions, with parliaments operating through committees on a more consensual basis.

The UK Parliament, however, is not seen as the weakest legislature in the category of policy-influencing legislatures. In western Europe, the weakest in this category are the French and Irish parliaments.

The categories identified in Box 15.1 cover legislatures in relation to public policy. Most legislatures fulfil a range of other functions. The UK Parliament is distinctive, but not unique, for the emphasis that its members give to constituency work. In common with other parliamentary – as opposed to presidential – systems, it serves as the route for advancement to executive office. It shares many of its functions with other policy-influencing legislatures. As with many other legislatures, it is under threat from the expansion of executive power. Where it is distinctive is in terms of its size. There are more than 1,400 parliamentarians (MPs and peers) at Westminster, making the UK Parliament the largest in the democratic world. (The US Congress, by contrast, has a total of 535 members; some legislatures in small states have fewer than 100 members.) Both chambers, in terms of sitting hours, are also among the busiest legislative chambers in the world.

Chapter summary

Parliament is an institution at the heart of the British political system. It forms a body of elected Members, the number varying over time, through the territorial basis of representation – the constituency – being long established. The principal role of the House of Commons is one of scrutinising government. Various means are available to MPs to undertake this role. They have expanded in recent decades, not least with the introduction of departmental select committees, and greater use is made of them than ever before. In combination, they make for a very active House – one of the busiest in the world – with MPs using both formal and informal mechanisms for calling government to account.

Discussion points

- What are the most important functions of the House of Commons?
- Should MPs be drawn from a more varied range of backgrounds?
- What purpose is served by select committees? Should they be strengthened?
- Should, and can, the House of Commons improve its scrutiny of government legislation?
- Is the increase in the constituency work of MPs a good or a bad thing?

Further reading

The most recent text on Parliament, useful for the student, is Norton (2013). Also available are Grant (2009), Rogers and Walters (2006) and Rush (2005). There is also a wide range of essays, by practitioners and academics, on different aspects of Parliament in Baldwin (2005). Riddell (2011) and Flynn (2012) are useful complements to works on Parliament.

The socio-economic background of MPs is covered by Rush (2001), the socialisation of MPs in Rush and Giddings (2011), and the behaviour of MPs in recent parliaments by Cowley (2002, 2005), Cowley and Stuart (2008, 2012) and Norton (2012b). The largely neglected relationship of Parliament to pressure groups is the subject of Rush (1990) and the report of the Public Administration Committee (2008). Parliamentary questions are considered extensively in Franklin and Norton (1993) and briefly in Giddings and Irwin (2005). The Procedure Committee of the House of Commons has also published a number of reports on parliamentary questions: the most recent, on written questions, was published in 2009 (Procedure Committee 2009). MPs' constituency service is covered in Norton and Wood (1993), Power (1998), Norton (2012a), and Chapter 11 of Norton (2013). Parliamentary scrutiny of executive agencies is the subject of Giddings (1995). The relationship of Parliament to the law is discussed in Oliver and Drewry (1998). The relationship of Parliament to the European Union is covered comprehensively in Giddings and Drewry (2004). Many of these books are the products of research by study groups of the Study of Parliament Group (SPG), a body that draws together academics and clerks of Parliament. A reflective set of essays, by members of the SPG, on parliamentary change and the issues facing Parliament in the twenty-first century is to be found in Giddings (2005). The relationships of Parliament to the European Union, government, pressure groups and citizens are put in comparative context in Norton (1996), Norton (1998), Norton (1999) and Norton (2002) respectively.

Bibliography

Baldwin, N.D.J. (ed.) (2005) *Parliament in the 21st Century* (Politico's).

Ball, J. and Beleaga, T. (2012) 'MPs' £1.8m in perks revealed', the *Guardian*, 10 April.

Brazier, A. (2004) 'Standing Committees: Imperfect Scrutiny', in Brazier, A. (ed.) *Parliament, Politics and Law Making* (Hansard Society).

Constitution Committee, House of Lords (2004) *Parliament and the Legislative Process*, 14th Report, Session 2003–4, HL Paper 173–I (The Stationery Office).

Constitution Committee, House of Lords (2010) *Pre-Legislative Scrutiny in the 2008–09 and 2009–10 Sessions*, 8th Report, Session 2009–10, HL Paper 78 (The Stationery Office).

Cowley, P. (ed.) (1998) *Conscience and Parliament* (Cass).

Cowley, P. (2002) *Revolts and Rebellions* (Politico's).

Cowley, P. (2005) *The Rebels* (Politico's).

Cowley, P. and Stuart, M. (2008) 'A Rebellious Decade: Backbench Rebellions under Tony Blair, 1997–207', in Beech, M. and Lee, S. (eds) *Ten Years of New Labour* (Palgrave Macmillan).

Cowley, P. and M. Stuart (2012) 'A Coalition with Two Wobbly Wings: Backbench Dissent in the House of Commons', *Political Insight*, Vol. 3.

Criddle, B. (2002) 'MPs and Candidates', in Butler, D. and Kavanagh, D. (eds) *The British General Election of 2001* (Macmillan).

Criddle, B. (2010) 'More Diverse, Yet More Uniform', in Kavanagh, D. and Cowley, P. (eds) *The British General Election of 2010* (Palgrave Macmillan).

Flynn, P. (2012) *How to be an MP* (Biteback Publishing).

Franklin, M. and Norton, P. (eds) (1993) *Parliamentary Questions* (Oxford University Press).

Giddings, P. (ed.) (1995) *Parliamentary Accountability* (Macmillan).

Giddings, P. (ed.) (2005) *The Future of Parliament* (Palgrave Macmillan).

Giddings, P. and Drewry, G. (eds) (2004) *Britain in the European Union* (Palgrave).

Giddings, P. and Irwin, H. (2005) 'Objects and Questions', in Giddings, P. (ed.) *The Future of Parliament* (Palgrave Macmillan).

Grant, M. (2009) *The UK Parliament* (Edinburgh University Press).

Griffith, J.A.G. and Ryle, M. (1989) *Parliament* (Sweet & Maxwell).

Hansard Society (2004) *Issues in Law-Making 5. Pre-Legislative Scrutiny* (Hansard Society).

Hansard Society Commission on the Communication of Parliamentary Democracy (2005), *Members Only?* (Hansard Society).

Hansard Society Commission on Parliamentary Scrutiny (2001) *The Challenge for Parliament: Making Government Accountable* (Vacher Dod Publishing).

Kennon, A. (2004) 'Pre-legislative Scrutiny of Draft Bills', *Public Law*, Autumn, pp. 477–94.

King, A. (1981) 'The Rise of the Career Politician in Britain – and its Consequences', *British Journal of Political Science*, Vol. 11.

Levy, J. (2009) *Strengthening Parliament's Powers of Scrutiny?* (The Constitution Unit, University College London).

Levy, J. (2010) 'Public Bill Committees: An Assessment. Scrutiny Sought: Scrutiny Gained', *Parliamentary Affairs*, vol. 63, no. 3.

Mezey, M. (1979) *Comparative Legislatures* (Duke University Press).

Norton, P. (1979) 'The Organization of Parliamentary Parties', in Walkland, S.A. (ed.) *The House of Commons in the Twentieth Century* (Oxford University Press).

Norton, P. (ed.) (1990) *Legislatures* (Oxford University Press).

Norton, P. (1994) 'The Parliamentary Party and Party Committees', in Seldon, A. and Ball, S. (eds) *Conservative Century: The Conservative Party since 1900* (Oxford University Press).

Norton, P. (ed.) (1996) *National Parliaments and the European Union* (Cass).

Norton, P. (ed.) (1998) *Parliaments and Governments in Western Europe* (Cass).

Norton, P. (1999) 'The United Kingdom: Parliament Under Pressure', in Norton, P. (ed.) *Parliaments and Pressure Groups in Western Europe* (Cass).

Norton, P. (ed.) (2002) *Parliaments and Citizens in Western Europe* (Cass).

Norton, P. (2012a) 'Parliament and Citizens in the United Kingdom', *The Journal of Legislative Studies*, Vol. 18.

Norton, P. (2012b) 'Coalition Cohesion', in Heppell, T. and Seawright, D. (eds) *Cameron and the Conservatives* (Palgrave Macmillan).

Norton, P. (2013) *Parliament in British Politics*, 2nd edn (Palgrave Macmillan).

Norton, P. and Wood, D. (1993) *Back from Westminster* (University Press of Kentucky).

Oliver, D. and Drewry, G. (eds) (1998) *The Law and Parliament* (Butterworth).

Power, G. (1998) *Representing the People: MPs and their Constituents* (Fabian Society).

Procedure Committee, House of Commons (2009) *Written Parliamentary Questions*, Third Report, Session 2008–09, HC 859 (The Stationery Office).

Public Administration Committee, House of Commons (2008) *Lobbying: Access and Influence in Whitehall*, First Report, Session 2008–09, HC 36–I (The Stationery Office).

Riddell, P. (1993) *Honest Opportunism* (Hamish Hamilton).

Riddell, P. (2011) *In Defence of Politicians* (Biteback Publishing).

Rogers, R. and Walters, R. (2006) *How Parliament Works*, 6th edn (Longman).

Rush, M. (ed.) (1979) 'Members of Parliament', in Walkland, S.A. (ed.) *The House of Commons in the Twentieth Century* (Oxford University Press).

Rush, M. (1990) *Pressure Politics* (Oxford University Press).

Rush, M. (2001) *The Role of the Member of Parliament Since 1868* (Oxford University Press).

Rush, M. (2005) *How Parliament Works* (Manchester University Press).

Rush, M. and Giddings, P. (2011) *Parliamentary Socialisation* (Palgrave Macmillan).

Somit, A. and Roemmele, A. (1995) 'The Victorious Legislative Incumbent as a Threat to Democracy: a Nine Nation Study', *American Political Science Association: Legislative Studies Section Newsletter*, vol. 18, no. 2, July.

Useful websites

Parliamentary websites

Parliament: www.parliament.uk

Parliamentary committees:
    www.parliament.uk/business/committees.cfm

Guide to parliamentary committees:
    www.parliament.uk/about/how/committees.cfm

Factsheets: www.parliament.uk/parliamentary_
    publications_and_archives/factsheets.cfm

Parliamentary education service:
    www.parliament.uk/education/index.htm

Register of Members' Interests:
    www.publications.parliament.uk/pa/cm/cmregmem.htm

Hansard:
    www.publications.parliament.uk/pa/cm/cmhansrd.htm

Other related websites

Hansard Society for Parliamentary Government:
    www.hansard-society.org.uk

CHAPTER 16

The House of Commons under pressure

Philip Norton

> " The British public has always displayed a healthy cynicism of MPs. They have taken it for granted that MPs are self-serving imposters and hypocrites who put party before country and self before party "
>
> Ivor Crewe

Learning objectives

- To identify contemporary challenges faced by the House of Commons.

- To describe and analyse pressures on Members of Parliament.

- To describe and analyse pressures on the House of Commons.

- To detail different schools of thought on the reform of the House.

- To identify different approaches to parliamentary power.

The House of Commons fulfils a range of functions, but its capacity to do so effectively has been the subject of controversy. Members of Parliament individually are having difficulty coping with the demands placed on them. The House of Commons collectively is under strain. The resources available may not be sufficient to meet the expectations placed on the House. Criticisms have led to demands for reform, with different schools of thought emerging. Much of the discussion, though, takes place within a pluralist view of power. Different views of power can result in the House being seen as more powerful than is often popularly recognised.

Members under pressure

Members of Parliament are called on to carry out the functions of the House of Commons. As we have seen (Chapter 15), the resources available to them to carry out those tasks have increased in recent years. MPs have more resources than before. They have a better salary than before, and they have office and support facilities far in excess of those available to their predecessors. However, the demands on MPs have increased massively in recent decades, on a scale that challenges their capacity to cope with them, even with increased resources. The increase in demands on MPs' time can be ascribed to four sources: public business, organised interests, constituents and MPs themselves.

Public business

The volume of business has increased in recent decades. This is particularly pronounced in terms of legislation. The number of bills introduced by the government is nowadays not much greater than it was in earlier decades. What has increased is the volume. Bills are much longer than they used to be. They are also more complex. Before 1950 no more than 1,000 pages of public Acts were passed each year. Before 1980 no more than 2,000 pages were passed each year. Since 1980 the figure has usually been in excess of 2,500 pages and on occasion has surpassed 3,000 pages. In the twenty-first century some bills – such as the Financial Services Bill in 2012 – have been so big that they have had to be published in two parts. This increased volume places a significant strain on parliamentary resources. Most bills go to public bill committees. The longer and more complex the bill, the more time it needs in committee. Given that several public bill committees will normally be in existence at the same time – bills frequently go for committee consideration at the same time in the session – there is a tremendous strain on the finite resources of MPs, in terms of both their number and the time they have at their disposal.

In addition to the greater volume of public legislation, there is also the burden of other business. This includes, for example, having to scrutinise EU legislation, a task that falls principally on the European Scrutiny Committee (which considers all EU documents submitted to the House) and three European committees, responsible for discussing documents that the House considers worthy of further consideration. It also includes the work of the select committees. The departmental select committees take up the time of 217 MPs. There are then the other investigative select committees, such as Public Accounts and Public Administration. Committee work, which often requires reading a substantial amount of paperwork submitted by witnesses and outside bodies, can be time-consuming. Some of the material can be detailed and complex. All this work – in terms of the European committees and the departmental and other investigative select committees – represents a relatively recent increase in the workload of MPs; there were no European committees prior to the 1970s and, as we have seen, only a few investigative select committees. Some MPs not only serve on an investigative select committee, but may also be appointed to a domestic committee and to a public bill committee. Keeping on top of all the work can prove a daunting, if not impossible, task. Even if Members attend committee meetings, they may not have done the preparatory reading, instead glancing at the paperwork while the meeting is in progress.

Organised interests

MPs have always been subject to lobbying by outside groups – groups wanting members to push for a particular outcome in terms of public policy. However, that lobbying has become pronounced in recent decades (Norton 2013: Ch. 12). Since 1979 organised interests – firms, charities, consumer groups, professional bodies, pressure groups – appear to have 'discovered' Parliament. Government after 1979 appeared to adopt more of an arm's-length relationship with outside bodies. The departmental select committees came into being and provided particular targets for organised interests. The 1970s had also seen something of a growth in the voting independence of MPs. As a consequence of these several developments, the House of Commons looked far more attractive than ever before to organised interests wanting to influence public policy (Rush 1990; Norton 1999a). One survey of organised interests found that, by the mid-1980s, three-quarters had 'regular or frequent contact with one or more Members of Parliament' (Rush 1990: 280). Of the groups that had such contact, more than 80 per cent had asked MPs to table parliamentary questions, and almost 80 per cent had asked MPs to arrange meetings at the House of Commons. Over half had asked MPs to table amendments to bills and to table a motion. It is common to hear MPs in debates refer to material they have received from interest groups (see Norton 2013: Ch. 12). This contact between organised interests and MPs has a number of beneficial consequences. Among other things, Members are provided with advice and information that can prove useful in questioning government and in raising new issues. However, it also has some negative consequences. One is the demand on MPs' time. One survey of 248 MPs in 1992 found that on average an MP spent over three-and-a-half hours a week meeting group representatives (Norris 1997: 36–7). Further time is taken up by acting on the requests of such groups and by reading and, if necessary, responding to the mass of material that is mailed by the groups. MPs now have difficulty coping with the sheer volume of lobbying material that is sent to them.

Constituents

Organised interests have been responsible for a marked increase in the mailbag of MPs. So too have constituents. We have touched already on the volume of mail received in the House of Commons in the twenty-first century. For the MP, constituency work takes priority and can occupy a large portion of the day in dictating replies to constituents' letters and e-mails. It can also occupy most of every weekend, through both appearances at constituency functions and holding constituency surgeries – publicly advertised meetings at which constituents can see the MP in private to discuss particular concerns.

When an MP receives a letter or e-mail from a constituent that raises a particular grievance (failure to receive a particular state benefit, for example) or issue of public policy, the MP will normally pursue the matter with the government through writing to the relevant minister. Ministers answer in the region of 250,000 letters a year, mostly from MPs. Some constituents are persistent. As one MP recounted, 'A tiny number of constituents and campaigners can hi-jack the attention of the office with a relentless flow of letters and calls . . . Often they have a single all-consuming problem and fail to understand the mass of daily demands on an MP's time' (Flynn 2012: 143).

The burden of constituency demands continues to increase, and MPs have difficulty finding the time to cope with constituency demands and the demands of public business (see Norton and Wood 1993; Norton 2013). By 1996 it was estimated that MPs devoted almost 40 per cent of their time to constituency business (Power 1996: 14). In 2006 MPs who had been elected for the first time in 2005 put the figure at 49 per cent (Rosenblatt 2006: 32) and in 2011 MPs first elected in 2010 put it at 59 per cent (Hansard Society 2011: 6). The problem is particularly acute for MPs with constituencies close to Westminster: constituents expect them to find the time to be at constituency events, even when the House is sitting. MPs are not only recipients of communications but are themselves generators of communications to constituents. MPs have made use of new social media, utilising not only websites but also blogs, Facebook and, increasingly, Twitter (Norton 2007, Williamson 2009, Jackson and Lilleker 2011, Norton 2012a). For many, this adds considerably to their workload.

MPs themselves

MPs are also responsible for adding to their own burden and to that of the resources of the House. As we have seen, recent years have seen the growth of the career politician. There is a greater body of members who are keen to be re-elected and to achieve office. They are keen to be noticed in the House. Achieving a high profile in the House helps them to be noticed locally. Utilising new social media also contributes to profile raising. This may help, albeit at the margins, with re-election (see Norton and Wood 1993) and, indeed, may help with reselection by the local party. It is also considered necessary for the purposes of promotion, given the growing number of career politicians and hence the more competitive parliamentary environment. The tendency of the career politician is to table as many questions as is permissible: research assistants will variously be asked to come up with suitable drafts (see Franklin and Norton 1993). The career politician will try to intervene as often as possible in the chamber and will table early day motions to raise issues. There is also likely to be an allied tendency to attract media attention, not least with frequent press releases and tweets.

All these pressures add up to create a particular burden for MPs. Surveys by the senior salaries review body have shown that, over the decades, the amount of time devoted to parliamentary duties has increased. One study in the 1990s suggested that MPs typically work in excess of a 70-hour week. It is difficult for MPs to keep pace with all the demands made of them. Their resources have improved in recent years, and they have been aided considerably by new technology, but the resources have not kept pace with the demands made of members. For many MPs it is a case of running in order to stand still. For others it is a case of slipping backwards. There is a particularly important conflict between trying to find time for constituency work and finding time for dealing with public business in the House (Norton and Wood 1993; Norton 2013: Ch. 11). So long as constituency work takes priority, then the time needed for public business is under particular pressure.

The House under pressure

The fact that MPs work hard for their constituents is frequently acknowledged by constituents. Assessments of the role of the local MP tend to be positive (twice as many people saying the local MP did a good job as the proportion saying the MP did a bad job) and consistent, having shown little change over a number of years. However, the view held by citizens about the House of Commons appears more ambivalent, certainly more volatile, than the views they hold of the local MP. The proportion of people thinking that the House of Commons is doing a good job has varied over the

Table 16.1 Views on the efficacy of Parliament, 1995–2010

Q. Are you satisfied or dissatisfied with the way that Parliament works?

	21 April– 8 May 1995[1]	17–21 August 2000[1]	9–15 May 2001[2]	6–17 December 2003	23–28 November 2006	29–31 May 2009[3]	13–19 November 2009	3–9 December 2010
	%	%	%	%	%	%	%	%
Very satisfied	2	4	4	1	2	2	1	1
Fairly satisfied	32	39	41	35	33	18	32	26
Neither satisfied nor dissatisfied	27	19	16	27	24	11	24	33
Fairly dissatisfied	22	21	19	23	24	30	25	24
Very dissatisfied	9	8	11	9	9	33	13	11
No opinion	8	10	9	5	8	6	4	4
Satisfied	34	43	45	36	35	20	33	27
Dissatisfied	31	29	30	32	33	63	38	35
Not satisfied	+3	+14	+15	+4	+2	−43	−5	−8

1 In 1995 and 2000, asked as 'To what extent are you satisfied or dissatisfied with the way each is doing its job these days? The way Parliament works'.

2 In 2001, asked as 'To what extent are you satisfied or dissatisfied with the way each is doing its job these days? The way the Westminster Parliament works'.

3 In May 2009, asked as 'To what extent are you satisfied or dissatisfied with the way each is doing its job these days? The Westminster Parliament'.

Base: c. 1,500–2,000 UK (GB & NI) adults aged 18+ (2001–6) or c. 1,000–2,000 GB adults aged 18+ (1995, 2000, 2009, 2010).

Source: Ipsos MORI

years, sometimes quite substantially. In a 1991 MORI poll, for example, 59 per cent of those questioned thought that Parliament worked well or fairly well. Four years later, in 1995, those very or fairly satisfied with the way Parliament works stood at 34 per cent. The figure increased in later years (though never reaching 50 per cent), before slumping to 20 per cent in May 2009. As shown in Table 16.1, the proportion increased later that year, but then slipped back in 2010, with only 27 per cent very or fairly satisfied with the way Parliament works. The percentage fairly or very dissatisfied reached an unprecedented 63 per cent in 2009, the only bright spot for Parliament in 2010 being that the difference between satisfied and dissatisfied responses fell from a massive −43 in 2009 (having previously been positive) to −8 in December 2010, the most significant increase being in those neither satisfied nor dissatisfied.

What, then, might explain why attitudes towards Parliament are not more positive? The House of Commons has seen major changes in recent decades. Some of these changes, such as the creation of the departmental select committees and the introduction of public bill committees, have reinforced the capacity of the House to fulfil a number of its functions. The creation of the Backbench Business Committee in 2010 has also had a notable effect in terms of the expressive function of the House. However, other

changes – internal as well as external to the House – have served to challenge its public standing and its capacity to fulfil the tasks expected of it. These can be summarised under the headings of partisanship, executive dominance, the creation of other policy-making bodies, and sleaze.

Partisanship

The clash between the parties is a characteristic of British political life. It is a long-standing feature of the House of Commons. There is a perception that, in recent years, it has become more intense. This is reflected, for example, in the nature of Prime Minister's Question Time, where the desire for partisan point-scoring has largely squeezed out genuine attempts to elicit information (see Franklin and Norton 1993). However, perhaps most important of all, partisanship is now more publicly visible. The presence of television cameras means that, in a single news broadcast covering the House, more people will see the House in that broadcast than could ever have sat in the public gallery of the House. Although there is general support for broadcasting proceedings among public and politicians, the focus on the chamber has tended to encourage a negative perception. As the

Table 16.2 Perceptions of MPs

Q In general, whose interests do you think MPs put first: their own, their constituents', their party's, or the country's?

	10–11 January 1994	23–26 May 1996	12–17 January 2006	3–6 January 2008[1]	29–31 May 2009
	%	%	%	%	%
Their/his own	52	56	45	55	62
Their/his party's	26	27	28	34	21
Their/his constituents	11	7	9	6	7
The country's	5	5	14	4	5
Other	1	1	1	n/a	1
None of these/don't know	5	4	3	1	4

Base: c. 800–1,600 GB adults aged 18+, except
1 Base: c. 1,070 UK (GB & NI) adults aged 16+.

Source: Ipsos MORI

author of a 1999 Hansard Society study of the broadcasting of Parliament noted:

> The overwhelming perception of parliamentarians as point-scoring, unoriginal and dogmatically partisan can not be blamed entirely on negative reporting by journalists. If one purpose of broadcasting Parliament was to allow people to judge it for themselves, the low esteem MPs are held in by the public has not been elevated by ten years of live exposure.
>
> (Coleman 1999: 21)

When people see the House on television, they see either a largely empty chamber – MPs are busy doing things elsewhere – or a body of baying MPs, busy shouting at one another and cheering their own side. That is particularly noticeable at Prime Minister's Question Time. One Gallup poll in 1993 found that 82 per cent of those questioned agreed that what took place 'sounds like feeding time at the zoo'. As Peter Riddell noted of Prime Minister's Question Time, 'no other aspect of parliamentary life generates more public complaints' (*The Times*: 4 April 1994). For MPs who want to win the next election, supporting their own side in the chamber takes precedence over maintaining public trust in the institution (see Norton 1997: 365). Given that the television coverage focuses on the chamber and not on the committee work of the House, the enduring perception that viewers have is of a House of noisy, point-scoring MPs, contributing little new to political debate.

The activity of MPs appears to contribute to a public perception that, after their own interests, MPs put their party interests ahead of those of their constituents and the country (Table 16.2). By 2009 fewer than one in eight people thought that MPs gave priority to the interests of constituents and the country.

Executive dominance

There has been a perception of a growth in executive dominance in the UK (see Allen 2001). The effect of this, it is argued, is a greater marginalisation of Parliament. Party dominates the House, and this stranglehold has been exacerbated as more and more power has been concentrated in Downing Street. This perception of executive dominance was marked when Margaret Thatcher occupied Downing Street and was revived under the premiership of Tony Blair and his successors, Gordon Brown and David Cameron. The extent to which Parliament is marginalised has been the subject of academic debate, but the perception of a peripheral legislature resonates with the public. The MORI state of the nation polls in the 1990s and in 2000 found a growing body of respondents who believed that Parliament did not have sufficient control over what the government does. By 2011 only 38 per cent of those questioned agreed or agreed strongly that Parliament holds government to account. More than a quarter – 29 per cent – neither agreed nor disagreed and 21 per cent disagreed or disagreed strongly (Hansard Society 2012: 50).

The popular perception during the Blair premiership of Labour MPs slavishly voting as they were told was encapsulated by a *Guardian* cartoon showing a Labour MP holding an electronic voting device displaying two options: 'Agree with Tony [Blair]' and 'Strongly Agree with Tony'. As research by Philip Cowley (2002, 2005) and Cowley and Stuart (2008) has shown, this perception is overstated. The Blair and Brown governments faced unprecedented rebelliousness from backbenchers. The three most notable occasions were in 2002 when 122 Labour MPs voted against government policy on Iraq, the biggest rebellion on foreign policy faced by any Labour government; in 2005 when the Blair Government suffered its first defeat on a whipped vote, MPs voting down a government proposal to allow detention without charge for 90 days; and in 2009 when the Brown Government was defeated on the rights of former Gurkha soldiers to settle in Britain. Nor was dissent stilled with the return of a coalition government in 2010 – quite the reverse – with dissent by government backbenchers proving unprecedented in a first session of a parliament under a new government (Cowley and Stuart 2012; Norton 2012b).

However, the perception of executive dominance persists – the Prime Minister governing with little regard to Parliament – and it remains the case that the government will almost always get its way in a parliamentary vote. The defeat in 2005 was the first in more than 2,000 votes to take place in the Commons since the Labour Government was returned in 1997. There remains a popular view of a House of Commons that it is not calling government to account. The House is seen as weak in the face of a strong executive.

Creation of other policy-making bodies

The capacity of the House to fulfil its functions is undermined not only by executive domination of the House but also by the creation of other policy-making bodies. Even if MPs had the political will to determine outcomes, their capacity to do so is now limited by the seepage of policy-making powers to other bodies, what has been termed the 'hollowing out' of the state. There are three principal bodies or rather three collections of bodies involved: the institutions of the EU, the courts and the devolved assemblies.

The effect of membership of the European Union will be touched on in Chapter 27. We shall return to its legal implications in Chapter 21. Membership has served to transfer policy competences in various sectors to the institutions of the European Union: they have increased in number with subsequent treaty amendments. Other than being able, under the Lisbon Treaty, to challenge a proposal on the grounds that it breaches subsidiarity, Parliament has no formal role in the law-making process of the EU. It seeks to influence the British minister prior to the meeting of the relevant Council of Ministers, but – if qualified majority voting (QMV) is employed – the minister may be outvoted. There is nothing that Parliament can do to prevent regulations having binding effect in the UK or to prevent the intention of directives from being achieved.

The courts have acquired new powers as a result of British membership of the EU as well now as a consequence of the incorporation of the European Convention on Human Rights (ECHR) into British law and as a consequence of devolution. The effect of these we shall explore in greater depth in Chapter 21. Various disputed issues of public policy are now resolved by the courts, which have the power to suspend or set aside British law if it conflicts with EU law. The courts are responsible for interpreting the provisions of the ECHR. The courts are also responsible for determining the legal limits established by the Acts creating elected bodies in Scotland, Wales and Northern Ireland. The capacity of the House of Commons to intervene or to overrule the courts is now effectively limited.

The devolution of powers to elected assemblies in different parts of the United Kingdom also limits the decision-making capacity of Parliament. Parliament is not expected to legislate on matters devolved to the Scottish Parliament. The Scottish Parliament has been given power to legislate in areas not reserved under the Scotland Act and has also been given power to amend primary legislation passed by Parliament. Legislative powers are also held by the Northern Ireland Assembly, other than for 'excepted matters' (powers that may never be transferred from Westminster) and 'reserved matters' (which may at some stage be transferred). The powers of the National Assembly for Wales have been extended under the terms of the Government of Wales Act 2006 and, following a referendum in the principality in 2011, power to legislate other than in reserved matters passed to the Assembly. The scope of decision making by Parliament is thus constricted.

Sleaze

Throughout the twentieth century there were various scandals involving politicians accepting illicit payments in return for some political favour. In the 1970s and 1980s there was criticism of MPs for accepting payment to act as advisers to lobbying firms or hiring themselves out as consultants. One book, published in 1991, was entitled *MPs for Hire* (Hollingsworth 1991). At the time it was published, 384 MPs held 522 directorships and 452 consultancies. In 1994 the issue hit the headlines when a journalist, posing as a businessman, offered 20 MPs £1,000 each to table parliamentary questions. Two Conservative MPs did not immediately say no to the offer. The story attracted extensive media coverage and the two MPs were briefly suspended from the service of the House. The subject received a further boost later in the year when the *Guardian* claimed that two ministers had, when backbenchers, accepted money to table questions; one, Tim Smith, promptly resigned as a minister and the other, Neil Hamilton, was eventually forced to leave office. The furore generated by the stories led the Prime

Minister, John Major, to establish the Committee on Standards in Public Life, under a judge, Lord Nolan. In 1995 the House accepted the recommendations of the committee about payment from outside sources, though not without opposition from some Conservative Members. MPs went further than the committee recommended in deciding to ban any paid advocacy by MPs: members cannot advocate a particular cause in Parliament in return for payment. Members were also required to disclose income received from outside bodies that is paid to them because they are MPs (for example, money from a company for advice on how to present a case to government). The House also approved the recommendation to establish a code of conduct and appoint a Parliamentary Commissioner for Standards to ensure that the rules are followed. The code was subsequently drawn up and agreed. It is accompanied by a guide to the rules of the House relating to members' conduct.

The effect of the 'cash for questions' scandal was reflected in opinion polls. In a 1985 MORI poll, 46 per cent thought that 'most' MPs made a lot of money by using public office improperly. In 1994 the figure was 64 per cent, and 77 per cent agreed with the statement that 'most MPs care more about special interests than they care about people like you'. Continuing allegations of breaches of the rules after the return of a new government in 1997 did nothing to help Parliament's reputation (see Doig 2001, 2002). However, what was to precipitate the slump in the reputation in the House of Commons in 2009 was a scandal over MPs' expenses. The House in 1971 introduced an additional cost allowance to assist MPs with maintaining a second home. Initially a modest sum, the amount that an MP representing a seat outside London could claim had reached £24,222 for 2009–10. Though the amount claimable was known, details about claims were not made public. In 2009 details were to be released under the Freedom of Information Act, but the *Daily Telegraph* got hold of advance and unexpurgated copies of the claims made by MPs and published details over a number of weeks. Publication of details of some of the claims – most prominently for a duck house, clearing a moat, in two instances claiming for mortgages that had already been paid off, and in another claiming for, even though not having, a second home – led to a public scandal. There was public dissatisfaction with the ease with which MPs could claim money for a whole range of items (furniture, household goods and repairs, food), often without receipts, and, in effect, supplement their salaries. The scandal led to the police investigating the actions of some MPs (such as those claiming to cover non-existent mortgages) and to the Speaker of the House of Commons, Michael Martin, resigning: he had resisted attempts to make public details of the claims and was the target of much of the criticism of how the House had responded to the crisis. Several

MPs who had made claims that attracted particular public opprobrium announced that they would not be seeking re-election; some Labour MPs were brought before a party 'star chamber' and told that they would not be permitted to stand again as Labour candidates. The Government achieved enactment of the Parliamentary Standards Act 2009, transferring responsibility for policing and paying allowances to an independent body. The Committee on Standards in Public Life was given responsibility for making other recommendations to address the problem. The public reaction was unprecedented in living memory. Gordon Brown described it as 'the biggest parliamentary scandal for two centuries' (Winnett and Rayner 2009: 349). It served not to destroy trust in parliamentarians, which was already low, but rather to reinforce it (see Hansard Society 2010: 3). All MPs were essentially tarred with the same brush. As Tony Blair recorded (quoted in Riddell 2011: 27):

> As ever with such an outpouring of outrage, the innocent or the mildly stupid have been executed along with those who really did cross the line. It is a real shame that no one stuck up for the MPs. Instead, everyone competed in condemnation of them.

Pressure for change

These variables combine to produce a House of Commons that is under pressure to restore public confidence and to fulfil effectively the functions ascribed to it. There are various calls for reform of the House in order to address both problems. However, there is no agreement on what should be done. Even in the wake of the scandal over MPs' expenses in 2009, not all those demanding reform were agreed on the scale of the problem, and they came up with very different proposals for reform.

There are, put simply, three principal approaches to reform. Each derives from a particular perception of the role of the House of Commons in the political system. They can be related very roughly to the three types of legislature identified at the beginning of the chapter.

1 *Radical*: The radical approach wants to see Parliament as a policy-making legislature. Parliament is seen as weak in relation to the executive – and is seen to be getting weaker. Reform of the House of Commons within the present constitutional and political framework is deemed inadequate to the task. Without radical constitutional reform, the House of Commons will remain party-dominated and under the thumb of the executive. To achieve a policy-making legislature, the radical approach not only supports reform within the institution but also

wants major reform of the constitution in order to change fundamentally the relationship between Parliament and government. Such change would include a new electoral system as well as an elected second chamber. As such, this radical approach can be seen to fit very much within the liberal approach to the constitution (see Chapter 13). The most extreme form of this view advocates a separation of powers, with the executive elected separately from the House of Commons. Only with radical reform, it is argued, can high levels of public trust in Parliament be achieved.

2 *Reform*: This approach wants to strengthen the House of Commons as a policy-influencing body, the onus for policy-*making* resting with government but with the House of Commons having the opportunity to consider policy proposals in detail and to influence their content. As such, it falls very much within the traditional approach to constitutional change (see Chapter 15), although it is not exclusive to it. Traditionalists, for example, can find common cause with adherents to the socialist approach in respect of some reforms. Even adherents of the liberal approach will support reform, although arguing that it does not go far enough. (For traditionalists, reform is both necessary and sufficient. For liberals, it is necessary but not sufficient.) Reformers favour structural and procedural changes within the House. They want to strengthen committees. They want more time for legislative scrutiny. Given the collapse in trust in the Commons, they also want to enhance the relationship between Parliament and the public, with greater scope for members of the public to make their views known – for example through e-petitions and online consultations. Reducing the size of the House was also seen as making more efficient use of resources, not least through reducing the pressure created by members themselves. The sorts of reforms that are advocated are listed in Table 16.3.

3 *Leave alone*: This approach, as the name suggests, opposes change. It is the stance of a High Tory (see Chapter 13) although it is not exclusive to the High Tory approach. Some Labour MPs have opposed reform, wanting to retain the chamber as the central debating forum. Those who support this stance stress the importance of the chamber as the place where the great issues of the day are debated. Committees and greater specialisation detract from the fulfilment of this historical role, allowing MPs to become bogged down in the detail rather than the principle of what is proposed by government. Providing MPs with offices takes them away from the chamber. Although not quite envisaging a House with little or no policy effect, advocates of this approach see the role of the House as one of supporting government. They emphasise that there is no great public demand for change, with scandals such as those of MPs' expenses in 2009 constituting, in their view, essentially transient and ultimately marginal events. Most people want a government that can govern, and the House of Commons is there to support that government in carrying out the programme it laid before the electors.

For radicals, the contemporary emphasis on constitutional reform gives them hope that their stance may be vindicated. The creation of new elected assemblies in Scotland, Wales and Northern Ireland will, they hope, act as a spur to radical change in England. Not only do these parts of the UK have their own elected assemblies, they also have electoral systems that are different to that employed for the House of Commons. With the use also of different electoral systems for the Greater London Assembly and the European Parliament, the House of Commons remains the only legislative body in the UK elected by the first-past-the-post system. Those who adopt this radical stance view electoral reform as a crucial mechanism for revitalising the House of Commons. The campaign took a knock in 2011, with the rejection of the Alternative Vote (AV) in a national referendum,

Table 16.3 Reform of the House of Commons: proposals to strengthen the House

- Make pre-legislative scrutiny the norm by publishing most bills, before their introduction into Parliament, in draft form and allowing select committees to study them.
- Create more time in public bill committees for consideration of evidence.
- Introduce a committee on legislative standards.
- Provide a systematic means for post-legislative scrutiny by Parliament.
- Establish a petitions committee to consider issues raised by the public, supplementing the work of the Backbench Business Committee.
- Make greater use of online consultations for select committee enquiries.
- Give each investigative select committee a research budget.
- Give select committees the power to summon ministers.
- Create new procedures for examining delegated legislation and give the House the power to amend statutory instruments.

but they argue that this does not affect the campaign to introduce a system of proportional representation.

For reformers, reform constitutes a practical as well as a desirable option. They point to what has happened in recent years as well as to various reform tracts identifying the case for further change. The introduction of the departmental select committees in 1979 showed what could be achieved in strengthening Parliament as a policy-influencing legislature. Further reforms have been carried out since 1997. These have included the creation of the 'parallel chamber' in Westminster Hall, the creation of public bill committees, the election by the House of chairs of select committees, and the introduction of regular post-legislative review by government departments. More modest changes have included the introduction of payment for those who chair both select and public bill committees.

Reformers want to see more significant changes, and recent years have seen the publication of various reform tracts, including the reports of the Conservative Party's Commission to Strengthen Parliament (the Norton Report) 2000, the Hansard Society's Commissions on Parliamentary Scrutiny (the Newton Report) 2001 and on the Communication of Parliamentary Democracy (the Puttnam Report) 2005, as well as reports from the Modernisation Committee, the Reform of the House of Commons Committee (the Wright Committee) in the Commons and the Constitution Committee in the House of Lords. The Constitution Committee's report, *Parliament and the Legislative Process* (2004), advocated not only reform of the legislative process, but also more extensive pre-legislative and post-legislative scrutiny. The report has led to the introduction of post-legislative review as a standard procedure, most Acts to be reviewed three to five years after enactment.

Those who want to leave the House of Commons alone take heart from the fact that they frequently succeed, not least by default (see Norton 1999b). Many ministers are not too keen on any significant reform that will strengthen the capacity of Parliament to criticise government or prevent it having its way. They want Parliament to expedite government business, not have it delayed. Robin Cook, when he was Leader of the House (2001–3), had notable difficulty in carrying his colleagues with him in pursuing a reform agenda. The whips have proved reluctant to see change. Also, MPs – once a parliament is under way – become too tied up with the day-to-day demands of constituency work and public business to stand back and address the issue of parliamentary reform. The 'leave alone' tendency may not be strong in its advocacy but can be quite powerful in achieving the outcome it wants.

Parliamentary reform has been a feature of debates over the past 40 years. However, the problem in achieving reform is the classic one. Most MPs are elected to support the party in government. At the same time, they are members of a body that is supposed to subject to critical scrutiny the very government they are elected to support. Are they going to vote to strengthen the House of Commons if the effect is to limit the very government they were elected to support? The options are not necessarily mutually exclusive – reformers argue that good government needs an effective Parliament – but perceptions are all-important. If ministers think a strengthened Parliament is a threat, will they not be inclined to call on their parliamentary majority to oppose it? In those circumstances, backbenchers may have to choose between party and Parliament. Some recent reforms have been important, but none challenges the basic capacity of government to get its way. At the end of the day, the government achieves passage of its measures.

Explaining parliamentary power

As is apparent from the data in Table 16.1, as well as the demands for reform made by observers and many politicians, there is a widespread perception that Parliament is not doing as good a job as it should be doing. The House of Commons is seen as weak in the face of executive dominance. Yet Parliament has survived for several centuries; it is at the heart of our political system. Just how powerful is it? On the face of it, not very, yet much depends on how power is defined. There are different approaches. The three principal approaches derive from explaining the capacity to affect outcomes in terms of observable decision making (the pluralist approach), non-decision making (deriving from elite theory) and institutional constraints (Norton 2013: Ch. 1).

Decision making

This approach focuses on how issues are resolved once they are on the political agenda. Once a government brings forward a proposal, what difference does Parliament make to it? Does the measure emerge in the form in which the government introduced it or at least in the form it wants? From this perspective, Parliament exercises some power, but it is limited. Parliament has the coercive capacity to say 'no' to government. Legislation is dependent on the assent of Parliament. If MPs vote down a bill, then it cannot proceed. However, as we have seen, the use of this coercive capacity is rare.

MPs also have a persuasive capacity: that is, they may induce government not to proceed with a measure (or to change it) even though it has the option of proceeding. Ministers may be persuaded by the force of argument, by a desire to maintain goodwill on the part of their own supporters, by the desire to avoid embarrassing publicity (the public appearance of a divided party), or by the threat of defeat. Even with large majorities in the 1997 and 2001 parliaments, Labour ministers occasionally made concessions to their own backbenchers. Thus, for example, Jack Straw as Home Secretary made changes to the Criminal Justice (Terrorism and Conspiracy) Bill as well as to the Immigration and Asylum Bill in order to assuage the criticisms of Labour MPs (Cowley 2002: 32, 52–4). When one Labour MP opposed to provisions for incapacity benefit embodied in a welfare bill went to see the then Social Security Secretary, Alistair Darling, he was asked 'What's your price?' (Cowley 2002: 47). This persuasive capacity became more pronounced in the 2005–10 parliament, when – with a reduced overall majority – the threat of defeat became more potent. It has also been pronounced in the parliament returned in 2010. In July 2012 the Government decided not to move a timetabled motion for the House of Lords Reform Bill, fearing that a combination of the Opposition and Conservative MPs opposed to the bill would have resulted in it being voted down. Recognising that they could not impose a timetable, and that opponents would talk at length on the bill, the Government decided not to proceed with it.

MPs thus have the capacity to affect the outcome of measures, but that capacity is extremely limited. Most bills will clear the Commons in the form they were introduced or at least in the form preferred by government. Amendments made in response to backbench pressure – or from members of other parties – are few and far between. Concessions are occasionally offered in order to ensure that enough MPs are prepared to vote for the bill. Ministers generally opt for the minimum they can get away with in terms of concessions; in the 1997–2001 parliament, for example, negotiations 'rarely yielded anything that discontented backbenchers wanted' (Cowley 2002: 180). The House of Commons *can* make a difference and occasionally the difference is significant and high-profile, as on the House of Lords Reform Bill, but on the whole it is usually at the margins. From this perspective, Parliament is not a particularly powerful body and certainly not as powerful as many would wish it to be.

Non-decision making

Non-decision making is the capacity to keep certain things off the political agenda. The pluralist, or decision making, approach is concerned with outcomes once an issue is on the agenda. The elitist, or non-decision making approach, focuses on how issues get on to the agenda in the first place. Non-decision making is when an issue is kept off the agenda. In elite theory, there is a body that acts as a gatekeeper, ensuring that certain fundamental matters never become

the subject of political debate. Parliament is not seen as part of such an elite, but the concept of non-decision making is relevant in so far as it relates to anticipated reaction. An issue may be kept off the political agenda because those responsible for agenda setting realise that it would encounter significant and possible fatal opposition. There may be occasions, therefore, when the government decides not to bring forward a bill because it does not believe it could get it through Parliament. On occasion, the adverse reaction may be so obvious that ministers do not even need to discuss it. As a consequence, there are obvious problems in detecting instances of non-decision making. There have been cases, though, where a government has been known not to proceed with a measure because of anticipated reaction. When she was Prime Minister, Margaret Thatcher once said that she had not been as radical in economic policy as she would have liked: the reason, she said, was because she would not have been able to get the approval of Parliament. That may have been a post hoc rationalisation for not being more radical rather than the actual reason, but it points to the potential power of Parliament.

Anticipation of how MPs may behave thus has some influence on government. It is a feature not confined to the UK. As Cox and Morgenstern (2002: 446) have observed, 'the venerable "rule of anticipated reactions" makes even primarily reactive legislatures . . . relevant'. If government becomes too extreme, then Parliament may act to constrain it. Knowing that, government avoids the extremes. As such, Parliament is powerful, though the number of occasions when ministers have actually contemplated introducing a measure but then decided not to because of anticipated parliamentary reaction is likely to be very small. Given the problems of identifying non-decision making, that can only be surmised, but the existence of overall majorities for government and the willingness of MPs to vote loyally with their party make it plausible.

Institutional constraints

The institutional approach is not so much concerned with the substance of a measure but rather with the institutional structures and norms that determine how an issue is resolved. Here the concern is not with how MPs behave – whether they vote for a bill or not – but with the rules (and the acceptance of those rules) that determine how a bill becomes law. However large the government's parliamentary majority, it cannot simply get all the measures it wants passed by Parliament within a matter of days or weeks. Each bill, as we have seen, has to go through a set procedure. There are several stages each bill has to go through and there are gaps between each stage. As we have seen, there is limited parliamentary time available. The finite number of MPs available to serve on public bill committees may be seen as a problem for Parliament but it also limits the number of bills that can be considered at the same time. Government thus has to consider which bills it wishes to introduce each year. There is not sufficient parliamentary time to deal with all the bills it would like to introduce and only a minority of bills put forward by departments are accepted for introduction in a particular session. Even then, there is the problem of miscalculation and a bill may not get through in the time available. A bill is more likely to fail because of misjudgements about timing (or previously the calling of a general election, prematurely bringing a parliament to an end) than it is because MPs have voted it down.

From this institutional perspective, Parliament is a notably powerful body. For bills to become law and be enforced by the courts, they have to be assented to by Parliament. There is no alternative process. The parliamentary *process* is thus crucial, and that process is governed by a large body of often complex rules. The book embodying all the rules and precedents, known as *Erskine May* (the name of the clerk who first produced it in the nineteenth century), runs to more than 1,000 pages. Though the House of Commons is master of its procedure, and the government could use its majority to change the rules (and sometimes does), it cannot embark on wholesale change. Ministers are not procedural experts – they rely on the clerks, who are politically neutral – and the House proceeds on the basis of a common acceptance of the rules. There is a general acceptance that government is entitled to get its business done and the Opposition is entitled to be heard.

Parliament thus functions on the basis of a consensus on the rules. If government tried to manipulate the rules excessively in its favour, opposition parties may refuse to continue playing by those rules. There is thus what has been termed an 'equilibrium of legitimacy' (Norton 2001a: 28), each side accepting the legitimacy of the other in what it seeks to do. That acceptance allows the process to function effectively. It is an acceptance that underpins the institutional power of Parliament. It is an acceptance that shapes ministers' behaviour. Bills have to be drawn up in a particular form for introduction to Parliament. Ministers are not only drawn from Parliament – and remain constituency MPs – they also have to appear in Parliament to justify their measures and their policies and to answer MPs' questions. There is no legal requirement for ministers to turn up at Question Time to answer questions, but the accepted rules of procedure ensure that they do. Whether they like it or not, Parliament shapes what they do. As an *institution*, Parliament is a powerful body.

Chapter summary

The capacity of the House of Commons to carry out its functions has been the subject of criticism for many years. Those criticisms have become more strident as the demands on MPs individually and collectively have increased. Some politicians see no need for change. Others advocate reform of the House, some through radical constitutional change, others through reform from within the institution. The debate itself takes place within a particular perspective of what constitutes power. Viewed from an institutional perspective, the House remains an essential and entrenched element of the British polity.

Discussion points

- Will reforming the practices and procedures make any difference to public perceptions of the House of Commons?
- What should be done to restore public confidence in the House of Commons?
- Which approach to reform of the House of Commons is the most persuasive?
- How powerful is the House of Commons?
- What would you do with the House of Commons – and why?

Further reading

A critique of Parliament's scrutiny of the executive is to be found in Weir and Beetham (1999). On parliamentary reform since 1900, see Kelso (2009). On proposals for reform of the House of Commons, see the Commission to Strengthen Parliament (2000), Norton (2001b), the Hansard Society Commission on Parliamentary Scrutiny (2001), the Constitution Committee of the House of Lords (2004), Brazier (2004), the Modernisation Committee of the House of Commons (2006, 2007), and the House of Commons Reform Committee (2009).

Bibliography

Allen, G. (2001) *The Last Prime Minister* (Graham Allen).

Brazier, A. (2004) 'Standing Committees: Imperfect Scrutiny', in Brazier, A. (ed.) *Parliament, Politics and Law Making* (Hansard Society).

Coleman, S. (1999) *Electronic Media, Parliament and the Media* (Hansard Society).

Commission to Strengthen Parliament (2000) *Strengthening Parliament* (Conservative Party).

Constitution Committee, House of Lords (2004) *Parliament and the Legislative Process*, 14th Report, Session 2003–4, HL Paper 173–I (The Stationery Office).

Cowley, P. (2002) *Revolts and Rebellions* (Politico's).

Cowley, P. (2005) *The Rebels* (Politico's).

Cowley, P. and Stuart, M. (2008) 'A Rebellious Decade: Backbench Rebellions under Tony Blair, 1997–207', in Beech, M. and Lee, S. (eds) *Ten Years of New Labour* (Palgrave Macmillan).

Cowley, P. and M. Stuart (2012) 'A Coalition with Two Wobbly Wings: Backbench Dissent in the House of Commons', *Political Insight*, vol. 3.

Cox, G.W. and Morgenstern, S. (2002) 'Epilogue: Latin America's Assemblies and Proactive Presidents', in Morgenstern, S. and Nacif, B. (eds) *Legislative Politics in Latin America* (Cambridge University Press).

Doig, A. (2001) 'Sleaze: Picking up the Threads or "Back to Basics" Scandals?', *Parliamentary Affairs*, vol. 54, no. 2.

Doig, A. (2002) 'Sleaze Fatigue in "the House of Ill-repute"', *Parliamentary Affairs*, vol. 55, no. 2.

Flynn, P. (2012) *How to be an MP* (Biteback Publishing).

Hansard Society (2010) *Audit of Political Engagement 7: The 2010 Report* (Hansard Society).

Hansard Society (2011) *A Year in the Life: From Members of Public to Members of Parliament* (Hansard Society).

Hansard Society (2012) *Audit of Political Engagement 9: The 2012 Report Part One* (Hansard Society).

Hansard Society Commission on Parliamentary Scrutiny (2001) *The Challenge for Parliament: Making Government Accountable* (Vacher Dod Publishing).

Hollingsworth, M. (1991) *MPs for Hire* (Bloomsbury).

House of Commons Reform Committee (2009) *Rebuilding the House*, First Report, Session 2008–09, HC 1117 (The Stationery Office).

Jackson, N. and D. Lilleker (2011) 'Microblogging, Constituency Service and Impression Management: UK MPs and the Use of Twitter', *The Journal of Legislative Studies*, vol. 17.

Kelso, A. (2009) *Parliamentary Reform at Westminster* (Manchester University Press).

Modernisation of the House of Commons Select Committee (2006) House of Commons, *The Legislative Process*, First Report, Session 2005–06, HC 1097 (The Stationery Office).

Modernisation of the House of Commons Select Committee (2007) House of Commons, *Revitalising the Chamber: The Role of the Back-bench Member*, First Report, Session 2006–07, HC 337 (The Stationery Office).

Norris, P. (1997) 'The Puzzle of Constituency Service', *The Journal of Legislative Studies*, vol. 3, no. 2.

Norton, P. (1997) 'The United Kingdom: Restoring Confidence?', *Parliamentary Affairs*, vol. 50, no. 3.

Norton, P. (1999a) 'The United Kingdom: Parliament Under Pressure', in Norton, P. (ed.) *Parliaments and Pressure Groups in Western Europe* (Cass).

Norton, P. (1999b) 'The House of Commons: The Half Empty Bottle of Reform', in Jones, B. (ed.) *Political Issues in Britain Today*, 5th edn (Manchester University Press).

Norton, P. (2001a) 'Playing by the Rules: The Constraining Hand of Parliamentary Procedure', *The Journal of Legislative Studies*, vol. 7.

Norton, P. (2001b) 'Parliament', in Seldon, A. (ed.) *The Blair Effect* (Little, Brown).

Norton, P. (2007) 'Four Models of Political Representation: British MPs and the Use of ICT', *The Journal of Legislative Studies*, vol. 13.

Norton, P. (2012a) 'Parliament and Citizens in the United Kingdom', *The Journal of Legislative Studies*, vol. 18.

Norton, P. (2012b) 'Coalition Cohesion', in Heppell, T. and Seawright, D. (eds) *Cameron and the Conservatives* (Palgrave Macmillan).

Norton, P. (2013) *Parliament in British Politics*, 2nd edn (Palgrave Macmillan).

Norton, P. and Wood, D. (1993) *Back from Westminster* (University Press of Kentucky).

Power, G. (1996) *Reinventing Westminster* (Charter 88).

Riddell, P. (2011) *In Defence of Politicians* (Biteback Publishing).

Rosenblatt, G. (2006) *A Year in the Life* (Hansard Society).

Rush, M. (1990) *Pressure Politics* (Oxford University Press).

Weir, S. and Beetham, D. (1999) *Political Power and Democratic Control in Britain* (Routledge).

Williamson, A. (2009) *MPs Online: Connecting with Constituents* (Hansard Society).

Winnett, R. and Rayner, G. (2009) *No Expenses Spared* (Bantam Press).

Useful websites

Parliamentary websites

Parliament: www.parliament.uk

Register of Members' Interests:
www.publications.parliament.uk/pa/cm/cmregmem.htm

Independent Parliamentary Standards Authority (IPSA):
www.parliamentary-standards.org

Committee on Standards in Public Life:
www.public-standards.gov.uk

Commission to Strengthen Parliament (the Norton Report):
www.conservatives.com/pdf/norton.pdf

Constitution Unit, University College London:
www.ucl.ac.uk/constitution-unit/research/parliament

Hansard Society for Parliamentary Government:
www.hansard-society.org.uk

Unlock Democracy: www.unlockdemocracy.org.uk

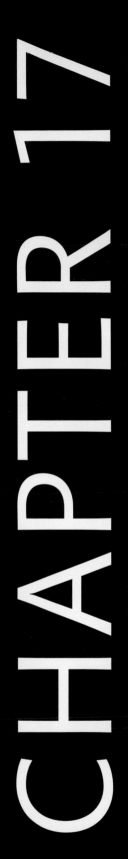

The House of Lords

Philip Norton

> **"The only justification of the [House of] Lords is its irrationality: once you try to make it rational, you satisfy no one "**
>
> Lord Campbell of Eskan

Learning objectives

- To describe the nature, development and role of the House of Lords.

- To identify the extent and consequences of fundamental changes made to the House in recent years.

- To assess proposals for further change to the second chamber.

The House of Lords serves as the second chamber in a **bicameral legislature**. The bicameral system that the United Kingdom now enjoys has been described as one of asymmetrical bicameralism: in other words, there are two chambers, but one is politically inferior to the other. The role of the second chamber in relation to the first moved in the twentieth century from being co-equal to subordinate. As a subordinate chamber, it has carried out tasks that have been recognised as useful to the political system, but it has never fully escaped criticism for the nature of its composition. It was variously reformed at different times in the twentieth century, the most dramatic change coming at the end of the century. Debate continues as to what form the second chamber should take in the twenty-first century.

The House of Lords is remarkable for its longevity. What makes this longevity all the more remarkable are two features peculiar to the House. The first is that it has never been an elected chamber. The second is that, until 1999, the membership of the House was based principally on the hereditary principle. The bulk of the membership comprised **hereditary peers**. Only at the end of the twentieth century were most of the hereditary peers removed. The removal of the hereditary peers was not accompanied by a move to an elected second chamber. Whether the United Kingdom is to have an elected or unelected second chamber remains a matter of dispute. It perhaps says something for the work of the House of Lords that the contemporary debate revolves around what form the second chamber should take rather than whether or not the United Kingdom should have a second chamber.

What, then, is the history of the House of Lords? How has it changed over the past century? What tasks does it currently fulfil? And what shape is it likely to take in the future?

Introduction

History

The House of Lords is generally viewed by historians as having its origins in the Anglo-Saxon *Witenagemot* and more especially its Norman successor, the *Curia Regis* (Court of the King). Two features of the King's *Curia* of the twelfth and thirteenth centuries were to remain central characteristics of the House of Lords. One was the basic composition, comprising the **lords spiritual** and the **lords temporal**. At the time of the Magna Carta, the *Curia* comprised the leading prelates of the kingdom (archbishops, bishops and abbots) and the earls and chief barons. The main change, historically, was to be the shift in balance between the two: the churchmen – the lords spiritual – moved from being a dominant to being a small part of the House. The other significant feature was the basis on which members were summoned. The King's tenants-in-chief attended court because of their position. Various minor barons were summoned because the King wished them to attend. 'From the beginning the will of the king was an element in determining its make up' (White 1908: 299). If a baron regularly received a summons to court, the presumption grew that the summons would be issued to his heir. A body thus developed that peers attended on the basis of a strictly hereditary dignity without reference to tenure. The result was to be a House of Lords based on the principle of heredity, with writs of summons being personal to the recipients. Members were not summoned to speak on behalf of some other individuals or bodies. Any notion of representativeness was squeezed out. Even the lords spiritual – who served by reason of their position in the established Church – were summoned to take part in a personal capacity.

The lack of any representative capacity led to the House occupying a position of political – and later legal – inferiority to the House of Commons. As early as the fifteenth century, the privilege of initiating measures of taxation was conceded to the Lower House. The most significant shift, though, took place in the nineteenth century. As we have seen (Chapters 15 and 16), the effect of the Reform Acts was to consign the Lords to a recognisably subordinate role to that of the Commons, although not until the passage of the Parliament Act of 1911 was that role confirmed by statute. Under the terms of the Act, the House could delay a non-money bill for no more than two sessions, and money bills (those dealing exclusively with money, and so certified by the Speaker) were to become law one month after leaving the Commons whether approved by the House of Lords or not. Bills to prolong the life of a parliament, along with delegated legislation and bills originating in the House of Lords, were excluded from the provisions of the Act. The two-session veto over non-money bills was reduced to one session by the Parliament Act of 1949.

The subordinate position of the House of Lords to the House of Commons was thus established. However, the House remained a subject of political controversy. The hereditary principle was attacked by those who saw no reason for membership of the second chamber to be determined by accident of privileged birth. It was attacked as well because the bulk of the membership tended to favour the Conservative cause. Ever since the eighteenth century, when William Pitt the Younger created peers on an unprecedented scale, the Conservatives enjoyed a political ascendancy (if not always an absolute majority) in the House. In other words, occupying a subordinate position did not render the House acceptable: the composition of the House, however much it was subordinated to the Commons, was unacceptable. There were some attempts in the period of Conservative government from 1951 to 1964 to render it more acceptable, not by removing hereditary peers or destroying the Conservative predominance but rather by supplementing the existing membership with a new type of membership. The Life Peerages Act 1958 made provision for people to be made members for life of the House of Lords, their titles – and the entitlement to a seat in the House of Lords – to cease upon their death. This was designed to strengthen the House by allowing people who objected to the hereditary principle to become members. Following the 1958 Act, few hereditary peerages were created. None was created under Labour governments, and only one Conservative Prime Minister, Margaret Thatcher, nominated any (and then only three – Harold Macmillan, who became the Earl of Stockton; George Thomas, former Speaker of the House of Commons; and William Whitelaw, her Deputy Prime Minister). The 1963 Peerages Act made provision for hereditary peers who wished to do so to **disclaim** their titles. Prior to 1999 these were the most important measures to affect the membership of the House. Although both measures – and especially the 1958 Act – had significant consequences, pressure continued for more radical reform. In 1999, acting on a commitment embodied in the Labour manifesto in the 1997 General Election, the Labour Government achieved passage of the House of Lords Act. This removed from membership of the House all but 92 of the hereditary members. The effect was to transform the House from one composed predominantly of hereditary peers to one composed overwhelmingly of **life peers**. However, the removal of the hereditary peers was seen as but one stage in a process of reform. The House of Lords created by their removal was deemed to be an interim House, to remain in place while proposals for a second stage of reform were considered. The issue of what should constitute the second stage of reform has proved highly contentious.

Membership

Until the passage of the House of Lords Act, which removed most hereditary peers from membership, the House of Lords had more than 1,000 members, making it the largest regularly sitting legislative chamber in the world. Its size was hardly surprising given the number of peers created over the centuries by each succeeding monarch, although the largest increase was in the twentieth century. In 1906 the House had a membership of 602. In January 1999 it had 1,296. Of those, 759 were hereditary peers. (The figure includes one prince and three dukes of the blood royal.) The remaining members comprised 485 life peers, 12 peers created under the Appellate Jurisdiction Act 1876 (the law lords, appointed to carry out the judicial business of the House) and 26 lords spiritual (the two archbishops and 24 senior bishops of the Church of England). With the removal of all but 92 of the hereditary peers, the House remains a relatively large one. In the immediate wake of the removal of the hereditary peers, the House had 666 members. With new creations and deaths, the figure has fluctuated since, but – as we shall see – with a marked upward trajectory. By July 2012 there were formally 816 members. The figure, though, includes 37 peers on leave of absence, 13 who were disqualified while holding senior judicial office and one disqualified while holding office as an MEP. The serving membership was thus 765 (Table 17.1). Of these 765, 650 were life peers created under the provisions of the 1958 Act.

The membership of the House has thus been affected dramatically by the 1958 Life Peerages Act and the 1999 House of Lords Act. In many respects, the former made possible the latter, creating a new pool of members who could serve once hereditary peers were removed. Indeed, the creation of life peerages under the 1958 Act had a dramatic effect on the House in terms both of composition and activity. The impact of the 1999 Act will be considered in greater detail later.

Composition

In terms of composition, the 1958 Act made possible a substantial increase in the number of Labour members. Previously, Labour members had been in a notable minority. In 1924, when Labour first formed a minority government, the party had only one supporter in the Upper House. The position changed only gradually. In 1945 there were 18 Labour peers. Forty-four Labour peers were created in the period of Labour government from 1945 to 1951, but their successors did not always support the Labour Party. By 1999 there were only 17 hereditary peers sitting on the Labour benches. Life peerages enabled Labour's ranks to be swelled over time. Prominent Labour supporters who objected to hereditary peerages were prepared to accept life peerages, so various former ministers, ex-MPs, trade union leaders and other public figures were elevated to the House of Lords. At the beginning of 1999 there were more than 150 life peers sitting on the Labour benches. Apart from former ministers and MPs, they included figures such as the broadcaster Melvyn Bragg, film producer David Puttnam, crime writer Ruth Rendell, and TV presenter, professor and doctor Robert Winston. Further creations helped bring the number above 200 and in the 2005–6 session the party became the largest single party in the House. In July 2012 (see Table 17.1), there were 226 Labour peers as against 213 Conservatives.

The creation of life peers from 1958 onwards served to lessen the party imbalance in the House. In 1945 Conservative peers accounted for 50.4 per cent of the membership. In 1998 the figure was 38.4 per cent (Baldwin 1999). Before 1999 the second largest category in the House comprised those peers who choose to sit independently of party ranks and occupy the cross-benches in the House. At the beginning of 1999 – that is, in the pre-reform House – the state of the parties was Conservative 473, Labour 168, Liberal Democrats 67 and cross-benchers 322. This left in excess of 250 other peers who did not align themselves with any of these groupings. The effect of the removal of most hereditary peers in 1999 was to create greater equality between the two main parties, leaving – as shown in Table 17.1 – the balance of power being held by the cross-benchers and the Liberal Democrats.

The creation of life peers drawn from modest backgrounds has also served to affect the social profile of the

Table 17.1 Composition of the House of Lords, 2 July 2012

By party				
Party	Life peers	Hereditary	Bishops	Total
Conservative	164	49	0	213
Labour	222	4	0	226
Liberal Democrat	86	4	0	90
Cross-bench	146	31	0	177
Bishops	0	0	26	26
Other[1]	32	1	0	33
Total	**650**	**89**	**26**	**765**

NB: Excludes 37 Members who are on leave of absence, and 14 disqualified as judges or MEPs.

1 These comprise non-affiliated peers and peers who sit as members of other political parties, such as Democrat Unionists and UKIP.

Source: www.parliament.uk

membership. Hereditary peers were typically drawn from the cream of upper-class society, including those who owned great estates. Life peers were drawn from a more diverse social background, ranging from some former miners who had served in the House of Commons to leading figures in business. However, even with the influx of life peers, the membership remained, and remains, socially atypical. Life peerages are normally conferred on those who have achieved some particular distinction in society, be it social, cultural, sporting, economic or political. By the time the recipients have achieved such a distinction, they are, by definition, atypical. There was therefore little chance of the House becoming socially typical. Members of the House are drawn notably from backgrounds in the law, the civil service and the teaching profession, these three categories accounting for nearly 40 per cent of the membership

(Criddle et al. 2005: 34–5). The next largest category – accounting for just nearly 5 per cent of the membership – is that of trade union officials. The House is also atypical in terms of age and gender. Given that peerages tend to be given to those who have already achieved something in life and that they entail service for life, it is not surprising that the average age of the membership is 69. It is rare for people to be made life peers while in their 20s or 30s. Television mogul Lord Alli (born 1964) was elevated to the peerage in 1998 at the age of 34. Lawyer and Conservative Party co-chair Baroness Warsi (b. 1971) became a peer in 2007 at the age of 36. The hereditary peerage produced some young peers, succeeding their fathers at an early age, but they were small in number and largely disappeared as a result of the House of Lords Act, though not entirely. One hereditary peer, Lord Freyberg (born 1970), entered the House at the

The Chamber of the House of Lords
Source: Rolf Richardson/Alamy

age of 23. Women, who were first admitted to the House under the provisions of the 1958 Life Peerages Act, also constitute a minority of the membership, but a growing one. In 1990, there were 80 women in the House, constituting 7 per cent of the membership. The removal of a large number of – overwhelmingly male – hereditary peers and the creation of more women life peers has meant that the number, and proportion, of women peers has increased notably. By July 2012 they constituted 22 per cent of the membership. Of these, all bar two held life peerages. Recent years have seen several black and Asian peers created; although they constitute a small proportion of the total, the proportion is greater than in the House of Commons. There are also a number of openly gay peers, including Lord Alli, former Cabinet ministers Lord Mandelson and Lord Smith of Finsbury, former head of BP Lord Browne of Madingley, former head of British Midlands airline Lord Glendonbrook, and executive director of the Telegraph Media Group Lord Black of Brentwood.

There has been another consequence of life peerages in terms of the membership of the House. It has brought into the House a body of individuals who are frequently expert in a particular area or have experience in a particular field. This claim is not exclusive to life peers – some hereditary peers are notable for their expertise or experience in particular fields – but it is associated predominantly with them. This has led to claims that when the House debates a subject, however arcane it may be, there is usually one or more experts in the House to discuss it (Baldwin 1985). Thus, for example, in a short debate held on 9 July 2012 on the long-term strategy for the arts and culture sector in the UK, those taking part included Lord Hall of Birkenhead, Chief Executive of the Royal Opera House; Lord Lloyd-Webber (Andrew Lloyd-Webber), the theatre impresario; Baroness Hooper, a former governor of the Royal Ballet; Baroness Young of Hornsey, a former actress and professor of cultural studies; Baroness McIntosh of Hudnall, who had been chief executive of the Royal National Theatre; former BBC producer Baroness Bonham-Carter of Yarnbury; and the actress and TV presenter Baroness Benjamin (Floella Benjamin). The same week the House was discussing the Justice and Security Bill. Among peers taking part in considering amendments to the Bill were those who had held the posts of Lord Chief Justice (Lord Woolf QC), Head of MI5 (Baroness Maningham-Buller), Lord Chancellor (Lord Falconer of Thoroton QC), Defence Secretary (Lord King of Bridgwater), the Government's independent reviewer of terrorism legislation (Lord Carlile of Berriew QC), and deputy high court judge (Lord Thomas of Gresford QC), as well as other leading lawyers such as Lord Faulks QC, human rights lawyer Lord Lester of Herne Hill QC and *Times* columnist Lord Pannick QC.

This claim to expertise in many fields is often contrasted with membership of the House of Commons, where the career politician – expert in the practice of politics – dominates. The body of expertise and experience serves, as we shall see, to bolster the capacity of the House to fulfil a number of its functions.

Activity

The creation of life peers also had a dramatic effect on the activity of the House. In the 1950s the House met at a leisurely pace and was poorly attended. Peers have never been paid a salary and many members, like the minor barons in the thirteenth century, found attending to be a chore, sometimes an expensive one: the practice, as in the thirteenth century, was to stay away. The House rarely met for more than three days a week, and each sitting was usually no more than three or four hours in length. For most of the decade, the average daily attendance did not reach three figures. Little interest was shown in its activities by most of its own members; not surprisingly, little interest was shown by those outside the House.

This was to change significantly in each succeeding decade (see Table 17.2). Life peers were disproportionately active. Although they constituted a minority of the House, they came to constitute a majority of the most active members of the House. The effect of the increasing numbers of life peers was apparent in the attendance of members. Peers attended in ever greater numbers and the House sat for longer. Late-night sittings, virtually unknown in the 1950s and for much of the 1960s, became regular features. In the 1980s and 1990s the average daily sitting was six or seven hours. By the end of the 1980s more than 800 peers – two-thirds of the membership – attended one or more sittings each year and, of those, more than 500 contributed to debate. By the time of the House of Lords Act in 1999, the House was boasting a better attendance in the chamber than the House of Commons. The effect of the 1999 Act was to result in a House in which the active members dominated. Although the membership halved in 1999, the daily attendance hardly changed. While the average daily attendance figure for 1992–3 constituted just under one-third of the membership, that for the post-reform 2003–4 session constitutes more than half. In the 2003–4 session 50 per cent of the members attended 65 per cent or more of the sittings – a remarkable achievement given that many members had full-time posts outside the House, attending in order to give the benefit of their expertise. The House now witnesses an average daily attendance that exceeds 450 (Table 17.2).

Table 17.2 House of Lords sittings and daily attendance

Session	Number of days sat	Average daily attendance	Number of hours sat	Number of peers
1960–61	125	142	599	918
1961–62	115	143	544	932
1962–63	127	140	698	987
1998–99	154	446	1,171	1,325
1999–00	177	352	1,325	693
2000–01[1]	76	347	508	679
2001–02[2]	200	370	1,395	694
2002–03	174	362	1,262	682
2003–04	157	368	1,094	707
2004–05[1]	63	388	459	706
2005–06[2]	206	403	1,372	751
2006–07	142	415	926	751
2007–08	164	413	1,110	744
2008–09	134	400	907	736
2009–10[1]	68	388	445	735
2010–12[3]	242	468	1,712	826

1 Short session.
2 Long session.
3 Long session: figures up to November 2011.

Source: House of Lords Library Note, *Work of the House of Lords: Statistics*, LLN 2012/009, 2012.

One other consequence of the more active House was that the number of votes increased. They were few and far between in the 1950s, about 10 to 20 a year. By the 1980s and 1990s, the figure was usually closer to 200. The political composition of the House meant that a Labour government was vulnerable to defeat. In the period of Labour government from 1974 to 1979, the government suffered 362 defeats at the hands of the House of Lords. However, Conservative governments were not immune. The preponderance of Conservative peers did not always translate into a majority for a Conservative government. In the period of Conservative government from 1979 to 1997, ministers suffered just over 250 defeats in the House. The government was vulnerable to a combination of opposition parties, the cross-benchers and, on occasion, some of its own supporters. The Labour Government elected in 1997 was vulnerable to defeat, at least for the first two sessions, because of the large number of Conservative peers. With the removal of most hereditary peers in 1999, it could not be defeated by the Conservatives alone but was vulnerable to defeat because of a combination of opposition parties or of the opposition and cross-benchers or of all the opposition parties and a preponderance of cross-benchers. In its 13 years in power (1997–2010), the Labour

Government suffered 528 defeats; of these, 458 took place in the post-1999 reformed House. With the formation of the Coalition in 2010, the Government was vulnerable to defeat by a combination of the Labour Opposition and a large number of cross-benchers. Under the Labour Government, the Liberal Democrats had been primarily the swing voters, whereas under the Coalition Government it was the cross-benchers. In the first, long session of 2010–12, the Coalition Government was defeated 48 times, primarily on occasions when large numbers of cross-bench peers attended and divided disproportionately against the Government.

The House also became more visible to the outside world. In 1985 television cameras were allowed to broadcast proceedings. There was a four-year gap before the televising of Commons proceedings began: in those four years, the House of Lords enjoyed exclusive television coverage. In the 1990s the House was also ahead of the House of Commons in appointing an information officer and seeking to ensure better public understanding of its role and activities. The Information Office of the House has been highly active in disseminating information about the work of the House, generating booklets and information packs for which the House of Commons has no equivalent.

BOX 17.1

The atmosphere in the House

The House of Lords is stunning in its grandeur. For some, it is awe-inspiring; for others, it is suffocating. The House combines crown, Church and a chamber of the legislature. The magnificent throne dominates the chamber. On entering the chamber, a peer bows to the cloth of estate – just above the throne – as a mark of respect. (Unlike the Commons, there is no bowing when leaving the chamber.) Look up and you see the magnificent stained glass windows. Look down and you see the red benches of a debating chamber. The House combines symbolism with the efficiency of a working body. From the bar of the House you see the throne: lower your eye-line and you see the laptop computer on the table of the House. The clerks sit in their wigs and gowns, using the laptop as well as controlling the button for resetting the digital clocks in the chamber.

On Mondays to Thursdays the benches are usually packed for the start of business. The combination of increasing attendance and a relatively small chamber means that peers often have to get in early to get their preferred spot on the benches. (Unlike the Commons, one cannot reserve a seat in advance.) The Lord Speaker's procession mirrors that of the Speaker of the House of Commons in its pomp and dignity. Peers bow as the mace passes. Once the Lord Speaker has taken her place on the Woolsack, prayers are said. Once these are over, members of the public are admitted to the gallery and other peers come into the chamber. At the start of Question Time, the Clerk of the Parliaments, sitting bewigged at the table, rises and announces the name of the peer who has the first question on the Order Paper. The peer rises and declares, 'I beg leave to ask the question standing in my name on the Order Paper'. The answering minister rises to the despatch box and reads out a prepared response. The peer rises to put a supplementary, followed later by others. If two peers rise at the same time, one is expected to give way; otherwise, as a self-regulating chamber, it is members who decide – usually by calling out the name of the peer they wish to hear, or else by shouting 'this side', indicating that the last supplementary was put by someone on the other side of the House. If neither gives way, the Leader of the House usually intervenes, but the Leader can be overruled by the House. Normally, but not always, good manners prevail.

Peers take a lively interest in questions. There are approximately seven or eight minutes available for each question. If time on a question goes beyond that, peers shout 'next question'. Ministers need to be well briefed. It is usually obvious when ministers are out of their depth or have been caught out. Question Time can be educational. The topics are diverse and usually there is knowledge on the part of questioners and ministers. If a minister runs into trouble, the fact that the chamber is packed adds to the tension. Question Time can also be funny. When a minister, questioned about the use of mobile phones on aeroplanes, faced a supplementary about the perils of mobile telephones 'on terra firma', he did not hear the full supplementary and had to ask a colleague. Realising he had taken some time to return to the despatch box, he rose and said: 'I am sorry, My Lords, I thought terra firma might be some obscure airline!' On another occasion, a question about the safety of a female chimpanzee that had been mistreated received a very detailed answer, which included the facts – as I recall – that the chimp was now in a sanctuary with other chimps, that the group was led by a male of a certain age and that the chimp was enjoying herself. Whereupon the redoubtable Baroness Trumpington got to her feet and declared: 'My Lords, she is better off than I am!'

The House of Lords is a remarkably egalitarian institution: members are peers in the true sense. The atmosphere of the House can be tense, sometimes exciting – the results of votes are frequently uncertain – and occasionally a little rough. Maiden speeches, given priority in debates and heard in respectful silence (peers cannot enter or leave the chamber while they are taking place), can be nerve-wracking, even for the most experienced of public speakers. Most of the time the House has the feel of what it is: a working body, engaged in debate and legislative scrutiny. The emphasis is on constructive debate and revision. Partisan shouting matches are rare. At times, especially at the committee stage of bills, attendance can be small, the main debate taking place between the two front benches, but the effect of the probing from the opposition benches ensures that ministers have to offer informed responses. Notes frequently pass from civil servants in the officials' box to the minister at the despatch box. The quality of ministers can be very good. Ministers who are well regarded and who take the House seriously can rely on the occasional indulgence of the House if they make a slip. The responsibilities of some ministers mean that they spend a great deal of time in the chamber.

The only way to appreciate the atmosphere, and the productive nature of the House, is to be there. One certainly cannot glean it from television – the House is squeezed out by the Commons – or from the official report. *Hansard* is good at tidying up speeches, correcting grammar and titles. The tidying-up can also have the effect of sanitising proceedings. During the passage of the Access to Justice Bill, Conservative Baroness Wilcox – a champion of consumers – moved an amendment dealing with consumer affairs. The Lord Chancellor, to the delight – and obvious surprise – of Lady Wilcox, promptly accepted the import of the amendment. Lady Wilcox rose and exclaimed 'Gosh. Thanks'. This appeared in *Hansard* as 'I thank the noble and learned Lord. He has pleased me very much today'! When the House collapses in laughter – as it did after the minister's terra firma remark or Baroness Trumpington's intervention – this either appears in *Hansard* as 'Noble Lords: Oh!' or else is ignored. No, one definitely has to be there to appreciate the atmosphere.

Procedures

The House differs significantly from the Commons not only in its size, composition and remuneration (peers can claim a daily attendance allowance – to cover accommodation, subsistence and some secretarial support – as well as travel costs, but they still receive no salary) but also in its procedures. The presiding officer of the House, who sits on the Woolsack, has no powers to call peers to speak or to enforce order. The maintenance of the rules of order is the responsibility of the House itself, although peers usually look to the Leader of the House to give a lead. Peers wishing to speak in a set-piece debate, such as a second reading debate, submit their names in advance (they can now do so electronically), and a list of speakers is circulated shortly prior to the debate. Peers then rise to speak in the order on the list. At other times, as in Question Time, if two peers rise at the same time, one is expected to give way. (If neither does so, other peers make clear their preference as to who should speak by shouting out the name of the person they wish to hear.) If a speaker strays from what is permissible, other peers shout 'Order'. If a speaker goes on for too long, it is always open to another peer to rise and call attention to the fact (a task normally undertaken by the government whip on duty) or, in extreme cases, to move the motion 'That the noble peer be no longer heard', but this is a device rarely employed. The Lords remains a more chamber-oriented institution than the Commons, although – as we shall see – it is making more use of committees than before. Although the House votes more frequently than it used to, the number of divisions in the Lords is fewer than in the Commons. (There will usually be about three times as many votes each year in the Commons as in the Lords.) This, in part, reflects the recognition by peers of the political predominance of the elected chamber. Peers are often reluctant to press issues to a vote and rarely do so on the principle of a measure. By virtue of an agreement reached between the two party leaders in the Lords in 1945, the House does not divide on the second reading of any bill promised in the government's election manifesto and, by extension now, any bill appearing in the government's programme for the session. This is known as the Salisbury convention, named after the Conservative leader in the Lords who enunciated it.

There are also two other features where it differs from the Commons and which enhance its capacity to affect the outcome of legislation. First, the House discusses all amendments tabled to bills. In the Commons the chair selects only a limited number for debate. Second, there are no timetable (guillotine) motions. Debate continues so long as peers wish to speak. There are also considerable opportunities for peers to raise issues in the House. Some debates are time-limited (although not the committee and report stages of bills) and a 15-minute time limit operates for backbench speeches in set-piece debates. Peers keep their speeches even shorter if a great many of them sign up to speak in a time-limited debate. Time limits force peers to think about what they want to say and ensure that they focus on the main points. The results tend to be a series of short, informed and often highly educative speeches.

Functions

The debate about reform of the House of Lords has focused largely, though not wholly, on its composition. The functions of the House – the tasks that it carries out – have not generated as much controversy. There has been a wide body of agreement that the functions it fulfilled in the twentieth century, and continues to fulfill in the twenty-first, are appropriate to a second chamber. As we shall see, this view is not necessarily held by all those expressing views on the House of Lords. Nonetheless, the view has tended to predominate among those engaged in the debate, including the government of the day. The functions are broadly similar to those of the Commons but not as extensive. The extent to which they differ derives from the fact that politically the House is no longer co-equal with the Commons.

Legitimisation

The House fulfils the functions of both manifest and latent legitimisation, but it does so on a modest scale. It is called upon to give the seal of approval to bills, but if it fails to give that approval, it can be overridden later by the House of Commons under the provisions of the Parliament Acts. Only in very rare circumstances – as in the case of a bill to lengthen the life of a parliament, secondary legislation or (somewhat more significantly) bills originating in the Lords – is its veto absolute. By virtue of being one of the two chambers of Parliament and by fulfilling the functions it does effectively, the House may have a limited claim to fulfilling a function of latent legitimisation. It is a long-established part of the nation's constitutional arrangements. However, such a claim is offset by the House having no claim to being a representative assembly – neither speaking for particular bodies in society nor being socially typical – and by its limited legislative authority. A claim to traditional authority has been superseded by a claim to specialised knowledge, the House being able to draw on experience and expertise in considering the measures before it, but that 'technocratic' legitimacy is not on a par with the legitimacy of the elected chamber.

Recruitment

The House provides some of the personnel of government. As we have seen (Chapter 9), ministers are drawn from Parliament and, by convention, predominantly now from the elected House.

The Prime Minister appoints a number of ministers from the Upper House primarily for political and managerial reasons. Although the government is normally assured of getting its bills through the House, it is not necessarily guaranteed getting them through in the form it wants them. It is therefore prudent to have ministers in the Lords in order to explain bills and to marshal support. In addition, the House provides a pool from which the Prime Minister can draw in order to supplement ministers drawn from the Commons. The advantage offered by peers is that, with no constituency responsibilities, they are able to devote more time to ministerial work than is the case with ministers who do have constituency duties. It also has the advantage of widening the pool of talent available to the Prime Minister. Someone from outside Parliament can be elevated to the peerage at the same time as being appointed to government office. Labour Prime Ministers Tony Blair and Gordon Brown

made use of this power to enhance the ranks of their ministerial team, each bringing in a range of people from industry, the law, broadcasting, the health service, finance, the military, the EU, the UN, as well as some Downing Street advisers, to serve as ministers. Conservative Prime Minister David Cameron has continued the practice, though not on quite the same scale. He brought in three people with City experience (Lord Sassoon, Lord Green of Hurstpierpoint, and Lord Freud, though the last of these was made a peer when the party was still in opposition) and a former member of the No. 10 Policy Unit under John Major (Lord Hill of Oareford).

Ministerial appointments in the Lords have also enabled women politicians to be promoted. Five women have served as Leaders of the House of Lords (Baroness Young 1981–2, Baroness Jay 1998–2001, Baroness Amos 2003–7, Baroness Ashton 2007–8, and Baroness Royall 2008–10). Baroness Amos was the first black woman to serve in the Cabinet. Of the ministers in the Lords in mid-2012, just under one-third were women, including the Chief Whip, Baroness Anelay of St Johns.

However, the number of ministers appointed in the Lords is relatively small. At least two peers have traditionally served in the Cabinet (Lord Chancellor and Leader of the House) but usually no more than four. Four is a rarity and two, until 2005, the norm. Under the Constitutional Reform Act 2005 the Lord Chancellor need no longer be a peer; Jack Straw was the first MP to be appointed to the post and his two Conservative successors – Kenneth Clarke (2010–12) and Chris Garyling (2012–) – also sat in the Commons. There is thus now only the Leader of the House who sits automatically in the Cabinet. However, there have been occasions when a peer has been appointed to head a department. Gordon Brown appointed two peers to head departments: Business Secretary Lord Mandelson and Transport Secretary Lord Adonis. Usually about 20 other ministers are drawn from the Lords, supplemented by eight whips (including the Chief Whip). The number of ministers does not match the number of ministries, with the result that the whips have to take on responsibility for answering for particular departments – another difference from the House of Commons, where the whips have no responsibility for appearing at the despatch box. Even with a small number of posts to be filled, governments have on occasion had difficulty in finding suitable peers for ministerial office. It used to be the case that Conservative governments had sometimes to draw on young hereditary peers. Labour governments were limited by the relatively small number of Labour peers. The creation of life peerages in recent years, quantitatively and qualitatively, has widened the pool of talent. Both sides have tended to use the Whips' Office as a training ground for substantive ministerial office.

Scrutiny and influence

It is in its remaining functions that the House of Lords is significant. The House performs an important role as an agent of scrutiny and influence. The House does not undertake the task of scrutiny on behalf of constituents, as peers have none. Rather, the House undertakes a more general task of scrutiny. Three features of the House render it particularly suitable for the detailed scrutiny of legislation. First, as an unelected House, it cannot claim the legitimacy to reject the principle of measures agreed by the elected House. Thus, basically by default, it focuses on the detail rather than the principle. Second, as we have noted already, its membership includes people who have distinguished themselves in particular fields – such as the sciences, the law, education, business, industrial relations – who can look at relevant legislation from the perspective of practitioners in the field rather than from the perspective of elected party politicians. And, third, the House has the time to debate non-money bills in more detail than is usually possible in the Commons – as we have seen, there is no provision for a guillotine, and all amendments are discussed. The House thus serves as an important chamber of legislative scrutiny, trying to ensure that a bill is well drafted and internally coherent. In order to improve the bill, it will often make amendments, most of which will be accepted by the Commons. In terms of legislative scrutiny, the House has thus developed a role that is viewed as complementary to, rather than one competing with (or identical to), that of the Commons.

The value of the House as a revising chamber is shown by the number of amendments it makes to legislation. Most of these are moved by the government itself, but a significant proportion of these are amendments promised by government in response to comments made by backbench members. Each session, the House will typically agree anything between 500 to 4,000 amendments to bills. (In the 1999–2000 session, the number of amendments made totalled 4,761, constituting an all-time record.) In the 2007–8 session, of 7,259 amendments that were tabled, 2,625 were agreed (House of Lords 2008). In the 2009–10 session, cut short by the 2010 General Election, 565 amendments were agreed. Most were agreed at committee stage (Table 17.3).

Even these figures do not do justice to the scrutiny undertaken by the Lords. The scrutiny is frequently constructive and is acknowledged as such by the government. Thus, for example, during the 1998–99 session, 108 non-government amendments were moved to the Access to Justice Bill. Of these, 71 received a ministerial response that was positive. The responses were important not only for their number but also for their range: they included promising to consider points raised in debate (28 occasions),

Table 17.3 Amendments agreed to Government Bills in the House of Lords, 2009–10

Stage	Amendments agreed
Committee	
Committee of Whole House	323
Grand Committee	32
Report	171
Third Reading	36
Consideration of Commons amendments	3

accepting the principle of an amendment (21 occasions) and promising to draw a point to the attention of those responsible for drafting the bill (three occasions) (Norton 1999). Ten amendments were accepted as they stood. The constructive work undertaken by the House was conceded by the Lord Chancellor, Lord Irvine of Lairg, at the conclusion of the bill's passage through the House. The importance of these figures lay not only in the number of constructive responses from government but also in the fact that it is difficult to envisage scrutiny in the House of Commons producing such a response.

This role in scrutinising legislation – in so far as it constitutes a 'second look' at legislation – is of special importance given that it has been characterised as one of the two core functions of the House (Norton 1999), meaning that it is a function that is particular to the House as the second chamber. It is not a function that the House of Commons can carry out, since it is difficult if not impossible for it to act as a revising chamber for its own measures; that has been likened to asking the same doctor for a second opinion. The role of the House as a revising chamber is thus offered as being central to the case for retaining a second chamber. It is also the role that occupies the most time in the House: usually about 50 to 60 per cent is devoted to considering legislation.

The House also scrutinises, and on occasion influences, government policy. Peers can debate policy in a less partisan atmosphere than the Commons and are not subject to the constituency and party influences that dominate in the elected House. They are therefore in a position to debate issues of public policy that may not be at the heart of the partisan battle and which, consequently, receive little attention in the Commons. Given their backgrounds, peers are also often – although not always – able to debate public policy from the perspective of those engaged in the subject. The House is able to debate higher education, for example, with considerable authority. The Lords contains several distinguished academics and members with experience in higher education (university chancellors, vice-chancellors and pro-vice-chancellors, masters of university colleges, peers who have chaired HE funding bodies, led enquiries into higher education, and former secretaries of state for education); although the House of Commons contains some former university lecturers, it does not have members with the same experience and status in education as those in the Upper House.

Expression

The House, like the Commons, also fulfils a number of expressive functions. It can bring issues onto the political agenda in a way not always possible in the Commons. MPs are wary of raising issues that may not be popular with constituents and that have little salience in terms of party politics. Peers can raise whatever issues they feel need raising. The House may thus debate issues of concern to particular groups in society that MPs are not willing to address. Formally, it is not a function the House is expected to fulfil. Indeed, according to *Erskine May*, the parliamentary 'bible' on procedure, Lords may indicate that an outside body agrees with the substance of their views, but they should avoid creating an impression that they are speaking as representatives of outside bodies. Thus, not only is the House not a representative assembly, it should avoid giving the impression of being one! In practice, peers take up issues that concern them, often alerted to the issue by outside bodies. Peers are frequently lobbied by outside organisations. One extensive survey in the 1990s found that half of the groups surveyed were in touch with peers at least once a month, and almost one in five were in contact on a weekly basis (Baggott 1995: 93, 164). Each peer receives letters each year usually running into four figures, most from outside organisations. Some groups write to ask peers to move amendments to bills, some merely keep members informed of what is happening, and some are keen that peers raise issues with government, if necessary on the floor of the House. Some peers are particularly active in raising the concerns of particular groups, such as farmers, the disabled, the terminally ill, or the people of Zimbabwe, or pursuing very particular issues, such as railways, the effects of smoking or the upkeep of war graves.

The House also has the potential to express views to citizens and influence their stance on public policy. The function is limited by the absence of any democratic legitimacy, the capacity to influence deriving from the longevity of the House and its place as one of the two chambers of Parliament, as well as from the authority of the individual peers who may be involved. However, the scope for fulfilling this function is somewhat greater than in the House of Commons, simply because more time is available for it in the House of Lords. Between 20 and 30 per cent of the time of the House is given over each session to debates on motions tabled by peers: about 20 per cent of time is given over to general

debates, and between 4 and 10 per cent of the time is given over to questions for short debate (QSDs), each lasting for 60 or 90 minutes.

Other functions

To these functions may be added a number of others, some of which are peculiar to the Upper House. Foremost among these historically has been the judicial function. The House until 2009 constituted the highest court of appeal within the United Kingdom. Although formally a function residing in the House as a whole, in practice it was carried out by a judicial committee comprising 12 **law lords** – judges specially appointed to the House to enable it to fulfil its judicial role – and peers who have held high judicial office. The law lords, though members of the House, avoided speaking on any matters that may be deemed partisan or involve measures on which they may later have had to adjudicate in a judicial capacity. They also normally abstained from voting, though on occasion a law lord voted on an issue that had been the subject of a free vote. However, this long-standing judicial function ceased to reside in the House in 2009, when a new Supreme Court, created under the Constitutional Reform Act 2005, came into being (see Chapter 13) and the law lords moved from the Palace of Westminster to form the justices of the new court.

Like the Commons, the House also retains a small legislative role, primarily in the form of private members' legislation. Peers can introduce private members' bills, and a small number achieve passage, but it is small – even compared with the number of such bills promoted by MPs. The introduction of such bills by peers is more important in fulfilling an expressive function – allowing views on the subject to be aired – than in fulfilling a legislative role. Time is normally found to debate each private member's bill and, by convention, the government – even if opposed to the measure – does not divide against it. Among contentious issues raised by such bills has been that of decriminalising the actions of those seeking to assist terminally ill individuals who wish to bring their lives to an end (assisted dying). The Assisted Dying Bill introduced by Lord Joffe in the 2004–5 session helped ensure that the issue was discussed and enabled people with views on the issue to make them known. The time given to private members' legislation is important but not extensive: as in the Commons, it occupies usually less than 5 per cent of the time of the House.

The House is also ascribed a distinct role, that of a constitutional safeguard. This is reflected in the provisions of the Parliament Acts. The House, as we have noted, retains a veto over bills to extend the life of a parliament. It is considered a potential brake on a government that seeks to act in a dictatorial or generally unacceptable manner: hence, it may use its limited power to amend or, more significantly, to delay a bill. In practice, though, the power is a limited one, as well as one not expected to require action by the House on any regular basis. The House lacks an elected base of its own that would allow it to act, on a substantial and sustained basis, contrary to the wishes of an elected government. Even so, it constitutes the other core function of the House in that it is a function that the House alone, as the second chamber, can fulfil: the House of Commons cannot act as a constitutional check upon itself.

In combination, these various functions render the House a useful body – especially as a revising chamber and for raising and debating issues on which peers are well informed – but one that is clearly subordinate to the elected chamber. The fact that the House is not elected explains its limited functions; it is also the reason why it is considered particularly suited to fulfil the functions it does retain.

Scrutiny and influence

The means available to the House to fulfil the tasks of scrutiny and influence can be considered, as with the Commons, under two heads: legislation and executive actions. The means available to the House are also those available to fulfil its expressive functions.

Legislation

As we have seen, 50 to 60 per cent of the time of the chamber is given over to legislation. Bills in the Lords have to go through stages analogous to those in the House of Commons. There are, though, differences in procedure. First readings are normally taken formally, but there have been rare occasions when they have been debated: on four occasions (in 1888, 1933, 1943 and 1969) first readings were actually opposed. Second readings, as in the Commons, constitute debates on the principle of the measure. However, votes on second reading are exceptionally rare. Because of the Salisbury convention, the House does not vote on the second reading of government bills. A vote may take place if, as exceptionally happens, a free vote is permitted. This happened in 1990 on the War Crimes Bill and in 1999 on the Sexual Offences (Amendment) Bill to lower the age of consent for homosexual acts to 16. Both bills had been passed by large majorities in the House of Commons but both were rejected, on free votes, in the House of Lords. Both occasions were exceptional. Both measures were later enacted under the provisions of the Parliament Act.

The main work of the House takes place at committee and report stages. For some bills, the committee stage is actually dispensed with. After second reading, a motion may be moved 'That this Bill be not committed' and, if agreed to, the bill then awaits third reading. This procedure is usually employed for supply and money bills when there is no desire to present amendments. For those bills that do receive a committee stage, it is taken either on the floor of the House or in grand committee. Virtually all bills used to be taken on the floor of the House, but now in order to ensure that the House continues to examine all bills in detail, several are considered in grand committee.

The grand committee is, in effect, something of a parallel chamber. It comprises all members of the House and can meet while the House is in session. In practice, attendance is relatively small – comprising those with a particular interest in the measure – permitting sessions to be held in the Moses Room, an ornate committee room just off the Peers' Lobby. Votes cannot take place in grand committee, so amendments can only be accepted if no member objects. (If objection is made, the matter has to be held over to report stage.) Of 1,769 amendments moved in grand committee in 2007–8, 357 were accepted.

More recently, the House has also experimented with sending a bill to a special procedure public bill committee, which is empowered to take oral and written evidence. Of longer standing is the power to refer a bill, or indeed any proposal, to a select committee for detailed investigation. It is a power that has been utilised when it has been considered necessary or desirable to examine witnesses and evidence from outside bodies. Between 1972 and 1991 seven bills were sent to select committees. All bar one of the bills were private members' bills. More recently, select committees have been appointed to consider a major government bill (the Constitutional Reform Bill) and a Private Member's Bill (the Assisted Dying for the Terminally Ill Bill).

Committee stage in the Lords differs notably from committee stage in the Commons. In the Lords, all amendments tabled are debated and – whether on the floor or in Grand Committee – any peer can attend the proceedings. All peers with an interest or expertise in a measure can thus take part, be it for the whole of the committee stage or on particular amendments of interest to them. There is thus the potential for a more thorough consideration than is possible in the Commons. The emphasis is on ensuring that the bill is well drafted and coherent.

Report and third reading provide further opportunities for consideration. Again, all amendments tabled are debated. Report may be used by government to bring forward amendments promised at committee stage and also to offer new amendments of its own. It is also an opportunity for members to return to issues that received an inadequate response by government at committee stage (although amendments rejected by the House at committee stage cannot again be considered). It is also possible for amendments to be made at third reading, and this opportunity is variously employed. The motion for third reading is put formally and agreed to and then amendments are taken. Once they have been dealt with, the motion 'That the Bill do now pass' is put. The result is that some bills, especially large or contentious bills, can and do receive a considerable amount of attention at different stages in the House of Lords.

Executive actions

As in the House of Commons, various means are available for scrutinising the actions of the executive. The principal means available on the floor of the House are those of debate and questions. Off the floor of the House, there are select committees and, at the unofficial level, party meetings.

Debates

Debates, as in the Commons, take place on motions. These may express a particular view or they may take the form of 'take note' motions. 'Take note' motions are employed in order to allow the House to debate reports from select committees or matters backbenchers wish to raise or to discuss topics on which the government wishes to hear peers' views.

All peers who wish to speak in debate do so, and there is a greater likelihood than in the Commons that the proceedings will constitute what they purport to be: that is, debates. Party ties are less rigid than in the Commons, though nonetheless still strong (see Norton 2003), and peers frequently pay attention to what is being said. Although in set-piece debates, such as Second Reading debates or Questions for Short Debate, the order in which peers speak is determined beforehand, it is common practice for a peer who is speaking to give way to interventions. Within the context of the chamber, the chances of a speech having an impact on the thought and even the votes of others are considerably greater than in the more predictable Lower House. Indeed, it is not unknown for peers when, uncertain as to how to vote, to ask 'what does X think about it?'

One day each week is given over to two general debates, up until the Whit recess. (The debate day used to be Wednesday but in 2005 the House agreed to change it to Thursday.) Once a month the debates are determined by ballot. Peers wishing to have debates submit motions which then appear on the order paper and two are drawn at random by the clerk on a set day. The topics on the remaining debate days are allocated to each of the parties in turn and to the cross-benchers. The two debates last up to a total of five hours. The balloted debates are automatically each of

two-and-a-half hours in length. On the party days, the time, within the five-hour maximum, is varied depending on the number of speakers. These general debates are occasions for issues to be raised by backbenchers rather than front-benchers. The purpose of each short debate is to allow peers to discuss a particular topic rather than to come to a conclusion about it. Topics discussed tend to be non-partisan, and the range is broad. On 28 June 2012, for example, Lord Addington (Liberal Democrat) moved a motion to call attention to accessible education and training for those with hidden disabilities and Lord Cormack (Conservative) moved a motion to call attention to the future of English cathedrals. Both motions provided the opportunity for interested peers to offer their views and for ministers to explain the government's position and to reveal what proposals were under consideration by the relevant department. The time devoted to each debate is divided equally among the number of backbench speakers (the opener and the minister replying have fixed time limits) and, in the event of many peers wishing to speak, the time available to each may be as little as four or five minutes.

Questions

Questions taken on the floor in the Lords are of two types: oral questions and questions for short debate (QSD). (Lords may also table questions for written answer, and nowadays they do so in increasing numbers: more than 5,000 in an average session.) Oral questions are taken in Question Time at the start of each sitting: the House sits at 2.30 pm on Monday and Tuesday, 3.00 pm on Wednesday and 11.00 am on Thursday. (If sitting on a Friday, it sits at 10.00 am but no questions are taken.) Question Time lasts for up to a maximum of 30 minutes and no more than four questions may be taken. Questions are similar to those tabled for oral answer in the Commons, although – unlike in the Commons – they are addressed to Her Majesty's Government and not to a particular minister (see Figure 17.1). Also, there is no departmental rota: the questions may be to different departments. A question to an environment minister, for example, may be followed by one to a defence minister. A peer rises to ask the question appearing in his or her name on the order paper, the relevant minister (or whip) replies for the government, and then supplementary questions – confined to the subject of the original question – follow. This procedure, assuming the maximum number of questions is tabled (it usually is), allows for seven to eight minutes for each question, the peer who tabled the motion by tradition being allowed to ask the first supplementary. Hence, although Question Time is shorter than in the Commons, the concentration on a particular question is much greater and allows for more probing.

NOTICES AND ORDERS OF THE DAY

Monday 10 December 2012 at 2.30 pm

*Oral Questions, 30 minutes

*__Lord Berkeley__ to ask Her Majesty's Government what proportion of the Highways Agency's budget is allocated to infrastructure for cycling.

*__Lord Roberts of Conwy__ to ask Her Majesty's Government what assessment they have made of the effect on the United Kingdom economy of the outcomes of the 'fiscal cliff' discussions in the United States of America.

*__Lord Trefgarne__ to ask Her Majesty's Government what are the respective numerical strengths of the medical services of the Royal Navy, Army and the Royal Air Force, and what proportion of those personnel are reservists.

*__Lord Barnett__ to ask Her Majesty's Government what action they propose with regard to the regulation of the banking industry.

†**Business of the House** Lord Strathclyde to move that Standing Order 46 (*No two stages of a Bill to be taken on one day*) be dispensed with on Tuesday 11 December to enable the Police (Complaints and Conduct) Bill to be taken through its remaining stages on that day; and that Standing Order 46 be dispensed with on Tuesday 18 December to enable the Small Charitable Donations Bill to be taken through its remaining stages on that day.

Partnerships (Prosecution) (Scotland) Bill [HL] Second Reading [Lord Wallace of Tankerness] (*Scottish Law Commission Bill*) (*Considered in Second Reading Committee on 4 December*)

†If the bill is read a second time, Lord Wallace of Tankerness to move that the bill be committed to a Special Public Bill Committee.

Crime and Courts Bill [HL] Report (day 3) [Lord Taylor of Holbeach]

Lord Teverson to ask Her Majesty's Government how they intend to implement their strategy for energy efficiency. (*Dinner break business, 1 hour*)

Grand Committee in the Moses Room at 3.30 pm

Enterprise and Regulatory Reform Bill Committee (day 3) [Lord Marland]

Figure 17.1 House of Lords Order Paper, 10 December 2012

At the end of the day's sitting, or during what is termed the 'dinner hour' (when the House breaks in mid-evening from the main business), there is also usually a QSD. If taken during the dinner hour, debate lasts for a maximum of 60 minutes. If taken as the last business of the day, it lasts for a maximum of 90 minutes. Peers who wish to speak do so – signing up in advance – and the appropriate minister replies to the debate. The advantages of QSDs are similar to those of the half-hour adjournment debates in the Commons, except that in this case there is a much greater opportunity for other members to participate. It is not unknown for the number of speakers to run into double figures. The topics are generally varied and non-partisan. On 28 June 2012, for example, Labour peer Lord Touhig raised the issue of support for people with dementia. In the example shown in Figure 17.1, Liberal Democrat Lord Teverson asked about the Government's strategy for energy efficiency.

Committees

Although the House remains a chamber-oriented institution, it has made greater use in recent years of committees.

Apart from a number of established committees dealing, for example, with the domestic function of the House, it has variously made use of ad hoc select committees. Some ad hoc committees have been appointed to consider the desirability of certain legislative measures. A number have been appointed to consider issues of public policy. (Some are also appointed to deal with essentially internal matters, such as the speakership of the House.) The House has also made use of its power to create sessional select committees, i.e. committees appointed regularly from session to session rather than for the purpose of one particular inquiry. The House has three long-established committees with reputations as high-powered bodies. They have been joined by three more, plus a joint committee.

The most prominent of the established committees is the *European Union Committee* (known, until 1999, as the European Communities Committee). Established in 1974, it undertakes scrutiny of draft European legislation, seeking to identify those proposals that raise important questions of principle or policy and which deserve consideration by the House. All documents are sifted by the chairman of the committee – who also holds the formal and salaried position

Table 17.4 Committees in the House of Lords, July 2012

Name of Committee	Chairman
Communications	Lord Inglewood (Con)
Constitution	Rt Hon. Baroness Jay of Paddington (Lab)
Delegated Powers and Regulatory Reform	Baroness Thomas of Winchester (Lib Dem)
Economic Affairs	Rt Hon. Lord MacGregor of Pulham Market (Con)
Subcommittee on the Finance Bill	Rt Hon. Lord MacGregor of Pulham Market (Con)
European Union Committee	Lord Boswell (Non-affiliated)
Subcommittees:	
A. Economic and financial affairs	Lord Harrison (Lab)
B. Internal market, infrastructure and employment	Baroness O'Cathain (Con)
C. External affairs	Lord Teverson (Lib Dem)
D. Agriculture, fisheries, environment and energy	Lord Carter of Coles (Lab)
E. Justice, institutions and consumer protection	Lord Bowness (Con)
F. Home affairs, health and education	Lord Hannay of Chiswick (Cross-bench)
Scrutiny of Secondary Legislation	Rt Hon. Lord Goodlad (Con)
Science and Technology	Lord Krebs (Cross-bench)
[Joint Committee on Human Rights	Dr Hywel Francis MP (Lab)]
Ad Hoc Committees:	
Adoption legislation	Rt Hon. Baroness Butler-Sloss (Cross-bench)
Public services and demographic change	Lord Filkin (Lab)
Small and medium-sized enterprises	Rt Hon. Lord Cope of Berkeley (Con)

of deputy chairman of committees – with those deemed potentially important being sent to a subcommittee. The committee works through six subcommittees (see Table 17.4), each subcommittee comprising two or more members of the main committee and several co-opted members. In total, the subcommittees draw on the services of 70 to 80 peers. Each subcommittee covers a particular area. Subcommittee E, for example, deals with justice, institutions and consumer protection. Members are appointed on the basis of their particular expertise. Members of the main or one of the subcommittees in 2012 included peers who had served as UK Ambassador to the United Nations, head of the Diplomatic Service, European Commissioner, as well as several who had been MEPs. A subcommittee, having had documents referred to it, can decide that the document requires no further consideration, or can call in evidence from government departments and outside bodies. If it decides that a document requires further consideration, then it is held 'under scrutiny' – that is, subject to the scrutiny reserve. The government cannot, except in exceptional circumstances, agree to a proposal in the Council of Ministers if it is still under scrutiny by Parliament.

Written evidence to a subcommittee may be supplemented by oral evidence and, on occasion (though not often), a minister may be invited to give evidence in person.

The subcommittees prepare reports for the House (in total, about 20 to 30 a year), including recommendations as to whether the documents should be debated by the House. (About 2 per cent of the time of the House is taken up debating EU documents, usually on 'take note' motions.) The EU Committee has built up an impressive reputation as a thorough and informed body, issuing reports that are more extensive than its counterpart in the Commons, and which are considered authoritative both within Whitehall and in the institutions of the EU. The House, like the chambers of other national legislatures, until the passage of the Lisbon Treaty, had no formal role in the European legislative process (see Norton 1996) and so has no power, other than that of persuasion, to affect outcomes. The significance of the reports, therefore, tended to lie in informing debate rather than in changing particular decisions (Norton 2013: Ch. 7). Though the Lisbon Treaty (2009) gives national parliaments a role in scrutinising legislative proposals to ensure they comply with the principle of subsidiarity, the role of reports in influencing deliberations at an early stage remains the most significant contribution.

The *Select Committee on Science and Technology* was appointed in 1979 following the demise of the equivalent committee in the Commons. (The Commons committee has since been recreated.) The remit of the committee – 'to consider science and technology' – is wide, and its enquiries have covered a broad range. The committee is essentially non-partisan in approach and benefits from a number of peers with an expertise in the subject. Recent chairmen have included the President of the Royal Academy of Engineers and a former rector of the Imperial College of Science, Technology and Medicine. The chairman in 2012, Lord Krebs, Principal of Jesus College, Oxford, is one of the world's leading experts in zoology. In recent sessions it has investigated science policy and government, nuclear research and development capabilities, science and heritage, and sports and exercise science and medicine. The committee has raised issues that otherwise might have been neglected by government – and certainly not considered in any depth by the Commons – and a number of its reports have proved influential (see Grantham 1993; Hayter 1992).

The *Delegated Powers and Regulatory Reform Committee*, previously known as the Delegated Powers and Deregulation Committee, looks at whether powers of delegated legislation in a bill are appropriate and makes recommendations to the House accordingly (see Himsworth 1995). It also reports on documents under the Regulatory Reform Act 2001, which allows regulations in primary legislation to be removed by secondary legislation. The committee has established itself as a powerful and informed committee, its recommendations being taken seriously by the House and by government. Indeed, it is standard practice for the government to accept its recommendations.

These committees have been supplemented by three more investigative committees. The *Constitution Committee* was established in 2001 to report on the constitutional implications of public bills and to keep the operation of the constitution under review. It regularly issues reports on the constitutional implications of bills and has published major reports on, among other topics, the surveillance society, the process of constitutional change, the use of referendums, the relationship between the executive, the judiciary and Parliament, the regulatory state, and Parliament and the legislative process. It also reports on bills of constitutional significance. The *Economic Affairs Committee* was also appointed in 2001. It has published reports in recent sessions on private finance projects, the economic outlook, auditors, and the economic implications for the UK of Scottish independence. It has also established a subcommittee to consider the annual Finance Bill. The *Communications Committee* is the most recent of the committees, having been appointed in 2007. It succeeded an ad hoc committee on the BBC Charter Renewal. Since its creation, it has undertaken a number of in-depth studies, publishing reports on the chairmanship of the BBC, the ownership of the news, government communications, and public service broadcasting.

The House in 2006 also appointed another committee concerned with legislative scrutiny: the *Select Committee on the Merits of Statutory Instruments*. While the Delegated Powers Committee examines delegated powers embodied in a bill, this committee considers the use of those powers. It examines statutory instruments to determine whether they are flawed – for example, by imperfectly achieving their objectives or, because of their importance, whether they should be drawn to the special attention of the House. In 2012 the remit of the committee was extended to encompass orders modifying or abolishing public bodies made under the Public Bodies Act 2011. As a result, the committee was renamed the *Scrutiny of Secondary Legislation Committee*.

As a consequence of the passage of the Human Rights Act 1998, the two Houses have also created a *Joint Committee on Human Rights*. The committee is chaired by an MP, but it follows Lords procedures. It has six members drawn from each House. It considers matters relating to human rights and has functions relating to remedial orders (bringing UK law into line with the European Convention on Human Rights) under the 1998 Act. Its main task is reporting to the House on bills that have implications for human rights. It was particularly influential, for example, in reporting on the Anti-Terrorism, Crime and Security Bill in 2001. In the light of the committee's report, and pressure from members in both chambers, the government agreed to make changes to the bill.

These permanent committees are variously supplemented by ad hoc committees, appointed to consider particular issues. Committees appointed in recent years have covered economic regulators (2007), intergovernmental organisations (2008), and the Barnett formula (2009). At the start of the 2012–13 session, the House appointed three ad hoc committees (see Table 17.4): on adoption legislation, public services and demographic change, and small and medium-sized enterprises.

The committees thus constitute a valuable and growing supplement to the work undertaken on the floor of the House. They allow the House to specialise to some degree and to draw on the expertise of its membership, an expertise that cannot be matched by the elected House of Commons. Like select committees in the Commons, the committees choose their own topics of enquiry. However, unlike the Commons committees, there is no government majority. A typical 12-member committee will comprise four Labour peers, four Conservatives, two Liberal Democrats and two cross-benchers. The composition in terms of expertise and political affiliation encourages a notable bipartisan approach.

The committees also fulfil an important expressive function. They take evidence from interested bodies – the submission of written evidence is extensive – thus allowing groups an opportunity to get their views on the public record. Given the expertise of the committees, reports are treated as weighty documents by interested groups; consequently, the committees enjoy some capacity to raise support for particular measures of public policy. Committees also have the capacity to elicit a government response at the despatch box as well as in writing. The government provides a written response to each committee report – agreeing in 2005 to do so within two months, bringing it into line with the Commons – but if the committee recommends that a report be debated in the House, then time is found to debate it. The House has agreed that such debates should be in prime time, but this is not always possible to achieve.

Party meetings

The parties in the Lords are organised, with their own leaders and whips. Even the cross-benchers, allied to no party, have their own elected leader (known as the convenor) and circulate a weekly document detailing the business for the week ahead. (They even have their own website: www.cross-benchpeers.org.uk.) However, neither the Conservative nor the Labour Party in the Lords has a committee structure. Instead, peers are able to attend the Commons backbench committees or policy group meetings, and a number do so. Any attempt at influence through the party structure in the Lords, therefore, takes the form of talking to the whips or of raising the issue at the weekly party meeting.

Party meetings, as well as those of cross-bench peers, are held each week. (The meeting day has changed in recent years, following changes to the arrangement of business in the House.) Such meetings are useful for discussing future business as well as for hearing from invited speakers. For example, in meetings of the Association of Conservative Peers (ACP) – the Lords equivalent to the 1922 Committee – the business usually comprises a short talk by a member of the executive of the 1922 Committee about developments in the Commons, the Chief Whip announcing the business for the following week, and a discussion on a particular issue or a talk from a frontbencher or expert on a particular subject. When a major bill is coming before the House, the relevant member of the Shadow Cabinet (or, if in government, minister) may be invited to attend, along with a junior spokesperson, to brief peers on the bill. Sometimes party meetings have the characteristics of a specialist committee, since often peers with an expertise in the topic will attend and question the speaker. For a minister or shadow minister, or even an expert speaker, the occasion may be a testing one, having to justify a measure or proposal before an often well-informed audience.

Party meetings are useful as two-way channels of communication between leaders and led in the Lords and, in a wider context, between a party's supporters in the Lords and the leadership of the whole party. Given the problems of ensuring structured and regular contact between whips and their party's peers, the party meetings provide a useful means of gauging the mood of the regular attenders. They are also useful ways of enhancing communication with the Commons, former MPs often being active in the membership.

Reform: stage one

Demands for reform of the House of Lords were a feature of both the late nineteenth century and the twentieth century. As the democratic principle became more widely accepted in the nineteenth century, so calls for the reform of the unelected, Conservative-dominated House of Lords became more strident. Conservative obstruction of Liberal bills in the 1880s led the Liberal Lord Morley to demand that the Upper House 'mend or end', an approach adopted as Liberal policy in 1891. In 1894 the Liberal conference voted in favour of abolishing the Lords' power of veto. When the Lords rejected the Budget of the Liberal Government in 1909, the Government introduced the Parliament Bill. Passed in 1911, the preamble envisaged an elected House. An inter-party conference in 1918 proposed a scheme for phasing out the hereditary peers, but no time was found to implement the proposals. A 1948 party leaders' conference agreed that heredity alone should not be the basis for membership. Again, no action was taken. The Parliament (No. 2) Bill, introduced in 1968 by the Labour Government led by Harold Wilson, sought to phase out the hereditary element. The bill foundered the following year in the House of Commons after encountering opposition from Conservative MPs, led by Enoch Powell, who felt it went too far, and from Labour MPs, led by Michael Foot, who believed it did not go far enough. The willingness of the House of Lords to defeat the Labour Government in the period from 1974 to 1979 reinforced Labour antagonism. In 1983 the Labour Party manifesto committed the party to abolition of the Upper House. Under Neil Kinnock (leader 1983–92) this stance was softened. In its election manifesto in 1992, the party advocated instead an elected second chamber. This was later amended under Tony Blair's leadership to a two-stage reform: first, the elimination of the hereditary element; and, second and in a later parliament, the introduction of a new reformed second chamber. The Liberal Democrats favoured a reformed second chamber – a senate – as part of a wider package of constitutional reform. Charter 88, the constitutional reform movement created in 1988 (see Chapter 13), included reform of the Upper House 'to establish a democratic, non-hereditary second chamber' as a fundamental part of its reform programme.

The Labour manifesto in the 1997 General Election included the commitment to reform in two stages. 'The

House of Lords', it declared, 'must be reformed. As an initial, self-contained reform, not dependent on further reform in the future, the rights of hereditary peers to sit and vote in the House of Lords will be ended by statute.' That, it said, would be the first step in a process of reform 'to make the House of Lords more democratic and representative'. A committee of both Houses of Parliament would be appointed to undertake a wide-ranging review of possible further change and to bring forward proposals for reform.

The Labour victory in the 1997 General Election provided a parliamentary majority to give effect to the manifesto commitment. However, anticipating problems in the House of Lords, the Government delayed bringing in a bill to remove hereditary peers until the second session of the parliament. The bill, introduced in January 1999, had one principal clause which ended membership of the House of Lords on the basis of a hereditary peerage. It was passed by the House of Commons by a large majority. In the House of Lords peers adhered to the Salisbury convention and did not vote on second reading. However, they subjected it to prolonged debate at committee and report stage. In the Lords, an amendment was introduced – and accepted by the government – providing that 92 peers should remain members of the interim House. The 92 would comprise 75 chosen by hereditary peers on a party basis (the number to be divided according to party strength among hereditary peers), 15 to be chosen by all members of the House for the purpose of being available to serve the House (for example, as Deputy Speakers) and the Earl Marshal and the Lord Great Chamberlain, in order to fulfil particular functions associated with their offices. The government had indicated in advance that it would accept the amendment, on condition that the Lords did not frustrate passage of the bill. Although the House made various other amendments to the bill, against the government's wishes, the bill made it eventually to the statute book. All bar the 92 hereditary peers exempted by the Act ceased to be members at the end of the session.

When the House met for the state opening of Parliament on 17 November 1999, it was thus a very different House from that which had sat only the week before. It was still a House of Lords, but instead of a House with a membership based predominantly on the heredity principle, it was now primarily an appointed House, the bulk of the members being there by virtue of life peerages.

Reform: stage two

The passage of the 1999 Act did not end debate on the future of the second chamber. The years following the passage of the Act have seen continued and often heated debate. Figure 17.2 shows the key dates, but these are the principal dates in what has been a long and complex story.

After the return of the Labour Government in 1997, opponents criticised ministers for not having announced what form stage two of Lords reform would take. The Government responded by appointing a Royal Commission on Reform of the House of Lords to consider reform in the light of other constitutional developments while having regard to the need to maintain the Commons as the pre-eminent chamber. The Commission, chaired by a Conservative peer, Lord Wakeham (a former Leader of both the House of Commons and the House of Lords), was appointed at the beginning of 1999 and was required to report by the end of the year. It held a number of public meetings in different parts of the country and completed its report by the end of 1999: it was published in January 2000.

In its report, *A House for the Future* (Cmd 4534), the Royal Commission recommended a House of 550 members, with a minority being elected. The report was extensive, but the reaction to it focused on its recommendations for election. Supporters of an appointed second chamber felt that it went too far. Supporters of an elected second chamber

---

1999 House of Lords Act (removed most hereditary peers from House of Lords).

2000 Report of Royal Commission on the Reform of the House of Lords, *A House for the Future* (recommended a small elected element).

2003 House of Commons votes against status quo and against every reform option; House of Lords votes for all-appointed House.

2007 House of Commons votes for second chamber with 80% or 100% members elected; House of Lords votes for all-appointed chamber.

2011 Government publishes draft House of Lords Reform Bill, with 80% of members of the House of Lords elected. Draft Bill considered by a Joint Committee of the two Houses.

2012 Government introduces House of Lords Reform Bill. Given a Second Reading in House of Commons, but Government fails to move a timetable motion (for fear of defeat). Government announces Bill is not to be proceeded with.

Figure 17.2 Lords reform – key dates

argued that it did not go far enough. Many critics of the report felt that at least 50 per cent of the members should be elected. The report did not get a particularly good press.

Although not well received by the press, the Commission's report was received sympathetically by the government. Following its 1997 manifesto commitment, it sought to set up a joint committee of both Houses, but the parties could not agree on what the committee should do. The Labour manifesto in the 2001 General Election committed the government to completing reform of the House of Lords: 'We have given our support to the report and conclusions to the report of the Wakeham Commission, and will seek to implement them in the most effective way possible.' In November 2001 the Government published a White Paper, 'Completing the Reform', proposing that 20 per cent of the members be elected. It invited comments, and the reaction it got was largely unfavourable. In a debate in the House of Commons many Labour MPs argued that the White Paper did not go far enough. Both the Conservative and Labour parties supported a predominantly elected second chamber. The Public Administration Committee in the Commons issued a report, *The Second Chamber: Continuing the Reform*, arguing that, on the basis of the evidence it had taken, the 'centre of gravity' among those it had consulted was for a House with 60 per cent of the membership elected. An early day motion favouring a predominantly elected second chamber attracted the signatures of more than 300 MPs.

Recognising that its proposals were not attracting sufficient support in order to proceed, the Government decided to hand over responsibility to Parliament itself. It recommended, and both Houses agreed to, the appointment of a joint committee. The committee completed the first stage of its work at the end of 2002, when it published a report addressing functions and composition. It argued that the existing functions of the House were appropriate. On composition, it listed seven options – ranging from an all-appointed to an all-elected House – and recommended that each House debate the options and then vote on each one. Both Houses debated the joint committee's report in January 2003. Opinion in the Commons was divided among the several options. Opinion in the Lords was strongly in favour of an all-appointed House. On 4 February both Houses voted on the options. MPs voted down the all-appointed option but then proceeded to vote down all the remaining options favouring partial or total election (see Maclean et al. 2003; Norton 2004). (An amendment favouring unicameralism was also put and defeated.) Peers voted by a three-to-one majority in favour of the all-appointed option and, by a similar margin, against all the remaining options. Of the options, that of an all-appointed chamber was the only one to be carried by either House. The outcome of the votes in the Commons was unexpected – commentators had expected a majority in favour of one of the options supporting election (the vote on 80 per cent of members being elected was lost by three votes) – and it was widely assumed in the light of the votes that there was little chance of proceeding with moves towards a second stage of reform involving election (see Norton 2004: 195–7).

Instead, the Government decided to introduce a bill to remove the remaining hereditary peers from the House of Lords, establish a statutory appointments commission and provide that peers could be expelled if convicted of an offence subject to a certain term of imprisonment. However, the Government abandoned the idea when it failed to craft an amendment-proof bill: it feared that MPs might try to amend it by introducing provisions for election. Some parliamentarians sought to keep the issue on the political agenda. The debate divided between those who were interested in reforming the powers of the Upper House and those who wanted to change its composition.

Labour peers in the Lords established a working party to review the powers, procedures and conventions of the House. Its report, published in 2004, favoured a new Parliament Act, embodying a time limit for bills in the Lords (and for bills starting life in the Lords to be brought within the scope of the Act), as well as a codification of conventions (Labour Peers Group 2004). The recommendations received a mixed response from peers, but in replying the Lord Chancellor, Lord Falconer, indicated sympathy with the argument for putting a time limit on bills in the Lords.

The debate then switched to those who supported a reform of the composition of the House. In 2005 five prominent MPs – including former Conservative Chancellor Ken Clarke and former Labour Foreign Secretary Robin Cook – published a reform tract, *Reforming the House of Lords*, in which they argued the case for a 350-member second chamber, with 70 per cent elected, the elected members serving for the equivalent of three parliaments and with one-third of the membership being renewed at each general election (Clarke et al. 2005). Led by Liberal Democrat Paul Tyler, they introduced a private member's bill, the Second Chamber of Parliament Bill, designed to give effect to their recommendations. The bill made no progress.

Labour's 2005 election manifesto showed that the government was drawn more to a reform of powers than a major change in composition. Declaring that a reformed Upper House 'must be effective, legitimate and more representative without challenging the primacy of the House of Commons', it said that, following a review by a committee of both Houses, 'we will seek agreement on codifying the key conventions of the Lords, and developing alternative forms of scrutiny that complement rather than replicate those of the Commons; the review should also explore how the upper chamber might offer a better route for public engagement in scrutiny and policy making.' It also committed the party to legislate to place 'reasonable limits on the time bills spend in the second chamber – no longer than 60 sitting days for most bills'. The paragraph dealing with composition was short: 'As part of the process of modernisation, we will remove the remaining hereditary peers and allow a free vote on the composition of the House.'

In the new 2005 parliament a joint committee on conventions was appointed – it essentially endorsed the existing conventions, but made clear they would not necessarily be able to survive any substantial reform of the House – and the Government published another White Paper on Lords reform (HM Government 2007), this time indicating a preference for a House with 50 per cent of the members elected and 50 per cent appointed. In March 2007 both Houses were again invited to vote on various options. Peers repeated their votes of 2003, voting by three-to-one in favour of an appointed House and against all the other options. However, on this occasion, MPs voted in favour of an 80 per cent elected House (by 305 votes to 267) as well as for a wholly elected House (by 337 votes to 224), though the majority for a wholly elected House was inflated by a substantial number of Labour MPs who opposed an elected House voting for the option in order to sabotage election: they reasoned that the Government would find unacceptable a wholly elected House.

The Government responded by establishing a group of leading members of each party to discuss ways of implementing the decision of the Commons. The outcome was a white paper in July 2008 (Ministry of Justice 2008) which identified different options but which produced little by way of concrete recommendations: Justice Secretary Jack Straw conceded in the foreword that it was not 'a final blueprint for reform'. It was announced that the white paper would be debated in both Houses before the end of the session. The White Paper evoked a largely apathetic response and was overshadowed by a range of other contentious issues. The debates in the two chambers never materialised. The government conceded that it would not be possible to legislate in that Parliament in order to create an elected chamber.

The issue of an elected House returned in 2010 with the formation of a Coalition Government. It was known that, had the Conservatives been elected, it was not an issue likely to have been pursued. The Liberal Democrats, however, were strongly committed to an elected House. The Coalition Agreement said that the Government would establish a committee to bring forward proposals for an elected House. The Government in 2011 published a draft bill and submitted it to a joint committee of both Houses for pre-legislative scrutiny. The committee published its report in April 2012, agreeing with some of the Government's proposals but recommending that they be subject to a referendum. The

Government then published a House of Lords Reform Bill. It proposed a House with 360 elected members and 90 appointed – all to serve fixed, non-renewal 15-year terms – and with the elected members chosen by a semi-open regional list system. (The draft bill had proposed the single transferable vote.) There were also to be up to 12 Lords Spiritual and 8 ministerial members appointed to serve at any one time as ministers. The Government rejected the idea of subjecting the proposals to a referendum. The Bill attracted substantial opposition, not least from Conservative MPs and a large section of the media. Even 12 members of the 26-member joint committee that had considered the draft bill published an alternative report, arguing the case for a referendum and a constitutional convention. After a two-day debate on the Second Reading of the Bill in the Commons, the Government decided not to proceed with an attempt to timetable the bill. The Opposition was committed to voting against the timetable motion the Government had tabled, claiming it allowed insufficient time for debate; with a large number of Conservative MPs also opposed to the motion, it was clear that the Government would lose. The Second Reading vote was won by the Government, with the Opposition – supporting the principle of election – voting for it. However, 91 Conservative MPs voted against it and a further 19 abstained from voting. The scale of the dissent was a major embarrassment for the Government. It also signalled that, without a timetable motion, there would be endless debate on the Bill. The Prime Minister, David Cameron, explored the possibility of scaling down the proposals, providing for the election of a small number of members at the next election and then leaving it to future Parliaments to decide whether to extend the provision. However, soundings of Conservative MPs who had voted against the bill revealed they were not shifting in their opposition. The following month, the Deputy Prime Minister, Nick Clegg, announced that the Government was not proceeding with the Bill. Ministers conceded that the issue of an elected second chamber was off the agenda for the rest of the parliament.

The future of the second chamber?

The question of what to do with the House of Lords has thus been a notable item on the political agenda. Given that the removal of hereditary peers from membership of the House was intended as the first stage in a two-stage process, the future shape of the House remains a matter of debate. What are the options?

RETAIN: Maintain an all-appointed House.

REFORM: Take the existing House but inject some element of election.

REPLACE: Remove the existing House and replace it with a wholly or mainly elected House.

REMOVE ALTOGETHER: Abolish the second chamber and introduce a single-chamber Parliament.

Figure 17.3 The four Rs of Lords reform

In the period leading up to the reform of the House in 1999, four approaches to reform were identified (Norton 1982: 119–29). These were known as the four Rs – retain, reform, replace or remove altogether. With some adaptation, they remain the four approaches following the passage of the House of Lords Act.

Retain

This approach favours retaining the House as a non-elected chamber. It argues that the interim House, comprising predominantly life peers, is preferable to an elected or part-elected chamber. The House, it is argued, does a good job. It complements the elected House in that it carries out tasks that are qualitatively different from those of the House of Commons. It is able to do so because its members offer particular expertise. By retaining a House of life peers, one not only creates a body of knowledge and experience, one also creates a body with some degree of independence. The cross-benchers in the House hold the balance of power and are able to judge matters with some degree of detachment. If the House were to be elected, it would have the same claim to electoral legitimacy as the Commons and would either be the same as the Commons – thus constituting a rubber-stamping body and achieving nothing – or, if elected by a different method or at different times, have the potential to clash with the Commons and create stalemate in the political system. Election would challenge, not enhance, the core accountability of the political system (see Norton 2007). Who would electors hold accountable if two elected chambers failed to reach agreement?

This approach has been taken by a number of MPs and peers, indeed by a clear majority of peers. Support for the retain option has also taken organisational form. In 2002 a campaign to argue the case against an elected second chamber was formed within Parliament. Led by an MP (Sir Patrick Cormack, Conservative MP for Staffordshire South) and a peer (this writer), it attracted a growing body of cross-party support in both Houses (Norton 2004). The group argued for some change, including closing off the by-election provision for peers, removing from membership peers who failed to attend, expelling those who committed criminal offences, enabling peers to apply for permanent leave of absence, and putting the Lords appointments commission on a statutory basis. It supported a private member's bill to implement these changes, introduced by one of its supporters, former Liberal Party leader Lord Steel of Aikwood, who brought the bill forward in succeeding sessions. The changes advocated by the group were designed to strengthen, not destroy, the existing appointed House. For it, appointment was fundamental to maintaining the existing value of the House. It believes the House adds value to the political process; a partly or wholly elected House it views as value detracting.

Reform

This approach, advocated by the Royal Commission, favours some modification to the existing House, although retaining what are seen as the essential strengths of the existing House. It acknowledges the value of having a membership that is expert and one that has a degree of independence from government. At the same time, it argues that a wholly appointed chamber lacks democratic legitimacy. Therefore it favours a mix of appointed and elected members. The advantages of such a system were touched on in the government's 1998 White Paper, *Modernising Parliament* (pp. 49–50): 'It would combine some of the most valued features of the present House of Lords with a democratic basis suitable for a modern legislative chamber.' The extent of the mix of nominated and elected members is a matter of some debate. Some would like to see a small proportion of members elected. The Royal Commission, as we have seen, put forward three options. The Government, in its 2001 White Paper, recommended that 20 per cent of the membership be elected and in 2007 increased this to 50 per cent. Some reformers favour an indirect form of election, members serving by virtue of election by an electoral college comprising, say, members of local authorities or other assemblies.

Replace

This approach favours doing away with the House of Lords and replacing it with a new second chamber. Some wish to replace it with a wholly elected house. Election, it is contended, would give the House a legitimacy that a nominated chamber, or even a part-elected chamber, lacks (see Box 17.1). That greater legitimacy would allow the House to serve as a more effective check on government, knowing that it was not open to accusations of being undemocratic. It would have the teeth that the House of Lords lacks. Government can ignore the House of Lords: it could not ignore an elected second chamber. If members were elected on a national and regional basis, this – it is argued – would allow the different parts of the United Kingdom (Scotland, Wales, Northern Ireland and the English regions) to have a more distinct voice in the political process. This stance is taken by a number of organisations, including the Liberal Democrats and Unlock Democracy. Both favour an elected senate. It is also the stance taken by a former Labour Leader of the House of Lords, Lord Richard (see Richard and Welfare 1999), who chaired the joint committee in 2011–12, and, as we have seen, by some senior MPs (Clarke et al. 2005). It is also the stance taken by succeeding governments since 2007: the Labour Government following the vote of the House of Commons in 2007 and the Coalition Government formed in 2010.

Others who favour doing away with the House of Lords want to replace it not with an elected chamber but with a chamber composed of representatives of different organised interests – a **functional chamber**. This, it is claimed, would ensure that the different groups in society – trade unions, charities, industry, consumer bodies – had a direct input into the political process instead of having to lobby MPs and peers in the hope of getting a hearing. The problem with this proposal is that it would prove difficult to agree on which groups should enjoy representation in the House. Defenders of the existing House point out that there is extensive de facto functional representation in any event, with leading figures in a great many groups having been ennobled.

There is also a third variation. Anthony Barnett and Peter Carty of the think-tank Demos have made the case for a second chamber chosen in part by lot (see also Barnett 1997). In evidence to the Royal Commission in 1999, they argued that people chosen randomly would be able to bring an independent view.

> We want 'People's Peers' but they must come from the people and not be chosen from above, by an official body. It is possible to have a strong non-partisan element in the Second Chamber, and for this to be and to be seen to be democratic and lively.

The principle of public participation, they argued, should be extended to the national legislature.

BOX 17.2

An elected second chamber

The case for

- Allows voters to choose members of the chamber.

- Provides a limit on the powers of the first chamber.

- Provides an additional limit on the powers of government.

- Gives citizens an additional channel for seeking a redress of grievance or a change of public policy.

- Can be used to provide for representation of the different parts of the United Kingdom.

- Confers popular legitimacy on the chamber.

The case against

- Rids the second chamber of the expertise and the experience provided by life peers.

- Undermines accountability of government – who should electors hold accountable if the second chamber disagrees with the first?

- Superfluous if dominated by the same party that has a majority in the first chamber.

- Objectionable if it runs into frequent conflict with the popularly elected first chamber.

- Will not be socially representative – election tends to favour white, middle-aged and male candidates – and would thus, in any event, simply replicate the House of Commons.

- May prevent the elected government from being able to implement its manifesto commitments.

- Legitimacy of the political process will be threatened if conflict between the two chambers produces stalemate or unpopular compromise policies.

Remove altogether

Under this approach, the House of Lords would be abolished and not replaced at all. Instead, the UK would have a **unicameral legislature**, the legislative burden being shouldered by a reformed House of Commons. Supporters of this approach argue that there is no case for an unelected second chamber, since it has no legitimacy to challenge an elected chamber, and that there is no case for an elected second chamber, since this would result in either imitation or conflict. Parliament should therefore constitute a single chamber, like legislatures in Scandinavia and New Zealand. The House of Commons should be reformed in order to be able to fulfil all the functions currently carried out by the two chambers.

Opponents of this approach argue that a single chamber would not be able to carry the burden, not least given the volume of public business in a country with a population of 60 million, many times larger than New Zealand and the Scandinavian countries with unicameral legislatures. Furthermore, they contend, the House of Commons could not fulfil the task of a constitutional safeguard, since it would essentially be acting as a safeguard against itself. Nor would it be an appropriate body to undertake a second look at legislation, since it would not be able to bring to bear a different point of view and different experience from that brought to bear the first time around.

Although abolition has on occasion attracted some support – including, as we have seen, at one point from the Labour Party – it is not an approach that has made much of the running in recent debate. It did, though, attract 163 votes when MPs voted on it in March 2007.

Polls reveal that opinion on the Lords is mixed. Supporters of change cite opinion polls showing that most respondents generally favour the reform or replace options, though with no clear majority for either. The 2010 British Attitudes Survey found that, of those asked, 6 per cent wanted the second chamber to be wholly appointed, 31 per cent mainly/wholly elected, 28 per cent equally appointed/elected, and 22 per cent supported abolition. A 2012 YouGov poll found that 10 per cent supported a wholly appointed House, 39 per cent a fully elected House and 32 per cent a partially elected one. However, a 2006 Populus poll found that people were quite capable of holding contradictory positions on the subject. In the poll 72 per cent of respondents thought that at least half the members should be elected and 75 per cent thought that the Lords should remain a largely appointed chamber! Supporters of an appointed chamber cite polls which show that people view the work of the House of Lords in a positive light and do not regard reform as a priority for government. An ICM poll for the think tank *Politeia* in March 2005 found that 72 per cent of respondents thought that the House of Lords did a very or fairly good job; only 23 per cent thought that it did a fairly bad or very bad job. A similarly large majority – 71 per cent – thought that the House provided an effective check on the power of the government. Almost two-thirds – 63 per cent – believed that the powers of the Lords should not be reduced. Though there may be support for change, it appears not to be very deep: 59 per cent of those questioned agreed that reform of the Lords was not a priority for the next five years.

A 2007 Ipsos MORI poll carried out for the Constitution Unit at University College London also revealed that members of the public believed that in determining the legitimacy of the Lords, trust in the appointments process was most important (76 per cent listed it as very important), followed by the House considering legislation carefully and in detail (73 per cent), members being experts in their field (54 per cent), and the House acting in accordance with public opinion (53 per cent). Having some members elected by the public came fifth in the list of priorities. When asked to select the two most important factors, election again came fifth. Those who claimed to be knowledgeable about Parliament ranked the inclusion of elected members even lower still (Russell 2007: 6). The survey also found that a slightly higher proportion of the public consider the House of Lords is carrying out its policy role well than say the same about the Commons. As Meg Russell concluded:

> Contrary to expectations, given widespread support for elected members in many earlier surveys, this factor is not considered important in comparison with other factors such as careful legislative scrutiny, trust in appointments, and listening to public opinion. Even when offered two choices about what matters, relatively few members of the public pick election, with more supporting the factors already mentioned or inclusion of independent members . . . However, there is concern about the way in which members of the House of Lords are chosen. One solution to this problem is clearly to introduce elections for the upper house. But our results suggest that a reform to the appointments process might actually have more widespread support.
>
> (Russell 2007: 8)

The debate continues. The options in terms of the contemporary debate are those of retain, reform, replace or remove altogether. Each, as we have seen, has its proponents. The arguments for and against an elected chamber are considered in Box 17.2. The battle to determine the future shape of the second chamber continues. No side has emerged triumphant.

BOX 17.3

BRITAIN IN CONTEXT

A distinctive second chamber

The House of Lords is distinctive as a second chamber because of its existence as a second chamber, its membership and its size.

It is distinctive, but far from unique, in existing as a second chamber; that is, as part of a bicameral legislature. Almost two-thirds of countries have unicameral legislatures (Massicotte 2001). Bicameral legislatures are, however, common in Western countries, especially larger ones, and in federal systems.

It is distinctive, but again not unique, in that its members are appointed rather than elected. (It was unique in the period up to 1999, when most of its members served in the House by virtue of having inherited their seats; no other major national legislature had a chamber based on the hereditary principle.) Of the 76 second chambers that exist, 21 are wholly directly elected, 17 are wholly indirectly elected, 15 are wholly appointed – 16 if you include the UK – and the rest are selected by a variety of means, such as part elected, part appointed (Russell 2012).

The House of Lords is unusual in that it has no fixed membership – the membership varies as some members die and others are appointed at different times. Members are also exceptional in terms of their tenure. Though it is common for members of second chambers to serve longer terms than members of the first chamber, no other chamber is based predominantly on life membership. In the House of Lords all members serve for life other than the Lords Spiritual, who cease to be members when they retire as archbishops or bishops. The House is remarkable also in terms of its size. Whereas it is common for second chambers to have a smaller membership than the first, the House of Lords is larger than the first and, indeed, has a claim to be the largest second chamber in the democratic world; the House of Commons has a claim to be the largest first chamber. Together, they form the largest legislature in the democratic world.

Chapter summary

The House of Lords serves as a notable body of scrutiny – both of legislation and of public policy – and as a body for giving expression to views that otherwise would not be put on the public record. As such, it adds value to the political process. The fact that it is not elected means that it has limited significance as a body for legitimising government and measures of public policy and as a body through which politicians are recruited to ministerial office. The fact that it is not elected also makes it a target of continuing demands for reform.

The question of what to do with the House of Lords has been a matter of debate for more than a century. The election of a Labour government in 1997, committed to reform of the House, brought it to the forefront of debate. The removal in 1999 of most hereditary peers from membership fundamentally changed the composition of the House. It became a chamber composed overwhelmingly of life peers. For some, that was a perfectly acceptable chamber. For others, it was not. The House of Lords serves not only as a forum to discuss political issues. It is itself a political issue. That is likely to remain the case.

Discussion points

- What are the principal functions of the House of Lords? Are they appropriate functions for a second chamber of Parliament?
- Does the House of Lords do a better job than the House of Commons in scrutinising government legislation? If so, why?
- Should the institutions of the European Union pay attention to reports from the House of Lords?
- Would a reform of the appointments process to the House of Lords be preferable to having an elected House?
- What would *you* do with the House of Lords – and why?

Further reading

The main text on the House of Lords is Shell (2007). Crewe (2005) constitutes a fascinating anthropological study. On the work of the House, see also Part IV of Blackburn and Kennon (2003), Chapter 6 of Baldwin (2005), Norton (2013) *passim*. On peers' voting behaviour, see Norton (2003) and the work produced by the Constitution Unit at University College London (www.ucl.ac.uk/constitution-unit/research/parliament/house-of-lords.html).

On the history of Lords reform, see Dorey and Kelso (2011) and Ballinger (2012). On the continuing debate over Lords reform, see Kent (1998), Tyrie (1998), Richard and Welfare (1999), the Report of the Royal Commission on the Reform of the House of Lords, *A House for the Future* (2000), the Government White Paper, *The House of Lords: Completing the Reform* (2001), the report from the Public Administration Select Committee, *The Second Chamber: Continuing the Reform* (2002), Norton (2004), Shell (2004), Clarke et al. (2005), Norton (2007), HM Government (2007), Ministry of Justice (2008), Tyrie, Young and Gough (2009), HM Government (2011), Fitzpatrick (2011), and the Joint Committee on the Draft House of Lords Reform Bill (2012). Useful comparative information is to be found in Russell (2000, 2012). There is also valuable material on the website of the Royal Commission, www.archive.official-documents.co.uk/document/cm45/4534/4534.htm

Bibliography

Baggott, R. (1995) *Pressure Groups Today* (Manchester University Press).

Baldwin, N.D.J. (1985) 'The House of Lords: Behavioural Changes', in Norton, P. (ed.) *Parliament in the 1980s* (Blackwell).

Baldwin, N.D.J. (1999) 'The Membership and Work of the House of Lords', in Dickson, B. and Carmichael, P. (eds) *The House of Lords: Its Parliamentary and Judicial Roles* (Hart Publishing).

Baldwin, N.D.J. (ed.) (2005) *Parliament in the 21st Century* (Politico's).

Ballinger, C. (2012) *The House of Lords 1911–2011* (Hart Publishing).

Barnett, A. (1997) *This Time: Our Constitutional Revolution* (Vintage).

Blackburn, R. and Kennon, A. (2003) *Griffith and Ryle on Parliament: Functions, Practice and Procedures*, 2nd edn (Sweet & Maxwell).

Clarke, K., Cook, R., Tyler, P., Wright, T. and Young, G. (2005) *Reforming the House of Lords* (The Constitution Unit).

Constitution Unit (1996) *Reform of the House of Lords* (The Constitution Unit).

Constitutional Commission (1999) *The Report of the Constitutional Commission on Options for a New Second Chamber* (Constitutional Commission).

Crewe, E. (2005) *Lords of Parliament* (Manchester University Press).

Criddle, B., Childs, S. and Norton, P. (2005) 'The Make-up of Parliament', in Giddings, P. (ed.) *The Future of Parliament* (Palgrave Macmillan).

Dickson, B. and Carmichael, P. (eds) (1999) *The House of Lords: Its Parliamentary and Judicial Roles* (Hart Publishing).

Dorey, P. and Kelso, A. (2011) *House of Lords Reform Since 1911* (Palgrave Macmillan).

Drewry, G. and Brock, J. (1993) 'Government Legislation: An Overview', in Shell, D. and Beamish, D. (eds) *The House of Lords at Work* (Oxford University Press).

Fitzpatrick, A. (2011) *The End of the Peer Show?* (The Constitution Society/CentreForum).

Grantham, C. (1993) 'Select Committees', in Shell, D. and Beamish, D. (eds) *The House of Lords at Work* (Oxford University Press).

Hayter, P.D.G. (1992) 'The Parliamentary Monitoring of Science and Technology', *Government and Opposition*, vol. 26.

Himsworth, C.M.G. (1995) 'The Delegated Powers Scrutiny Committee', *Public Law*, Spring.

HM Government (2007) *The House of Lords: Reform*, Cm 7072 (The Stationery Office).

HM Government (2011) *House of Lords Reform Draft Bill*, Cm 8077 (The Stationery Office).

House of Lords: Completing the Reform (2001) Cmd 5291 (The Stationery Office).

House of Lords (2006) *House of Lords Annual Report and Accounts 2005–06* (The Stationery Office).

House of Lords (2008) *House of Lords: Public Bill Sessional Statistics for Session 2007–08* (Public and Private Bills Office, House of Lords).

House of Lords Information Office (2005) *The Work of the House of Lords* (House of Lords).

Joint Committee on the Draft House of Lords Reform Bill (2012) *Draft House of Lords Reform Bill*, Session 2010–12, vol. 1, HL Paper 284-I, HC 1313-I (The Stationery Office).

Kent, N. (1998) *Enhancing Our Democracy* (Tory Reform Group).

Labour Peers Group (2004) *Reform of the Powers, Procedures and Conventions of the House of Lords* (Labour Peers Group).

Maclean, I., Spirling, A. and Russell, M. (2003) 'None of the Above: the UK House of Commons Vote Reforming the House of Lords, February 2003', *Political Quarterly*, vol. 74.

Massicotte, L. (2001) 'Legislative Unicameralism: A Global Survey and a Few Case Studies', *The Journal of Legislative Studies*, vol. 7, no. 1, pp. 151–70.

Ministry of Justice (2008) *An Elected Second Chamber: Further Reform of the House of Lords*, Cm 7438 (The Stationery Office).

Modernising Parliament: Reforming the House of Lords (1999) Cm 4183 (The Stationery Office).

Morrison, J. (2001) *Reforming Britain: New Labour, New Constitution?* (Reuters/Pearson Education).

Norton, P. (1982) *The Constitution in Flux* (Basil Blackwell).

Norton, P. (ed.) (1996) *National Parliaments and the European Union* (Cass).

Norton, P. (1999) 'Adding value to the political system', submission to the Royal Commission on the House of Lords.

Norton, P. (2003) 'Cohesion Without Voting: Party Voting in the House of Lords', *The Journal of Legislative Studies*, vol. 9.

Norton, P. (2004) 'Reforming the House of Lords: A View from the Parapets', *Representation*, vol. 40.

Norton, P. (2007) 'Adding Value? The Role of Second Chambers', *Asia Pacific Law Review*, vol. 15.

Norton, P. (2013) *Parliament in British Politics*, 2nd edn. (Palgrave Macmillan).

Patterson, S.C. and Mughan, A. (eds) (1999) *Senates: Bicameralism in the Contemporary World* (Ohio State University Press).

Public Administration Select Committee (2002) *The Second Chamber: Continuing the Reform*, Fifth Report, Session 2001–2002, HC 494-I (The Stationery Office).

Richard, Lord and Welfare, D. (1999) *Unfinished Business: Reforming the House of Lords* (Vintage).

Royal Commission on the Reform of the House of Lords (2000) *A House for the Future*, Cm 4534 (The Stationery Office).

Rush, M. (ed.) (1990) *Parliament and Pressure Politics* (Clarendon Press).

Russell, M. (2000) *Reforming the House of Lords: Lessons from Overseas* (Oxford University Press).

Russell, M. (2007) 'Peers and Public Attitudes to the Contemporary House of Lords', www.ucl.ac.uk/constitution-unit/files/research/parliament/lords/survey-results2007.pdf.

Russell, M. (2012) 'Elected Second Chambers and Their Powers: An International Survey', *Political Quarterly*, vol. 83, no. 1, pp. 117–29.

Shell, D. (1983) 'The House of Lords', in Judge, D. (ed.) *The Politics of Parliamentary Reform* (Heinemann).

Shell, D. (2004) 'The Future of the Second Chamber', *Parliamentary Affairs*, vol. 57.

Shell, D. (2005) 'The House of Lords: A Chamber of Scrutiny', in Giddings, P. (ed.) *The Future of Parliament* (Palgrave Macmillan).

Shell, D. (2007) *The House of Lords* (Manchester University Press).

Shell, D. and Beamish, D. (eds) (1993) *The House of Lords at Work* (Oxford University Press).

Tyrie, A. (1998) *Reforming the Lords: A Conservative Approach* (Conservative Policy Forum).

Tyrie, A., Young, G. and Gough, H. (2009) *An Elected Second Chamber: A Conservative View* (The Constitution Unit).

White, A.B. (1908) *The Making of the English Constitution 1449–1485* (G.P. Putnam).

Useful websites

Parliamentary websites

Cross-bench peers: www.crossbenchpeers.org.uk
Government Whips' Office: www.lordswhips.org.uk
(provides details on future business, including speakers)
House of Lords: www.parliament.uk/lords/index.cfm
House of Lords Select Committees:
www.parliament.uk/business/committees/ld_select.cfm

The Work of the House of Lords:
www.parliament.uk/documents/upload/HoLwork.pdf
What Lords do:
www.parliament.uk/about/how/members/lords.cfm

Reform

HM Government, *The House of Lords: Reform*: www.official-documents.gov.uk/document/cm70/7027/7027.pdf
HM Government (2011) *House of Lords Reform Draft Bill*, http://www.cabinetoffice.gov.uk/sites/default/files/resources/house-of-lords-reform-draft-bill.pdf

Joint Committee on the Draft House of Lords Reform Bill, *Draft House of Lords Reform Bill* http://www.publications.parliament.uk/pa/jt201012/jtselect/jtdraftref/284/284i.pdf
Ministry of Justice, *An Elected Second Chamber: Further reform of the House of Lords*: www.official-documents.gov.uk/document/cm74/7438/7438.pdf
Report of the Royal Commission on the Reform of the House of Lords (Wakeham Commission): www.archive.official-documents.co.uk/document/cm45/4534/contents.htm
Unlock Democracy: www.unlockdemocracy.org.uk/

The House of Lords: reform, not elect

Given the claims made by proponents of an elected second chamber in the UK, one might be forgiven for thinking that the debate was one of supporters of election versus opponents of change. Ironically, those calling for election of the House of Lords have sometimes been the ones most opposed to reform.

Calls for an elected House have actually got in the way of reforming the existing House of Lords. Under the Coalition Government elected in 2010, Deputy Prime Minister Nick Clegg was among those arguing that electing the second chamber was necessary in a modern democracy and was the 'democratic option'. Election is not self-evidently the democratic option. Democracy is about how people choose to govern themselves and government in the UK is chosen through elections to the House of Commons and is accountable through that very same process. Election of the first chamber is essential – and it is sufficient. Electing a second chamber has the potential to undermine the accountability of government, since the second would have a claim to challenge the first and the policy pursued by government. This raises fundamental problems of accountability.

However, the Government ploughed ahead with proposals for a largely elected House. In so doing, they rejected calls for reform of the existing House. The House of Lords is effective as a complementary chamber to the first, especially in undertaking legislative scrutiny. However, members accept that it could do an even better job and are keen to see changes that would enable it do so. The Government has resisted calls for reform, contending that there was no point, as the matter would be moot once the second chamber was elected. This line was maintained until August 2012, when the Government decided not to proceed with its Bill for a largely elected House. In announcing that the measure was to be dropped, the Deputy Prime Minister declined the invitation to support proposals designed to reform the existing House. Sources in government subsequently confirmed that the Government had no interest at all in pursuing the matter.

The principal supporters of reform of the House of Lords are thus those who oppose an elected second chamber and have had to contend with the opposition or disinterestness of those who argue the case for an elected house.

In what ways, then, could the existing House of Lords be reformed? There are two principal sets of reforms. One focuses on the membership and is designed to facilitate public trust and make the House a working House. Most of these can be achieved only through legislation. The other set is designed to strengthen its capacity to fulfil its prime functions of legislative scrutiny and calling government to account. These reforms are largely within the control of the House itself.

Membership

The House has a large and growing membership. The House not only has no control over who are selected to become peers, but also lacks the power to remove members. In successive sessions of Parliament, the former Liberal leader, Lord Steel of Aikwood, has introduced a Bill, drafted by this writer, to address both aspects.

The first relates to the size of the House. The membership has grown significantly since the removal of most hereditary peers in 1999. Following the passage of the House of Lords Act 1999, there were 666 peers. By July 2012 there were 765 (and 816 if you include peers who are on leave of absence or excluded by virtue of posts they hold, such as Supreme Courts Justices or members of the European Parliament). This creates a large, unwieldy body, creating practical difficulties when there is a large attendance. (The average daily attendance is close to 500.) Peers favour reducing the size of the House. Some have supported Meg Russell of the Constitution Unit at University College London in calling for a moratorium on the creation of new peerages. The Steel Bill makes provision for removing from the membership of the House those peers who never attend, as well as empowering the House to make provision for the permanent retirement of peers who wish to leave – for example, for reasons of infirmity. Peers can take leave of absence, even announce their retirement, but the Bill is designed not only to entrench this, but also to enable the House to craft new schemes to achieve a greater rate of members leaving the House. The Steel Bill, as originally introduced, was also designed to limit the number of new peerage creations.

The other aspect is to make provision to remove peers who commit serious criminal offences. Once one becomes a member of the Lords, one is a member for life and there is no way in which one can be removed (other than by legislation). This has proved an embarrassment when peers have been convicted and imprisoned. The Steel Bill includes provision to bring the House of Lords into line with the House of Commons, providing that a member who is convicted and sentenced to one year or more of imprisonment is expelled. This is deemed necessary both on grounds of principle and in order to bolster trust in the institution. There is also a powerful case to empower the House to expel a member: a peer may commit an impropriety which does not constitute a breach of the law, but which justifies their removal. The House has the power to suspend a member to the end of a parliament – a power recently used, for the first time since the 1640s – but not to expel them from the House.

There is also a case for putting the independent appointments commission, which nominates people to be cross-bench (independent) peers, to be put on a statutory basis – protecting its independence – and requiring it to ensure that all nominations, including those made by party leaders, meet a consistently high quality threshold.

Enhancing what the House does

The House is generally accepted to do a good job, adding value to the political process, but there is always room for improvement. In the last parliament four informal working groups were established by the Lord Speaker to identify possible reforms, for example in dealing with legislation and in internal management. I was the only peer to serve on all four. The subsequent reports led, in the present parliament, to the Leader of the House setting up a working group to consider reform. Chaired by former Cabinet minister, Lord Goodlad, it came up with no less that 55 recommendations for improving the performance of the House. The proposals were wide-ranging, encompassing conduct within the chamber through to greater use of pre-legislative and post-legislative scrutiny. The more significant proposals were designed to enhance the detailed scrutiny of legislation.

Some of these proposals have been considered already by the House and there is pressure to ensure that others are pursued: some peers have established a cross-party working group to push for their implementation. One consequence of the Goodlad report has been the establishment of an ad hoc committee, under former judge Baroness Butler-Sloss, to undertake post-legislative scrutiny of laws on adoption. This sets a valuable precedent. Another proposal, to establish a legislative standards committee, has been endorsed by various bodies and in 2012 the Constitutional and Political Reform Committee in the House of Commons undertook an inquiry into whether such a committee should be established. The Goodlad report argued that such a committee could play a crucial role in ensuring that bills brought forward by the government met certain criteria. These included a clear and unambiguous statement of the policy intention of the legislation and the desired outcomes, as well as why legislation was necessary. The purpose was to impose a discipline on government in bringing forward legislation and to discourage it from trying to rush legislation through Parliament in response to a feeling that 'something must be done' when a particular problem arises.

This illustrates some of the reforms that could be made to strengthen the House in fulfilling its functions. They build on a raft of changes carried through in recent decades, including greater specialisation through committees. The House has established a number of cross-cutting investigative select committees – designed to complement, and not duplicate, the departmental select committees in the Commons – and made greater use of grand committees for the committee stage of Bills. These play to the strengths of the House in enabling it to draw on the experience and expertise of its members.

Such reforms would strengthen the second chamber in carrying out tasks that complement the work of the elected chamber. MPs do a difficult and demanding job. There is little point in seeking to duplicate or undermine what they do. The House of Lords performs a role that is qualitatively distinctive. Electing the second chamber would be value detracting and not value adding. The most powerful case is one for reforming the existing House and strengthening it in the tasks that it fulfils. That is also now the most practical option.

by Philip Norton

PART 5

THE EXECUTIVE PROCESS

CHAPTER 18

The core executive: the Prime Minister and Cabinet

Philip Norton

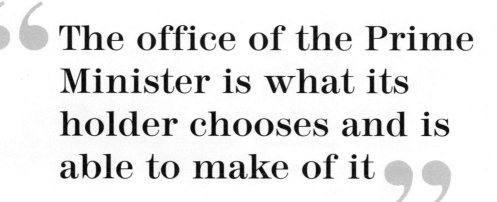

> **The office of the Prime Minister is what its holder chooses and is able to make of it**
>
> Herbert Asquith

Learning objectives

- To describe the development of the office of Prime Minister.

- To identify the nature of prime ministerial power and the significance of the individual in the office.

- To describe the development and role of the Cabinet.

- To assess different explanations of the location of power at the heart of British government.

The fount of policy making in Britain has always been the **executive**. Initially the crown was all-powerful, but then the powers of the crown came to be exercised by bodies on behalf of the crown. The king's justice came to be dispensed by his courts. Generating measures of public policy moved to the king's ministers, especially in the eighteenth century with the arrival of the Hanoverian kings, who had little interest in domestic politics. As we have seen (Chapter 14), the monarch moved from being at the heart of public policy to being, by the twentieth century, above the political fray, giving assent to what is decided but not interfering in the process. Political power came to be exercised by the king's ministers, the leading ministers drawn together in a **Cabinet** and headed by the king's principal, or prime, minister. Though political power passed to the Prime Minister and Cabinet, the form of monarchical government remained and continues to provide the legal framework within which government is conducted.

The emergence of a powerful Prime Minister and Cabinet was marked in the nineteenth century. Collective responsibility became a convention of the constitution. Although the legal authority of ministers rested on their position as servants of the crown, their political authority came to rest on the fact that they commanded a majority in the House of Commons. After the 1840s, the monarch's choice of ministry was constrained by the votes of the electors. The combination of legal and popular authority made for a powerful executive. The head of the party commanding a majority in the House of Commons was invited to become Prime Minister and, by the very reason he became Prime Minister, was able to exercise considerable power through the party's majority in the House. By virtue of the doctrine of parliamentary sovereignty (see Chapters 15 and 16), the outputs of Parliament were binding and could be set aside by no body other than Parliament itself. Whoever commanded a majority in the House of Commons could thus wield considerable power. The Prime Minister and Cabinet came to form the heart of government – the **core executive** – in the United Kingdom. Though recent pressures – the hollowing out of the state and multilevel governance (discussed later) – have led to the core executive operating in a more crowded and fragmented political environment, the Prime Minister and Cabinet remain at the heart of British government.

The Prime Minister

The first person generally held by historians to be the first Prime Minister was Robert Walpole (1721–41). As Stephen Taylor has written,

> Robert Walpole is one of the most remarkable figures of modern British politics. He is commonly regarded not only as the first prime minister, but also as the longest serving holder of that office, his twenty-one years far exceeding the tenure of any of his successors. He was the dominant figure of the early Hanoverian period.
>
> (Taylor 1998: 1)

He also came to live in 10 Downing Street, a house given to him by George II. However, the term 'prime minister' had been employed before and it was not one that Walpole favoured. The term entered common use following Walpole's tenure, but not until the twentieth century was it referred to in statute. The formal title held by the king's first minister was First Lord of the Treasury, a title still held by the occupant of 10 Downing Street.

Walpole established the basic features of the office and under him one can see the essential constitutional division between the monarch and the monarch's first minister: the former remained as head of state, but the latter became the head of government. For another century the monarch was to exercise the freedom to select the Prime Minister, but it was the selection of someone who was to head the King's government. The Prime Minister had arrived. Since Walpole's lengthy tenure as the king's principal minister, the office has undergone some significant change. The office itself has also seen an array of office holders (Englefield et al. 1995). Up to 2012, 52 men and one woman have been appointed Prime Minister, serving a total of 75 ministerial terms: some, of course, have held the office on more than one occasion. William Gladstone, for example, held the post on four separate occasions. Lord Derby and the Marquess of

Salisbury each held it on three separate occasions in the nineteenth century, as did Stanley Baldwin in the twentieth. Some have been short-lived premierships. The Duke of Wellington's second term in office lasted less than one month (17 November to 9 December 1834). In the twentieth century Andrew Bonar Law served for the shortest period of time – seven months, from October 1922 to May 1923 (he was dying from throat cancer) – and the longest serving was Margaret Thatcher: a total of 11.5 years, from May 1979 to November 1990.

Some prime ministers have gone down in history as major figures: William Pitt the elder (the Earl of Chatham), William Pitt the younger (Prime Minister at the age of 24), William Gladstone, Benjamin Disraeli, David Lloyd George and Winston Churchill among them. Others, including some of the early occupants of the office, have faded into obscurity and some never really emerged from it. Seven prime ministers have died in office, though the last was Lord Palmerston in 1865. Of the seven, one was assassinated (Spencer Perceval, in 1812). In the eighteenth and nineteenth centuries it was not uncommon for the Prime Minister to sit in the House of Lords. The last to do so was the Third Marquess of Salisbury, who left office in 1902 (being succeeded by his nephew, Arthur Balfour); since then, the convention has been that the prime ministers must sit in the House of Commons. Most prime ministers have entered office having served an apprenticeship in other senior ministerial offices. A few have entered No. 10 with no previous ministerial experience, including the first Labour Prime Minister, J. Ramsey MacDonald, in 1924 as well as two of the most recent prime ministers – Tony Blair in 1997 and David Cameron in 2010.

The Prime Minister heads the government. To understand the premiership, it is necessary to look at the powers that inhere in the office, as well as the constraints that operate. However, while necessary, it is not sufficient. To understand how those powers are deployed, it is necessary to look at who holds the office.

Downing Street
Source: Alamy Images/Justin Kase z01z

The office of Prime Minister

In the eighteenth century the person holding the premiership had little by way of a formal office: that is, a significant body of administrative support. The position became more significant in the nineteenth century with the development of a unified ministry, ministers becoming bound by the convention of collective ministerial responsibility. However, the body at the heart of government – the Cabinet – suffered from a lack of basic organisation. It was a collection of senior ministers, coming together for meetings; members took it in turn to be the host and the implementation of decisions was dependent on the individuals attending to remember what had been agreed. Civil servants had to approach ministers to see if they knew what had been decided. The waiters variously leaked what had been discussed and it was not unknown for some members to be asleep when important decisions were taken.

The situation changed notably in the twentieth century with the creation in 1916 of a Cabinet Secretariat and the appointment of a Cabinet Secretary. The impetus for the change was the need for efficiency in time of war, but the structure was maintained in peacetime. The use of the Secretariat initially attracted criticism.

The criticisms primarily grew out of the fact that the attachment of the Secretariat to the Cabinet had been carried out by Lloyd George and that he had then tied that body to his own person, thus effectively increasing his own power vis-à-vis the other members of the Cabinet.

(Carter 1956: 202)

The Secretariat served to ensure the recording and coordination of decisions, operating under the person who chaired the Cabinet – the Prime Minister. The position of the Prime Minister was also strengthened in 1919 with the creation of a unified civil service, under a Permanent Secretary as its head. A regulation 'laid down that the consent of the Premier (which in practice meant the head of the civil service) would be required in all departments to the appointment of permanent heads and their deputies' (Blake 1975: 46–7). It is a power that was to become a particularly important one under some later prime ministers, notably Margaret Thatcher, Tony Blair and David Cameron.

Over time, Downing Street has expanded. In addition to the private office, linking the Prime Minister to Whitehall, the PM's Office has acquired a political office, linking the PM to the party, and a press office, linking the PM to the media. It has also acquired a body of policy advisers. Prime Ministers variously appointed advisers, or drew on the advice of the Cabinet Secretary or other senior civil servants. In 1970 a small body of advisers – the Central Policy Review

Staff (CPRS), commonly known as 'the think tank' – was established. It comprised some political appointees and seconded civil servants to advise the Cabinet on policy issues. It answered to the Cabinet through the Prime Minister, but came to be overshadowed by a body of advisers answering solely to the PM, the No. 10 Policy Unit. The CPRS was wound up in 1983. The Policy Unit comprised a body of high-flying political advisers, including some policy specialists, though under David Cameron it has been staffed by civil servants, the Prime Minister drawing for political advice on a team of special advisers.

Margaret Thatcher also appointed a Chief of Staff. Tony Blair, Gordon Brown and David Cameron also did so, though each entrusted the holder with differing degrees of power; under Blair, the Chief of Staff was especially important and was empowered to give instructions to civil servants (a power rescinded by Gordon Brown). Tony Blair also created various units, such as a Performance and Innovation Unit, Delivery Unit and the Forward Strategy Unit, which were formally housed in the Cabinet Office but in many cases reported directly to the Prime Minister. They were designed to enhance joined-up government. Gordon Brown rescinded some of the changes introduced by his predecessor, but retained some units to provide advice. David Cameron has proved less prone to utilise such units, establishing only one, an Implementation Unit, designed to monitor progress of departments in delivering the commitments embodied in the Coalition Agreement.

The powers of the Prime Minister

The Prime Minister is the most powerful person in government, but exercises no statutory powers. Rather, his powers exist by convention. His power as the monarch's first minister confers considerable sway not only over Cabinet and all ministers, but also over the civil service, a raft of public bodies, and people seeking preferment through the award of honours. His principal powers can be listed as follows (see Figure 18.1).

Appoints, shuffles and dismisses ministers. The Prime Minister chooses who else will be in government. A new Prime Minister appoints over 100 ministers. Which ministers will form the Cabinet, and their ranking within Cabinet, is a

matter for the PM. The Prime Minister can also move or dismiss ministers. Some may be deemed to have earned promotion and others not to have lived up to expectations. Appointing and moving ministers may be undertaken not only for the purposes of reward (or indicating dissatisfaction in the case of demotion or dismissal) but also to reflect the PM's political values. Appointing ministers sympathetic to a particular philosophic strand within the party may demonstrate the PM's desire for that philosophy to dominate in a particular ministry. Margaret Thatcher, for example, appointed neo-liberal supporters to head the key economic ministries. When David Cameron became Prime Minister in 2010, his capacity was constrained by the fact of a Coalition Government, Liberal Democrat ministers being nominated by the Deputy Prime Minister (Liberal Democrat leader Nick Clegg) and the Prime Minister consulting the Deputy Prime Minister on other appointments.

Chairs the Cabinet. The PM not only decides who will be in the Cabinet, but also decides when it will meet, what it will discuss, and what it has decided. The Cabinet normally meets once a week, but under some PMs it has met more frequently. Under Tony Blair, it rarely met more than once a week and even then it was for a brief meeting, sometimes lasting less than an hour. Gordon Brown was keen to place more emphasis on the role of Cabinet and, in order to distinguish his approach from that of Blair, moved Cabinet meetings from Thursdays to Tuesdays. The creation of a Coalition Government in 2010 also enhanced the status of Cabinet as the body for clearing major government policy.

The agenda is determined by the PM. The inclusion or exclusion of certain issues can be politically contentious. The manner of discussion is also influenced by the PM. Some premiers encourage free-ranging discussion, others prefer more concise contributions. Cabinet under John Major was said to resemble a seminar. Under Tony Blair, the items tended to be for report rather than discussion. It is rare for votes to be taken. The PM normally sums up a discussion and it is the PM's summary that forms the basis of the minutes. The summing-up may not necessarily reflect the full tenor of the discussion and may not always coincide with some ministers' recollections of what was said, but it is the Prime Minister's summary that counts.

The PM not only decides the composition of Cabinet but also what **Cabinet committees** will be created. The Cabinet, a large body meeting once a week, is not in a position to transact all the business of government. Most policy proposals are considered by Cabinet committees. Only if there is disagreement in committee (and if the chair of the committee agrees) is an issue referred to Cabinet. The PM decides who will chair the committees as well as who will serve on them. Which minister is appointed to chair the most committees is often taken as a sign of which minister enjoys the PM's confidence.

Appoints, shuffles and dismisses ministers

Chairs the Cabinet

Controls Whitehall

Dispenses honours and public appointments

Figure 18.1 Principal powers of the Prime Minister

Controls Whitehall. The Prime Minister not only decides who shall be the ministerial heads of departments, he can also create, abolish or merge departments, as well as determine who shall be the civil service heads of those departments. The structure of government is a matter for the PM and some have created giant departments. Under Gordon Brown, a massive department, the Department for Business, Innovation and Skills, was created, with no less than 10 ministers under a Secretary of State. It remained the largest Department under the Coalition Government formed in 2010, but with only seven ministers. Responsibility for transport policy is sometimes included in a large department, such as the Department for the Environment, and at other times is handled by a free-standing Ministry of Transport.

The senior civil service appointments are also the responsibility of the Prime Minister. The PM used to leave this responsibility to others and promotion was usually on the basis of seniority. More recent Prime Ministers have taken an interest in who occupies the top positions. Margaret Thatcher ensured that some senior civil servants were promoted over the heads of more senior officials because they were seen to be capable of effective policy delivery. Tony Blair was also keen to press for civil service change in order to enhance policy delivery and to combat what he termed 'departmentalitis' – the tendency for ministers and officials to act in the interests of their department rather than deliver what the PM wanted (see Chapter 22). This led to David Cameron as Prime Minister to pursue the cause of civil service reform. In 2012 he also made major changes to the leading posts in the civil service, separating the leadership of the civil service into three positions: Cabinet Secretary, Permanent Secretary in the Cabinet Office, and Head of the Home Civil Service.

Dispenses honours and public appointments. The PM formally advises the monarch on who should receive particular honours and who should be appointed to public posts in the gift of the crown. In effect, he thus determines who will be honoured. The range of honours and appointments is substantial. It encompasses peerages. Though proposals for cross-bench (that is, non-party affiliated) peerages are now made by an independent appointments commission, the PM can still determine who shall be elevated on a party basis. He can appoint ministers from outside Parliament and make sure they are offered peerages, thus ensuring they are within Parliament. He can determine who shall hold various public appointments, including the heads of the security services, the armed forces, and the BBC. Even when appointments are formally in the gift of other ministers, the PM may intervene to make sure a favoured candidate is appointed. The Prime Minister's patronage extends even to certain professors (regius professors) at Oxford and Cambridge universities

and bishops of the Church of England. The archbishops and bishops of the Anglican Church are crown appointments, with the appointments process traditionally handled by an official in No. 10.

These are the main powers, but they are not the only ones. One particularly important power until 2011 was to advise the monarch as to when a general election should be held. Until 1918 this was a decision taken by the Cabinet, but from then until 2011 the final decision rested with the Prime Minister (Hennessy 2000: 68). A parliament was limited to a maximum term of five years, but within that period the PM could ask Her Majesty to call an election. This was seen as a useful political weapon, but it was ended by the Fixed-term Parliaments Act 2011, providing for a fixed term of five years, with only limited opportunities for an early election.

The PM's political capital is also enhanced by other aspects of his office as well as by the fact that he is party leader. As head of government, the PM attends various international gatherings, including the European Council and summits of heads of government of the leading economic nations. This gives him not only a voice in international deliberations but also raises his political profile. He can be seen to be striding the world stage, on behalf of the United Kingdom, in a way no other minister can. The Foreign Secretary or Chancellor of the Exchequer play essentially supporting roles when the Prime Minister is present to represent the UK.

The fact that the PM is head of government, and holder of an office held by a number of political greats, also enhances the media attention accorded the office holder. A report from outside 10 Downing Street is more likely to be carried by the broadcast media than one from outside a government department. Even if the report is of Cabinet proceedings, it will be broadcast in front of the place where the Cabinet meets – 10 Downing Street. There is no other obvious place. The backdrop of the Cabinet Office in Whitehall would have little resonance. The development of a rolling 24-hour news media increases the media focus on No. 10. Other developments also result in the PM being seen as standing apart from the rest of government. Security considerations mean that he travels with a security escort, setting him aside from others. Though some senior ministers have security protection, it is not on the scale accorded the Prime Minister.

These are all features deriving from the Prime Minister's status as Prime Minister. However, he also has political clout by virtue of the political position that propelled him to office and which he retains after he has entered No. 10: that of party leader. As party leader, he commands both a party apparatus, especially important when it is a Conservative Prime Minister, and can draw on the support of his parliamentary party. MPs want their party to succeed and it is the party leader who is crucial in delivering success. This can have its downsides for the PM if success is not forthcoming, but if it is (and if the party's standing in the opinion polls is strong) then the Prime Minister is usually unassailable within the party.

The Prime Minister is thus a powerful figure, standing at the apex of government. The powers that inhere in the office are considerable. However, the way in which those powers are exercised will not necessarily be the same under succeeding prime ministers. To understand how the powers are wielded, one has to look at *who* is Prime Minister.

The person in No. 10

The reasons why people become Prime Minister vary from PM to PM. The skills necessary to exercise the powers of the office also vary. One way of looking at why politicians become Prime Minister is to look at their purpose in being in office. Some seek office in order to achieve a particular programme of public policy. Some enter No. 10 out of a sense of public duty or simply because they are ambitious for office. To give some coherence as to the motivation for entering office, a fourfold typology of prime ministers has been created

(Norton 1987, 1988). The four types of prime ministers are *innovators*, *reformers*, *egoists*, and *balancers* (Box 18.1).

The categories shown in in Box 18.1 are ideal types and some prime ministers have straddled categories or moved from one to the other: Churchill, for example, was a very different Prime Minister in peacetime (1951–55) from the one he had been in wartime (1940–45). He had been an innovator in wartime, having a very clear understanding of what he wished to achieve, and in peacetime was a balancer, keen to maintain social stability and having little comprehension of domestic policy. Some commentators viewed Edward Heath as straddling the categories of reformer and egoist. David Cameron may sit astride the categories of reformer and balancer, one commentator identifying him as 'one of life's satisfiers rather than maximisers' (Montgomerie 2012: 21).

How the Prime Minister operates in office will thus vary from PM to PM. So too does the extent to which they achieve their goals. They may know what they want to achieve, but that does not guarantee that they will get their way. Prime ministers need a range of skills in order to get what they

---

BOX 18.1

Types of prime ministers

Innovators seek power – they fight to become Prime Minister – in order to achieve a particular programme, one that they have crafted. If necessary, they are prepared to push and cajole their party into supporting them in carrying out the programme. A leading example is Margaret Thatcher. She embraced a neo-liberal philosophy and pursued it with great vigour, sometimes in the face of much opposition from within her own party. She had a clear future goal.

Reformers seek power in order to achieve a particular programme of public policy, but one essentially dictated by the party itself. Prime Minister Clement Attlee led a reforming postwar Labour government, but under him the programme that was carried out was that embodied in Labour's 1945 election manifesto, *Let Us Face the Future*. David Cameron arguably falls under this heading, but is distinctive in that the programme is not one imposed by the party but by an agreement reached by the two parties to the coalition formed in May 2010.

Egoists seek power for the sake of having power. They are principally concerned with the here and now of British politics, operating in order to maintain their occupancy of No. 10. They will take whatever action they consider

necessary to protect their position. Harold Wilson was a good example of an egoist, variously contending with what he saw as attempts by other ministers to oust him. Tony Blair also falls primarily in this category. His period as Leader of the Opposition suggested he may be an innovator, but once in office his prime goal, especially in his first term, was to continue his tenure of office. Gordon Brown also falls principally into this category. Though he entered office with policy goals, his principal focus once in office was to maintain power.

Balancers seek to maintain stability in society. They are concerned with the current state of society, seeking to ameliorate tensions and avoiding policies that may prove socially divisive. They fall into two types: those who seek power and those who are conscripted; the latter are usually compromise choices for party leader. Balancers by their nature tend to be Conservatives, such as Harold Macmillan, but the category also includes Labour Prime Minister James Callaghan. Both Macmillan and Callaghan were power-seekers. An example of a conscript was Sir Alec Douglas-Home (then the Earl of Home) chosen by the Queen, after taking advice, in preference to power-seeking rivals.

A unique occasion when the Queen sat in on a Cabinet meeting

Source: Press Association/Jeremy Slewyn

want (Norton 1987). They have the powers of the office, but some may be more proficient than others in the exercise of those powers. Some PMs have been able to appoint ministers who have delivered what is expected of them. Some have been good in their management of government; others have not. Sir Anthony Eden, for example, was notoriously bad in his management of his ministers. Some know when to provide leadership and when to go ahead with something – and when not to go ahead with a particular policy. For much of her premiership, Margaret Thatcher demonstrated effective political antennae. As one of her Cabinet colleagues put it, she knew what she wanted to achieve, but she also recognised a brick wall when she saw one (former Cabinet minister to author). If there was a clear obstacle, she sought to work round it (as on limiting the powers of the trade unions) or, if necessary, abandoned the policy (as on post office closures). Others have sometimes just ploughed on.

Some prime ministers have adopted an oratorical approach in order to get their way – an approach favoured, for example, by Tony Blair – whereas others have tended to focus on detailed policy reflections and seeking to impose their decisions on Cabinet, an approach taken by Edward Heath and Gordon Brown. They have also differed in the extent to which they have left ministers to get on with their jobs or sought to micro-manage the affairs of government. Some have proved good at seeing backbenchers regularly in order to ensure they remain supportive of the government's aims; others have tended to distance themselves from their supporters, sometimes – as in the case of Edward Heath

(Norton 1978) – with disastrous consequences for their continuation as party leader.

The powers of the Prime Minister are thus substantial, though how and why they are utilised will differ from one Prime Minister to another. The extent to which a Prime Minister achieves desired outcomes will also be dependent on others. The occupant of 10 Downing Street does not live in a vacuum. The Prime Minister has to work in a political environment that includes a large number of political actors, and their number – as we shall see – has increased in recent years. One of those actors is the Cabinet.

The Cabinet

The King used to appoint people to key offices, such as Chancellor, Treasurer and Secretary of State. They came to meet in a council of the King, the Privy Council, though the number of people invited to it was such that it became too large for the purposes of maintaining secrets and moving quickly. In the latter half of the seventeenth century the principal ministers came to be drawn together in the Foreign Committee of the Privy Council: this in time came to be known as the junto, or Cabinet Council, or Cabinet (Macintosh 1977: 35–7). By the end of the century, such a body was meeting frequently. The appointment of Whig leaders in 1694, when there was a Whig majority in the Commons, was seen by some historians as constituting the first modern

Cabinet. The Cabinet developed in the eighteenth century and, under the Hanoverian kings, it met regularly without the King being present. There was also a smaller inner or working group of lords or an inner cabinet and at times, especially when the King withdrew from Cabinet, the influence of the Cabinet declined. Under George III the term 'Cabinet' came to be employed for the inner cabinet. Royal appointment was the crucial feature. 'Once a Cabinet was appointed and given royal support, it could normally rely on a majority in both houses and a victory at the next general election' (Macintosh 1977: 63). Though the Cabinet came to work as a distinct body, the membership nonetheless was determined by the King.

The political developments of the nineteenth century changed fundamentally the nature of politics. The extension of the franchise and the growth of mass-membership political parties served to transfer power from crown to Parliament and, within Parliament, to confirm the supremacy of the House of Commons. The outcomes of general elections came to determine which party was in power and, hence, which party leader was to be Prime Minister and form a Cabinet. The Cabinet could not necessarily take the House of Commons for granted, though by the end of the century the hold of party on the House had grown. By the twentieth century, political control in the House was essentially top-down rather than bottom-up. The convention of collective ministerial responsibility had also developed: ministers were bound by the decisions taken by Cabinet. This applied to all ministers and not just those who formed the Cabinet.

The Cabinet, as we have seen, was not a highly organised body prior to the twentieth century. When the Cabinet developed as a recognisable body, the practice tended to be to keep minutes, but the practice was not maintained during the nineteenth century. As we have noted, the Cabinet met regularly at dinner, with members taking it in turn to be host. These were not the most efficient means of despatching business. One member thought 'we should have no Cabinets after dinner. We all drink too much wine, and are not civil to each other' (cited in Gilmour 1971: 221). Sleeping was common and it is claimed that most members were asleep when the decision to invade the Crimea was taken. There were problems with maintaining secrecy, not least as the body grew in size (to about 15 members by 1850) and because waiters would hear what was discussed. The meetings themselves could be fairly discursive as there was relatively little business to discuss. 'The pressure of government business was slight . . . Even under Rosebery, at the end of the century, a large part of a Cabinet session could be spent discussing the exact text of one of Juvenal's satires' (Daalder 1964: 27). There was no infrastructure. Ministers had their own departments. There was no dedicated support structure

and no consistent records were kept. Implementation rested on ministers' recollections of what had been decided. As one commentator, himself later to be a Cabinet minister, recorded 'The Lord of Chaos himself could hardly have devised more suitable arrangements for the furtherance of his own objectives' (Gilmour 1971: 222).

Some structure was provided, as we have seen, by the creation in 1916 of a Cabinet Secretariat. This ensured there was administrative support and a means of ensuring decisions were recorded and transmitted to departments. The functions of the Cabinet were also authoritatively delineated two years later in the report of the Machinery of Government Committee (see Le May 1964: 237–42). These were listed as (a) the final determination of the policy to be submitted to Parliament; (b) the supreme control of the national executive in accordance with the policy prescribed by Parliament; and (c) the continuous coordination and delimitation of the authorities of the several departments of state. The Cabinet is thus, formally, the collective body that determines the policy of government and has the machinery to ensure that its writ runs throughout Whitehall. It operates within limits set by Parliament, but that is a body in which it usually enjoys the support of most MPs. It is chaired by the Prime Minister, but the conclusions, as summarised by the PM, are deemed to be those of the Cabinet.

Though the work of the Cabinet was not unduly onerous in the nineteenth century, it became notably more demanding in the twentieth. There were particular demands placed on it in wartime: the need for secrecy and despatch led to the creation of inner, or war, Cabinets. The main permanent development in peacetime occurred after 1945. The state sector expanded considerably and more demands were made of government. The business of government grew, making it difficult for the principal policies to be decided in a body meeting only once or sometimes twice a week. The use of Cabinet committees became more extensive. Committees were variously employed in the nineteenth century and the first permanent committee – the Committee of Imperial Defence – was created in 1903; it was also the first to have a secretariat. Many committees were established in the First World War, but the number receded in peacetime: in an average year, about 20 would be in existence (Gordon Walker 1972: 39). The number burgeoned in the Second World War, but – unlike in the aftermath of the First World War – the basic structure was retained in peacetime. 'Attlee was thus the first Prime Minister to have in peacetime a permanent structure of Cabinet Committees' (Gordon Walker 1972: 41). The structure was maintained under succeeding prime ministers. The extent of the committees, both in terms of number and activity, was such that from the Attlee Government onwards there were concerns as to the sheer volume of work being undertaken by committees and the consequent problem of overload. In 1951 there were 148 standing committees and 313 ad hoc committees (Hennessy 1986: 45). In 1967 the Prime Minister, Harold Wilson, enhanced the status of the committees by saying that a matter could only be taken from committee to Cabinet with the agreement of the committee chairman. Previously, any member of the committee could insist a matter dealt with in committee be considered in Cabinet.

The stress on Cabinet committees, however, was to decline towards the end of the twentieth century. The number of committees came down under Margaret Thatcher (just over 30 standing committees and just over 120 ad hoc committees in the period up to 1986) and also under Tony Blair. There was a greater reliance on bilateral meetings, or ad hoc meetings with senior ministers, or the Prime Minister determining the matter without recourse to the Cabinet. This was seen by commentators as confirming a trend towards prime ministerial government and away from **Cabinet government**.

Despite the perceived emphasis on the role of the Prime Minister, the Cabinet nonetheless remains a core component of British government. The functions ascribed to it in 1918 remain relevant and, in practice, are complemented by important political roles. The principal roles are essentially five (Figure 18.2).

Approves policy. Although policy does not originate in Cabinet, it is nonetheless the body, operating through its committees, that approves the policies that are to be laid before Parliament. Ministers serving on Cabinet committees do not necessarily agree proposals without commenting on them and sometimes inviting the minister to come back with a reworked policy. The Cabinet's Parliamentary Business and Legislation Committee is especially important for determining which measures shall be laid before parliament in the next session of Parliament. The Devolution Committee was also extremely important in the 1997–2001 parliament in drawing up measures to give effect to the Government's policy on devolution. The then Cabinet Secretary, Sir Robin Butler, was later to say: 'I have always held out that the operation of the Devolution Committee

Approves policy

Resolves disputes

Constrains the Prime Minister

Unifies government

Unifies the parliamentary party

Figure 18.2 Principal roles of the Cabinet

which Lord Irvine chaired after the 1997 election, was a model of how cabinet committees ought to work' (Butler 2009). The committee resolved most issues, which were then reported to Cabinet.

Resolves disputes. There are sometimes clashes between departments. A dispute may sometimes go to the Prime Minister, but the role of Cabinet is to act as an arbiter. This role is usually carried out by the Cabinet Office. For example, if there are differences between some departments as to the stance to be taken in an EU negotiation, the Cabinet Office seeks to iron out the differences and ensure – in the words of Cabinet Secretary Sir Gus O'Donnell – 'that the government goes with a single position' (O'Donnell 2009). However, serious policy disputes between ministers have to be ironed out in Cabinet or Cabinet Committee. As another former Cabinet Secretary, Lord Wilson of Dinton, put it:

> There is still an enormous amount of decision-taking that is circulated to Cabinet or circulated to Cabinet committees and where someone is unhappy they have the opportunity to bring it up and for a discussion to take place, and that does happen.
>
> (Wilson 2009)

One of the committees created in May 2010 was a Coalition Committee, established in order to resolve disputes between the two parties forming the Coalition Government, though in practice it has rarely met. A rare occasion when it did was in 2012 over the issue of reform of the House of Lords.

Constrains the Prime Minister. Although the Prime Minister chairs the Cabinet and usually achieves desired outcomes, there are occasions when members may not be prepared to go along with the PM. Even powerful prime ministers such as Winston Churchill and Margaret Thatcher could not always get their way with Cabinet colleagues. Thatcher was notable in that she sometimes summed up discussions at the beginning. This could be portrayed as a sign of a dominating Prime Minister, but it was just as much a sign of weakness. She could not be certain that ministers would agree with her and so she had to try to steer them in the direction she favoured. Tony Blair kept meetings short, reducing the opportunity for discussion, but there were occasions when he ran into opposition from members. Thus, for example, the lead headline in the *Independent on Sunday* on 8 May 2005 was 'Cabinet defies Blair in power struggle'. Even the most persuasive of premiers cannot always ensure that the Cabinet will go along with the policy favoured by No. 10.

Unifies government. The Cabinet formally has responsibility, as we have seen, for coordinating government. The Cabinet Office is the key body for monitoring what goes on in Whitehall and ensuring that Cabinet decisions are relayed to officials. However, there is also an important political dimension. The Cabinet is the body through which the Prime Minister can reach out to the rest of government. It is essentially a means of conveying the collective will of government and not only informing departments but, in effect, enthusing them. An astute Prime Minister can work through Cabinet to lead rather than direct.

Unifies the parliamentary party. The Prime Minister can work through Cabinet to reach the rest of government, but can also work through Cabinet to reach the party in Parliament. The Cabinet is described by some commentators as a committee of Parliament. It is not a committee of Parliament – it is a committee of government – but it comprises parliamentarians. Cabinet ministers remain within Parliament and see backbench members on a regular basis. Ministers have offices in the Palace of Westminster as well as in their departments. Some Cabinet ministers may also have their own power base within the House, having the support of like-minded MPs. Cabinet discussions can help ensure that ministers feel that they have been involved and are thus willing to embrace the outcomes of Cabinet deliberations, taking those decisions back to party colleagues and persuading them to support them. In 2010 this unifying role extended to the two parties forming the Coalition Government.

The Cabinet may thus be seen as a buckle between party leaders and Whitehall and between party leaders and Westminster. The extent to which it is an effective buckle depends in large measure on the extent to which it is fully utilised.

Under the Blair premiership in particular, it was open to accusations that it was not being fully utilised. Cabinet meetings were short and, according to one member, achieved little. 'Occasionally, people would express concern, or a little doubt about an issue raised, but only in a very mild way and others rarely took up such comments' (Short 2004: 70). Another, David Blunkett, wrote of Cabinet committees: 'Some are more useful than others. Where something has to be collectively agreed, then they are worthwhile, but where it is just a rubber stamp or where people just read out their departmental brief, then they are a complete waste of time' (Blunkett 2006: 564). According to James Naughtie, 'No Prime Minister since the nineteenth century has spent more time avoiding formal meetings with cabinet colleagues than Tony Blair' (Naughtie 2001: 104). He was seen as distancing himself not only from Cabinet, but from the civil service and Parliament (Norton 2008: 92–100). His premiership seemed to epitomise the presidentialisation of British politics. Though Cabinet and Cabinet committees retained relevance – they were still the sites on occasion of collective deliberation – the Cabinet system has given way to a debate over the extent to which power in British government is concentrated in No. 10 Downing Street.

Presidential government?

The debate as to whether Britain has prime ministerial or Cabinet Government is not new. It was being hotly debated 50 years ago (see Norton 1982: Chapter 1). What is remarkable is that some commentators thought that there was anything approaching government by the Cabinet (see, for example, Jones 1965; Brown 1968; Gordon Walker 1972). By its nature, a body of over 20 people meeting once and sometimes twice a week is not in a position to engage in policy making on a consistent basis. The Cabinet can give assent to policy proposals, its committees fulfil important tasks of scrutiny and approval, but it is not a body for the initiation or formulation of measures of public policy. Some prime ministers have been more dependent on their Cabinets, or some of their Cabinet colleagues, than others, but the Prime Minister has usually been the central figure of government. If the PM has been overshadowed in government, it has not usually been by the Cabinet but by one or more senior members of the Cabinet.

The thesis of a presidential premiership in UK government has grown in recent years. The thesis has been challenged, but not on the grounds of a powerful Cabinet but rather because of a more crowded political environment. The Prime Minister has had to contend with more powerful political actors. The territory in which the Prime Minister's writ runs has contracted. The Prime Minister operates in a shrinking world.

Presidential or constrained?

The thesis of a *presidential premiership* rests on the Prime Minister becoming more detached from Cabinet, party and Parliament and operating as if the occupant of the office is elected directly by the people (see Foley 1993, 2000, 2004). The PM acts as the embodiment of the national will and intervenes within government to ensure a particular outcome is achieved (Thomas 1998: 79). Detachment, or what Bennister has termed 'institutional stretch', is not confined to the UK (Bennister 2007: 2–19) but under Tony Blair it was arguably taken to unprecedented levels (Norton 2003a, 2003b, 2008). Though Gordon Brown and David Cameron sought to be more collegial than Blair, decision making has remained heavily concentrated in 10 Downing Street. The occupant of No. 10 is surrounded by key advisers, personally appointed by the Prime Minister and thus owing their positions to him. He may occasionally consult with senior ministers, or (as in David Cameron's case) with a particular senior minister, but it is usually the Prime Minister who determines the policy to be pursued; that policy is then

David Cameron and Nick Clegg
Source: Press Association/Nick Ansell

announced or reported to Cabinet before being put in the public domain. The style of government under Tony Blair was characterised as 'sofa government', comprising informal meetings with other senior ministers and/or key advisers. David Cameron was to find himself more constrained by the imperatives of a coalition government, but No.10 has remained the heart of governmental decision making.

However, the thesis has not gone unchallenged. The Prime Minister is dominant within British government, but not all-powerful, and the territory within which he is powerful is becoming smaller. He is constrained to some degree within government and, increasingly outside government.

Constraints within government. The Prime Minister may exercise considerable powers. Ministers are dependent on him for their positions and some commentators see them as agents of the Prime Minister. We shall examine the claims of a *principal–agent* relationship in the next chapter. However, there are other studies which suggest that policy-making power is not concentrated in Downing Street. The *baronial* model posits that much policy making is done by senior ministers. No statutory powers are vested in the Prime Minister, or in the Cabinet. The powers are vested in senior ministers. Though the Prime Minister may take an interest in particular sectors, he has limited time and is usually not a policy polymath. As a result, senior ministers are often left to generate policy initiatives within their departments. Again, we shall examine this model in the next chapter. We shall consider it alongside the *bureaucratic* model, which identifies the capacity of civil servants to shape policy outcomes. There are various means available to officials to influence what a minister sees and considers. Civil servants carry out the decisions of ministers, but they may have a considerable influence over those decisions. Indeed, in some cases, it was argued that 'in certain departments, for example the Home Office, it appeared that officials effectively ran the

department, and ministers were seen as obstacles to its smooth running' (Richards and Smith 2002: 61). Claims of excessive civil service influence became pronounced on the part of some Conservatives under the Coalition Government formed in 2010, prompting the Government to announce proposals in 2012 for a reform of policy making within Whitehall, including hiving off some policy advice to think tanks and universities.

The essential point is that the Prime Minister does not exist in a vacuum and, though some decisions may be taken unilaterally, nonetheless he has to work with ministers and officials in order to deliver public policy. The different parts of government will normally work together, but there may be times when they are not in harmony. The Prime Minister may face resistance within Cabinet. Particular Cabinet colleagues may refuse to go along with a particular proposal. He may be advised by the Cabinet Secretary that a particular proposal may not work or may best be achieved by some other means. As former Cabinet Secretary, Lord Wilson of Dinton, put it: 'I think you may take it that we have all of us, in our time, had to be firm' (Wilson 2009). There may be times when the Prime Minister may not be able to take Parliament for granted. All prime ministers since Edward Heath onwards have suffered one or more defeats in the House of Commons (and considerably more in the House of Lords); Margaret Thatcher's Government actually lost a bill – the Shops Bill in 1986 – when 72 Conservative MPs voted with the Opposition to defeat it. The Prime Minister may be able to achieve what he wants by adopting a detached and confrontational stance, but it is difficult to maintain that approach indefinitely without inciting a backlash. The Prime Minister is an integral part of government rather than a free-standing and all-powerful office standing apart from it.

Constraints outside government. However, perhaps the most powerful constraint on the Prime Minister in the twenty-first century is the fact that his capacity to achieve desired outcomes is limited by policy-making power becoming more dispersed. There has been what has been termed a 'hollowing-out' of the state (see Rhodes 1997: 17–18). Whereas policy-making power was previously concentrated at the centre – that is, within the core executive at the heart of a unitary nation state – it is now shared among a number of bodies at sub-national, national and supranational level.

Prime Minister and Cabinet

Cabinet Secretary Sir Gus O'Donnell in evidence to the House of Lords Constitution Committee 2009:

I worked with John Major who had a very collegiate style. He used the Cabinet committees in that way. Tony Blair, when he came in in 1997 – not that I was there at the time – had a strong emphasis on stock takes and delivery. He wanted to get specific deliveries on things like literacy and numeracy, specific items. That was his very big emphasis. With Gordon Brown coming in as Prime Minister, it is difficult to separate him coming in from global events. It has been dominated by an economic agenda and that has worked mainly through the National Economic Council. What this tells me is that it is partly the style of the Prime Minister, partly events. This is what I mean about being flexible.

Constitution Committee, House of Lords, *Cabinet Office Inquiry: Minutes of Evidence, Wednesday 4 November 2009* http://www.publications.parliament.uk/pa/ld/lduncorr/const041109ev10.pdf

Some policy-making competence has been transferred to elected bodies in Scotland, Northern Ireland and Wales. Some has passed to other bodies at national level, including regulators and the courts. The courts are now important actors in determining whether provisions of UK law are in conflict with European law or with the European Convention on Human Rights. Some has passed upwards to supranational bodies, such as the institutions of the European Union. The government also operates as but one of several participants in international gatherings such as the meetings of leaders of the key economic nations (G7, G20, the World Trade Organisation). The capacity to achieve desired outcomes is also increasingly limited by globalisation, reducing the barriers that each nation can erect to protect its own internal economic activity. The Prime Minister cannot dictate the flow of global markets. Policy is thus made by different bodies at different levels. Various terms have been utilised to describe this, but the most commonly used phrase now is that of 'multi-level governance' (see Bache and Flinders 2004).

The importance of this for British government is that, whereas the Prime Minister has been described (albeit ironically) as 'first among equals' in Cabinet, in international gatherings he is not first among equals, but at best an equal among equals. If anyone is pre-eminent in such gatherings, or first among equals as heads of government, it is the President of the United States. While in Cabinet the Prime Minister is dealing with members who are appointed by him, in summits of heads of government he is dealing with members who have their own national power base. Other than in bilateral meetings, he can find himself in a minority. Decisions may be taken with which the Prime Minister disagrees, but which he may find it politic to go along with. In the EU Council of Ministers the UK minister may lose out through qualified majority voting, a decision being taken which has effect in the UK even though it lacks the support of the British government and Parliament.

The consequence of these developments for the Prime Minister is encapsulated in the title of a study by Professor Richard Rose (2001): *The Prime Minister in a Shrinking World*. The world is getting smaller in terms of communication and economic developments. There is a growing interdependence and a growing trend towards seeking to address global problems through international meetings and agreement. When policy competences were concentrated in national government, the Prime Minister could exercise considerable power in determining outcomes. In the twenty-first century he has to try to accumulate more powers to his office in order to cope with a rapidly changing political environment, one in which his political writ does not run as far as it once did. It is thus possible to characterise the Prime Minister as having to run in order to stand still. Given the extent and speed of globalisation, it may be seen by some as a losing battle. The world may, in Rose's terms, be shrinking: a corollary is that so is the Prime Minister's kingdom.

Chapter summary

The Prime Minister stands at the apex within British government. The occupant of the office leads the Cabinet and heads the party that usually enjoys a clear majority in the House of Commons. A strong Prime Minister may thus be in a position to achieved desired outcomes. However, the extent to which prime ministers actually achieve what they want varies. Prime ministerial power is variable and not a constant.

The extent to which prime ministers can achieve their goals depends in part on who the Prime Minister is: what they want to achieve, and their skills in getting their way, will – as we have seen – vary from premier to premier. The political climate, not least the relationship between different political bodies, can change. A Prime Minister may enjoy a good parliamentary majority and be returned at the next election with a small and potentially difficult majority. Events at an international or national level may blow a government off course. John Major as Prime Minister led his party to victory in 1992, but with a much reduced majority: the same year, his Government was forced to withdraw from the European exchange rate mechanism, triggering a collapse in confidence in the Government's ability to handle the economic affairs of the nation. A 'no' vote in Denmark in a referendum on the Maastricht treaty emboldened Conservative MPs opposed to the treaty to try to defeat passage of the bill to give legal effect to it in the UK. Shortly after becoming Prime Minister, Gordon Brown was seen as a powerful Prime Minister, riding high in the opinion polls. His popular support plummeted later in the year when he decided not to call a general election. He reclaimed some support for his initial response to the global 'credit crunch' in 2008, but that then receded as the UK economy went into recession.

Prime ministerial power thus varies not only from premier to premier but also within a premiership. There were times when Margaret Thatcher was dominant as Prime Minister and at other times, as during the Westland crisis in 1986 or in her last year in office (1989–90), when she was politically vulnerable. Tony Blair, similarly, was usually powerful but nonetheless experienced phases when he was politically weak. He was also at times constrained by his Chancellor of the Exchequer, Gordon Brown. 'For such a so-called presidential figure Blair was blocked in key areas. The Chancellor carved out a measure of autonomy hardly ever achieved by a minister' (Kavanagh 2007: 7). David Cameron exercises the powers of the premiership but is limited by having a Deputy Prime Minister who, as the leader of the other party in coalition, can seek to block proposals unacceptable to Liberal Democrats.

The variability of prime ministerial power was well expressed in 2009 by former Cabinet Secretary, Lord Wilson of Dinton:

> You may have times, as we had times, when prime ministers have been so strong that their colleagues accepted anything they wanted to do; they had a parliamentary back bench which was supportive of whatever they did; public opinion was happy; the economy was going well. Their ability to get their way was therefore unparalleled, but that does not alter the fundamental fact that if circumstances are different and a prime minister is in a weak position, his cabinet colleagues are debating the issues strongly, it is not possible for the prime minister to have his way and we are not in a country where the prime minister is a president and can just say 'This is what happens and this is what goes'. We are always fundamentally in a position where if cabinet ministers wish to assert themselves then the power of the prime minister will be checked and balanced in that way.
>
> (Wilson 2009)

The variability of prime ministerial power is further exacerbated by international developments, over which the Prime Minister may have little or no influence. The Prime Minister can be and frequently is powerful, but ultimately is dependent on what one Prime Minister, Harold Macmillan, summarised as 'events, dear boy, events'.

Discussion points

- What are the main tasks of the Prime Minister? To what extent have they changed in recent decades?
- To what extent does it matter *who* is Prime Minister?
- Does the Cabinet still have a significant role in British government?
- What are the principal constraints on prime ministerial power?
- Has the United Kingdom seen the growth of a 'presidential' Prime Minister?
- To what extent is prime ministerial power variable?

Further reading

There are various books on prime ministers and the premierships. Among the most recent are Leonard (2005), Rose (2001) and Hennessy (2000). Foley (1993, 2000, 2004) examines the presidentialisation of the premiership. For a comparative study, see Helms (2005). On the premiership of Tony Blair, see Powell (2010), Beech and Lee (2008), Seldon (2007a, 2007b, 2004), Riddell (2005), Beckett and Hencke (2004), and Rentoul (2001). Campbell (2007, 2011, 2012a, 2012b) also gives a fascinating insight into what went on in Downing Street under Blair. On the Brown premiership, see Seldon and Lodge (2010), and on the Conservative-Liberal Democrat Coalition Government, see Heppell and Seawright (2012) and Lee and Beech (2011). On multilevel governance, see Bache and Flinders (2004). There is no one good recent work on the Cabinet: valuable material on Cabinet and relations between ministers and the PM may be found in the diaries of former Cabinet ministers, such as Straw (2012), Darling (2011), Mandelson (2010), Blunkett (2006) and Short (2004).

Bibliography

Bache, I. and Flinders, M. (2004) (eds) *Multi-Level Governance* (Oxford University Press).

Beech, M. and Lee, S. (2008) (eds) *Ten Years of New Labour* (Palgrave Macmillan).

Beckett, F. and Hencke, D. (2004) *The Blairs and their Court* (Aurum).

Bennister, M. (2007) 'Tony Blair and John Howard: Comparative Predominance and "Institution Stretch" in the UK and Australia', *British Journal of Politics and International Relations*, vol. 7, pp. 2–19.

Blake, R. (1975) *The Office of Prime Minister* (Oxford University Press).

Blunkett, D. (2006) *The Blunkett Tapes* (Bloomsbury).

Brown, A.H. (1968) 'Prime Ministerial Power (Part II)', *Public Law*, Summer, pp. 96–118.

Butler, Lord (2009) Evidence, Constitution Committee, House of Lords, *Cabinet Office Inquiry: Minutes of Evidence, Wednesday 24 June 2009*, http://www.publications.parliament.uk/pa/ld/lduncorr/const240609ev4.pdf

Campbell, A. (2007) *The Blair Years* (Hutchinson).

Campbell, A. (2011) *Diaries Volume 2: Power and the People* (Hutchinson).

Campbell, A. (2012a) *Diaries Volume 3: Power and Responsibility* (Hutchinson).

Campbell, A. (2012b) *The Burden of Power* (Hutchinson).

Carter, B.E. (1956) *The Office of Prime Minister* (Faber and Faber).

Daalder, H. (1964) *Cabinet Reform in Britain 1914–1963* (Stanford University Press).

Darling, A. (2011) *Back from the Brink* (Atlantic Books).

Englefield, D., Seaton, J. and White, I. (1995) *Facts About The British Prime Ministers* (Mansell).

Foley, M. (1993) *The Rise of the British Presidency* (Manchester University Press).

Foley, M. (2000) *The British Presidency: Tony Blair and the Politics of Public Leadership* (Manchester University Press).

Foley, M. (2004) 'Presidential Attribution as an Agency of Prime Ministerial Critique in a Parliamentary Democracy: The Case of Tony Blair', *The British Journal of Politics and International Relations*, vol. 6, no. 3, pp. 292–311.

Gilmour, I. (1971) *The Body Politic*, 3rd revised edn (Hutchinson).

Gordon Walker, P. (1972) *The Cabinet*, revised edn (Fontana).

Helms, L. (2005) *Presidents, Prime Ministers and Chancellors* (Palgrave Macmillan).

Hennessy, P. (1986) *Cabinet* (Basil Blackwell).

Hennessy, P. (2000) *The Prime Minister: The Office and its Holders since 1945* (Allen Lane, The Penguin Press).

Heppell, T. and Seawright, T. (2012) (eds) *Cameron and the Conservatives* (Palgrave Macmillan).

Jones, G.W. (1965) 'The Prime Minister's Powers', *Parliamentary Affairs*, vol. 18, pp. 167–85.

Kavanagh, D. (2007) 'The Blair Premiership', in Seldon, A. (ed.) *Blair's Britain 1997–2007* (Cambridge University Press).

Le May, G. (1964) *British Government 1914–1963*, 1964 edn (Methuen).

Lee, S. and Beech, M. (2011) (eds) *The Cameron-Clegg Government* (Palgrave Macmillan).

Leonard, D. (2005) *A Century of Premiers* (Palgrave Macmillan).

Macintosh, J.P. (1977) *The British Cabinet*, 3rd edn (Stevens).

Mandelson, P. (2010) *The Third Man* (HarperPress).

Montgomerie, T. (2012) 'Cameron fiddles while the Tory brand burns', *The Times*, 18 June, p. 21.

Naughtie, J. (2001) *The Rivals* (Fourth Estate).

Norton, P. (1978) *Conservative Dissidents* (Temple Smith).

Norton, P. (1982) *The Constitution in Flux* (Martin Robertson/Basil Blackwell).

Norton, P. (1987) 'Prime Ministerial Power: A Framework for Analysis', *Teaching Politics*, vol. 16, no. 3, pp. 325–45.

Norton, P. (1988) 'Prime Ministerial Power', *Social Studies Review*, vol. 3, no. 3, pp. 108–15.

Norton, P. (2003a) 'Governing Alone', *Parliamentary Affairs*, vol. 56, no. 4, pp. 543–59.

Norton, P. (2003b) 'The Presidentialisation of British Politics', *Government and Opposition*, vol. 38, pp. 274–8.

Norton, P. (2008) 'Tony Blair and the Office of Prime Minister', in Beech, M. and Lee, S. (eds) *Ten Years of New Labour* (Palgrave Macmillan).

O'Donnell, G. (2009) Evidence, Constitution Committee, House of Lords, *Cabinet Office Inquiry: Minutes of Evidence, Wednesday 4 November 2009*, http://www.publications.parliament.uk/pa/ld/lduncorr/const041109ev10.pdf

Powell, J. (2010) *The New Machiavelli* (The Bodley Head).

Rentoul, J. (2001) *Tony Blair: Prime Minister* (Little, Brown and Company).

Rhodes, R.A.W. (1997) *Understanding Governance: Policy Networks, Governance, Reflexivity and Accountability* (Open University Press).

Riddell, P. (2005) *The Unfulfilled Prime Minister* (Politico's).

Richards, D. and Smith, M.J. (2002) *Governance and Public Policy in the UK* (Oxford University Press).

Rose, R. (2001) *The Prime Minister in a Shrinking World* (Polity).

Seldon, A. (2004) *Blair* (Free Press).

Seldon, A. (2007a) *Blair Unbound* (Simon & Schuster).

Seldon, A. (2007b) (ed.) *Blair's Britain, 1997–2007* (Cambridge University Press).

Seldon, A. and Lodge, G. (2010) *Brown at 10* (Biteback Publishing).

Short, C. (2004) *An Honourable Deception?* (Free Press).

Straw, J. (2012) *Last Man Standing* (Macmillan).

Taylor, S. (1998) 'Robert Walpole, First Earl of Orford', in Eccleshall, R. and Walker, G. (eds) *Biographical Dictionary of British Prime Ministers* (Routledge).

Thomas, G.P. (1998) *Prime Minister and Cabinet Today* (Manchester University Press).

Wilson, Lord (2009) Evidence, Constitution Committee, House of Lords, *Cabinet Office Inquiry: Minutes of Evidence, Wednesday 24 June 2009*, http://www.publications.parliament.uk/pa/ld/lduncorr/const240609ev4.pdf

Useful websites

No. 10 Downing Street: www.number10.gov.uk

Deputy Prime Minister: www.dpm.cabinetoffice.gov.uk

Cabinet Office: www.cabinetoffice.gov.uk

Ministerial Code: www.cabinetoffice.gov.uk/resource-library/ministerial-code

Previous prime ministers: www.number10.gov.uk/history-and-tour/past-prime-ministers/

Government departments and structures: www.number10.gov.uk/transparency/org-charts/

Political and Constitutional Reform Committee, House of Commons – 2012–13 enquiry into role of Prime Minister: www.parliament.uk/business/committees/committees-a-z/commons-select/political-and-constitutional-reform-committee/news/role-of-prime-minister-further-call-for-ev/

Appendix

Prime ministers since 1900

Marquess of Salisbury (Con)	1895–1902
Arthur J. Balfour (Con)	1902–5
Sir Henry Campbell-Bannerman (Lib)	1905–8
Herbert H. Asquith (Lib)	1908–16
David Lloyd George (Lib)[1]	1916–22
Andrew Bonar Law (Con)	1922–3
Stanley Baldwin (Con)	1923–4
J. Ramsay MacDonald (Lab)	1924
Stanley Baldwin (Con)	1924–9
J. Ramsay MacDonald (Lab/Nat Lab)[2]	1929–35
Stanley Baldwin (Con)	1935–7
Neville Chamberlain (Con)	1937–40
Winston Churchill (Con)	1940–5
Clement Attlee (Lab)	1945–51
Winston Churchill (Con)	1951–5
Sir Anthony Eden (Con)	1955–7
Harold Macmillan (Con)	1957–63
Sir Alec Douglas-Home (Con)	1963–4
Harold Wilson (Lab)	1964–70
Edward Heath (Con)	1970–4
Harold Wilson (Lab)	1974–6
James Callaghan (Lab)	1976–9
Margaret Thatcher (Con)	1979–90
John Major (Con)	1990–7
Tony Blair (Lab)	1997–2007
Gordon Brown (Lab)	2007–10
David Cameron (Con)[3]	2010–

1   Led Conservative-dominated coalition from 1918
2   Led Conservative-dominated coalition from 1931
3   Led Conservative-dominated coalition from 2010

The Cabinet, June 2012

Prime Minister, First Lord of the Treasury and Minister for the Civil Service – The Rt Hon David Cameron MP

Deputy Prime Minister, Lord President of the Council (with special responsibility for political and constitutional reform) – The Rt Hon Nick Clegg MP

First Secretary of State, Secretary of State for Foreign and Commonwealth Affairs – The Rt Hon William Hague MP

Chancellor of the Exchequer – The Rt Hon George Osborne MP

Chief Secretary to the Treasury – The Rt Hon Danny Alexander MP

Lord Chancellor, Secretary of State for Justice – The Rt Hon Kenneth Clarke QC MP

Secretary of State for the Home Department; and Minister for Women and Equalities – The Rt Hon Theresa May MP

Secretary of State for Defence – The Rt Hon Philip Hammond MP

Secretary of State for Business, Innovation and Skills, and President of the Board of Trade – The Rt Hon Dr Vincent Cable MP

Secretary of State for Work and Pensions – The Rt Hon Iain Duncan Smith MP

Secretary of State for Energy and Climate Change – The Rt Hon Edward Davey MP

Secretary of State for Health – The Rt Hon Andrew Lansley CBE MP

Secretary of State for Education – The Rt Hon Michael Gove MP

Secretary of State for Communities and Local Government – The Rt Hon Eric Pickles MP

Secretary of State for Transport – The Rt Hon Justine Greening MP

Secretary of State for Environment, Food and Rural Affairs – The Rt Hon Caroline Spelman MP

Secretary of State for International Development – The Rt Hon Andrew Mitchell MP

Secretary of State for Culture, Olympics, Media and Sport – The Rt Hon Jeremy Hunt MP

Secretary of State for Northern Ireland – The Rt Hon Owen Paterson MP

Secretary of State for Scotland – The Rt Hon Michael Moore MP

Secretary of State for Wales – The Rt Hon Cheryl Gillan MP

Minister without Portfolio (Minister of State) – The Rt Hon Baroness Warsi

Leader of the House of Lords, Chancellor of the Duchy of Lancaster – The Rt Hon Lord Strathclyde

Attends Cabinet

Leader of the House of Commons, Lord Privy Seal – The Rt Hon Sir George Young Bt MP

Minister for the Cabinet Office, Paymaster General – The Rt Hon Francis Maude MP

Minister of State (providing policy advice to the Prime Minister in the Cabinet Office) – The Rt Hon Oliver Letwin MP

Attorney General – The Rt Hon Dominic Grieve QC MP (attends Cabinet when ministerial responsibilities are on the agenda)

Minister of State (Minister for Universities and Science) – The Rt Hon David Willetts MP

CHAPTER 19

Ministers, departments and civil servants

Philip Norton

> " In this country we prefer rule by amateurs "
>
> Clement Attlee

Learning objectives

- To promote an understanding of the place and significance of government departments in British government.

- To identify the role and political impact of ministers in policy making.

- To assess the relationship between ministers and civil servants.

- To summarise and assess competing models of policy making.

Departments form the building blocks of British government. Each is headed by a minister, who has responsibility for government policy in the sector covered by the department. Each is staffed by a body of professional civil servants, responsible for advising the minister on policy and for ensuring that policy is implemented. The capacity for ministers to determine policy has been increasingly constrained by external pressures, but ministers remain significant players in policy making.

Introduction

Ministers

Ministers stand at the heart of British government. In legal terms, they are the most powerful figures in government. When an Act of Parliament confers powers on government to do something, it does not say 'The Prime Minister may by order . . . [do this or that]'; nor does it say 'The Cabinet may by order . . .'. What it says is 'The Secretary of State may by order . . .'. In other words, legal powers are vested in senior ministers, not in the Prime Minister or Cabinet. Senior ministers are those appointed to head government departments. Their formal designation is Ministers of the Crown. Most will be given the title of Secretary of State (Foreign Secretary, Secretary of State for Home Affairs – popularly known as the Home Secretary – and so on). Originally, there was only one Secretary of State to assist the King. The post was subsequently divided, but the fiction was maintained that there was only one Secretary of State, and that fiction is maintained to the present day. That is why Acts of Parliament still usually stipulate that 'The Secretary of State may by order . . .' or 'The Secretary of State shall by order . . .'. There is no reference to 'The Secretary of State for Transport' or 'The Foreign Secretary' but simply 'The Secretary of State'.

Each Minister of the Crown heads a government department. Each has a number of other ministers, known as *junior ministers*, to assist in fulfilling the responsibilities of the office. Each senior minister has one or more political advisers. Each has a body of civil servants – permanent, non-political professionals – to advise on policy and to ensure the implementation of policy once it is agreed on. The number of civil servants in a department will sometimes run into many thousands.

Each Minister of the Crown is thus vested with important legal powers. Each has a department to assist in carrying out the policy or decisions that he or she has made. Each is thus, in formal terms, an important political figure, vital to the continuation of government in the United Kingdom. However, in the view of many commentators, the legal position does not match the political reality. Although legal power may be vested in senior ministers, the real power, it is argued, is exercised elsewhere. The capacity to determine policy has, on this argument, passed to other political actors, not least the European Union, the Prime Minister, civil servants, and the courts. One argument is that senior ministers are now not principals in terms of policy making but rather agents, be it of the Prime Minister, of the civil servants in their department or of the European Union.

What, then, is the structure and operation of government departments? What are the powers of a senior minister? What are the limitations? To what extent is a senior minister able to deploy the powers of the office to achieve desired outcomes? And what is the best model that helps us to understand the position of senior ministers in British government? Are they agents of other actors in the political system? Or are they powerful independent figures?

Departments

Each Minister of the Crown heads a **department**. The structure is essentially hierarchical. Those working in a department fall into one of two categories, the political or the official. At the head of the department is the minister, assisted by a number of junior ministers. The senior minister will have a parliamentary private secretary (PPS) as well as one or more special advisers to assist. Ministers of state will also normally appoint a PPS and some may also have special advisers. The minister and these other appointees constitute the political part of a department. The official part of the department comprises civil servants, headed by the Permanent Secretary. Civil servants in the department answer to the minister through the Permanent Secretary. There is now usually a management board, chaired by the Permanent Secretary and comprising the senior civil servants of the department. The department is usually divided into divisions, headed by a secretary-general or director. Each department will also usually have one or more **executive agencies** for which it is the sponsoring department. The structure differs from department to department, not least depending on the number and complexity of responsibilities within each department.

There has been a significant change since the mid-twentieth century in that departments have become less in number and greater in size. They have reduced by about a third in number, with some substantial departments being created – currently, for example, the Department for Business, Industry and Skills (BIS) – and with the large departments having far more ministers than any department had in the mid-twentieth century. In 1945 a department typically had two or three ministers. By the twenty-first century the number varied from two or three in the smaller departments and up to nine or ten in the largest. In 2009, when the Department for Business, Innovation and Skills was created, it had 11 ministers.

Political appointees

Junior ministers

There are three ranks of junior minister: ministers of state, parliamentary under-secretaries of state and parliamentary secretaries. (Because the acronym for the parliamentary under-secretaries of state is PUSS, they are known in Whitehall as 'pussies'.) They are appointed to assist the senior minister in carrying out the minister's responsibilities. They will normally be allocated particular tasks. Thus, for instance, in the Department for Culture, Media and Sports, one of the junior ministers is designated as Minister for Sport. In the Foreign and Commonwealth Office, one of the ministers of state is Minister for Europe. In the Department for Business, Innovation and Skills, one minister is the Minister for Universities and Science.

Junior ministers are appointed by the Prime Minister, although sometimes after consultation with the minister heading the department. Their authority derives from the senior minister. It is the senior minister who decides what responsibilities they shall have and, in effect, how powerful they shall be in the department. They act on behalf of the senior minister. They have no formal line control over civil servants. A junior minister, for example, cannot overrule the Permanent Secretary. A dispute between a junior minister and the Permanent Secretary would have to be resolved by the senior minister.

The number of ministers has grown over the decades. In 1945 there were a total of 76 members of the government, comprising senior ministers, junior ministers and whips. In October 2012 the figure was 119, comprising 22 Cabinet ministers, 71 junior ministers, and 26 whips. The number of ministerial posts was greater, as some ministers held posts in more than one department. As we have noted, it is not unusual for a department now to have several ministers; in 2012 three departments – the Foreign Office, the Department for Business, Innovation and Skills (BIS) and the Department for Communities and Local Government – each had seven, though some of the ministers held joint posts with other departments.

Serving as a junior minister is usually a prerequisite for serving as a senior minister. It is rare for an MP to be appointed to the Cabinet straight from the backbenches. An ambitious backbencher will normally hope to be appointed as a parliamentary under-secretary of state and then as a minister of state before being considered for appointment to the Cabinet. Not all aspiring politicians make it beyond the ranks of junior minister. Some are dismissed after two or three years; some serve for a decade or more without making it to the Cabinet.

The sheer number of junior ministers has been a cause of some controversy. Although their number helps to spread the workload within a department, some observers and former ministers have argued that there are too many of them. The Public Administration Committee of the House of Commons in 2011 argued that the rise in the number of ministers had outstripped the functional needs of government and recommended a reduction in numbers, especially if the number of MPs was reduced (Public Administration Committee 2011). As the committee recognised, the reason

for the growth may be the Prime Minister's desire to reward supporters and because the more junior posts there are the greater the size of the government's payroll vote in Parliament.

Parliamentary private secretaries

Traditionally, one route to reaching junior ministerial office has been through serving as a parliamentary private secretary (PPS). A parliamentary private secretary is appointed to assist a minister. The post is unpaid, the holder is not officially a member of the government and the tasks undertaken are largely determined by the minister. A PPS may serve as the minister's principal link with backbenchers, listening to what has been said and transmitting the views of MPs to the minister. The PPS will also normally help with arranging friendly parliamentary questions and act as a message carrier between the minister and the officials' box in the House of Commons during a parliamentary debate.

The PPS is selected by the minister, although subject to confirmation by the Prime Minister. In some cases, ministers will use their PPSs as trusted advisers. They may also arrange for them to have desks in their departments and may include them in the regular meetings (known as 'prayers') held with junior ministers and senior civil servants in the department. They thus learn how a department works, and if they perform especially well the senior minister may recommend them for promotion to junior ministerial office.

The number of PPSs has grown over the decades. Whereas only senior ministers used to appoint PPSs, it is now the practice for other ministers to appoint them as well. In 1950 there were 27 PPSs; since the 1990s the number has exceeded 40. Such appointments may be helpful to ministers. They are also helpful to government. Although PPSs are not paid, they are nonetheless usually treated as being part of the government when it comes to votes in the House of Commons. The ministerial code makes clear that 'Parliamentary Private Secretaries are expected to support the Government in important divisions in the House. No Parliamentary Private Secretary who votes against the Government can retain his or her position' (Cabinet Office 2010). The result is, in effect, to increase by almost 50 per cent the block vote that the government whips in the House of Commons can rely on in a parliamentary vote.

Special advisers

Unlike ministers and PPSs, special advisers are not drawn from the ranks of parliamentarians. There are two types of special adviser. One is the expert, appointed because of an expertise in a particular subject. The other – the more common type – is the political, appointed to act as an adviser to the minister on a range of issues, to assist with speech writing and to act as a political link between the minister and the party and with other bodies outside the department. They are typically young, bright graduates who are politically ambitious. (One of the special advisers appointed in 1992 by Conservative Chancellor Norman Lamont was David Cameron, later to become Prime Minister; one of Labour Chancellor Gordon Brown's advisers was Ed Balls, later to be a Cabinet minister.) Their loyalty is to the minister, who is responsible for appointing them and to whom their fortunes are linked: if the minister goes, the special adviser goes as well. A minister may, and frequently does, invite the special adviser to stay with them if they are moved to another post. Sometimes an incoming minister may invite the special adviser to the previous incumbent to stay on. However, the link is normally with one minister. It is thus in the interests of the special adviser to be loyal to the minister and to work hard to ensure the minister's success.

Like junior ministers and PPSs, the number of special advisers has grown in recent years. Special advisers have their origins in the 1960s, but they became important figures in the 1970s: then, only very senior ministers were permitted to have a special adviser, and no more than one. The number expanded in the 1980s and early 1990s and there was a further expansion with the return of a Labour government in 1997, with some departments permitted to have more than two special advisers. Two remains the norm, though with some senior ministers having more.

The appointment of special advisers has proved controversial. Some critics are wary of political appointees who are not answerable to Parliament having such a role close to ministers. Some see them as being too powerful and undermining the role of civil servants. 'They seem to have taken over the Prime Minister's office and largely run the Treasury' (Denman 2002: 254). Chancellor Gordon Brown dealt with civil servants largely through his special advisers (Darling 2011: 6–7). Supporters point out that special advisers are actually of value to civil servants in that they can absorb political work that civil servants should not be asked to do (such as liaising with party bodies and replying to correspondence that has a partisan flavour). However, if they encroach on functions assigned to civil servants, or seek to give orders to civil servants, then problems may arise and, as we shall see, in recent years have arisen.

The officials

The bulk of the people working in government departments are **civil servants**. Since 1996 the most senior posts have been brought together to form the 'Senior Civil Service', presently comprising just under 4,000 officials (3,800 in

2011). A new pay and performance management system was introduced in April 2002, with new salary bands introduced on the basis of recommendations from the Senior Salary Review Body. At the end of 2011 the salary range for Permanent Secretaries was £140,000 to £240,000 and for Pay Band 3, occupied by those immediately below Permanent Secretaries, it was £101,500 to £208,000. The base salary for a member of the senior civil service is £58,200. Salary increases are performance related.

Permanent Secretary

The Permanent Secretary is the permanent head of a department. He (occasionally she – just under a quarter of Permanent Secretaries are now women) will usually have spent his entire career in the Civil Service, rising up the ranks in the service before being appointed Permanent Secretary in a department. Formally, the Permanent Secretary has line control within a department. That is, all communication between civil servants and a senior minister is formally channelled through the Permanent Secretary. In practice, that is now administratively impossible. Instead, submissions will normally go straight to the minister, and the minister may call in the relevant civil servants to discuss particular issues for which they have responsibility. Nonetheless, submissions will be copied to the Permanent Secretary, and the Permanent Secretary will normally sit in on all discussions concerning important policy and administrative matters.

The Permanent Secretary is answerable to the minister for what goes on in the department. However, there is one exception. The Permanent Secretary is the accounting officer for the department. That means that responsibility for ensuring that money is spent for the purposes for which it has been voted by Parliament rests with the Permanent Secretary. The Permanent Secretary is answerable for the accounts, and if those accounts are the subject of an investigation and report by the National Audit Office, then it is the Permanent Secretary who appears before the Public Accounts Committee of the House of Commons to answer questions raised by the report.

The Permanent Secretary is, in effect, the chief executive of the department, but training for the role has usually been acquired over 20 or 30 years in the Civil Service. One study of 111 permanent secretaries in four periods between 1945 and 1993 found that all bar three were men (Theakston 1995: 36–43). They were usually educated at public school or grammar school before going on to Oxford or Cambridge University. Most went straight from university into the Civil Service and spent 25 years in Whitehall before taking up their present positions. Most had also served in more than one department, a feature especially of the latter half of the century. They were also predominantly 'generalists' – with degrees in classics or the arts – rather than specialists in law or economics; occasionally, a Permanent Secretary would be appointed who had some specialist knowledge of the subject covered by the department, but such figures were – and remain – rare. Just as ministers are normally generalists rather than specialists in a subject, so too are the civil servants who run the department. Their specialist knowledge is of how the machinery of government operates.

Various changes, though, have taken place in recent years. More permanent secretaries are now women – as we have noted, just under a quarter – and there is now open recruitment, with a number being appointed from outside the civil service or having spent part of their careers in the private sector or other parts of the public sector. Of the two top civil servants in 2012, Cabinet Secretary Sir Jeremy Heywood had previously left the civil service to be managing director of the UK Banking Division at the banking firm of Morgan Stanley, before returning to the service, and the head of the home civil service, Sir Bob Kerslake, had earlier been Chief Executive of Sheffield City Council.

Civil servants

A similar pattern is to be found for those below the rank of Permanent Secretary. The typical senior civil servant is a white male; recent years have seen an increase in the number of women entering the senior Civil Service, though two-thirds of posts are held by men. In 2011, 34 per cent of senior civil servants were women, up from 18 per cent in 1999; 5 per cent were drawn from ethnic minorities and the same proportion had a declared disability. However, the senior Civil Service remains the least diverse section of the civil service. While only one-third of senior civil servants are women, 53 per cent of all civil servants are female.

The Civil Service has a less rigid hierarchy than it had in the 1970s and 1980s. There is less rigidity in terms of the positions held by senior civil servants (titles are now likely to be more managerial, such as director, than bureaucratic, such as assistant secretary) and responsibility for pay and recruitment is no longer centralised but instead delegated to individual departments. Each department also has responsibility for training, although courses have been provided centrally. These used to be provided by the Civil Service College. The college was incorporated by the incoming 1997 Labour Government in a Centre for Policy and Management Studies (the CPMS). The CPMS was itself incorporated in the National School of Government, established in June 2005 to help public sector organisations build capacity in good governance. The School linked with academic bodies to provide training in management and offered senior manager workshops for senior civil servants as well as programmes in, for example, people management, leadership, financial management and policy delivery. In 2012, in order to reduce costs, the National School of Government was succeeded by Civil Service Learning, based primarily on e-learning with a limited number of face-to-face courses.

The senior civil service accounts for just under 1 per cent of civil servants. In March 2011 there were 498,433 full-time equivalent posts in the civil service. Most of these were in executive agencies. These agencies, such as Jobcentre Plus, the Driver and Vehicle Licensing Agency (DVLA), the Highways Agency, and the UK Border Agency, began to be created in 1988 following publication of a report, *Improving Management in Government: the **Next Steps***, by Sir Robin Ibbs. Most executive responsibilities of government have been hived off to such agencies, and today four out of five civil servants are employed in executive agencies. The intention behind the agencies has been to separate the service-delivery responsibilities of government from policy making. Those senior civil servants responsible for policy advice to ministers remain at the heart of government departments.

Two features of the Civil Service over the past three decades are of particular relevance in studying government departments. The first is the greater emphasis on managerial and business skills. This emphasis developed under the Conservative governments of Margaret Thatcher and John Major and has been maintained by succeeding governments. There is demand on the part of the government for the Civil Service to have much clearer goals, to operate in terms of performance indicators and to deliver on targets that are set for it. Prime Minister Tony Blair was particularly keen to shake up Whitehall and to ensure that civil servants were capable of delivering on the goals set by government (see Mandelson 2010: 222). This line was also taken under the Coalition Government formed in 2010, with Cabinet Office minister, Francis Maude, publishing a Civil Service reform plan in 2012. There has been a greater emphasis on efficiency and commissioning services from outside bodies. The 2012 reforms included opening policy development to competition from external sources, greater scrutiny and testing of major projects and an academy to train senior leaders responsible for such projects. A fund was set up (the Contestable Policy Fund) for the purpose of commissioning policy advice, and in September 2012 the Government announced that the Institute for Public Policy Research (IPPR), a left-leaning think tank, had won a contract to carry out a review into how other civil services work, with a particular focus on accountability systems.

The second change is less often commented on but is more central to explaining the relationship between ministers and civil servants: that is, the less rigid structure within the 'core' of each department. The old hierarchical structure, policed and protected by senior civil servants who had been in place for years, has given way to a more flexible arrangement, not just in terms of formal structure but also in terms of the contact that ministers have with civil servants (see Page and Jenkins 2005: 112–4). Permanent Secretaries tend no longer to be the gatekeepers of what advice is or is not sent to a minister. The change in the structure of the Civil Service has not only made departments more open in terms of the people recruited to serve in senior posts but has also coincided with changes introduced by ministers. In recent years ministers have been more prone to move away from a culture of paperwork – making decisions based on papers placed before them by officials – and towards a more open and interactive culture, calling in civil servants to discuss with them the proposals embodied in their papers.

Senior ministers thus head departments that have a more managerial and business-oriented ethos than before. Those departments, although they have shrunk in staff terms over recent decades (the privatisation of various agencies has led to a reduction in the size of the civil service, down from over 750,000 in 1968) can still be significant employers. Most civil servants work in one of four departments: the Department for Work and Pensions (with over 90,000 working in Jobcentre Plus), HM Revenue and Customs, the Ministry of Justice (with over 50,000 in the National Offender Management Service) and the Ministry of Defence. However, the policy-making side of each department is relatively small. Those employed in the top echelons of the Civil Service – the senior civil service and the ranks immediately below them – comprise no more than 20,000 people.

Ministerial power

It has been argued that ministerial power – the power to determine particular outcomes – derives from several variables (Figure 19.1). One is specific to the office: the legal, departmental and political powers of the office deriving from the convention of individual ministerial responsibility. Two others are specific to the individual: the purpose of the incumbent in taking office, and the skills of the incumbent. And there are three that are essentially external to the office: the power situation, the climate of expectation and international developments.

The office

Ministers are powerful by virtue of the constitutional convention of individual ministerial responsibility (see Norton 1997b). The doctrine confers important legal, departmental and even parliamentary powers.

The legal dimension is central. We have touched on this at the beginning of this chapter. No statutory powers are vested in the Prime Minister or Cabinet. As Nevil Johnson observed, 'the enduring effect of the doctrine of ministerial responsibility has been over the past century or so that the powers have been vested in ministers and on a relentlessly increasing scale' (Johnson 1980: 84). Postwar years have seen a substantial increase in the volume of legislation passed by Parliament. Bills are not more numerous, but they are longer and more complex. It is common for bills to confer powers on ministers and to do so in broad terms.

The doctrine confers important departmental powers in that it asserts ministerial line control. The focus of much of the writing on the doctrine has often been the culpability of ministers for the actions of their civil servants, but more importantly and more pervasively, the doctrine establishes that civil servants are answerable to the minister and to no one else. Civil servants answer to the minister formally through the Permanent Secretary. The minister answers to Parliament for what happens in the Department.

The creation of executive agencies and the demands made of government in recent years have not destroyed the convention, but they have affected the relationship between ministers and officials. Ministers cannot be expected to know everything that happens within their departments. As former Cabinet minister, John Redwood, has observed 'The doctrine of implied proportionality has emerged, where the decision has to be large enough to warrant personal intervention by the politician prior to it being taken' (Redwood 2012). Ministers can delegate management functions to senior civil servants and expect them to be responsible for delivering policies. The heads of executive agencies have responsibility for budgets and what happens in their agencies. They variously appear before parliamentary select committees.

The doctrine nonetheless remains important. The senior minister is the ultimate head of the department.

> The Minister is clearly responsible for setting the main policies of the department, on advice from officials

The office
    Legal, departmental and political powers

The individual in the office
    Purpose in taking office
    Skills of the incumbent

External environment
    The power situation
    Climate of expectation
    International developments

Figure 19.1 The components of ministerial power

Source: Adapted from Norton (1997a) 'Leaders or led? Senior ministers in British government', *Talking Politics*, vol. 10, no. 2, pp. 78–85. Reproduced with permission of The Politics Association

and the wider public the department serves. The Minister is solely responsible for representing the department in the Commons and satisfying the Commons concerning its budgets and actions . . . The Minister is primarily responsible for representing the department to the wider world through the media, conferences and the like. Senior officials play a supporting role.

(Redwood 2012)

The minister alone is answerable to Parliament. Civil servants who advise ministers are not answerable to Parliament. They cannot appear at the despatch box. They may be summoned before a select committee, but they have no independent voice before that committee.

Parliamentary powers also derive from being Her Majesty's ministers. Since the crown alone can request money, money resolutions have to be moved by a minister. Parliamentary rules also provide that certain other motions can be moved only by ministers. Parliamentary business proceeds on the basis of an agenda set largely by government, and that business largely entails bills and motions brought forward by government. That business is normally departmental business: bills are brought forward by individual departments and steered through Parliament by the ministers of that department. Ministers generally have a far greater opportunity to speak than is the case with other parliamentarians.

Ministers, then, enjoy considerable formal powers. They also enjoy some public visibility – itself a potential source of power – deriving from their position in government. A senior minister will have a greater chance of persuading a newspaper editor to come to dinner than will a member of the Opposition front bench or a humble backbencher. A minister will be able to attract publicity by virtue of exercising the power of the office or by announcing an intention to exercise that power. Even if no formal power to act yet exists, a minister may attract publicity by making a statement or letting the press know informally what is planned. Departments have press officers, but ministers may also use their special advisers to brief journalists. Press officers are civil servants. Special advisers, as we have seen, are political appointees.

Senior ministers also have some power by virtue of their political position. That is, they will be drawn (by convention) from one of the two Houses of Parliament. Unlike ministers in some other countries, they retain their seats in the legislature. More important, though also subject to much greater variability, they may also enjoy a power base in Parliament. They may seek to build that power base, for instance through regular contact with backbenchers. Under the Labour Government of Tony Blair, the Chancellor of the Exchequer, Gordon Brown, acquired a reputation for assiduously courting backbenchers and newly appointed ministers. Such a power base may give them leverage in relation to other ministers and to their departments. It may also make it very difficult for a Prime Minister to sack them.

The individual in the office

There are two dimensions to the individual in the office: purpose and skills. A minister may have important powers as a minister, but knowing that fact tells us little about how and why those powers are exercised. For that, we have to turn to the person in the office. Ministers become ministers for a variety of reasons. Some simply want to be ministers. Some want to achieve particular policy outcomes. Some want to be Prime Minister. What they want will determine how they act.

Consequently, how ministers act varies considerably. As one former cabinet minister recorded in her memoirs, 'there are as many ministerial styles as there are ministers' (Shephard 2000: 105). However, it is possible to identify different types of minister. One study has identified five types of senior minister – team player, commander, ideologue, manager and agent (Figure 19.2) (Norton 2000). The types relate to different locations of decision-making power. With commanders, ideologues and managers, power-making power is retained in the office but exercised in different ways. With team players and agents, policy is 'made' elsewhere, either because ministers cannot prevent it or because they prefer to abdicate power to these sources.

Team player

A team player is someone who believes in collective decision making and wants to be part of that team. This correlates more or less precisely with the concept of Cabinet government. Proposals may be put by a minister to Cabinet, but it is the Cabinet or rather a Cabinet committee that deliberates and decides on the policy. In practice, there is very little evidence to suggest that many senior ministers see themselves primarily as team players. Ministers will normally have a clear policy they wish the relevant Cabinet committee to approve. Rather than acting collegially, they prefer to operate as discrete policy-makers.

Figure 19.2 Types of senior minister

Commander

Commanders are those who have very clear ideas of what they want to achieve, and those ideas derive from their own personal preferences and goals. (Preferences should be taken to include ambition.) These may derive from their own past experiences in business or government, or simply from their personal reflections. When they accept a particular office, they usually have some idea of what they want to achieve. Individuals may not be consistent commanders throughout their ministerial career. They may have a very clear idea of what they want to achieve in one or more particular office but not in another. For example, one politician who held five Cabinet posts during the Thatcher and Major premierships had a clear idea of what he wanted to achieve in three of them (one was the post he had always wanted); in another he had a general idea (even though it was a post he had not wanted) and in the other – a rather senior post – he had no clear perception of what he wanted to achieve. Rather, he assumed one of the other roles: that of 'manager'.

There are normally commanders in each era of government. There were a number of commanders in the Labour Government of 1997–2010, including Gordon Brown as Chancellor of the Exchequer, David Blunkett as Education Secretary, and Robin Cook as Leader of the House of Commons. Under the Coalition Government formed in 2010, commanders have included Education Secretary Michael Gove, Work and Pensions Secretary Iain Duncan Smith, and Secretary of State for Communities and Local Government, Eric Pickles.

Ideologue

An ideologue is someone who is driven by a clear, consistent philosophy. Thus, whatever office they occupy, the policies they pursue will derive from that philosophy. There were some ideologues – pursuing a neo-liberal philosophy – in the period of Conservative government from 1979 to 1997. These included Sir Keith Joseph, Nicholas Ridley and John Redwood. However, they were not as numerous as is often supposed. This, in part, reflects the fact that prime ministers have rarely appointed ministers on purely ideological grounds. Prime Minister Margaret Thatcher largely left junior ministerial appointments to others, thus restricting her choice when it came to choosing Cabinet ministers. Some ministers who may appear to be ideologues are not; rather, their views in particular sectors coincide with those of a particular ideological strand. One minister who held office under Margaret Thatcher conceded that in one particular post he had what he described as 'Thatcherite priorities'; but when he occupied another more senior post later, he was certainly not seen as a Thatcherite but rather viewed by Thatcherites as having 'gone native'. There were few ideologues in the Cabinet under Tony Blair and Gordon Brown, other than members with a preference to side with either Blair ('Blairites') or Brown ('Brownites'), and few in the Cabinet formed by David Cameron.

Manager

Here the minister takes the decisions but is not driven by any particular ideology or personal world-view. Instead, the approach is pragmatic, sometimes Oakeshottian: that is, helping to keep the ship of state afloat and operating efficiently. Ministers may anticipate issues; more frequently they respond to them. They do not necessarily take the departmental line but decide it for themselves. When several competing demands are made of them, they act as brokers, listening and weighing the evidence and then taking a view. A good example of a manager during the period of Conservative government in the 1990s was Foreign Secretary Douglas Hurd. There were several managers in the Blair and Brown governments. One minister who attended Cabinet, and was a former parliamentary private secretary to Tony Blair, confided in a colleague that, with a few exceptions, members of the Cabinet were 'managerial types – capable, efficient, but without an ideological anchor' (Mullin 2009: 526). Managers were also to the fore in the Coalition Government of David Cameron.

Agent

Here the minister essentially acts on behalf of another body. There are two principal types of agent: those of the Prime Minister and those of the Civil Service.

1 *Prime ministerial*: The minister is appointed to ensure that the wishes of the Prime Minister are carried out. (This is distinct from an ideologue, who may share the Prime Minister's ideology but is an enthusiast for the ideology and will give that preference over the Prime Minister's wishes.) Occasionally, a Prime Minister may decide, in effect, to be their own Foreign Secretary or Chancellor of the Exchequer, although that depends on the willingness of the minister in question to comply: Margaret Thatcher had an easier time influencing economic policy with Sir Geoffrey Howe as Chancellor than she did when that office was held by Nigel Lawson. During the Thatcher era there were various media reports that some ministers were put in at middle-ranking level to act as the Prime Minister's eyes and ears in a department. Several 'Blairite' members of the Cabinet under Tony Blair were viewed as being there to deliver the vision of the Prime Minister. Similar claims were made under the Coalition Government of David Cameron: some Conservative junior ministers appointed to departments

headed by a Liberal Democrat – and some Liberal Democrats appointed by Deputy Prime Minister Nick Clegg to departments headed by Conservatives – in order to keep an eye on the Secretary of State. In a ministerial reshuffle in 2012 the appointment of Conservative Michael Fallon to the Department of Business, Innovation and Skills, headed by Liberal Democrat Vince Cable, was seen in this light.

2 *Civil Service*: Here the minister essentially adopts the departmental brief and does what the officials in the department want the minister to do. Ministers may adopt this role because they want a quiet life – some actually move up the 'greasy pole' of government despite being remarkably lazy – or because they do not have the personal will or intellect to resist the persuasive briefings of officials. Civil servants can be remarkably persuasive, and indeed devious (papers put in late, or among a mass of papers in the red box), and one or two departments, such as the Foreign Office, do have reputations for pursuing a particular departmental ideology. On some issues, ministers don't take a stand, and, as Gerald Kaufman recounts in *How to Be a Minister*, will read out their departmental brief in Cabinet committee (Kaufman 1997).

Ministers, then, have important powers and some of them want to exercise those powers. However, whether they do so successfully depends on their skills and the political environment they occupy.

Skills

In one study of prime ministerial power it was argued that the essential skills needed by a Prime Minister, in addition to those of selection, were those of leadership, anticipation and reaction, and that a number of strategic options were available to them to achieve the desired outcome (Norton 1987: 325–45). The strategic options were those of command, persuasion, manipulation, and hiding. These skills and options also apply to senior ministers:

1 *Command*: Ministers may have a clear intellectual view of what they want to achieve, but actually taking decisions to ensure that view is realised may be difficult. One Cabinet minister in the early 1980s, Sir Keith Joseph, was notorious for having difficulty making decisions to achieve his ideological goals. Despite being viewed as a strong minister, Gordon Brown as Chancellor of the Exchequer, and as Prime Minister, had a reputation for procrastination. Conversely, some ministers have no difficulty making decisions: examples in the 2010 parliament have included Education Secretary Michael Gove, Justice Secretary Kenneth Clarke and Communities Secretary Eric Pickles.

2 *Persuade*: Some ministers may know what they want to achieve and take a clear view. However, they need on occasion to be able to carry colleagues and others – MPs, outside organised interests, the public – with them. There are different devices that ministers may employ to bring the different actors onside: meetings with the relevant backbench committee, for example; a 'dear colleague' letter to the party's MPs; a press conference; private briefings for journalists; and 'keeping No. 10 briefed' ('No. 10' meaning principally the Prime Minister but also, on occasion, other actors in Downing Street, such as the Prime Minister's principal advisers). Some ministers will also spend time meeting affected bodies – for example, by making an effort to attend their annual conferences and accepting invitations to speak. Some ministers in the Blair and Brown governments had reputations as persuaders, being willing to see MPs privately to discuss their concerns and if necessary agree compromises. They included Justice Secretary Jack Straw and Chancellor of the Exchequer Alistair Darling.

3 *Manipulate*: The Prime Minister is sometimes devious, and the same applies to senior ministers. On occasion, one may have to play off one body against another. Manipulation may entail 'kite flying' in the media, feeding a misleading story that can be denied and then using it as leverage to achieve a particular outcome. Manipulation may be met by manipulation. Downing Street may leak a story, only for a member of the Cabinet to then provide an alternative view or to deny the story, or a minister may leak details of discussions in order to invoke media coverage and generate public opposition to what has been discussed.

4 *Hide*: Ministers need to know when to avoid a particular problem. Sometimes it is better to keep one's head below the parapet rather than risk putting it above the parapet and getting shot at by the media and disgruntled MPs. One of the values of having junior ministers is that they can be put up to take the flak. In 2009 public criticism of the Government's failure to extend settlement rights in the UK to all former Gurkha soldiers was fielded not by a Cabinet minister but by a junior Home Office minister.

These are strategic options. However, there are two other skills that ministers need in order to achieve their goals: they need to be good time managers, and they need to understand how the system – and their particular department – works.

1 *Effective time management*: The work of a senior minister is extraordinarily time-consuming. One Scottish Secretary was told by his private office that on average 1,000 items passed through the office every week, of

which he saw 700 – in other words, 100 items a day (Lang 2002: 65). Dealing with such items is in addition to a range of meetings, preparation for speeches and being in the House. For ministers, it is therefore essential to organise their time effectively. Some former Cabinet ministers have admitted that they had difficulty prioritising their activities and saying 'no' to various activities. Some expressed admiration for their colleagues who managed to organise their time and stay on top of their departments. One minister was described as 'superbly professional. Those who worked with him . . . say that he was ruthless in doing only what he considered essential' (Shephard 2000: 118). One means of relieving some of the pressure is by delegation. Some ministers are good at delegating and making use of junior ministers. One Conservative Cabinet minister in the Thatcher government, for example, gave his junior ministers particular responsibilities and then had them draw up a work programme for the next two years, and every three months he had a meeting with each minister to discuss progress. Others are less well organised, and some have difficulty delegating tasks effectively.

2 *Understanding the system*: Ministers need to know how the process works.

> The nature of a department and the tools at its disposal to achieve change are important factors in the exercise of power. Understanding them is necessary to achieve change, and to respond to pressure, whether of politics, circumstance or crisis.
>
> (Shephard 2000: 114–15)

Very occasionally some ministers are appointed without any prior experience of Parliament, but the experience has rarely been a happy one, those involved displaying a lack of sensitivity to the needs of a department and of the parliamentary environment. One way to understand the system – the most obvious and long-standing – is by ministerial apprenticeship. Holding junior ministerial office is useful as a way of seeing how the system works from the inside. One of the points made by one former minister was that in order to be effective in achieving your goals as a senior minister it helped, first, to have been a junior minister in the department that one was appointed to head; and, second, to have served in the Whips' Office. As a junior minister, one gets to know how the particular department works (departments differ enormously), and as a whip one gets to know how to handle MPs and to anticipate what is likely to cause trouble in the House. Understanding of a department may also derive from longevity in the office, but that is something largely beyond the control of the incumbent. Another, more recent, way is by study. Prior to the 1997 General Election, seminars were organised for shadow ministers on the workings of government. Training is now available to ministers through Civil Service Learning. Such training provides access to sources and best practice that may not be achieved by personal experience in junior office.

Without some (ideally, all) of these skills, a minister – however intelligent and self-driven – is not likely to succeed and may find their ministerial career stunted or destroyed altogether.

External environment

Ministers may also find that their capacity to achieve desired outcomes is enhanced by the environment external to their department. This environment includes the power situation, the climate of expectations and international developments:

1 *Power situation*: The power situation overlaps with the powers and constraints of the office but provides a dynamic element. Power relationships are not static. And what the 'power situation' refers to is the relationship between different bodies in the immediate political environment. In terms of ministers, this covers especially Downing Street, Cabinet, Parliament, the Civil Service and the media.

A previously popular Prime Minister may lose support among the parliamentary party or the public and start to seek support from particular ministers, doing so through being more supportive of their policies. A minister may find it easier to push a policy through as the authority of a Prime Minister wanes. There may be a shift in the power situation as a result of a Cabinet reshuffle. A minister may find that colleagues opposed to a particular policy have been moved or sacked. Elections of officers of backbench party committees may result in opponents of a minister's policy being replaced by supporters. Changes of ownership of particular newspapers may result in greater media support for a policy. Changes may occur that make the power situation unfavourable, but at times it may be highly favourable to a particular minister and the policies of that minister. Martin Smith sums up the difficulties faced by Prime Minister John Major compared with Margaret Thatcher not in terms of weak and strong personality but in terms of a changed power situation: 'Major had no majority in parliament, the government was divided, and the popular perception was that his government lacked economic competence – circumstances created Major's indecisiveness; it was not indecisiveness that led to the Conservative defeat' (quoted in Morrison 2001: 279). Prime Minister Gordon Brown also witnessed a significant shift in the power situation following his decision in 2007 not to call an election in that autumn and following the sudden economic downturn of 2008–9. He moved from being seen as an invulnerable premier to one who was highly vulnerable, with various ministers and backbenchers seeking to engineer his resignation (Straw 2012: 519–24).

2   *Climate of expectation*: The expectations of citizens are clearly important and change over time. The Conservative Party was the beneficiary of a particular climate of expectation in 1979 and the victim of a very different climate in 1997. The popular mood may initially be hostile to a particular proposal and then, perhaps induced by particular events, swing in support of it. Particular ministers may benefit from a particular climate of expectation, a popular mood favouring what they want to achieve. That mood can be a political resource for the minister, making it difficult for the Cabinet to resist a proposal for which there is clearly overwhelming popular support. Alternatively, the climate may change, constraining ministers in what they want to achieve. After 2003 there was a change of mood towards war, with popular support for continued involvement in war in Iraq, and later Afghanistan, seeping away.

3   *International developments*: What happens elsewhere in the world, such as a global economic recession, may limit ministers in terms of what they wish to achieve but on occasion may also make it possible for ministers to achieve what they want. A natural disaster or civil war may strengthen the position of a minister who wishes to increase foreign aid or to intervene militarily in a conflict. A shift in power or in policy in another state may facilitate a minister achieving a particular outcome. A change of government in another EU country may enable a minister to get a particular proposal adopted by the EU Council of Ministers.

Two conclusions can be drawn from the foregoing analysis. The first is that senior ministers have the potential to be significant figures in determining public policy. The second is that ministerial power is variable, not constant. It can be subject to a wide range of constraints. Let us consider in a little greater depth the constraints.

Constraints

Ministers labour under a number of constraints. The most important are constitutional, legal and managerial. Constitutionally, they are constrained by the doctrine of collective ministerial responsibility. Major decisions have to percolate up for Cabinet approval, which means, in practice, Cabinet committee; and approval may not always be forthcoming. The constitutional power exercised by the Prime

Minister to hire, fire and shuffle ministers may also be a powerful constraint on ministerial policies, and it may be exercised in order to reflect the Prime Minister's policy preferences.

At the individual level, there are two important constitutional constraints. One is the convention of individual ministerial responsibility. The other is the ministerial code. The convention of individual ministerial responsibility is one that, as we have seen, ensures that statutory powers are vested in ministers and that they have line control within their departments; it is also one that renders ministers answerable for what takes place within their departments. This is often assumed to mean that, in the event of an error within a department, the minister resigns. Although ministers may be deemed culpable for what goes on in their departments, this has rarely meant having to resign if mistakes are made. Ministers have variously resigned because of personal scandal, such as David Blunkett in 2004 (allegations of seeking preferential treatment for a nanny in gaining a visa), David Laws in 2010 (misuse of parliamentary expenses) and Liam Fox in 2011 (over inappropriate use of an unofficial adviser), or disagreement with government policy, such as Robin Cook in 2003 (over war with Iraq), or disagreement with the Prime Minister's style of leadership, as with Works and Pensions Secretary James Purnell and Europe Minister Caroline Flint in 2009, but very rarely because of a mistake made within their department (see Norton 1997b; see also Woodhouse 1994). A distinction is frequently drawn between policy and operation: if the policy is right but is not carried out, then those public officials who have failed to carry it out are the ones who are disciplined. However, the dividing line is not always clear. Conservative Home Secretary Michael Howard dismissed the head of the Prison Service, Derek Lewis, in 1995 over prison escapes, but was accused by the Opposition of being responsible for a failure of policy. Transport Secretary Patrick McLoughlin suspended three officials in 2012 over mistakes made in allocating the West Coast mainline railway franchise, but was also criticised by the Opposition for the overall policy. This reflects the weakness as well as the strength of the convention: ministers may not necessarily resign but they have to answer for what happens in their department. Even if the minister does not resign, the minister's career may be adversely affected.

Ministers are also constrained by the ministerial code. This is a code of conduct drawn up by the Prime Minister. The first modern version was drawn up by Clement Attlee in 1945 and was variously revised by his successors. It was formally a secret document until John Major agreed to its declassification in 1992. The code stipulates how ministers should conduct themselves in their dealings with others, including the Civil Service and Parliament, and how they should conduct their personal life in order to avoid conflicts of interest (Cabinet Office 2010). The code shapes ministers' behaviour and breaches may be punished by the Prime Minister. It was a failure to comply with one of the recommendations of the code that led to David Blunkett's second resignation from the Cabinet in 2005. Following accusations that the Prime Minister was both prosecutor and jury in respect of the code, Tony Blair in 2006 announced that he was appointing an external adviser to assist in considering complaints about ministerial conduct, a practice adopted by his succesors.

Legal constraints exist in that ministers may be limited by the powers conferred on them by Parliament. They have increasingly to be sensitive to the risk of acting *ultra vires* (beyond powers). A greater degree of judicial activism in recent decades may be the product of a change of judicial culture (or of those who are affected by government being more prepared to seek judicial review) or a change in the nature of government; but whichever it is, the courts are now more willing than previously to review the legality of ministerial actions.

The courts, as we shall see in Chapter 21, are also more active as a consequence of various constitutional changes. Ministers are constrained by the conditions of membership of the European Union, by the incorporation of the European Convention on Human Rights (ECHR) into British law, and by the devolution of powers to elected assemblies in different parts of the United Kingdom. In policy areas that fall within the competence of the EU, ministers can no longer exercise power unilaterally but rather form part of a collective decision-making body (the Council of Ministers) in which they may be overruled. As their responsibilities have increased as a consequence of the UK's membership of the EU, so their capacity to affect outcomes has decreased. Ministers are constrained by the provisions of the ECHR and in introducing bills now have to confirm that they comply with the provisions of the ECHR. Devolution has moved certain policy areas to the competence of elected assemblies, especially the Scottish Parliament, and a UK minister may have difficulty moving ahead with a policy without the support of one or more of the devolved executives.

Ministers are also subject to what may be termed managerial constraints. Ministers have a mass of responsibilities and duties: they are departmental ministers; they are members of the Cabinet; they are members of the appropriate EU Council of Ministers; they are party and political figures (invited to attend and address a mass of meetings); they are ministers answerable to Parliament; they are (except for those ministers who are peers) constituency MPs; and they are party MPs who have to attend Parliament to vote for their party. Ministers have difficulty managing their time. Their evenings are taken up reading and signing the papers that are crammed into their ministerial red boxes. Their days may be full of meetings with officials and representatives of outside bodies, leaving little time for sustained reflection. Time spent travelling between meetings is variously spent texting, catching up on business via Blackberries, or dictating constituency correspondence into a dictaphone.

Ministers are also public and political figures, driven increasingly by the demands of a 24-hour news service. The media demand instant comments, and there are now the means for immediate communication. Ministers – and those wanting to interview them – are rarely without their mobile telephones. Some ministers also maintain their own blogs and use Twitter.

The consequence of these demands is that ministers are frequently in a reactive, rather than a pro-active, mode, having to rush to deal with problems and queries placed before them – on a relentless scale – and with little time to stand back and to think through what they want to achieve and whether they are on the path to achieving it.

Explaining ministerial power

Ministers are powerful figures in government. At the same time, they are subject to remarkable constraints. How, then, can one make sense of their role in British government? Various models have been created to help us to understand the role of ministers in policy making. Let us assess three that provide very different perspectives: the principal–agent model, the power-dependency model and the baronial model.

Principal–agent model

This stipulates that ministers are essentially the agents of a principal. Thus, although some ministers may be commanders, ideologues or managers, most fall under the category, identified earlier, of agents. One school of thought contends that the UK has **prime ministerial government**, and thus that ministers are agents of the Prime Minister. Another school of thought advances the proposition that the UK has Civil Service government, and thus that ministers are agents of civil servants.

The prime ministerial government school of thought argues that the powers of the Prime Minister are such that the Prime Minister is in a position to determine public policy. He or she makes policy preferences through the choice of senior ministers. If the Prime Minister wishes to achieve a particular policy outcome, he can effectively require a senior minister to agree to that policy. A minister failing to comply with prime ministerial wishes may cease to be a minister. Furthermore, the Prime Minister can ensure particular outcomes through control of the Cabinet agenda and through chairing the Cabinet. Tony Blair in particular was accused of marginalising his Cabinet in order to ensure he got his way (see Kavanagh and Seldon 1999; Foster 2005). The Prime Minister can keep a tight rein on ministers through monitoring their speeches and through requiring the text of speeches to be cleared by Downing Street. Government policy, it is argued, is increasingly being made in Downing Street and not in the individual government departments.

The Civil Service school of thought argues that it is the Civil Service that determines policy outcomes. Working through departments, civil servants can help to shape, even determine, the minister's agenda. 'In practice', according to Weir and Beetham (1999: 167), 'ministers rely almost wholly on their departments, senior bureaucrats and private offices, and the resources and advice they can provide.' Civil servants have an advantage over ministers in terms of their numbers, permanence, expertise and cohesion. There is one senior minister heading a department. The number of senior civil servants in the department may run into three figures. A minister, even with the help of a number of junior ministers, cannot keep track of everything that is going on in a department. A senior minister will, on average, serve in one ministerial post for about two years. (In the decades before the Second World War, the average was four years.) Civil servants will be in place in the department before a minister arrives and will usually still be in place once a minister has departed. A new minister provides civil servants with an opportunity to fight anew battles that may previously have been lost. One former minister recounted:

> Lunch with my successor at Environment, Bob Ainsworth, who seems more at home in the job than I was. As I suspected, soon after I was out of the door, aviation officials came back to him with a modified version of the expensive and pointless research into night-flight sleep disturbance which I had refused to endorse . . .
>
> (Mullin 2009: 181)

Furthermore, their permanence also allows civil servants to build up a body of administrative expertise that is denied to a transient minister. Civil servants may be in a position to know what is achievable, and what is not, in a way that ministers cannot. Civil servants, it is argued, are also more politically and socially cohesive than ministers: politically cohesive in that they imbue a particular Civil Service and departmental ethos, and their approach is shaped by that ethos. Permanent Secretaries meet together informally once

a week to discuss current issues. They also tend to be socially cohesive in that they are mostly drawn from the same or similar social backgrounds and are members of the same London clubs. Ministers, on the other hand, imbue no particular ethos and are drawn from somewhat disparate backgrounds. They do not tend to mix socially together in the way that senior civil servants do.

Civil servants are in a position to influence, even control, the flow of information to a minister. A minister may not always receive every piece of information relevant to a particular proposal. The minister's diary may be filled with meetings that are largely inconsequential or so numerous as to squeeze out time to do other things (see Shephard 2000: 119). The minister's red boxes may be filled with a mass of papers, the more important tucked away at the bottom. Officials may put up position papers, outlining various options, but omitting others or skewing the material in support of each in such a way that only one option appears to be viable. Indeed, ministers may have little chance to think and write anything of their own. One Cabinet minister, deciding that he wanted to jot down some thoughts of his own, looked for some clean paper and found that there was none in his office. He asked his private secretary for some.

> He went out and came back after a pause, holding in front of him like a dead rat, one single sheet of plain white paper, which he solemnly laid on the desk. After an apprehensive glance at me he left and I suddenly realised how civil servants controlled their masters: always keep them supplied with an endless supply of neatly prepared memoranda. Never give them time to think for themselves. Above all, never give them paper with nothing on it.
>
> (Lang 2002: 65)

Civil servants also monitor ministers' calls and may seek to limit formal contact between one minister and another and, indeed, between ministers and people outside the department. One minister encountered opposition when she decided to hold a series of breakfasts for businesswomen: 'The roof fell in. There was strong Treasury resistance – "But why, Minister?" – and a total inability to provide a tablecloth or anything to eat or drink, much less to get anyone else to do so' (Shephard 2000: 112). If a minister takes a view contrary to that adopted by civil servants in the department, the civil servants may ask civil servants in other departments to brief their ministers to take a contrary line when the matter comes before Cabinet committee. There is also extensive contact between officials in the UK government and in the EU Commission. Ministers, with little time to prepare for meetings, often have to be briefed on the plane to Brussels. On this line of argument, ministers have little scope to think about policy goals and to consider information and advice other than that placed before them by their officials. Sometimes the limitations are purely those of time. In other cases, they may be intellectual, ministers not having the mental capacity to challenge what has been laid before them. As one Chief Secretary to the Treasury once recorded, on complex issues ministers not directly involved in an issue would read the briefs, prepared by civil servants, the night before or as the argument proceeded. 'More often that not . . . they would follow the line of the brief' (Barnett 1982: 41). The dependence on the papers prepared by officials can occur at the highest levels. The Cabinet Office prepares a brief for the Prime Minister for Cabinet meetings indicating, on the basis of papers circulated and knowledge of those involved, the line the PM may wish to take ('Subject to discussion, the Prime Minister might wish to conclude . . .'). This is a form of prompt to the PM, who may or may not choose to utilise it. However, one senior civil servant records the occasion when Prime Minister Harold Wilson had to leave during a discussion and handed over to his deputy, Edward Short:

> Short was a Bear of Little Brain and would have been as capable of understanding, let alone summarising, the previous discussion as he would have been at delivering a lecture on quantum mechanics. He presided wordlessly over the discussion for a further five minutes, then spoke. 'I find we have agreed as follows' – and read out the draft conclusions penned before the discussion had begun . . . Not without a modest satisfaction, the Secretariat recorded the conclusions read out by the Deputy Prime Minister.
>
> (Denman 2002: 169)

This view of the power of the Civil Service over ministers has been voiced by former ministers – among them Tony Benn – and was famously encapsulated in a popular television series, *Yes Minister*, in the 1980s. The Permanent Secretary, Sir Humphrey Appleby, and other civil servants were able to out-manoeuvre the minister, Jim Hacker, in a way that finds resonance in the memoirs of some ministers.

However, both schools of thought have been challenged. The prime ministerial government model overlooks, according to critics, the limited time, resources and interest of the Prime Minister. The Prime Minister occupies a particular policy space – that of high policy (dealing with the economic welfare and security of the nation) – and has limited time to interfere in middle-level policy generated by ministers (see Norton 1997a, 2000). Furthermore, despite an extension of policy resources in Downing Street under successive occupants, the resources available to a Prime Minister in Downing Street are limited. A senior minister has more advisers than the Prime Minister has in the minister's sector of public policy. Even when material has to be cleared

through Downing Street, some ministers are slow in submitting texts of speeches; some may never even reach Downing Street. Ministers may brief the press, or even give interviews, without clearance from No. 10 (see Short 2004: 177). Prime ministers rarely have a grasp of, or a deep interest in, every sector of public policy. Instead, they leave it to ministers to get on with their jobs, frequently free of interference from Downing Street. Indeed, one of the most remarkable findings of recent research into senior ministers was that it is very rare for a Prime Minister, when appointing ministers to Cabinet office, to tell them what is expected of them (Norton 2000). The advice offered to John Major when he was appointed Foreign Secretary was brief and unrelated to specific policy: 'You had better hang on to your seatbelt' (Seldon 1997: 87). When Clare Short was offered the post of International Development Secretary by Tony Blair, they discussed who she wanted as her junior minister and what to call the new department: 'I was then whisked off to my new department' (Short 2004: 56). It appeared to be a not dissimilar experience with John Prescott: 'We discussed briefly what the big new department would contain' (Prescott 2008: 212).

The Civil Service school of thought is challenged by the claim that civil servants are not as proactive and as cohesive as proponents of this thesis suggest. The demands made of civil servants are such that they too have little time for sustained thought and reflection. Although research suggests that civil servants in some departments imbue a particular departmental ethos, most civil servants seek to carry out the wishes of their ministers, regardless of their own views or prior departmental preferences. Indeed, recent research points to the extent to which civil servants are loyal to their ministers (Norton 2000). Far from seeking to impede them, they work hard to carry out their wishes. 'Good officials respect the right of an elected government to implement new policies which they have sold to the electors or which they believe will improve the lives of people' (Redwood 2012). Furthermore, as Page and Jenkins found in their study of middle-ranking civil servants, 'where ministerial and departmental priorities conflicted, and the minister has expressed a clear view on the matter, there was no question but that the minister's view prevailed' (Page and Jenkins 2005: 133). Ministers are also now more likely to call civil servants in to quiz them about the papers they have submitted. Ministers themselves may also discuss matters privately, free from Civil Service involvement. Some of these meetings are bilateral rather than multilateral. One minister, interviewed by this author, recalled with wry amusement how his civil servants tried to limit his contacts with other ministers, largely oblivious to the fact that once he was in his minister's room in the Commons he could quite easily pop to see other ministers, in adjoining offices, to have a quiet chat.

Civil Service cohesion, and the ethos attached to the service and to particular departments, is also being eroded by the people from outside the Civil Service being brought in to senior posts and also by the greater emphasis being placed on managerial skills. Civil servants are being trained to deliver certain specified goals. A perceived failure to deliver under the Labour Government of Tony Blair resulted in pressure being put on senior civil servants to improve their performance in meeting the government's targets (see Gray and Jenkins 2005). This has also been a feature of the Coalition Government formed in 2010. As civil servants are under greater pressure to deliver what ministers expect of them, so ministers are also bringing in more political appointees in order to provide advice and to handle their relations with the media (see Foster 2005: 207–22). That greater dependence on special advisers has been marked in recent years, generating public controversy and creating a grey area between civil servants and special advisers. Relations became especially strained in 2001–2 in the Transport Department between civil servants and the minister's special adviser, Jo Moore. Relationships broke down in the department, leading to the resignation of not only the special adviser but also the minister, Stephen Byers. Under the Blair Government, his chief of staff (Jonathan Powell) and communications secretary (Alastair Campbell), both special advisers, were given executive powers, allowing them to give instructions to civil servants, a position that led to criticism and claims of a politicisation of the civil service. These powers were rescinded when Gordon Brown became Prime Minister. There has also been a tendency to seek advice from a range of bodies outside government – think tanks, advisory committees and task groups. Under the Government of David Cameron, as we have seen, there has been pressure to hive off some policy-advising tasks to external bodies. In many cases, civil servants are not seen as being in the decision-making loop.

A seminal work on Cabinet ministers by Bruce Headey found that civil servants looked to ministers for leadership. They preferred ministers who could take decisions and fight (and win) departmental battles (Headey 1974: 140–53). That appears to remain the case. As one former Permanent Secretary put it, 'To some it might seem like heaven on earth to have a Minister who has no ideas and is endlessly open to the suggestions or recommendations of officials. But that is not the case. Officials need ministers with ideas . . . Officials need stimulus; need leadership; and, on occasion, conflict' (Holland 1995: 43). Middle-ranking civil servants work on policy detail, but they do so on the basis of a ministerial 'steer' (Page and Jenkins 2005: 136–40). This suggests that civil servants are more likely to welcome an effective commander, ideologue or manager as their minister than an agent or team player.

Power-dependency model

This model has been developed by R.A.W. Rhodes (1981, 1997). Although used to cover particularly, but not exclusively, centre–local relations, it is relevant for a study of the relationship between ministers and other actors in the political system. It is based on several propositions. One of the principal propositions is that any organisation is dependent upon other organisations for resources. Thus, the Prime Minister is dependent on the resources available in government departments; he does not have all the resources he needs in Downing Street. Ministers are dependent on their departments: they need civil servants to provide advice and to carry out their decisions. Civil servants need ministers to deliver resources through fighting battles with the Treasury and in Cabinet. Far from being in conflict with one another, the relationship may be closer to a partnership (Weir and Beetham 1999: 172–5). A second proposition is that in order to achieve their goals, organisations have to exchange resources. In other words, the relationship may not be as hierarchical as the formal structure may suggest. Actors within the political system need others in the system to help them to achieve their goals. It is not simply a case of demanding resources. There is a dependence on others (see Norton 2003). That means that alliances have to be created. The model recognises that there may be a body or group of bodies that dominate in the relationship but that the relationship may change as actors fight for position.

The relevance for understanding the role of senior ministers is that it stands as something of a corrective to the principal–agent model. Although there may be times when the Prime Minister or civil servants are to the fore in determining policy outcomes, ministers are not relegated to some supporting role. They need the Prime Minister and civil servants, but conversely the Prime Minister and civil servants need them: they are an important resource, and they cannot necessarily be taken for granted. A Prime Minister may thus need to build support in Cabinet to get a controversial measure approved: the support of senior ministers thus constitutes a vital, indeed a necessary, resource. It may be necessary, but it may not be sufficient. Statutory powers, as we have seen, are vested in senior ministers. The Prime Minister, and Cabinet, thus need to ensure that the relevant minister is willing to exercise those powers. Others may thus depend on the resources at the disposal of ministers. At the same time, ministers themselves are dependent on the resources of others. They need the political support of the Prime Minister. They need their civil servants to carry out their wishes. They also need different bodies outside government to accept and to help to implement their policies. The Justice Secretary, for example, may need to mobilise the support of the Bar in order to achieve reform of the legal system.

The power-dependency model thus suggests a more complex and less hierarchical political process than that advanced by the principal–agent model. Although the Prime Minister may predominate, it is not to the extent that we can claim the existence of prime ministerial government. Ministers are more important players in the process than the principal–agent model suggests. Although important, ministers themselves are not dominant either. They too depend on others in the political process. The process of policy making is thus an essentially crowded and interactive one.

The power-dependency model has been variously criticised (see Rhodes 1997: 37). In terms of understanding the place of senior ministers in government, it does not necessarily help to explain who is predominant at any one time. Extensive empirical research would be necessary to do that. It also runs foul of objections from advocates of the principal–agent model. They contend that senior ministers may be resources that a Prime Minister needs, but they are subordinate resources that can be drawn on by the Prime Minister without the need for persuasion. The power-dependency model does not help to explain cases where the Prime Minister has achieved a particular outcome by adopting a confrontational stance rather than an alliance-building one. As various Cabinet ministers noted, Margaret Thatcher as Prime Minister was not noted for seeking to build alliances in Cabinet. Similarly, Tony Blair was criticised for distancing himself from the Civil Service and others, substituting detachment and prime ministerial instructions for mutual dependence (Norton 2003: 543–59; Norton 2008). It also does not help to explain those cases where ministers can, and do, ignore civil service advice and act unilaterally and, on occasion, go beyond the bounds of normal ministerial powers. In the words of one former civil servant, 'We have to recognise that the assumption that the civil service is there to keep the government within the bounds of constitutional propriety is so threadbare it would be unwise to rely on it' (Jenkins 2004: 807).

Baronial model

This model has been developed by this writer. It posits that ministers are like medieval barons in that they preside over their own, sometimes vast, policy territory. Within that territory they are largely supreme. We have identified the formal and informal underpinnings of this supremacy. Ministers head their respective departments. They have the constitutional authority and the legal power to take decisions. No one else enjoys that power. Junior ministers have no formal power and can act only on the authority of the senior minister. Once the minister has taken a view – that is, made a decision – the civil servants in the department implement it. The ministers have their own policy space, their own

castles – even some of the architecture of departments (such as the Ministry of Defence and the Ministry of Health, both in Whitehall) reinforces that perception – and their own courtiers. Indeed, recent years have seen a growth in the coterie of courtiers appointed by some senior ministers, some – such as Gordon Brown when Chancellor of the Exchequer – being seen almost as having an alternative court to that of the Prime Minister (see Naughtie 2001: 124–5). The minister's baronial position is also protected to some degree by what is termed a 'silo mentality' in the Civil Service (Page 2005): officials want to protect their particular departmental turf and will support the minister in seeking to protect or extend the responsibilities, and budget, of the department. The ministers fight – or form alliances – with other barons in order to get what they want. They resent interference in their territory by other barons and will fight to defend it.

The analogy is not altogether accurate in that the barons have no responsibility for raising taxes. (The exception is the Chancellor of the Exchequer, who has become more powerful than the original holders of the ancient office.) The Prime Minister also has greater power than a medieval monarch to dispense with the services of the barons, although the differences are not as great as may be supposed: a Prime Minister has difficulty dispensing with the services of powerful barons. He has his court and they have theirs. Despite the absence of a precise fit, the model has utility for understanding the nature and fluidity of power relationships within government. It has found resonance in various works on the Blair premiership, as in Francis Beckett and David Hencke's *The Blairs and their Court* (2004). Far from Cabinet being a homogeneous body of prime ministerial agents, it is a heterogeneous gathering and usually includes some powerful individuals.

Furthermore, reinforcing the baronial model is the approach taken by ministers to their jobs. Although prime ministers can use ministerial appointments as a way of changing or confirming their own policy preferences, they rarely choose a Cabinet of similar ministerial types. A Cabinet typically contains a mix of commanders, managers and ideologues, with the interests of the individual ministers around the table, and their particular departmental territories, taking precedence over any concept of altruistic collective decision-making.

This provides a distinct perspective on the relationship between senior ministers and the Prime Minister. Rather than being able to give directions, as in a principal–agent relationship, a Prime Minister has to be prepared to bargain with the more powerful barons in his government. He may be able to control some of the weaker members of the Cabinet, but others may be too powerful to be subject to prime ministerial direction. Reducing the power of the Cabinet may not necessarily have diminished the position of individual ministers, with whom the Prime Minister has to deal directly. At a minimum, ministers have an important gatekeeping role. To follow the analogy, they can close their departmental drawbridges and deny the Prime Minister entry to their policy domain. If the Prime Minister wants a particular policy implemented, the relevant minister has the formal power to say no, and a strong-minded commander or ideologue, even a determined manager may have the political will to exercise that power.

A Prime Minister has limited scope to act unilaterally. He has no departmental responsibilities. Furthermore, the Prime Minister has limited resources to ensure that ministers act in accordance with his wishes. His own court, as we have noted, is a relatively small one. Attempts by Tony Blair and Gordon Brown to strengthen the coordination and oversight of Downing Street are testimony to this limited capacity. The more cunning of senior ministers can frequently circumvent attempts to limit what they say and do. Speeches may be sent late to Downing Street. Backbenchers or the media may be mobilised in support of a particular policy. Cabinet ministers often have their favoured lobby journalists. Outside bodies may come to the defence of a minister they believe to be sympathetic to their cause.

The senior barons are thus able to plough their own furrows, making their own speeches, leaking – through their courtiers – their own side of a particular argument and their own perception of what has taken place in Cabinet or Cabinet committee. They can and do form alliances to achieve the approval of measures subject to Cabinet – which usually means Cabinet committee – approval (middle-level policy) and may operate unilaterally in laying orders that they are empowered by statute to make (low-level policy). Sometimes prime ministers – especially at times when their political authority is weakened – are in a constricted position, having to remind their ministers not to leak details of what has taken place and not to speak to the press without clearance.

Ministers develop their own ways of preserving their territorial integrity. Some adopt an isolationist stance, others a confrontational stance (see Norton 2000). The stances taken reflect both the variety of approaches taken by ministers and the fact that they cannot be characterised as agents. They are barons, and in order to get their way they sometimes have to fight other barons as well as the monarch.

Characterising senior ministers as barons is also appropriate in that, like medieval barons, they are powerful but not all-powerful. They are constrained by other powerful actors, including the monarch (Prime Minister) and other barons (senior ministers), and by a recognition that they have to abide by laws and conventions. Indeed, as we have seen, they are increasingly constrained as the political environment has become more crowded, with groups coming into existence and making more demands of them – groups that they may need to cooperate with in implementing policy – and with more actors with the power to take decisions of their own. Ministers may thus find their time consumed by fighting battles with other political actors, be it bodies within the European Union or within the UK. Consequently, to provide a dynamic of the present state of senior ministers in British government, one can offer a model of barons operating within a shrinking kingdom (Norton 2000).

This model is compatible with the power-dependency model, but it provides a greater emphasis on the role of ministers and encompasses the different strategies adopted by ministers, including fighting battles as well as alliance building. It is geared more directly than the power-dependency model to senior ministers. However, it has been criticised on the grounds that the fit with medieval barons is far from perfect – that the power and activity of the barons bears little relevance to senior ministers today. It can also be challenged on the grounds that it underestimates the power of the Prime Minister. As someone close to Tony Blair said while Labour was still in Opposition: 'You may see a change from a feudal system of barons to a more Napoleonic system' (Hennessy 2000: 478; Naughtie 2001: 96). Napoleon, though, needed his generals and his form of rule was, and is, difficult to sustain.

The model also has the same drawback as the other models in that they are models rather than theories. However, it stands as a useful counterpoint to the principal–agent model. It provides a new perspective on the role of senior ministers, emphasising the role played in government by ministers as ministers, rather than seeing them solely as a collective body, subsumed under the heading of government or Cabinet. This model suggests that senior ministers are more important figures in British government than is generally realised.

BOX 19.1

BRITAIN IN CONTEXT

Bureaucrats and politicians

The distinction between ministers and civil servants – that is, elected politicians and full-time officials – is not distinctive to the UK. What is notable is the extent to which the integrity of the Civil Service is maintained. Despite accusations of a creeping politicisation of the Civil Service, the extent to which the Civil Service in the UK is a body of permanent public servants, there to serve the government whichever party is in power, is remarkable in comparative context. The distinction is one that has been exported to many Commonwealth countries, though not necessarily maintained to the same degree as in the UK.

In some countries, the senior administrative posts in government are essentially patronage posts. In the USA, not only are Cabinet ministers, and their juniors, appointed by the President, but so too are the administrative posts below them; the President has more than 2,000 administrative posts in his gift. In some countries, such as France, the distinction is not always a clear one to draw, with senior civil servants sometimes being appointed to senior ministerial posts, including that of Prime Minister.

The relationship between the head of government and cabinet ministers also differs, especially depending on the type of government that exists. In presidential systems, Cabinet members are usually dependent solely on the patronage of the President. They typically enjoy no separate political legitimacy of their own, since – under the separation of powers – they are not members of the legislature. In parliamentary systems, Cabinet members may be drawn from and remain within the legislature; in some, they may be drawn from, but are precluded from remaining in, the legislature. The principal difference between the two systems, though, is that a President cannot usually be brought down by the legislature. In a parliamentary system, the head of government is dependent on the confidence of the legislature. That dependence may sometimes give other members of the leader's party significant political clout, especially if they have a following of their own in the legislature. Relationships between the Prime Minister and Cabinet may thus be more complex, potentially rendering the Prime Minister vulnerable to a Cabinet coup or challenge by a senior member.

Chapter summary

Ministers of the Crown head government departments. Those departments are extensive and complex bodies. Ministers enjoy substantial formal as well as political powers. The extent to which they are able to utilise those powers will depend upon the purpose and skill of the individual minister as well as the power situation, the climate of expectation and international developments. Ministers face considerable constraints, especially in recent years as the domain in which they operate has been constricted.

Ministers operate in a complex political environment. Different models seek to locate the place of ministers in that environment. The principal–agent model contends that ministers are agents of the Prime Minister or of civil servants. The power-dependency model posits an environment in which ministers have to negotiate with other actors in order to achieve desired outcomes. The baronial model posits that ministers have their own policy territory, castles and courtiers and fight or build alliances in order to get their way. The last two models suggest that ministers enjoy a greater role in policy making than is generally realised in the literature on British politics.

Discussion points

■ Is there an ideal type of senior minister?

■ Why are departments the basic building blocks of British government?

■ What should be the relationship between a minister and civil servants?

■ What is the relationship between ministers and civil servants?

■ Which model best explains the position of senior ministers in British government?

Further reading

Former ministers variously publish memoirs or diaries. Among those by former Cabinet ministers are Lawson (1992), Hurd (2003), Cook (2003), Short (2004), Blunkett (2006), Mandelson (2010), Darling (2011), and Straw (2012). Shephard (2000) provides a succinct, and very readable, commentary in her section on 'Ministers and Mandarins'. Mullin (2009) provides excellent insights into the role of a junior minister. Kaufman (1997) provides a humorous but pertinent guide as to how to be a good minister. However, very few academic works have appeared, and none in recent years, that look exclusively and conceptually at the role of ministers. Rose (1987) provides a functional analysis, and Brazier (1997) offers a more formal analysis. A broader analysis, encompassing the dynamics of ministerial office, is provided by Norton (2000). Junior ministers are covered by Theakston (1987). The relation of ministers to Parliament is dealt with by Woodhouse (1994, 2002). Political, and judicial, accountability is also covered by Flinders (2001).

There are various works on departments and, more especially, civil servants. A massive work, looking at departments and the civil servants that work in them, is that of Hennessy (2001). Other works include Theakston (1995, 1999), Barberis (1997), Richards (1997), Rhodes (2001), Gray and Jenkins (2005), Page and Jenkins (2005), Richards (2007), Burnham and Pyper (2008) and, for a useful historical overview, Bogdanor (2003) and Lowe (2011); see also Chapter 15 of Foster (2005). Lipsey (2000) provides a useful analysis of relationships in the Treasury. Jenkins (2004) offers a useful and brief overview from the perspective of a former civil servant. Denman (2002) offers a wonderfully readable and insightful view from the perspective of a senior civil servant. Stanley (2004) provides the civil servant equivalent to Kaufman's book: Chapter 1 covers working with ministers. For more material, see Chapter 21 of the present volume.

Bibliography

Barberis, P. (ed.) (1997) *The Civil Service in an Era of Change* (Dartmouth).

Barnett, J. (1982) *Inside the Treasury* (André Deutsch).

Beckett, F. and Hencke, D. (2004) *The Blairs and their Court* (Aurum Press).

Blunkett, D. (2006) *The Blunkett Tapes* (Bloomsbury).

Bogdanor, V. (2003) 'The Civil Service', in Bogdanor, V. (ed.) *The British Constitution in the Twentieth Century* (The British Academy/Oxford University Press).

Brazier, R. (1997) *Ministers of the Crown* (Clarendon Press).

Burnham, J. and Pyper, R. (2008) *Britain's Modernised Civil Service* (Palgrave Macmillan).

Cabinet Office (2010) *Ministerial Code* (Cabinet Office).

Cook, R. (2003) *Point of Departure* (Simon & Schuster).

Darling, A. (2011) *Back from the Brink* (Atlantic Books).

Denman, R. (2002) *The Mandarin's Tale* (Politico's).

Flinders, M. (2001) *The Politics of Accountability and the Modern State* (Ashgate).

Foster, C. (2005) *British Government in Crisis* (Hart Publishing).

Gray, A. and Jenkins, B. (2005) 'Government and Administration: Public Service and Public Servants', *Parliamentary Affairs*, vol. 58.

Headey, B. (1974) *British Cabinet Ministers* (George Allen & Unwin).

Hennessy, P. (2000) *The Prime Minister: The Office and its Holders since 1945* (Allen Lane/Penguin Press).

Hennessy, P. (2001) *Whitehall*, revised edn (Pimlico).

Holland, Sir G. (1995) 'Alas! Sir Humphrey, I Knew him Well', *RSA Journal*, November.

Hurd, D. (2003) *Memoirs* (Little, Brown).

Jenkins, K. (2004) 'Parliament, Government and the Civil Service', *Parliamentary Affairs*, vol. 57.

Johnson, N. (1980) *In Search of the Constitution* (Methuen).

Kaufman, G. (1997) *How to be a Minister* (Faber and Faber).

Kavanagh, D. and Seldon, A. (1999) *The Powers Behind the Prime Minister* (HarperCollins).

Lang, I. (2002) *Blue Remembered Years* (Politico's).

Lawson, N. (1992) *The View from no. 11* (Bantam Press).

Lipsey, D. (2000) *The Secret Treasury* (Viking).

Lowe, R. (2011) *The Official History of the British Civil Service: Reforming the Civil Service*, vol. 1 (Routledge).

Mandelson, P. (2010) *The Third Man* (HarperPress).

Morrison, J. (2001) *Reforming Britain: New Labour, New Constitution?* (Reuters/Pearson Education).

Mullin, C. (2009) *A View from the Foothills* (Profile Books).

Naughtie, J. (2001) *The Rivals* (Fourth Estate).

Norton, P. (1987) 'Prime Ministerial Power: A Framework for Analysis', *Teaching Politics*, vol. 16, no. 3, pp. 325–45.

Norton, P. (1997a) 'Leaders or Led? Senior Ministers in British Government', *Talking Politics*, vol. 10, no. 2, pp. 78–85.

Norton, P. (1997b) 'Political Leadership', in Robins, L. and Jones, B. (eds) *Half a Century in British Politics* (Manchester University Press).

Norton, P. (2000) 'Barons in a Shrinking Kingdom? Senior Ministers in British Government', in Rhodes, R.A.W. (ed.) *Transforming British Government*, vol. 2 (Macmillan).

Norton, P. (2003) 'Governing Alone', *Parliamentary Affairs*, vol. 56.

Norton, P. (2008) 'Tony Blair and the Office of Prime Minister', in Beech, M. and Lee, S.D. (eds) *Ten Years of New Labour* (Palgrave Macmillan).

Page, E.C. (2005) 'Joined-up Government and the Civil Service', in Bogdanor, V. (ed.) *Joined-Up Government* (The British Academy).

Page, E.C. and Jenkins, B. (2005) *Policy Bureaucracy* (Oxford University Press).

Parkinson, C. (1992) *Right at the Centre* (Weidenfeld & Nicolson).

Prescott, J. (2008) *Prezza* (Headline Review).

Public Administration Committee, House of Commons (2011) *Smaller Government: What Do Ministers Do?*, Session 2010–12, HC1540 (The Stationery Office).

Pyper, R. (1995) *The British Civil Service* (Prentice Hall/Harvester Wheatsheaf).

Redwood, J. (2012) http://johnredwoodsdiary.com/2012/10/06/who-runs-a-whitehall-department/

Rhodes, R.A.W. (1981) *Control and Power in Centre–Local Government Relationships* (Gower).

Rhodes, R.A.W. (1997) *Understanding Governance* (Open University Press).

Rhodes, R.A.W. (2001) 'The Civil Service', in Seldon, A. (ed.) *The Blair Effect* (Little, Brown).

Richards, D. (1997) *The Civil Service under the Conservatives, 1979–1997* (Academy Press).

Richards, D. (2007) *New Labour and the Civil Service* (Palgrave).

Rose, R. (1987) *Ministers and Ministries* (Clarendon Press).

Seldon, A. (1997) *Major: A Political Life* (Weidenfeld & Nicolson).

Shephard, G. (2000) *Shephard's Watch* (Politico's).

Short, C. (2004) *An Honourable Deception?* (The Free Press).

Stanley, M. (2004) *Politico's Guide to How to be a Civil Servant* (Politico's).

Straw, J. (2012) *Last Man Standing* (Macmillan).

Tebbit, N. (1989) *Upwardly Mobile* (Futura).

Theakston, K. (1987) *Junior Ministers* (Blackwell).

Theakston, K. (1995) *The Civil Service since 1945* (Blackwell).

Theakston, K. (1999) *Leadership in Whitehall* (Macmillan).

Weir, S. and Beetham, D. (1999) *Political Power and Democratic Control in Britain* (Routledge).

Woodhouse, D. (1994) *Ministers and Parliament* (Clarendon Press).

Woodhouse, D. (2002) 'The Reconstruction of Constitutional Accountability', *Public Law*, Spring.

Useful websites

Ministers

List of government ministers: www.parliament.uk/mps-lords-and-offices/government-and-opposition1/

Ministerial responsibilities: www.cabinetoffice.gov.uk/resource-library/government-ministers-and-responsibilities

Ministerial Code: www.cabinetoffice.gov.uk/sites/default/files/resources/ministerial-code-may-2010.pdf

Civil service

Civil Service: www.civil-service.gov.uk

Civil Service Code: http://resources.civilservice.gov.uk/wp-content/uploads/2011/09/civil-service-code-2010.pdf

First Division Association of Civil Servants: www.fda.org.uk

Cabinet Office: www.cabinetoffice.gov.uk/content/about-cabinet-office

Civil Service Learning: www.civilservice.gov.uk/networks/hr/civil-service-learning

Related websites

Public Administration Committee of the House of Commons: www.parliament.uk/business/committees/committees-a-z/commons-select/public-administration-select-committee/

Guide to being a civil servant: www.civilservant.org.uk

Local government

Colin Copus

> " **Local institutions are to liberty what primary schools are to science; they put it within the peoples' reach** "
>
> De Tocqueville, 1835

Learning objectives

- To consider the dual role of local councils in acting as politically representative institutions and as the providers or facilitators of public services.

- To explore whether public apathy about local government undermines local democracy.

- To consider changes in the political decision-making process in local government: directly elected mayors, indirectly elected leaders and cabinets.

- To examine whether local councils should have more freedom from central control.

- To examine whether councillors represent the community or their party.

- To explore the relationship between local government and the European Union's policy-making network.

There are 20,638 councillors in Britain and at the beginning of 2013 just over 88 per cent of them come from the Conservative and Labour parties and the Liberal Democrats. There are however, a large array of councillors who are not members of one of the three main British parties and they have varying levels of success in fighting and winning council seats. The figures for the number of councillors by political affiliation are shown in Table 20.4 by the countries of the British state.

Local councils are politically representative and democratically elected bodies that play a vital role in ensuring the provision of a wide range of public services. The chapter will explore the tensions that exist between local government as a political institution and as a local authority that manages and administers local services. It will concentrate more closely on the political role of local government because, given the importance of public services, it is easy to forget that councils are elected bodies with their own political and policy agenda. The politics of local government often become submerged under discussions about running schools, providing social care, the lighting, repairing and sweeping of the streets and the emptying of dustbins (the latter is an issue in which even secretaries of state in the Cabinet will become involved). These are vital public services, of course, but, if all councillors disappeared tomorrow, these services would still continue to be provided. The chapter will concentrate on the politics of local government and the role councillors play as elected representatives, rather than the role they often find themselves playing – that of elected service managers.

Introduction

The first section of the chapter will explore the development and structure of local government; the second will examine the relationships between local and central government and will consider the Coalition Government's policies on localism and the new power of general competence given to councils. The third section will consider the policy environment of local government; the fourth will examine the development of party politics at the local level; the fifth will consider the introduction of directly elected mayors by the last Labour Government and how the Coalition has sought to increase the number of elected mayors. The final section will look at the relationship between local government and the European Union.

Background

Local government has always been subordinate to central control and, unlike many of its continental counterparts, it remains constitutionally unprotected from central government. The shape, size, structure, functions, powers, duties and very existence of local councils rest in the hands of central government to decide and the courts to interpret. Indeed, central government could abolish all local government and replace it with a system of central administration by passing an Act of Parliament. The abolition of local government would simply have to pass the same parliamentary procedures as any other bill – it would not have to navigate some special constitutional procedure. Moreover, at any point before April 2012 after the passage of the Localism Act 2011, councils could only do that which the law gave them permission or powers to do and any action not sanctioned by law was *ultra vires* (beyond the powers) and liable to be quashed or rendered null and void by the courts. We shall see later whether the new general power of competence introduced by the 2011 Act has changed this situation or just made things more uncertain.

The constitutionally subordinate role of local government to Westminster and Whitehall has led many to regard the work of local councils as no more than an administrative process – devoid of its own political life. Indeed, as Gyford (1976: 11) points out, some maintain that it is management and administration that solves local problems, not political and party political choices. Questions are raised, however, about the continued existence of, or need for, independent local government (Byrne 1983: 24); about central government interference in the way councils administer and provide public services across the country (what's often called the 'postcode lottery'); and about public apathy at local elections. To the litany of criticism often heaped upon local government can be added time-consuming and opaque decision-making structures; the supposedly poor calibre of many councillors; party politics leading to unnecessary conflict; large and remote units of local government which are distant from communities represented and served; the

tension between political and community representation and the technical efficiency of service administration; and the constraint on local action and decision-making arising from wider economic and social factors (Stanyer 1976; Dearlove 1979; Elcock 1982; Hampton 1987; Wolman and Goldsmith 1992). Despite questions as to its value and relevance, local government and indeed, local democracy and autonomy hold an important position in the governance of the country. Indeed, democratically elected councils provide an all too vital, if fragile, safeguard against an over-powerful central government and ensure that political space and positions exist for those not sharing the political affiliation of the government of the day. Local government and locally elected councillors are vital for any democratic country.

The decisions made by councillors come with a legitimacy that flows from the electoral process. Local elections produce a layer of political representatives able to claim a mandate for their policies and decisions. Moreover, councillors operate in greater proximity to the citizen than Members of Parliament. While the local electoral mandate theory has been criticised, councillors acting as elected representatives of the people provide an important legitimacy to the activities of local government (Wolman and Goldsmith 1992). It is the people's vote that prevents local government from being wholly an administrative arm of central government.

Local government: from confusion to cohesion

The current map of local government structure looks fairly, though not completely, uniform. However, it is a map that has been designed to reflect the demands of service management and administration rather than of recognisable communities of place and identity. Local government has gone through evolution interspersed with periodic revolution. Growing from the naturally formed communities of Anglo-Saxon England, local government took on a shape, size and structure that reflected its roots in very local communities. Parishes, boroughs and counties developed over time, sharing the provision of services and local administrative matters with an often confusing mix of other statutory, non-statutory and private providers, alongside magistrates and sheriffs appointed by the monarch.

As new problems for government arose, dealing with the impact of an increasingly complex world became the responsibility of a range of local bodies and appointed boards. Parishes, boroughs and counties overlapped in area and responsibilities with a host of boards and commissions such as those for improvement, street paving, drainage, public health and Poor Law relief (the last being a system of providing support to the poor that began in the Elizabethan period and, in one form or another, lasted until the formation of the modern welfare state in the 1940s). So, what we would today call 'councils' existed, at various times, alongside single-purpose bodies, formed variously by statute, appointment, self-selection or election.

It was the reforming zeal and legislative whirlwind of the Victorian period that began to give national coherence to the shape and responsibilities of local government. At the same time reform was often ad hoc when dealing with many of the problems generated by, and for, the developing capitalist system. The 1835 Municipal Corporations Act has been described by Wilson and Game (2002) as the 'foundation of our present day local government'. The Act introduced the idea of elected councils and was followed by an Act of 1888 which democratised the county councils. The Victorians gave a basis to local government of popular – although not yet universal – election, financial responsibility and uniformity of purpose, shape and process. By the turn of the century, local authorities looked and felt like the 'governments' of their localities but were, ironically, increasingly being controlled by the centre (see Chandler 2007). The structure of counties, districts, non-county boroughs and all-purpose county boroughs, with parishes as a fourth sub-tier, promoted some uniformity, but it left unanswered the question of how many layers (tiers) of local government there should be to meet the often conflicting requirements of political representation, identity with a place and well-run services.

The legislatively enforced uniformity of local government continued throughout the twentieth century, as did the preoccupation of central governments, of all colours, with the regulation of local activity and the diminution of local autonomy. After the Second World War policy-makers were grappling with rapidly changing demographic, political, social and technological developments and an expanding welfare state, which meant that the demands of efficient service administration and responsive, democratic local govern-

ment had to be reconciled (Young and Rao 1997). However, technocratic and democratic needs are driven by different factors, with technocracy requiring bigger and bigger units of local government and local democracy requiring smaller and more cohesive communities. Throughout the twentieth century, the technocratic arguments about efficiency and effectiveness won a series of important battles over the needs of local democracy and representation. These victories become very apparent when looking at the shape, size and structure of local government.

In 1966 the Labour Government set up a Royal Commission on Local Government in England, with separate enquiries into local government in Wales and Scotland. The Report of the Royal Commission (Cmnd 4040), while accepting the importance of democratic local government, expressed the belief that it was then too numerous and fragmented, but it was unable to agree a blueprint for change. The majority report suggested a unitary solution (single-tier councils providing all services) with 58 authorities across the country outside London. A minority report argued for a two-tier division of function and structure based on city regions and 'shire' and 'district' councils. The Labour Government accepted the majority report, but its Conservative successor, elected in 1970 and mindful of its strengths in the shires, introduced a new two-tier structure through the 1972 Local Government Act.

As a consequence, on 1 April 1974 the map of local government changed dramatically (Figure 20.1). The systems of local government for the big cities and the more rural areas were the inverse of each other. In the major conurbations of England six metropolitan counties were created alongside 36 metropolitan districts. The metropolitan counties were major strategic authorities, while the metropolitan districts had responsibility for the large-spending services such as education, social services and housing.

Outside the urban areas the situation was almost reversed; the counties – 47 of them across England and Wales (reduced from 58) – were the education and social service authorities as well as having a wider strategic remit. The districts were responsible for housing, with leisure as the other major spending service, alongside planning and waste-removal functions. In England and Wales the districts were reduced in number from 1,249 to 333. As a result of the Wheatley Commission (Cmnd 4159, HMSO 1969), local government in Scotland was reorganised on a two-tier basis with nine large regional councils and 53 districts, alongside three island authorities. In 1974 British local government became less local and more subject to division of function between increasingly large and remote units.

In the 1960s and 1970s the Labour and Conservative parties saw the structure of local government, the allocation of services between tiers and the drawing of authority boundaries as important political considerations – not a

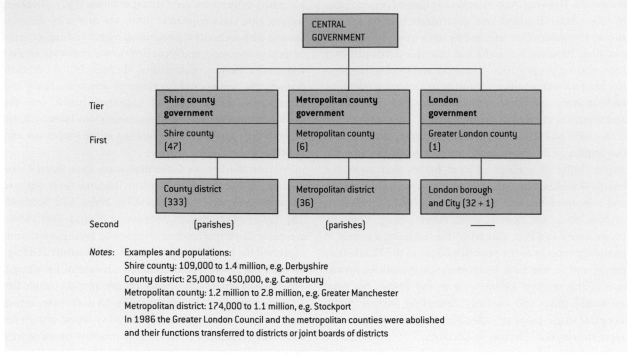

Figure 20.1 The structure of local government in England and Wales after 1974
Source: Adapted from Gray (1979).

new phenomenon but one shared by Victorian Conservative and Liberal governments. Labour's support for unitary local government is based on the creation of large, urban-centred councils running all services, and because of the party's urban base, these would be mainly Labour-controlled. Conservative support for two-tier councils, and the 1970 Government's allocation of services between the tiers, equally displayed its party political preoccupations. Shire counties received the more powerful and expensive services, as by and large these would be Conservative-dominated. The metropolitan districts were given similar functional responsibilities, which would enable Conservatives in some of the more affluent metropolitan areas to control significant local services. Thus, for the Labour and Conservative parties, the importance of the structure of local government rested not only on the technocratic and democratic arguments but on the realities of political control and power. Yet, there has been a shift in how the parties see the best way of organising local government, which first manifested itself over the issue of unitary councils and then the formation of city-based regions.

The reorganisations of the 1990s display similar political and party political undercurrents as well as an interesting shift by the Conservatives towards unitary councils. In 1992 John Major's Conservative Government established a Local Government Commission, chaired by Sir John Banham (former Director of Audit at the Audit Commission and

Director General of the Confederation of British Industry) to review the structure of local government. Government guidance to the commission favoured the unitary system and stressed the importance of local government efficiency, accountability, responsiveness and localness, criteria that display the contradictions inherent in the technocratic–democratic arguments that had been played out since 1945 (Young and Rao 1997).

The commission rejected the production of a national blueprint for local government structure and instead recommended the creation of all-purpose, single-tier **unitary authorities** in some areas and the retention of the two-tier system or a modified version of it in other areas. The commission justified its recommendations, which often conflicted with the favoured approach of the Government, on the basis of cost, community identity and local geography, and the degree of local support for change. The Secretary of State's replacement of Sir John Banham as chairman of the Commission with Sir David Cooksey, again from the Audit Commission, resulted in the formation of a few more unitary authorities than otherwise would have been the case, but no new nationwide reorganisation resulted.

The next big crop of unitary councils were formed by a Labour Government which in April 2009 replaced 44 councils with 9 new unitaries, with a loss of over 1,300 councillors (for an excellent analysis of the process, see Chisholm and Leach 2008).

Table 20.1 New unitary councils, 2009

County area unitary proposal (number of districts in brackets)	New unitary structure	Change in number of councils
Bedford (3)	2 Unitary Bedford	4 reduced to 2
Chester (6)	2 Unitary Chester	7 reduced to 2
Cornwall (6)	County Unitary	7 reduced to 1
Durham (7)	County Unitary	8 reduced to 1
Northumberland (6)	County Unitary	7 reduced to 1
Shropshire (5)	County Unitary	6 reduced to 1
Wiltshire (4)	County Unitary	5 reduced to 1

Each of theses new councils came into existence on 1 April 2009.

Things have been somewhat simpler in Wales and Scotland. The 1992 Local Government Act abolished the county and district councils in Wales and the regional and district councils in Scotland, replacing them with 22 unitaries in Wales and 32 in Scotland. Neither the Welsh Assembly or the Scottish Parliament have seriously sought to change their current structure of local government. Local government in Northern Ireland had been reorganised in 1972, when 26 district councils were created. As a result of the 'review of public administration' in Northern Ireland, launched in 2002, these 26 councils were to be replaced by seven councils (an arrangement forced though by the then secretary of State for Northern Ireland, Peter Hain). That proposal was later changed and following elections in 2011, the Northern Ireland Executive is committed to a model of 11 councils to be in place by 2015. However, the nature of politics in Northern Ireland and the difficulty of forming agreement between the parties in the Assembly may see that deadline slip.

A word about London

London has always posed particular problems for how the British unitary state would deal with the government of the most powerful city in the country. The economic, political and cultural power and sheer size of the city meant it could pose problems even for central government and particularly if it had its own elected government. The Victorians dealt with this by first of all avoiding any directly elected governing body for London. The Metropolis Local Management Act 1855 created the Metropolitan Board of Works for London, indirectly elected from parish and boards in London. Its job was to deal with the infrastructural development of London and not to act so much as a governing body. It was not until the London Government Act 1899 that the city was given its own elected council: the London County Council. The initials LCC can still be found on buildings and other structures across the centre of London.

The LCC lasted until the Herbert Commission Report on London Government (Cmnd 1164) resulted in its replacement in 1965 as the strategic authority by the geographically much larger Greater London Council (GLC). In addition, across London 32 boroughs and the City of London Corporation had responsibility for the provision of day-to-day services (replacing the 28 boroughs introduced in 1899) (see Pimlott and Rao 2002; Travers 2004). As with other reorganisations, size mattered and local cohesion and community representation lost out.

The life of the GLC was short lived, compared to its forerunner. By the mid-1980s the GLC, led from 1981 by Ken Livingstone, had become troublesome for the Thatcher Government. The Conservatives' 1983 manifesto had pledged to abolish these authorities, and after the publication of a White Paper, *Streamlining the Cities* (Cmnd 9063, HMSO 1983), this was duly accomplished in 1986. The responsibilities of the GLC and six metropolitan counties (which were abolished at the same time) were transferred to the boroughs below them, or to a series of joint boards. As a consequence for some 14 years London stood alone as the only West European capital city without an elected government of its own.

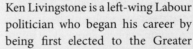

Ken Livingstone (1945–)

Ken Livingstone is a left-wing Labour politician who began his career by being first elected to the Greater London Council (GLC) in 1973. He went on to become the leader of the GLC in 1981 after Labour won control with a majority of six seats. Livingstone was not expected to become the leader of the GLC: that role was supposed to have gone to Andrew McIntosh, a more moderate candidate. But, Livingstone emerged as the new leader and stayed in that job until the GLC was abolished by the government of Margaret Thatcher in 1986.

Livingstone's 'Red Ken' nickname, given to him by the press because of his left-wing views, did not prevent him from being elected the MP for Brent in 1987 until 2001.

After failed attempts by the leadership of the Labour Party to prevent him from being selected as the Labour candidate for the first elections for the mayor of London, Livingstone served two 4-year terms from 2000 to 2008. In 2008 he was defeated by Conservative candidate, Boris Johnson. Johnson again defeated Livingstone at the 2012 London mayoral elections.

PROFILE

Boris Johnson (1964–)

Boris Johnson is a Conservative politician who was elected as the MP for Henley in the 2001 General Election and he has served as the shadow minister for the Arts and shadow minister for Higher Education. In 2007 he was selected as the Conservative candidate for mayor of London. By doing this he became notable as an MP who wished to leave Parliament to serve in local government – although the office of Mayor of London is by no means a traditional council appointment.

Johnson was elected in 2008, beating sitting Labour mayor Ken Livingstone; he defeated Livingstone again in the 2012 mayoral elections.

Johnson is a flamboyant and high-profile Conservative politician with a ready wit and keen intellect. As mayor of London during the London Olympics, he made some stirring Churchillian speeches before and after the events – noticeably criticising US presidential candidate, Mitt Romney, for suggesting that London might not be ready to stage such an international event.

Johnson was pictured famously dangling from a 150-foot high zipwire during the Olympic Games – very few politicians could survive such a media mistake. Johnson is, however, being spoken about as a future leader of the Conservative Party and potential Prime Minister.

The Blair Government elected in 1997 moved quickly on its promise to reintroduce elected local government for the whole of London, and did so with the Greater London Authority Act 1999. The Act created the new Greater London Authority, consisting of the London Assembly and the directly elected mayor of London. The Assembly has 25 elected members, 14 of whom are members elected from constituencies formed from the London boroughs and elected by the first-past-the-post system, while 11 are members from across London, with no specific constituencies, elected from a party (or independent) list. The London mayor is elected by the supplementary vote system and, if no candidate receives over 50 per cent of the votes on the first round of counting, all but the top two candidates are eliminated and the second preferences given by the voters are redistributed to the remaining two. The first elected mayor of London (2000), who served two consecutive terms in office, was Ken Livingstone – the last leader of the GLC. He was defeated in the 2008 elections by the Conservative candidate Boris Johnson. In the May 2012 elections for mayor of London Ken and Boris faced each other once again as well as five other candidates, and this time just before the London Olympics. The result was as follows:

Boris Johnson: Conservative: 971,931 first preference votes

Ken Livingstone: Labour: 889,918 first preference votes

The final tally of votes after second preferences were counted was;

Boris Johnson: Conservative: 1,054,811 votes

Ken Livingstone: Labour: 992,273 votes.

Boris Johnson was therefore declared a 'fit and proper person' to be mayor of London and re-elected to office.

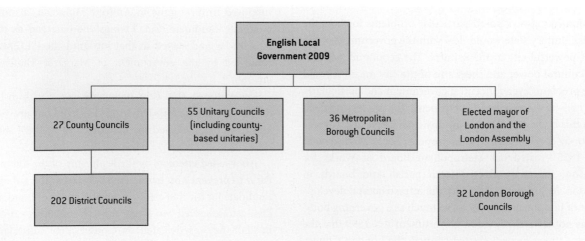

Figure 20.2 The structure of English local government

The Coalition Government is currently consulting on ways to make it easier to form parish councils.

If we look at the overall structure of local government we see a picture that is very different from the unitary system that exists in Scotland and Wales

The structure of local government in England

The gradual creep towards an all unitary system of local government goes hand-in-hand with an increase in the size of councils. Indeed, it is questionable whether the term 'local' can be applied to some units of local government, particularly when compared to the size of councils across Europe.

From Table 20.2 it can be seen that Britain has the largest average population size but the fewest councillors per citizen (representative ratio); the situation remains more or less the same whatever European nations are included in the table. Local government in Britain has increasingly become larger, and more remote and distant from the communities it serves. As Stewart reminds us, '[the] average population of shire districts is over 10 times the average of the lower tier in Europe' (Stewart 2003: 181). It is likely

Table 20.2 Local government scale

	Population (millions)	Number of lower tier councils	Average population per council	Total number of councilors 000s	Persons per council
France	59	36,700	1,600	515	120
Spain	40	8,100	4,900	65	620
Germany	83	12,400	6,600	200	420
Italy	57	8,000	7,200	100	600
Belgium	10	589	18,000	13	800
Sweden	9	290	31,000	46	200
The Netherlands	16	443	36,000	10	1,700
Denmark	5	98	51,000	5	1,200
UK 1974	56	520	108,000	26	2,150
UK 2008 (changes in England only)	60	468	128,000	22	2,730
UK 2009 (changes in England only)	61	433	140,000	21	2,900

Source: Adapted from: Chris Game, 'Lost! 90 per cent of councillors in 35 years: Are county-wide unitaries effectively the end of UK local government?' Paper presented to the PSA Local Politics Specialist Group University of Birmingham – 30 January 2009.

Table 20.3 Key legislation in the creation/abolition of councils

Act	Effect of the Act
Municipal Corporations 1835	The right to petition for an elected council
Local Government Act 1888	51 county councils; 62 county boroughs (and the London County Council)
London Government Act 1899	Creates 28 Metropolitan boroughs within the LCC
Local Government Act 1894	688 Urban District Councils; 692 Rural District Councils
London Government Act 1963	Greater London Council and 32 London boroughs
Local Government Act 1972	46 counties and 296 districts (excludes London)
Local Government Act 1985	Abolishes 6 metropolitan councils and the GLC
Local Government Act 1992	34 County Councils; 36 Metropolitan Borough Councils; 238 Districts; 46 Unitary councils
Greater London Authority Act 1999	Creates the London Assembly and the directly elected Mayor of London
Local Government and Public Involvement in Health Act 2007	Loss of 44 councils replaced by 9 new unitary councils
Localism Act 2011	Gives English councils general power of competence (ability to act without legislative permission) but the Act did not change the number of councils

that neither the Conservatives or Labour has finished with the unitarisation of English local government, nor with the increase in council size associated with it; English local government may not remain local at all. It is now necessary to consider whether we can, indeed, call it 'government' either.

Inter-governmental relations: general competence or general dogsbody?

The chapter has already set out British local government's subordinate role to central government. Such an arrangement is not the only relationship between national and sub-national governments, and this section will consider, in the light of the Coalition Government's policies on localism, how the centre and the localities could interact on a more equal footing.

The British unitary state and unwritten constitution, resting on the doctrine of parliamentary supremacy, ensures that the party with a majority in Parliament is able to legislate as it thinks fit, unhindered by any mechanisms for constitutional restraint. While the courts may interpret government legislation and even find that ministers have acted illegally, they cannot hold legislation unconstitutional and unenforceable, effectively striking legislation down as the US Supreme Court may do. Thus, intergovernmental relations in Britain are conducted in an environment where political control of the machinery of central government allows national political concerns and policy to supersede local discretion, although bargaining between central and local government is the norm.

We are left pondering whether councils should be subordinate to central control and regulation and only be able to act in cases where Parliament gives express authority. Councils are elected bodies, so should they not have the powers to act accordingly? Moreover, councils and councillors are closer to the people they represent than central government, MPs and civil servants. The issues they deal with often have a more immediate and greater specific impact on the day-to-day wellbeing of local citizens than the activities of central government. In addition, strong and independent councils can act as a counterbalance to the political power of central government and are a means by which local voices can be heard at the heart of government. We are left with the question: should local councils be granted a power of general competence (a widespread

power across Europe) (Wilson and Game 2011) to govern their own localities as they think fit and in accordance with the wishes of their electorate?

The last Labour government answered this question with a highly qualified 'maybe'. After displaying its views on local government in a number of publications – *Renewing Democracy: Rebuilding Communities* (Labour Party 1995); the 1997 and 2001 Labour Party election manifestos; and the Green and White Papers *Local Democracy and Community Leadership* (DETR 1998b), *Modern Local Government: In Touch with the People* (DETR 1998a), *Local Leadership: Local Choice* (DETR 1999) – it settled, in the Local Government Act 2000, on giving councils a duty to promote the social, economic and environmental wellbeing of local communities. (For a detailed exploration of how sub-national governments can affect the welfare or well-being of citizens, see Wolman and Goldsmith 1992.) As Wilson and Game (2011) point out, section one of the Act enabled local government to become involved in areas such as tackling social exclusion, reducing health inequalities, promoting neighbourhood renewal and improving local environmental quality. It did not, however, bestow a general power on councils to act as they think fit.

The Coalition Agreement (2010: 11) which formed the basis of the arrangement between the Conservative Party and Liberal Democrats to form a government stated the following aims:

- to shift power from Westminster to people (and councils);
- to promote decentralisation and democratic engagement;
- to end top-down government by giving new powers to local councils, communities, neighbourhoods and individuals.

It further boldly stated (p. 12) that: 'We will give councils a general power of competence'. It duly completed on that promise and section 1(1) of the **Localism Act 2011** states that: 'A local authority has power to do anything that individuals generally may do': general competence has arrived for English local government. Now, rather than having to find statutory authority for any action a councils wishes to conduct, it can point to section 1(1) and claim that it is acting under the **'general power of competence'** it has been granted by Parliament. Section 2, however, starts to set out what are a list of exceptions to the general power – things councils can still not do, but the Act has provided the beginnings of a new framework within which councils can operate – we have yet to see if councillors will act with boldness and imagination when it comes to the power, or, as no doubt their legal advice will suggest, they are reluctant and cautious in using the power. A cautionary tale is set out in Box 20.1.

Box 20.1

Praying for Bideford

Bideford Town Council, in Devon, always started its formal council meetings with prayers. An atheist member of the council, who objected to this, took the council to court, backed by the National Secular Society. The judge ruled that under the Local Government Act 1972 there was no statutory power permitting councils to say prayers as part of a formal meeting. Despite well over a thousand years of Christianity in England and despite there being no constitutional separation between church and state in England – unlike in the US – the judge effectively banned prayers at council meetings. As a result of the outrage caused by this judgement, Eric Pickles, MP, the Secretary of State for Communities and Local Government, in what he called 'a blow for localism over central interference' brought forward the signing of an order that brought into being the 'general power of competence'. Bideford and any other council could pray again. However, in an interesting twist the Mayor of Bideford believes that the judiciary are the highest authority, above government, and that the Government cannot overturn the judiciary. With an elected councillor having so little faith in government and forgetting that it is the legislature that changes the law, it bodes ill for the use of the 'general power of competence'.

We wait to see if the general power of competence results in a fundamental shift in the relationship between local and central government. It is unlikely that the courts will willingly give up their control over local government and abandon the principle of *ultra vires*. Indeed, lawyers are already saying that the new power doesn't mean what it says on the tin! One thing is sure, there will be a test case and it is possible that test case will say that when Parliament said a council can do anything that a person could do – it didn't mean what the council in the dock was doing. We will then see if the government rushes to the defence of general competence and clarifies and strengthens the law, thus placing democratically elected councils in a stronger position in relation to the unelected judges.

Local government: a changing policy environment

So far we have seen the power of the central government over councils and that the policy landscape within which councils operate is constantly changing. Central government allocates new roles and responsibilities to councils, takes away roles and gives them to other bodies, generally altering local government to suit its own policy agenda. Thus, it is of no surprise that the Coalition Government has introduced a range of policies to which local government must comply. Despite the need for councils to comply with government legislation, as we have seen this government has loudly trumpeted its commitment to localism.

Big society

The Localism Act 2011 is the centrepiece of the Government's commitment to localism and provides the framework within which the much vaunted, but less articulated policy of the 'Big Society' will operate. It applies to England alone as it covers a policy area that has been devolved to the Scottish and Welsh regional chambers. It forms part of the Conservative Party's policy of reducing the power and role of the state in the provision of public services by building on and supporting the role of communities, neighbourhoods, clubs, volunteer groups and other organisations and citizens in creating a vibrant and active engagement in local life. For the Conservatives the 'Big Society' is about getting the state off the back of the citizen and encouraging citizens to take responsibility for the way in which their communities develop. For Labour however, the 'Big Society' is a smokescreen for cuts in public expenditure, reductions in public services, redundancies in the public sector and a dismantling of the welfare state.

The Government has found it difficult to fully articulate – at least to the satisfaction of the media and its political opponents – exactly what the 'Big Society' is, which has meant the Prime Minister has been called upon to re-state and re-emphasise the nature of the 'Big Society'. One thing is clear and that is that the 'Big Society' has an impact on the role of local government. The Localism Act, through which the Government aims to give life to the 'Big Society', gives local communities a new set of powers that they can use in relation to their local council:

- *Community right to challenge* (enshrined in the Act) gives communities, voluntary groups, parish councils and other 'relevant bodies' the right to express an interest in taking over the running of a council service. The purpose is to ensure that those with ideas about how services can be improved can act on those ideas. The council will have to comply with procurement rules before a service becomes the responsibility of those outside the council.

- *Community right to express an interest* is linked to the right to challenge because it is how communities exercise the right to challenge. They must express their interest in providing or helping the council in providing a particular service and there are now legal requirements on councils to act when such an expression is received.

- *Community right to bid* allows voluntary groups, community groups and parish councils to nominate to the council a community asset. The council must keep a list of community assets, which might include community centres, a pub, a particular local shop or some other asset the community feels would be a major loss should it close or be sold. Any owner of such an asset must wait six months before it can be sold, thus giving any local group time to raise the finance to purchase that asset.

While we do not yet know how these very new powers will operate they have the potential to change the relationship between communities and their council, but we are left wondering exactly how many communities will use these powers and what part they will play in building the 'Big Society'.

The new planning framework

Planning issues are at the heart of much of what local government does in terms of the way in which communities develop and change physically and the nature of their infrastructural development. Amid much controversy and debate the Coalition Government introduced a new 'National Planning Policy Framework' which sets out the way in which councils must address the planning and development issues with which they must deal. Most of the controversy and argument was focused on the presumption in the framework in favour of 'sustainable development'. Critiques of the Government's proposals pointed out that this could lead to the erosion of the greenbelt and uncontrolled development of factories, offices and housing despite the objections of local people. Moreover, it was claimed that it contradicted the Localism Act 2011 which allows local people to produce neighbourhood plans which the council would have to consider in their own planning process. The Government argues that pursuing **sustainable development** involves seeking positive improvements in the quality of the built, natural and historic environment, as well as in people's quality of life, including (but not limited to):

- making it easier for jobs to be created in cities, towns and villages;
- moving from a net loss of bio-diversity to achieving net gains for nature;
- replacing poor design with better design;
- improving the conditions in which people live, work, travel and take leisure; and
- widening the choice of high quality homes.

(DCLG 2012: 3)

The outrage caused by the original proposals, which were seen as a blueprint for unrestricted development and which led even papers like the *Daily Telegraph*, which normally supports the Government, to demand changes, had its effect. The Government changed its definition of 'sustainable development' to what is know as the *Brundtland definition* (a more environmentally focused approach); emphasised 'Brownfield' development (land already built on rather than undeveloped land); and, stressed the importance of local plans and local decision-making. It now appears that councils, the House of Commons Communities and Local Government Select Committee, developers, planners and the Government are happy. We wait to see exactly how happy all those interested in planning turn out to be with this new policy.

A time of austerity

The Coalition Government has as a major plank of its policy platform the introduction of measures to reduce and control national public expenditure as a way of getting the economy back on track. Each year central government allocates money to each council though the Local Government Financial Settlement, using the formula grant system, which is made up of:

- revenue support grant;
- redistributed business rates;
- specific grants (for certain services);
- Home Office Police Grant.

Around 60 per cent of all local government income comes from central government and in 2011/12 central government allocated £73 billion to councils. Yet, the amount of money councils receive from government fell by 9.9 per cent in 2011/12, and by 7.3 per cent in 2012/13. Councils have little discretion in replacing any financial support they lose from the government with other income streams – certainly not to the extent of making up all the losses. Changes again introduced by the Localism Act require councils to hold a binding referendum of local people if they wished to increase council tax levy by 2 per cent in the 2013–14 financial year (House of Commons SN05682). The government offered councils a grant to freeze council tax for another year and 85 per cent of councils accepted that grant (HM Treasury http://www.hm-treasury.gov.uk/ press_89_12.htm).

Councils across the country have been forced into a series of reductions in their own expenditure which is already having an effect on the services that they provide. In times of economic downturn and austerity and with unemployment figures creeping upwards, public services become ever more important and it is at this time they face their own challenges. The councillors elected across the country are grappling with difficult choices about the level of services their councils can continue to provide. They are supported in that process by the officers that work for the council, who will be providing them with the information needed to decide the level of public services provided to local communities.

Councillors and officers navigating the changes

While councillors have links to the external environment through their parties and communities, and business, professional and political organisations, the decisions they take rest heavily on the advice they receive from officers employed by the authority. These professionals and managers provide important antennae for councillors on the outside world and are the key source of advice and expertise they rely on when responding to changes in legislation and government policy. Local government officers coming from a range of professional backgrounds, mainly associated with the specialist services provided by local authorities or from the wider professions such as the law, interact with colleagues whose profession is management. The professional as expert and the professional manager now operate in what is the accepted principle of local government management: the corporate approach. This approach was championed in 1972 by the Bains Report, which challenged the then dominant functional approach to local government organisation and management.

The Bains Report took a managerial perspective towards the role of the officer, but as Stewart (1986: 132) reminds

us, 'decisions made by a manager can have important and unexpected political consequences'. Indeed, it is senior officers and senior councillors acting as a 'joint elite' (Stoker 1991) that is at the heart of local government political management. While tensions may exist between the elite of senior councillors and officers, the carving-out of spheres of influence enables an uneasy alliance between officers and members to contribute a dynamic tension to local policy processes.

Many alternative sources of information exist for councillors to that received from officers, but, as the paid employees and advisers to the council, senior officers are a potentially powerful influence on councillors' final decisions. Indeed, for the vast majority of councillors the advice received from officers is among the most important and influential they receive. Even the overview and scrutiny committees formed by councils under the 2000 Act have yet to provide councillors with much direct access to sources of information and advice apart from local government officers.

Moreover, officers can influence councillors in their private discussions in the party group through the production of council minutes and reports that councillors consider in their group meetings, and, by attendance at those meetings, on request, to answer questions and give advice, which until quite recently was largely accepted. In 1990 Young and Laffin indicated that party politics has radically altered the patterns of interaction between officers and councillors and that the task of advising councillors no longer comes with the certainty of officer influence that it once had. Copus (2004) shows the powerful influence of national political parties in local government and it is to those parties we now turn.

Local government and local politics

Despite folklore to the contrary, local government and local and national politics have had a long and intertwined association, one stretching back much further than the 1974 local government reorganisation, often wrongly identified as the point when national politics invaded local council chambers. Indeed, prior to the 1835 Municipal Corporations Act, which democratised municipal boroughs and allowed towns to petition Parliament for an elected council, local government was already party politicised. It was controlled, for the most part, by what Fraser (1979) described as 'self-perpetuating Tory–Anglican élites'. Moreover, the first municipal elections after the 1835 Act were essentially party battles between the holders of, and contenders for, local political power. Even in the towns that did not immediately incorporate after the 1835 Act, the campaign for municipal status often divided along party lines. Similar party battles occurred throughout the nineteenth century over the reform, and control, of London government (Young 1975).

Gyford (1985) summarised the long-term process of the party politicisation of local government, identifying five distinct stages:

> Diversity (1835–65) – Crystallisation (1865–1905) – Realignment (1905–45) – Nationalisation (1945–74) – Reappraisal (1974 onwards).

The stages chart the gradual solidification of the party system in local government and how party activity strengthened itself in local government.

Local politics has moved from a time when candidates and councillors often disguised their national party allegiances (see also Grant 1973; Clements 1969) to today, where political party involvement in local government has been described as almost 'universal', with 'seven-eighths' of all councils having fully developed party systems (HMSO 1986b; see also Wilson and Game 2011: 309–12).

As representative bodies, with the ability to distribute scarce local resources and decide broad policy approaches to important local services, councils are inherently political bodies. It is therefore no surprise that members and supporters of national political parties have had an interest in securing representation on and control of councils. Hennock (1973), Jones (1969) and Lee (1963) indicate not only the long association between local government and political parties but also the different texture that party politics has taken and the varied relationships that have existed within and between parties.

Bulpitt (1967) has summarised these differences into a typology of local party systems as either negative or positive, the main distinction between the systems being the degree to which councillors act as coherent political groupings to accept responsibility for the control of council policy and the settling of patronage issues. What has varied over time and place is the nature of the relationship between the parties and the degree to which councillors sharing the same political allegiance cohere as distinct party groups. It is the rigidity with which party groups cohere to provide a council with a governing administration, or an opposition bloc, that distinguishes the conduct of party politics in council chambers from its more fluid predecessors (Young and Davis 1990).

Today the overwhelming majority of council elections are contested by members of national political parties, and for some time local elections have had the flavour of a series of mini general elections (Newton 1976). Indeed, on 18 April 2012 the Labour Party dedicated an entire party political broadcast for the English local elections to the National Health Service: an important political issue, yes; but not something in which local government has any real role as a provider. On the doorstep party activists will be talking about the economy, the health service, the EU, immigration, what promises the Prime Minister has broken, or what a mess the last Labour government made of the economy (depending on the activist's party); by this means national parties squeeze local issues out of local elections, when the voter should really be looking at what their local councillor and local council has or has not done.

A casual glance at the election-night programmes covering the results will give you constant analysis by the experts of what this, or that, result means for the Government, or for the recovery of the Labour Party, or for the fortunes of the Liberal Democrats in the Coalition and far less about what the results in Amber Valley, Adur, Barnsley, Blackburn with Darwen, Wyre Forest, Wokingham or Wolverhampton mean for local citizens and for the way in which those councils had hitherto been run. One thing is sure, however: local election turnout in Britain bumps along at around 40 per cent (36 per cent in 2008) (Rallings and Thrasher 2012). Indeed, in some by-elections turnout has fallen to single figures. Poor turnout raises serious questions about the democratic legitimacy of local government and the ability of councillors to claim an electoral mandate for their policies. Turnout figures for local elections have been lovingly kept by Rallings and Thrasher at the Local Government Elections Centre at: www.research.plymouth.ac.uk/elections and their database shows the average turnout for the 2011 local elections was 42.6 per cent.

Poor turnout no doubt damages local accountability and legitimacy, but, added to this is the party group system and the loyalty and discipline groups expect of, and by and large receive, from councillors. That system further damages local accountability and representation (Copus 1998, 1999a, 1999b). Political parties bind councillors to the decisions of their groups, taken in private and closed meetings, to which councillors are expected to publicly lead support, or at least acquiesce in, irrespective of how he or she may have spoken or voted in those meetings and of the views of the voters.

The organisation and activity of party groups varies depending on the party concerned, but each of the three main national and two nationalist parties produces model standing orders for their council party groups. Patterns of party interaction will vary depending on the type of council concerned but, largely, groups are well organised and structured, with a range of officers undertaking different tasks and clearly identified expectations of loyalty from their membership (Rallings and Thrasher 1997; Wilson and Game 2011). In addition, party groups have a range of

Table 20.4 Councillors by party and country, 2012

	Conservative	Labour	Lib Dem	Nationalists	Independents and smaller parties (incl. BNP & Gns)
England	8,746	5,599	2,535	2	1,273
Wales	108	581	72	167	335
Scotland	116	393	70	424	217

Source: http://www.gwydir.demon.co.uk/uklocalgov/makeup.htm

disciplinary procedures and sanctions available to use against recalcitrant members, making it now the most important setting for the conduct of local representation and for council decision making (Hampton 1970; Saunders 1979; Stoker 1991; Game and Leach 1995).

The way in which party groups conduct council business can be problematic, because local government is overwhelming dominated by the main three national political parties; in England alone, for example, almost 93 per cent of all councillors are from the Conservative and Labour parties or the Liberal Democrats (calculations based on the web data: http://www.gwydir.demon.co.uk/uklocalgov/makeup.htm).

With such a deep penetration into local town halls by the main parties it is all the more important to emphasise the 'local' element of local government and, if parties continue in the town hall setting their wider national political battle, we are left asking again, where is the 'local' in local government?

Yet, is it fair to say that if national political parties have such control of local government it is the voter that gave it to them and at least voters can express dissatisfaction with the way in which they make decisions? Indeed, the way in which councils make decisions has undergone a radical transformation from the committee system which developed from the Victorian period. Local councils now have executive leaders, and elected mayors and local cabinets – similar to the Westminster Cabinet – are now the norm.

Creating a new form and approach to local politics

When it was elected in 1997, the Blair Government was already committed to a widespread review of the British constitution; in opposition Labour had recognised the importance to political pluralism of a vibrant, healthy and vigorous local government and local politics. The reform agenda was displayed in a series of publications: a Green Paper, three White Papers, a discussion paper and two Acts of Parliament: *Local Democracy and Community Leadership* (DETR 1998b), *Modern Local Government: In Touch with the People* (DETR 1998), *Local Leadership: Local Choice* (DETR 1999), and *Strong Local Leadership: Quality Public Services* (DTLR 2001) and *Vibrant Local Leadership* (ODPM 2005); and the 1999 London and 2000 Local Government Acts.

The Local Government Act 2000 radically transformed the structure of political decision-making in local government, and Part II of the Act required all councils with populations above 85,000 to introduce one of three new-style executive political decision-making arrangements. Three executive options available under the Act were:

1 a directly elected executive mayor and cabinet;

2 a mayor and council manager (an option removed by the Local Government and Public Involvement in Health Act 2007); and,

3 an indirectly elected executive leader and cabinet.

The indirectly elected leader and cabinet option has been the one preferred by the overwhelming majority of councils, which is not surprising as this option represents the least change to existing practices and structures. Here, the council, but in reality the ruling party group, selects one of its members to be the leader of the council. A cabinet of up to nine councillors (plus the leader of the council) is formed, again normally from the majority party group unless the council has no overall control; the leader and cabinet form the council's political executive. The system is not dissimilar to that existing prior to the 2000 Act, when the ruling group would ensure that the council appointed its leader as council leader and went on to elect a number of committee chairs and vice-chairs from among its number. The main difference is that individual councillors can now have decision-making delegated directly to them – much like government ministers.

A directly elected mayor is the executive political head of the council, but unlike a council leader, he or she is elected by all the voters of a council area. There are two ways in which an elected mayor can be introduced by the council's executive arrangements:

1 A referendum is held after the collection of a petition signed by 5 per cent of local people and, if that referendum delivers a 'yes' vote, then an election for a mayor must be held within six months.

2 A council meeting can vote to introduce an elected mayor – without a referendum.

Much debate has centred on the directly elected mayor, a political office very different from the current ceremonial mayor that chairs council meetings. Despite many councillors complaining that the mayoral office would see the concentration of power in the hands of a single individual, the reality is different from that which is often claimed. The directly elected mayor has broadly similar powers to those of the indirectly elected leader. Moreover, as a result of the Local Government and Public Involvement in Health Act 2007, indirectly elected leaders are appointed by their councils for a four-year term.

The elected mayor is elected by all the voters of a council area, not just by councillors, and thus they have a direct electoral mandate which is far more powerful and legitimate than the indirect one granted to a council leader by fellow councillors.

The directly elected mayor is elected by the supplementary vote system, where voters place a cross in a first- and second-preference column against their preferred two candidates. After the first count, if no one candidate achieves 50 per cent of the votes cast, all but the top two candidates are eliminated and the second-preference votes redistributed to the remaining candidates.

The mayor becomes a highly visible political head of the council with responsibility for providing political leadership, proposing the policy framework for the council, preparing the council's budget and taking executive decisions. The council is responsible for scrutinising the work of the mayor and cabinet and proposing amendments to policy and the budget. It is fair to say that giving the public the right to select directly the political head of the council, rather than having the choice made for them by councillors, has failed to ignite a blaze of interest in the mayoral option. Only 14 of the 40 referendums held outside London returned a 'yes' vote. Table 20.5 displays the results of referenda held before May 2012. Leicester City Council joined the ranks of directly elected mayors after a vote by the full council in December 2010. Sir Peter Soulsby was elected mayor of Leicester in May 2011. Liverpool City Council also resolved, at a meeting of the council in February 2012, to have an elected mayor. On 3 May 2012 Joe Anderson, the Labour candidate, became the first directly elected mayor of Liverpool.

In May and October 2002 the first elections for directly elected mayors were held, and Table 20.6 shows the outcomes of these first contests. What is clear from the results is that voters in at least half the mayoral contests have taken the opportunity the new arrangements have given them to reject candidates from political parties and often from the party that has long controlled the council.

Indeed, elections for these new political leaders have thrown up some interesting results. June 2009 saw mayoral contests in Doncaster, Hartlepool and North Tyneside. In Doncaster the sitting Labour mayor was replaced as Labour candidate, which did Labour no good, as Peter Davies, the candidate for the English Democrats was elected mayor after the counting of second preference votes. The Doncaster result is a major victory for the English Democrats, a new party formed in 2002; it currently only has two councillors across the country and none in Doncaster, but the Doncaster result has given this new English party effective control of a major metropolitan borough.

In 2009 in Hartlepool, independent, Stuart Drummond, was re-elected to serve for his third term – he had won notoriety at his first election in 2002 by standing as 'hangus

A shrinking electorate

1 Birmingham City Council, the largest local authority in the country, has 120 elected councillors.

2 To control the council a party needs 61 seats.

3 To become leader of the council a councillor needs then to convince 32 of the councillors from the same party to vote for him or her – he or she would then become the single candidate from that party to lead the council and the entire group would vote for him or her.

4 The electorate of Birmingham is just over 650,000 people – but, under the council leader system the electorate shrinks to just 61 – all councillors.

5 Under the elected mayor system all 650,000 get a say in who runs the council

Table 20.5 Mayoral referenda 2001 to May 2012

Council	Date	R	Yes	%	No	%	Turn out	Type
Berwick-upon-Tweed	7 Jun 2001	No	3,617	26%	10,212	74%	64%	Poll with GE
Cheltenham	28 Jun 2001	No	8,083	33%	16,602	67%	31%	All postal
Gloucester	28 Jun 2001	No	7,731	31%	16,317	69%	31%	All postal
Watford	12 Jul 2001	Yes	7,636	52%	7,140	48%	24.5%	All postal
Doncaster	20 Sep 2001	Yes	35,453	65%	19,398	35%	25%	All postal
Kirklees	4 Oct 2001	No	10,169	27%	27,977	73%	13%	Normal
Sunderland	11 Oct 2001	No	9,593	43%	12,209	57%	10%	Normal
Hartlepool	18 Oct 2001	Yes	10,667	51%	10,294	49%	31%	All postal
LB Lewisham	18 Oct 2001	Yes	16,822	51%	15,914	49%	18%	All postal
North Tyneside	18 Oct 2001	Yes	30,262	58%	22,296	42%	36%	All postal
Middlesbrough	18 Oct 2001	Yes	29,067	84%	5,422	16%	34%	All postal
Sedgefield	18 Oct 2001	No	10,628	47%	11,869	53%	33.3%	All postal
Brighton and Hove	18 Oct 2001	No	22,724	38%	37,214	62%	32%	All postal
Redditch	8 Nov 2001	No	7,250	44%	9,198	56%	28.3%	All postal
Durham	20 Nov 2001	No	8,327	41%	11,974	59%	28.5%	All postal
Harrow	7 Dec 2001	No	17,502	42%	23,554	58%	26.06%	All postal
Plymouth	24 Jan 2002	No	29,553	41%	42,811	59%	39.78%	All postal
Harlow	24 Jan 2002	No	5,296	25%	15,490	75%	36.38%	All postal
LB Newham	31 Jan 2002	Yes	27,163	68.2%	12,687	31.8%	25.9%	All postal
Shepway	31 Jan 2002	No	11,357	44%	14,438	56%	36.3%	All postal
LB Southwark	31 Jan 2002	No	6,054	31.4%	13,217	68.6%	11.2%	Normal
West Devon	31 Jan 2002	No	3,555	22.6%	12,190	77.4%	41.8%	All postal
Bedford	21 Feb 2002	Yes	11,316	67.2%	5,537	32.8%	15.5%	Normal
LB Hackney	2 May 2002	Yes	24,697	58.94%	10,547	41.06%	31.85%	All postal
Mansfield	2 May 2002	Yes	8,973	54%	7,350	44%	21.04%	Normal
Newcastle-under-Lyme	2 May 2002	No	12,912	44%	16,468	56%	31.5%	Normal
Oxford	2 May 2002	No	14,692	44%	18,686	56%	33.8%	Normal
Stoke-on-Trent	2 May 2002	Yes	28,601	58%	20,578	42%	27.8%	Normal
Corby	3 Oct 2002	No	5,351	46%	6,239	53.64%	30.91%	All postal
LB Ealing	12 Dec 2002	No	9,454	44.8%	11,655	55.2%	9.8%	Combination postal and ballot
Ceredigian	20 May 2004	No	5,308	27%	14,013	73%	36%	n/a
Torbay	14 July 2005	Yes	18,074	55%	14,682	45%	32.1%	n/a
Isle of Wight	06 May 2005	No	28,786	44%	37,097	56%	60.4%	n/a
Fenland	15 July 2005	No	5509	24%	17,296	76%	33.6%	n/a
Crewe and Nantwich	4 July 2006	No	11,808	39%	18,786	61%	35.3%	n/a
Darlington	27 Sept 2007	No	7981	42%	11,226	58%	24.65%	n/a
Bury	03 July 2008	No	10,338	40%	15,425	60%	18.25%	n/a
LB Tower Hamlets	06 May 2010	Yes	60,758	60.3	39,857	39.7	62.1	
Great Yarmouth	06 May 2011	No	10,051		15,595			
Salford	26 January 2012	Yes	17,344		13,653		18.1	

Source: New Local Government Network 2003 (updated 2012)

Table 20.6 Mayoral election results, May and October 2002

Council	Winning candidate	Political affiliation	Elected on 1st or 2nd count	Electorate	Turnout
May 2002					
Doncaster	Martin Winter	Labour	2nd	216,097	58,487 (27.07%)
Hartlepool	Stuart Drummond	Independent	2nd	67,903	19,544 (28.78%)
LB Lewisham	Steve Bullock	Labour	2nd	179,835	44,518 (24.75%)
Middlesbrough	Ray Mallon	Independent	1st	101,570	41,994 (41.34%)
LB Newham	Robin Wales	Labour	1st	157,505	40,147 (25.49%)
North Tyneside	Chris Morgan	Conservative	2nd	143,804	60,865 (42.32%)
Watford	Dorothy Thornhill	Liberal Democrat	2nd	61,359	22,170 (36.13%)
October 2002					
Bedford	Frank Branston	Independent	2nd	109,318	27,717 (25.35%)
LB Hackney	Jules Pipe	Labour	2nd	130,657	34,415 (26.34%)
Mansfield	Tony Egginton	Independent	2nd	72,242	13,350 (18.48%)
Stoke-on-Trent	Mike Wolfe	Mayor 4 Stoke	2nd	182,967	43,985 (24.04%)

Source: New Local Government Network website: nlgn.org.uk

the monkey' and wearing the costume of the mascot for Hartlepool Town Football Club; he had been re-elected for a second term in 2005 with a 10,000 majority; his majority in 2009 was just 800 after the second preference count, but he was elected over another independent candidate; neither of the candidates from the two main parties made it to the second count. A sad end, however, has happened to this particular mayoralty. In August 2012 councillors on Hartlepool council, who have been unable to defeat the mayor in an election, voted to hold a referendum to ditch the mayoral system and return to the old-fashioned committee system of decision-making. The referendum was held on 15 November and on an 18 per cent turnout the result was: 7,366 for a committee system and 5,177 votes for continuing with an elected mayor. Mayor Drummond will see out his term of office which ends in May 2013.

In other areas, such as North Tyneside in 2009, Conservative candidate Linda Arkley, who had lost the mayoralty in 2005, was elected for a second time, defeating the sitting Labour mayor. In 2011 independents Ray Mallon and Tony Egginton were re-elected as the mayors of Middlesbrough and Mansfield respectively; a Liberal Democrat was re-elected in Bedford and the Conservatives to the mayoralty of Torbay.

Table 20.7 shows the current incumbent elected mayors and their political affiliations.

The Coalition Government which took power in 2010 has great interest in the mayoral model introduced by the forerunner Labour Government. Indeed, the idea has long been a favourite of Lord Michael Heseltine who first floated the idea

when a member of Margaret Thatcher's Cabinet. The Coalition Government required all 10 largest English cities to hold referenda on introducing an elected mayor. The referenda took place on 3 May 2012 and Table 20.8 shows the results.

Doncaster, which returned a 'Yes' vote in the May 2012 referendum was voting on whether or not to keep its existing elected mayor system or follow in the footsteps of Stoke-on-Trent which voted in 2008 to go back to a council leader system. Voters in Doncaster seem to like an elected mayor. The 2012 referendum campaigns in the 10 English cities (plus Doncaster which was holding a referendum anyway) show just how hard and desperately councillors will fight to make sure they and not the voters get to choose who will run the council. Even with Prime Minister David Cameron and senior ministers throwing their weight behind a 'Yes' vote for continuing the policy first introduced by Tony Blair, councillors and voters overwhelmingly rejected this way of governing locally. Indeed, the Prime Minster's pre-referendum pledge to create a cabinet of mayors to meet nationally, with him chairing its first meeting, failed to sway the voters.

Directly elected mayors may on the surface appear to be a radical change for local government, but the mayors and the councils on which they serve were given no new powers that would clearly distinguish them and their councils from any non-mayoral council. It is not the power of the mayor that is different, so much as how they get the job; and here it is the voters that decide rather than a handful of councillors from the ruling group on the council. One thing is clear

Table 20.7 Current mayoral incumbents, 2012

Council	Mayor	First elected
Bedford	Dave Hodgson: Lib Dem	2009
Bristol	George Ferguson: Independent	2012
Doncaster	Peter Davies: English Democrat	2009
Hackney	Jules Pipe: Labour	2002
Hartlepool	Stuart Drummond: Independent	2002
Leicester	Sir Peter Soulsby: Labour	2011
Liverpool	Joe Anderson: Labour	2012
Lewisham	Steve Bullock: Labour	2002
Mansfield	Tony Eggerton: Independent	2002
Middlesbrough	Ray Mallon: Independent	2002
Newham	Robin Wales: Labour	2002
North Tyneside	Linda Arkley: Conservative	2003; defeated 2005; elected for a second time 2009
Salford	Ian Stewart: Labour	2012
Torbay	Gordon Oliver: Conservative	2011
Tower Hamlets	Lutfur Rahman: Independent	2010
Watford	Dorothy Thornhill: Liberal Democrat	2002

Table 20.8 Mayoral referenda, 3 May 2012

Council	Yes (%)	No (%)	Turnout (%)	Electorate	No. of councillors
Birmingham	88,085 (42.2)	120,611 (57.8)	28.35	653,164	120
Bradford	53,949 (44.9)	66,283 (55.1)	35	341,126	90
Bristol	41,032 (53)	35,880 (47)	24	318,893	70
Coventry	22,619 (36.4)	39,483 (63.6)	26.6	236,818	54
Doncaster	42,196 (61.7)	25,879 (37.8)	30.5	224,678	63
Leeds	62,440 (36.7)	107,910 (63.3)	31	562,782	99
Manchester	42,677 (46.8)	48,593 (53.2)	24	370,453	96
Newcastle	24,630 (38.1)	40,089 (61.9)	32	203,512	78
Nottingham	20,943 (24.5)	28,320 (57.5)	23.9	207,312	55
Sheffield	44,571 (35)	82,890 (65)	32	390,890	84
Wakefield	27,610 (37.8)	45,357 (62.2)	28.84	257,530	63

however: as the referendum results show, voters across the country do not appear all that interested in having that power! However many elected mayors arrive over the following years, the move to the direct election of the political leader of the council is one of the most controversial changes to councils for some years and the debate is set to continue, as local government in this country struggles to come to terms with a model of governance that is widespread across Europe.

Local government and the European Union

The relationship between local government and the European Union (EU) has come a long way since a 1991 Audit Commission report drew attention to its often 'blinkered' approach to EU matters. Relationships between sub-national government such as councils and supra-national bodies such as the EU will always be conducted in a complex environment and through a complex system. John (1996) describes this system as 'triadic' – that is, conducted between three groups of actors at each of the three levels of governmental interaction. Indeed, the relationship between the EU and local government is influenced by two major factors: European law and policy; and the relationships between local and national government. Moreover, some local governments see the EU as a way around problematic relationships with national government and economic and political constraints, a situation that applied particularly in the UK throughout the 1980s and early 1990s (John 1996).

The impact of the EU on local government is less clear than the impact of national government, but is just as important. The EU affects local councils through a range of policy initiatives and demands: environmental health, consumer protection, public protection and even social and human rights legislation. The EU is also leading the charge for the use of e-government as a way of improving governance at all levels (Centeno et al. 2005).

Even so, many local authorities have recognised the importance of securing funding from the EU and contributing to the EU policy-making process, to the extent that some UK councils employ specialist staff to deal with European issues and negotiate with the EU (Goldsmith and Sperling 1997). Indeed, some have formed special committees of the council to deal with European matters and have European liaison officers, often with an economic development specialism, and located within economic development departments (Preston 1992a, 1992b). Moreover, the Local Government Association, the national body which represents all local government in England, also has a Brussels-based office. It is the larger, more urban councils with the greatest social problems to tackle that, not surprisingly are most likely to access EU funds (De Rooij 2002).

Some councils have established Brussels offices, either individually or as part of a consortium, and, while often small-scale affairs, they can disseminate information and establish links with the EU and other European national and sub-national governments. These offices are able to prepare funding bids, lobby for policy initiatives or changes, work with other bodies attempting to influence the EU, draw the private and voluntary sector closer into the EU policy network and place their local authority at the heart of the EU. John (1994) sees such Brussels offices as a cross-national marketplace to develop partnership funding bids and to indulge in informal lobbying of EU officials – a process in which many British councils lose out compared with their European counterparts, who place far more emphasis on resourcing such offices.

Local government placing itself at the heart of the EU serves three main purposes:

1 Authorities can develop a range of funding partnerships with a diverse group of organisations.

2 It enables councils, across Europe to communicate with each other and learn from each others experiences.

3 It enables regions and councils to learn of, and shape, new EU policy initiatives (Ercole et al. 1997).

Preston (1992b) indicates why local government is anxious to develop good relationships with the EU, highlighting the financial and policy benefits that flow from successful applications for European Social Fund and European Regional Development Fund support. The financial resources available from these programmes have enabled British local councils to pursue expansionist economic development policies in spite of tight controls from central government. Indeed, something like 74 per cent of British councils have applied for EU structural funds (Goldsmith and Sperling 1997).

Another reason for the popularity of the EU within local government is that element of the Maastricht Treaty concerning **subsidiarity**. This is popularly taken to mean by local councils that decisions should be decentralised to the lowest appropriate level of government, thus locating functions and powers with sub-national governments. However, John (1996) points out that this is a matter of political interpretation, as the treaty itself refers to relations between member states and the EU, not between states and local government. On the other hand, the Council of European Municipalities and Regions is campaigning for changes to the treaty that will clarify the meaning of subsidiarity in relation to the role of sub-national governments in policy and decision-making. The European Charter of local self-government, which the Blair government signed up to immediately after the 1997 election as a sign of commitment to local government, already recognises that many areas of public policy and political affairs are properly administered at the local or regional level.

The EU provides British local government with:

- access to funding;

- an opportunity to pursue its own policy agenda despite central government restrictions and direction – indeed, the possibility of a way around the unitary British state;

- political influence in important EU policy networks, linkages with other European local governments and local government consortiums;

- opportunities to strengthen its role, functions, powers and responsibilities.

As British local government comes to terms with devolved parliaments and chambers, it may find valuable resources in the EU that will enable it to ward off the possible reductions in council finances and the inevitably centralising tendencies of Westminster and Whitehall.

Box 20.2

BRITAIN IN CONTEXT

Councils and Country Constitutions

If you want to see what other countries say about their local government and the nature of the relationship between central government and local government, and between central government and local government and the citizen, then go to: http://www.politicsresources.net/const.htm

Here you can view the written constitutions of countries across the globe; note after the UK the site refers to Magna Carta. Yet, a random glance at some of the constitutions provides stark evidence of the context within which UK local government sits:

Ireland

Article 28A

- The state recognises the role of local government in providing a forum for the democratic representation of local communities, in exercising and performing at local level powers and functions conferred by law and in promoting by its initiatives the interests of such communities.

Poland

Article 16

- The inhabitants of the units of basic territorial division shall form a self-governing community in accordance with law.

- Local government shall participate in the exercise of public power. The substantial part of public duties which local government is empowered to discharge by statute shall be done in its own name and under its own responsibility.

Croatia

- Citizens shall be guaranteed the right to local self-government.

  The right to local self-government shall include the right to decide on needs and interests of local significance, particularly on regional development and town planning, organisation of localities and housing, public utilities, child care, social welfare, culture, physical culture, sports and technical culture, and the protection and promotion of the environment.

Germany

Article 28

- Article 28 (federal guarantee concerning Laender constitutions, guarantee of self-government for local authorities)

- The constitutional order in the Laender must conform to the principles of republican, democratic, and social government based on the rule of law, within the meaning of this Basic Law. In each of the Laender, counties and communities, the people must be represented by a body chosen in universal, direct, free, equal and secret elections. In the communities the assembly of the community may take the place of an elected body.

  (2) The communities must be guaranteed the right to regulate on their own responsibility all the affairs of the local community within the limits set by law. The associations of communities also have the right of self-government in accordance with the law within the limits of the functions given them by law.

These, and the other constitutions you can access, give to local government in the countries concerned something that is lacking in the UK: the constitutional right for local self-government to exist, in one form or another. Moreover, they provide a clear set of principles on which the relationship between the central government and local sub-national government will be conducted and what central government can and cannot do to local government. In Britain no such restraint exists on what central government can do to the localities, from rearranging responsibilities for certain services, to large-scale re-organisation of the size and shape of councils, to outright abolition of councils, such as in the 1974 re-organisation and the abolition of the metropolitan counties in 1986, as well as the forced merger and effective abolition of councils replaced by unitary authorities. Moreover, citizens have no say over the shape, size, responsibilities or powers of councils as, for example, is the case in many US states. In Britain local government is subservient to central government and the citizen subservient to both, at least in constitutional terms.

Unlike much, though by no means all, local government elsewhere, UK local government is heavily constrained by the law and the doctrine of *ultra vires*: that is, acting beyond powers specifically granted to it by statute. Before a council in Britain can do anything, it must be certain that there is legislation in existence saying it can do what it proposes to do. Other nations have a different approach to power and the role of local government, granting, often in a written constitution, the power of general competence. General competence means that local government can do whatever it wishes to do for the good of its citizens, so long as any actions are not prohibited by law. Put simply, British local government can do only what the law says it can do; elsewhere local government can do anything so long as the law does not say that it cannot. However, this picture is now becoming cloudier as the relationship between local government in Scotland and Wales takes on a different form with the Scottish and Welsh devolved chambers to that between England and the UK government. Looking at the UK, it is often easy to conclude that the words 'local government' are a misnomer; maybe we now have a situation where councils are too large to be local and have too little power to be government.

Different nations come to different constitutional settlements between the centre and the localities, and we have an arrangement that emerged over time from our histories and traditions, but one which was shaped to reflect the power of the centre; other nations, at various times, have had the opportunity to sit down and devise a system of government and to write a constitution and thus have created something different from our own approach to the power of government. Who is to say who has it right? Nonetheless, there is a choice to be made between an all-powerful central government which can control the localities, and powerful councils that can react to the wishes of local citizens – even if they conflict with the government's policies. If your council wanted to double the level of council tax, you might want the government to be able to stop it; or, you might want your council to be able to spend as much as it likes on local services, whatever the tax. Or, you might want to be able to force a local referendum on the issue, or be able to remove your councillors from office before the next election.

What do you think?

Chapter summary

This chapter has considered British local government as a politically representative set of arrangements designed to ensure responsiveness to the demands of local citizens. It has also outlined the constitutionally subordinate nature of local government to central control, but indicated that this need not be the only constitutional settlement available between the localities and the centre. This chapter has investigated the role of political parties in local government and the wider political process of local democracy as they are enacted through local councils. As well as a political process, it has considered local government as a set of institutional relationships between citizens, the centre and the EU. It has also discussed the main elements of the government's modernising agenda.

This chapter has also emphasised the politically dynamic nature of local government, which exists not only as a means of providing services – important though that may be – but also as a means by which the will of local people can be expressed and realised.

Discussion points

- Has the British system of local government been over-reformed since the early 1970s?
- Should local government get bigger or smaller, or stay the same size, and why?
- Should we have a tiered or unitary structure of local government?
- Should local government have more or less freedom to do what it wants to?
- Are directly elected mayors, elected by all the voters, a better way of running local government than a council leader chosen by councillors?
- Is it best to have councils run by national political parties or by local groups and independents?

Further reading

Party politics has had a long and contentious involvement in local government and Copus (2004) charts and explains that involvement and the effect it has had on local government and local democracy. Copus (2004) provides a full and detailed examination of the way in which party politics is organised in local government and how it operates. Wilson and Game (2011) provide a comprehensive overview of local government in the UK and explores its history, relationship with central government, financing, structure, politics and potential future – it is an indispensable read for students of local government in the UK. To fully understand local government as a politically representative institution and as an organisation with responsibility for and oversight of vast tracks of import public services, an international perspective is vital. Loughlin et al. (2011), Swianiewicz (2010) and Hendriks and Lidstrom (eds) (2010) more than offer that important international perspective. These three texts provide the student with sufficient examples and explanations of differences and similarities between and within systems of local government, to be able to place our own system into a much broader context.

Bibliography

Audit Commission (1991) *A Rough Guide to Europe: Local Authorities and the EC* (HMSO).

Bains, M.A. (1972) *Working Group on Local Authority Management Structures, The New Local Authorities: Management and Structure* (HMSO).

Bulpitt, J.J.G. (1967) *Party Politics in English Local Government* (Longman).

Byrne, T. (1983) *Local Government in Britain* (Pelican).

The Coalition: our programme for government: Freedom, Fairness, Responsibility (2010) (The Cabinet Office).

Centeno, C., van Bavel, R. and Burgelman, J.C. (2005) 'A Prospective View of e-Government in the European Union', *The Electronic Journal of e-Government*, vol. 3, no. 2, pp. 59–66, available online at www.ejeg.com.

Chandler, J.A. (2007) *Explaining Local Government: Local Government in Britain since 1800* (Manchester University Press).

Chisholm, M. and Leach, S. (2008) *Botched Business: The Damaging Process of Re-organising Local Government, 2006–2008* (Douglas McLean).

Clements, R.V. (1969) *Local Notables and the City Council* (Macmillan).

Copus, C. (1998) 'The councillor: representing a locality and the party group', *Local Governance*, vol. 24, no. 3, Autumn, pp. 215–24.

Copus, C. (1999a) 'The political party group: model standing orders and a disciplined approach to local representation', *Local Government Studies*, vol. 25, no. 1, Spring, pp. 17–34.

Copus, C. (1999b) 'The councillor and party group loyalty', *Policy and Politics*, vol. 27, no. 3, July, pp. 309–24.

Copus, C. (2000) 'Consulting the public on new political management arrangements: a review and some observations', *Local Governance*, vol. 26, no. 3, Autumn, pp. 177–86.

Copus, C. (2004) *Party Politics and Local Government* (Manchester University Press).

Dearlove, J. (1979) *The Reorganisation of British Local Government: Old Orthodoxies and a Political Perspective* (Cambridge University Press).

DCLG (2012) *National Planning Policy Framework*.

DETR (1998a) *Improving Local Services through Best Value*.

DETR (1998b) *Local Democracy and Community Leadership*.

DETR (1998) *Modern Local Government: In Touch with the People*.

DETR (1999) *Implementing Best Value: A Consultation Paper on Draft Guidance*.

DETR (1999) *Local Leadership: Local Choice*.

DETR (2000) *New Council Constitutions: Consultation Guidelines for English Local Authorities*, C. Copus, G. Stoker and F. Taylor.

DTLR (2001) *Strong Local Leadership: Quality Public Services*.

De Rooij, R. (2002) 'The impact of the European Union on local government in the Netherlands', *Journal of European Public Policy*, vol. 9, no. 3, pp. 447–67.

Elcock, H. (1982) *Local Government: Politicians, Professionals and the Public in Local Authorities* (Methuen).

Ercole, E., Walters, M. and Goldsmith, M. (1997) 'Cities, networks, EU regions, European offices', in Goldsmith, M.

and Klausen, K. (eds) *European Integration and Local Government* (Edward Elgar), pp. 219–36.

Fraser, D. (1979) *Power and Authority in the Victorian City* (St Martins Press).

Game, C. and Leach, S. (1995) *The Role of Political Parties in Local Democracy*, Commission for Local Democracy, Research Report No. 11 (CLD).

Goldsmith, M. and Sperling, E. (1997) 'Local government and the EU: the British experience', in Goldsmith, M. and Klausen, K. (eds) *European Integration and Local Government* (Edward Elgar), pp. 95–120.

Grant, W.P. (1973) 'Non-partisanship in British local politics', *Policy and Politics*, vol. 1, no. 1, pp. 241–54.

Gray, A. (1979) 'Local Government in England and Wales', in Jones, B. and Kavanagh, D. (eds) *British Politics Today* (Manchester University Press).

Green, G. (1972) 'National, City and Ward Components of Local Voting', *Policy and Politics* vol. 1, no. 1, September 1972, pp. 45–54.

Gyford, J. (1976) *Local Politics in Britain* (Croom Helm), p. 11.

Gyford, J. (1985) 'The Politicisation of Local Government', in Loughlin, M., Gelfand, M. and Young, K., *Half a Century of Municipal Decline* (George Allen and Unwin), pp. 77–97.

Hampton, W. (1970) *Democracy and Community: A Study of Politics in Sheffield* (Oxford University Press).

Hampton, W. (1987) *Local Government and Urban Politics* (Longman).

Hennock, E.P. (1973) *Fit and Proper Persons: Ideal and Reality in Nineteenth-Century Urban Government* (Edward Arnold).

HMSO (1960) *Royal Commission on Local Government in Greater London, 1957–60* (The Herbert Commission), Cmnd 1164.

HMSO (1967a) *Report of the Royal Commission on Local Government* (Redcliffe-Maud Report), Cmnd 4040.

HMSO (1967b) *Committee on the Management of Local Government*, Research Vol. III, *The Local Government Elector*.

HMSO (1969) *Royal Commission on Local Government in Scotland* (The Wheatley Commission), Cmnd 4159.

HMSO (1986a) *Committee of Inquiry into the Conduct of Local Authority Business*, Research Vol. III, *The Local Government Elector*, Cmnd 9800.

HMSO (1986b) *Committee of Inquiry into the Conduct of Local Authority Business*, Research Vol. I, *The Political Organisation of Local Authorities*, Cmnd 9798, pp. 25, 197.

HMSO (1997) *Committee on Standards in Public Life*, Vol. II, *Standards of Conduct in Local Government in England and Wales*, Cmnd 3702 – II.

HMSO (1998) *Modern Local Government: In Touch with the People*, Cmnd 4014.

HMSO (1999) *Local Leadership: Local Choice*, Cmnd 4298.

House of Commons (2013) Standard Note: SN/PC/05682, *Council tax: local referendums*.

Institute for Public Policy Research (1991) *The Constitution of the United Kingdom*.

John, P. (1994) 'UK sub-national offices in Brussels: diversification or regionalism?', Paper presented to the ESRC Research Seminar: British Regionalism and Devolution in a Single Europe, LSE.

John, P. (1996) 'Centralisation, decentralisation and the European Union: the dynamics of triadic relationships', *Public Administration*, Vol. 74, Summer, pp. 293–313.

Jones, G.W. (1969) *Borough Politics: A Study of Wolverhampton Borough Council 1888–1964* (Macmillan).

Keith-Lucas, B. (1952) *The English Local Government Franchise* (Basil Blackwell).

Lee, J.M. (1963) *Social Leaders and Public Persons: A Study of County Government in Cheshire since 1888* (Clarendon Press).

Local Authorities (Model Code of Conduct) (England) Order 2001, Statutory Instrument 2001 no. 3575, HMSO, 2001

Newton, K. (1976) *Second City Politics: Democratic Processes and Decision-Making in Birmingham* (Clarendon Press).

Office of the Deputy Prime Minister (ODPM), *Vibrant Local Leadership*, 2005.

Pimlott, B. and Rao, N. (2002) *Governing London* (Oxford University Press).

Preston, J. (1992a) 'Local government and the European Community', in George, S. (ed.) *Britain and the European Community: The Politics of Semi-Detachment* (Clarendon Press).

Preston, J. (1992b) 'Local government', in Bulmer, S., George, S. and Scott, J. (eds) *The United Kingdom and EC Membership Evaluated* (Pinter).

Rallings, C. and Thrasher, M. (1997) *Local Elections in Britain* (Routledge).

Rallings, C. and Thrasher, M. (2012) *Local Elections Handbook* (Biteback Publishing).

Regional Development Agencies and Regional Chambers (1999) (Ludgate Public Affairs).

Saunders, P. (1979) *Urban Politics: A Sociological Interpretation* (Hutchinson).

Stanyer, J. (1976) *Understanding Local Government* (Fontana).

Stewart, J. (1986) *The New Management of Local Government* (Allen & Unwin).

Stewart, J. (2003) *Modernising British Local Government: An Assessment of Labour's Reform Programme* (Palgrave).

Stoker, G. (1991) *The Politics of Local Government* (Macmillan).

Travers, T. (2004) *The Politics of London: Governing an Ungovernable City* (Palgrave).

Wilson, D. and Game, C. (2011) *Local Government in the United Kingdom*, 5th edn (Palgrave Macmillan).

Wolman, H. and Goldsmith, M. (1992) *Urban Politics and Policy: A Comparative Approach* (Blackwell).

Young, K. (1973) 'The politics of London government 1880–1899', *Public Administration*, vol. 51, no. 1, Spring, pp. 91–108.

Young, K. (1975) *Local Politics and the Rise of Party: The London Municipal Society and the Conservative Intervention in Local Elections 1894–1963* (Leicester University Press).

Young, K. and Davies, M. (1990) *The Politics of Local Government since Widdicombe* (Joseph Rowntree Foundation).

Young, K. and Laffin, M. (1990) *Professionalism in Local Government* (Longman).

Young, K. and Rao, N. (1997) *Local Government since 1945* (Blackwell).

Useful websites

Office of the Deputy Prime Minister: odpm.gov.uk
Local Government Association: lga.gov.uk
Improvement and Development Agency: idea.gov.uk
Local Government Information Unit: lgiu.gov.uk
New Local Government Network: nlgn.org.uk
National constitutions: www.constitution.org
For a directory of all local council websites, try: tagish.co.uk/tagish/links/localgov.htm
The Labour Party: labour.org.uk
The Conservative Party: conservativeparty.org.uk
The Association of Liberal Democrat Councillors: aldc.org.uk
The Green Party: greenparty.org.uk
Local Government Elections centre: research.plymouth.ac.uk/elections
The National Standards Board: standardsboard.co.uk
The Lyons Inquiry: lyonsinquiry.org.uk
http://www.unece.org/oes/nutshell/2004-2005/focus_sustainable_development.html

CHAPTER 21

The judiciary

Philip Norton

> " The keystone of the rule of law in England has been the independence of judges. It is the only respect in which we make any real separation of powers "
>
> Lord Denning

Learning objectives

- To identify the relationship of the judicial system to other parts of the political process.

- To describe the basic structure of that system, and how it has changed in recent years as a result of a greater willingness of judges to undertake judicial review, and as a consequence of constitutional change.

- To consider demands for change because of perceived weaknesses in the system.

Britain does not have a system like the USA, where the Supreme Court acts as ultimate interpreter of the constitution and pronounces upon the constitutionality of federal and state laws together with the actions of public officials. Since 1688 British courts have been bound by the doctrine of parliamentary sovereignty. They have been viewed as subordinate to the Queen-in-Parliament and detached from the political process. However, the received wisdom has not always matched the reality, and recent years have witnessed a growth in judicial activism. British membership of the European Union has added a significant juridical dimension to the constitution. So too has the incorporation of the European Convention on Human Rights (ECHR) into British law and legislation providing for devolution of powers to elected bodies in different parts of the United Kingdom. The UK has also acquired a Supreme Court, which came into being in October 2009, replacing the appellate committee of the House of Lords as the highest domestic court of appeal. The United Kingdom now has a court that has a physical similarity to, though not the powers of, its US namesake. The courts have become important political actors. Recent years have also seen criticism of the way the courts dispense justice. This chapter explores the nature of the British judicial system and growing concern about its powers and competence.

The judicial process

The literature on the judicial process in Britain is extensive. Significantly, most of it is written by legal scholars: few works on the courts or judges come from the pens of political scientists. To those concerned with the study of British politics, and in particular the process of policy making, the judicial process has generally been deemed to be of peripheral interest.

That this perception should exist is not surprising. It derives from two features that are considered to be essential characteristics of the judiciary in Britain. First, in the trinity of the executive, legislature and judiciary, it is a subordinate institution. Public policy is made and ratified elsewhere. The courts exist to interpret (within defined limits) and apply that policy once enacted by the legislature; they have no intrinsic power to strike it down. Second, it is autonomous. The independence of the judiciary is a much vaunted and essential feature of the rule of law, described by the great nineteenth-century constitutional lawyer A.V. Dicey as one of the twin pillars of the British constitution. The other pillar – parliamentary sovereignty – accounts for the first characteristic, the subordination of the judiciary to Parliament. Allied with autonomy has been the notion of political neutrality. Judges seek to interpret the law according to judicial norms that operate independently of partisan or personal preferences.

Given these characteristics – politically neutral courts separate from, and subordinate to, the central agency of law enactment – a clear demarcation has existed for some time, the study of the policy-making process being the preserve of political scientists, that of the judiciary the preserve of legal scholars. Some scholars – such as the late J.A.G. Griffith, formerly Professor of Law at the University of London – have sought to bridge the gap, but they have been notable for their rarity. Yet in practice the judiciary in Britain has not been as subordinate or as autonomous as the prevailing wisdom assumes. The dividing line between politics and the law is blurred rather than rigid and it is becoming more blurred.

A subordinate branch?

Under the doctrine of parliamentary sovereignty, the judiciary lacks the intrinsic power to strike down an Act of Parliament as being contrary to the provisions of the constitution or any other superior body of law. It was not always thus. Prior to the Glorious Revolution of 1688 the supremacy of **statute law** was not clearly established. In *Dr Bonham's Case* in 1610, Chief Justice Coke asserted that 'when an Act of Parliament is against common right and reason, or repugnant, or impossible to be performed, the common law will control it, and adjudge such act to be void'. A few years later, in *Judge* v *Savadge* (1625), Chief Justice Hobart declared that an Act 'made against natural equity, as to make a man judge in his own case' would be void. Statute law had to compete not only with principles of common law developed by the courts but also with the prerogative power of the King. The courts variously upheld the power of the King to dispense with statutes and to impose taxes without the consent of Parliament.

The Glorious Revolution put an end to this state of affairs. Thereafter, the supremacy of statute law, under the doctrine of parliamentary sovereignty, was established. The doctrine is a judicially self-imposed one. The common lawyers allied themselves with Parliament in its struggle to control the **prerogative** powers of the King and the prerogative courts through which he sometimes exercised them. The supremacy of Parliament was asserted by the Bill of Rights of 1689. 'For the common lawyers, there was a price to pay, and that was the abandonment of the claim that they had sometimes advanced, that Parliament could not legislate in derogation

The Middlesex Guildhall, Supreme Court entrance
Source: Alamy Images

of the principles of the common law' (Munro 1987: 81). Parliamentary sovereignty – a purely legal doctrine asserting the supremacy of statute law – became the central tenet of the constitution (see Chapter 15). However, the subordination of the common law to law passed by Parliament did not – and does not – entail the subordination of the judiciary to the executive. Courts retain the power of interpreting the precise meaning of the law once passed by Parliament and of reviewing the actions of ministers and other public agents to determine whether those actions are *ultra vires*: that is, beyond the powers granted by statute. The courts can quash the actions of ministers that purport to be, but that on the court's interpretation are not, sanctioned by such Acts.

If a government has a particular action struck down as *ultra vires*, it may seek parliamentary approval for a bill that gives statutory force to the action taken; in other words, to give legal force to that which the courts have declared as having – on the basis of existing statutes – no such force. But seeking passage of such a bill is not only time-consuming; it can also prove to be politically contentious and publicly damaging. It conveys the impression that the government, having lost a case, is trying to change the rules of the game. Although it is a path that governments have variously taken, it is one they prefer to – and often do – avoid.

The power of judicial review thus provides the judiciary with a potentially significant role in the policy cycle. It is a potential that for much of the twentieth century was not realised. However, recent decades have seen an upsurge in judicial activism, judges being far more willing both to review and to quash ministerial actions. The scope for judicial activism has also been enlarged by three other developments: British membership of the European Union, the incorporation of the European Convention on Human Rights (ECHR) into British law and the devolution of powers to elected assemblies in different parts of the UK. Indeed, the first two of these developments have served to undermine the doctrine of parliamentary sovereignty, giving to the courts a new role in the political process. Whether they wanted to or not, the courts now find themselves playing a more central role in the determination of public policy. That role is likely to become more visible now that there exists a dedicated Supreme Court, housed in its own building in Parliament Square.

An autonomous branch?

The judiciary is deemed to be independent of the other two branches of government. Its independence is, in the words of one leading textbook, 'secured by law, by professional and public opinion' (Wade and Bradley 1993: 60). Since the Act of Settlement, senior judges hold office 'during good behaviour' and can be removed by the Queen following an address by both Houses of Parliament (see Jackson and Leopold 2001: 433–4). (Only one judge has ever been removed by such a process. Jonah Barrington, an Irish judge, was removed in 1830 after it was found that he had misappropriated litigants' money and had ceased to perform his judicial duties.) Judges of inferior courts enjoy a lesser degree of statutory protection. Judges' salaries are a charge upon the consolidated fund: this means that they do not have to be voted upon each year by Parliament. By its own resolution, the House of Commons generally bars any reference by MPs to matters awaiting or under adjudication in criminal and most civil cases. By convention, a similar prohibition is observed by ministers and civil servants.

For their part, judges by convention refrain from politically partisan activity. Indeed, they have generally refrained from commenting on matters of public policy, doing so not only of their own volition but also for many years by the direction of the Lord Chancellor. The Kilmuir guidelines issued in 1955 enjoined judges to silence, since 'every utterance which he [a judge] makes in public, except in the course of the actual performance of his judicial duties, must necessarily bring him within the focus of criticism'. These guidelines were relaxed in the late 1970s but then effectively reimposed by the Lord Chancellor, Lord Hailsham, in 1980. For judges to interfere in a contentious issue of public policy, one that is not under adjudication, would – it was felt – undermine public confidence in the impartiality of the judiciary. Similarly, for politicians to interfere in a matter before the courts would be seen as a challenge to the rule of law. Hence the perceived self-interests of both in confining themselves to their own spheres of activity.

However, historically the dividing line between judges and politicians – and, to a lesser extent, between judicial and political decision making – is not quite as sharp as these various features would suggest. In terms of personnel, memberships of the executive, legislature and judiciary are not mutually exclusive. Particularly in the higher reaches, there has been some overlap, though the degree of overlap has declined considerably in the twenty-first century. The most obvious and outstanding historical example of overlap is to be found in the figure of the Lord Chancellor. Prior to the passage of the Constitutional Reform Act 2005, he was head of the judiciary, the presiding officer of the House of Lords, and a member of the Cabinet. The 2005 Act changed this situation, providing for the transfer of his judicial role to the Lord Chief Justice – the transfer took place in 2006 – and enabling someone other than a peer and senior lawyer to hold the post. The post of Lord Chancellor remains, as a conjoined role with that of Secretary of State for Justice, and has responsibility for the management of the courts system.

Other executive office holders with judicial appointments are the Law Officers: the Attorney General and the Solicitor General. They serve as legal advisers to the government and lead for the Crown in major prosecutions, especially where state security is concerned. The consent of the Attorney General is required for certain prosecutions to be launched. Within government the legal opinion of the Law Officers carries great weight and, by convention, is treated in confidence.

The highest court of appeal in the United Kingdom was, until 2009, the House of Lords. For judicial purposes, this constituted an appellate committee of the House, comprising the law lords – appointed to the House for the purpose of fulfilling its judicial functions – and peers who had held high judicial office. Some Members of Parliament serve or have served as recorders (part-time but salaried judges in the Crown Court) and several sit as local magistrates. Judges in the High Court, Court of Appeal and Court of Session are barred by statute from membership of the Commons, and any MP appointed to a judgeship becomes ineligible to remain in the House. In 2009 the prohibition was extended to the House of Lords, so that some peers who were senior judges, such as the Lord Chief Justice, were excluded from membership for the period that they held judicial office.

Although those holding political office seek as far as possible to draw a clear dividing line between political and judicial activity, that line cannot always be maintained. At times, they have to take judicial or quasi-judicial decisions. However, they remain members of an executive accountable, unlike judges, to Parliament. This remains the case with the Law Officers. (There are separate law officers for Scotland.) It used to be the case also with the Lord Chancellor and, to some extent, the Home Secretary, who exercised quasi-judicial functions, but the functions involved in both cases have now been transferred to the courts. The Attorney General may intervene to prevent prosecutions being proceeded with if he considers such action to be in the public interest. Under powers introduced in 1989 he may refer to the Appeal Court sentences that appear to the prosecuting authorities to be unduly lenient. He also has responsibility in certain cases for initiating proceedings, for example under the Official Secrets Act, and although he takes decisions in such matters independently of government colleagues, he remains answerable to Parliament for her decisions. These powers, along with the Attorney General's role as legal adviser to the government, can bring the Law Officers into the realms of political controversy. This was the case most notably with the Attorney General's advice to the Government in 2003 that it was lawful for it

to commit troops to the invasion of Iraq. Some lawyers questioned the legality of the war, and rumours that the Attorney's advice had raised some doubts about the legality generated demands that it be published – the advice is normally confidential – and led eventually to it being put in the public domain.

Judges themselves do not completely stand apart from public controversy. Because they are detached from political life and can consider issues impartially, they are variously invited to chair public inquiries into the causes of particular disasters or scandals and to make recommendations on future action. This practice has been employed for many years. Examples over the past 25 years have included the inquiries into the collapse of the BCCI bank (Sir Thomas Bingham, 1991), into standards in public life (Lord Nolan, 1995), into the sale of arms-making equipment to Iraq (Sir Richard Scott, 1996), into the police handling of the murder of black teenager Stephen Lawrence (Sir William Macpherson of Cluny, 1999), into the death of Dr David Kelly (Lord Hutton, 2003–4), into the shootings during 'Bloody Sunday' in Northern Ireland (Lord Saville of Newdigate, 2000–10) and into the ethics of the press (Lord Justice Leveson 2011–12). The inquiries or the reports that they issue are often known by the name of the judge who led the inquiry (the Nolan Committee, the Scott Report, the Hutton Report, the Leveson Report). The reports are sometimes highly controversial and may lead to criticism of the judge involved (see McEldowney 1996: 138). One irate Conservative MP berated Lord Nolan outside the Palace of Westminster in 1995, and his report was the subject of heated debate in the House of Commons. Sir Richard Scott was heavily criticised by many Conservative MPs and by a former Foreign Secretary, Lord Howe of Aberavon, for the way he conducted his inquiry. Lord Hutton's report, which led to the resignation of the director general of the BBC (Greg Dyke), was largely discredited when a subsequent report (the Butler Report) found that there had been significant changes to the government's dossier making the case for war with Iraq.

Judges themselves have also been more willing in recent years to enter public debate of their own volition. The past two decades have seen a tendency on the part of several judges to justify their actions publicly. In 1988 Lord Chancellor Mackay allowed some relaxation of the Kilmuir rules in order that judges may give interviews. One judge in particular – Judge Pickles – made use of the opportunity to appear frequently on television. A greater willingness to comment on issues of public policy has also been apparent on the part of the most senior judges. The appointment of Lord Justice Bingham as Master of the Rolls and Lord Justice Taylor as Lord Chief Justice in 1992 heralded a new era of openness. Both proved willing to express views on public policy, both advocating the incorporation of the European Convention on Human Rights into British law. Taylor not only gave press interviews but also used the floor of the House of Lords to criticise government policy. Their successors have maintained a similar degree of openness and this to some degree has become institutionalised: the Lord Chief Justice now publishes an annual report and usually appears annually before the Constitution Committee of the House of Lords to discuss any issues of concern. The judges have also appointed a spokesperson who can respond to public concerns or media criticism and explain the role of judges in the judicial process.

Thus, although the two generalisations that the judiciary constitutes a subordinate and autonomous branch of government – subordinate to the outputs of Parliament (Acts of Parliament) but autonomous in deciding cases – remain broadly correct, both are in need of some qualification. The courts are neither as powerless nor as totally independent as the assertion would imply. For the student of politics, the judiciary is therefore an appropriate subject for study. What, then, is the structure of the judicial system in Britain? Who are the people who occupy it? To what extent has the judiciary become more active in recent years in reviewing the actions of government? What has been the effect of membership of the EC/EU, the incorporation of the ECHR into British law, and of devolution? And what pressure is there for change?

The courts

Apart from a number of specialised courts and tribunals, the organisational division of courts is that between **criminal law** and **civil law**. The basic structure of the court system in England and Wales is shown in Figure 21.1. (Scotland and Northern Ireland have different systems.) Minor criminal cases are tried in the magistrates' courts, minor civil cases in county courts. Figure 21.1 also shows the higher courts that try serious cases and the routes through which appeals may be heard. The higher courts – the Crown Court, the High Court and the Court of Appeal – are known collectively, as the Senior Courts of England and Wales. At the head of the system stands the Supreme Court.

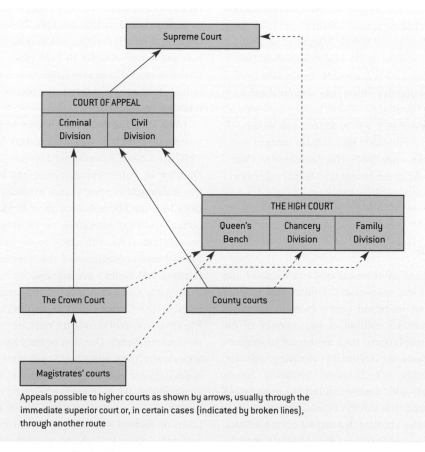

Appeals possible to higher courts as shown by arrows, usually through the immediate superior court or, in certain cases (indicated by broken lines), through another route

Figure 21.1 The court system in England and Wales

PROFILE

Lord Neuberger of Abbotsbury (1948–)

President of the Supreme Court, the son of a professor of chemical pathology, David Neuberger studied chemistry at Oxford and worked for three years at the bankers N.M. Rothschild & Sons before being called to the Bar in 1974. He became a QC in 1987 and served as a Recorder from 1990 to 1996. He was a High Court Judge (Chancery Division) from 1996 to 2004. He was made a Lord Justice of Appeal in 2004 and became a Law Lord in 2007, making him the youngest member of the highest court. When the Supreme Court was created in 2009 – a move that he criticised (describing it 'as a result of what appears to have been a last-minute decision over a glass of whisky') – he moved from being a Law Lord to serving as Master of the Rolls, the second highest judge in the country. Some of his comments attracted attention, including when he said in 2011 that social media sites (such as Twitter) were 'totally out of control' and society should consider ways to bring such websites under control. In 2012 he succeeded Lord Phillips of Worth Matravers as President of the Supreme Court. He was knighted in 1996 and joined the Privy Council in 2004: he became Lord Neuberger of Abbotsbury upon his appointment as a law lord.

Married – his wife is a TV producer and writer – with two sons and a daughter, he has been chair of the Schizophrenia Trust since 2003. His three brothers are all professors and he is the brother-in-law of the rabbi and broadcaster Baroness Neuberger.

Criminal cases

More than 95 per cent of criminal cases in England and Wales are tried in local magistrates' courts. The number of cases has dropped in recent years, from in excess of 2 million to just over 1.5 million, a consequence of the use of out-of-court resolutions, such as the use of cautions and fixed-penalty fines for summary motoring offences. Summary proceedings, which cover relatively minor offences and are dealt with entirely within the magistrates' courts, make up around two-thirds of cases. The courts have power to levy fines, the amount depending on the offence, and to impose prison sentences not exceeding six months. The largest single number of cases tried by magistrates'

courts comprises motoring offences. Other offences tried by the courts range from allowing animals to stray onto a highway and tattooing a minor to burglary, assault, causing cruelty to children and wounding. On average it takes just over 140 days from commission of an offence to completion of a case. Once before a court, a majority of minor offences are each disposed of in a matter of minutes; in some cases, in which the defendant has pleaded guilty, in a matter of seconds.

Magistrates themselves are of two types: professional and lay. Professional magistrates are legally qualified (usually barristers or solicitors prior to appointment) and are now known, under the provisions of the 1999 Access to Justice Act, as district judges (magistrates' courts); they were previously known as stipendiary magistrates. There are approximately 140 district judges and 170 deputy district judges; the former are full-time whereas the latter are fee-paid and sit for a minimum of 15 days a year. These professional magistrates sit alone when hearing cases. Lay magistrates, of whom there are just over 24,000, are part-time and, as the name implies, are not legally qualified, although they do receive some training. Their number has declined in recent years as a result of court closures, bench mergers and a reduction in workload. Lay magistrates are drawn from the ranks of the public, typically those with the time to devote to such public duty (for example, housewives, local professional and retired people), and they sit as a bench of between two and seven in order to hear cases, advised by a legally qualified clerk. Cities and larger towns tend to have district judges (magistrates' courts); the rest of England and Wales relies on lay magistrates.

Until 1986 the decision whether to prosecute – and the prosecution itself – was undertaken by the police. Since 1986 the Crown Prosecution Service (CPS), headed by the Director of Public Prosecutions, has been responsible for the independent review and prosecution of all criminal cases instituted by police forces in England and Wales, with certain specified exceptions. In Scotland, responsibility for prosecution rests with the Crown Office and Procurator Fiscal Service. Members of this service – like the CPS in England and Wales – are lawyers.

Appeals from decisions of magistrates' courts may be taken to the Crown Court or, in matrimonial cases, to the Family Division of the High Court, or – on points of law – to the Queen's Bench Division of the High Court. In practice, appeals are rare: less than 1 per cent of those convicted appeal against conviction or sentence. The cost of pursuing an appeal would, in the overwhelming majority of cases, far exceed the fine imposed. The time of the Crown Court is taken up instead with hearing the serious cases – known as indictable offences – which are subject to a jury trial and to penalties beyond those that a magistrates' court can impose.

In 2011 there were just over 148,000 cases received by the Crown Court. Most, though, do not result in a trial, most defendants who enter a plea – 70 per cent in 2010 and 2011, up from 56 per cent in 2001 – pleading guilty.

The Crown Court is divided into 92 courts. The most serious cases will be presided over by a High Court judge, the most senior position within the court; a circuit judge or a recorder will hear other cases. High Court and circuit judges are full-time, salaried judges; recorders are legally qualified but part-time, pursuing their normal legal practice when not engaged in court duties.

Appeals from conviction in a Crown Court may be taken on a point of law to the Queen's Bench Division of the High Court but usually are taken to the Criminal Division of the Court of Appeal. Appeals against conviction are possible on a point of law and on a point of fact, the former as a matter of right and the latter with the leave of the trial judge or the Court of Appeal. Approximately 10 per cent of those convicted in a Crown Court usually appeal. The Appeal Court may quash a conviction, uphold it or vary the sentence imposed by the lower courts. Appeals against sentence – as opposed to the conviction itself – are also possible with the leave of the Appeal Court and, as we have already seen, the Attorney General now has the power to refer to the court sentences that appear to be unduly lenient. In cases referred by the Attorney General, the court has the power to increase the length of the sentence imposed by the lower court.

The Court of Appeal is divided into two divisions, the criminal and the civil. The court comprises the Lord Chief Justice, the Master of the Rolls and 37 Lord Justices of Appeal. Appeals in criminal cases are usually heard by three judges, presided over by the Lord Chief Justice or a Lord Justice. Judges of the Queen's Bench may also sit on the court. In 2011 almost 7,500 applications for leave to appeal were made to the court. Most appeals are against the sentence rather than against conviction.

From the Court of Appeal a further appeal is possible to the Supreme Court if the court certifies that a point of law of general public importance is involved and it appears to the court, or to the Supreme Court, that the point ought to be considered by the highest domestic court of appeal. Given this limited scope, the number of cases heard by the court is small: 208 in 2011 for example. The Supreme Court is presided over by a President and 11 Justices of the Supreme Court.

One other judicial body should also be mentioned. It does not figure in the normal court structure. That is the Judicial Committee of the Privy Council, essentially a product of the country's colonial history. This committee was set up in 1833 to exercise the power of the Privy Council in deciding appeals from colonial, ecclesiastical and admiralty courts. It comprises usually three Justices of the Supreme Court and some other senior judges. Most of its functions have disappeared over time, though it has retained a limited role in considering particular appeals in certain criminal cases from a number of Commonwealth countries (it is the final court of appeal for 23 Commonwealth territories and four independent republics within the Commonwealth) and from certain ancient and ecclesiastical courts. It assumed a new – though, in the event, short-lived – significance as a consequence of devolution. Until 2009 legal challenges to the powers exercised by the devolved bodies were heard by the Judicial Committee. It lost these powers to the new Supreme Court. Five judges normally preside in cases involving appeals from Commonwealth courts and three in other cases. The court used to meet in 10 Downing Street but now sits in the Supreme Court building in Parliament Square.

Civil cases

In civil proceedings some minor cases (for example, involving the summary recovery of some debts) are dealt with in magistrates' courts. However, most cases involving small sums of money are heard by county courts; more important cases are heard in the High Court.

County courts are presided over by circuit judges. The High Court is divided into three divisions, dealing with **common law** (the Queen's Bench Division), equity (Chancery Division) and domestic cases (Family Division). The Court comprises the three judges who head each division and just over 100 judges known as 'puisne' (pronounced 'puny') judges. In most cases judges sit alone, although a Divisional Court of two or three may be formed, especially in the Queen's Bench Division, to hear applications for writs requiring a public body to fulfil a particular duty (*mandamus*), to desist from carrying out an action for which it has no legal authority (prohibition) or to quash a decision already taken (*certiorari*). Jury trials are possible in certain cases tried in the Queen's Bench Division (for example, involving malicious prosecution or defamation of character) but are now rare.

Appeals from magistrates' courts and from county courts are heard by Divisional Courts of the High Court: appeals from magistrates' courts on points of law, for example, go to a Divisional Court of the Queen's Bench Division. From the High Court – and certain cases in county courts – appeals are taken to the Civil Division of the Court of Appeal. In the Appeal Court, cases are normally heard by the Master of the Rolls sitting with two Lords Justices of Appeal.

From the Court of Appeal an appeal may be taken – with the leave of the Court or the Supreme Court – to the Supreme Court. In rare cases, on a point of law of exceptional difficulty calling for a reconsideration of a binding precedent, an appeal may go directly, with the leave of the Supreme Court, from the High Court to the Supreme Court.

Cases brought against ministers or other public bodies for taking actions that are beyond their powers (*ultra vires*) will normally be heard in the Queen's Bench Division of the High Court before being taken – in the event of an appeal – to the Court of Appeal and the Supreme Court. The government has suffered a number of reverses in the High Court as a result of ministerial decisions being judicially reviewed.

Tribunals

Many if not most citizens are probably affected by decisions taken by public bodies – for example, those determining eligibility for particular benefits or compensation for compulsory purchase. The postwar years have seen the growth of administrative law, providing the legal framework within which such decisions are taken and the procedure by which disputes may be resolved.

To avoid disputes over particular administrative decisions being taken to the existing, highly formalised civil courts – overburdening the courts and creating significant financial burdens for those involved – the law provides for a large number of tribunals to resolve such disputes. There are now tribunals covering a wide range of issues, including unfair dismissal, rents, social security benefits, immigration, mental health and compensation for compulsory purchase. Those appearing before tribunals will often have the opportunity to present their own case and to call witnesses and cross-examine the other side. The tribunal itself will normally – although not always – comprise three members, although the composition varies from tribunal to tribunal: some have lay members, others have legally (or otherwise professionally) qualified members; some have part-time members, others have full-time members. Employment tribunals, for example, each comprise an independent chairman and two members drawn from either side of industry.

The activities of tribunals are normally dull and little noticed. On rare occasions, though, decisions may have political significance. In January 1996 an employment tribunal in Leeds held that the policy of the Labour Party to have women-only shortlists for some parliamentary seats breached sex discrimination legislation. Rather than pursue an appeal, which could take up to 20 months to be heard, the party decided not to proceed with such shortlists.

The judges

The most senior judges are the 12 members of the Supreme Court. They are eminent lawyers, normally drawn from the ranks of the Court of Appeal. The other most senior judicial appointments – the Lord Chief Justice (head of the judiciary and of the Appeal Court in criminal cases), Master of the Rolls (head of the Appeal Court in civil cases), President of the Family Division and the Lord Justices of Appeal – are drawn from High Court judges or from barristers of at least 10 years' standing, although solicitors are now also eligible for consideration. Other judges – High Court judges, circuit judges and recorders – are drawn principally from barristers of at least 10 years' standing, although solicitors and circuit court judges may be appointed to the High Court. Nominations for judicial appointments are made by an independent Judicial Appointments Commission.

The attraction in becoming a judge lies only partially in the salary (see Table 21.1) – the top earners among barristers can achieve annual incomes of several hundred thousand pounds. Rather, the attraction lies in the status that attaches to holding a position at the top of one's profession. For many barristers, the ultimate goal is to become Lord Chief Justice, Master of the Rolls or a Justice of the Supreme Court.

Table 21.1 Judicial salaries, 2010

Group	Annual salary (£) from
1 (Lord Chief Justice)	239,845
1.1 (Lord Chief Justice of Northern Ireland, Master of the Rolls, President of the Supreme Court)	214,165
2 (Justices of the Supreme Court, President of the Queen's Bench Division, President of the Family Division)	206,857
3 (Lord Justices of Appeal)	196,707
4 (High Court judges)	172,753
5 (Senior Circuit Court judges, certain Tribunal Presidents, certain senior Recorders)	138,548
6.1 (Circuit judges, certain Tribunal Presidents)	128,296
6.2 (Deputy Senior District Judge [Magistrates' Court])	120,785
7 (District Judges [Magistrates' Courts], Immigration Judges)	102,921

Source: Ministry of Justice, *Judicial Salaries from 1 April 2010*

Judges, by the nature of their calling, are expected to be somewhat detached from the rest of society. However, critics – such as J.A.G. Griffith, in *The Politics of the Judiciary* (1997) – contend that this professional distance is exacerbated by social exclusivity, judges being predominantly elderly upper-class males.

The UK does not have a career judiciary – that is, beginning a career as a judge following graduation – but instead, as we have seen, judges are drawn from lawyers of several years' standing. They will typically be appointed to the bench when they are middle aged. The career trajectory is reflected in the retirement ages, which are generous compared to other professions. High Court judges retire at age 75, circuit judges at 72. By the time they reach the Supreme Court, judges may only have a few years of service remaining.

Concerns about the limited gender and racial background of judges have been expressed not only by academics such as Griffith but also by government and by parliamentary committees. In 2011 the Ministry of Justice launched a consultation on judicial diversity, and in its 2012 report on the subject, the Constitution Committee of the House of Lords observed:

> Despite concerns raised over the last few decades, the proportion of women judges, black, Asian and minority ethnic (BAME) judges and others from under-represented groups has increased too slowly. Many of the causes for this appear to stem from the structures of the legal professions (barristers and solicitors) and the pool of available mid-career legal professionals eligible and interested in putting themselves forward for selection. However, other barriers arise as a result of the appointments process itself or of the structures of the courts and tribunals in which judges work.
>
> (Constitution Committee 2012: 25)

Less than 25 per cent of judges are female (see Table 21.2). The percentage decreases the higher the court. In 2012 there was only one female Justice of the Supreme Court – Baroness Hale of Richmond, the first ever female to be appointed to the highest court of appeal (initially the House of Lords) – and four women among 37 Lord Justices of Appeal. Those from Black, Asian and minority ethnic (BAME) backgrounds are even scarcer (Table 21.2): only one in 20 judges is drawn from such a background and most sit as Recorders or Deputy District Judges (County Courts). There are no BAME judges in the Supreme Court or Court of Appeal and only four among 108 High Court judges.

In their educational backgrounds, judges are also remarkably similar. The majority went to public school (among Supreme Court Justices and Lord Justices, the proportion

Table 21.2 Women and ethnic minority judges in the UK, 1998–2011

Year	Judges in post	Women (%)	BAME (%)
1998	3,174	10.3	1.6
1999	3,312	11.2	1.7
2000	3,441	12.7	2.1
2001	3,535	14.1	1.9
2002	3,545	14.5	2.0
2003	3,656	14.9	2.2
2004	3,675	15.8	2.5
2005	3,794	16.9	2.9
2006	3,774	18.0	3.8
2007	3,545	18.7	3.5
2008	3,820	19.0	4.1
2009	3,602	19.4	4.5
2010	3,598	20.6	4.8
2011	3,694	22.3	5.1

Source: Appointments and Diversity: A Judiciary for the 21st Century, Ministry of Justice, Consultation Paper CP19/2011, November 2011, p. 7

exceeds 80 per cent) and the vast majority graduated from Oxford and Cambridge universities; more than 80 per cent of circuit judges did so, and the proportion increases the further one goes up the judicial hierarchy.

Senior judgeships are the almost exclusive preserve of barristers. It is possible for solicitors to become judges, though few have taken this route.

Judges thus form a socially and professionally exclusive or near-exclusive body. This exclusivity has been attacked for having unfortunate consequences. One is that judges are out of touch with society itself, not being able to understand the habits and terminology of everyday life, reflecting instead the social mores of 30 or 40 years ago. Courts that do not reflect society may undermine trust in the judicial process. As the Constitution Committee of the House of Lords recorded in its report on judicial diversity in 2012: 'we received evidence, with which we concur, arguing that diverse courts are better equipped to carry out the role of adjudicating than courts that are not diverse and that the public will have greater trust and confidence in a more diverse judiciary' (Constitution Committee 2012: 11). The background of the judges has also led to allegations of inbuilt bias – towards the government of the day and towards the Conservative Party. Senior judges have been accused of construing the public interest as favouring law and order and upholding the interests of the state (Griffith 1997). The claim of deference to the executive is also one that has been pursued by Keith Ewing (Ewing 2004; Ewing and Tham 2008). Though accepting courts may be an irritant to the executive, he has argued that they are not an obstacle (Ewing and Tham 2008: 691).

Such concerns exists at a time when the judiciary has become more active. There has been a greater willingness on the part of judges to review the actions of ministers (Stevens 2003: 358–9). There has also been increased activity arising from the UK's membership of the European Community/ Union. The incorporation of the ECHR into British law and the creation of devolved assemblies have also widened the scope for judicial activity. In combination, these developments have raised the courts in Britain to a new level of political activity – and visibility.

Judicial activism

The common law power available to judges to strike down executive actions as being beyond powers granted – *ultra vires* – or as contrary to natural law was not much in evidence in the decades prior to the 1960s. Courts were generally deferential in their stance towards government. This was to change in the period from the mid-1960s onwards. Although the judiciary changed hardly at all in terms of the background of judges – they were usually the same elderly, white, Oxbridge-educated males as before – there was a significant change in attitudes. Apparently worried by the perceived encroachment of government on individual liberties, they proved increasingly willing to use their powers of judicial review.

In four cases in the 1960s the courts adopted an activist line in reviewing the exercise of powers by administrative bodies and, in two instances, of ministers. In *Conway* v *Rimmer* in 1968, the House of Lords ruled against a claim of the Home Secretary that the production of certain documents would be contrary to the public interest; previously, such a claim would have been treated as definitive. Another case in the same year involved the House of Lords considering why, and not just how, a ministerial decision was made. It was a demonstration, noted Lord Scarman (1974: 49), that judges were 'ready to take an activist line'.

This activist line has been maintained and, indeed, become more prominent. Successive governments have found ministerial actions overturned by the courts. There were four celebrated cases in the second half of the 1970s in which the courts found against Labour ministers (Norton 1982: 138–40), and then several in the 1980s and the 1990s, when they found against Conservative ministers.

Perceptions of greater judicial activism derive not just from the cases that have attracted significant media attention. They also derive from the sheer number of applications for **judicial review** made to the courts (Stevens 2003: 358). At the beginning of the 1980s there were about 500 applications

a year for leave to apply for judicial review. In the 1990s it generally exceeded 3,000 and by the start of the new century regularly exceeded 4,000. In 2007 it reached 6,690 and four years later the number had reached five figures. In 2011, 11,200 applications were made.

Each year, a number of cases brought before the courts have attracted media attention and been politically significant. In 1993 Lord Rees-Mogg challenged the power of the government to ratify the Maastricht Treaty which formed the European Communities into the European Union (EU) and transferred various policy competences to the EU. His case was rejected by a Divisional Court of the Queen's Bench Division. The same month – July 1993 – saw the House of Lords find a former Home Secretary, acting in his official ministerial capacity, in contempt of court for failing to comply with a court order in an asylum case. The ruling meant that ministers could not rely on the doctrine of crown immunity to ignore the orders of a court. *The Times* reported (28 July 1993):

> Five law lords declared yesterday that ministers cannot put themselves above the law as they found the former home secretary Kenneth Baker guilty of contempt of court in an asylum case. The historic ruling on Crown immunity was described as one of the most important constitutional findings for two hundred years and hailed as establishing a key defence against the possible rise of a ruthless government in the future.

Ironically, the case was largely overshadowed by attention given to the unsuccessful case pursued by Lord Rees-Mogg. Kenneth Baker's successor as Home Secretary, Michael Howard, also variously ran foul of the courts, the Appeal Court holding that he had acted beyond his powers. Indeed, tension between government and the courts increased notably in 1995 and 1996 as several cases went against the Home Secretary (Woodhouse 1996). In July 1996 the court found that he had acted unlawfully in taking into account a public petition and demands from members of the public in increasing the minimum sentence to be served by two minors who had murdered the two-year-old Jamie Bulger. After the return of the Labour Government in 1997, successive Home Secretaries fell foul of the courts. In July 1999, for example, Jack Straw's attempts to retain his power to ban journalists who were investigating miscarriages of justice from interviewing prisoners was declared unlawful by the House of Lords. The same month, the Court of Appeal found against him after he sought to return three asylum seekers to France or Germany. In 2001 an order made by Mr Straw, and approved by Parliament, designating Pakistan as a country that presented no serious risk of persecution was quashed by the Court of Appeal. In a judgment at the end of 2004, in the *Belmarsh case*, the law lords held that powers in

Part 4 of the Anti-Terrorism, Crime and Security Act 2001 were disproportionate and discriminatory because they applied only to foreign nationals. The Coalition Government returned in 2010 also encountered problems with judicial decisions. The Government fell foul of some judicial decisions – though being successful in some cases – in seeking to deal with individuals suspected of being engaged in terrorist activity, including in their attempts to deport them to countries where they may face torture. There were also other clashes with the courts. In June 2012 a High Court judge held the Home Secretary, Theresa May, in contempt of court for failing to abide by an undertaking to release a foreign criminal. She thus became only the second Home Secretary, after Kenneth Baker, to be held in contempt of court. (As the foreign national was then released, no penalty was imposed.) In July 2012 Mrs May had to take emergency action when the Supreme Court declared unlawful recent changes to the UK Border Agency's points-based system of skilled migration, visitor's visas and family migration rules because they had not been directly approved by Parliament.

All these cases, along with several other high-profile judgments – including a number by European courts – combined to create a new visibility for the judiciary.

The courts, then, are willing to cast a critical eye over decisions of ministers in order to ensure that they comply with the powers granted by statute and are not contrary to natural justice. They are facilitated in this task by the rise in the number of applications made for judicial review and by their power of statutory interpretation. As Drewry (1986: 30) has noted:

> Although judges must strictly apply Acts of Parliament, the latter are not always models of clarity and consistency . . . This leaves the judges with considerable scope for the exercise of their creative skills in interpreting what an Act really means. Some judges, of which Lord Denning was a particularly notable example, have been active and ingenious in inserting their own policy judgements into the loopholes left in legislation.

Judicial activism is thus well established. The courts have been willing to scrutinise government actions, and on occasion strike them down, on a scale not previously witnessed. Some commentators in the 1990s saw it as a consequence of the Conservative Party being in government for more than a decade. However, the courts maintained their activism under a Labour government, much to the displeasure of some ministers and resulting, as we shall see, in some high-profile clashes between ministers and the courts.

However, the extent and impact of such activism on the part of judges should not be exaggerated. There are three important caveats that have to be entered. First, statutory interpretation allows judges some but not complete leeway. They follow well-established guidelines. Second, the majority of applications for judicial review concern asylum and immigration cases. Third, most applications made for judicial review fail.

Even so, activism on the part of the courts constitutes a problem for government. Even though the percentage of applications where leave is given to proceed has declined, the absolute number has increased. And even though government may win most of the cases brought against it, it is the cases that it loses that attract the headlines.

Enforcing EU law

The United Kingdom signed the treaty of accession to the European Community in 1972. The European Communities Act passed the same year provided the legal provisions necessary for membership. The UK became a member of the EC on 1 January 1973. The European Communities Act, as we have seen in Chapter 13, created a new juridical dimension to the British constitution.

The 1972 Act gave legal force not only to existing EC law but also to future law. When regulations have been promulgated by the Commission and the Council of Ministers, they take effect within the United Kingdom. Parliamentary assent to the principle is not required. That assent has already been given in advance by virtue of the provisions of the 1972 Act. Parliament may be involved in giving approval to measures to implement directives, but there is no scope to reject the purpose of the directives. And, as we recorded in Chapter 15, under the provisions of the Act, questions of law are to be decided by the European Court of Justice (ECJ), or in accordance with the decisions of that court. All courts in the United Kingdom are required to take judicial notice of decisions made by the ECJ. Cases in the UK that reach the Supreme Court are, unless the justices consider that the law has already been settled by the ECJ, referred to the European Court for a definitive ruling. Requests may also be made by lower courts to the ECJ for a ruling on the meaning and interpretation of European treaties. In the event of a conflict between the provisions of European law and those of an Act of Parliament, the former are to prevail.

The question that has most exercised writers on constitutional law since Britain's accession to the EC has been what British courts should do in the event of the passage of an Act of Parliament that expressly overrides European law. The question remains a hypothetical one. Although some doubt exists – Lord Denning when Master of the Rolls appeared to imply on occasion that the courts must apply EC law, Acts of Parliament notwithstanding – the generally accepted view among jurists is that courts, by virtue of the doctrine of parliamentary sovereignty, must apply the provisions of the Act of Parliament that expressly overrides European law (see Bradley 1994: 97).

Given the absence of an explicit overriding of European law by statute, the most important question to which the courts have had to address themselves has been how to resolve apparent inconsistencies or conflict between European and domestic (known as municipal) law. During debate on the European Communities Bill in 1972 ministers made clear that the bill essentially provided a rule of construction: that is, that the courts were to construe the provisions of an Act of Parliament, in so far as it was possible to do so, in such a way as to render it consistent with European law. However, what if it is not possible to construe an Act of Parliament in such a way? Where the courts have found UK law to fall foul of European law, the UK government has introduced new legislation to bring domestic law into line with EC requirements. But what about the position prior to the passage of such legislation? Do the courts have power to strike down or suspend Acts of Parliament that appear to breach European law? The presumption until 1990 was that they did not. Two cases – the *Factortame* and *Ex Parte EOC* cases – have shown that presumption to be false. The former case involved a challenge, by the owners of some Spanish trawlers, to the provisions of the 1988 Merchant Shipping Act. The High Court granted interim relief, suspending the relevant parts of the Act. This was then overturned by the House of Lords (predecessor of the Supreme Court), which ruled that the courts had no such power. The European Court of Justice, to which the case was then referred, ruled in June 1990 that courts did have the power of injunction and could suspend the application of Acts of Parliament that on their face appeared to breach European law until a final determination was made. The following month the House of Lords granted orders to the Spanish fishermen preventing the Transport Secretary from withholding or withdrawing their names from the register of British fishing vessels, the orders to remain in place until the ECJ had decided the case. The case had knock-on consequences beyond EU law: having decided that an injunction could be granted against the crown in the field of EU law, the courts subsequently decided that it could then be applied in cases not involving EU law (Jacobs 1999: 242). However, the most dramatic case in terms of EU law was to come in 1994. In *R. v Secretary of State for Employment, ex parte the Equal Opportunities Commission* – usually referred to as *Ex Parte EOC* – there was a challenge to provisions of the 1978 Employment Protection (Consolidation) Act. The House of Lords held that the provisions of the Act effectively excluded many part-time workers from the right to claim unfair dismissal or redundancy payments and were as such unlawful, being incompatible with EU law (Maxwell 1999). Although the *Factortame* case attracted considerable publicity, it was the *EOC* case that was the more fundamental in its implications. The courts were invalidating the provisions of an Act of Parliament. Following the case, *The Times* declared 'Britain may now have, for the first time in its history, a constitutional court' (5 March 1994, cited in Maxwell 1999: 197).

The courts have thus assumed a new role in the interpretation of European law, and the court system itself has acquired an additional dimension. The ECJ serves not only to hear cases that emanate from British courts but also to consider cases brought directly by or against the EC Commission and the governments of the member states. Indeed, the ECJ carries a significant workload, so much so that it has to be assisted by another court, the Court of First Instance, and both are under considerable pressure in trying to cope with the number of cases brought before them. In the twenty-first century, the ECJ alone receives 800 to 900 cases a year.

There is thus a significant judicial dimension to British membership of the European Union, involving adjudication by a supranational court, and the greater the integration of member states the greater the significance of the courts in applying European law. Furthermore, under the Maastricht Treaty, which took effect in 1993, the powers of the ECJ were strengthened, the court being given the power to fine member states that did not fulfil their legal obligations. Although the cases heard by the ECJ may not often appear to be of great significance, collectively they produce a substantial – indeed, massive – body of case law that constitutes an important constraint on the actions of the UK government. Each year, that body of case law grows greater.

Against this new judicial dimension has to be set the fact that the doctrine of parliamentary sovereignty remains formally extant. Parliament retains the power to repeal the 1972 Act. The decisions of the ECJ have force in the United Kingdom inasmuch as Parliament has decreed that they will. When Lord Rees-Mogg sought judicial review of the government's power to ratify the Maastricht Treaty, the Speaker of the House of Commons, Betty Boothroyd, issued a stern warning to the courts, reminding them that under the Bill of Rights of 1689 the proceedings of Parliament could not be challenged by the courts. (Lord Rees-Mogg, whose application was rejected, emphasised that no such challenge was intended.) And it was the British government that instigated the provision in the Maastricht Treaty for the ECJ to fine member states. The number of cases brought in the ECJ against the UK, alleging a failure to fulfil its obligations, is a relatively small one. Out of 207 cases brought before the ECJ in 2009, for example, only 13 were brought against the UK and even this constituted a high number compared to previous years. Even so, the impact of membership of the EU should not be treated lightly. It has introduced a major new judicial dimension to the British constitution. It has profound implications for the role of the courts in influencing public policy in the United Kingdom. That was emphasised by the ruling of the House of Lords in the *Ex Parte EOC* case. The courts now appear to have acquired, in part, a power that they lost in 1688.

Enforcing the European Convention on Human Rights

Reinforcing the importance of the courts has been the incorporation of the European Convention on Human Rights (ECHR) into British law. Although not formally vesting the courts with the same powers as are vested by the 1972 European Communities Act, the incorporation nonetheless makes British judges powerful actors in determining public policy.

The European Convention on Human Rights was signed at Rome in 1950 and was ratified by the United Kingdom in March 1951. It came into effect in 1953. It declares the rights that should be protected in each state – such as the right to life, freedom of thought and peaceful assembly (see Figure 21.2) – and stipulates procedures by which infringements of those rights can be determined. Alleged breaches of the Convention are investigated by the European Commission on Human Rights and may be referred to the European Court of Human Rights.

The convention is a treaty under international law. This means that its authority derives from the consent of the states that have signed it. It was not incorporated into British law, and not until 1966 were individual citizens allowed to petition the commission. In subsequent decades a large number of petitions were brought against the British government. Although the British government was not required under British law to comply with the decisions of the court, it did so by virtue of its international obligations and introduced the necessary changes to bring UK law into line with the judgment of the court. By 1995 over 100 cases against the UK government had been judged admissible, and 37 cases had been upheld (see Lester 1994: 42–6). Some of the decisions have been politically controversial, as in 1994 when the court decided (on a ten–nine vote) that the killing of three IRA suspects in Gibraltar in 1988 by members of the British security forces was a violation of the right to life.

The decisions of the court led to calls from some Conservative MPs for the UK not to renew the right of indi-

- O Article 1 – respecting rights
- O Article 2 – life
- O Article 3 – torture
- O Article 4 – servitude
- O Article 5 – liberty and security
- O Article 6 – fair trial
- O Article 7 – retrospectivity
- O Article 8 – privacy
- O Article 9 – conscience and religion
- O Article 10 – expression
- O Article 11 – association
- O Article 12 – marriage
- O Article 13 – effective remedy
- O Article 14 – discrimination
- O Article 15 – derogations
- O Article 16 – aliens
- O Article 17 – abuse of rights
- O Article 18 – permitted restrictions

Convention protocols

- O Protocol 1
  - ■ Article 1 – property
  - ■ Article 2 – education
  - ■ Article 3 – elections
- O Protocol 4 – civil imprisonment, free movement, expulsion
- O Protocol 6 – restriction of death penalty
- O Protocol 7 – crime and family
- O Protocol 12 – discrimination
- O Protocol 13 – complete abolition of death penalty
- O Procedural and institutional protocols

Figure 21.2 Articles of the European Convention on Human Rights

viduals to petition the commission. Liberal Democrats and many Labour MPs – as well as some Conservatives – wanted to move in the opposite direction and to incorporate the ECHR into British law. Those favouring incorporation argued that it would reduce the cost and delay involved in pursuing a petition to the commission and allow citizens to enforce their rights through British courts. It was also argued that it would raise awareness of human rights. This reasoning led the Labour Party to include a commitment in its 1997 election manifesto to incorporate the ECHR into British law. Following the return of a Labour government in that election, the government published a White Paper, *Rights Brought Home*, and followed it with the introduction of the Human Rights Bill. The bill was enacted in 1998.

The Human Rights Act makes it unlawful for public authorities to act in a way that is incompatible with convention rights. It is thus possible for individuals to invoke their rights in any proceedings brought against them by a public authority or in any proceedings that they may bring against a public authority.

> Courts will, from time to time, be required to determine if primary or secondary legislation is incompatible with Convention rights. They will decide if the acts of public authorities are unlawful through contravention, perhaps even unconscious contravention, of those rights. They may have to award damages as a result.
>
> (Irvine of Lairg 1998: 230)

Although the courts are not empowered to set aside Acts of Parliament, they are required to interpret legislation as far as possible in accordance with the convention. They look to the jurisprudence of the European Court on Human Rights, but can build on it: the standards set out in case law by the Strasbourg court constitute a floor rather than a ceiling (Wright 2009). The higher courts can issue declarations of incompatibility where UK law is deemed incompatible with the ECHR: it is then up to Parliament to take the necessary action. The Act makes provision for a 'fast-track' procedure for amending law to bring it into line with the ECHR.

The incorporation of the ECHR into British law creates a new role for British judges in determining policy outcomes. In the words of one authority, 'it gives the courts an increased constitutional role, moving them from the margins of the political process to the centre and increasing the underlying tension between the executive and the judiciary' (Woodhouse 1996: 440). Indeed, the scale of the change was such that senior judges had to be trained for the purpose and, in order to give the courts time to prepare, the principal provisions of the Act were not brought into force until October 2000. (One effect, though, was immediate. The provision requiring ministers to certify that a bill complies with the provisions of the ECHR was brought in immediately following enactment.) By May 2007 the courts had issued 24 declarations of incompatibility, though six of these were overturned on appeal and one remained subject to appeal. Twelve were dealt with by legislation or remedial orders and the government had yet to decide how to remedy the incompatibility in the remaining cases.

In April 2003, for example, in the case of *Bellinger* v *Bellinger*, the courts held that section 11(c) of the Matrimonial Causes Act 1973 was incompatible with Articles 8 and 12 of the Convention. This led to Parliament enacting the Gender Recognition Act conferring rights on those who changed gender, including the right to a new birth certificate. Also in April 2003 the courts in *Blood and Tarbuck* v *Secretary of State for Health* issued a declaration in respect of a provision of the Human Fertilisation and Embryology Act 1990 which prevented the use of a dead husband's sperm to be used by the mother to conceive. A private member's bill was employed, with government assistance, to change the law. However, the most significant case was to come in December 2004, in the *Belmarsh case*, to which we have already referred, when the House of Lords held that powers in Part 4 of the Anti-Terrorism, Crime and Security Act breached the provisions of the convention in that they were disproportionate and discriminatory in applying only to foreign nationals. The decision, as we shall see, caused a political storm and contributed to a major clash between executive and judiciary. The Government nonetheless introduced a Terrorism Bill with new provisions in place of those embodied in the 2001 Act. However, provisions in the new Act, providing for control orders on individuals, also fell foul of the courts, the House of Lords holding that impositions of 18-hour curfews constituted a deprivation of liberty under Article 5 of the convention.

The Act has thus had a major effect on the relationship of Parliament and the executive to the courts. Parliament has, in effect, handed over its traditional power of protecting rights to the courts. One study, covering the period 1994 to 2007, found a notable increase in human rights cases being considered by the highest court of appeal (then the House of Lords) following enactment of the Act (Shah and Poole 2009). Enforcing the rights embodied in the Act has on occasion brought the courts into conflict with the executive. Though the courts have not gone as far as some critics would wish, they have used their powers to limit the executive (Kavanagh 2009). The position was summarised by Jeffrey Jowell, in writing that the Human Rights Act 'may on the face of it be just another unentrenched statute, but its effect is to alter constitutional expectations by creating the presumption across all official decision making that rights do and should trump convenience' (Jowell 2003: 597). It is the courts that decide when such trumping should take place.

The impact of devolution

The devolution of powers to elected assemblies in different parts of the United Kingdom (see Chapter 15) has also enlarged the scope for judicial activity. The legislation creating elected assemblies in Scotland, Wales and Northern

Ireland – the Scotland Act, the Government of Wales Act and the Northern Ireland Act – stipulates the legal process by which the powers and the exercise of powers by the assemblies can be challenged.

There are complex provisions for determining whether a particular function is exercisable by a devolved body, whether it has exceeded its powers, whether it has failed to fulfil its statutory obligations or whether a failure to act puts it in breach of the ECHR. These are known as 'devolution issues'. A law officer can require a particular devolution issue to be referred to the Supreme Court (before 2009, it was to the Judicial Committee of the Privy Council). It is also open to other courts to refer a devolution issue to higher courts for determination. Devolution issues considered by the High Court or the Court of Appeal may be appealed to the Supreme Court, but only with the leave of the court or the Supreme Court. If a court finds that a devolved body has exceeded its powers in making subordinate legislation, it can make an order removing or limiting any retrospective effect of the decision, or suspend the effect of the decision for any period and on any conditions to allow the defect to be corrected. A law officer can also make a pre-enactment reference to the Supreme Court to determine whether a bill or a provision of a bill is within the competence of the devolved body. In other words, it is not necessary for the measure to be enacted: a law officer can seek a determination while the measure is in bill form.

The provisions of the devolution legislation create notable scope for judicial activity. There is scope for the courts to interpret the legislation in a constrictive or an expansive manner. The approach taken by the courts has major implications for the devolved bodies. There is also scope for the courts to move away from the intentions of the Westminster Parliament. The longer an Act of constitutional significance survives, the intent of Parliament in passing it gradually loses its significance (Craig and Walters 1999: 289). Policing powers of the devolved bodies by the courts has political as well as legal implications. The point has been well put by Craig and Walters. As they note, the Scotland Act, while giving the Scottish Parliament general legislative powers, also limits those powers through a broad list of reservations.

> At the minimum, this means that the Scottish Parliament will have to become accustomed to living with the 'judge over its shoulder'. Proposed legislation will have to be scrutinised assiduously lest it fall foul of one of the many heads of reserved subject matter . . . The need for constant recourse to lawyers who will, in many instances, indicate that proposed action cannot be taken, is bound to generate frustration and anger in Scotland.
>
> (Craig and Walters 1999: 303)

As they conclude,

> The courts are inevitably faced with a grave responsibility: the way in which they interpret the SA [Scotland Act] may be a significant factor in deciding whether devolution proves to be the reform which cements the union, or whether it is the first step towards its dissolution.
>
> (Craig and Walters 1999: 303)

As with the Human Rights Act, the cases may be more significant for their quality, and their deterrent effect, than for their number. The number of 'devolution issues' brought before the courts is relatively rare. From the inception of devolution and the transfer of responsibility for devolution issues to the Supreme Court in 2009, the Judicial Committee of the Privy Council decided 20 cases brought before it, some of them incorporating more than one appeal. In 2001, for example, the Judicial Committee dealt with ten appeals in five cases. All of them were brought under the Scotland Act, and all but one group involved claims made in Scottish criminal proceedings that the Lord Advocate (the Scottish equivalent of the Attorney General), as prosecutor, was infringing their human rights. One group related to proceedings arising from a law passed by the Scottish Parliament that prevented the discharge from hospital, where the safety of the public so required, of a patient suffering from a mental disorder even if not detained for medical treatment. Of the ten appeals, five were dismissed and five were allowed. Since then, the court had no more than three cases brought before it in any one year.

Demands for change

Recent years have seen various calls for change in the judicial process. Some of these have focused on the court's constitutional role in relation to government and the protection of rights. Others have focused on decisions of the courts in domestic criminal and civil cases.

Constraining the executive

In terms of the place of the courts in the nation's constitutional arrangements, there have been various demands to strengthen the powers of the courts, and some of these calls have borne fruit, primarily with the incorporation of the ECHR into British law. Some want to go further. Some want to see a more inclusive document than the ECHR. The ECHR, for example, excludes such things as a right to food or a right of privacy (see Nolan and Sedley 1997). The Liberal Democrats, Unlock Democracy and a number of jurists want to see the enactment of an entrenched Bill of Rights. In other words, they want a measure that enjoys some degree of protection from encroachment by Parliament. Formally, as we have seen, Parliament does not have to act on declarations of incompatibility issued by the courts. Under the proposal for an entrenched Bill of Rights, the courts would be able to set aside an Act of Parliament that was in conflict with the ECHR, rather in the same way that the courts have set aside the provisions of an Act deemed to be incompatible with EU law.

The powers acquired by the courts – and the calls for them to be given further powers – have not been universally welcomed (see Box 21.1). Critics view the new role of the courts as a threat to the traditional Westminster constitution

---

BOX 21.1

More power to judges?

The European Convention on Human Rights has been incorporated into British law. This gives a new role to judges. Some proposals have been put forward to strengthen the courts even further by the enactment of an entrenched Bill of Rights, putting fundamental rights beyond the reach of a simple parliamentary majority. Giving power to judges, through the incorporation of the ECHR and, more so, through an entrenched document, has proved politically contentious. The principal arguments put forward both for and against giving such power to the courts are as follows:

The case for

- A written document, such as the ECHR, clarifies and protects the rights of the individual. Citizens know precisely what their rights are, and those rights are protected by law.

- It puts interpretation in the hands of neutral judges, independent of the political process.

- It prevents encroachment by politicians in government and Parliament. Politicians will be reluctant to tamper with a document, such as the ECHR, now that it is part of the law. **Entrenchment** of the measure – that is, imposing extraordinary provisions for its amendment – would put the rights beyond the reach of a simple majority in both Houses of Parliament.

- It prevents encroachment by other public bodies, such as the police. Citizens know their rights in relation to public bodies and are able to seek judicial redress if those rights are infringed.

- It ensures a greater knowledge of rights. It is an educative tool, citizens being much more rights-conscious.

- It bolsters confidence in the political system. By knowing that rights are protected in this way, citizens feel better protected and as such are more supportive of the political system.

The case against

- It confuses rather than clarifies rights. The ECHR, like most Bills of Rights, is necessarily drawn in general terms and citizens therefore have to wait until the courts interpret the vague language in order to know precisely what is and what is not protected.

- It transfers power from an elected to a non-elected body. What are essentially political issues are decided by unelected judges and not by the elected representatives of the people.

- It does not necessarily prevent encroachment by public bodies. Rights are better protected by the political culture of a society than by words written on a document. A written document does not prevent public officials getting around its provision by covert means.

- It creates a false sense of security. There is a danger that people will believe that rights are fully protected when later interpretation by the courts may prove them wrong. Pursuing cases through the courts can be prohibitively expensive; often only big companies and rich individuals can use the courts to protect their interests.

- If a document is entrenched, it embodies rights that are the product of a particular generation. A document that is not entrenched can be modified by a simple majority in both Houses of Parliament. If it is entrenched – as many Bills of Rights are – it embodies the rights of a particular time and makes it difficult to get rid of them after their moral validity has been destroyed, as was the case with slavery in the United States.

(see Chapter 15), introducing into the political process a body of unaccountable and unelected judges who have excessive powers to interpret the provisions of a document drawn in general terms. Instead of public policy being determined by elected politicians – who can be turned out by electors at the next election – it can be decided by unrepresentative judges, who are immune to action by electors. As we have seen, the powerful position of the courts has not commended itself to all ministers. In 2001 Home Secretary David Blunkett attacked the interference by judges in political matters and even raised the possibility of 'suspending' the Human Rights Act (Woodhouse 2002: 261). In December 2004, following the decision of the House of Lords to issue a declaration of incompatibility in respect of certain provisions of the Anti-Terrorism, Crime and Security Act, Foreign Secretary Jack Straw said that the law lords were 'simply wrong' to imply that detainees were being held arbitrarily; it was for Parliament and not the courts to decide how best Britain could be defended from terrorism (see Norton 2006). Following terrorist bombings in London in July 2005, ministers wanted new anti-terrorist legislation but were worried it might fall foul of the courts. In announcing a series of measures to address the terrorist threat, Prime Minister Tony Blair in August 2005 stirred controversy by declaring 'the rules of the game are changing'. He conceded it was likely that the legislation would be tested in the courts. 'Should legal obstacles arise', he said, 'we will legislate further including, if necessary, amending the Human Rights Act in respect of their interpretation of the European Convention on Human Rights and apply it directly in our own law.' In 2008, Justice Secretary Jack Straw reiterated his 'great frustration' with the way the Act had been interpreted by the courts and wanted to 'rebalance' the legislation with an emphasis on responsibilities. Both Prime Minister Gordon Brown, in his *Governance of Britain* agenda, and Conservative leader David Cameron raised the prospect of a British Bill of Rights of Duties and Responsibilities. Following the formation of the Coalition Government in 2010, a Commission on a Bill of Rights was established the following year to 'investigate the creation of a UK Bill of Rights that incorporates and builds on all our obligations under the European Convention on Human Rights, ensures that these rights continue to be enshrined in UK law, and protects and extend our liberties'.

Portraying the courts as part of the problem, rather than as part of the solution, meant the government was drawing the courts into the political fray, essentially anticipating conflict and doing so at a time of major change in the highest echelon of the judicial system.

Applying the law

The courts have thus proved controversial in terms of their constitutional role. They have also been the subject of debate in terms of their traditional role in interpreting and enforcing the law. The debate has encompassed not only the judges but also the whole process of criminal and civil justice.

In 1999 the usually sure-footed law lords encountered criticism when they had to decide whether the former Chilean head of state, General Augusto Pinochet, who had been detained in the UK, should be extradited from Britain to Spain. The first judgment of the court had to be set aside when one of the law lords hearing the case was revealed to have been a director of a company controlled by a party (Amnesty International) to the case. It was the first time that the law lords had set aside one of their own decisions and ordered a rehearing. Especially embarrassing for the law lords, it was also the first case in which an English court had announced its decision live on television (see Rozenberg 1999).

Lower courts, including the Court of Appeal, came in for particular criticism in the late 1980s and early 1990s as a result of several cases of miscarriages of justice (see Mullin 1996; Walker and Starmer 1999). In 1989 the 'Guildford Four', convicted in 1975 of bombings in Guildford, were released pending an inquiry into their original conviction; in 1990 the case of the Maguire family, convicted of running an IRA bomb factory, was referred back to the Appeal Court after the Home Secretary received evidence that the convictions could not be upheld; and in 1991 the 'Birmingham Six', convicted of pub bombings in Birmingham in 1974, were released after the Court of Appeal quashed their convictions. The longest-running case was the Bridgewater case, in which several men had been convicted in 1979 of the murder of newspaper boy Carl Bridgewater. The Court of Appeal refused leave to appeal in 1981 and had turned down an appeal in 1987, before the case was again brought back in 1996. The men were released in 1997. In 1998 the Court of Appeal decided to set aside posthumously the conviction of Derek Bentley, hanged in 1953 for murder, after deciding that he had been deprived of a fair trial. Several previous attempts to get the conviction set aside had failed. Various lesser-known cases have also resulted in earlier convictions being overturned. By the end of August 2009 the Court of Appeal had quashed a total of 280 convictions referred to it by the Criminal Cases Review Commission.

The judges involved in the original cases were variously criticised for being too dependent on the good faith of prosecution witnesses – as was the Court of Appeal. The

Appeal Court came in for particular criticism for its apparent reluctance even to consider that there might have been miscarriages of justice. As late as 1988 the court had refused an appeal by the 'Birmingham Six', doing so in terms that suggested that the Home Secretary should not even have referred the case to the court. When lawyers for the 'Birmingham Six' had earlier sought to establish police malpractice by bringing a claim for damages, the then Master of the Rolls, Lord Denning, had caused controversy by suggesting, in effect, that the exposure of injustice in individual cases was less important than preserving a façade of infallibility (Harlow 1991: 98). By the 1990s that façade had been destroyed. The cases were few in number and only a small proportion of the applications made to the Criminal Cases Review Commission result in cases being referred to the Appeal Court: of 14,778 applications made to the commission (up to 31 May 2012), only just under 500 cases had been referred. It has been the high-profile cases that have undermined the position of the courts.

Another criticism has been the insensitivity of some judges in particular cases, notably rape cases. A number of judges have been criticised for their comments and lenient sentence handed out in such cases. In one case, for example, the judge had said that he received evidence that the girl in the case was 'no angel herself'. The comment attracted widespread and adverse criticism. The Appeal Court, while asserting that the judge had been quoted out of context, nonetheless condemned the sentence as inappropriate and increased the sentence. An earlier case, in which another judge had awarded a young rape victim £500 to go on holiday to help her to forget about her experience, attracted even more condemnation. Such cases highlighted a problem that appears pervasive. Although the maximum sentence for rape is life imprisonment, and guidelines recommend that a five-year sentence should be the starting point after conviction in contested rape cases, there has been a substantial proportion of cases where the sentence has been less than five years. Lenient sentences in a number of cases involving other offences have also fuelled popular misgivings about the capacity of the courts to deliver appropriate sentences.

In 2000 the European Court of Human Rights ruled that the minimum term of imprisonment (or 'tariff') for murder committed by juveniles should be set by the courts and not by the Home Secretary. In effect, the power thus passed to the Lord Chief Justice. It was first used in the case of two young men, Thompson and Venables, who as minors had abducted and killed two-year-old Jamie Bulger. Lord Woolf recommended a reduction in the tariff set by a previous Home Secretary, a reduction that meant that both became eligible for parole immediately. The case had aroused strong feelings, and the Lord Chief Justice's decision was unpopular. Equally unpopular was a subsequent granting by a senior judge of an injunction, which remains in place, preventing publication of any information that might lead to the identity or future whereabouts of the two.

The result of such cases may have limited public regard for judges, albeit not on a major scale. MORI polls have tended to show that around 60 per cent of those questioned express satisfaction with the way judges do their job. In 2004, the last year for which we have data, it was 58 per cent. However, the figure is less than for most of the other professions mentioned. In 2004, although 58 per cent were satisfied or very satisfied with the way judges did their job – against 18 per cent who were fairly or very dissatisfied – the figure was notably below that for nurses (96 per cent), doctors (92 per cent), teachers (86 per cent), and dentists (82 per cent). The police (67 per cent) also came out ahead of the judges. Only lawyers (54 per cent), politicians generally (27 per cent), and government ministers (27 per cent) received lower satisfaction ratings. Nonetheless, the figures show more than three times as many people satisfied than dissatisfied. The figures remained reasonably consistent, apart from a notable dip in 2003. Polls also show that, perhaps not surprisingly, most people trust judges to tell the truth.

Other aspects of the criminal justice system have also attracted criticism. The activity and policy of the Crown Prosecution Service have also been particular targets. The CPS has been largely overworked and has had difficulty since its inception in recruiting a sufficient number of well-qualified lawyers to deal with the large number of cases requiring action. The CPS has also been criticised for failing to prosecute in several highly publicised cases where it has felt that the chances of obtaining a conviction were not high enough to justify proceeding. Despite reforms to the service following damning reports on the organisation and leadership of the CPS in 1998 and 1999, criticisms continue to be levelled. At times, these are because of a failure to prosecute and at other times because of a decision to prosecute when it was felt the case did not justify such action. In 2012, for example, a leading football player, John Terry, was prosecuted for allegedly racially abusing a black player on the pitch. He was acquitted and the CPS criticised for adopting what was seen as a heavy-handed approach. Though the case revealed a disturbing feature of behaviour in football, it was felt it was predominantly a matter for the sport itself to address rather than the courts.

Another problem has been that of access to the system. Pursuing a court case is expensive. In civil cases, there is often little legal aid available. Those with money can hire high-powered lawyers. In cases alleging libel or slander, or claiming invasion of privacy, only those with substantial wealth can usually afford to pursue a case against a well-resourced individual or organisation, such as a national newspaper. Millionaires such as motor racing executive Max Moseley have pursued cases successfully, but for anyone without great financial resources the task is virtually impossible. Cases can also be delayed. Many individuals have neither the time nor the money to pursue matters through the courts.

Implementing change

Various proposals have been advanced for reform of the judiciary and of the system of criminal justice. A number, as we have seen, have been implemented. There have been moves to create greater openness in the recruitment of senior judges as well as to extend the right to appear before the senior courts. A Commissioner for Judicial Appointments, to oversee judicial appointments, was put in place in 2001. The Constitutional Reform Act 2005 created a Judicial Appointments Commission. This has been active in seeking to achieve greater judicial diversity. Although most judges are still white, male and middle aged, there has been progress (as can be seen in Table 21.2) in promoting women and members of Black, Asian and minority ethnic backgrounds to the bench.

In 1998 new judges were required to reveal whether they were freemasons. (It was feared that membership of a secret society might raise suspicions of a lack of impartiality.) The 1999 Access to Justice Act created a community legal service (CLS) to take responsibility for the provision of legal advice and for legal aid. It also created a criminal defence service, to provide that those charged with criminal offences receive a high-quality legal defence. Legal language has also been simplified. The Crown Prosecution Service has also undergone significant change.

There have also been various reforms to criminal law in terms of sentencing and the management of cases in the magistrates' courts. In 2002 the Government published a White Paper, *Justice for All*, proposing further changes to the criminal justice system. These included changing the rules as to what evidence may be presented, having judge-only trials in serious and complex fraud cases, removing the double jeopardy rule (preventing someone from being tried twice for the same offence), and creating a Sentencing Guidelines Council to ensure more uniformity in sentencing. Some of these have been implemented, including the ending, in certain exceptional circumstances, of the double jeopardy rule and the creation of a Sentencing Guidelines Council. Attempts to reduce the number of jury trials have variously fallen foul of opposition in the House of Lords. And, as we have seen, the Lord Chancellor's position as head of the judiciary has been transferred to the Lord Chief Justice and, in 2009, the Supreme Court came into being.

The courts are undergoing significant change – the changes of the past decade probably surpassing anything experienced in the previous half-century – but the pressure for reform continues. As the constitution has acquired a new judicial dimension, so the courts have become more visible and embroiled in political controversy. The creation of a Supreme Court, in the eyes of some, strengthens the position of the judiciary. The court, according to former Lord Chancellor Lord Falconer, 'will be bolder in vindicating both the freedoms of individuals and, coupled with that, being willing to take on the executive' (BBC News Online, 8 September 2009; http://news.bbc.co.uk/1/hi/uk/8237855.stm). A law lord, Lord Neuberger, who declined to move to the new Supreme Court and was instead appointed Master of the Rolls (though later becoming President of the Supreme Court in 2012), said in September 2009 that there was a real risk of 'judges abrogating to themselves greater power than they have at the moment' (BBC News Online, 8 September 2009). Others have argued that the court may actually become exposed and vulnerable to attack by ministers, lacking the buffer provided by the House of Lords (Norton 2005: 321–3). The presence of the law lords enabled peers to understand and appreciate their role, and provide something of a protective shield; the law lords, for their part, were able to understand the nature of the parliamentary system. The Lord Chancellor has also traditionally been in a position to protect the interests of the judicial system within government. The creation of a Supreme Court, and the ending of the traditional role of the Lord Chancellor, may leave senior judges isolated and hence more exposed to attack from senior ministers. The judges have become more important political actors and, as such, more significant targets of political attack. One cannot now study the making of public policy in the United Kingdom with the courts left out.

BOX 21.2

BRITAIN IN CONTEXT

Common law versus civil law

Courts in the UK differ from those in most other countries in that they do not have responsibility for interpreting a codified constitution. Their role has principally been that of engaging in statutory, not constitutional, interpretation; courts in other countries generally engage in both (though not always: there are countries with codified constitutions, such as the Netherlands, which maintain the principle of parliamentary sovereignty). The role of the courts in the UK has changed significantly as a consequence of the UK's membership of the EC/EU and the passage of the Human Rights Act 1998 – the treaties of the EU and the European Convention of Human Rights having the characteristics of higher law documents – but the basic distinction still remains. In so far as the courts are empowered to interpret such documents, they do so under the authority of Parliament and not a written constitution.

They also differ from their continental counterparts in that – along with the USA and most Commonwealth jurisdictions – they are based on the principles of common law rather than civil (or Roman) law. The common law tradition is based on law deriving from particular measures and their interpretation by the courts; much rests on judge-made law. The civil law tradition rests on a particular legal code stipulating the general principles of law that are to apply.

Not all systems follow the British in adopting an adversarial format – a feature of the common law tradition, the case being argued by competing counsel – nor in the presumption of being innocent until proven guilty.

Some systems adopt a form of religious or socialist law, in some cases requiring the accused to prove their innocence or simply presuming guilt, with the accused having no real opportunity to put their case.

Though generalisations can be drawn about courts in the United Kingdom, these can only be taken so far. Scotland has its own legal system. Though the Act of Union 1707 resulted in a unitary state, Scotland nonetheless retained its legal system. There is thus one court system, and body of law, for England and Wales and another for Scotland.

However, though there are significant differences between the legal system (or rather systems) in the UK and those in other countries, there are also features that are increasingly common. The effect of international treaties is to create common obligations. Thus, for example, the United Kingdom is a signatory to the European Convention on Human Rights; so too are more than 40 other countries. The European Court of Human Rights is ultimately responsible for the interpretation of the convention. Though the British courts are now empowered to consider convention rights, their interpretation can be challenged in the European Court in Strasbourg. The UK is one of 27 members of the European Union and each is bound by the treaties establishing the Union. The interpretation of the treaties lies ultimately with the European Court of Justice, which sits in Luxembourg. European countries are witnessing what, in effect, constitutes a common juridicalisation of their political systems.

Chapter summary

Although not at the heart of the regular policy-making process in Britain, the courts are nonetheless now significant actors in the political system. Traditionally restricted by the doctrine of parliamentary sovereignty, the courts have made use of their power of judicial review to constrain ministers and other public figures. The passage of two Acts – the European Communities Act in 1972 and the Human Rights Act in 1998 – has created the conditions for judges to determine the outcome of public policy in a way not previously possible. Judges now have powers that effectively undermine the doctrine of parliamentary sovereignty, with the outputs of Parliament not necessarily being immune to challenge in the courts. The passage of devolution legislation, creating elected bodies in Scotland, Wales and Northern Ireland, has also enlarged the scope for judicial activity, with potentially significant constitutional and political implications. The Constitutional Reform Act 2005 has resulted in the creation of a Supreme Court. The greater willingness of, and opportunity for, the courts to concern themselves with the determination of public policy has been welcomed by some jurists and politicians while alarming others, who are fearful that policy-making power may slip from elected politicians to unelected judges. The courts are having to meet the challenge of a new juridical dimension to the British constitution while coping – not always successfully – with the demands of an extensive system of criminal and civil justice.

Discussion points

- Why should the courts be independent of government?
- What role is now played by judges as a result of Britain's membership of the European Union?
- Can, and should, judges be drawn from a wider social background?
- Is the incorporation of the European Convention on Human Rights into British law a good idea?
- Has the creation of a Supreme Court strengthened or weakened the position of the senior judiciary?

Further reading

Basic introductions to the legal system can be found in student texts on constitutional and administrative law, such as Alder (2005) and Bradley and Ewing (2007). The most recent and succinct analysis of the changing role of judges in the nation's constitutional arrangements is Stevens (2002); see also Stevens (2003). On independence and accountability, see Bradley (2008). On possible future developments, see Le Sueur and Malleson (2008).

On judicial review, see Forsyth (2000). On the impact of membership of the EC/EU on British law, see Fitzpatrick (1999), Maxwell (1999) and Loveland (2003). On the incorporation of the ECHR, see Woodhouse (2002), Klug and O'Brien (2002), Shah and Poole (2009), Kavanagh (2009) and Wright (2009); for a critical view, see Ewing (2004) and Ewing and Tham (2008). On the implications for the courts of devolution, see especially Craig and Walters (1999). On the implications of the creation of the Supreme Court, see Le

Sueur (2004) for a detailed legal analysis of its role in the United Kingdom and Norton (2005) for a brief consideration of its constitutional implications. On the Constitutional Reform Act, see Windlesham (2005). On the abolition of the role of Lord Chancellor, see Oliver (2004).

Bibliography

Alder, J. (2005) *Constitutional and Administrative Law*, 5th edn (Palgrave Macmillan).

Banner, C. and Deane, A. (2003) *Off with their Wigs: Judicial Revolution in Modern Britain* (Imprint Academic).

Bingham, Lord (2002) *A New Supreme Court for the United Kingdom* (The Constitution Unit).

Blackburn, R. (1997) 'A Bill of Rights for the 21st Century', in Blackburn, R. and Busuttil, J. (eds) *Human Rights for the 21st Century* (Pinter).

Bradley, A.W. (1994) 'The Sovereignty of Parliament – in Perpetuity?', in Jowell, J. and Oliver, D. (eds) *The Changing Constitution*, 3rd edn (Oxford University Press).

Bradley, A.W. (2008) 'Relations Between the Executive, Judiciary and Parliament: an Evolving Saga?' *Public Law*, Autumn.

Bradley, A.W. and Ewing, K.D. (1997) *Constitutional and Administrative Law*, 12th edn (Longman).

Bradley, A.W. and Ewing, K.D. (2007) *Constitutional and Administrative Law*, 14th edn (Longman).

Constitution Committee, House of Lords (2012) *Judicial Appointments*, 25th Report, Session 2010–12, HL Paper 272 (The Stationery Office).

Craig, P. and Walters, M. (1999) 'The Courts, Devolution and Judicial Review', *Public Law*, Summer.

Drewry, G. (1986) 'Judges and Politics in Britain', *Social Studies Review*, November.

Drewry, G. (1991) 'Judicial Independence in Britain: Challenges Real and Threats Imagined', in Norton, P. (ed.) *New Directions in British Politics?* (Edward Elgar).

Ewing, K. (2004) 'The Futility of the Human Rights Act', *Public Law*, Winter.

Ewing, K. and Tham, J. (2008) 'The Continuing Futility of the Human Rights Act', *Public Law*, Winter.

Fitzpatrick, B. (1999) 'A Dualist House of Lords in a Sea of Monist Community Law', in Dickson, B. and Carmichael, P. (eds) *The House of Lords: Its Parliamentary and Judicial Roles* (Hart Publishing).

Forsyth, C. (ed.) (2000) *Judicial Review and the Constitution* (Hart Publishing).

Griffith, J.A.G. (1997) *The Politics of the Judiciary*, 5th edn (Fontana).

Harlow, C. (1991) 'The Legal System', in Catterall, P. (ed.) *Contemporary Britain: An Annual Review* (Blackwell).

Home Office (1998) *Rights Brought Home: The Human Rights Bill*, Cm 3782 (Stationery Office).

Irvine of Lairg, Lord (1998) 'The Development of Human Rights in Britain under an Incorporated Convention on Human Rights', *Public Law*, Summer.

Jackson, P. and Leopold, P. (2001) *O. Hood Phillips and Jackson, Constitutional and Administrative Law*, 8th edn (Sweet & Maxwell).

Jacobs, F. (1999) 'Public Law – the Impact of Europe', *Public Law*, Summer.

Jowell, J. (2003) 'Judicial Deference: Servility, Civility or Institutional Capacity?' *Public Law*, Winter.

Kavanagh, A. (2009) 'Judging the Judges under the Human Rights Act: Deference, Disillusionment and the "War on Terror"', *Public Law*, April.

Klug, F. and O'Brien, C. (2002) 'The First Two Years of the Human Rights Act', *Public Law*, Winter.

Klug, F. and Starmer, K. (2001) 'Incorporation Through the "Front Door": The First Year of the Human Rights Act', *Public Law*, Winter.

Le Sueur, A. (ed.) (2004) *Building the UK's New Supreme Court: National and Comparative Perspectives* (Oxford University Press).

Le Sueur, A. and Malleson, K. (2008) 'The Judiciary', in Hazell, E. (ed.) *Constitutional Futures Revisited* (Palgrave Macmillan).

Lester, Lord (1994) 'European Human Rights and the British Constitution', in Jowell, J. and Oliver, D. (eds) *The Changing Constitution*, 3rd edn (Oxford University Press).

Loveland, I. (2003) 'Britain and Europe', in Bogdanor, V. (ed.) *The British Constitution in the Twentieth Century* (British Academy/Oxford University Press).

Maxwell, P. (1999) 'The House of Lords as a Constitutional Court – the Implications of *Ex Parte EOC*', in Dickson, B.

and Carmichael, P. (eds) *The House of Lords: Its Parliamentary and Judicial Roles* (Hart Publishing).

McEldowney, J. (1996) *Public Law* (Sweet & Maxwell).

McEldowney, J. (1998) 'Legal Aspects of Relations Between the United Kingdom and the Scottish Parliament: the Evolution of Subordinate Sovereignty?', in Oliver, D. and Drewry, G. (eds) *The Law and Parliament* (Butterworth).

Mullin, C. (1996) 'Miscarriages of Justice', *The Journal of Legislative Studies*, vol. 2, no. 2.

Munro, C. (1987) *Studies in Constitutional Law* (Butterworth).

Munro, C. (1992) '*Factortame* and the Constitution', *Inter Alia*, vol. 1, no. 1.

Nolan, Lord and Sedley, Sir S. (1997) *The Making and Remaking of the British Constitution* (Blackstone Press).

Norton, P. (1982) *The Constitution in Flux* (Blackwell).

Norton, P. (2005) 'Parliament and the Courts', in Baldwin, N.D.J. (ed.) *Parliament in the 21st Century* (Politico's).

Norton, P. (2006) 'The Constitution: Selective Incrementalism', in Rush, M. and Giddings, P. (eds) *The Palgrave Review of British Politics* (Palgrave Macmillan).

Oliver, D. (2004) 'Constitutionalism and the Abolition of the Office of the Lord Chancellor', *Parliamentary Affairs*, vol. 57.

Rozenberg, J. (1999) 'The *Pinochet* Case and Cameras in Court', *Public Law*, Summer.

Scarman, Lord (1974) *English Law – The New Dimensions* (Stevens).

Shah, S. and Poole, T. (2009) 'The Impact of the Human Rights Act on the House of Lords', *Public Law*, April.

Stevens, R. (2002) *The English Judges* (Hart Publishing).

Stevens, R. (2003) 'Government and the Judiciary', in Bogdanor, V. (ed.) *The British Constitution in the Twentieth Century* (British Academy/Oxford University Press).

Wade, E.C.S. and Bradley, A.W. (1993) *Constitutional and Administrative Law*, 11th edn, A.W. Bradley and K.D. Ewing (eds) (Longman).

Walker, C. and Starmer, K. (1999) *Miscarriages of Justice* (Blackstone Press).

Windlesham, Lord (2005) 'The Constitutional Reform Act 2005: Ministers, Judges and Constitutional Change', *Public Law*, Winter.

Woodhouse, D. (1996) 'Politicians and the Judges: A Conflict of Interest', *Parliamentary Affairs*, vol. 49, no. 3.

Woodhouse, D. (2002) 'The Law and Politics: In the Shadow of the Human Rights Act', *Parliamentary Affairs*, vol. 55, no. 2.

Wright, J. (2009) 'Interpreting Section 2 of the Human Rights Act 1998: Towards an Indigenous Jurisprudence of Human Rights', *Public Law*, July.

Zander, M. (1989) *A Matter of Justice*, revised edn (Oxford University Press).

Useful websites

Judicial process in the UK

Court Service: www.hmcourts-service.gov.uk/

Criminal Cases Review Commission:
www.ccrc.gov.uk/index.htm

Criminal Justice System – England and Wales:
www.cjsonline.gov.uk/

Judicial Committee of the Privy Council:
www.privy-council.org.uk/output/page5.asp

Judiciary of England and Wales:
www.judiciary.gov.uk/index.htm

Magistrates' Association: www.judiciary.gov.uk/index.htm

Ministry of Justice: www.judiciary.gov.uk/index.htm

Supreme Court: www.supremecourt.gov.uk/index.html

Other relevant sites

European Court of Justice (ECJ):
http://europa.eu/institutions/inst/justice/index_en.htm

European Court of Human Rights: www.echr.coe.int/echr/

Why do governments always disappoint?

Enoch Powell famously said, 'All political lives, unless they are cut off in midstream at a happy juncture, end in failure, because that is the nature of politics and of human affairs'. The same is true of governments. They come in on a wave of euphoria, with high expectations riding on their shoulders, and depart one, two or three terms later compromised and riddled with distrust. Why do governments always disappoint?

Partly it is our fault as electors. We expect too much. Even when governments make relatively modest promises, as we did with our five pledges in 1997, the public project on to a new government all their hopes and wishes, and not all of them can be delivered. Voters often wish for contradictory things, like higher spending and lower taxes. When politicians make the difficult choices between those options they inevitably lose the support of part of the population. And if they make no difficult choices, they rapidly lose the support of all the population. We expect governments to be able to solve complex problems in modern society that often can't be solved by the state, or at least not by the state alone.

When we arrived in No. 10 Downing Street in May 1997 I was struck by the illusory nature of power. Before the election I thought it would be easy to make a difference, but once we came to pull on the levers of power we rapidly realised they weren't connected to anything. That realisation leads politicians to believe that real power lies somewhere else, and they start eyeing newspaper proprietors enviously, convinced they possibly have it. Bill Clinton famously said a couple of years after becoming President that he hoped when he died he would be reborn as someone with real power, like a member of a focus group in Macomb County (the key swing district of Michigan).

In *The Prince* Niccolo Machiavelli describes with admiration the way in which Cesare Borgia was able to wield power absolutely and make decisive moves that left his opponents paralysed. In developed democracies, however, power is not in the hands of the leader but widely diffused throughout society. Other members of the government, the civil service, Parliament, interest groups and the press act as a complicated system of checks and balances to prevent radical change happening. They are deliberately, and happily, built into our system to prevent dictatorship but they lead to the sort of sclerosis Mancur Olson describes in mature economic systems. The guilty secret of the British political system is that, far from a Prime Minister with a large majority in Parliament having untrammelled power, he is actually enormously constrained. He has to govern by influencing people, building coalitions and cajoling his colleagues into doing what he wants.

One of the biggest constraints on action by governments is the civil service. The frustration in dealing with the mandarins led Tony Blair to speak in 1999 about 'the scars on his back' and David Cameron in 2010 to attack the 'risk averse culture' of the civil service. The problem is that the civil service resembles a monastic order. Its members still, by and large, join after university and retire at 60. They have no experience of the outside world and they are remarkably resistant to change, so that 'Yes, Prime Minister' often seems to those inside the system more like a documentary than a farce. Civil servants have seen it all before and it is hard for them not to become cynical. Soon after we had arrived in Downing Street the Home Office gave us a presentation in the Cabinet Room, complete with coloured graphs, showing that crime would rise inexorably during our time in government. Tony asked why crime was projected to rise, and they replied because the economy would grow and there would be more to steal. I asked what would happen if there was a recession and, without missing a beat, they replied that crime would grow because there would be more poor people who needed to steal to get by.

We tried to change the one-way bet that civil servants face: if they change things and it goes wrong they are punished, but if they change things and it succeeds they get no recognition. Naturally they avoid taking risks. The answer is to make named individuals responsible for delivering the implementation of policies. They should be rewarded if they succeed and held accountable if they fail, rather than allowing everyone just to blame the system.

The problem with the civil service is not just their mind set but also their skill set. The main way to advancement is still through the traditional policy skills of the mandarin, and there are not enough project managers or those versed in IT. If we ever hired anyone from outside with those skills and paid them the market rate, we would be attacked by the *Daily Mail* in full baying-for-blood mode. But it is well worth the taxpayer paying an expert £1 million a year to sort out the Immigration and Nationality Department in terms of the savings it would make.

It is not good enough, however, just to blame the civil servants for the failure of government to deliver. It is also the fault of politicians. Machiavelli advises princes to be bold and take difficult steps all at once rather than spin them out agonisingly over years. We didn't take that advice and were too timid when we came to office. We were desperate to be the first Labour government to be elected for two full terms. As a result we hoarded political capital rather than spending it. We should have taken advantage of the political momentum provided by our election victory and pressed ahead with radical reform of the public services, but we were frightened of provoking a row within the party by attempting to be too radical and tried to do it instead by gradual steps. Over time opposition builds up, and steps that would have been easy in the first flush of victory become increasingly difficult. There is also a learning process in government. After we had been in power a few months, Tony remarked to me that it felt as if the government machine was a shiny Rolls-Royce parked outside Downing Street which he was not allowed to drive. By the time we left government we had mastered it.

Machiavelli accurately describes the challenge facing reformers: 'He who innovates will have as his enemies all those who are well off under the existing order of things, and only lukewarm supporters in those who might be better off under the new.' The problem is that in an endeavour like reforming the health or education systems the government faces strong vested interests opposed to reform for self-interested reasons. But the public, who will gain from the reforms, are not convinced of the advantages till they have seen them first hand. It is particularly complicated when it is the very vested interests you are taking on that are the same people that have to implement the reforms. Then you have to cajole them and persuade them into taking steps that may hurt their interests.

In government it is all too easy as Harold Macmillan said to be driven by 'events, dear boy, events', and to let the urgent crowd out the important. If a government is to change anything in a lasting way, it needs to be strategic and proactive, rather than merely reactive. That means choosing a very limited number of priorities, something politicians find hard to do when they are constantly under pressure to make everything better. One of the only sound bites I ever came up with for Tony Blair was 'education, education, education'. It set out pithily what I thought our top three priorities should be, and we would probably have been better off if we had kept that unyielding focus. But strategy is also a matter of time management. When we came into power we discovered that John Major had been scheduled with meetings every half hour from nine in the morning till nine at night. He had no time to stand back and think about where he was going. We insisted on reserving time for Tony to think about the big picture every day and even inserted fake meetings into his diary to keep the time blocked out.

Politicians and civil servants and we, the public, are therefore all to blame for the fact that governments always disappoint in the end. What has changed in the modern world in particular is the speed of events. It used to take two or three years before we became tired of celebrities. Now it is two or three months, and the same is true of governments. Our attention span is much reduced, and our patience wears out much more rapidly. Even though they are not enshrined in law, we now have de facto term limits which mean that no government can last more than 10 years. So, governments may always disappoint, but at least they can't disappoint us for very long.

by Jonathan Powell

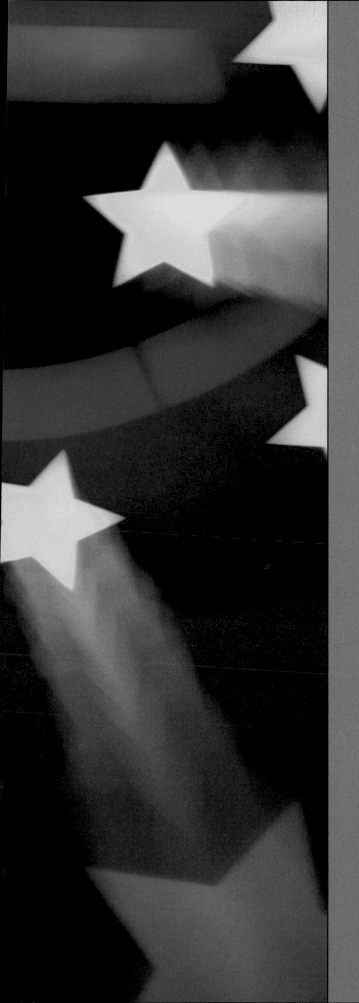

PART 6

THE POLICY PROCESS

CHAPTER 22

The policy-making process

Bill Jones

> " Surround yourself with the best people you can find, delegate authority, and don't interfere as long as the policy you've decided upon is being carried out "
>
> Ronald Reagan

Learning objectives

- To define policy in government.
- To encourage familiarity with the most popular models of policy making.
- To examine the notion of the policy process.
- To give some examples of questionable policy making.

This chapter examines the anatomy of policy and policy making in central government, focusing on its stages together with some theories relating to the process before concluding with a look at two case studies where outcome failed to match expectations. Accordingly, the chapter delves briefly into the complex area of policy studies, an area that has attracted attention, because it deals with political outcomes and draws together so many elements, embodying so much of the political universe: process, influence, power and pressure as well as the impact of personality. Consequently, policy studies has emerged as a kind of sub-discipline with some claim to be a focus for a social science approach to human interaction involving such subjects as psychology, sociology, economics, history, philosophy and political science. Policy studies was essentially born in the USA, so much of it focuses on American examples and policy environments; but more generally it draws on public policy in Western liberal democracies as a whole. The Bibliography provides an introduction to some of the voluminous literature in the field.

Introduction

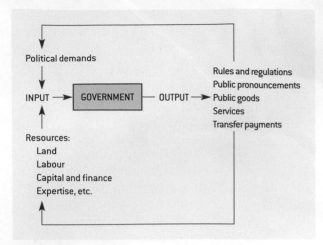

Figure 22.1 The policy process
Source: Burch (1979)

How policy is made

Policy can be defined as a set of ideas and proposals for action culminating in a government decision; to study policy, therefore, is to study how decisions are made. Government decisions can take many forms: Burch (1979: 108) distinguishes between two broad kinds, as follows:

1 Rules, regulations and public pronouncements (e.g. Acts of Parliament, Orders in Council, White Papers, ministerial and departmental circulars).

2 Public expenditure and its distribution: the government spends some £700 billion per annum, mostly on public goods and services (e.g. education, hospitals) and transfer payments (e.g. social security payments and unemployment benefit).

Figure 22.1 portrays the government as a system that has as its input **political demands** together with resources available and its 'output' as the different kinds of government decision. The latter impact on society and influence future 'inputs', so the process is circular and constant.

Both Burch and Wood (1990) and Jordan and Richardson (1987) review a number of different analyses as 'models': possible or approximate versions of what happens in reality. Eight of these are summarised below. For a fuller account of the available models, see Parsons (1995), John (1998), Hill (2000) and Dorey (2006).

Models of policy making

1 *The conventional model*: This is the 'official' explanation of policy making found in Central Office of Information publications and the utterances of civil servants in public (though seldom in private). This maintains that Parliament represents and interprets the public will through its representatives, who support government ministers, who formulate executive policies, which are thereupon faithfully and impartially implemented by civil servants. The notion that a 'thin red line' of democracy connects voters with civil servants via the nominee of a political party in Parliament strikes many as tenuous but this is the officially sanctioned theory of how policy is made.

2 *The ruling-class model*: This is effectively the Marxist assertion, that those empowered with taking key decisions in the state – civil servants and politicians – subscribe consciously or unconsciously to the values of the dominant economic class, the property-owning upper middle classes. It follows that 'the executive of the modern state is but a committee for managing the common affairs of the whole bourgeoisie' (Marx and Engels 1848). According to this view, most policy outputs will have the effect of protecting dominant group interests. It also assumes that the superstructure of democracy is all false, hiding the true 'hegemony' of the economic class. Ralph Miliband (1969) provides a good analysis of this approach (though, ironically, one of his sons is now a key person in this very system); for a summary of the argument see John (1998: Chapter 5).

The following two models attribute decisive importance to differing elements within the political system.

3 *The pluralist model*: This is often associated with the US political scientist Robert Dahl. It assumes that power is dispersed within society to the various interest groups that constitute it – business, labour, agriculture, and so forth – and that they can 'make themselves heard effectively at some crucial stage in the process of decision' (Jordan and Richardson 1987: 16). According to this view, interest groups interact and negotiate policy with each other in a kind of free market, with government acting as a more or less neutral referee.

4 *Corporatism*: This is associated with the work of Philippe Schmitter and is offered as an alternative to pluralism. This model perceives an alliance between ministers, civil servants and the leaders of pressure groups in which the latter are given a central role in the policy-making process in exchange for exerting pressure upon their members to conform with or accept government decisions. In this view, therefore, interest groups become an extension – or even a quasi-form – of government. Corporatism has also been used pejoratively by British politicians of the left (Benn), right (Thatcher) and centre (Owen) to describe the decision-making style of the much criticised 1974–9 Labour Government.

The next two models ascribe key importance to two specific elements of the system.

5 *The party government model*: The stress here is on political parties and the assertion that they provide the major channel for policy formulation. Some, like Wilensky (1975), regard 'politics' as peripheral to the formation of policy, while others, like Castles (1989) maintain that the agenda is shaped by the processes of liberal democracy (Parsons 1995: section 2.11).

6 *The Whitehall model*: This contends that civil servants either initiate major policy or so alter it as it passes through their hands as to make it substantially theirs – thus making them the key influence on policy. Allison (1971) argued that bureaucracies do not meekly do the bidding of elected masters but are fragmented, competing centres of power: in John's words, 'Policy often arrives as the outcome of an uncoordinated fight between government bureaus' (John 1998: 44). Ministers discuss possible future actions with their very experienced and able advisers. If a trusted senior civil servant advises against a new initiative, this is bound to give the minister pause for more thought and adjustments might be made or the idea might even be dropped completely. Whitehall is not just 'in the loop' of policy making, *it is an essential part* of this loop.

The final two theories concentrate upon the way in which decision makers set about their tasks.

7 *Rational decision making*: This approach assumes that decision makers behave in a logical, sequential fashion. Accordingly, they will identify their objectives, formulate possible strategies, think through their implications and finally choose the course of action that on balance best achieves their objectives. This approach is consistent with the traditional model in that civil servants undertake the analysis and then offer up the options for popularly elected politicians to take the decisions (see Parsons 1995: section 3.4; John 1998: Chapter 6).

8 *Incrementalism*: This approach, associated with the hugely influential work of Charles Lindblom, denies that policy makers are so rational and argues that in practice they usually try to cope or 'muddle through'. They tend to start with the status quo and make what adjustments they can to manage or at least accommodate new situations. In other words, policy makers do not solve problems but merely adjust to them. The case of privatisation argues against this 'adjusting' approach in that when Nigel Lawson came to consider it in the early 1980s the cupboard, in terms of relevant files and experience, was totally bare. Instead, Conservative ministers had to devise wholly new approaches and, whatever one's views on the outcome, it is perhaps to their credit that – even

allowing for a determined Prime Minister and a large majority – they succeeded in a government culture so resistant to radical innovation.

It is clear that most of these models are basically descriptive, while others, like the rational choice and conventional models, are also partially prescriptive – they offer an ideal approach as to how policies should be made – but cannot necessarily tell us how decisions are actually made.

It is also obvious that echoing somewhere within each approach is the ring of truth. It would not be too difficult to find examples in support of any of the above models. The truth is that policy making is such a protean, dense area of activity that it is extremely difficult to generalise and be accurate in all cases. Nevertheless, the search for valid statements is worth the effort, otherwise our political system will remain incomprehensible. We will therefore look at the process in greater detail in a search for some generally true propositions about it.

The policy cycle

If they agree on nothing else, policy study scholars seem to agree that policy making can be understood better as a **policy cycle**; a problem arrives on the agenda and is processed by the system until an answer is found. Analyses of the cycle can be quite sophisticated. Hogwood and Gunn (1984) discern a number of stages: deciding to decide (issue search and agenda setting); deciding how to decide; issue definition, forecasting; setting objectives and priorities; options analysis; policy implementation, monitoring and control; evaluation and review; and policy maintenance, succession or termination. However, Lindblom disagrees. He argues that 'Deliberate or orderly steps . . . are not an accurate portrayal of how the policy process actually works. Policy making is, instead, a complexly interactive process without beginning or end' (Lindblom and Woodhouse 1993: 11, quoted in Parsons 1995: 22). However, policy studies can appear overly abstract and removed from reality at times; for the limited purposes of this chapter, three easily understood stages will suffice: initiation, formulation and implementation. These are considered below, but first a brief look at how 'problems' come to be defined as such and how they come to be seen as requiring solutions.

'Social construction' of problems

This concept appears in Dorey (2006: 8–11) and relates to the evolving nature of things requiring action. In the nineteenth century women were denied certain basic rights and could even be beaten or raped by their husbands. It has taken a long while, but societal values have changed so that women have acquired the vote and legal protection against what is now seen as abuse. Similarly homosexuals – once persecuted and imprisoned – are now allowed to be themselves outside the reach of the criminal law. Attitudes towards legal drug use (alcohol, nicotine) and illegal use (cannabis, heroin, cocaine) are also in a constant state of change and influence related frameworks (for example, smoking is now seen as seriously unhealthy and is banned in workplaces).

Dorey also points out how wider values and ideological changes influence political action. Poverty was once not seen as a problem – prosperity was a personal responsibility – but by the twentieth century Liberal ideology was becoming the new orthodoxy; tax-funded state assistance began to be introduced to alleviate problems of old age, illness and unemployment. Moreover, the extension of the vote to lower socio-economic strata, meant 'inaction' – which favoured employers and owners of property – was no longer so easy to maintain.

Agenda setting

John Kingdon (1995, see Dorey 2006: 27–31) perceived it necessary for three 'streams' to conjoin for an item to be added to public policy: the recognition of something as a problem (problem stream); the identification of possible solutions (policy stream); and the requisite opportunities – time, accession to power of a party prepared to act and so forth (political stream). For example, poverty was not seen as a legitimate concern of government until Liberalism and Socialism emerged to suggest it might be and no action was taken until the Liberal and Labour parties gained power for periods in the twentieth century.

Policy initiation

Agenda setting

Each government decision has a long and complex provenance, but all must start somewhere. It is tempting to think that they originate, eureka-like, in the minds of single individuals, but they are more often the product of debate or a general climate of opinion involving many minds. Policy initiatives, moreover, can originate in all parts of the political system. Setting the political agenda is a curiously elusive process. Items can be deliberately introduced by government, and clearly it has many routes available to it: for example, Tony Blair in the summer of 1999 announcing in an interview that fox hunting really *would* be banned; or Blair again, announcing, in the wake of the 'cash for peerages' scandal in March 2006, that greater transparency would be introduced regarding loans to political parties. The media too have enormous power to set the agenda: Michael Buerk's reports from Ethiopia detailing a scale of famine that touched the nation and initiated assistance; Alan Milburn, in an interview on 9 April 2006, refusing to say he would not be a candidate for the leadership when Blair stood down.

Figure 22.2 depicts six groups of possible policy initiators placed on a continuum starting from the periphery and moving in towards the nerve centre of government in No. 10. The figure uses the idea of 'distance from the centre', capturing the truth that the routes into policy making are many and varied (see also Parsons 1995: section 2.4).

General public

The public's role in policy making is usually limited to (the democratically vital function of) voting for a particular policy package at general elections. They do have other

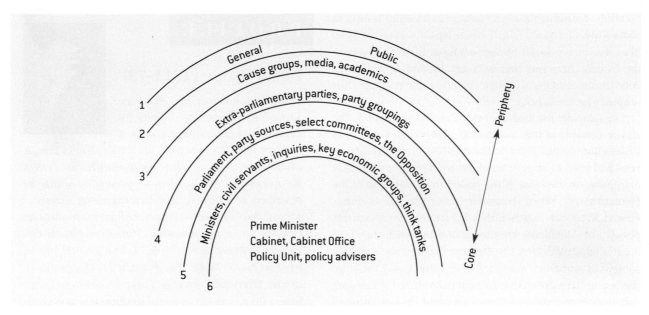

Figure 22.2 Policy initiatives

occasional opportunities, however – for example, the referenda on the EC and Scottish and Welsh devolution in the 1970s, and pressures can be built up through lobbying MPs, as when, in the mid-1980s, Sir Keith Joseph was forced to withdraw his proposals to charge parents for a proportion of their children's university tuition fees. Occasionally, events occur that create widespread public concern, and governments often take action in the wake of them. For example, legislation on dogs was enacted after a spate of attacks by dogs on children one summer in the 1980s, and handguns were banned after the Dunblane shootings of March 1996. In many cases – as in the two just cited – such precipitate action, in reaction to the sudden rousing of public opinion, proves to be poorly framed and receives much criticism. In more recent years public opinion has been roused by the proposed fox hunting ban and the war in Iraq in spring 2003. Both attracted huge demonstrations in London; in the former case they had some observable effect in delaying and altering proposed measures, but in the latter case Tony Blair carried on, convinced that he was right, and ignored the public outcry. However, the repercussions and damage of ignoring public and party opposition may take years to make themselves felt; what is without doubt is that Blair paid a heavy price in political support for ignoring the Iraq outcry.

Cause groups, media and academic experts

Many cause groups (see also Chapter 10) operate in the 'wilderness' – their values antithetical to government and not listened to – and many also stay there, but some do influence public opinion and decision makers and after years of struggle achieve action on issues such as abortion,

capital punishment and the environment. Others achieve success on specific issues after an extended period of campaigning, such as Des Wilson's 1960s and 1970s campaign to reduce lead in petrol. Some groups achieve success via a single, well-publicised event such as the Countryside Alliance's march on the Labour Party conference in 1999, which caused the government to postpone action on fox hunting during the succeeding session (despite Blair's assurances that he would act). Certain policy 'environments' will include a bewildering array of pressure groups, all of which seek to lean on the policy-making tiller. Local government associations, for example, are particularly important in areas like education, housing and social services.

Media coverage heavily affects the climate in which policy is discussed, and important policy proposals occasionally emerge from television programmes, newspaper editorials, articles in journals and so forth. One editorial on its own would have little effect, but a near consensus in the press might well stimulate action. Occasionally ideas are picked up from individual journalists – Mrs Thatcher used to be advised regularly by right-wing journalists such as Woodrow Wyatt, Paul Johnson and Simon Heffer. Other media figures who used to be consulted regularly on policy matters by Margaret Thatcher included the press magnates Rupert Murdoch and Conrad Black. Murdoch was also rumoured to advise Blair whenever he chose to visit Downing Street and where, because of his massive media clout, he was assured of a warm welcome. One commentator even argued Murdoch was virtually an additional member of the Cabinet (Wilby 2006). We also know that a wide range of influential people were regularly invited to dine with the Blairs at the PM's official rural retreat, Chequers, and almost certainly dinner-table conversation occasionally results in some kind of action. Lord Levy, a tennis partner of Tony Blair, eventually found himself acting as Blair's emissary to the Middle East and later as a key fundraiser (in March 2006 controversially so, when the 'loans for peerages' row erupted) for the Labour Party.

Occasionally the media provide crucial information. The classic example of this was in 1987, when Nigel Lawson, as Chancellor, denied entry to the ERM by prime ministerial veto, had tried to achieve his object by other means, namely manipulating the value of the pound to shadow that of the Deutschmark. When *Financial Times* journalists interviewed Margaret Thatcher, they questioned her about this policy. She denied any knowledge of it but when they produced definitive evidence in the form of charts she accepted, somewhat surprised, that they were correct, and the stage was set for the mammoth argument that resulted in Lawson's damaging resignation two years later and the beginning of the end of her reign in No. 10 (for more on the media and agenda setting, see Parsons 1995: section 2.3).

All these agencies in the 'outer rim' (see Figure 22.2) interact to provide that intangible climate of discussion that encourages the emergence of certain proposals and inhibits others. Each policy environment has its own climate created by its specialist press, pressure groups, academics, practitioners and the like, who frequently meet in conferences and on advisory committees. Specific policy environments therefore exist in their 'own' world but also exist in a wider, overarching reality – e.g. an economic recession, an overseas war – which sets limits to and influences policy content.

However, an interesting feature of these peripheral bodies is that from time to time they are blessed with favour, their arguments listened to, their proposals adopted, their leaders embraced by government and given advisory or even executive status. It is almost as if, godlike, the government has reached down and plucked them up to place them – albeit temporarily – on high.

Part 2 of this book explained how policy emerged out of an ideological framework and pointed out how academics, philosophers and other thinkers had contributed towards these frameworks. The most obvious influences on the Left would include Karl Marx, R.H. Tawney, Harold Laski, William Beveridge and, incomparably in the economic sphere, J.M. Keynes. Right-wing writers would include figures such as David Hume and Michael Oakeshott and (on economics from the 1970s onwards) the two overseas academics Friedrich Hayek and Milton Friedman. Academics specialising in specific policy areas such as transport, housing, criminology and so forth also regularly come up with proposals, some of which are taken up or drawn upon. John Major welcomed the views of the so-called 'seven wise men' (selected academics) on economic policy. Blair

PROFILE

David Hume (1711–73)

Scottish philosopher and historian. Studied in Edinburgh – where his depressive temperament meant it took time for him to settle – but went to live in France, where he wrote his *Treatise on Human Nature* (1739). He questioned the validity of principles, which he described as 'artificial', and challenged the notion of natural law as well as the social contract ideas of Hobbes, Locke and Rousseau. Hume was bitterly disappointed when his opus failed to make much impact, but his *Essays Moral and Political* (1743), produced shortly afterwards, was an instant success and confirmed his reputation as one of the founding, and greatest, British empiricist philosophers of his age.

PROFILE

Michael Oakeshott (1901–90)

Conservative philosopher. Educated at Cambridge, where he taught until 1949. *Experience and its Modes* (1933) was his first notable work. His writings lie within the pragmatic, sceptical traditions of Conservative thinking. He did not believe the purpose of politics was to achieve any particular end; rather, he saw the politicians' role as guiding the ship of state, enabling people to live their lives. He was a professor at the London School of Economics from 1950 to 1969.

and Brown established a formal committee called the Monetary Policy Committee comprising academics and financial experts who every month advise the Bank of England on interest rates. On other occasions, academics can suddenly be welcomed in by leading figures in government, as when sociologist Anthony Giddens was used by Blair as a kind of 'guru' regarding the formulation of 'Third Way' thinking.

Extra-parliamentary parties and party groupings

Both the Labour and Conservative extra-parliamentary parties find it easier to influence their respective leaders in opposition than in government. As Chapter 10 noted, Labour's system of internal democracy gave a substantial

Lord Giddens, Blair's sociologist guru on Third Way thinking
Source: Press Association Images/Associated Press

policy-making role to the trade unions, the National Executive Committee and the party conference during the 1930s and up until the 1970s (New Labour somewhat emasculated conference during and since the 1990s). The Conservative Party is far less democratic, but conference can set the mood for policy formulation, the research department can initiate important proposals, and the Advisory Committee on Policy did much to reformulate the main outlines of Conservative policy in the late 1970s.

Party groupings – many of which have contacts with Parliament – can also exert influence. The Fabian Society, founded in 1884, has long acted as a kind of left-wing think tank (see Box 22.2), and in the 1980s the once left-wing Labour Coordinating Committee was influential in advising Neil Kinnock as he shifted Labour's policies towards the centre. Similarly, the No Turning Back Group in the Conservatives sought to keep the party on the right-wing track indicated by their heroine Margaret Thatcher, both before and after her fall from power, and it took the 'Cameron uprising' in the autumn of 2005 to remove what many perceived as its dead hand. The Institute for Public Policy Research (IPPR) has established itself over the past decade as a kind of Labour think tank, constantly on hand to feed in relevant ideas and research findings.

Parliament

The role of Parliament in initiating policy can be considered under two headings: party sources and party groups, and non-party sources. In government, parliamentary parties have to work through their backbench committees, although individual MPs seek to use their easy access to ministers to exert influence and press their own solutions. One Conservative MP, David Evans, pulled off the remarkable coup of convincing his Prime Minister that the identity card system introduced by Luton Town Football Club should be compulsorily introduced nationwide. His success was short-lived: the scheme was dropped in January 1990 (though it did not die – see the section on identity cards towards the end of this chapter).

The Opposition is concerned to prepare its policies for when and if it takes over the reins of government. Neil Kinnock wrested future policy making out of the party's NEC with his policy review exercise (1987–9), involving leading members of his frontbench team in the process. However, the Opposition also has to make policy 'on the hoof' in reaction to political events. It is their function and in their interests to oppose, to offer alternatives to government – but this is not easy. Opposition spokesmen lack the detailed information and support enjoyed by government; they need to react to events in a way that is consistent with their other policy positions; they need to provide enough detail to offer a credible alternative, yet avoid 'hostages to fortune' and closing options should they come to power. The Conservatives after 1997 found it hard to perform as an effective Opposition, through splits in their ranks and uncertain leadership. Most commentators judged that this was not good for the health of the nation's democracy; the election of the young and dynamic new leader, David Cameron, in

BOX 22.2

Think tanks

Mrs Thatcher regained her momentum partly because she discovered 'Thatcherism': a new set of ideas comprising the abolition of constraints in the economy, privatising state-owned enterprises and reform of the public sector. These ideas were provided by the intelligentsia of the 'New Right', many of them working through think tanks (*The Economist*, 18 November 1992).

After the demise of Thatcher in 1990 these American-style independent hot-houses of ideas receded. The Centre for Policy Studies (CPS) used to issue a report every fortnight, but with Major in power rather than its original patron, its output slowed to zero. The output of the Adam Smith Institute (ASI), once a pioneer in privatisation ideas, also slowed and with Blair in power it was reduced to producing a complimentary report on his first 200 days. The Institute for Economic Affairs (IEA) was the oldest right-wing think tank, but it also curtailed its activities once Thatcher had gone. It also has to be said that the disaster of the 'poll tax', a product of the ASI, contributed to its declining respect. And the splits did not help: Graham Mather left the IEA to form his own European Policy Forum, while David Willetts at the CPS left after criticism to become an MP and director of the Social Market Foundation.

Labour was relatively light on think tanks, but the Fabian Society, set up by the Webbs in 1884, has effectively been a highly influential think tank for over 100 years. It still exists with an impressive membership from the public and the parliamentary party. It organises seminars and conferences and keeps up a good flow of pamphlets and serious studies, a post-1997 one being the work of a certain Tony Blair. In addition, at the current time there is the Institute for Public Policy Research (IPPR), which is seen as a Labour–learning think tank. Demos – initially headed by Geoff Mulgan before he became a No. 10 adviser is now led by David Goodhart. Are think tank personnel merely seeking to enter politics and become MPs? According to Tom Clougherty, the young director of the ASI, during a student study group visit in March 2009, his role gave him far more influence than any MP might exert. Certainly many think-tank personnel have made the journey into senior advisory or ministerial positions – for example, David Miliband (IPPR), John Redwood (Centre Policy Studies) and Geoff Mulgan (Demos) (see Dorey 2006: 19–26).

December 2005 transformed this situation. Unsurprisingly, he initially poured energy into changing the unpopular image and 'brand' of his party, and his policy statements were little more than statements of intent, designed to drag the party into the middle ground on social justice and the environment. Creating detailed policies, announced Oliver Letwin in April 2006, would take another 18 months of focused effort. Received wisdom for oppositions is that such exercises are best left until close to the election; an abiding problem for oppositions is that any good ideas they might come up with can be stolen by government and represented as its own.

Party groups (some of which have membership outside Parliament) such as the Bow Group, Monday Club, Tribune and Campaign Group can all have peripheral – but rarely direct – influence on policy making.

The 17 departmental select committees regularly make reports and recommendations, some of which are adopted. Most experts agree that these committees are much more important now that their proceedings can be televised, especially the Treasury Committee which summoned so many senior finance people for interrogation in the wake of the banking collapse in 2008. Most reports represent cross-party consensus on specific issues but others, such as the Social Services Committee, once chaired by the much admired (and briefly a minister) Frank Field, can offer wide-ranging and coherent alternatives to government policy. Individual MPs probably have a better chance of influencing specific, usually very specific, policy areas through the opportunities available to move private members' bills (see Chapter 15).

Failure to utilise the policy-making machinery provided by the governing party can lead to dissent. In May 2003 certain Labour MPs were complaining that the Prime Minister, set on ignoring Parliament, was now introducing policy – especially that relating to universities – that had originated wholly in his own office and not at all in the governing party. Party critics claimed 'top-up fees' in higher education in the autumn of 2003 was the product of Downing Street adviser Andrew Adonis – appointed and not elected, of course. After a cliff-hanging process of accommodation by the government of these internal criticisms, the bill eventually became an Act on 27 January 2004 by a majority of only five. Adonis was later elevated to the peerage and made Schools Minister after the 2005 election.

Ministers, departments, official inquiries and 'think tanks'

Strong-minded ministers will always develop policy ideas of their own either as a reflection of their own convictions or to get noticed and further their ambitions. Michael Heseltine, in the wake of the Toxteth troubles, probably shared both motivations when he submitted a paper to the Cabinet called 'It Took a Riot', proposing a new and un-Thatcherite approach to inner-city regeneration: the policy was not accepted by Cabinet but was partially implemented in Merseyside, though not elsewhere. Such major initiatives are not the province of civil servants, but through their day-to-day involvement in running the country they are constantly proposing detailed improvements and adjustments to existing arrangements. Such initiatives are not necessarily the preserve of senior officials: even junior officers can propose changes that can be taken up and implemented.

A Royal Commission can be the precursor to major policy changes (for example, the Redcliffe–Maud Royal Commission on Local Government, 1966–69), but Margaret Thatcher was not well disposed towards such time-consuming, essentially disinterested procedures – she always felt she knew what needed doing – and during the 1980s none was set up. Major, however, set up the Royal Commission on Criminal Justice, and Blair the Royal Commission on the House of Lords in 2000 chaired by Lord Wakeham. He also initiated scores of task forces and inquiries to prepare the ground for new legislation. Departments regularly establish their own inquiries, often employing outside experts, which go on to make important policy recommendations.

Right-wing think tanks were especially favoured by Margaret Thatcher (see Box 22.2). *The Economist* (6 May 1989) noted how she spurned Oxbridge dons – the traditional source of advice for No. 10 – and suggested that 'the civil service is constitutionally incapable of generating the policy innovation which the prime minister craves'. Instead, as a reforming premier she instinctively listened to the advice of 'people who have been uncorrupted by the old establishment'. Think-tank advice was often channelled to Margaret Thatcher via the No. 10 Policy Unit. Their radical suggestions acted as a sounding board when published and helped to push the climate of debate further to the right. If new ideas are received in a hostile fashion, ministers can easily disavow them. The 'privatisation' of government advice in the form of think tanks was a striking feature of Margaret Thatcher's impact upon policy making.

Prime Minister and Cabinet

This is the nerve centre of government, supported by the high-powered network of Cabinet committees, the Cabinet Office, the No. 10 Policy Unit and policy advisers. After a period of 10 years in office, it is likely that any Prime Minister will dominate policy making. Chapter 18 made it clear that, while many sought to whisper policy suggestions in her ear, Margaret Thatcher's radical beliefs provided her with an apparently full agenda of her own. The evidence of her extraordinary personal impact on major policy areas is plain to see: privatisation, trade union legislation, the environment, the exchange rate, sanctions against South Africa, the poll tax and Europe – the list could go on. However, she was also unusual in taking a personal interest in less weighty matters such as her (ill-starred) attempt to clean up litter from Britain's streets following a visit to litter-free Israel. Harold Wilson saw himself as a 'deep lying halfback feeding the ball forward to the chaps who score the goals'. Thatcher was not content with this role: she wanted to score the goals as well. Wilson also said that a Prime Minister governs by 'interest and curiosity': Thatcher had insatiable appetites in both respects and an energy that enabled her to feed them to a remarkable degree. Under her, assisted by her own relentless energy and a constitution that delivers so much power to the executive, the office of Prime Minister took on a policy-initiating role comparable, perhaps, with that of the US President. John Major was also exceptionally hard-working, as premiers must be, but he was happy to delegate more than his predecessor and to listen to voices around the Cabinet table, especially that of his powerful deputy, Michael Heseltine. Blair proved to be a premier more in the Thatcher mould, by-passing Cabinet and making decisions in small groups of close advisers (allegedly sitting on the sofa in No. 10 Downing Street), especially his 'kitchen cabinet', which originally included Alastair Campbell, Jonathan Powell and, more often than not, other unelected aides rather than elected politicians (see Chapter 18). Blair continued the 'presidentialising' tendency in British politics, dominating the spotlight of national attention and conducting a very personal style of government. The decision to back George W. Bush in his assault on Iraq in 2003 was very much the result of Blair's own passionate determination that this policy was the morally correct one. In her evidence to the Foreign Affairs Select Committee on 17 June 2003, Clare Short claimed a 'shocking collapse in proper government procedure' in that all the main decisions were made by Blair and a small unelected entourage of Blair, Alastair Campbell, Lady (Sally) Morgan, Jonathan Powell and adviser David Manning. Throughout the process, Foreign Secretary Jack Straw had been a mere 'cypher'. Gordon Brown claimed he would seek a return to more traditional policy making, but in practice – for example over the 2008 economic crisis – this did not appear to be the case (see Box 22.3 later in this chapter).

The concept of the core executive

This approach to understanding the nerve centre of British government has come into its own in recent years as it provides a clearer picture of how decision making occurs while supplying a number of useful correctives to more traditional thinking (for a fuller discussion see Chapter 18). The basic idea of the core executive is that decision making takes place at the highest level, constituted by a body of leading figures drawn, depending on the issue, from the Prime Minister's Office, the Cabinet and Cabinet Office plus the head officials of the departments concerned with the particular issue. This is a more helpful concept in that it reduces the notion of a simple hierarchy and replaces the idea of a tip to the pyramid with that of a halo or circle of key people. This is also useful in that it avoids the diversion of the difference between the political and administrative, the minister and civil servant. Anyone who has been involved in policy making will describe how civil servants – in theory policy 'eunuchs' who merely stand by loyally while politicians undertake this democratically driven function – participate in its evolution as centrally as any politician. And the same goes, in recent years, for the top political advisers like Alastair Campbell. It also embraces the idea of a permanent core of central 'players' on the policy-making stage plus a regular cast who visit according to the issue on the agenda. One of the best short accounts of the core executive – Moran (2005), *Politics and Governance in the UK* – elaborates usefully on the modern PM's office:

> The details [of the PM's Office] constantly change, partly because prime ministers constantly worry about whether they are being adequately served, and partly because life at the centre has a frenetic, hothouse quality: little empires are constantly being built (and dismantled) as different people struggle for the ear of the prime minister and for their own personal advancement. The atmosphere is rather like that of the court of a monarch, where the skill lies in catching the ear and the eye of the powerful one.
>
> (Moran 2005: 118)

So, private secretaries will process the information and paper which goes before the top person; combinations of civil servants and political advisers will feed in policy advice; and the press office will seek to ensure that what disseminates out to the wider political system, and beyond that to voters themselves, is formulated – with great sensitivity and sophistication – in a way which will advance policy objectives and not undermine them.

From this brief and admittedly selective description it is clear that:

- Policy can be initiated at both the micro and macro levels from within any part of the political system, but the frequency and importance of initiatives grow as one moves from the periphery towards the centre.

- Even peripheral influences can be swiftly drawn into the centre should the centre wish it.

- Each policy environment is to some extent a world unto itself with its own distinctive characteristics.

- The core executive, comprising the system's top decision makers, will be complicit in formulating high policy and directing it outwards and downwards to the relevant parts of the government machine.

Higher education policy making, for example, will include, just for starters, the Prime Minister, the Cabinet, the No. 10 Policy Unit, plus senior officials from Education (the core executive) assisted by think tanks, numerous parliamentary and party committees, more middle-ranking officials from the Departments of Education and Skills, the Treasury, the funding councils for the universities, the Committee of Vice-Chancellors and Principals, the University and College Union and other unions, and *The Times Higher Education Supplement*, together with a galaxy of academic experts on any and every aspect of the subject. Downing Street policy – not just the PM but his network of aides and advisers – is now of key importance in this high-profile policy area.

Policy formulation

Once a policy idea has received political endorsement it is fed into the system for detailed elaboration. This process involves certain key players from the initiation process, principally civil servants, possibly key pressure group leaders and outside experts (who usually are also political sympathisers) and, usually at a later stage, ministers. In the case of a major measure, there is often a learning phase in which civil servants and ministers acquaint themselves with the detail of the measure: this may require close consultation with experts and practitioners in the relevant policy environment. The measure, if it requires legislation, then has to chart a course first through the bureaucracy and then the legislature.

The bureaucratic process

This will entail numerous information-gathering and advisory committee meetings and a sequence of coordinating meetings with other ministries, especially the Treasury if finance is involved. Some of these meetings might be coordinated by the Cabinet Office, and when ministers become involved the measures will be progressed in Cabinet committees and ultimately full Cabinet before being passed on to parliamentary counsel, the expert drafters of parliamentary bills.

The legislative process

As Chapters 15, 16 and 17 explained, this process involves several readings and debates in both chambers. Studies show that most legislation passes through unscathed, but controversial measures will face a number of hazards, which may influence their eventual shape. Opposition MPs and peers may seek to delay and move hostile amendments, but more important are rebellions within the government party: for example, determined backbench Labour opposition to the university top-up fees legislation in January 2004 produced a series of amendments to the measure which made the original proposal almost unrecognisable – though such examples are rare. The task of piloting measures through the legislature falls to ministers, closely advised by senior officials, and this is often when junior ministers can show their mettle and make a case for their advancement.

From this brief description it is clear that four sets of actors dominate the policy formulation process: ministers, civil servants, pressure group leaders and an array of experts appropriate to the subject. Some scholars calculate that the key personnel involved in policy formulation might number no more than 3,500. As in policy initiation, Margaret Thatcher also played an unusually interventionist role in this process. Reportedly she regularly called ministers and civil servants into No. 10 to speed things up, shift developments on to the desired track or discourage those with whom she disagreed. It would seem that Tony Blair was in the same mould and maybe more so, raging in public and private at the inertia of the public sector and the more general 'forces of conservatism' he criticised at the 1999 Bournemouth party conference. Dynamic politicians like Thatcher and Blair become impatient at the slowness with which the wheels of government turn and so seek to catalyse its progress through personal interventions. In her resignation speech Clare Short, who resigned in May 2003 over the role of the UN in reconstructing Iraq, bitterly attacked Blair's centralisation of policy making in a fashion which was still valid in 2006:

> I think what's going on in the second term in this government, power is being increasingly centralised around the prime minister and just a few advisers, ever increasingly few. The Cabinet is now only a 'dignified' part of the constitution. It's gone the way of the Privy Council. Seriously, various policy initiatives are being driven by advisers [in No. 10] who are never scrutinised, never accountable.

Lord Butler of Brockwell, former Cabinet Secretary, was a well-known sceptic of Blair's methods involving political aides and meetings on the Number 10 sofa. His July 2004 *Review of Intelligence on Weapons of Mass Destruction*, arising from the decision to invade Iraq alongside US forces, contained a section on the machinery of government. In it the report cited evidence from two former Cabinet members who 'expressed their concern about the informal nature of much of the Government's decision-making process, and

the relative lack of use of established Cabinet Committee machinery' (pp. 146–7). Specifically, the report pointed out that from April 2002 to the outbreak of hostilities, the Defence and Overseas Policy Committee did not meet once, yet there were 'some 25 meetings attended by key Ministers, officials and military officers most closely involved [who] provided the framework of discussion and decision making within Government'.

Policy implementation

It is easy to assume that once the government has acted on something or legislated on an issue it is more or less closed. Certainly the record of government action reveals any number of measures that have fulfilled their objectives: for example, the Attlee Government wished to establish a National Health Service and did so; in the 1980s Conservative governments wished to sell off houses to council tenants and did so. But there are always problems that impede or sometimes frustrate implementation or that produce undesired side effects. Between legislation and implementation many factors intervene. Jordan and Richardson (1982: 234–5) quote the conditions that Hood suggests need to be fulfilled to achieve perfect implementation:

1 There must be a unitary administrative system rather like a huge army with a single line of authority. Conflict of authority could weaken control, and all information should be centralised in order to avoid compartmentalism.

2 The norms and rules enforced by the system have to be uniform. Similarly, objectives must be kept uniform if the unitary administrative system is to be really effective.

3 There must be perfect obedience or perfect control.

4 There must be perfect information and perfect communication – as well as perfect coordination.

5 There must be sufficient time for administrative resources to be mobilised.

To fulfil wholly any, let alone all, of these conditions would be rare indeed, so some degree of failure is inevitable with any government programme. Examples are easy to find.

Education

The 1944 Education Act intended that the new grammar, technical and secondary modern schools were to be different but share a 'parity of esteem'. In practice this did not happen: grammar schools became easily the most prestigious and recruited disproportionately from the middle classes: the government could not control parental choice. To remedy this, comprehensive schools were set up in the 1950s and 1960s, but it was the middle-class children who still performed best in examinations. Reformers also neglected one crucial and in retrospect blindingly obvious factor: comprehensive schools recruit from their own hinterlands, so inner-city schools draw children from predominantly working-class areas with a culture tending to produce lower educational standards, while suburban schools are drawn from more middle-class families who place a high value on education and whose children consequently achieve higher standards. The government made policy on the basis of inadequate information and awareness.

Poll tax

The euphemistically named 'community charge' – known as the 'poll tax' – was the brainchild variously of right-wing think tanks, Kenneth Baker, William Waldegrave and others (although following its collapse most people were keen to disclaim parentage – political failures, unsurprisingly, are always 'orphans'). The rationale behind it was logical: local taxes – the '**rates**' – were based on property but penalised the wealthy, who paid more on big properties. However, over half were either exempted or received rebates yet still enjoyed the benefits of local services; consequently, they had no reason to vote for lower rates and were not 'accountable' for them in the opinion of Conservatives like Thatcher, a keen supporter of the scheme. The new tax was to be a flat-rate one and payable by all to some degree, even students and the unemployed. The obvious unfairness of taxing the poor as heavily as the rich was widely recognised, even by Conservative voters. Yet Thatcher's personal support, defiant style and the pusillanimous nature of many MPs and ministers – Michael Portillo informed conference that he was not daunted but 'delighted' to be placed in charge of it – let a clearly flawed law onto the statute book. In March 1990 polls showed a huge majority opposed to it and on 7 April a riot erupted in London. When John Major succeeded Thatcher, he quickly replaced the measure with one more closely resembling the old property-based rates, and the heat soon left the issue of local government finance. Programme failure also often results from the operation of constraints that constantly bear upon policy makers.

Constraints upon policy makers

Financial resources

Policy makers have to operate within available financial resources, which are a function of the nation's economic health at any particular time, and the willingness of key decision makers, especially in the Treasury, to make appropriate provision from funds available to government.

Political support

This is initially necessary to gain endorsement for a policy idea, but support is also necessary throughout the often extended and complex policy-making process. Lack of it, for example, characterised the tortured birth of the poll tax as well as its ignominious demise. Support at the political level is also crucial, but it is highly desirable within the bureaucracy and elsewhere in the policy environment. Resistance to policies can kill them off *en route*, and anticipated resistance is also important; as Jordan and Richardson (1982: 238) hypothesised: 'There are probably more policies which are never introduced because of the anticipation of resistance, than policies which have failed because of resistance.' Some departments now seek to gauge levels of popular support through the use of focus groups, a technique borrowed from commercial and political marketing (see Chapter 19 and below).

Competence of key personnel

An able, energetic minister is likely to push policy measures through; a weak minister is not. Civil servants are famously able in Britain, but even they need to work hard to be up to the task of mastering rapidly the detail of new measures; their failure will impede the progress of a measure and limit its efficacy. Tony Blair created (maybe necessary) waves in the civil service by emphasising the primacy of 'delivery'. Civil servants must be able to achieve practical things as well as advise ministers.

Time

New legislative initiatives need to carve space out of a timetable so overcrowded that winners of private members' ballots are lobbied by departments themselves to adopt bills awaiting parliamentary consideration. Moreover, the whole system is arguably over-centralised and, some would say, chronically overloaded.

Timing

Measures can fail if timing is not propitious. Just after a general election, for example, is a good time to introduce controversial measures. Margaret Thatcher, it will be recalled, was unable to secure the sale of British Leyland to an American company in the spring of 1986 because she had lost so much support over the Westland episode.

Coordination

Whitehall departments divide up the work of government in a particular way: proposals that fall between ministries are often at a disadvantage, and the job of coordinating diverse departments is not, in the view of critics, managed with particular efficiency. Burch (1979: 133) also notes that:

> Too often policy making becomes a conflict between departments for a share of the limited resources available. This is . . . especially true of expenditure politics when departments fight for their own corner at the cost of broader policy objectives.

Personality factors

Key decision makers are not as rational as perhaps they ought to be. They might have personal objectives – ambition, desire for image and status, and rivalries – which lead them to oppose rather than support certain policy objectives. The best recent examples concern rows between Prime Ministers and their Chancellors: Margaret Thatcher and Nigel Lawson in the late 1980s; Blair and Brown clashed bitterly over very many issues – for example, entering the single currency – the euro, Blair was enthusiastic and Chancellor Brown cautious to the point of applying a veto to such a move.

Geographical factors

A bias in favour of the South-east is often detectable in government policies – for example, in the granting of defence contracts – partly because decision makers in our centralised system live in the home counties, partly because the South-east has a more buoyant economy and partly as a result of political factors: this after all is the heartland of the traditional party of government. (For a subtle and controversial analysis of territorial politics in the UK, see Bulpitt 1983.)

International events

The increasing interdependence of the large economies has made events such as the quadrupling of oil prices in the early 1970s major constraints upon policy making. In some cases these constraints are formal, as when the International Monetary Fund attached strict public expenditure conditions to its 1976 loan to Callaghan's Labour Government. Political events such as the Falklands War can clearly have an enormous impact upon major policy areas, while the 1989 revolutions in the communist countries changed the whole context within which foreign policy is formulated. The greatest perturbations in the present century were caused initially by the terrorist attacks of 11 September 2001 followed by the successive US-led wars in Afghanistan and Iraq.

The influence of Europe

Treaty obligations and the growing power of Community institutions have imposed increasingly powerful constraints upon the freedom of action that British policy makers have enjoyed (see Chapter 27). British policy making is now well embedded into the Brussels machinery with senior civil servants constantly travelling on the shuttle to Brussels, Strasbourg and Luxembourg.

Policy networks

Jordan and Richardson (1987) argued that policy making in Britain is not uniform; every aspect has its own specific characteristics. They lay less stress on manifestos or the activities of Parliament but point to the mass of interconnecting bodies that have an interest in the policy area: the 'policy community'.

To some extent this is a theory about how interest groups interact with government to help formulate policy. Access to the policy community is restricted to actors prepared to play the game: act constitutionally, accept that the government has the last word, keep agreements and make reasonable demands. These rules automatically exclude radical groups with high-profile campaigning styles in most cases, although the accession to power of a radical political message can alter this, as in the case of Thatcherism. To exercise real clout, a group has to become an 'insider' (see Chapter 10). Communities have a core and a periphery – rather like that suggested in Figure 22.3 – with the stable core continuously involved in the policy process and a secondary group, less stable in membership, involved from time to time but lacking the resources to be in the core.

Professor Rod Rhodes developed this idea but saw that often the policy community was not cohesive or sharply defined; he began to discern a more fragmented and more accessible form: a 'policy network' with a very large and constantly changing membership, often with conflicting views. Baggott's diagram (Figure 22.3) shows the contrast between the two ideas with some clarity. Baggott (1995: 26) criticises the approach for not explaining the provenance of the networks and over-concentrating on the group–government nexus to the exclusion of the broader political environment.

Comprehensive political marketing

Jennifer Lees-Marchment wrote a book in 2001 which argued that marketing had become so all-pervasive in modern politics that politicians now 'design' policies for the electoral market and then deliver them once in power. She claims parties no longer dispense 'grand ideologies' striving to convert voters to their faiths. Instead, they have adjusted

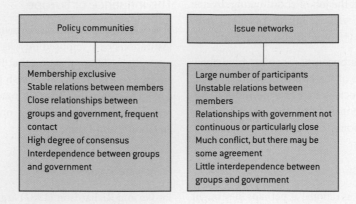

Figure 22.3 Policy networks
Source: Baggott (1995: 24)

to the way we now vote: instrumentally, expecting parties to deliver on promises made in the marketplace of election campaigns. She argued that initially Labour was 'product-based' in the early 1980s when it persisted in selling something no one wanted. The result was failure. Then the party tried a 'sales-oriented' approach, improving its campaigning capacity through advertising, direct mailings and so forth. The result was better but still not enough to win. Then, as New Labour, it began to listen to 'market' demands via focus groups and polls, and fashioned a 'product' the market, i.e. voters, really wanted. The result was the 1997 landslide. The thesis has been criticised as showing politics as devoid of real passion, or any meaning at all; but the analysis is sufficiently acute for much of it to emit the ring of truth.

Case studies in policy making

This chapter concludes with two case studies: an examination of policy formulation and implementation in the Millennium Dome; and the ongoing issue of identity cards.

The Millennium Dome

A Conservative project

The provenance of this idea is to be found in John Major's 1992 administration: to celebrate the new millennium in a way that would capture the imaginations of the British people, rather as the Festival of Britain had done in 1951. The Millennium Commission was set up in 1993 and received substantial funding from the National Lottery. Various ideas

were mooted to celebrate the event, some located outside the capital – one in Birmingham being the strongest rival to the London region. Michael Heseltine was keen on an exhibition based on the site of an old gasworks on the Greenwich peninsula on the prime meridian (0 degrees longitude). He became the driving force behind it, being appointed to the Millennium Commission when it was set up in 1994 and continuing in this role after becoming Deputy Prime Minister in 1995. In 1996 he set up a Cabinet subcommittee to progress the idea and to raise capital from bankers and businessmen. Crick (1997: 430) tells how the DPM bullied and twisted arms, holding a series of weekly breakfast meetings to ensure that the project would be embraced by the Government. The problem was that financing the project was very problematic, more so than the rejected Birmingham option. However, Heseltine was totally committed to the idea and steamrolled the doubters. In 1997 it seemed that the forthcoming election might imperil the project, so he personally lobbied Blair before the election (Heseltine 2000: 513) and won his agreement to continue with it (should he win the election), subject to a review.

New Labour adopts the Dome

New Labour considered the Dome in an early Cabinet. Blair, it seemed, was uncertain and dithered for a month over a decision. Peter Mandelson, grandson of Herbert Morrison, architect of the 1951 Festival, was the chief proponent of the project but was opposed by Gordon Brown, who scorned such PR approaches and was worried that the Treasury would have to bail out a possible failure. With a week to go, 'the costings were dubious; the sponsorship was absent; the contents were vague when not non-existent' (Rawnsley 2000: 54). Moreover, the press was mostly derisive and other ministers were highly sceptical, including Chris Smith, Frank Dobson (who said that the Dome should be 'fired into outer space'), Clare Short and David Blunkett. However, Blair was taken by Mandelson's flamboyant vision of a huge, symbolic, all-inclusive dome to celebrate the 'rebirth of Britain under New Labour'. It seems that the initial doubts of John Prescott had been won over by the regeneration aspects of the scheme. At a pre-Cabinet meeting on 19 June 1997, moreover, he insisted that abandonment of the project at this early stage would make them look 'not much of a government'. When Blair had to leave the meeting early, Prescott took over and faced so much criticism that he dared not take a vote. Instead, 'Tony wants it' was enough for the project to be approved. Blair chose to ignore the Dome's critics in the press, Parliament and Cabinet and to press on with the (destined) national 'folly'.

In a *Guardian* article (13 May 2003) following her resignation as International Development Secretary, Clare Short recalled the decision on the Dome being taken:

> We went around the table and everyone spoke. I remember Donald Dewar saying you could have a party and free drink for everyone in the country and still save a lot of money. Then Tony said 'I've got to go' and went out and announced we were going ahead with the dome. John Prescott was left there to sum up and that's how we learned that Cabinet government was coming to an end.

Short added that this was too often the way in which bad decisions were taken.

The Dome

The structure was designed by the Richard Rogers Partnership and became the world's largest dome, covering, remarkably, nearly 20 acres. It was divided into six zones for the purposes of the exhibition, including a Learning Zone, a Body Zone, a Talk Zone and a Faith Zone. Mandelson was the first minister to be in charge of the project, Blair's former flatmate Lord Falconer the next in line. Jenny Page, a former civil servant, was made chief executive of the government-owned Millennium Experience Company. In 1997 the first of many public controversies was caused when Stephen Bayley, the somewhat volatile consultant creative director, resigned. Critics fastened onto the lateness of the project and the inaccessibility of the site plus the paucity of displays to fill the vast new arena. Mandelson's visit to Disneyland in January 1998 gave out all the wrong signals. Through the fog of government pronouncements the press delightedly began to discern something decidedly pear-shaped. Mandelson's 'it's going to knock your socks off' merely added fuel to negative expectations. The cost soon escalated from £200 million closer to £1 billion, and the undoubted quality of the Dome's structure – completed, astonishingly, on time –

did not silence the critics, many of whom were invited to the opening celebration on New Year's Eve 1999. The evening's performances were rated as good but, by the greatest ill fortune, transport to the Dome broke down and huge crowds of key opinion formers were left waiting for three hours at a freezing East London station during which they sharpened their pens and then dipped them in vitriol for the next day's papers. Even New Labour's spin machine could not save the Dome from a comprehensive panning.

From then on it was downhill. The exhibitions were open to the public for the space of a year, and to meet financial targets 12 million members of the public were expected to pay the £20 entrance fee. However, actual attendance figures were half that, and while most who visited claimed that it was value for money, a vociferous minority insisted that it was not. Rawnsley comments acidly that 'The Dome was the vapid glorification of marketing over content, fashion over creation, ephemera over achievement . . . It was a folie de bombast' (2000: 327–30). Even a Dome supporter, Polly Toynbee in the *Guardian*, had to confess that it was 'a lemon'. Within weeks, the Dome had to be subsidised with a further £60 million of lottery money. In February Jenny Page resigned, to be replaced by a Frenchman from Eurodisney, Pierre-Yves Gerbeau. The press assiduously reported the poor attendance and the breakdowns. In May the chairman of the Millennium Company resigned. Poor 'Charlie' Falconer – the fall guy once Mandelson had departed – was forced to sustain a false enthusiasm for an unconscionable period. Eventually, the Government came to sell the structure but found few takers. In the end, it gave the building away – in exchange for a share of putative profits – to a company which successfully turned it into a venue for rock concerts. A 'vacuous temple to political vanity' (Rawnsley 2000: 331) had lost the nation a sum of money that could have built many schools and hospitals.

What went wrong?

- *Icon politics*: The government opted for a vanity project with little focus or meaning. Moran (2001) calls this 'icon politics', projects chosen merely for their symbolic significance. Inevitably it was decided by those occupying the inner sanctum of government – it was intended to be Blair's opening manifesto ploy in his re-election campaign.

- *Entertainment ill-suited to government*: The project was entertainment-based, and governments are not designed or equipped to succeed in such a fickle area. Desperate attempts to please a huge audience almost inevitably turned into banality; whatever the media advisers might have sought to feed to the nation, no amount of spin could change this.

- *Financial warnings*: From early days, warnings regarding uncertain finances were ignored.

- *Cabinet doubts* were voiced but overruled because of the iconic significance of the project. Fear of damaging criticism from the Opposition meant that such high-level criticism failed to enter the public domain.

- *Abandonment* of the project at an early stage might have minimised the damage but the Government – Blair to the fore – determined not to admit defeat and to brazen out the hurricane of flak.

All these factors contributed to the digging of an ever deeper hole by the Government: a classic case of policy making gone horribly wrong.

Postscript: a happier ending?

The future of the Dome itself hung in the balance for a while. John Prescott was associated with a scheme inspired by billionaire Philip Anshcutz to turn it into a mega casino but opposition to such establishments eventually scuppered it. The US businessman was behind Meridian Delta, the company which bought the Dome in 2001. If permission can be obtained, part of the Dome is still in theory available for a super casino but the rest of it has been converted into a leisure facilities centre and an arena for music concerts. Bon Jovi provided the opening concert in June 2007 but the O_2 arena has now become a well-recognised facility, meaning that not all of the Millennium Dome concept has crumbled into dust and ridicule.

Identity cards

This second case study is different because it is an issue only recently resolved. This policy saga – for that is what it has become – first entered the public domain in February 2002 when David Blunkett, the then Home Secretary, announced an 'entitlement card' to prevent benefit fraud and deter terrorism. The idea soon attracted vitriolic criticism for its estimated cost of over a billion pounds and its erosion of civil liberties. In consequence, the idea was repackaged to be introduced in stages with a full decision on a compulsory scheme delayed until 2013. Many suggested the idea should be dropped, but instead of dropping the scheme after the 2005 election it was submitted to Parliament at the end of June. This time, however, the card was to include biometric information relating to the subject's face, fingerprints and iris; it was passed on its second reading but the Government's slimmed majority was further reduced by rebels – mostly from the left-wing Campaign Group – to a mere 31. In the *Guardian* on 28 June 2005 Martin Kettle discussed objections by David Davis,

Charles Clarke's Conservative Shadow Home Secretary, who had suggested that the idea had to pass the test of four questions:

1 Will it work to achieve its stated goals? Certainly it would help prevent benefit and identity fraud but few believe, even in government, that it would deter terrorists, producing an (at best) opaque case for the innovation in the first place. Debates in the Lords during January made the case seem more 'dubious' the longer they continued, according to the *Guardian* on 18 January 2006. In a letter to the same paper on 23 January 2006, the minister in charge, Tony McNulty, argued that the card would be a major blow against financial and benefit fraud: 'linking a unique biometric to personal data means people have control over access to their details'.

2 Is the government capable of introducing such a system? IT-based schemes have turned out to be notoriously difficult to introduce successfully and huge amounts had been wasted by the NHS on new data processing which had proved calamitous, as had the tax credit scheme which had resulted in huge overpayments being claimed back from recipients.

3 Is it cost-effective? Initial estimates of the cost exceeded £1 billion but that soon tripled, with the government's best estimate of the cost to the public of the card – in combination with a passport – being £93 per person. Over half of respondents to an ICM poll supported the scheme at such a price in June 2005. The Home Office calculated the cost at £6 billion over 10 years, but a careful study by the LSE placed the total cost at £19 or even £24 billion. While dismissing the LSE estimate as absurd, the Government resisted giving detailed costings on the grounds that such commercially sensitive information would prevent the public from receiving the best possible deal when contracts were issued. Lord Crickhowell in the Lords debate inevitably accused the Government of offering the taxpayer a 'pig in the poke'.

4 Can civil liberties be safeguarded? The Information Commissioner, Richard Thomas, thinks not. He addressed the Home Affairs Select Committee in June 2004 and confessed himself 'increasingly alarmed' by the plan. He did not see a 'sufficient rationale' for recording for the whole population: their name, address, date of birth, gender, nationality and biometric details from finger and eye scans. The idea had 'potential for significant detrimental impact on the day-to-day lives of individuals'.

So, ID cards appear to be too expensive, too riskily experimental, and far too dangerous a violation of civil liberties. But the Government – convinced that these

BRITAIN IN CONTEXT

Policy making in the USA

Each political system produces different patterns of policy making. To some extent this is a direct reflection of system 'mechanics', but political culture and personalities as well as international factors often play important roles. So, we see that in the USA policy emerges via a route very different from that in the UK. At heart the British Prime Minister dominates the executive, like the President, but as long as his party is behind him, he also dominates the legislature. The US chief executive, however, is separately elected and has responsibility for initiating and implementing policy: on the face of it a more powerful figure. However, the US system is complex with myriad checks and balances.

The President is Head of State, Commander in Chief of the Armed Forces, Chief Appointing Officer, Chief Diplomat and, effectively, Chief Legislator. The President can veto any Congressional bill with which he disagrees; in addition to this he has responsibility for the successful implementation of policy. But these powers are balanced by the sole ability of Congress to declare war, the requirement for many appointments to be confirmed by the Senate, the need for a two-thirds majority to ratify treaties, the power of Congress over the making of new laws and the raising of revenue, the ability of Congress to override the veto with a two-thirds majority, and the ability of Congress to impeach the President for 'high crimes and misdemeanors'.

The President faces substantial foreign policy constraints from the Senate, made even more restrictive after the War Powers Act in 1973 in the wake of the Vietnam War. He has more freedom of action domestically but cannot set interest rates and is dependent on Congress for revenue. For a long time after the Constitution deemed that Congress would check the President, Congress was perceived as the more powerful institution, but in 1933 Roosevelt successfully extended presidential powers in a bid to overcome the problems created by the

Depression. Since then the relationship has ebbed and flowed. Presidential success is crucially dependent on the President's ability to negotiate successfully with Congress; he often has to persuade dissident legislators from his *own* party to give him the support he needs to push measures through; party discipline is nowhere near as strong as in the UK. Congress may also, of course, be of a different political complexion, as Clinton found to his cost towards the end of his time in power.

The President appoints Cabinet members to lead departments but shares one much criticised feature of British politics: he tends to rely a great deal on personal aides and advisers. Both Thatcher and Blair were criticised for allowing their 'kitchen cabinets' to assume too much power, as were Nixon, Carter, Reagan and Clinton. George Bush Jr also attracted some criticism but perhaps tended to give secretaries of state like Rumsfeld and Rice relatively more room in which to operate. So, a constant tension exists between departments and White House advisers as to whom the President listens and whose advice he follows.

The President has two other powerful weapons at his disposal. First, he can appoint to the Supreme Court judges who tend to reflect his political views, thus influencing the context in which laws will be made over the next two to three decades. Second, he has unrivalled access to public opinion which he uses to encourage or even bully Congress into passing his laws. Roosevelt, when negotiating with unsympathetic Congressional leaders, used to glance meaningfully at the microphone placed on his desk in the Oval Office – it often did the trick. Public opinion is a constant resource available to the President as voters can be thus mobilised to put pressure on Congress to follow the presidential lead. This explains why presidential ratings are often taken more seriously in the US than those of the Prime Minister in the UK.

judgements would be proved wrong – was determined to push through a 'flagship' piece of legislation. On 29 March 2006 votes in both Houses appeared to end the conflict between the two Houses. Despite the opposition of the Liberal

Democrats, the measure was passed in the House of Lords 287–60. MPs later approved it 301–84. From 2008 everyone renewing a passport were to be issued an ID card and have their details placed on the National Identity Register.

Through a legislative compromise, people would have the right, until 2010, not to be given a card; however, they would still have to pay for one and have their details placed on the NIR. Anyone seeking a passport after 2010 would be obliged to have an ID Card.

However, 'implementation' was subject to all kinds of pressures as we have seen. Public support for the idea was damaged by the loss of 25 million names by HMRC in November 2007. In March 2008 the Home Office announced that as a result of this loss plans had been put back by two years to 2012. In November it was announced that foreign nationals living in the UK could apply for identity cards at a variety of centres thoughout the country. Eventually all foreign nationals would have to have such cards and, by 2015, 90 per cent would have been issued with one. In March 2008 the Home Office announced future plans on ID cards.

From 2011–12 everyone over 16 who applies for a passport would have fingerprints and facial scans added to a National Identity Register. From 2010 students were be encouraged to acquire ID cards. The aim was that everyone would eventually carry an ID card and the Government hoped the nation would come to accept this as normal, just as it is in other European countries. However, the Conservatives and Liberal Democrats were strongly opposed on civil liberties grounds and when they formed their coalition after the May 2010 election, their Queen's Speech contained an 'Identity Documents Bill' to cancel the programme and destroy all data on the National Identity Register. So, this substantial piece of policy making had a somewhat tortured history and fell at the last through that oldest of democratic reasons: the election of a new government. ID cards were finally made null and void in January 2011.

Chapter summary

Policy can be defined as either rules and regulations or public expenditure and its distribution. There are various theories about or models of policy making, including the pluralist, corporatist, ruling-class and Whitehall models, plus the rational choice and incrementalist perspectives on decision making. Policy can be seen to pass through three stages: initiation, formulation and implementation. 'Core' decision makers have a constant control of the process, but elements from the 'periphery' are brought in from time to time. The concept of policy networks is useful in analysing policy making. Extra-parliamentary parties and think tanks can have considerable influence, depending on the issue and the situation. Implementation can be very difficult and result in policy objectives being missed or even reversed. Policy makers face many restraints upon their actions, including timing, coordination and international events.

Discussion points

- Which model of policy making seems closest to reality?
- Should there be more popular control over policy making?
- How persuasive is Lindblom's theory of incrementalism?
- What lessons can be learned from the process whereby the Millennium Dome project was brought into being?

Further reading

Building on the foundation texts of Lasswell, Simon, Lindblom, Etzioni, Dror and Wildavsky, the field of policy studies has spawned a substantial literature over the past 40 years or more. In recent decades, Burch and Wood (1990) and Ham and Hill (1993) have provided good introductions to the denser studies available. Hogwood and Gunn (1984) is well written and interesting, as is Jordan and Richardson (1987). For a penetrating analysis see Smith (1993). The best comprehensive study of policy studies used to be Wayne Parsons' *Public Policy* (1995), but that role has been thankfully superseded by Peter Dorey's excellent shorter and more accessible *Policy Making in Britain* (2006). Peter John's *Analysing Public Policy* (1998) and Michael Hill's *The Policy Process in the Modern State* (2000) are both short, competent, clear, though now slightly dated treatments. For a very good shorter introduction to the topic, Moran's *Politics and Governance in the UK* (2005: 412–50) has not been bettered.

Bibliography

Allison, G.T. (1971) *The Essence of Decision: Explaining the Cuban Missile Crisis* (Little, Brown).

Ashbee, E. and Ashford, N. (1999) *US Politics Today* (Manchester University Press).

Bachrach, P.S. and Baratz, M.S. (1970) *Power and Poverty, Theory and Practice* (Oxford University Press).

Baggott, R. (1995) *Pressure Groups Today* (Manchester University Press).

Bulpitt, J. (1983) *Territory and Power in the United Kingdom* (Manchester University Press).

Burch, M. (1979) 'The Policy Making Process', in Jones, B. and Kavanagh, D. (eds) *British Politics Today* (Manchester University Press).

Burch, M. and Wood, B. (1990) *Public Policy in Britain*, 2nd edn (Martin Robertson).

Butler, Lord of Brockwell (2004) *Review of Intelligence on Weapons of Mass Destruction*, HC898, July.

Castles, F. (1982) *The Impact of Parties* (Sage).

Castles, F. (1989) *The Comparative History of Public Policy* (Oxford University Press).

Crick, M. (1997) *Michael Heseltine* (Hamish Hamilton).

Dorey, P. (2006) *Policy Making in Britain* (Sage).

Downs, A. (1957) *An Economic Theory of Democracy* (Harper & Row).

Easton, D. (1965) *A Framework for Political Analysis* (Prentice Hall).

Etzioni, A. (1964) *A Comparative Analysis of Complex Organisations* (Prentice Hall).

Etzioni, A. (1968) *An Active Society: A Theory of Societal and Political Processes* (Free Press).

Franklin, B. (1998) *Tough on Soundbites, Tough on the Causes of Soundbites*, Catalyst paper 3 (Catalyst).

Hague, R., Harrop, M. and Breslin, S. (1998) *Comparative Government and Politics* (Macmillan).

Ham, C. and Hill, M. (1993) *The Policy Process in the Modern Capitalist State* (Harvester Wheatsheaf).

Heseltine, M. (2000) *Life in the Jungle: My Autobiography* (Coronet).

Hill, M.J. (ed.) (1993) *New Agendas in the Study of the Policy Process* (Harvester Wheatsheaf).

Hill, M. (2000) *The Policy Process in the Modern State* (Prentice Hall).

Hogwood, B. (1992) *Trends in British Public Policy* (Open University Press).

Hogwood, B. and Gunn, L.A. (1984) *Policy Analysis in the Real World* (Oxford University Press).

Jessop, B. (1990) *State Theory: Putting Capitalist States in Their Place* (Polity Press).

John, P. (1998) *Analysing Public Policy* (Pinter).

Jones, B. (1986) *Is Democracy Working?* (Tyne Tees TV).

Jordan, G. and Richardson, J.J. (1982) 'The British Policy Style or the Logic of Negotiation', in Richardson, J.J. (ed.) *Policy Styles in Western Europe* (Allen & Unwin).

Jordan, G. and Richardson, J.J. (1987) *Governing Under Pressure* (Martin Robertson).

Lee, G. (1989) 'Privatisation', in Jones, B. (ed.) *Political Issues in Britain Today*, 3rd edn (Manchester University Press).

Lees-Marchment, J. (2001) *Political Marketing and British Political Parties: The Party's Just Begun* (Manchester University Press).

Lindblom, C.E. (1959) 'The Science of Muddling Through', *Public Administration Review*, Vol. 19.

Lindblom, C.E. and Woodhouse, E.J. (1993) *The Policy Making Process*, 3rd edn (Prentice Hall).

Marx, K. and Engels, E. (1848) *The Communist Manifesto* (Oxford University Press).

McKay, D. (2001) *American Politics and Society* (Blackwell).

Miliband, R. (1969) *The State in Capitalist Society* (Weidenfeld & Nicolson).

Moran, M. (2001) 'Not Steering but Drowning: Policy Catastrophes and the Regulatory State', *Political Quarterly*, Autumn, pp. 414–27.

Moran, M. (2005) *Politics and Governance in the UK* (Palgrave).

National Audit Office, *The Millennium Dome: report by the Comptroller and Auditor General*, HC936 1999–2000, accessible at www.open.gov.uk/nao

Naughtie, J. (2001) *The Rivals* (Fourth Estate).

Parsons, W. (1995) *Public Policy* (Edward Elgar).

Platt, S. (1998) *Government by Task Force*, Catalyst paper 2 (Catalyst).

Rawnsley, A. (2000) *Servants of the People* (Hamish Hamilton).

Rawnsley, A. (2010) *The End of the Party: The Rise and Fall of New Labour* (Viking).

Rowlands, D. and Pollock, A. (2004) 'Choice and Responsiveness for Older People in the "Patient Centred" NHS', *British Medical Journal*, January.

Schmitter, P.C. (1979) 'Still the Century of Corporatism', in Schmitter, P.C. and Lembruch, G. (eds) *Trends Towards Corporatist Intermediation* (Sage).

Schnattschneider, E.E. (1960) *The Semisovereign People* (Holt, Reinhart & Winston).

Simpson, D. (1999) *Pressure Groups* (Hodder & Stoughton).

Smith, M. (1993) *Pressure, Power and Policy* (Harvester Wheatsheaf).

Watts, D. (2003) *Understanding US/UK Government and Politics* (Manchester University Press).

Wilby, P. (2006) 'Rupert Murdoch is Effectively a Member of Blair's Cabinet', the *Guardian*, 1 July 2006.

Wildavsky, A. (1979) *Speaking the Truth to Power* (Little, Brown).

Wilensky, H. (1975) *The Welfare State and Equality* (University of California Press).

Useful websites

Fabian Society: www.fabian-society.org.uk

Demos: www.demos.co.uk

Catalyst: www.catalystforum.org.uk

10 Downing Street: www.number10.gov.uk

Anti-ID Card Group: www.no2id.net

CHAPTER 23

The politics of law and order

Bill Jones

> " **The mood and temper of the public with regard to the treatment of crime and criminals is one of the unfailing tests of the civilization of a country** "
>
> Winston Churchill, as Home Secretary, 1911, quoted in Jenkins (2001: 180)

Learning objectives

- To explain the connection between political ideas and the problem of law and **order**.
- To consider the causes of crime and its profile as a political issue.
- To examine some related issues like punishment.
- To explain and analyse the secret security services.

This chapter examines a political issue that affects everyone: crime and punishment. Opinion surveys show that concern on this topic has been steadily rising throughout the 1980s and 1990s as crime figures have soared and in some cases, for example property crime, even exceeded American levels. Anticipating a general election, Prime minister Tony Blair packed his Queen's Speech in autumn 2004 with even more proposals to crack down on crime. This chapter examines the subject within the context of political ideas; assesses the extent of the current problem; discusses some of the probable causes of crime and concludes with a brief examination of the security services and other Home Office issues.

Political ideas context of law and order

Ever since humankind began to live together over 9,000 years ago, the question of law and order has been of central concern. Solitary cave dwellers did not need a code of law, but any group of humans living as a community did. Fundamental to such a code was property. From the earliest times this included food, clothes, homes and utensils, joined later by money once it had become a medium of exchange. Also highly important was physical safety – one of the reasons, after all, why people lived together in the first place. The Babylonian king, Hammurabi (d. 1750 BC) established a body of law famously based on the notion of retribution: 'an eye for an eye, a tooth for a tooth'; Islamic ('*sharia*') law, in some respects, tends to perpetuate such principles.

Legal systems in developed Western countries still seek to defend property and the person, but an extremely large variety of considerations have been embodied in pursuit of that elusive concept, 'justice'. Political thinkers have also wrestled with these problems. Aristotle recognised the necessity of law and governments that apply it with wisdom and justice. In the wake of the English Civil War, the philosopher Thomas Hobbes rested his whole justification for 'the state' on its ability to provide physical protection for its citizens. Without such protection, he argued, life would be a brutal process of destructive anarchy; Conservative philosophers have always stressed the need for such protection. Conservative Party policy still reflects this powerful emphasis: 'The Conservative Party has always stood for the protection of the citizen and the defence of the rule of law' (1992 election manifesto).

Another group of philosophers approach the issue from a different angle. They argue that people are naturally inclined to be law-abiding and cooperative. They only transgress, so the argument runs, when the social environment in which they grow up damages them and makes deviation both inevitable and understandable. It follows from this that social re-organisation can alleviate the problem of anti-social actions. Foremost among these thinkers was Karl Marx, who attributed most of what was wrong with society to the corrupting and debilitating effect of a vicious capitalist economic system.

A kind of continuum is therefore recognisable: pessimists, who see criminals as reflections of man's innate imperfections; and optimists, who believe that as crime reflects social effects it can be attacked and remedied by social action. In British politics the Tories have tended to occupy a position towards the pessimistic end of the spectrum and Labour the optimistic one.

In 1979 Margaret Thatcher made great play of how hers was the party of law and order. Studies showed this benefited her enormously in the election of that year. Moreover, there is reason to believe that most uninformed voters tend in any case towards the pessimistic end of the spectrum and respond to tough remedies that hark back to Hammurabi (if not the American Wild West). The Thatcherite analysis – still very influential in the Conservative Party – is that humans are basically weak and sinful creatures who need all the support of Church, family, school and community to keep them on the straight and narrow. During the 1960s ('that third-rate decade', according to Norman Tebbit), Labour's over-liberal approach tipped the balance of socialisation towards an absence of individual responsibility. Parents were encouraged to slough off their responsibility in favour of an insidiously vague concept of 'society', which took the blame for a whole portmanteau of things and destroyed the notion of 'personal accountability', that crucial binding quality in any functioning society. Consequently, according to this analysis, children grew up expecting and exercising free licence – 'doing their own thing' in the argot of the time – moving on to become juvenile offenders and then hardened criminals. Back in 1993 the *Sunday Telegraph* neatly summarised the Thatcherite critique of the left's approach (15 August):

> It is the very beliefs of those theorists [left-wing academics who maintain that crime is caused by social conditions] that are responsible for our present malaise. They preach, in a doctrine which first became prominent during the sixties but stretches back to Rousseau, that man is inherently good, and that he must cast off the chains of conventional behaviour and morality that enslave him.

The unlimited flow of immigrants, the argument continues, causes more tensions and contributes to crime, while the abrogation of personal responsibility which they alleged Labour accepted and encouraged, was nourishing a crime wave.

Labour rejected this view of the world. Their Home Office spokesmen and spokeswomen preferred to concentrate on the roots of crime, which they believed lay in poor economic and social conditions. The first element of this is seen as the huge inequality between rich and poor that the free-enterprise economic system invariably creates. Such social gulfs create anger and frustration: members of the favoured elite are able to progress smoothly through privileged education to highly paid and influential jobs. Meanwhile, poor people face vastly inferior life chances and huge, often insurmountable, challenges if they wish to succeed. They are surrounded by images that equate personal value with certain symbols such as expensive cars and clothes: when they cannot acquire them legally, it is a small step to breaking the law to redress the balance. So, the system itself causes crime by encouraging people to want things that they have to steal to acquire. When they do not, the result is often poverty and hopelessness: the breeding ground of crime for successive generations of people at the bottom of the pile. Richard Wilkinson and Kate Pickett, authors of *The Spirit Level* (2010), argue that study of social inequalities worldwide show, beyond any doubt, that those countries with the highest rates of inequality display the greatest degree of dysfunction (see below).

Left-wingers also point to how the law favours the rich and protects their property, imprisoning petty burglars for long stretches yet letting off city fraudsters with suspended sentences or fines. In his book on the 2007–9 greed-fuelled bankers crash, *Inside Job*, Charles Ferguson points out that in spite of clear breaches of the law, nobody has yet been prosecuted for them (2012: 1–24).

Interestingly, the positions of both major parties began to converge in the early 1990s. The Tories had long insisted that social conditions were not connected with crime: how else did figures stay stable during the Depression years of the 1930s? However, the massive increase in crime during the 1980s and early 1990s and a series of studies by the Home Office (especially those of Simon Field, who plotted graphs of property crime and consumption in 1900–88, finding a close correlation between unemployment and property crime) encouraged a change of heart. Eventually, the government abandoned this untenable position: on 28 October 1992 Home Office minister Michael Jack accepted that recession had played its part in pushing up the crime figures, saying that downturns in the economy were traditionally accompanied by increases in crime.

For its part, Labour responded to the spate of fearsome juvenile crime in 1993 – including the horrific murder of toddler James Bulger by two young boys – by expressing a tougher line on sentencing and the treatment of young offenders. The two big parties, especially with Kenneth Clarke as Home Secretary and Tony Blair as Shadow Home Secretary, found a surprising amount upon which to agree. Blair's soundbite 'tough on crime – tough on the causes of crime' (allegedly coined by Gordon Brown) was Labour's attempt to be true to its old social analysis of crime while exploiting the popular animus against law breakers. Arguably, the former emphasis came to eclipse the latter as time went by, so that Home Secretaries like Blunkett and Straw were as right-wing as any Conservative equivalent.

As the 1997 General Election approached, both parties targeted crime as a campaign priority, adopting tough postures on handguns and combat knives in the autumn of 1996, for example. Indeed, Michael Howard, the populist Conservative Home Secretary, sought to play to the right-wing gallery in his own party; what was more surprising was that his Labour shadow, Jack Straw, sought to match him and even exceed him in right-wing zeal, so sensitive had the opposition become to the need to attract floating votes, especially middle-class ones, in order to end 18 years out of power (see also Reiner 2006a).

PROFILE

Two Tory Home Secretaries

Michael Howard (1941–)

Former Conservative Home Secretary. Educated at Cambridge. Became MP in 1983, and was Minister of Local Government, Employment and Environment Secretary before Home Secretary (1993–97). Stood in leadership election in 1997 but, after being criticised in a Commons speech by former junior understudy Ann Widdecombe, saw the man he asked to run as his deputy, William Hague, go on to win. When Ian Duncan Smith's period of leadership came to an undistinguished end, Howard was elected unopposed to take IDS's place. He led his party into the May 2005 election, but when Labour won its third term, Howard resigned, leaving the field open for a new generation of younger Conservatives. He never quite lost the negative aura he acquired while Home Secretary.

Theresa May (1955–)

A grammar school girl who went on to Oxford, May worked for the Bank of England while serving eight years as a local councillor. She became an MP in 1997 and soon was promoted to a variety of senior Shadow Cabinet roles. On 12 May 2010 she became only the fourth woman to hold one of the great offices of state when David Cameron made her Home Secretary. As the person who had controversially argued the Conservatives were seen as 'The Nasty Party', she might have been expected to pursue an overtly 'moderniser', liberal agenda, but in the light of threats to law and order like the August 2011 riots, she has pursued a fairly traditional tough Tory law and order line.

Defining crime

Legal: In one sense crimes are anything which are so described by legal statute, but this is too broadbrush a classification:

1 Criminal law is itself a subdivision of the law, relating to those rules society as a whole have judged to be offences: burglary, assault, homicide, for example. They are crimes against 'everyone' and so are dealt with separately from 'civil' law which concerns differences at a more private, individual level – for example: disputes about contracts, landlords seeking back-rent from tenants, divorce settlements and the like. For this reason criminal law has a stricter standard of evidence – 'beyond reasonable doubt' – than civil law's 'on the balance of probabilities'.

2 Definitions of law change over time. Reiner (2008) mentions a study of 3,514 people prosecuted by Essex quarter sessions 1628–32:

> . . . 144 were thefts and 48 were assaults. But these figures were dwarfed by the 480 prosecutions for allowing bridges or roads to fall into decay, 229 for keeping a disorderly alehouse, and, by far the biggest category – 684 prosecutions for failing to attend church.
>
> Reiner 2008: 25

3 If a law is considered 'unjust' it is possible to argue its invalidity, as champions of justice, like Martin Luther King or Nelson Mandela did in relation to laws discriminating on the grounds of race.

4 Moral values change slowly but sometimes massively over time, so laws discriminating against women and homosexuals, for example, no longer feature on the statute book.

Causes of crime

Some of the causes of crime have already been touched on. Politicians, it has been shown, argue either that people have become, or have been allowed to become, less law-abiding, more 'evil' even (though this is a much-contested concept), or that society has become a forcing ground for such deviancy. Causes inevitably reflect political prejudices, but there are other possible causes.

The huge gap between rich and poor

One view is that all forms of private property constitute a form of theft, that all property by rights belongs to everyone. According to this view, everyone who is rich has 'appropriated' their property from others, leading to the position espoused by the American radical Angela Davis: 'The real criminals in this society are not the people who populate the prisons across the state but those who have stolen the wealth of the world from the people'. It remains a fact that the gap between rich and poor in Britain over the last 20 years has grown faster than in any other developed Western country.

A vividly clear recent contribution to this literature was made by the already mentioned book *The Spirit Level*. This book, based on painstaking research across international borders, suggests that the greater the relative inequality within a country, the more acute is its range and intensity of social dysfunction. Their figures proved this to be true in relation to trust levels, education, teenage pregnancies, life expectancy, obesity and violence. Their scatter graph, Figure 23.1, illustrates how imprisonment rates closely follow this index from the least unequal countries – Japan, Scandinavia, northern Europe – to the most unequal: UK, Australia, Israel, Portugal, and, by a distance, the biggest imprisoner, the USA whose rate is four-and-a-half times that of the UK and 14 times that of Japan.

There are now many more potential crimes

In the old days family arguments were ignored by police as 'domestics'. Since the law has changed, crimes of violence have registered an increase. Furthermore, the proliferation of consumer goods has increased the opportunity for crime: there are simply more things to steal, especially valuable portable objects like ipods and mobile phones.

Young people are faced with a difficult world in which to grow up

1 Many young people are increasingly the products of fragmented families and have lacked the emotional security of a proper home.

2 Unemployment – likely to increase following the deep depression beginning in 2009 – has replaced valuable socialisation through work with despair. As a consequence, young people lose out, as American sociologist Charles Murray (1990) observes, 'acquiring skills and the network of friends and experiences enable them to establish a place for themselves – not only in the workplace but a vantage point from which they can make sense of themselves and their lives' (1990: 25).

3 In consequence, youngsters find life infinitely grey and pointless. Crime can seem like the ultimate rebellion and excitement. John Purves, a solicitor who has defended many young joyriders in the North-west and the North-east, explains that it 'provides an escape from their humdrum existences. They are thrilled by the speed of these flying machines and the more dangerous it gets the more

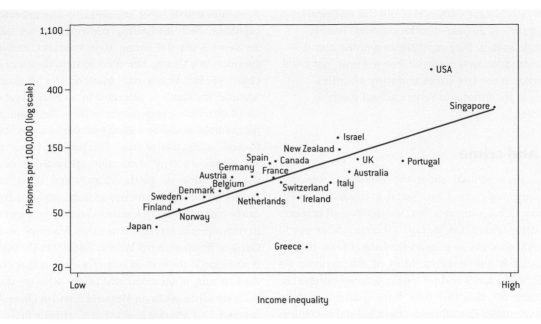

Figure 23.1 More people are imprisoned in more unequal countries
Source: Wilkinson and Pickett, 2008

excited they become. It's an addiction . . . The press call them "deathriders"; that's the real thrill' (*Observer*, 25 June 1994).

Growth of an underclass

Charles Murray, quoted above, has written that he thinks the UK is well on the way to developing its own underclass of disaffected poor living in the inner cities, often in council housing and unemployed, eking out their lives on

benefits and crime. Any youngster living in such an area finds it very difficult to resist the allure and rewards of crime and the attractions of drugs, easy living and violence.

Values have declined

This view is especially popular with Conservatives, who hark back to a golden age when it was possible to live without fear of crime. Geoff Pearson's brilliant book *Hooligan* (1983) disposes of this myth:

BOX 23.1

What really causes crime?
Polly Toynbee's view

In 1988 a piece of Home Office research fell on stony ground, out of kilter with the ruling ideology of the times. *Trends in Crime and their Interpretation* plotted crime figures in the last century against the economic cycles, with graphs tracking crime against boom and bust. Its evidence is conclusive: in good times, when *per capita* consumption rises with higher employment, property crime falls. When people have money their need is less great, so burglary and theft trends drop. However, theft rises as soon as consumption falls when the economy dips and people on the margins fall out of work. But that is not the

whole picture. Something else happens in good times. People have more money in their pockets, they go out and their consumption of alcohol rises. The result? They hit each other more and personal violence figures rise. Exactly this is happening now with near full employment and soaring drink consumption, creating a rise in assaults, mainly young men hitting each other at night (mainly not very hard, only 14 per cent visited a doctor afterwards).

Source: Polly Toynbee, 'What Really Causes Crime?', *Guardian*, 12 July 2002 © Guardian Newspapers Limited 2002, reprinted with permission

Conservatives have enthused about this mythical law abiding society 20 years ago for decades. Twenty years ago, in fact, they were just as worried about crime and disorderly youth as they are now, panicked by hippies in the late sixties and early seventies, by Teds in the fifties and 'Americanised youth' in the forties.

Drugs and crime

Much has been written about the complex connection between drugs and crime. Chris Nuttal, in charge of research at the Home Office, estimates that two-thirds of all property crime is drug-related. On average a heroin addict has to raise £13,500 annually to support the habit, £8,000 more if crack cocaine is also involved. Most of this is raised via shoplifting, and a series of drug tests in different parts of the country have revealed that over three-quarters of those arrested were under the influence of alcohol and two-thirds other drugs. In July 2005 the press revealed that a suppressed report on the war on drugs showed it was being lost. Traffickers made so much money out of their trade that seizures of 60–80 per cent were needed to turn the tide; in reality seizures amounted to a mere 20 per cent. An increasingly influential argument has emerged pressing for control of recreational drugs through legalisation, but most politicians shy away from a policy which superficially appears to advocate easier access to dangerous drugs.

Anti-social behaviour

Much has been written about the rise of anti-social behaviour or 'yob culture' of the kind which makes town and city centres unwelcome to families, women on their own or middle-aged people wishing to go to theatres and cinemas. For the general public this is possibly the major cause of crime and source of apprehension. The source of the problem, most agree, is excessive consumption of alcohol and the further liberalisation of drinking hours which took place in November 2005 was not thought to be an especially intelligent piece of government. To be fair, however, to date it has been hard to ascribe the increase in the crime rate to it.

Neo-liberal economic policies and 'anomie'

Reiner (2007) argues that the chief wellspring of crime is the eclipse of consensus Keynesian welfare thinking by neo-liberal ideas from the mid-1970s onwards. In the 1980s this produced 'the massive social dislocations of de-industrialisation and resurgent mass unemployment . . . for increasing numbers of young men, especially among ethnic minorities and in inner city areas . . .' The unbridled turbo capitalism had 'devastating consequences for order that far outweighed the strong state measures introduced to control it in a Canute-like effort to stem the social tsunami' (2007: 95–96). Reiner cites Merton's idea of alienation or 'anomie': the conflicts generated by a desire to get on combined with lack of opportunity to do so. Being unemployed, for example, would be a good example of a condition likely to create such a state of mind. This problem is exacerbated in a consumerist society where values are rooted in materialism, the acquisition of goods, chattels and other inanimate articles. Such a society provides no finite limit whereby 'success' can be measured: the rich want to become the super rich who in turn aspire to exceed the wealth of Microsoft founder Bill Gates or finance wizard Warren Buffet. On the other hand, if someone at the bottom end of society cannot even reach the first rung of the materialist ladder, what are they to do? A Liverpudlian youth on *Weekend World* in December 1985 expressed his reaction simply but eloquently thus:

> Some people have got jobs, they can go out and buy things they want. But we're on the dole, we haven't got the money so we go out robbing to get the money.

The work of Box, Erlich and the already mentioned Field did much to establish the once disputed nexus between economic downturns and increases in crime, whether against property or indeed violence against the person. A distinction also needs to be made between 'core' employment where, for example, skilled workers enjoy relative employment and financial security and the 'secondary' or peripheral sector where workers are poorly paid and lack employment rights. The latter kind of employment is much less likely to reduce crime rates though there is evidence the introduction of the minimum wage in 1999 helped bring down crime in previously low-wage areas (Reiner 2007: 101).

Possible role of lead poisoning

This might seem at first sight a ludicrous suggestion: that traces of lead ingested into the bodies of young children, could play a role in the incidence of crime. George Monbiot in the *Guardian*, 8 January 2013 was himself sceptical:

> Studies between cities, states and nations show that the rise and fall in crime follows, with a roughly 20-year lag, the rise and fall in the exposure of infants to trace quantities of lead. But all that gives us is correlation: an association that could be coincidental.

However, having studied the thoroughly respectable academic papers on the subject, Monbiot writes:

The curve is much the same in all the countries these papers have studied. Lead was withdrawn first from paint and then from petrol at different times in different places (beginning in the 1970s in the US in the case of petrol, and the 1990s in many parts of Europe), yet despite these different times and different circumstances, the pattern is the same: violent crime peaks around 20 years after lead pollution peaks. The crime rates in big and small cities in the US, once wildly different, have now converged, also some 20 years after the phase-out.

Clearly, more research will need to be undertaken but the sudden fall in crime on both sides of the Atlantic has never been adequately explained, even by the most learned criminologists. Could this be the explanation?

Conviction rates

Reiner (2007) explains how the volume of crime is much greater than that formally registered by the police. The British Crime Survey (BCS), now called the Crime Survey of England and Wales, gives a more reliable snapshot of how crime is being experienced 'at ground level':

> Only 2 per cent of crimes measured by the BCS end up with a convicted offender, and another 1 per cent in a caution. The proportion of known crimes leading to someone being sentenced to custody is 0.3 per cent. And they are mainly for a variety of street crimes . . . The imbalance begins with what is reported (or more often not reported) by victims and more marked as the cases go through the criminal justice system.

Figure 23.2 illustrates this tendency vividly.

'Dark crime figure' (unreported offences)

Why are less than half of this true 'dark figure' of offences ever reported to the police? There are several reasons. Some victims are not aware they have become victims – especially children; some choose not to report the offence because they consider it too minor or it entails insufficient loss to justify the trouble. In a fair number of violent crimes the victim saw the matter as 'private' to be resolved independently; in other cases victims might fear reprisals for going to the police. Some offences also do not have a victim in that the person against whom the 'offence' is committed – for example a drug or prostitution offence – are willing participants. Police officers, for their part, fail to record over half of all crimes reported to them, according to the 1981 BCS. Another consideration is the reclassifications of crime introduced by the Home Office on a fairly regular basis.

Who are the perpetrators?

One longitudinal survey of all people born in 1953 revealed that by the age of 30 one in three men had been convicted of a crime; one in 16 had been to prison; and, significantly, the 7 per cent who had been convicted six or more times accounted for two-thirds of all offences. The survey also showed that violence was on the increase: one in eight men convicted of an offence had committed a crime of violence by the age of 20. For those born in 1963, the proportion had risen to one in five. Certainly young

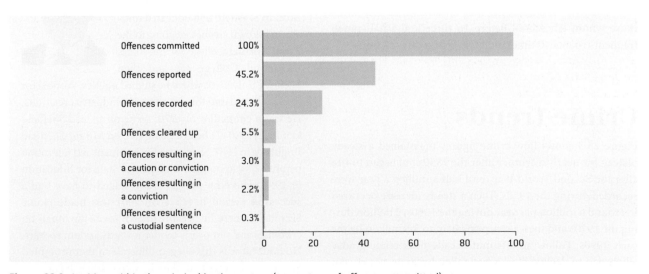

Figure 23.2 Attrition within the criminal justice system (percentage of offences committed)
Source: G. Barclay and C. Tavares, *Digest 4: Information on the Criminal Justice System in England and Wales* (London: Home Office, 1999: 29)

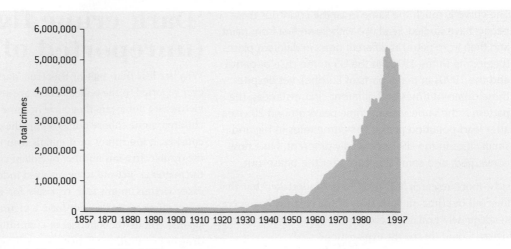

Figure 23.3 Crimes recorded by the police, 1857–1997

Source: G. Barclay and C. Tavares, *Digest 4: Information on the Criminal Justice System in England and Wales* (London: Home Office, 1999: 2)

criminals seem to abound. Most crimes are committed by people aged 14 to 20; over 90 per cent of all 15- to 16-year-old offenders re-offend within four years. On 20 November 1996 the Audit Commission reported on juvenile justice. Its document, *Misspent Youth*, revealed that the 150,000 teenage offenders commit 7 million crimes every year, only 19 per cent of which are recorded by police and only 5 per cent cleared up, with a mere 3 per cent resulting in arrest and action.

Predominantly those in prison are the products of poor, badly parented families, afflicted by economic problems. If those in prison are compared with society in general, studies have shown that while around 17 per cent of the general population are under 25, the percentage of those in prison is more than twice that figure. Other disproportionate figures include the fact that men are doubly represented – ethnic minorities, also; unemployed four times, homeless 30 times; those whom left school before 16 three and a half times; frequent truants 10 times; and taken into care, 13 times.

Crime trends

Figure 23.3 shows how crime figures maintained a steady plateau for nearly a century after the 1850s but began to rise after the Second World War until half a million a year were recorded during the 1950s. Then a steady increase occurred to around a million per year during the 1960s, 2 million during the 1970s and then a sharp spike up to 5.5 million by the early 1990s. Following this mid-decade peak crime gradually began to decline until it had fallen by some 40 per cent by 2008. Criminologists mostly attribute the fall to the prosperity associated with the 'boom years' of the first decade of the new century, but they also have doubts (see Box 23.3).

Getting tough on crime

As explained earlier on in the chapter, after 1979 crime, by virtue of its huge increase, became a potent factor in voter choice. The Conservatives under Michael Howard led the charge, as Box 23.2 explains.

PROFILE

David Blunkett (1947–)

Born in Sheffield and educated initially in his own city before going to the Royal Normal College for the Blind, Richmond College FE and then Sheffield University, where he studied politics. Worked for the Gas Board and then as a tutor in industrial relations. He was a councillor in 1970, going on to lead Sheffield Council (1980–7) before being elected MP for Sheffield Brightside in 1987. Shadowed Environment and Education before being appointed Secretary of State for Education in 1997, where he was generally judged to have had a successful period in office. In 2001 was made Home Secretary, where he became known for being tough on criminals and not overly tender towards asylum seekers. No doubt it was this alleged illiberalism that prompted Sir John Mortimer to declare in March 2003: 'It is so sad to learn, as a lifelong Labour voter, that our Home Secretaries are worse than the Conservative ones.'

BOX 23.2

Howard's measures to curb crime

At the 1993 Conservative Party conference in Blackpool, Home Secretary Michael Howard unveiled 'the most comprehensive programme of action against crime' announced in Britain, including abolition of the right to silence for defendants; new measures against terrorism; tougher penalties for persistent young offenders; the building of six new prisons; new powers to evict squatters and for police to stop trespassers; automatic custody for anyone convicted of rape, manslaughter or murder or attempting the offence who is subsequently accused of any of these crimes; a review to toughen sentences in the community; and accepting all 16 proposals of review on cutting paperwork to let police do more active duties.

Howard told the conference:

> There is a tidal wave of concern about crime in this country. I am not going to ignore it. I am going to take action. Tough action.

However, the reaction to Howard's line was not as warm outside the conference chamber as it was within. Lord Justice Woolf threw in a firecracker when he said publicly that these 'get tough' policies would not work and were 'short-sighted and irresponsible'. On 17 October 1993 the *Observer* led with the views of no fewer than seven judges, all of whom attacked the idea asserted by Howard that 'prison works' through taking criminals off the street and providing a deterrent to others.

Lord Ackner said the causes of crime 'lay deep in society, in the deterioration of personal standards, the family and the lack of self-discipline'. Lord Justice Farquharson, chairman of the Judicial Studies Board said:

> The idea that we are building more and more prisons appals me. I have never believed prison rehabilitates anyone.

Lord Bruce Laughland was even more explicit:

> The effectiveness of the deterrent diminishes the more an individual goes to prison. People fear hearing the gates shut behind them for the first time. Prison may satisfy public opinion and the victims' understandable feelings, but it has no rehabilitation effect whatsoever . . . a great deal of dishonesty is contributed by politicians.

Labour get even tougher

New Labour under Tony Blair was desperate to match Conservative toughness on crime and a virtual 'bidding war' on tough measures got under way. Reiner, writing in The *Guardian*, 25 November 2005, saw the tipping point occurring in the early 1990s when New Labour accepted the 'economic and social framework of Thatcherism', meaning that the second part of Blair's mantra on crime – 'tough on the causes of crime' – was likely to be vestigial; now the police had to try to be 'tough on crime' to substitute for the vanished social cohesion which had previously helped to keep crime at bay. Throughout Labour's tenure in power, prison populations continued to soar. Despite falling crime figures, the public, made sceptical by dodgy official statistics, continued to believe they were going up. The very precautions against crime, which ironically were helping to reduce it, encouraged citizens to retain a heightened awareness of crime and its likelihood. The onset of the economic recession beginning in 2008 saw property crime figures spike for the first quarter of 2009, but only mildly so.

The crime wave: its rise and decline

The huge explosion in crime figures occurred in the 1980s and was a consequence, argues Robert Reiner, of neo-liberal economic policies (see above). In 1921 a mere 193,000 **notifiable** (i.e. serious) **offences** were recorded; by 1979 the figure was 2.5 million and by 1993 had increased by a further 128 per cent to 5.7 million. Then crime figures began to decline steadily so that by the middle of the first decade of the new century Labour was claiming credit for a 40-plus

percentage reduction in serious crime with the BCS figures reflecting similar falls. Reiner (see Box 23.3) rejects as the explanation for this the increased punitiveness which has characterised penal policy for the last two decades and, while he confesses criminologists have no definitive answer, he thinks it is related to the relatively high levels of prosperity during the 'consumer boom' years 1995–2007.

Crime figures, summer 2012

Quarterly BCS figures in October 2009 showed that for the first time 50 per cent of respondents felt that councils and police are dealing with crime and anti-social behaviour – up from 45 per cent in 2008. However, the recession was thought to have been responsible for a spike in property crime (for example, robberies and cycle theft) in the first quarter of 2009. Crime figures some three years on however registered reductions of overall police recorded crime of 4.2 per cent for the year March 2011–12. Reductions occurred in nine of the ten main crime categories with criminal damage showing a substantial 10 per cent reduction, homicides at their lowest level since 1983 and violence against the person down 7.2 per cent. These figures are the more remarkable in that, according to a report published Her Majesty's Inspectors of Constabulary (HMIC, 11 September 2012), nearly 6,800 frontline officers had been lost because of economy cuts since May 2010.

Guardian journalist Alan Travis notes that both police statistics and the CSEW indicate a continued decrease despite an ongoing economic recession. He adds: 'One of the most interesting figures is about the perception of crime. The Crime Survey asks people whether they think crime is getting worse where they live and nationally. So people think crime is getting worse – but not where they live' (19 July 2012). Such a discontinuity of perception is not uncommon regarding the public sector and has been duplicated, for example in perceptions of the NHS.

Elected Police Crime Commissioners (PCCs)

Elections for Police Commissioners took place on 15 November 2012. The origins of this idea lie in a decision by Home Secretary Theresa May to scrap Home Office targets for police forces nationwide. This left an absence of an external body to drive up police performance. It was believed PPCs would fill this gap. The new PCCs, it is intended, will hire and fire top policemen in the 41 police areas, establish local policing priorities and budgets and advise on council tax rates.

However, the run-up to the elections witnessed much criticism of arrangements. Candidates required a deposit of £5,000, returnable only if they polled above 5 per cent of the vote; candidates for the Commons only have to find £500 and for local councils none at all. Further, candidates with minor juvenile convictions were in some cases barred from standing and very little funding for publicising the elections was made available. The Electoral Reform Society warned that turnout might be as low as 18 per cent and a poll in May had shown less than a fifth of respondents knowing about the elections at all, let alone understanding the role of the new commissioners. In the event turnout was a pathetic 15 per cent; the Home Secretary suggested it would increase once

the new roles had bedded down and become more familiar. It was perhaps significant that of the 41 commissioners elected, 12 were not overtly connected with a political party.

The security services and related Home Office matters

As well as the law enforcement agencies of the courts, supported by the police, there are the security services, much loved by novelists and screenwriters as sources for their plot lines. People who have worked for these services usually puncture the popular illusion of mystery, excitement and glamour by claiming that such work is mostly routine and often very boring. Most of us, perhaps, would be surprised that defending the state against enemies within or without is not inherently exciting.

Three pieces of legislation authorise the security services:

1 *Security Service Act 1989 (amended in 1996)*: This placed the services under the control of the Home Office and laid out the duties of the Director General.

2 *Intelligence Services Act 1994 (ISA)*: This established the Intelligence and Security Committee, a Commons Committee that oversees the expenditure, administration and policy of the intelligence and security services.

3 *Regulation and Investigatory Powers Act 2000 (RIPA)*: The Act that set up the Commissioner of Interception, a Commissioner for the intelligence services and a tribunal to hear complaints under the Human Rights Act.

The last two Acts allow warrants to be issued by the Home Secretary to intercept communications, interfere with property and undertake 'intrusive surveillance'.

There are four main elements to the security services: MI5, Special Branch, MI6 and GCHQ.

MI5

The existence of MI5 is well known, but until recently most of its activities were shrouded in secrecy. The most we knew officially was that it was set up in 1909 to counter the activity of German spies in the run-up to the First World War. We now know, since 1993, that it employs 2,000 personnel and has a budget of £150 million per year, most of which is spent on counter-terrorism and the bulk of the rest on counter-espionage. After the end of the Cold War, it was perhaps a little short of things to do and in 1992 it was tasked with gathering intelligence about the IRA. In 1996 it was given the further responsibility of helping to counter 'serious crime'.

For most citizens the closest they are likely to get to the agency is if they are vetted for a sensitive post in government. Physically, however, they can now easily see from where this very secret work is controlled: from its headquarters on the banks of the Thames not far from the Houses of Parliament. Political control is exercised by the Home Secretary.

Special Branch

This is a branch of the police force, again ultimately under Home Secretary control, tasked with combating terrorism, espionage, sabotage and subversion. In addition, it provides security for important people, watches the ports and airports and makes arrests for MI5. Like MI5, it employs 2,000 personnel but at £20 million per year spends much less.

MI6

MI6 deals with political and economic intelligence abroad. It works mostly through agents attached to British embassies overseas, although it maintains close liaison with the Defence Intelligence Service. It comes under the authority of the Foreign Secretary. From 1994 it has added serious crime to its portfolio of responsibilities, including money laundering and drug smuggling as well as illegal immigration.

Government Communications Headquarters (GCHQ)

This 'listening post' organisation originated from the famously successful code-breaking service based in Bletchley Park during the war. It operates under a treaty signed with the USA in 1947 and seeks to monitor international radio communications utilising communication satellites and listening posts worldwide. Its base in the UK is in Cheltenham and it has over 6,000 employees with an annual budget of £500 million. In 1984 the Thatcher Government controversially banned membership of trade unions – allegedly at US request – on security grounds; trade union rights were restored by Labour in 1997.

Apart from the 1994 Act mentioned above, the security services are not accountable to Parliament; the Prime Minister is ultimately responsible for their actions, and the respective heads of the services report directly to him. The PM also chairs the Cabinet Committee on the Security and Intelligence Services. One of the six secretariats in the Cabinet Office is concerned with security and intelligence and serves to coordinate relevant information for feeding into Cabinet. This secretariat contains the Coordinator of Intelligence and Security, who is another official in this important area who reports directly to the PM. The Joint Intelligence Committee comprises (among others) the secret service heads; it supplies the Cabinet with security information. The security services do not come under the jurisdiction of any complaints procedure, and they do not need to inform the police of their operations. When security service personnel have had to give evidence in court, they have done so with their identities concealed. Critics point out that those tasked with controlling these services have little time to do so and in practice know very little of what goes on. The Security Commission was established in 1964 and investigates security lapses and shortcomings.

The Home Affairs Select Committee in 1993 asked for the right to investigate the activities of the security services in order to guard against abuses of power. The Government went some of the way towards meeting its critics in 1994 when it set up, via the Intelligence Services Act, the Intelligence and Security Committee. This comprises nine members drawn from both Houses of Parliament and is charged with scrutiny of the expenditure, administration and policy of MI5, MI6 and GCHQ. It meets weekly and occasionally issues critical reports like the one (1995) in which the service heads were criticised for not being aware of the adverse effects of the spying activities of CIA agent Aldrich Ames. Critics argue that the new committee has too few powers to be effective: it cannot call witnesses or relevant papers and is able to investigate only that which the security service heads allow.

In May 2012 the Government announced plans to allow GCHQ to demand access to individual online accounts. This proposal was met with substantial opposition, including from the Conservatives, just as it had when the previous Labour Government made the same suggestion. Tory MP David Davis called it 'an unnecessary extension of the ability of the state to snoop on ordinary people' (BBC, April 2012).

Transfer of constitutional responsibilities to Lord Chancellor's department

Following the 2001 General Election, Tony Blair transferred a number of constitutional functions to the office of his former boss, the Lord Chancellor Lord Irvine. These covered human rights, House of Lords reform, freedom of information, data protection, the crown dependencies (Channel Isles, Isle of Man), royal, hereditary and Church matters, civic honours (city status and lord mayoralties) and the Cenotaph ceremony (an annual service to honour the war dead led by the Queen).

Terrorism Acts, 2000–9

The 2000 Act preceded the attack on the World Trade Center, although those horrific events prompted some additional toughening up of the earlier measure. The Act defined 'terrorism' as any threat to influence the government of the UK 'for the purpose of advancing a political, religious or ideological cause'. Civil rights campaigners point out that the Act's scope is dangerously wide. Taken with its detailed provisions, it empowers police to make arrests without warrants, enter buildings without court orders (if they reasonably suspect terrorists are to be found within) and prosecute people for holding information likely to be useful to terrorists. People can be stopped at random, and if they refuse to give their names can be sent to prison. Police can also seize any cash that they think 'is intended for the purposes of terrorism' without specific authorisation. The Liberal Democrats in the form of Simon Hughes MP attacked the definition of terrorism as 'far too wide'. In the event of someone being found in possession of something likely to be used for the purposes of terrorism, then it is up to the accused to prove his or her innocence. In April 2004 the Government announced CONTEST, a new cross-departmental strategy aiming to counter sources of terrorism and related acts at home and abroad.

In June 2005 the European Commisioner of Human Rights, Alvaro Gil-Robles, published a damning report on Britain's anti-terror laws. He perceived an attitude in which 'human rights are frequently construed as, at best, formal commitments and, at worst, cumbersome obstructions'. He concluded that such rights were not luxuries but 'the very foundation of democratic societies'. Particularly in mind were the long-term detention of terrorist suspects in Belmarsh prison and their treatment while in custody. Then came the July bombings on the London Underground which launched another wave of get-tough initiatives against possible terrorists. In the autumn of 2005 Tony Blair launched yet another Terror Bill which sought to exclude from the UK any people 'glorifying' or inciting terrorist acts, disseminating publications to the same end, or preparing such acts and training others to do so. But the most draconian and controversial measure proposed was the detention of suspects for up to 90 days. Blair and Clarke, his Home Secretary, were warned this was more than their party could accept, but they pressed on regardless and in November 2005 the measure was defeated when 49 Labour MPs refused to support the government. Blair was unrepentant, saying sometimes it was right to lose if the issue was the right course of action. The eventual 28-day period of detention was still longer than most other EU countries had thought wise to impose. In the autumn

of 2008 Home Secretary Jacqui Smith attempted to amend the detention time to 42 days, but after a crushing defeat in the House of Lords on 13 October she made a humiliating about-turn, announcing she was withdrawing the proposal. The Coalition Government avoided the kind of emphasis its Labour predecessor had given the issue. In January 2011 the Government reduced the 28 days to 14; the minister involved, Damian Green, told the Commons that the order, which elapsed on 20 January, would not be extended.

The security services and 'dodgy dossiers' on Iraq

In September 2002 the Government published a dossier on Iraqi 'weapons of mass destruction' that embodied a substantial amount of intelligence services information. Later, in February 2003, another dossier was published focusing on the Iraqi regime's concealment of such weapons. Neither dossier was considered convincing at the time, especially when the latter was damagingly revealed to include a plagiarised section of a 12-year-old PhD thesis, but in the wake of the war, critical scrutiny intensified. In May 2003 it was alleged by a BBC journalist Andrew Gilligan, that senior intelligence officers were accusing New Labour's spin-meister, Alastair Campbell, of adding his own material to the September dossier to 'sex it up' to make more compelling the case for a war his master strongly favoured. In the ensuing furious row, which involved the suicide of Dr David Kelly, the MOD officer alleged to be Gilligan's source, many observed that the intelligence services had been involved closely, and unhealthily, in the presentation of what were in essence political arguments. Lord Hutton took extensive evidence in the ensuing inquiry, some of which seemed to support the Gilligan case, but his report surprisingly exonerated government and accused only the BBC, leading to several resignations. The Butler Report on the intelligence services' failure over the non-existent weapons of mass destruction in Iraq also cleared the government of any major wrong-doing, but was critical of several areas of poor intelligence; it criticised Blair's description of the Iraq intelligence and warning that the country had weapons which could reach British-controlled areas within 45 minutes as 'authoritative'. Critics of the government were outraged that the man at the centre of much of the intelligence furore, John Scarlett, was allowed promotion to head of MI5. The Chilcot Inquiry into the Iraq war opened in July 2009; by May 2013 it still had not published its report.

BOX 23.3

BRITAIN IN CONTEXT

Crime and punishment

The Economist (23 August 2003) reacted to the news that 11.3 per cent of American boys born in 2001 will go to jail (33 per cent of black boys) with the comment that 'conservative politicians are on their way to creating a criminal class of unimaginable proportions'.

Every society on the planet suffers from problems of crime. Part of this is due to the fact that drugs are, albeit illegally, one of the world's major traded commodities. Crime in the USA has a well-known international profile, as so many Hollywood movies have chosen stories about gangsters, bank robbers or gang violence. Some sociologists have argued that countries with a very high Gini coefficient – relationship of rich to poor – were likely to attract the highest crime rates, as relative differences fuel resentment and – when in the same society – opportunity. Figures available suggest there may be much in such calculations.

The nation with the best rating on this index is Japan with a ratio of richest 10 per cent to poorest 10 per cent of 4.5. The crime rate in Japan is, accordingly, relatively low. The equivalent ratio for the UK is 13.8, placing it 51st in the international rankings. The USA comes in at 15.9 and 92nd. Countries like Brazil and South Africa, both notorious for their crime rates, come even lower down at ratios of 33.1 and 68, respectively: 116th and 117th overall. Murder figures in the USA have been astonishingly high by British or European standards. For many years visitors to New York expected to encounter muggers on every street corner or a Los Angeles blazing with gang warfare.

Crime is still a major problem in the USA with, in 2002, nearly 5,000 cases of aggravated assault in Washington alone, a sexual assault every two minutes somewhere in the country, and 42 murders for every 100,000 people in Detroit. But then came a rather unexpected fall in crime levels. According to the FBI, the crime rate per 100,000 inhabitants was just under 2,000 in 1960, rose to nearly 6,000 in 1990, but began to fall in the nineties, ending up at about 4,000 in 2004. Why did crime increase?

Professor Robert Reiner, from the London School of Economics (Reiner 2006b), analyses the changing patterns of crime, noting that similar patterns of crime occurred in the USA and industrialising European countries: an increase during the late eighteenth and early nineteenth centuries during the early Industrial Revolution followed by 'a long-term process of inclusion of the majority of the population in legal, political and, to a lesser extent, economic and social citizenship'. The late twentieth century saw a sharp upturn in crime in these same countries. Reiner identifies two explanations, one favoured by the Left and the other by the Right: the return to a tougher form of capitalism–neo-liberalism, replacing welfarism and causing hardship; and the erosion of social values by the '**permissiveness**' of liberalism, expressed most typically during the sixties.

Reiner quotes another criminologist, Elliot Currie who attributed the rise to:

> great structural inequalities and community fragmentation and weakened ability of parents to monitor and supervise their children – and a great many other things all going on at once, all entwined with each other, and all affecting the crime rate – with the combination having an impact that is much greater than its parts.

Why did crime fall? Reiner dismisses 'zero tolerance' as other cities in the US experienced similar falls to the home of this approach: New York. He also dismisses the 'enormous expansion of punitiveness, above all the staggering and gross levels of imprisonment' as a major cause. Numbers of US citizens in jail are indeed horrendous – a higher percentage than in any other country: 2 million are in jail, with nearly half of them drawn from the 12 per cent of the population which is black. More likely an explanation for the downturn, he thinks, was the upturn in the economies of these nations which reduced the need for property crime, but he has to conclude: 'The crime drop remains something of a mystery, defying any simple account.'

Chapter summary

Conservative thinkers have tended to base their law and order policies on a pessimistic view of human nature, while Labour has tended to be more optimistic. However, both views began to converge in the late 1980s and early 1990s. Crime figures suggest a crime wave, but there are many qualifications to bear in mind. It is doubtful whether the Conservatives substantially reversed the crime wave in the early 1990s. It seems likely that crime breeds in poor, rundown areas of big cities. Police attempts to control crime have not been very successful and have received much criticism, even from the Conservatives. Tougher prison sentences are favoured by the Conservatives, but experience suggests that this is no real answer.

The Home Office is the department in charge of the security services, although it has transferred constitutional responsibilities to the Lord Chancellor's Department. The 2000 and 2005 Terrorism Acts offended those concerned with the defence of human rights though polls show considerable support for tough laws against terrorism and terrorists.

Postscript

Crime statistics spring 2013 register further falls.

When the financial crisis arrived in 2007 many criminologists expected crime to soar, as it has in the past during tough financial times. However, even with increased levels of young males aged 15–24, the most likely offenders, youth unemployment doubled since 2001; big cuts in police numbers and an economy mired in stagnation, crime rates continue to fall. Over the past two decades, it has halved in England and Wales, falling by 8% in a single year to 2011–12. The murder rate has fallen to its lowest point – 540 in 2012 – since 1978; even anti-social behaviour fell from 4 m incidents in 2007 to 2.4 m in 2012. Why?

The Economist (20 April 2013) suggests that people are buying less therefore there is less to steal, people are more home bound so deter break-ins; but most important people have less money to spend on alcohol – a 16% drop in consumption since 2004 – so are less inclined to become involved in brawls. Moreover, car crime, often the gateway to more serious crimes, has been cut by better car security and the market for household goods, microwaves, televisions and the like, seems to have faded away. Criminals appear to have moved into such things as cloning credit cards or online crime, crimes which do not show up in crime reports. Crime might inch up again as further cuts bite even deeper but for the time being nothing seems to be slowing down the rate of criminal offending.

Discussion points

- Which analysis of human nature seems closer to the truth, the pessimistic or optimistic version?

- How reliable are crime figures?

- Would more widely spread prosperity solve the crime problem?

- Are too many criminals locked up?

- What alternative forms of punishment would you advocate?

Further reading

By far the best single book on this subject, and drawn on heavily in this chapter, is Reiner (2008); it is warmly recommended. On race riots, Michael Keith (1993) is worth reading; and on penal policy, Windlesham (1993) is authoritative and interesting. *The Economist*'s reports on crime are always well informed and well written, as are those of the quality press whenever crime moves to the top of the political agenda.

Bibliography

Box, S. (1987) *Recession, Crime and Punishment* (Oxford University Press).

Dorling, D. (2005) 'Prime Suspect', in Hilliard, P., Pantazis, C., Tombs, S. and Gordon, D. *Beyond Criminology* (Pluto).

Dunning, E.G., Gaskell, G. and Benewick, R. (eds) (1987) *The Crowd in Modern Britain* (Sage).

Ferguson, C. (2012) *Inside Job: The Financiers who Pulled Off the Heist of the Century* (Blackwell).

IPPR (2006) *Crime-share: The Unequal Impact of Crime* (Institute of Public Policy and Research).

Jenkins, R. (2001) *Churchill* (Pan).

Jones, B. (1999) 'Crime and Punishment', in Jones, B. (ed.) *Political Issues in Britain Today* (Manchester University Press).

Keith, M. (1993) *Race Riots and Policing* (UCL Press).

Lea, J. and Young, J. (1984) *What is to be Done about Law and Order?* (Penguin).

Mawby, R.I. (1999) *Policing Across the World* (UCL Press).

Murray, C. (1990) *The Emerging British Underclass* (IEA Health and Welfare Unit).

Pearson, G. (1983) *Hooligan: A History of Respectable Fears* (Macmillan).

Rawnsley, A. (2010) *The End of the Party: The Rise and Fall of New Labour* (Viking).

Reiner, R. (1993) *The Politics of the Police*, 2nd edn (Harvester Wheatsheaf).

Reiner, R. (2006a) 'The Social Democratic Criminology', in Newburn, T. and Rock, P. (eds) *The Politics of Crime Control* (Oxford University Press).

Reiner, R. (2006b) 'Law and Order', in *Current Legal Problems* (published via UCL by Oxford University Press).

Reiner, R. (2007) *Law and Order: An Honest Citizen's Guide to Crime and Control* (Polity).

Reiner, R. (2008) *Law and Order* (Polity).

Reiner, R. (2012) 'What's Left? the prospects for social democratic criminology', *Crime, media, culture*, vol. 8, no. 2, pp. 135–50.

Toynbee, P. (2002) 'What Really Causes Crime?' *Guardian*, 12 June 2002.

Travis, A. (2009) 'Crime Down 4%, Police Figures Show and Murders with Knives Decline 35%', *Guardian*, 23 October 2009.

Travis, A. (2012) *Crime Statistics for England and Wales*, 19 July 2012, Guardian Datablog.

Wilkinson, R. and Pickett, K. (2010) *The Spirit Level* (Penguin).

Windlesham, Lord (1993) *Responses to Crime*, Vol. 2 (Clarendon Press).

Useful websites

Home Office: http://www.homeoffice.gov.uk/
Prison Service: http://www.hmprisonservice.gov.uk/
Police Service: http://www.police.uk/

CHAPTER 24

Social policy in the UK

Anneliese Dodds

> " **Power has only one duty – to secure the social welfare of the People** "
>
> Benjamin Disraeli

Learning objectives

- To define 'social policy' and explain how it is composed of a variety of different types of public, private, voluntary and occupational provision as part of a 'mixed economy of welfare'.

- To describe the history of social policy within the UK, as well as more recent trends over the past 30 years.

- To consider in detail the different elements of current UK social policy, including transfer payments like pensions and unemployment benefit, and services like health and social care.

- To identify and assess current challenges for UK social policy, including the challenges of population ageing and of hardening public opinion towards benefits recipients.

This chapter examines those policies enacted by UK governments ostensibly to improve population wellbeing, including transfers and tax expenditures, and services like health and social care, social housing and education. Many policies in these areas are paid for and delivered directly by government. Nonetheless, UK governments have sometimes required individuals to contribute to the costs of social policy, or to deliver it themselves (as with families caring for older or younger relations when they become ill, for example). UK governments have also used non-governmental actors (like the voluntary and private sectors) to deliver services, even while they are paid for by government. This chapter therefore considers the broad range of government activities in the provision of social policy, including cases where government is no longer the sole provider of welfare services.

The chapter first considers the development of social policy in the UK. It then sets out some broad trends in social policy through the 1980s–2000s, and considers the UK in its international context. The chapter next moves on to detail developments in core areas including pensions, unemployment benefit, family support, tax credits, health and social care, housing, and education. The chapter ends with a consideration of key challenges for social policy in the UK, including the impact of demographic change and changes in public attitudes towards the welfare state.

Introduction

Readers should note that social policy in the UK is in a state of flux, following radical new plans proposed by the Conservative/Liberal Democrat Coalition Government. This chapter presents a picture of developments at the time of writing, but in order to be completely up-to-date on developments beyond March 2012, readers are advised to consult the sources referred to at the end of this chapter.

What is social policy?

There are numerous definitions of 'social policy'. Some authors focus only on the provision of government funds to needy individuals (like pensioners and the unemployed) – what are conventionally known as '**transfer payments**' (see Esping-Andersen 1990). Others argue that 'social policy' goes far wider, encompassing everything governments do to improve the wellbeing of their populations, by boosting incomes and also providing health, housing and education services (Wilensky 1975). Yet others would argue that social policies do not have to be delivered by governments, but can be provided by employers, as what is known as '**occupational welfare**'. As a result of the existence of 'occupational' (work-related) and voluntary systems of welfare in many nations alongside public provision, some authors have talked of a '**mixed economy of welfare**' (Powell 2007).

We generally think of social policies as in some way stemming from a desire to improve citizens' wellbeing. While some social policies may be motivated by altruism, others may have different motives at their root. Indeed, one of the reasons for the introduction of improved public health measures in the late-nineteenth century was concern over the poor health of recruits for the Boer War (Williams 2008: 161), rather than reflecting sympathy towards the poor. Furthermore, while social policies may be presented by politicians as increasing wellbeing, in practice they may harm some individuals' interests. Social policies in the UK have arguably promoted the interests of particular groups over others, affecting social classes, ethnic and racial groups, and men and women, differently (Ginsburg 1992).

Social policies have strong connections with other areas of public policy. This is for two reasons, one direct and the other indirect. First, some social policies are also delivery vehicles for other policy goals. For example, people who have untreatable mental disorders and are viewed as posing a potential risk to the community are subject to detention in secure hospitals within England (Cairney 2009). As a result, these hospitals have come to function effectively as an arm of criminal justice policy. Second, social policy affects other policy areas because it regularly consumes well over half of all government spending (see Table 24.1 below). So, it constrains governments' room for manoeuvre in other areas of spending. In addition, social policy can have a considerable impact on the economy as a whole by increasing or decreasing aggregate demand, through increasing or decreasing the amount of money in people's pockets.

Finally, the state employs a large proportion of the population in the delivery of social policies across the UK (see Figure 24.1). The percentage of the workforce employed in the health and social sectors has increased marginally over recent years, from 10.7 per cent of the population in 1995 to 12.9 per cent in 2007 (OECD 2011a).

Table 24.1 Social policy spending in relation to total government spending, in millions

Year	2005	2006	2007	2008	2009	2010
Housing and community amenities	13,471	14,468	15,635	16,794	19,493	18,565
Health	87,095	94,598	99,646	108,009	117,538	120,188
Education	77,590	81,560	86,709	92,309	97,060	101,794
Social protection (covering pensions, unemployment and family benefits, etc.)	197,597	203,847	215,446	229,984	250,932	262,563
Total government spending	**553,045**	**586,956**	**617,265**	**686,186**	**716,432**	**735,606**

Source: OECD, 2012, *Government expenditure by function*

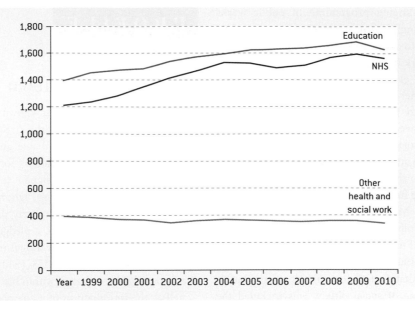

Figure 24.1 Employment within education, health and social work, in 1000s

Source: Based on data from Office for National Statistics, 2011a

The development of social policy in the UK

While the rest of this chapter details recent developments in social policy, this section provides some background on its historical development.

The term 'social policy' is closely allied to the notion of the **welfare state**. 'Welfare states' can be described as particularly well-developed systems of social policies which operate in democratic capitalist nations. As T.H. Marshall famously argued (1963), the development of the UK 'welfare state' occurred in parallel to the development of the UK's democratic parliamentary system. As individuals came to enjoy political rights with the extension of the franchise, they were increasingly provided with 'social rights' through the developing welfare state.

Nonetheless, while we generally associated the term 'welfare state' with a centralised system of provision, the first social policies in the UK were delivered locally, rather than by central government.

The beginnings of UK social policy

The origins of social policy can be traced back to systems of social assistance regulated by the 'Poor Laws' enacted from the mid-sixteenth century onwards. '**Social assistance**' refers to transfers available for those with no other forms of support. The Poor Laws required all parishes (the areas surrounding different churches) to collect and distribute contributions to aid the 'deserving poor'. Those classified as 'undeserving' (beggars) were subject to harsh punishment, including banishment from the parish and, in extreme cases, hanging. Every town was also required to provide work for the unemployed, through so-called 'Workhouses' or 'Poorhouses'.

Growing pressure on parishes due to increasing food prices and reduced local employment opportunities led to new approaches being adopted towards the end of the eighteenth century and start of the nineteenth. One of the most notorious was the so-called 'Speenhamland' approach, whereby Poor Law contributions were used to top up wages to help pay for the rising cost of bread. Unsurprisingly, this led to downward pressure on wages, since employers knew that below-subsistence wages would be subsidised by the parish. This exacerbated rather than diminished poverty.

Modern social policy

By the late nineteenth century more coordinated approaches were being pursued, again often by local authorities, but this time on a far larger scale. For example, the municipality of Birmingham, under Joseph Chamberlain as mayor, introduced a wide-ranging programme of public works during the 1870s ranging from slum clearance to public health and hygiene. In some areas these programmes were prompted by the work of social researchers, whose reports had highlighted the extent of crushing poverty amongst working, as well as unemployed, people. Pioneers in the area of social research were Joseph and Seebohm Rowntree and Charles Booth, who investigated poverty in York and London, respectively. Their work reflected the negative side of the abolition of feudalism and increasing industrialisation, which eventually led to two-thirds of the UK's population living in urban areas for the first time by the start of the twentieth century (Szreter and Mooney 1998). To put this into perspective, as of 2010, fully 85 per cent of the UK's population lived in urban areas (Eurostat 2012).

It was not until 1906 with the landslide election of a Liberal government that central government committed to a national programme of social policy. This included the provision of free school meals (made compulsory in 1914), relatively minimal means-tested pensions for the over 70s (from 1908, albeit under strict eligibility conditions), and the provision of 'labour exchanges' (the ancestors of today's 'Jobcentres') from 1909.

Most important, the Liberal Government also instituted the first system of **national insurance** in the UK under the National Insurance Act 1911. This combined contributions from workers, employers and government to provide a limited system of sick pay, unemployment payments for up to 15 weeks, and health services. Conservative opposition in the House of Lords to the 1909 Budget used to finance many of these reforms eventually led to the passing of the Parliament Act 1911, which established the formal supremacy of the Commons over the Lords.

Beveridge and the consolidation of national insurance

The core elements of the current UK welfare state were not, however, put into place until the end of the Second World War, following the publication in 1942 of William Beveridge's proposals for a programme of social provision to protect citizens 'from the cradle to the grave'. As a result, the UK welfare state is often described as **Beveridgean**, to differentiate it from welfare states drawing on the **Bismarckian** German model, designed by General Otto von Bismarck. While Beveridgean systems provide benefits to all contributors at the same rate, Bismarckian systems pay out different amounts depending on individuals' economic status, providing an occupation-based system (Bonoli 1997).

The Beveridge plan extended the previous system of national insurance to all workers, who would pay a flat rate contribution to cover expanded pensions, unemployment

PROFILE

William Henry Beveridge (1879–1963)

Lord Beveridge is now best known for his 1942 report to the UK Parliament on 'Social Insurance and Allied Services'. This report set the foundations for a limited system of national insurance designed to prevent the five 'giant evils' of want, disease, ignorance, squalor and idleness. When the Labour Party defeated Churchill's Conservative Party in 1945, it pledged to introduce the proposals set out within Beveridge's report. This resulted in the creation of the NHS (which Beveridge had acknowledged as essential within his 1942 proposals), as well as the introduction of a comprehensive system of national insurance.

Beveridge initially trained as a lawyer, but he soon tired of work as a barrister and abandoned the law to work at Toynbee Hall in East London. Toynbee Hall was, and still is, a 'university settlement' which brings students from Oxford University to experience the hardships of life in one of the most deprived areas of London. Whilst at Toynbee Hall, Beveridge met the social reformers Sidney and Beatrice Webb. From that point onwards, he concentrated his energies on the fields of manpower planning and social amelioration. These interests led to a varied career; Beveridge served as, variously, a government advisor, civil servant, Director of the London School of Economics, MP, and finally as the leader of the Liberal Party in the House of Lords.

Over recent years, the extent of transfer payments provided by national insurance has declined in relation to social assistance in areas like unemployment support. Nonetheless, Beveridge's 1942 proposals still continue to provide the overall framework for the UK welfare state.

insurance and health services. However, despite Beveridge's radical vision, the financial constraints facing the Labour Government of 1945 meant that his plan was supplemented by means-tested benefits such as social assistance (in its then form of 'National Assistance') from its very beginnings. Nonetheless, Beveridge's plan revolutionised the provision of health care, albeit after Nye Bevan, the then Labour Health Minister, had to 'stuff' GPs' mouths 'with gold' by letting them undertake private practice in addition to NHS work in exchange for them supporting the new system.

The UK's NHS was not the first 'national' and universal health service. The first had been put into place seven years earlier in New Zealand, albeit only for a more limited range of health care services (Blank and Burau 2004: 24). However, the NHS is undoubtedly the best-known example of a 'universal' health care system. The UK's 'Beveridgean' welfare state is often described as 'single payer', referring to the fact that, within it, government pays for the vast bulk of health care services and for unemployment insurance through the national insurance system, rather than this being paid for by social or private insurance schemes as occurs in many other countries (Flood 2000).

Social policy trends in the 1980s, 1990s and 2000s

Three core trends can be identified in the delivery of social policy over the past 30 years: changes in the nature of social policy spending, with a greater burden being shouldered by private individuals; a changed approach to the family, with women being viewed as increasingly likely to work as well as the 'male breadwinner'; and the introduction of competition and choice in the delivery of social policy.

Social policy expenditure

Early attempts to explain social policy development suggested that welfare states would grow steadily as economies modernised and industrialised (Wilensky 1975). This did initially occur in the UK, as in other industrialised nations. However, by the late 1970s new patterns of social policy started to form as welfare states matured (Alber 1981).

In the UK attempts were made under the Thatcher and Major Conservative governments to reduce the size of the welfare state. As discussed below, these attempts arguably bore fruit in relation to housing and pensions, but had less of an effect on other parts of the welfare state. Although welfare expenditure fluctuated to an extent throughout the 1980s, the overall direction of travel was towards an increase in the percentage of GDP devoted to public (i.e. government) social spending, from 16.5 per cent in 1980 to 18.7 per cent in 1997, and 20.5 per cent in 2007 (OECD 2012). It is important to remember, however, that increased spending may merely signify increased demand for welfare (as occurs when the level of unemployment increases), rather than higher levels of provision (Clayton and Pontusson 1998).

It should also be noted that the private contribution from individuals themselves to their own welfare has significantly increased over time. Figures 24.2 and 24.3 indicate the percentage of welfare provision coming from public and private sources, and from publicly mandated provision (where the state requires individuals or employers to pay into insurance funds, for example), in 1980 and 2007. They show clearly that individuals are increasingly contributing to their own pensions and paying for personal services like social care.

The pie charts also show areas where public social spending has increased and decreased over the last three decades. While public transfers to the unemployed and survivors (like widows' benefits) have decreased significantly, public spending to support those incapacitated and thus unable to work (such as the long-term sick) and to support housing costs have increased substantially.

Social policy and gender

Social policies frequently have differential impacts on men and women, yet the gendered nature of welfare states has only started to be seriously researched over the last quarter-century.

The UK's Beveridgean system of national insurance provided support like pensions only to those who had contributed, who were typically male workers for much of the twentieth century. As a result, the UK's welfare state has traditionally been described as a 'strong male breadwinner' model (Lewis 1992). According to this model, it was assumed that women would receive social protection through their relationship with men. Clearly, this created problems for those women who were not married.

Family structures have changed substantially since Beveridge's time. Now, only around a quarter of families approximate to a 'male sole earner' model, with the father being the sole breadwinner (Lewis 2009: 50). Some reforms have been made to social protection, including pensions, to improve coverage of those who have spent time out of the formal labour market, predominantly women who were raising families. Nonetheless, given women's low rates of pay and lower working hours than men, it may be most appropriate to describe the UK as exemplifying a 'one and a half earner' model (Pascall 2008) rather than a 'dual earner' model as exists in some Scandinavian countries. In addition, women still undertake the vast bulk of unpaid work within UK families, covering both housework and childcare, with no significant redistribution having occurred in this area (Pascall 2008).

Competition and choice in the delivery of social policy

Social policies have been traditionally controlled and delivered by a combination of central government departments such

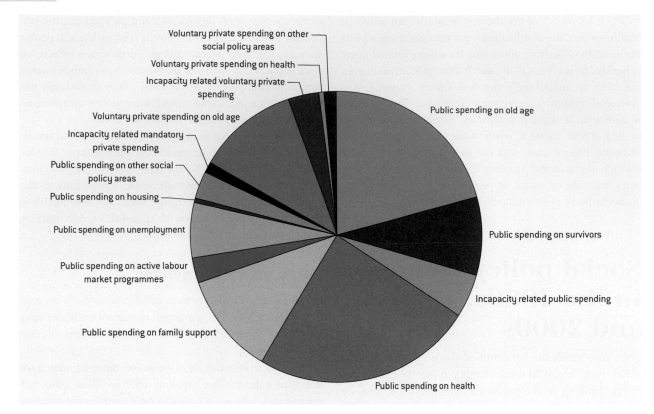

Figure 24.2 Social expenditure in 1980
Source: Based on data from OECD, 2012

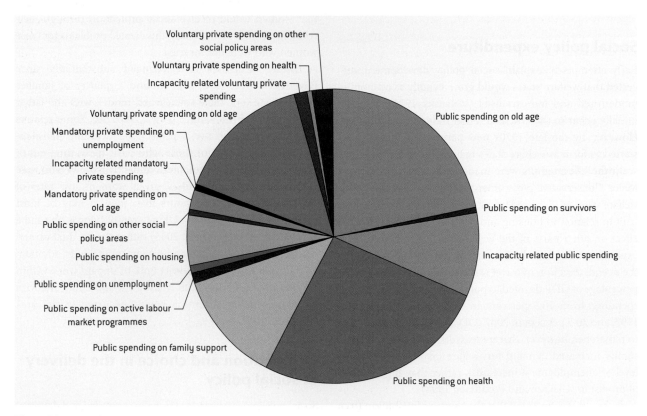

Figure 24.3 Social expenditure in 2007
Source: Based on data from OECD, 2012

as the Department for Work and Pensions, local authorities (covering housing and education policies and social services), and other public bodies such as health authorities. However, the delivery of many areas of social policy has changed markedly through the 1980s, 1990s and 2000s.

First, an increasing number of welfare services have been opened up to *competition*, with private and voluntary sector providers able to obtain service contracts as well as public providers. This situation has been described as a '*quasi-market*' (Bartlett and Le Grand 1993). It is not a 'full' market since services are still paid for by government, and free at the point of use.

A good example of the introduction of competition comes from the field of health policy (considered in more detail below). An **internal market** has been created in the NHS, with 'purchasers' of services being separated from 'providers'. The 'internal market' approach in the UK is associated with the US Professor Alan Enthoven, who proposed its introduction in Britain in the mid-1980s (O'Neill 2000). Although the UK's internal market system was reformed under the New Labour Government of 1997–2010, the Conservative/Liberal Democrat Government is currently introducing reforms which would effectively reintroduce, and intensify, the internal market in the NHS.

Within the NHS those doing the 'purchasing' have generally comprised GPs in some form or another (initially, what were described as 'GP fundholders', then 'Primary Care Trusts', and which have now been named Clinical Commissioning Groups). Providers have included voluntary and private sector bodies. 'Internal market' approaches within public health care systems like the NHS, where the public sector undertakes all purchasing, contrast with 'managed competition' systems, whereby different insurers purchase care (as in the US and Netherlands).

The evidence on whether competition has improved efficiency appears rather mixed. Allsop and Saks (2002), for example, argue that the 'purchaser/provider split' in healthcare effectively had limited impact. Similarly, Harrison argues that, in practice, competition-based reforms were often 'watered down' as policy-makers became faced with the difficulties of implementing radical change in complex healthcare systems. Harrison (2004) does suggest, however, that reforms have increased the power of heathcare managers in relation to other staff, and altered opinions about the role of the market and 'business' in healthcare systems. Greer argues that alternative approaches to administration and delivery have been, in any case, adopted across the UK's component territories, with competition only being embraced wholeheartedly in England (2004: 2).

In addition to the introduction of competition, recent governments have also been concerned to increase '*choice*' for service users in a range of areas, from healthcare to social care and housing to education. For example, in healthcare, service users have become less deferent to medical professionals following an explosion in the availability of information about medical conditions and treatments, particularly through the media and internet.

This has the potential to put tremendous pressure on the NHS, where services are implicitly 'rationed' to restrain costs (Blank and Burau 2004: 12). In apparent response to these pressures, patients have been given increasing control over which procedures they undergo, where, and when. A special website ('NHS Choices') has been introduced, which provides overall hospital 'scorecards' and 'performance data' on survival rates for particular operations and treated conditions, to enable patients to decide where they wish to be treated. This follows on from a 'charter' of patient rights introduced under John Major's Government. However, it appears that only a minority of patients 'actively' exercise 'choice', with most, for example, simply using their local hospital for any operations (Dixon et al. 2010).

There has been extensive debate around whether 'choice' improves or decreases the quality of services. In education some have argued that 'school choice' reinforces class inequalities, with wealthier parents more able to manipulate admissions procedures and even move house in order to get their children into what they perceive as a 'good' school,

Box 24.1

Recent controversies over competition

The introduction of competition has been subject to intense controversy over the last few years, following the apparent failure of a number of private providers. In social care, the largest provider of care homes in the UK, Southern Cross Healthcare, collapsed in 2011 after running into financial difficulties. This left the future of 750 care homes for elderly and disabled people in jeopardy, before other providers stepped in. In the area of work activation for unemployed people, the Chief Executive of one of the largest providers of welfare to work services, A4e, resigned following extensive (unproven) allegations of fraud in February 2012. This was despite the company retaining contracts with the government's 'Work Programme' worth £478 million (McSmith and Milmo 2012).

while poorer parents are more likely to choose local schools (Burgess et al. 2009). In social care individualised 'budgets', which enable service users to decide between competing providers, have been welcomed by many service users (Glendinning et al. 2008). However, it is unclear whether the aspirations associated with this 'personalisation' of social care will be fulfilled under conditions of extensive cuts to local authority budgets (Needham 2011).

The different elements of UK social policy

This section moves beyond broad trends to consider specific developments in different areas of social policy, covering both transfers and services.

Transfers

Pensions

In common with many developed nations, pensions constitute the largest single element of the UK social security budget, taking up around a third of transfer expenditures overall. Despite Beveridge's relatively clear vision for a Basic State Pension (BSP) paid for through national insurance, the BSP has been subject to extensive tinkering over recent decades, and has had additional schemes layered on top of it.

The BSP is a *'contributory'* scheme, since a history of payments into national insurance is required in order for individuals to be able to access it. However, the money that individuals pay in national insurance when working does not go towards their pension, but to paying for the pensions of current retired people; what is known as 'pay as you go'. This approach, where today's workers pay for today's pensioners, can effectively be viewed as a 'social contract between the generations' (Walker and Maltby 2008: 398).

The Basic State Pension rate paid to single people as at October 2012 was £107.45 per week, although due to erratic contributions histories, many people do not qualify for the full amount. Recent changes to the BSP have come from three directions. First, the age at which individuals can receive the BSP is being increased to 66 by 2020, going up from 65 for men and 60 for women.

Second, changes have been made to the rate at which the BSP is uprated to reflect the cost of living. The changes have been rather technical and complicated. In essence, pensions have gone from being uprated in line with both prices and earnings, to only reflecting increases in prices in the 1980s (calculated according to one 'basket' of prices, the Retail Price Index). Most recently, the Coalition Government linked pension uprating to increases in *either* one 'basket' of prices (the Consumer Price Index), earnings, or 2.5 per cent, whichever is the highest.

Third, the length of time during which individuals have had to contribute to national insurance in order to qualify for the BSP has been reduced, from initially 49 years for men and 44 for women, to only 30 years for both. However, the legacy of previous policies, and the fact that women work far less than men in the formal economy, meant that as at 2005 only a third of women received the full BSP (Barr 2009: 216; Frericks et al. 2009; Bardasi and Jenkins 2010). The 'gender gap' in UK pensions is worse than in the US, Germany, and France, and women make up the vast majority of those receiving means-tested benefits as pensioners (Walker 2009).

In addition to these changes to the BSP, successive governments have attempted to incentivise people to take on additional pensions. The 'State Earnings-Related Pension Scheme' (SERPS) introduced a second tier of state provision in 1975. However, from 1986 onwards those enrolled within SERPS were encouraged to leave the scheme and have the resultant rebate of national insurance paid directly into a personal or occupational pension. This approach was widely discredited after scandals concerning the 'mis-selling' of pensions to individuals who would have been better off staying within SERPS. SERPS was then transformed into the State Second Pension ('S2P') in 2002. The latest reform to take place, the Pensions Act 2008, requires employers to enrol eligible employees into a qualifying pension scheme, with a special occupational scheme, the 'National Employment Savings Trust', having been created for the low to moderate paid.

Within already existing occupational pension schemes, the general trend has been towards 'defined contribution' schemes, which require employees to pay in a set amount, and away from 'defined benefit' schemes, which guarantee a certain pay-out in the future for current contributors, as well as towards calculating pensions in relation to individuals' average salaries across their careers, rather than their final salaries. Certain groups have however been less affected by these changes, such as senior executives (Waine 2008). Although public sector pensions have been relatively more generous than those in the private sector, recent proposals appear likely to level these down by increasing eligibility ages and other structural changes.

Other transfers

Beveridge's initial desire to minimise reliance on means testing within the UK welfare state has not been fulfilled, with access to a number of transfers becoming increasingly

Box 24.2

Changes to Jobseekers' Allowance

The relative value of Jobseekers' Allowance has fallen over time, from 18.7 per cent of average earnings in 1981 to 10.5 per cent in 2007 (McNulty 2009). At the same time, the proportion of national insurance taken up with the contribution-based element of Jobseekers Allowance has also fallen, being estimated at less than 1 per cent of all payments from the National Insurance Fund for 2008–9 (Kenway 2009).

restricted. It is not possible in this short chapter to give the full picture of transfers, so this section concentrates on the most significant in financial terms: child benefit, benefits for unemployed and disabled people, help to deal with the costs of housing, and tax credits.

All these benefits are currently subject to radical reform, which it is difficult to summarise within the scope of a brief chapter. Essentially, virtually all means-tested benefits for people of working age are to be folded into a single benefit – the 'Universal Credit'. The process of transferring claimants to the new system will begin in October 2013. However, uncertainty remains over how the new system will be implemented in practice, and in particular how it will ensure that those in work will be automatically better off than the unemployed – a major aim of the reform.

Child Benefit

Child Benefit was traditionally a universal, rather than means-tested, benefit. As at October 2012 it is paid at £20.30 a week for a family's eldest child, and £13.40 a week for any other children. It is paid until children reach the age of 16, unless they are in particular kinds of education when they may receive it for longer. The Coalition Government announced during its 2012 Budget that it would remove child benefit from higher-income families (those earning £50,000 and above). As a result, this benefit is no longer 'universal'.

Unemployment benefit

Alongside pensions, the unemployment cover provided through national insurance was a core element of Beveridge's scheme. Over time, however, unemployment insurance has been supplemented by a range of additional, means-tested benefits. The unemployment insurance available from contributions to national insurance, 'Contribution-based Jobseekers Allowance', is available at a flat rate for up to 26 weeks. Following that period, 'Income-based Jobseekers Allowance' can be claimed, but not if you have savings above £16,000.

Another significant development in relation to unemployment insurance has been the imposition of conditions on those trying to claim the benefit. This draws on the legacy of what are known as 'Active Labour Market Policies' ('ALMP') which have been a feature of Scandinavian welfare states for many decades. ALMP were initially adopted 'to promote labour-force mobility, education and occupation flexibility' (Salonen 2009: 134). In this context ALMP enabled the reconciliation of 'structural economic change with social protection' (Wincott 2003: 548).

In the UK context, however, participation in the training and job preparation schemes allied with ALMP has become a condition for the continued receipt of benefits. To continue to receive the benefits available within the British New Deal for Young People, for example, individuals must undertake education or training, subsidised work in the private or voluntary sectors, or placement on an environmental task-force (Deacon 2008: 313). Similarly, those claiming Jobseekers' Allowance are required to sign a Jobseekers' Agreement which indicates how they will actively seek work for the duration of the period they receive the benefit.

As a result, an element of compulsion has been introduced, and such schemes in the UK (and other countries with similar approaches such as the US) have become described as 'workfare' (Peck 2001). Nonetheless, the UK approach involves significantly less compulsion than some US schemes, with lone mothers (for example) able to choose between work and staying at home to care for children below the age of five, and no limits on the amount of time during which individuals can claim unemployment benefits, unlike in many US states.

Benefits for disabled people and the incapacitated

A range of benefits are available to disabled people, such as Disability Living Allowance, Attendance Allowance, and Employment and Support Allowance. The relative significance of Disability Living Allowance has increased substantially since its introduction in the early 1990s, with the number of claimants trebling since 1992–3. Disability Living Allowance is to be replaced with a new 'Personal Independence Payment' from 2013, which will require potential claimants to undergo regular medical tests to ensure they are still entitled to the benefit. Employment Support Allowance, similar to Jobseekers' Allowance (see above), contains both national

Group of people outside a Jobcentre
Source: Getty Images/Cart de Souza/AFP

insurance-funded elements and taxation-funded (means-tested) elements. Recent reforms by the Coalition Government have reduced to one year the period for which the insurance-based element can be claimed. Beyond this time, claimants' incomes, assets, and those of their partners will be taken into account when deciding how much tax-based funding they will be able to claim.

Housing Benefit

Support to cover the costs of housing has become an increasingly important element of assistance to those on low incomes in the UK, with real house prices having increased by at least 90 per cent between 1980 and 2008 (OECD 2011b: 6) alongside stagnating real wage levels. The proportion of social spending allocated to cover housing costs has increased exponentially as a result.

Radical plans to reduce spending on this benefit are currently being implemented by the Coalition Government. Many of these are complex, reflecting the fact that the benefit is based on the cost of housing rather than being paid at a flat rate. Amongst other changes, the reforms involve: individuals from 25–34 being expected to share accommodation, rather than to rent a flat of their own; the rent levels which Housing Benefit can subsidise being reduced; and Housing Benefit being restricted to the level of four-bedroom houses for large homes.

Tax credits

'*Tax credits*' are a relatively new type of transfer introduced by the Labour Government from 1999 onwards. There are three main types of tax credit: Working Tax Credit and Child Tax Credit (which replaced the previous Working Families Tax Credit), and Pension Credit (which replaced the previous Minimum Income Guarantee). Essentially tax credits work as an '*income guarantee*', topping up incomes and reducing gradually as individuals' income rises. As at December 2011 it was estimated that 5.7 million families, containing 9.2 million children, would be receiving tax credits or the equivalent child support through benefits (HMRC/National Statistics 2011). This is greater than the number of recipients of Housing Benefit (4.94 million), and marginally less than the number of recipients of council tax benefit (5.87 million) as at November 2011 (DWP 2012).

Tax credits in the UK are often compared with the older US Earned Income Tax Credit, although it is arguable that the UK's Working Families Tax Credit built on existing UK provisions like 'Family Credit' rather than constituting a simple imitation of the US version (Page and Mark-Lawson 2007: 57).

Box 24.3

Tax credits: lifting families out of poverty, or subsidising poverty pay?

Although tax credits have been credited with lifting many people out of poverty (particularly those with children), they have also been accused of enabling employers to pay below subsistence-level wages. With current plans afoot to ensure that benefits will always 'make work pay' by subsidising low wages, the UK's welfare system has been described as rehabilitating the 'Speenhamland principle' referred to above. This contrasts with Beveridge's original plan for welfare, whereby national insurance would ensure the pooling of risks across all workers (Byrne 2011).

Services

Healthcare

The UK healthcare system can be divided into 'primary care' (general practitioner services and health education), 'acute' care (mainly delivered in hospitals and delivered to those who are severely unwell – sometimes described as 'secondary care'), and 'chronic' care (provided to those with long-term conditions, covering palliative care, hospices, and elements of 'social care').

The provision of healthcare has changed radically since the creation of the NHS, reflecting the changing nature of the disease burden. The incidence of chronic disease has come to outweigh that of communicable diseases, with the exception of new epidemics such as AIDS, and the resurgence of resistant strains of diseases like tuberculosis (Mechanic and Rochefort 1996). Healthcare policies have also had to incorporate rapid technological developments, from the development of organ transplants from the 1950s onwards to new innovations like foetal and keyhole surgery and nano-technology.

As previously mentioned, the UK's Beveridgean history means that it is a 'single-payer' system, where government is the near-exclusive funder of the majority of health services. Public spending on healthcare gradually increased over time in the UK, but not to the same level as many other EU countries. Indeed, some calculations suggest that in real terms, public expenditure on healthcare diminished in the UK through the 1980s and 1990s (Jordan 2011: 125–6). Public spending on healthcare then increased through the 2000s, with Tony Blair's commitment to move towards the EU average. While UK health spending did increase between 2000 and 2010 by nearly 3 per cent, spending in the other EU countries also increased, so the UK remains slightly below the EU average in health spending terms (see King's Fund 2010). Under the current Coalition Government, healthcare spending has been 'ringfenced', one of the few areas protected from cuts alongside international development funding and some universal benefits available to older people.

In comparative terms the UK's healthcare system has always been highly centralised (Freeman and Frisina 2010: 172–3). Nonetheless, following devolution, healthcare policies are starting to vary across the UK, with free prescriptions, for example, available in Scotland and Wales but not in England.

Other trends within the UK NHS include the increasing use of internal markets (separating 'purchasers' and 'providers'), mentioned above, and of private provision of healthcare. An example of the latter is provided by Independent Sector Treatment Centres, nicknamed 'cataract caravans', which were used under New Labour to cut waiting lists by undertaking routine operations such as the removal of cataracts and hip replacements. Relatively few UK patients, however, decide to take on private insurance so that they can use private rather than NHS services. As at 2005, for example, private insurance amounted to 7.9 per cent of overall spending on health (World Health Organization 2008) – a relatively small, if still significant, proportion.

Radical changes in the NHS are being pursued by the Coalition Government at the time of writing. These include changing who 'purchases' within the NHS (devolving this to groups of GPs and some other health professionals), and enabling all services to be open to the private sector, if the 'purchasers' decide to buy its services. Debate continues to rage about whether this will lead to the 'privatisation' of the NHS, with cheaper private services being purchased rather than state services, or to a more balanced outcome.

Social care

'Social care' covers services, beyond healthcare, received by older and disabled people. These include help in the home (for example, with cooking and cleaning), and, where necessary, residential care. Two developments are particularly significant in this area.

First, the availability of social care across the UK has changed substantially. While in Scotland personal care for older people has been made completely free, both in the home and in care homes, this is not the case in the rest of the UK. In England the provision of social care varies substantially across local council areas. As at May 2011 four English councils had scaled back their provision of social care so that it only covered 'critical' needs (and not 'substantial' or 'moderate' needs, which had previously been covered). Many other councils have also reduced provision, if not so drastically.

Second, attempts have been made to increase choice for older and disabled people in the social care they receive, especially through the provision of individual 'budgets'. These can be spent by recipients however they like, whether this be on a season ticket for the football, attendance at a day centre, or help in the home. Nonetheless, the level of take-up of individual budgets has been patchy, and some have argued that having to negotiate such a budget places extra stress on service users and their carers.

The future of social care services remains uncertain, in the face of a growing older population (see below) and significant reductions in local authorities' budgets. Attempts have been made to reach a cross-party consensus on a new financing mechanism for social care, but initial proposals by New Labour for all older people to pay into a special fund to cover the costs of future care were described as a 'death tax' by the Conservatives and fell by the wayside. The latest attempt to cobble together a consensus came with a Commission under the economist Andrew Dilnot, which proposed a cap on the amount individuals could contribute to social care costs and an increase in the means-tested threshold above which individuals have to start paying for their own social care. The Dilnot review is currently being considered by the Coalition Government, although it has stated that it will not be able to offer a comprehensive response until the time of the next Spending Review, which is not expected until 2015.

Housing

In 1981 nearly a third of the UK's housing stock was provided by the state – what is known as 'council housing'. By 2011 that proportion had diminished to less than a fifth. One of the most significant reasons for the reduction was Margaret Thatcher's programme enabling council tenants to buy their properties on favourable terms, the so-called 'right to buy' scheme. It has been estimated that around 2 million former council homes have been removed from the social housing sector through 'right to buy' (Inside Housing 2012). In addition, successive governments have encouraged councils to transfer ownership of their stock to not-for-profit housing associations. The council housing stock is likely to diminish further, with recent changes to the scheme having made purchases of council houses even more attractive to tenants.

As the size of the social housing stock (provided by councils and housing associations) has reduced, waiting lists have increased substantially. While around 250,000 new lettings were available each year for new social tenants during the 1980s and 1990s, only 170,000 were available in 2005 (Hills 2007). Partly as a result, social housing has become increasingly 'residualised', with new tenants tending to suffer from multiple disadvantage. This contrasts with Nye Bevan's original vision of social housing estates enabling 'the working man, the doctor and the clergyman [to] live in close proximity to each other'.

Education

There are four different types of educational provision in the UK: 'pre-school education', primary and secondary education, tertiary education (also known as 'further' and 'higher' education), and continuing and vocational education and training. It is not possible within this brief chapter to provide a detailed survey of educational developments. Readers requiring more information should refer to the 'further reading' sources at the end of this chapter.

Trends in education spending

Unlike spending on health and social care, education expenditure remained relatively stable until the election of the first New Labour government in 1997. Between 1999–2000 and 2009–2010, education spending then grew by over 5 per cent in real terms. Current reforms to education spending involve an estimated 3.5 per cent cut in spending up to 2014–15, constituting the 'largest cut in education spending over any four-year period since at least the 1950s' (Chowdry and Sibieta 2011: 1). Nonetheless, the distribution of cuts will be highly uneven, with school-building projects and higher education affected significantly more than other areas of the education budget.

Trends in pre-school education

The UK pre-school system is characterised by a division between 'educational' and 'care-based' providers, who are operated by the state, the voluntary sector, private companies and individuals ('childminders'). Those providers of pre-school services designated as 'educational' have become increasingly subject to quality control, coming under the purview of the Ofsted educational inspectorate in 2001.

Access to free pre-school education was considerably increased under New Labour, being extended to all three- and four-year-olds. Nonetheless, this provision remains 'part-time' (up to 15 hours per week), which is insufficient to enable many parents to work.

Trends in primary and secondary education

The major trend affecting primary and secondary education has been a reduction in local education authorities' control, and an increase in both the autonomy of schools and the powers of central government.

In comparison with many other countries' education systems, the UK is relatively decentralised. As in Germany, a patchwork of different approaches to selection exists, with some areas routinely separating off around a fifth of pupils to attend grammar schools, while other areas operate completely integrated, 'comprehensive', educational systems. Attempts to introduce or remove selection have proved highly politically charged in some areas, especially in Northern Ireland where selection continues to apply, and support for it is split along community lines.

While this patchwork of approaches has existed for some time, differences between areas of the UK appear to be widening. Gaps in performance linked to regional disparities in wealth have intensified. In addition, the UK's component nations also appear to be performing variably. For example, Wales received particularly low scores in the OECD's 'PISA' survey of educational attainment when compared with England, Scotland and Northern Ireland.

At the same time, local authorities' control over education providers has been reduced, with the advent of the then 'grant-maintained' schools in the 1980s and 1990s, new 'academies' in the 1990s and 2000s, and proposals for 'free' schools under the current Coalition Government. All of these schools have 'opted out' of control by local education authorities, being self-governing and funded directly by central government. Both academies and free schools can receive funds from private or voluntary sector sponsors (who have some influence on the management and 'ethos' of the school), as well as from government. The shift away from local education authority-controlled schools towards 'autonomous' schools has occurred relatively quickly, with one in six secondary schools having become academies by April 2011, and academies constituting the majority of schools in some local authority areas.

As described above, this has been accompanied by an increase in parents' and children's 'choice' over which school they can attend, and an intensification in parents' efforts to get their children into what they perceive is a 'good school'. In an attempt to overcome this, 'lottery' systems were introduced by up to a third of local authorities, which allocated school places randomly. The Coalition Government has banned lotteries, and instead allowed popular schools to expand beyond a threshold of 30 pupils per class, if necessary.

Trends in higher education

Until the 1970s British higher education was restricted in scope and scale, and explicitly elitist in orientation. However, it became subject to extensive reform from the 1980s onwards, and student numbers increased substantially. Between 1994–5 and 2008–9 undergraduate numbers increased by 51 per cent (see Figure 24.4).

By 2008–9 over 50 British higher education institutions (HEIs) had more than 20,000 students (see Figure 24.5).

The area of higher education has become heavily contested, with student fees forming a core political issue within the last general election. New Labour introduced tuition fees directly payable by students in the late 1990s, following the

Figure 24.4 The increase in undergraduate numbers at UK universities

Dearing Report on university funding. This followed a threat by the peak association for universities that its members would move to introduce 'top up' fees in the absence of government action to increase funding for the sector (Shattock 2008). Following successive increases in the tuition fee, an additional review was commissioned by Labour just before it left office, the Browne review, to be chaired by Lord Browne, formerly Chief Executive of the oil company British Petroleum. This recommended the removal of any cap on tuition fees for English universities. The Coalition Government did not heed this part of Browne's proposals, and instituted a £9,000 cap on tuition fees, which was nevertheless three times higher than the previous cap. The Coalition Government also retained Browne's proposal to remove state funding for teaching in the humanities, arts and social sciences.

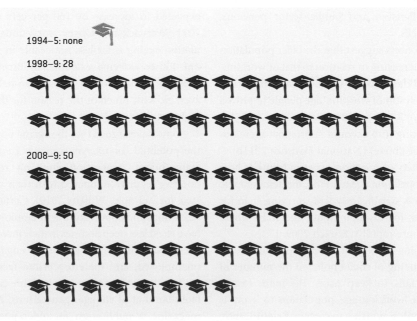

Figure 24.5 The increase in size of UK higher education institutions

Box 24.4

The impact of devolution on higher education

Along with social care, higher education is one area of social policy where the differences across the UK's component nations have become increasingly stark. In Scotland tuition fees were abolished following devolution. Initially, ex-students were required to make a contribution through a 'graduation endowment'. This was abolished in 2007, and since then Scottish students studying in Scotland have not been required to pay anything towards the cost of their tuition. Tuition fees were introduced in Wales, but the system of student support is slightly different, with the Welsh government reintroducing means-tested maintenance grants for Welsh students in 2002 – earlier than was the case in England. In addition, until 2010–11 the Welsh Assembly provided all Welsh students with a grant of almost £2,000 to offset the tuition fee costs.

As tuition fees tripled in England from September 2012, the differences in student support systems across the United Kingdom are becoming more marked. In particular, while applications from English students to study at Scottish universities have increased, fewer Scottish students appear to be choosing to study in England.

Looking forward: demographic change?

Discussions about the reform of social policy have been dominated by claims about the impact of demographic change. These have focused on what is often described as a 'demographic' or even 'dependency time bomb' – the fact that people are living longer, and thus the population is ageing rapidly. The ageing population has been used by politicians to justify increases in the retirement age, both for the Basic State Pension and public sector pensions, and reforms to the NHS.

Certainly, all projections suggest that the older population is likely to continue increasing in relation to that of working-age people, at least in the medium term. In concrete terms, it is estimated that the ratio of working-age people to retired people will decline from 3.16:1 as at 2010 to 2.87:1 in 2035 (see Figure 24.6), even taking into account substantial increases in the pension age (see above) (National Statistics 2011b).

Nonetheless, a variety of questions arise in terms of how we should interpret population ageing. First, the demographic 'challenge' for Britain is significantly less worrying than for many other countries, for example Spain and Italy, where ageing is occurring more rapidly (Börsch 2009: 173).

Second, the increasing number of older people only causes problems for the financing of social policy if the number of working-age people fails to keep pace. The main reason for this failure of the working-age population to grow is decreasing rates of fertility, which have received significantly less emphasis at a policy level. Following the 'baby boom' through the 1940s–60s, fertility declined in the UK from the 1970s onwards but has recently picked up, reaching 2.06 children per woman in Northern Ireland in 2010, 2.00 in England, 1.98 in Wales and 1.75 in Scotland (National Statistics 2011c). This constitutes a 25-year high in England and Wales. Nonetheless, given the previous decline, it appears that new births will be insufficient to balance out the growing number of older people, at least over the next few decades.

Third, the impact of population ageing will vary significantly across the UK. Some areas have rapidly ageing populations. For example, the number of people over 85 is expected to increase by 160 per cent in Warwickshire by 2031 (Warwickshire Observatory, undated). However, population ageing is far less noticeable in many cities. To take one rather extreme example: in Birmingham population ageing is likely to occur at less than half the rate of the UK average, with much of the reason for this lying in relatively high fertility rates.

Some have argued that the ageing population exacerbates the potential for *intergenerational conflict*, with the older, 'baby boom' generation enjoying relative income and housing security compared with their children's generation (see, for example, Willetts 2010). Certainly, compared with reductions in support for the unemployed, most pensioners have faced less steep declines in their income levels. Pensioners are considerably more politically engaged than the young unemployed, and therefore prima facie arguments would suggest that politicians might be more concerned about their fate than that of younger generations. As the editor of *Saga* magazine, a publication for older people, pointed out in the run-up to the 2010 General Election, the 'over-50s form

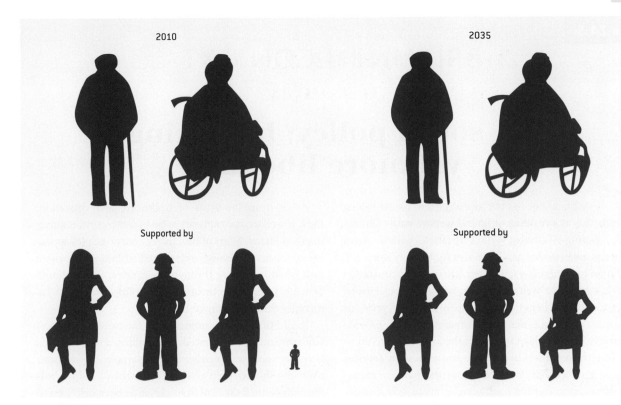

Figure 24.6 The increasing 'dependency ratio' of retired to working people

the majority of those who vote and their opinions must count . . .'

However, pensioners do not benefit uniformly from social policies, and some groups have seen their real incomes decline substantially. If we include a consideration of the services and transfers consumed by poorer older people (like social care and Housing Benefit), and the increased cost of living (with rises in VAT and fuel costs), the poorest fifth of older people have become increasingly worse off (AgeUK 2010). Older people are also significantly less likely to claim for means-tested benefits than younger people, particularly the 'oldest old' (Hill et al. 2007).

Looking forward: public support for the welfare state?

The American political scientist Paul Pierson has argued that attempts by governments to cut back on social spending will be resisted strongly by the beneficiaries of social policy (1994). He used this argument to explain why, despite numerous attempts to reform the welfare state, successive Thatcher and Major governments failed to significantly dent the public contribution to social policy. Certainly, some

areas of welfare expenditure have been relatively impervious to cuts, such as the UK health budget. Similarly, the core architecture of the Basic State Pension has been retained, although its value has been eroded through the technical changes described above.

However, the current UK governing coalition has not shied away from radical changes to other benefits, particularly means-tested transfers like housing and unemployment benefit. This has gone in tandem with an apparent decline in public support for benefits. In 1991 the British Social Attitudes survey suggested that 58 per cent of people thought the government should increase spending on benefits, but by 2009 only 27 per cent of people felt this (National Centre for Social Research 2012).

At the same time evidence suggests that most people support progressive tax and benefit systems, and that when people are presented with evidence about inequalities, they support interventions to improve disadvantaged individuals' life chances (Bamfield and Horton 2009). Similarly, there is evidence that those who are more 'interested' in social policy issues are more likely to be against cuts in benefits, suggesting that once people understand more about this highly technical area, they are less likely to be swayed by arguments in favour of retrenchment (Giger 2012). Regardless of the reasons for the change in public attitudes, it is clear that a shift towards a less 'collectivist' mindset has occurred within the British public.

Box 24.5

BRITAIN IN CONTEXT

UK social policy: becoming yet more liberal?

The UK's welfare state has traditionally been classified along with the US as a **residual** or **liberal welfare state** (Titmuss 1974; Esping-Anderson 1990). In these welfare states transfers are provided as a last resort for the very worst-off, and tend to be highly stigmatised. These can be contrasted with 'conservative' welfare regimes, which use social insurance to provide benefits based on individuals' previous incomes, and social democratic regimes, which provide relatively high levels of benefit at the same value to all.

Nonetheless, the UK's health and education services appear to contradict this 'liberal' classification. For example, if taxpayer-funded healthcare is taken into account when assessing the UK's welfare state, it can be viewed as possessing a 'hybrid' regime, with a liberal approach to benefits but a social democratic approach to healthcare (Bambra 2005). Others would argue, however, that certain areas of UK health policy reflect a 'liberal' approach. For example, Goodwin argues that when it comes to mental health policy, the UK has demonstrated a 'liberal' approach by moving patients out of institutions and into the community in order to reduce expenditure and ensure their insertion into the labour market (1997).

Aside from the areas of healthcare and education, the UK welfare state appears to be becoming more rather than less liberal. Many of Beveridge's core principles appear to have been abandoned, with the redistribution of income now often occurring through tax-funded, means-tested benefits, rather than through the pooling of individuals' incomes through national insurance.

In addition, some innovations by the current Coalition Government can be viewed as signalling a shift towards US-style 'localised' provision. For example, the decision over who should receive help to cover their local tax bills through council tax benefit has recently been devolved to local authorities (Turner 2011). In addition, discretionary social assistance, mainly used by very low-income individuals to pay for emergency requirements, is being devolved to local authorities (in England – alternative arrangements apply to the devolved nations). This contrasts with the current situation, where discretionary, non-interest-bearing loans like Crisis Loans and Funeral Payments are delivered by Jobcentres but within the national parameters set by the 'Social Fund'.

Chapter summary

Social policy is a very complex area, and this chapter has only offered a brief summary of the most significant recent changes to the UK welfare state. Social policy expenditure has fluctuated over time, with considerable increases through the late 1990s and 2000s, but reductions planned in many areas by the current Coalition Government. The UK welfare state has slowly come to terms with women's engagement in the labour market, but failed to overcome the persistent inequality between male and female incomes. While competition and choice have been introduced in many areas of the welfare state, their impacts have been varied and contested.

Aside from health and education, UK social policy has become increasingly 'residualised', with many transfers now means-tested and services like social housing becoming less widely available. At the same time, however, different patterns can be observed across the UK, particularly in the fields of social care and education, where different arrangements apply in different nations. Future developments in social policy are likely to be shaped by the challenge of an ageing population, and the recently hardened public attitude towards particular groups of social policy beneficiaries.

Discussion points

- Can the British welfare state still be described as 'Beveridgean'?
- To what extent has the introduction of competition and choice affected the quality of services like health and education?
- Why has more conditionality been introduced into areas like unemployment support? Has this been successful?
- Will the 'ageing society' lead to a demographic 'time bomb', or could older people become viewed as an asset, rather than a drain on social policy resources?

Further reading

There is a huge volume of literature available on the UK welfare state. Good textbooks which provide a consistently high-quality overview include Alcock et al. (2012) and Baldock et al. (2007). Dean's 'short introduction' to social policy (2006) is an enjoyable, lively and quick read. Lister's book on 'theories and concepts in social policy' provides a good overview of the ideological underpinnings of different approaches to welfare provision (2010). Timmins' magisterial 'biography of the welfare state' (2001) offers a clear and well-written history of the development of UK social policy. For the most up-to-date view of developments in UK social policy, it is often worth consulting journals in the field (such as the *Journal of Social Policy*, *Social Policy Review* or *Social Policy and Administration*) or the websites of expert bodies in this area (see 'useful websites' below).

Bibliography

AgeUK (2010) *How the Government's planned cuts will affect older people*, a report by Howard Reed and Tim Horton for Age UK, London (AgeUK).

Alber, J. (1981) 'Government responses to the challenge of unemployment: the development of unemployment insurance in Western Europe', in Flora, P. and Heidenheimer, A.J. (eds) *The Development of Welfare States in Europe and America* (Transaction Books).

Alcock, P., May, M. and Wright, S. (eds) (2012) *The Student's Companion to Social Policy*, 4th edn (Blackwell).

Allsop, J. and Saks, M. (2002) *Regulating the Health Professions* (Sage).

Baldock, J., Manning, N. and Vickerstaff, S. (2007) *Social Policy*, 3rd edn (Oxford University Press).

Bambra, C. (2005) 'Worlds of welfare and the health care discrepancy', *Social Policy and Society*, vol. 4, no. 1: 31–41.

Bamfield, L. and Horton, T. (2009) *Understanding Attitudes to Tackling Economic Inequality* (Joseph Rowntree Foundation).

Bardasi, E. and Jenkins, S.P. (2010) 'The gender gap in private pensions', in Blood, I. and Bamford, S.-M. (2010) *Equality and Diversity and Older People with High Support Needs* (Joseph Rowntree Foundation).

Barr, N. (2009) 'International trends in pension provision', *Accounting and Business Research*, vol. 39, no. 3, International Accounting Policy Forum, 211–25.

Bartlett, W. and Le Grand, J. (1993) *Quasi-markets and Social Policy* (Palgrave Macmillan).

Blank, R.H. and Burau, V. (2004) *Comparative Health Policy* (Palgrave Macmillan).

Bonoli, G. (1997) 'Classifying welfare states: a two-dimension approach', *Journal of Social Policy*, vol. 26, no. 3: 351–72.

Börsch, A. (2009) 'Many roads to Rome: Varieties of funded pensions in Europe and Asia', *Pensions*, 14, 172–80.

Burgess, S., Greaves, E., Vignoles, A. and Wilson, D. (2009) *Parental Choice of Primary School in England: What 'Type' of School Do Parents Choose?* (Centre for Market and Public Organisation).

Byrne, D. (2011) 'The "Speenhamland" poor laws were not about supporting the unemployed', the *Guardian*, 20 June.

Cairney, P. (2009) 'The "British policy style" and mental health: Beyond the headlines', *Journal of Social Policy*, vol. 38, no. 4: 671–88.

Chowdry, H. and Sibieta, L. (2011) 'Trends in education and schools spending', IFS Briefing Note BN121 (Institute for Fiscal Studies).

Clayton, R. and Pontusson, J. (1998) 'Welfare-state retrenchment revisited: entitlement cuts, public sector restructuring, and inegalitarian trends in advanced capitalist societies', *World Politics*, vol. 51, no. 1: 67–98.

Deacon, A. (2008) 'Employment', Ch.39, 311–17, in Alcock, P. May, M. and Rowlingson, K. (eds) *The Student's Companion to Social Policy* (Blackwell).

Dean, H. (2006) *Social Policy: a short introduction* (Polity Press).

Department for Work and Pensions (DWP) (2012) *First Release, DWP Statistical Summary*, 15 February.

Dixon, A., Robertson, R., Appleby, J., Burge, P., Devlin, N. and Magee, H. (2010) *Patient Choice: How patients choose and how providers respond* (King's Fund).

Dunleavy, P. (1980) 'The Political Implications of Sectoral Cleavages and the Growth of State Employment', Parts I and II, *Political Studies* 2, 364–83 and 527–49.

Esping-Andersen, G. (1990) *The Three Worlds of Welfare Capitalism* (Polity Press).

Eurostat (2012) *Population by Sex, Age Groups, Degree of Urbanisation of Residence and Labour Status Dataset* (Eurostat).

Flood, C.M. (2000) *International Health Care Reform: A legal, economic and political analysis* (Routledge).

Freeman, R. and Frisina, L. (2010) 'Health Care Systems and the Problem of Classification', *Journal of Comparative Policy Analysis: Research and Practice*, vol. 12, no. 1: 163–78.

Frericks, P., Knijn, T. and Maier, R. (2009) 'Pension Reforms, Working Patterns and Gender Pension Gaps in Europe', *Gender, Work and Organization*, vol. 16, no. 6: 710–30.

Giger, N. (2012) 'Is social policy retrenchment unpopular? How welfare reforms affect government popularity', *European Sociological Review*, vol. 28, no. 5: 691–700.

Ginsburg, N. (1992) *Divisions of Welfare: A critical introduction to comparative social policy* (Sage).

Glendinning, C., Challis, D., Fernandez, J., Jacobs, S., Jones, K., Knapp, M., Manthorpe, J., Moran, N., Netten, A., Stevens, M. and Wilberforce, M. (2008) *Evaluation of the Individual Budgets Pilot Programme: Final Report* (Social Policy Research Unit, University of York).

Goodwin, S. (1997) *Comparative Mental Health Policy: From institutional to community care* (Sage).

Greer, S.L. (2004) *Territorial Politics and Health Policy: UK health policy in comparative perspective*, (Manchester University Press).

Harrison, M. (2004) *Implementing Change in Health Systems: Market reforms in health systems in the United Kingdom, Sweden and the Netherlands* (Sage).

Hill, K., Kellard, K., Middleton, S., Cox, L. and Pound, E. (2007) *Understanding Resources in Later Life: Views and experiences of older people* (Joseph Rowntree Foundation).

Hills, J. (2007) *Ends and Means: The future roles of social housing in England* (Centre for the Analysis of Social Exclusion, LSE).

HMRC/National Statistics (2011) *Child and Working Tax Credits Statistics*, December 2011.

Inside Housing (2012) 'SALE! (while stocks last)', 13 January, www.insidehousing.co.uk.

Ipsos MORI (2011) Poll conducted for *The Future State of Welfare*, with John Humphrys (9.00 pm, BBC Two, Thursday 27 October).

Jordan, J. (2011) 'Health care politics in the age of retrenchment', *Journal of Social Policy*, vol. 40, no. 1: 113–34.

Kenway, P. (2009) *Should Adult Benefit for Unemployment Now Be Raised?* (Joseph Rowntree Foundation).

King's Fund (2010) 'How much has been spent on the NHS since 2005?', available at www.kingsfund.org.uk/current_projects/general_election_2010/key_election_questions/how_much_has_been.html.

Lewis, J. (1992) 'Gender and the development of welfare regimes', *Journal of European Social Policy*, vol. 2, no. 3: 159–73.

Lewis, J. (2009) *Work–Family Balance, Gender and Policy* (Edward Elgar).

Lewis, J. and Campbell, M. (2007) 'Work/family balance policies in the UK since 1997: a new departure?' *Journal of Social Policy*, vol. 36, no. 3: 365–81.

Lister, R. (2010) *Understanding Theories and Concepts in Social Policy* (Policy Press).

Marshall, T.H. (1963) *Sociology at the Crossroads* (Heinemann).

McNulty, T. (2009) 'Response to question on Jobseeker's Allowance', *Hansard*, 2 April 2009: Column 1401W.

McSmith, N. and Milmo, C. (2012) 'Harrison hired despite A4e fraud warning', the *Independent*, 27 February.

Mechanic, D. and Rochefort, D.A. (1996) 'Comparative Medical Systems', *Annual Review of Sociology*, 22: 239–70.

National Centre for Social Research (2012) *British Social Attitudes Survey, 2010*, Colchester, Essex: UK Data Archive.

National Statistics (2011a) *Public Sector Employment by Industry*, December.

National Statistics (2011b) *Fertility Summary – 2010*, 6 October.

National Statistics (2011c) *2010-based national population projections – principal projection and key variants*, London: ONS.

Needham, C. (2011) *Personalising Public Services: Understanding the Personalisation Narrative* (Policy Press).

OECD (2012) *Social Expenditure Database* (OECD).

OECD (2011a) *Health at a glance* (OECD).

OECD (2011b) *Economic Policy Reforms 2011: Going for Growth* (OECD).

O'Neill, F. (2000) 'Health, the internal market and the reform of the national health service', in D. Dolowitz (ed.) *Policy Transfer and British Social Policy. Learning from the USA?* (Open UP), pp. 59–76.

Page, E.C. and Mark-Lawson, J. (2007) 'Outward-looking policy making', Ch.3, pp. 47–64 in Bochel, H. and Duncan, S. (eds) *Making Policy in Theory and Practice* (Policy Press).

Pascall, G. (2008) 'Gender and New Labour: after the male breadwinner model?', in Maltby, T., Kennett, P. and Rummery, K. (eds) *Social Policy Review*, 20 (The Policy Press), pp. 215–40.

Peck, J. (2001) *Workfare states* (Guilford Press).

Penhale, B. and Manthorpe, J. (2004) 'Older people, institutional abuse and inquiries', in Stanley, N. and Manthorpe, J. (eds) *The Age of Inquiry: learning and blaming in health and social care* (Routledge), Chapter 12, pp. 257–72.

Pierson, P. (1994) *Dismantling the Welfare State? Reagan, Thatcher, and the politics of retrenchment* (Cambridge University Press).

Powell, M. (2007) *Understanding the Mixed Economy of Welfare* (The Policy Press).

Salonen, T. (2009) 'Sweden: between model and reality', Ch.7, in Alcock, P. and Craig, G. (eds) *International Social Policy: welfare regimes in the developed world*, 2nd edn (Palgrave Macmillan).

Shattock, M. (2008) 'The change from private to public governance of British higher education: its consequences for higher education policy making 1980–2006', *Higher Education Quarterly*, vol. 62, no. 3: 181–203.

Szreter, S. and Mooney, G. (1998) 'Urbanization, mortality, and the standard of living debate: new estimates of the expectation of life at birth in nineteenth-century British cities', *Economic History Review*, vol. 51, no. 84: 112.

Timmins, N. (2001) *The Five Giants: A biography of the welfare state* (Harper Collins).

Titmuss, R.M. (1974) 'What is social policy?', in Abel-Smith, B. and Titmuss, K. (eds) *Social Policy* (Pantheon), pp. 23–33.

Titmuss, R. (1958) *Essays on the Welfare State* (Allen and Unwin).

Turner, E. (2011) 'From co-operative to competitive localism? The changing balance between equity and efficiency in local government under the Conservative/Liberal Democrat coalition', paper presented to the Public Administration Committee conference, Birmingham.

Waine, B. (2008) 'Rules for the Rich? Contemporary Trends in Executive Pensions', *Competition and Change*, vol. 12, no. 3: 281–86.

Walker, A. and Maltby, T. (2008) 'Older People', Ch. 49, pp. 394–401 in Alcock, P. May, M. and Rowlingson, K. (eds) *The Student's Companion to Social Policy* (Blackwell).

Walker, A. (2009) 'Why is ageing so unequal?', in Cann, P. and Dean, M. (2009) *Unequal Ageing: The untold story of exclusion in old age* (Policy Press).

Warwickshire Observatory (undated) *Mid-2009 population estimates, by local authority district, by sex and five year age group*, obtained from ONS data, Warwickshire County Council.

Wilensky, H.L. (1975) *The Welfare State and Equality: Structural and ideological roots of public expenditures* (University of California Press).

Willetts, D. (2010) *The Pinch: How the baby boomers took their children's future – and why they should give it back* (Atlantic Books).

Williams, F. (2008) 'Culture and Nationhood', Ch. 20, pp. 159–65, in Alcock, P. May, M. and Rowlingson, K. (eds) *The Student's Companion to Social Policy* (Blackwell).

Wincott, D. (2003) 'Beyond social regulation? New instruments and/or a new agenda for social policy at Lisbon?', *Public Administration*, vol. 81, no. 3: 533–54.

World Health Organization (2008) *World Health Statistics* (World Health Organization).

Useful websites

The King's Fund – www.kingsfund.org.uk/publications/index.html – offers a wealth of expert and high-quality commentary, particularly on recent health reforms.

The Child Poverty Action Group – www.cpag.org.uk – provides well-informed commentary on benefits, an area where good-quality information is often lacking.

The Joseph Rowntree Association – www.jrf.org.uk/publications – reports on a variety of social policy topics.

The OECD – www.oecd.org – provides a wealth of statistics and commentary on all of the social policy areas touched on in this chapter.

CHAPTER 25

Economic policy

Wyn Grant

> " **Practical men, who believe themselves to be quite exempt from any intellectual influences, are usually the slaves of some defunct economist** "
>
> J.M. Keynes, *The General Theory*, 1936

Learning objectives

- To identify the nature of economic policy.
- To explain the economic policy-making process.
- To explain shifts over time in the conduct of economic policy.

Economic policy has a far broader significance than the technicalities of macroeconomic management suggest. It is at the heart of the central question of politics: who gets what, when, how. Decisions on taxation and the budget make citizens poorer and richer. The gap between rich and poor in the world has widened and has become the focus of increasing controversy. If the market fails, as happened in the global financial crisis (GFC), the consequences can be far reaching for everyone. In the GFC a variety of **financial institutions** could no longer carry out their functions, leading to a fall in confidence and a reduction in the availability of credit which produced a prolonged economic slump. The austerity policies of the Coalition Government after 2010 were at the heart of political controversy. The Government argued that the policies were unavoidable to close the gap between tax revenues and expenditure, but its critics maintained that the policies undermined economic growth which would boost tax revenues. Underlying this debate was a dispute how much government should intervene in the economy and how far it could do so effectively.

The nature of economic policy

Economic policy seeks to achieve objectives such as a high rate of growth, a low and stable rate of **inflation** and high levels of employment. These objectives are important to governments both for their own sake and because they influence their chances of re-election. Some critics would question the desirability of a high rate of economic growth as a primary objective because of its effects on the environment, particularly on tackling climate change. They would argue that, in any case, conventional measures of national income such as Gross Domestic Product (GDP) per capita are not a good measure of happiness or wellbeing. However, with the economy flatlining after the GFC, the need for growth became more evident.

Governments seek to manage the economy through using a number of tools or *policy instruments*. The mix of policy instruments used varies over time both in response to changes in economic thinking and current economic circumstances. For example, in the 1960s and 1970s prices and incomes policies were a favoured policy instrument because these policies were seen as the best available method for reducing the rate of inflation.

In the 1990s and the first decade of the twentieth century manipulation of the interest rate became the favoured policy instrument. However, with the onset of the global financial crisis (GFC) from 2007 this policy instrument no longer had the desired effect in terms of stimulating the economy and avoiding deflation: hence, the resort to a new policy instrument by the Coalition Government – quantitative easing – which involved pumping money into the economy.

The impact of globalisation

Over time it has become more difficult for governments to control what happens in their domestic economies because of a process that is often referred to as 'globalisation'. What happens under globalisation is that economies become integrated with each other. This is particularly relevant in the case of Britain which has always been highly integrated in the global economy. Under globalisation trade tends to grow faster than national input, so that a higher proportion of national production is exported and a higher proportion of consumption is imported.

Foreign investment also grows, leading to a greater presence in the economy of multinational companies which often integrate their production across several countries so that, for example, different parts of a car may be made in different locations before being assembled in one country. Multinational companies need new kinds of internationalised financial services to meet their needs. These in turn may acquire a momentum of their own, creating new and often not well-understood forms of finance – for example, those based on debt, which was to play an important role in the GFC. They may also offer multinationals opportunities to avoid taxation, an issue which became increasingly controversial in 2012. These developments would not have been possible to the extent that they have occurred without the development of new forms of instantaneous forms of communication of information based on electronic technology.

As economies become more integrated, shocks transmit more rapidly between them so that a crisis in one country can rapidly spread to others. The GFC started with a crisis in the 'sub-prime' housing market in the United States – i.e. mortgages granted to individuals with poor credit histories whose ability to repay was in question. The granting of mortgages to these individuals had wider repercussions because the loans were repackaged and sold as debt-based financial instruments. Because of the central position of the US in the world economy, and the fact that other economies had also over-borrowed, the crisis rapidly became a global one.

One response to such a crisis is to try and create new mechanisms to coordinate international economic management such as the G20 summit held in Britain in the spring of 2009. Countries may also come together to coordinate their economic policies on a regional basis, exemplified by the Eurozone within the European Union (EU) which seeks to create a zone of regional economic stability organised around the single currency, the euro. As the Eurozone crisis, driven by the indebtedness of southern European countries, has developed, efforts have been made to move towards a fiscal government in Europe which would influence taxation and spending decisions by individual member states. Britain has, however, chosen not to become a member of the Eurozone, although it does coordinate some aspects of economic policy with other member states in the EU.

However, the development of these forms of global and regional coordination does not mean that economic policy is no longer made at a national level. In particular, national governments make important decisions about taxation and the budget. These affect the distribution of wealth and income in society and the availability of public services such as health and education. Because Britain still controls its own currency, it can also manipulate the exchange rate as a policy instrument. If the pound falls against other currencies, imports become more expensive, but British exports become cheaper and hence more competitive. In the wake of the GFC, Britain was accused by other EU member states of engaging in a competitive devaluation against the euro, an option not available to member states within the Eurozone such as Ireland.

The boundaries of economic policy are not entirely clear or fixed. At the heart of economic policy is the management

Box 25.1

Areas of policy that are related to economic policy

Competition policy – preventing the emergence of monopolies and cartels and removing barriers to the operation of a competitive free market as well as the regulation of 'natural monopolies' or public utilities.

Industrial policy – providing assistance to firms or sectors in difficulty but also encouraging innovation and new industries.

Research and development policy – ensuring that sufficient research and development is undertaken to sustain a competitive economy and that research results are transmitted into commercial innovations.

Regional policy – promoting and developing the economies of less favoured regions which may, for example, be geographically remote, have poor communications links or outdated industrial structures.

Education policy – ensuring that the economy has available to it a workforce with the right mix of skills and the capability to enhance them in response to changing needs.

Labour market policy – encompasses what was known as training policy (the transmission of vocational skills), but also seeks to ensure that the workforce is flexible and available for work.

Trade policy – negotiating international trade agreements to open up new markets for domestic production and services, but also to secure greater social justice for the Global South.

Transport policy – ensuring that national transport infrastructure is modern and efficient and does not impose costs on the economy through delays or other problems. Its economic significance has grown with the development of 'just in time' manufacturing and new logistical systems for retailers.

---

of what are known as the 'macroeconomic aggregates' such as inflation, employment and growth. However, the success of an economy depends on many other factors than how these macroeconomic aggregates are managed. For example, workers in the economy have to have the right mix of skills and the capacity to develop new ones. There has to be sufficient investment in new plant and machinery and research and development to discover and develop new products, materials and technologies. In the GFC, the Labour Government effectively became involved once more in forms of industrial policy that provided funds for particular firms as it sought to secure the future of the motor industry.

Any policy can potentially affect the economy – e.g. environmental policy – but Box 25.1 identifies the policies that are particularly relevant to the management of the economy. There may be tensions between some of these policies and their objectives. For example, industrial or research and development policy may seek to promote European or national 'champion' firms, while competition policy would seek to restrain them. Regional policy generally favours taking work to the workers, while an active labour market policy would prefer taking steps to ensure that workers can move to where there is work.

All forms of economic policy are invariably influenced by the fact that their success or otherwise may have an influence on a government's political fate. Indeed, this is why there has been a trend to take some economic policy decisions away from politicians, often referred to as *depoliticisation*. As a generalisation, it can be said that electorates punish governments for poor economic performance, but are less inclined to reward them for good economic performance as, after a while, they tend to take good economic times for granted and focus on other issues.

Decisions on economic policy may be distorted by political considerations. Consider, for example, interventions by governments to support firms or sectors in difficulty which were popular with both Conservative and Labour governments in the 1960s and 1970s and have enjoyed something of a revival in the GFC. This type of policy carries with it a number of risks:

1 It enables multinational companies to play one country off against another to extract funds.

2 It is very difficult to demonstrate 'additionality', i.e. that the additional funds made available lead to investment that would not otherwise occur.

3 It is very difficult for politicians and bureaucrats to pick winners (or 'losers').

4 Often decisions are made on electoral grounds – e.g. the sensitivity of a particular constituency or region.

5 Often investments were replicated in different parts of the country for political reasons when there was no good economic case: steel and aluminium provide good examples in the case of Britain.

6 Large companies were generally favoured over smaller companies.

7 Outdated industrial structures were preserved, hindering modernisation.

The machinery of economic policy

The making of economic policy lies at the very heart of the government machine, what is sometimes referred to as the 'core executive'. The machinery of economic policy-making is not simply a neutral set of procedures for making decisions. It changes in a way that reflects changing perspectives on policy and fluctuations in the distribution of power within government.

It involves some of the most powerful figures in politics, in particular the Prime Minister and Chancellor and much depends on the relationship between them. It also involves powerful individuals outside the government itself, most importantly the Governor of the Bank of England.

The Prime Minister

Not all prime ministers take an active part in the management of economic policy, despite its electoral importance. They may choose to be less involved in economic policy because they have other priorities, doubt their competence to deal with economic matters or because of the nature of their relationship with the Chancellor. Thus, Margaret Thatcher felt that she had a good understanding of what was needed in economic policy and intervened a lot, while David Cameron was prepared to leave a lot more to his Chancellor, George Osborne. When Tony Blair was Prime Minister, he and Gordon Brown operated what was sometimes referred to as a 'dual monarchy' in which Brown was given considerable authority over wide areas of domestic policy and in particular the management of the economy. It has even been suggested that Brown kept the contents of the Budget to himself until the very last minute.

Box 25.2

Involvement of postwar Prime Ministers in the economy

Prime Minister	Level of involvement
Attlee	Moderate
Churchill	Low
Eden	Low
Macmillan	High
Douglas-Home	Low
Wilson (1)	High
Heath	High
Wilson (2)	Moderate
Callaghan	High
Thatcher	High
Major	Moderate
Blair	Moderate
Brown	High
Cameron	Moderate

Even so, Blair set the general strategy of economic policy, which involved the creation of a social market economy in which economic competition was encouraged and the acquisition of wealth was seen as desirable, but where government would intervene to help the less well off in society – for example, through tax credits and a minimum wage. Blair also sought to pursue his ambition to make Labour 'the natural party of business', meeting frequently with business leaders.

The Prime Minister–Chancellor relationship

This relationship is at the heart of the economic policy-making process. If it starts to break down, as it did between Margaret Thatcher and Nigel Lawson, then the whole stability of the government and certainly its capacity to make economic policy is threatened. On the one hand, it has been argued that the working relationship between George Osborne and David Cameron is too close so that the Prime Minister has been insufficiently questioning of the Chancellor's economic strategy, although the Liberal Democrats have sometimes been critical and have modified policy content.

The average time in office of chancellors is tending to lengthen. In part this is because it is recognised that it is politically damaging for a Prime Minister to remove or lose a Chancellor. It is also reflects the increased emphasis on stability in the conduct of economic policy. There is unlikely to be a repetition of the Macmillan premiership when there were three chancellors. John Major was damaged by the necessity to remove Norman Lamont as Chancellor after the exchange rate mechanism crisis. Lamont became a thorn in his side, while Major had to be circumspect in his dealings with Lamont's successor, Ken Clarke.

Leaving aside the special case of Iain Macleod, who died after a few weeks in office, there have now been six post-war administrations that have had the same chancellor for the whole of their period in office (Churchill/Butler; Home/Maudling; Heath/Barber; Wilson and then Callaghan/Healey; Blair/Brown; Brown/Darling) and it looks as if there will be a seventh (Cameron/Osborne). How does this important and often durable relationship work? It should be noted that a harmonious relationship does not mean that a Prime Minister and Chancellor never disagree, or that they are personal friends, but that they can work effectively together and resolve their differences amicably.

In many ways the ideal relationship is where the Chancellor is a political figure in his own right, can challenge the Prime Minister if necessary, but where the relationship is characterised by mutual respect and trust. In general, the relationship between James Callaghan and Denis Healey in the 1970s fits this pattern.

In contrast, over time, the relationship between Tony Blair and Gordon Brown moved from the top left-hand to the bottom right-hand corner of Table 25.1 as it became more strained. This was not because there were significant ideological differences. Both of them were fully signed up members of the New Labour project. However, Brown's ambition to become Prime Minister, and Blair's reluctance to leave, placed increasing strains on the relationship which affected the whole conduct of government policy. Brown had a significant base of support in the parliamentary party and, although the idea of moving him to Foreign Secretary was mooted, Blair lacked the political confidence to do it. After Brown became Prime Minister, his relationship with his Chancellor, Alastair Darling, became more strained over time as it became clear that Darling was not prepared to be a mere subordinate but would develop and implement his own ideas about economic policy.

The Treasury

One of the reasons why the Chancellor is such an important figure is because of the special position of **the Treasury** in the British policy-making process. The Treasury wants a strong Chancellor because it is always concerned that the Prime Minister may give way to the pleas of spending departments, placing the public finances under strain.

The role that the Treasury plays in the policy-making process is rather different from that of equivalent departments in other advanced industrial countries. In many such countries (for example, Germany and the United States), the roles of raising revenues, overseeing the financial system and economic stability, and making budgetary decisions are split between two different departments. In Britain these functions are all concentrated in one powerful department. This has led to criticisms that the Treasury is too powerful in economic policy-making, that it has been insufficiently concerned with economic performance (particularly of manufacturing industry) and that it has contributed significantly to poor economic performance.

Table 25.1 Prime Minister–Chancellor relationships

	Chancellor as political figure in own right	Chancellor lacks independent political base
Harmonious relationship	Chancellor enjoys autonomy and support from PM	Chancellor faithfully executes PM's policies
Difficult relationship	Clashes over policy affect work of government	Leads to resignation or dismissal

Three decision rules in government underpin the ability of the Treasury to exercise control over the conduct of economic policy. A standing order of the House of Commons which dates back to 1713 prevents an MP proposing a measure which would cost the Treasury money, without government consent. A second rule, formalised in 1924, requires that no proposal for additional expenditure can be circulated to the Cabinet before it has been discussed in draft with the Treasury. A third rule, dating from 1884, is that any proposal involving an increase in expenditure or any new service requires Treasury sanction. Harold Wilson, in his second term as Prime Minister, promulgated a new ruling to the effect that Treasury ministers could not be overruled on financial matters in Cabinet committees, which Wilson described as giving the Treasury 51 per cent of the votes. Appeals could only be made to the full Cabinet if the chair of the Cabinet committee agreed. This arrangement was written into the rules for ministers by Margaret Thatcher when she was Prime Minister.

The prestige of the Treasury and its influence on economic policy has fluctuated considerably over time. Before the Second World War, the Treasury was principally concerned with the 'candle ends' task of balancing the budget and exercising restraint in public expenditure. It was heavily wedded to financial orthodoxy and had no solutions to offer to the depression of the 1930s. Indeed, it was the Bank of England which took a more proactive role in seeking to reorganise and stimulate manufacturing industry.

The position of the Treasury was changed by the publication of Keynes' *General Theory of Interest, Employment and Money* in 1936 and the outbreak of the Second World War, which required extensive government intervention in the economy. Keynes served as an adviser to the Treasury and his ideas on how a new recession could be avoided gradually won acceptance, although the Treasury never was (or is) monolithic in its views and some officials clung to the view that the restraint of public expenditure should be paramount.

The economists in the Economic Section of the Treasury played an important role in disseminating and establishing Keynes' ideas (or rather his ideas as interpreted by his disciples after his untimely death in 1946). The general view in the civil service was that experts should be on tap rather than on top and there was certainly some scepticism about the input of economists among generalist civil servants who at that time were often recruited from a humanities background. Nevertheless, with the establishment of the Government Economic Service economists became more influential both in the Treasury and other departments. By 2009 there were over one thousand of them employed in various branches of government.

The postwar economy in the 1950s and most of the 1960s was characterised by relatively high rates of growth compared with Britain's historical experience, low unemployment and acceptable rates of inflation. Against the background of a fixed exchange rate regime, there were recurrent balance of payment crises. Nevertheless, the Treasury was credited with contributing to an economy that was performing better than in the inter-war period. Its reputation within the civil service was reinforced by the fact that it was able to recruit the brightest and best among incoming civil servants.

However, the Treasury faced increasing difficulty in keeping inflation under control. Its preferred least-bad policy option of prices and incomes policy was insufficient in the face of the rapid rise in commodity prices, especially oil, in the early 1970s. One consequence of rapid inflation was that it lost its ability to keep public expenditure under control and the so-called 'missing billions' of the mid-1970s did considerable damage to the Treasury's reputation. It had to introduce new methods of controlling public expenditure known as 'cash limits'. Although interpretations of these events vary, it is generally accepted that the Treasury used the International Monetary Fund (IMF) intervention in the British economy in 1976 to restore its authority and impose cuts in public expenditure which went beyond what the IMF actually required.

Despite the revival of its authority, suspicions of the Treasury remained. Reformist critics from the left argued that it was short-termist, arrogant, cut off and incapable of seeing the bigger economic picture. However, the Thatcher Government which came into office in 1979 was also suspicious of the Treasury mandarins whom (with some justification) it saw as being too wedded to interventionist Keynesian approaches to economic policy. It was only during the chancellorship of Nigel Lawson that the authority and prestige of the Treasury within the Government was restored. The Treasury then suffered another blow with the exchange rate mechanism (ERM) crisis of 1992 when Britain had to leave the ERM in circumstances not of its own choosing known as 'Black Wednesday'. In fact, the subsequent devaluation of the pound provided a stimulus to the economy so an alternative interpretation of the events was that they were 'Golden Wednesday'. After Norman Lamont resigned as Chancellor, Ken Clarke helped to build a new approach to economic policy that saw performance improve and consequently rebuilt the Treasury's reputation.

However, what appeared to be the golden age of the Treasury in modern times was under the Chancellorship of Gordon Brown from 1997 to 2007. Because of the 'dual monarchy' character of the Government, the Treasury enjoyed considerable authority over other departments concerned with domestic policy through the use of mechanisms such as public service agreements. Substantial additional funding was made available to public services, but this was made conditional on achieving performance targets with the Treasury, although these targets subsequently became the subject of criticism because of what was argued to be their distorting effect on the way in which services were delivered.

The reputation of the Treasury was also enhanced by a period of good economic performance, made possible in large part by a boom in the world economy that ultimately turned out to be unsustainable. Unemployment declined and, more significantly, employment levels (the proportion of the eligible population in work) increased. Inflation was low and growth rates were good. The one black spot was that Britain's productivity performance continued to be relatively poor, not just in manufacturing but also in services. The Treasury paid considerable attention to this problem and suggested a number of reforms that were controversial because they impinged on the turf of other departments – for example, reforms in the planning system. However, productivity performance failed to respond sufficiently, suggesting that the economy displayed structural weaknesses that were to some extent being concealed by a consumer boom fuelled by high levels of personal debt and government spending.

The outbreak of the GFC saw renewed criticism of the role and performance of the Treasury, and in particular the tripartite division of economic management after 1997 between the Treasury, the Bank of England and the Financial Services Authority (FSA) (discussed further below). It was argued that the Treasury had paid insufficient attention to the stability of the financial system and was ill-prepared for the GFC. As part of the continuous search for efficiency savings in the civil service, the size of the Treasury staff had been reduced, making it more difficult for it to conduct detailed surveillance of some areas of policy.

The capacity of the Treasury to act effectively has been undermined by a high rate of turnover in staff. Less than half of its staff in 2012 had joined the Treasury before the GFC began. Turnover was 28 per cent in 2011 alone. The average Treasury employee is just 32 years old compared with 45 years across Whitehall as a whole. Staff leave because pay is relatively poor and career progression is limited. Salaries can be as much as 50 to 100 per cent higher in the Bank of England and even more in financial services.

Controversy over the place of the Treasury in economic policy-making will no doubt continue. Its defenders will portray it as a Rolls-Royce machine which permits an integrated approach to the conduct of economic policy that is paralleled in only one other major advanced industrial country (France). Its critics will argue that it has excessive influence which is informed by a narrow view of economic policy which leads to serious errors.

The Bank of England

An old Treasury joke refers to the **Bank of England** as the 'Treasury's East End branch', but the Bank of England has always been a power centre in its own right, a role that was enhanced after 1997. The Bank's nationalisation in 1947 made relatively little difference to the way in which it operated: it continued to regard itself as the guardian of the City of London and its representative to government. However, as the City changed and the financial services sector became more differentiated and lost its 'club' atmosphere, the representative role of the Bank came to be shared with professional trade organisations such as the British Bankers' Association. Nevertheless, when the Governor of the Bank speaks, people listen as they did in spring of 2009 when Mervyn King made it known that he did not think that it would be possible to afford another fiscal stimulus to the economy in that year's Budget.

Relations between the Bank and Treasury reached perhaps their lowest ebb in 1976 when the Bank was accused of having mismanaged the foreign exchange markets. A no-doubt apocryphal story which has nevertheless entered the folklore is that, having been instructed to bring about a devaluation of sterling, senior Bank officials set sales of the currency in motion and went out to lunch leaving a junior official in charge. He continued to sell on a falling market which initiated a collapse of the pound. However, the general stance of the Bank in terms of the need to cut public spending and to negotiate an IMF loan to end speculation against sterling was vindicated by events.

Relations between Margaret Thatcher as Prime Minister and the Bank were initially strained. She took the view that her door plate said that she was First Lord of the Treasury and the Governor of the Bank must do as she said, which was not how he understood the relationship to work. Margaret Thatcher could not understand why the monetary indicators were not working as monetarist theory predicted and came to the view that the Bank was either technically incompetent or subversive.

Nevertheless, the emphasis of the Thatcher Government on monetary indicators gave the Bank a more central role in the Government's economic strategy. Nigel Lawson as Chancellor came round to the view that the Bank's performance would be improved if it had more independence. He made it a feature of his resignation speech and the case for greater central bank independence began to win wider support.

It was argued that politicians were susceptible to a 'political budget cycle', although the empirical evidence for this effect was ambiguous at least. Politicians could not be trusted to run the economy, because they would give undue weight to short-term electoral considerations. Central bankers were independent of such considerations, sympathetic to the market mechanism, either possessed or had ready access to relevant expertise and could be trusted to make prudent judgements. Credibility with the markets would thus be established and the chances of success in the fight against inflation increased. An independent central bank could take speedier action to anticipate and choke off the threat of higher inflation.

Politicians and Treasury officials were understandably reluctant to surrender a key policy instrument, the setting of interest rates, to the Bank. John Major's view as Prime Minister was that these decisions should be taken by someone answerable to Parliament. A broader argument was that the Bank would be more cautious (even alarmist) about the prospect of inflation than a politician would be. As a consequence, interest rates would go up relatively quickly and fall slowly.

Nevertheless, Major allowed Ken Clarke as Chancellor to take two small steps towards greater Bank independence which paved the way for the more radical step taken in 1997 by the New Labour Government. The minutes of the Chancellor's monthly meeting with the Governor of the Bank, one of the most crucial economic policy-making events, were to be published six weeks in arrears, so that the arguments made by both sides could become public knowledge. It was agreed that the Bank could publish its regular inflation report without prior approval by the Treasury. This was a symbolic recognition of greater Bank autonomy. Clarke, however, continued to set the interest rates, generally a little below the level that the then Governor, 'Steady' Eddie George, thought prudent.

Within a few days of coming into office, the Blair Government took one of the most significant economic policy decisions of the postwar period by transferring responsibility for interest rate policy to the Bank. The letter from Gordon Brown announcing the decision is displayed in a glass case in the Bank's museum. It should be emphasised that this policy change gave the Bank operational rather than goal independence. It is government that sets the inflation policy target and it retains emergency powers to intervene and set the interest rate itself, although those have never been used. In practice, the dense network of relationships between the Treasury and the Bank allows the Treasury to give some signals about its views on monetary policy. In particular a non-voting representative of the Treasury sits on the Bank committee that sets interest rates, the Monetary Policy Committee (MPC). The Treasury is still responsible for fiscal policy (taxation and spending) and this aspect of policy needs to be coordinated with monetary policy (conventionally pursued through setting the interest rate).

The government influences the appointment of the nine members of the MPC. Candidates for the governorship and deputy governorships of the Bank are recommended by the Prime Minister. These all sit on the committee, along with the Bank's Chief Economist and the Executive Director for Markets. The Chancellor selects the four members appointed from outside the Bank who are generally economists with relevant expertise. The Bank has a voting majority, but does not vote as a bloc and financial journalists spend a lot of effort analysing the minutes of the MPC's meetings to determine who can be classified as 'hard' or 'soft' on interest rates.

These arrangements worked well up until the GFC. Inflation was lower and generally more stable, but this was assisted by the benign economic environment. The Bank encountered criticism for failing to anticipate the extent of the GFC, which was directed particularly at the then Governor, Mervyn King. The interest rate policy instrument quickly failed to work as an instrument to regulate the economy, with the MPC rate falling to historically unprecedented levels with little immediate effect.

The Bank had to resort from March 2008 to a novel policy of 'quantitative easing' which in effect means printing electronic money and using it to buy up assets such as gilt-edged stock (government bonds that pay an interest rate) and corporate bonds. In the first month of this policy the Bank spent £21 billion on purchasing securities, principally gilt-edged stock. This increases the quantity of money in the economy and should give it a stimulus, although monetarist theory emphasises the velocity at which money is exchanged as well as its quantity. A downside risk of this exceptional policy was that inflation could accelerate as the economy emerged from recession.

These unprecedented events raised questions about the role of both the Bank and the MPC given that the interest rate, for the time being anyhow, had reduced policy relevance. The MPC was left to discuss the operation of the quantitative easing programme, a much more limited and less high-profile role than it had enjoyed. However, this did not mean the importance of the Bank in economic policy-making had declined: rather the contrary. The boundary between fiscal and monetary policy has been blurred and it was the Bank that took a major responsibility for reviving the economy. Cooperation between the Treasury and the Bank became more vital than ever and the Governor's role became pivotal. The appointment of Mark Carney, the Governor of Bank of Canada, as Governor from 2013 suggested that a new approach to the role might be needed. What was clear was that Carney would be a key actor in making economic policy – as important as the Chancellor.

The Financial Services Authority

The so-called 'Big Bang' of 1986 represented a major step in the **liberalisation** of financial services in Britain. It ended the traditional demarcation lines in the financial sector. However, it was recognised that there was inadequate protection for investors, something that has been confirmed by a number of subsequent scandals in which investors have lost money and have found it difficult to obtain compensation. The Conservative Government, however, did not want to impose a strict regulatory regime that might drive business away from London, and the tension between investor protection and securing highly mobile business has proved to be a recurrent one. Critics have argued that the interests of domestic investors have been sacrificed to the needs of international financial markets. After the GFC the reputation of the financial services sector was in tatters, it being argued that retail investors paid high fees and were given poor value in return.

Under the 1986 Financial Services Act the Conservatives set up a series of self-regulatory bodies with the Securities and Investment Board (SIB) at its core. This body was accountable to government, but was funded by a series of Self-Regulatory Organisations (SROs) which placed a levy on the firms for which they were responsible. This system was beset by a series of tensions and criticisms and there were many criticisms of its performance. When Labour came into office in 1997 the name of the SIB was changed to the Financial Services Authority (FSA).

The FSA was given statutory powers by the Financial Services and Markets Act 2000. Its principal statutory responsibilities are maintaining market confidence (probably the most important); public awareness; consumer protection; and reduction of financial crime. With the outbreak of the GFC there was considerable criticism of the FSA's performance, but in particular of the tripartite structure that had been created by the Labour Government in terms of the distribution of responsibility for supervision of the financial services sector between the Treasury, the Bank and the FSA. The first stage of the reform of financial services regulation was completed in June 1998, when responsibility for banking supervision was transferred to the FSA from the Bank of England. In May 2000 the FSA took over the role of UK Listing Authority from the London Stock Exchange. The 2000 legislation transferred to the FSA the responsibilities of several other organisations such as the Building Societies Commission. In October 2004 the FSA was given responsibility for mortgage regulation and in 2005 it became responsible for the regulation of general insurance business.

The FSA thus acquired a wide range of additional functions, but concern was expressed about whether it was equipped to deal with them. It was difficult for the FSA to compete with the salaries offered in the financial services sector before the GFC, leading to questions about whether its staff matched the calibre of those employed in City firms. It also lacked the traditional authority and network of contacts of the Bank. The FSA's credibility was tarnished by the collapse in the financial services sector, which seemed to take it by surprise. The underlying problem, which had been present in the regulation of the financial services sector since it was liberalised, was prioritising the international competitiveness of the financial services sector over the protection of consumer investors.

The Coalition Government introduced a new set of arrangements. The Bank of England's involvement in supervision of the financial services sector was restored with a new Financial Policy Committee within the Bank to spot and manage threats to financial stability. The FSA will be replaced by a 'twin peaks' system. A new arm of the Bank, the Prudential Regulatory Authority, will supervise banks for safety and soundness. An independent Financial Conduct Authority will protect investors and regulate markets.

Competition agencies

The competition agencies constitute another set of bodies that have a considerable impact on economic policy. Competition policy has been given a greater emphasis in British economic policy since the 1980s. This is partly a consequence of the need to regulate utilities which have been privatised but enjoy 'natural' monopolies – i.e. a situation where having just one firm is the most efficient solution as in the provision of transmission networks for electricity and gas. However, it also reflects the market-driven emphasis of the Blair Government's policies which saw an effective competition policy as an important factor in improved economic performance. Two key pieces of legislation, the Competition Act 1998 and the Enterprise Act 2002, greatly extended the powers of the competition authorities and in particular the range and size of penalties available to them. Some forms of anti-competitive behaviour can now be subject to criminal prosecution leading to prison sentences.

The key body is the Competition Commission (CC) which has around 150 staff, although it works in tandem with the Office of Fair Trading (OFT), but these two bodies will be merged from 2014. The CC has three main functions:

- To regulate mergers when large companies will gain more than 25 per cent market share and where a merger looks likely to undermine competition.

- To tackle the prevention, distortion or restriction of competition in particular markets.

- To oversee the operation of the regulatory system in regulated sectors.

The CC has carried out its work in cooperation with the EU competition authorities who have a particular role in dealing with mergers that affect more than one member state, EU-wide cartels and breaches of the EU's state aid rules. The OFT has seen its central task as making markets work well for consumers.

The GFC somewhat undermined the effectiveness and credibility of UK competition policy. The Enterprise Act 2002 was meant to ensure that ministers were largely removed from the merger control process. Ahead of the Act, the Government had maintained that decision-making would become more predictable if mergers were no longer influenced by political considerations. The old test of whether a merger was in the public interest would be replaced with an independent decision on whether there would be a substantial lessening of competition because rivals had joined forces. Even so, ministers may still intervene in mergers that raise public-interest considerations. Moreover, the minister can redefine the public interest with parliamentary approval. The then Business Secretary, John Hutton, announced in September 2008 that he would specify the stability of the UK financial system as a public-interest consideration.

The merger between Lloyds Bank and HBOS would not have normally been permitted under competition policy legislation. Moreover, the Banking (Special Provisions) Act of 2008 gave additional powers to government. It means that the Treasury can make an order transferring one bank to another and setting aside UK merger control legislation. This is exactly what happened with the transfer of the assets of Bradford and Bingley to the Spanish bank, Santander. Exceptional circumstances may be said to justify exceptional measures, but the advances made in competition policy were one of the unsung achievements of the Blair Government which have now been undermined by the consequences of the GFC.

From 2014 the CC and the OFT will be brought together in a new Competition and Market Authority. The Coalition Government claims that this will improve the quality of decisions and strengthen the regime, some criticism having been directed at the effectiveness of the OFT. Equally, there have been complaints from business that the CC has been too powerful and one of the objectives of the new regime is to increase its speed and predictability for business.

The changing conduct of economic policy

Five principal phases can be distinguished in postwar British economic policy:

1   A neo-Keynesian phase from 1945 to 1979.

2   The Conservative governments from 1979 to 1997.

3   New Labour from 1997 to 2007.

4   The financial crisis from 2007.

5   Austerity under the Coaliton Government.

The neo-Keynesian phase from 1945 to 1979

The wartime coalition government accepted a commitment to maintain **full employment**. Exactly what 'full employment' meant was never defined, but the postwar boom kept unemployment at relatively low levels until the late 1960s. Most unemployment during this period was 'frictional': i.e. it was made up of people changing jobs, although there were some pools of structural, long-term employment in particular localities. Maintaining full employment was essential to the success of the new welfare state as it prevented the cost of unemployment benefit causing too great a burden on the public finances. This is why the term 'Keynesian welfare state' is sometimes used, even though it is somewhat misleading as Keynes, the architect of the full employment economy, and Beveridge, who devised the plan for the welfare state, largely worked separately of each other.

Keynes considered that by a judicious use of government spending it would be possible to run the economy at a higher level of employment than had been possible in the recession of the 1930s. As interpreted by his disciples after his death, this meant 'fine tuning' the economy largely through the fiscal policy instruments of public expenditure and taxation. One of the problems caused by this fine tuning of the economy, which in any case was based on an inadequate set of statistics to measure its performance or the means to analyse such data as were available, was that it tended to produce 'stop go' cycles in the economy. This created uncertainty, which made it more difficult for businesses to engage in investment planning.

Another problem with running the economy at near the full employment ceiling was that it tended to create wage push inflation as labour was generally in relatively short supply. Keynes himself admitted that he had no answer to this problem. The solution that was favoured by the Treasury, and employed by both Conservative and Labour governments at various times between 1945 and 1979, was wage restraint in the form of incomes policies. These policies really only had an impact as short-term emergency measures. In the longer run they increased industrial unrest, particularly by eroding differentials between skilled and unskilled workers. They also tended to be more strictly enforced in the public sector, whereas ways were found of evading them in the private sector. They increased the influence of the trade unions in the running of the economy as their consent was needed to make the policies effective.

By the end of the 1950s it was becoming apparent that the British economy was lagging behind the performance of its major competitors. This led to the 'Brighton Revolution' of 1960 which has been described as an economic coup d'état. A conference of the country's economic establishment in

Brighton decided that the country needed to move towards a more interventionist economic policy model based on that of France, although it is clear with the benefit of hindsight that the French model was misunderstood at the time. This led to a great reliance on indicative planning in which government set economic targets and the creation of new institutional devices such as the National Economic Development Council (NEDC) which brought together government, the unions and employers to discuss the management of the economy. There was also a resort to more interventionist forms of industrial policy, particularly under the Labour Government from 1964 to 1970.

The high (or low) point of this tripartite (government/ unions/employers) model of running the economy was reached under the Conservative Government of 1970–4, particularly after its policy **U-turn** of 1972 which ushered in much more interventionist policies. In effect, the trade unions were offered a partnership to run the economy with government. They were tempted, but relations between them and the Government had been soured by controversial industrial relations legislation. The Government lost the 'Who governs?' election which it called in February 1974 amidst a miners' strike which had reduced the economy to a three-day week.

The Labour Government of 1974–9 continued with interventionist policies, although not as interventionist as some of the left-wing members of the Cabinet such as Tony Benn would have liked. However, it was clear that the neo-Keynesian model was no longer delivering against a background of 'stagflation': high unemployment, historically high rates of inflation and low growth. Alternative monetarist recipes began to be advocated in the financial press. In 1976 the Prime Minister, James Callaghan, made a speech which questioned Keynesian demand management by stating that it was no longer possible for the country to spend its way out of a recession. The Government subsequently started to monitor the monetary aggregates, although this was as much to reassure the markets as to guide its economic policy. It persisted with the neo-Keynesian device of prices and incomes policy and opposition to this policy led to widespread industrial unrest in the so-called 'winter of discontent' of 1978–79 and the defeat of the Labour Government in the 1979 General Election.

The Conservative Government, 1979–97

It is very easy in retrospect to portray Margaret Thatcher who became Prime Minister in 1979 as someone driven by ideological considerations. In fact, until her final years in office, she was a very shrewd politician who made tactical retreats when she had to. Nevertheless, she did have a clear vision of where she wanted to take the country. In particular,

she subscribed to the view held by Sir Keith Joseph that successive Conservative governments had moved away from fundamental Conservative principles and had subscribed to a 'corporatist' version of economic management which had contributed to the country's decline. One of her fundamental principles was that she was not prepared to accept the country's economic decline as an irreversible condition which had to be managed as best as could be achieved. She was determined to reverse that decline by putting new policies in place. She also saw economic management as a means of achieving broader objectives such as a freer society. As she said, 'Economics are the method, the objective is the soul.'

One of the most fundamental changes brought about by the Government was the effective replacement of the full employment objective which had prevailed since 1945. The control of inflation was seen as the principal goal and this was to be achieved by control of the money supply and restraint in public expenditure. A rapid appreciation of sterling, which the Government did not seek to control, after it came into office made it more difficult for British industry to export its goods and contributed to a rise in unemployment. Unemployment continued to rise for much of the 1980s and reached unprecedented levels for the postwar period. The Government's view, however, was that interventions to raise unemployment above its 'natural' level would only further undermine economic performance. Inflation fell, but then rose again, so that by the time Mrs Thatcher left office the 'misery index' that added together inflation and unemployment was higher than when she had become Prime Minister.

A key aspect of the Thatcher Government's approach was the emphasis on the **supply side** of the economy rather than the manipulation of the demand side as emphasised in the neo-Keynesian model. Contrary to the conventional postwar wisdom, the creation of conditions conducive to growth and employment should be the objective of microeconomic rather than macroeconomic policy. In particular, efforts were made to create a more flexible labour market by reducing the power of the trade unions, which were seen as having the ability to force up the cost of labour. The influence of the unions was reduced by facing down major strikes, passing new legislation to control them and privatising the nationalised industries which were one of the main bases of union power. The Government also sought to encourage entrepreneurship, particularly through smaller firms, by reducing punitive levels of taxation on income and placing greater emphasis on indirect – for example, Value Added Tax – rather than on direct taxation.

The consequences of these policies remain a matter of controversy, but what cannot be disputed is that Margaret Thatcher made a difference to the conduct of British economic policy, in particular by emphasising the centrality of sound money. Productivity performance did improve relative to

Britain's competitors, although some of this was due to a 'batting average' effect which saw the least efficient firms and plants closed. A more efficient economy was produced, but at some social cost, in particular the creation of an 'underclass' of long-term unemployed.

John Major, Mrs Thatcher's successor, consolidated her policies by undertaking further privatisations. He got rid of the last vestige of **tripartism** by abolishing the NEDC. After Britain was forced out of the ERM, he used an inflation target as the main driver of economic policy. He also placed more emphasis on what are known as active labour market policies designed to cajole those dependent on long-term benefits to enter the labour force, a policy that was developed further by New Labour.

New Labour from 1997 to 2007

New Labour's economic policies built on Thatcherite foundations, but took them in a new direction. They emphasised the value of a competitive market economy, sound money, low and stable inflation and a flexible labour market in which the unions had limited influence on wage bargaining and policy. With the approval of business, the Government sought derogations from EU legislation designed to enhance employment rights. The Government inherited and put into practice the Private Finance Initiative (PFI) developed by the Major Government which funded major construction projects for hospitals and schools and their subsequent maintenance and operation through agreements with the private sector, which critics argued were good deals for firms and poor ones for the taxpayer.

Conservative spending plans were accepted for the Government's first two years in office, although the Conservatives would have almost certainly have revised them upwards. In the 2000 Comprehensive Spending Review, however, the Government announced substantial increases in public expenditure and the tax take as a share of GDP started to increase. In part this was achieved by maintaining and increasing various indirect 'stealth' taxes introduced by the Conservatives, although the Blair Government had to abandon the fuel duty tax escalator after direct action protests. Part of the increase in taxes was brought about by 'fiscal drag' (i.e. tax allowances do not increase as fast as wage increases). As wages and salaries increased, more people found themselves in the higher-rate, 40 per cent tax band.

The most radical step taken by the Government was giving control of the interest rate to the Bank of England. The Government generally favoured the 'depoliticisation' of difficult issues, but this was inherently more difficult in the case of fiscal policy. The Government did devise a Code of Fiscal Stability. At the centre of the Code were two rules governing fiscal management. The so-called 'golden rule'

required that government will borrow only to invest and not to fund current spending. The second rule was a debt rule that required the ratio of GDP to public-sector debt to be held at a prudent and stable level, interpreted somewhat arbitrarily as below 40 per cent.

One consequence of the Thatcher Government's policies had been that the Gini coefficient for the UK had risen: that is, society had become more unequal in terms of the distribution of income. Indeed, Britain was the most unequal advanced industrial country alongside the United States. Labour sought to reverse this trend by introducing a minimum wage and instituting a generous policy of tax credits for working families with particular help for parents with young children. Eliminating child poverty was a long-term New Labour goal. This was often referred to as 'redistribution by stealth', but the Gini coefficient remained stubbornly unresponsive. In large part this was because of the effects of globalisation with international competition and possibly migration adversely affecting the wages of the lower paid. In the absence of New Labour's policies, inequality may have grown even more.

Critics of the Coalition Government argue that its policies have adversely affected the low paid with a decrease in the number of workers paying income tax offset by decreases in tax credits, below inflation wage increases and steep rises in the cost of travel, energy and food. It was argued that the minimum wage was inadequate, especially in London, and pressure was put on companies to pay a 'living wage' at a higher level.

One of the most difficult economic policy decisions that faced Britain was membership of the euro. Tony Blair was in favour of membership as he wanted Britain to be at the heart of Europe. However, he had agreed to a referendum on the subject to appease media critics. If this referendum had been held immediately after Labour had won the 1997 election, it is possible that it could have been won. However, Gordon Brown was not in favour of membership and set up the five tests which had to be met before Britain applied for membership. These were essentially a political device to block membership. The only one that mattered was that related to convergence between the British and continental European economies, not just in terms of the economic cycle but also structural convergence.

This raised one of the key problems about British membership. Britain has much higher levels of home ownership than most other European countries. Consumer activity in the economy more generally is strongly influenced by the housing market. Hence, variations in a 'one size fits all' European interest rate might have broader consequences in Britain than elsewhere. Supporters of British membership of the euro pointed to the boost that the removal of the uncertainty caused by fluctuations of the pound against the euro would give to trade and investment. Transaction costs would be reduced and price comparisons across the internal market would be made easier, delivering benefits to consumers.

Many of the arguments for and against the euro are political rather than economic. Its supporters are concerned that Britain will be excluded from the economic policy-making process at European level that involves the Eurozone countries, although Britain had to be brought into decisions about the GFC in the autumn of 2008. Opponents are concerned about what they see as the further loss of British sovereignty. In more practical terms, the UK government would lose a policy instrument, the ability to influence the exchange rate. There were also concerns about the decision-making mechanisms, priorities and accountability of the European Central Bank. There was a revived flurry of interest in British membership of the euro in the most severe phase of the GFC in the autumn of 2008, but the majority of voters remained opposed to membership, a view reinforced by the prolonged Eurozone crisis.

New Labour had promised an end to 'boom and bust' economics. For a time, it seemed as if this might have been achieved. The Government interpreted a rise in tax revenues after 2000 as a permanent one and started to ratchet up public expenditure, failing to put away a sufficient reserve for harder times. The onset of the GFC demanded a range of emergency measures which had to be developed over a short period of time. Many of Labour's economic policy innovations had to be jettisoned, including the fiscal rules.

The financial crisis from 2007

The financial crisis can be dated from the collapse of Northern Rock in September 2007 which saw a run on a bank in Britain for the first time since the nineteenth century. However, the full force of the GFC did not develop until 2008. All the long-run consequences are far from clear, but by 2009 it was evident that the bank bailout would cost the Government and the taxpayer at least £50 billion and possibly more. The Coalition Government's deficit reduction plan was more stringent than that set by the last Labour Chancellor, Alastair Darling, but not by much.

Long-time cycles can be discerned in economic policy. For example, between 1945 and 1979 the state's involvement in economic policy tended to increase, more or less regardless of which party was in office. Planning and regulation of the economy was seen as an inevitable feature of modern European societies, although Britain retained aspects of a more liberal outlook that it shared with the United States. After 1979 the state began a long-term retreat from involvement in the economy under the Conservatives and this trend was continued rather than reversed by New Labour.

Following the GFC, there were demands for a renewal of state involvement in the economy. There was a broad consensus that there needed to be tighter regulation of the financial system, at a national, European and global level. There was also much discussion of 're-balancing' the UK economy in favour of manufacturing. Both Labour and the Conservatives signed up to this rather vague notion without offering very much idea of how it was going to be achieved.

Beyond that it was evident that the Labour Government wanted to retain a largely hands-off relationship with the economy. It saw its interventions as temporary measures to dealing with an emergency. Even where the state had majority shares in a bank, the Government did not want to get dragged into decisions about whether a particular company or individual should receive a loan, although it did involve itself in the storm of complaint about banker's salaries, bonuses and pensions.

The Government's 'hands-off' approach to bank ownership is exemplified by the new arm's-length company it set up in November 2008 to manage its shareholdings in banks subscribing to its recapitalisation fund, UK Financial Investments Ltd. The company is required to act on a commercial basis and to ensure management incentives for banks. The board is made up of a private sector chair, three non-executive private sector members with relevant commercial skill and experience and two senior government officials.

Austerity under the Coalition Government

PROFILE

George Osborne (1971–)

George Osborne was only elected as a MP in 2001, but was associated with the 'Notting Hill Set' of Conservatives and became Shadow Chancellor in 2005 at the young age of 33. From 1994 he held various posts as a political researcher and adviser, becoming secretary to the Shadow Cabinet and political secretary to the Leader of the Opposition from 1997 to 2001. There is no doubt that Osborne was an effective critic of Labour policies, aided by the events of the GFC. Appointed Chancellor in the Coalition Government, he was initially seen as more effective in the role than expected. However, as the economy failed to grow, criticism of him increased, particularly in terms of his involvement in wider party management and the absence of a 'Plan B' to stimulate the economy. His stock as a potential future party leader fell.

The Coalition Government placed considerable emphasis on bringing the deficit in the public finances under control to the exclusion of the prioritisation of other economic policy objectives, notably economic growth. The Government's argument was that the deficit was unsustainable and if measures were not taken to deal with it, Britain would lose its triple A rating with credit agencies, forcing it to pay more to borrow money. By 2013 the rating had been lost from two agencies, but the consequences could be less serious than thought, given that very few other countries had retained such a rating. As it was, the cost of servicing the debt was considerable.

Quite a large part of the deficit was cyclical, the result of the recession – for example, greater spending on benefits. The Government was only targeting the structural deficit, the gap between taxation and spending that was not recession related. Even so, it made less progress than it would have liked in reducing the gap which was still over £100 billion a year at the end of 2012. It was also clear that the least painful cuts had been made and that further cuts would impact considerably on public services and the living standards of working families. The Government tried to deflect some criticism and save some more money by reducing benefit increases below the rate of inflation. Even so, bigger cuts in the welfare bill, which (including state pensions) accounted for around a third of all expenditure, would be necessary, particularly if major budgets such as those of the National Health Service were to continue to be 'ring fenced' from cuts. It was evident that whichever party was in office in 2015, there would have to be further tax rises and cuts in public expenditure.

By 2012 this policy was facing considerable criticism, both from backbenchers of the two governing parties and from economists who had originally supported it. The UK had faced a 'double dip' recession and growth prospects in the medium term were bleak. Economic output had not risen above its 2008 level and was estimated by 2012 to be 14 per cent below what was expected before the banking crisis. Admittedly, some of the figures were contradictory, with relative buoyancy in the labour market raising questions about the reliability of the GDP figures. Employment increased and the claimant count was relatively stable. However, some of this reflected a transfer to self-employment by those losing their jobs and an increase in part-time employment for people who would prefer to work full time. Productivity performance was also poor, although there was considerable disagreement about the reasons for this. Some thought that firms were holding on to skilled labour, a stance made easier by the fall in real wages, despite a fall in output so that it would be available to them when the economy recovered. Others thought that the switch by many workers from employment to self-employment led to them being less productive.

In 2012 the National Institute for Economic and Social Research attempted to estimate the effects of the policy of cutting back public expenditure or 'fiscal consolidation'. The work confirmed that 'doing nothing' was not an option as this scenario would have led to unsustainable debt ratios. However, the estimates suggested that the impact on the economy would have been much less, and less prolonged, if consolidation had been delayed until the economy had had a chance to recover.

Policy relied on very low interest rates and the use of quantitative easing by the Bank of England, although this was criticised for its focus on buying government bonds. Increasing doubts were expressed about how far monetary policy could be used to boost demand, given that households were squeezed by pay settlements below the rate of inflation, while small businesses were finding finance very difficult to obtain. Some analysts favoured cutting VAT as a short-term stimulus to consumer demand, arguing that increasing spending would offset the lost revenue. However, attention increasingly focused on giving a boost to the construction industry and in particular the housing market where results could be achieved more quickly than through large-scale infrastructure projects. The uncertainty produced by the Eurozone crisis made economic policy making more difficult.

Chapter summary

Economic policy went through a long period when it was 'depoliticised', particularly after the transfer of the setting of interest rates to the Bank of England. This reflected the influence of the 'rules v. discretion' debate in economics which argued that the more policy decisions that were rules-based the better as politicians were liable to be influenced by short-term electoral considerations. The GFC has seen a reintroduction of politics into economic policy which has become more central to the political process once again, very likely to be a central issue in the general election scheduled for 2015. Depoliticisation analysts would argue that in the long run politicians will want to transfer the responsibility elsewhere for unpopular decisions. There may also be more debate about whether growth should be a central objective of policy, given the importance of mitigating climate change and the questionable relationship between higher income and happiness beyond a level which meets basic human needs.

Discussion points

- Can government help the economy to perform more effectively or does it cause damage through its interventions?
- Does globalisation mean that national governments cannot conduct independent economic policies?
- Should Britain have joined the euro?
- Were the austerity policies of the Coalition Government too harsh and should there have been a clearer growth strategy?

Further reading

Although now somewhat dated, Grant (2002) provides an overview of British economic policy within the context of the global economy. Gamble (2009) provides a thorough and authoritative overview of the GFC. Gamble's (1994) book on Thatcherism remains one of the best treatments. Coates (2005) provides an excellent treatment of New Labour policies. Davies (ed. 2006) allows successive Chancellors to tell their own stories about how they tried to manage the British economy. Grant and Wilson (2012) look at why the GFC has not produced more change in economic policy and includes a chapter by Gamble on the case of Britain.

Bibliography

Coates, D. (2005) *Prolonged Labour: the Slow Birth of New Labour in Britain* (Palgrave Macmillan).

Davies, H. (ed.) (2006) *The Chancellors' Tales* (Polity Press).

Gamble, A. (1994) *The Free Economy and the State*, 2nd edn (Macmillan).

Gamble, A. (2009) *The Spectre at the Feast* (Palgrave-Macmillan).

Grant, W. (2002) *Economic Policy in Britain* (Palgrave-Macmillan).

Grant, W. and Wilson, G. (eds) (2012) *The Consequences of the Global Financial Crisis* (Oxford University Press).

Keynes, J.M. (1936) *The General Theory of Employment, Interest and Money* (Macmillan).

Useful websites

The website of HM Treasury is an essential reference point for current developments in economic policy (www.hm-treasury.gov.uk) as is that of the Bank of England (www.bankofengland.co.uk). The Institute of Fiscal Studies provides high quality independent assessment of the economy and economic policy (www.ifs.org.uk), as does the National Institute of Economic and Social Research (www.niesr.ac.uk), many of whose warnings have been vindicated by events.

CHAPTER 26

British foreign and defence policy

Bill Jones

> " We have no eternal allies, and we have no perpetual enemies. Our interests are eternal and perpetual, and those interests it is our duty to follow "
>
> Lord Palmerston

Learning objectives

- To explain the nature of foreign policy and, particularly, the 'idealist' and 'realist' approaches to it.

- To discuss the idea of an 'ethical foreign policy' and its viability since 1997.

- To assess defence policy in the post-Cold War world.

- To analyse relations with the USA and the UK's foreign policy options.

In this chapter, we study British foreign policy (mostly excluding the European issue) since the election of the Labour Government in May 1997 under three headings. The first is that Government's 'ethical' foreign policy, introduced as part of the FCO mission statement as early as 12 May 1997, days after the election; an extension of this was Blair's policy of 'liberal interventionism'. The second is the Strategic Defence Review, also announced within days of coming into office, conducted by Secretary of State for Defence George Robertson and completed in July 1998; further defence cuts were made by the Coalition Government after May 2010. The third heading is the government's relationship with the United States. This is the most familiar theme in foreign policy since the Second World War. Blair sought to repair a slackening of the relationship after the Major years; Brown tried hard to relate to Obama after 2008, as did Cameron after 2010.

Background

The study of British foreign policy has become increasingly problematical because of the difficulty of defining an arena or 'sphere' of foreign policy that is distinct from domestic policy. The internationalisation of government activity means that there are no longer, if indeed there ever were, clearly defined areas of domestic policy and of foreign policy. In the 1960s this internationalisation was often characterised by the perceived growth and alleged political influence of the multinational corporation in impacting on national political and economic life. In the 1970s and 1980s the development of the European Community and of the single market blurred enormously the boundaries between the British polity and a wider European sphere of policy making. Since the 1990s, the favoured term for this process has been 'globalisation', emphasising the consequences of the revolution in information and communications technology on the behaviour of the money and financial markets. The 'global village' predicted in the 1960s appears to have arrived, although some caution is required in interpreting these developments. For instance, the wars fought in former Yugoslavia throughout most of the 1980s were widely reported on our television screens, and commentators have often referred to these horrors taking place only two hours' flying time from Britain and in areas familiar to British holidaymakers. Nevertheless, at crucial times information about developments on the ground was lacking, air strikes were based on poor information, and the difficulties confronting the Western powers in influencing events were not dissimilar to those confronting the Western allies in 1945.

Practically all departments of government are involved in making European Union policy; the Foreign and Commonwealth Office is not the most important. See Figure 26.1 for a clear diagrammatic chart of the elements involved in making foreign policy.

For instance, policy on British membership of the euro, perhaps the single most important strategic issue that faced the Labour Government after its election in 1997, was tightly controlled not by the Foreign Secretary but by the Prime Minister and the Chancellor of the Exchequer. The Chancellor famously laid down five key criteria to determine the merits of British membership in October 1997, and Foreign Secretary Robin Cook was for long careful not to transgress any of the boundaries established by a colleague concerned principally with domestic matters.

'Idealist' versus 'realist' approaches

These two broad categories represent points on a continuum whereby such policies can be analysed. 'Idealist' approaches had some origin in the Manchester Radicals but emerged more fully following the disastrous Great War. It was felt that the traditional assumptions of foreign policy and practice of diplomacy had helped cause much tragic loss of life and that a radically new approach was required. This would seek to establish international management of disputes between nations, to gradually reduce the extent of armaments and conduct relations between states on the basis of moral principles and international law.

The 'Realist' approach represents the inherited wisdom of foreign policy practice over the last several centuries. It is based on the assumption that the key element in foreign relations is security of the state against attack, followed by defence and pursuit of its essential national interests. Since interstate relations do not operate within a framework which allows rules to be reliably enforced, as in the case of domestic law, every state has to appreciate that they are basically 'on their own' in an anarchic world. States will therefore seek alliances with others to guard against possible threats and to rectify any dangerous balances of power which are perceived. The bottom line of national defence is thus 'self-defence': a reliance on good military resources – men in uniform, aircraft, naval forces.

Realists believe they see the world as it is rather than how it ought to be and argue that idealism helped allow Hitler to emerge during the interwar years by exploiting the myths of idealism – including the toothless League of Nations and wishful thinking about Nazi objectives – to establish a momentum of conquest which led to the outbreak of war in 1939. They argue the business of diplomacy is to protect and advance the interests of the state and that if everyone acts in this fashion a kind of stability – albeit fragile at times – is achieved. The alternative idealist approach, argue realists, is based on false premises and will inevitably make matters worse. A basic tenet of this approach is non-intervention; if everyone cultivates and defends their own gardens there will, with luck and good judgement, be peace; intervention, on the other hand usually runs the risk of widening conflicts.

During the Great War the Union for Democratic Control, a body of liberal intellectuals, urged the idealist solution to world conflict. After the Second World War a similar effusion of idealism occurred resulting in the United Nations, but this improved version of its prewar League has not been notably successful either. Ernest Bevin, Labour's Foreign Secretary after 1945, had little truck with the Soviet Union, despite earlier claiming that 'left can speak unto left' and facing substantial support for the so-called 'socialist sixth of the world' within his own party. Instead he pursued a fundamentally 'realist' path, allying with the USA to form NATO in defensive alliance against the perceived aggression of the USSR (Jones 1977). The only real legacy of the idealist phase was to clothe foreign policy statements in lip-service

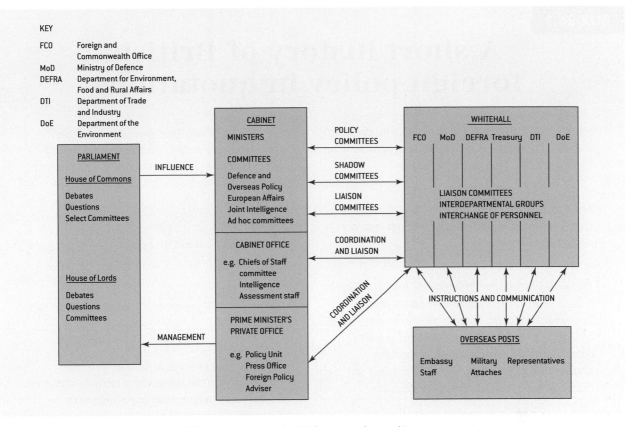

Figure 26.1 Schematic representation of the contemporary British foreign policy-making process

Source: Michael Clarke, 'The Policy-Making Process' in Michael Smith, Steve Smith and Brian White (eds) *British Foreign Policy: Tradition, Change and Transformation* (London: Unwin Hyman, 1988) p. 86 (Figure 4.1), reproduced by kind permission of UnwinHyman Ltd; © M. Smith, S. Smith and B. White 1988.

statements of support for collective security, the need for disarmament and the like.

British national interests

'Our interests are eternal and perpetual' said Lord Palmerston, Foreign Secretary for long periods in the nineteenth century, but he was less specific about what they might be. When he was in his pomp they would have included:

1   Security against attack and integrity of frontiers.

2   The primacy of trade. Britain was the world's foremost trading nation in the nineteenth century. It followed that naval supremacy was a prerequisite at that time to protect shipping lanes, especially the English Channel.

3   A favourable balance of power in Europe. Britain feared a dominant power which might encroach upon her trade interests or, at worst, contemplate an invasion as Spain

under Phillip II or Napoleon had done. The strategy had been to align with powers also opposed to the dominant power, whoever they might be. Palmerston also maintained that, 'We have no eternal allies, and we have no perpetual enemies'; we would side with those who best protected our interests.

4   Peace: a trading nation thrives on peaceful conditions; Britain always regarded war as a last resort.

5   Empire: Britain had created an extraordinary empire comprising one quarter of both the world's landmass and population. Trade within the Empire provided an integral part of the home country's prosperity and so defence of the Empire was seen as synonymous with the shores of Britain itself.

Modern conditions have caused British interests to change. Peace and security remain clearly as bedrock interests but trade is now much reduced in extent and its defence is closely related to the worldwide role of the EU and the USA. The UK is less crucially concerned about a European balance of power but shifting alliances in the EU continue and British

BOX 26.1

A short history of British foreign policy in quotations

We have no eternal allies, and we have no perpetual enemies. Our interests are eternal and perpetual, and those interests it is our duty to follow.

Lord Palmerston

The Foreign Office and the Colonial Office are chiefly engaged in finding new markets and in defending old ones.

Joseph Chamberlain (1896)

The general character of England's foreign policy is determined by the immutable conditions of her geographical situation on the ocean flank of Europe as an island state with vast overseas colonies and dependencies whose existence and survival as an independent community are inseparably bound up with the possession of preponderant sea power.

Sir Eyre Crowe (1907)

The policy of England takes no account of which nation it is that seeks the overlordship of Europe. It is concerned solely with whoever is the strongest or the potentially dominating tyrant. It is a law of public policy which we are following, and not a mere expedient dictated by accidental circumstances or likes or dislikes.

Sir Winston Churchill (twentieth century)

Foreign policy isn't something that is great and big, it's common sense and humanity as it applies to my affairs and yours.

Ernest Bevin (1950)

You will realize that I am speaking of the frequent suggestions that the United Kingdom should join a federation on the continent of Europe. This is something which we know, in our bones, we cannot do. We know that if we were to attempt it, we should relax the springs of our action in the Western democratic cause and in the Atlantic association which is the expression of that cause. For Britain's story and her interests lie far beyond the continent of Europe. Our thoughts move across the seas to the many communities in which our people play their part, in every corner of the world. These are our family ties. That is our life: without it we should be no more than some millions of people living on an island off the coast of Europe, in which nobody wants to take any particular interest.

Anthony Eden (1952)

Great Britain has lost an Empire and not yet found a role.

Dean Acheson (1962)

We are a world power, and a world influence, or we are nothing.

Harold Wilson (1965)

British foreign policy is defined as 'first, the commitment to an increasingly integrated Western Europe on as wide a basis as possible, with the European Common Market as its core, and secondly a commitment to a North Atlantic Alliance under US leadership as the main instrument for the conduct of East–West relations . . . Other broad aims on which there is general agreement are the reduction of East–West tension, whenever circumstances in the Soviet bloc permit this without weakening the Atlantic Alliance; the sustaining of Commonwealth links in a form appropriate to contemporary requirements, including our relations with a number of small dependent territories for which the British Government will continue to be responsible; the improvement of economic conditions in the less developed countries; and the strengthening of international organisations in which an effective dialogue can take place on issues which cause conflicts between nations.'

Duncan Report (1969)

Our destiny is in Europe, as part of the Community. That is not to say that our future lies only in Europe.

Margaret Thatcher (Bruges, 1988)

Foreign and defence policy essentially has to be about the obtaining and management of influence.

Lord Carrington, *Reflect on Things Past* (1988)

> *My aims for Britain in the community can be simply stated. I want us to be where we belong.*
> *At the very heart of Europe. Working with our partners in building the future. That is a challenge we take up with enthusiasm.*
>
> John Major (1991)
>
> *British foreign policy exists to protect and promote British interests. Despite all the changes in the world that underlying truth has not changed.*
>
> Douglas Hurd (1993)

> *We live in a modern world in which nation states are interdependent. In that modern world foreign policy is not divorced from domestic policy but a central part of any political programme.*
>
> Robin Cook (1997)
>
> *Our foreign policy must have an ethical dimension and must support the demands of other peoples for the democratic rights on which we insist for ourselves.*
>
> Foreign and Commonwealth Office

diplomats might find themselves wooing France one year, Germany the next, depending on the evolving politics of the organisation.

The Empire, of course, faded away after 1945 when it became clear an impoverished Britain could no longer defend its far-flung territories. India, the jewel in the imperial crown, was granted its independence in August 1947 and after the 1956 disastrous attempt to seize back the Suez Canal in alliance with France and Israel, the retreat from empire took on the appearance of a rout. By the end of the 1960s all but a few elements of the Empire had been granted independence, with Hong Kong transfering back to China in 1997. Accordingly, Britain sharply reduced its defence commitments east of Suez in the late 1960s, though the percentage of annual expenditure allocated to defence remained higher than most European countries.

In 1962 US Secretary of State Dean Acheson famously said, 'Britain has lost an empire and not yet found a role'. Adjusting to a more modest role proved difficult for British governments. In 1965 Prime Minister Harold Wilson declared, 'We are a world power and a world influence or we are nothing'. However, the only way British leaders were able to maintain the pretence of being a 'world power' was by sticking really close to their American allies. This was the case when Margaret Thatcher had to rely on them for support during the Falklands war and when Tony Blair sought to win Bill Clinton's support for his policy of intervention in Kosovo.

An ethical dimension to foreign policy

A foreign policy based on general principles was not something new as the more idealistic interwar years had shown. Indeed, in 1945 there was some talk that 'Left can talk unto left', in terms of Labour's supposed ability to do business with

Stalin but, as the latter's designs became clearer, Foreign Secretary Ernest Bevin found himself moving closer to the US in the hope of receiving support against a potentially dangerous enemy. This provoked a discordant protest on Labour's crowded left-wing benches, but Bevin steadfastly ignored them and pursued a virtually traditional rather than a 'socialist' foreign policy (Jones 1977). Similar eruptions occurred during the 1960s when Wilson supported US actions in Vietnam, though he was careful to stop short of sending any troops.

Nevertheless, the belief that Labour could and should offer a different and morally superior direction in foreign policy persisted. Robin Cook, when made Foreign Secretary on 12 May 1997, embodied such a concept in his 'mission statement' as a commitment to 'promote the national interests of the United Kingdom and contribute to a world community'. This would include to 'spread the values of human rights, civil liberties and democracy which we demand ourselves'. Senior mandarins in the Foreign Office were known to be sceptical of such an approach, and others claimed it was in any case an irrelevant sophistry, of no consequence. Certainly instances of arms sales by the UK to autocratic regimes did not advance the cause.

Sierra Leone

This action was important to Tony Blair as it preceded his Chicago Speech later that year which elaborated the idea of 'liberal intervention'. Sierra Leone had been racked by a brutal civil war in which Foday Sankoh's Revolutionary United Front (RUF), was raping, mutilating and killing thousands of innocent and helpless people. When they captured 500 members of a UN force in May 1999, Blair ordered a small British force to intervene. This they did with clinical efficiency, defeating the RUF, freeing the hostages and preventing the advance on Freetown. This experience was possibly 'fatally successful', in as much that a problem was presented to Blair on which he consulted military advisers. Such people always try to be helpful and persuasive too – it was

PROFILE

Robin Cook
(1946–2005)

Labour Foreign Secretary. Educated at Edinburgh University, MP in 1974, where he made his name as a clever left-winger. He shadowed Treasury, Health and Social Security in opposition but was made Foreign Secretary in 1997. He was recognised as the best parliamentarian of his party, but Jonathan Powell, Blair's Chief of Staff, judged him to be not especially effective in the office of Palmerston and Eden. It is hard to say whether his widely publicised affair with his secretary and subsequent divorce damaged him politically, but Blair replaced him after 2001 with Jack Straw, moving Cook to the less prestigious role of Leader of the House, where he proved to be a force for reform of the Commons before resigning over the war against Iraq in March 2003. He died tragically of a heart attack while walking in the Scottish mountains in 2005. Some believed his red hair, spiky Scottishness and less than classical good looks precluded him from ever reaching the premier rank of politics in this image-dominated age and there is probably some truth in this. However, the presentational gifts which made him Parliamentarian of the Year twice over, not to mention his determined insistence on a clear left-of-centre direction to New Labour's administration, meant that his absence was sorely felt during the remainder of New Labour's period in power.

an admiral who did much to persuade Thatcher to invade the Falkland Islands – and Blair took a gamble which paid off handsomely. However, early easy success – as Gamblers Anonymous will testify ad nauseam – can often nourish the confidence which leads to addiction and ruin. It is not impossible that Blair's success led him to believe the application of force is easier and more expedient than it really is. Iraq was some time in the future, but Blair felt confident enough to offer the world a lecture on the necessary virtue of doing good in the world.

Chicago Speech, 1999

Around the time of the successful military actions in Kosovo and West Africa, Blair was emboldened to elaborate a framework for his ideas on 'International Community' at a speech in Chicago. It is worth quoting from the speech itself:

> At the end of this century the US has emerged as by far the strongest state. It has no dreams of world conquest and is not seeking colonies. If anything Americans are too ready to see no need to get involved in affairs of the rest of the world. America's allies are always both relieved and gratified by its continuing readiness to shoulder burdens and responsibilities that come with its sole superpower status. We understand that this is something that we have no right to take for granted, and must match with our own efforts.
>
> We may be tempted to think back to the clarity and simplicity of the Cold War, but now we have to establish a new framework. No longer is our existence as states under threat. Now our actions are guided by a more subtle blend of mutual self-interest and moral purpose in defending the values we cherish.
>
> The most pressing foreign policy problem we face is to identify the circumstances in which we should get actively involved in other people's conflicts. Non-interference has long been considered an important principle of international order. And it is not one we would want to jettison too readily. But the principle of non-interference must be qualified in important respects. Acts of genocide can never be a purely internal matter. When oppression produces massive flows of refugees which unsettle neighbouring countries then they can properly be described as 'threats to international peace and security'.
>
> Looking around the world there are many regimes that are undemocratic and engaged in barbarous acts. If we wanted to right every wrong that we see in the modern world then we would do little else than intervene in the affairs of other countries. We would not be able to cope.
>
> So how do we decide when and whether to intervene. I think we need to bear in mind five major considerations:
>
> First, are we sure of our case? War is an imperfect instrument for righting humanitarian distress; but armed force is sometimes the only means of dealing with dictators.
>
> Second, have we exhausted all diplomatic options? We should always give peace every chance, as we have in the case of Kosovo.
>
> Third, on the basis of a practical assessment of the situation, are there military operations we can sensibly and prudently undertake?

Fourth, are we prepared for the long term? In the past we talked too much of exit strategies. But having made a commitment we cannot simply walk away once the fight is over; better to stay with moderate numbers of troops than return for repeat performances with large numbers.

Finally, do we have **national interests** involved? The mass expulsion of ethnic Albanians from Kosovo demanded the notice of the rest of the world. But it does make a difference that this is taking place in such a combustible part of Europe.

Arms sales

Despite UK government condemnation of the Indonesian government's support of the militias terrorising the autonomy-seeking East Timorese, the order for Hawk military aircraft was not cancelled. On 21 July 2002 the *Independent on Sunday* published an investigation that showed Britain selling arms to nearly 50 countries where conflict was endemic. These included Israel, Pakistan, Turkey, China, India, Angola and Colombia. The paper commented: 'Under its "ethical" foreign policy the Government bans arms sales to countries already at war, but instead arms manufacturers actively target countries where ethnic conflict is likely to explode.' For example, sales to Turkey in 2000 approached £200 million: 'Amnesty International has accused Turkey of suppressing its Kurdish minority population and of sustained persecution of orthodox Muslim groups, left-wing opponents and human rights activists.' Even more reprehensible was the suspension of a legal inquiry into allegations that BAE had paid bribes to senior members of the Saudi establishment in order to secure the huge Al Yamamah arms deals stretching from 1985–2006. The official explanation that the decision was in the interests of 'national security' sounded suspiciously like a covering-up of very murky dealings.

Kosovo

Kosovo is the most dramatic example of a major foreign policy issue in which there is a strong ethical dimension arising from the prominence given to human rights. The British intervention in Kosovo was the most important, and arguably most successful, foreign policy initiative of the Labour Government. Throughout the Kosovo crisis in 1999, Britain adopted a clear leadership role within the European Union and the Atlantic Alliance, dragging behind it reluctant alliance partners. In Kosovo, Britain 'punched above its weight' and exercised power within a complex alliance setting.

Throughout 1998 the situation in Kosovo worsened as the Serbian military and political machine exercised increasingly tight control over the province, in which over 90 per cent of the population was Albanian. NATO repeatedly pushed President Milosevic of Yugoslavia towards an agreement with the Kosovar nationalist opposition. Air strikes were threatened, much as they had been earlier in coercing Milosevic into agreement in Bosnia. Eventually, at Rambouillet in January 1999 an agreement was brokered by NATO between Milosevic and his Kosovar opponents to provide for a degree of self-rule within a larger Serbia. The agreement was short-lived. The Kosovar opposition was tentative in its support for the terms, and Milosevic denounced the terms that his negotiators had secured. On 24 March, without seeking UN support, NATO launched a strategic bombing campaign to force Milosevic back to the table.

The bombing, code-named *Operation Allied Force*, lasted until 10 June when, after 34,000 sorties had been flown, President Milosevic signalled that he would accept an allied army in Kosovo and withdraw his own forces. During the air campaign the war aims of the alliance expanded beyond the Rambouillet settlement to include an international force to be deployed on the ground to guarantee security for the Kosovars. As the scale of the expulsions from Kosovo grew, the British Government stated that the removal from power of Milosevic, indicted as a war criminal, had become a necessary guarantee of future stability. Nevertheless, full independence for Kosovo was not a war aim for NATO.

Why did Milosevic agree to NATO's demands and pull out of Kosovo? The continued resolve of the alliance may have persuaded him that eventually he would be forced to give way and that he could not rule out completely the possibility of a land war. However, the British argument that such a war should be planned and threatened was consistently met by American refusal to contemplate such an outcome. Internal opposition to Milosevic may also have played a part. The best explanation is probably that Milosevic was urged to back down by the Russians. His Russian allies could not afford to lose cooperation with the West, despite their opposition to the bombing campaign, and needed an end to the war. In an immediate sense, therefore, it was thus the persuasion of an ally rather than the coercion of an enemy that determined the outcome of the war.

The British Government, and its allies, resisted the demands of the Kosovo Liberation Army for an independent Kosovo, preferring weak multinational states in the Balkans to a multiplicity of nation states. Homogeneous nation states would, in any case, require further population movements, probably taking the form of 'ethnic cleansing' in a never-ending cycle of misery.

As in the case of President Carter's human rights policy of 1977, it is possible to argue that the war's consequences, as opposed to motives, for human rights were mixed or even counterproductive. The launch of the bombing campaign precipitated the forcible expulsion of the Kosovars from

Kosovo. The expulsion campaign was a macabre, larger-scale version of the ethnic cleansing earlier practised by Milosevic. As the bombing continued, the expulsions escalated. After the successful liberation of Kosovo, the refugees were able to return, in many cases only to find burnt-out homes. They paid a very high price for their right to remain. Unfortunately, but perhaps inevitably, the returning Kosovars began to practise similar tactics against their erstwhile Serb neighbours, about 180,000, precipitating a second exodus of refugees from Kosovo.

Nevertheless, it can be argued that, on balance, the consequences of the war are justified in terms of ethical foreign policy. The war improved the human rights situation for the majority of the population of Kosovo by eventually ending the Serb oppression. If the consequences of the war can be justified in ethical foreign policy, can the conduct of the war? There is a complex debate within the tradition of the 'just war' about strategic bombing and, in particular, the requirements under just war to avoid or at the very least to minimise the risk of unintended (collateral) damage to the innocent. Aerial bombardment tends to be indiscriminate unless the attacker accepts very high risks to himself to aim his bombs with precise accuracy. At the start of the air war, NATO attacked the Serb air-defence systems but thereafter continued to minimise the risk of damage to its own forces by confining itself to high-level bombing from about 14,000 feet. The effect of high-level bombing, together with inadequate ground-level information about Serb deployments, certainly minimised NATO's losses (zero in the case of Britain) but on the other hand increased collateral damage from inaccurate bombing or misinterpreted targets. Kosovar refugees were themselves bombed and many killed. Blair was later feted when he visited Kosovo; his success must have further reinforced his belief in the virtues of humanitarian intervention

The attacks on the World Trade Center, New York, 11 September 2001

When the devastating Osama bin Laden-inspired attacks on the twin towers of the World Trade Center occurred, Tony Blair was quick to stand 'shoulder-to-shoulder' with our American ally. At the Labour Party conference in October 2001, Blair excelled himself with an idealistic speech in which he envisaged a kind of ethical Anglo-US-led campaign to make the world better: 'more aid untied to trade'; 'write off debt'; 'encouraging the free trade we are so fond of preaching'. If the world as a community focused on it, 'we could defeat climate change . . . find the technologies that create energy without destroying the planet'. He described Africa as a 'scar on the conscience of the world' that the

world could, if it so chose, 'heal'. 'Palestinians', he declared, 'must have justice, the chance to prosper in their own land.' He finished by claiming 'The world community must show as much capacity for compassion as for force.' However, his hopes that the USA would rally to his clarion call were rapidly disappointed: US national interests were paramount for George W. Bush. He had already refused to ratify the hard-won international agreements on climate change signed at Kyoto in 1997. Moreover, he refused to send any representative to the world environment conference in Johannesburg. Tariffs were slapped on European steel products to protect US steel producers, many in regions electorally desirable to the Republicans. And the USA proved unmoved by the continuing refusal of Israel's right-wing government to adopt a conciliatory attitude towards the Palestinians; progress in resolving this conflict has always been high on the European list of priorities, particularly Britain's.

In the wake of '9/11', Blair made a number of visits to see the President and was, to be fair to his strategy, received with a warmth denied any other country. But did Blair receive any payoff for his loyalty? Apart from the warmth of his receptions, this was not easy to argue.

Afghanistan

British troops joined in the attack on Afghanistan in October 2001 and shared the deceptive initial sense of victory, despite Bin Laden's escape from pursuing Western forces. However, the country has a long history of resisting conquest, including the Mongols, British and Russians, and suppressing the fundamentalist Taliban, who had supported Al-Qaeda's activities, was always going to be difficult. The Taliban soon recovered their ability to fight, fostered by the support of sympathisers over the Pakistan border and began to inflict casualties on NATO (mostly US and British forces) which had come to provide the aegis under which the Western effort was made. The main policy dilemmas related, perhaps, to the objectives of the conflict: was it to support the resistance of the corrupt Karzai government, perceived by some as a Western puppet, or destroy the Taliban as a military force? The latter objective is still proving virtually impossible after eleven years of bitter conflict (making it the USA's longest-ever war) while the former is undermined by the fact that Western troops are dying in the cause of an undemocratic and unworthy government. Doubts also exist at all levels as to whether the battle can be won and whether it is worth fighting in the first place. For the UK this policy area in the run-up to the 2010 election was plagued by: accusations that the Labour Government was not providing adequate equipment, especially helicopters and vehicles able to withstand the deadly roadside bombs; open conflict between government ministers and the army top brass; the need to rein back military spending to reduce debt levels; a tragically rising death toll; and demands from President Obama that European forces increase their commitment to win the war. The growing tendency of insurgents dressed in Afghan army or police uniforms to kill US, British and other NATO troops has not helped public opinion in the UK to regard the war as worth any continued effort.

In November 2009 former Labour Foreign Office Minister Kim Howells, broke with his party's official views on the war:

> It would be better to bring home the great majority of our fighting men and women and concentrate, instead, on using the money saved to secure our own borders, gather intelligence on terrorist activities inside Britain.

He went on to argue that, as Al-Qaeda had been banished from the country and could easily set up bases in other countries, good reasons for keeping troops there no longer existed.

In September 2012 the Defence Secretary Philip Hammond raised the possibility of a withdrawal earlier than the planned 2014 on the grounds that the Afghans were increasingly able to defend themselves against the Taliban. Hammond also indicated that the only way to bring fighting to an end is through 'Northern Ireland style' talks with the moderate elements of the Taliban.

Iraq

After Afghanistan, the next on the agenda was the proposed war on Iraq. This created a series of dilemmas: Blair was intent on obtaining UN legitimacy for any invasion but, despite desperate flights to lobby members of the Security Council, he failed, with France playing a distinctly unhelpful role. Everyone agreed Saddam Hussein was a monstrous ruler who should be deposed but to do so would violate international law. The *casus belli* was eventually narrowed down to the fact that Saddam had 'weapons of mass destruction' (WMD) but, despite their best efforts, UN inspectors failed to find any. On 15 February 2003 there were demonstrations all over the world against the war with close on a million people marching in London. Yet this did not stay the invader's hand: on 20 March 2003 the troops moved in. After a few days fighting Saddam was toppled and Bush indulged in some premature triumphalism when he claimed 'Mission Accomplished' on 1 May 2003.

In fact, his troubles were only just beginning. By disbanding the army and police the invaders were allowing chaos to reign from the start as looters ran wild throughout Iraq.

Next came the guerilla attacks on US forces and the murderous feuds between militias belonging to rival Shia and Sunni Muslims. Moreover, by economising on the initial number of troops, Rumsfeld, the Defence Secretary, had hugely underestimated the numbers required to complete the job. British forces were relatively free of the worst trouble having been given the southern city of Basra to look after. Everyday television brought horrific images into US and UK homes of suicide bombers killing scores of people in Baghdad and elsewhere; reports persisted of night-time murders by one sect against another until the alleged death toll ran into hundreds of thousands.

A democratic framework was introduced by the occupiers and a government elected, but its legitimacy was fragile and its future uncertain. A senior advisory group led by James Baker urged a new **multilateral** approach, but Bush refused and initiated a 'surge' of new troops who actually managed to reduce the killings and begin a process leading to something akin to normalisation.

PROFILE

Jack Straw (1946–)

Foreign Secretary 2001–5. Educated at Leeds University, where he became President of the National Union of Students. Called to the Bar in 1972. Served as councillor for Islington, 1971–78; became MP for Blackburn in 1979. Served in a number of senior Shadow roles before becoming Home Secretary in 1997, where his reputation was as a tough though not illiberal minister. In 2001 he was surprised to be appointed Foreign Secretary, usually regarded as the third most important role in government. Straw proved an effective supporter of Blair's foreign policy, especially over Iraq, but inevitably was overshadowed by his boss over the big issues and on the big occasions. Former ambassador to Washington, Sir Christopher Meyer, in his memoir *DC Confidential*, damned Straw with faint praise in describing him as 'more to be liked than admired'. He was sacked in May 2005.

It is too early to judge how Iraq will be perceived by history, but from the present perspective it still looks like an ill-thought-through policy which was appallingly executed by the US at least and not significantly better by the UK. It was conceived by Blair as a justifiable intervention but its failure has probably scotched any further 'humanitarian interventions' being considered for many a year. Looking back at the Chicago speech of 1999 (see p. 542) can it be argued Iraq met Blair's five criteria?

1 *'Are we sure of our case?'* This has to be a 'no'. The invasion was never endorsed by the United Nations Security Council and the ostensible *casus belli*, the 'weapons of mass destruction', proved to be non-existent.

2 *'Have we exhausted all diplomatic options?'* It seemed clear that many wished the search for a diplomatic solution to continue; it was Bush and his advisers who were keen to get on with a unilateral action; strategic and military factors had made a US invasion inevitable by then, anyway.

3 *'Are there military operations we can sensibly and prudently undertake?'* In terms of defeating Saddam 'yes', but it became clear that little thought had been directed towards winning the peace.

4 *'Are we prepared for the long term?'* As events proved, it became crystal clear that neither of the two principal allies had looked into the future and solved problems which in retrospect seem blindlingly obvious.

5 *'Do we have national interests involved?'* Britain had scarcely any *direct* economic or military national interests involved, yet for Blair there were, on the grounds that Saddam was a leader of a 'rogue state', likely to host terrorists and support their efforts to create mayhem in the world. He and Bush argued that a democratic Iraq would provide a beacon to authoritarian Middle Eastern states and therefore encourage democratic developments in that area, together with a related softening of attitudes towards the West.

On 9 October 2009 a service was held in London to commemorate the thousands killed in Iraq. The Archbishop of Canterbury made some scathing criticisms of Tony Blair's leadership now that UK involvement was at an end; Blair was also snubbed by a father of a soldier killed in the struggle when he refused to shake the hand of someone he accused of being a 'war criminal'. For himself, Blair still argues Iraq is now better off than it was under Saddam Hussein, and he may be right. However, few agree the action was justified in view af the appalling casualties suffered and calls are regularly made (for example Desmond Tutu in September 2012) for him to be tried for war crimes in the International Court at the Hague.

Middle East

The Middle East has provided a cockpit for conflict ever since the end of the Second World War. Israel's determina-tion in the wake of the Holocaust to establish a national home in the Holy Land required that its former tenants be dislodged. This was essentially achieved after the conflict in 1948, but the price was the permanent enmity of the Arab world which, with varying degrees of hostility, resolved to drive the Israeli interlopers into the sea. Arab countries argued, with some justification, that Israel had used force to remove the original Palestinian inhabitants and caused thousands of them to flee as refugees into neighbouring countries. For its part Israel, argued it was an elected demo-cracy with a modern economy whilst many of the Arab nations were repressive, military-backed autocracies with ruling elites accumulating huge fortures at the expense of their impoverished populations.

Arab Spring 2011: Libya's revolution

Social and economic inequality and autocratic rule had persisted for several decades in Middle Eastern Arab coun-tries until a series of revolts in favour of democracy ensued following the self-immolation of a street vendor in December 2010. By 14 January 2011 President Ben Ali had stepped down and fled. Egypt's revolution quickly followed. Libya's, revolution, however, was to prove a protracted event, beginning February 2011 only to run up against a dictator in the person of Colonel Mu'ammer Gaddafi who refused to go quietly, and a civil war resulted. His threats to cleanse Benghazi of rebels 'street by street' finally registered in Europe when David Cameron and President Sarkozy of France led a movement to counter the attacking govern-ment forces.

For once the Russians and Chinese did not exercise their vetoes and air support was provided by NATO. After a bitter civil war the rebels finally defeated Gaddafi in October 2011. David Cameron had, surprisingly to some, revived a version of Blair's much criticised interventionism.

As the conflict dragged on, some commentators argued it had been ill-advised but success stilled such voices. No intervention was seriously contemplated, however, in Syria, where President Bashar al Assad proved equally intractable and prepared to use bloody repression against the rebels. Russia made it clear it was standing by its only real ally in the Middle East, while China joined in vetoing any attempts to isolate or even condemn Assad's excesses. Faced with these difficulties and the complex, combustible nature of Syrian politics located at the heart of the region, the West was forced to stand impotently by as the Syrian Free Army fought for the cities with rifles against tanks and helicopter gunships.

In a speech to the UN in September 2012 David Cameron condemned Russian and Chinese opposition to intervention against Assad as 'a stain on the reputation of this United Nations', saying they had 'aided and abetted Assad's reign of terror'.

New Labour's foreign policy assessed

On 10 September 2009 *The Economist* considered how well Labour's declared 'ethical dimension' in foreign policy had been pursued. It argued that 'the assumption that Labour promised much on ethics abroad but delivered little seems overdone'. It went on to point out that: arms sales to Indonesia had terminated in 1999; arms sales were made more transparent; the Kyoto Protocol had been warmly supported; and the International Criminal Court supported together with the Hague trials of war crimes in Yugoslavia.

> Mr Blair's 'Chicago Doctrine' was an attempt to insert a norm of ethical intervention into a world long dominated by the principle of state sovereignty. The 'responsibility to protect', an evolving humanitarian concept embraced by the UN, owes something to his words and deeds around the turn of the millennium.

This direction in foreign policy definitely went off track once the Iraq decisions were taken. As David Clark, Cook's adviser noted, it 'shattered the post-Kosovo consensus for ethical intervention'. It seems likely, at the time of writing, that any residual faith in such an ethical dimension will be obliterated by the painful experience of Afghanistan

Defence policy: the Strategic Review

Much is made of 'soft' power in the modern world. The American Joseph Nye invented the term and his book, *Soft Power, the Means to Success in World Politics*, elaborated its scope. The essence of this idea is that states do not necessarily need to achieve their objectives through the threat of military action. Similar results can often be won though the attractions of one's culture, persuasive power, national values and the power of example. Obama currently, for example, exercises considerable soft power through his inspirational life story (of overcoming the disadvantage of racism and winning the presidency); his oratorical abilities which draw upon black religious preaching; and his promise to change things for the better. All this is in addition to America's existing advantages as the perceived land of

opportunity, economic freedom and prosperity, not to mention Hollywood, jazz and popular music which have a worldwide reach. Britain is less well equipped but her status as the home of the English language as well as a literary tradition and a leading role in world cinema bestows considerable advantages.

However, the options actually available to a British Foreign Secretary are still substantially defined by what military hardware is available and how many troops are potentially available on the ground. In his day Palmerston could send a gunboat to achieve his objective, but in the present day such a gesture is no longer suggestive of the world's biggest navy, nor are there thousands of troops ready to respond to orders. The 1990 *Options for Change* document foresaw an overall reduction of the military, so that by 1998 it had reduced by over 20 per cent as measured by GDP.

By 1997 defence policy had entered a period of relative stability within ever-declining budgets. Three main defence roles had been identified. The first is the defence of the UK and its territories, even when there is no overt external threat. This core defence capability included the retention of the nuclear deterrent, untargeted in the absence of a clear nuclear enemy. This 'existential deterrent' (deterrence from mere possession) is similar to the traditional French policy of nuclear dissuasion, in contrast to Britain's previous strategy of deterrence through an overt threat of retaliation. The second defence role is insurance against a major attack on the UK or its allies and encompasses the NATO commitment and NATO force structures. The third defence role is the contribution to wider security interests through the maintenance of peace and stability. This is the extended concept of security including peace-keeping and peace enforcement through the UN and NATO, involving British forces even where no national security interests are immediately at stake.

The new Defence Secretary in 1997, George Robertson, set in train a Strategic Review in an effort to sculpt a coherent policy to meet Britain's defence needs within a reasonable budget.

Robertson largely confirmed Conservative procurement plans and added one major new project. The order for 386 Challenger 2 tanks would be completed and two armoured divisions established. The major new weapon for the army would be a battlefield helicopter to deploy against armoured forces in the form of the American Apache, to be built under licence in Britain. The Gulf War in 1991 had demonstrated the value of such a capability, at least against a weak opponent and in open desert country, although the American Apache force deployed during the Kosovo war made no impact at all and proved difficult to deploy against the

BOX 26.2

The changing pattern of world power

Barack Obama has to decide what to do in a world made unstable by terrorism, economic meltdown and shifts in the balance of power. A report appeared shortly after his election which explained how difficult his foreign policy role would be.

National Intelligence Council (NIC):
A Transformed World
In November 2008 this report revealed just how far-reaching the changes to American status in the world will be: in effect the end of American supremacy.

No longer unipolar
'By 2025 the international system will be a global **multipolar** one with gaps in national power continuing to narrow between developed and developing countries.' The 'unipolar' world, argues the report, which followed the end of the Cold War and the collapse of the USSR has now passed – arguably an opportunity bungled by George Bush – leaving the USA moving into a relative long-term decline. It is still by far the biggest military power, but as the NIC observes: 'advances by others in science and technology, expanded adoption of irregular warfare tactics by both state and non-state actors, proliferation of long-range precision weapons, and growing use of cyber warfare attacks increasingly will constrict US freedom of action'.

China
China, says the report, is 'poised to have more impact on the world over the next 20 years than any other country'. It is already a major economic power – due to become the world's second-largest economy by 2025 as well as a growing military one. By 2025 it will have replaced Europe as the second most powerful economic region.

Shift of wealth West to East
High oil prices and the growth of manufacturing in the East is causing economic power to shift eastwards. At the same time prosperity has ceased to be associated so much with democracies and more with state-run enterprises: 'state capitalism'. It by no means follows that democracy is bound to extend and take over such countries.

Failed states and failure of international organisations
The NIC predicts more anarchic states like Somalia with a growth of non-state actors like corporations, terrorists and religious groups. Some countries might be taken over by criminal gangs and some states might well wither away, unable to provide for their citizens. Attempts to reform the UN have been tried but it exhibits considerable 'institutional inertia'.

Climate change and scarcity
Finite resources might become a *casus belli* between states – India and China, for example, as their economies continue to grow rapidly. Water and arable land might also become bones of contention – especially in Africa – as states adjust to a less abundant world. James Lovelock recently predicted that once global warming advances, thousands of refugees from Europe will wish to emigrate to our less overheated climes. This, if it happens, will certainly cause conflict.

Serbian forces. Robertson committed the Government to completion of the full contract for 232 new Euro-fighters. This was the weapon that the RAF had set its heart on. Since the early 1980s it had lacked a specialist air defence fighter aircraft, relying on the ineffective Tornado F3, which had singularly failed to distinguish itself in the Gulf War. The Eurofighter contract had been subject to constant threats since being developed in the early 1980s with Germany, Italy and Spain, with the German government in particular perennially hovering on the point of cancellation.

The Royal Navy would reduce its declining submarine capability still further to a force of only ten nuclear-powered submarines, plus the four Trident ships. Robertson's major new procurement project, and in one sense the main outcome of the whole review, was the proposal to build two new large aircraft carriers, capable of carrying 50 aircraft, to replace the ageing fleet of three small warfare carriers built in the 1970s. These ships had evolved since the 1970s towards a general air attack role but were too small to carry adequate numbers of aircraft. The two new carriers, together with two new assault ships already on order and the recently completed helicopter carrier HMS *Hero*, would enable rapid deployment of a range of forces by sea. The navy would regain some of its traditional 'blue waters' capability of projecting power globally and flexibly. New naval capabilities complement the army's new emphasis on airmobile forces, in turn supported by heavier forces deployed by sea or by new heavy airlift capabilities.

The rationale for these new capabilities rests on a broad conception of Britain's security interests. What was the case for this? First, there is no immediate direct military threat to British security other than from the IRA, currently signed up to a ceasefire. However, conflicts in one area may spill over into other areas closer to home. Second, the emphasis on an ethical foreign policy and defence of humanitarian interests requires flexible capabilities. Third, it can be argued that Britain benefits by accepting responsibilities and duties that contribute to a stable world, which is itself a British interest. In the short run Britain could act, like Japan, as a free rider and obtain the benefits of stability without making a military contribution towards ensuring it. However, the Government thought that influence and prestige would decline if such an policy were adopted. In short, there is an unquestioned assumption within government that, through punching above its weight, prestige and influence are maximised and that straining expenditure to its limits brings its own reward. An activist policy increases influence with the United States and Germany and within NATO. NATO remains, on this analysis, the key to security policy, and Britain plans to remain at the centre of it.

British forces are highly professional and effective but, given high levels of specialisation, also small and expensive, operating without any economies of scale. Under Robertson's plans they had also to be prepared to take on a variety of roles. Given their small size, one particularly awkward question is raised. Can British military power aspire to be a premier-division force capable of fighting a high-intensity war, or is it now a second-division force whose effectiveness is confined to such lower-intensity wars as Bosnia or Kosovo? Forces capable of high-intensity warfare can be deployed on lower-intensity operations, even if their training and equipment are not exactly suited. On the other hand, forces only capable of lower-intensity warfare cannot be used in a high-intensity battle. British forces have clung persistently to the notion that they are small but capable of high-intensity warfare – in the premier division – and unique among other high-intensity forces in also being trained for low-intensity warfare as a result of the Northern Ireland situation and post-colonial wars. Kosovo does not answer the question. The air force participated on a very small scale, and apparently ineffectively, in an American-led,

high-intensity bombing campaign. On the ground below, the army prepared for a lower-intensity campaign, though one that was overtly coercive and, potentially, of higher intensity.

The Defence White Paper in July 2002 reflected the new realities following the 9/11 attacks on the World Trade Center. New weapons were envisaged for the armed forces that would enable them to identify and strike at terrorist enemies within minutes. Geoff Hoon, the Defence Secretary, explained a scenario where very mobile, lightly armed forces would be able to identify the enemy, acquire authority to act and strike in 'near real time'. Apache helicopters armed with Hellfire missiles would be instrumental in this new capacity. Plans to develop a new pilotless reconnaissance aircraft, the Watch-keeper, would be speeded up. Hoon told the Commons:

> Terrorism thrives on surprise and one of the key ways to defeat it is to take the fight to the terrorist. We must be able to deal with threats at a distance: hit the enemy hard in his own backyard – not in ours – and at a time of our choosing – not his – acting always in accordance with international law.

Defence overstretch

The Select Committee on Defence, reporting in March 2005, warned that overstretch of resources had reached dangerous levels:

> Many frontline units in the army have been experiencing an operational and training cycle whose intensity is unsustainable in the longer term.

MPs also warned that the Government may have underestimated the role armed forces may have to play in defending the 'homeland' against international terrorism. Because defence spending had been kept steady at about 2.5 per cent of GDP, a number of measures had been found necessary:

1 Delaying of two new aircraft carriers until the end of the decade or later.

2 Delaying of the Eurofighter (or Typhoon as it is now called) and the Joint Strike Fighter Programme, meaning existing carriers will be at sea without them for a period.

3 Delaying of new helicopters, badly needed by the army and air force.

However, the committee endorsed the decision to merge certain regiments, with some famous single-battalion regiments, like the Black Watch, being merged into bigger regiments.

Cuts continued to achieve economy targets. One journalist, James Meek, reflected in the *Guardian* on 21 January 2004 that the Royal Navy had 900 ships in 1945. In 2010 the number of frigates, destroyers and carriers stood at 36. He went on to question whether even these were needed. Wars fought in recent years had been located in land-locked regions – Afghanistan, Iraq – and even sophisticated high-tech ships like the US Navy's *Cole* had been nearly sunk in 2000 by a few terrorists on a small launch stacked with explosives.

Trident

The one aspect of naval renewal which is guaranteed to cause more controversy is the replacement of the Trident submarine-borne nuclear deterrent. In November 2005 Defence Secretary John Reid was forced to give a pledge that MPs be allowed to vote on the possible purchase of a replacement from the US with a new weapons system estimated to cost £20–25 billion. Reid agreed to hold the debate in a transparent fashion but insisted: 'I defy anyone here to say we will not need a nuclear weapon in 20–50 years' time.' He added that the UK was not planning to place its deterrent into multilateral disarmament negotiations until the US and Russians did likewise.

An opinion poll in November 2005 showed that when told of the cost of replacement, only 33 per cent declared support and 54 per cent opposed. As long as nuclear weapons continue to proliferate – with Iran being perceived as a dangerous impending candidate – retention of the deterrent is likely to be supported by a majority of MPs. However, Labour MPs, with their history of supporting the Campaign for Nuclear Disarmament, found replacement difficult to accept given the imperative to reduce public spending in the light of the 2008–9 economic crisis. In September 2012 former Lib Dem defence minister Sir Nick Harvey suggested a compromise might be made whereby Trident warheads might be stood down from active patrols but 'locked in a cupboard' for when international tension might rise during a crisis. He argued that a deterrent devised for the USSR was no longer justified in the same form for present-day Russia.

The Coalition and defence policy

The Defence Select Committee might have complained of 'overstretch' in defence back in 2005 (see above), but most of those MPs would have accepted the then status quo compared to the cuts made by the Coalition Government after May 2010. Forced to accept its share of cuts, in the autumn of 2012 defence faced a cut of 7.5 per cent or, the equivalent of 30,000 jobs in the armed forces. Army numbers would be cut to 82,000, the lowest since the Napoleonic Wars and the RAF and Navy will both shed 5,000 personnel. Particular concern was voiced about aircraft carriers. With the Ark Royal taken out of service the two new carriers will not come into service until the end of the present decade. A critical report by the Public Accounts Committee stated:

> The UK will have no carrier aircraft capability from 2011–20. While two carriers are still being built, only one will be converted to launch the planes that have now been selected, and the other will be mothballed.
>
> The UK will only have one operational carrier with a significantly reduced availability at sea when Carrier Strike capability is reintroduced in 2020.
>
> The government was also embarrassed when its cancellation of jump jets to replace the discarded Harriers was suddenly reversed in May 2012. It was further embarrassed when The National Defence Association, containing former defence chiefs and ministers predicted history would view Cameron as a 'guilty man' who left Britain vulnerable just as Baldwin and Chamberlain had done.

Co-author of the report, Air Commodore Lambert, said the effects of the cuts would be the 'slow but inevitable decline in to irrelevancy' for the UK's standing on the world stage. He warned as the country's reputation fell it would face having to fight more wars. And as Argentina continues to step up its rhetoric over the Falklands, he added: 'One of the reasons that the Argentinians took us on in 1982 was because we looked weak. Were that situation to occur again then the opportunities (for another conflict) are there.' (*Daily Telegraph*, 18 September 2012).

The charitable body, Drone Wars UK, focused attention in September 2012 on one area where defence spending has substantially increased: over £2 billion on developing unmanned drone aircraft as well as using them in the front line in Afghanistan.

Relations with the developing world

Since the world banking crisis and subsequent economic recession of 2007–9, the increased importance of the developing world has been recognised by the replacement of the **G8** as the world's primary managing group by the G20. It is inevitable that Britain will now seek to establish improved relations with these emergent powers as economic and political power moves from West to East (see Box 26.3). Foreign Secretary William Hague declared in July 2010 that he wanted the UK to reach out beyond the EU to emerging nations in Asia, Latin America and the Middle East.

China

As the most important of the emergent powers and the one destined perhaps to replace the USA as the world's premier economy, it follows that the UK should have worked very hard to woo for its favours. The Foreign Office has made clear its aim to 'step up our engagement with China across the board. This reflects China's increasing economic weight and political influence and our desire to work with China to tackle the many and complex challenges the international community face today.' Britain has become Europe's largest investor in China and there are more Chinese students in the UK than any other overseas group. In 2004 Tony Blair and premier Wen Jaibao agreed annual summit meetings between the two prime ministers. In addition the *China Task Force*, chaired by the Chancellor and comprising leading business and other public figures provides high-level advice to government. A similar body advises Chinese leaders on the UK. The UK–China Economic and Financial Dialogue is also chaired by the Chancellor and provides a high-level strategic forum; the sector-specific Ministerial Discussions provide contacts on education and sustainable development; and the UK–China Human Rights Dialogue provides a forum for, given China's repressive record, this more controversial topic. For all these efforts to edge closer, China can be a difficult partner to woo, often blaming Britain for any relationship problems Moreover, as its own reserves dry up, Chinese reliance on Iranian oil led to a recent new alliance and explains why China, to the discomfort of the UK and USA, supports Iran's nuclear programme.

India

In September 2005 the UK Government spelled out a new strategic partnership with India on foreign and defence policy; immigration, counter-terrorism, economic and trade issues, sustainable development and educational links. The 2006 White Paper on British Diplomacy stated that 'As the world's largest democracy, India will have a growing influence in international affairs and on the global economy.' This last point is reinforced by the fact that India's economic growth was 9.1 per cent in 2007–8, second only to China's rate of growth. The UK supports India's permanent seat on the UN Security Council and invited it to attend the G8 meeting in Gleneagles in 2005. In 2011 UK India bilateral trade grew by 26 per cent bringing the total to £16.4 billion (£13 billion in 2010). In 2011 the UK remains the chief destination for Indian companies setting up within the EU – India's familiarity with the English language undoubtedly being a factor. Despite its burgeoning economy, India is also a significant recipient of overseas aid from the British government and a close collaborator in the fields of education, health, the fight against HIV and Aids and climate change.

Brazil

As the major economic power in Latin America, Britain has been assiduous in establishing educational, sporting and ministerial contacts, as it has with a raft of other emerging nations in Asia, Latin America and Africa. Prince Harry made an official visit to Brazil in 2012, as did Hague and Deputy Prime Minister Clegg in 2011. In September 2012 Cameron made an official visit to Brazil accompanied by a large team of businessmen in an effort to encourage more trade with this rapidly expanding economy.

USA or EU?

Having said all this about the developing nations, however, British foreign policy at the end of the first decade of the twenty-first century still grapples with the dilemma which has dominated its concerns since the end of the Second World War: whether to continue seeking to exercise a world role via the proxy of US power, or investing more commitment in a unified EU foreign policy position. Links with the USA since the Second World War have been fondly regarded by Britain's political class as constituting a 'special relationship', but American insistence on debt repayment when Britain was bankrupt in 1945, the Suez debacle and the 1983 invasion of Grenada without consultation should put this into a wider and less special perspective. Tony Blair seemed almost manic in his desire to please George Bush by joining him in his ill-fated Iraq adventure, but received nothing tangible in return. Defence Secretary of State Rumsfeld was contemptuous of the need for UK support, and scrutiny of memoirs of America's main players in the Iraq drama reveals scant evidence that Blair exercised any real influence or any role apart from being a supportive voice. Gordon Brown was keen to draw back somewhat from Blair's position after he became Prime Minister in 2007, but joined in the general lionising of Obama with everyone else after his election in November 2008.

Downsizing Britain's role from a world to a medium power has not been easy for Britain. Holding on to her Security Council seat and nuclear weapons have provided two almost credible routes but, for the most part, it has sought to manage the transition by adhering, wherever possible, to US policy. Some critics argue that a more fruitful direction for foreign policy would be a serious attempt to engineer a more coherent common EU position. With a population of 500 million and the biggest unified market in the world, the EU is often said to be an 'economic giant but a political pygmy' with no common defence or foreign policy. During the crises caused by the break-up of Yugoslavia, this lack proved embarrassing and harmful as Milosevic's forces operated without scruple. The UK is, however, hopelessly divided over the EU with a large swath of voters suspicious or hostile of possible federal EU intentions to the extent that support for a unified foreign policy is not even on the distant horizon. Interestingly, David Miliband, Brown's Foreign Secretary, abandoned Blair's idea of the UK being a 'bridge' between the two continents; it was 'never quite right' he commented dismissively. Contrasting with Blair, again, who took his country to war five times, Miliband stressed soft power and multilateralism in his speech on 12 February 2008 as well as the new primacy of 'citizen issues like climate change, global poverty and human rights'. Meanwhile, Iraq is no longer such a divisive issue now that British troops have withdrawn.

The Coalition and the EU

Of the many fault lines underlying the UK's Coalition Government – environment, welfare spending, constitutional reform – the vexed question of the EU must be close to most contentious. The Lib Dems have always been an internationalist party, reflecting and continuing the traditions of Lowes Dickinson, Leonard Woolf and the cause of the United Nations. The Conservatives, despite taking Britain into the European Union under Heath in 1973, veered away from the loss of sovereignty and identity this entailed and, whipped on by Margaret Thatcher from the late 1980s onwards, developed a substantial 'Eurosceptic' wing, reflecting similar trends in public opinion.

At the height of the Eurozone crisis a summit was held in Brussells 8–9 December 2011. In advance of it David Cameron was known to be worried about his Eurosceptic right wing which had mobilised 81 hostile votes on the 25 October 2011 debate over a referendum on withdrawal. In addition, a number of them asked coordinated questions on Wednesday 7 December, before Cameron departed for the summit, urging him to summon up the 'bulldog' spirit together with other similar metaphors. The summit was aiming to amend EU treaties so that increased discipline could be exerted over member countries of the euro to prevent future accumulations of debt. Cameron decided the terms of the amended treaties were antithetical to British interests and applied a veto. This caused huge celebrations among Eurosceptics but outraged the Lib Dems. Nick Clegg declared himself 'bitterly disappointed' and feared Britain would now be 'isolated and marginalised' within the EU. In September 2012 Cameron announced he thought a referendum on membership of the EU would be possible if his party won a majority in 2015. This was clearly an attempt to woo those Tory anti-EU voters who were tempted to vote for UKIP.

During 2012 pressure built up on the Tory right for an in–out referendum on the EU. Cameron, personally believed to favour continued EU membership (though on renegotiated terms), was forced to concede such a referendum might take place in the event of a Tory victory in 2015. However, in a rebuff to those Conservatives who favour closer relations with the US rather than the EU, a senior official in the White House warned on 10 January 2013 that, 'referendums have often turned countries inward'; the US wanted a strong UK presence in the EU.

BOX 26.3

BRITAIN IN CONTEXT

UK's relationship with US foreign policy in a changing world

Foreign policy is usually founded on defence policy: the ability of a country both to defend itself from harm and to inflict harm in its own right. As defence policy reflects how much a country feels it can afford to pay on military hardware, foreign policy is also based, at root, on economic power. The USA is the world's only superpower and no country can currently match its expenditure on armaments. It spends over $400 billion a year on defence, a sum which has ratcheted up dramatically since the 9/11 attacks. The US spends as much on defence as the rest of the world combined and twice as much as the EU. In addition to this, US arms technology is years ahead of the rest of the world.

However, being a superpower militarily is only one facet of US power. America is aided by the huge advantage of a massive economy which stretches out to every corner of the world and a media industry which mass-markets American values and culture to the same places. And yet the superpower is not and does not feel safe. For years it did, and a strong strand of opinion – isolationism – wished to keep it even safer by avoiding major foreign commitments. Indeed, George W. Bush himself, when running for President in 2000, expressed mildly isolationist views. But its huge economic strength and international interests made such objectives unachievable for the USA, especially as some elements in the world, especially fundamentalist Muslims, saw the US as the source of great evil and corruption worldwide.

The attacks by al-Qaeda upon the World Trade Center in 2001 signalled the opening of a new war which the US could not avoid, as this time the fight, traumatic for Americans, had been taken onto their own soil. The 'War on Terror' became the main driver of US foreign policy and, via close association, of UK policy as well. However, the inability of the US to impose its will by brute force and the revulsion of the world at its treatment of prisoners discredited the idea of such a war, and the term ceased to be used once Barack Obama was elected president in 2008. Experience in Vietnam in the 1960s and in Iraq since 2003 reveals that mastery of the air and huge military superiority on the ground are no guarantors of successful containment of a determined, irregular enemy armed merely with small arms and suicide bombs.

US foreign policy strategists are highly aware of the changing geopolitical nature of world power. Defending Europe against a predatory USSR used to be its main priority, but now the EU is regarded as of waning importance. The new suitors wooed by the USA are all found in Asia. The fastest-rising economic power is China, a country of well over a billion people which has been expanding economically at some 10 per cent a year for the past two decades. It has now left the dark ages of Maoist communism way behind and is beginning to flex its own muscles. It is seen as the major long-term military and economic threat to the USA, already winning manufacturing business from the higher-waged superpower and holding vast sums of US currency, which potentially gives it a lever over US economic policy. Bush's visit to India in March 2006 revealed how the US sees the world's biggest democracy – also emerging as an economic superpower in its own right – as a possible counter to China.

In February 2006 Condoleeza Rice announced a major redeployment of diplomatic personnel: 61 posts in the 'old' world of the EU were to be dropped while 74 new posts were to be established in Asia. The UK also has done something similar: Sir Michael Jay, head of the Diplomatic Service, said on 3 March 2006: 'We are making sure our resources are deployed so the right people are in the right places to promote Britain's interests around the world. Among other things, this means shifting resources from our European to our Asian network.' China too has been readjusting to her nascent superpower status, sending scores of diplomats, inevitably, to the USA but also substantial delegations to other countries where she seeks to increase influence: Pakistan, Japan (despite the appalling historical record) and selected African countries like Angola.

Chapter summary

British foreign policy is based upon what it can afford economically and the Strategic Defence Review in the late 1990s did much to adapt defence policy to what could be afforded and what was needed to maintain national security in a rapidly changing world. Labour's attempt to introduce an 'ethical foreign policy' was controversial but was probably justified and successful in terms of the Kosovo crisis. Britain's traditional closeness to US foreign policy was reinforced by Blair when Clinton was president and he was quick to establish close relations with George Bush in 2000. However, the difficulties encountered following the joint invasion of Iraq caused Blair considerable political problems at home.

Discussion points

- Criticise the 'realist' approach to foreign policy.
- Should Britain have avoided involvement in Kosovo?
- Does the world need a new form of international government?
- Is Britain too keen to support the USA in all situations?
- Was the Iraq war justified?
- Should the UN have intervened in the Syrian civil war?

Further reading

Since the 7th edition when I complained there were not many good up-to-date analyses of this aspect of British policy, two books have appeared: Daddow and Gaskarth's, *British Foreign Policy – The New Labour Years* (2011), and Peter Self's, *British Foreign and Defence Policy Since 1945* (2010). Little and Whickham-Smith's *New Labour's Foreign Policy: a New Moral Crusade?* (2000) is very useful, especially Chapter 1 by Whickham-Smith, but Chapters 2–6 are all acutely analysed and worth reading. See also the dated Sanders (1990) and the more recent book by Paul Williams, *Britain's Foreign Policy under New Labour* (2006). See also Lord Butler's report from 2004 and Sir Christopher Meyer's enjoyably indiscreet memoirs (2005).

Bibliography

Butler, Lord (2004) *Review of Intelligence on Weapons of Mass Destruction*, HC 898.

Byrd, P. (1988) *British Foreign Policy Under Thatcher* (Philip Allan).

Carrington, Lord (1988) *Reflect on Things Past* (Collins).

Cook, R. (1997) 'British foreign policy' statement, 12 May.

Cornish, P. (2012) Strategy in Austerity, Chatham House.

Economist (2006) 'Fighter Jets: Keeping Secrets', 28 January.

Daddow, O. and Gaskarth, J. (2011) *British Foreign Policy – The New Labour Years* (Palgrave).

Freedman, C. and Clark, M. (1991) *Britain in the World* (Cambridge University Press).

Gamble, A. (2003) *Between Europe and America: The Future of British Politics* (Palgrave).

Hartley, K. (2002a) 'UK Defence Policy: An Economist's Perspective', www.york.ac.uk/depts/econ/research/documents/defence.pdf.

Hartley, K. (2002b) 'UK Defence Policy: A Triumph of Hope over Experience?', www.york.ac.uk/depts/econ/research/documents/ipr.pdf.

Harvey, M. (2009) 'Notes on a Post-Blair Foreign Policy', *New Statesman*, 15 February.

House of Commons Library Research Papers: Defence Policy Since 1997 (08/58, 2008); The Arab Uprisings, BP11/73, 2011;

UK Defence and Security Policy: A New Approach, BP 11/10, 2011.

Jones, B. (1977) *The Russia Complex: The British Labour Party and the Soviet Union* (Manchester University Press).

Kampfner, J. (1998) *Robin Cook* (Gollancz).

Labour Party (1997) *New Labour because Britain Deserves Better* (Labour Party).

Little, R. and Whickham-Smith, M. (2000) *New Labour's Foreign Policy: a New Moral Crusade?* (Manchester University Press).

Martin, L. and Garnett, J. (1997) *British Foreign Policy: Challenges for the Twenty First Century* (Royal Institute of International Affairs).

Meyer, C. (2005) *DC Confidential* (Weidenfeld & Nicolson).

Nye, J. (2004) *Soft Power: The Means to Success in World Politics* (Public Affairs).

Oborne, P. (2009) 'Cameron has only Himself to Blame for this Mess on Europe', *Observer*, 1 November.

Owen, D. (1978) *Human Rights* (Jonathan Cape).

Sanders, D. (1990) *Losing an Empire, Finding a Role* (Macmillan).

Self, P. (2010) *British Foreign and Defence Policy Since 1945* (Palgrave).

Smith, S. and White, B. (eds) (1988) *British Foreign Policy: Tradition, change and transformation* (Unwin Hyman).

Wheeler, N.J. and Dunne, T. (1998) 'Good International Citizenship: A Third Way for British Foreign Policy', *International Affairs*, vol. 74, no. 4, pp. 847–70.

Williams, P. (2006) *Britain's Foreign Policy under New Labour* (Palgrave).

Useful websites

Amnesty International: www.amnesty.org

Domestic sources of foreign policy: www.apsanet.org/-state

Foreign and Commonwealth Office: www.fco.gov.uk

Ministry of Defence: www.mod.uk

EU common security policy:
www.europa.eu.int/pol/cfsp/index-en.htm

NATO: www.nato.int

Organisation for Security and Cooperation in Europe:
www.osce.or.at/

CHAPTER 27

Britain and the politics of European integration

Michael Holmes

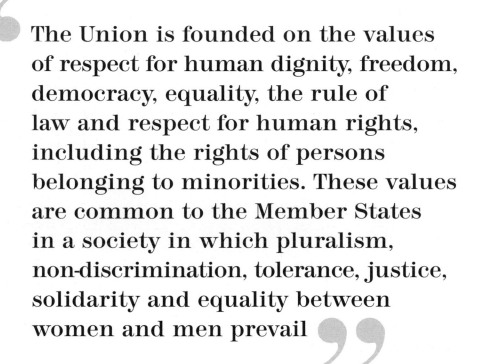

> The Union is founded on the values of respect for human dignity, freedom, democracy, equality, the rule of law and respect for human rights, including the rights of persons belonging to minorities. These values are common to the Member States in a society in which pluralism, non-discrimination, tolerance, justice, solidarity and equality between women and men prevail

Article 2, Treaty on European Union (consolidated version), 2010

Learning objectives

- To explain the background of European integration.
- To outline how the European Union works and what it does.
- To evaluate Britain's relationship with European integration.
- To discuss recent developments in the EU–British relationship.

On 1 January 1973 the United Kingdom joined what was then called the European Community. Instead of being the start of a strong and productive relationship, the decision to join became the start of a new debate, and the relationship between Britain and Europe has remained fractious and difficult. Outright critics have compared it to a 'doomed marriage' (Hannan 2012), while more balanced analyses have portrayed Britain as an 'awkward partner' (George 1998) in what is now called the European Union, as 'reluctant Europeans' (Gowland and Turner 1999), as a 'stranger in Europe' (Wall 2008).

This British ambivalence about Europe is captured nicely by contrasting pairs of quotes from the two most successful postwar British Prime Ministers. Margaret Thatcher can legitimately be portrayed as 'a ferocious anti-European' (Young 1998: 242), and indeed argued that 'to try to suppress nationhood and concentrate power at the centre of a European conglomerate would be highly damaging and would jeopardise the objectives we seek to achieve'. But in the very same speech, she also clearly espoused a place for Britain in a framework of European cooperation, declaring that 'Britain does not dream of some cosy, isolated existence on the fringes of the European Community. Our destiny is in Europe, as part of the Community'.

Partly in contrast, partly in concert with such views, Tony Blair was someone who was 'entirely comfortable to be a European' (Young 1998: 513) and was happy to declare 'I am a passionate pro-European. I always have been . . . I believe in Europe as a political project'. But at the same time, he was also prepared to berate the EU for refusing to change. 'We risk failure. Failure on a grand, strategic, scale. This is not a time to accuse those who want Europe to change of betraying Europe. It is a time to recognise that only by change will Europe recover its strength, its relevance, its idealism and therefore its support amongst the people.'

This captures the tensions in the relationship between Britain and the European Union. This chapter explores the relationship. It begins by setting out the emergence of European cooperation and integration in the postwar era, before summarising the present-day European Union in terms of its political structures, its policy competencies and its membership. It then examines the British path to membership and the subsequent development of the political relationship between the two, before concluding with an examination of Britain's response to the Eurozone crisis.

From European war to European Union

It was a European war that led to the foundation of what is now the European Union. Of course, World War Two was far more than just a European war. But it was a conflict that started in Europe and that affected virtually every European country in some form or other, and it was in Europe that some of the worst atrocities of the war occurred. In the aftermath of the war, there was a determination to find a way of preventing such a devastating conflict from happening again. The political, economic and social mood in many European countries demanded change and innovation and fresh approaches to problems, both among political leaders and in terms of general public attitudes.

Of course, the European integration project that emerged was not the only way in which this demand was expressed. In Britain, the election of Clement Attlee's Labour Government in 1945 and its creation of the welfare state is an example

of this desire for a new approach to politics and policies. Another new approach that appeared in the postwar years was the idea of greater cooperation and integration among Europe's nations. Since nationalism was widely blamed as a principal cause of the war, the aim was to transcend nationalism through international cooperation and integration.

This took a number of different forms, and what we now call the European Union grew out of one of the later projects to appear in this postwar European environment. Organisations intended to promote cooperation sprang up in a number of fields. In economics, the United States proposed the Marshall Plan in 1947 to provide loans and grants to help rebuild Europe's economies. Britain responded enthusiastically to the Plan and was its largest single beneficiary, receiving over $3 billion in aid from the US. The Plan came with the proviso that the aid should be disbursed by agreement among the recipient states, which in turn led to the creation of the Organisation for European Economic Cooperation (OEEC), which was established in 1948. Britain was a founder member of the OEEC.

Box 27.1

The Marshall Plan

The Marshall Plan was officially known as the European Recovery Program, or ERP. It was announced by US Secretary of State George Marshall in a speech at Harvard University in June 1947. The plan proposed that the US would provide European countries with loans and grants to speed up their economic reconstruction and recovery after the war. Almost all western European

countries took part. Indeed, the USSR and its East European allies were invited to join, but it was clear that the Plan was dependent on having a capitalist economy, so they did not join in. In the four years of operation of the Plan, from 1948 to 1951, a total of approximately $13 billion was dispensed, one of the biggest-ever programmes of foreign assistance.

Box 27.2

The Organisation for European Economic Cooperation (OEEC)

The OEEC was established to allow countries receiving support from the Marshall Plan to coordinate the distribution of the aid. It was established in April 1948, with its headquarters in Paris. After the Marshall Plan had ended, the OEEC sought to coordinate further economic cooperation among European countries. In 1960 it was agreed that the OEEC should be made into a much more global body to promote economic cooperation among developed states, and in 1961 it became the Organisation for Economic Cooperation and Development (OECD) – see www.oecd.org.

That west–east split was also at the heart of the emergence of another organisation, which dealt with cooperation in the field of defence. The North Atlantic Treaty Organisation (NATO) was founded in 1949, and Britain was once again involved in this initiative right from the outset. In 1947 Britain and France had signed a mutual defence pact, the Dunkirk Treaty. The following year, this was expanded by the inclusion of the three 'Benelux' countries (Belgium, the Netherlands and Luxembourg) through the Brussels Treaty, before the signing of the full North Atlantic Treaty the next year. NATO was particularly significant because of its extra-European dimension: the United States and Canada were both members, committed to a mutual defence agreement. NATO's primary focus when it was established was to defend western Europe against the Soviet Union.

Finally, there was an initiative which had a much more explicit political dimension. In May 1948 political leaders from across western Europe assembled in The Hague to attend the Congress of Europe. This was intended to discuss options for closer cooperation among European states, and it led to the foundation of the Council of Europe in 1949, with its headquarters in Strasbourg. The aim of the Council of Europe was to promote cooperation in a range of fields, but especially democracy and human rights. Once more, Britain took part from the outset. Indeed, it is often argued that one of the main inspirations for the convening of the Congress of The Hague was a speech made by Winston Churchill to the University of Zurich in 1946. Churchill called for the creation of a Council of Europe as the first step towards a possible United States of Europe:

> We must build a kind of United States of Europe . . . The structure of the United States of Europe, if well and truly built, will be such as to make the material strength of a single state less important.

Thus, by the end of 1949 there were three significant new organisations aiming to bring about European cooperation in a range of areas. Yet, within a few months some countries were already pushing ahead with further, more ambitious plans. To understand why this came about, it is necessary to look at the decision-making systems that were being used and to consider their strengths and weaknesses. Put simply,

Box 27.3

The North Atlantic Treaty Organisation (NATO)

NATO is an organisation for collective security with its headquarters in Brussels. It was founded in 1949, with 12 member states initially. The aim was mutual defence: an attack on any member state of NATO was to be considered as an attack on all of them. To begin with, NATO was focused on orthodox military defence against possible Soviet aggression. With the collapse of the USSR, NATO has redefined its role to become involved in peace enforcement, and its membership now stands at 28 states. See www.nato.org.

Box 27.4

The Council of Europe

The Council of Europe was established by the Treaty of London in 1949 with 10 founding members, including Britain. It now has 47 member states, and its headquarters are in Strasbourg. The main objectives of the organisation are to promote democracy, human rights and the rule of law throughout Europe, and to promote closer cultural cooperation. It is perhaps best known for the European Convention on Human Rights, overseen by the European Court of Human Rights. See www.coe.int.

the OEEC, NATO and the Council of Europe all made use of a system where, essentially, the governments of each member state retained control over how far and how fast they moved. This is what is known as an inter-governmental system, where power is held by member-state governments.

It has the advantage that states cannot be forced into decisions they are not in favour of – they have a veto over policies. However, it has the disadvantage that this veto means that the organisation can only progress at the pace of the most reluctant member state. The benefits of being in a convoy are compromised by the fact that to keep all the ships together, the convoy can only travel at the speed of the slowest craft. Even at the Congress of Europe it was clear that, while some countries were content to adopt the slower and more limited approach, others felt that in order to achieve meaningful change in Europe something more ambitious was required. By the end of the 1940s they were becoming increasingly frustrated at the slow pace of progress, and began to explore plans for a more radical transformation.

On 9 May 1950, a date now celebrated as 'Europe Day', French Foreign Minister Robert Schuman announced a plan for countries to give control of their coal and steel industries to a new authority that would act independently of the member states. This became the Treaty of Paris, establishing the European Coal and Steel Community (ECSC) which came into operation in 1952. Obviously, economic coopera-tion was at the heart of this project. But it also had an explicit political dimension, and that brings us right back to the dominant concern of the postwar era: how could states avoid another European war? The ECSC project sought to contribute to an answer in two main ways. First of all, by bringing coal and steel under international authority, it was taking control of the means of making war – you could not build tanks or guns without coal and steel. Second, the ECSC project was centred on France and West Germany, and thus put European reconciliation at its heart.

This did not mean that Europe fell into instant agreement on everything. Indeed, as the ECSC project was getting under way, a similar scheme for European cooperation in the areas of defence and foreign policy – the European Defence Community and European Political Community – was attempted but did not get off the ground. However, rather than acting to discourage people, this setback served to motivate them, particularly since the ECSC was proving very successful. Within a few years there was a proposal to build on the economic model of the ECSC, and in the 1957 Treaty of Rome the ECSC member states agreed to set up two further communities: the European Economic Community (or EEC) and the European Atomic Energy Community (EAEC or Euratom).

Since then European integration has developed signi-ficantly. There has been a sequence of further treaties that

Table 27.1 Key treaties of European integration

Signed	Title of treaty	Main developments	Into effect
1951	Treaty of Paris	Created European Coal and Steel Community	1952
1957	Treaty of Rome	Created European Economic Community (EEC Treaty) and European Atomic Energy Community (Euratom Treaty)	1958
1965	Merger Treaty	Merged the three communities into a single European Community	1967
1986	Single European Act	Created Single Market	1987
1992	Treaty on European Union (aka Maastricht Treaty)	Established European Union; Economic and Monetary Union; Common Foreign and Security Policy	1993
1997	Treaty of Amsterdam	Revision of structures; employment policy	1999
2001	Treaty of Nice	Institutional reform to cater for enlargement	2003
2007	Treaty of Lisbon	Further institutional reform intended to democratise the EU	2009

have added new powers and competences, altered the institutional structures, absorbed new members and changed the name of the organisation. Let's clarify the last of those first. From 1958 onwards the ECSC, the EEC and Euratom formed three parallel if very closely linked communities, so that throughout most of the 1960s the correct appellation was the European Communities. In 1967 the Merger Treaty was signed which effectively brought the three communities together into a single European Community. Then in 1992 the Maastricht Treaty declared a European Union, and this title came into effect on 1 January 1993. These name changes were not just cosmetic; they reflected a genuine transformation of policies and membership. In the next section we examine how the EU has grown, what it does, and most important, how it works.

How the European Union works

What makes the EU distinctive is its institutional structure. The EU has five core institutions: the **European Council**, the Council of Ministers, the European Commission, the European Parliament and the Court of Justice. These reflect a carefully constructed balance between the interests of each member state on the one hand and the collective European interest on the other. Member-state interests are protected and promoted through the European Council, which consists of the heads of government from each state, and the Council of Ministers, which is made up of the ministers and civil servants from each member state. These have to share power with the other institutions, however. In particular, the Commission is the source of EU legislation, the Parliament participates in decision-making and the Court referees the process.

The decision-making system is one of the most unique and distinctive features of the EU. It represents a compromise between two models: the inter-governmental one that we have already mentioned, and a supranational model. The basic feature of **inter-governmentalism** is that power remains under the control of each of the national governments, while under **supranationalism**, power is transferred – at least partially – to institutions that are independent of the control of the national governments.

The EU is neither one thing nor the other – it is a hybrid, a mixture of these two. On the one hand, decision-making is still primarily held by national governments through the Council of Ministers and the European Council, and any decision to expand the power of the EU can only be taken by unanimous agreement of all member states. Unanimity can be a strength, but it can also produce situations where the will of the majority can be baulked by a minority. The EU

gets around that by including some supranational features. Supranationalism prevents that from happening by removing that power of veto. The main supranational components of the EU are the Commission, the Parliament and the Court, all three of which have some independence from the national governments, and also the system of weighted voting that is used in the Council of Ministers, which means that individual states can be outvoted.

It is important to add that the EU does not have one single system for making decisions. This depends strongly on the policy area under discussion. In some areas, the Commission and Parliament play an important role and the Union's decision making is best characterised as a hybrid of supranational and inter-governmental features. This would apply, for example, in relation to policies connected with the core common market provisions. However, in other areas, the inter-governmental aspects of the Union come to the fore, and the Commission and Parliament are marginalised. This applies, for example, in areas such as foreign policy cooperation. It is also worth re-emphasising that for the EU to gain responsibility for any new area of policy, a new treaty must be negotiated and must be ratified by every member state. This can be taken as another inter-governmental feature, as it essentially means that each state has a veto over any new policies, though once they have been approved that veto disappears.

The EU's decision-making system has been criticised for a number of flaws. It is undoubtedly complicated and difficult for ordinary citizens to comprehend, though this is perhaps inevitable when trying to assemble a choir where so many competing voices have to be heard. More seriously, the complexity of the EU's structures has created problems for democracy. What has been called a 'democratic deficit' has emerged, meaning that national parliaments have lost power to the EU, but the European Parliament has been unable to compensate for this. The result is a system where the decision makers – and again, remember that this means predominantly the national governments, working together in the Council of Ministers – are not subject to the same levels of scrutiny, transparency and accountability that would be expected at national levels. Indeed, one underlying flaw is the absence of one single body which could be termed 'the government'. Instead, power is shared in an obtuse manner between 28 governments, the European Commission and the European Parliament, with 28 national parliaments also trying to contribute. This complexity is captured by the fact that the EU has three different presidents – a president of the Commission, one for the European Council, and one for the Parliament – and none of these really comes near to being the head of an EU government in power or authority.

This also means that the EU can at times seem to lack political cohesion and direction. There is no requirement for the three presidents to be from the same party family – indeed, in 2012 the European Parliament president was

Table 27.2 Institutions of the European Union

European Council

Membership:	The heads of government of all the member states
Leadership:	Since 2009 national governments have appointed a President of the European Council
Where does it meet?	No fixed headquarters – meetings are rotated around all member states
How often does it meet?	Usually three times a year
Key powers:	In principle, if everything is working smoothly in the Union, then the European Council has nothing to do other than allow heads of government to meet for a chat. However, it exists to resolve intractable problems and to give initial approval to any new treaties
How does it take decisions?	There is no formal system of decision taking at this level; problems are dealt with by political negotiation and bargaining.
Website:	www.european-council.europa.eu

Council of the European Union

Membership:	Ministers from each of the member states, supported by their national civil service staff. The Council of Ministers meets in many different guises: agriculture ministers on agricultural issues, trade ministers on trade issues and so on
Leadership:	There is a 'presidency' system, where responsibility for managing the Council is rotated around each member state every six months
Where does it meet?	The Council of the EU has a headquarters in Brussels, but also rotates its meetings around all member states
How often does it meet?	This depends on the subject area. Some meet (at the staff level) virtually on a daily basis, others less frequently
Key powers:	The Council makes the main decisions on EU policy
How does it take decisions?	Depends on the topic area, but it usually involves a system of weighted votes (giving bigger states like the UK more power)
Website:	www.consilium.europa.eu

European Commission

Membership:	28 Commissioners, who oversee a professional staff of about 18,000. Each member state nominates a Commissioner for a five-year term of office
Leadership:	One of the 28 is chosen by the national governments as President of the Commission.
Where does it meet?	Headquarters are in Brussels
How often does it meet?	All 28 Commissioners hold a weekly meeting
Key powers:	The Commission has the sole power to initiate legislation in the EU, so long as the policy area has been mandated in a treaty
How does it take decisions?	It doesn't – all Commission proposals are submitted to the Council and the Parliament for consideration, amendment and approval
Website:	www.europa.eu

European Parliament

Membership:	725 members, directly elected every five years
Leadership:	The MEPs elect a President of the EP, though this role is more akin to being speaker of the house
Where does it meet?	In Brussels for three weeks out of every four, in Strasbourg for the other week – and with some sessions held in Luxembourg
Key powers:	The Parliament has the power of co-decision with the Council, meaning that it must be consulted on all legislation and included in all decisions
How does it take decisions?	By votes of MEPs
Website:	www.europarl.europa.eu

Table 27.2 (*continued*)

Court of Justice	
Membership:	28 judges, one appointed from each member state, appointed for renewable six-year terms. They are supported by eight Advocates-General, with the five largest EU states always nominating one and the smaller states rotating the other three. The Court of Justice consists of: the European Court of Justice, the General Court and the Civil Service Tribunal
Leadership:	One of the 28 is chosen as President of the Court of Justice, who presides over the workings of the Court
Where does it meet?	The Court is based in Luxembourg
Key powers:	To interpret and apply the treaties
How does it take decisions?	By unanimity – the Court does not publish minority opinions. The Court can sit in various permutations, from three or five judges hearing a case, to the more usual Grand Chamber of 13 judges or even the full court of 28.
Website:	www.curia.europa.eu

Table 27.3 The EU's three presidents, 2012

President of the European Council	
Herman Van Rompuy	
	Christian Democrat
	Formerly Prime Minister of Belgium
Roles:	Chairing meetings of the European Council
	Promoting the work of the European Council
	Facilitating consensus and cohesion in the European Council
	Liaising with the European Commission and the Council of Ministers
	Reporting annually to the European Parliament
Appointment:	Elected by a majority vote of the European Council
	Serves a 2½-year term, which can be renewed
President of the European Commission	
José Manuel Barroso	
	Christian Democrat (member of Portuguese PSD)
	Formerly Prime Minister of Portugal
Roles:	Leading the Commission and chairing its meetings
	Promoting the cause of European integration
	Representing the Commission in meetings with Council, Parliament and other bodies
Appointment:	Appointed by the heads of government of the EU member states
	Approved by a vote in the European Parliament
	Serves a 5-year term, which can be renewed
President of the European Parliament	
Martin Schulz	
	Social Democrat
	MEP for the German SPD
Roles:	Chairing the Parliament and ensuring it abides by its rules
	Liaison with the European Council and Council of Ministers
	Representation of the Parliament internationally
	Signing into effect the annual EU budget
Appointment:	Elected by a majority vote of the Parliament
	Can serve up to a 5-year term, and can be re-elected

from the centre-left Party of European Socialists, while the presidents of the Commission and Council were both from the centre-right European Peoples' Party. And this situation is made worse by the fact that each of the three institutions has a multiplicity of parties. We would expect a parliament to contain a lot of different parties, but the Commission and Council also include a mix of centre-right, centre-left, green, liberal and conservative politicians. This makes it harder for them to develop a strong political vision or direction.

Of course, this is not to say that the EU does not pursue a political agenda. It certainly tries to promote the cause of further integration. It also has a political policy impact, but there is disagreement about the nature and direction of that impact. Margaret Thatcher famously railed against what she saw as 'socialism by the back door', in other words the maintenance through European regulations of the kinds of social and environmental protections she was trying to dismantle in the UK. However, the left is equally adamant in viewing the EU as 'neo-liberalism by the front door', in other words that EU treaties have promoted a particularly pro-market set of policies. For example, they argue that the EU has embedded neo-liberal policies favouring privatisation, low taxation, cutbacks in public expenditure and so on. Examples include the criteria for the single currency, the rules governing the single market and the austerity programmes being pushed through as a result of the financial crisis. Alongside these features, they argue that the social protections are minimal.

While it is relatively easy to identify problems in the decision-making structure of the EU, it is far more difficult to find an alternative. Remember, the EU is a compromise between supranational and inter-governmental approaches, and its institutions are a hybrid of these elements. Criticisms of the EU tend to depend on whether one is viewing the EU from a supranational or an inter-governmental perspective. One side argues that the flaws in the system are the result of an incomplete construction, and claim that the democratic deficit is best addressed by strengthening the European Parliament and creating a clear EU government. This, of course, is anathema to the other side, who see the problems as being due to too much integration, and who argue for powers to be taken back from the EU and returned to national political systems.

What the European Union does

At this point, it is worth explaining the breadth and range of policies for which the EU has responsibility. The EU has a very clear economics cornerstone, being founded as it was on establishing a common market, initially in coal and steel and then covering all trade. The basic principles of the common market are the four freedoms: free movement of goods, of labour, of capital and of services. And the common market has in turn led to the adoption of further policies: a common external trade policy, a common agricultural policy and fisheries policy, then movement towards harmonisation of exchange rates, and in 2000 a common currency. Nor have these economic developments come to an end. Clearly, the single currency project is in turmoil due to the financial crisis, and there is a prospect of a significant move towards further integration covering fiscal policies. This is also moving the EU closer to a debate about some degree of harmonisation of tax policies.

But that is just the economic aspect of integration. By the 1970s it began to develop a common social policy, launching a Social Fund and providing aid for less well-off regions through the Regional Development Fund. In the 1980s this evolved further into extensive cooperation on environmental policies. A political aspect has also emerged. A common foreign policy began to appear in the 1970s, and this has developed into a common security policy. In addition, police and judicial cooperation has developed as the European Union has begun to build a system of open internal borders. So, today's EU has changed considerably from the ECSC of the 1950s.

The EU has also evolved considerably in terms of membership. The ECSC started with just six member states, but with the entry of Croatia in 2013 had expanded to 28 member states, with a queue of countries that have either already applied to join or are considering such a move.

The Union has set out a number of criteria for membership. Countries must be European – though the EU is careful to avoid being too dogmatic about where, exactly, Europe begins and ends. Countries must also be democratic. This was made very clear in the 1960s, when the Community quickly and explicitly rejected overtures from Franco's Spain about submitting an application to join. The democratic component is defined not just in terms of holding free and fair elections but also in terms of defending human rights and protecting minorities. The EU has also adopted the European Convention of Human Rights, which was originally promulgated by the Council of Europe. Next, countries must be capitalist. Indeed, not only do they have to be capitalist, they must have a robust economy sufficiently strong to cope with the competitive pressures involved in the EU market. Finally, countries must accept all of the existing treaties – something known by the French term *acquis communautaire*. They cannot pick and choose which bits of the Union they sign up to, and that means they must accept the commitment in the Treaty of Rome to work towards an 'ever-closer union'.

Clearly, one of the strongest motivations for joining is that the EU is seen as producing benefits. These are primarily

Table 27.4 European Union member states and candidates

1952	Founder members (6)	Belgium; France; West Germany; Italy; Luxembourg; Netherlands
1973	First enlargement (+3)	Denmark; Ireland; United Kingdom
1981	Second enlargement (+1)	Greece
1986	Third enlargement (+2)	Portugal; Spain
1992	de facto enlargement	East Germany (incorporated into Germany and thus into the EC)
1995	Fourth enlargement (+3)	Austria; Finland; Sweden
2004	Fifth enlargement (+10)	Cyprus; Czech Republic; Estonia; Hungary; Latvia; Lithuania; Malta; Poland; Slovakia; Slovenia
2007	Sixth enlargement (+2)	Bulgaria; Romania
2013	Seventh enlargement (+1)	Croatia
2013	Current candidates	Iceland; Macedonia; Montenegro; Serbia; Turkey

economic – the advantages of access to a large market, the stability and security provided by agreed social provisions, the direct gains available through social, regional and agricultural funding. However, for a number of member states, accession was also of considerable political benefit, as membership was seen as a means of copper-fastening democracy after the collapse of right-wing (in the cases of Greece, Portugal and Spain) and communist (in the case of former Soviet satellites) dictatorships. Other countries undoubtedly join less to gain benefits than to minimise disadvantages. As the Union has expanded, smaller neighbouring economies have become increasingly dependent on it, and membership in such cases is more a case of trying to regain some control over economic decisions. But finally, it should be noted that for many states, joining the EU is as much a cultural assertion as anything else. Membership of the EU is seen as a means of demonstrating 'Europeanness'.

So why have some countries chosen to remain outside the Union? Prosperous, democratic and undoubtedly European states like Norway and Switzerland have not joined. The main reason is that the economies of these countries are strongly dependent on one particularly successful economic sector – oil in Norway, banking in Switzerland. As a result, the economic costs of membership are thought to outweigh the economic advantages of joining. Of course, there is at least one prosperous, democratic and undeniably European country which has joined the EU but where there has always been a strong antipathy to membership. The rest of this chapter focuses on Britain and the EU.

Britain's path to membership

As we have already seen, Britain was centrally involved in the initial stages of European cooperation in the postwar era. It was a founder-member of the OEEC, NATO and the Council of Europe. It also had the opportunity to participate in the initial steps of European integration. It was sounded out about joining the ECSC, and a British government representative attended the initial discussions that were to lead to the Treaty of Rome. However, despite Churchill's rhetoric about a United States of Europe, Britain dithered about joining the EEC. Why did Britain remain outside the initial stages of the project? Three major reasons can be put forward:

1 *International role.* Britain felt that it had alternative focuses, and was more than just a European power. In particular, in the 1950s the Empire and the Commonwealth was still seen as a major cultural and economic partnership, and there was also the so-called 'special relationship' with the United States.

2 *Economic interests.* There was a perception that Britain had separate economic interests. One big factor in the decision to remain outside the ECSC was the fact that the Labour Party had only just nationalised the coal and steel industries in Britain. Another example of a separate economic interest was in the financial sector. The British pound had a role as a global currency, and the British economy already depended strongly on financial services based in the City of London.

3 *Political distinctiveness.* British politicians and the public alike disliked supranationalism, and there was something of a conceit that Britain had a superior political culture: the UK did not *feel* itself to be very European.

As Labour leader Hugh Gaitskell noted in 1962, talking about the prospect that the European Community might develop towards some form of federal United States of Europe:

What does federation mean? . . . It does mean the end of Britain as an independent nation state.

Box 27.5

The European Free Trade Association (EFTA)

The European Free Trade Association was set up in response to the creation of the EEC. It brought together seven non-EEC states, including Britain, to promote free trade. However, over time six of its member-states have ended up leaving EFTA and joining the EC/EU. Although a few other states have joined, it still leaves EFTA with just four states as members today. Its headquarters are in Geneva. See www.efta.int.

Nevertheless, there was awareness that cooperation – particularly in the economic sphere – could bring significant benefits. Faced with the common market being constructed by its neighbours and some of its main trading partners, Britain responded by leading the establishment of a rival organisation, the European Free Trade Association (EFTA). Founded in 1960, this brought together a number of small and medium-sized economies, such as Sweden, Switzerland and Portugal. But this was always going to be of secondary importance to the EEC Six. In August 1961 Britain applied for membership of the EEC. In 1962 Conservative Prime Minister Harold Macmillan stated:

> For Britain to stay out and isolate herself from the mainstream of European strength would, I believe, have very damaging results both for ourselves and for the whole of the Commonwealth.

What had changed to bring this about? First of all, it was becoming evident Britain had backed the wrong horse – the British economy was growing, but at nothing like the rate of its major European trading partners. At this time the Community's growth rate was about two and a half times that of the UK. In addition, other motivations were changing. The Suez Crisis of 1956 had indicated that the 'special relationship' with the United States was rather more lopsided than British leaders might have desired. It was also clear that the days of empire were numbered, as decolonisation began to sweep the world. So, although the distaste for supranationalism remained, it was harder to justify such particularism in the light of the cold economic reality of falling further and further behind countries like Germany and the Netherlands, and of seeing others like France and Italy catch up and forge ahead.

Of course, applying to join is one thing. But every applicant must be accepted, and that requires initial agreement to commence membership negotiations, then the successful conduct and completion of those negotiations, and then a final ratification process where all member states must give final approval for each applicant. By the time Britain applied, the political landscape had changed. While most of the six member states welcomed the application, one did not. France had undergone a significant political transformation in 1958, with Charles de Gaulle becoming president of the country.

De Gaulle was no advocate of a supranational Europe – his aim was *l'Europe des patries*, or 'Europe of the nations', and throughout his presidency he sought, with some success, to turn the European Community towards a more inter-governmental path. He was wary of British entry into the EEC, essentially because he felt that this would dilute French influence and leadership. De Gaulle vetoed the British application to join at the first hurdle. In his memoirs, he declared:

> Having failed, from the outside, to prevent the birth of the Community, they [the British] now plan to paralyse it from within.

Britain applied again in May 1967, but once more de Gaulle refused to allow negotiations to commence. It was not until de Gaulle resigned from office in 1969 that there was any chance of breaking this political stalemate. But once De Gaulle had left office, negotiations got under way and progress was rapid. They were successfully completed within two years, and Britain joined the Community on 1 January 1973 under the government of Edward Heath. Prior to accession, Heath re-emphasised the fundamental economic rationale for membership:

> It is common knowledge that our prosperity as a nation, and indeed our very existence, depends on exporting our goods abroad. The countries of the European Community, with their rapidly expanding economies, would provide us with that market. This is one of the strongest arguments for going in and competing on level terms.

Britain's accession

This was still not yet the end of the story of the path to accession. The following year was one of political turmoil in Britain, with two general elections, and the European issue was dragged into the debates. Throughout the 1960s, while there had been supporters and opponents of membership in both major parties, the Conservatives had generally been the more enthusiastic. The initial application in 1961 had come from Macmillan's Government, the third application and the negotiations for membership had been carried out under Heath's leadership, and it was Heath who signed the Accession Treaty. But Labour won slim majorities in the two 1974 elections. While Labour was not uniformly anti-European – after all, Britain's second application to join had been submitted by the Harold Wilson Government – nonetheless there was stronger opposition to membership in some quarters in Labour at that time.

Labour had contested both 1974 elections on a policy of withdrawal from the EEC. Of course, the realities of being in office soon led to a watering-down of this commitment. Labour sought renegotiation of the terms of British membership. While the outcome of this process produced little other than some cosmetic changes, nonetheless it was enough to allow Labour to put the amended terms to a public referendum. In 1975 the British public voted on British membership. Perhaps slightly surprisingly, given the lugubrious stance adopted up till then, the vote was quite strongly in favour. With a turnout of 64.5 per cent, the electorate endorsed membership by a margin of two-to-one – 67.2 to 32.8 per cent. Fourteen years after its first application to join the EEC, it seemed that the issue of British membership had finally been settled. Of course, this proved to be far from the case. But for the moment, it is worth summarising the main impacts associated with the British path to membership through the 1950s and 1960s:

1 First of all, it is important to underline that Britain was central to the discussions about European cooperation and integration in the postwar era. However, through its own equivocation and through the hesitations of others, Britain became confined to the margins of European integration. The whole to-and-fro process of applications, rejections, negotiations, renegotiations and referendums left a legacy of suspicion on both sides, with a concern that Britain showed a distinct lack of commitment to the principle of European integration.

2 Second, the path to membership shows how European integration has brought about a political transformation in the UK. Even if it was deployed somewhat belatedly (all the other applicant countries had held one in advance of joining), the use of a referendum for the first time was a significant departure from the political principle of parliamentary sovereignty that supposedly underpins the British political system. We can also see the way in which Europe has affected the party system. European issues cut across the traditional left–right divide in British politics, and even in this early period had begun to cause problems for internal party cohesion and coherence.

3 Above all, the early path to membership underlines the extent to which political interests were becoming subservient to economic ones. The traditional political-legal understanding of sovereignty – the capacity of a state to govern itself – was being subverted as patterns of economic sovereignty – the capacity of a state to manage its economy – shifted. There is an extensive debate as to whether European integration is a cause of changing patterns of economic sovereignty or a response to it. But what is evident is that economics was increasingly having an effect on politics.

This latter point is crucial for understanding one final feature of the British relationship with European integration. The long and winding road to British membership was not just a political affair; it also had implication for public attitudes. Public opinion in Britain has never evinced great enthusiasm for the whole European project. Various explanations have been advanced – that parties have never tried hard enough to sell the European idea; that British people value their independence more than others; that it is a legacy of the fact that Britain avoided invasion during the Second World War. But certainly, as Britain sought to take its place alongside its European partners, the public response was characterised as being at best cautiously supportive.

The impact of membership: the marginal member-state?

The three themes just outlined have remained present in Britain's relations with the EU. Membership has undoubtedly had a significant impact on British politics, economy and society – not always beneficially so, but it would also be misleading to suggest that no benefits have accrued. However, a mutual suspicion and lack of commitment has persisted. At its heart is the tension between perceptions of political and economic sovereignty.

There is no doubt that Britain has remained an awkward partner in Europe. We have already recounted how Britain demanded a renegotiation of its terms of accession within a year of joining the EEC, and put these to a referendum – hardly a resounding endorsement of membership. However, rather than settle the issue of British membership, the referendum simply deferred further problems. Within a few years a major row erupted between Britain and its European partners. Margaret Thatcher had been an enthusiastic advocate of membership and of a 'Yes' vote in the referendum in the 1970s, but after she came to power at the end of the decade, she began to adopt a much more critical tone in her dealings with the Community. The first target concerned the perceived imbalance between the amount of money that Britain was contributing to the Community and the amount it was receiving.

It is important to bear in mind that Europe is not supposed to work on the basis of equal pots of money for each state. Nor should the economic benefit of membership be measured in terms of monies received from EU funds – instead, the main economic advantage lies in the indirect effect of the common market allowing companies to grow. With that being said, there was a noticeable disparity between the British contribution and its direct receipts. This was recognised by the other Community states, but instead of resolving the issue through one of the usual EC compromises, Thatcher adopted a very confrontational stance. In the end, a rebate was agreed, but this was as much despite Thatcher's intransigence as because of it. And the rebate was won at the expense of a further souring of relations. As one commentator put it, 'Britain's European partners were in turn shocked, repelled and alienated' (Pilkington 2001: 19).

Thatcher wanted European integration to focus on creating a free market. Therefore, she was reasonably content with the 1987 Single European Act (SEA), which consolidated the basic market approaches of the Community, though it also paved the way for much more extensive use of qualified majority voting. Subsequent treaties were to prove

more controversial. Thatcher's aversion to the social and environmental regulation aspects of the EU has already been noted, and that attitude was to set the tone for the next phase of British truculence. In 1992 the member states negotiated the Treaty on European Union, and this included a commitment to a common set of social standards, the Social Charter. These amounted to little more than a consolidation of the rules already in operation in the member states, but Britain, by now under the leadership of John Major, chose to opt out of these social commitments.

The other big issue in the Treaty on European Union was Economic and Monetary Union, a plan to create a single currency. Once again, the Major Government sought and acquired an opt-out clause, so that Britain did not join the euro when it came into full circulation in 2002. In some ways the **euro** encapsulates much about European integration and about Britain's lack of enthusiasm for it. The single currency is an excellent example of an economic project which has very clear political overtones. It was founded as a means of tying Germany more firmly to its European partners in the wake of reunification. But this manner of using economic means to achieve political goals is the kind of ambitious and far-reaching initiative that successive British governments have loathed.

Although the Labour Government that came to power in 1997 promised to bring Britain to the heart of Europe, it only partially delivered on this pledge. While Tony Blair was happy to sign up for the Social Chapter, Britain remained outside the euro. Gordon Brown, as Chancellor of the Exchequer, set out five 'economic tests' that would need to be satisfied before Britain would consider joining the euro (see Box 27.6). While these might seem to be objective, in reality there is a very strong subjective and political tone to them.

In any case, Labour's defeat in the 2010 General Election and the Eurozone crisis has pushed the prospect of British membership of the euro out of consideration for the foreseeable

Box 27.6

The five 'economic tests' for British membership of the euro

1 There must be sufficient convergence between British and European economies.

2 There must be sufficient flexibility in how the euro operates.

3 The euro must be structured in a way that encourages investment into Britain.

4 Euro membership should benefit the financial services sector in the City of London.

5 Euro membership should enhance British growth and employment prospects.

future. However, even though membership of the euro was no longer at issue, other topics emerged to continue the confrontational rhetoric. First of all, at a summit of EU leaders in Brussels in December 2011 the Conservative Prime Minister David Cameron vetoed the idea of drafting a new EU treaty to try to deal with the escalating euro-crisis. In June 2012 Cameron indicated that a referendum would be held on the EU, and in January 2013 he announced that, if the Conservatives were returned to power in the next general election, he would seek to renegotiate the terms of British membership and would then hold an 'in/out' referendum on the basis of that renegotiation.

The impact of membership: Euroscepticism or Europeanisation?

To understand why these patterns of constant EU-critical rhetoric and the drawing of lines in ever-shifting sands exist, we need to look in more depth at the political aspects of the British relationship with the EU. There is no doubt that membership has had a significant impact on British politics. The difficulty lies in gauging what the direction of impact has been. Two vectors can be picked out. First of all, there is plenty of evidence of a strong and growing Eurosceptic dimension in British politics, which has had an effect on party politics and on public opinion. But second, there is also a pro-European dimension, with parties, pressure groups and some quarters of the public showing strong and increasing support for and enthusiasm for European integration.

Euroscepticism does not simply mean opposition to integration; it can be defined in a number of ways. Indeed, outright rejection of integration is a relatively rare stance. Instead, the idea of Euroscepticism includes positions ranging from criticism of selected EU policies through to more comprehensive critiques of the EU's institutional mechanisms. The most obvious indicator of Euroscepticism in Britain comes from public opinion polls. This is clearly shown in various public opinion surveys. The EU's Eurobarometer surveys provide data for all EU states, allowing comparisons of attitudes in the UK with those in the rest of the Union. Undoubtedly, public opinion in the UK is more cautious and critical about membership of the EU than in virtually any other EU country.

Such Eurosceptic attitudes among the public undoubtedly has an effect on political parties. Again, there is clear evidence of a Eurosceptic streak in most British parties. Notably, both of the two largest political parties have had to try to deal

with significant internal divisions and disputes on the European issue. The Labour Party suffered an actual split triggered at least in part by differences of opinion over European policy when a number of leading members left to form the Social Democratic Party in 1981. The underlying motivation was a concern at what was felt to be a general leftwards drift in the Labour Party, but the two catalytic factors were Labour's anti-Europeanism and its commitment to unilateral nuclear disarmament. More recently, the Conservative Party has had to deal not only with a strong anti-EU faction within the party, but also the emergence of a rival right-wing anti-EU party. The UK Independence Party (UKIP) was founded in 1993, and has won seats in several EP elections, as well as luring some Conservative Party members to join its ranks.

On the evidence above, European integration has been arguably the most politically divisive issue in British politics over the past 60 years. Nonetheless, it is important to consider the ways in which the opinions and attitudes of both public and parties can be formed and influenced. In particular, the media have played a significant role in Britain. There is a strong Eurosceptic tone to much of the British press, most notably in the *Daily Mail* and the *Daily Express*, but also evident throughout the News International/News Corporation stable of newspapers. These are dominated by owners and editors that have been very strongly critical of the EU. The EU-critical stances reflect personal preferences of those owners and editors and their interpretation of their business interests.

However, alongside these Eurosceptic elements in parties, in the press and in the wider public, there is also evidence of what has been termed '**Europeanisation**'. This refers to the process by which the political and economic policy-making dynamics of the EU become embedded into national political and economic policy-making structures. 'Europeanisation' can be taken to mean two distinct things. First of all, it can simply refer to adaptation to the existence of the EU through participation in EU activities and institutions. Thus, the fact of political parties taking part in European elections and in the Parliament is an instance of this form of 'Europeanisation'. However, the term also has a stronger meaning, implying a policy shift towards a more pro-European position. So parties or pressure groups or other public bodies such as courts or administrations adopting a position of advocacy towards the EU would be an example of this form of 'Europeanisation'.

The first form is clearly evident in British politics. There are virtually no groups that refuse to have anything to do with the EU. Even those parties and groups that advocate British withdrawal from the Union tend to do so on the grounds that Britain can build a better relationship with Europe from the outside – and in the meantime, they are quite prepared to engage with and participate in European

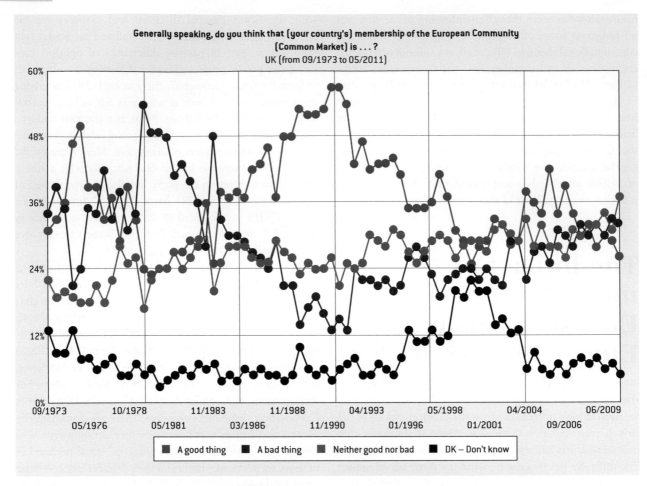

Figure 27.1 British attitudes towards European integration
Source: © European Union, 1995–2010

institutions. Thus, UKIP contests EP elections and takes its seats in the Parliament, even if it seeks to use this position to criticise the Union.

The EP works on the basis of transnational party groups, and most British parties have found a place alongside allies from other European countries. This has been easiest for Labour, the Liberal Democrats and the Greens, who have had ready-made European federations of like-minded parties to slot into. Even UKIP has a small group of Eurosceptic partners to sit with in the Parliament. But the Conservatives have had far greater problems finding a comfortable European home. Its natural partner on many policy fronts is the European People's Party, which includes the conservative and Christian Democratic parties from all European countries. Indeed, the Conservatives were affiliated to the EPP throughout the 1990s and early 2000s. But the EPP is also a strongly pro-integration party, and this led the Conservatives to leave and form their own EP group.

However, their problems did not end there, because in their efforts to construct a viable new group they ended up

including parties against whom there were allegations of anti-immigrant and anti-gay policies. Indeed, in a similar vein UKIP suffered defections among its MEPs, as some of them were unhappy to be included with a number of far-right parties in their Europe of Freedom and Democracy group.

Clearly, while it possible to use UKIP's presence in the EP as an example of the first kind of 'Europeanisation', this does not include the second usage of the term – there is not much evidence of UKIP becoming pro-EU. However, in other organisations in the British political structures, there is some evidence of a tendency for regular involvement in the running of policy through the EU to result in personnel being persuaded that integration can – and does – work.

One area of the British political system which has had a great deal of contact with the European Union is the civil service. As we have seen, the Council of Ministers involves a great deal of contact and coordination between the national administrations. In Britain the Foreign and Commonwealth Office carries much of the primary responsibility for dealing with EU affairs. In addition, most ministries and depart-

Table 27.5 European Parliament party groups and British parties, 2012

Party group	Total seats	British members	Seats
European People's Party	271	No current British member party	–
Progressive Alliance of Socialists and Democrats	189	Labour Party	13
Alliance of Liberals and Democrats for Europe	86	Liberal Democrats	12
Greens/European Free Alliance	59	Green Party Scottish Nationalist Party Plaid Cymru	2 2 1
European Conservatives and Reformists	52	Conservative Party Ulster Unionist	25 1
Europe of Freedom and Democracy	34	UK Independence Party	10
Confederal Group of the United Left/Nordic Green Left	34	Sinn Féin	1
Non-attached	29	UK Independence Party British National Party Democratic Unionist Party We Demand a Referendum Party	2 2 1 1

Source: European Parliament Information Office in the UK (www.europarl.org.uk)

ments have some degree of contact with the Union, whether it is the kind of intensive and regular contact required of the Department of Environment, Food and Rural Affairs, which deals with the Common Agriculture Policy, or the less demanding European responsibilities of a portfolio like education, where policy remains largely in national hands.

Partly, this activity requires a constant shuttle of various British ministry officials back and forth between London and Brussels and other European cities. In addition, there is a full-time team of British civil servants based in Brussels, attached to the UK's Permanent Representation to the EU and led by the Permanent Representative (a post equivalent to being an ambassador). The Permanent Representation works closely with colleagues from the other member states in a constant process of consultation, negotiation and compromise. While, of course, the civil servants act to defend and promote Britain's interests, they are also exposed to – and can become accustomed to – a very different style of politics and public administration.

There are also many British people working directly for the European institutions, including the European Commission. Indeed, British Commissioners have played a significant role in the development of integration. However, it should be kept in mind that Commissioners and their European civil servants, from whatever country, are legally obliged to act from a European perspective rather than protect their 'national' interests. Although Commissioners are appointed by national governments, those governments have no subsequent power to terminate their appointment early. It is a little bit like being a chief executive of a multinational corporation, who would be expected to act in the interests of the corporation, not in the interests of whatever country they came from.

Another type of organisation that has developed close working relations with the European Union over the past 40 years is pressure groups. Of course, this is a term that covers a vast number of groups, and it would be ridiculous to imagine that all of them are engaged with EU issues. Even among those that are involved with the European Union, there are Eurosceptic as well as Euro-enthusiastic ones. But some of them provide an interesting example of 'Europeanisation'. The European Union is a policy-making framework, and therefore groups interested in influencing public policy are going to seek involvement. Indeed, the EU recognises this, and provides formal channels for the involvement of pressure groups.

In the British case, one interesting example is the approach taken by the trade union movement towards European integration. As with the Labour Party, the trade unions drifted towards a more critical stance in the 1970s and 1980s. However, that stance changed significantly when Commission President Jacques Delors addressed the TUC annual conference in Bournemouth in 1988. His arguments in support of the social benefits of integration persuaded many in the British trade union movement to soften their stance on Europe, and contributed in turn to a shift on the part of the Labour Party as well. But it is not just trade unions that support Europe; a number of business organisations do so as well, such as the Business for New Europe group.

Thus, both pro-integration and anti-integration opinions can be found in Britain. The position adopted depends on two factors. First of all, the ideological disposition of the group is important. For example, parties and groups that are strongly nationalist or strongly pro-American in their outlook are less likely to view the EU positively, while those that regard international cooperation as an intrinsically good thing are likely to see it in a much more positive light. Second,

Table 27.6 Britain's European Commissioners, 1973 to date

From 1973 to 2004, the UK had the right to appoint two Commissioners, with an agreement between Labour and the Conservatives that there would be one from each party. Since 2004, as a result of enlargement, the British allocation was reduced to one Commissioner.

Christopher Soames	Con	1973–7	External Relations and Trade
George Thomson	Lab	1973–6	Regional affairs
Roy Jenkins	Lab	1977–81	Commission President
Christopher Tugendhat	Con	1977–85	Budget and Finance
Ivor Richard	Lab	1981–5	Employment and Social Affairs
Stanley Clinton Davis	Lab	1985–8	Environment, Consumer Protection and Transport
Arthur Cockfield	Con	1985–9	Internal Market and Services
Leon Brittan	Con	1989–99	Competition (1989–93); Trade (1993–9); External Relations (1995–9)
Bruce Millan	Lab	1989–95	Regional Policy
Neil Kinnock	Lab	1995–2004	Transport (1995–9); Administrative Reform (1999–2004)
Chris Patten	Con	1999–2004	External Relations
Peter Mandelson	Lab	2004–8	Trade
Cathy Ashton	Lab	2008 to date	Trade (2008–9); Foreign Affairs (2009–)

Sources: European Commission (2010–14) *Members of the Barroso Commission* (http://ec.europa.eu/commission_2010-2014/index_en.htm) and *List of European Commissioners* (http://ec.europa.eu/commission_2010-2014/pdf/composition_de_la_commission_europeenne_1958_2004_fr.pdf)

it depends on whether the parties or groups think that Britain has benefited from membership or not. To explore that, we need to summarise the impact of membership.

The impact of membership: politics, economics and society

Clearly, EU membership has had a political impact. The sections above have indicated how political parties and pressure groups have responded to it. Membership has also altered some basic structures of the British political system. It did so right at the outset of membership by triggering a referendum, a political device that had not been used in the UK before then. Also, the prospect of further referenda on European issues moved closer with the EU Act of July 2011, which required that, if there is any further transfer of powers to the EU, there must automatically be a referendum to endorse this – a kind of institutionalisation of Euroscepticism in the British case.

Membership altered the basic structures of British politics again through European elections. Direct elections to the EP were introduced in 1979 – prior to that, British MEPs were seconded from the House of Commons. In 1999 the electoral system was changed for European elections, with

Britain switching from first-past-the-post to proportional representation by regional lists. This has produced a far greater range of representation, giving the Liberal Democrats a greater share of seats and allowing other parties like UKIP, the Greens and the BNP to gain representation.

Third, the role of the Houses of Parliament has been altered. More and more legislation emanates from shared decision-making at the EU level, and it is difficult for Parliament to deal with this. This is partly because of the sheer volume of EU legislation and partly because much EU decision making takes place by complex trade-offs and bargains that cannot readily be unpicked back in the national parliament. This is by no means something unique to the UK, but it does leave questions over the accountability of the EU.

While the political consequences for Britain and for Europe are important, at core the EU remains an economic project. Britain is a net contributor to the EU budget but, as already noted, membership should not be solely measured in terms of contributions and returns. The EU is the largest single trading block in the world (and it is on Britain's doorstep), so to ignore it would be foolish to the point of wilfulness. Its impact varies considerably. Unsurprisingly, those companies with strong links to the European market are the ones most in favour of very strong ties to the EU, but not all companies are EU-focused.

Of course, the counter-argument is not that the EU should be ignored, but that a different relationship is possible. The situation has changed since the 1970s. The World Trade Organization (WTO) seeks to ensure access to markets internationally, making the EU somewhat less special. The

Table 27.7 European Parliament election results[1] in Great Britain[2], votes and seats by party, 1979–2009

Year	GB seats	Con		Lab		Lib Dem[3]		UKIP		Green[4]		SNP		PC		BNP		Other		Turnout (%)
		V (%)	S	V (%)	S	V (%)	S	V (%)	S	V (%)	S	V (%)	S	V (%)	S	V (%)	S	V (%)	S	
1979	78	51	60	33	17	13	0			0	0	2	1	1	0			1		32.1
1984	78	41	45	37	32	19	0			1	0	2	1	1	0			0		32.1
1989	78	35	32	40	45	6	0			15	0	3	1	1	0			1		36.5
1994	84	28	18	44	62	17	2	1	0	3	0	3	2	1	0			3		36.2
1999	84	28	36	36	29	13	10	7	3	6	2	2	2	3	2	1	0	5		23.1
2004	75	27	27	23	19	15	12	16	12	6	2	1	2	1	1	5	0	6		38.2
2009	69	28	25	16	13	14	11	17	13	9	2	2	2	1	1	6	2	8		34.3

1 Electoral system: first-past-the-post 1979–94, PR by regional list, 1999 to date.
2 Not including Northern Ireland (3 seats, electoral system: PR by single transferable vote).
3 Liberal Party in 1979; Lib/SDP Alliance in 1984.
4 Ecology Party in 1979 and 1984.

Source: McGuinness 2012: 33–34

European Economic Area agreements signed between the EU and other states like Norway and Switzerland suggest a model that some believe the UK could emulate, which would mean the country could dispense with what some see as the unsavoury social and supranational elements of membership.

Equally, however, there are those in the UK who consider exactly those elements to be very good reasons for supporting the EU, for being in favour of integration, for wanting more Europe, not less. In particular, the social and environmental regulation of the EU is seen as a hindrance by some but as a bulwark by others. In these cases there is a recognition that, for an economic and social model to work across so many different countries, and for the benefits to continue to flow from the EU, it might be necessary to see greater sharing of sovereignty. And as Europe struggles to deal with the financial crisis and the Eurozone crisis, this becomes a very real prospect.

Britain and the future of Europe

Since the late 2000s the EU has been dominated by one concern: the global financial crisis, and in particular the problems of the Eurozone. Starting in 2007, a massive crisis unfolded. It was triggered by a series of banking collapses, beginning in the United States with companies like Lehmann Brothers, and also affecting Britain, where Northern Rock went bankrupt and had to be rescued by state intervention. The crisis was not of the EU's making, but its financial system was unusually vulnerable to the crisis because of the adoption of the euro. The single currency had brought together economies with considerable differences, and the crisis brought those differences to the fore. In particular, the banking sector in weaker economies in places like Ireland, Greece, Portugal and Spain ran into serious difficulties. Rather than let the banks fail, the European Central Bank and the International Monetary Fund intervened by providing bailouts which were conditional on the adoption of very restrictive (and deeply unpopular) austerity programmes.

Although the UK is not part of the Eurozone, nonetheless it was strongly affected by these events. UK banks were among those that had lent to the countries now in difficulties, so the bailout in effect constituted a safeguard for their investments. Therefore, although the bailout was dominated by contributions from the ECB and the IMF, the UK government also contributed towards the fund; and, of course, although the EU was suffering a particularly severe crisis, the UK economy was by no means invulnerable, so it was in the UK's interest to contribute to collective responses. Globalisation has made it much more difficult for any country to run its economic affairs in isolation.

On previous occasions a crisis in the process of European integration has proved to be the spur for a further initiative, for deeper integration. This was also the reaction to the Eurozone crisis. Alongside the fire-fighting plans to try to deal with the immediate crisis, there were several calls for a new initiative to significantly alter the long-term basis of the single currency. The euro was launched on the basis of economic and monetary unity, but not a full fiscal union. Proposals emerged in 2012 that would move the Eurozone countries towards a full fiscal union, involving greater control of budgetary policies and tax harmonisation.

These proposals produced a very mixed reaction in the EU in general. While some felt that the austerity programmes and fiscal control were necessary, there were also huge public protests in the bailout countries, where many people felt that the bailouts were effectively subsidies being given to banks at the expense of public services.

The proposals also met with a predictably negative reaction in the UK. While the crisis underlined the interconnectedness of economic relations in the world today, the political reaction in the UK treated it as Europe's problem, not Britain's. This was reflected in the responses to the idea of a new fiscal union, which ranged from cautious support on the condition that it would be purely for Eurozone states and would not involve any consequences for the UK, to the more forthright position that the proposed new union represented a further dangerous and unnecessary expansion of powers by the EU.

Once again, Britain responded to a European initiative with caution and scepticism. However, while there might well have been very good reasons for such an attitude, it highlights once more the extent to which Britain remains on the sidelines of events. Britain cannot prevent other EU states from pressing ahead. It can make life more awkward for them and put up obstacles, but that simply exacerbates the problem. There is no such thing as a perfect political system, and the EU is certainly far from perfect. But it does work, and it functions on the basis of cooperation and consensus-building. That has always sat uneasily with the more competitive winner-takes-all style of British politics, and perhaps explains why Britain has never fully been comfortable with its place in the European Union.

Chapter summary

The development of European integration and the emergence of the European Union is one of the most significant features of European politics in the past 60 years. This chapter has sought to illustrate the significance of that development and to highlight some of the strengths and weaknesses of the EU, examining its historical origins, looking at how the EU's institutions function to make decisions, and summarising its main policies. Integration has also been a very major bone of contention in British politics, from the initial debates about whether or not to seek membership in the 1950s through to the arguments about whether or not to hold a referendum on continued British membership in the present day. The chapter has shown the importance of the EU dimension for British politics and policies.

Discussion points

- Why has the UK been so hesitant about participating in European integration?
- What are the main reasons for UK membership of the European Union?
- In what ways can UK politicians influence policy making in the European Union?
- To what extent has the EU changed British politics?
- What are the probable future challenges that the UK will face from European integration?

Further reading

If you want to get a good overview of the European Union, there are a number of textbooks that summarise the key features of institutions, policies and politics of the Union, such as Dinan (2010), Nugent (2010) and McCormick (2011). Good historical analyses are provided by Dinan (2004) and Dedman (2009). More detailed texts on the EU's

institutions and politics include Cini and Perez-Solorzano Borragan (2009), Bomberg, Petersen and Corbett (2011) and Peterson and Shackleton (2012), while good evaluations of EU policies are provided by Wallace, Pollack and Young (2010) and Senior Nello (2011). The *Journal of Common Market Studies* produces an annual review of the EU which provides an up-to-date summary of developments.

Specifically on Britain and Europe, there are worthwhile general texts by Geddes (2003), Jones (2007) and Gowland, Turner and Wright (2009). Both Bache and Jordan (2008) and Mannin (2009) look at Europeanisation in the British context, while Forster (2002) examines British Euroscepticism. The history of the British relationship with Europe is covered well in Young (1998), Young (2000), Wall (2008) and Daddow (2011a). Crowson (2005) and Daddow (2011b) explore the EU policies of the Conservative Party and the Labour Party respectively, while Anderson and Weymouth (1999) look specifically at the role of the British press. Finally, Liddle (2013) looks ahead to the future of the relationship between Britain and European integration.

There are also a range of excellent web resources. The European Union's own website contains huge amounts of information, including the Eurobarometer opinion poll surveys.

The excellent CVCE site (*Centre Virtuel de la Connaissance sur l'Europe*) contains a superb online archive on all aspects of the history of integration – and despite the name, it's not just in French! A handy site for keeping up to date with EU politics is the *EU Observer*, an online news magazine on EU issues. The UK Office of the European Parliament provides a useful online booklet, *Britain and Europe in ten speeches*, from which the quotes in this chapter from Churchill, Gaitskell, Macmillan, Heath, Thatcher and Blair are taken.

Bibliography

Anderson, P. and Weymouth, A. (1999) *Insulting the Public? The British press and the European Union* (Longman).

Bache, I. and Jordan, A. (eds) (2008) *The Europeanisation of British Politics* (Palgrave Macmillan).

Bache, I., George, S. and Bulmer, S. (2011) *Politics in the European Union*, 3rd edn (Oxford University Press).

Baker, D. and Seawright, D. (1998) *Britain for and against Europe: British politics and the question of European integration* (Clarendon Press).

Bomberg, E., Peterson, J. and Corbett, R. (eds) (2011) *The European Union: How does it work?*, 3rd edn (Oxford University Press).

Cini, M. and Perez-Solorzano Borragan, N. (2009) *European Union Politics*, 3rd edn (Oxford University Press).

Crowson, N.J. (2005) *The Conservative Party and European Integration since 1945: At the heart of Europe?* (Routledge).

Daddow, O. (2011a) *Britain and Europe since 1945: Historiographical perspectives on integration* (Manchester University Press).

Daddow, O. (2011b) *New Labour and the European Union: Blair and Brown's logic of history* (Manchester University Press).

Dedman, M. (2009) *The Origins and Development of the European Union 1945–2008: A History of European Integration*, 2nd edn (Routledge).

Dinan, D. (2004) *Europe Recast: A history of European Union* (Palgrave Macmillan).

Dinan, D. (2010) *Ever Closer Union: An introduction to European integration*, 4th edn (Palgrave Macmillan).

Forster, A. (2002) *Euroscepticism in Contemporary British Politics: Opposition to Europe in the Conservative and Labour Parties since 1945* (Routledge).

Geddes, A. (2003) *The European Union and British Politics* (Palgrave Macmillan).

George, S. (1998) *An Awkward Partner: Britain and the European Community*, 3rd edn (Oxford University Press).

Gowland, D. and Turner, A. (1999) *Reluctant Europeans: Britain and European integration, 1945–96* (Longman).

Gowland, D., Turner, A. and Wright, A. (2009) *Britain and European Integration since 1945: On the sidelines* (Routledge).

Hannan, D. (2012) *A Doomed Marriage: Britain and Europe* (Notting Hill Editions).

Hix, S. and Høyland, B. (2011) *The Political System of the European Union*, 3rd edn (Palgrave Macmillan).

Jones, A. (2007) *Britain and the European Union* (Edinburgh University Press).

Liddle, R. (2013) *Engaging with Europe: Britain and the future challenges of European integration* (I.B. Tauris).

Mannin, M.L. (2009) *British Government and Politics: balancing Europeanization and independence* (Rowman & Littlefield).

McCormick, J. (2011) *European Union Politics* (Palgrave Macmillan).

McGuinness, F., Cracknell, R., Davies, M. and Taylor, M. (2012) *UK Election Statistics: 1918–2012* (House of Commons Library Research Paper 12/43).

Nugent, N. (2010) *The Government and Politics of the European Union*, 7th edn (Palgrave Macmillan).

Pilkington, C. (2001) *Britain in the European Union Today*, 2nd edn (Manchester University Press).

Peterson, J. and Shackleton, M. (eds) (2012) *The Institutions of the European Union*, 3rd edn (Oxford University Press).

Senior Nello, S. (2011) *The European Union: economics, policy and history*, 3rd edn (McGraw Hill).

Wall, S. (2008) *A Stranger in Europe: Britain and the EU from Thatcher to Blair* (Oxford University Press).

Wallace, H., Pollack, M. and Young, A. (eds) (2010) *Policy-making in the European Union* (Oxford University Press).

Young, H. (1998) *This Blessed Plot: Britain and Europe from Churchill to Blair* (Papermac).

Young, J.W. (2000) *Britain and European Unity 1945–1999*, 2nd edn (Palgrave Macmillan).

Useful websites

The European Union's own website: www.europa.eu

The European Parliament: www.europarl.eu

EU Observer (online news magazine): www.euobserver.com

CVCE (EU online archive): www.cvce.eu

UK Representation to the EU: http://ukeu.fco.gov.uk/en/

Can we buck the markets?

For four decades until the end of the 1970s markets were in retreat: that was an age of expanding public ownership, active government management of the economy, a growing welfare state and an intellectual climate that emphasised the limits, and indeed the failures, of markets. The election of Mrs Thatcher's first administration in 1979 marked the end of that era and began nearly three decades of market triumphalism. The mantra of the early Thatcher years – TINA, 'there is no alternative' – was another way of saying 'you can't buck the markets'. Over the following decades the market rolled on apparently remorselessly. Key publicly owned industries and services, like steel, telecoms, electricity, gas and water were privatised. Key markets – labour markets, financial markets – were freed from controls. Mrs Thatcher, while rhetorically hostile to European economic integration, passed the Single European Act in 1986 – a huge advance in diminishing national barriers to the creation of a single competitive market covering the whole of the European Union. Perhaps the single most striking sign of the triumph of the market occurred, though, not in government but within the Opposition. On Tony Blair's accession to the leadership of the Labour Party in 1994 the Party amended Clause four of its constitution – a clause that committed the Party to public ownership – to include a tribute to 'the enterprise of the market and rigour of competition'. Labour's first 10 years in office after 1997 were the high point of market triumphalism. The financial services industries in the City of London were the centrepiece of the new dynamic service-led economy that Labour claimed to be pioneering. And London financial markets were supposed to exemplify the superiority of market processes over administrative controls: 'light touch regulation' was practised because it was believed that freely functioning markets were better at recognising risk, and at creating instruments that could manage risk. Drawing on the most fashionable theories in economics, the idea of 'efficient markets' argued that free market mechanisms were the most effective way of allocating resources and anticipating and coping with risk.

The great financial crisis which began publicly in the UK in September 2007 with the collapse of the Northern Rock bank ended this era of triumphalism. But even before the crisis the idea that 'you can't buck the markets' had met some important limitations. The conversion to theories of market superiority was, for a start, largely an elite conversion. One of the striking features of the Thatcher Revolution was that, while it achieved a revolution in ownership and market organisation, it made little impact on the core values of the population. Survey data showed that attachment to the key institutions of the age preceding market triumphalism, like the welfare state with its principles of universal entitlements, remained widespread among the people at large. That explains why, for all the rhetoric, neither Thatcherism nor its spiritual successor, New Labour, did more than nibble away at key welfare state institutions, like the National Health Service. Moreover, not only did market values have weak popular roots; the actual practice of market liberalisation was fraught with contradictions. The contradictions are nicely caught in the title of the best study of Thatcherism yet written, Gamble's *The Free Market and Strong State* (Gamble 1994). To create a free market required a large amount of state intervention. The contradiction was well illustrated by the case of Europe. Creating a single market after 1986 did indeed abolish many national barriers; but it also involved a huge increase in Brussels-led regulation in order to create a 'level playing field' – to create the circumstances where competitive conditions would be equalised between the different national economies of the member states of the European Union. The contradiction explains why in the age of the single market, the Conservatives, once the leading Europhile party in the UK, fell out of love with the EU.

Thus even before the great financial crisis there were important areas where markets were indeed limited. But the crisis brought the age of market triumphalism to an end. It greatly damaged the intellectual dominance of market theories. It turned out that 'efficient markets', far from ensuring stability, were actually part of the cause of the crisis: the sophisticated financial instruments that were supposed to package and contain risk, were actually so sophisticated and complicated that they created illusions of stability and encouraged massive risk taking. Far from being a highway to prosperity and stability, 'efficient markets' in finance were a road to perdition. But the change was more than intellectual. The years since then have seen recurring scandals about practices in financial markets, once the 'poster boy' of market theory. The crisis also revived the state as an owner and active manager. The global financial system was only saved in 2007–8 by government interventions involving the commitment of huge amounts of public money. In the UK the state has ended up owning a sizeable chunk of the banking system, nationalised as part of the 2007–8 rescues. Moreover, it has also ended up caring for much of the rest of the banking system by feeding cheap assets to ailing private banks, notably through the policy of quantitative easing. In 1983, after the Labour Party disastrously lost the general election, its election manifesto was described as 'the longest suicide note in history', principally because it contained radical proposals for bank nationalisation. Yet it was precisely this 'suicidal' measure that New Labour enacted in the great financial crisis.

Is the age of market triumphalism therefore now at an end? In some domains, notably in the regulation of financial markets, it has indeed been succeeded by a commitment to tight controls and a tough approach to enforcement. But in wider issues of economic policy the belief that 'you can't buck markets' remains highly influential. It still lies at the heart of the economic strategy of the Coalition Government. The most important shaper of that policy is the Chancellor, George Osborne. Central to Mr Osborne's strategy is the policy of debt reduction – of cutting spending so as to reduce public borrowing. And the strategy is central because Mr Osborne is convinced that there is one set of markets – the markets in government debt – that cannot be 'bucked'. He is committed to debt reduction to reassure bond markets – the markets where most government borrowing is raised – that Britain is unlike Ireland, or Greece, or Spain or Italy: that it can contain its future borrowing, and service its existing debts. The success of that strategy is much disputed, even within the Coalition, and even at the time of writing there are calls for Mr Osborne to be replaced as Chancellor and for a shift away from the strategy of giving top priority to debt reduction. But the focus on Mr Osborne's personal position misses the point. Whoever is Chancellor, the Conservatives are the dominant partners in the Coalition,

and the majority of Conservative MPs still believe that 'you cannot buck markets'. After his election as leader in 2005 David Cameron famously set about 'detoxifying' the Conservative image – making it more voter friendly. But that detoxification concerned what might be called broad cultural matters: notably making the Conservatives more liberal on gender issues, such as the recruitment of women parliamentary candidates, on attitudes to gay people, and on attitudes to ethnic minorities. On economic policy, most Conservative MPs are still proud to be Thatcher's children. Had the Conservatives won a parliamentary majority in 2010 we would undoubtedly have seen a still more market-friendly response to the management of the crisis than we have witnessed under the Coalition. And if the Conservatives succeed in winning a majority in 2015 we will hear much more of the mantra that 'you can't buck markets'. In their sights are a range of barriers to market forces. A recent publication by the Free Enterprise Group – a ginger group mostly of new Conservative entrants to the Commons in 2010 – gives a flavour of what to expect (Kwarteng et al. 2012.) It argues that the only way to meet the challenge of global market competition, from economies like the Chinese, is further wholesale deregulation. Among the targets are the minimum wage, legal protection against dismissal, and large parts of the welfare state budget, notably benefits for the unemployed.

The question of whether or not 'you can't buck markets' is therefore not just an abstract question in economic theory. It is a political question. Whether markets will be further constrained, or will resume the triumphant progress that marked the decades after 1979, will depend on political outcomes: on the choices that political elites make in the coming years; and on what electors decide about those choices.

by Michael Moran

References

Gamble, A. (1994). *The Free Market and Strong State: the politics of Thatcherism* (Macmillan).

Kwarteng, K., Patel, P., Raab, D., Skidmore, C. and Truss, E. (2012). *Britannia Unchained: global lessons for growth and prosperity* (Palgrave Macmillan).

Coalition government in the UK: how has it been?

Bill Jones, May 2013

> **The Coalition Parties will work together effectively to deliver our programme, on the basis of goodwill, mutual trust and agreed procedures which foster collective decision-making and decision-making while reflecting each party's identity.**
> (Coalition Agreement for Stability and Reform, May 2010)

> **It's because the Conservatives really know capitalism doesn't work and the Liberal Democrats think it actually does, that the coalition government has survived so far.**
> (Jeremy Hardy, comedian, 24 November 2012, York Theatre Royal)

> **The initial bright-eyed vow that served as the defining mission of the coalition – to eradicate the deficit by 2015, thereby winning re-election as a reward for clearing up the economic mess – has turned to dust.**
> (Jonathan Freedland, the *Guardian*, 6 December 2012)

When the 6 May election results produced no overall winner, a rather unseemly wrestling match took place between the three biggest parties in the Commons as to who would ally with whom. David Cameron, as leader of the biggest party, could have claimed the right to lead a minority government and to try and hang on until another election would have given him a chance to achieve a workable majority. However, this would not have been a strong government, and it was widely appreciated that the nature of Britain's economic crisis required a government able to take unpopular measures. Cameron came to favour a coalition, as linking with the Lib Dems would have given him protection against his dissatisfied right wing which felt strongly – still does – that his *Big Society*-themed election campaign 'lost' them an election

against a failing Labour government led by the disastrously unpopular Brown that they should have won easily. So, he made his 'big, open and comprehensive offer' to the Liberal Democrats and talks began.

Brown, no doubt devastated at losing the election, must have been surprised to still be 'in play' the day after polling. But his position was much less favourable. First, to assemble a majority he would need to do deals with a rainbow-coloured group of smaller parties, some of whom – the SNP for instance – would be likely to pull the plug if their demands were ignored. Second, by any commonsense measure Labour had 'lost' the election and, as several of the party's leading figures made clear during Brown's negotiations, voters were unlikely to accept the continuation in government of a party which had served 13 years, had been seriously unpopular for some time and had been soundly beaten in the national contest for control of Westminster.

The 'consummation' of the Tory–Lib Dem love affair in the Rose Garden of Number 10 was much lampooned as a 'gay' political marriage, so affectionate did Nick and Dave appear to be. The ridicule concealed not a little astonishment also as the Lib Dems had operated politically to the left of Labour post 2005 with reasonably well-entrenched positions on: favouring welfare payments and redistributing wealth; being opposed to increased tuition fees for university study; stoutly defending civil liberties and opposing New Labour's tightening of the screw on terrorist suspects; encouraging closer integration of the UK with the EU; and forging ahead with constitutional change, especially voting reform.

Given that the Conservatives had been moving to the right on most of these issues for some years, the emergence of a Coalition Agreement, somewhat grandly entitled a 'Programme for Government', did cause eyebrows to be raised and pundits to predict a short shelf life for this highly unusual experiment. However, with Labour not really in the game, the real choice was between a minority Conservative government with Lib Dems tacitly offering support, or a straightforward coalition to address the economic crisis. The Lib Dems were bitterly criticised subsequently by those who had voted for them in order to keep the Conservatives out. They were soon to be excoriated by former supporters for reneging on their promise – many Lib Dem MPs had made it in public by signing a pledge – to resist increased tuition fees. But Nick Clegg's party faced an impossible dilemma: to be howled down for swallowing traditional anti-Tory principles, or to be condemned for passing up the first chance of government since David Lloyd George. If they had refused the 'coalition offer', the accusation of running away from the responsibility of governing would have been hung around their necks for years to come. Besides, 13 years of New Labour rule had more or less ended Lib-Dem empathy with the party of Attlee, Wilson and Blair. Crucially, moreover, the heavyweight Lib Dem authors of *The Orange Book* – especially David Laws, were much closer to the Tories economically.[1]

At the time of writing, Cameron's joint administration with Nick Clegg's Liberal Democrats is still in place, though it has had to cope with some extremely embarrassing and painful disagreements. Assessing how the Government has performed falls under two headings: how the two parties have handled the joint activity, the consultation, joint policy making and so forth; and how the Coalition has coped with the acute stresses of policy disagreements.

Political issues dividing Coalition partners since May 2010

Those who predicted a difficult relationship between the two partners were not wrong. Below I pick out the major points of difference between the two parties.

1   *Tuition fees*: this row escalated rapidly at the expense of the Lib Dems. The increase in fees to around £9,000 per student per year, albeit without the requirement of upfront money, was blamed on Clegg and his party who had nailed their colours to its mast in an attempt to win student votes, sometimes with public signings of the

pledge to reinforce the message. Once in the Coalition, this backfired badly. It was bad enough to see a Tory PM, but to lose out on this issue infuriated many younger voters. Though equally responsible, the Tories seemed not to get the blame.

2   *Economy*: Osborne's determination to cut deeply and quickly was condemned by Labour as an ideologically inspired 'coup' attempt to shrink the state in line with Conservatives' longstanding objective. Lib Dems, including Vince Cable, had excoriated this idea in the election campaign. However, the Lib Dem negotiators proved tractable on this point, perhaps because they included David Laws and Danny Alexander, both closer to the Tory economic position than Cable, who was not a negotiation team member.

3   *AV referendum*: Clegg's ambition was to show the efficacy of his party by pushing though sweeping constitutional changes. Maybe even the holy grail of voting reform was a possibility? Cameron had allowed a referendum on the partial measure of the Alternative Vote, a non-proportional system which would only eliminate minority-elected MPs. But at least it was a start. The unspoken assumption of LDs was that Cameron would go easy on his campaigning to allow his partner party some slack after a bruising start to their experience in government. However, right-wing Tories grew alarmed and put pressure on the PM to front the 'No' campaign, which he then did to great effect. The Lib Dems were humiliated and felt let down by Cameron though Clegg did not complain in any discernible, public way.

4   *EU veto*: this came about when the EU summit in Brussels introduced a bill to tighten up financial arrangements in the Eurozone. Cameron was worried UK banking would suffer, so he used his veto to pre-empt it. Clegg was furious with this and had known nothing about it. He was left looking foolish, while Cameron rode a wave of support by looking tough on the EU.

5   *Banking*: this was just one of the many issues on which there were differences of opinion. Widespread public anger at how the bankers had behaved in causing the crisis in 2008, and then the ensuing recession, had not been quelled or even addressed properly when Osborne announced that the separation of retail from investment banking recommended by the Vickers Report would only involve some 'ring fencing'. Lib Dem MPs complained loudly.

6   *NHS*: this surprise reform proposal from the Tories proved unacceptable to the Lib Dems who voted to oppose it at their spring conference in 2011. In consequence, the bill was halted for a space of three months while its

---

1   David Laws, Paul Marshall (eds) (2004) *The Orange Book*: *Reclaiming Liberalism*.

terms were studied anew. The principal objection from Labour and Lib Dem was the opportunities it would give for private sector takeovers of health services. In the end the reform was passed, but if it results in bad reports or financial problems, there might be a popular revolt along the lines of Kidderminster in 1997 when an independent MP was elected purely on the basis of a hospital closure.

7   *House of Lords reform*: denied any progress on voting reform, LDs had great hopes of solving the perennial problem of the Lords. Clegg came up with a plan to reduce the size of the Lords, introduce 15-year terms and elections based on PR. There was a revolt among Tory MPs and the bill was defeated.

8   *Boundary revisions*: the idea here was to reduce the number of MPs to 600 and to make constituencies more equal in population. Clegg responded to right-wing Tory scuppering of his Lords plan by withdrawing support from a boundary revision plan which might have gained the Tories an additional 20 invaluable seats.

9   *Environment*: in May 2010 Cameron promised the 'greenest government ever', but by December 2012, this promise looked tattered: the Sustainable Development Commission had been abolished; Osborne and Cameron seemed determined to go ahead with the third Heathrow runway; wind farms had been rubbished by the Lib Dem energy secretary's junior minister; and David Kennedy's appointment as permanent secretary to the department was vetoed by Number 10 as too 'green'.

10   *Leveson Inquiry and Report*: the Leveson Inquiry into press practices and ethics recommended a regulatory framework reinforced by legislation. On 29 November 2012 David Cameron, while endorsing the report's principles, refused to accept any statutory underpinning for regulation of the press. In an unprecedented departure from previous Coalition practice, Nick Clegg, along with Ed Miliband and the victims of press excesses, made his own separate statement endorsing the need for a legislative foundation for regulation.

Practising coalition government

The book by Robert Hazell and Ben Young (2012) *The Politics of Coalition* (Hart Publishing) provides valuable insights into how the two parties have managed to work together when so much of their respective histories has been one of fractious and occasionally bitter disagreement. It has to be said that the research for the book took place during the first 18 months of the Cameron–Clegg partnership; since then more division has set in.

Just like coalitions on the continent the current one is based on written agreements: in the UK case, two key documents.

Interim Agreement

The title of this is pretty self-explanatory: a 3,000-word document in seven sections focusing on deficit reduction and reducing public spending.

Programme for Government (PfG)

This 16,000-word, 36-page document compares with equivalent recent coalition agreements of 200 words (Finland) and 43,000 (Belgium). It was negotiated in detail by Danny Alexander and Oliver Letwin respectively, in charge of their party manifestos. They were assisted by two special advisers and a small team of Cabinet Office civil servants to assist with drafting and policy advice. The PfG included some items not in the earlier document – for example, NHS reform. In the end the PfG comprised 400 pledges, which the authors reckon embraced 75 per cent of Liberal Democrat ideas and 60 per cent Conservative. However, as the latter is the bigger party and had a bigger manifesto, the weight of the document was more 'Conservative' than 'Liberal Democrat'.

Having said that, some sections reflected almost wholly a party view – for example, Lib-Dem on civil rights and Conservative on the economy. The Lib Dems had four key pledges: take poorer people out of tax altogether, put forward more green policies, provide more help for poor children in schools and undertake a 'cleaning-up' of politics. Two pledges were soon delivered on tax and the 'pupil premium', but during the first 18 months the story was of Lib Dem policy failure regarding tuition fees and the loss of the referendum on AV. Conservatives gave economic policy its direction; it did not help the Lib Dems that Vince Cable – a fierce opponent of cutting too far and too fast – was not part of the negotiating team, while City experts Chris Huhne and David Laws were.

Some policy areas were recognised as disputed, and an 'agree to disagree' position on things like Trident and tuition fees was allowed, though it extended only to abstaining, not to voting against. On those areas where there was sharp disagreement policy reviews were set up – 25 of them – plus five commissions. Despite its attempt to embrace different traditions and policy positions, Hazell and Young concede the PfG was essentially a 'Conservative flavoured' document which conceded control of the economy to the bigger party.

Coalition Agreement for Stability and Reform

This 1,300-word document was at heart a procedural agreement, vowing to reach agreement on policy through 'close consultation' between the Prime Minister, the Deputy Prime Minister and both parties in both houses of the legislature. The next election will not be until 7 May 2015, and this gives the prospect of good continuity and makes a snap election difficult (the Fixed Term Parliament Act was passed in September 2011).

The DPM has the right to be consulted on all issues and on some he has a veto in effect. He agrees all ministerial appointments even including whips and special advisers. He nominates Lib Dem ministers, as one might expect, and they cannot be removed without his agreement.

Two committees were set up to deal with coalition issues: Coalition Committee and Coalition Operation and Strategic/Planning Group (COSPG). In practice, this machinery was supplanted by more informal mechanisms.

Appointments

Clegg and Cameron nominated ministers and agreed which jobs they were to do. Hague, Ed Llewellyn and Osborne advised as did Danny Alexander. Lib Dems got 22 per cent of Cabinet posts drawn from their 16 per cent of MPs. Lib Dems did slightly better than their seats allocation merited, but this is not unusual for smaller parties which make government possible. If they had been given posts according to votes they would have done much better: 2–3 ratio. LDs went for a wide spread rather than focusing; perhaps if they had, they would have done better in terms of public perceptions of their role in government. Departments with no Lib Dem minister tended to be in those where there were no disagreements. Anger was felt in the Tory party, however, because there were fewer jobs to go around for them. Resentment of LDs, therefore, had many sources, especially on the right wing of the party. Lib Dems were left under-represented in the Lords where they had only two ministers, so that party whips have had to stand in for ministers. This has reinforced the Lib Dem feeling that the Lords is not a democratic chamber and needed reform.

Government at the centre

In theory both parties were liable to disagree and quarrel, but in practice this did not happen. 'Far from being quarrelsome, slow and indecisive, it proved remarkably harmonious, smooth and effective in its decision-making' (Hazell and Young 2012: 68). This was achieved through a number of informal means. The official Coalition Committee was

not used as 'no disputes escalated to that level'. Smaller meetings brokered agreement before issues entered the usual machinery. The Cabinet office was unusually effective as it supported the DPM. The need for both sides to endorse decisions led to a revival of genuine Cabinet government which had been in decline since John Major.

Emerging out of the fog of joint decision-making were the weekly meetings of the so-called *Quad* (Cameron, Osborne, Clegg and Danny Alexander) plus *bilaterals* between Alexander and Oliver Letwin. Interviews by Hazell and Young with key players suggested that 'disagreements between ministers of the same party were more frequent and more serious than those between coalition partners.' However, the authors note that on balance the Lib Dems lost out in terms of public perceptions. While they were loyal and diligent partners, their poll standing plummeted. Conservative ratings, however, survived reasonably well.

Ministerial clashes with civil servants – *Times* report, January 2013

Contrary to the 'peace, love and harmony' conclusions reached by Hazell and Young in their study mentioned above, a substantial journalistic investigation suggested an alternative narrative.

The Time's two-page spread collated views from a wide range of luminaries including: Tony Blair (advises Asian heads of government not to follow the British model); Andrew Adonis ('We have a non-expert civil service, characterised by very poor training'); Margaret Hodge ('there's a pervading sense that it is not their money . . . they escape responsibility'); Steve Hilton ('When you try and make change happen, that's not easy'); Jonathan Powell ('The Civil Service is much too closed'); and Peter Hennessy ('There's too much management speak. If the Sermon on the mount had been written in Whitehall, none of us would be Christian').

The trigger for much of this occasionally bilious comment was the recent series of mistakes made over the West Coast Mainline Rail Franchise disaster, the errors made in the 'omnishambles' 2011 Budget and other mishandlings like that of the ash die-back tree disease. The Coalition ministers worry that the reputation for incompetence resulting from such mistakes has tainted the administration unfairly, since civil service shortcomings have mostly been to blame.

'According to the goverment's own figures' says *The Times*, 'only about a third of major projects have been delivered on time and to budget. Disagreements are simmering about the way in which Britain should be run and the scale and speed of reform. A breach of trust has developed in some departments between ministers and mandarins.'

Lord (Peter) Hennessy, doyen of Whitehall watchers, said: 'It's as bad as I've ever known it. The governing marriage between the civil service and the politicians is in real trouble.'

Future Coalition prospects: Conservatives

Obama's victory was the first by an incumbent government since economic recession removed 17 elected governments in Europe and other developed countries.

Writing in the *Sunday Times* on 11 November 2012, Martin Ivens saw only slight comfort to the Coalition in the re-election of an incumbent government. Obama, he pointed out, had merely to *defend* a majority; Cameron must *manufacture* one. In 2010 the Conservatives won 37 per cent of the vote; to win an overall majority next time, they need to achieve 42 per cent.

> No governing party has achieved this since Lord Palmerston led the Liberals to victory in 1857 on a wave of jingoism. 'Pam' had beaten the Russians and bashed the Chinese. I wouldn't advise Cameron to try to emulate his achievement today.

He pointed out that Cameron has already suffered a great defeat which might have already scuppered any chance of victory: Clegg's refusal to support their plan to equalise constituency boundaries.

> The Tories will now need an 11% swing not 2.7% as they would have on new boundaries.

It's worth mentioning an article in the *Guardian* on 12 November which suggests the Tories tried to do a deal with the eight-strong Democratic Unionists to gain their support for the boundary deal. The Coalition has a majority of 86 in the Commons with the Conservatives three short of a majority if Labour and Lib Dems voted against it. At the time of writing it seemed nothing had come of this initiative.

Without new boundaries, Cameron has to broaden the appeal of his party beyond the South-east. Working-class voters in the South are more likely to vote Conservative than middle-class voters are in the North. With 8 per cent of the British population comprising ethnic minorities, only 4 per cent of black voters and 7 per cent of Asians say they identify with Conservative aspirations. Lord Ashcroft has pointed out the crucial importance of these minorities when in the 20 most vulnerable Labour marginals, the average non-white population is 15 per cent and within London 28 per cent.

Things look very bad on the gender front too. Up to last Christmas, wrote Ivens, women voters favoured the Conservatives but the lead had evaporated. Women, in particular, are reluctant to accept that expenditure cuts are either fair or necessary. Cameron needs to argue such cuts are necessary in order to help women cope with the high costs of raising children. If the double-dip recession is finally over, and even modest growth returns, Cameron will have much to smile about. Voters are receptive to the argument that 'the worst is over – don't let the other party spoil it.' A majority of American voters believed their economic problems were the fault of George Bush, four years after he left office. The Conservatives are bound to deploy, with much enthusiasm, the 'Labour to Blame for the Economy' line to see if it gains the same traction.

Economy

This will almost certainly be the main issue in 2015 and, until the Office of National Statistics results from the third economic quarter, things looked very bad for the Coalition. However spirits rose, headily, when a 1 per cent rate of growth was reported. This spelt a 4 per cent annual growth rate and seemed to augur very well for the future of both the economy and the Coalition. Cameron's triumphalism at PMQs, however, was short-lived. On 15 November Mervyn King, Governor of the Bank of England, referred to the last growth figure as a 'one-off' and unlikely to indicate a future trend. This was instead likely to be predominantly low and to 'zig-zag' in character; he thought it possible that growth in the final quarter of 2012 would be negative. Larry Elliott reported that, according to King:

> Growth will remain below its historic trend for the next two years and the level of national output in late 2014 will still be below where it was before the recession started in early 2008.
>
> (L. Elliot, the *Guardian*, 14 November 2012)

The economy in 2012, according to the Office for Budget Responsibility (OBR), would shrink by 0.1 per cent and grow by 1.2 per cent in 2013, making this the weakest post-recession recovery since the end of the Second World War.

Worse was still to come. Osborne's Autumn Statement in 2012 included an admission that the plan so confidently announced in May 2010 had not worked. The plan had been to clear the structural deficit by 2015 after a period of necessary spending cutbacks and tax increases. Instead of engineering a fall in the nation's debt as a share of GDP by 2015 as promised, Osborne was forced to admit this would not be achieved until 2016–17. Austerity would now last until at least 2018. This transforms the hoped-for slogan for the Coalition in 2015's election from 'job done' to 'We're on the right track – don't turn back' with an unspoken rider of 'Don't let Labour spoil it again'. Lack of growth caused the UK to lose the support of two of the rating agencies. Moody's valued triple A credit rating was lost in February 2013 and in April, Fitch's followed suit.

Political prospects

As discussed above, the prospects of the two coalition parties hangs squarely on the state of the economy. On top of that only a quarter of the anticipated cuts have so far been made, and it is unlikely that further austerity will do much for the electoral chances of the Conservative Party (already addressed above). As for the Liberal Democrats, their poll ratings have fallen into single figures and there is a real danger that they will disappear completely as an effective political force.

Lib Dems

Traditionally the repository of 'protest' votes against the government of the day, the Lib Dems was now part of government and suffered greatly thereby. In the Rotherham by-election (30/11/12) the party came a dismal eighth; Nigel Farage, leader of the United Kingdom Independence Party claimed, with some justification, to have taken on the role of Britain's 'third party'. Clearly concerned at the party's poll rating of 8 per cent on 16 December 2012, Nick Clegg made an effort on the following day to highlight those occasions when Lib Dem influence had moderated the intentions of their Conservative partners. Reducing the severity of the cuts announced in the Autumn Statement in December 2012 was one claim made; Richard Reeves, a former advisor to Nick Clegg, claimed, in a *Guardian* article on the same day that from now on his party would openly reveal the extent of their differing policy positions in an attempt to win back the millions of voters who had deserted them since May 2010. If the party's fortunes refuse to improve, this could bring about either the premature ending of the Coalition or a change in its *modus operandi* whereby both parties, rather than agreeing their compromises in private, seek to set out their positions clearly on issues in advance of decisions and votes. A parting of the ways is probably going to occur sometime before the five years is up to enable separate campaigns to be run. But, despite manifold stresses and anxieties, the Coalition seems set fair, at the time of writing and baning unforeseen developments, to survive until that point is reached.

UKIP

A senior Tory MP, Michael Fabricant, suggested in November 2012 that an electoral pact might be agreed with UKIP so that they would avoid competing in certain marginal constituencies. Fabricant calculated some 40 seats might be saved for his party in this way. However, the Tory leadership dismissed the idea, as did UKIP itself. Tories think a pledge to hold an 'in-out' referendum would win back voters inclined to vote UKIP; other Tories worry that UKIP's policy stance on a number of issues – for example, by opposing gay marriage – will do great damage to fervent Tory hopes that they can win an overall majority in 2015. The idea of such an electoral pact might well re-emerge as the election approaches.

Labour

For its part, Labour must have at least a chance of winning the next election, though it will have to steer a careful course. Ed Miliband's rating as 'prime minister in waiting' still lags behind Cameron's and the party's economic competence ratings, while hugely improved, are no higher than the Conservatives'. But the party will aspire to winning another overall majority as in 1997, 2001 and 2005. It hopes the Coalition's economic policies will have demonstrated the incompetence of Tory thinking and that public indignation at the pain inflicted by deep cuts will render a harvest of votes for the party led by Ed Miliband.

Some psephologists predict a repeat of the big '*third party*' vote which precluded an overall majority in 2010 but this might depend on how an imploded Liberal Democrat vote – 24 per cent of the vote in 2010 – redirects itself: if to one of the major parties, we might return to one-party government, but disillusionment with traditional politics might squeeze disaffected voters into new party categories, perhaps strengthening the Greens or UKIP to the extent that they win substantial representation in the Commons.

Mid-term report

On Monday 7 January 2013, Cameron and Clegg sought to re-launch the Coalition via the device of a half-way report on how it was doing. The media reception of the event was not good, with references being made to Tony Blair's short-lived attempt to spin the success of his government with annual reports after 1997. 'David Cameron and Nick Clegg need not feel they have to trouble everyone with a repetition,' advised *The Times*' editorial.

Yet the influential Simon Jenkins in the *Guardian* (9 January 2013) could be found praising Cameron and Clegg as:

> Two leaders who have serious differences on many topics still stand shoulder to shoulder on essentials and seem likely to do so for a full five years. They have carved out areas of agreement and disagreement and, like political grownups, have seen that they publicly agree on what currently matters. This is mature politics. On any showing, this has been a rare period of political discipline.

The fact that at its halfway stage the Coalition had defied critics by still being alive and likely to survive more or less its full term gives the lie to those who argued Britain would never be able to make work such an 'alien' concept as a coalition government. Given the distinctly real chance of future hung parliaments, this is perhaps an encouraging sign for the future of British politics.

However, the elevation of UKIP into a genuine threat to Conservative votes tended to pull Cameron's policy back towards the right-wing end of the spectrum. The full extent of the Coalition's subsequent fragility is reflected in this quotation by Nick Clegg in *The Guardian* on the eve of the 2013 local elections:

> '. . . the Conservative emphasis before 2010 was to be centrist, compassionate, green party, but it is returning to some pretty traditional Conservative signature tunes that I totally understand they think are necessary to strengthen Conservative defences against Ukip. There is a real struggle on the right of British politics'.
>
> *The Guardian*, 2 May 2013

GLOSSARY

301 Group: Set up in 2012 by Conservative MPs loyal to David Cameron, aiming to ensure party unity. Takes name from number of Conservative MPs needed for outright Conservative victory at next general election (assuming planned boundary changes took place).

adversarial politics: a theory popularised by (among others) Professor S.E. Finer in the 1970s which portrayed politics at Westminster as a gladiatorial combat between Labour and the Conservatives with disastrous consequences for the national interest.

affiliated: the way in which an organisation associates itself with a political party by paying a fee and gaining influence in the party's affairs. In Britain, a number of trade unions are affiliated to the Labour Party; members pay the 'political levy' which makes them affiliated members of the party.

alignment: a situation when the electorate is divided into reliable and stable support for the various parties. The British electorate was said to be aligned in both class and partisan terms from 1945 to 1970.

authority: the acceptance of someone's right to be obeyed.

backbencher: the name given to all MPs who are not members of the government or the Opposition Front Bench.

Bank of England: the institution concerned with the government's management of all financial markets, and after the Treasury the most important institution in economic policy.

Beveridgean welfare system: a 'universal' system of social policy provision which provides transfer payments to all people at the same rate, regardless of their previous economic status.

Beveridge group: faction within Liberal Democrats who see the party as a force for progressive, centre-left politics. Linked to politicians like Charles Kennedy and Simon Hughes; sceptical of the Coalition.

bicameral legislature: a legislature that consists of two houses. Most Western industrialised countries have a bicameral legislature, with the second or Upper House having a more limited role than the Lower, perhaps being composed of appointed rather than elected members, although in a few countries, most notably the United States, both are of more or less equal significance.

Bismarckian welfare system: an occupationally based system of social policy provision where the amount of transfer payments relate to individuals' previous economic status.

Black Labour: Group of Labour Party academics who argue that Labour will lack credibility until it has its own ideas for tackling the national deficit.

block vote: the system under which affiliated trade unions cast votes at Labour Party conferences and in party elections. Unions cast votes on the basis of the numbers of members paying the political levy. These votes may or may not reflect the views of union members.

Blue Collar conservatism: formed by group of Conservative MPs in 2012, designed to reconnect Conservative Party with 'aspirational' working class voters.

Blue Labour: a Labour Party tendency, embodied by MPs like Jon Cruddas, arguing that Labour could and should address key conservative themes (such as immigration and the EU) from a centre-left perspective.

bottom-up: the idea that power in the Labour Party is dispersed throughout the party, with the final say in the choices of policy and party organisation being vested in the annual conference.

Bright blue: a group of Conservative modernisers, strongly supportive of Boris Johnson, who want the party to be socially as well as economically liberal.

broadsheets: large-format newspapers, which aim at the better-educated and more affluent readers, with a particular interest in influencing the opinion-formers.

Cabinet: the Cabinet consists of the leading members of the government, chosen by the Prime Minister. It is the place where major decisions are taken or ratified and where disagreements within government are resolved.

Cabinet committees: Cabinet committees are appointed by the Prime Minister and are composed of cabinet ministers (sometimes with junior ministers) to consider items of government business. Some are standing committees, some are ad hoc, to deal with specific problems or issues.

Cabinet government: the view that collective government survives and that the Prime Minister is not the dominant force within government. Decisions are taken by a group of colleagues after discussions in Cabinet according to this view.

capital expenditure: expenditure on long-term projects such as buildings, large items of equipment, etc.

capitalism: an economic and political system in which property and the means of production and distribution are in private ownership (rather than in the hands of the state) and goods are produced for private profit.

cause or promotion groups: these groups promote some particular cause or objective, perhaps the protection of some vulnerable section of society, or seek to express the attitudes and beliefs of members. They tend to concentrate on a single issue.

Chancellor of the Exchequer: the political head of the Treasury, and with the Prime Minister the most important elected politician concerned with economic policy.

charismatic: having a natural attraction as a quality of leadership.

civil law: the law governing the rights of individuals and their relationships with each other rather than the state.

civil servants: servants of the crown, other than holders of political or judicial offices, who are employed in a civil capacity and whose remuneration is paid wholly and directly out of moneys voted by Parliament.

class: distinctions made between people on the basis of their social origins, education and occupation.

Clicktivists: A new breed of party activists operating mainly via the electronic media (e.g. those involved in *ConservativeHome*)

Cold War: the state of hostility between nations or alliances without actual fighting. Usually applied to USA–USSR relationships after 1945.

collective responsibility: all members of the government are collectively responsible for its decisions. Members, whatever their private reservations, must be prepared to defend government policy. If unable to do so, they must resign or be dismissed.

colonialism: the extension or retention of power by one nation over another.

Committee of the Whole House: a sitting of the House of Commons presided over by the Chairman of Ways and Means (Deputy Speaker) which hears the Budget speech and debates the committee stage of important bills, especially those affecting the constitution. It deals with matters where, in principle, any member should be allowed to participate.

common law: the body of law, distinct from statute law, based on custom, usage and the decisions of the law courts in specific cases brought over time.

Communism: an economic and political system which aimed at the abolition of capitalism, the establishment of the dictatorship of the proletariat and the eventual 'withering away' of the state.

community charge (poll tax): a flat-rate local tax introduced to replace the rates by the Thatcher Government. It was intensely unpopular because of its perceived unfairness, in that the amount paid was not related to income. It was a factor in Mrs Thatcher's downfall.

Compass: A Labour Party pressure group, linked to politicians like Ken Livingstone, and often referred to as the 'new left'. Keen to advocate racial, sexual and cultural equality, as well as economic equality.

consensus: an agreement. In British politics it describes the general continuity and overlap between economic, social, defence and foreign policies of postwar Labour and Conservative governments.

conservation: care and protection of natural resources.

Conservative Voice: Conservative Party pressure group, set up in 2012 by David Davies and Liam Fox. Seeks to ensure that the party upholds the political ideas of Margaret Thatcher.

constituency Labour parties (CLPs): responsibilities include the selection of Labour candidates and casting a third of the votes in Labour leadership contests (see electoral college).

constitution: the system of laws, customs and conventions which defines the composition and powers of organs of the state, and regulates their relations with each other and with the citizens. Constitutions may be written or unwritten, codified or uncodified.

constitutional: doing things according to agreed written or legal authority within the state.

constitutional monarchy: while the monarch is the titular head of state invested with considerable legal powers, these powers are exercised almost without exception on 'advice' (i.e. by ministers); and the monarch has a largely symbolic role.

conventions: unwritten rules of constitutional behaviour; generally agreed practices relating to the working of the political system, which have evolved over time.

core executive: the group of people and institutions in Whitehall around the Cabinet and Prime Minister who decide most key policies. They include No. 10 staff, the Cabinet Office and senior civil servants, particularly those in the Treasury.

corporatism: A corporatist economic model is one in which there is close collaboration between the government, labour and business. In Britain after 1945 a more corporatist model of economic management was used to try to reverse British economic decline with governments regularly consulting the trade unions. The government, trades unions and business leaders were brought together in new institutions to try to plan economic activity in the early 1960s. This system came under great strain in the 1970s and was abandoned in 1979 when the Conservative Government of Margaret Thatcher was elected.

cosmopolitan: here meaning a world free from national interests and prejudices.

council tax: the local tax introduced by the Major Government in 1993 to replace the poll tax. It is a property-based tax with reductions and exemptions for a number of categories of residents.

criminal law: law determining the acts and circumstances amounting to a crime or wrong against society as defined by the terms of law.

dealignment: a situation when there is a weaker relationship between occupational class and party support and when a declining percentage of the electorate identify with a party.

decommissioning: removal from use of paramilitary arms in Northern Ireland.

deference: a propensity to believe that people who have good education or connections with well-established families have more right to be in positions of authority than those who lack these characteristics.

de-industrialisation: the process by which manufacturing industries decline and close.

democracy: a political system in which a government is removable by the people, and in which they should be the ultimate decider of who should govern, thus enabling all adults to play a decisive part in political life.

democratic: a form of decision making in which the wishes of the adult population are claimed to be of decisive importance.

democratic deficit: the argument that reforms to the management of public services have reduced the accountability of government and diminished the democratic rights available to the citizen.

department (also known as ministry): the principal organisation of central government, responsible for providing a service or function, such as social security or defence, and headed (usually) by a secretary of state or minister.

dependency culture: the growth in the sense of dependence by users on the welfare services.

devolution: creating government institutions that exercise power locally rather than centrally.

direct rule: ruling an area directly from the capital of a country rather than through a local or regional government.

disclaim: under the 1963 Peerage Act, a hereditary peer can give up his or her title (and thus, until 1999, the right to sit in the Lords) without affecting the claim of the next heir.

divine right: the belief that monarchs derive their power and position from God and that Parliament is dependent on the will of the monarch.

ecology: an approach to politics centred around the importance of the environment.

election pacts: an arrangement made at either national or local level between two parties for a mutual withdrawal of candidates in the hope of maximising their strength vis-à-vis a third party.

electoral college: mechanism used for Labour leadership contests; includes Labour's constituency members, MPs, MEPs and affiliated trade unions.

electoral quota: the average number of electors per constituency. There are separate electoral quotas for England, Wales, Scotland and Northern Ireland. Parliament decides the number of constituencies in each part of the United Kingdom and the *Boundary Commission* is then responsible for drawing constituency boundaries as near the electoral quota as possible.

electoral register: the list of those entitled to vote. It is compiled on a constituency basis by the Registrar of Electors, an official of the local authority, through forms distributed to homes and by door-to-door canvassing. Although it is supposed to be 100 per cent accurate, there are doubts about its comprehensiveness, an issue highlighted by the poll tax.

electoral system: a set of rules enabling voters to determine the selection of the legislature and/or the executive. Electoral systems have several often incompatible aims: to produce a legislature that is proportional to the distribution of votes; to produce a government that represents the majority of voters; and to produce strong, stable and effective government.

emerge: the process by which leaders of the Conservative Party were chosen prior to the adoption of a system of elections in 1965. The new leader would 'emerge' following secret discussions between leading members of the party, with the monarch's private secretary acting as a go-between.

entrenchment: the idea that the constitution is protected in some way against amendment by a temporary majority in the legislature. There may be provision for judicial review, i.e. that courts can review the constitutionality of statutes.

environmentalism: the belief that protection of the environment is a political issue of central importance.

equality: the belief that people should all be treated in the same way and have the same rights.

equality of opportunity: the idea that there should be no legal or formal barriers to advancement in the world between citizens.

euro: the short name for the single European currency which since 2002 has been the only currency used in most member states of the European Union. Whether Britain abolishes sterling and joins the Eurozone will be the most important issue in British politics in the near future.

European Council: the European Council is made up of all the heads of government of the member states of the European Union.

Europeanisation: a term with a number of meanings, including the impact of membership of the European Union on British society and politics; the European Union expanding its boundaries through enlargement; the development of institutions of governance at the European level; adapting national and subnational systems of governance to Europe-wide institutions and Europe-wide norms; a political project aiming at a unified and politically stronger Europe; and the development of a sense of identity with Europe, the EU, etc.

Eurosceptic: a person with the view that the process of European integration has been moving too fast.

Euroscepticism: a shorthand expression for a set of complex feelings that sees closer economic and political integration in Europe as damaging to national independence. Commonly associated with, but by no means confined to, sections of the Conservative Party in the UK.

executive: the body in a political system responsible for the day-to-day running of the state.

executive agencies: an office performing a function of government, subordinate to but not wholly controlled by the parent department. They perform the *executive* as opposed to the *policy making* functions of government.

fascism: the right-wing nationalist ideas espoused by Mussolini and adapted by Hitler as the basis of his own Nazi ideology.

feminism: the advocacy of women's rights on the grounds of equality of the sexes.

financial institutions: institutions such as pension funds and insurance companies, identified as the largest holders of shares in British companies.

first-past-the-post: the name given to the electoral system used in Britain and a few other Commonwealth countries such as Canada, in which the country is divided into single-member parliamentary constituencies and the winner is the candidate with the largest number of votes, irrespective of whether he or she gains an absolute majority. This can often produce highly disproportionate election results.

fiscal: relating to public revenue, e.g. taxes.

flexible constitution: a constitution with no formal method of amendment. The British constitution is amended either by an ordinary Act of Parliament or by a change in convention.

foreign policy: a shorthand term designating the external diplomatic and diplomacy-related activities of a given state in the international arena. Foreign policy activity in the UK is nominally in the hands of the Foreign Office in Whitehall and its embassies abroad. Given its politically sensitive nature, the Prime Minister usually keeps a very close watch on foreign policy activity, particularly at times of perceived crisis when it relates to defence and security interests.

free market: a doctrine that believes that the economy operates best when it is subject to the 'laws' of supply and demand and when government interferes and regulates as little as possible. The capitalist market system is the best supplier of goods and services and allocator of rewards; the role of government is minimal and is restricted to those things that only it can do, such as national defence and internal law and order.

Fresh Start group: set up in 2012 by Conservative MPs seeking a radical renegotiation of Britain's relationship with the European Union.

front bench: the leaders of the main parties in Parliament, derived from the fact that the leadership groups sit on the front benches of parliamentary seats in the chamber.

frontbencher: the name given collectively to members of the government, who sit on the front bench on their side of the House, and to members of the Shadow Cabinet, who sit opposite.

full employment: a political and economic doctrine which advocates that everyone seeking work should be able to find a job within their capacities at a wage that would enable them to live an adequate life.

functional chamber: a legislative body composed of representatives of various interests in society, such as business, trade unions, the churches and so on.

G8: the seven major world economies – G7 (The United States, Japan, Germany, UK, France, Italy and Canada) plus Russia.

general power of competence: a new power for councils introduced by the Localism Act 2011. Prior to the 2011 Act the legal doctrine of *ultra vires* (beyond the powers) meant that councils could only carry out actions that were specifically permitted by law. Section 1 of the Localism Act 2011, which introduced the new power, states that: a local authority has power to do anything that individuals generally may do. In other words, councils can now take any actions they want, so long as there is not legislation saying they can not take that action.

gerrymandering: the practice of rigging electoral boundaries or affecting the social composition of electoral districts to ensure the success of the governing party, whatever level of support it receives. The term derives from Elbridge Gerry, Governor of Massachusetts, who in 1812 drew a congressional district shaped like a salamander so as to maximise the advantage for his party.

globalisation: processes whereby the world is less dependent on traditional nation-states. It can refer to the globalisation of political issues such as terrorism and ecological issues but most commonly refers to the economy. Trade, investment and finance have become more global with multinational corporations and finance markets. New technology means that money can be moved around the global system much more easily. Some argue that globalisation has fundamentally changed the economic context as nation-states have been hollowed out. Governments are now forced to comply with the wishes of finance markets or risk currency flight. Multinational corporations will relocate to countries where there is a cheaper labour supply. However, some would dispute this and argue that nations and international regional blocs such as the European Union have more power.

Golden Age: the period from 1832 to 1867 when, some commentators claim, there was a balance between the executive and the legislature and when Parliament was a significant influence on government policy and actions.

governance: the act or manner of governing within or across territorial jurisdictions.

hegemony: the dominant military and economic state that uses its power to force a world order conducive to its own interests.

hereditary peers: a member of the aristocracy whose title has been inherited from the nearest relative. Very few peerages are inheritable through the female line.

home rule: the transfer of independence by a sovereign parliament to former territories.

identifiers: voters who have a continuing relationship with a party and consider themselves partisans who identify with its beliefs and policies.

ideology: a system of beliefs embodying political, social and economic ideas and values.

imperialism: the policy of acquiring power over other countries, usually neighbouring ones, by political and economic exploitation.

Industrial Revolution: the period in the late eighteenth and early nineteenth centuries when mass production techniques were invented and introduced into what became known as factories.

industrialism: Jonathan Porritt's term for the present attitude of political parties to unlimited production and consumption.

inequality: differences in wealth and opportunity between different groups in society.

inflation: the increase in the amount of money in circulation producing rising prices and falls in value.

influence: the ability to have some bearing on the outcome of a decision.

inner city: the areas that surround the centres of cities, usually comprising older housing in poor condition and acting as 'reception' areas for immigrant groups.

integration: full unity of one territory with another. The cooperative process whereby countries move closer together on economic and other areas of policy.

interest: a stake, or a reason for caring about the outcome of a particular decision.

interest groups: *see* Sectional or interest groups.

intergovernmentalism: primacy of national governments in decision making.

internal market: when an artificial separation between users and providers is invented to try to introduce some of the discipline of the free market into a public service.

international organisation: states create and sign up to international organisations, to which they delegate the power and authority to act at international level, usually for some perceived collective gain. International organisations work across some or all of the following realms of international life – economic, political, environmental or security. The UN, EU and ASEAN are examples of international organisations, showing that they can have regional and global memberships and remits.

internationalism: the view that foreign policy should be based on the idea of cooperation between countries all over the world.

intervention: usually refers to a period of international activity when political, economic and military instruments are used by one state or a group of states acting in concert, to intervene in the affairs of a state. This might be for humanitarian reasons (such as in Libya) or for much more contentious reasons such as regime change. There is inevitably a blurred line between invasion and intervention, when seen in critical context, or when all motives are perceived to be at work in political rhetoric and practice (such as the last Iraq War).

issue voting: voting on the basis of issues presented at an election rather than on the basis of class or party preference.

judicial review: the ability of the courts to declare illegal any government action that they deem to be unauthorised by the terms of law.

judiciary: the body in a political system responsible for interpreting and enforcing laws.

Keynesian/Keynesianism: named after the economic theories and prescriptions for government action of John Maynard Keynes (1883–1946). These advocated a role for vigorous government action to stimulate economic growth through high levels of spending and the control of aggregate demand in order to avoid slumps and booms.

law lords: lords of appeal in ordinary are senior judges who have been given a life peerage so that they can carry out the judicial work of the Lords. There are currently 12 law lords.

legislature: the body in a democracy responsible for discussing and creating laws.

legitimacy: the right to govern.

liberal Conservatives: linked to groups like Bright Blue and Policy Exchange, and Tory 'modernisers' like George Osborne and Michael Gove, the term refers to Conservatives who want to combine liberal/laissez-faire economics with a more liberal/laissez-faire approach to culture and lifestyle (supporting, for example, gay marriage). Liberal Conservatives thus uphold the economic aspects of Thatcherism while rejecting its social conservatism.

liberalisation: literally to make freer or less restrictive, as in 'liberalisation of trade'.

liberal welfare state: a system of social provision where transfer payments are provided only as a last resort to the very worst-off, and are often highly stigmatised.

liberty: freedom from slavery, captivity or any other form of arbitrary control.

life peers: since the 1958 Life Peerages Act, most peers have been created for their lifetime only. Until 1999, life peers constituted around one-third of the nominal membership of the Lords.

lobby: the general term used to describe the activities of pressure groups, so called because lobbyists seek to waylay MPs as they pass through the lobby of the Commons. It also refers to the off-the-record briefings given by government spokespeople to journalists.

Localism Act 2011: an Act of Parliament which decentralises powers and responsibilities to councils and local communities, introduces changes to the planning system to make it more democratic and reforms the way decisions are taking locally about housing matters. The key element of the Act is the introduction of the general power of competence which changes the legal position of local government from one where councils could only do what the law specifically states they could do to one where councils can take any action so long as that action is not prohibited in law.

lords spiritual: the Archbishops of Canterbury and York and the 24 most senior diocesan bishops of the Church of England who sit in the Lords until they cease to hold their post.

lords temporal: all those peers who are not lords spiritual.

mandate: the idea that winning the general election gives the government the authority to put its policies, either as stated in the campaign or as required by circumstances, into effect. It can also mean that the government is expected to put its manifesto into action, that it has made a binding contract with the electors.

manifesto: a document issued by a political party containing a list of policy pledges which will be implemented if the party wins the election.

manipulation: the ability to influence someone else involved in a decision.

media: the collective name for the press, radio and television. Sometimes called the 'Fourth Estate' to represent its powerful position in the political system.

mercantilism: the doctrine that state power and security were enhanced by a favourable balance of trade. Popular in Britain between the mid-sixteenth and the mid-eighteenth centuries, when policy was directed to reducing imports and increasing national self-sufficiency at the expense of free trade.

ministerial responsibility: ministers are responsible to Parliament for their ministerial conduct, the general work of their departments and the actions or omissions of their officials.

ministry: *see* department.

mixed economy: the existence of a substantial public sector in the economy alongside a substantial private one. An economic system combining public ownership (most commonly of certain infrastructure industries and services) with the private ownership of the rest of the economy.

mixed economy of welfare: the mixture of public, private, voluntary and occupational social provision which characterises many modern welfare states, including that of the UK.

Modernising Government: White Paper published in March 1999, which encapsulates a range of managerial and service delivery themes with a focus on updating and modernising the basic functioning of the government machine. The White Paper and the subsequent implementation programme contained many modish concepts including 'government direct', 'joined-up government' and 'information-age government'.

motion of no confidence: a motion tabled (usually by the Leader of the Opposition) stating that 'This House has no confidence in Her Majesty's Ministers'. If passed, the government must, by convention, resign or request a dissolution of Parliament.

multilateral: agreements between two or more states.

multilateralism: attempting to solve international problems through collective approaches.

multinational companies/firms: organisations that operate in a wide range of companies/firms across several national boundaries, shifting economic activity around them in order to exploit the best conditions for producing profit.

multi-polar: an international system where there are more than two dominant powers, or no dominant powers at all.

national identity: a shared sense by a group of people – usually citizens of a state – as to their own history and character.

national insurance: a system of social policy provision where some transfer payments and welfare services are paid for through contributions from employees, employers and government.

national interest: the calculation by its government of what constitutes the best course of action for a nation in international affairs.

nationalisation: the act of transferring a part of the economy to state ownership, usually by establishing a nationalised corporation. Usually associated with the postwar 'socialist' political device of placing sections of the economy under the control of the government, so that privately owned assets such as buildings, equipment etc., or shares in a company are transferred by law from private into public ownership.

nationalism: the belief that one's country is worth supporting strongly in most situations.

natural rights: the belief that everyone is born with certain basic rights regarding freedom, citizenship and law.

negative constitutionalism: a belief in a constitution serving as a constraining mechanism, giving precedence to enduring principles over the transient will of the majority.

neo-liberal: in this usage refers to the doctrine which advocates individual autonomy and market principles over state control.

New Labour: the summary label to describe the economic policies devised by the Labour Party in the 1990s to ensure a departure from traditional ('old') Labour economic policies.

Next Steps: stemming from the Ibbs, or Next Steps, Report in 1988, a programme of managerial and structural reform which transformed the civil service through the creation of new executive agencies to carry out central government services and functions.

notifiable offences: those offences that are sufficiently serious to be tried by a judge.

occupational class: the method of assigning individuals to class groups on the basis of their occupational classification – manual working class, and so on.

occupational welfare: types of social support (e.g. health insurance) that are provided by employers, rather than governments.

oligarchy: a political system in which power is exercised by a group or committee of people.

one member, one vote (OMOV): the process of reform in the Labour Party by which party members vote as individuals instead of having their views represented by unions, constituency parties, etc.

Orange Book: Title of book written by leading Liberal Democrats in 2004, arguing the party should be more supportive of free market economics.

order: the degree of calm and law-abidingness present in society.

pacifist: someone opposed to the conduct of war.

paramilitaries: groups of supporters for a cause who accept violence as a method, accept military discipline and often wear neo-military dress.

paramilitary organisations: armed organisations not recognised by the state.

Parliamentary Labour Party (PLP): enfolding Labour's MPs and peers.

parliamentary sovereignty: the doctrine that Parliament is the supreme law-making body in the United Kingdom, with absolute *legal* right to make any law it chooses, subject only to those restrictions imposed by the membership of the EU, itself an expression of parliamentary sovereignty. The sovereignty of Parliament is subject to a host of practical and political limitations.

participatory democracy: a political system in which everyone is allowed and encouraged to take part in making decisions.

partisan dealignment: the declining number of voters over the past three decades who are identifying with political parties.

perestroika: the Russian word for reconstruction, popularised by Mikhail Gorbachev.

permissive: the alleged characteristic of Labour social policy in the 1960s when it was first believed that anything goes and that 'doing your own thing' was good.

pluralism: a political system in which power is diffused into several different centres within society and thus there are competing centres of power and authority rather than one in which the state is dominant. Pluralists argue that power is and should be dispersed in society, thus ensuring that freedom is maintained.

pluralist: a form of political decision making in which a variety (a plurality) of interests are held to contest outcomes.

plurality: electoral systems (especially 'first-past-the-post') that require only that the winning candidate has more votes that his or her nearest rival rather than an absolute majority. Such systems tend to produce disproportionate results.

policy cycle: the process of policy initiation, formulation and implementation.

political demands: the requirements made upon political systems by the societies they regulate.

political participation: the act of taking part in politics.

political party: an organised group of people sharing common policy preferences and a general ideological position. It seeks to possess or share political power, usually by nominating candidates for election and thus seeking a place in the legislature.

polluted: made unclean, corrupt or defiled.

positive constitutionalism: a belief in a constitution serving as a mechanism through which the will of the people is paramount.

power: the ability to make someone do as one wishes.

pragmatism: the belief that problems should be solved on their unique merits rather than according to some pre-ordained ideological pathway.

prerogative: prior or exclusive privilege often associated with rank or position.

press barons: newspaper proprietors who have been raised to the peerage either out of gratitude for services rendered to the governing party or because of the hope that they will omit to bite the hand that feeds them.

pressure group: a body possessing both formal structure and common interests which seeks to influence government at the national, local and international level without normally seeking election to representative bodies.

prime ministerial government: the view most associated with Richard Crossman and John Mackintosh that the Prime Minister has become dominant, almost a President, and that the Cabinet has become part of the 'dignified' aspects of the system.

private member's bill: a public bill promoted by a member of the Commons who is not a minister. They have a variety of purposes; several pass into law each year, though most fail. The opposition of the government is usually fatal.

private sector: the part of the economy that is the product of market forces alone.

privatisation: the process of transferring state-owned enterprises to the private sector, mainly by the sale of shares. The term also refers to other aspects of the reduction of the economic role of the state, such as liberalisation policies to encourage greater reliance on the market including deregulation of business, contracting out of services and the opening of the public sector generally to market forces.

professional politicians: the small minority of citizens who devote their whole life to politics, and who make a livelihood from it.

Progress: Labour Party pressure group, linked to supporters of Tony Blair and New Labour.

promotion groups: *see* Cause or promotion groups.

proportional representation (PR): a system of election that attempts to relate votes cast for the various parties to the number of seats won in the legislature. There are various forms of PR, with widely differing consequences.

psephological: to do with the study of voting behaviour as shown in elections and opinion polls. The word derives from the Greek word *psephos*, a pebble. Classical Athenians voted by putting a pebble into one of two jars, one for the 'yes' votes, the other for the 'no' votes. It was a form of direct democracy.

public bills: bills that must relate to a matter of public (general) interest and be introduced by an MP or a peer. Any bill proposed by the government, regardless of its content or intent, is a public bill.

public sector: that part of the economy which is in state ownership and is funded substantially by money originating from taxation of some kind.

Purple Labour: Tendency within Labour Party, represented by those close to Tony Blair. Keen that Labour should update and not abandon New Labour ideas.

quango: a quasi-autonomous non-governmental organisation, independent (at least in theory) from the department that created it, nominally under the control of the minister who appoints its members, sets its budget and establishes its aims, and with little responsibility to Parliament. Quangos are public bodies which advise on or administer activities and which carry out their work at arm's length from government.

radical feminism: argues that society is dominated by men who use their power to oppress women into occupying suborinate gender roles. They urge proactive action to challenge and overcome such oppression.

rates: a form of local taxation based upon the notional value of a property which was used until replaced by the community charge or poll tax.

rationality: a belief that the exercise of reason is superior to other ways of finding the truth.

reactionary: right-wing policies held to be harsh and unfeeling. Strictly speaking support for the status quo ante (that which previously existed).

recession: a period of economic downturn, usually defined as two consecutive quarters of zero growth. Features of a recession include rising unemployment, declining investment and falling consumer spending. It also has psychological features, most notably a lack of confidence in the economy generally. Recessions are described as being V, U, W or L-shaped depending on the nature of the recovery.

Red Tory: term coined by philosopher Philip Blond, denoting how Conservatism could and should give greater focus to social cohesion and communities.

referendum: a ballot in which the people at large decide an issue by voting 'yes' or 'no', although multi-outcome referenda are possible. The matter may be referred to the people by the government, perhaps because it is unable to make a decision, the law or the constitution may require such a reference, or there may be a mechanism by which the people can demand a referendum. Britain's only national referendum, that of 1975 over continued membership of the EC, was *advisory* only.

representation: the notion that those who are governed should be involved in the process of government.

representative government: government whereby decisions are taken by representatives who are (normally) elected by popular vote. The people do not take decisions directly.

residual welfare state: see 'liberal welfare state'.

responsibility: the accountability of government to the people.

Royal prerogative: powers that legally are in the hands of the crown, having been accepted by the courts over time as rightfully belonging to the monarch in his or her capacity as ruler. Most prerogative powers are now exercised by ministers (particularly the Prime Minister) who 'advise' the monarch as to their use.

rule of law: the idea that human activity should be controlled within a framework of agreed rules.

sectional or interest groups: these groups represent the interests (particularly economic) of their members. They include business, labour and professional organisations and often have close links with political parties.

select committee: a committee chosen by the House to work according to specific terms of reference. It may be given special powers to investigate, examine and report its findings to Parliament. Some are concerned with the working of Parliament itself; others scrutinise the activities of the executive.

separatist feminism: radical feminists who do not believe men can ever disinterestedly introduce genuine equality and conclude women need to achieve equality separately. This could entail women withdrawing from working, casual or intimate relationships with men.

social assistance: transfer payments provided to those without any other available means of support.

socialism: an economic system in which everyone benefits from the labour of others.

soundbite: a brief quote that is intended to make the maximum possible political impact. Research indicates that most listeners and viewers can absorb information for some 30 seconds, a theory that has influenced politicians on both sides of the Atlantic.

sovereignty: autonomy over national decision making. The ultimate legal authority in a state.

special relationship: the close feeling between US and British governments based on common culture and alliance in warfare.

spin doctor: a party official or public relations consultant whose job is to influence the media and put the best possible construction on events, by getting the party or candidate's message over by any possible means.

standing committee: usually a small group of MPs reflecting party strength in the Commons which takes the committee stage of bills that have received their second reading. They scrutinise the bills and can propose amendments to the House.

state: a commonly governed group of people all living within a defined territory.

statute law: those laws deriving their authority from Acts of Parliament and subordinate (delegated) legislation made under authority of the parent Act. Statute law overrides common law.

subsidiarity: the general aim of the principle of subsidiarity is to guarantee a degree of independence for a lower authority in relation to a higher body or for a local authority in respect of a central authority. It therefore involves the sharing of powers between several levels of authority, a principle which forms the institutional basis for federal states. When applied in an EU context, the principle means that the member states remain responsible for areas which they are capable of managing more effectively themselves, while the Community is given those powers which the member states cannot discharge satisfactorily.

subvention: government subsidy.

suffrage: the right to vote. The extension of the suffrage was a gradual process, culminating in 1969 when 18-year-olds were enfranchised. The suffrage is unusually wide in this country, including British subjects, resident Commonwealth citizens and citizens of the Irish Republic who have been resident for three months.

supply-side economics: provided the political and theoretical foundation for a remarkable number of tax cuts in the United States and other countries during the 1980s. Supply-side economics stresses the impact of tax rates on the incentives for people to produce and to use resources efficiently.

supranationalism: the character of authority exercised by European Union bodies that takes precedence over the autonomy of the member states.

sustainable development: the capability of the current generation to ensure it meets the need of the present without compromising the ability of future generations to meet their own needs.

sustainable economic growth: one in which resources are used more efficiently so that pressures on the environment do not increase as the economy grows.

swing: the way in which the switch of voters from one party to another on a national or constituency basis can be calculated. It is worked out by adding the rise in one party's vote to the fall in the other party's and then dividing by two.

tabloids: small format newspapers, usually aimed at the bottom end of the market with an informal style, use of large and often sensational headlines and many photographs.

Thatcherism: the economic, social and political ideas and particular style of leadership associated with Margaret Thatcher, Prime Minister from 1979 to 1990. It was a mixture of neo-liberal beliefs in the free market and

neo-conservative social attitudes and beliefs about the limited role of government.

the Treasury: the most important department of government concerned with economic policy.

think tanks: the name give to specialist organisations that frequently research and publish on policy and ideological matters.

toleration: accepting the legitimacy of views with which one does not necessarily agree.

top-down: the term used to denote power residing in the leading figures of an organisation, control over organisation being exercised by those figures over the ordinary members.

transfer payments: a method of transferring money from one group of citizens to another: for instance, taxing those in work and transferring the money raised to the unemployed in the form of unemployment benefits.

Tribune group: Gathering of the 'old left' within the Labour Party. Anti-capitalist and resentful of New Labour's legacy.

tripartism: a variant of *corporatism* in which economic policy is made in conjunction with business and labour groups to the exclusion of Parliament and other interests.

turnout: the measure, usually expressed as a percentage, of registered voters who actually vote. The average turnout in postwar elections has been around 75 per cent, generally lower than in most other EU countries.

tyranny: a political system in which power is exercised harshly without any consideration for the citizenry.

unicameral legislature: legislatures made up of one chamber are to be found mainly in smaller countries such as Israel and New Zealand or in smaller states in federal systems, such as Nebraska in the United States.

unitary authorities: a local government structure in which all services are provided by a single-tier authority as opposed to a structure in which powers and functions are divided between two tiers.

U-turn: a fundamental change of policies or philosophy by a political party or leader. The term is used to describe Heath's abandonment in 1971/72 of the free-market policies on which he was elected in 1970.

welfare state: the system of comprehensive social security and health services which was based on the Beveridge Report of 1942 and implemented by the postwar Labour Government. Often referred to as 'cradle to grave' security.

welfarism: the idea that the government should take some responsibility for the health and well-being of its citizens.

whip: this term has several meanings: (a) parliamentary business managers found in all parties, responsible for maintaining party discipline and ensuring a maximum turnout in the division lobbies; (b) the summons to vote for an MP's party, with the importance of the issue indicated by a one-, two- or three-line whip, sent out weekly to members of the parliamentary party; (c) membership of an MP's party – withdrawal of the whip means that the MP concerned is no longer recognised as a member in good standing.

world role: a term used to express the expectations on a nation when it acts on the international stage: diplomatically, economically and militarily. The UK's world role is said to derive strongly from its democratic history and role as promoter of human rights and the rule of law.

INDEX